THE ART
OF INDIAN
VEGETARIAN
COOKING

LORD KRISHNA'S CUISINE

THE ART
OF INDIAN
VEGETARIAN
COOKING

YAMUNA DEVI

BALA BOOKS

ANGUS
& ROBERTSON
PUBLISHERS

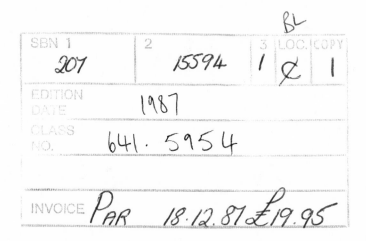

ANGUS & ROBERTSON PUBLISHERS

Unit 4, Eden Park, 31 Waterloo Road,
North Ryde, NSW, Australia 2113, and
16 Golden Square, London W1R 4BN,
United Kingdom

First published in Australia
by Angus & Robertson Publishers in 1987
First published in the United Kingdom
by Angus & Robertson (UK) Ltd in 1987

Published by arrangement with
Bala Books, Inc., USA

Copyright © Yamuna Devi 1987

ISBN 0 207 15594 1

Typeset in Palatino
Printed in the United States of America

Dedicated To Srila Prabhupada:

"Whatever actions a great man performs,
common men follow.
And whatever standards he sets by exemplary acts,
all the world pursues."

Bhagavad Gita 3.21

ACKNOWLEDGMENTS

This book has been brought to life by the efforts of people who deserve special mention. Lifetime friend Dina Sugg has collaborated on the project for years, giving it her invaluable support, guidance and hard work. From the typing of the original hand-written manuscripts to the final keying-in of the computer corrections, she has sacrificed more than just her time.

Bala Books publisher Joshua M. Greene years ago shared my vision of seeing this cuisine in America's kitchens. His intelligent structuring cut the unwieldy 1,400 page manuscript down to size and greatly improved its contents. Bala Books production manager Phillip Gallelli's enthusiasm and helpful attitude kept the pressure of deadlines at bay. His dedication and enthusiasm leveled mountainous obstacles during production.

Photographer Vishakha Dasi is a patient friend who not only shot the cover photo and more than 300 others as reference for the illustrations, but also spent months collecting props and testing recipes. Illustrator David Baird met every deadline and painstakingly turned the photographs into works of art.

Book designer Marino Gallo's graphic artistry is evidenced on each spread. Gilda Abramowitz exercized sensitivity and skill in her copy-editing. Special friend Farnie Spottswood shared her culinary knowledge and expertise through months of recipe testing, and her husband, John Sims, provided support and encouragement. Patricia Gallelli contributed exacting work on metric weights and measurements. Design consultant Barbara Berasi and computer typist Michelle Farkas also have my deepest thanks. I am indebted to Amy Mintzer and her industrious staff at E.P. Dutton. A special and heartfelt thanks goes to Jonathan Rice for having made the entire effort possible.

It is not possible to mention everyone who has helped on this project, but I offer them all my thanks.

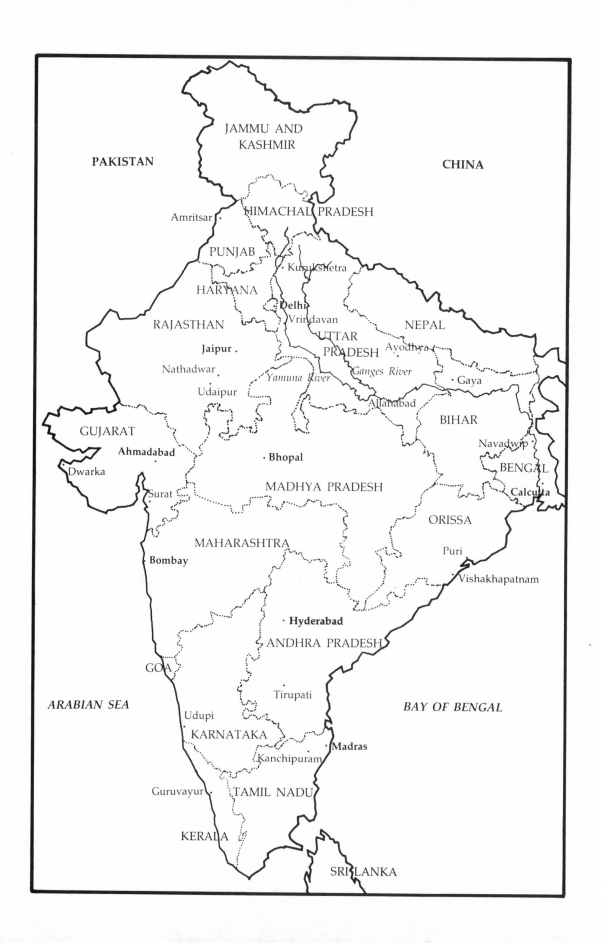

TABLE OF CONTENTS

INTRODUCTION

Every cookbook author must feel that there is something unique in his or her work that justifies the effort of producing it. I'm no exception. My feeling is that in this book you will find the richly varied foods from India's regional cuisines presented in a unique way, a way that explains India's culinary heritage in a spiritual light.

My involvement with both an Indian and vegetarian lifestyle began in 1966 when my sister invited me to attend her wedding in New York. She informed me that she and her fiancé had met an Indian Swami, called Srila Prabhupada, and were taking Sanskrit classes and studying *Bhagavad Gita* with him.

I arrived the day before the wedding and was unexpectedly whisked to lunch at the Swami's apartment. Everything about the experience was exotic, even though I was told it was an everyday meal: nutrition from grains, protein from beans, and vitamins from fresh vegetables. There were two hot vegetable dishes, *dal* soup, rice and buttered wheat flat breads. A yogurt salad and chutney served as accompaniments. They were ordinary vegetables, but cooked extraordinarily well. This meal bore little resemblance to the Indian restaurant food I had experienced—it was light, vibrant and subtly seasoned. As a cook, I was fascinated.

At the close of the meal, Prabhupada explained to me that it was the custom for the family members of the bride to prepare the wedding feast and, although he would be doing the cooking, he invited me to assist him in the task. The irony of the situation was almost comical to me. Here I was, with my inexorable apathy toward anything "spiritual," having come to New York expecting a traditional wedding, and finding instead an Indian "swami" performing a "hindu" marriage ceremony with me helping to cook the wedding feast! Yet my curiosity was roused and his sincerity was infectious, so I gladly accepted.

The day of the wedding, I arrived at Srila Prabhupada's apartment and was met with genuine hospitality. Prabhupada escorted me in and immediately served refreshments. More new tastes: flaky lemon-flavored crackers laced with crushed peppercorns and a frothy chilled yogurt drink sprinkled with sugar and rose water. As we spoke, I relished the sensational new flavors. He was a gentleman, a patient listener and an interesting speaker. He did not try to overwhelm me with emotional charisma, nor did he drone on with dry philosophy. He was quite unlike any religious man I had ever met.

Within an hour of my arrival at his apartment, I was introduced to numerous new spices and seasonings, unfamiliar ingredients and foreign cooking techniques. Given the stationary task of shaping potato-stuffed pastries, called *aloo kachoris*, I observed him from the adjoining room. Working in a narrow galley kitchen, he was organized and impeccably clean, simultaneously preparing up to four dishes at a time. His flow of activity was efficient and graceful, and, save for his instructions to me, his attention focused solely on his craft. He performed a number of tasks by hand, without the help or likely hinderance of tools. Each spice was measured in his left palm before use. Dough was hand-kneaded, *bada* dumplings hand-shaped, and fresh cheese hand-brayed until smooth—and, despite his advanced age, all with lightning speed. I was intrigued by the obvious satisfaction he experienced in every task he undertook. After having cooked all day, he performed the wedding ceremony that evening—the event culminating with the lavish eighteen-course feast he had prepared.

My planned two week stay in New York lengthened to nearly three months. When I returned to the West Coast with my sister and brother-in-law, we enlisted our friends to help bring Srila Prabhupada to San Francisco. In January, l967, he left New York's Lower East Side and moved into San Francisco's Parnassus Hill District. During the following months, prompted largely by my inquiries on morning walks, cooking classes or informal visits, Srila Prabhupada explained the workings of a Vaishnava kitchen in India. He explained that cooking was a spiritual experience for a Vaishnava, much like meditation—a means of expressing love and devotion to the Supreme Lord, Krishna. He touched on more than external standards, relating the subtle effects a Vedic lifestyle creates in the kitchen.

No matter what its size, the Vaishnava kitchen is divided into two areas: one for preparation and cooking and another for storage of staples, cookware, implements, and cleanup. The first area could take up only a few square feet—often a bare space devoid of anything except a stove. A cook bathes and puts on clean clothes before entering the kitchen, then sits comfortably on a low stool and uses the floor as countertop space. Only kitchen shoes or no shoes are allowed in this area, as it is kept spotlessly clean. Cooks develop a sixth sense for their ingredients, and, without assistance from recipes or measuring tools, they prepare sumptuous meals, never tasting the foods while cooking. While I resided in India, I learned to apply these principles in my kitchen, and, though much of what I learned is impractical in my American kitchen, the basic lessons in cleanliness and purity in the ingredients, cooking procedures and hygiene have become an integral part of my life.

In March of 1967, I asked Prabhupada to take me as his disciple, and that is how Joan Campanella became Yamuna Devi. Off and on over the next eight years, I was fortunate enough to serve as his personal cook. During some of this time, we traveled the length and breadth of India, giving me the invaluable opportunity to study in depth the country's varied regional cuisines. For two years I was part of a group that accompanied Srila Prabhupada on extensive tours of the subcontinent. This gave me the opportunity of learning from scores of famous temple *brahmana* cooks. In some cases, I was privileged to be the first Westerner allowed in previously restricted temple kitchens. Lavish royal kitchens sometimes engage as many as fifty such cooks and 100 servers for festival events—and though thousands of dialects are spoken in India, kitchen language is universal.

Of the 760 million residents in India today, more than eighty percent, or 600 million people, are vegetarian. Hundreds of thousands of these vegetarians are Vaishnavas or devotees of Lord Krishna, and their homes all have small temples in them. Further, there are thousands of established public Krishna temples in cities and villages across the country. Traveling with Srila Prabhupada afforded me the opportunity of visiting these Vaishnava devotees in their homes.

Sometimes I was able to attend fairs or *melas* devoted to reading sacred texts and the chanting of sacred songs. Such festivals around the pastimes of Lord Krishna are attended by millions of pilgrims and provide yet more opportunity to learn about the dietary habits and the roots of Lord Krishna's cuisine at its source.

Looking back, I can only say that when I first climbed the stairs to Prabhupada's apartment, I could never have imagined the treasure of transcendental philosophy, music, art and cuisine that awaited me. In the ten years since I first started writing this book, several very qualified people have brought India's fine cuisines to the attention of the world. My hope is that this humble effort will add meaningfully to theirs.

HOW TO MEASURE AND USE THE RECIPES

India, like most of the world, uses the metric system for measurement today. Most Indian cooks do not rely on cookbooks or volume measurements for accuracy; rather, they choose to measure by weight ratios. A dozen or so memorized formulas enable a cook to demonstrate versatility in thousands of ways. For instance, the formula for a moderately sweet Bengali *sandesh* is: for each given weight of *chenna* cheese, add one-quarter of that weight in sugar.

If you use recipes, accurate measuring techniques and equipment are essential to prevent culinary disasters and avoid guesswork. America is the only country that has not converted to the metric system, though there is little justification for the holdout. The metric system is easy and accurate. Americans use the customary volume measurements with graduated spoons and cups; British cooks use both the Imperial and metric systems, while Australians and Canadians exclusively use metric weights and measurements.

Both American and metric measurements are given in this book, and both systems use graduated spoons to measure small quantities of liquids or solids. A basic set of measuring spoons includes four spoons: the American set measures from ¼ teaspoon to 1 tablespoon; the metric set measures from 1 ml to 15 ml. All measurements are level unless otherwise specified.

Liquid measuring containers, made of clear glass or strong plastic, usually contain both cup and liter markings. The best metric liquid container I have come across is the Metric Wonder Cup by Wecolite, available at better cookware stores. With 10 ml gradations from 10 ml to 500 ml (½ liter), it meets all metric requirements. For accuracy, read the container at eye level.

Measuring dry ingredients by weight is far more accurate than measuring by volume, especially for main ingredients like flour and sugar. Accurate spring balance scales are available in better cookware stores, and many have dual American ounce/pound and metric gram/kilogram markings.

If you are using American cups for measuring dry goods, it is important to know how ingredients are handled in this book. Cereals, legumes and whole grains can be scooped out of containers and leveled off with your fingers. Before measuring, whole wheat and *chapati* flours are sieved to remove bran, and chickpea flour, icing or other lumpy sugars are sifted to lighten them and remove lumps. These ingredients, along with all other flours, are then spooned into an appropriate cup and then leveled with a spatula or knife. If you shake a cup to level an ingredient, the measurement will be inaccurate.

To get the most out of the recipes, try the following suggestions:

1. Read through the entire recipe—from the initial description of the dish through its final stages—to make sure you understand it. Unfamiliar ingredients, equipment and cooking terms or techniques are explained in the A–Z General Information section at the back of the book. When trying out a complicated recipe, allow a little extra time for preparation, organization and cleaning up.

2. Estimated preparation time does not include the time needed to assemble the ingredients. Therefore, soak, chill, cut or cook ingredients in advance when indicated. Next, arrange the ingredients near your cooking area to assure a smooth, uninterrupted work flow. Many cooks find it helpful to measure all the spices and ingredients beforehand and set them where they can be easily reached.

3. Pan size is specified whenever important. When too little food is cooked in a large pan, the ingredients spread out, liquids evaporate faster than desired and foods easily scorch on high heat. To increase or decrease the amount of servings, refer to the recipe converter in the A–Z General Information section and adjust the pan size and cooking times accordingly.

4. The recipes were tested on varied heat sources: electric stoves, household and restaurant gas stoves, electric glass cooktops and even cast-iron wood stoves. The cooking times are based on the average cumulative times and serve only as guidelines. Whatever your heat source, take its capabilities and liabilities into consideration and adjust cooking times accordingly. Keep in mind that, compared to gas, electric burners are slow to warm up and cool down.

A certain amount of repetition has been necessary in the forwards and recipes in order to prevent referrals from one chapter to another. For example, when the success of a recipe depends on freshly made warm *chenna* cheese, the process for making the cheese is included to assure every possible success.

Rice

You are what you eat. Many people have come to agree with George Bernard Shaw that our bodies and minds are greatly affected by the things we eat. If this is true, then few foods have influenced the development and character of humankind more than rice. Throughout history it has been a staple food for three-fourths of the world's population, remaining so even today—and with good reason. Rice is easy to grow, inexpensive and almost always available. Nutritionally, rice complements the proteins in other foods, and when eaten together with dried beans, nuts or dairy products, rice increases their combined food value by up to forty-five percent. Rice is a versatile grain that can be almost habit-forming, especially when accompanied by the salad, vegetable or *dal* dishes in this book.

Regional rice dishes are both varied and delicious. Plain rice, perfectly cooked, served steaming hot and garnished with a drizzle of melted *ghee* or butter, is the center of innumerable luncheon and dinner plates. It is surrounded by *dal* soup, vegetables, yogurt, chutney, pickles or salad, and is alternately married with each. Rice may also be cooked with herbs, spices, seasonings, nuts, raisins, *panir* cheese, *dals* and succulent vegetables to make the consummate pilaf entrée. Yogurt folded into cooled, seasoned rice makes an ideal side dish for a warm summer's day. When dried split *dals* or beans and vegetables are simmered with rice and seasonings, the result is a delicious all-in-one easy meal. And rice boiled with milk and sweet spices yields a creamy, scrumptious pudding. Rice can be pressed into flakes, heated into puffs or ground to a flour to make pancakes, dumplings, snacks and sweets.

Rice is selected and graded with careful attention to shape, color, fragrance, age, taste and cooked texture. Although there are a purported 10,000 varieties of rice cultivated worldwide, from a cook's point of view all rice is classified according to length and width: short-, medium- or long-grain, and then coarse, fine or extra-fine. Like their ancestors, Vedic cooks almost exclusively use polished, or white, rice, *arwa chaval*. It has a significantly longer storage life than *ukad chaval*, unpolished, or brown, rice. Indian brown rice has a strong flavor which even seems to overpower seasonings. So great is the preference for white rice that only the poorest eat brown rice and, more often than not, the brown rice available at bazaar grain shops is an inferior strain, with a large percentage of broken or cracked grains and a considerable amount of roughage.

Polished short-grain rice, fat or oval, white and somewhat chalky in appearance, is glutinous when cooked, and used primarily in southern and eastern cuisines. Medium-grain rice, about three times as long as it is wide, holds its shape when cooked, but is soft-textured. Over half of India's short- and medium-grain rice is parboiled and called *sela chaval*. Long-grain rice, four to five times as long as it is wide, when properly cooked is transformed into fluffy, well-separated grains. *Basmati* long-grain rice was used in all recipe testing, and all the recipes are written exclusively for long-grain varieties. Easy-to-cook, instant rices are completely shunned in the Vedic tradition for reasons of both taste and nutrition.

Three recommended long-grain rice varieties are widely available: North Indian *patna*, American Carolina and—the one rice rated par excellence—Indian or Pakistani *basmati*. *Patna* and Carolina rices are similar in flavor, and both cook into dry, fluffy long grains. Less readily available but worth searching for is brown *basmati*, or Calmati, a cross between brown rice and Indian *basmati* grown in the cool climate of California's Sacramento Valley. Texmati—a flavorful long-grain grown in Texas—and wild pecan from Louisiana are also delicious. Cooking times differ depending on processing. The slightly amber-colored Carolina, Texmati and wild pecan varieties do not require washing or soaking before cooking, and experience will teach you the exact amount of liquid that each variety absorbs. *Patna* rice has a soft white color and is noted for its mild bouquet and long, thin grains. I recommend that you give *patna* a good washing to remove surface starch and small bits of husk. It does not, however, require soaking before cooking.

For authentic, delectable Vedic rice cooking, *basmati* is the highly recommended choice. It is a relative newcomer to most Americans but is widely available in Indian and Middle Eastern grocery stores, specialty or gourmet stores and some health food shops and co-ops. This rice is prized for its good-looking kernels, pale yellow to creamy white color, fragrant bouquet and faintly nutlike flavor. For centuries, *basmati* rice has been harvested, husked and winnowed by hand, with minimal processing, in an efficient collective village ritual. Extended processing is avoided. Bleaching, pearling, oiling and powder-coating may produce more appealing commercial products, but such refinements diminish both flavor and nutritional value. Most imported *basmati* rice has been aged from six months to a year to enhance and intensify its flavor, bouquet and cooking characteristics. For this reason, and because of limited cultivation, *basmati* rice will usually cost a little more than Carolina or *patna*, but the difference is only pennies per pound.

The imported *basmati* rice available in America comes from three places. The best, hard-to-find Dehradhun *basmati*, comes from Dehradhun in North India. The others are *patna basmati* from Bihar State in North India and Pakistani *basmati* from Pakistan. Each of these rices is graded according to its percentage of unbroken, long, pointed grains; translucent milk-white color; delicate perfume; and buttery, nutlike flavor. To ensure fluffy and tender *basmati* rice, it is necessary to follow the time-honored ritual of cleaning, washing and soaking the rice before use. Brown *basmati* has a coarser grain, with typical brown-rice flavor and nutrition, and takes approximately 45 minutes to cook.

CLEANING INDIAN *BASMATI* RICE: Spread the rice out on a clean table, countertop or large metal tray so that all of the grains are visible. Working on a small portion at a time, pick out all foreign matter such as pieces of dirt, bits of stone, stems and unhulled rice grains. Push the finished portion to one side and continue until the rice is free of impurities.

WASHING *PATNA* AND INDIAN *BASMATI* RICE: Place the rice in a large bowl and fill it with cold water. Swish the rice around to release starches clinging to the grains and to encourage any husk and bran flakes to float to the surface. Pour off the milky residue and repeat the process several times until the washing water remains clear. Drain in a strainer.

SOAKING INDIAN AND BROWN *BASMATI* RICE: Soak the washed and drained *basmati* rice in warm water for 10 minutes to allow the long, pointed grains to absorb water and ''relax'' before cooking. This warm water is drained off and used as the cooking water after the rice has been soaked. Valuable nutrients and flavors are preserved by this process. Drain the rice in a strainer, collecting the premeasured water for cooking. Air-dry the rice for 15–20 minutes before cooking.

COOKING RICE: Rice is not hard to cook, and there are several methods. Some cooks prefer to cook rice like pasta, boiling it in large quantities of salted water until it is just over half done. It is then drained and cooked until tender in the oven. Rice can also be partially steamed on top of the stove and then finished off in the oven, using the exact amount of water needed for absorption. There are also different ways to steam rice completely on top of the stove. You'll find several methods of rice cooking in this chapter.

Since there are thousands of varieties of rice, is there one foolproof method for steaming long-grain rice on top of the stove? Is it safer to follow package instructions or rely on the proverbial ratio of two parts water to one part rice? The answer depends on three variables: the strain of rice you use, the type of pan you select and your heat source. As a general rule, I find that the two parts water is more than required for the rices I have mentioned. In most of the recipes I have suggested 1⅔–1¾ cups (400–420 ml) of water to 1 cup (95 g) of rice, no matter what type. This is only a general guideline, since only you can determine whether you prefer a softer or firmer consistency. I find that *basmati* requires slightly less water than Carolina, *patna* or Texmati, while all brown rice requires more, especially medium-grain.

Use a heavy pot for good heat distribution and make sure the lid fits tightly. Since rice is cooked in the minimum amount of water, it is important that the precious steam inside the pot not escape. Three types of pots are excellent for cooking rice: Silverstone on heavy aluminum, Cuisinart or Revere Ware stainless steel and Le Creuset enameled cast-iron pots. The rice should steam over very low, evenly distributed heat. If you cannot reduce your heat to a very low setting on gas, improvise by raising your pot above the heat source. Place a pair of tongs or a Chinese wok ring over the burner and place the pot on it. On electric stoves use heat diffusers.

Here are a few reminders for cooking the rice dishes in this chapter:

1. Always use long-grain rice.

2. A sprinkle of lemon or lime juice or a dab of *ghee*, butter or oil added during cooking helps the grains to remain separate and light.

3. Generally, 1 cup (95 g) of uncooked rice yields 2¾–3 cups (650–710 ml) of cooked rice. The ratio of water to rice varies not only with the type of rice used but also according to the degree of firmness desired. Brown rice absorbs more water than white rice.

4. Thick walls on your pot will help distribute the heat evenly throughout the rice, bringing all the grains to the same degree of tenderness. If your rice is cooking unevenly (perhaps the top layer is not cooked enough while the rest of the rice is tender), it is likely that your lid does not fit tightly enough. Try covering the pot with a tight sheet of aluminum foil, then replace the lid. Good-quality nonstick cookware is excellent for preventing rice from burning or scorching once the liquid is absorbed. A golden crust will form, but the rice will not burn if kept over low heat.

5. Once the lid has been placed on the rice, the heat must remain very low, just high enough to maintain a very gentle simmer. If you cannot achieve a sufficiently low setting from your burner, try cooking the rice in a well-covered, ovenproof dish in a preheated 325°F (160°C) oven for 25 minutes.

6. Never stir or otherwise disturb the rice while it is covered and steaming. Keep the rice well covered with a tight-fitting lid and let it cook undisturbed until all the water is absorbed and the rice is tender and fluffy. Removing the lid will allow precious steam to escape and make the rice cook unevenly.

7. Rice is at its best when prepared just before serving. Try to time your rice so that it has cooked and rested before fluffing. A rice pilaf or simple rice dish will remain piping hot for up to 20 minutes, provided you've used a heavy pot with a tight-fitting lid. If there is an unavoidable delay and the rice must sit before serving, transfer the entire dish into a wire-mesh strainer and set it over barely simmering water. Place a folded kitchen towel over the saucepan and replace the lid. This can save you from a disaster for up to an hour.

Buttered Steamed Rice
SADA CHAVAL

Though rice is generally steamed in a tightly closed pan over direct heat, in this recipe I recommend a "double-steamed" procedure. Measured rice and water rest in a closed pan which rests in a larger steamer pan. Steam surrounds the entire closed rice pan, producing very soft, evenly cooked rice with well-separated, unsplit grains.

My spiritual master, Srila Prabhupada, was expert in all kitchen matters and very particular about his daily steamed rice. One cooking utensil which always accompanied him in his world travels was a three-tiered brass steamer, known simply as "Prabhupada's cooker" by his resident cooks. At each port of entry, the cooker was unpacked and polished until it shone like gold. An entire lunch for four people—*dal* or *shukta* in the bottom chamber, assorted vegetables in the middle and double-steamed rice in the top—cooked in about 45 minutes. The tempered heat in the top of the steamer yielded the butter-soft grains he preferred.

More and more, cooks' catalogs and better cookware stores are offering two- and three-tiered steamers. Italian stainless steel steamers are available in various sizes and, though costly, will prove invaluable. Calphalon and enamel steamers are also excellent. Those who don't foresee using steamers on a regular basis can improvise by making a rice steamer with available pots and pans. I've used a covered Pyrex dish resting on a cake rack in an electric frying pan filled with water ½ inch (1.5 cm) deep. Or try putting any 4-cup (1 liter) ovenware dish with a tight-fitting lid on a vegetable steaming rack or steaming trivet inside a 5–6-quart/liter pot filled with water 1 inch (2.5 cm) deep. This will suffice for steaming up to 2 cups (180 g) of raw rice.

Preparation time (after assembling ingredients): 5 minutes
Cooking time: 35–45 minutes
Serves: 3 or 4, depending on accompanying dishes

1 cup (95 g) *basmati* or other long-grain white rice
1½–1¾ cups (360–420 ml) water
1 teaspoon (5 ml) salt
1–2 tablespoons (15–30 ml) *ghee* or butter (optional)

1. If *basmati* rice is used, clean, wash, soak, and drain as explained on page 6.

2. Combine the water (or reserved soaking water if you are using *basmati* rice), salt, half of the *ghee* or butter and the rice in a pan or dish capable of being steamed. Cover tightly with heavy-weight aluminum foil or a secure lid.

3. Set up your steaming equipment in any pan that can easily hold the rice dish. Bring the water to a boil. Add your steaming tier to the steamer, or place a trivet in the large pan which clears the water by at least ½ inch (1.5 cm). Reduce the heat to low once the water boils. Place the covered rice in the steamer or on the trivet and cover the steaming pan. Cook the rice very slowly over simmering water for 35–45 minutes, depending on the texture desired. Remove the rice from the heat, uncover, add the remaining *ghee* or a butter pat and gently fluff with a fork.

Sautéed Rice
KHARA CHAVAL

This simple way of steaming rice works equally well with either washed and drained *basmati* or unwashed American long-grain. By frying the rice in butter or *ghee* for a few minutes, you can keep the grains distinct, unsplit and fluffy. You may, of course, omit the frying step if you prefer: simply put all the ingredients except butter or *ghee* in a saucepan or electric rice cooker and cook as directed. Depending on the type of electric rice cooker, the rice will firm up 5–10 minutes after the red light goes off.

Preparation time (after assembling ingredients): 5 minutes
Cooking time: 25–35 minutes
Serves: 3 or 4

1 cup (95 g) *basmati* or other long-grain white rice
1½ tablespoons (22 ml) unsalted butter or *ghee*
1⅔–2 cups (400–480 ml) water
1 teaspoon (5 ml) fresh lemon or lime juice
¾ teaspoon (3.5 ml) salt

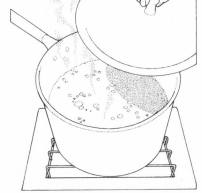

1. If *basmati* rice is used, clean, wash, soak and drain as explained on page 6.

2. Heat the butter or *ghee* in a heavy 1½-quart/liter nonstick saucepan over moderate heat until the butter froths or the *ghee* is hot. Pour in the rice and gently stir-fry for about 2 minutes.

3. Add the water, lemon juice and salt, increase the heat to high and quickly bring the water to a full boil.

4. Immediately reduce the heat to very low, cover with a tight-fitting lid and gently simmer without stirring for 20–25 minutes or until the rice is tender and the water is fully absorbed. Turn the heat off and let the rice sit, covered, for 5 minutes to allow the fragile grains to firm up.

5. Just before serving, uncover and fluff the piping-hot rice with a fork.

Simple Boiled Rice

OBLA CHAVAL

Indian rice pots are very heavy, giving excellent heat distribution. They are usually made of tinned brass or bell metal and have round bottoms, narrow necks and saucerlike lids. When rice is cooked in these pots, it is boiled until about half done. Then muslin cloth is tied over the neck and the water is drained off. Next, the lid is put in place, live coal embers are put in the lid and the pot is set on dying coal embers. The rice slowly dries off and cooks until tender. In the villages, the cooking water is often reserved and used to starch cotton garments or fed to the calves and cows as extra nourishment.

Whether the quantity of rice is small or large, it is easy to control the degree of tenderness by first boiling the rice and then finishing it in the oven. When done, the long, slender grains should be separate, fluffy and soft. Test by pressing a grain between the thumb and finger: it should have no hard core. It can be either firm, *al dente,* or very soft. When you serve steaming-hot portions of rice along with vegetable dishes and soups, it is not necessary to serve a flatbread.

Preparation time (after assembling ingredients): 5 minutes
Cooking time: 25–35 minutes
Serves: 4 or 5

1½ cups (130 g) *basmati* or other long-grain white rice
8–10 cups (2–2.5 liters) water
½ teaspoon (2 ml) fresh lemon or lime juice
1 teaspoon (5 ml) salt (optional)
2 tablespoons (30 ml) butter or *ghee* (optional)

1. Preheat the oven to 300°F (150°C). If *basmati* rice is used, clean, wash, soak and drain as explained on page 6.

2. Bring the water, lemon juice and salt to a full boil in a 5-quart/liter pan. Stirring constantly, slowly pour in the rice and return the water to a full boil. Boil rapidly, without stirring, for 10–12 minutes or until the rice is no longer brittle though still firm.

3. Pour the cooked rice into a strainer and drain. Quickly transfer the rice to a flat ovenproof dish and spread it out evenly. Put half of the butter or *ghee* over the hot rice and cover tightly. Place in a preheated 300°F (150°C) oven for 15–20 minutes or until the rice has dried out and is tender. Add the remaining butter, gently toss with a fork and serve piping hot.

Simple Yellow Rice
HALDI CHAVAL

Turmeric lends a glimmer of yellow to this rice dish. The herbs and seasonings are elusive, and they complement the *basmati*'s naturally nutty flavor. This is quick, easy and delicately flavored and goes nicely with any soup and salad. You could also try it with *Nutritious Whole Grain Split Pea and Vegetable Soup* for a superb visual and taste delight.

Preparation time (after assembling ingredients): 5 minutes
Cooking time: 35–40 minutes
Serves: 3 or 4

1 cup (95 g) *basmati* or other long-grain white rice
2 tablespoons (30 ml) *ghee* or vegetable oil
1 teaspoon (5 ml) cumin seeds
¼ teaspoon (1 ml) *ajwain* seeds
6 whole cloves
1-inch (2.5 cm) piece of cinnamon stick
1⅔–1¾ cups (400–420 ml) water (as desired)
½–1 teaspoon (2–5 ml) salt
¼ teaspoon (1 ml) coarsely ground black pepper
½ teaspoon (2 ml) turmeric
3 tablespoons (45 ml) chopped celery leaves, parsley,
    coriander or other fresh herbs

1. If *basmati* rice is used, clean, wash, soak and drain as explained on page 6.
2. Heat the *ghee* or oil in a heavy 1½-quart/liter nonstick saucepan until it is hot but not smoking. Add the cumin seeds, *ajwain* seeds, whole cloves and cinnamon. Fry until the cumin seeds turn brown.
3. Pour in the rice and stir-fry for about 2 minutes. Add the water, salt, pepper, turmeric and celery leaves or herbs. Increase the heat to high and bring the water to a full boil.
4. Immediately reduce the heat to very low, cover with a tight-fitting lid and gently simmer for 20–25 minutes or until the rice is tender and the water is fully absorbed. Turn the heat off and let the rice sit, covered, for 5 minutes to allow the fragile grains to firm up. Just before serving, remove the whole cloves and cinnamon stick and fluff the piping-hot rice with a fork.

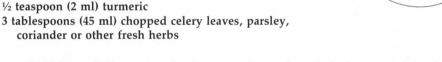

Savory Rice and Green Pea Pilaf
MASALA HARI MATAR PULAU

A savory, eye-catching centerpiece, this rice pilaf is perfect for the buffet table or as an adaptable main dish for a light luncheon or dinner. It is rich with color, texture and flavor. Try it with *Tomato Broth with Spicy Paparh Noodles, Glazed Carrots* and *Deep-Fried Whole Wheat Bread* for a special, light lunch.

Preparation time (after assembling ingredients): 5 minutes
Cooking time: 30–40 minutes
Serves: 4

1 cup (95 g) *basmati* or other long-grain white rice
3 tablespoons (45 ml) *ghee* or vegetable oil
¼ cup (35 g) raw cashew, almond or peanut bits or halves
1 teaspoon (5 ml) cumin seeds
1–2 teaspoons (5–10 ml) minced seeded hot green chilies
½ tablespoon (7 ml) scraped, finely shredded or minced fresh ginger root
1⅔–1¾ cups (400–420 ml) water
¾ cup (180 ml) shelled fresh green peas or frozen baby peas, defrosted
1 teaspoon (5 ml) turmeric
½ teaspoon (2 ml) *garam masala*
¼ cup (35 g) raisins or currants
½–1 teaspoon (2–5 ml) salt
3 tablespoons (45 ml) mixed fresh herbs (basil, oregano, thyme, etc.) or
    1½ tablespoons (22 ml) mixed dried herbs

   1. If *basmati* rice is used, clean, wash, soak and drain as explained on page 6.
   2. Heat the *ghee* or oil in a heavy 1½-quart/liter nonstick saucepan over moderately low heat. Add the cashew, almond or peanut bits or halves. Fry, stirring constantly, until the nuts are golden brown. Remove the nuts with a slotted spoon.
   3. Raise the heat to moderate and toss in the cumin seeds, green chilies and ginger root. Fry until the cumin seeds turn brown. Pour in the rice and stir-fry for about 2 minutes.
   4. Pour in the water, fresh peas (if you are using them), turmeric, *garam masala*, raisins, salt and herbs. Raise the heat to high and bring to a full boil.
   5. Immediately reduce the heat to very low, cover with a tight-fitting lid and gently simmer without stirring for about 20–25 minutes, depending on the type of rice, or until all the water is absorbed and the rice is tender and fluffy. If you are using frozen peas, defrost them in a strainer under hot running water. After the rice has cooked for 15 minutes, remove the lid and quickly sprinkle the peas on top. Replace the cover and continue cooking for 5–10 minutes, until all the water is absorbed and the rice is tender and fluffy.
   6. Turn the heat off and let the rice sit, covered, for 5 minutes to allow the fragile grains to firm up. Just before serving, remove the cover, pour in the fried nuts and fluff the piping-hot rice with a fork.

Rice and Cauliflower Pilaf
GOBHI PULAU

   Butter-soft cauliflower flowerets, delicately seasoned, are nestled in this succulent rice dish. For best results, take care to cut the buds and stalks uniformly; odd sizes do not cook evenly. The cauliflower is stir-fried until slightly golden. A coconut-yogurt mixture is folded in and the vegetable is cooked until half tender, then finally steamed to tenderness with the seasoned rice. You will be amazed at this cauliflower-rice combination, and you will find it a superb dish for entertaining. For a really special dinner, try it with *Pineapple and Peas in Almond Broth*, *Shallow-Fried Batter-Coated Chenna Cheese Patties* with a dab of *Sour Cream Parsley Sauce* and *Green Beans with Water Chestnuts*.

Preparation time (after assembling ingredients): 10 minutes
Cooking time: 35–45 minutes
Serves: 6 to 8

For the Cauliflower:

¼ cup (25 g) fresh or dried grated coconut, lightly packed
1 tablespoon (15 ml) minced seeded hot green chilies (or as desired)
1 tablespoon (15 ml) scraped, finely shredded or minced fresh ginger root
3 tablespoons (45 ml) minced fresh parsley or coarsely chopped coriander
½ cup (120 ml) plain yogurt
½ teaspoon (2 ml) turmeric
1 teaspoon (5 ml) salt
¼ teaspoon (1 ml) freshly ground black pepper
3 tablespoons (45 ml) *ghee* or vegetable oil
1 small cauliflower (about ¾ pound/340 g), washed,
    trimmed and cut into 1 x ¾ x ½-inch (2.5 x 2 x 1.5 cm) flowerets

For the Rice:

1 cup (95 g) *basmati* or other long-grain white rice
3 tablespoons (45 ml) *ghee* or a mixture of
    vegetable oil and unsalted butter
1 small cassia or bay leaf
1½ teaspoons (7 ml) cumin seeds
½ teaspoon (2 ml) black mustard seeds
2 large black or 4 large green cardamom pods, slightly crushed
1¾–2 cups (420–480 ml) water
1 teaspoon (5 ml) raw sugar
lemon or lime wedges or twists for garnishing

To Cook the Cauliflower:

    1. Combine the coconut, green chilies, ginger, parsley or coriander and yogurt in a blender. Cover and blend until smooth. Scrape into a small bowl, add the turmeric, salt and pepper, and mix.

    2. Heat 3 tablespoons (45 ml) of *ghee* or oil in a heavy 2-quart/liter saucepan over moderately high heat until it is hot but not smoking. Drop in the cauliflower flowerets and stir-fry for about 5 minutes or until the cauliflower has light brown edges. Pour in the yogurt mixture and stir well. Reduce the heat slightly and fry until the vegetable is dry and half-cooked.

    3. Remove the pan from the heat and transfer the contents to a small bowl. Wipe the pan clean.

To Cook the Rice:

    1. If *basmati* rice is used, clean, wash, soak and drain as explained on page 6.
    2. Heat 1½ tablespoons (22 ml) of *ghee* or oil-butter mixture in a heavy 2-quart/liter nonstick saucepan over moderate heat. Fry the cassia or bay leaf, cumin seeds, black

mustard seeds and cardamom pods until the mustard seeds turn gray and sputter and pop. Pour in the rice and stir-fry for 2–3 minutes.

3. Add the water and sweetener, raise the heat to high and bring the liquid to a full boil. Stir in the seasoned cauliflower, immediately reduce the heat to very low and cover with a tight-fitting lid. Simmer gently, without stirring, for 20–25 minutes or until the liquid is absorbed and the rice is tender and fluffy. Turn the heat off and let the rice sit, covered, for 5 minutes to allow the fragile grains to firm up. Just before serving, remove the cover, add the remaining 1½ tablespoons (22 ml) of *ghee* or oil-butter mixture and fluff the piping-hot rice with a fork. Garnish with a lemon or lime wedge or twist.

Curried Eggplant Rice
BAIGAN PULAU

Golden brown cashews and butter-soft eggplant spears are embedded in this succulent rice dish. The eggplant spears are flavorful to the the core because they are first tossed in turmeric and salt. A freshly made dry-roasted spice powder complements the faintly nutlike flavor of the *basmati* rice and does wonders for American supermarket long-grain rice. It is a good idea to collect all of the ingredients beforehand. This is an ideal main dish rice for any full luncheon or dinner menu. Try it with a spoonful of *Homemade Yogurt* or *Homemade Sour Cream*, *Spiced Green Beans*, *Gold Broth with Julienne Cucumbers* and *Griddle-Baked Yogurt Whole Wheat Bread*. From the sweets corner, round off the meal with a serving of *Shredded Carrot Halva with Pistachios* or delicate *Nut-Stuffed Chenna Balls in Rose Syrup*.

Preparation time (after assembling ingredients): 15 minutes
Cooking time: 35–45 minutes
Serves: about 6

1¼ cup (105 g) *basmati* or other long-grain white rice
1 teaspoon (5 ml) turmeric
2 teaspoons (10 ml) salt
2–2¼ cups (480–530 ml) water
1 small eggplant (about ½ pound/230 g), washed but not peeled, and evenly cut into
    2 x ½ x ½-inch (5 x 1.5 x 1.5 cm) strips
3 tablespoons (45 ml) sesame seeds
12 black peppercorns
1½ tablespoons (22 ml) coriander seeds
8 whole cloves
¼ teaspoon (1 ml) cinnamon
5 tablespoons (75 ml) *ghee* or a mixture of sesame oil and unsalted butter
½ cup (75 g) raw cashew bits or halves
½ tablespoon (7 ml) scraped, finely shredded or minced fresh ginger root
2 teaspoons (10 ml) minced seeded hot green chilies (or as desired)
½ teaspoon (2 ml) black mustard seeds
2 large black or 4 large green cardamom pods, slightly crushed
5–6 curry leaves, preferably fresh
½ tablespoon (7 ml) fresh lemon or lime juice

For information about unfamiliar ingredients or techniques, see A-to-Z

1 teaspoon (5 ml) raw sugar
3 tablespoons (45 ml) minced fresh parsley or coarsely chopped coriander

1. If *basmati* rice is used clean, wash, soak and drain as explained on page 6.

2. Combine the turmeric, 1 teaspoon (5 ml) of salt and 1 tablespoon (15 ml) of the water in a shallow bowl. Add the eggplant strips and coat well. The flavors will mingle while you prepare the rice.

3. Pour the sesame seeds, peppercorns, coriander seeds and whole cloves into a heavy frying pan over low heat. Dry-roast, stirring occasionally, until the sesame seeds are golden brown. Transfer the roasted seasoning to a small coffee mill or stone mortar and grind to a powder. Add the cinnamon, mix well and set aside.

4. Heat the *ghee* or oil-butter mixture in a heavy 2-quart/liter nonstick saucepan over moderate heat. Fry the cashew nuts until golden brown. Remove with a slotted spoon and set aside. Raise the heat to moderately high and drop in the ginger root, chilies, black mustard seeds and cardamom pods. Fry until the mustard seeds turn gray and sputter and pop. Add the curry leaves and immediately drop in the marinated eggplant spears. Gently stir-fry for a few minutes until the strips of eggplant begin to brown.

5. Pour in the rice and continue to fry for 2 minutes or until the grains glisten with the *ghee*. Add the water, spice-powder blend, remaining teaspoon (5 ml) of salt, lemon juice, sweetener, the fried cashew nuts and half of the fresh herb. Raise the heat to high and quickly bring to a full boil.

6. Immediately reduce the heat to very low, cover with a tight-fitting lid and gently simmer, without stirring, for 20–25 minutes or until the liquid is absorbed and the rice is tender and fluffy. Turn off the heat and let the rice sit, covered, for 5 minutes to allow the fragile grains to firm up.

7. Just before serving, remove the cover, sprinkle in the remaining fresh herb and with a wide spoon or fork gently fluff the piping-hot rice from the bottom to evenly mix the ingredients.

Rice with Stuffed Baby Eggplant
CHOTI BAIGAN PULAU

This is a delicate, mildly seasoned rice coming from the South Indian and Maharashtrian tradition, unique in its garnish of whole pan-fried stuffed eggplants. The special appeal of this recipe is in the tiny eggplants, only 2–3 inches (5–7.5 cm) long and weighing about 2 ounces (60 g) each. The white or purple oval types are occasionally found in Indian grocery stores or gourmet greengrocers. An alternative is the slim, 4-inch (10 cm) purple-black Japanese variety. The egg-plants are slit into quarters and stuffed with a mixture of pan-roasted spices, chickpea flour and yogurt. Serve this scrumptious main dish rice with a fresh tossed green salad, *Spicy Cauliflower with Braised Tomato, Double-Dal Soup* and *Griddle-Baked Whole Wheat Bread* for a nutritious lunch or dinner.

Preparation time (after assembling ingredients): 40 minutes
Cooking time: 50–60 minutes
Serves: 5 or 6

1½ cups (130 g) *basmati* or other long-grain white rice
5–6 baby oval eggplants, 2½–3 inches (6.5–7.5 cm) long,
    or 5–6 slim 4-inch (10 cm) eggplants
1 teaspoon (5 ml) fennel seeds
1 teaspoon (5 ml) cumin seeds
2 teaspoons (10 ml) coriander seeds
1½ tablespoons (22 ml) chickpea flour
¾ teaspoon (3.5 ml) turmeric
¼ teaspoon (1 ml) paprika or cayenne pepper (or as desired)
3 tablespoons (45 ml) plain yogurt
⅓ teaspoon (1.5 ml) salt for the eggplant
5 tablespoons (75 ml) *ghee* or vegetable oil
1 teaspoon (5 ml) split *urad dal*, if available
1 teaspoon (5 ml) black mustard seeds
8–10 curry leaves, preferably fresh
1–2 hot green chilies, stemmed, seeded and cut
    lengthwise into long slivers
2⅓–2⅔ cups (550–630 ml) water
1 teaspoon (5 ml) salt for the rice
¼ teaspoon (1 ml) freshly ground black pepper
5 or 6 lemon or lime wedges or twists for garnishing
a few sprigs of fresh parsley or coriander leaves for garnishing

1. If *basmati* rice is used, clean, wash, soak, and drain as explained on page 6.

2. Cut the eggplants lengthwise into quarters, from the round end two-thirds of the way down toward the stem, so that they can be stuffed with spices yet still remain whole. Soak them in a bowl of slightly salted water for 20 minutes, then drain in a wire-mesh strainer.

3. Meanwhile, combine the fennel seeds, cumin seeds, coriander seeds and chickpea flour in a heavy frying pan and, stirring, dry-roast them over moderately low heat for about 5 minutes or until the seeds are toasted and the chickpea flour turns reddish-brown. Transfer the mixture to an electric coffee mill or a stone mortar and reduce to a powder.

4. Combine the roasted spices, turmeric, paprika or cayenne, yogurt and ⅓ teaspoon (1.5 ml) of salt in a small bowl and mix into a smooth paste. With a knife blade, gently smear the paste equally into the cuts in the eggplants.

5. Heat 3 tablespoons (45 ml) of the *ghee* or oil in an 8-inch (20 cm) nonstick frying pan over low heat. Place all of the eggplants in the pan, cover with a lid and cook for about 8 minutes. Remove the lid and turn the eggplants over. Cover and cook for about 8 more minutes. Remove the lid. The eggplants should be butter-soft and evenly browned. If not, turn the eggplants and let them cook for an additional few minutes. Remove and set aside in a warm oven.

6. Heat the remaining 2 tablespoons (30 ml) of *ghee* or oil in a heavy 2-quart/liter nonstick saucepan over moderate heat until it is hot but not smoking. Toss in the split *urad dal* and mustard seeds and fry until the *dal* is reddish-brown and the mustard seeds turn gray and sputter and pop. Drop in the curry leaves and green chilies and fry for

2–3 seconds, following immediately with the rice. Stir-fry for 2 minutes or until the rice grains glisten with *ghee*. Add the water, salt and pepper and bring to a full boil. Reduce the heat to very low and cover with a tight-fitting lid. Gently simmer without stirring for 20–25 minutes or until the rice is dry, tender and fluffy. Turn off the heat and let the rice sit, covered, for 5 minutes to allow the fragile grains to firm up.

7. Remove the cover and fluff the rice with a fork immediately before serving. Spoon into a warmed flat chafing dish or serving platter and garnish the top with a ring of the cooked eggplants, the lemon or lime wedges or twists, and parsley or coriander in the center.

Herbed Rice with Mixed Vegetables
SABJI-KI CHAVAL

This is a quick and easy recipe made with a fresh ginger-flavored stock known in Bengal as *akhnir jhol*. The rice is fried with the whole spices in *ghee* or vegetable oil, then cooked in the stock until tender. Vegetables, either fresh or frozen, are then folded into the pilaf. The whole spices are not meant to be eaten, so remove them when fluffing the rice prior to serving. For a light lunch, serve this pilaf with *Greens and Plantain with Toasted Almonds, Cucumber and Coconut in Dill Yogurt Cream, Herbed Cornmeal Pakora* and a fresh flatbread or whole grain bread rolls.

Preparation time (after assembling ingredients): 15 minutes
Cooking time: 35–45 minutes
Serves: 6

1 cup (95 g) *basmati* or other long-grain white rice
3 medium-sized firm ripe tomatoes
6 black peppercorns
¾ cup (180 ml) water or unsalted vegetable stock (pages 227–28)
2 teaspoons (10 ml) scraped, finely shredded or minced fresh ginger root
2 tablespoons (30 ml) *ghee* or vegetable oil
2-inch (5 cm) piece of cinnamon stick
6 whole cloves
2 large black or 4 large green cardamom pods, slightly crushed
1 cassia or bay leaf
½ teaspoon (2 ml) turmeric
1 teaspoon (5 ml) salt
1 cup (240 ml) fresh or frozen diced mixed vegetables
    (corn, peas, carrots, zucchini, etc.), steamed until tender
6 lemon or lime wedges or twists for garnishing

1. If *basmati* rice is used, clean, wash, soak and drain as explained on page 6.
2. Cut the tomatoes into quarters. Place the tomatoes, peppercorns, water or stock and ginger root in a small saucepan over high heat and bring to a boil. Reduce the heat to low, cover and gently boil for 10–12 minutes. Remove from the heat, mash the tomatoes and force them through a strainer to remove the seeds, skins and spices. Add

enough water to the remaining tomato stock to make 1¾ cups (420 ml). Set aside.

3. Heat the *ghee* or oil in a heavy 1½-quart/liter nonstick saucepan over moderate heat until it is hot but not smoking. Toss in the cinnamon stick, whole cloves, cardamom, and cassia or bay leaf. Fry for just a few seconds. Then pour in the rice and stir-fry for about 2 minutes.

4. Pour in the tomato stock, turmeric and salt. Raise the heat and rapidly bring to a boil. Immediately reduce the heat to very low and cover with a tight-fitting lid. Gently simmer without stirring for 20–25 minutes or until the rice is tender and fluffy and the liquid is fully absorbed.

5. Remove from the heat, uncover and sprinkle the steamed vegetables over the rice. Cover immediately, and let the rice sit for 5 minutes to allow the fragile grains to firm up. Remove the cover, gently fluff the rice and mix in the vegetables. Garnish each serving with a wedge or twist of lemon or lime.

Almond Rice with Mixed Vegetables
BADAAM SABJI-KI CHAVAL

This is a very delicate rice and vegetable dish with lively colors and textures. The potato, peppers, zucchini, carrots and green beans must be fresh, but the green peas can be frozen. The mild seasoning allows the rich flavor of the vegetables to be the main feature of the dish. Golden-brown almonds are folded into the rice before serving, adding even more texture and flair to an already lovely dish. This wonderful rice may be eaten with any soup and salad, or with a Vedic menu. For lunch, try it with *Deep-Fried Chickpea-Flour Pearls in Creamy Yogurt, Mung Dal Purée with Sliced White Radishes* and *Sweet 'n' Sour Eggplant*. At dinner, you could add *Potato Pakora with Dried Pomegranate Seeds* and a *chutney*. From the pastry corner, you could add *Flaky Pastry Diamonds with Fennel Milk Glaze* or the elegant *Super-Flaky Pastry Swirls with Cardamom Glaze*.

Preparation time (after assembling ingredients): 20 minutes
Cooking time: 30–40 minutes
Serves: 8

1 cup (95 g) *basmati* or other long-grain white rice
5 tablespoons (75 ml) *ghee* or vegetable oil
½ cup (55 g) slivered or sliced almonds
⅛ teaspoon (0.5 ml) salt for the almonds
1 medium-sized all-purpose potato, peeled and cut into ½-inch (1.5 cm) dice
1 teaspoon (5 ml) cumin seeds
1 dried red chili or ½ teaspoon (2 ml) crushed dried red chili (or as desired)
½ green or red bell pepper, seeded and diced
½ cup (120 ml) zucchini cut into ½-inch (1.5 cm) dice
2–2¼ cups (480–530 ml) water
¼ cup (25 g) ground almonds
1½ teaspoons (7 ml) salt for the rice

For information about unfamiliar ingredients or techniques, see A-to-Z

½ teaspoon (2 ml) *garam masala* or ¼ teaspoon (1 ml) each
    ground nutmeg and ground cloves
⅓ cup (80 ml) fresh young carrots, scraped and thinly sliced
⅓ cup (80 ml) fresh green beans, washed and sliced into ¼-inch (6 mm) pieces
⅓ cup (80 ml) shelled fresh green peas or frozen baby peas, defrosted
1 tablespoon (15 ml) butter or *ghee* (optional)
2 tablespoons (30 ml) minced fresh parsley or coarsely chopped coriander leaves

1. If *basmati* rice is used, clean, wash, soak and drain as explained on page 6.

2. Heat 3 tablespoons (45 ml) of *ghee* or oil in a 2-quart/liter nonstick saucepan over moderately low to moderate heat. Slowly fry the almonds until golden brown. Remove with a slotted spoon and set aside to drain. Lightly salt.

3. Raise the heat to moderately high and add 1 more tablespoon (15 ml) of *ghee* or oil. Drop in the potato and stir-fry until golden brown. Remove with a slotted spoon and set aside.

4. Add the remaining 1 tablespoon (15 ml) of *ghee* or oil and heat until hot but not smoking. Drop in the cumin seeds and red chili. Fry until brown. Then stir in the bell pepper, zucchini and rice. Fry for about 2 minutes.

5. Add the water, ground almonds, salt and *garam masala* or nutmeg and cloves. Bring to a full boil over high heat. Add the carrots and green beans. If using fresh peas, add them now. Immediately reduce the heat to very low. Cover with a tight-fitting lid and gently simmer without stirring for 20–25 minutes or until the rice is fluffy, the vegetables are tender-crisp and all of the liquid has been absorbed. If using frozen peas, defrost them in a strainer under hot running water while the rice is cooking, and after the rice has cooked for 15 minutes remove the lid and quickly sprinkle them on top. Replace the cover and let the rice finish as described above.

6. Turn the heat off and let the rice sit, covered, for 5 minutes to allow the fragile grains to firm up. Remove the cover and drop the fried almonds and potatoes into the rice. Fluff the rice and vegetables gently with a fork to mix evenly. Serve piping hot. An additional tablespoon (15 ml) of butter or *ghee* may be drizzled over the surface before serving. Garnish each serving with parsley or coriander.

Rice with Shredded Carrots and Coconut
GAJAR PULAU

This is a pale golden rice marbled with shredded carrots and toasted shredded coconut. A touch of raisins adds a little sweetness. You may want to remove the whole cloves, peppercorns and cinnamon stick before serving, as they are not meant to be eaten. This is a good choice for luncheon or evening menus along with any *dal* soup or tossed salad. This dish is quick, colorful, aromatic and, most important, delicious.

Preparation time (after assembling ingredients): 5 minutes
Cooking time: 25–35 minutes
Serves: 3 or 4

1 cup (95 g) *basmati* or other long-grain white rice
2 tablespoons (30 ml) *ghee* or vegetable oil
1½ tablespoons (22 ml) sesame seeds
6 whole cloves
6 black peppercorns
1½-inch (4 cm) piece of cinnamon stick
3 tablespoons (45 ml) fresh or dried shredded coconut
1⅔–2 cups (400–480 ml) water
1½ cups (360 ml) scraped and shredded carrots (about 8 ounces/230 g)
1¼ teaspoons (6 ml) salt
2 tablespoons (30 ml) raisins or currants

1. If *basmati* rice is used, clean, wash, soak and drain as explained on page 6.

2. Heat the *ghee* or oil in a heavy 1½-quart/liter nonstick saucepan over moderate heat until it is hot but not smoking. Add the sesame seeds, cloves, peppercorns, cinnamon stick and coconut. Stir-fry until the coconut turns light brown. Stir the rice into the mixture and fry for a few minutes until the rice grains are slightly translucent.

3. Add the water and the remaining ingredients, raise the heat to high and bring to a full boil.

4. Reduce the heat to low, cover with a tight-fitting lid and gently simmer without stirring for 20–25 minutes or until the rice is fluffy and the vegetables are tender-crisp and all of the liquid has been absorbed.

5. Turn the heat off and let the rice sit, covered, for 5 minutes to allow the fragile grains to firm up. Just before serving, remove the cover and fluff the piping-hot rice with a fork.

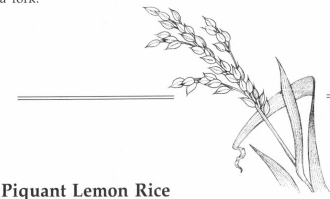

Piquant Lemon Rice
NIMBU BHAT

This light, mildly piquant lemon-flavored rice dish is enlivened with crunchy bits of cashew nuts. The final burst of flavor comes from a fried seasoning called *chaunk*, made of mustard seeds and split *urad dal* fried in *ghee* or sesame oil until the aromatic oils in the seeds are released and the *dal* turns golden brown. This South Indian delight is simple to make and can be served at any time and at any occasion, from a simple noonday lunch to an elaborate banquet.

For information about unfamiliar ingredients or techniques, see A-to-Z

Preparation time (after assembling ingredients): 5 minutes
Cooking time: 25–35 minutes
Serves: 4

1 cup (95 g) *basmati* or other long-grain white rice
1⅔–2 cups (400–480 ml) water
1 teaspoon (5 ml) salt
3 tablespoons (45 ml) *ghee* or sesame oil
½ cup (75 g) raw cashew bits or halves
½ tablespoon (7 ml) split *urad dal*, if available
1 teaspoon (5 ml) black mustard seeds
⅓ teaspoon (1.5 ml) turmeric
⅓ cup (80 ml) fresh lemon or lime juice
3 tablespoons (45 ml) minced fresh parsley or
    coarsely chopped coriander
¼ cup (25 g) fresh or dried shredded coconut for garnishing

1. If *basmati* rice is used, clean, wash, soak and drain as explained on page 6.

2. Bring the water to a boil in a heavy 1½-quart/liter nonstick saucepan. Stir in the rice, salt and ½ tablespoon (7 ml) of the *ghee* or oil. Cover with a tight-fitting lid. Reduce the heat to very low and gently simmer without stirring for 20–25 minutes or until the rice is fluffy and tender and the water is fully absorbed. Set aside, still covered.

3. Heat the remaining 2½ tablespoons (37 ml) of *ghee* or oil in a small saucepan over moderately low heat until it is hot. Drop in the cashew nuts and stir-fry until golden brown. Remove with a slotted spoon and pour them over the cooked rice. Cover the rice again.

4. Raise the heat under the saucepan slightly, toss in the *urad dal* and the mustard seeds and fry until the mustard seeds turn gray and sputter and the *dal* turns reddish-brown.

5. Pour the fried spices into the cooked rice and sprinkle with the turmeric, lemon or lime juice and parsley or coriander. Gently fold until well mixed.

6. Remove from the heat and garnish each serving with a sprinkle of coconut.

Rice with Ginger-Seasoned Yogurt
DAHI BHAT

This dish is centuries old and is mentioned in the ancient Vedic texts. It is nutritious and easy to digest. It is served at room temperature or slightly chilled and is a good selection on a light summer luncheon menu with any vegetable or salad. It is also good on a dinner menu, because the rice can be cooked and cooled or chilled beforehand and finally assembled at the last moment. Try it with *Zucchini Boats Stuffed with Herbed Buckwheat Pilaf, Fresh Coriander Chutney* and *Spinach Pakora with Ajwain Seeds* for a special evening meal or dinner.

Preparation time (after assembling ingredients): 5 minutes
Cooking time: 25–35 minutes
Serves: 4

1 cup (95 g) *basmati* or other long-grain white rice
1⅔–2 cups (400–480 ml) water
2 tablespoons (30 ml) butter or *ghee*
1 teaspoon (5 ml) salt
1¼ cups (300 ml) plain yogurt, buttermilk or sour cream,
    at room temperature or chilled
¼ teaspoon (1 ml) ground ginger or 1 teaspoon (5 ml) scraped,
    finely shredded or minced fresh ginger root

1. If *basmati* rice is used, clean, wash, soak and drain as explained on page 6.

2. Bring the water to a boil in a 1½-quart/liter nonstick saucepan. Add the rice, stir, reduce the heat to very low and cover with a tight-fitting lid. Simmer gently without stirring for 20–25 minutes or until the rice is soft and fluffy and the water is fully absorbed. Remove from the heat and let the rice sit, covered, for 5 minutes to allow the fragile grains to firm up.

3. Spoon the cooked rice into a flat dish. Add the butter or *ghee* and the salt. Mix gently.

4. When the rice has cooled to room temperature or been chilled, and you are ready to serve it, gently fold in the yogurt, buttermilk or sour cream and ginger.

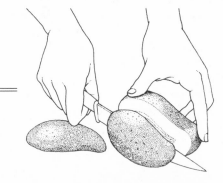

Chilled Yogurt Rice with Shredded Mango
DADHYODHANA

This moist, pleasantly seasoned rice and yogurt dish in the South Indian tradition takes only a short time to prepare. Whenever rice is combined with yogurt, the result is refreshing, nutritious and easy to digest. The combination may be served either chilled or at room temperature, so it fits into many different menus. This particular rice dish is a welcome favorite, especially in the summer season, when a light rice is preferred. For a luncheon, try it with *Sprouted Mung Bean Salad with Water Chestnuts and Toasted Almonds* and chilled grape juice. For a formal dinner menu, try it with *Toovar Dal with Chopped Spinach, Green Beans with Coconut* and *Deep-Fried Shredded Plantain Clusters* and garnish with *Fresh Mint Chutney*. For dessert, serve *Dainty Chenna Cheesecakes with Almond Frosting*.

For information about unfamiliar ingredients or techniques, see A-to-Z

Preparation time (after assembling ingredients): 5 minutes
Cooking time: 20–30 minutes
Serves: 5 or 6

1 cup (95 g) *basmati* or other long-grain white rice
1⅔–2 cups (400–480 ml) water
1½ cups (360 ml) plain yogurt or mixture of sour cream and yogurt
1 teaspoon (5 ml) salt
1¼ teaspoons (6 ml) ground ginger
¼ teaspoon (1 ml) freshly ground black pepper
⅔ cup (160 ml) peeled, shredded green raw mango, firm but underripe
   (cucumber or carrot can be substituted for the mango)
1½ tablespoons (22 ml) *ghee* or sesame oil
½ tablespoon (7 ml) split *urad dal*, if available
1 teaspoon (5 ml) black mustard seeds
6–8 curry leaves, preferably fresh
a few sprigs of fresh parsley or coriander for garnishing

1. If *basmati* rice is used, clean, wash, soak and drain as explained on page 6.

2. Bring the water to a boil in a heavy 1½-quart/liter nonstick saucepan. Stir in the rice and reduce the heat to very low. Cover and gently simmer without stirring for 20–25 minutes or until the rice is tender and fluffy and all of the water is absorbed. Remove from the heat and let the rice sit, covered, for 5 minutes to allow the fragile grains to firm up.

3. Spoon the cooked rice into a flat dish. Let cool to room temperature. Gently fold in the yogurt, salt, ginger, pepper and mango until evenly mixed.

4. Heat the *ghee* or oil in a small saucepan over moderate heat until it is hot but not smoking. Toss in the *urad dal* and mustard seeds. Fry until the *dal* is richly browned and the mustard seeds turn gray and sputter and pop. For the last 3–5 seconds of frying the spices, toss in the curry leaves. Pour the fried spices into the rice and mix gently. Chill if desired.

5. Garnish each serving with parsley or coriander.

Herbed Rice with Julienne Potatoes
ALOO PULAU

Rice and potatoes? A unique and surprisingly delicious pilaf. In this recipe, julienned strips of potatoes are marinated in yogurt and grated coconut and sautéed with seasonings until they are richly browned. Next, rice and peas are added, then cooked with the potatoes to make a delicious dish of richly varied textures and colors—a dish especially suitable for entertaining. For an every-day lunch or dinner, serve it with a steamed green vegetable. For entertaining, combine it with *Okra Supreme, Butter-Soft Zucchini and Tomatoes, Shallow-Fried Batter-Coated Chenna Cheese Patties, Currant and Date Chutney* and *Deep-Fried Sesame Whole Wheat Bread*. Top it off with *Pistachio Milk Fudge*.

Preparation time (after assembling ingredients): 10 minutes
Cooking time: 35–45 minutes
Serves: 5 or 6

1 cup (95 g) *basmati* or other long-grain white rice
2 medium-sized all-purpose potatoes, peeled
½ tablespoon (7 ml) scraped and finely shredded or minced fresh ginger root
2 teaspoons (10 ml) minced seeded hot green chilies (or as desired)
¼ cup (25 g) fresh or dried grated coconut, lightly packed
2 tablespoons (30 ml) minced fresh parsley or coarsely chopped coriander
3 tablespoons (45 ml) plain yogurt
3 tablespoons (45 ml) *ghee* or peanut oil
6 whole cloves
1½-inch (4 cm) piece of cinnamon stick
1 small cassia or bay leaf
1½ teaspoons (7 ml) cumin seeds
½ cup (120 ml) shelled fresh peas or frozen peas, defrosted
1 teaspoon (5 ml) salt
¾ teaspoon (3.5 ml) turmeric
1 teaspoon (5 ml) fresh lemon or lime juice
2–2¼ cups (480–530 ml) water
1 teaspoon (5 ml) raw sugar
1 tablespoon (15 ml) butter or *ghee*
5 or 6 lemon or lime wedges or twists for garnishing

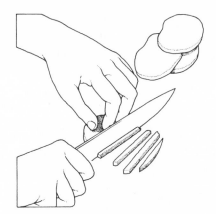

1. If *basmati* rice is used, clean, wash, soak and drain as explained on page 6.

2. Wash the peeled potatoes and cut them evenly into julienne strips, 1½ inches (4 cm) long and ⅓ inch (1 cm) wide and thick.

3. Combine the ginger root and green chilies, coconut, parsley or coriander and yogurt in a bowl. Mix well. Drop in the potato strips. Stir and allow them to marinate while you prepare the seasoning.

4. Heat the *ghee* or oil in a heavy 2-quart/liter nonstick saucepan over moderately high heat. Drop in the whole cloves, cinnamon stick, cassia or bay leaf and cumin seeds. Fry until the cumin seeds brown. Add the marinated potatoes and stir-fry until they are lightly browned.

5. Add the rice, fresh peas, salt, turmeric, lemon or lime juice, water and sugar. Stir and quickly bring to a full boil. (If using defrosted frozen peas, add them to the rice about 5 minutes before the end of cooking.)

6. Reduce the heat to very low and cover with a tight-fitting lid. Simmer gently without stirring for 20–25 minutes or until the rice is tender and fluffy and all of the liquid is absorbed.

7. Remove the lid, turn off the heat and add 1 tablespoon (15 ml) of butter or *ghee*. Cover and let the rice sit for 5 minutes to allow the fragile grains to firm up. Fluff and serve piping hot, each portion garnished with a wedge or twist of lemon or lime.

Cashew Rice with Diced Potatoes

KAJU ALOO PULAU

In Vedic cuisine, rice can be combined with any vegetable, seasoning, nut or dried fruit. Here, it joins forces with the potato. This may seem like a lot of starch for one dish, but the starch content of potatoes and rice is about the same, so whether you have a portion of plain rice or a portion of rice with potatoes, you have the same amount of starch. For this delightful combination, you first make a *garam masala* featuring coconut. Then you quickly fry the seasonings, nuts and potato cubes and simmer them with the rice. This is one of the tastiest ways to serve rice, primarily because of the custom-made *garam masala*. Try it with a green salad, *Mung Dal Soup with Tomatoes* and *Griddle-Baked Village-Style Corn Bread* for a special family lunch or dinner.

Preparation time (after assembling ingredients): 15 minutes
Cooking time: 35–40 minutes
Serves: 4 or 5

For the Garam Masala:

5 black peppercorns
6 whole cloves
2-inch (5 cm) piece of cinnamon stick
½ tablespoon (7 ml) coriander seeds
1 teaspoon (5 ml) cumin seeds
1 tablespoon (15 ml) sesame seeds
2 tablespoons (30 ml) fresh or dried shredded coconut

For the Rice:

1 cup (95 g) *basmati* or other long-grain white rice
3 tablespoons (45 ml) *ghee* or vegetable oil
½ cup (75 g) raw cashew halves or bits
1 teaspoon (5 ml) fresh scraped and finely shredded or minced ginger root
1–2 teaspoons (5–10 ml) minced seeded hot green chilies
½ teaspoon (2 ml) cumin seeds
½ teaspoon (2 ml) black mustard seeds
8–10 curry leaves, preferably fresh
1 large boiling potato, peeled and cut into ½-inch (1.5 cm) cubes
½ teaspoon (2 ml) turmeric
1 teaspoon (5 ml) salt
2–2½ cups (480–600 ml) water
1 tablespoon (15 ml) butter or *ghee*
3 tablespoons (45 ml) fresh or dried shredded coconut for garnishing
2 tablespoons (30 ml) minced fresh parsley or coarsely chopped coriander for garnishing

To Make the Garam Masala:

   1. Combine the peppercorns, whole cloves, cinnamon stick, coriander seeds and cumin seeds in a small heavy iron frying pan. Place over low heat and, stirring occasionally, roast for 4–5 minutes or until the cumin seeds darken one or two shades.
   2. Remove from the heat. Remove the cinnamon stick and reduce it to coarse bits in a mortar or with a kitchen mallet or rolling pin.

3. Place all the ingredients, including the cinnamon, sesame seeds and coconut, in a small electric coffee mill or stone mortar and reduce them to a powder. Transfer to a small cup and set aside.

To Cook the Potato Rice:

1. If *basmati* rice is used, clean, wash, soak and drain as explained on page 6.

2. Heat the *ghee* or vegetable oil in a heavy 2-quart/liter nonstick saucepan over moderately low heat until it is hot but not smoking. Fry the cashew nuts until golden brown, remove with a slotted spoon and set aside.

3. Raise the heat to moderately high and add the ginger root, green chilies, cumin seeds and black mustard seeds. Fry until the mustard seeds turn gray and sputter and pop. Drop in the curry leaves and fry for just a few seconds. Immediately add the potato and stir-fry for 5–7 minutes or until the potato is golden brown.

4. Add the rice, turmeric and salt. Fry for 1–2 minutes. Add the water, *garam masala* and cashews. Raise the heat to high and quickly bring to a full boil.

5. Reduce the heat to very low, cover with a tight-fitting lid and gently simmer without stirring for 20–25 minutes or until the rice is tender and fluffy and all of the liquid is absorbed.

6. Remove from the heat and let the rice sit, covered, for 5 minutes to allow the fragile grains to firm up. Pour in 1 tablespoon (15 ml) of butter or *ghee*, fluff with a fork and serve piping hot, each serving garnished with coconut and parsley or coriander.

Toasted Coconut Rice
NARIYAL-KI CHAVAL

If you have a piece of fresh coconut in your refrigerator, try this recipe. It is quick, easy and delightful. The rice is cooked with whole sweet spices, and golden-fried coconut strips are folded in along with the *chaunk* (spices cooked in *ghee* or coconut oil), which adds to the flavor. Finally, the dish is garnished with more coconut strips. This is a most attractive rice dish, with a slightly crunchy texture and faintly sweet, toasty flavor. It can be served on any menu in any season. Try it with *Spiced Eggplant in Smooth Yogurt, Sliced White Radish with Golden Pumpkin* and *Three-Dal Delight* for a special family meal.

Preparation time (after assembling ingredients): 5 minutes
Cooking time: 25–30 minutes
Serves: 4 or 5

1 cup (95 g) *basmati* or other long-grain white rice
1⅔–2 cups (400–480 ml) water
¾ teaspoon (3.5 ml) salt
1½-inch (4 cm) piece of cinnamon stick
6 whole cloves
3 tablespoons (45 ml) *ghee* or coconut oil

For information about unfamiliar ingredients or techniques, see A-to-Z

¼ fresh coconut, peeled and cut into slices ⅛ inch (3 mm) thick
     and ½ inch (1.5 cm) long
1 teaspoon (5 ml) cumin seeds
½ teaspoon (2 ml) black mustard seeds

1. If *basmati* rice is used, clean, wash, soak and drain as explained on page 6.

2. Bring the water to a boil in a heavy 1½-quart/liter nonstick saucepan over high heat. Stir in the rice, salt, cinnamon stick and cloves. When the boiling resumes, reduce the heat to very low, cover with a tight-fitting lid and gently simmer without stirring for 20–25 minutes or until the rice is tender and fluffy and the water is absorbed.

3. Remove from the heat and let the rice sit, covered, for 5 minutes to allow the fragile grains to firm up. In the meantime, heat the *ghee* or oil in a small frying pan over moderate heat. Stir-fry the coconut strips until golden brown. Remove with a slotted spoon. Toss in the cumin seeds and black mustard seeds and fry until the mustard seeds turn gray and sputter and pop. Pour this seasoning into the rice, add two-thirds of the fried coconut, gently mix and remove the whole cloves and cinnamon stick.

4. Spoon the rice onto a serving platter and garnish with the remaining fried coconut.

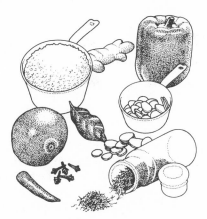

Savory Saffron Pilaf
KESAR PULAU

Saffron—the dried stigmas of the saffron crocus—has been widely used in Vedic cooking for more than fifty centuries, despite being the world's most costly seasoning. It is very potent: a good-sized pinch of high-quality saffron threads, with their brilliant orange hue and strong aroma, will flavor a whole dish. Poor-quality saffron, however (usually yellow, bleached or streaked with white), will add little flavor or color. When the stigmas are placed in hot water, they expand and release their color. Avoid inexpensive powdered saffron, as it is generally adulterated. In this savory rice dish, high-quality saffron transforms commonplace ingredients such as bell pepper and tomato into superior culinary components. First, the vegetables are sautéed in a lively combination of seasonings and spices. Then the rice is added; the mixture is fried briefly and finally cooked in fragrant saffron water. The saffron gives this rice dish extra warmth, making it perfect for those cold winter days. For a moist rice, use 2 cups (480 ml) of water; for a drier rice, use 1¾ cups (420 ml) of water. For a special dinner, try this rice with *Thin Karhi Sauce with Sprouted Mung Beans*, *Crunchy Chana Dal Patties with Coconut and Sesame Seeds*, *Pishima's Stuffed Okra* and *Fresh Mint and Green Mango Chutney*. For a simple luncheon menu, try it with a salad and whole wheat bread.

Preparation time (after assembling ingredients): 10 minutes
Cooking time: 30–40 minutes
Serves: 5 or 6

1 cup (95 g) *basmati* or other long-grain white rice
1¾–2 cups (420–480 ml) water
⅓ teaspoon (1.5 ml) high-quality saffron threads
3 tablespoons (45 ml) *ghee* or vegetable oil
¼ cup (35 g) raw cashew bits or ¼ cup (30 g) slivered or sliced raw almonds
1–2 teaspoons (5–10 ml) minced seeded hot green chilies (as desired)
1½ tablespoons (22 ml) scraped, finely shredded
    or minced fresh ginger root
6 whole cloves
1 teaspoon (5 ml) cumin seeds
½ teaspoon (2 ml) black mustard seeds
1 small cassia or bay leaf
½ cup (120 ml) cored, seeded and chopped green
    or red bell pepper
1 medium-sized firm ripe tomato, finely chopped
1 teaspoon (5 ml) salt
1 teaspoon (5 ml) raw sugar

1. If *basmati* rice is used, clean, wash, soak and drain as explained on page 6.

2. Bring the water to a boil in a small saucepan, remove from the heat, add the saffron and set aside for 10–15 minutes while preparing the rice.

3. Heat the *ghee* or oil in a heavy 2-quart/liter nonstick saucepan over moderate heat until it is hot but not smoking. Add the cashews or almonds and stir-fry until the nuts turn golden brown. Remove them with a slotted spoon and set aside. Drop in the chilies, ginger root, cloves, cumin seeds, black mustard seeds and cassia or bay leaf. Fry until the mustard seeds turn gray and sputter and pop.

4. Add the bell pepper and sauté for 4–5 minutes. Stir in the rice and fry for 1–2 minutes, stirring occasionally.

5. Add the saffron water, tomato, salt and sweetener. Quickly bring to a full boil. Immediately reduce the heat to very low, cover with a tight-fitting lid and gently simmer without stirring for 20–25 minutes or until the rice is tender and fluffy and all of the liquid is absorbed.

6. Remove from the heat and let the rice sit, covered, for 5 minutes to allow the fragile grains to firm up. Just before serving, remove the cover and fluff the piping-hot rice with a fork.

For information about unfamiliar ingredients or techniques, see A-to-Z

Sweet Saffron Rice with Currants and Pistachios
MEETHA KESARI BHAT

This relatively simple sweet rice is made regal by the color and flavor of saffron. The success of the dish depends on the delicate balance of flavors contributed by the rice, saffron and sweetener. *Jaggery*, light brown sugar, or maple sugar is the best sweetener for this dish. If you use maple syrup or honey, omit 2 tablespoons (30 ml) of water. *Basmati* rice is highly recommended. Serve this dish with *Golden Mung Dal Soup, Eggplant and Bell Pepper Stew with Fried Panir Cheese* and *Deep-Fried Potato Wheat Bread* for a special family dinner.

Preparation time (after assembling ingredients): 5 minutes
Cooking time: 25–30 minutes
Serves: 4 or 5

1 cup (95 g) *basmati* or other long-grain white rice
1¾–2 cups (420–480 ml) water
⅓ teaspoon (1.5 ml) high-quality saffron threads
1½-inch (4 cm) piece of cinnamon stick
6 whole cloves
¼ teaspoon (1 ml) salt
½ cup (75 g) crumbled *jaggery*, maple sugar or equivalent raw sugar, lightly packed
1 teaspoon (5 ml) cardamom seeds, coarsely crushed
2 tablespoons (30 ml) *ghee* or vegetable oil
3 tablespoons (45 ml) slivered or sliced raw pistachios or almonds
3 tablespoons (45 ml) raisins or currants
2 tablespoons (30 ml) blanched raw pistachios, sliced into thin curls for garnishing

1. If *basmati* rice is used, clean, wash, soak and drain as explained on page 6.
2. Bring the water to a boil in a heavy 1½-quart/liter nonstick saucepan. Place the saffron threads in a small bowl and add 2½ tablespoons (37 ml) of the boiling water. Allow the threads to soak for 10–15 minutes while cooking the rice.
3. Stir the rice into the boiling water and add the cinnamon stick, cloves and salt. When the water resumes boiling, reduce the heat to very low, cover with a tight-fitting lid and gently simmer without stirring for 20–25 minutes or until the rice is tender and fluffy and all of the water is absorbed. Remove from the heat and let the rice sit, covered, for 5 minutes to allow the fragile grains to firm up.
4. In the meantime, combine the saffron water, sweetener and cardamom seeds in a small saucepan. Place over moderate heat and stir until the sweetener is dissolved. Lower the heat slightly and simmer for about 1 minute. Pour the syrup into the rice and quickly re-cover.
5. Heat the *ghee* or oil in a small pan over moderately low heat until it is hot but not smoking. Fry the nuts and raisins until the nuts turn golden brown and the raisins swell. Pour the nuts, raisins and *ghee* or oil into the piping-hot rice and gently fluff with a fork to mix. Spoon onto a serving platter and sprinkle with the sliced pistachio nuts.

Rice with Crunchy Fried *Badis* and Green Beans
BADI BARBATTI PULAU

It is hard to translate the word *badi*, as there is no counterpart to the *badi* or ground *dal* cake in American or Continental cuisine. Selected legumes (*dals*) are soaked, drained and ground into either mild or highly seasoned paste. This is dropped on the drying trays in small mounds ½ inch–1½ inches (1.5–4 cm) in diameter and dehydrated into brittle cakes that can then be stored in airtight containers for up to 8 months if refrigerated. At a moment's notice *badis* can be fried into reddish-brown, crunchy and ever-so-tasty ingredients for rice dishes, vegetable dishes, soups and liquid *dals*. Ready-made *badis* are available from well-stocked Indian grocery stores, but if you have some warm sunshiny weather or a food dehydrator and a little time, you can make them at home. In this dish, the finely chopped green beans and small dried *dal*-cake bits add a delightful texture to the savory rice pilaf. For a light lunch, serve with a cool yogurt salad such as *Chopped Spinach in Smooth Yogurt* or *Tomatoes in Smooth Yogurt*, with chilled sparkling grape or apple juice.

Preparation time (after assembling ingredients): 10 minutes
Cooking time: 25–35 minutes
Serves: 5 or 6

1 cup (95 g) *basmati* or other long-grain white rice
3 tablespoons (45 ml) *ghee* or vegetable oil
½ cup (45 g) *moong dal badis*, broken into pea-sized bits
1¼ teaspoons (6 ml) cumin seeds
½ teaspoon (2 ml) black mustard seeds
6 ounces (170 g) (about 1 cup/240 ml) fresh green beans,
    trimmed and cut into ¼-inch (6 mm) pieces
1¾–2¼ cups (420–530 ml) water
¾–1 teaspoon (3–5 ml) salt
½ teaspoon (2 ml) turmeric
2 tablespoons (30 ml) minced fresh parsley or coarsely chopped coriander

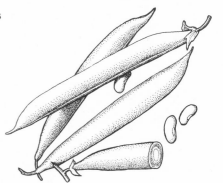

1. If *basmati* rice is used, clean, wash, soak and drain as explained on page 6.
2. Heat the *ghee* or oil in a heavy 1½-quart/liter nonstick saucepan over moderate heat until it is hot but not smoking. Drop in the *dal badi* bits. Stir-fry for 30–45 seconds or until they are nut-brown. Remove with a slotted spoon and set aside.
3. Add the cumin and black mustard seeds and fry until the mustard seeds turn gray and sputter and pop. Stir in the green beans and rice and sauté for 3–4 minutes, partially cooking the beans and fully coating the rice.
4. Add the fried *dal* bits and the remaining ingredients. Rapidly bring the liquid to a full boil. Reduce the heat to very low, cover with a tight-fitting lid and gently simmer without stirring for 20–25 minutes or until the rice is tender and fluffy and the water is completely absorbed. Remove from the heat and let the rice sit, covered, for 5 minutes to allow the fragile grains to firm up. Fluff with a fork and serve piping-hot.

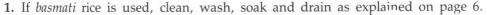

Rice with *Panir* Cheese and Bell Peppers
PANIR SIMLA MIRCH PULAU

Fried cubes of fresh homemade cheese add succulent, moist chunks of flavor and nutrition in the form of protein and calcium to this simple pilaf. The bell peppers and tomatoes add nuances of taste, texture and color, along with their own nutritional value. The result is a remarkably wholesome and elegant Sunday lunch rice dish that goes well with a cool yogurt salad such as *Seasoned Potatoes in Smooth Yogurt* and *Griddle-Baked Sourdough Bread* or *Deep-Fried Buttermilk Whole Wheat Bread*.

Preparation time (after assembling ingredients): 15 minutes
Cooking time: 35–40 minutes for white rice, 45–50 minutes for brown rice
Serves: 5 or 6

1 cup (95 g) Calmati or other brown *basmati* or long-grain white rice
2 medium-sized firm ripe tomatoes, quartered
2 teaspoons (10 ml) scraped, finely shredded or minced fresh ginger root
1½ teaspoons (7 ml) minced seeded hot green chilies (or as desired)
1–2 small cassia or bay leaves
6 black peppercorns
1½ cups (360 ml) water
2 tablespoons (30 ml) *ghee* or vegetable oil
fresh *panir* cheese (page 313) made from 4 cups (1 liter) milk,
    diced into ⅓-inch (1 cm) pieces (about 4 ounces/115 g)
1½ teaspoons (7 ml) cumin seeds
1 cup (240 ml) cored, seeded and chopped green or red bell peppers
½ teaspoon (2 ml) turmeric
½ teaspoon (2 ml) *garam masala*
1 teaspoon (5 ml) salt
2 tablespoons (30 ml) minced fresh parsley or coarsely chopped coriander

1. If *basmati* rice is used, clean, wash, soak and drain as explained on page 6.
2. Combine the tomatoes, ginger root, green chilies, cassia or bay leaves, peppercorns and water in a 1-quart/liter saucepan. Bring to a boil over high heat. Reduce the heat to moderately low, partially cover and gently boil for 10 minutes. Remove from the heat and force the liquid from the tomatoes and spices through a metal sieve into a bowl. Add enough water to make 1⅔–2 cups (400–480 ml) of tomato stock.
3. Put the *ghee* or oil in a 2-quart/liter nonstick saucepan over moderate to moderately high heat. When it is hot, add the *panir* cheese cubes and gently stir-fry until they are evenly browned on all sides. Remove the cubes with a slotted spoon and set them aside.
4. Drop the cumin seeds in and fry until richly browned. Stir in the bell pepper and sauté for 3–4 minutes.
5. Stir in the rice and fry for 2–3 minutes. Add all of the remaining ingredients, including the tomato stock, raise the heat to high and quickly bring the liquid to a full boil.
6. Reduce the heat to very low, cover and gently simmer, without stirring, for 30–40 minutes for brown rice or 20–25 minutes for white rice, or until the rice is tender and fluffy and all of the liquid has been absorbed. Remove from the heat and let the rice sit, covered, for 5 minutes to allow the fragile grains to firm up. Just before serving, remove the cover and fluff the piping-hot rice with a fork.

Herbed Rice with *Panir* Cheese and Zucchini
PANIR LOUKI PULAU

Panir cheese, which has no counterpart in Western cuisine, is made by adding a curdling agent to boiling milk and collecting and draining the resulting curds. In this recipe, the cheese is cut into cubes and fried in *ghee* or vegetable oil. *Panir* cheese is a surprisingly healthy food. A half cup (120 ml) provides twenty-five percent of the protein that an average adult needs in one day. In this easy-to-make pilaf, savory rice is embellished with cubes of juicy *panir* cheese and succulent pieces of zucchini and tomato. Try it with a chilled salad, such as *Creamy Potato Salad Surprise*, *Minted Cucumbers and Strawberries* or *White Radish Pickle*, and a cool beverage.

Preparation time (after assembling ingredients): 10 minutes
Cooking time: 35–40 minutes for white rice, 45–50 minutes for brown rice
Serves: 5 or 6

1 cup (95 g) Calmati or other brown *basmati* or long-grain white rice
3 tablespoons (45 ml) *ghee* or peanut oil
1½ teaspoons (7 ml) minced seeded hot green chilies (or as desired)
1½ teaspoons (7 ml) scraped, finely shredded or minced fresh ginger root
1¼ teaspoons (6 ml) cumin seeds
½ teaspoon (2 ml) black mustard seeds
1 large black or 2 large green cardamom pods, slightly crushed
8–10 curry leaves, preferably fresh
fresh *panir* cheese (page 313) from 4 cups (1 liter) milk,
    cut into ½-inch (1.5 cm) cubes (about 4 ounces / 115 g)
1 cup (240 ml) zucchini or other summer squash, cut into ½-inch (1.5 cm) cubes
1 teaspoon (5 ml) turmeric
1 teaspoon (5 ml) salt
1⅔–2 cups (400–480 ml) water
3 tablespoons (45 ml) chopped fresh herbs (coriander, parsley, basil,
    oregano and marjoram leaves) or 1 tablespoon (15 ml) mixed dried herbs
1 medium-sized firm ripe tomato, cut into 8–10 pieces

1. If *basmati* rice is used, clean, wash, soak and drain as explained on page 6.
2. Heat the *ghee* or oil in a 2-quart/liter heavy nonstick saucepan over moderate heat until it is hot but not smoking. Add the green chilies, ginger root, cumin seeds, mustard seeds and cardamom pod or pods. Fry until the mustard seeds turn gray and sputter and pop. Drop in the curry leaves and fry for a few seconds, then add the *panir* cheese cubes. Fry the cubes for 5–7 minutes, gently but continuously turning them with a spoon until evenly browned on all sides. Add the squash and stir-fry for 1–2 minutes.
3. Add the rice, turmeric, salt, water, mixed herbs and tomato pieces. Raise the heat to high and quickly bring to a boil. Reduce the heat to very low, cover with a tight-fitting lid and gently simmer without stirring for 30–40 minutes for brown rice or 20–25 minutes for white rice, or until the rice is tender and fluffy and all of the water is absorbed.
4. Remove from the heat and let the rice sit, covered, for 5 minutes to allow the fragile grains to firm up. Just before serving, remove the cover and fluff the piping-hot rice with a fork.

Cracked Black Pepper Rice

MOLA HORA

This zesty side dish is particularly pleasing in a large, full-course meal with two or more varieties of rice. It is served at room temperature, sometimes chilled, but it always retains a pungent warmth from its substantial quantity of cracked black pepper. The rice is best cooked *al dente*, so that the grains are not soft but remain just firm to the bite. This dish is traditionally served with a cool yogurt salad such as *Tomatoes in Smooth Yogurt* or *Fried Okra in Smooth Yogurt*. If it is part of a dinner menu, you can accompany it with a creamy yogurt soup such as *Tender Chickpeas in Golden Karhi Sauce*. Seasonal steamed vegetables—three or four varieties served with *Mint-Lime Butter*—would form the basis of an appealing meal.

Preparation time (after assembling ingredients): 5 minutes
Cooking time: 15 minutes
Serves: 5 or 6

1 cup (95 g) *basmati* or other long-grain white rice
8 cups (2 liters) water
1 tablespoon (15 ml) fresh lemon or lime juice
3 tablespoons (45 ml) butter or *ghee*
1 small cassia or bay leaf
½–1 teaspoon (2–5 ml) salt
1–1½ teaspoons (5–7 ml) cracked black pepper
5 or 6 lemon or lime wedges or twists for garnishing

1. If *basmati* rice is used, clean, wash, soak and drain as explained on page 6.
2. Bring the water, lemon or lime juice, ½ teaspoon (2 ml) of the butter or *ghee* and the cassia or bay leaf to a full boil in a large pan or stockpot over high heat. Stirring constantly, pour in the rice in a slow stream. Cook uncovered in briskly boiling water for 12–15 minutes or until the rice is just tender and fluffy.
3. Pour the rice into a strainer or colander and drain. Let cool for 1–2 minutes, pick out the cassia or bay leaf and spoon the rice onto a serving platter. Stir in the remaining butter or *ghee*, salt and black pepper. Toss gently to mix.
4. Chill or let cool to room temperature. Garnish with citrus wedges or twists.

Royal Rice

PUSHPANNA

In the heart of Central London, near the British Museum, there is a stately four-story building that in 1969 became the first temple of the International Society for Krishna Consciousness (ISKCON) in England. At the official opening ceremonies, Srila Prabhupada introduced this particular version of *pushpanna*. At this important event, covered by the BBC and other media and attended by thousands of guests, the temple kitchen distributed hundreds of servings of this delicacy.

Pushpanna is the consummate rice pilaf of Bengali cuisine, and although time-consuming, it is not difficult to prepare. Though the balance of flavors may vary, top-quality ingredients are a must: the best saffron, nuts and *basmati* rice give this dish its characteristic richness and elegance. The resulting dish has an aristocratic appearance and flavor, making it especially appropriate for weddings, special holiday feasts or important dinners. For a festive menu, try this pilaf with *Cauliflower Kofta* and *Seasoned Tomato Gravy*. Add a bowl of *Mellow Karhi with Spicy Paparh Noodles*. For vegetables try *Char-Flavored Eggplant and Green Peas*, *Bengali Spinach* and *Fried Bitter Melon with Ground Almonds*. Accompany with a yogurt dish such as *Shredded Cucumbers in Smooth Mint-Flavored Yogurt* or *Sliced Bananas in Smooth Tart Cream*. Piping-hot *pooris* or *pakoras* can be added as a fried item. Dessert could be simple fresh fruit and *Lemon-Lime Cheese Fudge* or *Heart-Shaped Cheesecakes with Saffron Frosting*.

Preparation time (after assembling ingredients): 30 minutes
Cooking time: 30 minutes
Serves: 8 to 10

1¼ cups (105 g) *basmati* or other long-grain white rice
freshly made *chenna* cheese (page 315) made from 6 cups (1.5 liters) milk (about 7½ ounces/215 g)
1 tablespoon (15 ml) all-purpose flour
¼ cup (30 g) slivered or sliced raw almonds
¼ cup (35 g) raw cashew bits or halves
2 tablespoons (30 ml) blanched raw pistachio nuts, split in half
¼ cup (25 g) dried coconut cut into ribbons
3 tablespoons (45 ml) raisins or currants
3 tablespoons (45 ml) melted butter or *ghee*
1 teaspoon (5 ml) turmeric
1½ tablespoons (22 ml) milk
¼ teaspoon (1 ml) high-quality saffron threads
ghee or vegetable oil for shallow-frying
6 whole cloves
2-inch (5 cm) piece of cinnamon stick
2 large black or 4 large green cardamom pods
1 whole dried red chili (or as desired)
1½ teaspoons (7 ml) cumin seeds
1 teaspoon (5 ml) coriander seeds
¼ teaspoon (1 ml) *kalonji*, if available
½ teaspoon (2 ml) yellow asafetida powder (*hing*)*
3 tablespoons (45 ml) sugar or equivalent sweetener
2 teaspoons (10 ml) salt
2¾–3 cups (650–710 ml) water
two 4-inch (10 cm) pieces of edible gold or silver foil for garnishing, if available

This amount applies only to yellow Cobra brand. Reduce any other asafetida by three-fourths.

1. If *basmati* rice is used, clean, wash, soak and drain as explained on page 6.
2. Place the warm *chenna* cheese on a countertop, break it apart and press it with absorbent towels to extract any excess moisture. Knead with your palms until the cheese is creamy and smooth. Knead in the flour. With the help of a spatula, scrape all of the smooth cheese into one round mass. Wash and dry your hands and the countertop.

Place a dry plate nearby. Rub a film of oil on your hands. Divide the cheese into 5 equal portions and then roll 10 smooth round pellets per portion, making a total of 50 cheese balls. Set aside on the plate.

3. Place the almonds, cashews, pistachios, coconut and raisins or currants in individual mounds on another plate and set aside.

4. Transfer the drained rice to a bowl. Add 1 tablespoon (15 ml) of the melted butter or *ghee* and the turmeric to the rice. Mix with your fingertips until all of the rice grains are coated with turmeric and *ghee*. Set aside.

5. Heat the milk in a serving spoon, transfer it to a small cup and soak the saffron threads in the hot milk until you cook the rice.

6. In the meantime, heat *ghee* or vegetable oil to a depth of 2 inches (5 cm) in a deep frying pan over moderately low heat. When the oil reaches about 325°F (160°C), fry one by one the mounds of nuts and coconut until each batch turns a nice golden brown. Fry the raisins until they turn plump and a few shades lighter. Remove each batch with a slotted spoon and place all of the ingredients in a medium-sized bowl. Raise the heat to moderate. Divide the cheese pellets into two batches and gently slip them into the hot *ghee* or oil, cooking one batch at a time. Let them cook for ½ minute, then constantly move the cheese balls with a chopstick until they rise to the surface. Continue frying, but now use a slotted spoon, and fry until they are a rich golden brown on all sides. Remove with the slotted spoon and set aside in a bowl.

7. Remove the *ghee* or oil from the heat, put 4 tablespoons (60 ml) of it in a heavy 3-quart/liter nonstick saucepan and set over moderate heat until it is hot but not smoking. Drop in the cloves, cinnamon stick, cardamom pods, chili, cumin seeds, coriander seeds and *kalonji*. Fry until the cumin seeds turn brown. Stir in the asafetida powder and then quickly add the turmeric-coated rice, sweetener and salt. Stir-fry for 2–3 minutes. Add the water, raise the heat to high and quickly bring to a boil.

8. Pour in the fried nuts, raisins, and coconut and the saffron milk and stir to mix. Reduce the heat to very low, cover with a tight-fitting lid and gently simmer without stirring for 20–25 minutes or until the rice is tender and fluffy and all of the water has been absorbed.

9. Remove from the heat and let the rice sit, covered, for 5 minutes to allow the fragile grains to firm up. Add the remaining 2 tablespoons (30 ml) of melted butter or *ghee* and the fried *chenna* cheese balls. Gently fluff the rice with a fork to mix all of the ingredients.

10. The rice should be served on a warmed serving platter or on individual plates and, if desired, the top can be garnished regally with sheets of special edible gold or silver foil.

Spinach Rice with *Panir* Cheese
PALAK PANIR PULAU

This is a nutritious, elegant pilaf with a delicious flavor. The rice is fried with spices, a sweetener and tomatoes. It is then cooked with chopped fresh spinach and, when it is done, golden fried nuts and *panir* cheese cubes are folded in. Add a sprinkle of lemon juice and listen to the exclamations of delight when you serve this richly satisfying dish. If fresh spinach is not available, you can use frozen chopped spinach. For a special brunch or luncheon, try this rice with *Mung Dal Balls in Herbed Yogurt* and *Jicama Salad with Snow Peas, Avocado and Watercress*.

Preparation time (after assembling ingredients): 10 minutes
Cooking time: 30–40 minutes
Serves: 5 or 6

1 cup (95 g) *basmati* or other long-grain white rice
3 tablespoons (45 ml) *ghee* or vegetable oil
⅓ cup (45 g) raw cashew bits or halves
fresh *panir* cheese (page 313) made from 4 cups (1 liter) milk,
    cut into ⅓-inch (1 cm) cubes (4 ounces/115 g)
1½ teaspoons (7 ml) cumin seeds
1 teaspoon (5 ml) black mustard seeds
2 tablespoons (30 ml) sugar or equivalent sweetener
2 medium-sized firm ripe tomatoes, diced
¾ teaspoon (3.5 cm) turmeric
2 teaspoons (10 ml) ground coriander
¼ teaspoon (1 ml) ground nutmeg
¼ teaspoon (1 ml) cayenne pepper or paprika (or as desired)
1¾–2 cups (420–480 ml) water
1 teaspoon (5 ml) salt
8 ounces (230 g) fresh spinach, washed, trimmed, patted dry
    and coarsely chopped, or ½ of a 10-ounce (285 g) package of frozen
    chopped spinach, thawed at room temperature.
1½ teaspoons (7 ml) lemon juice
5 or 6 lemon or lime wedges or twists for garnishing

1. If *basmati* rice is used, clean, wash, soak and drain as explained on page 6.

2. Heat the *ghee* or oil in a 2–3-quart/liter heavy nonstick saucepan over moderately low heat until hot. Drop in the cashews and stir-fry until golden brown. Remove with a slotted spoon and drain. Raise the heat to moderate and add the *panir* cheese cubes. Fry, gently turning the cubes, for 5–8 minutes or until golden brown on all sides. Remove with a slotted spoon and drain.

3. Add the cumin seeds, black mustard seeds and sweetener. Fry until the sweetener caramelizes and turns a rich reddish-brown. Immediately add the tomatoes to stop the fried seasonings from burning. Follow with the turmeric, coriander, nutmeg, cayenne or paprika and rice. Stir-fry for 2–3 minutes.

4. Pour in the water and salt. Quickly bring to a full boil. Stir in the fresh spinach. Reduce the heat to very low, cover with a tight-fitting lid and gently cook without stirring for 20–25 minutes or until all of the water is absorbed and the rice is tender and fluffy. If you are using defrosted frozen chopped spinach, press it between your palms to remove excess water and add it after the rice has cooked for 10–15 minutes.

5. Remove from the heat and let the rice sit, covered, for 5 minutes to allow the fragile grains to firm up. Gently fold in the fried nuts, *panir* cheese cubes and lemon juice. Garnish each serving with a wedge or twist of lemon or lime.

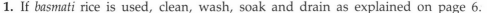

For information about unfamiliar ingredients or techniques, see A-to-Z

Dals

For centuries, dried peas and beans—now recognized as protein-rich staple foods—have been a part of the Vedic culinary tradition. In India, the generic name for all members of the dried pea and bean family, and the dishes made from them, is *dal*. The repertoire of *dal* dishes is so vast that you can make a different one every day, without repetition, for months. *Dals* can be made into liquid soups, thick purées, sauces, stews, fried savories, moist raw chutneys, crispy pancakes, sprouted salads and sweets. The thoughtful cook can select a *dal* dish to suit any meal, from breakfast to late dinner. You can also vary your *dal* dishes according to season: warm and hearty in winter, light and refreshing in summer. The *dal* dish you choose for any meal should complement the flavors, appearances and textures of the other dishes.

Nutritionists say that all dried beans are rich in iron, vitamin B and substantial amounts of incomplete proteins that yield their total nutritional value only when combined with other proteins. The Vedic tradition suggests that to obtain the maximum nutritional value from dried *dals* you should combine them with other protein-rich foods, such as grains, nuts, yogurt or milk. The harmonious blending of these simple ingredients will not only produce delicious meals but will also round out the full potential nourishment dormant in the *dal*. Although the world's agriculturists have produced numerous strains of dried beans, it was the Vedic vegetarians who cultivated the best ones—easily digested, highly nutritious and quickly prepared.

The fried seasoning called *chaunk* is especially important with *dals* because it stimulates the digestive processes and enhances the flavor, aroma and appearance of the dish. Fresh ginger root, long recognized as a digestive calmant, is invariably present. The *chaunk* is added sometimes at the beginning of cooking, sometimes at the end. The later it is added, the more it retains its own character. Its flavor depends on the ingredients and how long they are fried. How long the *chaunk* should brown and when it should be added depend largely on personal preference. Cooking the spices in *ghee* or oil until they are just lightly roasted produces a mild *chaunk*; slightly charring or blackening the spice seeds produces a pungent one.

There are two approaches to cooking *dal* in the Vedic tradition, which divides food into two classes: raw (*kacha*) and cooked (*pakka*). Raw foods include not only raw vegetables, fruits and grains, but also any foods cooked in water, whether boiled, steamed, stewed or soaked. The *dal* recipes in this chapter are the everyday *kacha* selections prepared in any wet cooking method. Only baked and fried foods are considered cooked or *pakka*. Pan-, shallow- and deep-fried *dal* dishes such as *Soft 'n' Savory Chickpea Kofta*, *Mung Dal Patties with Chopped Spinach* and *Delicate Rice and Urad Dal Dosa Pancakes* are among the cooked *dal* dishes found in "Light Meals and Savories" (page 442).

For information about unfamiliar ingredients or techniques, see A-to-Z

CLASSIFICATION OF *DALS*

Dals are available whole, split with skins, split without skins and ground into flour. Here is a short alphabetical list of the principal varieties of *dals* used in Vedic cooking and where to find them.

ADUKI BEANS: Also known as adzuki, adsuki and feijao beans. These are small, oblong, reddish-brown beans native to Japan and China. Called the "king of beans" in Japan, adukis were little known or used in the West until recently. They have an unusually sweet, quite strong flavor, and make excellent sprouts that are used raw in salads or briskly-sautéed in other dishes. The aduki bean is noted for its medicinal properties and is available at health food, specialty or gourmet stores and Chinese or Japanese grocery stores.

BLACK-EYED PEAS: Known as cowpeas in America. In India, when split and husked they are known as *chowla dal*. Whole, they are called *lobya*. Widely available in the southern United States and at health food stores.

CHANA DAL: A variety of small chickpea, sold split and without the skin. They are pale buff to bright yellow and about ¼ inch (6 mm) in diameter. *Chana dal* is classically used in thick-textured *dal* purées. It is also soaked, drained and deep-fried as a munchy snack, or ground into wet pastes to be seasoned and fried into savories. *Chana dal* is used raw in fresh chutney and ground into flour for extensive use in sweets and savories. It is available at Indian grocery stores.

CHICKPEAS (*KABLI CHANA*): Also known as garbanzo beans. A cousin to the smaller *chana dal*, chickpeas are pale buff to light brown and are used whole, without skins. They look like wrinkled peas and are about ⅓ inch (1 cm) in diameter. Chickpeas are popularly used as whole dried beans with potatoes, savory sauces, yogurt sauces or tomatoes. They can also be roasted and ground into flour for sweets and savories. Chickpeas are available at supermarkets and health food stores, Indian grocery stores and Latin American stores.

KALA CHANA: A cousin to the chickpea. *Kala chanas* are somewhat smaller and darker brown than chickpeas, but have the same shape. Despite their apparent similarities, these two beans are not interchangeable, as they have different flavors and cooking requirements. *Kala chanas* are popular in whole bean dishes and, like chickpeas, are exceptionally nutritious, providing more vitamin C than most other legumes and nearly twice as much iron. They are also very high in protein. *Kala Chanas* are available at Indian and Middle Eastern grocery stores.

KIDNEY BEANS (*RAJMA DAL*): Red-brown, oval beans. They are used in a spicy North Indian vegetarian chili and other whole bean dishes. They are available at Indian and Middle Eastern grocery stores as well as at health, specialty or gourmet food stores.

MUNG DAL: Also known as mung beans and green grams. Mung *dal* is popular in three forms:

1. Whole mung beans, with skins (*sabat moong*). These are BB-sized, pale yellow oval beans with moss-green skins, easy to digest and relatively quick to cook. They are used primarily for sprouts and dry bean dishes. You can get whole mung beans at Indian and Middle Eastern grocery stores, health food stores and specialty or gourmet food stores.

2. Split mung *dal* without skins (*moong dal*). These are used extensively in soups, stews and sauces. They become slightly glutinous when cooked into thick purées and make excellent *dal* soup. They can be soaked, drained and fried into crispy snacks. Mung *dal* is available at Indian grocery stores.

3. Split mung *dal* with skins (*chilke moong dal*). These are recommended whenever soaked beans are required for savories and chutneys. They too are available at Indian grocery stores.

MUTH **BEANS:** Known as dew bean. The beans are used fresh as a vegetable; dried in whole bean dishes; and soaked, drained and fried as crunchy snacks. The greenish-brown beans are available at Indian grocery stores.

SPLIT PEAS (*MATAR DAL*): There are two popular varieties—green and yellow. Both are about ¼ inch (6 mm) in diameter. The yellow can be used as a substitute for *chana dal* or *toovar dal*. The green is ideal for thin to medium soups or purées. Split peas are readily available at all supermarkets and health food stores and Indian grocery stores.

TOOVAR DAL: Also known as *arhar dal, tuar dal* and pigeon peas. The pale yellow to gold lentils, about ¼ inch (6 mm) in diameter, are sold split, without skins. Slightly sweet, they are popular in *dal* soups and purées and the South Indian daily staple known as *sambar*. They are available at some supermarkets and Latin American stores and all Indian grocery stores.

URAD DAL: Also known as black gram. These beans are popular in three forms, all available at Indian grocery stores:

1. Whole *urad* beans, with skins (*sabat urad*). These BB-sized, oval ivory beans have gray-black skins. They are used whole in dried bean dishes.

2. Split, without skins (*urad dal*). Used in purées and soups and ground into flour for savories and sweets.

3. Split, with skins (*chilke urad dal*). Used just like *urad dal*; many cooks prefer the lighter texture of fried savories made from soaked *chilke urad*.

HOW TO CLEAN AND WASH *DALS*

Imported *dals* arrive minimally processed and should be picked through for kernels that have become too hard and for foreign matter such as dried leaves, stems and stones. You can observe the time-honored ritual of cleaning *dal* by following these two steps:

1. Pour the *dal* onto one end of a large cookie sheet or metal tray. Working on a small amount, pick out the unwanted matter and move the clean *dal* to one side. Clean the rest of the *dal* the same way.

2. Put the *dal* in a sieve and lower it into a large bowl filled two-thirds with water. Rub the *dal* between your hands for about 30 seconds. Lift out the sieve, discard the water and refill the bowl. Repeat the process three or four times or until the rinse water is practically clear. Drain or soak as directed in the recipe.

For information about unfamiliar ingredients or techniques, see A-to-Z

GUIDE FOR PRESSURE COOKING *DALS*

TYPE OF *DAL*	SOAKING TIME	*DAL*-TO-WATER RATIO (*dal* measured before soaking)	COOKING TIME (under pressure)
Whole: chickpeas, kidney beans, black-eyed peas, *kala chana dal*	8 hours or overnight	1 to 3½	30–40 minutes
Whole: aduki beans, mung beans, *urad* beans, *muth* beans	5 hours or overnight	1 to 3	20–25 minutes
Split: mung *dal*, urad *dal*	no soaking required	1 to 6 for soup	20–25 minutes
Split: *toovar dal* *chana dal* split peas	3 hours 5 hours 5 hours	1 to 6½ for soup	25–30 minutes

The hardness or softness of the water will affect the cooking time. Because hard water increases cooking time, salt—a mineral—is never added during cooking.

COOKING *DALS*

The simplest way to cook split *dal* is to put it in a heavy saucepan with the suggested amount of water, a dab of butter or *ghee*, fresh ginger root and a dash of turmeric. Stirring occasionally, bring to a boil over high heat. Reduce the heat to moderately low, cover with a tight-fitting lid, and gently boil until the *dal* is thoroughly softened, anywhere from 45 minutes to 1½ hours. Cooking time varies with the type of *dal*, the hardness or softness of the water, and the age of the *dal*; old *dal* may take twice as long as new *dal*. The consistency of the *dal*—liquid or dry—is determined by the amount of water. Small whole beans—mung, aduki, *muth* and *urad*—take up to 45 minutes more.

Thin split *dal* soups and whole beans cook rapidly in a pressure cooker: a small amount of *dal* soup cooks to perfection in 20–25 minutes, and whole chickpeas become butter-soft in 30–40 minutes. For medium to thick *dal* purées and sauces, use the saucepan method described above, as they tend to stick to the bottom of the pressure cooker and clog the vent on the lid.

Some manufacturers caution against cooking dried peas and beans in a pressure cooker, because legumes cooked without enough water or insufficiently washed tend to froth up and clog the vent. To prevent this, fill the pressure cooker no more than half full; use at least 6 parts water to 1 part split *dal* or 3 parts water to 1 part whole beans; and keep the heat moderately low. The first few times you pressure cook *dals*, watch for signs of clogging, such as a suddenly still vent weight. If this happens, take the pan off the heat, put it in the sink and run lukewarm water over it, gradually changing to cold. After several minutes, tilt the weight and slowly reduce the pressure, aiming the release away from you. Finish cooking the *dal*, covered but not under pressure.

Bean Sprouts

Another way to prepare dried beans is to sprout them. The food value of beans skyrockets as they sprout, making them among the most vital and nutrition-packed of foods. Sprouting beans greatly multiplies their levels of vitamins C, E, and all of the B group. Their proteins become extremely digestible, and their starches turn to sugar, making them pleasantly sweet. Minerals, enzymes, and fiber combine to make bean sprouts a superfood, yet they are low-calorie. Moreover, sprouted beans are a very economical addition to the diet.

Eat sprouted beans as soon as they reach the desired size in order to enjoy the full nutritional benefits. They can be served raw in salads, sautéed with spices or briefly steamed to make a healthy and delicious breakfast, especially during winter. You can also add sprouts to stir-fried dishes, broths and *dal* soups just before serving, or use them as a garnish for many dishes.

To sprout ½ cup (100 g) whole beans, such as chickpeas, mung, aduki, *muth* or *urad* beans, you will need a medium-sized mixing bowl, a 1-quart/liter wide-mouthed jar, a doubled square of cheesecloth (4½ inches/11.5 cm square) and a strong rubber band. If you become fond of sprouts, you can buy a sprouter in a health food store.

1. Buy only those beans that are sold specifically for sprouting. They are available at health food stores and through mail order sources. Select clean, whole beans. Pick through them to remove broken beans, dead kernels, chaff, stones and other unwanted matter.

2. Thoroughly wash the beans. Soak for 8–12 hours, or overnight, in a bowl of lukewarm water. After soaking, drain the swollen beans and rinse them in clean water three or four times or until the rinse water is clear. Do not throw away the soaking water. It will be yellow, musky and none too fragrant, but just what your houseplants have been waiting for.

3. Put the beans in the jar, stretch the cheesecloth over the mouth of the jar, and secure it with the rubber band. Turn the jar upside down and set it at a 45° angle in the mixing bowl to give the excess water a place to drain into. Keep the jar this way in a cool, dark cupboard, and rinse the beans with fresh water three or four times a day. Depending on their size, the beans should sprout in three to five days.

4. Generally, sprouted beans are ready when the tails are ¼–½ inch (6 mm-1.5 cm) long. Serve at once or refrigerate, loosely covered, for up to 2 days.

For information about unfamiliar ingredients or techniques, see A-to-Z

DAL SOUPS

Simple Mung *Dal* Soup
SADA MOONG DAL

This smooth, liquid mung *dal* soup is seasoned with a simple *chaunk*. It is easy to prepare and easy to digest, and its light consistency makes it appealing in any season. Serve it accompanied by a wheat bread or rice and a vegetable. To complete the meal, serve yogurt or green salad.

Preparation time (after assembling ingredients): 10 minutes
Cooking time: 1¼ hours or 25 minutes in a pressure cooker
Serves: 4 to 6

⅔ cup (145 g) split *moong dal*, without skins
6½ cups (1.5 liters) water (5½ cups/1.3 liters if pressure-cooked)
1 teaspoon (5 ml) turmeric
2 teaspoons (10 ml) ground coriander
1½ teaspoons (7 ml) scraped, finely shredded or minced fresh ginger root
1 teaspoon (5 ml) minced seeded hot green chili (or as desired)
1¼ teaspoons (6 ml) salt
2 tablespoons (30 ml) *ghee* or vegetable oil
1 teaspoon (5 ml) cumin seeds
2 tablespoons (30 ml) coarsely chopped fresh coriander or minced fresh parsley

   1. Sort, wash and drain the split mung beans as explained on page 42.
   2. Combine the mung beans, water, turmeric, coriander, ginger root and green chili in a heavy 3-quart/liter nonstick saucepan. Stirring occasionally, bring to a full boil over high heat. Reduce the heat to moderately low, cover with a tight-fitting lid and boil gently for 1 hour or until the *dal* is soft and fully cooked. For pressure cooking, combine the ingredients in a 6-quart/liter pressure cooker, cover and cook for 25 minutes under pressure. Remove from the heat and let the pressure drop by itself.
   3. Off the heat, uncover, add the salt and beat with a wire whisk or rotary beater until the *dal* soup is creamy smooth.
   4. Heat the *ghee* or oil in a small saucepan over moderate to moderately high heat. When it is hot, toss in the cumin seeds. Fry until the seeds turn brown. Pour into the *dal* soup, immediately cover and allow the seasonings to soak into the hot *dal* for 1–2 minutes. Add the minced herb, stir and serve.

Golden Mung *Dal* Soup
KHARA MOONG DAL

This is a variation of the simple *dal* soup, using the same ingredients as the previous recipe, but a different seasoning procedure changes the flavor considerably. The contrast between these recipes shows the possibilities of using different procedures to produce varieties of flavors. This dish will go well in any lunch menu, such as a rice, salad and vegetable of your choice. For a special occasion, try it with *Lemons Stuffed with Almond-Chickpea Pâté, Simple Yellow Rice* and *Char-Flavored Spiced Eggplant and Potatoes.*

Preparation time (after assembling ingredients): 10 minutes
Cooking time: 1¼ hours or 25 minutes in a pressure cooker
Serves: 4

⅔ cup (145 g) split *moong dal*, without skins
6 cups (1.5 liters) water (5½ cups/1.3 liters if pressure-cooked)
½ teaspoon (2 ml) turmeric
2 tablespoons (30 ml) *ghee* or vegetable oil
½ tablespoon (7 ml) coriander seeds
½ tablespoon (7 ml) cumin seeds
1 teaspoon (5 ml) salt
2 teaspoons (10 ml) scraped, finely shredded or minced fresh ginger root
1 teaspoon (5 ml) minced seeded hot green chili (or as desired)
2 tablespoons (30 ml) minced fresh parsley or coarsely chopped coriander

1. Sort, wash and drain the split mung beans as explained on page 42.
2. Place the mung beans, water, turmeric and a dab of the *ghee* or oil in a heavy 3-quart/liter nonstick saucepan and, stirring occasionally, bring to a full boil over high heat. Reduce the heat to moderately low, cover with a tight-fitting lid and boil gently for 1 hour or until the *dal* is soft and fully cooked. For pressure cooking, combine the ingredients in a 6-quart/liter pressure cooker, cover and cook for 25 minutes under pressure. Remove from the heat and let the pressure drop by itself.
3. Meanwhile, slowly dry-roast the coriander and cumin seeds in a heavy iron frying pan for about 8 minutes. Remove and coarsely crush with a mortar and pestle, kitchen mallet or rolling pin.
4. Off the heat, uncover the *dal* and add the salt and roasted spices. Beat with a wire whisk or rotary beater until the *dal* soup is creamy smooth.
5. Heat the *ghee* or oil in a small saucepan over moderately high heat. When it is hot, toss in the ginger root and green chili. Fry until golden brown, then pour into the soup. Cover immediately and let the seasonings soak into the hot *dal* for 1–2 minutes. Sprinkle in the minced herb, stir and serve.

Creamy Mung *Dal* with Chopped Spinach
PALAK MOONG DAL

Moong, North India's most popular *dal*, was a great favorite of my spiritual master, Srila Prabhupada. It is easy to digest and has a good flavor and high vitamin content. The spinach, preferably fresh, enhances the texture and marbled color of this power-packed *dal* soup, and the fried spices poured in at the end of the cooking add lashings of flavor. This dish goes well with *Sautéed Rice* or *Griddle-Baked Chickpea and Whole Wheat Bread*. To complete your menu, serve with any seasonal steamed fresh vegetable drizzled with a flavored *ghee* such as *Cumin-Flavored Ghee*. For a sweet touch add *Cardamom Shortbread Cookies*.

Preparation time (after assembling ingredients): 10 minutes
Cooking time: 1¼ hours or 25 minutes in a pressure cooker
Serves: 5 or 6

⅔ cup (145 g) split *moong dal*, without skins
8 ounces (230 g) fresh spinach, washed, trimmed, patted dry
    and coarsely chopped, or ½ of a 10-ounce package
    of chopped frozen spinach, defrosted (140 g)
6½ cups (1.5 liters) water
    (5½ cups/1.3 liters if pressure-cooked)
1 teaspoon (5 ml) turmeric
½ tablespoon (7 ml) ground coriander
½ tablespoon (7 ml) scraped, finely shredded
    or minced fresh ginger root
2 tablespoons (30 ml) *ghee* or vegetable oil
1¼ teaspoons (6 ml) salt
1 teaspoon (5 ml) cumin seeds
¼ teaspoon (1 ml) yellow asafetida powder (*hing*)*
¼–½ teaspoon (1–2 ml) cayenne pepper or paprika
½ tablespoon (7 ml) lemon juice

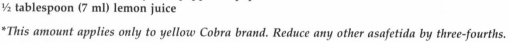

This amount applies only to yellow Cobra brand. Reduce any other asafetida by three-fourths.

    1. Sort, wash and drain the split mung beans as explained on page 42. If you are using frozen spinach, defrost it at room temperature, place it in a strainer and press out all excess water.
    2. Place the mung beans, water, turmeric, coriander, ginger root and a dab of *ghee* or oil in a heavy 3-quart/liter nonstick saucepan. Stirring occasionally, bring to a full boil over high heat. Reduce the heat to moderately low, cover with a tight-fitting lid and gently boil for 1 hour or until the *dal* is soft and fully cooked. For pressure cooking, combine the ingredients in a 6-quart/liter pressure cooker, cover and cook for 25 minutes under pressure. Remove from the heat and let the pressure drop by itself.
    3. Off the heat, uncover and add the salt. Beat with a wire whisk or rotary beater until the *dal* soup is creamy smooth. Add the fresh spinach, cover and boil gently for 5–8 minutes more; or cook frozen spinach for 2–3 minutes.
    4. Heat the *ghee* or oil in a small saucepan over moderate to moderately high heat. When it is hot, pour in the cumin seeds and fry until they are brown. Add the asafetida and cayenne or paprika and fry for just 1–2 seconds more. Then quickly pour the fried seasonings into the soup. Cover immediately. Let the seasonings soak into the hot *dal* for 1–2 minutes. Add the lemon juice, stir and serve.

Mung *Dal* Purée with Sliced White Radishes
MOOLI MOONG DAL

If you live in a large city, you are likely to find the white cooking radishes called *mooli* in an Indian or Chinese grocery store. They may be a bit difficult to find in other areas, so for a similar but milder flavor, you may substitute the smaller red salad radishes. This surprisingly delicious combination will greatly raise your estimation of the common radish. You can vary the texture of the *dal* by varying the amount of water. This recipe yields a thinnish purée. Try this Bengali *dal* with a Bengali vegetable such as *Char-Flavored Vegetable Medley with Crunchy Dal Badi* and *Buttered Steamed Rice*.

Preparation time (after assembling ingredients): 10 minutes
Cooking time: 1¼ hours
Serves: 6 or 7

¾ cup (170 g) split *moong dal*, without skins
6¼–7 cups (1.5–1.75 liters) water
½ teaspoon (2 ml) turmeric
1 teaspoon (5 ml) scraped, finely shredded or minced fresh ginger root
1 teaspoon (5 ml) minced seeded hot green chili (or as desired)
2 tablespoons (30 ml) *ghee* or vegetable oil
1 cup (240 ml) thinly sliced scraped white cooking radishes or red salad radishes
1¼ teaspoons (6 ml) salt
1 tablespoon (15 ml) minced fresh parsley or coarsely chopped coriander
1 teaspoon (5 ml) cumin seeds
¼ teaspoon (1 ml) fenugreek seeds
¼ teaspoon (1 ml) black mustard seeds
1 tablespoon (15 ml) sugar
¼–½ teaspoon (1–2 ml) yellow asafetida powder (*hing*)*
6–8 small curry leaves, preferably fresh
1 tablespoon (15 ml) fresh lemon or lime juice

*This amount applies only to yellow Cobra brand. Reduce any other asafetida by three-fourths.

1. Sort, wash and drain the split mung beans as explained on page 42.
2. Place the mung beans, water, turmeric, ginger root, green chili and a dab of the *ghee* or oil in a heavy 3-quart/liter nonstick saucepan. Stirring occasionally, bring the mixture to a full boil over high heat. Reduce the heat to moderately low, cover with a tight-fitting lid and boil gently for 30 minutes. Add the radishes, cover and continue to cook for 30–45 minutes more or until the *dal* is soft and fully cooked. Add the salt and half of the parsley or coriander, stir, and set aside.
3. Combine the cumin seeds, fenugreek seeds, and mustard seeds in a small bowl. Heat the *ghee* in a small frying pan over moderate to moderately high heat. When it is hot, stir in the seeds and sweetener. Stir-fry until the sweetener caramelizes and turns a rich reddish-brown. Drop in the asafetida powder and curry leaves, and fry for just 1–2 seconds. Immediately add a large spoonful of the cooked *dal* to the frying pan to stop the spices from burning. Stir, remove from the heat and pour the seasonings into the *dal*. Cover immediately and let the seasonings soak into the hot *dal* for 1–2 minutes. Add the remaining minced herb and the lemon juice, stir and serve.

For information about unfamiliar ingredients or techniques, see A-to-Z

Simple Mung *Dal* Soup with Radishes
KHARA MOOLI MOONG DAL

As the personal cook of my spiritual master, Srila Prabhupada, who was himself a superb cook, I took every opportunity to learn from his expertise in both simple and complicated dishes. Often, especially when traveling, he would come into the kitchen to check on the progress of lunch and, in some cases, give instructions. He used to make this *dal* in his tiered steamer. With the *dal* cooking in the bottom chamber, the vegetables in the middle chamber, and the rice gently steaming in the top chamber, the entire lunch cooked in one hour.

In India white *mooli* radishes are used, but icicle, salad or red radishes may be substituted. The white icicle radish, cultivated in many countries, is usually at its best in the spring. Its typically strong, pungent flavor blends remarkably well with the mild flavor of split mung beans. A few simple spices round out the flavor of this pleasing thick *dal* soup.

Preparation time (after assembling ingredients): 10 minutes
Cooking time: 1¼ hours
Serves: 4 to 6

⅔ cup (145 g) split *moong dal*, without skins
6 cups (1.5 liters) water
1 teaspoon (5 ml) turmeric
3 tablespoons (45 ml) *ghee* **or vegetable oil**
**1 cup (240 ml) thinly sliced, scraped white cooking radishes
    or red salad radishes**
1–2 whole dried red chilies, broken into small bits
1½ teaspoons (7 ml) cumin seeds
¼ teaspoon (1 ml) yellow asafetida powder (*hing***)***
1 teaspoon (5 ml) salt
**3 tablespoons (45 ml) minced fresh parsley
    or coarsely chopped coriander**

**This amount applies only to yellow Cobra brand. Reduce any other asafetida by three-fourths.*

1. Sort, wash and drain the split mung beans as explained on page 42.

2. Combine the mung beans, water, turmeric and 1 tablespoon (15 ml) of the *ghee* or oil in a heavy 3-quart/liter nonstick saucepan. Stirring occasionally, bring to a full boil over high heat. Reduce the heat to moderately low, cover with a tight-fitting lid and boil gently. After 30 minutes, add the radishes and cover. Continue to cook for 30–45 minutes more or until the *dal* is soft and fully cooked.

3. Heat the remaining 2 tablespoons (30 ml) of *ghee* or oil in a small saucepan over moderately high heat. When it is hot, drop in the chilies and cumin seeds and fry until they turn brown. Add the asafetida powder, fry for just 1–2 seconds and quickly pour into the soup. Cover immediately and allow the seasonings to soak into the hot *dal* for 1–2 minutes. Add the salt and minced herb, stir and serve.

Mung *Dal* Soup with Tomatoes
TAMATAR MOONG DAL

Dals are perhaps the most popular and the most economical foods in Vedic cuisine. They are relished by everyone, rich and poor, and are part of almost every Vedic lunch. A bouquet of delicate flavors in this creamy *dal* soup comes from the spices, seasonings, tomatoes and sweetener added in the final stages of cooking. The recipe comes from the skilled hands of a great devotee of Krishna from West Bengal, Srila Prabhupada's younger sister, Bhavatarini, lovingly known to his disciples as Pishima (Aunt). Try it with *Spiced Creamed Spinach* and *Cracked Wheat Salad* for a well-balanced lunch or dinner.

Preparation time (after assembling ingredients): 10 minutes
Cooking time: 1¼ hours
Serves: 4 to 6

¾ **cup (170 g) split *moong dal*, without skins**
7¼ **cups (1.75 liters) water**
¾ **teaspoon (3.5 ml) turmeric**
2-inch (5 cm) piece cinnamon stick
3 tablespoons (45 ml) *ghee* or vegetable oil
2 teaspoons (10 ml) coriander seeds
1 teaspoon (5 ml) cumin seeds
½ **teaspoon (2 ml) fennel seeds**
½ **tablespoon (7 ml) sesame seeds**
3 whole cloves
4 green cardamom pods
5 black peppercorns
1½ **teaspoons (7 ml) salt**
1–2 seeded hot green chilies, cut into large pieces
1 tablespoon (15 ml) sugar or equivalent sweetener
2 medium-sized firm ripe tomatoes, coarsely chopped
3 tablespoons (45 ml) minced fresh parsley or coarsely chopped coriander

1. Sort, wash and drain the split mung beans as explained on page 42.

2. Combine the mung beans, water, turmeric, cinnamon stick and a dab of the *ghee* or oil in a heavy 3-quart/liter nonstick saucepan over high heat. Reduce the heat to moderately low, cover with a tight-fitting lid and boil gently for 1 hour or until the *dal* is soft and fully cooked.

3. While the *dal* is cooking, warm a heavy iron frying pan over low heat. Add the coriander seeds, cumin seeds, fennel seeds, sesame seeds, cloves, cardamom pods and peppercorns. Dry-roast, stirring occasionally, for 8–10 minutes or until the sesame seeds are golden brown. Remove and set aside.

4. Take out the cardamom pods. Remove the black seeds and put them with the other roasted spices. Discard the pods. With an electric coffee mill or a stone mortar and pestle, reduce the spices to a powder. Add enough water to make a moist paste.

5. When the *dal* is cooked, remove from the heat and take out the cinnamon stick. Add the salt and beat with a wire whisk or rotary beater until the *dal* is smooth.

6. Heat the *ghee* or oil in a small frying pan over moderate to moderately high heat. When it is hot, add the chilies and the moist spice paste. Stir-fry for about 30 seconds.

For information about unfamiliar ingredients or techniques, see A-to-Z

Pour in the sweetener and stir. As soon as the sweetener turns a rich reddish-brown, toss in the chopped tomatoes and sprinkle liberally with water. Fry for about 4 minutes or until the tomatoes are reduced to a purée. Remove the pieces of chili and pour the spiced tomato seasoning into the *dal*.

7. Bring the finished *dal* to a boil once more, turn off the heat and cover. Let the seasonings soak into the hot *dal* for 1–2 minutes. Add the minced herb, stir and serve.

Toasted Mung *Dal* Soup with Tender Eggplant Cubes
BAIGAN MOONG DAL

Dry-roasted split mung beans lend a distinctive flavor to this thick, textured *dal*. The recipe comes to me from Pishima. It is simple to make and perfect for persons new to cooking with eggplant. Be sure *not* to wash and drain the *dal* until after the dry-roasting, as explained below.

Preparation time (after assembling ingredients): 15 minutes
Cooking time: 1¼ hours
Serves: 6 or 7

¾ cup (170 g) split *moong dal*, without skins
7 cups (1.75 liters) water
½ tablespoon (7 ml) scraped, finely shredded
    or minced fresh ginger root
7 tablespoons (105 ml) *ghee* or peanut oil
⅓ teaspoon (1.5 ml) cayenne pepper or paprika
1 teaspoon (5 ml) turmeric
1½ teaspoons (7 ml) *garam masala*
3 tablespoons (45 ml) water for the spice paste
1½ teaspoons (7 ml) salt
1 small eggplant (about ½ pound/230 g) with skin,
    washed and cut into 1-inch (2.5 cm) cubes
1–2 teaspoons (5–10 ml) minced hot green chilies
1 teaspoon (5 ml) cumin seeds
¼–½ teaspoon (1–2 ml) yellow asafetida powder (*hing*)*
1 teaspoon (5 ml) ground coriander
2 tablespoons (30 ml) minced fresh parsley or
    coarsely chopped coriander leaves
1 teaspoon (5 ml) fresh lemon juice

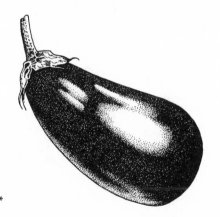

*This amount applies only to yellow Cobra brand. Reduce any other asafetida by three-fourths.

1. Sort the split mung beans as explained on page 42, but do not wash them.
2. Place the mung beans in a heavy 3-quart/liter nonstick saucepan and dry-roast them over moderately high heat, stirring frequently, until the *dal* assumes a faint reddish color. Remove the pan from the heat and pour the *dal* into a strainer. Wash under running water until the rinse water is clean.
3. Return the *dal* to the saucepan and add the water, ginger root and a dab of *ghee*

or oil. Stirring frequently, bring to a full boil over high heat. Reduce the heat to moderately low, cover with a tight-fitting lid and boil gently.

4. Meanwhile, combine the cayenne or paprika, turmeric, *garam masala*, 3 tablespoons (45 ml) of water and half of the salt in a shallow bowl. Mix into a thin paste. Rub the eggplant pieces with this spice paste.

5. Heat the remaining *ghee* or oil in a large frying pan over moderate to moderately high heat. When it is hot, add the chilies and cumin seeds. Fry until the cumin seeds are brown. Add the asafetida powder, and after just 1–2 seconds pour in the spiced eggplant cubes to stop the powder from burning. Stir-fry for 7–10 minutes, turning the cubes with a wooden spatula to brown them evenly.

6. When the *dal* has gently boiled for about 45 minutes, add the eggplant. Stir, cover again and gently boil for another 25 minutes or until the *dal* is soft and fully cooked and the eggplant is butter-soft.

7. Just before serving, sprinkle in the remaining salt, ground coriander, minced herb and lemon juice. Stir well and serve.

Double-*Dal* Soup
MOONG TOOVAR DAL

Toovar dal is also known as *arhar* or *tuar dal* and pigeon peas. The mildly seasoned combination of *moong* and *toovar dals* in this recipe is popular in cool-weather months.

Dal soaking time: 3 hours for *toovar dal*, 5 hours for yellow split peas
Preparation time (after assembling ingredients): 10 minutes
Cooking time: 1½ hours
Serves: 4 to 6

⅓ cup (75 g) split *moong dal*, without skins
⅓ cup (70 g) split *toovar dal* or yellow split peas
5¾ cups (1.5 liters) water
½ teaspoon (2 ml) turmeric
1 teaspoon (5 ml) scraped, finely shredded or minced fresh ginger root
1 teaspoon (5 ml) minced seeded hot green chili (or as desired)
3 tablespoons (45 ml) *ghee* or vegetable oil
2 tablespoons (30 ml) minced fresh parsley or coarsely chopped coriander
1 tablespoon (15 ml) fresh lemon or lime juice
1 teaspoon (5 ml) salt
1 teaspoon (5 ml) black mustard seeds
4–6 small curry leaves, preferably fresh

1. Sort, wash, and drain the split mung beans and *toovar dal* or split peas as explained on page 42. If using *toovar dal*, soak in 2 cups (480 ml) of hot water for 3 hours; if using yellow split peas, soak in 2 cups (480 ml) of hot water for 5 hours. Drain well.

2. Place the water, turmeric, ginger root, green chili and 1 tablespoon (15 ml) of the *ghee* or oil in a heavy 3-quart/liter nonstick saucepan. Bring to a boil over high heat. Stir in the *dals*, cover with a tight-fitting lid and reduce the heat to moderately low. Simmer for 1½ hours or until the *dals* are soft and fully cooked. Remove from the heat and beat with a wire whisk or rotary beater until the *dal* soup is creamy smooth. Stir in the fresh herb, lemon juice and salt.

3. Heat the remaining *ghee* or oil in a small saucepan over moderate to moderately high heat. When it is hot, add the black mustard seeds. Fry until they turn gray and sputter and pop. Remove from the heat and add the curry leaves. Fry for 1–2 seconds. Pour this hot seasoning into the cooked *dal* and cover immediately. Allow the seasonings to soak into the hot *dal* for 1–2 minutes, then stir and serve.

Three-Vegetable *Urad Dal* Soup
SABJI URAD DAL

Although one type of *dal* can be successfully substituted for another in many recipes, the particular flavor and texture of the *urad dal* in this recipe, enhanced by the combination of selected seasonings and vegetables, cannot be obtained with any other. The combination of vegetables is typically Bengali—spinach, sliced plantains and white cooking radishes. As an alternative, use any type of fresh greens, parsnips and red salad radishes. In the final step a wet paste of spices and seasonings is cooked in *ghee* and added to the soup. This *chaunk* makes the *dal* soup not only delicious but also easier to digest. Try this Bengali *dal* with refreshing *Rice and Ginger-Seasoned Yogurt, Crispy Deep-Fried Eggplant Slices* and a tossed green salad.

Preparation time (after assembling ingredients): 15 minutes
Cooking time: 1½ hours
Serves: 6 or 7

⅔ cup (145 g) split *urad dal*, without skins
7 cups (1.75 liters) water for the *dal*
1–2 minced seeded hot green chilies
½ teaspoon (2 ml) turmeric
½ cup (120 ml) thinly sliced scraped white cooking radishes or red salad radishes
8 ounces (230 g) fresh spinach, washed, patted dry, trimmed and coarsely chopped,
    or ½ of a 10-ounce package of frozen chopped spinach, defrosted (140 g)
1 small plantain or parsnip, peeled and cut into ¼-inch (6 mm) slices
1 teaspoon (5 ml) salt
1 teaspoon (5 ml) cumin seeds
1 teaspoon (5 ml) coriander seeds
½ teaspoon (2 ml) fennel seeds
3 black peppercorns
⅓ cup (80 ml) water for the spice paste
2 teaspoons (10 ml) scraped, finely shredded or minced fresh ginger root
2 tablespoons (30 ml) *ghee* or vegetable oil
¼ teaspoon (1 ml) yellow asafetida powder (*hing*)*

*This amount applies only to yellow Cobra brand. Reduce any other asafetida by three-fourths.

1. Sort, wash and drain the split *urad dal* as explained on page 42.

2. Pour the water for the *dal* into a heavy 3-quart/liter nonstick saucepan and bring to a rapid boil over high heat. Stir in the *urad dal*, green chilies, turmeric and vegetables. Bring to a boil again. If you are using frozen leaf spinach, let it thaw at room temperature and then press between your palms to remove all excess water before adding.

3. Reduce the heat to moderately low, cover with a tight-fitting lid and boil gently for 1 hour or until the *dal* is soft and fully cooked. Remove from the heat, uncover, add the salt and stir.

4. While the *dal* is cooking, reduce the cumin seeds, coriander seeds, fennel seeds and black peppercorns to a smooth powder with an electric coffee mill or a stone mortar and pestle. Transfer to a small bowl.

5. Blend the ⅓ cup (80 ml) of water and the ginger root in a blender at high speed until the mixture is thoroughly reduced to a smooth ginger water. Pour the liquid into the freshly powdered spices and mix well to make paste *masala*.

6. Heat the *ghee* or vegetable oil in a small frying pan over moderate heat. When it is hot, drop in the asafetida powder and paste *masala*. Fry for 1–2 minutes. If necessary, add sprinkles of water to keep the paste from drying out. Pour a spoon of the cooked *dal* into the spices and stir well. Then pour the seasonings into the cooked *dal*. Allow the seasonings to soak into the hot *dal*, then cover for 1–2 minutes. Stir and serve.

Urad Dal with Tomatoes
URAD TAMATAR DAL

My cinematographer friend, Yadubara Das, was part of a small traveling party that accompanied Srila Prabhupada to Rishikesh in May 1977. Though Srila Prabhupada's health was not good on this trip, he took the time to show Yadubara how to make this *urad dal*. Since the recipe was spoken rather than demonstrated, the measurements given are mine, as is the addition of the fresh ginger and herb. It is important that the dish be highlighted with the heat from red chili and the flavor of asafetida—two musts in many *urad dal* recipes from Rajasthan.

This is a good, simple, medium-consistency *dal* that requires up to 1½ hours of cooking time but very little attention—so little that you can make it on the side while you are cooking the rest of the meal. This protein-rich *dal* packs even more power when served with rice, bread and yogurt. For a special meal, you might also try it with *Piquant Lemon Rice* and *Zesty Mashed Potatoes*.

Preparation time (after assembling ingredients): 10 minutes
Cooking time: 1½ hours
Serves: 4 or 5

⅔ cup (145 g) split *urad dal*, without skins
6 cups (1.5 liters) water
½ teaspoon (2 ml) turmeric
3 tablespoons (45 ml) *ghee* or vegetable oil
3 medium-sized tomatoes, each cut into 8 pieces

For information about unfamiliar ingredients or techniques, see A-to-Z

1¼ teaspoons (6 ml) salt
1½ teaspoons (7 ml) scraped, finely shredded or minced fresh ginger root
1¼ teaspoons (6 ml) cumin seeds
1–2 whole dried red chilies broken into bits (use as desired)
¼–½ teaspoon (1–2 ml) yellow asafetida powder (*hing*)*
2 tablespoons (30 ml) minced fresh parsley or coarsely chopped coriander

This amount applies only to yellow Cobra brand. Reduce any other asafetida by three-fourths.

1. Sort, wash and drain the split *urad dal* as explained on page 42.

2. Bring the water, turmeric and a dab of the *ghee* or oil to a boil in a heavy 3-quart/liter nonstick saucepan over high heat. Stir in the *dal* and again bring to a boil.

3. Reduce the heat to moderately low, cover with a tight-fitting lid and gently boil for about 30 minutes. Add the tomatoes. Cover and continue cooking for 1 hour or until the *dal* is soft and fully cooked. Remove from the heat, uncover, add the salt and stir.

4. Heat the *ghee* or oil in a small pan over moderate to moderately high heat. When it is hot, add the ginger root, cumin seeds and red chili in rapid succession. Fry until the cumin seeds and chili turn brown. Add the asafetida powder, and after just 1–2 seconds quickly pour the fried seasonings into the *dal*. Immediately cover and allow the seasonings to soak into the *dal* for 1–2 minutes.

5. Add the parsley or coriander, stir and serve.

Fennel-Flavored *Urad Dal* Soup
SADA URAD DAL

This is my favorite *urad dal* recipe, given to me by Srila Prabhupada. The seasoning combination in this recipe best highlights the flavor of *urad dal*. Although Srila Prabhupada told me to grind the seasonings with a stone mortar and pestle, the blender is an effective and time-saving alternative. The spices, especially the fennel, asafetida, ginger and mint, combine beautifully with *urad dal*. Be sure to use fresh mint, since the dried leaves are ineffectual by comparison. Even if you don't like *urad dal*, you'll like this dish—and if you do like *urad dal*, you will love it. For a Bengali menu, try this *dal* with *Buttery Mashed Potatoes with Crispy Fried Bitter Melon, Succulent Summer Squash and Green Peas with Poppy Seeds, Coconut and Cucumber Salad* and any bread. For a sweet, try *Classic Juicy Chenna Balls*.

Preparation time (after assembling ingredients): 5 minutes
Cooking time: 1½ hours
Serves: 4 to 6

⅔ cup (145 g) split *urad dal*, without skins
1 tablespoon (15 ml) scraped, coarsely chopped fresh ginger root
1 teaspoon (5 ml) fennel seeds
6 cups (1.5 liters) water
⅓ cup (80 ml) coarsely chopped trimmed fresh mint
1¼ teaspoons (6 ml) salt
3 tablespoons (45 ml) *ghee* or peanut oil
1 whole dried red chili, broken into bits (use as desired)
1½ teaspoons (7 ml) cumin seeds
¼–½ teaspoon (1–2 ml) yellow asafetida powder (*hing*)*
2 medium-sized firm ripe tomatoes, diced

This amount applies only to yellow Cobra brand. Reduce any other asafetida by three-fourths.

1. Sort, wash and drain the split *urad dal* as explained on page 42.
2. Combine the ginger root, fennel seeds and 1 cup (240 ml) of the water in a blender. Blend at high speed for 1 minute.
3. Place the spiced water, remaining plain water, *urad dal* and half of the mint in a heavy 3-quart/liter nonstick saucepan over high heat and bring to a boil. Reduce the heat to moderately low, cover with a tight-fitting lid and boil gently for 1 hour or until the *dal* is soft and fully cooked.
4. Remove from the heat, uncover, add the salt and beat with a wire whisk or rotary beater until the *dal* soup is creamy smooth.
5. Heat the *ghee* or oil in a small saucepan over moderate to moderately high heat. When it is hot, drop in the chili pieces and cumin seeds in rapid succession and fry until the cumin seeds turn brown. Add the asafetida powder and after just 1–2 seconds add the tomatoes. Cook for 3–4 minutes or until the tomatoes are reduced to a purée. Pour into the *dal*, cover immediately and allow the fried seasonings to soak into the hot *dal* for 1–2 minutes. Add the remaining mint, stir and serve.

Chana Dal Purée with Tender Bottle Gourd Cubes
LOUKI CHANA DAL

I first came across this dish at the famous Radha-Ramana Temple in Vrindavan, India. The cooks there are excellent and the kitchen standards are high. The balance of textures and flavors so impressed me that I immediately inquired about the recipe. The two featured ingredients—bottle gourd and *chana dal*—can be replaced by zucchini and yellow split peas, and if adjustments are made in cooking times, you'll get a good copy of the original. Bottle gourd, called *louki* or *ghiya* in Hindi, is a fine-grained, white-fleshed summer squash that does not become waterlogged or mushy when cooked to tenderness. It is not a common supermarket item but is often available in

For information about unfamiliar ingredients or techniques, see A-to-Z

Indian, Chinese and Italian grocery stores. By the time the squash reaches the market, it usually requires peeling and seeding. The soft green outer skin can be removed with a potato peeler and the seedy inner core discarded. The firm flesh is then ready to be cut. Alternatively, any young, tender summer squash can be used—green or yellow zucchini or summer pattypan. Try this *dal* with *Savory Saffron Pilaf, Sautéed Spinach* and *Dal Noodles with Herbed Tomato Sauce* and *Cauliflower Pakora*. If you want a sweet, try *Almond Milk Fudge Diamonds*.

Dal soaking time: 5 hours
Preparation time (after assembling ingredients): 10 minutes
Cooking time: 2 hours in a saucepan or 1¼ hours
    using pressure cooker and saucepan combination
Serves: about 6

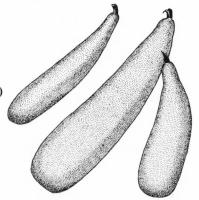

1 cup (195 g) split *chana dal* or yellow split peas
7 cups (1.75 liters) water (5½ cups/1.3 liters if pressure-cooked)
½ teaspoon (2 ml) turmeric
2 teaspoons (10 ml) ground coriander
1 tablespoon (15 ml) scraped, finely shredded
    or minced fresh ginger root
4 tablespoons (60 ml) *ghee* or a mixture of vegetable oil
    and unsalted butter
12 pieces peeled, seeded bottle gourd or young zucchini
    (about 1¼ pounds/570 g), 1½ inches (4 cm) long and ¾ inch (2 cm) thick
1½ teaspoons (7 ml) *garam masala*
1¼ teaspoons (6 ml) salt
½ tablespoon (7 ml) fresh lemon or lime juice
1¼ teaspoons (6 ml) cumin seeds
1–2 whole dried red chilies
¼–½ teaspoon (1–2 ml) yellow asafetida powder (*hing*)*
6–8 curry leaves, preferably fresh

**This amount applies only to yellow Cobra brand. Reduce any other asafetida by three-fourths.*

1. Sort, wash and drain the split *chana dal* as explained on page 42. Place the *chana dal* or yellow split peas in a bowl, cover with 3 cups (710 ml) of hot water and let soak for 5 hours. Drain.
2. Place the *chana dal* or split peas, 7 cups (1.75 liters) of water, turmeric, coriander, ginger root and a spoonful of the *ghee* or oil-butter mixture in a heavy 3-quart/liter nonstick saucepan over high heat. Stirring frequently, bring to a full boil. Reduce the heat to low, cover with a tight-fitting lid and boil gently for 1½ hours. For pressure cooking, combine the ingredients in a 6-quart/liter pressure cooker, cover and cook for 25 minutes under pressure. Remove from the heat and allow the pressure to drop by itself. Off the heat, uncover and add the squash and *garam masala*. Stir and continue to cook gently for 30 minutes or until the *dal* is soft and fully cooked and the vegetables are butter-soft. Stir in the salt and lemon or lime juice.
3. Heat the remaining *ghee* or oil-butter mixture in a small saucepan over moderate to moderately high heat. When it is hot, add the cumin and red chilies. Fry until the cumin seeds turn brown. Add the asafetida powder and curry leaves, cook for just 1–2 seconds and then quickly pour the fried seasonings into the cooked *dal*. Cover immediately and allow the seasonings to soak into the hot *dal* for 1–2 minutes. Stir. Serve with 2 pieces of squash in each portion.

Golden Pumpkin *Toovar Dal* Soup

TOOVAR KADDU DAL

This creamy smooth pumpkin and *dal* soup of the Gujarati cuisine has a rich reddish-gold color and a distinctive flavor. The lemon juice and bay leaves introduce a tart, pleasantly bitter element in contrast to the mildly sweet burst of flavor from the warm *chaunk* added at the end. If you are substituting yellow split peas for the *toovar dal*, allow a little extra cooking time. This golden *dal* goes well with either a simple or an elaborate menu, but for a special main meal, try it with *Stuffed Eggplant Supreme with Panir Cheese and Chickpeas, Deep-Fried Baby Potatoes in Seasoned Yogurt Broth* and *Cucumber and White Radish Salad.* For a sweet as beautiful as it is delicious, try the *Grand Caramel Milk Fudge Cake.*

Dal soaking time: 3 hours for *toovar dal*, 5 hours for yellow split peas
Preparation time (after assembling ingredients): 10 minutes
Cooking time: 1½ hours
Serves: 5 or 6

⅔ cup (135 g) split *toovar dal* or yellow split peas
6½ cups (1.5 liters) water
1 cup (240 ml) peeled pumpkin or other winter squash
    cut into ½-inch (1.5 cm) cubes
1 teaspoon (5 ml) scraped, minced fresh ginger root
1 teaspoon (5 ml) minced hot green chili (or as desired)
3 tablespoons (45 ml) fresh lemon or lime juice
1 cassia or bay leaf
½ teaspoon (2 ml) turmeric
3 tablespoons (45 ml) *ghee* or vegetable oil
1 teaspoon (5 ml) salt
1 teaspoon (5 ml) cumin seeds
¼ teaspoon (1 ml) fenugreek seeds
1 teaspoon (5 ml) black mustard seeds
1 whole dried red chili (or as desired)
1 tablespoon (15 ml) sugar or equivalent sweetener
¼ teaspoon (1 ml) yellow asafetida powder (*hing*)*
6–8 small curry leaves, preferably fresh
2 tablespoons (30 ml) minced fresh parsley or coarsely chopped coriander

*This amount applies only to yellow Cobra brand. Reduce any other asafetida by three-fourths.

1. Sort and wash the *toovar dal* as explained on page 42. Soak in 3 cups (710 ml) of hot water for 3 hours. If using yellow split peas, soak in 3 cups (710 ml) of hot water for 5 hours. Drain well.

2. Place the *dal*, water, pumpkin, ginger root, green chili, lemon juice, cassia or bay leaf, turmeric and ½ tablespoon (7 ml) of the *ghee* or oil in a heavy 3-quart/liter nonstick saucepan. Stirring frequently, bring to a full boil over high heat. Reduce heat to moderately low, cover with a tight-fitting lid and boil gently for 1 hour or until the *dal* is soft and fully cooked. Remove from the heat, pick out the cassia or bay leaf and add the salt. Beat with a wire whisk or rotary beater until the *dal* is creamy smooth.

For information about unfamiliar ingredients or techniques, see A-to-Z

3. Heat the remaining *ghee* or oil in a small pan over moderate to moderately high heat. When it is hot, stir in the cumin seeds, fenugreek seeds, black mustard seeds, dried red chili and sweetener in rapid succession. Stir-fry until the sweetener caramelizes and turns a rich reddish-brown. Remove the pan from the heat, drop in the asafetida powder and curry leaves and after just 1–2 seconds quickly pour the fried seasonings into the cooked *dal*. Cover immediately and allow the spices to soak into the hot *dal* for 1–2 minutes. Add the minced herb, stir and serve.

Vishakha's Cream of Vegetable *Dal* Soup
SABJI DAL SHORBA

Here is a quick pressure-cooker soup. The rice and legumes complement each other nutritionally and—with the vegetables, seasonings and powdered spices—make a full-bodied creamy soup. Practically a meal in itself, this dish needs only a fresh flatbread and salad to make an excellent light lunch. If the vegetables listed are not available, you can substitute peeled Jerusalem artichokes, winter squash, summer squash or fresh peas in equivalent amounts. For a quick lunch, try this nutritious soup with either a bowl of *Tomatoes in Smooth Yogurt* or a tossed salad, and a whole wheat bread.

Dal soaking time: 1 hour
Preparation time (after assembling ingredients): 10 minutes
Cooking time: 25 minutes
Serves: 4 or 5

3 tablespoons (45 ml) yellow or green split peas
3 tablespoons (45 ml) split *moong dal* or *toovar dal*,
    or 3 more tablespoons (45 ml) of split peas
3 tablespoons (45 ml) *basmati* or other long-grain white rice
2 tablespoons (30 ml) butter or *ghee*
½ teaspoon (2 ml) turmeric
¼ teaspoon (1 ml) yellow asafetida powder (*hing*)*
½ seeded small hot green chili (or as desired)
½-inch (1.5 cm) piece of fresh ginger root, peeled
2 medium-sized carrots, peeled and cut into 1-inch (2.5 cm) pieces
½ small cauliflower, stemmed and cut into flowerets
6 whole red radishes
5¼ cups (1.25 liters) water
1 tablespoon (15 ml) ground cumin
1 tablespoon (15 ml) ground coriander
1 teaspoon (5 ml) *garam masala*
½ teaspoon (2 ml) freshly ground black pepper
1½ teaspoons (7 ml) salt
2 tablespoons (30 ml) fresh minced parsley or coriander

*This amount applies only to yellow Cobra brand. Reduce any other asafetida by three-fourths.

1. Soak the split peas in hot water for 1 hour, then drain. Sort, wash and drain the split *moong* or *toovar dal* as explained on page 42.

2. Combine the rice, legumes, butter or *ghee*, turmeric, asafetida, green chili, ginger root, vegetables and water in a 6-quart/liter pressure cooker. Cook under pressure for a little more than 20 minutes. Remove from the heat and allow the pressure to drop.

3. Blend half of the cooked vegetables and 2½ cups (600 ml) of broth from the pressure cooker in a blender. Blend at high speed to make a creamy smooth soup. Transfer to a heavy 2-quart/liter nonstick saucepan. Blend the other half of the cooked vegetables with the remaining broth plus enough water to make 2½ cups (600 ml) of liquid and add to the soup.

4. Sprinkle in the ground coriander, cumin and *garam masala*. Bring the soup to a gentle boil, stirring occasionally to prevent sticking, and boil for 1–2 minutes. Remove from the heat.

5. Add the black pepper, salt and minced herb. Stir and serve.

Quick Cream of Split Pea Soup with Sliced Carrots
GAJAR MATAR DAL

Here is an elegant, mildly seasoned *dal* soup that is good the whole year round. The ingredients are easily obtained, and the texture is light and pleasant. Yellow or green split peas are transformed into a smooth, creamy soup, and sliced carrots lend color and nutrition. This *dal* is pleasant with *Curried Eggplant Rice* and *Crisp Apple Salad*. For a larger Vedic vegetarian meal, try adding *Seasoned Spinach with Julienne Potatoes* and *Crackling Crispy Dal Wafers*.

Dal soaking time: 5 hours
Preparation time (after assembling ingredients): 10 minutes
Cooking time: 1½ hours or 30 minutes in a pressure cooker
Serves: 6 to 8

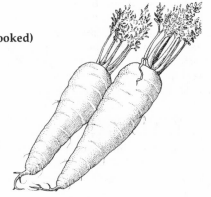

1 cup (210 g) yellow or green split peas
7½ cups (1.75 liters) water (6¾ cups/1.5 liters if pressure cooked)
1 teaspoon (5 ml) scraped, minced fresh ginger root
1–2 hot green chilies
½ teaspoon (2 ml) turmeric
1 tablespoon (15 ml) ground coriander
4 tablespoons (60 ml) *ghee* or a mixture of
    vegetable oil and unsalted butter
4 medium-sized scraped carrots, sliced
1¼ teaspoons (6 ml) salt
2 tablespoons (30 ml) minced fresh parsley
    or coarsely chopped coriander
1¼ teaspoons (6 ml) cumin seeds
¼–½ teaspoon (1–2 ml) yellow asafetida powder (*hing*)*

This amount applies only to yellow Cobra brand. Reduce any other asafetida by three-fourths.

For information about unfamiliar ingredients or techniques, see A-to-Z

1. Soak the split peas in 3 cups (710 ml) of hot water for 5 hours, then drain.

2. Combine the split peas, water, ginger root, green chilies, turmeric, ground coriander and a dab of the *ghee* or oil-butter mixture in a heavy 3-quart/liter nonstick saucepan. Bring to a boil over high heat.

3. Reduce the heat to moderately low, cover with a tight-fitting lid and boil gently for 1 hour. Add the carrots, cover and continue to cook for 30 minutes or until the split peas are soft and fully cooked. For pressure cooking, combine the ingredients in a 6-quart/liter pressure cooker, cover and cook for 30 minutes under pressure. Remove from the heat and let the pressure drop by itself.

4. Off the heat, uncover and stir in the salt and herb.

5. Heat the remaining *ghee* or oil-butter mixture in a small saucepan over moderate to moderately high heat. When it is hot, toss in the cumin seeds and fry until they turn brown. Sprinkle in the asafetida and fry for just 1–2 more seconds, then quickly pour the fried seasonings into the *dal*. Cover immediately and allow the *chaunk* to soak into the *dal* for 1–2 minutes. Stir and serve.

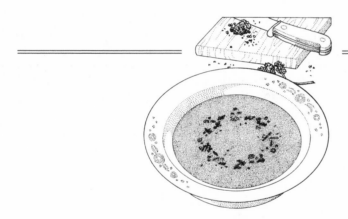

Nutritious Whole Grain, Split Pea and Vegetable Soup
SABJI MATAR DAL

This is a quick pressure-cooker soup that is warming, nutritious and very welcome on cold winter days. You can vary this recipe by substituting parsnips, green beans, zucchini or corn for any of the suggested vegetables. A nice stew can be obtained by adding large, even-sized pieces of potato or winter squash. (You will need to increase the amount of water a bit when cooking these starchy vegetables.) Try your own favorite combinations according to the season and time of day. You can get whole grains and split peas at most health food stores and co-ops, so the next time you are out shopping pick up a pound (455 g) each of whole barley, wheat, rye, brown rice, millet and split peas. At the rate of only 1–2 tablespoons (15–30 ml) per pot of soup, you will be able to stretch these wholesome ingredients over many meals. This soup is a meal in itself, and it also goes especially well with *Buttered Steamed Rice*, a bowl of *Homemade Yogurt* and a tossed green salad.

Grain and *dal* soaking time: 2 hours
Preparation time (after assembling ingredients): 5 minutes
Cooking time: 25 minutes in a pressure cooker
Serves: 6 to 8

2 tablespoons (30 ml) each barley, wheat, rye, brown rice,
    wild rice, millet and split peas
7 cups (1.75 liters) water
1 medium-sized carrot, scraped and cut into ¼-inch (6 mm) rounds
1 medium-sized celery stalk and leaves, sliced
1 large firm ripe tomato, cut into 8 pieces
a generous handful of spinach (about 1 ounce/30 g), washed, dried, stemmed and coarsely
    chopped
½ tablespoon (7 ml) scraped, finely shredded or minced fresh ginger root
1 teaspoon (5 ml) minced seeded hot green chili (or as desired)
1 teaspoon (5 ml) turmeric
½ tablespoon (7 ml) ground coriander
1½ teaspoons (7 ml) salt
2 tablespoons (30 ml) minced fresh parsley or coarsely chopped coriander
4 tablespoons (60 ml) *ghee* or vegetable oil
1 teaspoon (5 ml) cumin seeds

1. Mix together the grains and split peas and soak in hot water for 2 hours. Drain.

2. Combine them with the remaining ingredients except the salt, parsley or coriander, 2 tablespoons (30 ml) of the *ghee* or vegetable oil and the cumin seeds in a 6-quart/liter pressure cooker. Cover and cook under pressure for 20 minutes. Remove the pan from the heat and allow the pressure to drop. Uncover and stir in the salt and herb.

3. Heat the remaining 2 tablespoons (30 ml) of *ghee* or vegetable oil over moderate heat in a small saucepan. When it is hot, add the cumin seeds and fry until they are brown. Pour them into the soup and cover immediately. Allow the seasonings to soak into the hot *dal* for 1–2 minutes. Stir and serve.

Herbed Split Pea Soup with Apple and Coconut
MASALA MATAR DAL

Split peas are economical and require no sorting or washing. In this unusual dish, the flavors of the split peas, apples, coconut, spices and seasonings intermingle through very slow cooking. The result is a zesty, naturally sweet soup that's very satisfying on blustery winter days. Try it with a *Griddle-Fried Potato-Stuffed Whole Wheat Bread* and a green salad for lunch or dinner.

Dal soaking time: 5 hours
Preparation time (after assembling ingredients): 10 minutes
Cooking time: 1½ hours
Serves: 4 to 6

⅔ cup (145 g) green or yellow split peas
1 teaspoon (5 ml) scraped, finely shredded or minced fresh ginger root
1–2 hot green chilies, minced
1¼ teaspoons (6 ml) cumin seeds
2-inch (5 cm) piece of cinnamon stick
8 whole cloves
4 black peppercorns
4 tablespoons (60 ml) *ghee* or vegetable oil
1 teaspoon (5 ml) turmeric
7 cups (1.75 liters) water
1 large cooking apple, cored and cut into 16 pieces
¼ cup (25 g) fresh or dried shredded coconut
2 tablespoons (30 ml) minced fresh parsley
    or coarsely chopped coriander leaves
1½ teaspoons (7 ml) salt

1. Soak the split peas in hot water for 5 hours. Drain.

2. Combine the ginger root, green chili, cumin seeds, cinnamon stick, cloves and peppercorns in a small bowl. Heat the *ghee* or oil in a heavy 3-quart/liter nonstick saucepan over moderate heat. When it is hot, sprinkle in the combined seasonings. Fry until the cumin seeds turn brown. Add the turmeric and follow immediately with the water. Bring the liquid to a full boil and stir in the split peas, apple and coconut.

3. Reduce the heat to moderately low, cover and gently boil for 1½ hours or until the *dal* is soft and fully cooked. Remove from the heat and stir in the herb and salt. Then cover and allow the added seasonings to soak into the hot *dal* for 1–2 minutes. Stir and serve.

Three-*Dal* Delight
MOONG URAD TOOVAR DAL

As vegetarian cooking increases in popularity, so will the use of *dals*, since they are cheap and high in protein. As people begin to explore the world of *dals*, they will find that each variety has its own taste, texture and appearance, creating a tremendous range of culinary possibilities. This variety can be increased by combining different *dals* in the same dish. In this recipe, *moong*, *urad* and *toovar dals* share the cooking pot and when finished are crowned with a fried seasoning of cumin, coriander and fennel seeds. It takes some time to cook but needs hardly any attention. For a special lunch, try it with *Deep-Fried Fenugreek Whole Wheat Bread*, *Baked Eggplant Purée with Seasoned Yogurt*, a green salad and *Maple Cream Simply Wonderfuls*.

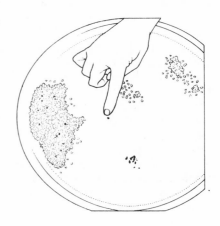

Dal soaking time: 3–5 hours
Preparation time (after assembling ingredients): 10 minutes
Cooking time: 1½ hours
Serves: 6 to 8

⅓ cup (75 g) split *moong dal*, without skins
⅓ cup (70 g) split *urad dal*, without skins
⅓ cup (70 g) split *toovar dal* or yellow split peas
7 cups (1.75 liters) water
¾ teaspoon (3.5 ml) turmeric
3 tablespoons (45 ml) *ghee* or vegetable oil
1½ teaspoons (7 ml) salt
1¼ teaspoons (6 ml) cumin seeds
1 tablespoon (15 ml) coriander seeds
½ teaspoon (2 ml) fennel seeds
1–2 whole dried red chilies, broken into small bits
¼–½ teaspoon (1–2 ml) yellow asafetida powder (*hing*)*
1 cassia or bay leaf
2 tablespoons (30 ml) minced fresh parsley or coarsely chopped coriander

This amount applies only to yellow Cobra brand. Reduce any other asafetida by three-fourths.

1. Sort, wash and drain the *moong* and *urad dals* as explained on page 42. Then soak all three *dals* in 3 cups (710 ml) of hot water for 3–5 hours. Rinse well and drain.
2. Place the *dals*, water, turmeric and a dab of the *ghee* or oil in a heavy 3-quart/liter nonstick saucepan. Stirring occasionally, bring to a boil over high heat. Reduce the heat to moderately low, cover with a tight-fitting lid and boil gently, stirring occasionally, for 1½ hours or until the *dals* are soft and fully cooked. Remove from the heat and uncover. Add the salt and beat with a wire whisk or rotary beater until the *dal* soup is creamy smooth.
3. Combine the cumin, coriander and fennel seeds and red chilies in a small bowl. Heat the remaining *ghee* or oil in a small saucepan over moderately high heat. When it is hot, toss the seasonings in and stir-fry until the seeds are brown. Add the asafetida powder and the cassia or bay leaf and quickly pour the fried seasonings into the cooked *dal*. Cover immediately and let the seasonings soak into the hot *dal* for 1–2 minutes. Uncover and garnish with minced herb. Stir and serve.

Hearty Five-*Dal* Soup
PANCH DAL SHORBA

Here is a hearty, wholesome, thick *dal* soup. Although the cooking time is long, this recipe is by no means laborious, and the delicious result is well worth the time. Some of the spices and seasonings are cooked along with the *dals* to allow their qualities to permeate the dish; the others are fried in *ghee* or vegetable oil and added at the end for a burst of flavor. There are innumerable ways to assemble a five-*dal* soup, but this variation was given to me by Srila Prabhupada in Delhi. Though I have tried many variations since then, this one remains my favorite. The first time I cooked it, the *chana dal* was far from broken down when the other *dals* were cooked. Should this happen to you, note that in the future the *dal* must be soaked or cooked longer. If the *chana dal* takes longer than the others to cook, it may be old. Old *dal* can take up to twice the recommended cooking time to break down.

You can serve this dish in a bowl or spooned over hot rice. Try it with *Shredded Cabbage with Green Peas, Clear Broth with Potatoes and Urad Badi* and *Carrots, Cashews and Dates in Smooth Yogurt.* Piping-hot *Griddle-Baked Paper-Thin Whole Wheat Bread* is a perfect bread if you are having a full Vedic lunch.

Dal soaking time: 3–5 hours
Preparation time (after assembling ingredients): 10 minutes
Cooking time: 1½ hours
Serves: 6 to 8

3 tablespoons (45 ml) split *moong dal*, without skins
3 tablespoons (45 ml) split *urad dal*, without skins
3 tablespoons (45 ml) split *toovar dal* or yellow split peas
3 tablespoons (45 ml) green or yellow split peas
3 tablespoons (45 ml) split *chana dal*
7 cups (1.75 liters) water
1 teaspoon (5 ml) turmeric
1 tablespoon (15 ml) ground coriander
1 tablespoon (15 ml) scraped, finely shredded or minced fresh ginger root
3 tablespoons (45 ml) *ghee* or vegetable oil
1¼ teaspoons (6 ml) salt
4 ounces (115 g) fresh spinach or Swiss chard, washed, dried, stemmed and coarsely chopped
1¾ teaspoons (8 ml) cumin seeds
2 teaspoons (10 ml) minced seeded hot green chilies (or as desired)
1 cassia or bay leaf
⅓ teaspoon (1.5 ml) yellow asafetida powder (*hing*)*
¼ teaspoon (1 ml) cayenne pepper or paprika (or as desired)
½ teaspoon (2 ml) *garam masala*
2 tablespoons (30 ml) minced fresh parsley or coarsely chopped coriander

*This amount applies only to yellow Cobra brand. Reduce any other asafetida by three-fourths.

1. Sort, wash and drain the split *dals* as explained on page 42. Combine in a bowl, cover with hot water and soak for 3–5 hours. Drain.

2. Combine the five *dals*, water, turmeric, coriander, ginger root and a tablespoon (15 ml) of the *ghee* or vegetable oil in a heavy 3-quart/liter nonstick saucepan. Bring to a boil over high heat. Reduce the heat to moderately low and cover with a tight-fitting lid. Cook gently, stirring occasionally, for 1½ hours or until the *dals* are soft and fully cooked.

3. Remove the pan from the heat, add the salt and beat with a wire whisk or rotary beater until the *dal* soup is creamy smooth. Add the spinach or Swiss chard and cover. Cook gently for 5–10 minutes longer.

4. Heat the remaining *ghee* or oil in a small pan over moderate to moderately high heat. When it is hot, toss in the cumin seeds and green chilies. Fry until the cumin seeds turn brown. Toss in the cassia or bay leaf, powdered asafetida and cayenne pepper or paprika, and just 1–2 seconds later add about 3 tablespoons (45 ml) of water. After 15–20 seconds, pour the fried spices into the cooked *dal*, sprinkle in the *garam* *masala* and cover. Allow the seasonings to soak into the hot *dal* for 1–2 minutes. Stir in the minced herb and serve.

Toovar Dal with Chopped Spinach
TOOVAR PALAK DAL

As opposed to thinnish *dal* soup, this dish is "dry" and "textured": each bit of *dal* stands tender yet plump, separate from the others. To achieve this, the *dal* is cooked in a small quantity of water until it is soft but not broken down. This dish contains fresh spinach or Swiss chard, giving a beautiful marbled effect. You can also use other types of green vegetables: peas, sliced green beans or sliced broccoli, for example. If *toovar* or *moong dal* is not available, use yellow split peas. They will give an equally delicious result. You will have to soak the split *dal* or legumes for 3–5 hours in hot water before cooking them and perhaps increase the cooking time for split peas to achieve the desired results. For a full Vedic menu, try *Rice and Cauliflower Pilaf, Spicy Potato-Stuffed Green Peppers, Spicy Okra with Coconut, Sweet 'n' Sour Broth with Cabbage and Carrots* and *Deep-Fried Whole Wheat Bread*. For a sweet, try quick and easy *Pistachio Milk Fudge*.

Dal soaking time: 3–5 hours
Preparation time (after assembling ingredients): 10 minutes
Cooking time: 40 minutes
Serves: 4

1 cup (200 g) split *toovar dal* or *moong dal*
1½ cups (360 ml) water
5 tablespoons (75 ml) *ghee* or a mixture of vegetable oil and unsalted butter
1½ teaspoons (7 ml) cumin seeds
¼ teaspoon (1 ml) yellow asafetida powder (*hing*)*
1 large firm ripe tomato, cut into 8 pieces
1½ teaspoons (7 ml) ground coriander
⅛ teaspoon (0.5 ml) cayenne powder or paprika (or as desired)
½ teaspoon (2 ml) turmeric
1 teaspoon (5 ml) salt
½ pound (230 g) spinach or Swiss chard, washed, dried, stemmed and coarsely chopped
1 teaspoon (5 ml) fresh lemon juice
2 tablespoons (30 ml) minced fresh parsley or coarsely chopped coriander
⅛ teaspoon (0.5 ml) freshly ground nutmeg

This amount applies only to yellow Cobra brand. Reduce any other asafetida by three-fourths.

1. Sort, wash and drain the *dal* as explained on page 42.
2. Place the *dal*, water and a tablespoon (15 ml) of the *ghee* or oil-butter mixture in a heavy 3-quart/liter nonstick saucepan over high heat. Stirring occasionally, bring to a boil. Reduce the heat to moderately low and cover with a tight-fitting lid. Boil gently for 30 minutes or until the *dal* is tender and plump. When finished, each bit of *dal* should be

soft and separate; do not allow it to cook so long that they begin to fall apart. Remove from the heat and drain.

3. Heat the remaining *ghee* or oil-butter mixture in a large frying pan over moderate to moderately high heat. When it is hot, toss in the cumin seeds and fry until they turn brown. Add the asafetida powder and then immediately add the tomato, ground coriander, cayenne or paprika, turmeric and salt. Cover and cook for 3 minutes. Stir in the spinach or Swiss chard, cover and cook for another 5 minutes. If you are using another vegetable, add it now and cook until it is tender.

4. Pour in the *dal*, lower the heat slightly and add the lemon juice. Cook briefly until dry and richly textured. Garnish with minced herb and a sprinkle of nutmeg just before serving.

Sweet 'n' Sour *Dal* Soup with Mixed Vegetables
SAMBAR

In South India, *sambar* is always made with *toovar dal* but it can be combined with almost any vegetable. Besides the green beans, carrots and eggplant suggested in this recipe, you could try broad beans, radishes, fennel root, kohlrabi, parsnip, cauliflower, summer or winter squash, snow peas or lima beans. It is traditionally fiery hot (I have seen cooks add handfuls of dried red chilies and spoonfuls of cayenne as well!). This recipe uses green chilies and cayenne, but it is entirely up to you to decide how much heat you wish to add. For authenticity I suggest that you allow the dish at least a hint of heat. The ingredient *sambar masala* can be purchased ready-made at an Indian grocery store. If you want to serve a festive South Indian meal for entertaining, try *Sambar* with *Buttered Steamed Rice* or *Rice and Urad Dal Iddli*. Add *Green Beans with Crunchy Fried Mung Badi*, *Savory Urad Dal Doughnuts* and *Fresh Coconut, Tamarind and Coriander Leaf Chutney*. For condiments, try *Deep-Fried Stuffed Green Chilies* and a bowl of buttermilk, sour cream or *Homemade Yogurt*. To complete the menu, try *Date–Rice Pudding* or *Melt-in-Your-Mouth Chickpea Flour Fudge*—or both.

Dal soaking time: 3–5 hours
Preparation time (after assembling ingredients): 15 minutes
Cooking time: 1½ hours or 40 minutes in a pressure cooker
Serves: 6 or 7

⅔ cup (135 g) split *toovar dal* or yellow split peas
6½ cups (1.5 liters) water (5½ cups/1.3 liters if pressure-cooked)
½ teaspoon (2 ml) turmeric
1 tablespoon (15 ml) butter or *ghee* for *dal*
1½-inch (4 cm) ball of dried tamarind pulp
1 cup (240 ml) boiling water for tamarind
½ cup (45 g) fresh or dried shredded coconut
2 tablespoons (30 ml) raw sugar or *jaggery*
¼–½ teaspoon (1–2 ml) cayenne pepper
⅔ cup (160 ml) water for coconut purée
4 tablespoons (60 ml) *ghee* or vegetable oil
½ tablespoon (7 ml) black mustard seeds
1–2 teaspoons (5–10 ml) minced seeded hot green chilies
¼ teaspoon (1 ml) fenugreek seeds
¼ teaspoon (1 ml) yellow asafetida powder (*hing*)*
12–15 curry leaves, preferably fresh
1 cup (240 ml) green beans cut into 1-inch (2.5 cm) pieces
1 cup (240 ml) carrots cut into ¼-inch (6 mm) slices
1 small eggplant, cut into ¾-inch (2 cm) cubes
2 medium-sized firm ripe tomatoes, cut into quarters
½ tablespoon (7 ml) *sambar masala*
2 teaspoons (10 ml) salt
2–3 tablespoons (30–45 ml) minced fresh parsley or coriander

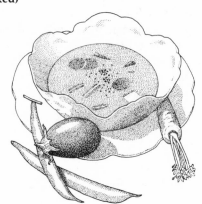

*This amount applies only to yellow Cobra brand. Reduce any other asafetida by three-fourths.

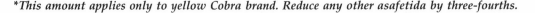

1. Sort, wash and drain the *toovar dal* as explained on page 42. Place the *toovar dal* (or yellow split peas) in a bowl, cover with hot water and soak for 3–5 hours. Drain.

2. Combine the *dal*, 6½ cups (1.5 liters) of water, turmeric and 1 tablespoon (15 ml) of butter or *ghee* in a 3–4-quart/liter nonstick saucepan and bring to a boil over high heat. Reduce the heat to moderately low, cover with a tight-fitting lid and gently simmer for about 1½ hours or until the *dal* is soft and broken down. For pressure cooking, combine the ingredients in a 6-quart/liter pressure cooker, cover and cook under pressure for 20–25 minutes. Remove the pan from the heat and let the pressure drop by itself before removing the lid.

3. Meanwhile, soak the tamarind in 1 cup (240 ml) of boiling water in a small bowl for 20 minutes. Squeeze the tamarind through your fingers to separate the pulp from the seeds and fiber. Force the pulp through a sieve, pressing out all of the juice. Discard any seeds and fiber.

4. Put the coconut, sugar, cayenne pepper and ⅔ cup (160 ml) of water in a blender, cover and blend at high speed until smooth.

5. Heat the 4 tablespoons (60 ml) of *ghee* or oil in a heavy 2½–3-quart/liter saucepan over moderate to moderately high heat. When it is hot, stir in the black mustard seeds, green chilies and fenugreek seeds and fry until the mustard seeds turn gray and sputter and pop and the fenugreek seeds darken a few shades.

For information about unfamiliar ingredients or techniques, see A-to-Z

6. Add the asafetida and curry leaves, then immediately add the green beans, carrots, eggplant, tomatoes, and *sambar masala*. Stir-fry for about 10 minutes. Pour in the tamarind pulp and coconut purée, partially cover and gently cook for 10–15 minutes or until the vegetables are tender.

7. Add the *dal* and the salt and, stirring constantly, simmer for 5 minutes. Garnish with minced herb and serve.

WHOLE BEAN DISHES

Mung Beans with *Panir* Cheese
PANIR SABAT MOONG

This earthy, high-protein bean dish, typical in the Punjab, is ideal for the cold winter months, and can be the main attraction of lunch. Although it goes well with hot rice, I especially recommend it with hot flatbreads, perhaps *Griddle-Baked Paper-Thin Whole Wheat Bread* or *Griddle-Baked Sourdough Bread*. To round off a perfect lunch, try a beautiful *Whole Cauliflower Crowned with Creamy Avocado* and a green salad.

Dal soaking time: 5 hours or overnight
Preparation time (after assembling ingredients): 10 minutes
Cooking time: 1¼–1½ hours
Serves: about 6

1 cup (195 g) whole mung, aduki or *urad* beans
3 cups (710 ml) water
1 teaspoon (5 ml) turmeric
¼–½ teaspoon (1–2 ml) cayenne pepper or paprika
½ tablespoon (7 ml) brown sugar
1½ teaspoons (7 ml) scraped, finely shredded
    or minced fresh ginger root
6 tablespoons (90 ml) *ghee* or a mixture of
    vegetable oil and unsalted butter
fresh *panir* cheese made from 6 cups (1.5 liters) milk (page 313),
    cut into ⅓-inch (1 cm) cubes (about 6 ounces/170 g)
½ teaspoon (2 ml) cumin seeds
¼–½ teaspoon (1–2 ml) yellow asafetida powder (*hing*)*
1 teaspoon (5 ml) *garam masala*
2 medium-sized firm ripe tomatoes, diced
3 tablespoons (45 ml) yogurt or sour cream
2 teaspoons (10 ml) salt
1 teaspoon (5 ml) fresh lemon juice
3 tablespoons (45 ml) minced fresh parsley or coriander
6 lemon or lime wedges or twists for garnishing
6 tomato flowers for garnishing

*This amount applies only to yellow Cobra brand. Reduce any other asafetida by three-fourths.

1. Sort and wash the beans as explained on page 42. Place the beans in a bowl, cover with at least 1½ inches (4 cm) of hot water and soak for 5 hours or overnight. Drain.

2. Bring 3 cups (710 ml) of water to a boil in a heavy 2–3-quart/liter saucepan over high heat. Add the turmeric, cayenne or paprika, sweetener, ginger root and 1 table-spoon (15 ml) of the *ghee* or oil-butter mixture. Add the beans, reduce the heat to low and partially cover. Gently simmer for 1–1¼ hours or until the beans are butter-soft but not mashed or broken. Remove from the heat. Place 1 cup (240 ml) of the cooked beans and liquid in a blender or food processor and blend until smooth. Pour this paste back into the pot of beans.

3. Heat the remaining *ghee* or oil-butter mixture in a wok or frying pan over moderate heat. When it is hot, add the cheese cubes and stir-fry for about 5 minutes, constantly turning the cubes to brown them evenly on all sides. As they turn crisp and golden brown, remove them with a slotted spoon and drop them into the cooked beans.

4. Fry the cumin seeds until they turn brown. Toss in the asafetida powder and *garam masala* and immediately add the tomatoes. Cook the tomatoes until they dry into a thick, moist paste that separates from the *ghee* or oil. Scrape the tomatoes into the cooked *dal*, add the yogurt or sour cream and salt, and gently mix.

5. Pour into a serving dish and sprinkle with lemon juice and minced herb. If desired, drizzle with melted *ghee* or butter. Serve with lemon or lime wedges or twists, alternating them with small tomato flowers, arranged around the edge of the serving dish.

Sautéed Sprouted Mung Beans with Julienne Ginger Root
SABAT MOONG USAL

This Gujarati specialty requires home-sprouted mung or aduki beans in order to be authentic, because the market variety, with 2–3-inch (5–8 cm) tails, is waterlogged. Ideally, the sprouted beans should barely measure ½ inch (1.5 cm). Sprouting increases the vitamin and mineral content of mung or aduki beans and does not take much effort: a little water, up to 2 days' sprouting time, and only a few moments of attention. The sprouts are dressed with complementary flavors: fried spices, lemon juice, shredded mint leaves and a hint of heat. Health enthusiasts may prefer to cook the sprouts only slightly, for a crunchy texture and full food value, while others may prefer to stir-fry them until they are tender-crisp. This dish is a popular breakfast in India, and is adaptable to any season. In winter, accompany it with a hot cup of *Cardamom Milk* or herb tea and fruit compote. In the summer, serve with fruit and a glass of frosted *Papaya Yogurt Shake*, or try a chilled, savory *Cumin-Flavored Yogurt Shake*.

Ginger marinating time: 30 minutes
Preparation time (after assembling ingredients): 5 minutes
Cooking time: 5 minutes
Serves: 4 or 5

For information about unfamiliar ingredients or techniques, see A-to-Z

1½-inch (4 cm) piece of scraped fresh ginger root
1¼ teaspoons (6 ml) salt
3 tablespoons (45 ml) fresh lemon juice
¼ teaspoon (1 ml) yellow asafetida powder (*hing*)*
1 tablespoon (15 ml) ground coriander
¼ teaspoon (1 ml) cayenne pepper or paprika
½ teaspoon (2 ml) turmeric
3 tablespoons (45 ml) *ghee* or vegetable oil
1½ teaspoons (7 ml) cumin seeds
1½ teaspoons (7 ml) black mustard seeds
1½ cups (305 g) whole mung beans, sorted, washed and sprouted
    until the tails are ¼ inch (6 mm) long (page 44)
    (about 3½ cups/830 ml sprouted beans)
1–2 tablespoons (15–30 ml) water
2 teaspoons (10 ml) raw sugar or equivalent sweetener
3 tablespoons (45 ml) minced fresh mint
1 tablespoon (15 ml) butter or *ghee*
4 or 5 radish roses and celery curls for garnishing (optional)

This amount applies only to yellow Cobra brand. Reduce any other asafetida by three-fourths.

1. Cut the ginger root into paper-thin slices, stack and cut again into paper-thin julienne strips. Place all of the strips in a small bowl, sprinkle with ¼ teaspoon (1 ml) of the salt and ½ teaspoon (2 ml) of lemon juice and set aside for 30 minutes.

2. Mix the asafetida powder, ground coriander, cayenne or paprika and turmeric in a small bowl. Heat the *ghee* or oil in a heavy 3–4-quart/liter casserole over moderate to moderately high heat. When it is hot, stir in the cumin seeds and black mustard seeds. Fry until the cumin seeds turn brown. Toss in the powdered spices, and 2 or 3 seconds later stir in the sprouts.

3. Add the 1–2 tablespoons (15–30 ml) of water and cover. Cook for a few minutes if you want your sprouts crunchy, or up to 10 minutes if you want them tender-crisp. Then stir in the sweetener and the rest of the lemon juice and salt.

4. Pour onto a warmed platter or individual plates. Sprinkle with the marinated ginger strips, mint and a drizzle of melted butter or *ghee* and serve immediately. If you like, garnish each serving with a crisp radish rose and celery curl.

Tender-Crisp Sprouted *Urad* Beans in Sesame-Yogurt Sauce
SABAT URAD USAL

Whole *urad* or *muth* beans are the traditional favorites, but you can also use sprouted chickpeas, aduki or mung beans in this dish. Sprouted beans are bursting with nutrition because they are a living, growing food. When left raw, their flavor may be unpalatable to the newcomer. In this dish, however, flavor is obtained without sacrificing the nutritive value of the sprouts. First, a combination of sweet and savory spices is dry-roasted along with shredded coconut and sesame.

When toasted and golden, the seasonings are powdered and blended with yogurt to make a smooth sauce. The sauce is then *chaunked* with spices fried in *ghee*, and finally the sprouts are added and cooked for only a short time, thus preserving their nutritional value. The result is a light, easy-to-digest breakfast dish, or a superb companion to a salad at lunch.

Preparation time (after assembling ingredients): 10 minutes
Cooking time: 5–10 minutes
Serves: 5 or 6

1½ teaspoons (7 ml) cumin seeds
2 teaspoons (10 ml) coriander seeds
6 black peppercorns
½ teaspoon (2 ml) fennel seeds
2 teaspoons (10 ml) sesame seeds
8 whole cloves
¼ cup (25 g) unsweetened shredded coconut, lightly packed
⅔ cup (160 ml) plain yogurt or sour cream
3–4 tablespoons (45–60 ml) *ghee* or vegetable oil
1½ teaspoons (7 ml) scraped, finely shredded
    or minced fresh ginger root
1½ teaspoons (7 ml) minced hot green chili (or as desired)
1 teaspoon (5 ml) black mustard seeds
12 small fresh or dried curry leaves, if available
1 cup (195 g) whole *urad* beans, *muth* beans, mung beans, or chickpeas, sorted, washed and
    sprouted until ⅓ inch (1 cm) long (page 44) (about 2½–3 cups/600–710 ml sprouted)
1 teaspoon (5 ml) salt
1 teaspoon (5 ml) sugar or equivalent sweetener
1 tablespoon (15 ml) fresh lemon juice
2 tablespoons (30 ml) coarsely chopped fresh coriander or minced parsley

   1. Place the cumin seeds, coriander seeds, black peppercorns, fennel seeds, sesame seeds and cloves in a heavy frying pan over moderately low heat. Dry-roast for about 5 minutes. Add the coconut and, stirring frequently, dry-roast it until golden brown. Transfer the roasted ingredients to a blender and blend on high speed until reduced to a powder. Add the yogurt or sour cream and blend on moderately high speed for about 1 minute. Transfer the mixture to a small bowl.
   2. Heat the *ghee* or oil in a large frying pan over moderate to moderately high heat. When it is hot, drop in the ginger root, green chili and black mustard seeds. Fry until the mustard seeds turn gray and sputter and pop. Add the curry leaves and immediately pour in the yogurt seasoning. Fry, uncovered, until half of the liquid has cooked away.
   3. Stir in the sprouts, salt and sweetener. Cover and reduce the heat to moderately low and cook until the sprouted beans are warmed through and slightly softened. How long you cook them is up to you, anywhere from 3 minutes (crunchy) to 10 minutes (tender-crisp).
   4. Pour onto a small serving platter or individual plates and sprinkle with lemon juice and chopped herb.

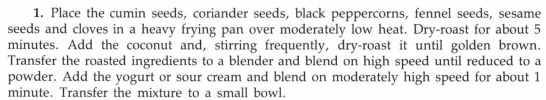

For information about unfamiliar ingredients or techniques, see A-to-Z

Curried Whole Brown Chickpeas
CHOLE

This dish features a small, dark brown chickpea called *kala chana dal*. Generally, it is hard to find, stocked only by Indian or Middle Eastern grocery stores, so it's a good idea to buy a few pounds at a time and keep it on hand for variety in your *dal* cooking. *Chole*, with its characteristic *garam masala* and mango-powder flavor, is both tart and hot—and a very popular dish throughout the Punjab in North India. The texture of the dish can be soupy, with whole beans or dry, with the beans absorbing the zesty sauce. Most often it is served with a puffy deep-fried bread called *bhatura*. This classic combination, *chole-bhatura*, is sold in street stalls and narrow-laned bazaars throughout Uttar Pradesh and Punjab. For contrast, crispy raw vegetable crudités are often served. For a traditional lunch or brunch, serve this dish with *Bhatura* and some of the decorative vegetable garnishes: radish roses, celery curls and cucumber, tomato or carrot flowers. To expand the menu, add a cool dish of *Tart Cream* and accompany with *Pan-Fried Baby Eggplants Stuffed with Ground Almonds.*

Dal **soaking time: 8 hours or overnight**
Preparation time (after assembling ingredients): 15 minutes
Cooking time: 2–3 hours or 1 hour in a pressure cooker
Serves: about 6

1¼ cups (235 g) whole *kala chana* beans or dried chickpeas
5½ cups (1.3 liters) water (4 cups/1 liter if pressure-cooked)
1 cassia or bay leaf
5 tablespoons (75 ml) *ghee* or a mixture of
    vegetable oil and unsalted butter
2-inch (5 cm) piece of cinnamon stick
6 black peppercorns
½ teaspoon (2 ml) cardamom seeds
8 whole cloves
1 tablespoon (15 ml) cumin seeds
1 tablespoon (15 ml) scraped, finely shredded or minced fresh ginger root
1 teaspoon (5 ml) minced seeded hot green chili (or as desired)
1 teaspoon (5 ml) turmeric
1½ teaspoons (7 ml) paprika
1 tablespoon (15 ml) ground coriander
¼–½ teaspoon (1–2 ml) cayenne pepper
¼–½ teaspoon (1–2 ml) yellow asafetida powder (*hing*)*
1 large firm ripe tomato, diced
1–1½ teaspoons (5–7 ml) salt
1 tablespoon (15 ml) *amchoor* powder or
    3 tablespoons (45 ml) fresh lemon or lime juice
3 tablespoons (45 ml) coarsely chopped fresh coriander or minced fresh parsley
6 lemon or lime wedges or twists for garnishing (optional)

This amount applies only to yellow Cobra brand. Reduce any other asafetida by three-fourths.

    1. Sort through the beans and remove any dead kernels or foreign matter. Then rinse and drain. Place the beans in a bowl, add 5½ cups (1.3 liters) of hot water and soak for at least 8 hours or overnight at room temperature.

2. Place the chickpeas and their soaking liquid in a heavy 3–4-quart/liter saucepan. Add the cassia or bay leaf and a dab of *ghee* or oil-butter mixture and bring to a full boil over high heat. Reduce the heat to moderately low, cover with a tight-fitting lid and gently boil for 1½–3 hours or until the beans are butter-soft but not broken down. The cooking time varies according to the freshness of the beans. For pressure cooking, combine the ingredients in a 6-quart/liter pressure cooker, cover and cook under pressure for 30 minutes. Remove from the heat and let the pressure drop by itself.

3. Drain the chickpeas, saving the liquid. Discard the cassia or bay leaf. Take out ⅓ cup (80 ml) of the soft beans and mash to a coarse paste.

4. To make fresh *garam masala*, pound the cinnamon stick into small bits in a stone mortar or with a rolling pin or kitchen mallet. Combine the cinnamon, peppercorns, cardamom seeds, cloves and cumin seeds in an electric coffee mill or stone mortar and grind to a powder.

5. Heat 3 tablespoons (45 ml) of the *ghee* or oil-butter mixture in a heavy 2½–3-quart/liter nonstick saucepan over moderate to moderately high heat. When it is hot, stir in the ginger root and green chili and fry until browned. Remove the pan from the heat and sprinkle in the turmeric, paprika, ground coriander, cayenne and asafetida. Stir well. Place the pan over the heat and immediately drop in the tomato. Stir-fry for 4–5 minutes or until the *ghee* or oil separates from the spices and tomato paste.

6. Stir in the salt, whole chickpeas, mashed chickpeas, ½ cup (120 ml) of the cooking water and the *amchoor* powder or lemon or lime juice. Reduce the heat to low, cover and simmer until the liquid is reduced to a thick sauce. Sprinkle the finished dish with the *garam masala* powder. Stir and sprinkle on the remaining *ghee* or oil and the chopped herb. Garnish, if desired, with lemon or lime wedges or twists.

Savory Chickpeas in Tangy Tomato Glaze
TAMATAR KABLI CHANA USAL

A buttery, spiced tomato glaze coats tender chickpeas in this delicious dried bean dish, ideal for a substantial warm breakfast or brunch with *Griddle-Fried Whole Wheat Bread*, seasonal fruits and a beverage.

Soaking time: 8 hours or overnight
Preparation time (after assembling ingredients): 10 minutes
Cooking time: 2–3 hours or 30–40 minutes in a pressure cooker
Serves: 6

1¼ cups (235 g) dried chickpeas
5½ cups (1.3 liters) water (4 cups/1 liter if pressure-cooked)
5 tablespoons (75 ml) *ghee* or peanut oil
1½ teaspoons (7 ml) scraped, minced fresh ginger root
1½ teaspoons (7 ml) minced hot green chili (or as desired)
1½ teaspoons (7 ml) cumin seeds

For information about unfamiliar ingredients or techniques, see A-to-Z

½ teaspoon (2 ml) black mustard seeds
8–12 small curry leaves, preferably fresh
5 medium-sized tomatoes, peeled, seeded and diced
1 teaspoon (5 ml) turmeric
1 teaspoon (5 ml) *chat masala* or 2 teaspoons (10 ml)
    fresh lemon juice
1 teaspoon (5 ml) *garam masala*
¼ cup (60 ml) minced fresh parsley or coarsely chopped coriander leaves
1¼ teaspoons (6 ml) salt
6 lemon or lime twists for garnishing

1. Place the chickpeas in a bowl, add 5½ cups (1.3 liters) of water and soak for at least 8 hours or overnight at room temperature.

2. Place the chickpeas and their soaking liquid in a heavy 3–4-quart/liter saucepan, add a dab of *ghee* or oil and bring to a full boil over high heat. Reduce the heat to moderately low, cover with a tight-fitting lid and gently boil for 2–3 hours or until the chickpeas are butter-soft but not broken down. For pressure cooking, combine the ingredients in a 6-quart/liter pressure cooker, cover and cook under pressure for 30 minutes. Remove the pan from the heat and allow the pressure to drop by itself before removing the lid. Drain the chickpeas, saving the cooking liquid.

3. Heat 3 tablespoons (45 ml) of *ghee* or oil in a heavy 3-quart/liter nonstick saucepan over moderate to moderately high heat. When it is hot, stir in the ginger root, green chili, cumin seeds and black mustard seeds. Fry until the cumin seeds turn brown.

4. Drop in the curry leaves, and just 1–2 seconds later stir in the tomatoes. Add the turmeric, *chat masala*, *garam masala*, and half of the minced herb. Stir-fry over moderate heat, adding sprinkles of water when necessary, for 3–5 minutes or until the *ghee* or oil separates from the sauce and the texture is smooth and even.

5. Add the chickpeas and ¼ cup (60 ml) of the saved cooking liquid. Reduce the heat to low, cover and gently simmer for about 10 minutes, stirring occasionally. If necessary, add small quantities of the cooking water to keep the mixture from sticking to the saucepan.

6. Remove from the heat and add the salt, the remaining *ghee* or oil and the remaining minced herb. Garnish each portion with a twist of lemon or lime.

Chickpeas and Potato Cubes in Creamy Coconut Sauce
NARIYAL KABLI CHANA USAL

Chickpeas, also known as garbanzo beans, are large beige legumes shaped like wrinkled hazelnuts. They have a faintly nut-like flavor and are naturally rich in protein-nitrogen compounds, important for muscle-building and body growth. When they are combined with this delicately seasoned coconut-yogurt sauce and fried potatoes, they make a sensational dish, bound to turn newcomers into chickpea lovers. If you want a less caloric dish, use steamed potatoes or even replace the potatoes with some type of cooked, chopped or diced green vegetable. This is a nice main-dish vegetable, from brunch to late supper. For a light meal, try it with *Griddle-Baked*

Papaya Whole Wheat Bread and a tossed green salad with *Safflower-Lime Vinaigrette*. For a main meal, you could add *Sweet Saffron Rice with Currants and Pistachios* and *Tomato Soup*.

Soaking time: 8 hours or overnight
Preparation time (after assembling ingredients): 15 minutes
Cooking time: 2–3 hours or 45 minutes in a pressure cooker
Serves: 6

1¼ cups (235 g) dried chickpeas
5½ cups (1.3 liters) water (4 cups/1 liter if pressure-cooked)
4 tablespoons (60 ml) *ghee* or vegetable oil
1½ teaspoons (7 ml) cumin seeds
2 teaspoons (10 ml) coriander seeds
½ teaspoon (2 ml) fennel seeds
8 black peppercorns
1½ tablespoons (22 ml) white poppy seeds or chopped cashews or almonds
1 cup (240 ml) plain yogurt, sour cream or buttermilk
2–3 teaspoons (10–15 ml) minced seeded hot green chilies
1 tablespoon (15 ml) scraped, finely shredded or minced fresh ginger root
1 cup (85 g) fresh or dried grated coconut, lightly packed
ghee or vegetable oil for deep-frying
2 medium-sized baking potatoes, peeled and cut into ½-inch (1.5 cm) dice
1 teaspoon (5 ml) black mustard seeds
6–8 curry leaves, preferably fresh
1¼–1½ teaspoons (6–7 ml) salt
1 teaspoon (5 ml) turmeric
2 tablespoons (30 ml) minced fresh parsley or coarsely chopped coriander
6 lemon or lime wedges or twists for garnishing

   1. Soak the chickpeas in 5½ cups (1.3 liters) of water for at least 8 hours or overnight at room temperature.
   2. Place the chickpeas and their soaking liquid in a heavy 3–4-quart/liter saucepan. Add ½ tablespoon (7 ml) of *ghee* or oil and bring to a full boil over high heat. Reduce the heat to moderately low, cover with a tight-fitting lid and gently boil for 2–3 hours or until the chickpeas are butter-soft but not broken down. For pressure cooking, combine the ingredients in a 6-quart/liter pressure cooker, cover and cook under pressure for about 30 minutes. Remove the pan from the heat and let the pressure drop by itself. Drain, reserving the cooking liquid.
   3. While the beans are cooking, combine the cumin seeds, coriander seeds, fennel seeds, black peppercorns, and poppy seeds or nuts in a heavy frying pan over moderately low heat. Slowly dry-roast until the spices and nuts darken a few shades. Transfer to a blender, electric coffee mill or mortar and reduce to a powder. Combine the yogurt, green chilies, ginger root, powdered spice mixture, dried coconut and ½ cup (120 ml) of the cooking liquid in a blender. Cover and blend on moderately high speed for about 1 minute or until the ingredients are reduced to a smooth sauce.
   4. Heat *ghee* or oil to a depth of 1½ inches (4 cm) in a deep frying pan over moderately high heat until the temperature reaches 365°F (185°C). Carefully put the diced potatoes in the hot *ghee* or oil and fry until crispy and golden brown. Remove, drain and set aside in a preheated 200°F (95°C) oven on a paper-towel-lined baking sheet.
   5. Heat the remaining 3½ tablespoons (53 ml) of *ghee* or oil in heavy 3–4-quart/liter

nonstick saucepan over moderate to moderately high heat. When it is hot, drop in the black mustard seeds and fry until they turn gray and sputter and pop. Stir in the curry leaves and quickly add the chickpeas. Then pour in the coconut-yogurt sauce, salt and turmeric. Reduce the heat to moderately low and cook, uncovered, stirring frequently, until the sauce is reduced to half its original quantity. Just before serving, fold in the fried potato cubes.

6. Garnish each serving with the minced herb and a wedge or twist of citrus.

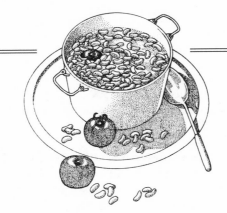

Curried Red Kidney Beans with *Panir* Cheese
RAJMA

If you like Mexican chili, you will love this Punjabi vegetarian specialty. It is robust, nutritious, filling and spicy. Several variations of *Rajma* are popular in Northern India, and this one is my favorite. I first had this dish in a village in Punjab. It was part of a simple, elegant meal served on leaf plates and unglazed clay dishes. At the end of the meal, we discarded the plates and dishes and washed our hands with lemon-scented warm water. The *Rajma* was served with *Deep-Fried Whole Wheat Bread* and *Spinach-Radish Salad*. The mingling of tastes is good for a brunch on a cold winter's day. You can also serve *Rajma* with any bread or rice selection as part of almost any menu.

Soaking time: 8 hours or 1 hour by quick method
Preparation time (after assembling ingredients): 15 minutes
Cooking time: 2½–3½ hours or 1 hour in a pressure cooker
Serves: 6 to 8

For the Beans:

2¼ cups (410 g) dried red kidney beans
6 cups (1.5 liters) water (5 cups/1.25 liters if pressure-cooked)
1 small cassia or bay leaf
¼ teaspoon (1 ml) turmeric
¼ teaspoon (1 ml) cayenne pepper or paprika
1 tablespoon (15 ml) butter or *ghee*

Remaining Ingredients:

2½ tablespoons (37 ml) coriander seeds
1 tablespoon (15 ml) cumin seeds
½ teaspoon (2 ml) fennel seeds
⅓ teaspoon (1.5 ml) *ajwain* seeds
2–3 tablespoons (30–45 ml) scraped, finely shredded
    or minced fresh ginger root
½ cup (120 ml) water
1 teaspoon (5 ml) *garam masala*
1 teaspoon (5 ml) turmeric
1 tablespoon (15 ml) salt
1½ tablespoons (22 ml) fresh lemon or lime juice
5 tablespoons (75 ml) *ghee* or peanut oil
fresh *panir* cheese made from 6 cups (1.5 liters) milk (page 313),
    cut into ½-inch (1.5 cm) cubes (about 6 ounces/170 g)
4 medium-sized firm ripe tomatoes, diced
1 tablespoon (15 ml) *ghee* or butter
¼ cup (60 ml) chopped fresh parsley or coriander

1. Soak the kidney beans in 4 cups (1 liter) of water for at least 8 hours or overnight at room temperature. A quicker method is to wash the beans in a colander under running water, place them in a 3–4-quart/liter saucepan with 3 cups (710 ml) of cold water, and bring to a full boil over high heat. Reduce the heat to moderate, cover and gently boil for 2 minutes. Remove the pan from the heat and allow the beans to soak, covered, for 1 hour.

2. Drain the beans in a colander, collecting the soaking water in a bowl. Add enough cold water to make 6 cups (1.5 liters) and put it, along with the beans and the other ingredients for cooking them, in a 3–4-quart/liter saucepan. Bring to a boil, cover and gently simmer over low heat for 1½–3 hours or until the beans are soft and tender but not broken down. For pressure cooking, combine the ingredients in a 6-quart/liter pressure cooker, cover and cook under pressure for 25–30 minutes. Let the pressure drop and uncover.

3. Mash ¾ cup (180 ml) of the cooked beans to a purée. The cooking liquid should be quite thick. If not, ladle out the tender beans with a slotted spoon and transfer them to a bowl. Gently boil the sauce until it is reduced to about 1½ cups (360 ml). Remove from the heat and set aside.

4. Combine the coriander seeds, cumin seeds, fennel seeds and *ajwain* seeds in an electric coffee mill or a stone mortar and reduce them to a powder. Transfer to a small bowl.

5. Place the ginger root and ½ cup (120 ml) of water in a blender, cover and blend on high speed until the mixture is a smooth liquid. Pour it into the powdered spices and add the *garam masala*, turmeric, salt and lemon or lime juice, then stir. The mixture should have the consistency of thin cream. Add water if it is too thick.

6. Heat 5 tablespoons (75 ml) of *ghee* or oil in a 3–4-quart/liter casserole or nonstick heavy saucepan over moderate heat. When it is hot, drop in the *panir* cheese and stir-fry for 5–7 minutes, carefully turning the cubes with a spatula or spoon until they are browned on all sides. As the cubes brown, transfer them to a dish.

7. Pour the spice paste into the *ghee* or oil and stir-fry for 1–2 minutes. Stir in the tomatoes and cook for about 8 minutes more or until the tomatoes are reduced to a thick paste and the *ghee* or oil separates from the mixture.

8. Add the whole cooked beans, mashed beans, fried cheese cubes and 1½ cups (360 ml) of the cooking liquid, reduce the heat to low and simmer for about 15 minutes. Before serving, stir in 1 tablespoon (15 ml) of *ghee* or butter and the minced herb.

DAL AND RICE DISHES

Khichari is a nutritious stew featuring *dals* and rice, heightened by exquisite spicing. When made properly, it is a dish you will never forget. *Khicharis* show amazing variety, but there are two main types. The moist, mildly seasoned type is called *geeli khichari* and is easily digestible. The dry kind, *sookha khichari*, is usually rich, thick and laced with a medley of nuts, dried fruits or vegetables. The cooking time and amount of water needed may vary according to the age of the *dal*. Some dry *khicharis* are substantial one-dish meals, finished slowly in an oven, like a casserole. Others, cooked entirely on top of the stove, will complement a multicourse meal. However you prepare your *khichari*, you may soon find it becoming an integral part of your daily diet—such is its irresistible taste and appeal.

Rice and Split Pea *Khichari* with Fried Cashews
KHARA MATAR DAL KHICHARI

Sometimes called *pongal*, this South Indian version of *khichari* is juicy, thick and mildly seasoned. It is an ideal way to combine the complementary proteins of yellow or green split peas and rice. When eaten together, the peas and rice supply 43 percent more usable protein than when eaten separately. A generous sprinkling of cashew bits further enriches this easy-to-make, high-protein dish. What is more, it is easy to digest and tastes wonderful. If you want to use less *ghee*, dry-roast the cashews and reduce the amount of *ghee* to as little as 1 tablespoon (15 ml). For a special luncheon, try it with *Crackling-Crispy Dal Wafers*, steamed spinach with *Basil Nutmeg Butter*, *Baked Bananas Stuffed with Tamarind-Flavored Coconut* and *Shredded Cucumbers in Smooth Mint-Flavored Yogurt*. If you want to add a sweet, try fresh fruit or the rich, elegant taste of *Sliced Oranges with Maple Cream*.

Dal soaking time: 3–5 hours
Preparation time (after assembling ingredients): 5 minutes
Cooking time: 1 hour
Serves: 5 or 6

⅓ cup (65 g) yellow or green split peas
7½ cups (1.75 liters) water
5 tablespoons (75 ml) *ghee* or a mixture of vegetable oil and unsalted butter
2 tablespoons (30 ml) scraped, finely shredded or minced fresh ginger root
2 teaspoons (10 ml) cumin seeds
6 whole cloves
¼ teaspoon (1 ml) yellow asafetida powder (*hing*)*
1 cup (95 g) *basmati* or other long-grain white rice
1 teaspoon (5 ml) turmeric
½ teaspoon (2 ml) freshly cracked black pepper
1½ teaspoons (7 ml) salt
⅓ cup (50 g) coarsely chopped or broken raw cashews
5 or 6 pats butter for garnishing (optional)
5 or 6 parsley sprigs for garnishing

This amount applies only to yellow Cobra brand. Reduce any other asafetida by three-fourths.

1. Soak the split peas in 2 cups (480 ml) hot water for 3–5 hours before use. If *basmati* rice is used, clean, wash, soak and drain as explained on page 6.

2. Partially cook the split peas in 3 cups (710 ml) of rapidly boiling water for 20 minutes. Drain.

3. Heat 3 tablespoons (45 ml) of the *ghee* or oil-butter mixture in a heavy 3-quart/liter nonstick saucepan over moderate to moderately high heat. When it is hot, stir in the ginger, cumin seeds and cloves. Fry until the cumin seeds turn brown.

4. Add the asafetida powder. Immediately stir in the rice and fry for 2–3 minutes. Pour in 4 cups (1 liter) of water and add the turmeric, black pepper and salt. Bring rapidly to a full boil. Stir in the split peas. Cover with a tight-fitting lid, reduce the heat to low and slowly cook for about 30 minutes or until the rice and *dal* are tender. Stir in part or all of the remaining ½ cup (120 ml) of water if the mixture is too thick. Remove from the heat.

5. Heat the remaining *ghee* or oil-butter mixture in a small frying pan over low heat. Stir-fry the cashew bits until golden brown and fold them into the rice and *dal* stew. Garnish each serving with a pat of butter and a sprig of parsley.

Rice and Mung *Dal Khichari* with Cauliflower and Peas
GOBHI MOONG DAL KHICHARI

In 1969, Srila Prabhupada and a handful of disciples were the guests of John Lennon and Yoko Ono at their estate near Ascot, England. During our stay, I was Prabhupada's cook. Every day he would give me his lunch menu, and one day he told me exactly how he wanted his *khichari*. He mentioned that the predominant seasonings—cumin, asafetida and turmeric—should be used liberally. The cauliflower should be browned quickly before the soaked rice and *dal* are added. The *khichari* should be served with a separate bowl of melted *ghee*. After lunch, Srila Prabhupada gave his critique and commented: "Very tasty *khichari*—yogurt and fried potatoes—and you have a poor man's feast, fit for a king!"

For information about unfamiliar ingredients or techniques, see A-to-Z

If you do not have split *moong dal* without skins but you really want to try this dish, use whole mung beans. Soak the beans in water overnight. Then rub off the skins, rinse well and drain. Parboil the beans for 20–25 minutes and set them in a strainer to air-dry for about 20 minutes. Continue the recipe as directed. Try this dish with a bowl of *Homemade Yogurt, Deep-Fried Julienne Potatoes and Carrots* and a mixed green salad with tarragon-lime vinaigrette. After dinner, serve crisp apples or a hot cup of *Spiced Apple Cider*.

Preparation time (after assembling ingredients): 5 minutes
Cooking time: 1–1½ hours
Serves: 4 to 6

1 cup (95 g) *basmati* or other long-grain white rice
1 small cauliflower, washed, dried and cut into 2 x ¾ x ¾-inch (5 x 2 x 2 cm) flowerets
¼–½ teaspoon (1–2 ml) yellow asafetida powder (*hing*)*
4 tablespoons (60 ml) *ghee* or a mixture of vegetable oil and unsalted butter
½ tablespoon (7 ml) scraped, finely shredded or minced fresh ginger root
1 tablespoon (15 ml) minced seeded hot green chilies (or as desired)
1 tablespoon (15 ml) cumin seeds
⅔ cup (145 g) split *moong dal*, without skins
¾ cup (180 ml) fresh green peas or frozen baby peas, defrosted
7 cups (1.75 liters) water
1¼ teaspoons (6 ml) turmeric
up to 2½ teaspoons (12 ml) salt
1 tablespoon (15 ml) butter or *ghee*

*This amount applies only to yellow Cobra brand. Reduce any other asafetida by three-fourths.

1. If *basmati* rice is used, clean, wash, soak and drain as explained on page 6.
2. Have the cauliflower and asafetida ready next to the stove. Heat 4 tablespoons (60 ml) of *ghee* or oil-butter mixture in a heavy 4–5-quart/liter nonstick saucepan over high heat. When it is hot but not smoking, stir in the ginger root, green chilies and cumin seeds. Fry until the cumin seeds turn brown (they will darken in seconds).
3. Quickly add the asafetida and immediately follow with the cauliflower. Turn it about with a spoon, frying for 4–5 minutes or until slightly browned and partially cooked. Stir in the rice and *dal*. Fry about 1 minute.
4. Pour in the fresh peas, water and turmeric and bring to a full boil over high heat. Reduce the heat to low, partially cover and slowly cook, stirring occasionally, for 1–1½ hours or until the rice and *dal* are soft and the mixture is similar to oatmeal in consistency. If you use frozen peas, add them during the last 5 minutes. As the *khichari* thickens, stir frequently to prevent sticking. Before serving, add the salt and 1 tablespoon (15 ml) of butter or *ghee*.

Simple Rice and *Chana Dal Khichari* with Dill and Tomatoes
GEELI CHANA DAL KHICHARI

This Gujarati dish takes up to an hour to cook but requires only a few minutes of preparation and very little attention. It is nutritious and exceptionally easy to digest. If you don't have *chana dal*, you could substitute yellow split peas. Try this with a green salad or *Raw Vegetables in Smooth Yogurt* and hot *Griddle-Baked Whole Wheat Bread* or whole wheat toast.

Dal soaking time: 5 hours
Preparation time (after assembling ingredients): 5 minutes
Cooking time: 1–1½ hours
Serves: 5 or 6

¾ cup (150 g) split *chana dal* or split peas
¾ cup (70 g) *basmati* or other long-grain white rice
6½ cups (1.5 liters) water
1 teaspoon (5 ml) turmeric
½ tablespoon (7 ml) dried dill weed or 3 tablespoons (45 ml) chopped fresh dill
½ teaspoon (2 ml) *garam masala*
3 tablespoons (45 ml) *ghee* or vegetable oil
2 teaspoons (10 ml) cumin seeds
½–1 whole dried red chili
¼ teaspoon (1 ml) yellow asafetida powder (*hing*)*
2 medium-sized tomatoes, each cut into 8 pieces
1 teaspoon (5 ml) salt

This amount applies only to yellow Cobra brand. Reduce any other asafetida by three-fourths.

1. Soak the *dal* or split peas in 3 cups (710 ml) of hot water for 5 hours, then drain. If *basmati* rice is used, clean, wash, soak and drain as explained on page 6.

2. Place the *dal*, rice, water, turmeric, dill and *garam masala* in a heavy 3–4-quart/liter nonstick heavy saucepan and bring to a boil over high heat. Reduce the heat to low, partially cover, and slowly cook for 1–1½ hours or until the *dal* is butter-soft and the liquid is absorbed. Remove from the heat.

3. Heat the *ghee* or oil in a small saucepan over moderate to moderately high heat. When it is hot, stir in the cumin seeds and red chili. Fry until the cumin seeds are brown. Sprinkle in the asafetida powder and immediately add the tomato pieces. Fry for 1–2 minutes or until the tomatoes soften and glisten with *ghee* or oil. Pour the fried seasoning into the cooked *dal*, stir in the salt and serve.

Lavish Rice and Mung *Dal Bunchi Khichari*
BUNCHI MOONG DAL KHICHARI

In the temple of Lord Jagannatha in Puri, Orissa, this *khichari* dish is served daily during the fortnight preceding the Festival of the Chariots. The Festival, which honors Lord Jagannatha as

For information about unfamiliar ingredients or techniques, see A-to-Z

Lord of the Universe, draws millions of pilgrims from across the subcontinent and has been held in Puri annually for the past two thousand years. Srila Prabhupada sent out two variations of this dish in letters, one to me personally, just prior to one year's Festival. This is my own rendition, based on his instructions, and one I made for him personally, which he claimed "was second to none." For a drier variation, you can reduce the water by one-third.

Few dishes are as visually and nutritionally well-balanced and appetizingly fragrant as *bunchi khichari*. It is not time-consuming to prepare, the most tedious part being the sorting and washing of the *basmati* rice (if you use it) and split mung beans. The rest is a simple matter of frying the nuts and spices, adding the rice and *dal* and simmering in a covered saucepan. Here is a main dish you can always count on for a warm reception. On the one hand, it is a full meal accompanied only by a tossed salad. On the other hand, it fits into numerous larger menus, such as summer or fall holiday fare. Try it with *Bitter Melon Chips with Ground Almonds; Summer Squash with Green Peas* or *Bottle Gourd and Green Peas in Tomato Broth; Mashed Potato Balls Spiked with Horseradish* or *Butternut Squash Purée with Coconut* and a small dish of cooling *Homemade Yogurt* garnished with freshly ground pepper. Add flair with piping-hot *Deep-Fried Whole Wheat Bread* or *Deep-Fried Banana Whole Wheat Bread*, and finish with a taste of *Lemon-Lime Cheese Fudge* or elegant *Rainbow Layered Cheese Fudge Bars*.

Preparation and cooking time (after assembling ingredients): 1¼ hours
Serves: 6

1 cup (95 g) *basmati* or other long-grain white rice
¾ cup (170 g) split *moong dal*, without skins, sorted, washed and drained
1½ teaspoons (7 ml) turmeric
about 8 cups (2 liters) water
½ cup (120 ml) *ghee* or a mixture of vegetable oil and unsalted butter
⅓ cup (45 g) raw cashew bits or halves
⅓ cup (40 g) sliced raw almonds
¼ cup (25 g) fresh or dried ribbon coconut
⅓ cup (45 g) raisins or currants
3-inch (7.5 cm) piece of cinnamon stick
8 whole cloves
1 tablespoon (15 ml) cumin seeds
1–2 whole dried red chilies
2 tablespoons (30 ml) raw sugar or equivalent sweetener
¼ teaspoon (1 ml) yellow asafetida powder (*hing*)*
1 cup (240 ml) fresh green peas or frozen baby peas, defrosted
2½–3 teaspoons (12–15 ml) salt
2 tablespoons (30 ml) butter or *ghee*
3 tablespoons (45 ml) minced fresh parsley or coarsely chopped coriander

*This amount applies only to yellow Cobra brand. Reduce any other asafetida by three-fourths.

1. If *basmati* rice is used, clean, wash, soak and drain as explained on page 6.
2. Combine the split *moong dal*, rice and turmeric in a bowl, sprinkle in about 1 teaspoon (5 ml) of the water and stir until the mixture is coated with the turmeric.
3. Heat the *ghee* or oil-butter mixture in a heavy 3–4-quart/liter nonstick saucepan over moderate heat. One after another, separately fry the cashew nuts, almonds and coconut, until they each become golden brown. As the batches brown, remove with a slotted spoon and transfer to paper towels to drain. Add the raisins and mix well.
4. Increase the heat to moderately high, add the cinnamon stick, cloves, cumin seeds, red chilies and sweetener and fry until the cumin seeds darken and the sweetener caramelizes and turns a rich reddish-brown.

5. Drop in the asafetida, stir in the rice and *dal* mixture and stir-fry for 2–3 minutes. Pour in the water, raise the heat to high and bring the liquid to a full boil. Mix in three-fourths of the fried nut, coconut and raisin mixture. If you are using fresh peas, add them now. Reduce the heat to moderately low and cover with a tight-fitting lid. Slowly cook, stirring occasionally, for about 1 hour or until the grains are soft and slightly broken down and all of the water has been absorbed. During the last 10–15 minutes you may need to add more water; stir frequently to distribute the small quantity of remaining liquid throughout the simmering mixture. If you are using frozen peas, add them during the last 5 minutes.

6. Before serving, stir in the salt and 2 tablespoons (30 ml) of butter or *ghee*. Garnish the top with the remaining nut mixture and the minced herb.

Rice and Toasted *Toovar Dal Khichari* with Mixed Vegetables
TOOVAR DAL SABJI KHICHARI

When I first met Srila Prabhupada's younger sister, Pishima, in 1972, I could not speak more than pidgin Bengali, nor could she speak English. But kitchen language is universal, and I was an eager student. She was silent as she cooked, usually making only Bengali dishes. Though she was expert in all phases of Bengali cuisine, her *khicharis*, *shuktas* and sweets stand out in my memory. This delightful dish is made special by dry-roasting the *toovar dal* before it is cooked. During the period of *Kartikka*, *khichari* was often an integral part of Pishima's noon menu. A typical November lunch might include *Pan-Fried Chenna Cheese Patties with Poppy Seeds*, *Crispy-Fried Diced Eggplant with Bitter Neem Leaves* and small bowls of *Sautéed Bell Peppers in Karhi Sauce*. For a sweet, she might add *Nut-Stuffed Chenna Balls in Rose Syrup*.

Dal soaking time: 3 hours for the *toovar dal*, 5 hours for the
    yellow split peas
Preparation time (after assembling ingredients): 15 minutes
Cooking time: 1–1½ hours
Serves: 6 to 8

1 cup (95 g) *basmati* or other long-grain white rice
¼ cup (40 g) raisins or currants
⅔ cup (135 g) split *toovar dal* or yellow split peas
2-inch (5 cm) piece of cinnamon stick
8 whole cloves
½ teaspoon (2 ml) black cardamom seeds
    (about 6 green cardamom pods)
3 tablespoons (45 ml) water for the ginger
½-inch (1.5 cm) scraped fresh ginger root, coarsely chopped
1 cup (240 ml) *ghee* or vegetable oil
½ small cauliflower, cut into 1-inch (2.5 cm) flowerets
⅔ cup (160 ml) sliced red or white radishes
2 teaspoons (10 ml) cumin seeds

1 small cassia or bay leaf
⅓–½ teaspoon (1.5–2 ml) yellow asafetida powder (*hing*)*
2 medium-sized tomatoes, each cut into 8 pieces
7½ cups (1.75 liters) water
1 teaspoon (5 ml) turmeric
⅔ cup (160 ml) green beans, washed, trimmed
    and cut into 1-inch (2.5 cm) lengths
1½ teaspoons (7 ml) salt
2 tablespoons (30 ml) minced fresh parsley or
    coarsely chopped coriander
6–8 pats of butter for garnishing (optional)
6–8 parsley sprigs for garnishing

*This amount applies only to yellow Cobra brand. Reduce any other asafetida by three-fourths.

  1. If *basmati* rice is used, clean, wash, soak and drain as explained on page 6.
  2. Soak the raisins꞉ in hot water for about 15 minutes, then drain. Remove any foreign matter from the *dal*. If using *toovar dal*, soak it in hot water for 3 hours; if using yellow split peas, soak them in hot water for 5 hours. Pour the soaked *dal* into a strainer and air-dry for 20–25 minutes. Dry-roast the *dal* in a heavy iron frying pan over low heat, stirring frequently, for 12 minutes or until the *dal* turns reddish-brown. Set aside.
  3. Pound the cinnamon stick into small bits with a mortar and pestle, kitchen mallet or rolling pin. Combine the cinnamon bits, whole cloves and cardamom seeds in an electric coffee mill or a stone mortar and reduce to a powder. Transfer to a small bowl. Blend the 3 tablespoons (45 ml) of water and the ginger root in a blender for 30 seconds. Pour the ginger water into the bowl of powdered spices and mix the paste *masala* well.
  4. Heat the *ghee* or oil in a medium-sized frying pan over moderately high heat. When it is hot, shallow-fry the cauliflower until slightly browned, then remove it with a slotted spoon to a bowl. Shallow-fry the sliced radishes until slightly browned, remove with a slotted spoon and transfer to the same bowl. Remove the *ghee* or oil from the heat. Measure out ⅓ cup (80 ml) of the hot *ghee* or oil and pour it into a heavy 3-quart/liter nonstick saucepan over moderate heat.
  5. Stir in the cumin seeds and fry until they turn brown. Toss in the cassia leaf and asafetida powder, then immediately follow with the paste *masala*. Fry for about 30 seconds, then stir in the tomato pieces and fry until they glisten with *ghee* or oil. Pour in the 7½ cups (1.75 liters) of water, toasted *dal*, rice, turmeric and raisins. Bring the liquid to a full boil over high heat.
  6. Reduce the heat to low or moderately low, cover with a tight-fitting lid and slowly cook for 15 minutes. Add the cauliflower, radishes and green beans. Cover again and cook for 30–40 minutes, stirring occasionally, until the grains and vegetables are soft and tender and the water is fully absorbed. Stir frequently during the last 10 minutes to avoid scorching and to distribute the remaining water throughout the simmering mixture. Stir in the salt and minced herb before serving. Garnish each portion with a pat of butter and sprig of parsley.

SUN-DRIED *DAL BADIS*

No presentation of *dal* cooking would be complete without mentioning sun-dried *dal badis*, also known as *warian* or sometimes *varhia*. A well-stocked Vedic larder is rarely without one or two selections of these staples. To make *badis*, *dals* are soaked, ground, mixed with spices and made into firm doughs or pastes. They are then shaped into dollops or hollowed-out knobs and sun-dried until thoroughly brittle. Though you need really hot summer temperatures to make them at home outdoors, you can effectively make them indoors in a food dehydrator. Once they are made or purchased, you can get away with using them for up to a year if they are kept in airtight containers in the refrigerator or a cool, dark cupboard. For occasional use, I suggest purchasing them ready-made from an Indian grocery store. Do not hesitate to inquire about the freshness of new stocks. Two types of *badis* are usually available. One, made from *moong dal*, is smallish and lightly seasoned; the other, made from *urad dal*, is walnut-sized and very hot and spicy. I have included recipes for both of these and others not available ready-made.

Before cooking any type of *badis*, break them into pieces roughly ¼ inch (6 mm) in diameter. Use any available tool—a kitchen mallet, a hammer or even a clean garden rock. Do not discard the splintered bits and pieces, as they can all be used. Nine times out of ten, *badis* are browned in hot *ghee* or vegetable oil before being cooked and softened. There is an occasional Bengali stew in which they are cooked whole, without browning, and broken up with a spoon when soft.

GRINDING *DALS*: Stone-grinding *dals* is time-consuming and requires considerable skill. If you have the equipment and the inclination, by all means go ahead and carry on with the traditional method. Most of us will prefer the food processor or blender, both of which yield smoothly ground, light pastes.

To grind *dal* in a food processor, first attach the metal cutting blade. Place up to 1½ cups (315 g) of soaked, well-drained *dal* in the work bowl, cover and process for about a minute. Scrape down the sides of the bowl with a spatula to keep the *dal* near the work blades. Process for up to 5 minutes, adding only enough water to facilitate grinding the *dal* to a thick paste. Stop to occasionally scrape down the sides of the work bowl. The final texture should be a fine but dense paste, resembling a heavy cornmeal muffin batter.

To grind *dal* in a blender, place up to 1 cup (210 g) of soaked, well-drained *dal* in the blender jar and add 1–2 tablespoons (15–30 ml) of water. Cover and blend on high speed for 15–20 seconds. Remove the lid, scrape down the sides of the jar with a rubber spatula, replace the cover and continue the process for 4–5 minutes or until a light, fine-ground paste is obtained. The idea is to use the minimum amount of water needed for grinding. When you have finished one batch, remove it and start another. This method takes a bit more time than the food processor, but gives good results.

For information about unfamiliar ingredients or techniques, see A-to-Z

DRYING *DAL BADIS*: There are two ways of drying *badis* at home: in the sun or with artificial heat. Sun-drying is practical, simple and, according to many, the most healthful if the weather is right. The ideal condition is a temperature of at least 100°F (40°C) and low humidity. Drying time varies but is measured only in days, not nights. This is because foods do not dry at night, when dew and condensation replace some of the moisture lost during the day. If you sun-dry, bring your drying trays indoors with the setting of the sun. Drying time will vary according to the size of the *badis* and the outside temperature, but the process should take no more than 3–4 days of hot sun. *Badis* must be thoroughly dried with no hint of moisture in the center; otherwise, there is every chance of spoilage. Break one apart to see if the center is absolutely dry, and store them only when all moisture has evaporated. For sun-drying, almost any clean, flat surface will do, but I prefer nylon-mesh screen. Once the *badis* have set into shape, turn them occasionally to allow them to breathe and to dry evenly. If you use a food de-hydrator, follow the manufacturer's instructions and check the *badis* after about 24 or 36 hours. Allow the dried *badis* to rest a bit at room temperature before storing; then store them in an airtight container labeled with the date.

Sun-Dried Mung *Dal Badi*
MOONG BADI

This variation of *badi* is mild and versatile. You can fry up to ½ cup (45 g) of *badi* bits in *ghee* or oil to brown them, add them to any pilaf, pan-fried vegetable or soup and cook them until softened. You will get an idea of how to use *badis* by trying one or two recipes such as *Rice with Crunchy Fried Badis and Green Beans* or *Green Beans with Crunchy Fried Mung Badis*. This recipe makes a small jar of *badis*, so if you really enjoy them you can double or triple the measurements to be assured of a good supply.

Dal soaking time: 8 hours or overnight
Preparation time (after assembling ingredients): 45 minutes
Resting time for ground *dal*: 4 hours
Drying time: 2–4 days
Makes: about 50–70 small knobs

1½ cups (325 g) split *moong dal*, without skins
water for soaking and grinding
1½ teaspoons (7 ml) salt (optional)
2 tablespoons (30 ml) minced hot green chilies
¼ teaspoon (1 ml) baking soda
1 tablespoon (15 ml) vegetable oil
up to ¼ cup (35 g) mung bean flour
   or whole wheat flour, if necessary

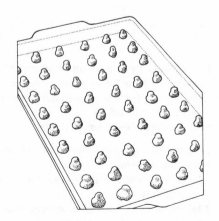

1. Pick over the *moong dal* to remove any foreign matter, then rinse. Place it in a bowl and cover with at least 1½ inches (4 cm) of water. Soak for 8 hours or overnight. Drain well in a wire-mesh strainer.

2. To grind the paste in a food processor, first attach the metal cutting blade. Place the *dal* in the work bowl, add enough water to facilitate grinding (starting with 2–3 teaspoons/10–15 ml) and process for about 5 minutes, turning the machine off to scrape the *dal* down the sides of the jar to the blades whenever necessary. This will grind the *dal* to a smooth texture and whisk air into it as well.

To grind the paste in a blender, place half of the *dal* in the blender jar and add 2 tablespoons (30 ml) of water. Cover and blend on high speed for 15 seconds, then turn off the machine and scrape the *dal* down the sides of the jar with a spatula. Continue this process of blending for 15 seconds, turning off the machine and scraping the *dal* down the walls into the center for about 5 minutes or until the *dal* has broken down into a perfectly smooth paste. Use only as much water as necessary to facilitate the grinding. Transfer the *dal* paste to a bowl and repeat the process for the remaining *dal*.

3. Gently blend in the remaining ingredients and, depending on the consistency of your paste, add flour if it needs thickening. You should have a paste that, when dropped from a teaspoon, will hold its shape. Cover the bowl and set in a warm nook for about 4 hours.

4. If you are drying the *badis* on trays, rub a thin film of oil over the surface with your palms. Using your fingertips or two teaspoons, drop small, even-sized dollops of the *dal* paste onto the trays or screens. Use a scant teaspoon (5 ml) of paste for each *badi*. Sun-dry as explained on page 87, or dry in a dehydrator until thoroughly brittle. Store in airtight containers. Label with the date, and use when desired.

Sun-Dried Tomato-Flavored Mung *Dal Badi*
MOONG TAMATAR BADI

In this second *badi* recipe, two kinds of chili are added for heat and a fresh tomato paste is added for robust flavor. If you use this *badi* in another dish which calls for chilies, remember that there is already a trace of heat, so adjust the particular recipe by reducing or eliminating the chilies or cayenne.

Dal soaking time: 8 hours or overnight
Preparation time (after assembling ingredients): 45 minutes
Resting time for the ground *dal*: 4 hours
Drying time: 2–4 days
Makes: about 50–70 small knobs

1½ cups (325 g) split *moong dal*, without skins
water for soaking and grinding
3 large firm ripe tomatoes (about 1¼ pounds/570 g), quartered
⅓ cup (80 ml) water
2 tablespoons (30 ml) *ghee* or vegetable oil
1½ tablespoons (22 ml) cumin seeds
1½ teaspoons (7 ml) salt

For information about unfamiliar ingredients or techniques, see A-to-Z

1 tablespoon (15 ml) *garam masala*
¼ teaspoon (1 ml) baking soda
½ teaspoon (2 ml) cayenne pepper
1–2 hot green chilies, seeded and finely chopped
up to ¼ cup (35 g) mung bean flour or whole wheat flour, if necessary

1. Pick over the *moong dal* to remove any foreign matter, then rinse. Place it in a bowl and cover with at least 1½ inches (4 cm) of water. Soak for 8 hours or overnight. Drain well in a wire-mesh strainer.

2. Place the tomatoes and water in a small saucepan, cover and simmer for 10 minutes to soften. Force the juice and tomato pulp through a fine strainer and collect in a bowl. Discard the skins and seeds.

3. Heat the *ghee* or oil in a small saucepan over moderate to moderately high heat. When it is hot, drop in the cumin seeds and fry until they are brown. Add the salt and tomato pulp. Stirring frequently, fry until the liquid has evaporated and the oil separates from the paste. Set aside to cool.

4. To grind the paste in a food processor, first attach the metal cutting blade. Place the *dal* in the work bowl and add enough water to facilitate grinding (starting with 2–3 teaspoons/10–15 ml). Process for about 5 minutes, turning the machine off to scrape the *dal* down the sides of the jar to the blades whenever necessary. This will grind the *dal* to a smooth texture and whisk air into it as well.

To grind the paste in a blender, place half of the *dal* in the blender jar and add 2 tablespoons (30 ml) of water. Cover and blend on high speed for 15 seconds, then turn off the machine and scrape the *dal* down the sides of the jar with a spatula. Continue this process of blending for 15 seconds, turning off the machine and scraping the *dal* down the walls into the center for about 5 minutes or until the *dal* has broken down into a perfectly smooth paste. Use only as much water as necessary to facilitate the grinding. Transfer the *dal* paste to a bowl and repeat the process for the remaining *dal*.

5. Gently combine the tomato paste, *garam masala*, soda, cayenne, green chilies and *dal* paste. Add flour, if necessary, to thicken the paste; when dropped from a teaspoon the paste should hold its shape. Cover the bowl and set in a warm nook for about 4 hours.

6. If you are drying the *badis* on trays, rub a thin film of oil on the trays with your palms. Using your fingertips or two teaspoons, drop small, even-sized dollops of the *dal* paste onto the trays or screens. Use a scant teaspoon (5 ml) of paste for each *badi*. Sun-dry as explained on page 87, or dry in a dehydrator until thoroughly brittle. Store in airtight containers, label with the date and use as desired.

Spicy Sun-Dried *Urad Dal Badi*
URAD BADI

Also known as Punjabi *urad badi*, this *badi* is available in Indian grocery stores. Black pepper, crushed red chilies and crushed spice seeds are combined with the *urad dal* paste before being shaped into large, hollow cakes about 2 inches (5 cm) in diameter. The spicy dried cakes are then cracked into pea-sized bits and added to rice or vegetable dishes, savories or *dal* soups for extra aroma and texture. Before adding the *badis*, remember to compensate for the considerable amount of spice that the *badi* will lend to this dish. One cake is usually enough to spice a totally unseasoned dish for as many as four persons, so make your adjustments accordingly. Try these *badis* in *Succulent Mixed Vegetables with Crunchy Fried Badis*, *Clear Broth with Potatoes and Urad Badis* or *Char-Flavored Vegetable Medley with Crunchy Dal Badis*.

Dal soaking time: 8 hours or overnight
Preparation time (after assembling ingredients): 45 minutes
Resting time for the *dal* paste: 4 hours
Drying time: 2–4 days
Makes: about 24 large knobs

1¼ cups (260 g) split *urad dal*, without skins
water for soaking and grinding
2 tablespoons (30 ml) coriander seeds
1½ tablespoons (22 ml) cumin seeds
1½ teaspoons (7 ml) fennel seeds
½ tablespoon (7 ml) cracked black pepper
1½ tablespoons (22 ml) crushed red chilies (or as desired)
½ teaspoon (2 ml) yellow asafetida powder (*hing*)*
scant ½ teaspoon (2 ml) baking soda
1½ teaspoons (7 ml) salt
up to 4 tablespoons (35 g) *urad* flour
    or whole wheat flour, if necessary

This amount applies only to yellow Cobra brand. Reduce any other asafetida by three-fourths.

  1. Pick over the *urad dal* to remove any foreign matter, then rinse. Place it in a bowl and cover with at least 1½ inches (4 cm) of water. Soak for 8 hours or overnight. Drain well in a wire-mesh strainer.
  2. Combine the coriander seeds, cumin seeds and fennel seeds in a heavy frying pan. Dry-roast over moderately low heat until the cumin seeds turn one or two shades darker. Remove and crush coarsely.
  3. To grind the paste in a food processor, first attach the metal cutting blade. Place the *dal* in the work bowl and add enough water to facilitate grinding (starting with 2–3 teaspoons/10–15 ml). Process for about 5 minutes, turning the machine off to scrape the *dal* down the sides of the jar to the blades whenever necessary. This will grind the *dal* to a smooth texture and whisk air into it as well.
  To grind the paste in a blender, place half of the *dal* in the blender jar and add 2 tablespoons (30 ml) of water. Cover and blend on high speed for 15 seconds, then turn off the machine and scrape the *dal* down the sides of the jar with a spatula. Continue this process of blending for 15 seconds, turning off the machine and scraping the *dal* down the walls into the center for about 5 minutes or until the *dal* has broken down into a perfectly smooth paste. Use only as much water as necessary to facilitate the grinding. Transfer the *dal* paste to a bowl and repeat the process for the remaining *dal*.
  4. Gently blend in the remaining ingredients, adding the flour if the paste needs thickening; dropped from a teaspoon, the paste should hold its shape. Cover the bowl and set in a warm nook for about 4 hours.
  5. If you are drying the *badis* on trays, rub a thin film of oil on the trays with

For information about unfamiliar ingredients or techniques, see A-to-Z

your palms. Divide the paste into 24 even-sized balls. Press your thumb halfway through each ball to hollow out the inside; then set it, round side up, on a tray. Sun-dry as explained on page 87, or dry in a dehydrator until thoroughly brittle. These *badis* take some time to dry. They will flatten out as they set, but once they begin to firm up, round them out again and turn them over. When completely dry, store in airtight containers. Label with the date and use as desired.

Sun-Dried *Urad Dal Badi* with White Poppy Seeds
URAD KHAS-KHAS BADI

Sometimes called *phoola badi*, these are found in many kitchens in Bengal. They are mildly spiced, with a hint of nut-like flavor from the poppy seeds.

Dal soaking time: 8 hours or overnight
Preparation time (after assembling ingredients): 45 minutes
Resting time for the *dal* paste: 4 hours
Drying time: 2–4 days
Makes: about 50–70 small knobs

1¼ cups (260 g) split *urad dal*, without skins
water for soaking and grinding
½ teaspoon (2 ml) yellow asafetida powder (*hing*)*
½ teaspoon (2 ml) cayenne pepper or paprika (or as desired)
⅔ cup (160 ml) white poppy seeds, soaked for 2 hours, then drained
1 teaspoon (5 ml) salt
¼ teaspoon (1 ml) baking soda
up to 4 tablespoons (35 g) *urad* flour or whole wheat flour, if necessary

*This amount applies only to yellow Cobra brand. Reduce any other asafetida by three-fourths.

1. Sort over the *urad dal* to remove any foreign matter, then rinse. Place it in a bowl and cover it with at least 1½ inches (4 cm) of water. Soak for 8 hours or overnight. Drain well in a wire-mesh strainer.

2. To grind the paste in a food processor, first attach the steel cutting blade. Place the *dal* in the work bowl, add enough water to facilitate grinding (starting with 2–3 teaspoons/10–15 ml) and process for about 5 minutes, turning the machine off to scrape the *dal* down the sides of the jar to the blades whenever necessary. This will grind the *dal* to a smooth texture and whisk air into it as well.

To grind the paste in a blender, place half of the *dal* in the blender jar and add 2 tablespoons (30 ml) of water. Cover and blend on high speed for 15 seconds, then turn off the machine and scrape the *dal* down the sides of the jar with a spatula. Continue this process of blending for 15 seconds, turning off the machine and scraping the *dal* down the walls into the center for about 5 minutes or until the *dal* has become a perfectly smooth paste. Use only as much water as necessary to facilitate the grinding. Transfer the *dal* paste to a bowl and repeat the process for the remaining *dal*.

3. Gently blend in the remaining ingredients, adding the flour if needed to thicken the paste; when dropped from a teaspoon, the paste should hold its shape. Cover the bowl and set in a warm nook for about 4 hours.

4. If you are drying the *badis* on trays, rub a thin film of oil on the trays with your palms. Using your fingertips or two teaspoons, drop small, even-sized dollops of the *dal* paste onto the trays or screens. Use a scant teaspoon (5 ml) of paste for each *badi*. Sun-dry as explained on page 87, or dry in a dehydrator until thoroughly brittle. Store in airtight containers, label with the date and use as desired.

Breads

Breads—nutritious, economical and delicious—are a challenge welcomed by cooks all over the world. And, if you'll pardon the enthusiasm, the breads in this chapter are some of the best. Once tasted, they will win their way into your heart and stay there.

Vedic breads have stayed close to their origins. Vedic literature even mentions the unpretentious *chapati*'s role in sumptuous *prasadam* feasts. As fundamental to Vedic cooking as the sacred *Bhagavad Gita* and Ganges River are to Vedic philosophy, these whole grain breads play an integral part in the world's oldest cuisine. Vedic breads are unleavened and flat, quite different from Western oven-baked, leavened loaves. There are, of course, other flat, unleavened breads in the world—Mexican corn or wheat *tortillas*, Norwegian potato *lefse*, Finnish rye *sultsinas* or graham *flatbrøt*—but they hardly compare in scope to the Vedic flatbreads.

In one sense, nothing could be more unsophisticated than Vedic flatbreads. What could be more straightforward than dough made from water and predominantly stone-ground whole wheat flour, rolled into thin circles and cooked on top of the stove for a few minutes? Yet they are unexcelled in nutrition, aroma, taste, and texture. Different flour mixtures, shaping techniques and cooking mediums produce a variety of tastes and textures. To introduce you to the classics, I have divided the breads roughly into five categories: griddle-baked, griddle-fried, shallow-fried, deep-fried and variations.

GRIDDLE-BAKED BREAD: The daily breads of India—*chapati, phulka* and *roti*—are usually made of finely milled whole wheat flour and water. Griddle-baked breads are typically made without salt or oil, but a touch of salt or a spoonful of *ghee* are used in some regional cuisines to round out flavors or tenderize the dough. Small amounts of maize, millet or chickpea flour, even shredded or mashed vegetables may be added for nutrition or flavor variation.

The cooking is in two phases: rounds of dough are baked on a hot griddle until three-quarters cooked, then held over direct heat, where they puff into steam-filled balloons. The open flame dots the breads with charcoal accents but does not burn them, and they remain soft and pliable.

Whether you serve these breads plain or brush them with melted butter or *ghee* (seasoned, if desired), they are at their best hot off the flame, or at least kept warm in towel-lined baskets. Allow 2–3 *chapatis* or *rotis* per person and 1–2 *phulkas*.

GRIDDLE-FRIED BREADS: These breads, called *parathas*, are flaky and somewhat more substantial than griddle-baked breads. The dough, usually made from wheat flour, is enriched with light to liberal amounts of melted butter or *ghee*. In their simplest form, *parathas* are layered: brush the rounds with *ghee*, fold, turn and roll out again. As the bread cooks on the hot griddle, steam makes the layers of dough swell and puff, resulting in flaky, pastrylike flatbreads. *Parathas* are sometimes stuffed with herbed potatoes, shredded radishes, minted peas or even jams or dried fruit pastes. They are perfect afternoon snacks, lunch-box favorites, light brunch items or traveling companions. Cut into wedges, they are excellent finger foods for parties. If *parathas* are a featured menu item, allow 2 per person; as part of a large meal, 1 per person.

SHALLOW-FRIED BREADS: These puff-pastry flatbreads are delicate, rich and elegant. The dough is light—usually a mixture of whole wheat *chapati* flour and unbleached white flour (sometimes only unbleached white flour) enriched with *ghee* and sweet spices such as cardamom, fennel or saffron. I find that a combination of three parts unbleached white flour and one part cake flour yields a particularly silky-textured dough for the delicate *paratha* variations. To achieve a flaky crumb, roll out the breads, twirl into spirals and roll out again before shallow-frying. They are basted as they cook. Save your shallow-fried *paratha* selections for a special late-morning Sunday breakfast, brunch or small-menu celebration. If *parathas* are a featured menu item, allow 2 per person; as part of a large meal, 1 per person.

DEEP-FRIED BREADS: These flatbreads are for festive occasions—parties and banquets. The simplest are whole wheat *pooris*: rounds of tenderized dough are slipped into hot oil or *ghee*, where they fill with steam and balloon in seconds. *Poori* crusts are thin, light and golden brown. The thicker *luchis* and *bhaturas* are usually made from unbleached white flour and have a pale gold, puffed crust. Allow 2–3 per person, depending on the size of the breads and the accompanying dishes.

BREAD VARIATIONS: This small category includes a sample of techniques—baked bread balls, flame-toasted *dal* wafers, a steamed savory cake and clay-baked flatbreads. The village bread ball delicacy, *baati*, is traditionally made by nestling balls of dough in dying coal embers, where they bake ever so slowly into smoke-flavored charred breads. The outer crust is scraped off and the balls are floated in *dal* soup to become part of a popular dish known as *dal baati*. Crispy-crackling *paparh* or *pappadam* wafers are part of a full dinner menu, usually as a closing item. They can be flame-toasted or deep-fried; both methods yield excellent results. The steamed Gujarati bread known as *dhokla* is reminiscent of an herbed corn bread and is delicious as a snack or with soup. *Naan* is the most popular flatbread in North Indian homes and restaurants equipped with a coal- or wood-fired clay *tandoor* oven, which produces an exceptionally flavorful crust and light crumb. Many city dwellers throughout Punjab and Uttar Pradesh take advantage of custom-order takeouts at neighborhood *tandoor* bakeries. Though the smoky *tandoor* is important for flavor, you can achieve a very good crust and crumb by baking the breads on an unglazed pizza stone (available at better cookware stores and from mail order kitchen suppliers).

FLOURS

Wheat, known as *gehun*, has been cultivated in northern India for over 5,000 years. Ancient cooks used it much as today's cooks do—coarsely cracked for pilafs, finely cracked and boiled in milk for puddings, or ground into flour for flatbreads. Though untreated whole wheat is widely regarded as the most nutritionally well-balanced flour, legume, vegetable and other grain flours play supporting roles in traditional bread making. Chickpeas, mung beans, *urad dal*, corn, water chestnuts, potatoes, rice, barley, millet and buckwheat flours are used in different regions for flavor, texture and nutritional variation. In the last decade all of these flours, including wheat *chapati* flour, have become available at Indian and Chinese grocery stores, health food stores and co-ops and through mail order specialty stores. In addition to these, contemporary cooks can take advantage of oat, sorghum, amaranth, and triticale flour to achieve astonishing variety.

Because wheat can be cultivated anywhere where there is adequate rainfall—from river bottom plains to 10,000-foot altitudes—it has long been the world's most popular grain for bread. Not only India, but China, Egypt, Syria and Palestine and much of Southwest Asia have taken advantage of this adaptable crop. Like vegetables, there are different varieties and types of wheat cultivated for different purposes. While the shape of whole wheat and grains vary, a cross section of their anatomy shows them to be similar. They are composed of three parts: the "germ" or seed at the core, a starchy endosperm which surrounds it, and multiple protective layers of bran. The germ—containing nearly all of the kernel's vitamin E, over 8 percent protein, high fiber and fatty acids—constitutes only about 3 percent by weight. The endosperm contains not only over 70 percent of the protein, but also gluten—an elastic network of complex proteins that allows wheat to respond to handling and determines its ability to rise. The endosperm constitutes about 82 percent of the kernel by weight. Bran, about 15 percent by weight, is an excellent source of natural fiber and contains nearly 20 percent of the protein.

Seasonal winter and spring wheat are called "hard" or "soft" according to gluten and starch content. For example, cold-climate spring wheat cultivated in northern Canada and America is generally higher in protein than winter wheat. With at least 12 percent protein, it forms a strong web of gluten, and makes outstanding yeast breads. Soft winter wheat, cultivated in warmer temperatures, has more starch than protein and, very finely milled, is best used in unleavened breads, cakes and pastries.

Vedic flatbreads are made from a stone-ground soft-wheat flour called *atta* or *chapati* flour. It is quite different from whole wheat flours sold at supermarkets and health food stores. The entire soft, golden kernel, including the bran and germ, is milled almost to a powder. The tan or buff flour makes light, delicate flatbreads that roll out and shape easily and cook quickly. Even the finest-milled American wheat flours yield heavier doughs and doughier breads.

To delve into authentic flatbreads, buy *chapati* flour from an Indian grocery store or through one of the mail order sources listed in the back of this book. As your first alternative, mix two parts whole wheat pastry flour (available at health food stores, co-ops and specialty food stores) with one part unbleached white flour or cake flour. To further lighten flatbread doughs, you can sift *chapati* flour through a fine-mesh sieve (such as an Indian *chalni*) to remove traces of fine bran particles. (French or Italian fine-mesh sieves, available at better cookware stores, are ideal substitutes for the *chalni*.)

If you are using supermarket whole wheat flour, there are two ways you can lighten the dough. The first is to sieve the flour, before measuring, through a *chalni* three or four times to remove coarse bran flakes. (Use the bran in cereal dishes, for muffins or granola.) The sieved flour will not have as high a proportion of finely milled germ and husk as *chapati* flour, but the evenly distributed, powdered roughage will balance the

For information about unfamiliar ingredients or techniques, see A-to-Z

starch and gluten in whole wheat flour and produce soft, pliable flatbreads. The second way is to mix one part whole wheat flour with one part unbleached white flour. In general, the higher the proportion of regular whole wheat flour, the stiffer and harder the dough and the resulting bread. Doughs with a high proportion of unbleached white flour yield flatbreads that cook quickly but have less flavor and texture than whole wheat breads.

Proportions of flour, therefore, are very much a matter of availability, nutrition and personal taste. Once you are familiar with the flavor, texture and feel of different flours, try varying the proportions. Keep in mind that wheat flour is your gluten source. Corn, millet, barley, potato and buckwheat are flavorful but poor in gluten, so they play subordinate roles to whole wheat flour.

Words cannot describe the taste of flatbreads made from freshly milled flour; you have to experience it for yourself. My introduction to it came a few days after I arrived in Bombay for the first time. Our Marawadi host employed eight family-trained cooks, who pampered us with excellent *prasadam*, using the finest fruits, vegetables and grains. Every day, 8 pounds (4 kg) of golden *pisi lahore* wheat were stone-milled in the large marble kitchen. Two *neem* wood fires were reserved for griddle-baking round after round of paper-thin *phulkas*. As each bread came off the coals, it was immediately buttered and whisked, steaming hot, to the dining room. Though not possible in many situations, this has been an aspired-to standard in my kitchen over the years.

Most grains and flours reach us with about 12 percent moisture content, and it is our job to keep it at that during storage. Airtight containers and cool, dark, dry pantries are ideal. If you live in an area that is hot and damp, refrigerate your flour.

MEASURING FLOUR: Before measuring, put *chapati* flour and regular whole wheat flour through a fine-mesh sieve, as explained above, to remove traces of bran. Chickpea flour is always sifted, not to remove roughage but because it tends to lump, much like confectioners' sugar. Unbleached white flour, cake flour, *masa harina*, corn flour, buckwheat flour, potato flour and others do not require sifting before measuring, just a light touch in handling. To measure flour, do not scoop it out, but spoon it lightly into a measuring cup, to overflowing, then level it gently with a knife. Shaking or packing the cup to level the flour gives an inaccurate measure.

DOUGH-MAKING TECHNIQUES

Flours vary in their capacity to absorb water. One type of flour may require as much as 20 percent more water than another to make a dough of the same consistency. In following a bread recipe, start by using the smallest amount of liquid suggested and add more in spoonfuls as needed, according to the feel of the dough.

Bread doughs fall roughly into three categories: soft, medium and stiff. When soft dough is ready for kneading, it is shaggy and sticky. As it is kneaded, the gluten develops and the dough becomes smooth and elastic. A soft dough will stretch out during its resting time, and may need extra flour during shaping. Medium dough is easy to mix and knead and will keep its shape during resting, while a stiff dough is firm and quite unyielding until it has been well kneaded and rested.

Unless otherwise stated, begin by bringing the dry ingredients and yogurt or buttermilk (if called for) to room temperature. The *ghee* or butter is melted, and the water is usually warm (about 100°F/38°C). In Western yeast doughs, small amounts of water or flour are routinely added after the initial mixing of the dough, but here the goal is to add the exact amount of water (or other liquid: milk, yogurt or a combination of liquids) to the dry ingredients *all at once* and *one time only*. Too much initial water makes the dough sticky and unmanageable; too little makes it rubbery. No matter what adjustments you make later, the results will not match those from a dough made with the right amount of liquid added only once. Initially, you will have to fine-tune your water-to-flour ratios by making adjustments, but feel and experience will soon guide you to the exact amount of liquid.

All bread doughs are made in a similar way, in three simple steps: mixing, kneading and resting.

MIXING AND KNEADING: Put the dry ingredients in a large bowl. If you are using *ghee*, butter or oil, work it in with your fingertips until well blended. Pour in a stream of measured water (or other liquid: milk, yogurt, or a combination of liquids) with one hand, and use the other in a brisk rotating motion to mix from the center of the bowl outward, until the dough is moist enough to be gathered into a rough mass. Continue adding the water more and more slowly, until the mixture cleans the sides of the bowl and has become a nonsticky, kneadable dough. Gather it into a ball and set it on a clean (unfloured) surface.

There are two kneading methods: push and fold or press and stretch; use whichever you prefer. In the push-and-fold method, the dough is kneaded on a flat work surface. Fold the far edge of the dough toward you and push it away from you with the heels and palms of your hands. Giving the dough small turns, fold and push for up to 10 minutes, adding minimal sprinkles of flour or water if necessary. In India kneading is usually done in a high-walled tray called a *paraath*, using the press-and-stretch method. Holding the *paraath* with one hand, with the other make a fist and, with your knuckles, press and stretch the dough into a round approximately 8 inches (20 cm) in diameter. Fold the dough into a quarter-circle and continue, pressing and stretching, for up to 10 minutes. By using the weight of your body, not just your hands and arms, you can increase the pressure and knead for up to 15 minutes without tiring.

When the dough is fully kneaded, it will be elastic and silky smooth. White flour doughs develop a satiny sheen, with blisters beneath the surface. To test the dough, press it lightly with a fingertip. If it springs back, it is ready to be rested.

Mixing and kneading in a food processor: I thoroughly recommend this alternative method. It takes less than one minute and is simple and clean. Fit the work bowl with the steel blade and add the dry ingredients. Cover and process for about 5 seconds to

---

For information about unfamiliar ingredients or techniques, see A-to-Z

blend them. If you are using *ghee*, butter or oil, add it now, cover and process for about 10 seconds. With the machine running, add about three-fourths of the water (or other liquid: milk, yogurt, or a combination of liquids) in a steady stream. As the flour begins to form into a mass, add the water in dribbles until the dough forms a ball that cleans the inside of the work bowl. If at any time the motor slows down, stop the machine, redistribute the partially mixed dough, and continue to process, adding water or flour only while the machine is running. Once the ball of dough has formed, process until it turns around the work bowl about 25 times; it should be smooth and elastic to the touch. Let the dough rest in the bowl for 1–2 minutes, then rub your hands with flour and carefully remove it. It is ready for resting.

RESTING THE DOUGH: This final step allows the kneaded dough to relax for a while. The elastic dough becomes light and springy, less resistant to being rolled out into thin rounds. The ideal temperature for this resting period is higher than for yeast doughs— between 100° and 110°F (38°–43°C). At this temperature a half-hour rest is all that is necessary. If you leave the dough at cooler room temperatures, 65°–70°F (18°–21°C), it can rest for up to 3 hours.

To rest the dough, shape it into a smooth ball and, to keep it from drying out, cover it with an inverted bowl or dampened tea towel, or put it in a lightly oiled plastic bag. Cover the bowl with plastic wrap, or deflate and seal the bag, and let it sit in a warm place for ½ hour–3 hours, depending on the environment.

Any bread dough can be mixed, kneaded, rested and then refrigerated, well wrapped, for 24 hours before being rolled out. About an hour before you are ready to roll out and cook the breads, take the dough out of the refrigerator and let it come to room temperature.

EQUIPMENT

If you cook at all, you probably have the necessary equipment. Since nearly all Vedic flatbreads are made on top of the stove, the basic items are a heavy cast-iron griddle and a high-walled deep-frying pan or Dutch oven.

The Indian version of a griddle is called a *tava*. It is usually 8–12 inches (20–30 cm) in diameter, with a smooth, slightly concave cast-iron surface and a wooden handle for ease in lifting. Any heavy griddle or skillet will make a good substitute.

The classic deep-frying vessel is called a *karai*. It is a bowl-shaped cast-iron pan with sloping sides a little higher than those of its relative, the popular wok. In the United States, stainless steel, Calphalon and cast-iron woks are sold in better cookware stores, and nonstick aluminum woks can be found even in chain stores.

To complete your essential equipment you will need a mixing bowl, a rolling pin and a rolling surface near the stove. The traditional Indian mixing bowls and rolling pins have been carefully designed for versatility and efficiency. The metal *paraath*—a tray 18–24 inches (45–60 cm) across, with sloping sides 2–3 inches (5–7.5 cm) high—is used for mixing, kneading and resting bread doughs. For shaping the flatbreads, most cooks prefer a tapered rolling pin called a *belan*; the gentle swell in the center greatly facilitates subtle adjustments in pressure to iron out uneven thickness and round shapes.

Again, any type of equipment will do, but if you want the classic utensils—*tava*, *karai*, *paraath* and *belan*—they are available at most Indian grocery stores and from the mail order sources listed in the back of this book.

HELPFUL HINTS FOR COOKING BREADS

The procedures in the recipes ensure that the flatbreads will balloon over gas or electric heat. Flatbreads can be placed directly on wood or coal embers, but not on hot gas or electric burners (the breads would burn immediately). Flatbreads should be held a little above a gas burner; rest them on either a metal cake rack, smooth round tongs or a *chapati* rack. To make a *chapati* rack that works remarkably well, bend the rounded corners of a metal coat hanger down about 4 inches (10 cm) to form a horseshoe; the neck becomes a handle. The rack easily holds up to a 10-inch (25 cm) flatbread over the heat.

Always keep the soft, hot breads wrapped in a tea towel to absorb the steam released as they collapse, or they can become soggy. Left uncovered, they dry out and toughen. If you are not going to serve the breads soon after they are cooked, let them cool, wrap them in a tea towel and store in a covered bread tin. To reheat, wrap them in double-thick paper towels, cover tightly with tinfoil and put them in a preheated 350°F (175°C) oven for 15 minutes.

Experienced cooks roll out, cook and balloon the breads simultaneously. As one bread griddle-bakes, the next is rolled out; as one balloons, the next is slapped on the griddle; then back to rolling out. When you have gained confidence in rolling out, try it. You will become absorbed in the rhythm of it.

Now you are ready to begin.

GRIDDLE-BAKED BREADS

Griddle-Baked Whole Wheat Bread
CHAPATI

This is the most popular of all Vedic breads. Every day in northern and central India the aroma of freshly made *chapatis* fills the air. They are utterly irresistible. The unpretentious *chapati* requires only finely milled wheat flour and water, though you may want to add a touch of salt to round out the flavor of the wheat and a touch of melted butter or *ghee* for a softer texture. The *chapati* is baked on a hot griddle until it is three-fourths cooked, with brown spots and small blisters of hot air on the surface; then it is exposed to an open heat source. It can be held directly over a gas flame or electric element with a small cake rack, smooth, unserrated tongs, or the homemade coat-hanger rack described above. (If you are using a coal or wood stove, the bread can be placed directly on glowing embers to swell or puff into a balloon.) Your first few batches of *chapatis* may be unevenly rolled out, and only a few may balloon, but with practice you will master the procedure. Do not lose heart; your *chapatis* will be delicious no matter what their shape.

For information about unfamiliar ingredients or techniques, see A-to-Z

I had the opportunity to be instructed in *chapati* cookery from Srila Prabhupada and to watch him instruct others. Simply by feeling wheat flour he knew what it would need to become the perfect dough for perfect flatbreads. At various times he would emphasize one technique or another. For example, as an alternative to resting dough under a bowl or damp cloth he suggested soaking it in water, much as the French proof yeast doughs.

As an alternative to the rolling pin, he gave two methods for hand-shaping breads. In the first, a ball of soft dough is stretched and patted into a medium-thick disk, then slapped back and forth between the palms to remove excess flour and further enlarge it. (Though Srila Prabhupada cooked this bread on a griddle, I have also seen it baked in a clay *tandoori* oven. The clay drum, about 2½ feet/75 cm in diameter and 4 feet/120 cm deep, is covered with a layer of fine mud, making the inside surface very smooth. At the top the opening narrows to only about 1 foot/30 cm. The rounds of dough are slapped onto the inside walls of the oven, where they bake for 7–10 minutes and puff into crusty flatbreads.) In the second method, Srila Prabhupada shaped two breads at once. Two patties of medium-soft dough were liberally dusted with flour and then finger-pressed out, one on top of the other, until they were quite thin. The breads were peeled apart, baked on a griddle and finished over direct heat. Sometimes he demonstrated griddle-baking three breads simultaneously, in a stack. This involved rhythmically turning the breads over so each surface could bake on the griddle before they were individually ballooned over direct heat. Srila Prabhupada preferred *chapatis* rolled very thin and, when possible, cooked on a wood fire. Thin breads are not only elegant but also easily digested. *Chapatis* go well with any lunch or dinner menu, whether you serve them with a salad, soup or five-course vegetable menu. For a salad-oriented luncheon menu try hot *chapatis* with *Whole Cabbage Stuffed with Carrot Coleslaw*, or *Mixed Bean Salad with Fennel* and a cup of refreshing, iced *Watermelon Sorbet*. For a soup-based luncheon, serve them with *Corn and Bell Peppers in Herbed Coconut Milk* or *Garden Tomato Soup*.

Preparation time (after assembling ingredients): 5–15 minutes
Dough resting time: ½–3 hours
Cooking time: 30–40 minutes
Makes: 14 *chapatis*

2¼ cups (295 g) sieved *chapati* flour, or 1½ cups
     (190 g) sieved whole wheat flour mixed with
   ¾ cup (95 g) unbleached white flour
1 tablespoon (15 ml) melted butter or *ghee* (optional)
½ teaspoon (2 ml) salt (optional)
⅔ cup (160 ml) warm water (about 100°F/38°C), or as needed
***chapati* or sieved wheat flour for dusting**
melted butter or *ghee* for brushing on the finished flatbreads (optional)

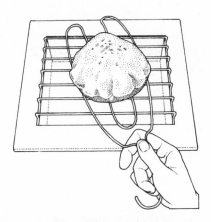

1. Place the flour in a large mixing bowl. If you are adding butter or *ghee* and salt, rub them into the flour with your fingertips until thoroughly incorporated. Add up to ⅔ cup (160 ml) of water, pouring fast at first, to moisten the flour until it adheres into a rough mass, then slowly, in dribbles, until you have a kneadable dough. (The amount of water may vary, depending on the flour.) Knead the dough on a clean work surface, adding flour or water if necessary, until silky smooth and pliable, about 8 minutes. You can also make the dough in a food processor (see page 100). Roll the dough into a ball, cover with an inverted bowl and let it rest, well covered, for ½ hour–3 hours. If you want to leave it longer, you can refrigerate it for up to 24 hours; let it come to room temperature before you start to roll out the breads.

2. Gather the items needed for rolling out and cooking: a rolling pin, dusting flour in a shallow plate or pie dish, a cake rack, a basket lined with clean tea towels, and a bowl of melted butter or *ghee* (if desired) and a pastry brush. Knead the dough briefly and divide it into 14 portions. Roll them into smooth balls, put them on a plate without letting them touch, and cover with a damp cloth.

3. Set a griddle over moderately low heat to preheat for 3–5 minutes. Flatten a ball of dough into a 2-inch (5 cm) patty and dip both sides in the dusting flour. Roll it out as evenly as you can into a thin round about 6 inches (15 cm) in diameter, dipping it in the dusting flour from time to time, just enough to keep it from sticking to the work surface (excess flour will make the *chapati* brittle). Roll with even, gentle pressure, easing the dough into a round rather than stretching it. (Experienced cooks rotate the breads as they flatten them, using a slightly clockwise back-and-forth motion.)

4. When the griddle is hot, pick up the *chapati* and slap it back and forth between your palms to shake off excess flour. Half-slap, half-slip the bread onto the griddle. It should lie flat, without any wrinkles. If there are wrinkles, do not try to press them out, as the bread would stick and burn. Wait until the bottom firms up, then shake the griddle to try to ease out the wrinkles. Cook for about 1 minute on the first side. (If you are using electric heat to balloon the bread, preheat a back burner on high.) When the top of the *chapati* lightens in color, small bubbles begin to form, and the bottom has small brownish spots, turn the *chapati* over with your fingertips or a spatula and cook on the second side for about half a minute. Take the griddle off the heat to keep it from overheating.

5. If you are using gas, turn a back burner on high. Place the *chapati* on the rack and hold it 2 inches (5 cm) over the burner. In seconds the *chapati* will swell, fill with steam and puff into a balloon. Continue to cook, turning it once, until it has charcoal-black flecks. Ballooning the bread takes only 10–15 seconds. (If you hold the bread over the heat too long, its surface tends to burn or become brittle.)

6. Slip the finished bread into the basket and cover. Set the griddle back over moderately low heat and repeat the process. If desired, brush one side with melted butter or *ghee* before serving.

For information about unfamiliar ingredients or techniques, see A-to-Z

Griddle-Baked Yogurt Whole Wheat Bread
DAHI CHAPATI

The texture of yogurt-enriched *chapati* dough is similar to that of plain *chapati* dough, but the cooked breads are a touch softer. Try this delicious bread with *Chana Dal Purée with Tender Bottle Gourd Cubes, Curried Cauliflower and Potatoes* and a tossed green salad.

Preparation time (after assembling ingredients): 5–15 minutes
Dough resting time: ½ hour–3 hours
Cooking time: 30–40 minutes
Makes: 14 *chapatis*

2¼ cups (295 g) sieved *chapati* flour, or 1½ cups (190 g) sieved whole
    wheat flour mixed with ¾ cup (95 g) unbleached white flour
½ teaspoon (2 ml) salt (optional)
⅓ cup (80 ml) plain yogurt, at room temperature
4–5 tablespoons (60–75 ml) warm water (about 100°F/38°C), or as needed
chapati or sieved wheat flour for dusting
melted butter or *ghee* for brushing on the finished flatbreads (optional)

1. Place the flour in a large mixing bowl. Add the salt, if desired, and yogurt, and rub them in with your fingertips until well blended. Add the water, pouring fast at first, to moisten the flour until it adheres into a rough mass, then slowly, in dribbles, until you have a kneadable dough. (The amount of water may vary, depending on the flour.) Knead the dough on a clean work surface, adding flour or water if necessary, until silky smooth and pliable, about 8 minutes. You can also make the dough in a food processor (see page 100). Roll the dough into a ball, cover with an inverted bowl and let it rest for ½ hour–3 hours. If you want to leave it longer, you can refrigerate it, well covered, for up to 24 hours; let it come to room temperature before you start to roll out the breads.

2. Gather the items needed for rolling out and cooking: a rolling pin, dusting flour in a shallow plate or pie dish, a cake rack, a basket lined with clean tea towels, and a bowl of melted butter or *ghee* (if desired) and a pastry brush. Knead the dough briefly and divide it into 14 portions. Roll them into smooth balls, put them on a plate without letting them touch, and cover with a damp cloth.

3. Set a griddle over moderately low heat to preheat for 3–5 minutes. Flatten a ball of dough into a 2-inch (5 cm) patty and dip both sides in the dusting flour. Roll it out as evenly as you can into a thin round about 6 inches (15 cm) in diameter, dipping it in the dusting flour from time to time, just enough to keep it from sticking to the work surface (excess flour will make the *chapati* brittle). Roll with even, gentle pressure, easing the dough into a round rather than stretching it. (Experienced cooks rotate the breads as they flatten them, using a slightly clockwise back-and-forth motion.)

4. When the griddle is hot, pick up the *chapati* and slap it back and forth between your palms to shake off excess flour. Half-slap, half-slip the bread onto the griddle. It should lie flat, without any wrinkles. If there are wrinkles, do not try to press them out, as the bread would stick and burn. Wait until the bottom firms up, then shake the griddle to try to ease out the wrinkles. Cook for about 1 minute on the first side. (If you are using electric heat to balloon the bread, preheat a back burner on high.) When the top of the *chapati* lightens in color, small bubbles begin to form, and the bottom has small brownish spots, turn the *chapati* over with your fingertips or a spatula and cook on

the second side for about half a minute. Take the griddle off the heat to keep it from overheating.

5. If you are using gas, turn a back burner on high. Place the *chapati* on the rack and hold it 2 inches (5 cm) over the burner. In seconds the *chapati* will swell, fill with steam and puff into a balloon. Continue to cook, turning it once, until it has charcoal-black flecks. Ballooning the bread takes only 10–15 seconds. (If you hold the bread over the heat too long, its surface tends to burn or become brittle.)

6. Slip the finished bread into the basket and cover. Set the griddle back over moderately low heat and repeat the process. If desired, brush one side with melted butter or *ghee* before serving.

Griddle-Baked *Chenna* Whole Wheat Bread
CHENNA CHAPATI

Winter days in Vrindavan—the birthsite of Lord Krishna in Uttar Pradesh—are crisp and bracing. It is not uncommon to see the first rays of the sun meet thin icicles hanging from the porch roof. On one of those cobalt-blue-sky mornings, Srila Prabhupada first asked me for these *chapatis* for his breakfast. He called them winter *chapatis*—warming and nutritious. I served them with fresh fruit, hot milk and a small piece of Bengali *tal gur* candy, much like maple sugar candy. The dough softens considerably while resting and is more difficult to handle than plain *chapati* dough. It is important to begin with a medium-stiff dough, roll out the rounds evenly to ensure ballooning, and to maintain the correct griddle temperature—a few extra degrees heat will quickly burn small holes in the bread's delicate surface.

Chenna chapatis are usually served at lunch or dinner, though you can serve them for a special breakfast or brunch. They are always good with soup or salad. For a light lunch, serve them with a seasonal vegetable dish such as *Curried Potatoes with Eggplant, Summer Squash and Green Peas with Poppy Seeds, Lima Beans with Golden Raisins* or *Spicy Cauliflower with Braised Tomato*, and accompany with a rice or whole grain dish and a cool yogurt salad.

Preparation time (after assembling ingredients): 10–20 minutes
Dough resting time: ½ hour–3 hours
Cooking time: 30–40 minutes
Makes: 12 *chapatis*

¾ cup (180 ml) milk
about 1 teaspoon (5 ml) fresh lemon juice
2¼ cups (295 g) sieved *chapati* flour,
    or 1¼ cups (160 g) sieved whole wheat
    flour mixed with 1 cup (120 g)
    unbleached white flour, or as needed
½ teaspoon (2 ml) salt (optional)
chapati or sieved wheat flour for dusting
melted butter or *ghee* for brushing on
    the finished flatbreads (optional)

1. Bring the milk to a boil in a large saucepan. Take the pan off the heat and immediately add the lemon juice. Swirl the milk to distribute the juice. Within a minute the milk will separate into solid curds and yellowish whey; if not, place the pan back over the heat until it curdles (adding sprinkles of additional juice) and again remove the pan from the heat. Add half of the flour into the hot cheese and whey and with a mixing spoon stir vigorously into a thick, smooth paste. When it is cool enough to handle, gather it into a mass and transfer to a work surface. Add the salt (if desired) and enough of the remaining flour to make a medium-stiff dough. Knead the dough until silky smooth and pliable, about 8 minutes.

To make the dough in a food processor, make the fresh cheese, let it cool for 3–4 minutes and pour both cheese and whey into the work bowl, fitted with the steel blade. Turn the machine on and off quickly three times to break down the cheese slightly. With the machine on, add the salt (if desired) and the remaining flour as needed, until the dough forms a ball that cleans the sides of the bowl. Process until the ball turns around the bowl 25 times. The dough should be a little firm, not sticky, and smooth and satiny to the touch. Let the dough rest in the bowl for 1–2 minutes, then dust your hands with flour and carefully remove it.

Shape the kneaded dough into a ball, cover with an inverted bowl and let it rest for ½ hour–3 hours. If you want to leave it longer, you can refrigerate it, well covered, for up to 24 hours; let it come to room temperature before you start to roll out the breads.

2. Gather the items needed for rolling out and cooking: a rolling pin, dusting flour in a shallow plate or pie dish, a cake rack, a basket lined with clean tea towels, and a bowl of melted butter or *ghee* (if desired) and a pastry brush. Knead the dough briefly and divide it into 12 portions. Roll them into smooth balls, put them on a plate without letting them touch, and cover with a damp cloth.

3. Set a griddle over moderately low heat to preheat for 3–5 minutes. Flatten a ball of dough into a 2-inch (5 cm) patty and dip both sides in the dusting flour. Roll it out as evenly as you can into a thin round about 6 inches (15 cm) in diameter, dipping it in the dusting flour from time to time, just enough to keep it from sticking to the work surface (excess flour will make the *chapati* brittle). Roll with even, gentle pressure, easing the dough into a round rather than stretching it. (Experienced cooks rotate the breads as they flatten them, using a slightly clockwise back-and-forth motion.)

4. When the griddle is hot, pick up the *chapati* and slap it back and forth between your palms to shake off excess flour. Half-slap, half-slip the bread onto the griddle. It should lie flat, without any wrinkles. If there are wrinkles, do not try to press them out, as the bread would stick and burn. Wait until the bottom firms up, then shake the griddle to try to ease out the wrinkles. Cook for about 1 minute on the first side. (If you are using electric heat to balloon the bread, preheat a back burner on high.) When the top of the *chapati* lightens in color, small bubbles begin to form, and the bottom has small brownish spots, turn the *chapati* over with your fingertips or a spatula and cook on the second side for about half a minute. Take the griddle off the heat to keep it from overheating.

5. If you are using gas, turn a back burner on high. Place the *chapati* on the rack and hold it 2 inches (5 cm) over the burner. In seconds the *chapati* will swell, fill with steam and puff into a balloon. Continue to cook, turning it once, until it has charcoal-black flecks. Ballooning the bread takes only 10–15 seconds; the bread burns easily if not constantly moved about over the heat.

6. Slip the finished bread into the basket. Set the griddle back over moderately low heat and repeat the process. If desired, brush one side with melted butter or *ghee* before serving.

Griddle-Baked Paper-Thin Whole Wheat Bread
PHULKA

Phulka dough resembles *chapati* dough in its softness and pliability, but it is usually enriched with a touch of butter or *ghee*. The real difference between *phulkas* and *chapatis*, however, is in the size. Plain *phulkas* are large (8–10 inches/20–25 cm in diameter) and paper-thin. *Phulkas* are a featured item at a typical Sunday brunch in central and southwestern India, often accompanying a *dal* dish and a creamy condensed-milk pudding. I have seen many temple kitchens turn out several hundred buttered, perfectly cooked *phulkas*, stack after stack, for Sunday guests of the Deity. If you are inexperienced at rolling out flatbreads, allow extra time or, better yet, try it with a help-er—one person can roll out as the other cooks. In keeping with the timeless brunch tradition of India, try serving *phulkas* with a *dal* dish such as *Toasted Mung Dal with Tender Eggplant Cubes*, *Hearty Five-Dal Soup* or *Curried Whole Brown Chickpeas*.

Preparation time (after assembling ingredients): 5–15 minutes
Dough resting time: ½ hour–3 hours
Cooking time: 35–45 minutes
Makes: 10–12 *phulkas*

2¼ cups (295 g) sieved *chapati* flour, or 1¾ cups (220 g) sieved whole
    wheat flour mixed with ½ cup (65 g) unbleached white flour

1 teaspoon (5 ml) salt (optional)
1½ tablespoons (22 ml) melted butter or *ghee*
⅔ cup (160 ml) warm water (about 100°F/38°C), or as needed
chapati or sieved wheat flour for dusting
melted butter or *ghee* for brushing on the finished flatbreads (optional)

1. Place the flour in a large mixing bowl. Add the salt, if desired, and melted butter or *ghee* and mix with your fingertips until well blended. Add the water, pouring fast at first, to moisten the flour until it adheres into a rough mass, then slowly, in dribbles,

For information about unfamiliar ingredients or techniques, see A-to-Z

until you have a kneadable dough. (The amount of water may vary, depending on the flour.) Knead the dough on a clean work surface, adding flour or water if necessary, until silky smooth and pliable, about 8 minutes. You can also make the dough in a food processor (see page 100). Shape the dough into a ball, cover with an inverted bowl and let it rest for ½ hour–3 hours. If you want to leave it longer, you can refrigerate it, well covered, for up to 24 hours; let it come to room temperature before you start to roll out the breads.

2. Gather the items needed for rolling out and cooking: a rolling pin, dusting flour in a shallow plate or pie dish, a cake rack, a basket lined with clean tea towels, and a bowl of melted butter or *ghee* (if desired) and a pastry brush. Knead the dough briefly and divide it into 10–12 portions. Roll them into smooth balls, put them on a plate without letting them touch, and cover with a damp cloth.

3. Set a griddle over moderately low heat to preheat for 3–5 minutes. Flatten a ball of dough into a 2-inch (5 cm) patty and dip both sides in the dusting flour. Roll it out as evenly as you can into a thin round at least 8 inches (20 cm) in diameter, dipping it in the dusting flour from time to time, just enough to keep it from sticking to the work surface (excess flour will make the *phulka* brittle). Roll with even, gentle pressure, easing the dough into a round rather than stretching it. (Experienced cooks rotate the breads as they flatten them, using a slightly clockwise back-and-forth motion.)

4. When the griddle is hot, pick up a *phulka* and slap it back and forth between your palms to shake off excess flour. Half-slap, half-slip the bread onto the griddle. It should lie flat, without any wrinkles. If there are wrinkles, do not try to press them out, as the bread would stick and burn. Wait until the bottom firms up, then shake the griddle to try to ease out the wrinkles. Cook for 45 seconds to 1 minute on the first side. (If you are using electric heat to balloon the bread, preheat a back burner on high.) When the top of the *phulka* lightens in color, small bubbles begin to form, and the bottom has small brownish spots, turn the *phulka* over with your fingertips or a spatula and cook on the second side for about half a minute. Take the griddle off the heat to keep it from overheating.

5. If you are using gas, turn a back burner on high. Place the *phulka* on the rack and hold it 2 inches (5 cm) over the burner. In 5 seconds the *phulka* will swell, fill with steam and puff into a balloon. Continue to cook, turning it once, until it has charcoal-black flecks. Ballooning the bread takes only 10–15 seconds. (If you hold the bread over the heat too long, its surface tends to burn or become brittle.)

6. Slip the finished bread into the basket and cover. Set the griddle back over moderately low heat and repeat the process. If desired, brush one side with melted butter or *ghee* before serving.

Freshly Ground Wheat Berry Bread
GEHUN PHULKA

I first tasted a variation of these breads in Bombay, at the home of Mr. and Mrs. Kartikeya Mahadevia. Both husband and wife are excellent cooks and sensitive to the health benefits of wheat grass and freshly milled wheat berry breads. Though I tried for several years to imitate their breads in the West, none of my attempts proved successful until the advent of the miraculous food processor. Now anyone can wet-grind wheat with ease, preserving all the proteins, vitamins, minerals and fiber—and flavor—that whole grains have to offer. Reddish-brown hard-wheat berries are good for yeast breads; golden soft wheat is preferred for flatbreads. Call your grain sources—health food stores, co-ops, gourmet stores, etc.—to check on the availability of soft wheat before going shopping. Most good stores offer a wide selection. You may even want to branch out into combinations of flours and different whole grains such as triticale, rye or oat.

For a really special breakfast or brunch, try these breads with a dab of *Golden Papaya Chip Chutney* or apple butter, *Creamy Scrambled Chenna Cheese with Tomatoes and Snow Peas* and a fresh summer fruit plate or winter fruit compote. On a hot day try a frosty glass of *Fennel Lemon-Lime Squash*; in winter, a cup of hot tisane.

Grain soaking time: 8 hours to overnight or 4 hours by quick method
Preparation time (after assembling ingredients): 20 minutes
Dough resting time: ½ hour–3 hours
Cooking time: 45 minutes
Makes: 18–20 *phulkas*

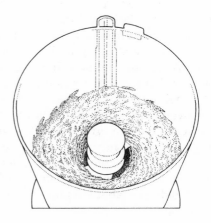

1 cup (230 g) whole wheat, rye, oat or
    triticale berries
3 cups (395 g) sieved *chapati* flour or
    3 cups (355 g) unbleached white flour
¼ cup (35 g) non-instant powdered milk or
    powdered buttermilk
2 tablespoons (30 ml) melted butter or *ghee*
1 teaspoon (5 ml) salt (optional)
⅔ cup (160 ml) warm water (about 100°F/38°C),
    or as needed
***chapati* or sieved wheat flour for dusting**
melted butter or *ghee* for brushing on the
    finished flatbreads (optional)

1. To soak and cook the berries in a bowl, add hot water to cover and let stand at room temperature for 8 hours or overnight. The whole grains will lighten a few shades and nearly double in volume. An alternative is to cover them with boiling water and let stand for 4 hours. Then transfer the berries with their soaking water to a saucepan and simmer for 10 minutes, uncovered. Remove the pan, drain, and let the grains cool on paper towels or absorbent kitchen towels. (Cooked grains can be kept refrigerated in a sealed plastic bag for 3–4 days.)

2. To make the dough, fit the work bowl of a food processor with the steel blade. Place the soaked grains with ½ cup (65 g) of flour in the bowl and process for 2–3 minutes or until very finely powdered. Add the remaining flour, powdered milk, butter or *ghee* and salt, if desired. Process for 1 minute. With the machine running, add the water through the feed tube and process for about 45 seconds, until the dough is smooth and elastic and cleans the sides of the bowl. If the dough is too dry, add water by teaspoons (5 ml); if it is too moist, add flour by tablespoons (15 ml), always with the machine running. Roll the dough into a ball, cover it with an inverted bowl and let it rest for ½–3 hours. If needed, you can refrigerate it, well covered, for up to 24 hours; let it come to room temperature before you start to roll out the breads.

For information about unfamiliar ingredients or techniques, see A-to-Z

3. Gather the items needed for rolling out and cooking: a rolling pin, dusting flour in a shallow plate or pie dish, a cake rack, a basket lined with clean tea towels, and a bowl of melted butter or *ghee* (if desired) and a pastry brush. Knead the dough briefly and divide it into 18–20 portions. Roll them into smooth balls, put them on a plate without letting them touch, and cover with a damp cloth.

4. Set a griddle over moderately low heat to preheat for 3–5 minutes. Flatten a ball of dough into a 2-inch (5 cm) patty and dip both sides in the dusting flour. Roll it out as evenly as you can into a thin round at least 8 inches (20 cm) in diameter, dipping it in the dusting flour from time to time, just enough to prevent it from sticking to the work surface (excess flour will make the *phulka* brittle). Roll with even, gentle pressure, easing the dough into a round rather than stretching it. (Experienced cooks rotate the breads as they flatten them, using a slightly clockwise back-and-forth motion.)

5. When the griddle is hot, pick up the *phulka* and slap it back and forth between your palms to shake off excess flour. Half-slap, half-slip the bread onto the griddle. It should lie flat, without any wrinkles. If there are wrinkles, do not try to press them out, as the bread would stick and burn. Wait until the bottom firms up, then shake the griddle to try to ease out the wrinkles. Cook for about 1 minute on the first side. (If you are using electric heat to balloon the bread, preheat a back burner on high.) When the top of the *phulka* lightens in color, small bubbles begin to form, and the bottom has small brownish spots, turn the *phulka* over with your fingertips or a spatula and cook on the second side for about half a minute. Take the griddle off the heat to keep it from overheating.

6. If you are using gas, turn a back burner on high. Place the *phulka* on the rack and hold it 2 inches (5 cm) over the heat. In seconds the *phulka* will swell, fill with steam and puff into a balloon. Continue to cook, turning it once, until it has charcoal-black flecks. Ballooning the bread takes only 10–15 seconds. (If you hold the bread over the heat too long, its surface tends to burn or become brittle.)

7. Slip the finished bread into the basket and cover. Set the griddle back over moderately low heat and repeat the process. If desired, brush one side with melted butter or *ghee* before serving.

Griddle-Baked Papaya Whole Wheat Bread
PAPITA PHULKA

Ripe papaya is a real tropical delicacy. The sweet, juicy fruit is orange-pink with a melonlike texture, and its flavor and fragrance are rivaled only by a good mango. *Papita phulka* is made by combining fresh puréed papaya with wheat flour. The results are outstanding: soft, sweetish, golden flatbreads excellent for breakfast, lunch or dinner. Make the dough firmer than for basic *chapatis*, as it tends to soften considerably while it rests. For a special lunch, try it with *Melon Bowl Supreme with Honey-Lime Dressing* and a *Sweet Yogurt Shake* or *Cumin-Flavored Yogurt Shake*. For a spectacular brunch, accompany the bread with *Creamy Pineapple and Rice Jubilee* and chilled sparkling grape juice. For a late-dinner treat, try these breads with *Semolina Uppma with Bell Peppers and Cabbage* and *Crème de la Crème*.

Preparation time (after assembling ingredients): 10–20 minutes
Dough resting time: ½ hour–3 hours
Cooking time: 30–40 minutes
Makes: 10–12 *phulkas*

2¼ cups (295 g) sieved *chapati* flour or a mixture of
    whole wheat flour and unbleached white flour
½ teaspoon (2 ml) salt (optional)
½ cup (120 ml) papaya purée or ⅔ cup (160 ml) finely chopped fresh papaya
chapati or unbleached white flour for dusting
melted butter or *ghee* for brushing on the finished flatbreads (optional)

1. Place the flour in a large mixing bowl. Mix in the salt (if desired) and make a well in the center. Pour the papaya purée into the well and work into a kneadable medium-stiff dough. (You may need more flour or purée, depending on the type of flour.) Knead the dough for 5–10 minute, until silky smooth and pliable.

To make the dough in a food processor, first fit the work bowl with the steel blade. Add the chopped papaya, cover and process on-off for a few bursts to reduce the papaya to a purée. With the motor running, add the flour and salt (if desired) through the feed tube in ⅓-cup (80 ml) amounts until the dough forms, then allow it to turn around the bowl about 25 times. Remove the dough, divide it into four parts, return it to the work bowl and process again for 10 seconds. The dough should be on the stiff side. If it is too soft, work in more flour.

Roll the kneaded dough into a ball, cover with an inverted bowl and let it rest for ½ hour–3 hours. If you want to leave it longer, you can refrigerate it, well covered, for up to 24 hours; let it come to room temperature before you start to roll out the breads.

2. Gather the items needed for rolling out and cooking: a rolling pin, dusting flour in a shallow plate or pie dish, a cake rack, a basked lined with clean tea towels, and a bowl of melted butter or *ghee* (if desired) and a pastry brush. Knead the dough briefly and divide it into 10–12 portions. Roll them into smooth balls, put them on a plate without letting them touch, and cover with a damp cloth.

3. Set a griddle over moderately low heat to preheat for 3–5 minutes. Flatten a ball of dough into a 2-inch (5 cm) patty and dip both sides in the dusting flour. Roll it out as evenly as you can into a thin round 6–8 inches (15–20 cm) in diameter, dipping it in the dusting flour from time to time, just enough to keep it from sticking to the work surface (too much flour will make the *phulka* brittle). Roll with even, gentle pressure, easing the dough into a round rather than stretching it. (Experienced cooks rotate the breads as they flatten them, using a slightly clockwise back-and-forth motion.)

4. When the griddle is hot, pick up a *phulka* and slap it back and forth between your palms to shake off excess flour. Half-slap, half-slip the bread onto the griddle. It should lie flat, without any wrinkles. If there are wrinkles, do not try to press them out, as the bread would stick and burn. Wait until the bottom firms up, then shake the griddle to try to ease out the wrinkles. Cook for about 1 minute on the first side. (If you are using electric heat to balloon the bread, preheat a back burner on high.) When the top of the *phulka* lightens in color, small bubbles begin to form, and the bottom has small brownish spots, turn the *phulka* over with your fingertips or a spatula and cook on the second side for about half a minute. Take the griddle off the heat to keep it from overheating.

5. If you are using gas, turn a back burner on high. Place the *phulka* on the rack and

---

For information about unfamiliar ingredients or techniques, see A-to-Z

hold it 2 inches (5 cm) over the burner. In seconds the *phulka* will swell, fill with steam and puff into a balloon. Continue to cook, turning once, until it has charcoal-black flecks. Ballooning the bread takes only 10–15 seconds. (If you hold the bread over the heat too long, its surface tends to burn or become brittle.)

6. Slip the finished bread into the basket, fold over the towel and loosely cover. Set the griddle back over moderately low heat and repeat the process. If desired, brush one side with melted butter or *ghee* before serving.

Griddle-Baked Fresh Corn Bread
TAZA MAKKAI ROTI

Just as Mexico has given the world corn tortillas, the Punjab in North India offers us many corn-based flatbreads. This delicious bread is made with fresh corn, cornmeal and *chapati* or whole wheat flour. In terms of flavor and nutrition, stone-ground or water-ground cornmeal is the best. It has guaranteed good fiber and calcium content and retains the valuable germ. Cornmeal and corn flour are available in several textures, from fine to coarse. For this bread I prefer a fine grind; if all you can find is coarse cornmeal, powder it in a coffee mill.

These golden flatbreads are softer than most *chapatis* and complement almost any menu. In rural India, from Amritsar to Varanasi, they are popular with leafy green vegetables and plain yogurt. Try them with *Curried Greens and Eggplant*, *Fresh Date Yogurt* and *Simple Rice and Chana Dal Khichari with Dill and Tomatoes*.

Preparation time (after assembling ingredients): 10 minutes
Dough resting time: ½ hour–3 hours
Cooking time: 30–40 minutes
Makes: 16 *rotis*

1¾ cups (420 ml) water
3 tablespoons (45 ml) butter or vegetable oil
1 cup (145 g) fine cornmeal
1 ear of corn, husked and cleaned
about 1⅓ cups (175 g) sieved *chapati* or whole wheat flour
¼ teaspoon (1 ml) cayenne pepper
1 teaspoon (5 ml) salt
1 tablespoon (15 ml) sugar
chapati or sieved wheat flour for dusting
melted butter or *ghee* for brushing on the finished flatbreads (optional)

1. Bring the water to a boil in a small saucepan. Take it off the heat and add half of the butter or oil. Pour in the cornmeal, stirring constantly to avoid lumps, cover and set over very low heat for 4–5 minutes. Add the remaining butter or oil, stir well and set aside to cool.

2. With the tip of a knife, slit down the center of each row of corn. With the dull edge of the knife, scrape out the pulp and juice into a strainer resting over into a bowl. Press out all the liquid; you should have 3 to 4 tablespoons (45–60 ml). Add the flour, cayenne pepper, salt and sweetener. Blend well. When the cornmeal is cool enough to handle, mix it in. On a clean work surface, knead into a medium-soft dough (about 5 minutes), adding water or flour if necessary. You can also make the dough in a food processor (see page 100). Roll the dough into a ball, cover with an inverted bowl and let it rest for ½ hour–3 hours. If you want to leave it longer, you can refrigerate it, well covered, for up to 24 hours; let it come to room temperature before you start to roll out the breads.

3. Gather the items needed for rolling out and cooking: a rolling pin, dusting flour in a shallow plate or pie dish, a cake rack, a basket lined with clean tea towels, and a bowl of melted butter or *ghee* (if desired) and a pastry brush. Knead the dough briefly and divide it into 16 portions. Roll them into smooth balls, put them on a plate without letting them touch, and cover with a damp cloth.

4. Set a griddle over moderately low heat to preheat for 3–5 minutes. Flatten a ball of dough into a 2-inch (5 cm) patty and dip both sides in the dusting flour. Roll it out as evenly as you can into a thin round about 6 inches (15 cm) in diameter, dipping it in the dusting flour from time to time, just enough to keep it from sticking to the work surface (excess flour will make the *roti* brittle). Roll with even, gentle pressure, easing the dough into a round rather than stretching it. (Experienced cooks rotate the breads as they flatten them, using a slightly clockwise back-and-forth motion.)

5. When the griddle is hot, pick up the *roti* and slap it back and forth between your palms to shake off excess flour. Half-slap, half-slip the bread onto the griddle. It should lie flat, without any wrinkles. If there are wrinkles, do not try to press them out, as the bread would stick and burn. Wait until the bottom firms up, then shake the griddle to try to ease out the wrinkles. Cook for about 1½ minutes on the first side. When the top of the *roti* lightens in color, small bubbles begin to form, and the bottom has small brownish spots, turn the *roti* over with your fingertips or a spatula and cook on the second side for another 1½ minutes. Usually it will balloon fully on the griddle. If the griddle is too hot, the bread will burn before it has finished cooking; if not hot enough, it will take so long to swell that it may burn first, and it will be dry and tough rather than flexible and soft. To encourage the bread to balloon, press the surface with a folded tea towel. When the *roti* balloons, take the griddle off the heat to keep it from overheating.

6. Slip the finished bread into the towel-lined basket and loosely cover. Repeat the process to cook the remaining breads. If desired, brush one side of the hot bread with melted butter or *ghee*.

Griddle-Baked Village-Style Corn Bread
MAKKAI ROTI

This second corn-based flatbread selection is made from a mixture of supermarket *masa harina* and wheat flour. As the main ingredient in ready-made Mexican tortilla flat breads, fresh *masa* is made from dry white field corn boiled with lime, washed and wet-ground. It's difficult for a novice to shape and cook flatbreads made from fresh *masa*, but this hurdle is circumvented by

For information about unfamiliar ingredients or techniques, see A-to-Z

using a combination of wheat and *masa harina* flour. This dough is not only easy to handle—the corn-wheat flavor is scrumptious. *Masa harina* can be found in the flour or foreign food sections at large supermarkets and at Latin or Mexican grocery stores.

Preparation time (after assembling ingredients): 5 minutes
Dough resting time: 15 minutes
Cooking time: about ½ hour
Makes: 12 *rotis*

1½ cups (180 g) *masa harina*
½ cup (70 g) sieved *chapati* flour or whole wheat flour
2 teaspoons (10 ml) minced seeded hot green chilies
1 cup (240 ml) warm water (about 100°F/38°C), or as needed
melted butter or *ghee* for brushing on the finished
    flatbreads (optional)

1. Combine the flours and chilies in a mixing bowl, add the water and mix until the dough is moist but holds its shape. Because most of the flour is *masa*, which has no gluten, the dough will be quite unlike wheat-based flatbread doughs and may need additional water or flour to achieve the desired moistness (like pastry dough). Roll the dough into a smooth ball, cover with a damp towel and let it rest for 15 minutes.

2. Gather the items needed for shaping and cooking: a tortilla press or flat-bottomed baking dish, two dozen 7-inch (17.5 cm) squares of waxed paper, and a basket lined with clean tea towels. Divide the dough into 12 portions. Roll them into smooth balls, put them on a plate without letting them touch, dampen slightly with water, and cover with a damp cloth.

3. Set a griddle over moderately low heat to preheat for 3–5 minutes. Place a ball of dough between two sheets of waxed paper. Using the tortilla press or baking dish, press into a 6-inch (15 cm) round, taking care not to wrinkle the paper. Repeat until all are shaped, stacking the paper-covered rounds.

4. Carefully peel off the top sheet of waxed paper from one of the rounds, place the bread on the griddle, paper side up, and gently peel off the other piece of waxed paper. Cook for ½–1 minute or until the edges begin to dry and the bottom of the *roti* has small brownish spots. Turn the *roti* over and cook until the surface puffs in a few places. Usually it will balloon fully on the griddle. If the griddle is too hot, the bread will burn before it has finished cooking; if not hot enough, it will take so long to puff that it will burn first, and it will be dry and tough rather than flexible and soft. To encourage the bread to balloon, press the surface with a folded tea towel.

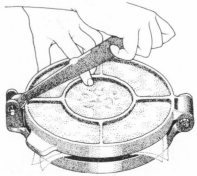

5. Slip the finished bread into the basket and cover. Repeat the process to cook the remaining breads. If desired, brush one side of the hot breads with melted butter or *ghee*.

Griddle-Baked Sourdough Bread
MOTI ROTI

This soft, chewy flatbread is not a genuine sourdough bread but a very pleasing facsimile. A yogurt-based dough is allowed to rest until it increases in volume and takes on a slightly sour flavor. Though the dough is usually made from unbleached white flour, it is equally delicious replacing ½ cup (65 g) of white flour with the same amount of whole wheat, barley, potato, chickpea or rice flour. Like all flatbreads, *moti roti* is torn into bite-sized pieces and used, in place of cutlery, to mop up juicy vegetable or *dal* dishes. The flat bread can also be deep-fried, like *bhatura*. Accompany it with *Bitter Melon Vegetable Soup with Dal Badi* or *Gingered Chickpeas with Eggplant, Spinach and Tomato* and a salad, and you have a satisfying lunch. For breakfast, try exotic *Spicy Guava Jam* or *Mild Plum Chutney* and seasonal fresh fruits.

Preparation time (after assembling ingredients): 15 minutes
Dough resting time: 8 hours or overnight
Cooking time: 40 minutes
Makes: 14 *rotis*

2 cups (235 g) unbleached white flour
1 teaspoon (5 ml) sugar
¼ teaspoon (1 ml) baking soda
1 teaspoon (5 ml) salt
¼ cup (60 ml) plain yogurt, at room temperature
3 tablespoons (45 ml) vegetable oil
6–8 tablespoons (90–120 ml) warm water (about 100°F/38°C)
unbleached white flour for dusting
melted butter or *ghee* for brushing on the finished breads (optional)

1. Blend the flour, sweetener, soda and salt in a bowl. Combine the yogurt with the oil and 6 tablespoons (90 ml) of warm water and pour it over the flour in a thin stream, then mix into a kneadable dough. (The amount of water may vary, depending on the flour.) Knead the dough on a clean work surface, adding flour or water if necessary, until silky smooth and pliable, about 8 minutes. You can also make the dough in a food processor (see page 100), adding the yogurt along with the 6 tablespoons (90 ml) of warm water. Roll the dough into a ball. Pour a little oil into a plastic bag and rub the sides together. Place the dough in the bag, push out all of the air, and close it with a twist tie. Set the dough in a warm nook (about 100°F/38°C) and in 8–12 hours it will slightly sour and expand in volume.

For information about unfamiliar ingredients or techniques, see A-to-Z

2. Gather the items needed for rolling out and cooking: a rolling pin, dusting flour in a shallow plate or pie dish, a cake rack, a basket lined with clean tea towels, and a bowl of melted butter or *ghee* (if desired) and a pastry brush. Knead the dough briefly and divide it into 14 portions. Roll them into smooth balls, put them on a plate without letting them touch, and cover with a damp cloth.

3. Set a griddle over moderately low heat to preheat for 3–5 minutes. Flatten a ball of dough into a 2-inch (5 cm) patty and dip both sides in the dusting flour. Roll it out as evenly as you can into a round about 5 inches (12.5 cm) in diameter, dipping it in the dusting flour from time to time, just enough to keep it from sticking to the work surface (excess flour will make the *roti* brittle). Roll with even, gentle pressure, easing the dough into a round rather than stretching it. (Experienced cooks rotate the breads as they flatten them, using a slightly clockwise back-and-forth motion.)

4. When the griddle is hot, pick up the *roti* and slap it back and forth between your palms to shake off excess flour. Half-slap, half-slip the bread onto the griddle. It should lie flat, without any wrinkles. If there are wrinkles, do not try to press them out, as the bread would stick and burn. Wait until the bottom firms up, then shake the griddle to try to ease out the wrinkles. Cook for about 1½ minutes on the first side. (If you are using electric heat to balloon the bread, preheat a back burner on high.) When the top of the *roti* lightens in color, small bubbles begin to form, and the bottom has small brownish spots, turn the *roti* over with your fingertips or a spatula and cook on the second side for about half a minute. Take the griddle off the heat to keep it from overheating.

5. If you are using gas, turn a back burner on high. Place the *roti* on the rack and hold it 2 inches (5 cm) over the burner. In seconds the *roti* will swell, fill with steam and puff into a balloon. Continue to cook, turning it once, until it has charcoal-black flecks. Ballooning the bread takes only 10–15 seconds. (If you hold the bread over the heat too long, its surface tends to burn or become brittle.)

6. Slip the finished bread into the basket or dish and cover. Set the griddle back over moderately low heat and repeat the process. If desired, brush one side with melted butter or *ghee* before serving.

Griddle-Baked Chickpea and Whole Wheat Bread
BESAN THEPLA

In western Gujarat, from Ahmedabad to Surat, this is a much-loved dish. Ground spices—turmeric, cumin and *garam masala*—mingle with fresh herbs, chickpea flour and wheat flour in this soft bread with a nutty wheat flavor. Try it with *Vegetable Chowder* or *Wholesome Whole Grain and Vegetable Soup* and a tossed green salad.

Preparation time (after assembling ingredients): 10–20 minutes
Dough resting time: ½ hour–3 hours
Cooking time: 30–40 minutes
Makes: 12 *theplas*

⅓ cup (30 g) sifted chickpea flour, dry-roasted *
1⅔ cups (215 g) sieved *chapati* flour, or
    1 cup (130 g) sieved whole wheat flour mixed
    with ⅔ cup (80 g) millet or barley flour
¼ teaspoon (1 ml) cayenne pepper
¼ teaspoon (1 ml) turmeric
2 teaspoons (10 ml) ground cumin
2 teaspoons (10 ml) *garam masala*
1 teaspoon (5 ml) herb or sea salt
2 tablespoons (30 ml) minced mixed fresh herbs—
    coriander, parsley, basil, savory, marjoram
2 tablespoons (30 ml) melted unsalted butter, *ghee* or nut oil
¼ cup (60 ml) plain yogurt, at room temperature
⅓ cup (80 ml) warm water (about 100°F/38°C)
chapati or sieved wheat flour for dusting
melted butter or *ghee* for brushing on the finished flatbreads (optional)

*Place the sifted flour in a heavy frying pan over low heat. Stirring constantly, toast the flour until it darkens a few shades and takes on a nutty aroma. Sift again before use.

1. Place the flours, spices, salt and herbs in a mixing bowl and blend well. Add the melted butter, *ghee* or oil and yogurt and mix in with your fingertips until thoroughly incorporated. Add the water, pouring fast at first, to moisten the flour until it adheres into a rough mass, then slowly, in dribbles, until you have a kneadable dough. (The amount of water may vary, depending on the flour.) Knead the dough on a clean work surface, adding flour or water if necessary, until silky smooth and pliable, 5–10 minutes. You can also make the dough in a food processor (see page 100). Roll the dough into a ball, cover with an inverted bowl and let it rest for ½ hour–3 hours. If you want to leave it longer, you can refrigerate it for up to 24 hours; let it come to room temperature before you start to roll out the breads.

2. Gather the items needed for rolling out and cooking: a rolling pin, dusting flour in a shallow plate or pie dish, a cake rack, a basket lined with clean tea towels, and a bowl of melted butter or *ghee* (if desired) and a pastry brush. Knead the dough briefly and divide it into 12 portions. Roll them into smooth balls, put them on a plate without letting them touch, and cover with a damp cloth.

3. Set a griddle over moderately low heat to preheat for 3–5 minutes. Flatten a ball of dough into a 2-inch (5 cm) patty and dip both sides in the dusting flour. Roll it out as evenly as you can into a thin round about 6 inches (15 cm) in diameter, dipping it in the dusting flour from time to time, just enough to keep it from sticking to the work surface (excess flour will make the *thepla* brittle). Roll with even, gentle pressure, easing the dough into a round rather than stretching it. (Experienced cooks rotate the breads as they flatten them, using a slightly clockwise back-and-forth motion.)

4. When the griddle is hot, pick up the *thepla* and slap it back and forth between your palms to shake off excess flour. Half-slap, half-slip the bread onto the griddle. It should lie flat, without any wrinkles. If there are wrinkles, do not try to press them out, as the bread would stick and burn. Wait until the bottom firms up, then shake the griddle to try to ease out the wrinkles. Cook for about 1 minute on the first side. (If you are using electric heat to balloon the bread, preheat a back burner on high.) When the top of the *thepla* lightens in color, small bubbles begin to form, and the bottom has small

For information about unfamiliar ingredients or techniques, see A-to-Z

brownish spots, turn the *thepla* over with your fingertips or a spatula. Cook on the second side for about half a minute. Take the griddle off the heat to keep it from overheating.

5. If you are using gas, turn a back burner on high. Place the *thepla* on the rack and hold it 2 inches (5 cm) over the burner. In seconds the *thepla* will swell, fill with steam and puff into a balloon. Continue to cook, turning it once, until it has charcoal-black flecks. Ballooning the bread takes only 10–15 seconds. (If you hold the bread over the heat too long, its surface tends to burn or become brittle.)

6. Slip the finished bread into the basket and cover. Set the griddle back over moderately low heat and repeat the process. If desired, brush one side with melted butter or *ghee* before serving.

GRIDDLE-FRIED BREADS

Griddle-Fried Whole Wheat Bread
PARATHA

Paratha dough is similar to *chapati* dough, except for a little *ghee* or butter to enrich it and less water, making a medium-stiff instead of medium dough. Salt is usually added to round out the flavor. The breads are fully cooked on the griddle, not puffed over an open flame, and during the cooking they are basted with *ghee* to make them crisp and rich. Plain *parathas* are folded and rolled out using several techniques, and during the cooking a multitude of layers separate and become flaky, like puff pastry. The classic finished shape for plain *parathas* is roughly triangular, with sides 6 inches (15 cm) long. Experienced cooks roll out and fry the breads simultaneously, but if you are new to the task it is best to roll them all out before beginning to cook them. You can cut cooking time to a minimum by using two, three or even four griddles.

Srila Prabhupada always refused to eat airplane food when traveling. "What is the use of artificial food when there is such variety in nature?" he once commented. "Why bother with frozen, canned and preserved ingredients—practically rotten foods—when fresh ingredients are available for the preparation of *prasadam*?" His traveling meal for intercontinental flights reflected this standard, often repeating a menu his mother made for childhood lunch boxes: a griddle-fried or deep-fried bread, a dry-textured vegetable dish (often potato-based), fresh chutney or jam, seasonal fruits, a sweetmeat and a chilled or hot beverage. Once, just before a long flight, he taught me how to make a fantastic *Spicy Guava Jam*, and requested plain *parathas* to complete the combination. For a typical brunch, lunch box or light meal, try *parathas* with exotic *Rose Petal and Fruit Jam*, *Pear Chutney with Dates and Pecans* or *Spicy Plum Chutney*. Add one or two seasonal fruits and you have a gem of a meal. *Parathas* also go well with small portions of fresh chutney or pickle. To round out a lunch or dinner menu, add a vegetable—perhaps *Deep-Fried Cauliflower and Potatoes in Spiced Tomato Broth* or *Pleasingly Bitter Vegetable Stew*.

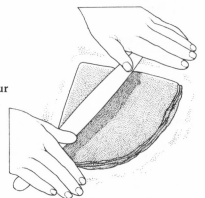

Preparation time (after assembling ingredients): 5–15 minutes
Dough resting time: ½ hour–3 hours
Cooking time: 35–45 minutes
Makes: 10 *parathas*

2⅓ cups (305 g) sieved *chapati* flour, or 1⅓ cups (165 g) whole
  wheat flour mixed with 1 cup (120 g) unbleached white flour
¾ teaspoon (3.5 ml) salt
2 tablespoons (30 ml) melted butter, *ghee* or oil
⅔ cup (160 ml) warm water (about 100°F/38°C), or as needed
chapati or sieved wheat flour for dusting
about ½ cup (120 ml) melted *ghee* or vegetable oil for cooking

1. Mix the flour and salt in a large bowl. Drizzle in the melted butter, *ghee* or oil and rub it in with your fingertips until the mixture has the consistency of coarse oatmeal. Add the water, pouring fast at first, to moisten the flour until it adheres into a rough mass, then more slowly, in dribbles, until it forms a medium-stiff dough. (The amount of water may vary, depending on the flour.) Knead the dough, dusting occasionally with flour to keep it from sticking to the work surface, until silky smooth and pliable, about 10 minutes. You can also make the dough in a food processor (see page 100). Shape it into a ball, rub it with *ghee* or oil, cover with an inverted bowl and let it rest for ½ hour–3 hours. If you want to leave it longer, you can refrigerate it, well covered, for up to 24 hours; let it come to room temperature before you start to roll out the breads.

2. Gather the items needed for rolling out and cooking—a rolling pin, dusting flour in a shallow plate or pie dish, a basket lined with clean tea towels, and a bowl of melted *ghee* or oil and a pastry brush and a teaspoon. Knead the dough briefly and divide it into 10 portions. Roll them into smooth balls, put them on a plate without letting them touch, and cover with a damp cloth.

3. To roll out the breads, flatten a ball into a 2-inch (5 cm) patty and dip both sides in the dusting flour. Roll it out as evenly as you can into a thin round about 6 inches (15 cm) in diameter, dipping it in the dusting flour from time to time, just enough to keep it from sticking to the work surface. With the pastry brush or your fingertips, brush the top of the round with *ghee* or oil, then fold it in half. Brush the top of the half-circle with *ghee* or oil, fold into a quarter-circle, and dip both sides in the dusting flour. Roll it out into a triangle 6 inches (15 cm) on a side, dipping it in the dusting flour from time to time, just enough to keep it from sticking to the work surface (excess flour will make the *paratha* brittle and will burn in the hot *ghee* or oil). As you shape the breads, put them in a single layer on wax-paper-lined cookie sheets, without letting them touch, or they will stick together and become impossible to separate. Cover with a damp cloth.

4. Preheat the griddle over moderate heat for 2–3 minutes (about 375°F/190°C on an electric griddle) and brush it with a little *ghee* or oil. Slip a bread onto the griddle and cook for 1½ minutes, then drizzle 1 teaspoon (5 ml) of *ghee* or oil around the edges and on top of the bread and cook for another minute or until the bottom has reddish-brown spots. Turn it over with a spatula and drizzle another teaspoon (5 ml) of *ghee* or oil on the surface. To encourage the *paratha* to cook evenly and puff up in places, rub the

---

For information about unfamiliar ingredients or techniques, see A-to-Z

bottom of a spoon over the bread in a circular motion. Cook for up to 2 minutes more or until it becomes crisp and shows reddish-brown spots on both sides. Slip it into the basket and fold a tea towel over the top. Repeat the process for the remaining breads.

Griddle-Fried Potato-Stuffed Whole Wheat Bread
ALOO PARATHA

Stuffed *parathas* take a bit more time to assemble than plain, so try them when you have plenty of time or an extra pair of helping hands, and use several griddles. Though nothing beats piping-hot *parathas*, they are fine kept warm or even served at room temperature.

Srila Prabhupada knew the nooks and crannies of Old Delhi, having lived there before coming to the United States in 1965. Many areas are so congested that foot travel is the only feasible transportation. I first found myself in *"Paratha Gully"* while heading for a famous *sari* shop in the Red Fort district—a compact, confined area with wall-to-wall shops, famous for its outdoor *paratha* stands. Family-trained specialists, young and old, sit hour after hour preparing fresh *parathas* for residents and tourists. After studying what I considered the best of them, I was ready the next time Srila Prabhupada requested a stuffed *paratha*. While the bread was still hot, with only a few bites gone, he asked where I had learned to make the variation. After hearing my story, he commented that he too had seen them making *parathas*, one after another. "An observant cook can learn simply by watching and hearing. As a child, I learned to cook by watching my mother, my maternal aunt and the street vendors." Everyone in Delhi has a favorite variation. This has always been one of mine.

For a real summer lunch-box treat, try potato *parathas* accompanied by *Mixed Vegetable Salad* and a thermos of cool *Minty Lemon-Lime Refresher*. When the weather turns nippy, *parathas* with fruit compote and a hot beverage makes a warm, satisfying breakfast. For a light brunch or lunch, try these *parathas* with *Shredded Cucumbers in Smooth Mint-Flavored Yogurt*.

Preparation time (after assembling ingredients): 15–30 minutes
Dough resting time: ½ hour–3 hours
Cooking time: 40 minutes
Makes: 10 stuffed *parathas*

For the Bread:

4 cups (520 g) sieved *chapati* flour, or 2⅔ cups (335 g) sieved whole
     wheat flour mixed with 1⅓ cups (155 g) unbleached white flour
½ tablespoon (7 ml) salt
⅓ cup (80 ml) melted unsalted butter or *ghee*
1⅓ cups (320 ml) warm water (about 100°F/38°C), or as needed
chapati or sieved wheat flour for dusting

For the Filling:

2 tablespoons (30 ml) *ghee* or vegetable oil
½ tablespoon (7 ml) scraped, minced fresh ginger root
½ tablespoon (7 ml) minced seeded hot green chili
½ tablespoon (7 ml) cumin seeds
2½ cups (600 ml) warm mashed potatoes
½ tablespoon (7 ml) ground coriander
¼ teaspoon (1 ml) paprika or cayenne pepper
scant ½ teaspoon (2 ml) turmeric
½ tablespoon (7 ml) salt
1 tablespoon (15 ml) lemon juice
2 teaspoons (10 ml) *jaggery* or brown sugar
3 tablespoons (45 ml) chopped fresh coriander,
    dill or parsley
chapati or sieved wheat flour for dusting
⅔ cup (160 ml) melted *ghee* or vegetable oil for cooking

    1. Mix the flour and salt in a large bowl. Drizzle in the melted butter or *ghee* and rub it in with your fingertips until the mixture has the consistency of coarse oatmeal. Add the water, pouring fast at first, to moisten the flour until it adheres into a rough mass, then more slowly, in dribbles, until it forms a medium-stiff dough. (The amount of water may vary, depending on the flour.) Knead the dough, dusting occasionally with flour to keep it from sticking to the work surface, until silky smooth and pliable, about 10 minutes. You can also make the dough in a food processor (see page 100). Shape it into a ball, rub it with *ghee* or oil, cover with an inverted bowl and let it rest for ½ hour–3 hours. If you want to leave it longer, you can refrigerate it, well covered, for up to 24 hours; let it come to room temperature before you start to roll out the breads.
    2. To make the filling, heat the *ghee* or oil in a large frying pan over moderate heat. Add the ginger root, chili and cumin seeds, and fry until the seeds brown. Stir in the mashed potatoes, ground coriander, paprika or cayenne, turmeric, salt, lemon juice, sweetener and herb. Stir-fry for a minute or so, and set aside to cool. (The filling can be made ahead of time and refrigerated. Let it come to room temperature before assembling the breads.) Divide into 10 portions on a plate.
    3. Gather the items needed for rolling out and cooking—a rolling pin, dusting flour in a shallow plate or pie dish, a basket lined with clean tea towels, and a bowl of melted *ghee* or oil and a pastry brush and a teaspoon. Knead the dough briefly, divide in half, roll each piece into a rope and cut into 10 portions. Roll them into smooth balls, put them on a plate without letting them touch, and cover with a damp cloth.
    4. To roll out the breads, flatten a ball into a 2-inch (5 cm) patty and dip both sides in the dusting flour. Roll it out as evenly as you can into a round about 6 inches (15 cm) in diameter, dipping it in the dusting flour from time to time, just enough to keep it from sticking to the work surface (excess flour will make the *paratha* brittle and will burn in the hot *ghee* or oil). Roll with even, gentle pressure, easing the dough into a round rather than stretching it. (Experienced cooks rotate the breads as they flatten them, using a slightly clockwise back-and-forth motion.) Repeat the process with another ball of dough. Dip a pastry brush in water and paint a border around the edges.
    5. To assemble, spread a portion of filling evenly over one round, leaving a ½-inch (1.5 cm) border around the edges. Carefully pick up the other round and lay it on top.

For information about unfamiliar ingredients or techniques, see A-to-Z

Gently smooth the surface, easing out air bubbles, and press around the edges to seal in the filling. If you have rolled even, round breads, they will not need trimming, but if there is too much overlap on top or bottom, simply cut off the excess with a sharp knife. As you assemble the breads, put them on waxed-paper-lined cookie sheets without letting them touch, or they will be impossible to separate.

6. Preheat a griddle over moderate heat for 2–3 minutes (about 375°F/190°C on an electric griddle) and brush with a little *ghee* or oil. Check the temperature by sprinkling a few drops of water on the surface; if the drops bounce and sputter, the griddle is ready. Carefully lay a stuffed bread on the griddle and cook for about 1½ minutes, then drizzle 1 teaspoon (5 ml) of *ghee* or oil around the edges and on top of the bread. When it has cooked for a total of 2–3 minutes and the bottom has reddish-brown spots, turn it over with a spatula, drizzle another teaspoon (5 ml) of *ghee* or oil on the surface and cook for up to 2 minutes more. When both sides of the bread puff in places, become crisp and show reddish-brown spots, it is done. You can encourage the bread to puff by gently rubbing the surface with the bottom of a spoon. Turn it over once again if it needs to brown a little more. Slip it into the basket and fold a tea towel over the top. Repeat the process for the remaining breads.

Griddle-Fried Caulifower-Stuffed Whole Wheat Bread
GOBHI PARATHA

All of the stuffed *paratha* recipes in this chapter call for similar shaping and cooking; the main difference is in the filling. Each features a special ingredient—mashed potatoes, grated radish or cauliflower, mashed peas, jam or raw sugar—and most of them are pleasantly hot or spicy. In the previous recipe, sugar and lemon juice gave the potato filling a piquant sweet-and-sour twist; here, the cauliflower is complemented by the nippy heat of fresh ginger root and the spice blend *garam masala*. They are delicious beyond words.

Since it is hard for two people to agree on the size of a medium-sized cauliflower, the recipe calls for 2¾ cups (650 ml) of finely chopped cauliflower. Of course, a food processor quickly shreds the exact amount, but a blender does the job quite adequately. Fill the jar one-third full of water and add small chunks of cauliflower, roughly ¾ inch (2 cm) square, to fill the jar to half. Cover and blend until finely chopped. Pour the contents into a strainer, drain and press out the water. To measure the cauliflower, pack it lightly.

Any type of *paratha* goes well with fresh or cooked chutneys. If you want to try a special combination, accompany the breads with a dab of cooked *Gooseberry Chutney, Fresh Pineapple and Raisin Chutney* or *Apricot Chutney with Currants*. They are also delicious finger-food appetizers for parties: cut them into wedges and arrange on a platter around a bowl of chutney.

Preparation time (after assembling ingredients): 15–30 minutes
Dough resting time: ½ hour–3 hours
Cooking time: 40 minutes
Makes: 10 stuffed *parathas*

For the Bread:

**4 cups (520 g) sieved *chapati* flour, or 2⅔ cups (335 g) whole
    wheat flour mixed with 1⅓ cups (155 g) unbleached white flour**
½ tablespoon (7 ml) salt
⅓ cup (80 ml) melted unsalted butter or *ghee*
1⅓ cups (320 ml) warm water (about 100°F/38°C), or as needed

For the Filling:

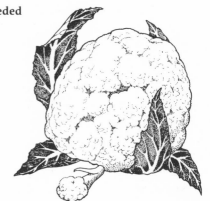

3 tablespoons (45 ml) *ghee* or vegetable oil
**2 tablespoons (30 ml) scraped, finely shredded
    or minced fresh ginger root**
**2¾ cups (650 ml) finely chopped or
    coarsely shredded cauliflower**
2 teaspoons (10 ml) *garam masala*
¼ teaspoon (1 ml) paprika or cayenne pepper
1¼ teaspoons (6 ml) salt
***chapati* or sieved wheat flour for dusting**
⅔ cup (160 ml) *ghee* or vegetable oil for cooking

   1. Mix the flour and salt in a large bowl. Drizzle in the melted butter or *ghee* and rub it in with your fingertips until the mixture has the consistency of coarse oatmeal. Add the water, pouring fast at first, to moisten the flour until it adheres into a rough mass, then more slowly, in dribbles, until it forms a medium-stiff dough. (The amount of water may vary, depending on the flour.) Knead the dough, dusting occasionally with flour to keep it from sticking to the work surface, until silky smooth and pliable, about 10 minutes. You can also make the dough in a food processor (see page 100). Shape it into a ball, rub it with *ghee* or oil, cover with an inverted bowl and let it rest for ½ hour–3 hours. If you want to leave it longer, you can refrigerate it, well covered, for up to 24 hours; let it come to room temperature before you start to roll out the breads.
   2. To make the filling, heat the *ghee* or oil in a large frying pan over moderate heat. Add the ginger and cauliflower and stir-fry for about 5 minutes or until the cauliflower softens and begins to look fried. Add the *garam masala*, paprika or cayenne and salt, stir well and take the pan off the heat. Divide the filling into 10 portions and set aside to cool. (The filling can be made ahead of time and refrigerated. Let it come to room temperature before assembling the breads.)
   3. Gather the items needed for rolling out and cooking—a rolling pin, dusting flour in a shallow plate or pie dish, a basket lined with clean tea towels, and a bowl of melted *ghee* or oil and a pastry brush and a teaspoon. Knead the dough briefly, divide in half, roll each piece into a rope and cut into 10 portions. Roll them into smooth balls, put them on a plate without letting them touch, and cover with a damp cloth.
   4. To roll out the breads, flatten a ball into a 2-inch (5 cm) patty and dip both sides in the dusting flour. Roll it out as evenly as you can into a round about 6 inches (15 cm) in diameter, dipping it in the dusting flour from time to time, just enough to keep it from sticking to the work surface (excess flour will make the *paratha* brittle and will burn in the hot *ghee* or oil). Roll with even, gentle pressure, easing the dough into a round rather than stretching it. (Experienced cooks rotate the breads as they flatten them, using a slightly clockwise back-and-forth motion.) Repeat the process with another ball of dough. Dip a pastry brush in water and paint a border around the edges.

For information about unfamiliar ingredients or techniques, see A-to-Z

5. To assemble, spread a portion of filling evenly over one round, leaving a ½-inch (1.5 cm) border around the edges. Carefully pick up the other round and lay it on top. Gently smooth the surface, easing out air bubbles, and press all around the edges to seal in the filling. If you have rolled even, round breads, they will not need any trimming, but if there is too much overlap on top or bottom, simply cut off the excess with a sharp knife. As you assemble the breads, put them on waxed-paper-lined cookie sheets without letting them touch, or they will be impossible to separate.

6. Preheat a griddle over moderate heat for 2–3 minutes (about 375°F/190°C on an electric griddle) and brush with a little *ghee* or oil. Check the temperature by sprinkling a few drops of water on the surface; if the drops bounce and sputter, the griddle is ready. Carefully lay a stuffed bread on the griddle and cook for about 1½ minutes, then drizzle 1 teaspoon (5 ml) of *ghee* or oil around the edges and on top of the bread. When it has cooked for a total of 2–3 minutes and the bottom has reddish-brown spots, turn it over with a spatula, drizzle another teaspoon (5 ml) of *ghee* or oil on the surface and cook for up to 2 minutes more. When both sides of the bread puff in places, become crisp and show reddish-brown spots, it is done. You can encourage the bread to puff by gently rubbing the surface with the bottom of a spoon. Turn it over once again if it needs to brown a little more. Slip it into the basket and fold a tea towel over the top. Repeat the process for the remaining breads.

Griddle-Fried Pea-Stuffed Whole Wheat Bread
HARI MATAR PARATHA

Whenever I am in Calcutta, my compass directs me to the well-tended kitchens of the C.L. Bajoria household. As well as maintaining the highest standard of garden-fresh produce, they keep an impeccable stock of fresh spices, nuts, grains and legumes. Mr. Sharma, the live-in resident chef, daily transforms commonplace items into masterpieces. His late-afternoon *tiffins* (similar to the high teas of England and served at about 5:00 pm) are feasts, consisting of at least seven different items. Every dish is first offered to Lord Krishna in the family temple and then enjoyed by family and guests.

When Mr. Sharma makes a pea filling for *parathas* or *kachoris*, he always uses oil, for an obvious but perhaps overlooked reason: in cool weather, *ghee* firms up at room temperature. Since *parathas* and *kachoris* are quite acceptable served at room temperature, he prefers not to use *ghee* in the filling, as it might coagulate into small flecks. He rounds out flavors in the peppery stuffing with a touch of sugar and lime juice.

In the Bajoria vegetable gardens, there are two seasons for growing peas. The peas for this filling are picked and shelled within an hour of cooking. They are sweet, and so tender that only a quick blanching is necessary. If you are using frozen baby peas, defrost and blanch for a minute or two. They are almost as good as garden peas, and often much better than the aging "fresh" peas at many stores. Pea *parathas* go well in menus from breakfast to late evening. I once served Srila Prabhupada these *parathas* upon his arrival in London late one afternoon. Along with the hot *parathas*, I served a typical Bengali *tiffin*: chilled mango slices, *Orange Zest Chenna Balls in Orange Flower Syrup* and *Raisin and Nut Milk Laced with Fennel*.

Preparation time (after assembling ingredients): 15–30 minutes
Dough resting time: ½ hour–3 hours
Cooking time: 30–40 minutes
Makes: 10 *parathas*

For the Bread:

4 cups (520 g) sieved *chapati* flour, or 2⅔ cups (335 g) whole wheat
    flour mixed with 1⅓ cups (155 g) unbleached white flour
½ tablespoon (7 ml) salt
⅓ cup (80 ml) melted unsalted butter or *ghee*
1⅓ (320 ml) cups warm water (about 100°F/38°C), or as needed

For the Filling:

2 tablespoons (30 ml) vegetable oil
1 tablespoon (15 ml) scraped, finely shredded or minced fresh ginger root
1–3 minced seeded hot green chilies (use as desired)
a generous ¼ teaspoon (1 ml) yellow asafetida powder (*hing*)*
2½ cups (600 ml) coarsely mashed cooked green peas
2 teaspoons (10 ml) *garam masala*
¼ teaspoon (1 ml) cayenne pepper or
    ½ teaspoon (2 ml) paprika
1¼ teaspoons (6 ml) salt
2 teaspoons (10 ml) lime or lemon juice
2 teaspoons (10 ml) *jaggery* or maple sugar
3 tablespoons (45 ml) minced fresh parsley or finely chopped coriander
chapati or sieved wheat flour for dusting
⅔ cup (160 ml) melted *ghee* or vegetable oil for cooking

*This amount applies only to yellow Cobra brand. Reduce any other asafetida by three-fourths.

1. Mix the flour and salt in a large bowl. Drizzle in the melted butter or *ghee* and rub it in with your fingertips until the mixture has the consistency of coarse oatmeal. Add the water, pouring fast at first, to moisten the flour until it adheres into a rough mass, then more slowly, in dribbles, until it forms a medium-stiff dough. (The amount of water may vary, depending on the flour.) Knead the dough, dusting occasionally with flour to keep it from sticking to the work surface, until silky smooth and pliable, about 10 minutes. You can also make the dough in a food processor (see page 100). Shape it into a ball, rub it with *ghee* or oil, cover with an inverted bowl and let it rest for ½ hour– 3 hours. If you want to leave it longer, you can refrigerate it, well covered, for up to 24 hours; let it come to room temperature before you start to roll out the breads.

2. To make the filling, heat the oil in a large frying pan over moderate heat. Toss in the ginger and chilies. Fry until the ginger starts to brown, then drop in the asafetida. A few seconds later, add the peas. Add the remaining ingredients and stir-fry for about 2 minutes. Remove the pan from the heat and divide into 10 portions. (The filling can be made ahead of time and refrigerated. Let it come to room temperature before assembling the breads.)

3. Gather the items needed for rolling out and cooking—a rolling pin, dusting flour in a shallow plate or pie dish, a basket lined with clean tea towels, and a bowl of melted

For information about unfamiliar ingredients or techniques, see A-to-Z

ghee or oil and a pastry brush and a teaspoon. Knead the dough briefly, divide in half, roll each piece into a rope and cut into 10 portions. Roll them into smooth balls, put them on a plate without letting them touch, and cover with a damp cloth.

4. To roll out the breads, flatten a ball into a 2-inch (5 cm) patty and dip both sides in the dusting flour. Roll it out as evenly as you can into a round about 6 inches (15 cm) in diameter, dipping it in the dusting flour from time to time, just enough to keep it from sticking to the work surface (excess flour will make the *paratha* brittle and will burn in the hot *ghee* or oil). Roll with even, gentle pressure, easing the dough into a round rather than stretching it. (Experienced cooks rotate the breads as they flatten them, using a slightly clockwise back-and-forth motion.) Repeat the process with another ball of dough. Dip a pastry brush in water and paint a border around the edges.

5. To assemble, spread a portion of filling evenly over one round, leaving a ½-inch (1.5 cm) border around the edges. Carefully pick up the other round and lay it on top. Gently smooth the surface, easing out air bubbles, and press around the edges to seal in the filling. If you have rolled even, round breads, they will not need trimming, but if there is too much overlap on top or bottom, simply cut off the excess with a sharp knife. As you assemble the breads, put them on waxed-paper-lined cookie sheets without letting them touch, or they will be impossible to separate.

6. Preheat a griddle over moderate heat for 2–3 minutes (about 375°F/190°C on an electric griddle) and brush with a little *ghee* or oil. Check the temperature by sprinkling a few drops of water on the surface; if the drops bounce and sputter, the griddle is ready. Carefully lay a stuffed bread on the griddle and cook for about 1½ minutes, then drizzle 1 teaspoon (5 ml) of *ghee* or oil around the edges and on top of the bread. When it has cooked for a total of 2–3 minutes and the bottom has reddish-brown spots, turn it over with a spatula, drizzle another teaspoon (5 ml) of *ghee* or oil on the surface and cook for up to 2 more minutes. When both sides of the bread puff in places, become crisp and show reddish-brown spots, it is done. You can encourage the bread to puff by gently rubbing the surface with the bottom of a spoon. Turn it over once again if it needs to brown a little more. Slip it into the basket and fold a tea towel over the top. Repeat the process for the remaining breads.

Griddle-Fried Radish-Stuffed Whole Wheat Bread
MOOLI PARATHA

White radishes vary considerably in size and taste, and there are usually three varieties available in the United States. The first, a summer-salad icicle radish, is a small finger-length type with a very mild flavor. It is usually on the produce shelves in the spring and summer months. By comparison, the Japanese *daikon* is a mild giant—invariably over a foot (30 cm) long and about 3 inches (7.5 cm) in diameter—and sometimes four times that size. These can usually be found in better supermarket produce departments and also at Japanese, Korean and Chinese grocery stores. Finally, the Indian white cooking radish, called *mooli*, is slender and 8–12 inches (20–30 cm) long. Offset with *ajwain* and coriander seeds, the nippy, rather pungent bite of *mooli* makes it not only traditional selection but exceptionally delicious   and lends authenticity and outstanding flavor to the *ajwain* and coriander stuffing. *Mooli* is available sporadically at Indian and Middle Eastern grocery stores. You can call to ask about incoming shipments. But do not despair if the main ingredient for this bread is not available; even though *moolis* are preferred, I have often used the common round red salad radish with success in this delicious and unusual bread, whose featured seasonings are whole coriander seeds and *ajwain* seeds.

Long white radishes can easily be shredded by hand or machine. To hand shred, wash the radishes and scrub or peel, then shred them on the medium holes of a hand grater. Drain in a strainer. If you use a food processor, fit the work bowl with a medium shredding disk and feed through the tube with steady pressure. To finely chop radishes in a blender, cut them into roughly ¾-inch (2 cm) chunks. Fill a blender jar one-third full of radishes and then fill to half full with water. Cover and pulse in bursts until finely chopped. Pour the contents through a strainer, and repeat until you have the required amount. Regardless of which method you use, squeeze the prepared radishes between your palms to extract excess liquid. For accurate measurement, loosely pack in cups or use a scale.

Radish *paratha* is popular throughout Kashmir, the Punjab and much of Northeastern India. This recipe, from the Hari Goswami family of Vrindavan, is more than 250 years old and perhaps my favorite variation, with a perfect balance of flavors from coriander and *ajwain* seeds. They can be made in advance and warmed up for a light, entertaining meal and are suited to any seasonal menu. For anything from a picnic to a Sunday brunch, try serving them with a spoonful of *Banana and Pomegranate Salad*, a dab of *Crab Apple or Green Apple Chutney* and *Fresh Orange Squash with Ginger*.

Preparation time (after assembling ingredients): 25 minutes
Dough resting time: ½ hour–3 hours
Cooking time: 30–40 minutes
Makes: 10 stuffed *parathas*

For the Bread:

4 cups (520 g) sieved *chapati* flour, or 2⅔ (335 g) cups whole wheat
  flour mixed with 1⅓ cups (155 g) unbleached white flour
½ tablespoon (7 ml) salt
⅓ cup (80 ml) melted unsalted butter or *ghee*
1⅓ (320 ml) cups warm water (about 100°F/38°C), or as needed

For the Filling:

2 tablespoons (30 ml) coriander seeds
½ teaspoon (2 ml) *ajwain* seeds
2½ cups (600 ml) shredded radishes, pressed dry
1–2 minced hot green chilies (use as desired)
½ tablespoon (7 ml) scraped minced fresh ginger root
1 teaspoon (5 ml) *garam masala*
2 tablespoons (30 ml) finely chopped fresh coriander
½ teaspoon (2 ml) salt
***chapati* or sieved wheat flour for dusting**
⅔ cup (160 ml) *ghee* or vegetable oil for cooking

For information about unfamiliar ingredients or techniques, see A-to-Z

1. Combine the flour and salt in a large bowl and mix well. Drizzle in the melted butter or *ghee* and rub it into the flour with your fingertips until the mixture takes on the consistency of coarse oatmeal. Pour in the water, quickly at first to moisten the flour enough to make it adhere into a rough mass, then more slowly, in dribbles, until it forms a medium-stiff dough. Knead the dough for 10 minutes or until it is silky smooth. You can also make the dough in a food processor (see page 100). Shape it into a ball, rub the dough with *ghee* or oil, cover with an inverted bowl and let it rest for ½ hour–3 hours. If you want to leave it longer, you can keep it well sealed in a refrigerator for up to 24 hours; let it come to room temperature before you start to roll out the breads.

2. Place the coriander and *ajwain* seeds in a small heavy pan and dry-roast over moderate heat until they begin to change color. Coarsely crush them with a mortar and pestle or in an electric coffee mill. In a bowl, mix the crushed spices with the remaining stuffing ingredients. Divide into 10 portions and set aside.

3. Knead the dough briefly. Divide in half, roll each piece into a rope and cut into 10 parts. Roll each part into a ball and set on a plate. Drape the balls with a damp towel. Flatten a ball into a 2-inch (5 cm) patty and dip both sides in the dusting flour. Roll it out as evenly as you can into a round about 6 inches (15 cm) in diameter. Dip the round in the dusting flour from time to time, but only enough to prevent the bread from sticking to the rolling surface; too much flour tends to make a brittle bread. Use even, gentle pressure during the rolling, easing the dough into a round rather than stretching it. (Experienced cooks rotate the breads as they flatten them, using a slightly clockwise back-and-forth motion.) Repeat the process with another round of dough.

4. To assemble, spread a portion of the filling evenly over one of the rolled-out breads; brush around the edges with a film of water. Carefully pick up another rolled-out bread and lay it over the filling-topped bread. Gently smooth the surface and then press all around the edges to seal in the filling. If you have rolled even, round breads, they won't need any trimming, but if there is too much overlap on top or bottom, simply cut off the excess so that your bread is round. Lay the breads on individual sheets of waxed paper on cookie sheets. Do not stack or overlap rolled breads; they are impossible to separate.

5. Preheat a griddle over moderate heat for 2–3 minutes (about 375°F/190°C on an electric griddle) and brush with a little *ghee* or oil. Check the temperature by sprinkling a few drops of water on the surface. If the water bounces and sputters, the griddle is ready. Carefully lay a stuffed bread on the griddle and cook for 1½ minutes, then drizzle 1 teaspoon (5 ml) of *ghee* or oil around the edges and on top of the bread. When it has cooked for a total of 2–3 minutes and has reddish-brown spots on the underside, flip it over with a spatula. Drizzle the surface with up to another teaspoon (5 ml) of melted *ghee* or oil around the edges and cook for up to 2 minutes more. When both sides of the bread puff in places, become crisp and show reddish-brown spots, it is finished. You can encourage the bread to puff up by gently rubbing the surface with the bottom of a spoon. Turn it over once again if it needs to brown a little more, then serve it at once or slip it into a tea-towel-lined basket, fold a tea towel over the top and start immediately to cook the remaining breads.

Griddle-Fried Sweet Stuffed Whole Wheat Bread
MEETHA PARATHA

In India, the raw sugars commonly known as *jaggery* and *gur* are sold in varying grades of texture, color and flavor. The textures range from solid lumps to semi-liquid, something like peanut butter. Some strains are honey-brown, while others are deep reddish-brown. Flavor is the biggest variable: each sugar has its own distinct aroma and taste, just like different varieties of honey. My favorite *gur* comes from Navadvipa in West Bengal. Each season has an excellent crop of high-quality *tal* palm sugar: a golden honey-colored solid cake of easily breakable, unrefined, raw sugar. Unfortunately, *tal gur* is not available in America, but you can still find good raw sugars in Middle Eastern and Indian grocery stores. Look for visibly clean sugar: some low grades show signs of unsophisticated handling and refining. Try to get a solid sugar, but not one that is rock hard. Generally, lighter-colored sugars have milder flavors.

Alternately, date sugar, grated maple candy, maple butter or maple granules make terrific sweet stuffings. For a sweet, but refreshingly sugar-free stuffing, use any one of the sugarless jams, preserves or jellies available in gourmet and health food stores.

These *parathas* are festive—pleasantly sweet and borderline rich—but certainly not injurious for an occasional special breakfast or late-dinner treat. Accompany with little more than a beverage and salad.

Preparation time (after assembling ingredients): 25 minutes
Dough resting time: ½ hour–3 hours
Cooking time: 30–40 minutes
Makes: 10 stuffed *parathas*

For the Bread:

4 cups (520 g) sieved *chapati* flour, or 2⅔ cups (335 g) whole
    wheat flour mixed with 1⅓ cups (155 g) unbleached white flour
½ tablespoon (7 ml) salt
⅓ cup (80 ml) melted unsalted butter or *ghee*
1⅓ cups (320 ml) warm water (about 100°F/38°C), or as needed
chapati or sieved wheat flour for dusting

For the Stuffing:

1 cup (155 g) shredded *jaggery*, maple sugar
    or equivalent jam, jelly or preserve
chapati or sieved wheat flour for dusting
⅔ cup (160 ml) *ghee* or vegetable oil for cooking

1. Combine the flour and salt in a large bowl and mix well. Drizzle in the melted butter or *ghee* and rub it into the flour with your fingertips until the mixture takes on the consistency of coarse oatmeal. Pour in the water, quickly at first to moisten the flour enough to make it adhere into a rough mass, then more slowly, in dribbles, until it forms a medium-stiff dough. Knead the dough for 10 minutes or until it is silky smooth. You can also make the dough in a food processor (see page 100). Shape the dough into a ball, rub it with *ghee* or oil, cover with an inverted bowl and let the dough rest for ½ hour–3 hours. If you want to leave it longer, keep it well sealed in a refrigerator for up to 24 hours. Remove it at least 1 hour before use.

For information about unfamiliar ingredients or techniques, see A-to-Z

2. Knead the dough briefly. Divide in half, roll each piece into a rope and cut into 10 parts. Roll each part into a ball and set on a plate. Drape the balls with a damp cloth. Flatten a ball into a 2-inch (5 cm) patty and dip both sides in the dusting flour. Roll it out as evenly as you can into a round about 6 inches (15 cm) in diameter. Dip the round in the dusting flour from time to time, but only enough to prevent the bread from sticking to the rolling surface; too much flour tends to make a brittle bread. Use even, gentle pressure during the rolling, easing the dough into a round rather than stretching it. (Experienced cooks rotate the breads as they flatten them, using a slightly clockwise back-and-forth motion.) Brush around the edges with a film of water.

3. To assemble, spread about 1½ tablespoons (22 ml) of the selected sweet filling evenly over one of the rolled-out breads, leaving a ½-inch (1.5 cm) border around the edges. Carefully pick up another rolled bread and lay it over the filling-topped bread. Gently smooth the surface and then press all around the edges to seal in the filling. If you have rolled even, round breads, they will not need any trimming, but if there is too much overlap on top or bottom, simply cut off the excess so your bread is round. Lay the assembled breads on individual sheets of waxed paper on cookie sheets. Do not stack or overlap rolled breads; they are impossible to separate.

4. Preheat a griddle over moderate heat for 2–3 minutes (about 375°F/190°C on an electric griddle) and brush with a little *ghee* or oil. Check the temperature by sprinkling a few drops of water on the surface. If they bounce and sputter, the griddle is ready. Carefully lay a stuffed bread on the griddle and cook for about 1 minute, then drizzle 1 teaspoon (5 ml) of *ghee* or oil around the edges and on top of the bread. Cook for up to 2 minutes more. Turn over and cook for an additional 2 minutes. When both sides of the bread puff in places, get crisp and have reddish-brown spots, it is finished. You can encourage the bread to puff by gently rubbing the surface with the bottom of a spoon. Turn it over once again if it needs to brown a little more, then serve it at once or slip it into a tea-towel-lined basket, fold a tea towel over the top and immediately start cooking the remaining breads.

Griddle-Fried Whole Wheat and Corn Bread
MAKKAI PARATHA

Just as Mexico has given the world corn tortillas, the Punjab in North India offers mouthwatering corn-based flatbreads. This version highlights corn and wheat flour with *ajwain* seeds and slivered green chilies. Creamy yellow, sweet-flavored corn flour is rich in oils and vitamin A. It is a relatively gluten-free flour and therefore requires the gluten in wheat to keep the dough easily workable. Straight corn doughs are tricky to roll and cook. If you cannot find corn flour, process cornmeal in a coffee mill or food processor and pass it through a fine sieve before measuring. These breads are wonderful accompaniments to moist vegetables such as *Bitter Melon Vegetable Stew in Poppy Seed Gravy* or the full-bodied *Curried Whole Mung Beans with Panir Cheese*.

Preparation time (after assembling ingredients): 10 minutes
Dough resting time: ½ hour–3 hours
Cooking time: 40 minutes
Makes: 10 *parathas*

1 cup (115 g) corn flour
2 cups (250 g) sieved whole wheat flour or *chapati* flour
1 teaspoon (5 ml) salt (optional)
1 tablespoon (15 ml) *jaggery* or brown sugar
2–3 hot green jalapeño chilies, halved, seeded and slivered
1 teaspoon (5 ml) *ajwain* seeds
3 tablespoons (45 ml) melted *ghee* or vegetable oil
¾ cup (180 ml) warm water (about 100°F/38°C), or as needed
chapati or sieved wheat flour for dusting
⅔ cup (160 ml) melted *ghee* or vegetable oil for cooking

1. Combine the flours, salt (if desired), sweetener, chilies and *ajwain* seeds in a mixing bowl. Blend well. Drizzle in the melted *ghee* or oil, and rub it into the flour with your fingertips until the mixture resembles coarse oatmeal. Pour in the water, quickly at first to moisten the flour enough to make it adhere into a rough mass, then more slowly, in dribbles, until it forms a medium-stiff dough. Knead the dough for 10 minutes or until silky smooth. You can also make the dough in a food processor (see page 100). Shape the dough into a smooth ball, rub it with *ghee* or oil, cover with an inverted bowl and let the dough rest for ½ hour–3 hours. If you want to leave it longer, keep well sealed in a refrigerator for up to 24 hours. Remove it at least 1 hour before use.

2. Collect all of the items you will need for rolling out and cooking: a rolling pin, dusting flour in a shallow plate or pie dish, a basket or bowl lined with clean tea towels, and a bowl of melted *ghee* or vegetable oil with a pastry brush and a teaspoon. Knead the dough briefly on a clean work surface and divide it into 10 portions. Roll the portions into smooth balls and place them on a plate without letting them touch. Then drape them with a damp cloth.

3. Flatten a ball of dough into a 2-inch (5 cm) patty, and dip both sides in the dusting flour. Roll it out as evenly as you can into a round about 6 inches (15 cm) in diameter. Dip the round in the dusting flour from time to time, but only enough to prevent the bread from sticking to the rolling surface; too much flour tends to make a brittle bread. Use even, gentle pressure during the rolling, easing the dough into its shape rather than stretching it.

4. Using the pastry brush or your fingertips, brush the top of the bread with melted *ghee* or oil, then fold the circle in half. Brush the top of the half-circle with *ghee* or oil and fold to make a quarter-circle. Dip the folded dough in the dusting flour and coat both sides. Return to the work surface and roll it out into a 6-inch (15 cm) triangle. Dip the dough in the dusting flour to keep it from sticking as you roll it, using only enough flour to facilitate rolling. Lay the breads on waxed-paper-lined cookie sheets without letting them touch; otherwise they will stick together and be impossible to separate.

5. Preheat a griddle over moderate heat for 2–3 minutes (about 375°F/190°C on an electric griddle) and brush with a little *ghee* or oil. Check the temperature by sprinkling a few drops of water on the surface; if the drops bounce and sputter, the griddle is ready. Brush the griddle with a little *ghee* or oil and slip a rolled bread onto it. Cook for 1 minute, then drizzle 1 teaspoon (5 ml) of *ghee* or oil around the edges and on top of the bread. When it has cooked a total of 2 minutes and has reddish-brown spots on the underside, flip it over with a spatula. Drizzle the surface with up to another teaspoon

(5 ml) of melted *ghee* or oil around the edges, and cook for up to 2 minutes more. When both sides of the bread puff in places, become crisp, and show reddish-brown spots, it is finished. You can encourage the bread to puff up by gently rubbing the surface with the bottom of a spoon. Turn it over once again if it needs to brown a little more; then serve it at once, or slip it into the towel-lined basket, fold a towel over the top and immediately continue to cook the remaining breads.

SHALLOW-FRIED BREADS

Shallow-Fried Flaky *Paratha*
WERKI PARATHA

I am not sure of the origin of this recipe. I learned it from a Marawadi cook in a Bengali kitchen who called them British *parathas*. This surely must be one of the flakiest, richest *parathas* in existence. First, the dough is shortened with *ghee*. Then it is brushed with a butter paste during shaping and rolling, and finally it is shallow-fried rather than griddle-fried. *Werki parathas* compare with the butter-rich brioches and croissants that the French relish, so try them when you want a Vedic counterpart to Western pastry breads.

For this recipe, use an 8- or 9-inch (20–22.5 cm) omelette pan with slightly sloping walls; you can make maximum use of the *ghee* and have easy access to the breads as they fry. Though I roll out the breads to about 6 inches (15 cm) in diameter (which is perfect for the recommended pan size), you could make larger or smaller breads and vary pan size. For best results, be sure to read through the instructions before beginning.

Preparation time (after assembling ingredients): 25 minutes
Dough resting time: ½ hour–3 hours
Chilling time: 2 hours or up to 24 hours
Cooking time: 30 minutes
Makes: 8 *parathas*

2½ cups (300 g) unbleached white flour, or 1 cup (110 g) cake flour
    mixed with 1½ cups (175 g) unbleached white flour
½ tablespoon (7 ml) baking powder
½ teaspoon (2 ml) salt
½ teaspoon (2 ml) sugar
3 tablespoons (45 ml) melted *ghee*
¾ cup (180 ml) warm water (about 100°F/38°C), or as needed
2½ tablespoons (37 ml) softened unsalted butter
1½ tablespoons (22 ml) cornstarch or arrowroot
unbleached white flour for dusting
ghee for shallow-frying

1. Combine the flour, baking powder, salt and sugar in a mixing bowl and blend well. Add the melted *ghee* and, using your fingertips, rub it into the flour until the mixture takes on the consistency of coarse oatmeal. Pour in the water, quickly at first, to moisten the flour enough to adhere into a rough mass, then more slowly, in dribbles, until it forms a medium-stiff dough. (The amount of water may vary, depending on the flour.) Knead the dough for 10 minutes, dusting occasionally with flour to keep it from sticking to the work surface, until the dough is silky smooth. You can also make the dough in a food processor (see page 100). Shape it into a ball, rub it with *ghee* or oil, cover with an inverted bowl and let it rest for ½ hours–3 hours.

2. Knead the dough again and divide it into eight portions. Roll them into smooth balls and set aside, covered with plastic wrap. Prepare the butter paste by creaming the softened butter with the arrowroot or cornstarch. Collect all of the items needed for rolling out: a rolling pin, dusting flour in a shallow plate or pie dish and a large plate.

3. Flatten a ball of dough into a patty, then dip both sides in flour and begin to roll into a round about 7 inches (17.5 cm) in diameter. Each time the bread begins to stick to the rolling surface, dip both sides in the dusting flour and roll it out again. Spread 1 teaspoon (5 ml) of butter paste on the round. With a sharp knife, cut from the center of the round to the outside edge. Roll tightly, from the cut, all the way around so that you end up with a neat little cone. Place the large end or base of the cone on a clean countertop and press the cone down into a patty. Place it on an oiled plate and cover with plastic wrap. Work the remaining pieces of dough into patties and keep them on the plate in a single layer, without touching. Refrigerate the patties, covered, for at least 2 hours or up to 24 hours, as desired.

4. About 10 minutes before cooking, remove the patties from the refrigerator. Pour *ghee* to a depth of ½ inch (1.5 cm) into an omelette pan and preheat over moderate to moderately low heat while you roll out the first bread. Dip both sides of a patty in flour. Roll it out until it is nearly 6 inches (15) in diameter, using only enough flour to facilitate rolling out and to keep it from sticking. When the *ghee* has reached about 330°F (165°C), gently slip in a bread. With a slotted spoon, immediately begin pressing down on the bread to keep submersed in hot *ghee* and prevent it from bobbing to the surface. This will cook the inside thoroughly and encourage the *paratha* layers to separate and become flaky. Fry for 2–3 minutes per side or until the crust is crisp and golden-brown. You can either serve the bread at once or put it in a basket or bowl lined with folded tea towels. Cook the remaining breads. If you are not going to serve the breads soon after cooking, let them cool, wrap them in a tea towel and store them in a covered bread tin. To reheat the *parathas*, wrap them in double-thick paper towels and cover tighly with tinfoil. Warm them in a preheated 350°F (175°C) oven for 15 minutes. Although these breads are delicious plain, I have experimented with a dusting of fine maple sugar, drizzles of warmed honey and a brushing of warmed apricot preserves. Try one, or use your imagination.

For information about unfamiliar ingredients or techniques, see A-to-Z

Shallow-Fried Chickpea *Paratha*
BESAN PARATHA

Although this bread takes more time than most, it is well worth it for a special brunch or a late-evening meal. The *paratha's* elusive nut flavor is from dry-roasted chickpea flour, an ingredient used in both North and South Indian confections. To develop full nut flavor from the flour, it must be toasted slowly and stirred constantly to prevent scorching. This aromatic brown flour is now blended with unbleached flour, heightened with *garam masala* and shortened with *ghee* before the mixing into a half-pastry, half-bread dough. The breads are shaped the same as in the previous recipe, an once again *ghee* is the essential cooking medium for authenticity. This is an appropriate finger food for parties: warm breads cut into wedges or, if you have the time for shaping, individual miniature breads. It is also a good afternoon or early-evening tea selection for terrace or backyard breaks.

Try these *parathas* with colorful accompaniments like a festive *Pineapple Tower Surprise, Khoa-Covered Cheese Balls Rolled in Coconut, Feather-Soft Urad Dal Doughnuts with Seasoned Yogurt* and a summertime tossed green salad. *Besan parathas* complement both sweets and savories.

Preparation time (after assembling ingredients): 40 minutes
Dough resting and chilling time: 1½ hours or up to 24 hours
Cooking time: 1 hour
Makes: 12 *parathas*

1½ cups (145 g) sifted chickpea flour *
1½ cups (175 g) unbleached white flour
2 teaspoons (10 ml) baking powder
½ tablespoon (7 ml) salt
½ tablespoon (7 ml) *garam masala*
3 tablespoons (45 ml) finely chopped fresh dill or fennel,
    or ½ tablespoon (7 ml) crumbled dried herbs
2 cups (480 ml) melted *ghee*, for the dough and frying
unbleached white flour for dusting
1 cup (240 ml) warm water (100°F/38°C), or as needed

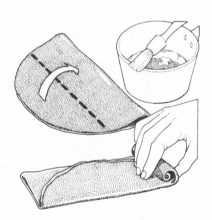

Sift the chickpea flour before measuring, then spoon into a measuring cup and level off with a knife. Avoid shaking or packing to level off. The flour is again sifted after toasting.

1. Place the chickpea flour in a heavy frying pan over moderately low heat. Dry-roast, stirring constantly, for 12–15 minutes or until the flour darkens several shades, from buff to rich tan. (Chickpea flour burns easily, even over moderate heat. If the flour even begins to smoke, remove the pan from the heat, and still stirring, continue to brown.)

2. Combine the toasted flour with the unbleached white flour, baking powder, salt and *garam masala* in a sifter and pass through into a mixing bow. Rub in the herbs and 2 tablespoons (30 ml) of melted *ghee* into the dry ingredients until it is evenly distributed. Add ¾ cup (180 ml) of water, pouring it fast at first, stirring to moisten the flour until it adheres into a rough mass, and then slowly, adding sprinkles of the remaining water up to 1 cup (240 ml), until it forms a dough you can knead. Knead the dough until it is silky smooth and pliable (about 8 minutes). Alternately, you can mix and knead the dough in a food processor (see page 100). Roll the dough into a smooth ball and cover it with an inverted bowl. Let it rest for ½ hour–3 hours. If you want to leave it longer, keep it well sealed in the refrigerator for up to 24 hours. Remove it at least 1 hour prior to rolling out.

3. Collect the items you will need for rolling out: a rolling pin, dusting flour in a shallow plate or pie dish and a basket or bowl lined with clean tea towels for stacking the cooked breads. Knead the dough again and divide it into 12 portions. Roll each portion into a smooth ball and set them aside, covered with plastic wrap.

4. Flatten a ball of dough into a patty, then dip both sides in flour and begin to roll it into a round about 7 inches (17.5 cm) in diameter. Each time the bread begins to stick to the rolling surface, dip both sides in the dusting flour and roll it out again. Brush melted *ghee* over the surface of the bread, fold in half and brush the half-circle with *ghee*. Fold the round over the top to meet the first fold and pat down with the rolling pin to seal. Fold over once again and pinch the edges to form a rope. With the seam facing inward, coil tightly into a jelly roll. Flatten slightly, place it on an oiled plate and cover with plastic wrap. Work each of the remaining patties in the same way, keeping them all on the plate in a single layer without touching. Refrigerate the patties, covered, for 1½– 24 hours, as desired.

5. About 10 minutes before cooking, remove the patties from the refrigerator. Pour ½–¾ inch (1.5–2 cm) of *ghee* into an 8- or 9-inch (20–22.5 cm) omelette pan. Place the pan over moderate to moderately low heat while you roll out the first bread. Dip the patty on both sides in flour and roll it out, using only enough flour to facilitate rolling and to keep it from sticking, until it is nearly 6 inches (15 cm) in diameter. When the *ghee* is about 335°F (170°C) on a frying thermometer, gently slip in a bread. Immediately begin pressing down on the bread to keep it in the hot *ghee* so it cannot bob to the surface. This will help to cook the inside thoroughly and encourage it to swell. Fry on both sides, for 2–3 minutes per side, until the bread is crisp and a glowing reddish-brown. Either serve the bread at once or slip it into the towel-lined basket and continue to cook the remaining breads. If you are not going to serve the breads soon after cooking, let them cool, wrap them in a tea towel and store them in a covered bread tin. To reheat the *parathas*, wrap them in double-thick paper towels and cover tightly with tin-foil. Warm them in a preheated 350°F (175°C) oven for 15 minutes.

DEEP-FRIED BREADS

Deep-Fried Whole Wheat Bread
POORI

Poori is *the* Vedic bread for entertaining—from a party of six to a crowd of six hundred. Once the dough is made, the breads can be rolled and cooked one after another in a matter of minutes. Traveling through India, from bazaar stalls to campsite festival kitchens, it is customary to see a bowl-shaped iron *karai*, at least 2½ feet (75 cm) in diameter, resting on a single-burner stove. Two or three men gather around the stove and cook *poori* after *poori*, which are then served, still filled with steam, in cups made from leaves. Though *poori* is generally made from whole wheat flour, especially in Northern India, it can also be made out of flour blends. The dough is almost the same as that for *chapatis*, with only minor changes. A little less water is added, so it is a firmer dough; and it is shortened with a touch of *ghee* or oil and salted to bring out the flavor.

Though it may take time to master the rhythm of simultaneously rolling out a perfectly round, evenly thick *poori* while frying another, don't lose heart. Perfection assuredly comes with determined practice. Your breads may initially be oblong or elongated, but if carefully fried, at the right temperature, they will balloon and taste delicious. If you are new to *pooris*, I suggest rolling them out ahead of time and giving all your attention to last-minute frying. This recipe yields 16 standard-size *pooris*, or 8 giant-sized breads and takes no more than a half hour rolling and frying time. Oversize *pooris* are festive and perfect when you want something spectacular, but they *must* be served piping hot and puffed—whisked from the pan to the table. If possible, schedule frying *pooris* just before serving. In a pinch, they can be held in warm oven for up to ½ hour. After that, the breads loose their sheen, soften and are called *baasi*—tired or deflated breads. In this still form, they are frequent traveling companions for train journeys, park or seaside outings and lunch boxes.

One of Srila Prabhupada's traveling cooks, Srutakirti Das, told me a story that confirmed Srila Prabhupada's appreciation of *pooris*. On an intercontinental flight, Srila Prabhupada was relishing a *baasi poori* from his lunch box. "When I was a boy," he said, "my father encouraged my favorite tastes. He would return home from work long after I had been sent to bed, would wake me up to sit together and relish our favorite combination: hot *pooris* and hot milk. Up until nearly my twentieth year, I only ate *pooris* as my bread—I had no taste for *chapatis* and practically refused to eat them. It was awkward to go to a friend's home for *prasadam* and not eat *chapatis* if they were served, but somehow I always managed to avoid having to eat them."

By the time I cooked for Srila Prabhupada, he was already more than seventy years old. He had long since cultivated a taste for *chapatis* at lunch, but occasionally he requested hot *pooris* for breakfast or late dinner, especially in colder climates. These sheer puffs of delight go well with almost any menu, from banquet spreads to late night twosomes.

Preparation time (after assembling ingredients): 15 minutes
Dough resting time: ½ hour–3 hours
Cooking time: ½ hour
Makes: 16 individual breads or 8 giant *pooris*

2 cups (260 g) sieved *chapati* flour, or 1 cup (130 g) whole wheat flour mixed with
either 1 cup (120 g) unbleached white flour or 1 cup (110 g) cake flour
½ teaspoon (2 ml) salt
2 tablespoons (30 ml) melted *ghee* or vegetable oil
⅔ cup (160 ml) warm water (about 100°F/38°C), or as needed
***ghee* or vegetable oil for deep-frying**

1. Place the flour and salt in a large mixing bowl and blend well. Drizzle in the *ghee* or oil and rub it into the flour with your fingertips until thoroughly incorporated. Add ⅓ cup (80 ml) water all at once and work the mixture into a mass. Then, while still mixing with your hand, add water slowly, in dribbles, until the dough is formed and kneadable. (You want a pliable, but moderately stiff dough; you may use more than ⅔ cup/160 ml of water to achieve this, depending on the flour.) Place the dough on a clean work surface, wash and dry your hands, rub them with oil and knead the dough until it is silky smooth and pliable (about 8 minutes). You can also make the dough in a food processor (see page 100). Form the dough into a smooth ball, rub it with *ghee* or oil and cover with an inverted bowl. Let the dough rest for ½ hour–3 hours. If you want to leave it longer, keep it well sealed in a refrigerator for up to 24 hours. Remove it at least 1 hour before use.

2. Collect the items you will need for rolling and cooking: a rolling pin, two or three cookie sheets, a slotted spoon for frying, a tray lined with double-thick paper towels for draining the fried breads, and a *karai*, wok or deep-walled Dutch oven.

Place the dough on a clean work surface and knead briefly. The dough should be stiff enough to roll out without extra flour. If it has softened too much during its rest period, knead in flour as necessary. To make 16 *pooris*, divide the dough in half and roll one portion into a rope 8 inches (20 cm) long. Cut into 8 pieces and roll each piece into a smooth ball. Place the balls on a plate without letting them touch and cover with a damp cloth. Repeat the procedure for the other half of the dough. To make 8 party *pooris*, divide the dough into 8 pieces and roll into smooth balls.

3. If you are experienced at rolling out and frying the breads one after another, pour melted *ghee* or oil to a depth of 3 inches (7.5 cm) in the frying pan and place it over moderately high heat. (If you are going to roll out all the breads first, do not place the pan on the heat yet.) Take one ball of dough, keeping the others covered, and flatten it into a ½-inch (1.5 cm) patty. Dip a corner of the patty in melted *ghee* or oil and roll it out, exerting firm but even pressure, into a 4½- to 5-inch (11.5–12.5 cm) or 10-inch (25 cm) round (you will need a roomy *wok* to fry the party-sized breads). Place it on a cookie sheet and roll out all of the *pooris* in this way. Do not allow the rounds to touch; lay them out in one layer on several cookie sheets or another clean, flat surface. Cover with plastic wrap.

4. Heat the *ghee* or oil over moderately high heat until it reaches about 365°F (185°C) on a deep-frying thermometer. Lift up a rolled-out *poori* and carefully slip it into the hot oil so it remains flat and does not fold over. The bread will sink to the bottom of the pan but quickly wants to bob to the surface. As it begins to rise, cover it with the back of the slotted spoon, and keep it submerged under the frying surface until it puffs into a steam-filled balloon. (Take care not to press the *poori* harshly; a tear in the delicate crust could fill the inside with oil.) When it is lighly browned on the first side, carefully turn it over and brown the second side. The frying time is under a minute for both sides. Remove the puffed bread with the slotted spoon and drain on paper towels. Repeat the procedure for all of the *pooris*, adjusting the heat to keep the oil at an even temperature. If it overheats, remove the pan from the burner.

Serve immediately or, to keep the batch warm for up to ½ hour, place the drained breads on paper-towel-lined cookie sheets, letting them overlap very slightly, and set in a preheated 275°F (135°C) oven. As *pooris* cool, they deflate. At room temperature, the *baasi pooris* can be stacked and kept wrapped in a clean tea towel for up to 12 hours.

For information about unfamiliar ingredients or techniques, see A-to-Z

Deep-Fried Buttermilk Whole Wheat Bread
DAHI POORI

Since the consistency of homemade and commercial buttermilk varies from batch to batch and from brand to brand, it is difficult to define accurate flour-buttermilk measurements; use what you need to make a fairly stiff dough. You can use black poppy seeds instead of crushed cumin to vary both appearance and taste.

Preparation time (after assembling ingredients): 15 minutes
Dough resting time: ½ hour–3 hours
Cooking time: ½ hour
Makes: 16 *pooris*

2 cups (260 g) sieved *chapati* flour, or 1 cup (130 g) whole wheat
    flour mixed with 1 cup (120 g) unbleached white flour
½ teaspoon (2 ml) salt
1 tablespoon (15 ml) coarsely crushed dry-roasted cumin seeds
    or whole black poppy seeds
1 teaspoon (5 ml) freshly cracked black pepper
2 tablespoon (30 ml) melted *ghee* or vegetable oil
¾ cup (180 ml) buttermilk, or as needed, at room temperature
ghee or vegetable oil for deep-frying

1. Place the flour in a large mixing bowl. Blend in the salt, seeds and black pepper, then dribble the melted *ghee* or oil over the flour and rub it in with your fingertips. Initially, add ⅔ cup (160 ml) buttermilk and work the mixture into a mass. Knead until you have a dough that is stiff yet pliable. More buttermilk may be used to obtain the right texture. Place the dough on a clean work surface. Then wash and dry your hands, rub them with oil and knead the dough until it is silky smooth and pliable (about 8 minutes). You can also make the dough in a food processor (see page 100). Rub the dough with *ghee* or oil and cover with an inverted bowl. Let the dough rest for ½ hour–3 hours. If you want to leave it longer, keep it well sealed in a refrigerator for up to 24 hours. Remove it at least 1 hour before use.

2. Collect the items needed for rolling out and cooking: a rolling pin, two or three cookie sheets, a slotted spoon, a tray lined with double-thick paper towels for draining the fried breads, and a *karai*, wok or deep-walled Dutch oven.

Place the dough on a clean work surface and knead briefly. The dough should be stiff enough to roll out without extra flour; if it has softened too much during its rest period, knead in flour as necessary. Divide the dough in half and roll one portion into a rope 8 inches (20 cm) long. Cut into eight pieces and roll each piece into a smooth ball. Place the balls on a plate without letting them touch and cover with a damp cloth. Repeat the procedure for the other half of the dough.

3. If you are experienced at rolling out and frying the breads one after another, pour melted *ghee* or oil to a depth of 3 inches (7.5 cm) in the frying pan and place it in over moderately high heat. (If you are going to roll out all of the breads first, do not heat the oil yet.) Take one ball of dough, keeping the remaining ones covered, and flatten it into a 2-inch (5 cm) patty. Dip a corner of the patty in melted *ghee* or oil and roll it out, exerting firm but even pressure, into a 5-inch (12.5 cm) round. Place it on a cookie sheet and continue to roll out all of the *pooris* in this way. Do not allow the rounds to touch. Lay them out in one layer on several cookie sheets or another clean, flat surface. Cover with plastic wrap.

4. Heat the *ghee* or oil over moderately high heat until it reaches about 365°F (185°C). Lift up a rolled-out *poori* and carefully slip it into the hot oil so that it remains flat and does not fold over. The bread will sink to the bottom of the pan but will quickly bob to the surface. As it begins to rise, cover it with the back of the slotted spoon, and keep it submerged under the frying surface until it puffs into a steam-filled balloon. (Take care not to press the *poori* harshly; a tear in the delicate crust could fill the inside with oil.) When it is lightly browned on the first side, carefully turn it over and brown the second side. The frying time is under a minute to brown both sides. Remove the puffed bread with a slotted spoon and drain on paper towels. Repeat the procedure for all of the *pooris*, adjusting the heat to keep the oil at an even temperature. If it overheats, remove the pan from the burner.

Serve immediately or keep the batch warm for up to ½ hour on paper-towel-lined cookie sheets, overlapping slightly, in a preheated 275°F (135°C) oven. At room temperature the *baasi pooris* can be stacked and kept wrapped in a clean tea towel for up to 12 hours.

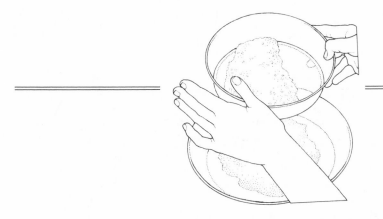

Deep-Fried Seasoned Whole Wheat Bread
MASALA POORI

During my first winter in Delhi, I met an old aquaintance of Srila Prabhupada, Sriman J. Dalmia, Sr. Though he was the director of numerous business concerns, and a very busy man, he was a gentleman host and interested in my pursuit of the Vedic culture. To my delight, he was also very knowledgeable about cooking, and during our first meeting he personally escorted me to his estate's "joint family kitchen" to answer questions about layout considerations, purchasing, food preparation and service. This deep-fried bread selection was the first of many recipes collected from resident chefs.

Seasoned *pooris* are very popular throughout much of North India—served at any time of the day, from breakfast to late dinner. In the Dalmia household, they were served with a vegetarian chili, in this book called *Curried Red Kidney Beans with Panir Cheese*. This combination—*Masala Puri and Rajma* is a nutrition-packed meal in itself, and in many Delhi homes, the basis of Sunday morning brunch. Round out the meal with an assortment of colorful vegetable crudités and a hot tisane.

For information about unfamiliar ingredients or techniques, see A-to-Z

Preparation time (after assembling ingredients): 15 minutes
Dough resting time: ½ hour–3 hours
Cooking time: ½ hour
Makes: 16 *pooris*

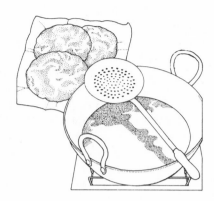

2 cups (260 g) sieved *chapati* flour, or 1½ cups (165 g) whole
   wheat pastry flour and ½ cup (85 g) fine-grain semolina*
½ teaspoon (2 ml) salt
¼ teaspoon (1 ml) cayenne pepper or paprika
scant ¼ teaspoon (1 ml) turmeric
2 teaspoons (10 ml) ground coriander
½ tablespoon (7 ml) ground cumin
2 tablespoons (30 ml) melted *ghee* or vegetable oil
⅔ cup (160 ml) warm water (about 100°F/38°C), or as needed
ghee or vegetable oil for deep-frying

*If you do not have fine semolina, reduce farina to a powder in an electric coffee mill, then sieve and
   measure.*

1. Place the flour, salt, cayenne or paprika, turmeric, ground coriander and ground
cumin in a large mixing bowl. Blend well. Drizzle in the *ghee* or oil and rub it into the
flour with your fingertips until thoroughly incorporated. Add ⅓ cup (80 ml) of water all
at once and work into a mass. Then, while still mixing with your hand, add water
slowly, in dribbles, until the dough is formed and is kneadable. (You want a pliable, but
moderately stiff dough; you may use more than ⅔ cup/160 ml of water to achieve this,
depending on the flour.) Place the dough on a clean work surface, wash and dry your
hands and rub them with oil. Knead the dough until it is silky smooth and pliable
(about 8 minutes). You can also make the dough in a food processor (see page 100).
Form the dough into a smooth ball. Rub it with *ghee* or oil and cover with an inverted
bowl. Let the dough rest for ½ hour–3 hours. If you want to leave it longer, keep it well
sealed in a refrigerator for up to 24 hours. Remove it at least 1 hour before use.
2. Collect the items needed for rolling out and cooking: a rolling pin, two or three
cookie sheets, a slotted spoon for frying, a tray lined with double-thick paper towels for
draining the fried breads, and a *karai*, wok or deep-walled Dutch oven.
Place the dough on a clean work surface and knead briefly. The dough should be
stiff enough to roll out without extra flour; if it has softened too much, knead in flour as
necessary. Divide the dough in half and roll one portion into a rope 8 inches (20 cm)
long. Cut into eight pieces and roll each piece into a smooth ball. Place the balls on a
plate without letting them touch and cover with a damp cloth. Repeat the procedure for
the other half of the dough.
3. If you are experienced in rolling and frying the breads one after another, pour
melted *ghee* or oil to a depth of 3 inches (7.5 cm) in the frying pan and place it over
moderately high heat. (If you are going to roll out all of the breads first, do not heat the
oil yet.) Take one ball of dough, keeping the others covered, and flatten it into a 2-inch
(5 cm) patty. Dip a corner of the patty in melted *ghee* or oil and roll it out, exerting firm
but even pressure, into a 5-inch (12.5 cm) round. Place it on a cookie sheet and continue
to roll out all of the *poris* in this way. Do not allow the rounds to touch. Lay them out in
one layer on several cookie sheets or on another clean, flat surface. Cover with plastic
wrap.

4. Heat the *ghee* or oil over moderately high heat until it reaches 365°F (185°C). Lift up a rolled-out *poori* and carefully slip it into the hot oil so it remains flat and does not fold over. The bread will sink to the bottom of the pan but quickly wants to bob to the surface. As it begins to rise, cover it with the back of the slotted spoon and keep it submerged under the frying surface until it puffs into a steam-filled balloon. (Take care not to press the *poori* harshly; a tear in the delicate crust could fill the inside with oil.) When it is lightly browned on the first side, carefully turn it over and brown the second side. The frying time is under a minute to brown both sides. Remove the puffed bread with the slotted spoon and drain on paper towels. Repeat the procedure for all of the *pooris*, adjusting the heat to maintain an even temperature. If the oil overheats, remove the pan from the burner.

Serve immediately or keep the batch warm for up to ½ hour on paper-towel-lined baking sheets, overlapping slightly, in a preheated 275°F (135°C) oven. At room temperature the *baasi pooris* can be stacked and kept wrapped in a clean tea towel for up to 12 hours.

Deep-Fried Potato Whole Wheat Bread
ALOO POORI

Though I have recommended a blend of whole wheat and barley flour, this *poori* is also excellent using all wheat or an unbleached white-wheat flour combination. Seasoned flour is bound with mashed potatoes, yielding an exceptional silky-smooth dough. Initially, keep this dough quite stiff, as it softens considerably upon resting. I prefer to let this type of *poori* brown more than other types, so they are especially crisp and golden-brown; they seem to hold a balloon shape longer than most breads.

For a late-morning breakfast or brunch, try them with *Panir Cheese and Green Peas in Mint Tomato Sauce, Broiled Bananas with Toasted Almonds* or seasonal fresh fruits and an herb tea. For a light lunch or dinner, they complement any number of salads or vegetables, such as *Whole Cauliflower Crown with Spiced Tomato Sauce*, and *Creamy Cheese Fudge*.

Preparation time (after assembling ingredients): 5–15 minutes
Dough resting time: ½ hour–3 hours
Cooking time: ½ hour
Makes: 16 *pooris*

2 medium-sized boiling potatoes (8 ounces/230 g),
    freshly boiled or steamed in skins
1 cup (135 g) sieved *chapati* flour or 1 cup (105 g)
    whole wheat pastry flour
1 cup (120 g) barley, soya or unbleached white flour
¾ teaspoon (3.5 ml) salt
1 teaspoon (5 ml) *garam masala*
1 teaspoon (5 ml) ground cumin
¼ teaspoon (1 ml) paprika or cayenne pepper
3 tablespoons (45 ml) melted *ghee* or vegetable oil
ghee or vegetable oil for deep-frying

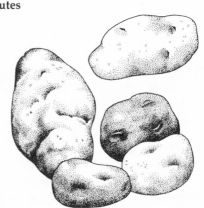

For information about unfamiliar ingredients or techniques, see A-to-Z

1. While the potatoes are still warm, peel them and press through a potato ricer or a coarse sieve. You should have about 1⅔ cups (400 ml), loosely packed. Set aside.

2. Combine the flours, salt, *garam masala*, cumin and paprika or cayenne (this much cayenne adds quite a bit of heat to the dish; add less for hinted heat) in a large mixing bowl. Blend well. Rub the potatoes and 3 tablespoons (45 ml) of *ghee* or oil into the flour until the ingredients are thoroughly blended. At this point, you may need to add dribbles of water or sprinkles of flour until you can form the mass into a ball of firm dough. Knead the dough (about 8 minutes). Form the dough into a smooth ball. Rub it with *ghee* or oil and cover with an inverted bowl. Let the dough rest for ½ hour–3 hours. If you want to leave it longer, keep it well sealed in a refrigerator for up to 24 hours. Remove it at least 1 hour before use.

3. Collect the items needed for rolling out and cooking: a rolling pin, two or three cookie sheets, a slotted spoon, a tray lined with double-thick paper towels for draining the fried breads and a *karai*, wok or deep-walled Dutch oven.

Place the dough on a clean work surface and knead briefly. The dough should be stiff enough to roll out without extra flour; if it has softened too much, knead in flour as necessary. Divide the dough in half and roll one portion into a rope 8 inches (20 cm) long. Cut into eight pieces and roll each piece into a smooth ball. Place the balls on a plate without letting them touch and cover with a damp cloth. Repeat the procedure for the other half of the dough.

4. If you are experienced at rolling out and frying the breads one after another, pour melted *ghee* or oil to a depth of 3 inches (7.5 cm) in the frying pan and place it over moderately high heat. (If you are going to roll out all of the breads first, do not heat the *ghee* or oil yet.) Remove one ball of dough, keeping the remaining ones covered, and flatten it into a 2-inch (5 cm) patty. Dip the corner of the patty in melted *ghee* or oil and roll it out, exerting firm but even pressure, into a 5-inch (12.5 cm) round. Place it on a cookie sheet and continue to roll out all of the *pooris* in this way. Do not allow the rounds to touch. Lay them out in one layer on several cookie sheets or another clean, flat surface. Cover with plastic wrap.

5. Heat the *ghee* or oil over moderately high heat until it reaches 365°F (185°C). Lift up the rolled-out *poori* and carefully slip it into the hot oil so it remains flat and does not fold over. The bread will sink to the bottom of the pan but quickly wants to bob to the surface. As it begins to rise, cover it with the back of the slotted spoon and keep it submerged under the frying surface until it puffs into a steam-filled balloon. (Take care not to press the *poori* harshly; a tear in the delicate crust could fill the inside with oil.) When it is lightly browned on the first side, carefully turn it over and brown the second side. The frying time is under a minute to brown both sides. Remove the puffed bread with the slotted spoon and drain on paper towels. Repeat the procedure for all of the *pooris*, adjusting the heat to maintain the oil at an even temperature. If it overheats, remove the pan from the burner.

Serve immediately or keep the batch warm for up to ½ hour on paper-towel-lined cookie sheets, overlapping very slightly, in a preheated 275°F (135°C) oven. As *pooris* cool they deflate. At room temperature the *baasi pooris* can be stacked and kept wrapped in a clean tea towel for up to 12 hours.

Deep-Fried Sesame Whole Wheat Bread
TIL POORI

This flavorful, nutty-tasting *poori* features sesame seeds—a good source of protein and calcium if they are unhulled. White, hulled seeds are sold in small tins and jars on supermarket spice shelves. For full flavor, the sesame seeds should be dry-roasted before being ground. Place them in a heavy pan over moderately low heat. Stirring frequently, roast them until they turn a few shades darker. When they are cool, grind them in an electric coffee mill or with a mortar and pestle. Aim for a medium to coarse powder; large pieces tend to keep the breads from puffing. Try these *pooris* with *Rice and Panir Cheese and Bell Peppers* and a light mixed green salad for a special lunch.

Preparation time (after assembling ingredients): 5–15 minutes
Dough resting time: ½ hour–3 hours
Cooking time: ½ hour
Makes: 16 *pooris*

2 cups (260 g) sieved *chapati* flour, or 1½ cups (165 g) whole wheat pastry flour mixed with ½ cup
(55 g) millet flour
⅓ cup (55 g) ground dry-roasted sesame seeds
½ teaspoon (2 ml) salt
2 tablespoons (30 ml) melted *ghee* or vegetable oil
⅔ cup (160 ml) warm milk (about 100°F/38°C), or as needed
ghee or vegetable oil for deep-frying

1. Place the flour in a large mixing bowl and blend in the sesame seeds and salt. Drizzle in the *ghee* or oil and rub it into the flour with your fingertips until thoroughly incorporated. Add ⅓ cup (80 ml) of milk all at once and work it into a mass. Then, while still mixing with your hand, add milk slowly, in dribbles, until the dough is formed and kneadable. (You want a pliable but moderately stiff dough; you may use more than ⅔ cup/160 ml of milk, depending on the flour.) Place the dough on a clean work surface, wash and dry your hands and rub them with oil. Knead the dough until it is silky smooth and pliable (about 8 minutes). You can also make the dough in a food processor (see page 100). Form the dough into a smooth ball. Rub it with *ghee* or oil and cover with an inverted bowl. Let the dough rest for ½ hour–3 hours. If you want to leave it longer, keep it well sealed in a refrigerator for up to 24 hours. Remove it at least 1 hour before use.

2. Collect the items needed for rolling out and cooking: a rolling pin, two or three cookie sheets, a slotted spoon, a tray lined with double-thick paper towels for draining the fried breads and a *karai*, wok or deep-walled Dutch oven.

Place the dough on a clean work surface and knead briefly. The dough should be stiff enough to roll out without extra flour; if it has softened too much, knead in flour as necessary. Divide the dough in half and roll one portion into a rope 8 inches (20 cm) long. Cut into eight pieces and roll each piece into a smooth ball. Place the balls on a plate without letting them touch and cover with a damp cloth. Repeat the procedure for the other half of the dough.

For information about unfamiliar ingredients or techniques, see A-to-Z

3. If you are experienced at rolling out and frying the breads one after another, pour melted *ghee* or oil to a depth of 3 inches (7.5 cm) in the frying pan and place it over moderately high heat. (If you are going to roll out all the breads first, do not heat the oil yet.) Remove one ball of dough, keeping the remaining ones covered, and flatten it into a 2-inch (5 cm) patty. Dip a corner of the patty in melted *ghee* or oil and roll it out, exerting firm but even pressure, into a 5-inch (12.5 cm) round. Place it on a cookie sheet and continue to roll out all of the *pooris* in this way. Do not allow the rounds to touch. Lay them out in one layer on several cookie sheets or another clean, flat surface. Cover with plastic wrap.

4. Heat the *ghee* or oil over moderately high heat until it reaches 365°F (185°C). Lift up a rolled-out *poori* and carefully slip it into the hot oil so it remains flat and does not fold over. The bread will sink to the bottom of the pan but quickly wants to bob to the surface. As it begins to rise, cover it with the back of the slotted spoon and keep it submerged under the frying surface until it puffs into a steam-filled balloon. (Take care not to press the *poori* harshly; a tear in the delicate crust could fill the inside with oil.) When it is lightly browned on the first side, carefully turn it over and brown the second side. The frying time is under a minute to brown both sides. Remove the puffed bread with a slotted spoon and drain on paper towels. Repeat the procedure to fry all of the *pooris*, adjusting the heat to maintain the oil at an even temperature. If it overheats, remove the pan from the burner.

Serve immediately or keep the batch warm for up to ½ hour on paper-towel-lined cookie sheets, overlapping slightly, in a preheated 275°F (135°C) oven. As *pooris* cool they deflate. At room temperature the *baasi pooris* can be stacked and kept wrapped in a clean tea towel for up to 12 hours.

Deep-Fried Fenugreek Whole Wheat Bread
METHI POORI

Most Americans have never seen fresh fenugreek leaves, though countless health enthusiasts have tasted the mildly bitter sprouts from germinated seeds. In Vedic cookery, the seeds are used both whole and ground, while the new leaves are a popular herb in vegetable dishes with new potatoes, greens or yams. If you are in a big city and lucky enough to come across an Indian, Chinese or specialty greengrocer who sells bunches of the herb, buy them and try this recipe. You can also grow the herb easily in a summer window box. Buy the flat brownish-yellow seeds (actually, legumes) at an Indian grocery store or health food store. Soak them in water for a few hours, then plant them in pots or small window boxes in a mixture of one part rich, friable soil to two parts sand. With a little luck, the seeds will germinate. The herb yields cuttable leaves when it is 6–8 inches (15–20 cm) high. You can let the plants grow to 12–15 inches (30–37.5 cm), and when they start to droop, cut and dry them. Alternately, I have made these breads with numerous leafy greens or herbs—wheat grass, mustard cress, finely chopped mixed herbs and garden spinach—each with excellent results. Use whatever is fresh, vibrant and available. Be sure to carefully wash leafy greens; trim and pat dry before measuring.

For a really special occasion, try these *pooris* with the elegant *Deep-Fried Cauliflower and Potatoes in Spiced Tomato Broth, Butter-Soft Eggplant Wedges*, a green salad and *Simple Mung Dal Soup with Radishes*.

Preparation time (after assembling ingredients): 25 minutes
Dough resting time: ½ hour–3 hours
Cooking time: ½ hour
Makes: 16 *pooris*

1 cup (240 ml) lightly packed fresh fenugreek leaves, spinach
    or other greens, trimmed, washed and patted dry
⅓ cup (80 ml) lukewarm water (about 100°F/38°C), or as needed
1–2 green chilies, seeded and cut into small pieces
2 tablespoons (30 ml) plain yogurt, at room temperature
2 tablespoons (30 ml) melted *ghee* or vegetable oil
2¼ cups (295 g) sieved *chapati* flour, or
    1¼ cups (160 g) whole wheat pastry flour
    and 1 cup (120 g) unbleached white flour
¼ teaspoon (1 ml) turmeric
1 tablespoon (15 ml) ground coriander
½ tablespoon (7 ml) *garam masala*
1 teaspoon (5 ml) salt
ghee or vegetable oil for deep-frying

1. Place the fenugreek leaves, spinach or greens in a heavy saucepan. Add 2 table-spoons (30 ml) of the water, cover the pan and place it over moderate heat. Cook for 2–3 minutes, then remove the pan from the heat, uncover and let the softened greens cool to near room temperature. (If you use fresh herbs, simply trim and chop.) Combine the green chilies, yogurt and melted *ghee* or oil in a blender or food processor, cover and pulse for three or four bursts. Add the cooked greens or herbs and process until puréed. Transfer the mixture to a small bowl.

2. Combine the flour, turmeric, coriander, *garam masala* and salt in a mixing bowl. Blend well. Add the purée and 2 tablespoons (30 ml) of melted *ghee* or oil. Mix thorough-ly. Depending upon the ratio of flour to liquid, you could end up with a shaggy mass or something near a dough. Add either the remaining water or additional flour, tablespoon by tablespoon (15 ml), then gather the dough into a firm ball so you can knead it. Knead and fold the dough by pressing and folding with your palms or knuckles until it is silky smooth and pliable (about 8 minutes).

You can also make the dough in a food processor (see page 100), adding the purée with the *ghee* or oil. Form the dough into a smooth ball. Rub it with *ghee* or oil and cover with an inverted bowl. Let the dough rest for ½ hour–3 hours. If you want to leave it longer, keep it well sealed in a refrigerator for up to 24 hours. Remove it at least 1 hour before use.

Dust your hands with flour and form the dough into a smooth ball. Rub the dough with a film of *ghee* or oil and cover with a bowl or damp cloth or place it in a zip-lock bag. Let the dough rest for ½ hour–3 hours. If you want to leave it longer, keep it well sealed in a refrigerator for up to 24 hours. Remove it at least 1 hour before use.

3. Collect the items needed for rolling out and cooking: a rolling pin, two or three cookie sheets, a slotted spoon for frying, a tray lined with double-thick paper towels for draining the fried breads, and a *karai*, wok or deep-walled Dutch oven.

Place the dough on a clean work surface and knead briefly. The dough should be stiff enough to roll out without extra flour; if it has softened too much, knead in flour as

For information about unfamiliar ingredients or techniques, see A-to-Z

necessary. Divide the dough in half and roll one portion into a rope 8 inches (20 cm) long. Cut into eight pieces and roll each piece into a smooth ball. Place the balls on a plate without letting them touch and cover with a damp cloth. Repeat the procedure for the other half of the dough.

4. If you are experienced at rolling out and frying the breads one after another, pour melted *ghee* or oil to a depth of 3 inches (7.5 cm) in the frying pan and place it over moderately high heat. (If you are going to roll out all of the breads first, do not heat the *ghee* or oil yet.) Remove one ball of dough, keeping the remaining ones covered, and flatten it into a 2-inch (5 cm) patty. Dip a corner of the patty in melted *ghee* or oil and roll it, exerting firm but even pressure, into a 5-inch (12.5 cm) round. Place it on a cookie sheet and continue to roll out all of the *pooris* in this way. Do not allow the round to touch. Lay them out, in one layer, on several cookie sheets or another clean, flat surface. Cover with plastic wrap.

5. Heat the *ghee* or oil over moderately high heat until it reaches about 365°F (185°C). Lift up a rolled-out *poori* and carefully slip it into the hot oil so it remains flat and does not fold over. The bread will sink to the bottom of the pan but quickly wants to bob to the surface. As it begins to rise, cover it with the back of a slotted spoon and keep it submerged under the frying surface until it puffs into a steam-filled balloon. (Take care not to press the *poori* harshly; a tear in the delicate crust could fill the inside with oil.) When it is lightly browned on the first side, carefully turn it over and brown the second side. The frying time is under a minute to brown both sides. Remove the puffed bread with the slotted spoon and drain on paper towels. Repeat the procedure for all of the *pooris*, adjusting the heat to maintain the oil at an even temperature. If it overheats, remove the pan from the burner.

Serve immediately or keep the batch warm for up to ½ hour on paper-towel-lined cookie sheets, overlapping very slightly, in a preheated 275°F (135°C) oven. As *pooris* cool, they deflate. At room temperature the *baasi pooris* can be stacked and kept wrapped in a clean tea towel for up to 12 hours.

Deep-Fried Banana Whole Wheat Bread
KELA POORI

The flavor in this bread is only faintly reminiscent of banana tea bread, but even the subtle similarity should make it appealing for a Sunday brunch or lazy morning breakfasts. Cardamom, coriander, nutmeg and grated lemon zest are combined with mashed bananas, wheat and barley flour to yield a fragrant dough, and slightly sweet finished flatbreads. I have also made the breads substituting mashed papaya and lime zest or mashed mango and orange zest for the bananas and lemon, and the results are excellent. Make a stiff, firm dough, since it softens considerably as it rests. If you fry the *pooris* until they turn golden brown, the flavors are enhanced. Hot off the flame, the breads are crisp and puffed, but they quickly deflate and soften because of the sugary bananas. Serve piping hot with a dusting of confectioners' sugar or wispy drizzles of maple syrup for a delectable treat. You might accompany the hot *pooris* with *Dainty Rose Water Drink* for a summer afternoon cooler.

Preparation time (after assembling ingredients): 10–25 minutes
Dough resting time: ½ hour–3 hours
Cooking time: ½ hour
Makes: 16 *pooris*

2 cups (260 g) *chapati* flour, or ¾ cup (95 g) whole wheat flour mixed with ¾ cup (95 g)
    unbleached white flour and ½ cup (55 g) barley flour
2 teaspoons (10 ml) grated lemon zest
½ teaspoon (2 ml) each ground cardamom and coriander
¼ teaspoon (1 ml) freshly ground nutmeg
¼ teaspoon (1 ml) salt
3 tablespoons (45 ml) melted *ghee* or vegetable oil
½ cup (120 ml) puréed banana, mango or papaya
enough warm water to make a stiff dough
ghee or vegetable oil for deep-frying

1. Place the flour, citrus zest, ground spices and salt in a large mixing bowl. Blend
well. Dribble the melted *ghee* or oil over the flour and rub it in with your fingertips. Add
the fruit and ¼ cup (60 ml) of water all at once and work into a mass. Then, while still
mixing with your hand, add water slowly, in dribbles, until a kneadable dough is
formed. Place the dough on a clean work surface, wash and dry your hands, rub them
with oil and knead the dough until it is silky smooth and pliable (about 8 minutes). You
can also make the dough in a food processor (see page 100), adding the fruit along with
the *ghee* or oil. Form the dough into a smooth ball. Rub it with *ghee* or oil and cover with
an inverted bowl. Let the dough rest for ½–3 hours. If you want to leave it longer, keep
it well sealed in a refrigerator for up to 24 hours. Remove at least 1 hour before use.

2. Collect items needed for rolling out and cooking: a rolling pin, two or three
cookie sheets, a slotted spoon for frying, a tray lined with double-thick paper towels for
draining the fried breads, and a *karai*, wok or deep-walled Dutch oven.

Place the dough on a clean work surface and knead briefly. The dough should be
stiff enough to roll out without extra flour; if it has softened too much, knead in flour as
necessary. Divide the dough in half and roll one portion into a rope 8 inches (20 cm)
long. Cut into eight pieces and roll each piece into a smooth ball. Place the balls on a
plate without letting them touch and cover with a damp cloth. Repeat the procedure for
the other half of the dough.

3. If you are experienced at rolling out and frying the breads one after another, pour
melted *ghee* or oil to a depth of 3-inches (7.5 cm) in the frying pan and place it over
moderately high heat. (If you are going to roll out all of the breads first, do not heat the
ghee or oil yet.) Remove one ball of dough, keeping the remaining ones covered, and
flatten it into a 2-inch (5 cm) patty. Dip a corner of the patty in melted *ghee* or oil and
roll it, exerting firm but even pressure, into a 5-inch (12.5 cm) round. Place on a cookie
sheet and continue to roll out all of the *pooris* in this way. Do not allow the rounds to
touch; lay them out, in one layer, on several cookie sheets or on another clean, flat
surface. Cover with plastic wrap.

4. Heat the *ghee* or oil over moderately high heat until it reaches 365°F (185°C). Lift
up a rolled-out *poori* and carefully slip it into the hot oil so it remains flat and does not
fold over. The bread will sink to the bottom of the pan but quickly wants to bob to the
surface. As it begins to rise, cover it with the back of a slotted spoon and keep it
submerged under the frying surface until it puffs into a steam-filled balloon. (Take care

For information about unfamiliar ingredients or techniques, see A-to-Z

not to press the *poori* harshly; a tear in the delicate crust could fill the inside with oil.) When it is lightly browned on the first side, carefully turn it over and brown the second side. The frying time is under a minute for both sides. Remove the puffed bread with slotted spoon and drain on paper towels. Repeat the procedure for all of the *pooris*, adjusting the heat to maintain the temperature of the oil. If it overheats, remove the pan from the burner.

Serve immediately or keep the batch warm for up to ½ hour on paper-towel-lined baking sheets, overlapping slightly, in a preheated 275° (135°C) oven. As *pooris* cool they deflate. At room temperature the *baasi pooris* can be stacked and kept wrapped in a clean tea towel for up to 12 hours.

Deep-Fried Sweet Potato Whole Wheat Bread
SHAKARKAND POORI

This delicious *poori* can also be made by substituting cooked yams, winter squash or pumpkin for sweet potato. The flat breads should *hint* of heat and spices—what is hot for a Punjabi is unbearable for most Westerners—and amounts are a matter of personal preference. Note that ¼ teaspoon (1 ml) of cayenne will yield noticeable heat, while the same amount of paprika is almost indiscernable; vary the red powder accordingly. To begin with, make a stiff dough; it softens considerably upon resting.

This is the ideal bread for an autumn dinner, during peak season for tubers and winter squash. Try it with *Succulent Rice and Mung Dal Khichari with Cauliflower and Green Peas, Red Bell Peppers with Roasted Chickpea Flour* and a salad.

Preparation time (after assembling ingredients): 5–15 minutes
Dough resting time: ½–3 hours
Cooking time: ½ hour
Makes: 16 *pooris*

1 large sweet potato (8 ounces/230 g), freshly boiled
    or steamed until tender
2 cups (520 g) sieved *chapati* flour, or 1⅓ cups
    (165 g) whole wheat flour mixed with ⅔ cups
    (80 g) unbleached white flour or potato flour
¾ teaspoon (3.5 ml) salt
¼ teaspoon (1 ml) yellow asafetida powder (*hing*)*
⅓ teaspoon (1.5 ml) turmeric
½ tablespoon (7 ml) ground coriander
¼ teaspoon (1 ml) cayenne pepper or paprika
3 tablespoons (45 ml) minced fresh coriander,
    parsley, dill or mixed herbs
3 tablespoons (45 ml) melted *ghee* or butter
ghee or vegetable oil for deep-frying

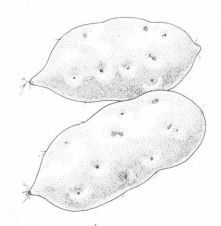

This amount applies only to yellow Cobra brand. Reduce any other asafetida by three-fourths.

1. While the sweet potato is still warm, peel and mash it (you should have about 1⅔ cups/400 ml, loosely packed). Set aside.

2. Combine the flour, salt, asafetida, turmeric, ground coriander, cayenne or paprika and minced herb in a large mixing bowl. Blend well. Rub the sweet potatoes and 3 tablespoons (45 ml) of *ghee* or oil into the flour until the ingredients are thoroughly blended. At this point you may need to add dribbles of water or sprinkles of flour until you can form the mass into a ball of firm dough. Knead the dough until it is silky smooth and pliable (about 8 minutes). You can also make the dough in a food processor (see page 100). Form the dough into a smooth ball. Rub it with *ghee* or oil and cover with an inverted bowl. Let the dough rest for ½–3 hours. If you want to leave it longer, keep it well sealed in a refrigerator for up to 24 hours. Remove it at least 1 hour before use.

3. Collect the items needed for rolling and cooking: a rolling pin, 2–3 empty baking sheets, a slotted spoon for frying, a tray lined with double-thick paper towels for draining the fried breads and a *karai*, wok or deep-walled Dutch oven filled with *ghee* or oil 3 inches (7.5 cm) deep.

Place the dough on a clean work surface and knead briefly. The dough should be stiff enough to roll out without using flour; if it has softened too much, knead in flour as necessary. Divide the dough in half and roll one portion into a rope 8 inches (20 cm) long. Cut into 8 pieces and roll each piece into a smooth ball. Place the balls on a plate without letting them touch each other and cover with a damp cloth. Repeat the procedure for the other half of the dough.

4. If you are experienced at rolling out and frying the breads one after another, pour melted *ghee* or oil to a depth of 3 inches (7.5 cm) in the frying pan and place it over moderately high heat. (If you are going to roll out all of the breads first, do not heat the *ghee* or oil yet.) Remove one ball of dough, keeping the remaining ones covered, and flatten it into a 2-inch (5 cm) patty. Dip a corner of the patty in melted *ghee* or oil and roll it, exerting firm but even pressure, into a 5-inch (12.5 cm) round. Place it on a cookie sheet and roll out all of the *pooris* in this way. Do not allow the rounds to touch. Lay them out in one layer on several cookie sheets or another clean, flat surface. Cover with plastic wrap.

5. Heat the *ghee* or oil over moderately high heat until it reaches about 365°F (185°C). Lift up a rolled-out *poori* and carefully slip it into the hot oil so that it remains flat and does not fold over. The bread will sink to the bottom of the pan but quickly wants to bob toward the surface. As it begins to rise, cover it with the back of the slotted spoon and keep it submerged under the frying surface until it puffs into a steam-filled balloon. (Take care not to press the *poori* harshly; a tear in the delicate crust could fill the inside with oil.) When it is lightly browned on the first side, carefully turn it over and brown the second side. The frying time is under 1 minute for both sides. Remove the puffed bread with a slotted spoon and drain on paper towels. Repeat the procedure for all of the *pooris*, adjusting the heat to maintain the oil at an even temperature. If it overheats, remove the pan from the burner.

Serve immediately or keep the batch warm for up to ½ hour on paper-towel-lined cookie sheets, overlapping slightly, in a preheated 275°F (135°C) oven. As *pooris* cool, they deflate. At room temperature the *baasi pooris* can be stacked and kept wrapped in a clean tea towel for up to 12 hours.

For information about unfamiliar ingredients or techniques, see A-to-Z

Deep-Fried Golden Puffs
LUCHI

In Bengal, the terms *luchi* and *poori* are almost synonymous. Technically, the only difference is the flour: *luchi* is always made with unbleached white flour, while *poori* is made from wheat flour or flour blends. The light, delicate *luchi* requires a fresh frying medium, and for the purist, *ghee* is the only choice. For many Western kitchens, this extravagance will be almost unthinkable, but personally I don't even include *luchi* in a menu unless I have a *karai* of fresh *ghee* on hand. Because the dough is only flour, *ghee* and water—sometimes with a pinch of baking soda, salt and sugar— the flatbreads clearly reflect the flavor and aroma of sweet clarified butter. Hot off the flame, a ballooned *luchi* has a crisp, thin crust, but quickly deflates and softens.

Luchi is sometimes tricky to puff. Unless you are quite experienced in making them, a good percentage of your batch may only blister into large bubbles rather than puff completely. I find that a mixture of unbleached white flour and soft wheat cake flour makes the best dough. A few opinionated chefs I know insist that baking powder in the dough and a slightly longer time in the *ghee* helps puffed breads to remain ballooned a few extra minutes. Though true, the *luchi* character is also changed—so it is a six-of-one-and-half-dozen-of-the-other situation. Try to roll the breads evenly; thick and thin spots will likely prevent ballooning.

These breads go well on any special-occasion menu and are pleasant for brunch or teatime, sweetened with a dusting of confectioner's sugar or superfine sugar or drizzles of maple syrup or honey.

Preparation time (after assembling ingredients): 15 minutes
Dough resting time: ½–3 hours
Cooking time: ½ hour
Makes: 14 *luchis*

1⅓ cups (155 g) unbleached white flour mixed with ⅔ cup (75 g)
    cake flour, or 2 cups (235 g) unbleached white flour
¼ teaspoon (1 ml) each salt and sugar (optional)
3 tablespoons (45 ml) melted *ghee*
½ cup (120 ml) warm water (about 100°F/38°C), or as needed
ghee for deep-frying

1. Blend the flours, salt and sugar in a large mixing bowl, then dribble the melted *ghee* over the flour and rub it in with your fingertips until thoroughly incorporated. Add ⅓ cup (80 ml) of water all at once and work the mixture into a mass. Then, while still mixing with your hand, add water slowly, in dribbles, until the dough is formed and is kneadable. (You want a pliable but moderately stiff dough and may need more water, depending on the flour.) Place the dough on a clean work surface, wash and dry your hands, rub them with a oil and knead the dough until it is silky smooth and pliable (about 8 minutes). You can also make the dough in a food processor (see page 100). Form the dough into a smooth ball. Rub it with *ghee* and cover with an inverted bowl. Let the dough rest for ½–3 hours. If you want to leave it longer, keep it well sealed in a refrigerator for up to 24 hours. Remove it at least 1 hour before use.

2. Collect the items needed for rolling out and cooking: a rolling pin, two or three cookie sheets, a slotted spoon for frying, a tray lined with double-thick paper towels for draining the fried breads and a *karai*, wok or deep-walled Dutch oven.

Place the dough on a clean work surface and knead briefly. Divide the dough in half and roll one portion into a rope 7 inches (17.5 cm) long. Cut into seven pieces and roll each piece into a smooth ball. Place the balls on a plate without letting them touch and cover with a damp cloth. Repeat the procedure for the other half of the dough.

3. If you are experienced at rolling out and frying the breads one after another, pour melted *ghee* or oil to a depth of 3 inches (7.5 cm) in the frying pan and place it over moderately high heat. (If you are going to roll out all of the breads first, do not heat the *ghee* or oil yet.) Remove one ball of dough, keeping the remaining ones covered, and flatten it into a 2-inch (5 cm) patty. Dip both sides of the patty in a dish of flour and roll it, exerting firm but even pressure, into a 5-inch (12.5 cm) round. (Dip the patty in flour only enough to facilitate rolling out; excess flour on the *luchi* simply burns in the ghee.) Place it on a cookie sheet and continue to roll out all of the *luchis* in this way. Do not allow the rounds to touch. Lay them out in one layer on several cookie sheets or another clean, flat surface. Cover with plastic wrap, and if possible, freeze for 10 minutes to firm up the rounds before frying.

4. Heat the *ghee* over moderately high heat until it reaches about 365°F (185°F). Lift up a rolled-out *luchi* and carefully slip it into the hot oil so that it remains flat and does not fold over. The bread will sink to the bottom of the pan but quickly wants to bob toward the surface of the *ghee*. As it begins to rise, cover with the back of a slotted spoon and keep it submerged until it puffs into a steam-filled balloon. (Take care not to press the *luchi* harshly; a tear in the delicate crust fills the inside with oil.) When it is lightly browned on the first side, carefully turn it over and cook the second side. The frying time is under a minute for both sides. Remove the *luchi* with a slotted spoon and drain on paper towels. Repeat the procedure for all of the breads, adjusting the heat to maintain an even temperature for the *ghee*. If it overheats, remove the pan from the burner and add a spoon of cold *ghee* to bring the temperature down.

Serve immediately, or within 10–15 minutes, keeping the batch warm for up to ½ hour on paper-towel-lined cookie sheets, overlapping slightly, in a preheated 275°F (135°C) oven. After the breads deflate and cool to room temperature, they are called *baasi luchis*, and can be stacked, wrapped in a clean tea towel and stored in a closed container for up to 12 hours.

Deep-Fried Leavened Bread
BHATURA

In central Delhi, especially around Connaught Circus, New Market and Jan Path, you are likely to see street vendors selling the popular combination of *chole aur bhatura*—brown chickpeas in a spicy tamarind gravy and hot fried bread. To the casual observer, the bustling street cook seems to deep-fry *bhatura* non-stop, the wafting aromas convincing any determined passerby that missing this treat is a loss indeed. A careful observer also notices a good *bhatura-wala* moving his stand here and there—wherever people congregate—cashing in on the snack mentality of shoppers and cinema goers.

Though quick-method *bhatura* dough—made from self-rising flour, is quite acceptable, bread connoisseurs prefer doughs made with a fermented-starter. Made on the same principle as sourdough, a culture of semolina flour and yogurt is allowed to grow and ripen in a warm nook until it rises and pleasantly ferments. It is then combined with flour, a little *ghee* and other ingredients, and kneaded into a velvety, elastic dough. *Bhatura* is rolled out a bit thicker than for *poori*, and the flatbread is not allowed to brown during frying. The finished color is fawn gold to biscuit.

Serve *Bhatura* and *Chole* with crunchy vegetable crudités—radish flowers, cherry tomatoes, snow peas, carrot flowers or celery curls—anything that strikes your fancy.

Preparation time (after assembling ingredients): 15–20 minutes
Dough resting time: 8–10 hours or overnight
Cooking time: ½ hour
Makes: 12 *bhaturas*

½ cup (85 g) fine-grained semolina flour or
   ½ cup (65 g) unbleached white flour
½ cup (120 ml) plain yogurt, at room temperature
1¾ cups (215 g) unbleached white flour
½ teaspoon (2 ml) salt
1 teaspoon (5 ml) sugar
½ teaspoon (2 ml) baking powder or soda
3 tablespoons (45 ml) melted *ghee* or vegetable oil
¼ cup (60 ml) warm water (about 100°F/38°C), or as needed
unbleached white flour for dusting
ghee or vegetable oil for deep-frying

1. To make the starter, combine the semolina or white flour with the yogurt in a small ceramic bowl or crock and mix thoroughly. Cover well and let the mixture rest in a warm place (about 100°F/38°C) for 8–10 hours or until it rises slightly.

2. To make the dough, combine the starter, flour, salt, sugar, baking powder, melted *ghee* or oil and enough water to make a medium dough. Place the dough on a clean work surface, wash and dry your hands, rub them with oil and knead the dough until it is silky smooth and pliable (about 8 minutes).

To make the dough in a food processor, fit the bowl with the steel blade. Place the starter in the bowl, add the water, melted *ghee*, salt and sugar, and pulse on-off to blend. Mix the flour and baking powder in a small bowl. With the processor on, feed the flour–baking powder mixture through the feed tube, and continue to process as directed on page 100.

Form the dough into a smooth ball. Rub it with *ghee* or oil and cover it with an inverted bowl. Let the dough rest for ½–3 hours.

3. Collect the items needed for rolling out and cooking: a rolling pin, a slotted spoon for deep-frying, a tray lined with double-thick paper towels for draining the fried breads and a *karai*, wok or deep-walled Dutch over.

Place the dough on a clean surface and knead briefly. *Bhatura* dough should be soft enough so that the breads can be rolled out in a light dusting of flour. Divide the dough in half and roll one portion into a rope 7 inches (17.5 cm) long. Cut into six pieces and roll each piece into a smooth ball. Place the balls on a plate without letting them touch and cover with a damp cloth. Repeat the procedure for the other half of the dough.

4. Pour *ghee* or oil to a depth of 3 inches (7.5 cm) in the deep-frying pan and begin heating it over moderate heat. Working with one ball of dough at a time, press it into the dusting flour and flatten it into a 2-inch (5 cm) patty. Roll the patty into a round 4 inches (10 cm) in diameter. Dust the bread in flour to keep it from sticking to the rolling surface, but use as little flour as possible.

When the frying temperature reaches (365°F/185°C), lift the bread, slap it back and forth between your palms to shake off excess flour, and carefully slip it into the hot oil so that it remains flat and does not fold over. The bread will sink to the bottom of the pan but quickly tends to bob toward the surface. As it begins to rise, cover with the back of the slotted spoon and keep it submerged under the frying surface until it puffs into a steam-filled balloon. (Take care not to press the *bhatura* harshly; a tear in the delicate crust causes the inside to fill with oil.) When the bread begins to color on the first side (about 1 minute), carefully turn it over and fry the second side. The bread should be a pale biscuit color, not brown or even golden brown. Remove the puffed bread with the slotted spoon and drain on paper towels, without overlapping. Repeat the procedure to fry all of the *bhaturas*, adjusting the heat to maintain the oil at an even temperature. If it overheats, remove the pan from the burner and add a cold oil or *ghee* to lower the temperature.

Serve immediately or soon thereafter, keeping the batch warm for up to ½ hour in a 250°F (120°C) oven.

BREAD VARIATIONS

Coal-Baked Whole Wheat Bread Balls
BAATI

For most Americans, outdoor cooking, especially with simple equipment at campsites, is a novelty—perhaps a once-a-year family indulgence with nature. But throughout India, even today, outdoor cooking is anything but novel. With staples from a basket and a few heavy pots and tongs, the open field or river bank is a frequent location of really delicious meals. The villagers from the arid northwest Indian state of Rajasthan have preserved, almost ritualistically, a time-honored meal centered around a dish called *dal baati*.

Preparation begins in the evening, with the building of a campsite stove. Ferreting out dry *neem* wood (margosa) and an assortment of rocks, a substantial fire is started. Then the meal is cooked: perhaps a vegetable dish of sun-dried lotus root, potatoes, peppers and *badis*, a *dal* and rice *khichari* dish and finally, griddle-baked flatbreads. Out come an assortment of pickles and relishes in clay pots, and, in the coolness of a starry night, the late meal is relished. When the fire has burned down, a bed of fresh *neem* leaves is placed on the hot rocks to add aromatic flavors. Simple bread balls, made only from wheat flour, *ghee* and water, are nestled in the fading embers to slowly bake overnight. In the morning, the smoke-scented bread balls are brushed off—along with at least some portion of the crisp charred crust—and set aside for the noon meal. The center of the lunch menu is a *dal* soup. When the cooked soup is creamy smooth, the bread balls are dropped in it to simmer until softened. To complete the dish, a fried seasoning, or *chaunk*, is added. No amount of luxurious city cuisine can replace the beautiful sight of camping villagers and the taste of their *dal baati*.

For information about unfamiliar ingredients or techniques, see A-to-Z

Many of us have had outdoor cooked bread balls, perhaps way back in scout outings as children. They were sometimes rock hard, sometimes chewy and firm, but always good. If you have the inclination to imitate the village method I have described, by all means try it on your next camping trip. You can also cook the balls in a half-covered cast-iron skillet to get smoky-tasting bread balls without direct contact on open coals.

If you have a backyard smoker, you can really control *baati* flavors. So many aromatic wood selections are available now—hickory, pecan, cherry, almond, and peach; I find mesquite overbearing for breads. (Soak the wood chunks in water for 20 minutes, and drain well before use.) Start with a very hot fire made from hardwood charcoal briquets. When it has died down, and the glowing embers are somewhat gray, add the drained wood chunks. Let the fire die down further, and while grilling corn, eggplants, potato slabs, and squash, add a cast iron skillet filled with *baati* dough balls, and covered, begin baking the balls. Cook, checking and turning the vegetables, and then the *baati*, until charred and cooked. Butter and serve immediatly. During my last Key West residence, I even baked *baati* in a domed La Cloche brick oven (sold by Sassafras). For flavor, I resorted to sprigs of herbs, mango or key lime leaves. The *baati* crust made on stoneware is sensational.

Whether on a camping trip or planning a backyard lunch, try *baati* on their own with herb butter or simmer small breads in *Simple Mung Dal Soup* or *Herbed Split Pea Soup with Apple and Coconut*. Bring out the pickles and relishes: mild *Cauliflower Pickle* or, for true pickle-lovers, *Sour Lemon or Lime Pickle* or a sweet spoonful of *Mango Jam*. At home, finish the meal with a red leaf, radicchio, arugula and tender spinach salad.

Preparation time (after assembling ingredients): 10–15 minutes
Baking time: 1 hour or up to several hours
Makes: 30 bread balls

For Light Bread Balls:

2¼ **cups (295 g) sieved** *chapati* **flour, or 1 cup (130 g) whole wheat**
  flour mixed with 1¼ (150 g) cups unbleached white flour
¼ **teaspoon (1 ml) each baking soda and baking powder**
⅓ **cup (45 g) powdered buttermilk**
½ **teaspoon (2 ml) smoked or herbed salt (optional)**
1 **tablespoon (15 ml) sugar (optional)**
⅓ **cup (80 ml) butter or** *ghee*
⅔ **cup (160 ml) warm water, or as needed**
fresh herb sprig (optional)

For Dense Bread Balls:

2¼ **cups (295 g) sieved** *chapati* **flour, or 1 cup (130 g) whole wheat**
  flour mixed with 1¼ cups (150 g) unbleached all-purpose flour
½ **teaspoon (2 ml) salt**
⅓ **cup (80 ml) butter or** *ghee*
⅔ **cup (160 ml) water or buttermilk, at room temperature**

To Make Light Bread Balls:

1. Combine the flour, soda, baking powder, powdered buttermilk, optional salt and sugar (if using) in a large mixing bowl. Add the butter or *ghee* and rub it into the flour with your fingertips until fully incorporated. Add up to ⅔ cup (160 ml) water, pouring it fast at first to moisten the flour until it adheres into a rough mass, and then more slowly, in dribbles, until a kneadable dough is formed.

To Make Firm Bread Balls:

1. Combine the flours and salt in a large mixing bowl. Rub the butter or *ghee* into the flour with your fingertips until fully incorporated. Add up to ⅔ cup (160 ml) water or buttermilk, pouring it fast at first to moisten the flour until it adheres into a rough mass, and then slowly, in dribbles, until a dough is formed that you can knead.

2. For both kinds, knead the dough briefly for a few minutes, then roll into 30 even-sized balls. If you are baking in an gas or electric oven, preheat it to 300°F (150°C). Place the balls in a greased cast-iron skillet, baking pan or corn-meal-sprinkled stoneware oven. If you like, lay herb sprigs over the bread balls, cover and bake for 1½ hours. If you bake in a skillet over an open fire, cover with aluminum foil and pierce holes in it every 2 inches (5 cm). Bake until the balls are cooked. If you venture to try coal-baked bread balls, let the fire die down and bake the balls slowly on a flat stone or dying embers until crisp and cooked.

Crackling-Crispy *Dal* Wafers
PAPARH AUR PAPPADAM

Wafers made from plain or seasoned *dal*-based doughs are time-consuming to shape and sun-dry. Even in India, it is a rare kitchen that bothers with the task. In the north of India, where they are called *paparh*, they are rolled out 6–8 inches (15–20 cm) in diameter and liberally spiced—with crushed red peppers, cracked black pepper or a spice blend. In South India, where they are called *pappadam*, they are usually smaller (3–5 inches/7–12 cm in diameter) and unseasoned. Fortunately, both these *dal* wafer varieties are readily available already shaped and sun-dried, in several flavors. For the newcomer, I suggest trying the plain, black pepper and red pepper varieties. Avoid the spice blends, which are sometimes overloaded with garlic and onions.

Though these are not technically breads, they are thin wafers eaten like breads, usually served at the beginning or end of a meal. There are two ways to cook them: deep-frying and open-heat toasting. Deep-frying allows them to nearly double in size and instantly become crisp and light. Open-heat toasting allows the wafers to expand slowly and develop charcoal flavors. This toasting method is excellent for low-salt, low-fat diets, providing really good nutrition with minimal calories.

**Cooking time: a few seconds each if deep-fried; a few minutes
    each if flame-toasted**
Allow: ½–1 wafer per person, depending on size

To Deep-Fry:

1. Pour *ghee* or oil into a large frying pan to a depth of 1 inch (2.5 cm) and place it over moderately high heat. When the oil is hot (360°F/180°C), slip in a *dal* wafer. It will immediately sizzle, begin to expand and tend to curl around the edges. With the back of a large spatula or slotted round frying spoon, exert gentle pressure on the top surface of

---

For information about unfamiliar ingredients or techniques, see A-to-Z

the wafer, and within 5 seconds it will turn crisp and slightly lighten in color. Remove at once and drain on its side, on paper towels or in a colander over paper towels. (Do not allow the wafer to turn brown; it should remain a light yellow-gold color.) Fry the remaining pieces, taking care not to let the hot oil reach its smoking point. The wafers will remain crisp for 1–2 hours.

To Toast:

1. Place a *dal* wafer on a rack and hold it 2 inches (5 cm) above an electric or gas burner set on high. The areas of the wafer exposed to heat will lighten in color, expand and become flecked with black spots. Constantly move the wafer around to cook it evenly and keep it from burning.

2. Flip the wafer over to cook the second side. The cooked wafer should be brittle but not brown—remaining yellowish with charred flecks on both sides. Stack as the wafers cook.

Steamed Chickpea Bread with Coconut Garnish
DHOKLA

This version of savory golden bread, also called *khaman dhokra* is made from a yogurt-chickpea flour batter. In Gujarat there are scores of variations—some batters made with flour blends and vegetables and others made entirely from wet-ground soaked rice and *dal*. Because it is steamed instead of baked, the top of *dhokla* is soft and shiny rather than browned and crisp. The bread is served warm or at room temperature, with meals or at snack time. It is usually steamed in stainless steel pans (similar to round cake tins), and cut into roughly 1½-inch (4 cm) pieces. No matter what the occasion, it is colorfully garnished with snowy fresh coconut, chopped fresh coriander and a fried sesame or mustard seed *chaunk*. Though not traditional, you could also try a fried seasoning with poppy or sunflower seeds.

Preparation time (after assembling ingredients): 15 minutes
Batter resting time: 8 hours or overnight
Cooking time: 20 minutes
Makes: about 24 pieces

For the Bread:

1½ cups (145 g) sifted chickpea flour (measure after sifting)
2 hot green chilies, finely chopped
1½ tablespoons (22 ml) scraped, minced fresh ginger root
¼ teaspoon (1 ml) cracked black pepper
¼ teaspoon (1 ml) turmeric
¾ teaspoon (3.5 ml) salt
¼ teaspoon (1 ml) yellow asafetida powder (*hing*)*
1 teaspoon (5 ml) *jaggery* or brown sugar
3 tablespoons (45 ml) melted *ghee* or sesame oil
    plus 1 tablespoon (15 ml)) for the pan
about ⅔ cup (160 ml) plain yogurt or buttermilk
½ teaspoon (2 ml) each baking powder and baking soda
3 tablespoons (45 ml) warm water (100°F/38°C)

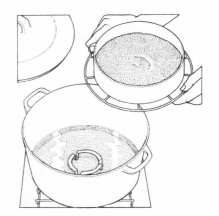

For the Garnish:

⅓ cup (35 g) grated fresh coconut
3 tablespoons (45 ml) coarsely chopped fresh coriander leaves
¼ cup (60 ml) *ghee* or unsalted butter and ½ tablespoon (7 ml)
    black mustard seeds, sesame seeds or black poppy seeds

*This amount applies only to yellow Cobra brand. Reduce any other asafetida by three-fourths.

1. Combine the flour, chilies, ginger, black pepper, turmeric, salt, asafetida and sugar in a medium mixing bowl and blend well. Stir in 3 tablespoons (45 ml) of *ghee* or oil and the yogurt or buttermilk and mix into a thick batter. Cover and set aside in a warm place for 8 hours or overnight.

2. Set up an arrangement for steaming, large enough to hold an 8-inch (20 cm) round or square cake pan. I use a trivet set inside a 6-quart/liter pot, filled with water to a depth of 1¼ inches (3.5 cm). (The bottom of the cake pan must rest a good ½ inch/1.5 cm above the boiling water.) Have a clean tea towel ready to line the inside of the lid during steaming. Pour 1 tablespoon (15 ml) melted butter or oil into the cake pan and tilt to spread it over the bottom and sides.

3. When you are ready to steam the bread, place the steaming pan over moderately high heat, covered to bring the water to a boil. Sprinkle the baking powder and soda into the chickpea-yogurt batter, and mix. Pour in the water and with a gentle hand, stir *in one direction* until the batter begins to froth. Immediately pour the batter into a prepared pan and set it in the steaming pot. Lay the tea towel over the large pot, and with the lid in place, stretch the towel out until it is taut, bringing the corners up over the lid. Put a heavy weight on the lid and steam for 8–12 minutes. Uncover and insert a toothpick in the bread: if it comes out clean, the bread is cooked. If not, steam a few more minutes. Remove the finished bread and set it aside, loosely covered, for 10 minutes.

4. Turn the bread out onto a cutting board and cut into roughly 1½-inch (4 cm) pieces. To get about 24 pieces, make two circular cuts from the edges, each about 1½ (4 cm) inches wide, and then cut across into squares. Place the *dhokra* pieces in a single layer on a serving tray. Sprinkle the bread with fresh coconut and coriander leaves. Heat the *ghee* or oil in a small pot over moderate heat. When it is hot, add the mustard seeds and fry until they sputter and pop. Pour over the bread. If you use sesame or poppy seeds, add the seeds to the pan and within 5 seconds, pour over the bread. Serve warm or at room temperature.

Baked Flatbreads with Nigella Seeds
NAAN

Many versions of coal and wood-fired clay ovens are found in Central Asia—east to Iran, west to India, and north to the U.S.S.R. The large *tandoori* clay ovens, found in Pakistan and northwest India, are especially suited for baking flatbreads. When the smooth clay walls of the oven are hot, thickish flatbreads are slapped right onto the inner walls, where they cook quickly, partially puff-

For information about unfamiliar ingredients or techniques, see A-to-Z

ing and taking on a smoky flavor. With a long metal skewer, each bread is pierced and carefully peeled off the wall. *Tandoori* breads have a trademark flavor combining the clay and smoke, with sensational crusts.

Whole wheat–based *tandoori* breads are often made with milk, even cream, and are layered during shaping, like *parathas*. But *naans* are leavened white flour breads, made simply by hand-slapping soft dough into large, roughly tear-drop shapes. They are traditionally leavened with a non-yeast starter, much like old-fashioned sourdough. The chancy wild yeast starter is made with only flour and water (I find that potato water helps the process along), mixed to a paste, covered and set in a warm nook, where it attracts the wild yeast organisms in the air, and begins to grow. From practical experience I can warn you that this fragile starter sometimes works and sometimes does not. Do not go any further if the culture turns black or doesn't froth and expand. Try again, or if you have an active sourdough culture in the fridge, that should save the day. Well-developed sourdough gives this flatbread excellent rising power and delicious flavor. If all else fails, go ahead and use yeast. I have suggested three methods to make the dough: traditional, sourdough and yeast.

Yeast, a single-celled fungus, floats about in the atmosphere, and in kitchens, attaches itself to any foods left uncovered—from raw vegetables and fruits to cooked dishes. Different species of yeast have different characteristics and are used for different purposes; wild yeast and bakers' yeast are used in baking, while wine and brewers' yeast are used for various alcoholic beverages. As living organisms, yeast feeds on sugars, or converts the starch in flour into necessary sugar. As yeast multiplies, much of the sugar is converted into carbon dioxide, CO_2 and alcohol. In fact, yeast varies in its tolerance to alcohol, so producers of beer, wine or spirits need a strain that thrives in an alcohol environment; the CO_2 gas is simply released. The needs of a baker are just the opposite: allowing the carbon dioxide's bubbles to give doughs a rise while the alcohol evaporates and escapes into the air during the baking. Bakers' yeast (*Saccharomyces cerevisiae*), in dry granules or solid cakes, contains active vegetive cells that need a warm sugar water (about 100°F/38°C) to grow and multiply, but are killed at temperatures over 120°F (50°C). Though Vedic cooks in the past had to rely on wild yeast for the occasional bread that used a sponge starter, modern alternatives are certainly more convenient.

To imitate a *tandoori* oven atmosphere, breads are initially baked in a hot oven and then toasted under a broiler. Preheated heavy iron pizza griddles yield good results, but Superstone pizza bricks, (made by Sassafras) are even better. These easy-to-handle brick slabs act much the same as gigantic ones used in old-world brick ovens—bakers have long appreciated the light crusts from stone baked breads. Superstone bricks are available in rounds and rectangles through better cookware stores and mail order sources such as William-Sonoma. Try *naan* on any North Indian lunch or dinner menu, or alone, with hearty soups or stews, such as nutritious *Mustard-Flavored Mixed Vegetable Soup* or *Hearty Chickpea Soup*.

Preparation and dough resting time: 2½ hours to 2 days
Cooking time: 40 minutes
Serves: 6

Traditional Sponge Starter Method :

½ **cup (65 g) unbleached white flour**
¼ **teaspoon (1 ml) salt**
1 **teaspoon (5 ml) sugar**
½ **cup (120 ml) water or potato water**
3 **cups (355 g) unbleached white flour**
1 **teaspoon (5 ml) baking powder**
½ **teaspoon (2 ml) salt**
1 **teaspoon (5 ml) sugar**
2 **tablespoons (30 ml) melted *ghee* or vegetable oil**
½ **cup (120 ml) plain yogurt, or as needed**
½ **teaspoon (2 ml) *kalonji* or black poppy seeds**

Combine ½ cup (65 g) flour, ¼ teaspoon (1 ml) salt and 1 teaspoon (5 ml) sugar in a crockery jar (do not use metal) and mix well. Add ½ cup (120 ml) water or potato water and mix well. Cover and set aside for 1½–2 days at about 100°F (38°C). The mixture should become light and expand in volume, with small cracks on the surface. If it has blackened, it must be discarded and made again. Mix the remaining flour, baking powder, salt and sugar in a large mixing bowl. Combine the starter, melted *ghee* or oil, 2–3 tablespoons yogurt and *kalonji* or black poppy seeds and mix. Add the liquid starter mixture to the flour all at once and work it well, using your hands. Continue mixing, adding flour or water as necessary, until the mixture leaves the sides of the bowl and becomes a nonsticky, kneadable dough. Knead for 6–8 minutes or until smooth and elastic. Set in a clean bowl, cover and let stand in a warm place for 2 hours.

Sourdough Starter Method :

½ cup (120 ml) ready-made sourdough starter, at room temperature
4 tablespoons (60 ml) melted *ghee* or vegetable oil
½ cup (120 ml) yogurt, or as needed
3 cups (355 g) unbleached white flour
2 teaspoons (10 ml) sugar
1 teaspoon (5 ml) salt
1 teaspoon (5 ml) baking powder
½ teaspoon (2 ml) *kalonji* or black poppy seeds

Mix the sourdough culture, melted *ghee* or butter and yogurt in a small bowl. Combine the flour, sugar, salt, baking powder and *kalonji* in a large mixing bowl. Add the sourdough-yogurt mixture and work it into the dry ingredients, using your hands. Continue mixing, adding flour or water, as needed, until the mixture leaves the sides of the bowl and becomes a nonsticky, kneadable dough. Knead for 6–8 minutes or until smooth and elastic. Place in a clean bowl, cover and let stand for about 4 hours in a warm place, until well risen.

Yeast Method:

1 package dry yeast
1 teaspoon (5 ml) sugar
2 tablespoons (30 ml) warm water (about 100°F/38°C)
¼ cup (60 ml) warm milk or half-and-half
¼ cup (60 ml) plain yogurt, at room temperature
4 tablespoons (60 ml) melted butter or *ghee*
3 cups (355 g) unbleached white flour
1 teaspoon (5 ml) salt
½ teaspoon (2 ml) baking powder
½ teaspoon (2 ml) *kalonji* or black poppy seeds

Combine the yeast, sugar and warm water in a small bowl. Set aside for 5–10 minutes or until it foams. Blend in the warm milk, yogurt and melted butter or ghee. In a large bowl, mix the flour, salt, baking powder and *kalonji* or black poppy seeds. Pour in the yeast-milk mixture all at once and work it into the flour mixture, using your hands. Continue mixing, adding flour or water, until the mixture leaves the sides of the bowl and becomes a nonsticky, kneadable dough. Knead for 6–8 minutes or until smooth and elastic. Place in a clean bowl, cover and let stand in a warm place for about 4 hours or until well risen.

To Shape and Bake the Breads:

1. Punch the dough down and knead briefly, adding a little flour if it is too sticky to handle. Divide into six pieces, pinching the bottom of each one to make a smooth round. Place them on an oiled plate and cover with lightly oiled plastic wrap. Let the balls rest for 10–15 minutes.

2. Preheat the oven to 550°F (290°C) or the highest setting and set a rack in the lower third of the oven, removing the upper shelves. Place two large cast-iron griddles or steel pizza trays or a large Superstone brick on rack and preheat while shaping the *naan*. Preheat the broiler.

3. Working with two balls at a time, roll and stretch each one into a teardrop shape about 10 inches (25 cm) long and 5 inches (12.5 cm) at its widest. When the pans have heated for about 10 minutes, remove them and brush with oil. Slap the shaped *naan* on the griddles or stone, and immediately return to the oven. Bake for 4–5 minutes or until they are puffed and have brown spots. Transfer the breads to a wire rack and return the pans to the oven to reheat. Now place the wire rack under the broiler, about 3 inches (7.5 cm) from the heat, and toast slightly until charcoal flecks appear on the surface. Slip the hot breads into a tea towel, cover and repeat the procedure for the remaining breads. Serve the oversized breads in a napkin-lined basket, allowing 1 per person, depending on the menu. To reheat, allow the *naan* to cool, then wrap in paper-towel-lined tinfoil. Place in a preheated 350°F (175°C) oven for 15 minutes.

Vegetables

The diversity of vegetables available to American cooks today is exhilarating. All across the country, a growing number of farms sell fresh produce, often organic, at roadside stands and farmers' markets. Even big-city shoppers can ferret out good local produce, though they may have to look around a bit; in New York City, outdoor greenmarkets offer variety and unusual specialties. More and more corner greengroceries and supermarkets offer European, Middle Eastern and Asian produce, while ethnic outlets tempt us with the exotic—bottle gourds and bitter melons, Italian and Japanese eggplants, water chestnuts and colocasia, Indian *mooli* and lotus root. This vegetarian cornucopia, along with other influences—travel abroad, interest in health and nutrition, and the inspiration provided by some outstanding restaurants—has sent cooks leafing through international cookbooks for new ideas. But although the French, Middle Easterners, Chinese and Japanese have an undeniable talent for vegetable cookery, the cradle of the art is India, the land of Lord Krishna's cuisine.

In a country housing over 500 million vegetarians—over 80 percent of the population—it is no wonder that India produces one of the largest assortments of vegetables, fruits and legumes in the world. Its *sabji* bazaars, or vegetable markets, are filled with freshly picked vegetables. Before dawn, workers unload bullock carts and arrange dew-covered squash, earth-speckled potatoes and washed spinach leaves in neat mounds for inspection. As in the open-air markets of Europe, early shoppers wander about, compare, poke here and there, and haggle for a good buy. The *subjiwalla* (greengrocer), sitting cross-legged behind a scale, calls out his wares. The prices vary according to quality and availability.

By and large, India's vegetarians embrace a diet similar to their ancient ancestors, and especially in the villages, cooks reflect regional standards and tradition. City vegetarians are far more creative, influenced by new trends, ingredients, and the current worldwide fascination for "light" and "healthy" cuisine. But it must be brought out that the major distinction between India's vegetarian cooks and others of fine stature is a reverence for God and His creation. A devotional attitude in the kitchen is as essential as organization. In particular, Vaishnavas—worshippers of Lord Krishna—take ultimate care in their cooking. Whether shopping, gardening or planning a menu, whether designing a clay stove or a sleek marble kitchen, Vaishnavas are veritable conductors of a culinary symphony. Because they cook as an offering to the Lord, their standard of cleanliness is not limited to the external: it includes speech, thought and action. It is not surprising to find out that this approach in the kitchen is not limited to cooking, but extends to all aspects of Vaishnava life.

While some of the recipes in this chapter are centuries old, others are contemporary variations of classic dishes. Hopefully it will put to rest the lingering myth that Indian vegetarian cuisine means overcooked, tongue-blistering concoctions from a poverty-stricken land. Although some of the ingredients may be unfamiliar to you, the recipes have been composed to preserve authenticity—a *shukta* must be bitter; a *charchari*, charred; fried plantain wafers, crispy—and they do not shock the palate. The recipes are arranged according to technique or texture. Aside from exploring numerous wet and dry cooking methods, they include diverse flavors—sweet, bitter, pungent, sour, and astringent. You can use them to add variety to a Western menu, or cook a surprisingly diversified three-course Vedic vegetable dinner, perhaps combining a purée, a stuffed vegetable and a sautéed vegetable.

Vedic purists do not believe in reheating vegetables, feeling that, like flat breads, they should be cooked to perfection and served immediately. This is especially true for stir-fried dishes cooked over moderately high heat. Some vegetable stews hold well over gentle heat, while others are served at room temperature or slightly chilled. Keep in mind that reheating breaks down vegetable fiber and increases nutrient loss—likewise for vegetables prepared for cooking long before use, or kept under prolonged refrigeration or light. If you must cook vegetables in advance, cool to room temperature, seal well and immediately refrigerate. Moist vegetables reheat with minimal changes in a double boiler or a steamer.

Heat and timing are important in vegetable cooking, but personal panache assuredly depends on spices, herbs and seasonings, over 50 of which are mentioned in this chapter. You will quickly notice the absence of onions, garlic, leeks, shallots and mushrooms, both as foods and as seasonings. Vedic vegetarians avoid them because they are considered *rajasic*, causing the same bodily distress as excessively salty or pungent dishes. Instead, you will find exotic flavor from ingredients such as fresh ginger root, coriander leaves, coconut milk, palm sugar, lime juice and hot chilies. From New Orleans cajun to Bombay Marawadi, heat belt cuisines invariably include chilies, not only for flavor, but to induce perspiration and relief from tropic temperatures. There is a considerable flavor and heat range in fresh green chilies, from smoky and sweet to mild or searing. I have used easy-to-seed jalapeños in recipe testing because they keep well, are medium-hot and are widely available. If you use smaller, lighter-green serranos, unseeded, expect the hotness to increase considerably, and use much less.

Look for young ginger root, also known as green ginger; it should have a thin, glossy, gossamer skin that can easily be scraped off. The roots are virtually fiberless and can be puréed or finely shredded. Old ginger is more pungent, with tough fibers, and the thick skin must be peeled off with a knife. Fresh coriander, also known as cilantro or Chinese parsley, is one of the world's most used herbs. Its indescribable flavor will grow on you. It is rich in vitamin C and worth the effort to locate. Though it can be used interchangeably with fresh parsley, it has a taste of its own and lends authenticity especially to Gujarati and Maharastrian dishes.

Far from stamping your meals with repetitive flavors, these wonderful flavor enhancers will bring out subordinate tastes from aromatics like cumin, turmeric, coriander, curry leaves, cardamom and asafetida. Because of the current popularity of Mexican, Chinese and Asian food, these ingredients are easy to find.

Fresh vegetables, properly cooked, are the basis of good eating anywhere in the world. They are bursting with energy-giving vitamins, minerals and carbohydrates. Wilted produce is never a bargain, even from your own garden. Vegetables start losing flavor and nutrients from the moment they are picked, so the sooner they are cooked, the more you are assured of tenderness, taste and nutrition.

Use most produce immediately or whisk it into storage. Sturdy tubers and winter squash will do well in paper bags in a cool, dark cupboard, but greens should be sealed in plastic and refrigerated. On the whole, small, slightly underripe produce is more succulent than oversized giants. The recipes in this chapter offer information on shopping, storage and preparation. Unripe mango or papaya is used while still very firm and should be kept in paper bags and refrigerated until use.

The peak season for any vegetable varies considerably according to the region, which makes the menu suggestions tentative. Everything ultimately depends upon the availability of seasonal produce. The following chart may help you in planning varied and balanced menus. Select a variety of vegetables from different groupings for color, texture and taste.

BEAN PODS AND SEEDS:		ROOTS AND TUBERS:
broad beans	corn	beets
green or snap beans	okra	carrots
(stringbeans)	green peas	celeriac
wax beans	snow peas	Jerusalem artichokes
butter beans	sprouts	parsnips
lima beans		potatoes: all-purpose (round or long white)
CABBAGE FAMILY:		mature baking (Russet or Idaho)
broccoli	cauliflower	boiling (round red or white)
green cabbage	kohlrabi	baby new potatoes
red cabbage	Brussel sprouts	yams
Savoy cabbage		sweet potatoes
		turnips
LEAFY GREENS AND STALKS:		**WINTER SQUASH:**
asparagus	collard greens	acorn
celery	mustard greens	Hubbard
fennel	kale	butternut
Swiss chard	sorrel	buttercup or Turban
(red or green)	spinach	pumpkin
Belgian endive	vine leaves	spaghetti
beet greens	watercress	
SUMMER SQUASH:		**SPECIALTY SELECTIONS:**
zucchini, green or yellow		bittermelon or bittergourd (*karela*)
crooknecks		bottlegourd (*louki*)
pattypan (cymling)		sponge gourd (*toray*)
cocozelle		round gourd or squash melon (*tinda*)
cucumber		green papaya or paw paw
VEGETABLE FRUITS:		jicama
tomatoes: salad, plum, baby, green		plaintain
bell peppers: red, yellow, green		colocasia (*arbi*)
stuffing peppers: banana, California,		horseradish root
Anaheim		lotus root (*bhain*)
eggplants: medium or large		white cooking radish (*mooli* or daikon)
Japanese or baby eggplants: narrow or		waterchestnuts (*singhara*)
small		chayote or vegetable pear

For information about unfamiliar ingredients or techniques, see A-to-Z

THREE METHODS OF COOKING VEGETABLES

VEGETABLE BASICS: People often ask me how I became involved in Vedic cooking. My first exposure to it was a luncheon hosted by Srila Prabhupada in 1966, an experience that unlocked a floodgate of questions in my mind. By early 1967 I was Srila Prabhupada's fortunate student, attending his small cooking classes every day for three months. As apprentices, his students were exposed to the basics: how to shop, organize, prepare ingredients, measure, use a knife and our hands, clean up and, ultimately, cook. Though I came from a family of serious cooks, some French-trained, this period was the most formative and thrilling of my life.

Our study of vegetable cooking began with the effects of seasoning and cooking methods on texture and taste. Using the world's best-known vegetable—the potato—we spent weeks exploring three basic methods of cooking, learning how to control the taste and appearance of a dish without diminishing its nutritive value. If you are new to Vedic cooking, you might like to start by exploring these three basic methods. When you are conversant with the variables, you can confidently and pleasurably improvise with seasonal fresh produce. Let's take a quick look at these three methods.

METHOD ONE—Sautéed and Braised Dry Vegetables (cooked without water): Small pieces of uniformly cut-up vegetables—dice, julienne, or diagonal slices—are briskly sautéed in seasoned *ghee* or oil in an open pan over brisk heat until they are partially cooked and slightly browned. As they cook they are turned frequently with a spoon, or the pan is shaken, to keep them from browning unevenly or sticking.

From here on, there are two options. The first, for vegetables with a substantial amount of moisture, is to reduce the heat slightly and stir-fry the vegetables until tender-crisp and lightly browned. The second is to cover the pan tightly, reduce the heat to low and cook the vegetables in their own juices.

If you want a crust on the cooked vegetables, raise the heat and quickly brown them, tossing gently. During this final stage you can drizzle in *ghee* or oil to prevent sticking.

Try this method with potatoes, yams, peas, snow peas, asparagus, okra, eggplants, cabbage, new carrots, green beans, bell peppers and spinach.

METHOD TWO—Sautéed and Braised Vegetables (cooked in broth): The vegetables are briskly sautéed and then simmered in an aromatic broth until tender. This method combines several procedures, with options as to the finished texture. The most engaging aspects of this method are the timing and heat control: it is a challenge to cook the vegetables just to the point of tenderness without overcooking. Vegetables cut into medium-sized chunks or cubes are sautéed in seasoned *ghee* or a mixture of oil and butter until partially cooked and slightly browned. At this point the liquid is added, the heat is reduced to low, the pan is covered and the vegetables are simmered to tenderness.

Four finished textures are possible: a vegetable stew, vegetables in a sauce, moist vegetables in a concentrated glaze, or crusty, dry vegetables. If all of the broth is to be cooked off, I find a nonstick pan helpful for putting a crust on the dry vegetables. Small quantities of *ghee* or butter help keep them from sticking to the pan while they become tender. The right heat, timing and pan size all play important parts in controlling the texture of the finished dish. Vegetables suitable for this method include cauliflower, carrots, eggplants, potatoes, winter and summer squash, yams, potatoes, peas, green beans, Swiss chard, broad beans, lima beans, chayote, bottle gourd and Jerusalem artichoke.

METHOD THREE—Precooked Vegetables in Seasoned *Ghee*, Sauce or Broth: In the first two methods, the vegetables are sautéed before being cooked to tenderness. In this method, the vegetables are first cooked to near tenderness, then pan-fried or sautéed in seasonings. Depending on the vegetable and the precooking technique, it can be cooked either whole or cut up, peeled or unpeeled, by boiling, steaming, pressure cooking, oven-baking, coal-baking, deep-frying or shallow-frying. If it has been cooked whole— say, by steaming or baking—it is then cut into uniform pieces and quickly browned with seasonings in *ghee* or a blend of oil and butter. It can be served dry or further finished in a prepared sauce, or it can be added to a light broth. In contrast to Methods One and Two, this method is broad enough to encompass almost any vegetable.

EXAMPLES OF USING THE THREE METHODS

To get a clearer idea of the three methods, let's carry potatoes through the steps. Depending on the spices on your shelves, pick one of the three sample seasoning combinations below and try each method with the same ingredients. You will notice the vast differences created by varying heat, timing and vegetable shape. With variations in seasoning, too, it is easy to see how you can create innumerable dishes from any vegetable.

Sometimes the *chaunk*, or fried spice seasoning, is added to the main ingredients; other times, the main ingredients are added to the *chaunk*. In either case, the seasoning greatly affects the flavor. The *chaunk*'s strength is determined by the heat and how long it is fried: the faster or longer you cook it, the more potent the flavor. Watch the color as it cooks; lightly browned seasonings impart mild flavor, dark brown bracing flavor and black a pungent, extreme taste. It is strictly a matter of personal preference.

For information about unfamiliar ingredients or techniques, see A-to-Z

Seasoning 1:

3 medium-sized all-purpose potatoes (about 1 pound/455 g)
3 tablespoons (45 ml) *ghee* or peanut oil
½–2 dried red chilies, broken into bits
1 teaspoon (5 ml) cumin seeds
½ teaspoon (2 ml) turmeric
2–4 tablespoons (30-60 ml) water or stock for Method One;
    1–2½ cups (240–600 ml) for Methods Two and Three
1 teaspoon (5 ml) salt
2 tablespoons (30 ml) chopped fresh coriander or minced parsley

Seasoning 2:

3 medium-sized all-purpose potatoes (about 1 pound/455 g)
3 tablespoons (45 ml) *ghee* or sesame oil
½ tablespoon (7 ml) minced green chilies (or as desired)
l teaspoon (5 ml) cumin seeds
½ tablespoon (7 ml) scraped, finely shredded or minced fresh ginger root
½ teaspoon (2 ml) turmeric
½ tablespoon (7 ml) ground coriander
2–4 tablespoons (30–60 ml) water for Method One;
    1–2½ cups (240–600 ml) for Methods Two and Three
1 teaspoon (5 ml) salt
2 tablespoons (30 ml) chopped fresh coriander or minced parsley

Seasoning 3:

3 medium-sized all-purpose potatoes (about 1 pound/455 g)
3 tablespoons (45 ml) *ghee* or a mixture of oil and unsalted butter
½ tablespoon (7 ml) minced green chilies (or as desired)
1 teaspoon (5 ml) cumin seeds
½ teaspoon (2 ml) black mustard seeds
½ tablespoon (7 ml) scraped, finely shredded or minced fresh ginger root
¼ teaspoon (1 ml) yellow asafetida powder (*hing*)*
½ teaspoon (2 ml) turmeric
½ tablespoon (7 ml) ground coriander
2–4 tablespoons (30–60 ml) water or stock for Method One;
    1–2½ cups (240–600 ml) for Methods Two and Three
1 teaspoon (5 ml) salt
½ teaspoon (2 ml) *garam masala*
2 tablespoons (30 ml) chopped fresh coriander or minced parsley

This amount applies only to yellow Cobra brand. Reduce any other asafetida by three-fourths.

Example of Method One
DRY POTATOES (COOKED WITHOUT WATER)

1. Cut the potatoes into ½-inch (1.5 cm) dice. Heat the *ghee* or oil in a heavy non-stick frying pan over moderate heat. When it is hot but not smoking, add the red or green chilies, whole spice seeds (cumin and perhaps black mustard seeds), ginger root and asafetida. Fry until the cumin seeds darken a few shades or the mustard seeds turn gray and pop. If you are using asafetida, add it, and in a few seconds stir in the potatoes. Sauté until they are partially cooked and slightly browned.

2. Reduce the heat to low and sprinkle in the ground spices (turmeric and perhaps coriander). Toss to mix. At this point you can sprinkle in 2–4 tablespoons (30–60 ml) of water or stock. Cover and cook, stirring once or twice, for about 15 minutes or until the potatoes are fork-tender. Uncover and add the salt, *garam masala*, if desired, and fresh herb. Toss to mix, and serve.

Example of Method Two
SUCCULENT BRAISED POTATOES (COOKED IN STOCK)

1. Cut the potatoes into 1-inch (2.5 cm) cubes. Heat 2½ tablespoons (37 ml) of *ghee* or selected alternative in a large heavy nonstick saucepan over moderately high heat. When it is hot but not smoking, drop in the green or red chilies, whole spice seeds—cumin and possibly black mustard seeds—and ginger root. Fry until the cumin seeds darken a few shades or the mustard seeds turn gray and pop. Sprinkle in the asafetida, and a few seconds later stir in the potatoes. Sauté until the cubes are lightly browned.

2. Sprinkle in the ground spices (turmeric and coriander if you are using them). Follow with half of the fresh herbs and 1¼ cups (300 ml) of water or stock. Partially cover, reduce the heat to low and gently cook until the potato cubes are just tender and the liquid has nearly cooked off. You will have to adjust the heat to coordinate these factors. When the potatoes are nearly dry, uncover, add the remaining ½ tablespoon (7 ml) of *ghee* or oil and raise the heat. Shake the pan to keep the potatoes from sticking to the bottom, and cook until a light crust forms. Complete the dish with salt, the remaining herbs and *garam masala* if you are using them.

Example of Method Three
BAKED POTATOES SAUTEÉD IN SEASONINGS (USING NO LIQUID)

1. Bake the potatoes until just tender, peel them, and cut into ¾-inch (2 cm) cubes.
2. Heat the *ghee* or oil in a large heavy frying pan over moderate heat. When it is

---

For information about unfamiliar ingredients or techniques, see A-to-Z

hot but not smoking, add the green or red chilies and whole spice seeds (cumin and possibly black mustard seeds) and ginger root. Fry the seasoning until the cumin seeds darken a few shades or the mustard seeds turn gray and pop. Sprinkle in the asafetida, if desired, and in seconds stir in the potatoes. Sprinkle with the ground spices (turmeric and perhaps coriander), and shake the pan or gently toss with a spatula until the potatoes brown slightly. Complete the dish with salt, *garam masala*, if desired, and fresh herb. Stir once before serving.

DRY-TEXTURED VEGETABLES

The vegetable dishes in this section are some of the most frequently prepared in India. In the north and west, they would be served with hot flat breads; in the east and south, with hot rice. These dishes are neither pan-fried nor braised nor sautéed, but prepared by a combination of techniques that yield dry-textured vegetables. Added liquids are reduced during the cooking and become an integral part of the finished dish.

Ghee is considered the most flavorful cooking medium in most regions, though I have indicated when mustard, sesame, peanut or coconut oil is a regional alternative. Butter cannot be used on its own for stir-fried recipes as it burns over even moderate heat. If you do not have *ghee* or the suggested oil in your kitchen, use a mixture of butter and light vegetable oil—sunflower, safflower, or corn.

Glazed Carrots
GAJAR SABJI

In India, carrots are more often used raw in salads, as crisp pickle spears or in sweet *halvas* than as a cooked vegetable. They are brilliant orange-red roots, harvested both young and sweet or oversized as giants. Most Americans have three choices: baby carrots 2–3 inches (5–7.5 cm) long, medium-sized carrots and large tapered carrots with a fibrous core. You can use any of them with slightly different preparation. Finger-thick babies require little preparation: simply trim the ends and slice in half lengthwise. To prepare medium-sized carrots, peel and trim the ends and slice on the diagonal about ½ inch (1.5 cm) thick. When dealing with mature carrots, peel, trim the ends, slice in half lengthwise and remove the core (insert a small pointed knife beneath the core at the thick end of the carrot and pry the core free). Cut the hollow carrots on the diagonal into ½-inch (1.5 cm) lengths.

I first had this dish while traveling through the Punjab. It was prepared in an alkaline Himalayan sparkling water, and terrific, though still water or water with a lemon or apple juice yields an equally flavorful cardamom glaze. For a typically North Indian lunch, accompany with a second contrasting-textured vegetable, say *Simple Potato and Green Pea Stew*. To round out the menu, add a *dal* such as *Fennel-Flavored Urad Dal Soup*, steamed rice and *Crackling-Crispy Dal Wafers*.

Preparation time (after assembling ingredients): 10 minutes
Cooking time: 20–40 minutes Serves: 4 or 5

30 baby carrots, about 1 pound (455 g), 6–8
    medium-sized or 4–5 large, cut as described above
3 tablespoons (45 ml) *ghee* or unsalted butter
2 tablespoons (30 ml) brown sugar or maple syrup
¼ teaspoon (1 ml) turmeric
½ teaspoon (2 ml) coarsely crushed cardamom seeds
½ teaspoon (2 ml) ground coriander
2 tablespoons (30 ml) orange or apple juice
⅔ cup (160 ml) still or sparkling mineral water
½ teaspoon (2 ml) salt
⅛ teaspoon (0.5 ml) freshly ground pepper
    or cayenne pepper
2 tablespoons (30 ml) coarsely chopped fresh coriander
    or minced fresh parsley
1 teaspoon (5 ml) fresh lime or lemon juice
¼ teaspoon (1 ml) freshly grated nutmeg

1. Place the carrots in a single layer in a roomy skillet or sauté pan. Add 2 tablespoons (30 ml) of *ghee* or butter and the sweetener, turmeric, cardamom seeds, ground coriander, orange or apple juice, water and salt. Bring to a boil, cover and reduce the heat to low. Simmer young carrots for as little as 20 minutes, older ones for up to 40 minutes.

2. When almost all of the water has evaporated, uncover and rapidly boil off the remainder. Shake the pan to keep the carrots from sticking. When the carrots are coated with a shiny glaze, remove the pan from the heat and add the remaining 1 tablespoon (15 ml) of *ghee* or butter and the pepper and fresh herb. Shake the pan to mix the ingredients. Just before serving, toss with lime or lemon juice and nutmeg.

For information about unfamiliar ingredients or techniques, see A-to-Z

Spicy Cauliflower with Braised Tomato
GOBHI TAMATAR SABJI

Snowy cauliflower and ripe tomatoes marry their colors and flavors over gentle heat until the cauliflower is butter-soft and the tomatoes are reduced to a seasoned glaze. The only liquid is the juice from the tomatoes, so the dish must be braised slowly. The result is a dry-textured, succulent everyday dish that can be featured on any lunch or dinner menu. This typically Maharashtrian dish makes a meal when served with *Griddle-Fried Whole Wheat Bread* or *Baked Buckwheat with Almonds* and a tossed green salad.

Preparation time (after assembling ingredients): 10 minutes
Cooking time: 25–30 minutes
Serves: 4 or 5

3–4 tablespoons (45–60 ml) *ghee* or vegetable oil
1-inch (2.5 cm) piece of fresh ginger root, scraped and cut into thin julienne
1–2 green jalapeño chilies, cored, seeded and slivered
½ teaspoon (2 ml) black mustard seeds
1 teaspoon (5 ml) cumin seeds
1 large cauliflower (about 3 pounds/1.5 kg), trimmed, cored and cut into flowerets 2 x 1 x ½
   inches (5 x 2.5 x 1.5 cm)
1 tablespoon (15 ml) ground coriander
½ teaspoon (2 ml) turmeric
1 teaspoon (5 ml) salt
3 medium-sized tomatoes, each peeled and cut into eighths (about 1 pound/455 g)
1 teaspoon (5 ml) *garam masala*
3 tablespoons (45 ml) coarsely chopped fresh coriander or minced parsley
butter (optional)

1. Heat the *ghee* or oil in a large nonstick casserole or sauté pan over moderate to moderately high heat. When it is hot but not smoking, drop in the ginger, chilies, mustard and cumin seeds. Fry until the mustard seeds pop and turn gray and the cumin seeds turn brown. Stir in the cauliflower, ground coriander, turmeric and salt. Stir-fry until the flowerettes are slightly browned, then stir in the tomatoes. Cover and reduce the heat to low. Cook for 15–20 minutes, shaking the pan occasionally to keep the vegetables from sticking, or until the cauliflower stalks are just tender.

2. Uncover, raise the heat and stir-fry to evaporate all the liquid. Just before serving, sprinkle with the *garam masala*, fresh herb, and add a knob of butter, if desired.

Sautéed Cauliflower and Green Peas
GOBHI HARI MATAR SABJI

In all cauliflower dishes, the quality of the vegetable is paramount. Look for crisp, tightly packed white flowerets and bright green leaves. It is important to cut the flowerets into uniform pieces, but the success of the dish really lies in slow, gentle braising; the cauliflower cooks in its own juice and seasonings until the flowerets are butter-soft and the stems tender-crisp. Garden-fresh peas are in a class of their own, but good-quality frozen baby peas are sometimes better than "fresh" peas from the store, and certainly much less work.

This type of dry cauliflower dish is popular for a simple lunch throughout Uttar Pradesh, served with little more than *chapatis* and a *kachambar*. For a more elaborate family dinner, try it with fried *Crispy Plantain Wafers* or *Pumpkin Wafers* or a light soup such as *Sweet 'n' Sour Broth with Cabbage and Carrots*. To complete a nutritious meal, add *Griddle-Fried Whole Wheat and Corn Bread*.

Preparation time (after assembling ingredients): 10 minutes
Cooking time: 25–30 minutes
Serves: 4 or 5

4 tablespoons (60 ml) *ghee* or vegetable oil
½ tablespoon (7 ml) scraped, finely shredded or minced fresh ginger root
1¼ teaspoons (6 ml) cumin seeds
8–10 curry leaves or 1 bay leaf
1 large cauliflower (about 3 pounds/1.5 kg), trimmed, cored and cut into flowerets 1½ x 1 x ½
    inches (4 x 2.5 x 1.5 cm)
½ teaspoon (2 ml) turmeric
¼ teaspoon (1 ml) paprika or cayenne pepper
3 tablespoons (45 ml) chopped fresh coriander, parsley or chervil
1 cup (240 ml) fresh peas (about 1 pound/455 g in pods) or frozen baby peas, defrosted
2–4 tablespoons (30–60 ml) water
1 teaspoon (5 ml) salt
⅓ cup (80 ml) plain yogurt, sour cream or cream
Brazil nut curls or parsley sprigs for garnish (optional)

1. In a heavy 5-quart/liter nonstick saucepan, heat the *ghee* or oil over moderately high heat until it is hot but not smoking. Fry the cumin seeds until they brown, then drop in the curry leaves or bay leaf, and in a few seconds stir in the cauliflower. Sprinkle with turmeric, paprika or cayenne and half of the fresh herb. Stir-fry until the cauliflower is lightly browned. Add the fresh peas and 2–4 tablespoons (30–60 ml) of water, cover and reduce the heat to low. Stirring occasionally, cook for 15–20 minutes or until the cauliflower is tender. If you are using frozen peas, drain well and add for the last 3–4 minutes of cooking.

2. Before serving, mix in the salt, remaining herb and yogurt, sour cream or cream. If desired, garnish each serving with Brazil nut curls or parsley sprigs.

For information about unfamiliar ingredients or techniques, see A-to-Z

Whole Cauliflower Crown with Spiced Tomato Sauce
KHASA OBLA GOBHI

This entertainment dish is famous in Rajasthan's "Pink City"—Jaipur. Home of the vibrant Shree Radha Govinda Temple, it is one of the most popular pilgrimage sites for Vaishnavas in North India. From dawn to late at night, a steady stream of Krishna devotees pour through the temple gates, exuberantly calling out the name of the presiding Deity. Directly across from the temple, in the ornate city palace, I was served this dish at the well-appointed table of the Maharani of Jaipur, Srimati Gayatri devi.

This is a beautiful centerpiece vegetable to bring to the table whole and cut into wedges for serving. Shop for unblemished snow- or cream-white cauliflower with compact flowerets tightly pressed together. You could use one large or two small cauliflowers, depending on availability. The cooked whole cauliflower is drizzled with a spicy tomato sauce, yogurt or sour cream, and chopped nuts. If you are entertaining, cook several and line them up on a large platter surrounded by decorative outer leaves of Savoy cabbage.

Preparation time (after assembling ingredients): 10 minutes
Cooking time: 30–50 minutes
Serves: 5 or 6

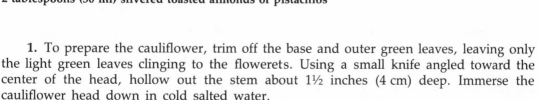

1 large cauliflower (about 3 pounds/1.5 kg)
    or 2 small (each 1 pound/455 g)
about 3 cups (710 ml) salted water for cooking the cauliflower
5 medium-sized tomatoes, peeled and quartered (1¼ pounds/570 g)
¼ cup (60 ml) plus 2 tablespoons (30 ml) water
1 bay leaf
6–8 peppercorns
4 tablespoons (60 ml) *ghee* or unsalted butter
½ teaspoon (2 ml) ground cumin
1 teaspoon (5 ml) ground coriander
¼ teaspoon (1 ml) cayenne pepper or paprika
¼ teaspoon (1 ml) ground fennel
¼ teaspoon (1 ml) ground yellow mustard
¼ teaspoon (1 ml) turmeric
½ teaspoon (2 ml) salt
½ teaspoon (2 ml) brown sugar
½ cup (120 ml) plain yogurt or sour cream, at room temperature
2 tablespoons (30 ml) slivered toasted almonds or pistachios

1. To prepare the cauliflower, trim off the base and outer green leaves, leaving only the light green leaves clinging to the flowerets. Using a small knife angled toward the center of the head, hollow out the stem about 1½ inches (4 cm) deep. Immerse the cauliflower head down in cold salted water.

2. Pour the 3 cups (710 ml) salted water into a saucepan slightly larger than the cauliflower and bring to a boil over high heat. Place the cauliflower in it, stem end down, and when the water returns to a boil, cover and boil for 15–25 minutes over moderate heat. (If you steam the cauliflower instead, allow 40–50 minutes, depending on the size.) Meanwhile, place the tomatoes in a small saucepan with the ¼ cup (60 ml) water and the bay leaf and peppercorns. Gently boil over moderate heat for 10 minutes.

Strain the juice through a sieve, discarding the seeds and spices.

3. When the cauliflower is almost tender, carefully lift it out and drain in a colander. Transfer it to a heated serving dish, rub with 1 tablespoon (15 ml) of the *ghee* or butter and set aside in a warm oven.

4. Combine the ground spices with the 2 tablespoons (30 ml) of water in a small dish. Heat the remaining 3 tablespoons (45 ml) of *ghee* or butter in a small saucepan over moderate heat. Add the spice water and fry for 30 seconds. Pour in the tomato juice, salt and sugar, bring to a boil and reduce until thick enough to coat a stirring spoon.

5. To serve, spoon the tomato sauce over the cauliflower, drizzle the yogurt or sour cream over the sauce and sprinkle with nuts. Serve immediately, cutting into wedges.

Curried Cauliflower and Potatoes
GOBHI ALOO SABJI

Potato spears and cauliflower flowerets are browned in spices over strong heat to bring out their rich, deep flavors and are then gently cooked to tenderness with tomatoes. Neither dry nor wet, this dish has a succulent, moist texture that is somewhere in between. You can vary the flavor with tomatoes, using green, Italian plum or ripe reds. This typically North Indian vegetable mixture is almost always served with flatbread. Simple *chapatis* or *pooris* are the Vedic favorites, but it is equally delicious with whole grain toast. It can be served anytime, from Sunday breakfast to late-night dinner, accompanied by a *dal* dish and yogurt salad.

Preparation time (after assembling ingredients): 5 minutes
Cooking time: 30 minutes
Serves: 5 or 6

2 hot green chilies, stemmed, seeded and cut lengthwise into long slivers (or as desired)
½-inch (1.5 cm) piece of scraped fresh ginger root, cut into thin julienne
1 teaspoon (5 ml) cumin seeds
½ teaspoon (2 ml) black mustard seeds
4 tablespoons (60 ml) *ghee* or a mixture of vegetable oil and unsalted butter
3 medium-sized potatoes (about 1 pound/455 g), peeled and cut
    into spears 2½ x ½ x ½ inches (6.5 x 1.5 x 1.5 cm) long
1 medium-sized cauliflower (about 2 pounds/1 kg), trimmed, cored
    and cut into flowerets 2½ x ½ x ½ inches (6.5 x 1.5 x 1.5 cm) long
2 medium-sized red or green tomatoes (about ½ pound/230 g), quartered
½ teaspoon (2 ml) turmeric
2 teaspoons (10 ml) ground coriander
½ teaspoon (2 ml) *garam masala*
1 teaspoon (5 ml) *jaggery* or brown sugar
1¼ teaspoons (6 ml) salt
3 tablespoons (45 ml) coarsely chopped fresh coriander or minced parsley
lime or lemon wedges (optional)

For information about unfamiliar ingredients or techniques, see A-to-Z

1. Combine the chilies, ginger, cumin seeds and mustard seeds in a small bowl. Heat the *ghee* or oil-butter mixture in a large nonstick saucepan over moderately high heat. When it is hot but not smoking, pour in the combined seasonings and fry until the mustard seeds turn gray, sputter and pop. Drop in the potatoes and cauliflower and stir-fry for 4–5 minutes or until the vegetables pick up a few brown spots.

2. Add the tomatoes, turmeric, coriander, *garam masala*, sweetener, salt and half of the fresh herb. Stir well, cover and gently cook over low heat, stirring occasionally, for 15–20 minutes or until the vegetables are tender. You may want to sprinkle in a few tablespoons (45 ml) of water if the vegetables stick to the bottom of the pan, but stir gently to avoid mashing or breaking them. Serve with the remaining fresh herb and garnish with lemon or lime wedges, if desired.

Crispy Diced Eggplant with Bitter *Neem* Leaves
NEEM BAIGAN

The ingredients for this dish are mentioned in the *Chaitanya Charitamrita*, a fifteenth-century Bengali text describing the pastimes and activities of Sri Chaitanya Mahaprabhu. The author describes a feast prepared in honor of the great saint: "Among the various vegetables offered were newly-grown leaves of *nimba* (*neem*) trees fried with eggplant."

Bitter-tasting vegetable dishes are popular in Bengal. They are known to stimulate a failing appetite and pleasantly contrast with other tastes. I suggest beginning with only a hint of this flavoring agent, enough to enliven and heighten the vegetable. Once overdone, nothing can remedy bitter seasonings. Bitter *neem* leaves (in English, margosa) are rarely, if ever, available at Indian grocery stores. A substitute is dry-roasted fenugreek seeds. Bengalis prefer to cook this dish in mustard oil, but you can use the oil of your choice. Serve the dish in portions of 2–3 tablespoons (30–45 ml) to complement a full lunch or dinner menu.

Preparation time (after assembling ingredients): 15 minutes
Cooking time: 10 minutes
Makes: 5 or 6 small servings

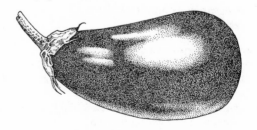

1 medium-sized eggplant (1¼ pounds/570 g)
½ tablespoon (7 ml) salt
1 teaspoon (5 ml) turmeric
½ cup (120 ml) *ghee*, mustard oil or vegetable oil
¼–½ teaspoon (1–2 ml) powdered bitter *neem* leaves or
½-1 teaspoon (2-5 ml) powdered roasted fenugreek seeds a sprinkle of lemon or lime juice

1. Dice the eggplant and transfer to a bowl. Sprinkle with 1 teaspoon (5 ml) salt and the turmeric, toss and set aside for 15 minutes. Toss again, then remove the eggplant with a slotted spoon and pat dry with paper towels.

2. In a frying pan, heat the *ghee* or oil over moderately high heat until it is hot but not smoking. (If you use mustard oil, let it smoke for 5 seconds before adding the eggplant. This makes the pungent oil docile.) Add the eggplant and stir-fry until browned and crisp. In the last minute of cooking, add the *neem* or fenugreek and the remaining salt. Toss well, drain in a strainer or on paper towels, and serve hot with a sprinkle of lemon or lime juice.

Okra Supreme
BHINDI SABJI

For many cooks okra is an unknown vegetable. If they have ever eaten it, it may have been in the American South as part of a gumbo or stew, or deep-fried in a corn batter. Few, however, would ever buy it and try to serve it to family or guests. Yet this stir-fried okra is easy to make, and so delicious that it will surprise even the reluctant. Okra is a summer vegetable, at its best in June or July, but you may find it as early as April and as late as September. The pods should be small—3–4 inches (7.5–10 cm) long—and the pointed end will snap off if fresh; when the pods are old, the ends will only bend. The cut pods release a glutinous sap, so the rinsed okra must be dried thoroughly on paper towels before it is cut, to prevent excessive stickiness. Since this is a pan-fried vegetable, cooked without water, a nonstick frying pan is ideal, using a minimal amount of oil to yield the lightly browned vegetable. Serve it on almost any Vedic lunch or dinner menu, including a flatbread or rice, a *dal* dish and a salad.

Preparation time (after assembling ingredients): 15 minutes
Cooking time: 25 minutes
Serves: 4

1 pound (455 g) fresh okra
3–4 tablespoons (45–60 ml) *ghee* or peanut oil
1½ tablespoons (22 ml) ground coriander
½ teaspoon (2 ml) ground cumin
¼ teaspoon (1 ml) paprika or cayenne pepper
½ teaspoon (2 ml) *garam masala*
½ teaspoon (2 ml) turmeric
1 teaspoon (5 ml) salt

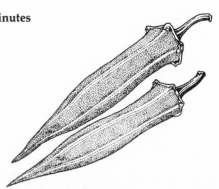

For information about unfamiliar ingredients or techniques, see A-to-Z

1. Wash the okra and dry *thoroughly* on paper towels. (If it is a warm day, air-dry in the sun.) Trim off the tip and stem, and slice into rounds ⅓ inch (1 cm) thick.

2. In a large, heavy frying pan, preferably nonstick, heat the *ghee* or oil over moderately high heat. When it is hot but not smoking, add the okra in a single layer and reduce the heat to moderate. Cook for about 20 minutes, stirring occasionally to brown the okra evenly. Toward the end, add the ground spices, raise the heat to moderately high and, stirring steadily, fry until golden brown and fully cooked. Remove the pan from the heat, sprinkle with salt, toss to coat the okra evenly, and let it sit, covered, for 1 minute before serving.

Spicy Okra with Coconut
MASALA BHINDI SABJI

Here is another easy and delicious okra dish, pan-fried with whole spices and grated coconut. As the okra browns lightly, the seasoned coconut forms a flavorsome crust. If you do not have fresh or frozen grated coconut on hand, substitute ground almonds—equally delicious. Keep in mind that okra releases a glutinous sap when cut and sweats when salted, so dry it thoroughly and salt after cooking.

You can serve this South Indian dish with practically anything. For a simple meal, try *Quick Cream of Split Pea Soup with Sliced Carrots* and plain rice, or *Cold Minty Yogurt Soup* and *Griddle-Baked Whole Wheat Bread*.

Preparation time (after assembling ingredients): 15 minutes
Cooking time: 20–25 minutes
Serves: 4

1 pound (455 g) okra, preferably small (3–4 inches/7.5–10 cm long)
4 tablespoons (60 ml) *ghee* or sesame oil
1 teaspoon (5 ml) black mustard seeds
1 teaspoon (5 ml) slightly crushed cumin seeds
¼ teaspoon (1 ml) yellow asafetida powder (*hing*)*
½ teaspoon (2 ml) turmeric
¼ teaspoon (1 ml) cayenne pepper or paprika
⅓ cup (35 g) grated fresh coconut or frozen coconut (55 g) , defrosted,
    or ½ cup (50 g) ground almonds
1 teaspoon (5 ml) salt

*This amount applies only to yellow Cobra brand. Reduce any other asafetida by three-fourths.

1. Wash the okra and dry *thoroughly* on paper towels. (If it is a warm day, air-dry in the sun.) Trim off the tips and stems and slice into rounds ¼ inch (6 mm) thick.

2. Heat the *ghee* or oil in a 10–12-inch (25–30 cm) nonstick frying pan over moderately high heat. When it is hot but not smoking, add the black mustard seeds and cumin seeds and fry until the mustard seeds turn gray and sputter and pop. Drop in the asafetida and immediately follow with the okra. Spread the okra into a single layer and reduce the heat to moderate. Stir in the turmeric, cayenne or paprika and coconut or almonds and cook for about 20 minutes, stirring occasionally to brown the okra evenly. You may want to add sprinkles of water if the okra dries out too much.

3. When the okra is golden brown and crusty, remove the pan from the heat, add the salt and cover for 1 minute before serving.

White Radish with Chopped Radish Greens
MOOLI SABJI

This typically North Indian radish dish is predominantly seasoned with whole cumin, corian- der and *ajwain* seeds, with a splash of lime juice and sweetener. In Kashmir the likely oil would be mustard; in the Punjab, peanut oil. The distinct appeal of the dish depends on the type of radish you use, as the varieties grown range enormously in pungency, color and size. Radishes, like beets, are at their best pulled fresh from the garden, so you will have to use fresh greens, which means a variety that is available locally—from pink-red round radishes to white icicles. If the commercially grown radishes where you shop come without the greens, fill in with a bunch of Swiss chard, spinach, mustard greens or kale. If you can find good *mooli* radish from Indian or Chinese greengrocers, by all means use it, the flavor is exceptional.

This dish goes well with *Griddle-Baked Village-Style Corn Bread*, *Deep-Fried Chenna Cheese Balls in Fragrant Tomato Gravy* and *Sprouted Mung Bean Salad with Water Chestnuts and Toasted Almonds*.

Preparation time (after assembling ingredients): 15 minutes
Cooking time: 15–20 minutes
Serves: 4

6 medium-sized white icicle radishes (about ½ pound/230 g),
    18–20 medium-sized round red radishes or
    4 medium-sized *mooli* or daikon radish
½ pound (230 g) radish greens, Swiss chard, spinach, or kale,
    washed, trimmed and chopped
1 teaspoon (5 ml) cumin seeds
½ tablespoon (7 ml) coriander seeds
¼ teaspoon (1 ml) *ajwain* seeds
3 tablespoons (45 ml) *ghee*, mustard or peanut oil
½ teaspoon (2 ml) turmeric
¼ teaspoon (1 ml) cayenne pepper or paprika
2 teaspoons (10 ml) maple or brown sugar
1 teaspoon (5 ml) salt
2 teaspoons (10 ml) fresh lime or lemon juice

1. Wash and trim the radishes, paring the long variety if necessary. Cut white radishes into ¼-inch (6 mm) dice; if using the round variety, thinly slice. Place the radishes in a steaming basket, lay the greens on top and steam for up to 15 minutes or until tender-crisp.

For information about unfamiliar ingredients or techniques, see A-to-Z

2. Combine the cumin, coriander and *ajwain* seeds in a small bowl. In a large heavy-bottomed nonstick pan, heat the *ghee* or oil over high heat. When it is hot but not smoking, (unless you are using mustard oil which you let smoke for a few seconds) add the spice seeds and fry until they darken a few shades. Seconds later, add the radishes and greens. Stir in the turmeric, cayenne or paprika and sweetener. Reduce the heat to moderate and fry for 4–5 minutes. Remove from the heat, add the salt and lime or lemon juice and toss to mix well.

Shredded White Radishes and Diced Potatoes
MOOLI ALOO SABJI

Lord Krishna's birthday—*Janamastami*—is celebrated on a grand scale in India. Taking advantage of the fall season, festivities are often outdoors, held in gigantic makeshift tents housing exhibits, theaters, food stalls and dining areas. In the central arena, guest speakers continue with nonstop discourses on the significance of the Lord's appearance. It is a joyous time for chanting, dancing and feasting.

Professional cooks are expert at setting up temporary kitchens or food stalls virtually *anywhere*, and almost every imaginable refreshment is available—from a glass of cold water or fried finger foods to full meals. This Bengali dish is from Sriman Ram Lal Dass, a relatively unknown, but none the less masterful vegetable chef.

With only one assistant to prepare vegetables, he made batch after batch of stir-fried vegetables, for hours on end. Prepared Bengali style, dishes were cooked over high heat, absorbing every drop of the cooking oil. Because the vegetables were cooked on an open fire, hints of smoky flavor accented the spice blends. This dish is best made with *mooli* radish, usually available at Asian and Chinese groceries; alternately use white daikon or icicle radishes.

Preparation time (after assembling ingredients): 10 minutes
Cooking time: 15 minutes
Serves: 5 or 6

2 tablespoons (30 ml) white poppy seeds
   (*khas khas*) or chopped almonds
1-inch (2.5 cm) piece fresh ginger root,
   scraped and coarsely chopped
2–3 hot green chilies (or as desired)
3 tablespoons (45 ml) coarsely chopped fresh
   coriander or parsley
⅛ teaspoon (0.5 ml) each ground
   cinnamon, cloves and nutmeg
⅓ cup (80 ml) water
½ teaspoon (2 ml) *kalonji*, if available
1 teaspoon (5 ml) cumin seeds
4 tablespoons (60 ml) *ghee*, mustard
   or vegetable oil
¼ teaspoon (1 ml) yellow asafetida powder (*hing*)*
3 medium-sized potatoes (about 1 pound/455 g),
   peeled and cut into ¼-inch (6 mm) dice
2½ cups (600 ml) shredded white radish
   (about 8 ounces/230 g)
1 teaspoon (5 ml) turmeric
2 teaspoons (10 ml) ground coriander
1¼ teaspoons (6 ml) salt
2 teaspoons (10 ml) lime or lemon juice

This amount applies only to yellow Cobra brand. Reduce any other asafetida by three-fourths.

   1. Combine the poppy seeds or almonds, ginger, chilies, 1 tablespoon (15 ml) of the herb and the ground spices with the water in a blender and process until smooth. Transfer to a small dish. Combine the *kalonji* and cumin seeds in a small dish.
   2. Heat the *ghee* or oil in a heavy-bottomed 5-quart/liter nonstick pan over high heat. When it is hot but not smoking (unless you are using mustard oil—let it smoke for a few seconds), add the *kalonji* and cumin seeds and fry until the cumin seeds darken a few shades. Immediately add the asafetida and then the potatoes, and stir-fry for 1–2 minutes. Follow with the radishes and poppy seed–spice blend and cook quickly for 2–3 minutes. Reduce the heat slightly and add the turmeric and coriander. Cook over moderately high heat, stirring almost constantly, until the potatoes are just tender. (Depending on the thickness of your pan and the source, sprinkle the vegetables with water to prevent sticking and scorching.) Before serving, fold in the remaining fresh herb, salt and lime or lemon juice.

Spiced Green Beans
MASALA BARBATTI SABJI

Here is a simple yet delicious way to cook green beans Marawadi style. If you are a gardener, try growing Thompson and Morgan's thin, long asparagus beans; they most resemble the type used in India. Beans are sweet and tender only when harvested immature and full of sugar. They are best cooked within hours after being picked, as are peas. If you are supermarket shopping, try to get locally grown, vividly green beans that break with a snap. Some strains of beans still have strings down the side of the pods, which should be pulled off. To complement this vegetable, try *Savory Mashed Yam Patties* with *Chickpea, Almond, Sesame Sauce, Bottle Gourd and Green Peas Cooked in Tomato Broth* and *Buttered Steamed Rice*. For a more elaborate meal, add *Crispy-Fried Eggplant Slices* and salad, and finish with *Rainbow-Layered Cheese Fudge Bars*.

Preparation time (after assembling ingredients): 10 minutes
Cooking time: 15 minutes
Serves: 4 or 5

4 tablespoons (60 ml) *ghee* or a mixture of light oil and unsalted butter
2 teaspoons (10 ml) black mustard seeds
1 teaspoon (5 ml) cumin seeds
¼–½ teaspoon (1–2 ml) crushed dried chilies
1 pound (455 g) green beans, trimmed and cut into ¼-inch (6 mm) pieces
½ cup (120 ml) water
1 teaspoon (5 ml) ground coriander
1 teaspoons (5 ml) salt
1 teaspoon (5 ml) sugar

1. Heat the *ghee* or oil-butter mixture in a large heavy-bottomed frying pan over moderate heat. When it is hot but not smoking, add the mustard seeds, cumin seeds and chilies and fry until the cumin seeds darken and the mustard seeds pop and turn gray. Add the beans and stir-fry for 2–3 minutes. Pour in the water, cover tightly and cook for 10–12 minutes or until the beans are tender-crisp.

2. Uncover, raise the heat and add the remaining ingredients. Raise the heat and boil until the water evaporates and the beans sizzle in the seasoned *ghee* or oil.

Green Beans in Yogurt–Poppy Seed Sauce
BARBATTI TARI SABJI

These beans can be cooked quite some time before needed and the final cooking completed just before serving. They are warmed in a velvety yogurt sauce made rich with puréed white poppy seeds or cashews. This nutmeg-laced sauce is as delicious as it is nutritious. For a light but elegant meal, accompany it with *Paper-Thin Dosa Stuffed with Herbed Potatoes* and *Delicious Chickpea Chutney*. I have also served this dish at room temperature or chilled as a salad on a bed of greens. If you want some crunch, blanched jicama slices are a delicious addition.

Preparation time (after assembling ingredients): 10 minutes
Cooking time: 5 minutes
Serves: 4 or 5

3 tablespoons (45 ml) white poppy seeds or chopped cashews
2 hot green chilies (or as desired)
½-inch (1.5 cm) piece of fresh ginger root, scraped and coarsely chopped
½ teaspoon (2 ml) cumin seeds
¼ cup (60 ml) coarsely chopped fresh coriander or parsley
¾ cup (180 ml) plain yogurt
1 pound (455 g) green beans, trimmed, cut into 3-inch (7.5 cm) pieces and
    steamed until tender- crisp
3 tablespoons (45 ml) *ghee* or unsalted butter
6 curry leaves, preferably fresh, or ½ cassia or bay leaf
1 teaspoon (5 ml) salt
¼ teaspoon (1 ml) freshly ground nutmeg

1. Put the poppy seeds or cashews in a food processor or blender, cover and pulse until powdered. Add the chilies, ginger, cumin, half of the fresh herb and the yogurt. Process until creamy smooth, then combine with the green beans in a bowl and toss well.

2. To assemble the dish, heat the *ghee* or butter in a large heavy-bottomed frying pan over moderate heat. Drop in the curry leaves or bay leaf and let sizzle for a few seconds. Pour in the beans and sauce, salt and nutmeg. Stir-fry until the sauce thickens, either slightly or until almost dry. Serve with the remaining herb, piping hot, at room temperature or chilled.

Green Beans with Crunchy Fried Mung *Badis*
BARBATTI BADI SABJI

Unless you've been to South India, it is unlikely that you have had a chance to taste this wonderful dish—it is not Indian-restaurant food, but home-style Madrasi cooking at its best. I first had it with freshly steamed *arhar dal badi*. More often mung *dal* or spicy *urad dal badis* are used to bring out the flavor of the fresh green beans. This combination is sure to win you raves and recipe requests. What are *badis*? In a word, dehydrated bits of seasoned *dal* paste. Nine times out of ten they are browned before they are added to a dish. Depending on the heat and spice blend already in *badis*, your finished vegetable will have varied personalities. Once you try *badis*, you'll likely be hooked and use them everywhere—from soups and pilafs to salads and stuffings. Also called *warian*, they can be purchased ready-made in Indian grocery stores. Or you can try making them at home, using the recipes starting on page 522.

You can serve this dish with either a pilaf, such as *Rice with Stuffed Baby Eggplants*, or a flatbread such as *Griddle-Baked Whole Wheat Bread* or *Deep-Fried Sesame Whole Wheat Bread*. *Mung Dal Soup with Tomatoes* and *Chickpeas and Potato Cubes in Creamy Coconut Sauce* are *dal* possibilities. For a nutritious and not too sweet ending, try elegant *Almond Cheese Fudge Delights*.

For information about unfamiliar ingredients or techniques, see A-to-Z

Preparation time (after assembling ingredients): 5 minutes
Cooking time: 15–20 minutes
Serves: 4 or 5

¾ cup (65 g) dried *moong dal badis*
4 tablespoons (60 ml) *ghee* or unsalted butter
1 pound (455 g) green beans, trimmed and cut
    into ¼-inch (6 mm) pieces
½ teaspoon (2 ml) turmeric
⅛ teaspoon (0.5 ml) freshly ground pepper
1 teaspoon (5 ml) salt
2 tablespoons (30 ml) minced fresh parsley
    or coarsely chopped coriander
¾ cup (180 ml) water
1 teaspoon (5 ml) crushed dry-roasted cumin seeds
1 tablespoon (15 ml) lemon juice

   1. Some ready made *badis* are already pea-sized; if yours are larger, place them in a mortar or bowl and crack into pea-sized bits with a heavy pestle or kitchen mallet. Gather up all the bits and pieces and transfer to a bowl.

   2. Heat the *ghee* or butter in a heavy saucepan over moderate heat. When just hot, drop in the *badis* and stir-fry until they turn reddish-brown. Add the beans, turmeric, pepper, salt, half of the herb and the water. Reduce the heat to low, cover and cook for 8–10 minutes or until the beans are tender.

   3. Uncover, add the crushed cumin, raise the heat and boil away all the remaining liquid, shaking the pan to prevent sticking. Before serving, sprinkle with the remaining herb and the lemon juice.

Green Beans with Coconut
BARBATTI NARIYAL SABJI

   There are innumerable popular green bean and coconut variations in Hyderabad's Vaishnava kitchens, this one from the home of S.K. Sethi. The contrast of bright green beans against snow-white coconut speckled with black mustard seeds and reddish *urad dal* makes this an attractive yet simple dish. For extra protein, if you do not have *urad dal*, use 3 tablespoons (45 ml) of chopped peanuts. You can steam the beans ahead of time and assemble the dish just prior to serving. For a nutritious lunch, serve with *Easy Rice and Split Pea Khichari with Fried Cashews* and *Tomatoes in Smooth Yogurt*. If you are having guests, add *Spicy Matchstick Potatoes*.

Preparation time (after assembling ingredients): 5 minutes
Cooking time: 10 minutes
Serves: 4 or 5

1 tablespoon (15 ml) each *chana dal* and raw rice
2 minced seeded hot green chilies (or as desired)
3 tablespoons (45 ml) water
5 tablespoons (75 ml) *ghee* or sesame oil
1 tablespoon (15 ml) split *urad dal* or 3 tablespoons
    (45 ml) chopped peanuts or almonds
1 teaspoon (5 ml) black mustard seeds
8–10 curry leaves, if available
¼ teaspoon (1 ml) yellow asafetida powder (*hing*)*
1 pound (455 g) green beans, trimmed and cut into ¼-inch (6 mm)
    pieces and steamed until nearly tender
1 teaspoon (5 ml) salt
⅛ teaspoon (0.5 ml) freshly ground black pepper
1 cup (85 g) grated fresh or defrosted frozen coconut (140 g)
3 tablespoons (45 ml) chopped fresh dill, fennel or coriander

This amount applies only to yellow Cobra brand. Reduce any other asafetida by three-fourths.

1. Grind the *dal* and rice in a spice mill until powdered. Transfer to a bowl and stir in the green chilies and water. Mix well. Heat the *ghee* or oil in a large heavy-bottomed nonstick frying pan over moderate heat. When it is hot but not smoking, add the *urad dal*, peanuts or almonds and fry for 15 seconds or until they begin to turn light brown. Follow with the mustard seeds and fry until they turn gray and pop. Drop in the curry leaves and asafetida and seconds later, pour in the *dal*-rice mixture. Cook until the mixture is dry, then follow with the green beans, salt and pepper. Sauté, shaking the pan, until the beans are heated through, adding the coconut and fresh herb at the last moment. Toss to mix.

Green Beans with Water Chestnuts
BARBATTI SINGHARA SABJI

The water chestnut is a floating water plant growing in lakes and ponds on several continents. The fruits are angular, with brown skins and a white, floury nut inside—refreshingly crisp and delicious. There are several kinds. *Singhara* nuts, grown in the lakes of Kashmir, are eaten as snacks or blanched, sliced, dried and ground into flour. Chinese water chestnuts, or *pi-tsi*, are not really nuts, but tubers, deriving their name from their resemblance to the water chestnut. They are available in small cans, sliced or whole, in supermarkets. The South American tuber called jicama is a readily available fresh substitute for canned water chestnuts. Use whichever kind you can find easily. To prepare fresh water chestnuts, cut with a sharp knife from the crown to the base and peel away the soft, brownish casing. Blanch, slice and soak in water until used.

This appealing vegetable dish goes with almost anything. I love it with *Lacy Semolina Dosa with Cumin Seeds and Bell Peppers* or *Herbed Mung Dal Cheela* with *Creamy Fresh Coconut Chutney*. Add *Sweet Potato Salad in Maple-Lemon Vinaigrette*.

For information about unfamiliar ingredients or techniques, see A-to-Z

Preparation time (after assembling ingredients): 5 minutes
Cooking time: 10 minutes
Serves: 4–6

1 teaspoon (5 ml) black mustard seeds
3 tablespoons (45 ml) melted *ghee* or unsalted butter
1-inch (2.5 cm) piece of fresh ginger root, scraped
    and cut into thin julienne
1 pound (455 g) green beans, trimmed, cut into ½-inch
    (1.5 cm) lengths and steamed until tender-crisp
¼ teaspoon (1 ml) paprika or cayenne pepper
1 teaspoon (5 ml) ground coriander
12 water chestnuts, peeled and sliced; or
    1 small jicama, peeled, trimmed and
    cut into pieces about 1 inch (2.5 cm)
    square by ⅛ inch (3 mm) thick; or
    one 10-ounce (285 g) can of sliced
    water chestnuts, drained and rinsed
2 tablespoons (30 ml) fresh lime juice
1 teaspoon (5 ml) salt
2 tablespoons (30 ml) chopped fresh coriander, basil or parsley

Preheat a large heavy-bottomed frying pan over moderate heat. Drop in the mustard seeds, and when they begin to pop add the melted *ghee* or butter. Drop in the ginger, green beans, paprika or cayenne, ground coriander and water chestnuts or jicama, and sauté until the green beans and water chestnuts are heated through. Add the lime juice, salt and fresh herb at the last moment.

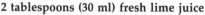

Crusty Potatoes with White Poppy Seeds
MASALA ALOO

Because these steamed potatoes are marinated in seasoned yogurt before they are browned, aromatic flavors seem to permeate every bite. The combination of potatoes and white poppy seeds is typical in Bengali cuisine. I have taken the liberty of suggesting almonds as a substitute for white poppy seeds, though they would not be used in the traditional Bengali recipe. The soaking and marinating time is not actual kitchen time, and the preparation requires very little time. This vegetable is almost always accompanied by a deep-fried bread, such as *Deep-Fried Seasoned Whole Wheat Bread* or *Deep-Fried Leavened Bread*. For entertaining you could add a mixed green salad, *Clear Soup with Spinach and Rice* and *Eggplant Fritters*. For a sweet, try *Glazed Flower Blossom Pastries*.

Poppy seed soaking time: 3 hours to overnight
Preparation time: 5 minutes
Marinating time: 1–3 hours
Cooking time: 10–15 minutes
Serves: 4–6

⅓ cup (45 g) white poppy seeds, cleaned, rinsed and soaked in water for 3 hours to overnight, or
    ⅓ cup (40 g) chopped almonds
2 hot green chilies (or as desired)
1-inch (2.5 cm) piece of fresh ginger root, scraped and cut into chunks
generous ¼ teaspoon (1 ml) cardamom seeds
3 tablespoons (45 ml) coarsely chopped fresh coriander
2 tablespoons (30 ml) grated fresh or dried coconut
¾ cup (180 ml) plain yogurt
10 medium-sized new potatoes (1½ pounds/685 g), peeled,
    steamed and cut into 1-inch (2.5 cm) cubes
4 tablespoons (60 ml) *ghee* or vegetable oil
½ tablespoon (7 ml) cumin seeds
¼ teaspoon (1 ml) *kalonji*, if available
1-inch (2.5 cm) piece of cinnamon stick
½ cassia or bay leaf
½ teaspoon (2 ml) turmeric
1 teaspoon (5 ml) salt
2 tablespoons (30 ml) lemon or lime juice

1. Drain the poppy seeds. Combine the poppy seeds or almonds, green chilies, ginger, cardamom, coriander, coconut and yogurt in a blender or food processor, cover and process until smooth. Mix the seasoned yogurt with the potatoes, cover and refrigerate for 1–3 hours.

2. Heat the *ghee* or oil in a large nonstick frying pan or wok over moderately high heat. When it is hot but not smoking, drop in the cumin seeds, *kalonji*, cinnamon stick and cassia or bay leaf and cook until the cumin seeds darken a few shades. Add the potatoes, turmeric and salt and toss.

Reduce the heat to moderate and cook until the potatoes dry and have a crusty golden surface. Sprinkle with lemon or lime juice before serving.

Cubed Potatoes with Fresh Fenugreek
KHATTE ALOO METHI

This everyday vegetable is popular throughout North and Central India. Earth-specked new potatoes—no bigger than marbles—and fresh fenugreek greens are sold in vegetable bazaars from Amritsar to Benares. New potato skins rub away easily during washing, and what little remains is paper thin and negligable. Fresh fenugreek greens vary from source to source—and no matter what the leaf size, be sure to trim off thick stems—they tend to toughen when cooked. The flavor from young leaves is pleasingly bitter, something like the nippy heat from sprouted mustard or cress, and are quite effortless to grow in a kitchen or windowsill herb garden. Fenugreek is usually available fresh at Indian groceries and is always available dried though the packages usually contain more stems than leaves. If you can't get the fresh greens, substitute spinach and add a pinch of powdered roasted fenugreek seeds for flavor. For variation, try the dish using different oils—*ghee*, mustard oil or peanut oil. All three are surprisingly different and tasty.

For information about unfamiliar ingredients or techniques, see A-to-Z

This potato dish goes well with any flat bread—in the winter you might try it with *Griddle-Baked Chenna Whole Wheat Bread*, and in the summer, *Griddle-Baked Yogurt Whole Wheat Bread*. Add *dal* and a salad and you have a well balanced meal. If you serve the dish for company, add a savory, chutney and sweet—say *Corn Kachori*, a touch of *Apricot Chutney with Currants* and *Honeycomb Coconut Candy*.

Preparation time (after assembling ingredients): 15 minutes
Cooking time: 15–20 minutes
Serves: 5 or 6

1½ pounds (685 g) medium-sized waxy red
    new potatoes or walnut-sized baby reds
5 tablespoons (75 ml) mustard oil,
    peanut oil or *ghee*
1 teaspoon (5 ml) cumin seeds
1 teaspoon (5 ml) black mustard seeds
1½ cups (360 ml) chopped fenugreek greens
    or leaf spinach, (washed and trimmed)
¼ teaspoon (1 ml) paprika or cayenne pepper
½ teaspoon (2 ml) turmeric
1 teaspoon (5 ml) salt
1 teaspoon (5 ml) *garam masala*
2 teaspoons (10 ml) lemon or lime juice

1. Wash the potatoes and boil them in their skins until they are just fork-tender. Do not overcook. Drain them and spread out to cool. Peel and cut into ¾-inch (2 cm) cubes.

2. Heat the oil or *ghee* in a heavy 12-inch (30 cm) nonstick frying pan. Let mustard oil reach the smoking point. Sauté the potatoes quickly until they begin to brown, then remove with a slotted spoon and set aside.

3. Add the cumin and mustard seeds to the hot oil and fry until the mustard seeds turn gray and sputter. Stir in the fenugreek greens or spinach, paprika or cayenne, turmeric and a sprinkle of water, cover and reduce the heat to moderately low. Cook for 8–10 minutes, then add the potatoes, salt and *garam masala*. Shake the pan or gently toss to mix, cover and cook until the potatoes are heated through. Sprinkle with lemon or lime juice before serving.

Baby Potatoes with Seasoned Tomato Sauce
ALOO TAMATAR SABJI

If you have a garden and can pull up really small marble-sized waxy-red potatoes, you have the perfect choice for this dish—the delicate skins almost float off during scrubbing. If you use larger new potatoes, red or white, cook them whole and slip off the skins when cool. Once cooked, the potatoes are warmed in an indescribably delicious fresh tomato sauce. Both the potatoes and sauce can be prepared ahead of time, and the dish assembled minutes before it is needed. These potatoes really need to be served with a bread—*Griddle-Baked Freshly Ground Wheat Berry Bread* or *Deep-Fried Seasoned Whole Wheat Bread* are great if you have the time. They go equally well with whole grain toast for a breakfast or brunch.

Preparation time (after assembling ingredients): 10 minutes
Cooking time: 15–20 minutes
Serves: 4 or 5

1½ pounds (685 g) waxy new potatoes, no
    more than 2 inches (5 cm) in diameter
3–4 whole cloves
6–8 whole black peppercorns
2 teaspoons (10 ml) coriander seeds
1 teaspoon (5 ml) cumin seeds
½ teaspoon (2 ml) fennel seeds
1-inch (2.5 cm) piece fresh ginger root,
    peeled and coarsely chopped
2–3 hot green chilies (or as desired)
3 tablespoons (45 ml) coarsely chopped
    fresh coriander leaves or parsley
2–3 tablespoons (30-60 ml) water
4 tablespoons (60 ml) *ghee*, or 2
    tablespoons (30 ml) each vegetable
    oil and melted unsalted butter
1 teaspoon (5 ml) black mustard seeds
6–8 curry leaves, preferably fresh
1 cup (240 ml) tomatoes, peeled, seeded and
    coarsely chopped (about ¾ pound/340 g)
scant ½ teaspoon (2 ml) turmeric
1 teaspoon (5 ml) *garam masala*
½ teaspoon (2 ml) *chat masala*
½ tablespoon (7 ml) salt

1. Boil the potatoes in their skins just until fork tender. Cool and peel if necessary and cut into ½-inch (1.5 cm) pieces.

2. Place the cloves, peppercorns, coriander seeds, cumin seeds and fennel seeds in a mortar or spice mill and grind to a powder. Transfer to a blender, add the ginger, chilies, 1 tablespoon (15 ml) of the fresh herb and the water, and blend until smooth.

3. Heat the *ghee* or oil in a heavy 12-inch (30 cm) nonstick frying pan over moderately high heat. When it is hot but not smoking, add the black mustard seeds and fry until they pop and turn gray. (If you are using oil, add the butter now.) Drop in the curry leaves and in seconds follow with the tomatoes and turmeric. Reduce the heat and, stirring now and then, cook until the juices cook off and the *ghee* separates from the tomatoes. Add the potatoes, *garam masala*, *chat masala* and salt, gently stir, and cook, covered, until the potatoes are hot. (You may need to add sprinkles of water if you do not use a nonstick pan.) Sprinkle with the remaining fresh herb before serving.

For information about unfamiliar ingredients or techniques, see A-to-Z

Curried Potatoes with Eggplant

ALOO BAIGAN SABJI

This is an example of the third method of cooking vegetables described in the introduction to this chapter. Both vegetables are steamed until tender. The potatoes are briskly stir-fried in seasoned *ghee* and then coated, along with the eggplant, in a delicately spiced yogurt-coconut sauce. Besides having a lovely flavor, this dish is light because the eggplant is steamed rather than fried. As a luncheon vegetable entrée, it can be accompanied by plain rice or *Almond Rice with Mixed Vegetables, Tender Chickpeas in Golden Karhi Sauce, Buttery Spinach* and a green salad.

Preparation time (after assembling ingredients): 5 minutes
Cooking time: 15 minutes
Serves: 5 or 6

⅓ cup (80 ml) plain yogurt
½-inch (1.5 cm) piece of fresh ginger root, scraped and coarsely chopped
2 seeded hot green chilies, broken into bits (or as desired)
¼ cup (25 g) shredded fresh or dried coconut
½ teaspoon (2 ml) *garam masala*
4 tablespoons (60 ml) *ghee* or a mixture
    of vegetable oil and unsalted butter
1 teaspoon (5 ml) black mustard seeds
½ tablespoon (7 ml) cumin seeds
8–10 curry leaves, preferably fresh
¼ teaspoon (1 ml) yellow asafetida powder (*hing*)*
6 medium-sized boiling potatoes (about 2 pounds/1 kg), steamed
    until tender, peeled and cut into ¾-inch (2 cm) cubes
1 teaspoon (5 ml) turmeric
1 tablespoon (15 ml) ground coriander
1 small eggplant (8–10 ounces/230–285 g) cut into
    1-inch (2.5 cm) cubes and steamed until tender
1¼ teaspoons (6 ml) salt
3 tablespoons (45 ml) chopped fresh parsley or coriander
1 tablespoon (15 ml) fresh lemon juice

*This amount applies only to yellow Cobra brand. Reduce any other asafetida by three-fourths.

1. Combine the yogurt, ginger green chilies and coconut in a food processor or blender, cover and process until smooth. Add the *garam masala* and pulse for a few seconds. Set aside.

2. Heat the *ghee* or oil-butter mixture in a heavy 4–5-quart/liter saucepan or 12-inch (30 cm) nonstick frying pan over moderately high heat. When it is hot but not smoking, drop in the mustard and cumin seeds and fry until the mustard seeds sputter and the cumin seeds turn golden brown. Stir in the curry leaves and asafetida, and immediately follow with the potatoes. Stir-fry for 3–4 minutes, then pour in the seasoned yogurt, turmeric, ground coriander, eggplant, salt and half of the remaining fresh herb. Gently toss to mix.

3. Reduce the heat to moderate, then fry, turning the vegetables very gently until they are dry. Before serving, mix in the lemon juice and remaining fresh herbs.

Sesame Yogurt Potatoes

EKADASEE TIL ALOO BHAJI

In the Hindi language, *eka* means "eleventh" and *dasee* means "day". The eleventh day after each full moon and the eleventh day after each new moon are called *Ekadasee*. All Vaishnavas observe *Ekadasee* by minimizing physical needs and increasing spiritual practices. Many Vaishnavas fast the whole day, taking only water or fruits. For practicality, Srila Prabhupada recommended light meals consisting of nuts, root vegetables, seeds and milk products. This dry potato dish was frequently on his *Ekadasee* menu, as was another classic choice, *Crusty Potatoes with White Poppy Seeds*. Not only on *Ekadasee*, but at any time, these delicious potatoes make any meal superb, from breakfast to late supper. They are best made in a nonstick frying pan or a well-used cast-iron skillet.

Preparation time (after assembling ingredients): 10 minutes
Cooking time: 30–40 minutes
Serves: 6

6 medium-sized all-purpose potatoes (about 2 pounds/1 kg),
    peeled and cut into ½-inch (1.5 cm) cubes
½ cup (120 ml) plain yogurt, whisked until smooth
½ tablespoon (7 ml) scraped, finely shredded or minced fresh ginger root
¼ teaspoon (1 ml) cayenne pepper or paprika
5 tablespoons (75 ml) *ghee* or sesame oil
3 tablespoons (45 ml) sesame seeds
1 teaspoon (5 ml) black mustard seeds
½ tablespoon (7 ml) cumin seeds
½ tablespoon (7 ml) salt
1 tablespoon (15 ml) fresh lemon juice
2 tablespoons (30 ml) chopped fresh coriander or parsley

1. Boil or steam the potatoes until they are fork-tender. Drain them and place in a mixing bowl. Add the yogurt, ginger and cayenne or paprika, and gently fold to coat the potatoes with seasoned yogurt. Set aside for ½–3 hours.

2. Heat the *ghee* or oil in a heavy 10–12-inch (25–30 cm) frying pan over moderate heat. When it is hot but not smoking, drop in the sesame seeds, black mustard seeds and cumin seeds. When the seeds begin to pop, add the potatoes and salt and fry, stirring occasionally, for 3–5 minutes or until the potatoes begin to brown. Sprinkle with lemon juice and fresh herb before serving.

For information about unfamiliar ingredients or techniques, see A-to-Z

Summer Squash and Green Peas
LOUKI HARI MATAR SABJI

Any young, seedless summer squash—such as green or yellow zucchini, pattypan, bottle gourd or yellow crookneck—will yield good results. Recognizing quality in raw zucchini will make all the difference between a successful dish and a tasteless one. Zucchini should be small, 3–6 inches (7.5–15 cm) long, with a bright color, firm, crisp texture and paper-thin glossy skin. Cooked zucchini is sweet and tender with a fine, distinct yet delicate flavor all of its own. This dish goes well with almost any other vegetable.

Preparation and cooking time (after assembling ingredients): 15–20 minutes
Serves: 5 or 6

3 tablespoons (45 ml) *ghee* or 1½ tablespoons
    (22 ml) each vegetable oil and unsalted butter
2 hot green chilies, stemmed, seeded and cut
    lengthwise into slivers (or as desired)
1 teaspoon (5 ml) cumin seeds
8–10 small zucchini (about 1½ pounds/685 g)
    cut into ½-inch (1.5 cm) cubes
½ teaspoon (2 ml) turmeric
1 tablespoon (15 ml) ground coriander
1½ cups (360 ml) fresh peas (1½ pounds/685 g in pods or
    one 10-ounce (285 g) package of frozen baby peas, defrosted
3 tablespoons (45 ml) chopped fresh coriander, parsley or mint
1 teaspoon (5 ml) salt

1. Heat the *ghee* or oil in a heavy 2–3-quart/liter nonstick saucepan over moderate heat. Add the chilies and cumin seeds and fry until they begin to darken. Stir in the zucchini, turmeric, ground coriander, fresh peas, half of the fresh herb, and the butter (if you used vegetable oil). Cover and cook for 10 minutes, stirring occasionally.

2. Uncover and sauté until the squash softens. If you are using frozen peas, add them 1–2 minutes before serving. Add the salt and the remaining fresh herb, gently stir and serve.

Red Bell Peppers with Roasted Chickpea Flour
SIMLA MIRCH SABJI

This dish is usually made with green bell peppers in North India, but I find American red or yellow more flavorsome. For real contrast you could use one of each color. Toasted chickpea flour binds the dish together with an elusive, nutty flavor. Serve with buttered rice, *Seasoned Potatoes in Smooth Yogurt* and *Panir and Spinach Salad with Walnut—Coriander Dressing*.

Preparation and cooking time (after assembling ingredients): 25–30 minutes
Serves: 5 or 6

½ cup (50 g) sifted chickpea flour (sift before measuring)
5 tablespoons (75 ml) *ghee* or mixture of vegetable oil and unsalted butter
¼ teaspoon (1 ml) paprika or cayenne pepper
¼ teaspoon (1 ml) yellow asafetida powder (*hing*)*
2 teaspoons (10 ml) coarsely crushed cumin seeds
3 large bell peppers (about 1¼ pounds/570 g) stemmed,
    seeded and cut lengthwise into thin strips
1 teaspoon (5 ml) salt
2 tablespoons (30 ml) chopped fresh coriander or minced parsley
2 tablespoons (30 ml) yogurt, at room temperature
¼ cup (60 ml) water

*This amount applies only to yellow Cobra brand. Reduce any other asafetida by three-fourths.

1. Place the chickpea flour in a heavy-bottomed 12-inch (30 cm) nonstick frying pan and dry-roast over moderately low heat until it darkens two or three shades. You must stir constantly with a spatula to keep the flour from burning. The kitchen will be filled with a nutty aroma. Transfer the flour to a bowl and set aside. Rinse the pan and dry it.

2. Heat the *ghee* or oil-butter mixture in the frying pan over moderate heat. When it is hot but not smoking, add the paprika or cayenne, asafetida and cumin seeds, and seconds later, drop in the peppers. Sauté until they are half-wilted but still have a touch of body, about 8 minutes. Reduce the heat to moderately low and add the salt, half of the fresh herb, and the yogurt and water. Stir well to mix and cook, gently tossing, for 2–3 minutes or until dry. Garnish with the remaining fresh herb. Remove the pan from the heat and let the dish rest for 2–3 minutes before serving.

MOIST VEGETABLES

Sautéed Brussels Sprouts with Coconut
CHAUNK GOBHI FOOGATH

Adapted from a recipe cooked by the residents of Udupi, in South India's Kanada district, this dish may be prepared with either *ghee* or coconut oil. In the fried seasoning, split *urad dal* is browned with spice seeds. Shop for baby Brussels sprouts, bright green and compact. If the sprouts are large, remove the tough outer leaves. If you want a creamy dish, fold in a spoonful of plain yogurt or sour cream just before serving.

Preparation time(after assembling ingredients): 30 minutes
Cooking time: 15–25 minutes
Serves: 4

1½ pounds (685 g) small Brussels sprouts
3 tablespoons (45 ml) *ghee* or coconut oil
1½ teaspoons (7 ml) black mustard seeds
2 teaspoons (10 ml) split *urad dal*, if available
8 curry leaves, preferably fresh
¼ teaspoon (1 ml) cayenne pepper or paprika
½ teaspoon (2 ml) *garam masala*
⅛ teaspoon (0.5 ml) freshly ground nutmeg
1 teaspoon (5 ml) salt
⅓ cup (35 g) shredded fresh coconut

1. Cut off the stem of the Brussels sprouts, along with any wilted, yellow or loose outer leaves. If the sprouts are large, remove the tough, outer leaves and use only the compact center. Cut a small cross in the base of each and soak in salted water for 15 minutes.

2. Drop the sprouts into a large pot of salted boiling water and cook, uncovered, for 5 minutes. Drain well. (These two steps can be done ahead of time.)

3. Heat the *ghee* or oil in a large frying pan over moderately high heat. When it is hot but not smoking, drop in the black mustard seeds and split *urad dal* and fry until the mustard seeds pop and turn gray and the *urad dal* turns reddish – brown. Add the curry leaves, Brussels sprouts, cayenne or paprika, *garam masala* and nutmeg. Sauté for 3–4 minutes, then cover and reduce the heat to low. Cook for 4–5 minutes longer if the sprouts are young, up to 10 minutes if they are old. When they are just tender, add the salt and coconut and gently toss.

Plantains in Seasoned Coconut Sauce
KACHA KELA FOOGATH

In tropical climates, many varieties of bananas are cultivated. Plantains are large cooking bananas, 9–12 inches (22–30 cm) long, with firm flesh and green skins. They have a higher starch and lower sugar content than yellow-skinned eating bananas and are baked, steamed or stir-fried as vegetables or deep-fried as wafers for snacks. When dried, plantains are ground into flour. The skins of ripe plantains turn black. This fragrant, crystallized ginger–flavored dish goes well with *Red Bell Pepper Uppma Stuffed Cabbage Leaves, Deep-Fried Fenugreek Whole Wheat Bread* and a small salad.

Preparation time (after assembling ingredients): 10 minutes
Cooking time: 40 minutes
Serves: 5 or 6

5 large ripe plantains
3 tablespoons (45 ml) melted *ghee* or butter
3 tablespoons (45 ml) chopped crystallized ginger
¼ cup (40 g) raw cashews
⅓ cup (35 g) grated fresh or dried coconut
¼ teaspoon (1 ml) cayenne pepper or paprika
½ teaspoon (2 ml) turmeric
2 teaspoons (10 ml) *jaggery* or brown sugar
½ cup (120 ml) plain yogurt or sour cream
½ tablespoon (7 ml) dry-roasted coarsely crushed cumin seeds
1¼ teaspoons (6 ml) salt
2 tablespoons (30 ml) coarsely chopped fresh coriander

1. Preheat the oven to 375°F (190°C). Cut off the ends of the plantains, peel, and cut in half crosswise, then lengthwise, and finally into 1-inch (2.5 cm) pieces. Place them on a large sheet of aluminum foil on a cookie sheet. Brush with 1 tablespoon (15 ml) of the melted *ghee* or butter and sprinkle with the crystallized ginger. Seal the foil and bake for 25–30 minutes or until tender.

2. While the plantains are baking, combine the cashews and coconut in a food processor or blender and process until ground. Add the cayenne or paprika, turmeric, sugar and yogurt or sour cream, and process briefly until smooth.

3. To finish the dish, heat the remaining 2 tablespoons (30 ml) of *ghee* or butter in a large nonstick frying pan over moderate heat. When it is hot, add the baked plantain. Toss gently, pour in the coconut mixture and heat thoroughly, but do not boil. Remove the pan from the heat and stir in the dry-roasted cumin seeds, salt and fresh coriander.

Curried Cabbage with Tender Whole Mung Beans
BANDHGOBHI MOONG TARKARI

This Bengali-style cabbage dish can be cooked in *ghee*, mustard oil or vegetable oil, yielding a sweet, pleasantly pungent or mild flavor. Mustard oil, unlike other oils, is always heated to the smoking point, to reduce its nose-tingling flavor. You can either cook the cabbage until it is quite tender or leave it bright green, with some crunch. You could also substitute 1½ cups (360 ml) of sprouted mung or aduki beans for the whole mung beans. Though it is not traditional, I have served this at room temperature, as a salad with sliced tomatoes. It is delicious hot, accompanied by hot flatbreads or rice and a soup.

Bean soaking and cooking time: about 2 hours
Preparation time (after assembling ingredients): 5 minutes
Cooking time: 15 minutes
Serves: 4 or 5

For information about unfamiliar ingredients or techniques, see A-to-Z

⅔ cup (135 g) whole green mung beans, sorted and cleaned
1 teaspoon (5 ml) cumin seeds
1 teaspoon (5 ml) black mustard seeds
2 hot green chilies, seeded and sliced lengthwise into slivers (or as desired)
1-inch (2.5 cm) piece fresh ginger root, scraped and cut into thin julienne
5 tablespoons (75 ml) *ghee*, mustard or vegetable oil
¼ teaspoon (1 ml) yellow asafetida powder (*hing*)*
10 curry leaves or 1 bay leaf
1 small green cabbage (about 1 pound/455 g), trimmed, cored and finely shredded
1 teaspoon (5 ml) turmeric
1 tablespoon (15 ml) ground coriander
1 teaspoon (5 ml) salt
2 teaspoons (10 ml) lemon juice
1 teaspoon (5 ml) maple syrup or honey

This amount applies only to yellow Cobra brand. Reduce any other asafetida by three-fourths.

1. To quick – cook the mung beans, wash well, then drop them into 2 quarts/liters of boiling water. Simmer over low heat for 2 minutes. Remove the pan from the heat, cover and set aside for 1 hour. Bring the water to a boil again and simmer for up to 1 hour or until just tender but not broken down. Drain the beans and set aside.

2. Combine the cumin seeds, black mustard seeds, green chilies and ginger in a small dish. Heat the *ghee* or oil in a wok or large, heavy casserole over moderately high heat (let the mustard oil reach the smoking point). When hot, drop in the spice-seed mixture and fry until the mustard seeds begin to sputter and pop. Immediately drop in the asafetida, curry leaves or bay leaf, cabbage, turmeric and coriander and cook, stirring frequently, for 10–20 minutes or until the cabbage is wilted, browned and crisp, or quite tender. The cooking time will depend on the size of your pan, the quantity of cabbage, heat intensity and the preferred degree of doneness.

3. In the last few minutes, add the beans, salt, lemon juice and sweetener. Serve piping hot or at room temperature.

Shredded Cabbage with Green Peas
BANDHGOBHI HARI MATAR TARKARI

In much of Northwest India, villagers still cook on open fires, and often in throwaway clay cooking pots. Because clay pots breathe, smoky flavors lend distinctive character to the finished dishes. This is especially noticeable in slowly cooked braised dishes. This dish was made that way by the priests of the Valmiki Ashram (Ramtirath) near Amritsar, and it is typical village fare.

This recipe combines cabbage and green peas in a glistening light tomato sauce—a dish that is rich in flavor, low-calorie and very economical. Try it with *Coconut Dosa Pancakes* offset with *Creamy Cashew Nut Chutney*. Include a crisp green salad with a light dressing.

Preparation and cooking time (after assembling ingredients): 45 minutes-1 hour
Serves: 5 or 6

¼ teaspoon (1 ml) caraway seeds
½ teaspoon (2 ml) coriander seeds
4–5 black peppercorns
3 whole cloves
1 teaspoon (5 ml) cardamom seeds
4 tablespoons (60 ml) *ghee* or unsalted butter
2 large tomatoes, peeled, seeded and chopped (1¼ pounds)
½ teaspoon (2 ml) turmeric
¼ teaspoon (1 ml) cayenne pepper or paprika
1 small cabbage (about 1 pound/455 g), cored,
    trimmed and shredded
1 cup (240 ml) fresh peas (1 pound/455 g in pods)
    or frozen baby peas, defrosted
2 tablespoons (30 ml) chopped fresh coriander or dill
1 teaspoon (5 ml) salt

1. Combine the caraway seeds, coriander seeds, peppercorns, cloves and cardamom seeds in a spice mill or mortar and grind to a powder. Set aside.

2. Heat the *ghee* or butter in a large, heavy casserole over moderately high heat. When it is hot, add the tomatoes, half of the powdered spices, and the turmeric and cayenne or paprika, and cook, stirring often, until the purée is reduced to a thick sauce. Add the cabbage and stir until it glistens. Cover and reduce the heat to low, or place in a preheated 325°F (160°C) oven, and cook for 15 minutes.

3 Add the fresh peas, stir and continue to cook for 15–30 minutes, stirring once or twice to check the liquid. If the dish becomes dry, add 2–3 tablespoons (30–45 ml) of water. Add frozen peas only in the last 2–3 minutes, along with the fresh herbs, salt and remaining powdered spices. Toss to mix.

Creamed Potatoes with Lemon Pepper
EKADASEE ROGAN ALOO

Root vegetables are popular on *Ekadasee* menus. This substantial variation is ideal for cold winter days, when everyone gravitates to the warmth of the kitchen. With *pooris*, hot rolls or toast, your family will likely find it a welcome change from Sunday hashbrowns. The potatoes can be half-cooked—either steamed or pan-fried the night before or early in the morning—and finished at mealtime.

Preparation time (after assembling ingredients): 10 minutes
Cooking time: 30 minutes
Serves: 6 to 8

For information about unfamiliar ingredients or techniques, see A-to-Z

12 small boiling potatoes (about 2 pounds/1 kg), peeled
5 tablespoons (75 ml) *ghee* or unsalted butter
½ bay or cassia leaf
3 whole cloves
¾ cup (180 ml) light cream or milk
½ teaspoon (2 ml) black lemon pepper
1 teaspoon (5 ml) freshly ground sea salt
2 tablespoons (30 ml) chopped fresh parsley or coriander
a sprinkle of paprika or cayenne pepper

1. Cut the potatoes into quarters and prick each piece in two or three places with the tip of a sharp paring knife or potato fork. Heat the *ghee* or butter in a large heavy-bottomed nonstick frying pan over moderate heat. Add the bay or cassia leaf and cloves and let them sizzle for several seconds. Add the potatoes and fry, stirring occasionally, until they are half-cooked and turning golden. Alternately, steam the potatoes, along with the bay or cassia leaf and cloves. (This can be done ahead of time.)

2. Pour in the cream or milk, reduce the heat slightly and cook, stirring now and then, until it has reduced by half into a thick sauce and the potatoes are fork – tender. Sprinkle with lemon pepper and salt. Remove the pan from the heat, cover and set aside for 1–2 minutes. Stir gently, remove the cloves and bay or cassia leaf, and serve piping hot sprinkled with the fresh herb and paprika or cayenne.

Gingered Chickpeas with Eggplant, Spinach and Tomato
KABLI CHANA BAIGAN TARKARI

This *mélange* of ingredients is as basic to North Indian cuisine as *ratatouille* is to *la cuisine provencale*, and every kitchen in North India has its own variation. It is a favorite for Sunday feasts, not only because it is easy to cook but because it is so delicious. It is always served with *pooris*. As with a braised stew, it may be left textured or cooked until the eggplant is almost puréed—cooked for as little as ½ hour or left in the oven for 2 hours. This dish goes splendidly with rice, *Gold Mung Dal soup, Creamed Potatoes with Lemon Pepper* and *Deep-Fried Chickpea Flour Pearls in Creamy Yogurt* and a mixed green salad. For adding a delightfully light and nutritious sweet, try *Orange Zest Cheena Balls in Orange Flower Syrup*.

Preparation and cooking time (after assembling ingredients): ½ hour-2 hours
Serves: 4 to 6

8 tablespoons (120 ml) *ghee*, or 6 tablespoons (90 ml)
    olive oil and 2 tablespoons (30 ml) vegetable oil
1 medium-sized eggplant (1–1¼ pounds/455–570 g),
    cut into 1-inch (2.5 cm) cubes
1½ tablespoons (22 ml) scraped, minced fresh ginger root
2 hot green chilies, stemmed, seeded and finely minced
½ tablespoon (7 ml) cumin seeds
¼ teaspoon (1 ml) yellow asafetida powder (*hing*)*
1½ cups (360 ml) peeled, seeded and chopped tomatoes
    (about 1 pound/455 g)
1 tablespoon (15 ml) ground coriander
1 teaspoon (5 ml) paprika
⅛ teaspoon (0.5 ml) each cayenne and black pepper
1 teaspoon (5 ml) turmeric
½ cup (120 ml) water
2 cups (480 ml) cooked chickpeas
1 pound (455 g) fresh spinach, washed, patted dry,
    trimmed and coarsely chopped, or one 10-ounce
    (285 g) package of frozen chopped spinach,
    defrosted and pressed dry
½ tablespoon (7 ml) salt
4 tablespoons (60 ml) chopped fresh coriander or parsley
1 teaspoon (5 ml) *garam masala*

This amount applies only to yellow Cobra brand. Reduce any other asafetida by three-fourths.

1. Heat 6 tablespoons (90 ml) of the *ghee* or olive oil in a large nonstick frying pan or wok over moderate heat. When it is hot but not smoking, add the eggplant and fry, stirring frequently, until it is browned and offers no resistance to the point of a knife. Remove with a slotted spoon and set aside.

2. Add the remaining 2 tablespoons (30 ml) of *ghee* or vegetable oil and raise the heat to moderately high. When it is hot but not smoking, add the ginger, chilies, and cumin seeds and fry until the seeds turn dark brown. Drop in the asafetida and seconds later the tomatoes. Stir well, then add the ground coriander, paprika, cayenne, black pepper and turmeric. Cook until the tomatoes are reduced to a sauce that separates from the oil (up to 10 minutes depending on the intensity of your heat).

3. Add the water and bring to a boil. Reduce the heat to low and add the eggplant, chickpeas, fresh spinach, salt and half of the the fresh herb. Cover and gently simmer, or bake in a preheated 325°F (160°C) oven, for about 30 minutes. If you are using frozen spinach, add during the the last 10 minutes of cooking. The dish is now cooked, but you could cook it for another 1½ hours if you want a sloppy joe consistency. Before serving, stir in the remaining fresh herb and the *garam masala*.

For information about unfamiliar ingredients or techniques, see A-to-Z

Sautéed Eggplant and Bell Pepper
BAIGAN SIMLA MIRCH TARKARI

This dish can be made with green, red or yellow bell peppers, all yielding wonderful flavor and color variations. The eggplant is steamed prior to its browning in seasoned *ghee*, a step that cuts calories to the minimum. Fresh *garam masala* puts a mark of distinction on the dish.

Preparation time (after assembling ingredients): 10 minutes
Cooking time: 15–20 minutes
Serves: 4 or 5

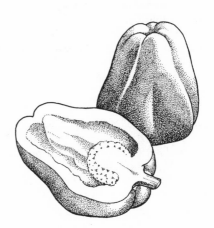

½ teaspoon (2 ml) caraway seeds
¼ teaspoon (1 ml) cardamom seeds
½-inch (1.5 cm) piece of cinnamon stick, crushed
½ teaspoon (2 ml) cumin seeds
½ tablespoon (7 ml) coriander seeds
3 whole cloves
6 black peppercorns
¼ teaspoon (1 ml) freshly ground nutmeg
3 tablespoons (45 ml) *ghee* or vegetable oil
1 teaspoon (5 ml) black mustard seeds
3 green, red or yellow bell peppers (about 1 pound/455 g),
    stemmed, seeded and cut lengthwise into thin strips
1 medium-sized eggplant (1–1¼ pounds/455–570 g) cut
    into ¾-inch (2 cm) cubes and steamed until tender
½ teaspoon (2 ml) turmeric
1¼ teaspoons (6 ml) salt
2 tablespoons (30 ml) chopped fresh coriander or parsley
¼ cup (60 ml) yogurt or sour cream, at room temperature (optional)

1. To make the *garam masala*, combine the caraway seeds, cardamom seeds, crushed cinnamon, cumin seeds, coriander seeds, cloves and peppercorns in a spice or coffee mill and grind to a powder. Add the nutmeg and blend well. Set aside.

2. Heat the *ghee* or oil in a large, heavy nonstick frying pan over moderately high heat. When it is hot, but not smoking, add the mustard seeds and fry until they sputter and turn gray. (You may want to use a lid or spatter screen to prevent the seeds from scattering on the stovetop.) Drop in the peppers and sauté until blistered and wilted (5–7 minutes). Remove and transfer to a plate.

3. Add the eggplant, freshly ground seasonings and turmeric to the pan, then, gently tossing, fry until slightly brown. Add the peppers, salt and fresh herb and toss to mix. If desired, fold in the yogurt or sour cream before serving.

Succulent Mixed Vegetables with Crunchy Fried *Badis*
SABJI BADI TARKARI

In India, every cook has a different conception of how to season this dish. Much depends on the type of dried *badi* used, and unless yours are homemade, you will have two ready-made choices: medium-hot serrano chili-laced *moong dal badi* or really hot and seasoned *urad dal badi*. Both types are available from Indian grocery stores. Let the seasonings in the *badi* control the end flavors in the dish. It should be zesty, but need not be volcanic to be authentic. This recipe is a blend of two Delhi kitchens, from a mother and her daughter. I have replaced two hard-to-find Indian squashes—round gourd (*tinda*) and bottle gourd (*louki*)—with pattypan and zucchini. Try this dish with *Griddle-Baked Chenna Whole Wheat Bread, Crusty Potatoes with White Poppy Seeds, Clear Soup with Spinach and Rice* and a green salad.

Preparation and cooking time (after assembling ingredients): 30 minutes
Serves: 5 or 6

2 tablespoons (30 ml) *ghee* or unsalted butter
½ cup (45 g) dried *moong dal badi* or 1½ (45 g) plum-sized
      urad dal badi, cracked into pea-sized bits
5 small zucchini (about ¾ pound/340 g), peeled
      and cut into ½-inch (1.5 cm) dice
4 small patty pan squash (about ¾ pound/340 g),
      peeled and cut into ½-inch (1.5 cm) dice
2 hot green chilies (or as desired)
½ cup (120 ml) fresh peas
4 whole cloves
½-inch (1.5 cm) piece of cinnamon stick
2 tablespoons (30 ml) chopped fresh mint
4 tablespoons (60 ml) coarsely chopped fresh coriander
⅔ cup (160 ml) half-and-half
1 teaspoon (5 ml) salt

1. Heat the *ghee* or butter in a heavy 3-quart/liter nonstick saucepan over moderate heat. When it is warm, add the *badis* and stir-fry until golden brown.
2. Add the remaining ingredients, except salt, turn the heat down to low, cover and cook for about 30 minutes or until the half-and-half has reduced and been absorbed into the vegetables. Stir gently, turning the vegetables to keep them from sticking. During the last 10 minutes of cooking, before serving, remove the whole green chilies and fold in the salt.

Butter Soft Zucchini and Tomatoes
LOUKI TAMATAR TARKARI

This recipe is an adaptation of a dish usually made with bottle gourd (*louki*) or round gourd (*tinda*). These squash are something like zucchini, only with tighter, firm flesh. Both are harvested immature, before seeds form. (The seeds are, however, as edible as those in zucchini.) In the Mediterranean, a type of bottle gourd is considered the best of all squash and preferred over baby zucchini. In America, bottle gourd and sometimes round gourd, are found at Chinese and Indian grocery stores. Do not bother to buy them if the skins are thick or if the squash are large or soft. Because varieties and names of Indian squash, marrow and gourds overlap from market to market, ask for *louki* or *tinda*. This dish is delicious using any young, soft squash—zucchini, pattypan or crookneck. Cooking times will vary considerably, for bottle gourd and round gourd take almost twice as long as zucchini and pattypan.

For a simple summer lunch, try it served with flatbreads—for example, *Griddle-Baked Paper-Thin Whole Wheat Bread*—or a pilaf such as *Sautéed Rice with Green Peas*. A *dal* dish such as *Curried Whole Mung Beans with Panir Cheese* or *Mung Dal Purée with Sliced White Radishes* would be a suitable accompaniment. For a salad, try *Carrot and Water Chestnut Salad* or *Papaya, Avocado and Jerusalem Artichoke Salad*.

Preparation time (after assembling ingredients): 5 minutes
Cooking time: 30–50 minutes
Serves: 4 to 6

2 seeded hot green chilies (or as desired)
¾-inch (2 cm) piece of fresh ginger root,
**   scraped and roughly chopped**
3 tablespoons (45 ml) cashews or almonds
1½ tablespoons (22 ml) coriander seeds
1 teaspoon (5 ml) cumin seeds
¼ teaspoon (1 ml) fennel seeds
¼ cup (60 ml) water
3 tablespoons (45 ml) *ghee* or unsalted butter
2 medium-sized tomatoes (about ¾ pound/340 g),
**   peeled, seeded and chopped**
1½ pounds (685 g) young squash, peeled
**   and cut into ¾-inch (2 cm) cubes**
½ teaspoon (2 ml) turmeric
1 teaspoon (5 ml) salt
3 tablespoons (45 ml) chopped fresh coriander, basil or parsley

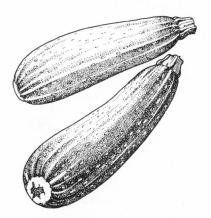

1. Combine the green chilies, ginger root, cashews or almonds, coriander seeds, cumin seeds, fennel seeds and water in a blender cover and process until smooth.

2. Heat the *ghee* or butter in a large heavy nonstick saucepan over moderate heat. Pour in the spice purée and fry until it thickens and separates from the *ghee*. Stir in the tomatoes and cook for a few minutes. Add the squash, turmeric, salt and half of the fresh herb, stir, cover and cook over low heat for 10 minutes. From time to time, stir and scrape the squash from the bottom of the pan to prevent sticking. If the squash is dry, add a little water. Cook until the squash is soft and succulent (20–40 minutes depending on the type you use). Before serving, sprinkle with the remaining fresh herb.

Garden Vegetable Stew with Crunchy Fried *Badis*
AVIYAL

In Tamil, *kuttu* means a combination, almost any *dal* and vegetable mixture. It is thicker than *sambar*, and much loved on festive menus. *Aviyal* is Kerala's version, thicker than *kuttu*, and made with or without *dal*. The vegetables are complemented by coconut, yogurt and, in this version, *dal badi*. If you live near a good Indian greengrocer, try some of South India's favorite vegetables—drumstick, plantain, colocasia, ash gourd, asparagus bean, tiny white eggplant and green mango.

Alternately, try *aviyal* with available local produce. Several vegetable combinations are possible. For the potatoes or carrots you can substitute parsnips or rutabagas; for the beans substitute fresh broad or lima beans; for the yam substitute sweet potato or firm-textured winter squash; and instead of the bell peppers, substitute snow peas, spinach or Swiss chard. No matter what vegetables you select, cut them so that they cook in the same amount of time. This should be a moist to semi dry stew, so the cooking time depends on the vegetables and your heat source.

The type of dried *dal* cakes you use will directly influence the flavor of the dish. Ready – made *urad* and *moong dal* cakes are almost always available at Indian grocery stores. Homemade dried *dal* cake recipes start on page 522.

This substantial vegetable dish can be served with either rice or flatbreads, such as *Steamed Chickpea Bread with Coconut Garnish* or *Coal-Baked Whole Wheat Bread Balls*. For a change from griddle-baked breads, try fried flatbreads. A special dessert could be a pastry and fruit combination, such as *Stuffed Pastries with Lemon Milk Glaze* and *Stuffed Dessert Grapes*, or *Sweet Rose-Flavored Crêpes with Fennel Seeds* and *Mango Fool*.

Preparation and cooking time: 30–45 minutes
Serves: 6

4 tablespoons (60 ml) coconut oil or *ghee*
2 dried *urad dal badis* (60 g) or ½ cup (45 g) dried
    moong dal badis , cracked into lima bean-sized bits
2 medium-sized boiling potatoes (about ½ pound/230 g),
    peeled and cut into ¾-inch (2 cm) cubes
2 medium-sized carrots (about 6 ounces/170 g),
    sliced ¼ inch (6 mm) thick
1 cup (240 ml) green beans (about 6 ounces/170 g),
    trimmed and cut into ½-inch (4 cm) pieces
1 medium-sized yam (about 6 ounces/170 g), peeled
    and cut into ¾-inch (1.5 cm) cubes
2–3 medium-sized zucchini (about ½ pound/230 g),
    sliced ¼ inch (6 mm) thick
1 small green, red or yellow bell pepper (about 4 ounces/115 g),
    stemmed, seeded and cut lengthwise into strips
½ cup (120 ml) fresh peas or frozen baby peas, defrosted
⅔ cup (160 ml) water
1 teaspoon (5 ml) turmeric
6–8 fresh curry leaves, if available
⅔ cup (60 g) shredded fresh coconut
½ cup (120 ml) plain yogurt
2 hot green chilies, seeded and minced (or as desired)
2 teaspoons (10 ml) salt

For information about unfamiliar ingredients or techniques, see A-to-Z

1. Heat the oil or *ghee* in a large heavy-bottomed, nonstick pan over moderate heat. Drop in the *dal badis* and stir-fry until they turn a nice reddish-brown.

2. Add all of the vegetables (if you are using defrosted peas, add them later), water, turmeric and curry leaves and bring to a boil. Reduce the heat to low, cover and simmer, stirring occasionally, for about 30 minutes or until the vegetables are fork-tender and have absorbed the liquid. If the dish becomes dry, add a little water.

3. Combine the coconut, yogurt and chilies in a dish and whisk until smooth. Add this mixture, along with the salt and defrosted peas, and gently stir to mix. Cover and set aside for a few minutes until the peas are warmed, then serve immediately.

Simple Potato and Green Pea Stew
ALOO HARI MATAR FOOGATH

This dish is popular throughout North India. If you use ¾ cup (180 ml) of water, the texture should be dry. If you want a stewlike consistency, add more water. This is an ideal accompaniment to steamed rice or flatbreads.

Preparation and cooking time: 30–40 minutes
Serves: 6

3 tablespoons (45 ml) *ghee* or vegetable oil
1 tablespoon (15 ml) scraped, finely shredded
    or minced fresh ginger root
2 hot green chilies, seeded and minced (or as desired)
½ tablespoon (7 ml) cumin seeds
1 teaspoon (5 ml) black mustard seeds
¼ teaspoon (1 ml) yellow asafetida powder (*hing*)*
8 curry leaves, preferably fresh
2 medium-sized tomatoes (about ¾ pound/340 g),
    peeled, seeded and chopped
1½ pounds (685 g) waxy new potatoes, peeled
    and cut into ¾ inch (2 cm) thick fingers
¾ teaspoon (3.5 ml) turmeric
1 tablespoon (15 ml) ground coriander
¾ -1½ cups (180–360 ml) water
1½ cups (360 ml) fresh peas (1½ pounds / 685 g in
    pods) or frozen baby peas, defrosted
1¼ teaspoons (6 ml) salt
3 tablespoons (45 ml) chopped fresh coriander or parsley

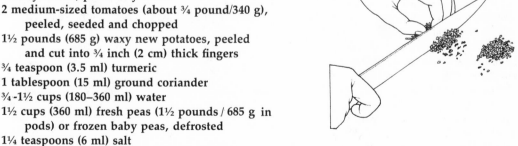

*This amount applies only to yellow Cobra brand. Reduce any other asafetida by three-fourths.

1. Heat the *ghee* or oil in a heavy-bottomed 5-quart/liter pan, preferably nonstick, over moderate heat. When it is hot but not smoking, add the ginger, chilies, cumin seeds and black mustard seeds and fry until the mustard seeds turn gray and pop. Immediately add the asafetida and curry leaves, and within seconds add the tomatoes. Fry for 2–3 minutes or until the *ghee* separates from the tomato purée.

2. Add the potatoes, turmeric, ground coriander and water and bring to a boil. Reduce the heat to moderately low, cover and cook for 15 minutes.

3. Add the fresh peas, salt and half of the fresh herb and continue cooking, partially covered, until the potatoes are soft but not broken down. If you are using frozen peas, add them in the last 2–3 minutes. Garnish with the remaining fresh herb and serve.

Sliced White Radishes with Golden Pumpkin
MOOLI KADDU FOOGATH

White cooking radishes (*mooli*) pleasantly contrast in color and taste with golden-red pumpkin. The flavor of radishes varies enormously, from the mild salad icicle type available in supermarkets to the slightly hot and pungent *mooli* sold in ethnic markets. Use whatever type is easily available, including Oriental *daikon*. When you fry fenugreek seeds in a seasoning, allow them to turn khaki-red but do not let them darken to deep brown, for at that stage flavor is excessively bitter. Quite amazingly, if you continue cooking the seeds until they blacken, they again lose their bitterness!

In Bengal, this dish might be accompanied by *Sesame Yogurt Potatoes*, *Fried Panir Cheese in Seasoned Tomato Sauce*, *Toasted Coconut Rice* and a tossed green salad served with *Savory Butter Crackers with Lemon*.

Preparation and cooking time: 30–40 minutes
Serves: 5 to 6

4 tablespoons (60 ml) *ghee* or corn oil
1 teaspoon (5 ml) scraped, finely shredded
  or minced fresh ginger root
1 teaspoon (5 ml) cumin seeds
½ teaspoon (2 ml) black mustard seeds
scant ½ teaspoon (2 ml) fenugreek seeds
8 curry leaves, preferably fresh
¼ teaspoon (1 ml) yellow asafetida powder (*hing*)*

For information about unfamiliar ingredients or techniques, see A-to-Z

2 cups (480 ml) ¼-inch (6 mm) thick sliced
    white radishes (about ¾ pound/340 g)
1½ pounds (685 g) peeled yellow pumpkin,
    Hubbard or butternut squash, peeled and
    cut into 1-inch (2.5 cm) cubes
½ cup (120 ml) fresh peas or frozen baby peas,
    (defrosted under hot water and drained)
¼ teaspoon (1 ml) cayenne pepper or paprika
1 teaspoon (5 ml) turmeric
2 teaspoons (10 ml) ground coriander
¼ cup (60 ml) water
½ teaspoon (2 ml) *amchoor* powder or
    2 tablespoons (30 ml) lemon juice
1 teaspoon (5 ml) salt
3 tablespoons (45 ml) coarsely chopped fresh
    coriander or minced parsley

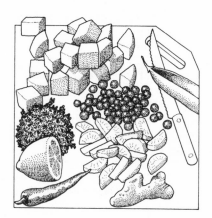

*This amount applies only to yellow Cobra brand. Reduce any other asafetida by three-fourths.

1. Heat the *ghee* or oil in a heavy-bottomed 5-quart/liter nonstick pan over moderately high heat until it is hot but not smoking. Add the ginger, cumin seeds, black mustard seeds and fenugreek seeds and fry until the fenugreek seeds darken to a golden red. Drop in the curry leaves and asafetida, and in seconds add the radishes. Sauté until they begin to brown, then stir in the pumpkin or squash, fresh peas, cayenne or paprika, turmeric, ground coriander and water. Cover, reduce the heat to low and cook until the pumpkin is fork-tender (anywhere from 20 to 30 minutes).

2. A few minutes before serving, fold in the *amchoor* or lemon juice, salt, fresh herb and frozen peas.

Julienne Potatoes and Whole Okra in Seasoned Cream Sauce
MASALA ALOO BHAJI

Dinatarine, my long-time friend and typist of the original cookbook manuscript, herself rarely cooks. One day, however, she offered this recipe as a contribution to the cookbook. It was tested and artistically presented in a two-compartment vegetable serving dish accompanied by the following recipes: *Buttered Steamed Rice, Lima Beans with Golden Raisins, Urad Dal Balls with Coriander Leaves* and *Sweet 'n' Sour Tamarind Sauce.*

Preparation and cooking time: 1 hour
Serves: 4 to 6

2 large baking potatoes (about 1 pound/455 g), peeled and cut
  into 2½ x ½-inch (6.5 x 1.5 cm) fingers
5 fresh mint sprigs
2 tablespoons (30 ml) unsalted butter
a few grinds of coarse salt and black pepper
⅔ cup (160 ml) cream or sour cream, slightly warmed
¼ teaspoon (1 ml) paprika
⅛ teaspoon (0.5 ml) yellow asafetida powder (*hing*)*
2 tablespoons (30 ml) minced pistachio nuts
1¼ teaspoons (6 ml) salt
3 tablespoons (45 ml) finely chopped fresh coriander or parsley
4 tablespoons (60 ml) *ghee* or a mixture of half
  unsalted butter and half vegetable oil
1 pound (455 g) okra, preferably small (3-inch/7.5 cm pods), trimmed
½ teaspoon (2 ml) turmeric
1 teaspoon (5 ml) *garam masala*

*This amount applies only to Cobra brand. Reduce any other asafetida by three-fourths.

1. Preheat the oven to 375°F (190°C). Place the cut potatoes on a large piece of aluminum foil on a cookie sheet. Nestle the mint sprigs among the potatoes, and dot the butter. Grind salt and pepper over the potatoes. Seal the foil tightly and bake for 45 minutes or until fork-tender.

2. Assemble the simple sauce, combining the cream or sour cream, paprika, asafetida, pistachios, ¼ teaspoon (1 ml) of the salt and the fresh herb in a bowl. Set aside.

3. While the potatoes are baking, heat the *ghee* or oil-butter mixture in a large frying pan over moderately high heat. When it is hot but not smoking, add the okra and spread it into a single layer. After a minute, reduce the heat to moderate and cook, tossing now and then, until the okra is fork-tender, anywhere from 20 to 35 minutes. When it is cooked, add the remaining 1 teaspoon (5 ml) salt, and the turmeric and *garam masala*, and toss well.

4. To serve, arrange the okra on one side of a serving tray and the potatoes, minus the mint, on the other side. Pour the sauce over both vegetables.

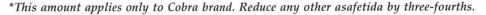

Lima Beans with Golden Raisins
SEM KISHMISH FOOGATH

Fresh lima beans are usually available as small "butter limas" or larger, as "potato limas." Shop for local produce—dark green pods, tightly closed and bulging with large beans. To free the beans from the pods, cut a strip along the inner edge of the pod, then with your thumbnail remove the beans. June, July and August yield the most profuse crops, yet at some specialty greengrocers the availability extends a month before and after. If you want to try this dish in the dead of winter, you can substitute frozen Fordhook limas. As the raisins plump, they impart a delicate sweetness to this dish. Serve this dish with *The Great Shallow-Fried Vine Leaf Rissole*, a dab of *Sour Cream Parsley Sauce*, and a tossed green salad .

For information about unfamiliar ingredients or techniques, see A-to-Z

Preparation and cooking time (after assembling ingredients): 30 minutes
Serves: 4

3 cups (710 ml) water
1½ cups (360 ml) fresh lima beans (about 2 pounds/1 kg in pods) or
    one 10-ounce (285 g) package of frozen Fordhook lima beans, defrosted
2 tablespoons (30 ml) *ghee*, unsalted butter or olive oil
¼ teaspoon (1 ml) paprika or ⅛ teaspoon (0.5 ml) cayenne pepper
¼ teaspoon (1 ml) ground mustard
¼ teaspoon (1 ml) turmeric
3 tablespoons (45 ml) golden raisins or currants
2 teaspoons (10 ml) *jaggery* or brown sugar (optional)
1½ tablespoons (22 ml) lime or lemon juice
½ teaspoon (2 ml) salt
1½ tablespoons (22 ml) finely chopped fresh coriander, dill or parsley
¼ cup (60 ml) water

1. Bring the 3 cups (710 ml) of water to a boil in a 3-quart/liter saucepan, preferably nonstick. Add the beans and cook over low heat for 10 minutes. Pour off the water.

2. Add the *ghee*, butter or oil and remaining ingredients (if you are using frozen beans, add at this stage). Simmer, partially covered, for 10–15 minutes or until the beans are tender. Uncover, raise the heat and reduce the remaining liquid to a glaze.

Note: Cooking times vary considerably depending on the size and freshness of the beans.

FRIED VEGETABLES

Crispy Deep-Fried Eggplant Slices
BAIGAN BHAJI

Though fried potatoes are welcome almost any time of day, fried eggplants are usually part of a meal, because they must be served just after they are fried. If they are held in a warmer, even for 10 minutes, the crispy crust softens and the overall effect is a soggy fritter. If you reuse the *ghee* or oil after frying, be sure to pass it through a fine filter to remove traces of flour; the inevitable residue would burn and shorten the life of the frying medium.

Preparation time (after assembling ingredients): ½ hour
Cooking time: 10 minutes
Serves: 6 to 8

1 medium-sized eggplant (1–1¼ pounds/455–570 g)
    cut crosswise into ¼-inch (6 mm) slices
salt
⅓ teaspoon (1.5 ml) paprika or cayenne pepper
whole wheat flour for dusting
ghee or vegetable oil for frying

1. Place the eggplant slices on a tray and sprinkle liberally with salt. Let them sit for at least ½ hour to draw out excess moisture. Rinse off the salt, then pat the slices dry with paper towels. Sprinkle the slices with paprika or cayenne.

2. Place a small quantity of flour in a plastic or paper bag and drop in as many eggplant slices as you will fry in a batch. Shake vigorously, then remove each piece, shake off the excess flour, and set on a plate.

3. Pour enough *ghee* or oil to measure 2–3 inches (5–7.5 cm) deep into a large, heavy deep-frying pan. Heat the oil to 375°F (190°C) and put in as many eggplant slices as will fit in a single layer. Fry each side until crisp and browned. Remove the slices with a slotted spatula and set aside on paper towels. Repeat for each batch.

Sweet 'n' Sour Eggplant

KHATTE BAIGAN BHAJI

This Bengali delicacy is not an everyday dish, but it is wonderful for company dinners and special occasions. Eggplant slices are fried, coated in a spicy glaze and finally broiled until warm and bubbly. Alternately, the fried vegetable can be served at room temperature, the glaze acting as a marinade.

Salting and preparation time: 30–40 minutes
Cooking time (after assembling ingredients): about 20 minutes
Serves: 5 or 6

1 large eggplant, (1½–2 pounds/685–900 g), cut lengthwise
    and then crosswise into 1-inch (2.5 cm) slices
salt
½ teaspoon (2 ml) cumin seeds
½ teaspoon (2 ml) black mustard seeds
½ teaspoon (2 ml) fennel seeds
¼ teaspoon (1 ml) fenugreek seeds
¼ teaspoon (1 ml) yellow asafetida powder (*hing*)*
¼ teaspoon (1 ml) cayenne pepper or paprika
¼ teaspoon (1 ml) *chat masala*, if available
3 tablespoons (45 ml) *jaggery*, maple syrup or brown sugar
3 tablespoons (45 ml) lemon juice
4 tablespoons (60 ml) water
ghee or vegetable oil for shallow-frying

This amount applies only to yellow Cobra brand. Reduce any other asafetida by three-fourths.

1. Place the eggplant slices on a tray and sprinkle them liberally with salt. Let them sit for ½ hour to draw out excess moisture.

2. Meanwhile, place the cumin, black mustard, fennel and fenugreek seeds in a small pan. Dry-roast over moderate heat until the seeds darken one or two shades. Transfer to a spice mill and grind to a powder. Transfer the powder to a small saucepan and add the asafetida, cayenne or paprika, *chat masala*, sugar, lemon juice and water. Bring to a boil, then simmer until the mixture is reduced to a shiny sauce. Set aside.

For information about unfamiliar ingredients or techniques, see A-to-Z

3. Rinse off the salt from the eggplant slices and pat dry with paper towels. Pour into a large heavy frying pan ½ inch (1.5 cm) *ghee* or oil and place over moderately high to high heat. When it is hot but not smoking, add as many eggplant pieces as will fit in a single layer. Fry on both sides until fork tender, reddish-brown and crisp. Remove with a slotted spoon and drain on paper towels. Fry the remaining eggplant, adding additional *ghee* or oil as necessary.

4. Place the fried eggplant in a single layer on a cookie sheet, brush or spoon on the sauce, and warm under the broiler just to let the flavors mingle. Serve hot.

Eggplant Fritters
KHASA BAIGAN BHAJI

These are more aptly called eggplant sandwich fritters. When I first served them to Srila Prabhupada, I had neither mozzarella cheese nor bread crumbs, so instead I used kneaded herbed *chenna* cheese patties and *iddli* crumbs blended with fine semolina. Much to my delight, he dubbed them "vegetable chops." These fritters can be served hot or at room temperature. For outdoor garden menus they can be served around a bowl of *Sour Cream Parsley Sauce* or *Velvet Tomato Catsup*. They also go well as an entrée for a late supper or afternoon tea.

Salting time: ½ hour
Preparation and cooking time: about 30 minutes
Serves: 4 to 6

1 large eggplant (about 2 pounds/1 kg), cut crosswise into ½-inch (1.5 cm) slices
salt
½ cup (50 g) chickpea flour (sifted before measuring)
3 tablespoons (45 ml) self-rising flour or whole wheat pastry
    flour mixed with a generous pinch of baking powder
2 tablespoons (30 ml) cornmeal
⅛ teaspoon (0.5 ml) cayenne pepper or paprika
¼ teaspoon (1 ml) turmeric
3 tablespoons (45 ml) finely chopped fresh coriander, basil or parsley
3 tablespoons (45 ml) water
6 ounces (170 g) mozzarella cheese, thinly sliced,
    or 6 ounces (170 g) kneaded *chenna* cheese (page 315)
1¼ cups (125 g) fresh or dry bread crumbs or ⅔ cup (115 g) fine semolina
ghee or vegetable oil for shallow-frying

1. Place the eggplant slices on a tray and sprinkle liberally with salt. Let them sit for at least ½ hour to draw out excess moisture.

2. Combine the flours, baking powder, cornmeal, cayenne or paprika, turmeric, fresh herb and ¼ teaspoon (1 ml) of salt with the water in a bowl and whisk into a smooth batter the consistency of thick cream. (You may have to add more water.)

3. Rinse the salt off the eggplant and pat the slices dry with paper towels. To obtain uniform rounds, cut out with biscuit rings about 2 inches (5 cm) in diameter. Pair eggplant slices of the same size, reserving the ends or trimmings for another use. Trim the cheese slices so they are slightly smaller than the eggplant rounds. Place 2 thin slices of cheese or a shaped *chenna* patty between a pair of eggplant slices. Dip the sandwich in the chickpea batter, lightly shake off the excess flour, then coat with bread crumbs or semolina and set aside on waxed paper. Make all of the eggplant sandwiches in this way.

4. Heat *ghee* or oil to a depth of ½ inch (1.5 cm) in a large heavy frying pan over moderate heat until it is hot but not smoking. Place the sandwiches in the pan and fry for 10–15 minutes on each side or until the eggplant is fork-tender and nicely browned. Adjust the heat carefully: if the temperature is too high, the cheese tends to burst through the batter–crumb casing; if it is too low, the fritters absorb excessive oil. Serve piping hot.

Butter Soft Eggplant Wedges
BHONA BAIGAN BHAJI

Srila Prabhupada gave us this recipe during his 1967 San Francisco cooking classes. In Bengal, *bhaji* is loosely defined as any fried vegetable, and while this variation has other names, such as Eggplant *Pukki*, one thing is constant: it must be served immediately after cooking, piping hot. To get authentic results, I recommend using fresh *ghee*; my second choice would be a newcomer on the market—avocado oil. It can be heated to a very high temperature without smoking, is very delicious, and one of the lowest of all unsaturated fats—actually helping to lower cholesterol in the blood. Olive oil would be the third choice. I like to use baby white or purple egglants, but large eggplants can be cut into wedges and used as well.

This dish is a natural with buttered rice, cracked wheat, buckwheat or mixed grain pilaf. You might also include *Tender-Crisp Sprouted Urad Beans in Sesame-Yogurt Sauce, Panir Cheese, Summer Squash and Red Bell Peppers*, a tossed green salad and fresh bread. For a sweet ending, try dainty *Pistachio Nut Milk Fudge* with a fresh fruit platter.

Salting time: 15–30 minutes
Preparation and Frying time: under 15 minutes
Serves: 6 to 8

1½ tablespoons (22 ml) turmeric
1½ tablespoons (22 ml) salt
3 tablespoons (45 ml) water
8–10 baby white or purple eggplants (about 1¼ pounds/570 g) or 1 medium-sized eggplant (about
    1¼ pound/570 g)
ghee or olive oil for frying

1. Combine the turmeric, salt and water in a bowl. Cut small eggplants in half, or cut larger ones into wedges roughly 2½ inches (6.5 cm) long and 1½ inches (4 cm) wide. Toss the eggplant with the turmeric-salt mixture and set aside for 15–30 minutes.

2. To remove the watery turmeric marinade, drain the eggplant in a paper towel-lined colander. Pour enough *ghee* or oil to reach a depth of ½ inch (1.5 cm) in a large heavy frying pan and place it over moderately high heat. When it is hot and nearly reaches its smoking point, carefully add a single layer of eggplant pieces. Fry, turning the pieces on all sides, until they assume a rich reddish-brown color and are fork-tender.

For information about unfamiliar ingredients or techniques, see A-to-Z

(The skin side of the eggplants requires less cooking time than do cut edges, and excessive frying tends to toughen them.) Remove the pieces and drain on paper towels. Serve at once, piping hot.

Cauliflower and Potato Surprise
GOBHI ALOO BHAJI

Although this was one of four cauliflower and potato vegetables served at a recipe testing banquet, it was unanimously voted the favorite. It is indeed popular throughout much of North India, this version a long-time secret from the Shashi Gupta family of Kurukshetra. I noticed that although undeniably rich, it is always one of the first to disappear at holiday dinners. I often use homemade yogurt, or good commercial yogurt like Brown Cow or Nancy's, instead of cream or sour cream. It is every bit as delicious and far less caloric.

For a gala menu, serve with *Herbed Rice with Panir Cheese and Zucchini* or *Lavish Rice and Mung Dal Bunchi Khichari* and *Deep-Fried Sweet Potato Whole Wheat Bread* or *Baked Flatbreads with Nigella Seeds*. For accompanying dishes, include *Green Beans with Water Chestnuts* and a salad. From the sweets department, try *Semolina and Chickpea Flour Halva with Almonds and Saffron*.

Preparation and cooking time (after assembling ingredients): 35 minutes
Serves: 5 or 6

2 large baking potatoes (about 1 pound/455 g) peeled
    and cut into rounds ¼-inch (6 mm) thick
ghee or vegetable oil for frying
1 medium-sized cauliflower (about 2 pounds/1 kg),
    trimmed and divided into flowerets
1 teaspoon (5 ml) dry-roasted coarsely crushed cumin seeds
¼ teaspoon (1 ml) fresh coarsely ground black pepper
⅛ teaspoon (0.5 ml) cayenne pepper or paprika
½ teaspoon (2 ml) turmeric
1 teaspoon (5 ml) salt
1 cup (240 ml) very fresh plain yogurt or sour cream, at room temperature
parsley sprigs for garnishing

1. Rinse the potatoes in cold water, rubbing the slices gently between your palms to remove surface starch. Pat the rounds dry with paper towels. This step is not essential, but helps to keep the potatoes white and prevents them from sticking together during frying.

2. Pour in enough *ghee* or vegetable oil to half fill a deep-frying vessel. Place over moderate heat and allow it to slowly reach 375°F (190°C). If you use a roomy wok or *karai*, you can fry all of the potatoes at once; if the pan is small, divide into two batches. Carefully add the potatoes and fry until golden brown (8–10 minutes). Remove the slices with a slotted spoon and drain on paper-towel-lined cookie sheets. Fry each batch of potatoes and cauliflower until tender and golden brown. (I keep the fried vegetables warm in a preheated oven.)

3. When all of the vegetables are fried and still warm, place them in a large bowl. Sprinkle with the cumin seeds, black pepper, cayenne or paprika, turmeric and salt. Gently toss the delicate vegetables to coat with the spices. Fold in the yogurt or sour cream, garnish with the parsley sprigs and serve piping hot.

Note: The yogurt or sour cream puts a glistening coat of sauce on the crisp vegetables, which must be served immediately. If the dish is kept warm or held before serving, the vegetables absorb the sauce and the dish becomes dry.

Double-Fried Potatoes
KHASA ALOO BHAJI

I remember watching my mother prepare *pommes soufflées* for an occasional dinner party. She began preparation in the morning and finished them off just before serving. I never expected to see the delicate operation in a New Delhi kitchen—but then, the Vijay Nagar household in Delhi possesses several excellent cooks. In this variation on a classic French dish, perhaps only 60 percent of your potatoes will fully puff, but the not-so-perfect rounds are more than acceptable and very delicious.

To make this dish, select mature, mealy varieties such as Idahos or Burbanks. To a certain degree, the finished result resembles soufléed potatoes. Before washing and drying, the potatoes are uniformly trimmed and sliced lengthwise on the grain. Then they are twice fried: the first time in 360°F (180°C) oil until cooked but not browned, and the second time in 375°F (190°C) oil until browned. Before the second frying, the soft potato rectangles are pressed into a seed mixture. Though this prevents many of the slices from puffing, it gives them a marvelous crunchy crust. Served piping hot, the potatoes are delicious sprinkled with lemon or lime juice, much in the same way that the British douse "chips" with vinegar.

Preparation time (after assembling ingredients): 25 minutes
Cooking time: about 30 minutes
Serves: 4

4 large mealy-type baking potatoes
    (about 2 pounds/1 kg), peeled
ghee or vegetable oil for frying
3 tablespoons (45 ml) sesame seeds
½ tablespoon (7 ml) each cumin seeds
    and coriander seeds, slightly crushed
½ teaspoon (2 ml) fennel seeds
½ teaspoon (2 ml) fine or herb salt
3 tablespoons (45 ml) lime or lemon juice (optional)

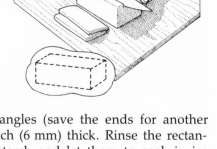

1. Cut the potatoes into the largest possible rectangles (save the ends for another use) and cut lengthwise, on the grain, into slices ¼ inch (6 mm) thick. Rinse the rectangular potato pieces in cold water to remove surface starch and let them to soak in ice cold water for at least 20 minutes. While they are soaking, combine the sesame seeds, cumin, coriander and fennel seeds in a shallow dish and mix. Set aside.

For information about unfamiliar ingredients or techniques, see A-to-Z

2. When you are ready to fry the potatoes, drain them and pat dry with paper towels. Half – fill your deep-frying vessel with *ghee* or oil and heat to 340°F (170°C) over moderate heat. Without crowding the pan, deep-fry the potatoes in small batches until they are blistered but not browned, about 6–7 minutes. Transfer to paper towels to drain, and fry the remaining potatoes. After they have cooled for at least 5 minutes, press each slice into the sesame seed mixture, and shake off loose seeds. (You can prepare the potatoes up to this stage and refrigerate, covered, for several hours. Before the second frying, bring them back to room temperature.)

3. Just before you are ready to serve the potatoes, heat the *ghee* or oil to 375°F (190°C) and fry the potatoes a second time until golden brown. Drain on a paper towel-lined cookie sheet to absorb excess oil. Salt and if desired, sprinkle with lime or lemon juice before serving.

Crisp 'n' Soft Mixed Vegetable Croquettes
EKADASEE ARBI ALOO BADA

This is a unique croquette dish, for it is neither bound with cream sauce nor breaded in crumbs, as are most. Instead, these croquettes are a combination of three starchy vegetables: potatoes, plantains and colocasia or *arbi*. They are cooked individually until soft, mashed or shredded, and blended with little more than salt, pepper, chilies and herbs. Don't let the simplicity fool you: these croquettes are nothing short of terrific. Very soft inside, with a thin, crisp deep-fried shell, they were a favorite of my spiritual master, Srila Prabhupada.

Known as *Ekadasee* croquettes, they are made without the addition of any form of grain. Fried carefully, the mixture is sufficiently starchy to remain intact, but if the temperature is either too high or low, the croquettes tend to disintegrate. To prevent this disaster, you may want to be on the safe side and bind the mixture with a generous spoon of arrowroot. No matter what your choice, do watch the frying temperature—it should not fall below 360°F (180°C) and avoid crowding the pan. For additional flavor, I like to place a pat of *Mint-Lime Butter* on them while they are piping hot. As the butter melts, the flavors are absorbed.

Preparation time (after assembling ingredients): 45 minutes
Cooking time: about 15 minutes
Serves: 6 or 7

¾ pound (340 g) colocasia corns (*arbi*), cut into 1-inch (2.5 cm) pieces
3 medium-sized waxy boiling potatoes (about ¾ pound/340 g), peeled
1 green plantain, about 10 inches (25 cm) long
1 teaspoon (5 ml) cracked black pepper
1 teaspoon (5 ml) salt
2 hot chilies, seeded and minced (or as desired)
1 tablespoon (15 ml) arrowroot (optional)
3 tablespoons (45 ml) chopped fresh coriander
ghee or oil for deep-frying

1. Boil the colocasia for 20–25 minutes or until fork-tender. If you have a tiered vegetable steamer, so much the better. You can cook all the vegetables simultaneously. Increase the cooking time by at least 15 minutes, then check to see if it is done every 5 minutes thereafter. Plunge then into cold water and peel off the starchy skins. Set aside to dry out.

2. Cut the potatoes into quarters and boil for 20–30 minutes or until fork-tender. Drain and set aside in a folded clean kitchen towel to dry out.

3. Cut the thick skin from the plantain, removing any fibers. Cut in half and boil for 25–30 minutes or until tender. Drain, and when cool enough to handle, shred through the coarse holes on a hand grater into a mixing bowl.

4. Mash together the colocasia and potatoes and add the plantain. Knead in the pepper, chilies, salt, arrowroot and coriander.

5. Wash your hands, rub them with a film of oil and divide the mixture into 14 even pieces. Roll, press and mold into smooth logs about 2 inches (5 cm) long or dough-nuts 2 inches (5 cm) in diameter and set aside on waxed paper.

6. Heat *ghee* or oil to a depth of at least 1½ inches (4 cm) in a deep-fryer until it reaches 370°F (190°C) on a frying thermometer. Add half of the croquettes, making sure not to crowd the pan, and fry until richly browned. Remove with a slotted spoon and drain on paper towels. Serve at once in a napkin-lined basket or fry the remaining batch and serve all together, piping hot.

Deep-Fried Julienne Potatoes and Carrots
ALOO GAJAR BHAJI

This is an easy dish for the kitchen with a good mandoline or a food processor. The peeled vegetables can be hand-cut across the julienne blade to yield perfectly uniform straws. Cuisinart has a blade that makes a reasonably fine julienne vegetables in seconds. Without a julienne blade, use a standard 3–4 mm slicing disk. Pre-cut the carrots and potatoes to fit horizontally into the feeding tube. Slice, then remove the slices and stack them, cut side up, in the feeding tube. Process again to yield fine julienne. This is not a main-dish vegetable but rather a little nibbler. Allow 3–4 tablespoons (45–60 ml) per serving.

Preparation time: 30 minutes by hand or 5 minutes with food processor
Soaking time: 30 minutes
Cooking time: about 15 minutes
Serves: 5 or 6

2 large carrots (about 6 ounces/170 g), peeled
2 medium-sized baking potatoes (about 12 ounces/340 g), peeled
ghee **or vegetable oil for deep-frying**
¼–½ teaspoon (1–2 ml) fine salt
¼ teaspoon (1 ml) cayenne pepper or paprika
1 tablespoon (15 ml) lemon juice

For information about unfamiliar ingredients or techniques, see A-to-Z

1. To cut the vegetables in a food processor, attach the fine julienne blade. Cut the carrots and potatoes into pieces 2½ inches (6.5 cm) long and load them horizontally in the processor chute. This will make 2½ inch (6.5 cm) long julienne.

To cut the vegetables by hand, first cut them lengthwise into slices about ⅛ inch (3 mm) wide. Then cut them crosswise into pieces 2½ inches (6.5 cm) long. Try to make all the pieces uniform in size so that they will take the same time to cook.

2. Soak the cut vegetables in separate bowls of ice water for 30 minutes. Pat thoroughly dry with paper towels.

3. Pour enough *ghee* or oil into a frying vessel to fill it to a depth of 2 inches (5 cm). Place the pan over moderately high heat until the temperature reaches 370°F (190°C) on a deep-frying thermometer. Fry a small handful of julienne carrots until golden brown and crisp. Remove with a slotted spoon and drain on paper towels. In batches, fry all of the carrots and potatoes.

4. Place the crisp straws in a bowl and sprinkle in the salt, cayenne or paprika and lemon juice and serve immediately. The vegetables will soften as they cool. Do not cover.

Deep-Fried Shredded Plantain Clusters
KHASA KACHA KELA BHAJI

These little finger foods work well as hor d'oeuvres and appetizers for any social occasion. If you want to try the dish but lack asafetida, omit the first three ingredients and use ¼ cup (60 ml) of *Mint-Lime Butter* instead.

Preparation time (after assembling ingredients): 15 minutes
Cooking time: up to 20 minutes
Makes: 10–12 clusters

4 tablespoons (60 ml) unsalted butter, at room temperature
¼ teaspoon (1 ml) yellow asafetida powder (*hing*)*
⅛ teaspoon (0.5 ml) paprika or cayenne pepper
2 large plantains, 9–12 inches (23–30 cm) long
ghee or oil for deep-frying
5 or 6 lemon or lime twists (optional)

*This amount applies only to yellow Cobra brand. Reduce any other asafetida by three-fourths.

1. Mix the butter, asafetida and paprika or cayenne in a bowl and set aside.

2. Peel the plantains with a knife, removing the tough green skins and stray strings. Shred through the large holes on a hand grater or in a food processor fitted with a coarse shredding disk. Press ¼ cup (60 ml) of shredded plantains firmly between your palms to flatten and mold into a tight 2-inch (5 cm) cluster. Arrange them on a plate in a single layer.

3. Pour *ghee* or oil into a large, heavy frying pan to a depth of 1½ inches (4 cm). Place over moderate heat until it reaches 365°F (185°C) on a deep-frying thermometer. When it is hot, place the clusters one at a time into the oil in a single layer. Fry on both sides until golden brown and crisp, about 3 minutes per side. Remove with a slotted spoon and drain on paper towels. Fry the remaining clusters. While they are still quite warm but not steaming hot, smear the top of each cluster with the seasoned butter.

Crispy Plantain Wafers
SADA KACHA KELA BHAJI

In South India these are as popular as potato chips are in America. It is a national snack pastime, and in much of the south, is almost always fried in coconut oil. This tasty oil is also highly saturated, and should be avoided if you are on a cholesterol reduced diet; try sunflower, safflower or soybean oil instead. South Indians, from roadside cooks to housewives, swear by a special frying treatment for the wafers. Since it involves sprinkling water in hot oil, it breaks all safety rules. To avoid splattering, use a spray bottle set on the finest mist. It will cause the oil to foam, but splatter no more than when adding potato straws for frying. Try a bowl of these wafers with homemade *Lime Ginger Ale* or a frosty *Lemon-Flavored Yogurt Shake* for a late-afternoon refresher or to entertain guests.

Preparation time (after assembling ingredients): 10 minutes
Soaking time: 30 minutes
Cooking time: 15 minutes
Serves: 4 or 5 as a nibbler

2 large unripe plantains, each 9–12 inches (23–30 cm) long
½ tablespoon (7 ml) salt
¼ teaspoon (1 ml) turmeric
2 tablespoons (30 ml) hot water
melted coconut or vegetable oil for frying

1. Cut away the hard skins from the plantains with a paring knife and slice crosswise, slightly on the diagonal, as thinly as possible. Soak the plantain in ice water for at least ½ hour, then drain and pat thoroughly dry with paper towels.

2. Dissolve the salt and turmeric in the hot water and place it in a spray bottle. Pour 2 inches (5 cm) of oil into a deep-frying vessel. Place the pan over moderate heat and slowly heat to 370°F (190°C) on a deep-frying thermometer. When it is hot, drop in enough plantain slices to float to a layer on top of the oil. The oil will froth and foam. Fry for about 2 minutes. Holding the spray bottle well above the pan, spray a fine mist into the pan. The oil will froth, but not splatter. (Experts feel this is the means to the crispiest wafers.) Fry, turning to cook on both sides, until they are very crisp, still yellow-colored, for another 1–2 minutes. Transfer with a slotted spoon to paper towels to drain. Fry the remaining wafers in the same way. Serve hot, or let cool and store in airtight containers. These wafers stay crisp indefinitely but are considered stale after a week or two.

Bitter Melon Chips with Coconut
BHONA KARELA NARIYAL

Srila Prabhupada was so fond of bitter melons that he requested them in one form or another nearly every day for lunch. Like most Bengalis, he regarded the vegetable as both a digestive aid and appetite stimulator. Because they are not always easily available, he requested his personal cook to keep a stock of dehydrated sliced bitter melons on hand for world wide traveling. To this

For information about unfamiliar ingredients or techniques, see A-to-Z

day, I try to keep a jar of dried bitter melon slices in the larder, used primarily for this recipe. Dried bitter melon is less pungent than fresh, and deep-fried, it is far crunchier. The wafers fry in seconds, and even for new comers, are quite irresistible.

Bitter melons, also called bitter gourds or balsam pears, are an important vegetable in eastern and southern cuisines. They are spiny melons, 4–8 inches (10–20 cm) long, thickish in the middle and pointed at both ends. Always look for small melons, picked immature, that are dark green in color and heavy for their size. In Bengal the bitter melons are fried in mustard or peanut oil until dark brown and crisp. To tone down the bitterness, the chips are coated with powdered fresh coconut and seasonings. Serve 4–6 chips per person as an appetizer-relish with a dab of pickle or chutney, such as *Sour Lemon or Lime Pickle* or *Zesty Green Tomato Chutney*, on a full Vedic lunch or dinner menu.

Preparation and salting time: 30 minutes
Cooking time: 10–15 minutes
Serves: 4 to 6

4 small or 2 medium-sized bitter melons (about ½ pound/230 g)
salt
4 tablespoons (60 ml) mustard or peanut oil
¼ teaspoon (1 ml) turmeric
¼ teaspoon (1 ml) paprika or cayenne pepper
¼ cup (25 g) grated fresh or dried coconut
½ tablespoon (7 ml) lemon or lime juice

    1. Trim the ends off the bitter melons and slice crosswise into rounds ¼ inch (6 mm) thick. Place them in a bowl, sprinkle liberally with salt and place a weight on them. Set aside for at least ½ hour. Rinse under running water, drain, and pat dry with paper towels.

    2. Heat the oil in a 7–9 inch (17.5–22.5 cm) frying pan over moderate heat. (If using mustard oil, allow it to reach the smoking point before adding the vegetables. This makes the pungent oil docile.) When it is hot, add the bitter melon rounds and stir-fry, cooking on both sides, until crisp and reddish-brown, from 10–15 minutes. Remove the pan from the heat, add the remaining ingredients and ¼ teaspoon (1 ml) salt, and toss well. Serve hot or at room temperature.

Fried Bitter Melon with Ground Almonds
BHONA KARELA BHAJI

Aside from the fact that no Bengali meal is complete without a bitter dish, Bengalis also assert that bitter melon dishes aid digestion, cleanse the blood and encourage a failing appetite. Because most Americans feel that bitter foods are akin to medicines, this version tones down the bitterness. The cut vegetables are parboiled in salted water before they are fried and then liberally coated with ground almonds, nut butter and a touch of seasoning. The finished product is perfect for newcomers to fresh bitter melon cookery. Serve as you would a little mound of seasoned potatoes, more as an appetizer than a vegetable dish, on a full lunch or dinner menu.

Preparation and blanching time: 30 minutes
Cooking time: 10–15 minutes
Serves: 4 to 6

4 small bitter melons, up to 4½ inches (11.5 cm)
　　long, or 2 medium-sized bitter melons, up to
　　6 inches (15 cm) long (about ½ pound/230 g)
2 tablespoons (30 ml) salt
3 cups (710 ml) warm water
4 tablespoons (60 ml) *ghee* or vegetable oil
2 tablespoons (30 ml) ground almonds or cashews
2 tablespoons (30 ml) almond or cashew butter
⅛ teaspoon (0.5 ml) paprika or cayenne pepper
⅛ teaspoon (0.5 ml) freshly ground nutmeg

1. Trim the ends off the bitter melons, slice lengthwise in half, then into quarters, and scoop out the yellow-orange seeds and pulp. Now cut crosswise at ¼-inch (6 mm) intervals. Combine the salt and water in a small saucepan and add the bitter melon. Set aside for 25 minutes, then bring to a boil over high heat. Parboil for 3 minutes, then rinse in a strainer under running water. Drain and pat dry with paper towels.

2. Heat the *ghee* or oil in a 7–9-inch (17.5–22.5 cm) frying pan over moderate heat. When it is hot but not smoking, add the bitter melon pieces and stir-fry until two-thirds cooked, about 8 minutes. Stir in the remaining ingredients and continue to cook for up to 5 minutes until well browned. Serve hot or at room temperature.

Sliced Okra in Seasoned Yogurt
BHINDI BHAJI

This typically Kashmiri dish, from the Srinagar kitchen of Dr. Karan Singh, is served at room temperature and assembled just before serving. For entertaining, I like to serve it garnished with toasted almonds or pine nuts and accompanied by *Mashed Potato Balls Spiked with Horseradish*. As the main-dish entrée, try *Spicy Potato-Stuffed Green Peppers* and *basmati* rice. Add a mixed green salad, *Munchy Chickpea Flour Spirals with Sesame Seeds* and, depending on the season, a summer cooler of *Fresh Coconut Ice Cream* with crushed *Sesame-Nut Nibbler* sprinkled on top or, in winter, *Sesame Seed Milk Toffee Balls* or *Creamy Saffron Cheese Fudge*.

Preparation time (after assembling ingredients): 15 minutes
Cooking time: under 15 minutes
Serves: 4 to 6

For information about unfamiliar ingredients or techniques, see A-to-Z

1 pound (455 g) okra
1 teaspoon (5 ml) salt
⅛ teaspoon (0.5 ml) yellow asafetida powder (*hing*)*
1 teaspoon (5 ml) *garam masala*
3 tablespoons (45 ml) finely chopped fresh coriander
⅔ cup (160 ml) plain yogurt, or half yogurt and half sour cream
2 tablespoons (30 ml) finely chopped toasted almonds or pine nuts
⅛ teaspoon (0.5 ml) freshly ground pepper
2 tablespoons (30 ml) toasted sliced almonds or pine nuts, as a garnish
melted *ghee* or vegetable oil for frying
This amount applies only to yellow Cobra brand. Reduce any other asafetida by three-fourths.

1. Wipe the okra with a slightly damp kitchen towel to brush off any dirt. Dry thoroughly with paper towels, then cut off the stems and tails and slice crosswise into rounds ½ inch (1.5 cm) thick. Pour *ghee* or oil to a depth of 1½ inches (4 cm) into a deep-frying vessel. Place over moderate heat until it reaches 365°F (185°C) on a deep-frying thermometer. Add the okra and fry until golden brown and crispy. Remove the okra with a fine-mesh frying spoon and transfer to a cookie sheet lined with paper towels. Sprinkle with ¾ teaspoon (3.5 ml) salt, and the asafetida, *garam masala* and coriander, and toss to mix.

2. Combine the yogurt with the chopped pine nuts, black pepper and the remaining ¼ teaspoon (1 ml) salt in a bowl and stir until creamy.

3. Drizzle portions of the fried okra with the yogurt sauce and garnish with whole pine nuts, or fold the okra into the sauce and gently blend.

Pumpkin Wafers
KADDU BHAJI

You can use any winter squash—butternut, acorn, banana, or Hubbard.

Preparation and salting time: 30 minutes
Cooking time: about 20 minutes
Makes: 4 to 6 small servings

1 pound (455 g) peeled, seeded pumpkin or
    squash, cut into wafers ¼ inch (6 mm)
    thick and 1½ inches (4 cm) across
1 teaspoon (5 ml) salt
1 teaspoon (5 ml) turmeric
¼ teaspoon (1 ml) cayenne pepper
3 tablespoons (45 ml) ground rice (coarse flour)
    or sifted chickpea flour
ghee or vegetable oil for deep-frying

1. Place the pumpkin wafers in a single, slightly overlapping layer on a tray, sprinkle with salt, turmeric and cayenne, and set aside for ½ hour.

2. Pat the slices dry with paper towels, place them in a paper or plastic bag containing the flour, and shake the bag to dredge the slices. Shake off the excess flour by slapping each piece sharply and then divide them into three batches.

3. Pour 2 inches (5 cm) of *ghee* or oil into a deep frying pan. Place over moderately high heat until the temperature reaches 360°F (180°C) on a deep-frying thermometer. Fry one batch for 4–5 minutes or until the slices turn a rich golden brown, then transfer with a slotted spoon to paper towels. Fry the remaining two batches in the same way. Sprinkle with additional salt, if desired.

Deep-Fried Stuffed Hot Green Chilies
HARI MIRCH BHAJI

Fresh hot green jalapeños, averaging 2½ inches (6.5 cm) long and 1 inch (2.5 cm) wide, are available in most areas. If their skin has begun to turn red but is still shiny and firm, they are still quite usable. Smaller chilies are inevitably the hottest, especially serranos, and they are next to impossible to seed and stuff. Use jalapeños or the conical fresnos (usually limited to California markets). Srila Prabhupada once commented to his servant-cook Srutakirti das, "Chili *pakori* and fried chilies are cooling in hot climates; they actually reduce the body temperature." They are also recognized as appetite stimulators by inhabitants of the tropics. If you fancy hot foods, by all means give this dish a try on a full Vedic menu. Warn the unseasoned newcomer, and, depending on personal tolerance, allow 1 or 2 per person.

Preparation time: 15 minutes
Cooking time: 10 minutes
Makes: 12 chilies

12 hot green jalapeño chilies, each about 2½ inches (6.5 cm) long
½ teaspoon (2 ml) ground mustard
½ teaspoon (2 ml) turmeric
¼ teaspoon (1 ml) salt
¼ teaspoon (1 ml) ground cumin
¼ teaspoon (1 ml) *garam masala*
1 tablespoon (15 ml) chickpea flour
about 1 tablespoon (15 ml) plain yogurt
1 cup (240 ml) *ghee* or vegetable oil for deep-frying

1. Wash the chilies and pat them dry. With a sharp paring knife, make a cut from the top to the bottom of each chili, cutting halfway through. Carefully pry out the seeds and membrane, then wash the cavity under running water and pat dry.

2. Combine the mustard, turmeric, salt, cumin, *garam masala*, chickpea flour and enough yogurt to make a paste. Mix well. Spread the paste evenly into the cavity of each chili.

3. Heat the *ghee* or oil in a 1-quart/liter saucepan over high heat until it reaches 360°F (180°C) on a deep-frying thermometer. Fry the chilies 4 at a time for 2–3 minutes or until they blister and turn brown. Remove with a slotted spoon and drain on paper towels.

For information about unfamiliar ingredients or techniques, see A-to-Z

VEGETABLE SOUPS

Seasoned Vegetable Stocks
AKHNIR JHOL

The Vedic axiom *"Annam Brahma"* or "Food is God" never leaves the mind of a Vaishnava cook. Following this concept in the kitchen, regional cooks have devised ingenious means of using often discarded produce—banana or potato skins and the outer leaves of cabbage and cauliflower. The Western philosophical counterpart might be "Waste not, want not," and if this is your motto, you are probably aware of the goodness of vegetable stock. It is natural to save trimmings, outer leaves and stalks, to be simmered along with seasonings into a pot of liquid nutrition. This is not a reject pot, but a reservoir of flavor to enhance soups, stews, pilafs, *dal* dishes and much more. The proportion of vegetables is roughly 1 pound (4 cups/455 g coarsely chopped) to 1 quart/liter water, with 1–2 teaspoons (5–10 ml) of salt. The secret is to very slowly cook the vegetables in butter until they soften and color, then cover and slowly "sweat" for about 15 minutes. Add water, herbs and spices, simmer until the liquid has reduced (about an hour), and strain. Let cool, pour into ice cube trays, freeze and pop out one or two as needed.

These three stocks have outstanding flavor and can be used in almost anything. Root vegetable stock is possible year-round, while green vegetable stock is a summer specialty with stronger flavor. Brown vegetable stock is enriched by cooking beans with vegetables, a technique also used in 17th-century French kitchens.

Root Vegetable Stock

Preparation time: about 10 minutes
Cooking time: 1½ hours
Makes: about 10 cups (2.5 liters)

2 tablespoons (30 ml) *ghee* or unsalted butter
3 large carrots, scraped and coarsely chopped
3 large celery stalks with leaves, coarsely chopped
1 medium-sized potato, cut into ½-inch (1.5 cm) cubes
1 large turnip, coarsely chopped
12 cups (3 liters) water
1 small cassia or bay leaf
2 tablespoons (30 ml) coriander seeds
1 teaspoon (5 ml) cumin seeds
½ teaspoon (2 ml) black peppercorns
½-inch (1.5 cm) piece of fresh ginger root, scraped and cut into thin julienne
3 whole cloves
2 teaspoons (10 ml) salt
2 overripe tomatoes, chopped

1. Melt the *ghee* or butter in an 8-quart/liter stockpot over moderately low heat. Add the vegetables and cook slowly, stirring now and then, for 15 minutes.

2. Stir in the water and remaining ingredients and bring to a boil over high heat. Reduce the heat to low, partially cover and simmer for 1¼ hours.

3. Strain. If you wish to freeze the stock, let cool to room temperature and pour into ice cube trays. Pop out cubes as they are needed.

Brown Vegetable Stock

This stock is enriched by adding whole beans for flavor and nutrition. The strained beans and vegetables can be puréed, thinned with cream, milk or stock, and seasoned to become a delicious bean soup.

Cooking time: 4½ hours
Makes: about 6 cups (1.5 liters)

2 cups (365 g) dried white beans
4 tablespoons (60 ml) *ghee* or unsalted butter
3 medium-sized carrots, coarsely chopped
1 medium-sized parsnip, coarsley chopped
2 celery stalks with leaves, diced
12 cups (3 liters) water
10 sprigs fresh parsley
10 sprigs fresh coriander
1 sprig fresh thyme or ¼ teaspoon (1 ml) dried thyme
3 whole cloves
1 small bay or cassia leaf
½-inch (1.5 cm) piece of fresh ginger root, scraped and cut into thin julienne
1½ tablespoons (22 ml) salt

1. Place the beans in a 3-quart/liter saucepan and add enough water to cover by 2 inches (5 cm). Bring to a boil over moderate heat and simmer for 2 minutes. Remove the pan from the heat and set aside, covered, while you cook the vegetables.

2. Heat the *ghee* or butter in a 6-quart/liter stockpot over moderate heat. Add the carrots, parsnip and celery and slowly cook for 20 minutes or until browned.

3. Stir in the water, parsley and coriander and bring to a boil over high heat. Discard any beans that float on the top of the water. Drain the beans in a colander and add to the stockpot. Tie the thyme, cloves, bay or cassia leaf and ginger in a piece of cheesecloth. Drop in this bouquet garni and the salt, and slowly simmer over low heat, covered, for 4 hours.

4. The stock is delicious served as is, simply strained and garnished with fresh herbs. To make a hearty bean soup, remove the bouquet garni and purée the vegetables and beans with stock, milk or cream to the desired consistency. Add salt, pepper or other seasonings as desired.

For information about unfamiliar ingredients or techniques, see A-to-Z

Green Vegetable Stock

Use whatever greens are locally available, of two different varieties. The flavor will be stronger or milder depending on your selection. Spinach, lettuce, Swiss chard, Belgian endive, kale, collard greens, mustard greens, turnip greens and sorrel are a few to try.

Cooking time: 2 hours
Makes: about 8 cups (2 liters)

8 cups (455 g) fresh greens, washed trimmed and coarsely chopped
½ cup (120 ml) chopped fresh parsley
¼ cup (60 ml) coarsely chopped fresh coriander
2 large celery stalks with leaves
8–10 pea pods, coarsely chopped
8–10 green beans, coarsely chopped
2 overripe tomatoes
12 cups (3 liters) water
4 whole cloves
2 teaspoons (10 ml) salt
1 small cassia or bay leaf
1-inch (2.5 cm) piece of cinnamon stick

Follow the same instructions as explained in *Root Vegetable Stock.*

Clear Soup with Spinach and Rice
PALAK CHAVAL SHORBA

This pleasantly hot South Indian Malabar dish is reminicent of Italy's *risi e bisi* and tastes as spectacular as it looks: a clear broth with snowy white rice and chiffonade ribbons of green spinach. In Malabar, the dish would derive its character more from chilies than any other ingredient—heat offset with flavor. I would suggest you allow at least a hint of warmth from the jalapeños—the amount recommended will do that just fine. To make the spinach chiffonade, stack several spinach leaves and roll them up lengthwise. Slice across the roll at ¼-inch (6 mm) intervals to make thin ribbons. You can also use a chiffonade of red or green swiss chard or ⅔ cup (160 ml) frozen baby peas, defrosted, instead of spinach.

Preparation time (after assembling ingredients): 10 minutes
Cooking time: about 30 minutes
Serves: 4

2 tablespoons (30 ml) *ghee* or olive oil
½ teaspoon (2 ml) black mustard seeds
1 hot green jalepeño chili, stemmed, seeded
    and cut lengthwise into long slivers
3 tablespoons (45 ml) *basmati* or other
    long-grain white rice
5 cups (1.25 liters) *Brown Vegetable Stock*
    (page 228) or other vegetable stock
¼ teaspoon (1 ml) turmeric
1 teaspoon (5 ml) ground coriander
20–22 spinach leaves, washed, stemmed
    and sliced into chiffonade
1 teaspoon (5 ml) salt
⅛ teaspoon (0.5 ml) freshly ground pepper
4 thin lemon slices for garnishing

1. Place the *ghee* or olive oil in a 3-quart/liter saucepan over moderate heat. When it is hot, drop in the black mustard seeds and fry until they turn gray, sputter and pop. Stir in the green chili, rice, stock, turmeric and coriander and bring to a boil over high heat. Reduce the heat to low, cover and simmer for 20 minutes.

2. Add the spinach and salt and simmer for 4–6 minutes or until dark green. Stir in the pepper and lemon juice and serve at once in warmed bowls. Garnish with lemon slices.

Gold Broth with Julienne Cucumbers
KHEERA SHORBA

Americans do not cook cucumbers often, except perhaps stuffed or creamed, but they are delicious and nutritious. One large cucumber contains not only iron, calcium, phosphorus, potassium and sodium, but also most of the vitamin C an average adult requires in one day. With a mixed green salad dressed with *Delicious Chickpea Chutney* thinned with buttermilk, you have the basis for a light, healthful lunch. Rather than crackers, you might take the time to try a whole wheat flatbread.

Preparation and soaking time: 25 minutes
Cooking time: 30 minutes
Serves: 4 or 5

For information about unfamiliar ingredients or techniques, see A-to-Z

2 large cucumbers (about 12 inches/30 cm long) or 4 medium-sized
    (6–7 inches/15–17.5 cm long)
3 tablespoons (45 ml) *ghee* or unsalted butter
½ red or yellow capsicum, seeded, trimmed
    and cut lengthwise into thin julienne
⅛ teaspoon (0.5 ml) cayenne pepper or paprika
¼ teaspoon (1 ml) turmeric
½ teaspoon (2 ml) *garam masala*
4 cups (1 liter) *Root Vegetable Stock*
    (page 227) or other vegetable stock
1 tablespoon (15 ml) chopped fresh parsley or coriander
1 tablespoon (15 ml) finely chopped fresh dill
    or ½ teaspoon (2 ml) dried dill weed
1½ tablespoons (22 ml) lime or lemon juice
1 teaspoon (5 ml) sugar
1 teaspoon (5 ml) salt
3 tablespoons (45 ml) sour cream, optional

1. Peel the cucumbers, quarter them lengthwise, and scoop out the seeds. Cut cross-wise into 2-inch (5 cm) pieces. Soak in salted water for 20 minutes. Rinse under running water and drain. Slice lengthwise into thin julienne.

2. Heat the *ghee* or butter in a 3-quart/liter saucepan over moderately low heat. When it is hot, stir in the capsicum, cucumbers, cayenne or paprika and *garam masala* and cook for 2–3 minutes. Pour in the vegetable stock, bring to a boil over high heat, then reduce the heat to low and simmer, covered, for 10 minutes or until the cucumber is fork-tender.

3. Add the parsley or coriander, dill, lime or lemon juice, sugar and salt. Remove the pan from the heat and let the flavors mingle for a few minutes. Garnish each serving with a spoonful of sour cream.

Zucchini Cubes in Light Tomato Broth
LOUKI SHORBA

In India this dish would be made with young bottle gourd (*louki*) or round gourd (*tinda*). If you live near a good Indian greengrocery, by all means try both kinds. Zucchini should be young and seedless. Basil complements any summer-type squash. Native to India, sweet basil is found profusely in one form or another throughout the country. It is not, however, commonly used in cooking. Two of the three most popular varieties—the purple-leafed *Krishna tulsi* (*Ocimum sanctum*) and the green-leafed *Rama tulsi* (*Ocimum albuin*)—are never used in cooking. They are sacred plants, kept for the worship of Lord Krishna, and are cared for with reverence. The shiny, pale-green-leafed variety of camphor basil (*Ocimum kilimandscharicum*) is used in cooking. It is always used fresh; in the Himalayan foothills, cooks purchase it daily, along with coriander, mint or curry leaves and a handful of green chilies and ginger root. In America, it is encouraging to see fresh herbs such as these becoming more common in supermarkets and specialty greengroceries. They are also easy to grow in a kitchen window sill garden and flourish in hydroponic containers.

This dish, laced with both fresh sweet basil and coriander, is an example of simple North Indian cooking at its best. Serve it with a grain pilaf and flatbreads for a light lunch. For a company dinner, serve it with *Cashew Rice with Diced Potatoes, Three-Vegetable Urad Dal Soup* and *Deep-Fried Sesame Whole Wheat Bread*. You could elaborate with *Pan-Fried Whole Bitter Melons with Cashew Stuffing* and *Fried Okra in Smooth Yogurt*. To complete the menu, include *Pistachio-Stuffed Chenna Patties in Cardamom Cream Sauce* or *Creamy Milk Pudding with Juicy Tangerine Segments*.

Preparation time (after assembling ingredients): 10 minutes
Cooking time: 15 minutes
Serves: 4 or 5

½ tablespoon (7 ml) scraped, minced fresh ginger root
2 hot green chilies, seeded and minced (or as desired)
2 tablespoons (30 ml) tomato paste
1¼ teaspoons (6 ml) crushed dry-roasted cumin seeds
1 teaspoon (5 ml) *garam masala*
⅛ teaspoon (0.5 ml) paprika or cayenne pepper
½–1 teaspoon (2–5 ml) salt
¾ cup (180 ml) water
¾ cup (180 ml) half-and-half or light cream
3 tablespoons (45 ml) *ghee* or unsalted butter
6–7 small zucchini (about 1 pound/455 g), trimmed
    and cut into ½-inch (1.5 cm) cubes
½ teaspoon (2 ml) turmeric
1½ tablespoons (22 ml) each chopped
    fresh sweet basil and coriander

1. Combine the ginger, chilies, tomato paste, cumin, *garam masala*, paprika or cayenne and salt in a mixing bowl. Slowly stir in ½ cup (120 ml) of the water, blending well, to make a seasoned tomato purée. Whisk in the remaining water and the half-and-half.

2. Heat the *ghee* or butter in a 3-quart/liter saucepan or sauté pan over moderate heat until it is hot or until the butter froths. Add the zucchini and turmeric and sauté, stirring, until the squash is soft, 8–10 minutes. *Louki* or *tinda* requires additional time to soften; cook until fork-tender.

3. Slowly add the tomato purée and simmer for 1–2 minutes. Remove the pan from the heat and stir in the basil and half of the coriander. Garnish with the remaining coriander.

Fried *Panir* Cheese in Seasoned Tomato Stock
PANIR MAHARANI

During his 1968 *Vyasa-Puja* celebration in Montreal, Srila Prabhupada took the time to teach us two dishes: this light soup and a Bengali sweet. The Montreal temple kitchen was small, and several disciples crowded around to catch a glimpse of their spiritual master cooking. I noted down the recipe as he cooked. In calculating ingredient measurements, I have tried to remain faithful to the essence of the dish. The only notable change is the addition of fresh herb—something that he requested but that wasn't available at the time.

This is a very quick soup to assemble if you have a generous cup of cubed fresh *panir* cheese on hand. Overall flavors in the dish vary with your choice of liquid: water, homemade vegetable stock or whey. Instant stock made from cubes is not suitable, as it tends to overpower the simple, clean flavors of the cheese and seasonings. For a healthful lunch or dinner, accompany this nutritious soup with a rice or whole grain pilaf, a green salad and a platter of steamed vegetables drizzled with *Black Pepper Ghee* and fresh lemon juice.

Preparation time (after assembling ingredients): 10 minutes
Cooking time: 25 minutes
Serves: 4 or 5

1¼ cups (300 ml) fresh *panir* cheese (page 313) made from
    8 cups (2 liters) milk, cut into ½-inch (1.5 cm) cubes
2 tablespoons (30 ml) sifted chickpea or whole wheat flour
½ cup (120 ml) *ghee* or vegetable oil for frying
1 teaspoon (5 ml) cumin seeds
1 cup (240 ml) coarsely chopped peeled tomatoes (about ¾ pound/340 g)
⅛ teaspoon (0.5 ml) cayenne pepper or paprika
¼ teaspoon (1 ml) turmeric
2¾ cups (650 ml) water, vegetable stock or whey
½–1 teaspoon (2–5 ml) salt
2 tablespoons (30 ml) coarsely chopped fresh coriander, dill or parsley

1. Lay the *panir* cheese cubes on waxed paper and sprinkle with flour. Toss gently and let them dry out for about 10 minutes.

2. Heat the *ghee* or oil in a 3-quart/liter nonstick saucepan over moderate heat until hot. Carefully drop in the cheese cubes and fry, gently tossing to ensure even browning, for about 8 minutes or until golden brown and crisp. Remove them with a slotted spoon and set aside.

3. Add the cumin seeds and fry until they darken a few shades. Stir in the tomatoes, cayenne or paprika and turmeric and cook for 3–4 minutes. Add the remaining ingredients and the fried cheese cubes, raise the heat to high and bring to a boil. Reduce the heat to low, partially cover and simmer for 10–12 minutes.

Clear Broth with Potatoes and *Urad Badis*
ALOO BADI SHORBA

Urad badi fried and simmered in broth with cubed potatoes is a traditional North Indian dish, now adopted throughout India. In some areas, roasted red peppers or chopped tomatoes are added, or the potatoes are deep-fried before simmering in the broth. This Vrindavan-area version, from the Vaishnava kitchen of the Dr. O.B.L. Kapoor family, has been one of my favorite winter-lunch soups for many years. The flavor of store-bought *urad badis* varies from batch to batch, but it is usually spicy and hot. It is unlikely that many cooks will want to add green chilies or cayenne; aficionados of North Indian cuisine may be the exception. I like to serve this dish with *chapatis*, *pooris* or *parathas*. You could add a yogurt salad and nutritious *Farina Uppma with Cashews and Coconut* for a special lunch or brunch.

Preparation time (after assembling ingredients): 5 minutes
Cooking time: 35–40 minutes
Serves: 5 or 6

2 plum-sized dried *urad dal badis* (about 2 ounces/60 g)
3 tablespoons (45 ml) *ghee* or unsalted butter
2 medium-sized potatoes, peeled and cut into ¾-inch (2 cm) cubes (about ¾ pound/340 g)
1 teaspoon (5 ml) ground coriander
½ teaspoon (2 ml) ground cumin
¼ teaspoon (1 ml) turmeric
1 teaspoon (5 ml) *garam masala*
¼ teaspoon (1 ml) paprika or cayenne pepper
3 cups (710 ml) vegetable stock or water
½–1 teaspoon (2–5 ml) salt
2 tablespoons (30 ml) coarsely chopped fresh coriander or minced parsley

1. Place the *badis* in a bowl or pan and tap with a heavy pestle or kitchen mallet, cracking them into pieces no larger than ½ inch (1.5 cm) in diameter.

2. Heat the *ghee* or unsalted butter in a 3-quart/liter sauté pan or saucepan over moderate heat. When the *ghee* is hot or the butter froths, add the *badis* and fry, tossing with a wooden spoon, for up to 1 minute or until they turn a few shades darker. Add the potatoes, ground coriander, cumin, turmeric, *garam masala* and paprika or cayenne and stir-fry for 2–3 minutes.

3. Pour in the stock or water and salt, stir and bring to a boil. Cover, reduce the heat to low and gently simmer until the potatoes are fork tender, up to ½ hour. Garnish with the fresh herb.

Sweet 'n' Sour Broth with Cabbage and Carrots
BANDHGOBHI GAJAR SHORBA

This light, coriander-flavored *toovar dal* broth complements everyday winter vegetables—carrots and cabbage. You can substitute yellow split peas or *moong dal* for variety.

Preparation and *dal* soaking time: 1 hour
Cooking time: 45 minutes
Serves: 6

For information about unfamiliar ingredients or techniques, see A-to-Z

3 tablespoons (45 ml) split *toovar dal*, washed
1½ tablespoons (22 ml) coriander seeds
1 cup (240 ml) boiling water
½-inch (1.5 cm) piece of fresh ginger root,
    scraped and cut into thin julienne
6 cups (1.5 liters) water
3 tablespoons (45 ml) *ghee* or sesame oil
¼ teaspoon (1 ml) caraway seeds
½ teaspoon (2 ml) cumin seeds
½ teaspoon (2 ml) black mustard seeds
6–8 curry leaves, preferably fresh
1 small green cabbage (about 1 pound/455 g),
    cored and finely shredded (if you use
    large, outer cabbage leaves or Savoy
    cabbage, cut the tough stem off before
    shredding)
2 medium-sized carrots (about 4 ounces/115 g),
    peeled and sliced on the diagonal into
    rounds ⅛ inch (3 mm) thick
3 tablespoons (45 ml) chopped fresh coriander or parsley
3 tablespoons (45 ml) fresh lemon juice
2 tablespoons (30 ml) *jaggery* or maple syrup
freshly ground black pepper
1¼ teaspoons (6 ml) salt

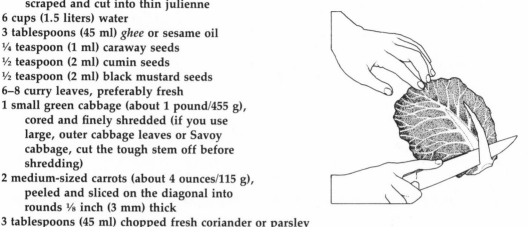

1. Place the *toovar dal* and coriander seeds in a bowl. Add the boiling water and set aside for 1 hour.

2. Combine the soaked beans and coriander seeds, soaking water and ginger in a blender or food processor, cover and process until smooth. Transfer to a 3-quart/liter saucepan, add 2 cups (480 ml) of water and boil over moderate heat until the liquid is reduced by half, to 1½ cups (360 ml). Strain.

3. Place the *ghee* or oil in a 4-quart/liter sauté pan or saucepan over moderately high heat. When it is hot but not smoking, add the caraway seeds, cumin seeds and black mustard seeds, and fry until the mustard seeds turn gray, sputter and pop. Drop in the curry leaves and fry for a few seconds, then drop in the cabbage and carrots. Reduce the heat to moderate and stir-fry until the cabbage is wilted and soft but not brown.

4. Pour in the *dal* broth, the remaining 4 cups (1 liter) of water and half of the fresh herb. Cover, lower the heat and simmer for about 20 minutes or until the vegetables are tender. Before serving, add the lemon juice, sugar or maple syrup and black pepper. Ladle into cups or bowls, and garnish with the remaining minced herb.

Tomato Broth with Spicy *Paparh* Noodles
PAPARH SHORBA

Paparhs, also called *pappadams*, are not really noodles, but they are a viable alternative for thin ribbon pasta. *Paparhs* are usually made from *urad* or mung *dal* dough, unseasoned or spiced. They are rolled into paper-thin wafers 3½–10 inches (9–25 cm) in diameter, and then dried in the sun. Sold in Indian grocery stores or specialty gourmet stores, these *dal* wafers can be deep-fried or flame-toasted for munching as crackers, or cut into ribbons and cooked as noodles. The smaller South Indian *pappadams* are unseasoned; the larger North Indian *paparhs* are spicy and hot. In this recipe, the noodles float in a light tomato broth. Reducing the liquid by half, adding 1½ cups (360 ml) defrosted frozen baby peas, 1½ cups (360 ml) steamed cut asparagus, and minced fresh sweet basil, you can make a terrific noodle vegetable.

Preparation time (after assembling ingredients): 10 minutes
Cooking time: 25 minutes
Serves: 4 or 5

1–2 hot green chilies, seeded and finely chopped
½ inch (1.5 cm) scraped, finely shredded or minced fresh ginger root
3 tablespoons (45 ml) blanched sliced almonds or pine nuts
½ tablespoon (7 ml) cumin seeds
1 tablespoon (15 ml) coriander seeds
½ teaspoon (2 ml) turmeric
2 medium-sized tomatoes (about ¾ pound/340 g),
      peeled, seeded and coarsely chopped
1 small red bell pepper (about 4 ounces/115 g),
      stemmed, seeded and coarsely chopped
3 tablespoons (45 ml) *ghee* or unsalted butter
3½ cups (830 ml) vegetable stock, *panir* whey or water
¾–1¼ teaspoons (3.5–6 ml) salt
3 large black pepper *paparhs* or 5 small plain *pappadams*,
      cut into ribbons ½ inch (1.5 cm) wide
2 tablespoons (30 ml) chopped fresh coriander, basil or parsley

1. Combine the green chilies, ginger, almonds or pine nuts, cumin seeds, coriander seeds, turmeric, tomatoes and bell pepper in a food processor or blender, cover and process to a paste. You will need to stop the machine and push the ingredients down the walls of the container once or twice during the processing.

2. Place the *ghee* or butter in a 3-quart/liter saucepan over moderate heat. When the *ghee* is hot or the butter froths, stir in the tomato-bell pepper paste and fry for about 5 minutes. Pour in the stock, whey or water and salt, and stir. Bring to a boil, reduce the heat to low and simmer for 15 minutes.

3. Add the *paparh* noodles and simmer for about 30 seconds. If you are using defrosted frozen peas, add them just 1–2 minutes before serving. Garnish each serving with fresh herb.

For information about unfamiliar ingredients or techniques, see A-to-Z

Pineapple and Green Peas in Almond Broth
ANANAS HARI MATAR SHORBA

This festive dish is from the southern region of Maharashtra and, so far as I know, is eaten only by the Vaishnava residents of the area. Though containing an unusual combination of flavors, this soup has garnered approval from many of my taste testers and dinner guests. Aside from terrific taste, the golden pineapple and baby green peas also make a visually beautiful contrast with the saffron broth. To fully appreciate this dish, use field ripened pineapple, ones shipped to market by air, and purchased for immediate use. Unripe pineapples never really sweeten, and, contrary to popular belief, do not ripen in a warm place. If necessary, you can keep a ripe pineapple for one or two days by refrigerating it in a plastic bag. Avoid overripe fruits and those with bruises, discolored patches or wilting leaves.

For a special occasion, serve with *Urad and Rice Flour Dosa with Cracked Black Pepper* and *Toasted Fresh Coconut and Tomato Chutney*. Add *Double-Fried Potatoes* or *Crisp 'n' Soft Mixed Vegetable Croquettes* and *Herbed Rice with Panir Cheese and Zucchini*. For a sweet duo, try *Semolina Halva with Golden Raisins*.

Preparation time (after assembling ingredients): 10–15 minutes
Cooking time: 30 minutes
Serves: 6 to 8

3 tablespoons (45 ml) blanched almonds, halved
3 tablespoons (45 ml) raw cashew halves
1 teaspoon (5 ml) sesame seeds
½ tablespoon (7 ml) coriander seeds
2 tablespoons (30 ml) grated fresh or dried coconut
1¾ cups (420 ml) water or coconut milk
½-inch (1.5 cm) piece of fresh ginger root,
    scraped and cut into thin julienne
1–2 hot green chilies, stemmed and seeded
3 tablespoons (45 ml) *ghee* or unsalted butter
½ teaspoon (2 ml) black mustard seeds
12 high-quality saffron threads
1¼ teaspoons (6 ml) salt
1 small pineapple, peeled, cored and
    cut into ½-inch (1.5 cm) cubes
1 cup (240 ml) fresh peas (about 1 pound/455g
    in pods) or frozen baby peas, defrosted
3 tablespoons (45 ml) cream
⅛ teaspoon (0.5 ml) freshly ground nutmeg
½ teaspoon (2 ml) *garam masala*

1. Place 1½ tablespoons (22 ml) each of the almonds and cashews and all of the sesame seeds, coriander seeds, and coconut in a blender or food processor, cover and pulse to a coarse powder. Add ½ cup (120 ml) of water or coconut milk and the ginger and chilies, cover and process until smooth. Pour through a fine-mesh strainer, pressing out all of the liquid.

2. Heat the *ghee* or butter in a 3-quart/liter saucepan over moderate heat. Add the remaining 1½ tablespoons (22 ml) each cashews and almonds and stir-fry until golden brown, then remove them with a slotted spoon and set aside. Drop in the black mustard seeds and fry until they turn gray and pop. Pour in the seed–nut milk and cook, stirring to prevent sticking, for 2–3 minutes. Pour in the remaining 1¼ cups (300 ml) water or coconut milk and the saffron threads and salt. Bring to a boil, then reduce the heat and simmer for 5 minutes.

3. Add the pineapple and fresh peas, cover and simmer for 20–25 minutes or until the pineapple and peas are tender. If you are using frozen defrosted peas, add only 1–2 minutes before serving. Remove the pan from the heat, stir in the cream, nutmeg and *garam masala*, and garnish each serving with the fried nuts.

Deep-Fried Baby Potatoes in Seasoned Yogurt Broth
ALOO DUM

This inexpensive but elegant North Indian dish has become popular worldwide. *Aloo* means potato and *dum* means the cooking technique—a tightly sealed pot and very gentle heat. This is a very good dish to make in quantity; I have made it on restaurant or banquet menus for up to 1,500 servings! Because the dish is finished off very slowly, it can be kept warm for up to 3 hours before serving and will not suffer in texture or taste, provided the pans and stoves are right.

For a quantity or holiday menu, start with the basics: rice, *dal* and flatbreads. Try colorful *Rice with Shredded Carrots and Coconut, Savory Chickpeas in Tangy Tomato Glaze* and *Deep-Fried Banana Whole Wheat Bread*. Add *Eggplant Pakora with Poppy Seeds* or *Pumpkin Pakora with Crushed Coriander Seeds* for your deep-fried vegetable fritter, or try a pastry—*Spicy Green Pea Kachori*. I would include a selection of seasonal raw vegetable crudités sprinkled with lemon juice, olive or walnut oil, and dry-roasted, coarsely crushed cumin seeds. One of the most popular sweet combinations is *ladoo* and *kheer*, such as *Melt-in-Your-Mouth Chickpea Flour Confections* served with *Simple Rice Pudding with Cashew Nuts*.

Preparation time (after assembling ingredients): 15 minutes
Cooking time: 45 minutes
Serves: 6 to 8

30 baby new potatoes (2 pounds/1 kg), each about walnut-sized,
     or 10 medium-sized boiling potatoes, peeled and cut into 1½-inch (4 cm) pieces
ghee or vegetable oil for deep-frying
3 tablespoons (45 ml) coarsely chopped blanched almonds
¼ cup (60 ml) water or vegetable stock
2–3 hot green chilies, cored and seeded
½-inch (1.5 cm) piece of scraped fresh ginger root, coarsely chopped
1 teaspoon (5 ml) turmeric
1 teaspoon (5 ml) *garam masala*
½ tablespoon (7 ml) ground coriander
½ teaspoon (2 ml) sugar
3 tablespoons (45 ml) *ghee* or unsalted butter
½ cassia or bay leaf

For information about unfamiliar ingredients or techniques, see A-to-Z

½ tablespoon (7 ml) cumin seeds
¼ teaspoon (1 ml) yellow asafetida powder (*hing*)*
1 cup (240 ml) plain yogurt, stirred until smooth, at room temperature
1–2 cups (240–480 ml) water
1½ teaspoons (7 ml) salt
⅓ cup (80 ml) cream (optional)
⅛ teaspoon (0.5 ml) freshly ground black pepper
3 tablespoons (45 ml) coarsely chopped fresh coriander or minced parsley

This amount applies only to yellow Cobra brand. Reduce any other asafetida by three-fourths.

1. If you use baby potatoes, scrub them to remove skins. Steam or parboil the potatoes until half-cooked. Then remove and plunge into cold water until cool enough to handle. Pierce each potato in 4 or 5 places to a depth of about ½ inch (1.5 cm). (For a simpler version of this recipe, you can omit the next step of deep-frying altogether and instead cook the potatoes until fork-tender.) Pat the potatoes dry with paper towels.

2. Heat *ghee* or oil to a depth of 2 inches (5 cm) in a deep-frying pan over moderately high heat until it reaches 365°F (185°C) on a deep-frying thermometer. Fry a batch of the potatoes, without crowding the pan, until they are golden brown. Then remove them with a slotted spoon and drain. Fry the remaining potatoes and set aside momentarily.

3. Place the almonds and water or stock in a blender or food processor, cover and process until smooth. Drop in the green chilies and ginger through the feed tube and continue to process—adding the turmeric, *garam masala*, ground coriander and sugar—until smooth.

4. Heat the 3 tablespoons (45 ml) of *ghee* or butter in a heavy 4-quart/liter casserole over moderate heat. Add the cassia or bay leaf and cumin seeds and fry until the cumin darkens a few shades, or until the butter froths. Sprinkle in the asafetida and then, in ¼-cup (60 ml) amounts, whisk in the yogurt until it is fully absorbed into the *ghee* or butter. Next, whisk in the seasoned almond milk, water and salt and bring to a simmer. Add the potatoes and remove the pan from the heat.

5. The dish can be finished off in a preheated 300°F (150°C) oven or rested on a raised pot rack over very low heat. Lay a sheet of aluminum foil over the pan and fold the edges under, crumpling and pressing them against the rim of the pan to form a tight seal. Cover with the lid. This prevents any steam from escaping and seals in flavor. Cook in the oven or over low heat for about 25 minutes. If you used only 1 cup (240 ml) of water, check the dish to see if the potatoes are sticking, and add a bit more water if needed. Stir in the black pepper and cream, if desired. Garnish with the fresh herb, and serve.

Note: If need be, you can keep this dish warm by placing it, covered, in a 200°F (100°C) oven for up to 2 hours.

Deep-Fried Cauliflower and Potatoes in Spiced Tomato Broth
GOBHI ALOO DUM

As in the previous recipe, this dish employs the *dum* process of cooking. Vegetables are deep-fried and cooked ever so slowly in a fennel-flavored cream and tomato broth. Because the casserole is tightly sealed and baked, flavors are dramatic and textures preserved. This is a classic company dish, either on a full menu or for a fireside supper. On a party menu, include a rice, *dal*, flatbread, salad, stuffed or braised vegetable and deep-fried savory. For a celebration brunch or supper, try it with *Shallow-Fried Chickpea Parathas*, *Char-Flavored Eggplant and Green Peas*, *Baked Buckwheat with Almonds* and *Simple Cucumber and Ginger Root Salad*. From the sweets corner, sample *Pineapple Tower Surprise*.

Preparation time (after assembling ingredients): 15 minutes
Cooking time: 45 minutes
Serves: 6 to 8

1 tablespoon (15 ml) sesame or white poppy seeds
½ teaspoon (2 ml) fennel seeds
½ tablespoon (7 ml) coriander seeds
3 whole cloves, crushed
3 tablespoons (45 ml) chopped cashew nuts
1 teaspoon (5 ml) sugar
1½ cups (360 ml) water or vegetable stock
2 tablespoons (30 ml) tomato paste
¾ cup (180 ml) cream
16 baby or 5 medium-sized new potatoes (1 pound/455 g), scrubbed
    or peeled and cut into 1¼-inch (3.5 cm) pieces
ghee or vegetable oil for deep-frying
1 small cauliflower (about 1 pound/455 g), trimmed,
    cored and divided into 2-inch (5 cm) flowerets
3 tablespoons (45 ml) *ghee* or sesame oil
2–3 hot green chilies, cored, seeded and slivered
¾-inch (2 cm) piece of fresh ginger root, scraped and cut into fine julienne
1 teaspoon (5 ml) black mustard seeds
6–8 curry leaves, preferably fresh
1 teaspoon (5 ml) *garam masala*
3 tablespoons (45 ml) coarsely chopped fresh coriander or minced parsley

1. To make the broth, combine the sesame or poppy seeds, fennel seeds, coriander seeds, cloves, nuts and sugar in a spice grinder or coffee mill and grind to a powder. Transfer to a bowl and add ⅓ cup (80 ml) of water or stock and the tomato paste. Whisk until blended, then add the remaining water and the cream and mix thoroughly.

2. Before frying the vegetables, pierce each potato piece in 3 or 4 places to a depth of about ½ inch (1.5 cm). Heat *ghee* or oil to a depth of 2 inches (5 cm) in a deep-frying pan over moderately high heat until it reaches 365°F (185°C) on a deep-frying thermometer. Fry in batches, without crowding the pan, until all the potatoes and cauliflower are golden brown. Drain each batch on paper towels.

3. Heat the 3 tablespoons (45 ml) of *ghee* or sesame oil in a heavy 4-quart/liter casserole over moderate heat. When it is hot but not smoking, add the chilies and ginger and

For information about unfamiliar ingredients or techniques, see A-to-Z

let them sizzle for several seconds. Add the mustard seeds and fry until they sputter and turn gray. Drop in the curry leaves, then slowly pour in the cream-tomato broth and, whisking constantly, bring to a simmer.

4. Add the fried vegetables and remove the pan from the heat. The dish can be finished off in a preheated 300°F (150°C) oven or rested on a raised pot rack over very low heat. Lay a sheet of aluminum foil over the pan and fold the edges under, crumpling and pressing them under the rim of the pan to form a tight seal. Cover with a lid. This prevents any steam from escaping and locks in the flavor. Cook in the oven or over low heat for about 25 minutes. Check to see if the vegetables are sticking, and add more water or stock if needed. Just before serving, fold in the *garam masala* and garnish with the fresh herb.

Note: If need be, you can keep this dish warm by placing it, covered, in a 200°F (100°C) oven for up to 2 hours.

Garden Tomato Soup
TAMATAR SHORBA

In India, most families do not need a garden. They buy produce daily at the *sabji* bazaar, a bustling farmers' market with hawkers and vendors bargaining over their goods. I first had this dish at the home of a Bengali gentleman, C.L. Bajoria, who had extensive family gardens. He had steady supplies of Thompson and Morgan, Parks and Burpee seeds, along with local favorites, and succeeded in cultivating outstanding produce. The family chef used Italian plum tomatoes, vine-ripened and bursting with flavor, but you could use any locally grown tomatoes that are fresh and very ripe. This turn-of-the-century Bengali recipe has a definite contemporary European influence (most likely from the Scottish business associates of my Bengali friend), as it is thickened with flour and enriched with cream. But, as in all Vedic cooking, ancient or contemporary, the soup is laced with chilies, herbs and spices. One of my favorite versions is made with yellow tomatoes, light and broth like—without flour and cream.

For most Americans, even delicious homemade tomato soup needs a special presentation to break the Campbells stereotype. Garnish each bowl with a swirl of crème fraîche or a dab of seasoned butter and sprinkle with fresh herbs. One of my favorite herb butters for tomato soup includes a pinch of cayenne pepper and yellow mustard, two pinches of shredded horseradish and a few twists of milled salt and pepper added to 1½ tablespoons (22 ml) of softened butter.

Preparation and cooking time (after assembling ingredients): 40 minutes
Serves: 4

4 tablespoons (60 ml) unsalted butter
8 medium-sized ripe red or yellow tomatoes (about
    2 pounds/1 kg), each cut into 8 pieces
1 small apple, peeled, cored and cut into 8 pieces
1-2 fresh hot red or yellow chilies (or as desired)
½ cassia or bay leaf
4–5 white, green or black peppercorns
½-inch (1.5 cm) piece scraped and sliced fresh ginger root
½ teaspoon (2 ml) cumin seeds
¼ cup (60 ml) water
2 cups (480 ml) vegetable stock
2 tablespoons (30 ml) whole wheat pastry flour
¼ teaspoon (1 ml) sugar
1 teaspoon (5 ml) salt
½ cup (120 ml) half-and-half or light cream
1 tablespoon (15 ml) herb butter, optional
2 tablespoons (30 ml) chopped fresh coriander, parsley or dill

1. Melt 1 tablespoon (15 ml) of butter in a 3-quart/liter saucepan over moderate heat. Add the tomatoes, apple, hot chilies, cassia or bay leaf, peppercorns, ginger and cumin seeds and cook for 1–2 minutes. Pour in the water, cover with a round of buttered parchment, and place the lid on the pan. Reduce the heat to low and gently cook for 20–25 minutes or until the tomatoes are very soft and pulpy.

2. Rub the tomato mixture through a fine-mesh sieve into a bowl with the stock and mix well.

3. Melt the remaining 3 tablespoons (45 ml) of butter in a saucepan over low heat, add the flour and cook, stirring, for 2–3 minutes. Pour in the tomato-vegetable broth, stirring as you pour, and bring to a simmer. Add the sugar and salt and continue to simmer for no more than 5 minutes. Before serving, add the half-and-half or cream and again heat (the soup will curdle if it is boiled). Place a dab of seasoned butter in each *katori* or warmed bowl, ladle in the hot soup, and garnish with a little circle of the fresh herb.

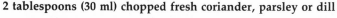

Wholesome Whole Grain and Vegetable Soup
SABJI SHORBA

Because it is pressure-cooked, this meal-in-one soup takes less than ½ hour to cook. Its nutritional value is as impressive as its flavor: the whole grains are rich in protein, iron and B vitamins; the vegetables are rich in A and C vitamins; and both grains and vegetables have minerals, iron and calcium. Eaten together, their nutrients complement each other to form a satisfying, nearly complete meal. Keep at least a small supply of whole cereals in your kitchen, espe-

For information about unfamiliar ingredients or techniques, see A-to-Z

cially good for winter stews and soups: barley, wheat, rye, wild rice, brown rice, millet and buckwheat. They will go a long way, as only a few spoons of each are needed at a time. To round out the meal, add a seasonal salad and crackers, toast or flatbreads.

Dal soaking time: 1 hour
Preparation time (after assembling ingredients): 5 minutes
Cooking time: 30 minutes
Serves: 5 or 6

6 cups (1.5 liters) hot water
2 medium-sized tomatoes, peeled and quartered (about ¾ pound/340 g)
1 medium-sized carrot, scraped and cut crosswise into ¼-inch (6 mm) rounds
1 medium-sized celery stalk with tops, cut crosswise into ⅓-inch (1 cm) slices
1 medium-sized boiling potato, scrubbed and cut into ½-inch (1.5 cm) dice
1 small zucchini or summer squash, cut into ½-inch (1.5 cm) dice
¼ cup (60 ml) corn kernels
⅓ cup (80 ml) green beans, trimmed and cut into 1-inch (2.5 cm) lengths (1½ ounces/45 g)
a few fresh spinach or Swiss chard leaves, washed, trimmed and coarsely chopped
1½ tablespoons (22 ml) whole barley
1½ tablespoons (22 ml) whole wheat
1½ tablespoons (22 ml) whole rye
1½ tablespoons (22 ml) long-grain rice
1½ tablespoons (22 ml) wild rice
¼ cup (55 g) green or yellow split peas, soaked in hot water for 1 hour and drained
½ tablespoon (7 ml) ground coriander
½ teaspoon (2 ml) turmeric
½ tablespoon (7 ml) of scraped, finely shredded or minced fresh ginger root
3 tablespoons (45 ml) unsalted butter
4 tablespoons (60 ml) coarsely chopped fresh coriander or minced parsley
½ tablespoon (7 ml) salt
1¼ teaspoons (6 ml) dry roasted coarsely crushed cumin seeds

1. Place the water, vegetables, whole grains, rice, wild rice, split peas, ground coriander, turmeric, ginger, 1 tablespoon (15 ml) of the butter and 2 tablespoons (30 ml) of the fresh herb in a 6-quart/liter pressure cooker. Cover and place over high heat.

2. When the pressure regulator begins to rock, reduce the heat to moderate and cook, letting the regulator rock very gently, for 20 minutes. Remove the pan from the heat, allow the pressure to fall according to the manufacturer's directions, and remove the lid.

3. Stir in the salt, the remaining 2 tablespoons (30 ml) of butter and the cumin seeds. Ladle into large *katoris* or warmed soup bowls, and garnish with the remaining 2 tablespoons (30 ml) of the fresh herb.

Mustard-Flavored Mixed Vegetable Soup
LAPHRA VYANJANA

In the sixteenth-century Bengali text *Shri Chaitanya Charitamrita*, there is a detailed description of the day Shri Chaitanya Mahaprabhu, in humble service to Lord Krishna, cleansed the Gundicha Temple. The joyous pastime spanned an entire day and includes scores of devotional scenarios, culminating in a gigantic feast. Held in the temple gardens, hundreds of His followers assembled for the occasion. The author, Krishnadas Kaviraj Goswami, relates that Chaitanya Mahaprabhu knew the preferences of all present and instructed the servers to deliver the dishes each person liked. In this way, there was a festive atmosphere and everyone ate to his full satisfaction.

For Himself, Lord Chaitanya requested this simple *laphra* dish over the scores of other lavish preparations. *Laphra* is a mustard-flavored cross between soup and stew. It can be made with any seasonal produce, although in Bengal tropical *portals*, *toray* and *bhatura* are favorites.

For a Bengali dinner sampler, serve *laphra* with fluffy steamed rice, *Urad Dal with Tomatoes*, *Yogurt Cheese Patties with Spicy Green Peas*, *Pishima's Stuffed Okra* and *Crackling-Crispy Dal Wafers* or *Deep-Fried Golden Puffs*. From the sweets department, few dishes can top the simple elegance of *Pistachio Cheese Fudge with Rose Water*. If you want a rich sweet dish, try *Chenna and Powdered Milk Pastries in Cardamom Syrup*.

Preparation time (after assembling ingredients): 10 minutes
Cooking time: 30–40 minutes
Serves: 6 to 8

2–3 hot green chilies, seeded
½-inch (1.5 cm) piece of fresh ginger root,
    scraped and cut into thin julienne
1 tablespoon (15 ml) black mustard seeds
¼ cup (40 g) chopped blanched peanuts
4 cups (1 liter) vegetable stock or water
½ teaspoon (2 ml) turmeric
1 tablespoon (15 ml) ground coriander
1 tablespoon (15 ml) *jaggery* or brown sugar
1½–2 teaspoons (7–10 ml) salt
1 tablespoon (15 ml) unsalted butter or
    ½ teaspoon (2 ml) sesame oil
1½ pounds (685 g) of 4 or 5 vegetables,
    washed, trimmed or peeled, and cut into
    stew-sized cubes, wedges or slices
1 cup (240 ml) peeled, seeded and coarsely
    chopped tomatoes (about 1 pound/455 g)
1¼ teaspoons (6 ml) cumin seeds
¼ teaspoon (1 ml) fennel seeds
¼ teaspoon (1 ml) *kalonji*, if available
½ cassia or bay leaf
2 tablespoons (30 ml) *ghee* or peanut oil
¼ teaspoon (1 ml) freshly ground black pepper
½ tablespoon (7 ml) lemon juice
3 tablespoons (45 ml) finely chopped fresh coriander or parsley

For information about unfamiliar ingredients or techniques, see A-to-Z

1. Combine the chilies, ginger, black mustard seeds and peanuts in a blender or food processor, cover and pulse until coarsely pulverized. Add 1 cup (240 ml) of the stock or water and the turmeric, ground coriander, sweetener and salt, cover and process until smooth.

2. Pour the remaining 3 cups (710 ml) of stock or water and the spicy mustard water into a large soup pot, add the butter or sesame oil, vegetables and tomatoes, and bring to a boil over high heat. Cover, reduce the heat to moderately low, and simmer until the vegetables are fork-tender. (The cooking time will vary according to the variety and size of the vegetables. Cut longer-cooking vegetables into small pieces and quick-cooking vegetables into large pieces.)

3. Combine the cumin seeds, fennel seeds, *kalonji* and cassia or bay leaf in a small dish. Heat the *ghee* or peanut oil in a small pan over moderately high heat. When it is hot but not smoking, add the spice blend and fry until the cumin and fennel seeds darken a few shades. Pour the spices and oil into the *laphra*, cover immediately and let the seasonings steep for 2–3 minutes. Before serving, stir in the black pepper and the lemon juice. Transfer to a warmed soup tureen, *katoris* or warmed soup bowls, and garnish with the fresh herb.

Bottle Gourd and Green Peas Cooked in Tomato Broth
LOUKI HARI MATAR SHORBA

All along the equator, from India through the Middle East and from Africa to Mexico, bottle gourd is a much-loved vegetable. Indeed, Italians prefer it to baby zucchini. When harvested immature, 6–8 inches (15–20 cm) long, the firm, tender flesh is seedless and the thin skins come off easily with a potato peeler. Older bottle gourds, 12–14 inches (30–35 cm) long, have skins nearly ⅛-inch (3 mm) thick which must be removed with a paring knife; the large seeds must be scooped out. Oversized, mature bottle gourds develop very woody shells, which are used to make bowls and even musical instruments. If you have a garden with hot sun, the plants will grow like wildfire. I have had the shoots crawl beyond the garden borders and climb 15 feet (5 meters) up pine trees! If you live in a city, phone Indian, Middle Eastern or Chinese greengrocers and inquire about shipment dates.

I like to serve this dish with *Delicious Mixed Vegetable Cutlets* and a dollop of *Velvet Tomato Catsup* or a ladle of *Pistachio Cream Sauce with Sesame Seeds*. Add a mixed green salad and *Creamy Pineapple and Rice Jubilee* for special company or family suppers.

Preparation and cooking time: 30–40 minutes
Serves: 4 to 6

2 tablespoons (30 ml) tomato paste
½ cup (120 ml) water or vegetable stock
½ cup (120 ml) cream
4 whole cloves
½-inch (1.5 cm) piece of cinnamon stick
1 teaspoon (5 ml) turmeric
1 tablespoon (15 ml) ground coriander
¼ teaspoon (1 ml) ground fennel
½ teaspoon (2 ml) *garam masala*
⅛ teaspoon (0.5 ml) mild asafetida powder (*hing*)*
¼ teaspoon (1 ml) paprika
2 tablespoons (30 ml) *ghee* or 1 tablespoon (15 ml) unsalted butter
1 fresh green serrano chili (or as desired)
6–8 curry leaves, preferably fresh
3 medium-sized tomatoes (about 1 pound/455 g), seeded and diced
2 small bottle gourds (about 1¼ pound/570 g), each 6–8 inches
        (15–20 cm) long, peeled and cut into ¾-inch (2 cm) cubes
1 cup (240 ml) fresh peas (1 pound/455 g in pods)
        or 1 cup (240 ml) frozen baby peas, defrosted
1 teaspoon (5 ml) salt
1 tablespoon (15 ml) each finely chopped fresh coriander and mint

*This amount applies only to yellow Cobra brand. Reduce any other asafetida by three-fourths.

1. Whisk together the tomato paste, water or stock and cream until smooth. Combine all of the ingredients (except defrosted peas) in a heavy-bottomed 3-quart/liter non-stick saucepan over low heat. Cover with a tight-fitting lid and simmer over low heat for 30–40 minutes or until the vegetables are butter-soft and the liquid is absorbed. Stir now and then, adding water if necessary, to prevent the dish from sticking. If you are using defrosted peas, gently stir them in now.

2. Remove the whole spices and green chili before serving.

Note: If the bottle gourd is old, it may require double the recommended cooking time to soften. To prevent an overcooked dish, I would suggest steaming it until half tender before assembling the *laphra*. As a second, considerably less worthy resort, slowly bake the already cooked dish in a covered casserole in a preheated 325°F (170°C) oven for up to 45 minutes, adding additional liquid and gently stirring once or twice during cooking.

For information about unfamiliar ingredients or techniques, see A-to-Z

Cold Minty Yogurt Soup
PODINA DAHI SHORBA

In nearly every regional cuisine, yogurt is a staple food that is used virtually every day in one form or another. This light soup from Madras is very pleasant during hot summer months. Mild homemade yogurt offers the best flavor. Though not traditional, I enjoy using hazelnut or walnut oil in the soup; light olive or almond oil are equally delicious. This soup could be served on almost any type of summer menu—Vedic or other.

Preparation time (after assembling ingredients): 5 minutes
Chilling time: at least 1 hour
Serves: 4

1 large cucumber (about 1 pound/455 g), peeled and seeded
2½ cups (600 ml) plain yogurt
⅓ cup (50 g) finely chopped toasted hazelnuts or walnuts
2 tablespoons (30 ml) minced fresh mint or ½ teaspoon (2 ml) dried mint
2 tablespoons (30 ml) hazelnut or above suggested oil
½ teaspoon (2 ml) salt
1 teaspoon (5 ml) coarsely ground, dry-roasted cumin seeds
4 sprigs mint for garnishing

1. Coarsely chop the cucumber and place it with the yogurt in a blender or food processor. Cover and process until smooth. Transfer to a bowl, add the hazelnuts or walnuts, minced mint, oil, salt and cumin seeds, and blend well. Cover and refrigerate for at least 1 hour.
2. Stir well and ladle into chilled bowls. Garnish with mint sprigs.

Vegetable Chowder
SABJI DOODH SHORBA

This is an exquisite, light cream soup with summer's tender offerings such as new potatoes, baby carrots, tiny zucchini, thin green beans, petite new peas and chiffonade of spinach. It resembles a dish popular in Scandanavia, but with the addition of fresh curry leaves and ground spices it is typically Gujarati. This recipe, from the Surti J. L. Lakshmann family kitchen, perks up any luncheon and supper menus. For backyard or patio fare, accompany it with fresh *Griddle-Baked Chickpea and Whole Wheat Bread* spread with *Delicious Chickpea Chutney* and toasted sesame seeds, and grilled vegetable cutlets.

Preparation time (after assembling ingredients): a few minutes
Cooking time: 30 minutes
Serves: 8

6–8 curry leaves or 3 sprigs fresh mint
6 green, black or white peppercorns
½-inch (1.5 cm) piece of cinnamon stick
1 teaspoon (5 ml) coriander seeds
2½ cups (600 ml) water or vegetable stock
2 tablespoons (30 ml) *ghee* or unsalted butter
6 baby new potatoes (about 1 pound/455 g), each about
    1½ inches (4 cm) in diameter, peeled and halved
12 very young carrots (about ½ pound/230 g)
3 small zucchini (about ½ pound/230 g), cut into julienne
    2 inches (5 cm) long and ⅓ inch (1 cm) thick
1 cup (240 ml) young green beans, trimmed and cut into 1-inch (2.5 cm) pieces (4 ounces/115 g)
1½ cups (360 ml) young peas (1½ pounds/685 g in pods) or
    one 10-ounce (285 g) package of frozen baby peas, defrosted
2 ounces (60 g) fresh spinach, washed and trimmed
2 tablespoons (30 ml) cornstarch or unbleached white flour
2 cups (480 ml) light cream
1 teaspoon (5 ml) salt

1. Wrap the curry leaves or mint, peppercorns, cinnamon and coriander seeds in cheesecloth to make a bouquet garni. Heat the water or stock and *ghee* or butter to boiling in a 5-quart/liter pan. Add the potatoes, reduce the heat, cover and simmer for 5 minutes. Add the carrots, zucchini and green beans and simmer for 8 minutes more. Add the peas, if using fresh peas, and simmer for another 4 minutes or until the vegetables are tender but still firm.

2. While the soup is simmering, prepare the spinach. Stack and roll the leaves into a scroll, then slice crosswise at ⅛-inch (3 mm) intervals. Combine the cornstarch and cream and blend until smooth.

3. Remove the bouquet garni. Add the spinach and frozen peas, if using them, and gradually stir in the cream. Cook, stirring often, until the soup has thickened slightly, for 4–5 minutes. Salt before serving.

Corn and Bell Peppers in Herbed Coconut Milk
MAKKAI SHORBA

This typically Gujarati dish comes from the Ahmadabad kitchen of Srimati Shyamadevi Patel. The coconut milk features flavor from curry leaves, a wonderful herb to serve with any sweet corn dish. Although it is almost unknown in America, it is as common to South Indian and Gujarati cuisine as basil is to Italian cooking. There is no substitute for the heady burst of flavor in fresh leaves, but dried ones will release some flavor when simmered. The other unusual ingredient is

For information about unfamiliar ingredients or techniques, see A-to-Z

coconut milk—made from scratch or instant. To make it at home, pour 2 cups (480 ml) of boiling water over 1 cup (85 g) of shredded fresh coconut. Process in a blender or food processor for 15 seconds, let cool to room temperature, then pour into a cheesecloth-lined colander resting over a bowl, gather the corners, and squeeze out all of the milk. For the instant version, pour 2 cups (480 ml) of boiling water over 4 ounces (115 g) of chopped solid white creamed coconut and blend or process until smooth. Alternately, mash the coconut with a fork, then whisk or blend until smooth. This product is sold in Indian grocery stores in solid or frozen cakes called "coconut cream" or "cream of coconut."

For an end-of-summer company lunch or supper, accompany with *Shallow-Fried Cabbage and Mung Dal Patties*, *Shredded Radish and Mung Dal Patties* or *Griddle-Fried Sweet-Stuffed Whole Wheat Bread* and a mixed green–sprout salad. For a sweet combination, try *Creamy Almond Pudding*.

Preparation time (after assembling ingredients): 15 minutes
Cooking time: 40 minutes
Serves: 4 or 5

4 large ears of corn or 2 cups (480 ml)
    frozen corn kernals, defrosted
½ tablespoon (7 ml) ground coriander
1 teaspoon (5 ml) ground cumin
¼ teaspoon (1 ml) turmeric
½ teaspoon (2 ml) *garam masala*
⅛ teaspoon (0.5 ml) cayenne pepper or paprika
1 tablespoon (15 ml) *ghee* or unsalted butter
8–10 curry leaves, preferably fresh
1 medium-sized red bell pepper (about 6 ounces/170 g),
    stemmed, seeded and cut lengthwise into strips
2 cups (480 ml) coconut milk as mentioned above
1 cup (240 ml) vegetable stock
1 cup (240 ml) light cream or milk
½ teaspoon (2 ml) salt
1 teaspoon (5 ml) sugar
a few sprigs fresh coriander or parsley

1. With a sharp knife, cut the kernels off of 3 ears of corn. To scrape the creamy pulp from the fourth ear, draw the knife lengthwise through each row of kernels, then scrape with the back of the knife to extract the pulp. If you use defrosted frozen corn, process in a blender until smooth. Press the corn through a strainer to extract the pulp; discard the roughage.

2. Combine the coriander, cumin, turmeric, *garam masala* and cayenne pepper or paprika in a small dish, add the water, and blend until smooth. Melt the *ghee* or butter in a 4-quart/liter pan over moderate heat. Add the wet spice mixture and fry until the liquid cooks off and the paste sizzles. Drop in the curry leaves, then 5 seconds later add the corn pulp, bell pepper, coconut milk and stock. Bring to a boil, then reduce the heat to low and gently boil for about 25 minutes. Add the cream or milk and leave the pan over heat only until it is hot, but do not allow it to boil. Remove the pan from the heat, stir in the salt and sweetener. Pour into a warmed serving bowl or individual dishes and garnish with fresh herb sprigs.

LEAFY GREEN DISHES

Greens, including the tops of root vegetables, the leaves of cabbages and grapevines, and, in warm climates, the fifty-plus species grown especially for tender leaves, constitute the basis of a group of loved dishes called *sak*. In India, these usually center around a strain of spinach called Malabar nightshade. In addition, mustard greens, fenugreek greens, collard greens, escarole and radish greens, to name a few, are added for seasonal variation. They offer a range of tastes from sweet to bitter, and textures from purées to wilted salads. Depending on regional customs, *sak* can be cooked in scantily seasoned *ghee*, mustard oil, sesame oil or ground nut oil. On one occasion when I served *sak* to Srila Prabhupada, he captivated me with histories detailing Lord Chaitanya's love for it. He related the *Shri Chaitanya Charitamrita* pastime in which Lord Chaitanya traveled from Jagannatha Puri to Vrindavan through the vast Jharikanda forests. His servant, Balabhadra Battacharya, would collect all kinds of forest greens, edible shoots and roots, and with only spices and oil prepare delicious *sak* for the Lord. Indeed, *sak* was so dear to the Lord that all the Vaishnavas receiving Him would invariably prepare *sak* as part of His meals.

The *sak* recipes in this section hail from several regional cuisines and illustrate variety in tastes and textures. So long as half of the greens are spinach, feel free to add fresh turnip, beet or radish tops, kale, collard or mustard greens, or cress, sorrel or stemmed Swiss chard. If possible, buy locally grown unpackaged leaves so you can examine what you purchase. Select brightly colored, crisp leaves that appear young and tender. Usually old greens are outsized, with thick stems and coarse veins on the leaves. Avoid yellow, spotted, wilted or bruised plants. Once picked, the leaves should be used as soon as possible. If you must keep them for up to 2 days, refrigerate, unwashed, in a plastic bag.

All greens must be trimmed and washed before cooking. Cut or tear off any bruised parts of the leaf, then remove the stem. Fold each leaf in half, glossy top side in. Grasp the thick stem at the base of the leaf and pull it off toward the tip, removing coarse veins. Plunge the leaves into a large bowl of cold water; press and swish to loosen the clinging sandy grit. Change the water 2 or 3 times, depending on quantity. If the leaves are mud-caked, they must be individually washed in cold water. Shake off excess water before placing them in a colander. (Do not try to wash them in a colander; the grit will remain nestled on the textured surfaces.) Avoid cooking greens in aluminum or cast iron, for they tend to discolor and absorb flavors from the pan. Stainless steel, enamel on iron or a nonstick surface is ideal.

For information about unfamiliar ingredients or techniques, see A-to-Z

Buttery Spinach
SAK

There are so many ways to season a simple *sak* that I find it difficult to select just one recipe to represent the possibilities. This variation could come from any region, from almost any kitchen, garnished with fried currants and cashew nuts. In Punjab and Gujarat, *sak* is routinely accompanied with corn dishes. Try this one with *Corn and Bell Peppers in Herbed Coconut Milk* and *Shallow-Fried Flaky Parathas* or *Griddle-Fried Whole Wheat Bread*.

Preparation time (after assembling ingredients): a few minutes
Cooking time: 15 minutes
Serves: 4

2 pounds (1 kg) fresh spinach, trimmed and washed
5 tablespoons (75 ml) *ghee* or unsalted butter
1–2 hot green chilies, cored, seeded and slivered
1½-inch (4 cm) piece of fresh ginger root,
    scraped and cut into thin julienne
2 whole cloves, crushed
¼ teaspoon (1 ml) each fennel seeds, black mustard
    seeds, and cumin seeds, crushed
1 teaspoon (5 ml) salt
¼ cup (35 g) raw cashew bits
⅓ cup (45 g) dried currants, soaked in warm water
    for 30 minutes, drained and dried on paper towels
½ teaspoon (2 ml) *garam masala*
a few butter pats (optional)
lemon or lime twists (optional)

1. Plunge the spinach into a large pot of salted boiling water. Cook for 8 minutes. Drain in a colander, pressing firmly with the back of a spoon to extract as much water as possible. Coarsely chop.

2. Melt 2½ tablespoons (37 ml) of the *ghee* or butter in a wide heavy casserole or sauté pan over moderate heat. Add the green chilies, ginger, cloves and spice seeds, and fry for about 1 minute. Stir in the spinach and salt and heat through. Cover and set aside.

3. Heat the remaining 2½ tablespoons (37 ml) of *ghee* or butter in a small saucepan over moderately low heat. Toss in the cashew bits and fry, stirring constantly, until they begin to color. Add the currants and continue to fry until they plump and brown. Remove the pan from the heat. Stir in the *garam masala* then pour the contents over the spinach. Finish with an additional pat of butter and lemon or lime twists, if desired.

Sautéed Spinach and *Dal* Noodles with Herbed Tomato Sauce
TAMATAR SAK

The combination of spinach and tomatoes is typical in many parts of India, but I must admit that I have taken liberties with a simple recipe and turned it into an elegant main-dish entrée. Flavors abound—not only does fresh sweet basil (*biswa tulasi*) account for part of the greens, but the tomato sauce is made with wonderful oven-roasted tomatoes. The dish is completed with the addition of thin *pappadam* noodles and enriched with sour cream All in all, this is one of my favorite spinach dishes, ideal for entertaining or Sunday dinner. Serve on a heated platter or plates. Accompany with *Butter Soft Eggplant Wedges, Buttered Rice* and sliced avocado and papaya salad on a bed of lettuce with a light dressing.

Preparation time (after assembling ingredients): a few minutes
Cooking time: 40 minutes
Serves: 5 or 6

4 medium-sized tomatoes
5 tablespoons (75 ml) *ghee* or olive oil
1–2 hot green chilies, seeded and finely chopped
1 teaspoon (5 ml) cumin seeds
6–8 curry leaves, preferably fresh
⅛ teaspoon (0.5 ml) yellow asafetida powder (*hing*)*
1 teaspoon (5 ml) each salt and sugar
5 plain *pappadams* (about 5 inches/12.5 cm in diameter),
    cut with scissors into noodles ⅓ inch (1 cm) wide
3 pounds (1.5 kg) fresh spinach, trimmed, washed and torn into large pieces
1 cup (240 ml) trimmed fresh basil, lightly packed, or 1 teaspoon (5 ml) dried basil
⅔ cup (160 ml) sour cream
5–6 sprigs of fresh coriander, basil or parsley

This amount applies only to yellow Cobra brand. Reduce any other asafetida by three-fourths.

1. Place the tomatoes on an aluminum-foil-lined cookie sheet and set under a pre-heated broiler, about 6 inches (15 cm) away from the heat. Broil, turning, until all sides of the tomatoes are charred, about 10 minutes. Set aside to cool, then remove the skins and coarsely chop.

2. Heat 2½ tablespoons (37 ml) of the *ghee* or oil in a 12-inch (30 cm) frying pan over moderate heat. When it is hot, add the green chilies and cumin seeds and fry until the cumin darkens a few shades. Drop in the curry leaves and asafetida and fry for a few seconds, then add the tomatoes, salt and sugar. Stirring, cook until thickened. Remove the pan from the heat, sprinkle half of the *pappadam* noodles over the top, cover and set aside for 3 minutes. Fold in the soft noodles and sprinkle with the remaining pieces. Cover and set aside.

3. Place the remaining 2½ tablespoons (37 ml) of *ghee* or oil in a large nonstick saucepan and pack the spinach and basil in the pan. Place the pan over moderately high heat, cover and cook until you hear a sizzling sound, then cook for 2–3 minutes more. Uncover and turn the leaves over with 2 forks, so that the uncooked leaves on the top

For information about unfamiliar ingredients or techniques, see A-to-Z

switch places with the cooked leaves underneath. Uncover and cook until the water has evaporated, tossing to prevent scorching.

4. Add the noodles and tomato sauce and mix very gently. Fold in half of the sour cream. Garnish each serving with a spoonful of sour cream and a sprig of the fresh herbs.

Seasoned Spinach with Julienne Potatoes
ALOO SAK

India's city dwellers have been influenced by numerous international cuisines, but the villagers are slow to accept change, if at all, and this recipe is real village-style cooking—simple and straightforward. Spinach is often coupled with mustard greens, kale or collard greens in this dish, and because of the potatoes, it is a good way to be introduced to new flavors. This is a "dry" dish, and the fried potatoes are added to the cooked greens just before serving to prevent them from losing their shape. For the North Indian villager, a simple, healthful lunch favorite is *aloo sak*, a bowl of homemade fresh yogurt and *Griddle-Baked Village-Style Corn Bread*. You might round off the menu with grilled tomatoes.

Preparation time (after assembling ingredients): 10 minutes
Cooking time: 30 minutes
Serves: 6 to 8

4 medium-sized new boiling potatoes (about
    1 pound/455 g), cooked until nearly fork-tender
½ teaspoon (2 ml) turmeric
½ teaspoon (2 ml) *garam masala*
½ teaspoon (2 ml) ground cumin
¼ teaspoon (1 ml) cayenne pepper or paprika
2 teaspoons (10 ml) ground coriander
1 teaspoon (5 ml) sugar
1½ tablespoons (22 ml) lemon juice
2½ tablespoons (37 ml) water
5 tablespoons (75 ml) *ghee* or sesame oil
1 pound (455 g) fresh spinach, trimmed, washed and coarsely chopped, or one
    10-ounce (285 g) package of frozen chopped spinach, defrosted and pressed dry
⅓ pound (150 g) each fresh collard greens, mustard greens and kale, stemmed,
    washed and chopped, or one 10-ounce (285 g) package of frozen mixed greens,
    defrosted and pressed dry
1–1½ teaspoons (5–7 ml) salt
6–8 lemon or lime wedges

1. Peel the potatoes and cut into coarse julienne—⅓ inch (1 cm) wide and thick by 1½ inches (4 cm) long. Combine the turmeric, *garam masala*, cumin, cayenne or paprika, coriander, sweetener, lemon juice and water in a small cup and mix well.

2. Heat the *ghee* or oil in a heavy 12-inch (30 cm) nonstick frying pan or sauté pan over moderately high heat. Add the potatoes and fry, gently turning, until they are golden brown. Remove with a slotted spoon and set aside.

3. Reduce the heat to low, add the spice blend and fry until all of the liquid has evaporated. Stir in the greens, cover and cook for 10–15 minutes; you may add a sprinkle of water during the cooking if the excess on the leaves has evaporated. Uncover, add the salt and stir well to blend in the spices.

4. Add the potatoes, cover and let them warm through, about 5 minutes. Gently fold the potatoes into the greens. Accompany each serving with a lemon or lime wedge, or arrange on a warmed platter garnished with citrus wedges.

Curried Greens and Eggplant
BAIGAN SAK

The "heat" in this *sak* should be noticeable. Fresh green chilies, though unpredictable in strength, are usually milder than dried red chilies. If you are very sensitive to chilies, try fresh Anaheims or yellow wax. To be authentic, this dish should be a bit hot and spicy. Bengalis sauté the greens quickly over high heat, allowing them to wilt, then soften, but still retain exuberant color and fresh flavor. This is a delightful contrast to the butter-soft bits of crispy eggplant. In Bengal, this is always served with rice, and often also with paper-thin flatbread. You can build your menu from there to suit the occasion, adding *dal*, a yogurt salad, chutney and a savory.

Preparation time (after assembling ingredients): a few minutes
Cooking time: 10–15 minutes
Serves: 4 or 5

4 tablespoons (60 ml) peanut oil plus
    2 tablespoons (30 ml) mustard oil, or
    6 tablespoons (90 ml) vegetable oil
1 small eggplant (8–10 ounces/230–285 g),
    cut into ¾-inch (2 cm) cubes
½ teaspoon (2 ml) *garam masala*
½ teaspoon (2 ml) turmeric
1–2 whole green jalapeño chilies, dried
    whole red chilies, Anaheim chilies or
    yellow wax chilies (or as desired)
1 teaspoon (5 ml) each crushed fennel seeds,
    coriander seeds and cumin seeds
½ cassia or bay leaf
1 pound (455 g) fresh spinach, trimmed, washed
    and coarsely chopped, or one 10-ounce (285 g)
    package of frozen chopped spinach, defrosted
    and pressed dry
1 teaspoon (5 ml) *jaggery* or maple syrup
½ tablespoon (7 ml) salt
1 tablespoon (15 ml) lemon or lime juice
4 or 5 lemon or lime wedges

1. Heat 4 tablespoons (60 ml) of peanut or vegetable oil in a nonstick wok or large frying pan over moderately high heat. When it is hot but not smoking, drop in the eggplant and stir-fry until reddish-brown and crisp. Remove with a slotted spoon and drain on paper towels. Sprinkle with *garam masala* and turmeric, and toss to coat the cubes with spices.

2. Add the mustard oil or the remaining 2 tablespoons (30 ml) vegetable oil to the pan. Heat the mustard oil to the smoking point for a few seconds, but only allow the vegetable oil to become hot. Immediately add the chilies, spice seeds and cassia or bay leaf, and in a few seconds add the greens, sugar and salt. Reduce the heat to moderate and cook for about 4 minutes, stirring frequently.

3. Add the lemon or lime juice and fried eggplant, toss gently and reheat the eggplant. Serve immediately, garnished with lemon or lime wedges.

Bengali Spinach
BADAAM SAK

Srila Prabhupada encouraged me to observe cooking techniques from the expert chefs at the C.L. Bajoria household in Calcutta. On one occasional visit, I arrived just after Mr. Bajoria had returned from his hill station resort and jute plantations in Bihar. He had brought back kilos of hand picked raw almonds. Each was encased in a soft, greenish skin with a texture somewhere between those of crisp apples and water chestnuts. They were served at breakfast as nibblers, accompanied by several varieties of seasonal fruit. For the evening meal, the ingenious cooks chose to contrast the crisp almonds with stir-fried spinach. As an alternative to almonds, try peanuts or pistachios.

Preparation and nut soaking time: at least 4 hours
Cooking time: 25 minutes
Serves: 4 or 5

⅔ cup (100 g) raw almonds, peanuts or pistachios, with skins
2 cups (480 ml) warm water
3 tablespoons (45 ml) *ghee* or sesame oil
1 teaspoon (5 ml) black mustard seeds
½ teaspoon (2 ml) cumin seeds
⅛ teaspoon (0.5 ml) fenugreek seeds
1½ tablespoons (22 ml) *jaggery* or dark brown sugar
½ tablespoon (7 ml) scraped, finely shredded or minced fresh ginger root
1 teaspoon (5 ml) seeded and minced hot green chilies
2 pounds (1 kg) fresh spinach, trimmed, washed and coarsely chopped, or two
    10-ounce (570 g) packages frozen chopped spinach, defrosted and pressed dry
⅓ cup (35 g) freshly shredded coconut, lightly packed
1 teaspoon (5 ml) salt
2 tablespoons (30 ml) heavy cream
⅛ teaspoon (0.5 ml) freshly ground nutmeg
butter and lemon twists for garnishing

1. Soak the nuts in warm water for 4 hours or overnight. Drain and slip off the loose skins. Wash in fresh water, then drain.

2. Heat the *ghee* or oil in a 5-quart/liter nonstick pan over moderate heat. When it is hot but not smoking, add the spice seeds and sugar and fry until the seeds darken and the sugar caramelizes. Add the ginger, chilies, spinach, nuts, coconut and salt, cover, reduce the heat to low, and cook for 10 minutes. Uncover and turn the spinach over with two forks, so that the cooked leaves on the bottom change places with those on the top. Add water if necessary, and cook for another 10 minutes.

3. Stir in the cream or and nutmeg and heat for 1–2 minutes. Serve immediately. Garnish each serving with a pat of butter and a lemon twist.

Broccoli and Spinach Purée
NARIYAL SAK

In India, spinach season is anticipated long before its arrival, and this thick, rich spinach dish is a particular favorite in the Punjab region of North India. In 1970 I traveled through this region with Srila Prabhupada as part of his *sankirtan* party, and during our two-week stay in Amritsar not a day passed when our hosts did not offer us some form of *sak*. The combination of broccoli and spinach is not as common as *panir* and spinach, but several households did serve some variation on this dish, and they were delicious. It is also outstanding as a gratin—sprinkled with buttered bread crumbs and shredded cheese and broiled until browned. To make the bread crumbs, melt 4 tablespoons (60 ml) of butter in a frying pan, add ¾ cup (120 g) of fresh crumbs, and toss over moderate heat until crisp. You will be surprised at how much butter the crumbs can absorb. Try it with *Sautéed Rice* or *Griddle-Fried Radish-Stuffed Whole Wheat Bread* and *Herbed Cracked Wheat Uppma with Mixed Vegetables* for a special lunch or dinner.

Preparation time (after assembling ingredients): a few minutes
Cooking time: 1–1½ hours
Serves: 6 to 8

½ cup (120 ml) water
1 pound (455 g) fresh spinach, trimmed, washed and coarsely chopped, or one
    10-ounce (285 g) package of frozen spinach, defrosted and pressed dry
1 pound (455 g) fresh mixed greens, trimmed, washed and coarsely chopped, or one
    10-ounce (285 g) package of frozen mixed greens, defrosted and pressed dry
1 pound (455 g) fresh broccoli, larger stalks trimmed and coarsely chopped,
    or one 10-ounce (285 g) package of frozen broccoli, defrosted and coarsely chopped
1 medium-sized potato, peeled and diced
2–3 hot green chilies
½-inch (1.5 cm) piece of fresh ginger root, scraped and sliced
½ teaspoon (2 ml) turmeric
2 teaspoons (10 ml) ground coriander

For information about unfamiliar ingredients or techniques, see A-to-Z

½ tablespoon (7 ml) salt
5 tablespoons (75 ml) *ghee* or peanut oil
1 teaspoon (5 ml) cumin seeds
1 teaspoon (5 ml) *garam masala*
3 tablespoons (45 ml) cream cheese or cream
a handful of buttered bread crumbs or shredded cheese (optional)

1. Bring the water to a boil in a 5–6-quart/liter nonstick pot. Pack in the spinach, greens, broccoli, potato, green chilies, ginger, turmeric, coriander and salt. Cover and cook over moderately low heat for 50–60 minutes, stirring after 20 minutes and every 10 minutes thereafter. You may have to add additional water to prevent scorching.

2. Process in batches in a food processor or blender, until all of the ingredients are reduced to a smooth purée.

3. Heat the *ghee* or oil in a heavy 12-inch (30 cm) nonstick frying pan or sauté pan over moderate heat. When it is hot but not smoking, drop in the cumin seeds and fry until they darken a few shades. Add the puréed greens, stir and reduce the heat to low. Cook, stirring occasionally, until all of the liquid has evaporated and the mixture begins to pull away from the sides of the pan. Stir in the *garam masala* and cream cheese or cream, and cook until thoroughly mixed.

4. Serve on a warmed platter, or transfer to a buttered gratin dish and smooth the surface. To finish the gratin, sprinkle the top with a mixture of buttered fresh bread crumbs and/or a handful of shredded cheese. Place 6 inches (15 cm) from a preheated broiler and brown until crisp and golden. Serve bubbling hot.

Greens and Plantain with Toasted Almonds
KACHA KELA SAK

Plantains, unlike their ubiquitous smaller cousins, bananas, must be cooked before eating. When they are not available, a good alternative is parsnips. Choose young, tender parsnips— about 8 inches (20 cm) long. In the North Indian style, the coarsely shredded plantains or parsnips and greens are cooked separately, then assembled. They are then thickened into a purée and flavor-enriched with spices and fine cornmeal or chickpea flour.

This is a beautiful dish to serve with *Cracked Black Pepper Rice*, *Crisp Lotus Root Salad* and *Stuffed Arbi Leaves in Tomato and Sour Cream Sauce*. For a delectable sweet, try *Coconut Cheese Fudge* with seasonal fresh fruits.

Preparation time (after assembling ingredients): 10 minutes
Cooking time: 30 minutes
Serves: 4 or 5

1 large plantain or two 8-inch (20 cm) parsnips
1 pound (455 g) fresh spinach, trimmed and washed,
    plus 1 pound (455 g) mixed fresh greens, trimmed
    and washed; or one 10-ounce/285 g) package of
    frozen leaf spinach plus one 10-ounce /285 g)
    package of frozen mixed greens
4 cups (l liter) water
5 tablespoons (75 ml) *ghee* or corn oil
3 tablespoons (45 ml) fine cornmeal or chickpea flour
1 teaspoon (5 ml) coarsely crushed black mustard seeds
1 teaspoon (5 ml) coarsely crushed cumin seeds
½ teaspoon (2 ml) turmeric
¼ teaspoon (1 ml) cayenne pepper or paprika
1 teaspoon (5 ml) *jaggery* or brown sugar
1 teaspoon (5 ml) salt
3 tablespoons (45 ml) toasted slivered almonds
4 or 5 lemon or lime wedges for garnishing

1. Cut off the skin from the plantain with a sharp paring knife, or peel the parsnips with a potato peeler. Shred through the coarse holes on a grater. Steam or blanch until soft. Drain well.

2. If you are using fresh spinach and mixed greens, bring the water to a boil in a large stockpot. Pack in the greens, reduce the heat, cover and simmer for 15 minutes. Drain well in a colander, pressing out excess moisture. Using two sharp knives scissors fashion, finely chop. Alternatively, cook the frozen spinach and greens according to package directions, drain and press out excess moisture.

3. Heat the *ghee* or oil in a large, heavy-bottomed nonstick frying pan or wok over moderate heat. Add the cornmeal or chickpea flour, black mustard seeds and cumin, and fry, stirring constantly, until the meal or flour darkens a few shades. Stir in the plantain or parsnip and stir-fry for 2 minutes. Add the turmeric, cayenne or paprika, sweetener, salt and greens. Gently stir until hot throughout. Serve on a warmed platter or on individual dishes with a sprinkle of almonds and a citrus wedge.

Spiced Creamed Spinach
MALAI SAK

Throughout India, districts, towns, even individual homes have their own distinct cuisines. This delicious creamed spinach hails from the community of Vaishnava *brahmins* of Delhi, and the final texture and richness are determined by the milk product you select: cream, sour cream, crème fraîche, cream cheese or plain yogurt. For a simple yet varied menu, try this spinach with *Shredded*

White Radish and Diced Potato, Curried Cabbage with Tender Whole Mung Beans and rice or flatbreads. For a light lunch, it is delicious with whole grain toast and *Potato Patties with Crunchy Bitter Melon Chips*.

Preparation time (after assembling ingredients): 5 minutes
Cooking time: 15 minutes
Serves: 4 or 5

⅛ **teaspoon (0.5 ml) cayenne pepper**
½ **tablespoon (7 ml) ground coriander**
¼ **teaspoon (1 ml) freshly ground pepper**
⅛ **teaspoon (0.5 ml) freshly grated nutmeg**
¼ **teaspoon (1 ml) turmeric**
1 **teaspoon (5 ml)** *garam masala*
3 **tablespoons (45 ml) water**
4 **tablespoons (60 ml)** *ghee* **or unsalted butter**
⅛ **teaspoon (0.5 ml) yellow asafetida powder (***hing***)***
2 **pounds (1 kg) fresh spinach, trimmed, washed and coarsely chopped**
1 **teaspoon (5 ml) salt**
½ **cup (120 ml) of any of the following: heavy cream, cream cheese**
     (cut into cubes), crème fraîche, sour cream or stirred yogurt

*This amount applies only to yellow Cobra brand. Reduce any other asafetida by three-fourths.

1. Combine the cayenne, coriander, black pepper, nutmeg, turmeric and *garam masala* in a small bowl, add the water, and mix well. Melt the *ghee* or butter in a 5-quart/liter nonstick pan over moderate heat. Add the asafetida and let it sizzle for a few seconds, then pour in the spice mixture. Fry for about 2 minutes.

2. Pack in the spinach and sprinkle with the salt. Cover and reduce the heat. Cover for 6–8 minutes, then turn the leaves over so that the uncooked layer on the top changes places with the cooked leaves underneath. Cook for an additional few minutes.

3. Remove the pan from the heat and stir in the desired milk product. Return the pan to the heat and rewarm briefly. (If the yogurt is allowed to simmer, it will curdle.) Serve immediately.

SEASONED VEGETABLE PURÉES

Why do potatoes baked in an oven and potatoes baked in ashes taste so different? Both are cooked by dry heat, but the latter allows charcoal flavors to permeate the skins, resulting in a smoky flavor that is incomparable. It is this taste that is essential to authentic *bhartas*, or vegetable purées.

Indian stoves today have changed little from their ancient past. The most popular household version is still a coal- or wood-burning model, usually custom-designed by the woman of the house, sitting as the only fixture in a near-empty kitchen. Known as a *choola*, it can accommodate up to four burners and be built right into the floor, or it may be a bucket-sized portable model that gets carried from kitchen to veranda. It is designed to hold pans or griddles on the top and allow vegetables or breads to toast or bake in a small ash-filled chamber on the floor of the stove. The other type of stove is a large, underground clay *tandoor*. This oven is beautifully designed for baking flatbreads such as *parathas* and *naan* which are slapped right onto the clay walls and cooked in smoky direct heat. Variations of these old-fashioned brick and clay ovens are in use today in many countries, and experts agree with Srila Prabhupada that the flavor of foods cooked outdoors, on the simplest equipment, is often the best.

Few vegetables can stand exposure to open heat without protective covers. Classic *bhartas* are therefore made from those limited few: mature potatoes, yams or sweet potatoes, winter squash and eggplants. If you have a hibachi, fireplace, campfire or pile of fall leaves that has been burning for some time and is covered with white ash, by all means take the opportunity to ash-bake a vegetable and try a *bharta*. Here are three methods of preparing the vegetables—in ashes, in an oven, or over open flame. Potatoes, sweet potatoes, yams and squash are ash- or oven-baked, while eggplant is best ash-baked or gas flame-roasted. Of course, they all can also be baked in an electric or gas oven.

Ash-Baked Vegetables: Wash and dry the vegetable and pierce the skin in a few places. Bake the root vegetables or squash, nestled in a bed of hot white ash. Cook yams and sweet potatoes for 1–1¼ hours, mature baking potatoes for 1½–1¾ hours, and squash, depending on size, for about 2½ hours. The eggplant should be laid on the ash and rotated intermittently until the outside is charred and the inside has become butter-soft throughout, anywhere from 45 minutes to 1 hour. Wearing thick gloves, dig out or lift off the vegetables, then brush off the ashes. Vegetables are done when they easily yield to pressure or can easily be pierced with a fork, offering no resistance. Cut in half, discarding seeds and fiber in squash, and scoop out the soft pulp.

Oven-Baked Vegetables: Wash and dry the vegetable, then pierce the skin in a few places. I like to rub butter on the root vegetables and eggplant and then rub with smoked salt before baking. Bake in a preheated 425°F (220°C) oven, allowing about 1 hour for mature baking potatoes, 45–50 minutes for yams or sweet potatoes, about 45 minutes for eggplants resting on a baking sheet. Remove the root vegetables or squash with a mitt. They are done when they easily yield to pressure or when the thick skins can be easily pierced with a fork. The eggplant is done when butter soft. Cut the baked squash in half, discarding the seeds and fibers, and scoop out the soft pulp.

Roasted or Broiled Eggplants: Wash and dry medium-sized eggplants, then prick the surface in seven or eight places. To roast on top of the stove, line the burner with aluminum foil. Turn the heat on low and set an eggplant, stem side up, directly on the burner. Roast for 5–6 minutes or until the skin is charred. Lay it on its side and cook until charred, then give it a quarter-turn and char, bit by bit, for 20 minutes or until the entire eggplant is blistered and charred and the flesh is butter-soft. To broil in an oven, preheat the broiler and lay the eggplant on a foil-lined tray. Broil until the skin is charred, then rotate and broil the eggplant, bit by bit, for about 15–20 minutes or until the entire skin is charred and the flesh is butter soft. Let cool briefly, then rinse with water and pat dry. Split open and scoop out the eggplant, discarding the skin.

Zesty Mashed Potatoes
ALOO BHARTA

Mature potatoes—large russets or Idahos, mealy and dry-fleshed, are ideal for mashing. Bake or boil them, mash them while hot, and season, allowing a little "heat" from the green chilies. I sometimes imitate ash-baked flavor by adding a sprinkle of smoked salt rather than using all sea salt. This is a good place to introduce *Ginger Ghee* or flavored butters.

Preparation time: (after assembling ingredients): a few minutes
Serves: 4

5–6 mature baking potatoes (about 2 pounds/1 kg),
    freshly ash- or oven-baked (page 260),
    or freshly boiled or steamed potatoes
3–4 tablespoons (45–60 ml) seasoned or plain
    butter or *ghee*
1 teaspoon (5 ml) salt
⅛ teaspoon (0.5 ml) freshly ground pepper
1–2 seeded and minced hot green chilies
3 tablespoons (45 ml) scalded cream or milk
fresh parsley or coriander sprigs for garnishing

1. Cut the warm baked potatoes and scoop out the pulp, or peel the skins from boiled or steamed potatoes. Mash with a potato masher or force through a food mill or potato ricer. Add the remaining ingredients and whisk with a fork until creamy and blended. Serve immediately or keep warm in a double boiler.

Mashed Potato Balls with Horseradish
MASALA ALOO BHARTA

Horseradish, a pungent tap root, is used primarily in Bengali and Orissan cuisines, though occasionally elsewhere. You can find the roots at Oriental and Indian grocery stores and sometimes even in supermarkets. Peel off the brownish skin and finely grate the outer part; discard the tough woody core. Since you are likely to use only a little at a time, you can freeze the unused portion in plastic bags for up to two months. At room temperature, freshly ground horseradish loses its "punch" within eight hours. In England, and in some American gourmet shops, plain grated horseradish is sold in small bottles.

This side dish is meant to be nose-tingling and buttery. It is served in smooth balls, 2 or 3 per person, at room temperature, with a wedge of lime. If you are considering a full-course Bengali meal, do give this delightful potato dish a try. It is also delicious for breakfast, spread on whole grain toast sprinkled with shredded cheese and broiled.

Preparation time (after assembling ingredients): a few minutes
Serves: 6 or 7

3 large baking potatoes (about 1½
    pounds/685 g) freshly ash- or oven-baked
    (page 260), or freshly boiled or steamed potatoes
4–5 tablespoons (60–75 ml) unsalted butter
2–3 teaspoons (10–15 ml) grated fresh horseradish
1 teaspoon (5 ml) salt
⅛ teaspoon (0.5 ml) freshly ground white pepper
⅛ teaspoon (0.5 ml) paprika or cayenne pepper
6 or 7 lime wedges, preferably Key lime

1. Cut and scoop out the warm baked potatoes, or peel the skins from boiled or steamed potatoes. Mash with a potato masher or force through a food mill or potato ricer. Add the butter, horseradish, salt and white pepper, and mash with a fork until well blended. Let cool to room temperature.

2. Divide into 12–15 portions and roll between buttered palms into smooth balls. Sprinkle with paprika or cayenne and serve at room temperature with lime wedges.

Note: This dish may be assembled up to 6 hours before serving, kept covered and refrigerated. Bring to room temperature before serving.

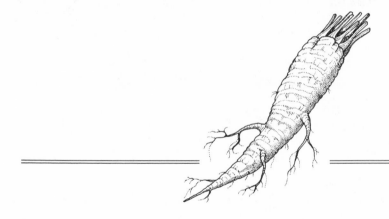

Baked Eggplant Purée with Seasoned Yogurt
BAIGAN BHARTA

Eggplant *bharta*, in one form or another, is a national favorite of India. I learned to make this variation during my first Bombay residence in the kitchen of the Kailash Seksaria family. The cooks excel at several regional cuisines, and this Punjabi-style presentation was a favorite of hosts and guests alike. Baby white eggplants were ever-so-slowly ash-baked on a nearly burned-out *neem* wood fire until they nearly fell apart. Chilies and seasonings gave the dish a feisty punch, and the yogurt added creamy distinction. *Bharta* goes well with any flatbread: griddle-baked, shallow-fried or deep-fried. It goes equally well on crackers, thin melba toast and fresh whole grain toast. It is an excellent sandwich spread as well.

For information about unfamiliar ingredients or techniques, see A-to-Z

Preparation time (after assembling ingredients): 5 minutes
Cooking time: 15 minutes
Serves: 4

1 medium-sized eggplant (1–1¼ pounds/455–570 g),
    freshly baked, roasted or broiled (page 260)
2 tablespoons (30 ml) *ghee* or vegetable oil
1–2 teaspoons (5–10 ml) hot green chilies, seeded and minced
¼ teaspoon (1 ml) yellow asafetida powder (*hing*)*
1 teaspoon (5 ml) cumin seeds
1 teaspoon (5 ml) ground coriander
1 teaspoon (5 ml) salt
2 tablespoons (30 ml) each finely chopped fresh coriander and mint
⅔ cup (160 ml) plain yogurt or sour cream
1 teaspoon (5 ml) *garam masala*

This amount applies only to yellow Cobra brand. Reduce any other asafetida by three-fourths.

1. Slice the eggplant in half lengthwise and carefully scoop out the pulp. Discard the skin and coarsely chop the pulp.

2. Heat the *ghee* or oil in a large nonstick frying pan over moderate heat. When it is hot but not smoking, add the green chilies, asafetida and cumin seeds and fry until the cumin seeds darken. Add the eggplant, ground coriander and salt, and cook, stirring frequently, until the mixture is dry and thick, about 10 minutes.

3. Remove the pan from the heat and let cool to room temperature. Stir in the fresh herbs, yogurt or sour cream and *garam masala*. (You may want to add a sprinkle of smoked salt if you baked the eggplant in an electric or gas oven.) Serve hot, at room temperature or chilled.

Butternut Squash Purée with Coconut
KADDU BHARTA

Pumpkin is the most popular winter squash in India. It is sold in cut pieces. This bright orange squash is more often boiled than baked. In the West, we can ash- or oven-bake whole smaller varieties, such as butternut, acorn, Hubbard or buttercup. Flavor and nutrition are locked within the tough, thick skin. A delicate blend of cardamom, fennel and lime juice beautifully offsets the sweet purée. Garnish with toasted coconut and/or hazelnuts.

Preparation time (after assembling ingredients): a few minutes
Cooking time: 15 minutes
Serves: 4

1 large butternut squash (about 1 pound/455 g), freshly baked or steamed
4 tablespoons (60 ml) unsalted butter
2 teaspoons (10 ml) fennel seeds, crushed
½ teaspoon (2 ml) cardamom seeds, crushed
1–2 teaspoons (5–10 ml) hot green chilies, seeded and minced
2–3 tablespoons (30–45 ml) *jaggery*, maple sugar or syrup
3 tablespoons (45 ml) cream (optional)
1 teaspoon (5 ml) salt
¼ cup (25 g) shredded coconut and/or chopped hazelnuts,
    toasted in a 300°F (150°C) oven until golden
2 tablespoons (30 ml) lime juice

   1. Cut open and peel the squash. If it has been baked whole, scoop out the seeds and fibers. Place the pulp in a bowl and purée with a potato masher or in a food processor.
   2. Heat 3 tablespoons (45 ml) of the butter in a 12-inch (30 cm) nonstick frying pan over moderate heat. When it is hot and frothing, add the fennel seeds, cardamom seeds and green chilies. Within seconds add the squash purée, sweetener, cream, if desired, and salt. Cook, stirring frequently, until thickened, about 5 minutes. Before serving, garnish with coconut or hazelnuts, the remaining butter and sprinkle with lime juice.

Buttery Sweet Potato Purée with Tomato Bits
SHAKARKAND BHARTA

   For this dish you can use either yams or sweet potatoes, depending on the degree of sweetness or moisture you prefer. It is little more than a seasoned mashed root vegetable dish, and is nice with a Vedic or Western dinner menu. To keep calories to a minimum, rely on the orange juice to make a buttery consistency. The sweet, firm flesh of Italian plum tomatoes is ideal for this *bharta*, though you can use any type; even green tomatoes are delicious.

Preparation time (after assembling ingredients): a few minutes
Cooking time: about 10 minutes
Serves: 6

6 medium-sized yams or sweet potatoes
    (about 2 pounds/1 kg) freshly ash-
    or oven-baked (page 260)
1 teaspoon (5 ml) salt
½ teaspoon (2 ml) turmeric
¼ teaspoon (1 ml) paprika or ⅛
    teaspoon (0.5 ml) cayenne pepper
¼ teaspoon (1 ml) ground nutmeg or mace
    or ⅛ teaspoon (0.5 ml) ground ginger

For information about unfamiliar ingredients or techniques, see A-to-Z

4 tablespoons (60 ml) orange juice
½ teaspoon (2 ml) orange zest
3 tablespoons (45 ml) *ghee* or butter
1½ tablespoons (22 ml) brown sugar or *jaggery*
2 medium-sized Italian plum tomatoes (about ¾
    pound/340 g), seeded and coarsely chopped
2 tablespoons (30 ml) sliced almonds, toasted

1. Cut and scoop out the yam or sweet potato pulp and mash with a potato masher or force through a food mill or potato ricer. Add the salt, turmeric, paprika or cayenne, nutmeg, mace or ginger, orange juice and orange zest, and whisk with a fork until well blended.

2. Heat the *ghee* or butter in a 12-inch (30 cm) frying pan over moderate heat. Add the sweetener and cook until it caramelizes and turns reddish-brown. Drop in the tomatoes and cook, gently tossing, just until they soften and glisten.

3. Add the yams or sweet potatoes and, using the back of a wooden spoon, mash and blend the ingredients. When warmed throughout, serve on a warmed platter, garnished with toasted almonds.

STUFFED VEGETABLES

Side Dishes

Pishima's Stuffed Okra
BHARA BHINDI

The size of okra pods determines which recipes they are best used in. Baby pods are perfect for slicing or leaving whole. Medium-sized pods, 4½–5 inches (11.5–12.5 cm) long, are still young and tender but large enough to endure stuffing. Though large pods may possess a fine flavor or shape, they usually have fibrous, tough spines running lengthwise along the sides from cap to tail, and should be avoided. This is a good recipe to select when you can hand pick even-sized pods. To reduce the mucilage that cut okra gives off, wash and pat each pod thoroughly dry. After that, you may want to further oven-dry them for 10 minutes in a preheated 200°F (100°C) oven. The stuffing is spicy and hot, but only enough is spread in the slit to excite the already delicious flavor of fresh okra.

This is my favorite stuffed okra recipe, and I have stuck as close as possible to the original version I learned from my well-wishing Vaishnava teacher and cooking inspiration, Pishima. Her Bengali lunch menu included steamed rice, *Fennel-Flavored Urad Dal Soup*, *Char-Flavored Curried Potatoes and Green Beans* and *Creamy Karhi with White Radishes*. Her savory and chutney added lively flavors: *Seasoned Chana Dal Patties and Tomatoes* and *Zesty Mint and Green Mango Chutney*. This lunch was completed by one of Bengal's most-loved cultured milk products, *Sweetened Condensed Yogurt*. You can copy the menu for a full Bengali luncheon, or pick 2 or 3 dishes to suit the occasion.

Preparation time (after assembling ingredients): 30 minutes
Cooking time: 20–30 minutes
Serves: 6

1½ pounds (685 g) tender okra, preferably 4-inch
    (10 cm) pods, washed and thoroughly dried
2 tablespoons (30 ml) coarsely crushed coriander seeds
1 tablespoon (15 ml) coarsely crushed cumin seeds
2 teaspoons (10 ml) fennel seeds
½ teaspoon (2 ml) freshly ground pepper
1 tablespoon (15 ml) *garam masala*
¼ teaspoon (1 ml) cayenne pepper or paprika
¼ teaspoon (1 ml) yellow asafetida powder (*hing*)*
½ teaspoon (2 ml) turmeric
1 tablespoon (15 ml) ground almonds
½ teaspoon (2 ml) *amchoor* powder or
    ½ tablespoon (7 ml) lemon juice
5 tablespoons (75 ml) *ghee* or sunflower oil
½ tablespoon (7 ml) salt

*This amount applies only to yellow Cobra brand. Reduce any other asafetida by three-fourths.

    1. Slice off the stem end and ⅛ inch (3 mm) off the tip of each okra pod. Slit each one lengthwise, leaving ¼ inch (6 mm) unslit at both ends, taking care not to cut the pods in half.

    2. Combine the crushed coriander seeds, cumin seeds, fennel seeds, black pepper, *garam masala*, cayenne or paprika, asafetida, turmeric, ground almonds and *amchoor* powder if you're using it. After mixing the ingredients together, drizzle in the lemon juice (if you haven't used *amchoor*) and 2 teaspoons (10 ml) of *ghee* or oil, and crumble through your fingers to blend well into a dry, oatmeal like consistency.

    3. Using a teaspoon or butter knife, ease about ¼ teaspoon (1 ml) of the stuffing evenly into each slit. Working one at a time, stuff, then press the cut edges closed and set aside, covered, until ready to cook.

    4. When you are ready to fry the okra, place the *ghee* or oil in a heavy-bottomed 12-inch (30 cm) frying pan over moderately high heat. When it is hot but not smoking, add the stuffed okra and spread the pods into one layer. Cover, reduce the heat to moderate and cook for about 5 minutes. Remove the lid, gently turn the okra to ensure even browning, and fry, turning frequently, for 20–25 minutes or until the okra is tender, golden brown and crisp. Depending on the size of the pods, cooking time will vary. Transfer the okra to paper towels, salt and gently toss. Serve piping hot.

For information about unfamiliar ingredients or techniques, see A-to-Z

Baked Bananas Stuffed with Tamarind-Flavored Coconut
NARIYAL BHARA KELA

Bananas are native to India and are one of the most popular fruits of the nation. There are said to be a staggering 400 varieties of bananas. Even so, they are divided into only two categories: eating and cooking. In this dish, a small, very sweet eating banana, either yellow- or red-skinned, is preferred. Known as *lady fingers* or *golden fingers*, they are often available in Mexican or Indian grocery stores. Though they are traditionally baked in softened banana leaf wrappers on a coal-fed oven, I find that they bake wonderfully in any oven and in almost any type of baking dish. This South Indian side-dish delicacy goes well on any warm weather lunch or dinner menu.

Preparation time (after assembling ingredients): 15 minutes
Cooking time: 20 minutes
Makes: 8 side dish servings

2 tablespoons (30 ml) instant tamarind concentrate (available at Indian groceries)
1½ tablespoons (22 ml) water
1 tablespoon (15 ml) minced fresh mint or ½ teaspoon (2 ml) dried mint
⅛ teaspoon (0.5 ml) cayenne pepper or ¼ teaspoon (1 ml) paprika
3 tablespoons (45 ml) grated fresh or dried coconut
1 teaspoon (5 ml) *garam masala*
½ teaspoon (2 ml) *ajwain* seeds or fennel seeds, crushed
¼ teaspoon (1 ml) salt
8 small firm ripe bananas, no more than 6–7 inches (15–18.5 cm) long, preferably
    "finger" bananas, red or yellow, 4–5 inches (10–12.5 cm) long
3 tablespoons (45 ml) slivered almonds
½ cup (120 ml) maple syrup
2 tablespoons (30 ml) finely chopped crystallized ginger
1 tablespoon (15 ml) each lime and orange juice
3 tablespoons (45 ml) slivered almonds
2 tablespoons (30 ml) melted butter

1. Combine the tamarind concentrate with water and whisk with a fork until blended. Add the mint, cayenne or paprika, coconut, *garam masala*, *ajwain* or fennel seeds and salt, and toss to mix.

2. Preheat the oven to 375°F (190°C). Peel the bananas and, using a sharp paring knife, cut a slit about two-thirds through the flesh lengthwise, leaving ¼ inch (6 mm) uncut at each end. Very carefully ease the tamarind-coconut mixture evenly into the slits. Arrange in a single layer in a baking dish and scatter slivered almonds over the bananas.

3. Combine the maple syrup, crystallized ginger, lime and orange juice and butter in a bowl and stir until blended. Pour the syrup over the bananas and bake for about 20 minutes, basting occasionally to keep them moist. Serve with a drizzle of the thickened syrup, either warm or at room temperature.

Pan-Fried Whole Bitter Melons with Cashew Stuffing
KAJU BHARA KARELA

Bitter melon or bitter gourd—called *karela* by many Indian and Chinese grocers—has a decidedly bitter taste that is startling but pleasing. For almost all Westerners, it is a cultivated taste, and this recipe is a good way to begin. The pungency is toned down by salting and parboiling the melons to extract the bitter juice. Purchase baby gourds, no more than 3 inches (7.5 cm) long, and fry them until richly browned and crisp. Vary the flavor in the stuffing by using almonds or hazelnuts instead of cashews. This Bengali side-dish delicacy goes well on any full-course Vedic menu. Allow 1 per person for newcomers, 2 for aficionados. Serve with lime wedges.

Salting and preparation time: about 1 hour
Cooking time: 30 minutes
Makes: 8 stuffed bitter melons

8 baby bitter melons (about 12 ounces/340 g
    each), 2½–3 inches (6.5–7.5 cm) long
1½ tablespoons (22 ml) salt
½ tablespoon (7 ml) sugar
3 cups (710 ml) water
½ cup (75 g) cashew halves, blanched
    almonds or hazelnuts
3 tablespoons (45 ml) shredded fresh coconut
    or shredded frozen coconut, defrosted
½ tablespoon (7 ml) dark brown sugar
½ teaspoon (2 ml) fennel seeds
1 teaspoon (5 ml) cumin seeds
l tablespoon (15 ml) coriander seeds
½ teaspoon (2 ml) turmeric
¼ teaspoon (1 ml) cayenne pepper or paprika
¼ cup (60 ml) plain yogurt
5 tablespoons (75 ml) *ghee* or vegetable oil
lime wedges for garnishing

1. Wash and dry the bitter melons. With a sharp paring knife, slit lengthwise, cutting halfway through each. Using a small melon baller, scoop out the pulp and seeds and discard. Rub each melon inside and out with salt and sugar, and set aside for 30 minutes. Bring the water to a boil in a 2-quart/liter saucepan and partially cook for 10 minutes. Remove them with a slotted spoon and plunge into cold water. After cooling for 5 minutes, drain and pat thoroughly dry, inside and out.

2. To make the stuffing, place the nuts, coconut, brown sugar, fennel seeds, cumin seeds and coriander seeds in a blender or food processor fitted with a metal blade. Cover and pulse until the nuts are powdered. Transfer to a bowl and add the turmeric, cayenne or paprika and enough of the yogurt to make a moist stuffing. Divide into 8 portions.

3. Using a butter knife, stuff each bitter melon, handling them carefully to avoid tearing the uncut side. Press the two cut melon edges together until they meet, then bind each one closed, wrapping them from one end to the other 5 or 6 times around with ordinary white sewing thread.

For information about unfamiliar ingredients or techniques, see A-to-Z

4. Heat the *ghee* or oil in a 8–9-inch (20–22.5 cm) frying pan over moderate heat. When it is hot but not smoking, add the melons in a single layer. After 2 minutes, reduce the heat slightly, then pan-fry, turning them as they brown, so that they are crisp and richly colored, about 20–25 minutes.

5. Remove with a slotted spoon and drain on paper towels. Snip the thread and unwind, removing all loose pieces. Serve hot and crispy with lime wedges.

Pan-Fried Baby Eggplants Stuffed with Ground Almonds
BADAAM BHARA BAIGAN

Eggplant is a native of India and is prepared in almost every conceivable way. As a side-dish vegetable, baby white or purple eggplants are slit, spread with spices and pan-fried until butter soft. Although baby whites (which look like large eggs) are only available at specialty greengrocers in large cities, the seeds are sold through numerous mail order and retail outlets. They are as easy to grow as tomatoes. You could also use small, narrow Japanese eggplants for this dish. Try this Marawadi side dish on a mixed Vedic menu with *Chickpea and Ginger Root Salad* with *Golden Pastry Chips*, *Cauliflower Kofta* with *Fragrant Tomato and Yogurt Gravy* and steamed rice and green beans with hazelnuts. Finish with tropical *Mango Fool* or a seasonal fruit plate and ice cream.

Preparation time: 15–20 minutes
Cooking time: about 30 minutes
Serves: 6

12 baby white or purple eggplants (2 ounces/60 g each)
3 tablespoons (45 ml) ground almonds
1 tablespoon (15 ml) ground coriander
1 teaspoon (5 ml) ground cumin
1 teaspoon (5 ml) *garam masala*
½ teaspoon (2 ml) turmeric
¼ teaspoon (1 ml) cayenne pepper
½ teaspoon (2 ml) *amchoor* powder or ½
　　tablespoon (7 ml) lime juice
¼ teaspoon (1 ml) yellow asafetida powder (*hing*)*
½ tablespoon (7 ml) salt
4 tablespoons (60 ml) *ghee* or vegetable oil
2 coin-sized slices of peeled fresh ginger root
6 sprigs fresh coriander or parsley for garnishing

*This amount applies only to yellow Cobra brand. Reduce any other asafetida by three-fourths.

1. Almost halve the eggplants, cutting from the rounded base end to within ½ inch (1.5 cm) of the stem and cap. Soak in cold water for 10 minutes or until they open up slightly. Drain in a colander, then pat the outsides dry with paper towels.

2. Combine the almonds, spices and salt in a small dish and mix well. Smear the stuffing on the cut surfaces of the eggplants until all the mixture is used. Gently press the eggplants together to reshape them, then bind them closed by winding 2 or 3 rounds of ordinary white sewing thead around the thick end, and twist to knot.

3. Combine the *ghee* or oil and sliced ginger root in a heavy-bottomed 12-inch (30 cm) nonstick frying pan. Place the pan over moderate heat and when the *ghee* or oil is hot but not smoking, drop in the eggplants and cook, gently tossing, for about 8 minutes or until they are glossy and lightly browned. Reduce the heat to low, cover and cook for about 20 minutes, turning the eggplants 3 or 4 times to brown evenly on all sides. Remove the threads and garnish with herb sprigs before serving.

Main Dishes

Stuffed Eggplant Supreme with *Panir* Cheese and Chickpeas
PANIR BHARA BAIGAN

Eggplants are one of the most popular vegetables in India, and the techniques and ingredients used in their preparation change from region to region, household to household. Villagers are likely to prefer simple, smoky-flavored eggplant *bharta*, while city dwellers are accustomed to international cuisines and mixed menus. I first had this stuffed eggplant dish in the home of a well-wishing friend, Mr. Kenneth Keating, America's ambassador to India in the early 1970s. With minor changes, this is my version. A blend of ten spices and fresh herbs seasons a filling of spinach, tender chickpeas and roasted red peppers. Two homemade cheeses—fried *panir* and melted light cheese—make this dish an outstanding choice for entertaining company or a special family occasion. This dish can be made ahead of time and baked just before serving. For an easy flow during preparation, read the recipe through and collect all your ingredients before you begin cooking. For a main dish entrée, serve half an eggplant on a small bed of buttered rice. A light soup such as *Clear Broth with Potatoes and Urad Badi*, a green salad and *Deep-Fried Leavened Bread* complete a meal of distinction.

Preparation and cooking time (after assembling ingredients): 1 hour
Baking time: 1 hour
Serves: 6 as a main dish

3 small eggplants (each 8–10 ounces/230–285 g)
salt
¼ teaspoon (1 ml) cayenne pepper or paprika
1 tablespoon (15 ml) scraped, finely shredded or minced fresh ginger root
2–3 seeded and minced hot green chilies
½ tablespoon (7 ml) cumin seeds
1 teaspoon (5 ml) black mustard seeds
¼ teaspoon (1 ml) fennel seeds
¼ teaspoon (1 ml) *ajwain* seeds
scant ½ teaspoon (2 ml) yellow asafetida powder (*hing*)*
10–12 curry leaves, preferably fresh
1 tablespoon (15 ml) arrowroot or flour
fresh *panir* cheese (page 313) made from 6 cups
    (1.5 liters) milk, cut into ⅓-inch (1 cm) dice
5 tablespoons (75 ml) *ghee* or vegetable oil
3 medium-sized tomatoes (about 1 pound/455 g),
    peeled, seeded and coarsely chopped
½ tablespoon (7 ml) ground coriander
½ teaspoon (2 ml) turmeric
1 teaspoon (5 ml) *garam masala*
1 medium-sized red bell pepper, roasted (see note at the end of the recipe)
1 cup (240 ml) cooked chickpeas; mash 2 tablespoons (30 ml)
½ pound (230 g) fresh spinach, washed, trimmed and coarsely
    chopped, or half of a 10-ounce (140 g) package of frozen
    chopped spinach, defrosted and pressed dry
½ tablespoon (7 ml) salt
2½ tablespoons (37 ml) each chopped fresh coriander and sweet basil
1 cup (240 ml) fresh curd cheese or ricotta cheese
paprika for garnishing
fresh coriander sprigs for garnishing

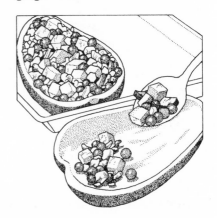

This amount applies only to yellow Cobra brand. Reduce any other asafetida by three-fourths.

   1. Cut the eggplants in half lengthwise. Using a paring knife and a spoon, carve and scoop out the eggplant centers, leaving shells with walls ⅓ inch (1 cm) thick on the sides and ½ inch (1.5 cm) thick on the bottom. Slice off a thin piece from the bottom of each shell so that it sits flat. Sprinkle the inside of the shells with salt and cayenne or paprika, and set aside to drain on several layers of paper towels. Coarsely chop the scooped-out eggplant and place it in the center of a clean tea towel. Gather the corners, twist, and extract as much liquid as possible.

   2. Combine the ginger, green chilies, cumin seeds, black mustard seeds, fennel seeds and *ajwain* seeds in a mound on a small plate. Place the asafetida and curry leaves in separate piles. Sprinkle the flour on the *panir* and toss to coat the pieces. Heat the *ghee* or oil in a large nonstick frying pan over moderate heat. Carefully add the *panir* dice to the hot oil, gently tossing with a wooden spoon to brown on all sides evenly. Fry for 10 minutes or until they are crisp and reddish-gold, then remove with a slotted spoon and set aside.

   3. While the *ghee* is still hot, drop in the combined seasonings and fry until the black mustard seeds begin to pop and turn gray. Stir in the asafetida and curry leaves, and in seconds follow with the chopped eggplant. Cook for about 5 minutes, stirring occasionally. Add the tomatoes, ground coriander, turmeric and *garam masala*, stir, cover and reduce the heat slightly. Cook for 10 minutes, stirring now and then. While the eggplant is cooking, cut the bell pepper into ⅓-inch (1 cm) dice. Combine in a bowl with the whole and mashed chickpeas and set aside.

4. After about 10 minutes of cooking, add the spinach and ½ tablespoon (7 ml) salt, cover and cook for up to 10 minutes. Uncover and stir, blending the ingredients well. Remove the pan from the heat. Add the fried *panir* cheese, the chickpea–bell pepper mixture and the fresh herbs, and gently mix. Finally, add ½ cup (120 ml) of fresh cheese or ricotta cheese and gently blend.

5. Pat the eggplant shells dry and brush the insides with a film of oil. Spoon in the stuffing, evenly distributing it among all the halves, and smooth the surface. Place a little of the remaining curd or ricotta cheese on each eggplant half. Lay the eggplants in a buttered baking dish. If making it ahead, cover and refrigerate. Let it return to room temperature before baking.

6. Bake in a preheated 350°F (180°C) oven for about 1 hour or until the shells are fork tender. Garnish with a sprinkle of paprika and a sprig of the fresh herb.

Note: To roast a pepper, place it in a baking pan and broil, turning frequently, about 2 inches (5 cm) from the heat source until it is charred and blistered on all sides. Place the pepper in a paper bag, close and allow it to sweat for 15 minutes. Strip off the charred skin, then quarter lengthwise. Remove the seeds and stems. If needed, this can be refrigerated in plastic bags for up to 2 days.

Spicy Potato-Stuffed Green Peppers
ALOO BHARA SIMLA MIRCH

In India, these stuffed peppers are always pan-fried until blistered and browned, usually in a bowl-shaped metal *karai*. I have chosen to bake them. It is a dish that is limited to stuffing peppers, medium-sized and mildly flavored. In American cities, you will likely find the best types to be California green Anaheims or Italian yellow banana peppers. According to the length and width of the peppers, you will need different amounts of stuffing. The variables are too great to pin down in accurate yields and measurements, but I do offer our test-kitchen results. This dish can be a side dish or a main dish, depending on the menu and occasion.

Preparation time (after assembling ingredients): about 15 minutes
Cooking time: 30–40 minutes
Serves: 6 to 8

8 peppers, 7–8 inches (17.5–20 cm) long and thinnish, or
      4–5 inches (10–12.5 cm) long and thickish; or
      15 smaller peppers 3–4 inches (7.5–10 cm) long
boiling water
2½ cups (600 ml) hot mashed potatoes
5 tablespoons (75 ml) *ghee* or unsalted butter
1 tablespoon (15 ml) dry-roasted coarsely crushed cumin seeds
½ teaspoon (2 ml) turmeric

For information about unfamiliar ingredients or techniques, see A-to-Z

1 teaspoon (5 ml) *chat masala* or *amchoor* powder
¼ teaspoon (1 ml) cayenne pepper or paprika
½ teaspoon (2 ml) sugar
1 teaspoon (5 ml) salt
3 tablespoons (45 ml) minced fresh coriander or parsley
2 tablespoons (30 ml) chickpea flour (dry-roasted until it
    darkens a few shades and gives off a fragrant aroma)
½ cup (120 ml) diced cheddar cheese (optional)

1. Cut a slice from the stem end of each pepper. Scoop out the seeds and rinse inside and out. Plunge into boiling water for 3–4 minutes, remove and drain, cut sides down.

2. Assemble the stuffing by mixing the mashed potatoes with 3 tablespoons (45 ml) of the *ghee* or butter and the cumin seeds, turmeric, *chat masala* or *amchoor*, cayenne or paprika, sugar, salt and fresh herb. Sprinkle with the chickpea flour and mix again. The mixture will be dry, but is less likely to ooze out during baking. Let cool to room temperature.

3. If you wish to use cheddar cheese, place about ½ tablespoon (7 ml) in each pepper and shake toward the pointed end. Carefully spoon in small amounts of the stuffing, packing lightly and take care not to tear the small opening. Replace the pepper caps.

4. Use a baking dish that will allow you to lay the peppers in a single layer, barely touching. Melt the remaining 2 tablespoons (30 ml) *ghee* or butter, brush the dish with it, add the stuffed peppers, and brush them with melted *ghee* or butter. Bake in a preheated 350°F (180°C) oven for 30–40 minutes, turning 2 or 3 times, or until the peppers are fork-tender and lightly browned.

Zucchini Boats Stuffed with Herbed Buckwheat Pilaf
KOTU BHARA LOUKI

One of India's most popular summer squashes, known as *tinda*, is actually a very tiny variety of watermelon, usually translated as "squash melon". The pale-green, round vegetables appear in the bazaar just after spring monsoons, at summer's onset. They are harvested before the seeds even form, allowing no chance for them to toughen and pervade the firm, sweet flesh. In some regional cuisines they are stuffed, but rarely with *dal* or grains. Because I have yet to see young, fresh *tinda* in America, even in large cities, I have substituted small, locally grown zucchini or pattypan. In keeping with tradition, the hollowed-out squash are stuffed with a light, non-cereal buckwheat pilaf. Accompany with a sauce—try *Fresh Tomato Sauce*. Ladle hot sauce in a warmed plate and allow ½ large zucchini or 2 smaller halves per serving. Garnish with tomato flowers.

Preparation and stuffing time: 45 minutes
Baking time: 30 minutes
Serves: 8

4 large zucchini, about 8½ inches (21.5 cm) long and 2 inches (5 cm) wide,
    or 8 smaller zucchini, each about 6 inches (15 cm) long
4 tablespoons (60 ml) unsalted butter or olive oil
1–2 seeded and minced hot green chilies
⅔ cup (105 g) kasha (buckwheat or quinoa
2 tablespooons (30 ml) chopped fresh coriander or dill
1⅓ cups (320 ml) boiling vegetable stock or water
⅛ teaspoon (0.5 ml) freshly ground pepper or cayenne pepper
6–8 high-quality saffron threads
1 teaspoon (5 ml) salt
½ cup (120 ml) sour cream or calorie-reduced cream cheese
¼ cup (30 g) sliced almonds
paprika or cayenne pepper for garnishing

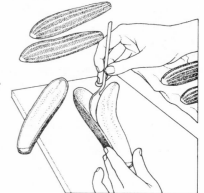

1. Cut each zucchini in half lengthwise, then cut ⅓ inch (1 cm) deep around the inside edge of each half, leaving a ¼-inch (6 mm) shell. Using a spoon, scoop out the loosened pulp, scraping and sculpting to leave an even ¼-inch (6 mm) shell. Coarsely chop the pulp, then place it in a clean tea towel and twist to extract as much moisture as possible. Sprinkle the inside of the shells with salt and place them upside down on several layers of paper towels.

2. Heat 3 tablespoons (45 ml) of the butter or oil in a 2-quart/liter pan over moderate heat. Add the zucchini pulp and green chilies and fry until softened and dry. Add the kasha and continue to fry for 2–3 minutes. Add the herb, stock or water, pepper or cayenne, saffron and salt. When the liquid begins to boil, cover, reduce the heat to very low and cook for 25–30 minutes. Remove the pan from the heat, fluff and fold in the sour cream or cream cheese.

3. Dry the inside of each zucchini half with paper towels, then spoon in the stuffing, distributing it evenly. Warm the remaining tablespoon (15 ml) butter or oil and brush it on each half. Sprinkle with sliced almonds and a touch of paprika. Place a rack in a baking dish and lay them in a single layer. Pour in water until it is ¼ inch (6 mm) deep. If making it ahead, cover and refrigerate. Let it return to room temperature before baking.

4. Bake in a preheated 350°F (180°C) oven until the shells are fork-tender, about 20–25 minutes. Serve with a light sauce.

Stuffed *Arbi* Leaves in Tomato and Sour Cream Sauce
URAD DAL BHARA ARBI PATTA

My friend Siddhartha das, former resident chef at Bombay's famous Sree Radha-Rasabehari Mandir, contributed the concept for this scrumptious, meal-in-itself main-dish entrée. I first tasted it at this temple, and was suitably impressed. The family recipe hails from Madhya Pradesh. In this region, Vaishnava cooks use *urad dal*, while farther west in Gujarat, they prefer *arhar dal*. I've tried it with others—*moong* and even split peas—each with delicious results. The basis of the dish is *arbi patta*—deep-green, heart-shaped leaves called "elephant ears," *dasheen* or taro leaves at Indian and Chinese grocery stores. They are periodically available, finding their way onto shelves in the summer months. Check with your grocer to see if and when he can get them for you, and then be sure to plan this dish. They vary from giant-sized, 14–18 inches (35–45 cm) long, to small, 8–10 inches (20–25 cm) long. So, depending on the varied sizes of available leaves, you may only need 5 large leaves or up to 12 small leaves for this recipe. Get a few extra in any case.

When you make the dish for the first time, read the instructions through until you have a feel for all of the steps involved; you will save time in the long run. Assemble all of your ingredients and equipment and then begin. This is a nice make-ahead main dish, good for company and holiday menus. You can make it well ahead of serving time and slip it into the oven when you need it. Once baked, allow it to rest and firm up, as you would lasagna, before cutting. For a gala occasion, try *Pumpkin Wafers*, *Clear Soup with Spinach and Rice*, *Papaya, Avocado and Jerusalem Artichoke Salad*, *Triangle Crisps* and *Green Beans with Coconut*. For a dessert selection, offer *Gingered Milk Fudge Confections* or *Deep-Fried Pretzel-Shaped Loops in Saffron Syrup* and *Pineapple Tower Surprise*.

Dal soaking time: 4–6 hours
Preparation time (after assembling ingredients): 40 minutes
Cooking time: 40 minutes
Serves: 6 to 8

1¼ cups (260 g) split *urad dal*, without skins
⅔ cup (160 ml) water
½ teaspoon (2 ml) yellow asafetida powder (*hing*)*
½ teaspoon (2 ml) freshly ground black pepper
½ teaspoon (2 ml) salt
arbi leaves (elephant ears), 5 large leaves, 14–18 inches (35–45 cm) long,
    or 8 medium-sized leaves, 10–12 inches (25–30 cm) long,
    or 12 small leaves, 7–8 inches (17.5–20 cm) long
10–12 medium-sized firm ripe plum tomatoes,
    blanched (about 2½ pounds/1.25 kg)
pinch of baking soda
about 1¼ cups (300 ml) *ghee* or safflower oil
½ tablespoon (7 ml) cumin seeds
1 teaspoon (5 ml) black mustard seeds
1 teaspoon (5 ml) turmeric
1 tablespoon (15 ml) ground coriander
½ tablespoon (7 ml) *garam masala*
¼ teaspoon (1 ml) paprika or cayenne pepper
1 teaspoon (5 ml) salt
1¼ cups (300 ml) plain yogurt or sour cream
3 tablespoons (45 ml) finely chopped fresh parsley or coriander

**This amount applies only to yellow Cobra brand. Reduce any other asafetida by three-fourths.*

1. Clean and wash the *urad dal*, following the directions on page 44. Place the drained *dal* in a bowl and cover with 2 inches (5 cm) of water. Soak for 4–6 hours, then rinse and drain.

2. To grind the *dal* to a purée in a food processor, first attach the metal blade to the work bowl. Add the *dal* and just under ⅔ cup (160 ml) of water, cover and process for 4–5 minutes or until the purée is smooth and fluffy. (You may need to use all of the water or even a splash more.) Transfer the paste to a mixing bowl.

To grind the *dal* in a blender, process half of the soaked *dal* and ⅓ cup (80 ml) of water for 10–15 seconds. Turn off the motor and scrape down the inside of the jar with a narrow rubber spatula to force the *dal* near the blades. Repeat the process for 5 minutes or until the paste is smooth. Transfer the purée to a bowl and repeat the process for the remaining *dal*. (Note: If you use split peas, *moong dal* or *arhar dal*, reduce the water by at least half.)

3. Mix the asafetida, black pepper and salt into the *dal* purée, then divide into as many portions as you have leaves.

4. Wash each *arbi* leaf and trim off the stalks. Fold each leaf in half, glossy side in. Using a sharp knife, cut away the thick central rib and discard it. Blanch the leaves in boiling water with a pinch of baking soda for 4–5 minutes to extract bitter juices and soften the leaves. Rinse well, then set aside, covered. Using a grapefruit knife, core the tomatoes, then squeeze into a strainer resting over a bowl. Force all of the pulp into the bowl and discard the seeds. Lay the tomatoes on their sides and slice thinly.

5. To assemble the leaves, lay half a large leaf or a whole small leaf in front of you, with the lighter side down and the point facing away from you. Spread an even layer of the purée, ⅛–¼ inch (3–6 mm) thick, over the leaf, leaving a ½-inch (1.5 cm) border at the edges. Fold the leaf in half lengthwise and spread the top with another layer of purée. Then fold the half into quarters so you have a small, nearly square packet. Pat the packet gently to evenly distribute the *dal* inside, and set the leaf aside. Stuff all of the leaves. Steam the packets in a steamer for 15 minutes. (This may be done several hours before cooking.) Refrigerate, covered, for up to 8 hours.

6. When you are ready to cook the leaves, fill a large frying pan with *ghee* or oil to a depth of ½ inch (1.5 cm) and heat over moderately high heat to just under the smoking point. Gently slip in enough of the packets to make a single layer in the pan. While pressing the leaf-packets firmly with the back of a slotted spoon, fry on each side until the leaves are richly browned, 5–6 minutes on each side. When the leaves are reddish-brown, transfer them to a strainer to drain. Repeat, frying batches of leaves until they are all cooked. Conclude by cutting each fried leaf into 1½ inch (4 cm) squares, and set them in a single layer in a buttered baking dish.

7. Add any remaining *ghee* or oil to the frying pan and place it over moderate heat. When it is hot but not smoking, add the cumin seeds and black mustard seeds and fry until the mustard seeds turn gray and pop. Drop in the tomatoes and pulp, turmeric, ground coriander, *garam masala*, paprika or cayenne and salt. Gently cook for 15 minutes. Pour the sauce over the leaves and spoon the yogurt or sour cream over the top. Serve with the minced herbs. You can also cover and refrigerate for several hours, then bake in a preheated 350°F (180°C) oven for 25 minutes, until the top is browned. Cool for 15 minutes before cutting. Serve as is, garnished with the fresh herbs.

For information about unfamiliar ingredients or techniques, see A-to-Z

Cabbage Leaves Stuffed with Red Bell Pepper *Uppma*
UPPMA BHARA BANDHGOBHI

Leaf-wrapped dishes are attractive entrées on mixed menus, ideal for entertaining. This is one of my own versions of stuffed leaves, nestled in a smooth bell pepper and tomato sauce. You could use Swiss chard leaves instead of cabbage, though they do require more care in stuffing. It is a light, relatively quick, make-ahead dish which can be baked just before serving. I allow 2 stuffed leaves per person, served on a shredded-potato pancake, which can also be made ahead and warmed. Accompany with a jicama, watercress and fried *panir* cheese salad, rice pilaf, creamy soup and hot bread—blending cuisines from several directions.

Preparation time (after assembling ingredients): 20 minutes
Cooking time: 1½ hours
Serves: 4

8 large cabbage leaves, blanched for 2 minutes, then drained

Filling:

3 tablespoons (45 ml) *ghee* or vegetable oil
1–2 hot green chilies, cored, seeded and slivered
½-inch (1.5 cm) piece scraped fresh ginger root, cut into thin julienne
1 teaspoon (5 ml) cumin seeds
6–8 curry leaves, preferably fresh
⅔ cup (160 ml) chopped red bell peppers
⅓ cup (60 g) Malt-o-Meal brand pretoasted farina
¾ cup (180 ml) buttermilk or a mixture of half
    yogurt and half water, at room temperature
3 tablespoons (45 ml) chopped fresh coriander or parsley
½ teaspoon (2 ml) salt
1 teaspoon (5 ml) lemon juice

Sauce:

2 tablespoons (30 ml) *ghee* or olive oil
2 medium-sized red bell peppers, seeded, stemmed and coarsely chopped (about ¾ pound/340 g)
3 large tomatoes, coarsely chopped
½ teaspoon (2 ml) sugar
1 teaspoon (5 ml) *garam masala*
1 cup (240 ml) vegetable stock
1 tablespoon (15 ml) chopped fresh dill or ½ teaspoon (2 ml) dried dill
½ teaspoon (2 ml) salt
⅛ teaspoon (0.5 ml) freshly ground pepper

Potato Pancakes:

1 large unpeeled baking potato (about 8 ounces/230 g), boiled for 10 minutes
melted butter
1 teaspoon (5 ml) poppy seeds
5 tablespoons (75 ml) sour cream or yogurt for garnishing
2 tablespoons (30 ml) blanched pistachio nuts, chopped

1. Place a cabbage leaf, stem side toward you, on a cutting board. Cut away the thick outside central rib from the base to the green leaf portion so that the pliable, soft leaves will be easy to roll. Prepare all the leaves and set aside.

2. To prepare the filling, heat the *ghee* or oil in a 3-quart/liter sauté pan over moderate heat. When it is hot but not smoking, add the hot chilies, ginger and cumin seeds and fry until the cumin seeds darken a few shades. Add the curry leaves and, a few seconds later, the bell peppers. Stir-fry until the peppers wilt and glisten with oil. Stir in the farina and cook for 1 minute. Remove the pan from the heat and pour in the cultured milk product, fresh herb, salt and lemon juice. Stir to mix, then cover the pan and set aside for 5 minutes. Fluff with a fork, divide into 8 portions, then gently press into logs about 2 inches (5 cm) long.

3. To stuff a leaf, lay it stem side down on the cutting board and place a portion of the filling at the base of the leaf. Fold the sides of the leaf over the filling and roll up from the base to make a neat parcel. Stuff and roll up the remaining leaves and place them in a single layer in a buttered casserole, close together, with the loose ends underneath so they cannot unroll. Cover and set aside.

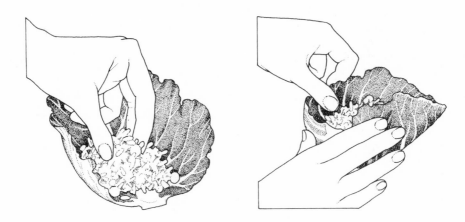

4. To make the sauce, heat the *ghee* or oil in a 3-quart/liter pan over moderate heat. Add all of the ingredients and when the liquid boils, reduce the heat and partially cover. Simmer for 30 minutes. Pour through a sieve or food mill, collecting the purée in a pan. Discard the seeds and skins.

5. Pour the sauce over the stuffed cabbage. Cover and bake in a preheated 350°F (180°C) oven for about 1 hour.

6. To make the pancakes, peel the potato and shred, using a coarse shredding disk, in a hand-operated Mouli machine or food processor. Heat two 8-inch (20 cm) nonstick frying pans over moderate heat and brush with butter. Strew in a handful of shredded potato and, using a fork or your fingertips, spread into a 7–8-inch (17.5–20 cm) layer. Sprinkle with poppy seeds and fry slowly for about 5 minutes per side or until both sides are golden brown and crisp. Depending on the size of the potato, you should be

For information about unfamiliar ingredients or techniques, see A-to-Z

able to make 4 pancakes. Set them on a cookie sheet without overlapping, and keep warm, uncovered, in a low oven.

7. To serve, place a crisp potato pancake on a warmed dinner plate. Place 2 baked cabbage leaves, along with some of the sauce, on top of the pancake. Garnish with a dollop of sour cream or yogurt and a sprinkle of pistachio nuts.

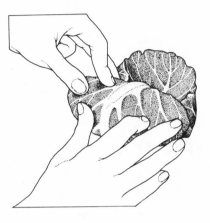

CHAR-FLAVORED *CHARCHARIS*

Charcharis are Bengali vegetable dishes that combine three cooking procedures: boiling, steaming and frying. Though other cuisines in the world use the same procedures, and in similar sequence, to my knowledge only *charcharis* are brought to the point of charring. During the entire procedure, the vegetable is never stirred—not even once! They are succulent vegetables, often rich and served as side dishes, but take little attention during cooking and are really delicious.

The dividing line between the cooking procedures is blurry. In the first stage, large pieces of vegetables are gently boiled in seasoned liquid. Sometimes sugar, tomatoes or lemon juice is added to provide a glaze, flavor or zest in the finished dish. In the second stage, the vegetables are steamed by the concentrated liquids barely boiling in the bottom of the pan. In the final stage, the vegetables should be butter soft, with all of the liquid completely absorbed, and browned in seasoned *ghee*. Because the dish is cooked without any stirring, and the liquid cooked off, a crust forms on the bottom of the pan. Srila Prabhupada described the final stages of cooking: "When the liquid is absorbed, there will be a little noise, a *hhhzzzz* sound, and then, just as the bottom crust browns, turn off the heat and it is done." The pan is covered and allowed to sit off the heat for a few minutes, until the crust softens and can easily be folded into the moist vegetables.

Since this final stage of cooking delicately borders on burning, it is important to convey that it should not come to that. No one wants to serve or eat burned vegetables. It is essential to use a very heavy, thick-bottomed pan such as enamel on steel, stainless steel or, better still, nonstick Silverstone on heavy aluminum. With good nonstick cookware and attention to heat control, perfect *charcharis* are possible even the first time around.

Char-Flavored Eggplant and Green Peas
BAIGAN HARI MATAR CHARCHARI

Like all *charcharis*, from beginning to end, this succulent vegetable is never stirred. During the cooking the eggplant is almost transformed into a buttersoft purée, contrasting texture with the still whole peas. The dish is complete when all of the liquid is cooked off, and a slightly charred crust rests on the bottom of the pan. The trick in finishing off this no fuss dish is to catch the crust before it burns: keep the heat low toward the end of cooking. This crust is folded back into the dish, lacing the vegetable with "outdoor" flavor. The chilies are left whole to add zest and flavor; they are not meant to overpower the dish and make it spicily hot. Do give green chilies a try and start with at least two small ones. Because of substantial quantities of *ghee*, the dish is very rich. Serve as a side-dish vegetable with rice or fresh hot bread. This is a good, left-over dish, one that seems to improve the second day. Reheat in a double boiler.

Preparation time (after assembling ingredients): a few minutes
Cooking time: 35–45 minutes
Serves: 6

1 medium-sized eggplant (1–1¼ pounds/455–570 g), cut into 1-inch (2.5 cm) cubes
2 cups (480 ml) fresh green peas (2 pounds/1 kg in pods) or
    one 10-ounce (285 g) package of frozen baby peas
4 tablespoons (60 ml) *ghee* or unsalted butter
1 tablespoon (15 ml) coarsely crushed coriander seeds
½ tablespoon (7 ml) coarsely crushed cumin seeds
1 teaspoon (5 ml) turmeric
1¼ teaspoons (6 ml) salt
1–3 whole hot serrano or jalapeño chilies
¼–½ teaspoon (1–2 ml) yellow asafetida powder (*hing*)*
3 or 4 sprigs fresh coriander leaves
2 cups (480 ml) water or unsalted vegetable stock

*This amount applies only to yellow Cobra brand. Reduce any other asafetida by three-fourths.

1. Place the eggplant in a heavy-bottomed 3-quart/liter nonstick pan. Sprinkle in the fresh peas, dot with *ghee* or butter and add the remaining ingredients. Bring the liquid to

---

For information about unfamiliar ingredients or techniques, see A-to-Z

a boil over moderate heat and cook for 3–4 minutes. Reduce the heat to low, partially cover and cook for about 30 minutes, shaking the pan from time to time. You should check to see if the water is drying up too fast; if so, add a little water and reduce the heat. When nearly all of the water has been absorbed, (add the defrosted peas if you are using them) reduce the heat again and fry until a crust has formed on the bottom of the pan and is just beginning to char.

2. Remove the pan from the heat and let the vegetable sit for 3–4 minutes, then gently stir in the crust. If desired, remove the whole chilies before serving.

Char-Flavored Curried Potatoes and Green Beans
ALOO BARBATTI CHARCHARI

Unlike the butter-soft, moist quality of many *charcharis*, in this recipe the potatoes are fork-tender but not broken down and the green beans barely tender; there is texture in the dish. At the precise time that the liquid has been absorbed, the vegetables must be completely cooked. The crust is achieved by raising the heat during the final moments of cooking. The keys to success are timing and knowing your heat source. Although the ingredients are important, the cooking times are, at best, only guidelines. You might serve this vegetable for a family brunch with hot toast or flatbreads, or make it a part of any lunch or dinner.

Preparation time: (after assembling ingredients): a few minutes
Cooking time: about 30 minutes
Serves: 6–8

2 medium-sized tomatoes, peeled, seeded and chopped
6–8 curry leaves, preferably fresh
5 medium-sized waxy boiling potatoes (1¼ pound/570 g),
    peeled and cut into 1-inch (2.5 cm) cubes
2½ cups (600 ml) trimmed green beans, cut into
    1½-inch (4 cm) pieces (about 1 pound/455 g)
3 sprigs fresh basil
1–2 dried whole red chilies
4 sprigs fresh coriander
½ teaspoon (2 ml) turmeric
¼ teaspoon (1 ml) yellow asafetida powder (*hing*)*
1¼ teaspoons (6 ml) salt
⅛ teaspoon (0.5 ml) freshly ground pepper
6 tablespoons (90 ml) *ghee* or butter
2⅔ cups (630 ml) water

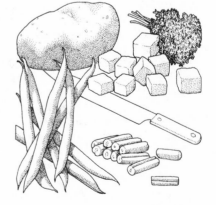

*This amount applies only to yellow Cobra brand. Reduce any other asafetida by three-fourths.

1. Place all of the ingredients in a heavy-bottomed 3-quart/liter nonstick pan, starting with the tomatoes and ending with the water. Bring to a boil over moderately high heat, then reduce the heat to moderate and boil for 5 minutes.

2. Reduce the heat again and gently boil, partially covered, for 20–25 minutes. From time to time, peek at the dish and check that the water is not disappearing too fast. You may have to adjust the heat, and perhaps add more water to see that the vegetables are just tender when the water is fully absorbed.

3. To finish the dish, raise the heat to moderately high and fry quickly, without stirring, to allow the crust to form and just begin to char. When you are satisfied with the texture, remove the pan from the heat and set aside, covered, for 5 minutes. Gently stir the crust into the tender vegetables before serving.

Note: Remove the red chilies before serving. They can be a shock to the unsuspecting newcomer.

Char-Flavored Spiced Eggplant and Potatoes
BAIGAN ALOO CHARCHARI

A penetrating combination of lemon zest and sweet, freshly ground spices make this a truly distinguished *charchari*. This version originated in the old world village of Bir Nagar in West Bengal. Like all *charcharis*, it should be allowed to char slightly.

Preparation time (after assembling ingredients): 5 minutes
Cooking time: 30–35 minutes
Serves: 6

6 tablespoons (90 ml) *ghee*, or 2 tablespoons (30 ml)
    peanut oil and 4 tablespoons (60 ml) melted butter
1 teaspoon (5 ml) black mustard seeds
1 tablespoon (15 ml) scraped, finely shredded or minced fresh ginger root
2–3 hot green chilies, cored, seeded and slivered
¼ teaspoon (1 ml) yellow asafetida powder (*hing*)*
6–8 curry leaves, preferably fresh
5 medium-sized waxy boiling potatoes (1¼ pounds/570 g),
    peeled and cut into 1-inch (2.5 cm) cubes
1 medium-sized eggplant (1 pound/455 g), cut into 1-inch (2.5 cm) cubes
1⅔ cups (400 ml) unsalted vegetable stock or water
10–12 fresh spinach leaves, washed, trimmed and coarsely chopped
½ teaspoon (2 ml) turmeric
¼ teaspoon (1 ml) lemon zest
1 tablespoon (15 ml) lemon juice
½-inch (1.5 cm) piece of cinnamon stick
3 freshly ground whole cloves
¼ teaspoon (1 ml) freshly ground fennel seeds
¼ teaspoon (1 ml) freshly ground nutmeg
1¼ teaspoons (6 ml) salt

*This amount applies only to yellow Cobra brand. Reduce any other asafetida by three-fourths.

For information about unfamiliar ingredients or techniques, see A-to-Z

1. Heat the *ghee* or 2 tablespoons (30 ml) of oil in a heavy-bottomed 3-quart/liter nonstick pan over moderate heat. When it is hot but not smoking, add the black mustard seeds, ginger and chilies and fry until the mustard seeds sputter and turn gray. Sprinkle in the asafetida and curry leaves and, within 5 seconds, stir in the potatoes (and the butter if you fried the spices in oil). Fry, tossing with a wooden spoon, for 2–3 minutes.

2. Add the remaining ingredients and bring to a boil. Reduce the heat to low, partially cover and gently cook for about 30 minutes. From time to time, check to see if the vegetables are drying up, and adjust the heat or liquid accordingly. When the vegetables are fork-tender, all of the liquid should be absorbed and the vegetables left sizzling in seasoned *ghee*.

3. Raise the heat to moderately high and fry, without stirring, until a slightly charred crust forms on the bottom of the pan. Stir the crust into the soft vegetables before serving.

Char-Flavored Vegetable Medley with Crunchy *Dal Badi*
SABJI BADI CHARCHARI

The *dal badi* called for in this recipe is made from *urad* or mung beans and is available at Indian grocery stores and from mail order sources. The flavors and "heat" vary considerably from batch to batch, so the seasoning in the dish is kept simple. If you want a robust, zesty dish, use large Punjabi *urad badi*; if you want a milder bit of crunch, use *moong badi*. The dish can also be made without the *badis*.

Preparation time (after assembling ingredients): a few minutes
Cooking time: about 30 minutes
Serves: 6

5 tablespoons (75 ml) *ghee*, or 2 tablespoons (30 ml)
    vegetable oil and 3 tablespoons (45 ml) butter
2 plum-sized dried *urad dal badis* (2 ounces/60 g), cracked into lima bean-sized
    bits, or ⅓ cup (30 g) raisin-sized dried *moong dal badi*
4 cups (455 g) mixed trimmed carrots, cauliflower, broccoli
    and zucchini cut into 1-inch (2.5 cm) pieces
1 cup (240 ml) fresh peas or trimmed green beans cut into 1-inch (2.5 cm) pieces
2 medium-sized tomatoes, peeled, seeded and chopped
2 cups (480 ml) water
½ teaspoon (2 ml) turmeric
1 teaspoon (5 ml) *garam masala*
½ tablespoon (7 ml) salt
3 tablespoons (45 ml) coarsely chopped fresh coriander or parsley
¼ cup (60 ml) sour cream or yogurt (optional)

1. Heat the *ghee* or oil in a heavy-bottomed 3-quart/liter nonstick pan over moderate heat. When it is hot but not smoking, add the *dal badis* and fry, stirring constantly, until they darken several shades or turn reddish-brown. Add the remaining ingredients except the sour cream or yogurt, and bring to a boil.

2. Reduce the heat to low, cover and simmer for 30 minutes. From time to time, check to see that the liquid is not drying up, and adjust the heat accordingly. The vegetables should be tender and all of the liquid absorbed at the same time.

3. When the vegetables are cooked and all of the liquid has been absorbed, raise the heat and cook without stirring until a crust forms and the vegetables begin to char. Remove the pan from the heat, cover and set aside for 3–4 minutes. Gently stir the crust into the soft vegetables. If desired, fold in (or garnish with) sour cream or yogurt.

Summer Squash and Green Peas with Poppy Seeds
TORAY HARI MATAR CHARCHARI

There are as many differences between varieties of the same species of squash as there are between zucchini, pattypan and yellow crookneck. The differences concern color, flavor and texture. In India, the two most popular summer-type squash are bottle gourd or snake gourd (called *louki*) and sponge gourd (*toray*). Both are available at Indian groceries and sometimes at Mexican and Chinese groceries. Both kinds are excellent when harvested immature. Old bottle gourds develop woody, tough skins which are used for bowls and musical instruments. Old sponge gourds develop tough skeletons, which are macerated and dried into the well-known *loofah*. No matter what type of summer squash you use, select baby vegetables with thin, glossy skins, a heavy weight for their size, and firm seedless flesh. This recipe requires that the vegetables simmer slowly with whole spices and cream. It is not allowed to char as much as most *charcharis*, because the cream would scorch. The squash is cooked until the cream is absorbed and it finally sizzles in seasoned butter or oil.

Preparation time (after assembling ingredients): a few minutes
Cooking time: 35 minutes
Serves: 6

1½ pounds (685 g) seedless young summer squash (any
    type mentioned above), cut into ¾-inch (2 cm) cubes
1½ cups (360 ml) fresh peas (1½ pounds/685 g
    in pods) or one 10-ounce (285 g) package of
    frozen peas, defrosted
1 medium-sized tomato, peeled, seeded and chopped (½ pound/230 g)
1½ tablespoons (22 ml) each chopped fresh coriander and mint
1-inch (2.5 cm) piece of cinnamon stick
1–2 hot green chilies
3 whole green cardamom pods
1 tablespoon (15 ml) unsalted butter or *ghee*
⅔ cup (160 ml) light cream, warmed
1 teaspoon (5 ml) salt
2 tablespoons (30 ml) toasted poppy seeds

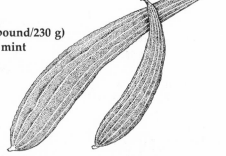

1. Combine all of the ingredients (keep the defrosted frozen peas aside if you use them) except the poppy seeds, in a heavy-bottomed 3-quart/liter nonstick pan. Bring to a boil, stirring, then cover and reduce the heat to low, giving it a stir with a wooden spatula to prevent the cream from catching on the bottom of the pan. When the dish is cooked, the squash should be butter soft and all of the cream absorbed, with the vegetables sizzling in seasoned butter. (Add the defrosted peas a few minutes before serving.)

2. Remove the cinnamon, chilies and cardamom pods before serving. Garnish with toasted poppy seeds.

SHUKTA: VEGETABLE STEWS

Among Bengalis, two types of foods are regional specialties: *chenna* cheese sweets and bitter vegetable *shukta* stews. There is mention in the Vaishnava texts compiled by Krishnadas Kaviraj that Lord Chaitanya favored the taste of *shukta* over even the nectar drink *panchamrita*, which is made with honey, yogurt and cardamom. For a Westerner, a taste for bitter-flavored dishes demands some cultivation but is well worth the effort.

At this very moment, across the length and breadth of Bengal, *shuktas* are simmering on the fire. This dish is characterized by large, tender chunks of vegetables—sometimes shallow- or deep-fried beforehand—floating in aromatic gravies or broths. Although many vegetables can be used, a few classic ones that are always appropriate are starchy potatoes, yams, plantains, pungent white radish, smooth eggplant or *toray* and textured *parval*, drumstick or green beans. This dish is always flavored with either a bitter spice, a bitter leaf or a bitter vegetable. Whole fenugreek seeds and leaves have a decidedly bitter flavor, and the most popular bitter vegetable found in the West is bitter melon or bitter gourd. These bumpy little green gourds are sporadically available at Chinese, Japanese and Indian grocery stores in the large cities. If you intend to delve into *shukta* cooking on a regular basis, you should find a source for high-quality young melons, purchase a whole box (usually 20-28 pounds/10-14 kg), cut them into slices and dehydrate. This supply should last for a few months of cooking. Out of necessity, I have learned to enjoy dried bitter melons as much as fresh ones. The flavor is milder, but they are ready to fry at a moment's notice. Simply wash the bitter melons, slice them into rounds about ¼ inch (6 mm) thick, and lay them out on screens or trays in the hot sun or a warm oven until they are thoroughly dried and brittle. The dehydrated rounds should be stored in an air-tight container in a cool, dry, dark cupboard. They will retain their flavor for 6 to 7 months. Since dried bitter melon is less pungent than fresh, increase the quantity for a heightened bitter flavor, according to your preference.

Pleasingly Bitter Vegetable Stew
SHUKTA

For open-minded, daring taste explorers, here is a welcome change from your favorite vegetable stew. It is a dish that explores the realm of bitterness through the spice seed fenugreek. The flavor here will be affected not only by how much of the seeds you use, but also by how much you brown them. The quantity I have suggested is not meant to overwhelm the other ingredients; rather, it is meant to be pleasingly complementary to them. Fry the seeds over moderate heat so you can watch them change color. Either allow the seeds to darken just a few shades to a golden brown, or let them actually blacken. (If you fry them somewhere in between, to a dark reddish-brown, they will release a powerfully bitter taste.) Serve with rice or fresh bread.

Preparation time (after assembling ingredients): 10 minutes
Cooking time: 45 minutes
Serves: 5 or 6

1-inch (2.5 cm) piece of fresh ginger root, scraped and coarsely chopped
2 teaspoons (10 ml) black mustard seeds
2½ cups (600 ml) vegetable stock or water
2 teaspoons (10 ml) cumin seeds
½ teaspoon (2 ml) fennel seeds
4 tablespoons (60 ml) *ghee* or vegetable oil
⅓-1 teaspoon (1.5-5 ml) fenugreek seeds
1 small cassia or bay leaf, crumbled
½ teaspoon (2 ml) turmeric
½ tablespoon (7 ml) brown sugar
3 medium-sized waxy boiling potatoes (¾ pound/340 g),
     peeled and cut into 1-inch (2.5 cm) cubes
2 medium-sized tomatoes (about ¾ pound/340 g), peeled, seeded and chopped
1 medium-sized sweet potato (about ¾ pound/340 g),
     peeled and cut into ¾-inch (2 cm) cubes
2 cups (480 ml) fresh green beans (8 ounces/230 g),
     trimmed and cut into 2-inch (5 cm) lengths
2 small Japanese eggplants (about 6 ounces/170 g), cut into 1-inch (2.5 cm) cubes
¼ cup (60 ml) shelled lima beans or fresh peas
2 tablespoons (30 ml) chopped fresh coriander or parsley
1½ teaspoons (7 ml) salt

1. Combine the ginger, black mustard seeds and ½ cup (120 ml) of stock or water in a blender, cover and process until the seeds are crushed. Pour in the remaining liquid and process for 30 seconds, then set aside.

2. Place the cumin seeds and fennel seeds in a small, cast-iron frying pan. Dry-roast over low heat until they darken a few shades. Let cool for a few minutes, then coarsely crush and set aside.

3. Heat the *ghee* or oil in a 4-quart/liter pan over moderate heat. When it is hot but not smoking, add the fenugreek seeds and fry until they darken a few shades to golden brown. Drop in the cassia or bay leaf, turmeric, sugar and potatoes. Fry the potatoes, tossing with a wooden spoon, for about 4-5 minutes. Add the tomatoes, sweet potato and green beans, stir-fry for a few minutes, then pour in the mustard-ginger water and bring to a full boil. Add the eggplants, lima beans or peas, half of the minced herb and the salt. Reduce the heat to low, cover and simmer for 30-35 minutes or until the

---

For information about unfamiliar ingredients or techniques, see A-to-Z

vegetables are fork-tender. Check from time to time to see if the vegetables are cooking in sufficient liquid.

4. Before serving, sprinkle with the remaining fresh herb and the dry-roasted seeds.

Bitter Melon Vegetable Soup with *Dal Badi*
DAL BADI SHUKTA

Shukta is alleged to stimulate a failing appetite and is customarily taken at the start of a meal. In this variation, the distinction between stew and thick soup is blurry. If it is part of a large meal, serve in small, custard cup sized portions. If it is the center of a simple lunch, serve in warmed roomy bowls. This variation is unique because of its delicate reduced yogurt broth and dried *dal* cakes. Yogurt is added, one spoonful at a time, so it is absorbed into seasoned *ghee* or oil. (If you add it too fast, it will curdle when heated.) This produces a pleasant tartness in the delicate broth. Dry *dal* cakes, called *badi*, are made from either *urad* or mung *dal*, and will directly affect the finished flavor of the dish. As a rule, large Punjabi *urad badi* are very hot and spicy, while mung *badis* are mild. These are usually sold at Indian grocery stores and are kept refrigerated, like valuable grains. Recipes for homemade *badi* begin on page 522. This *shukta* could be accompanied by *Rice and Cauliflower Pilaf* and *Steamed Chickpea Flour Bread with Coconut Garnish*.

Preparation and salting time: 30 minutes
Cooking time: 40 minutes
Serves: 6 to 8

2 small green bitter melons (each about 2 ounces/60 g) or
    20 slices of dried bitter melon, ¼ inch (6 mm) thick
½ tablespoon (7 ml) plus ½ teaspoon (2 ml) salt
4 tablespoons (60 ml) *ghee* or vegetable oil
2 plum-sized dried *urad dal badis* (60 g) cracked
    into lima-bean-sized bits, or ¼ cup (25 g) dried
    moong dal badis cracked into pea-sized bits
1 teaspoon (5 ml) cumin seeds
½ teaspoon (2 ml) black mustard seeds
¼ teaspoon (1 ml) *kalonji*
¼ teaspoon (1 ml) fennel seeds
1 cup (240 ml) plain yogurt, whisked
    until smooth, at room temperature
½ teaspoon (2 ml) turmeric
½ tablespoon (7 ml) ground coriander
½ teaspoon (2 ml) *garam masala*
3 medium-sized waxy boiling potatoes
    (about ¾ pound/340 g), peeled
    and cut into 1-inch (2.5 cm) cubes
1 small butternut squash (about ¾ pound/340 g),
    peeled, seeded and cut into 1-inch (2.5 cm) cubes
2½ cups (600 ml) water or unsalted vegetable stock
6-8 curry leaves, preferably fresh
1 cup (240 ml) broad beans (about 1 pound/455 g in shells)
20 spinach leaves, trimmed and washed
a few sprigs of fresh coriander or parsley for garnishing

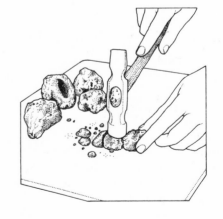

1. If you use fresh bitter melons, cut ¼ inch (6 mm) off both ends, then cut the bumpy little melon into slices ¼ inch (6 mm) thick. Sprinkle the ½ teaspoon (2 ml) of salt over the slices, toss and set aside for at least 20 minutes. Wash in fresh water, drain and pat thoroughly dry with paper towels.

2. Heat the *ghee* or oil in a 4-quart/liter saucepan over moderate heat. When it is hot but not smoking, place the fresh bitter melon rounds in a single layer on the bottom of the pan and shallow-fry on both sides until crispy and dark brown. As they brown, remove them with a slotted spoon and transfer to paper towels to drain. Dried bitter melon rounds brown within 30 seconds; simply drop them into the pan and, tossing with a spoon, fry until crisp.

3. While the oil is still hot, stir in the *dal* bits and fry until nicely browned, anywhere from 30 seconds to 1½ minutes. As they brown, remove them with a slotted spoon and drain on paper towels. Drop in the cumin seeds, black mustard seeds, *kalonji* and fennel seeds, and fry until the black mustard seeds crackle and turn gray. Put in a spoonful of yogurt and whisk until it is fully absorbed into the seasoned *ghee* or oil. Continue adding the yogurt, a spoonful at a time, until all of it has been incorporated into the *ghee*. Add the turmeric, ground coriander, *garam masala*, potatoes and squash, stir, and cook for about 5 minutes.

4. Slowly pour in the water or stock, curry leaves, fried *dal badi* and the remaining ½ tablespoon (7 ml) salt. Bring to a boil, cover tightly, reduce the heat to low, and simmer for 10 minutes. Add the broad beans and continue to simmer, covered, for about 20 minutes more or until the potatoes and squash are fork-tender. During the last 5 minutes of cooking, add the fried bitter melon and the spinach. Garnish with sprigs of fresh herb.

Bitter Melon Vegetable Stew in Poppy Seed Gravy
KHAS KHAS SHUKTA

No Bengali feast is complete without at least one type of *shukta*. When prepared properly, a cup of bitter-tasting *shukta* can convert people who once held their noses in disdain into *shukta* lovers and finally addicts. That is what happened to me. In this Bengali variation on bitter vegetable stew, the vegetables are deep-fried until partially cooked and then added to a poppy seed gravy, in which they finish cooking. The *shukta* gravy is thickened with cream-colored poppy seeds called *khas khas* or *posta* in Bengal (these are not the large blue-gray seeds often used in poppy seed cake or sprinkled on kaiser rolls). The off-white seeds have a pleasant nutty flavor and are used instead of flour to thicken and flavor gravies and stews. You can buy them at Indian and Middle Eastern grocery stores.

Preparation and soaking time: 4 hours or overnight
Cooking time: about 1 hour
Serves: 6

For information about unfamiliar ingredients or techniques, see A-to-Z

4 tablespoons (60 ml) white poppy seeds
½ tablespoon (7 ml) black mustard seeds
⅔ cup (160 ml) water
2 small green bitter melons (about 2 ounces/60 g each), or 25
    slices of dried bitter melon, ⅛-¼ inch (3-6 mm) thick
1 tablespoon (15 ml) salt
½-inch (1.5 cm) piece of fresh ginger root, scraped
1-2 hot green chilies, seeded
3 tablespoons (45 ml) chopped fresh coriander
⅓ cup (80 ml) cream or half-and-half
ghee or vegetable oil for deep-frying
3 medium-sized all-purpose potatoes (about ¾ pound/340 g),
    peeled and cut into 1-inch (2.5 cm) cubes
1 medium-sized yam (about ½ pound/230 g), peeled
    and cut into ¾-inch (2 cm) cubes
2 white icicle salad radishes or peeled carrots, cut
    on the diagonal into ½-inch (1.5 cm) slices
2 small Japanese eggplants (about 6 ounces/170 g),
    cut into 1-inch (2.5 cm) cubes
1½ cups (360 ml) green beans cut into 2-inch (5 cm) pieces
    (about 8 ounces/230 g), steamed until half-cooked
4 tablespoons (60 ml) *ghee* or a mixture
    of vegetable oil and unsalted butter
1 teaspoon (5 ml) *panch puran*
2½ cups (600 ml) water or vegetable stock
1 teaspoon (5 ml) *garam masala*

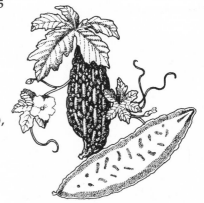

   1. Combine the white poppy seeds, black mustard seeds and ⅔ cup (160 ml) water in a small bowl, cover and set aside for at least 4 hours or overnight.
   2. Place the fresh bitter melon slices in a bowl and sprinkle with 1 teaspoon (5 ml) of the salt. Toss and set aside for at least 20 minutes. Rinse with fresh water, drain and pat thoroughly dry with paper towels.
   3. Place the soaked seeds and soaking water in a blender or food processor fitted with a metal blade. Cover and process for 1 minute. Add the ginger, chilies and 1 tablespoon (15 ml) of the coriander and process until smooth. Strain through a fine sieve placed over a bowl containing the cream or half-and-half. Blend with the poppy seed mixture and set aside.
   4. Pour *ghee* or oil to a depth of 2 inches (5 cm) into a deep-frying pan over moderate heat. When the temperature reaches 360°F (180°C) on a deep-frying thermometer, separately fry batches of bitter melons, potatoes, yam, radishes or carrots, and eggplant, until the vegetables are nearly tender and golden brown. Remove each batch with a large slotted spoon and set aside on paper towels to drain. Take the pan off the heat.
   5. Heat 4 tablespoons (60 ml) of *ghee* or an oil-butter mixture in a 4-quart/liter saucepan over moderate heat. When it is hot but not smoking, add the *panch puran* and fry until the fenugreek seeds turn golden brown. Pour in about ¼ cup (60 ml) of the poppy seed-cream mixture and fry, stirring, until absorbed into the *ghee* or oil. Continue adding the mixture in ¼-cup (60 ml) portions, stirring, until it is all accepted into the *ghee* or oil. Add the water or stock slowly and bring to a boil. Reduce the heat to low and simmer, stirring occasionally, for 10 minutes.

6. Add all of the vegetables, the remaining 2 teaspoons (10 ml) salt, and the *garam masala*. Gently stir, cover and reduce the heat to the lowest possible setting. Cook very gently for 10-15 minutes. Remove the pan from the heat and allow the dish to rest for 10 minutes before serving. Garnish with the remaining fresh herb.

Garden Vegetable Stew with Almond Pesto and Fried Dumplings
BADAAM SHUKTA

Bengalis love this dish as much as Italians love minestrone. Although it is a traditional dish, there are numerous ways to prepare it. The best *shuktas* are filled with fresh seasonal vegetables, so feel free to use the bounty of your garden. This variation is served with a type of fried *pakora*. You can serve them almost crisp, as a garnish, or allow them to soak and soften for 5 minutes before serving. The final touch is a spoonful of smooth fresh herb pesto. You could use toasted cashews or walnuts instead of almonds in the pesto and, to save calories, cottage cheese in place of cream. Serve with a *dal*, rice and fresh cheese dish for complementary nutrition.

Preparation and blanching time: 15 minutes
Cooking time: 45 minutes
Serves: 6 to 8

Dumplings:

½ cup (50 g) sifted chickpea flour (sifted before measuring)
¼ teaspoon (1 ml) salt
½ teaspoon (2 ml) baking powder
⅛ teaspoon (0.5 ml) cayenne pepper or paprika
1 teaspoon (5 ml) dry-roasted coarsely crushed cumin seeds
½ teaspoon (2 ml) melted butter or oil
about ⅓ cup (80 ml) water
ghee or vegetable oil for shallow frying

Pesto:

⅓ cup (80 ml) each trimmed fresh coriander and sweet basil, washed and patted dry
⅓ cup (40 g) toasted sliced almonds
3 tablespoons (45 ml) olive oil
⅛ teaspoon (0.5 ml) each freshly ground pepper and salt
½ cup (120 ml) heavy cream or low-fat cottage cheese

For information about unfamiliar ingredients or techniques, see A-to-Z

For the Stew:

2 small green bitter melons (each about 2 ounces/60 g) or
    20 dried bitter melon slices, ¼ inch (6 mm) thick
3 tablespoons (45 ml) *ghee* or unsalted butter
½ cassia leaf or bay leaf
2 medium-sized tomatoes (about ¾ pound/340 g), peeled and diced
2 medium-sized waxy boiling potatoes (about ¾ pound/340 g),
    cut into ¾-inch (2 cm) cubes
3½ cups (830 ml) vegetable stock or water
½ small head cauliflower (½ pound/230 g), broken into flowerets
2 small zucchini (½ pound/230 g)
½ cup (120 ml) fresh peas (½ pound/230 g in pods) or black-eyed peas
½ teaspoon (2 ml) turmeric
½ tablespoon (7 ml) ground coriander
1 teaspoon (5 ml) salt
½ teaspoon (2 ml) black mustard seeds
¼ teaspoon (1 ml) fennel seeds
¼ teaspoon (1 ml) fenugreek seeds
⅛ teaspoon (0.5 ml) *garam masala*
2 tablespoons (30 ml) chopped fresh coriander or parsley

1. To make the dumplings, combine the flour, salt, baking powder, cayenne or paprika and cumin seeds in a mixing bowl. Pour in the melted butter or oil and stir to blend. Add the water, using as much as necessary up to ½ cup (120 ml), to make a light, cake like batter.

2. Fill a small frying pan with *ghee* or oil to a depth of ½ inch (1.5 cm). Place the pan over moderate heat. When the *ghee* or oil is hot but not smoking, add 1 tablespoon (15 ml) of the batter at a time to make small dumplings. As the batter makes contact with the hot oil, it should immediately begin to puff. Fill the pan with 8-10 dumplings. Baste and fry on both sides until they are crisp and golden brown. As they brown, remove with a slotted spoon and set aside to drain. Shape and fry the dumplings until all of the batter has been used.

3. To make the pesto, combine the fresh coriander, fresh basil, almonds, olive oil, pepper, salt and cream or cottage cheese in a food processor or blender, cover and process until smooth. Cover and set aside. (If made ahead of time, it can be refrigerated and brought back to room temperature before using.)

4. To make the stew, drop fresh bitter melon slices into salted boiling water. Boil for 4 minutes, then remove to a strainer. Shake off the excess water and pat dry with paper towels.

5. Heat the *ghee* or butter in a 5-quart/liter pan over moderate heat. When it is hot but not smoking, add the fresh bitter melon slices and spread them into a single layer. Fry on both sides until reddish-brown. As they brown, remove with a slotted spoon and drain on paper towels. If you are using dried bitter melon slices, drop them into the pan, tossing them about with a spoon, and fry until crisp. They will brown within 30 seconds. Remove and drain. Add the cassia or bay leaf and tomatoes to the remaining hot oil and fry, stirring occasionally, for 3 minutes. Add the potatoes and stock or water and bring to a boil. Cover, reduce the heat slightly, and simmer for 15 minutes.

6. Add the cauliflower and zucchini and simmer for 10 more minutes, then add the peas, turmeric, ground coriander and salt. Simmer for another 10 minutes or until the vegetables are tender. Remove the pan from the heat, add the fried bitter melon and set aside, covered.

7. Combine the black mustard seeds, fennel seeds and fenugreek seeds in a small, heavy pan, place it over low heat and dry-roast the spices slowly until the fenugreek seeds turn golden brown. Grind to a coarse powder in an electric coffee mill or with a stone mortar and pestle.

8. Before serving the soup, stir in the *garam masala* and fresh herb. Ladle the hot soup into bowls, add a few fried dumplings to each serving, and finish with a generous spoonful of pesto.

Dairy Products and Dairy-Based Dishes

Perhaps you have traveled to India and, sitting in the back of a speeding cab, experienced something like this: Moving at a breakneck pace, the car approaches a trio of lotus-eyed white cows sleeping smack in the middle of the street. The driver toots his horn, people scatter, the driver deftly swerves, misses the cows and weaves on through a labyrinth of city congestion. That was no mere stroke of good luck. No one, taxi drivers included, would ever disturb the cows. In India, cows, calves and bulls are free to wander through the streets of cities and villages. Further, millions of residents, many very poor, share their meager sustenance with a pet cow or calf. Naturally, you may ask, why does an entire country maintain such reverence for cows?

The answer can be traced to the vast religio/philosophical texts of India known as the *Vedas*. Comprising voluminous *Puranas* (histories) and *Upanishads* (philosophic treatese), the *Vedas* detail the laws, morals and knowledge required to lead one to the ultimate stage of spiritual perfection. Each level of development, from social to intellectual to spiritual, is meticulously detailed so as to give the best chance for rapid spiritual development. The first stage of spiritual progress comes in learning to live in harmony with the land. India—still very much an agrarian culture—acknowledges the vital part cows play in the well-being of the community; indeed, the Sanskrit word *go* means both "cow" and "land". Protecting both is considered a religious duty and the secret to peace and prosperity. Both are also the basis of a vegetarian diet for hundreds of millions in India, providing milk products, grains, legumes, vegetables and fruits.

Milk is considered to be a perfect, complete food that nourishes the brain and calms the nerves, thus facilitating *yoga* practice. To own a cow is to possess great wealth, and despite suggestions by uninformed observers that reverence for cows impedes India's economic self-sufficiency, no one is willing to give up owning them.

The Puranic text *Srimad Bhagavatam* tells us something of cow protection in former ages. The First Canto describes the shock, anger and decisive reaction of Pariksit Maharaj, one of the last great kings of the Vedic period, when he discovered someone attempting to butcher a cow. Elsewhere in the *Bhagavatam*, The Eleventh Canto pays tribute to Nanda Maharaj of Vrindavan, whose immense wealth stemmed from his unflagging protection of the cows under his care: "The bodies of the cows, bulls and calves were painted with a mixture of oil and turmeric mixed with varieties of precious minerals. Their heads were bedecked with peacock feathers, and they were each garlanded with flowers and covered with cloth and golden ornaments." The cows sensed that they were protected, and in their happiness they saturated the pasturing fields with their milk.

The *Vedas* compare milk to nectar, and the cooks in India's Vedic times made full use of the creative possiblities of milk and its three main products—butter, fresh unripened cheeses and yogurt—both as raw ingredients and as the basis for thousands of sweet and savory dishes. The ancient process of sterilizing milk was very simple: twice a day, morning and evening, all of the milk was quickly brought to a boil three times. Milk was so abundant that it was considered stale at half a day old! Every drop was used; the whey left over from freshly churned butter, called *chaach*, was fed to domestic animals.

The milk most of us buy starts out as it always has, with the cow, but then it is subjected to the intricacies of modern processing technology. First, the milk is no longer drawn from the cows by hand but by machine, and pumped directly into 37°F (3°C) holding tanks, pending pasteurization and then homogenization. Then the milk is labeled according to its percentage of butterfat. Most American milk comes from Holstein cows and is pale and bland. Store-bought skim milk contains less than 0.5 percent butterfat; low-fat milk, 2 percent; whole milk, about 3.25 percent; extra-rich milk, 4 percent; half-and-half, at least 10.5 percent; light cream, at least 18 percent; whipping or heavy cream, 30–36 percent; and catering heavy cream, up to 40 percent. Certified raw milk—with the highest butterfat content of all—is available in Oregon and California. California's Alta Dena is the nations largest raw milk producer.

British milk has color-coded metallic caps on the bottle tops. Green means certified raw milk; silver, pasturized; red, homogenized; blue, sterilized; and gold, pasturized rich Guernsey or Jersey (at least 4 percent butterfat). Some outstanding European specialty milk products, such as England's Cornish clotted cream with 60 percent butterfat, and double cream, with 48 percent, as well as French crème fraîche, with 40 percent butterfat, are now sold at supermarkets in large cities.

Milk is dried or powdered by spray drying or roller drying. Spray-dried milk is made by spraying whole or skim milk into a large chamber of hot air. Powder forms and falls to the bottom of the chamber. Then it is processed (at temperatures lower than those for roller drying) into nutritious powdered milk. Roller-dried milk is made by putting a film of milk on a heated steel roller and scraping it off when dried. Although spray-dried non-fat, non-instant powdered milk is best for adding body to yogurt, it does not work well in quick and easy milk fudges. British whole milk powder is excellent for making shortcut milk fudge, but is not available in America. No matter what your choice, check the expiration date on powdered milks. If it is sold in bulk, give it a sniff: it should have virtually no smell. If it is old, it will have a "milky" odor.

Because milk and its products are as perishable as they are valuable, keep them refrigerated at 35–40°F (1–5°C). For each hour that milk is kept over 45°F (7°C), it loses one day of freshness.

Since most Vedic dishes call for milk that is heated at least to the boiling point, equipment is also important. Milk is sensitive to bacteria, and porous utensils such as wooden spatulas absorb bacteria easily. Heavy-bottomed thick stainless steel, enamel-covered cast iron, and nonstick heavy aluminum cookware are all better choices. If you delve into making *ghee*, yogurt or fresh cheese on a regular basis, buy one or two pans and reserve them exclusively for milk.

HOMEMADE BUTTER, *GHEE* AND SEASONED VARIATIONS

Understandably, village life in India centers on land and cows; but even in urban areas, the majority of households make their own fresh butter and *ghee* weekly. I was first inspired to make my own butter when living in southern Oregon's Rogue Valley. Fresh from a five-year stay in India, I settled into a small farm complete with garden plot, orchards and a family pet Guernsey cow named Bhimala. With the arrival of her first calf, Bhimala produced an astounding 4½ gallons (18 liters) of milk daily for three years non-stop—enough to supply five families and a local restaurant with whole and skimmed milk, yogurt, crème fraîche and seasoned butters. I am no longer on a farm. Gone are the milk separator and butter churn. Now I use cartons of store-bought heavy cream and a food processor.

Where I live now, heavy cream costs roughly $3.00 a quart/liter. That quart/liter churns into 1¼–1¾ pounds (570–795 g) of butter. As of this writing, a pound (455 g) of unsalted butter costs about $2.40 and it costs me $1.70–$2.40 a pound to make it at home. The savings are not great—maybe enough for a new food processor attachment or a knife now and then—but I much prefer the quality of the homemade. If you use fresh cream, the pure skim buttermilk that is left over will be sweet; if you use ripened cream, it will be tart. I prefer the sweet, but both are usable in breads, muffins, some soups and fruit drinks. So far as the cream is concerned, I find that the flavor depends mainly on the kind of pasture where the cows grazed. Bhimala grazed in alfalfa fields full of buttercups and wild lavender, and her milk was the sweetest imaginable. But no matter what your source, you are sure to be delighted with homemade fresh unsalted butter.

Homemade Butter
MAKHAN

In Indian homes, butter is churned today much as it has been for thousands of years. A large earthen pot called a *ghara* is half-filled with several days worth of ripened cream. By using a system of interconnected sticks and ropes, hand-agitation makes a wooden paddle whirl butter flecks into butter blobs. Our modern wonder the food processor has more than simplified the procedure. Depending on the size of your work bowl, you can process 1–2 quarts/liters at a time.

For information about unfamiliar ingredients or techniques, see A-to-Z

Preparation time (after ingredients are assembled): 10–20 minutes
Makes 1¼–1¾ pounds (570–795 g)

1 quart/liter heavy cream
½ cup (120 ml) ice water
2 ice cubes, cracked

Bring the refrigerated cream to about 60°F (15°C). Fit the food processor with a metal blade, add the cream, cover and process. That's all! As it is whipped, the cream gets thicker and thicker—like custard—then finally separates into flecks of butter. Add the ice water and cracked ice at this point to encourage the butter to form into large lumps. Strain off the buttermilk and, using your hands, knead the butter and squeeze out the milky whey. (Alternatively, work the butter with two grooved wooden butter paddles.) When it is clean and compact, rinse under very cold running water, then store in a well-sealed container. You can add salt or seasoned salt to taste, if desired. Well sealed, the butter can be kept frozen for up to 3 months.

Cardamom-Orange Butter

ELAICHE MAKHAN

This butter can be made with either orange juice concentrate or orange marmalade, both yielding vibrant results. Equally delicious is a variation made with rose petal jam. Both orange and rose are compatible with cardamom. Best served on morning breads, muffins or crackers.

Preparation time (after ingredients are assembled): a few minutes
Makes 1¼–1¾ pounds (570–795 g)

1–1½ pounds (455–685 g) unsalted butter, preferably homemade (page 298), at room temperature
3 tablespoons (45 ml) frozen orange or orange-pineapple juice concentrate or
    1½ tablespoons (22 ml) Seville orange marmalade or rose petal jam
1 tablespoon (15 ml) coarsely crushed cardamom seeds
1½ tablespoons (22 ml) orange flower or rose water (optional)

Cut the butter into 1-inch (2.5 cm) pieces and put them in a food processor fitted with a metal blade. Add the juice concentrate, marmalade or jam, cardamom and optional orange flower or rose water. Cover and process until the cardamom is ground and the butter is light and fluffy. May be used at room temperature or chilled, in molds or a butter crock. Well sealed, the butter can also be kept frozen for up to 3 months.

Mint-Lime Butter
PODINA MAKHAN

I feel that a splash of lime or lemon juice livens up almost any food, and for those who are cutting down on salt it is a flavor booster and natural salt substitute. The limes in India are most like our Key limes: yellowish-skinned, very juicy and sour. The dark green-skinned limes from Florida are quite acid by comparison. If you wish to control flavors, use lemon or lime juice for sourness, the zest for concentrated taste, and fresh lemon verbena or lemon balm leaves for a milder suggestion of a flavor. I like to serve this butter on almost any *dal* dish, wet or dry.

Preparation time (after ingredients are assembled): a few minutes
Makes: 1 pound (455 g)

1 pound (455 g) unsalted butter, perferably
   homemade (page 298), at room temperature
¼ cup (60 ml) chopped fresh mint
3 tablespoons (45 ml) lime or lemon juice or
   1 tablespoon (15 ml) grated lime zest or 3 tablespoons
   (45 ml) chopped fresh lemon verbena or lemon balm

Cut the butter into 1-inch (2.5 cm) pieces and put them in a food processor fitted with a metal blade. Add the mint leaves and citrus flavoring and process until the butter is fluffy and the leaves are finely chopped. Well sealed, it can be kept refrigerated for 1–2 weeks or frozen for up to 3 months.

Basil-Nutmeg Butter
JAIPHAL MAKHAN

I like to serve this butter with whole grain dishes—from steamed rice to cracked wheat, buckwheat, kasha or millet pilaf. It is equally a natural over blanched *paparh* or *pappadam* noodles. The possibilities are endless. Flavored butters are eye-catching when molded, dressing up even everyday dishes. For entertaining, take time to make individual molds, and keep any leftovers frozen for quick occasional garnishing of steamed vegetables.

Preparation time (after ingredients are assembled): a few minutes
Makes: 1 pound (455 g)

1 pound (455 g) unsalted butter, preferably
    homemade (page 298), at room temperature
⅓ cup (80 ml) chopped fresh basil
1 tablespoon (15 ml) freshly ground nutmeg
1 tablespoon (15 ml) chopped fresh coriander
1 teaspoon (5 ml) salt
1 tablespoon (15 ml) black poppy seeds (optional)

Cut the butter into 1-inch (2.5 cm) pieces and put them in a food processor fitted with a metal blade. Add the basil, nutmeg, coriander and salt. Cover and process until the leaves are finely chopped. For additional flavor, stir in the poppy seeds. Well sealed, the butter can be kept frozen for up to 3 months.

Mango–Maple Syrup Butter
AAM MAKHAN

For this recipe you can use mango, papaya, even peaches or pears. Maple syrup has a flavor reminiscent of *jaggery* from Bengal's date palm trees. This elegant butter is a natural for company brunch with assorted tea breads, muffins or biscuits.

Preparation time (after ingredients are assembled): a few minutes
Makes: about 1½ pounds (680 g)

2 tablespoons (30 ml) sugar
5 strips of orange zest, each 4
    inches x ½ inch (10 x 1.5 cm)
1 pound (455 g) unsalted butter, preferably
    homemade (page 298), slightly chilled
    and cut into 1-inch (2.5 cm) pieces
one 3½-ounce (100 g) package of cream cheese
    or neuchatel, brought to room temperature
    and cut into 1-inch (2.5 cm) pieces
1½ cups (360 ml) chopped mango,
    papaya, peach or pear
½ cup (120 ml) maple syrup

Fit a food processor with a metal blade. Add the sugar and orange zest and pulse the machine off and on until the zest is finely minced. Add the butter and cream cheese and process until smooth. Add the fruit and maple syrup and pulse until the fruit is finely chopped but not puréed. Well covered, the butter can be kept refrigerated for up to 3 weeks.

GHEE

For centuries *ghee* has been a sign of wealth in India, and in the Vedic times one who had ample stocks of *ghee* was said to possess liquid gold. Vedic literature actually refers to *ghee* as "food for the brain," a source of protein and energy. Though other oils are used for specific purposes—Bengalis use mustard oil for pickles and green leafy vegetables, coconut oil is favored in Gujarati and Maharastrian cooking, and ground nut or sesame oil is excellent in many dishes—*ghee* is the choice for those who wish to delve into the true Vedic tradition.

Unless you have particular dietary restrictions, cooking in moderate quantities of *ghee* is no more harmful than cooking in any other oil—in fact better, according to some researchers—and the taste cannot be imitated. Some describe it as "nutty and sweet," which I find an elusive description at best. There is something quite wonderful, however, about the caramel-like aroma of a pot of *ghee* simmering on the kitchen stove.

Though butter is an obvious choice for serving at the table and for baking, it cannot be used on the stove for most sautéing or frying. This is because it is composed of about 80 percent pure butterfat, 18 percent water and 2 percent protein solids, and above 250°F (120°C) the solids begin to burn. *Ghee* is the better choice, for it is free of the solids. French clarified butter (which comes closer than butter to being an acceptable sautéing or frying medium) is made by melting unsalted butter and separating the clear yellow butterfat from the milky protein solids. *Ghee* is made by further simmering the melted butter until the protein solids harden and darken slightly. All of the water evaporates, and the concentrated golden butterfat is carefully strained. Not only does the flavor intensify by this method, but the smoking point rises to nearly 375°F (190°C), at which frying and sautéing are fully possible.

Just as flavored butters lend character to the table, *ghee* is often simmered with curry leaves, fresh ginger root, turmeric, peppercorns or green chilies to add suggested flavors. These flavors, when added to the *ghee*, are the simplest way to liven up steamed vegetables, needing only the addition of a splash of lemon juice. You can purchase ready-made *ghee* at Indian and Middle Eastern grocery stores and many gourmet stores. Dutch *ghee* is excellent, Norwegian and Australian *ghee* are also very good, but these are much more costly than homemade. A six-month supply of homemade *ghee* takes very little effort and only a short time to make. For little more than the few minutes it takes to strain and bottle the *ghee* and label the containers, you can have a pure, golden oil that will keep for up to two months in a cool kitchen larder, up to four months if refrigerated, and six months or more when frozen.

In larger cities, health food stores and gourmet stores handle certified raw unsalted butter made from unpasteurized cream—about as close as you can get to the good old days. Because people are becoming more and more cautious about excess salt in their diet, most supermarkets now sell unsalted butter, either fresh or frozen. The third option is to make your own unsalted butter, using heavy cream and a food processor (see page 298). Making *ghee* is neither difficult nor complicated, but the larger the quantity,

---

the longer the cooking time. There are no shortcuts in preparing pure *ghee*. Only by slow cooking over gentle heat is all of the water driven off and the lactose sugar slightly caramelized, lending a sweet flavor to the butterfat.

You can make *ghee* either on the stove or in an oven. If you are in the kitchen anyway and have a free burner, up to 5 pounds (2.5 kg) can conveniently simmer on a back burner. Should you wish to make a stockpile or want to prepare for quantity cooking, you can make two, four, even six times that amount in a large oven overnight, with the *ghee* almost taking care of itself. The chart below gives you an idea of how long it takes to make various amounts by both methods. You will be amazed at how batch yields will vary, mostly because different butters have different liquid contents.

GRADE AA UN-SALTED BUTTER	OVEN METHOD	STOVE METHOD	APP. YIELD
1 pound (455 g)	1¼–1½ hours	1 hour	1⅔ cups/¾ pound (400 ml/340 g)
2 pounds (900 g)	1¾–2¼ hours	1½ hours	3 cups/1½ pounds (710 ml/685 g)
3 pounds (1.4 kg)	2¾–3¼ hours	2 hours	5 cups/2¼ pounds (1.25 lt/1 kg)
5 pounds (2.3 kg)	3½–4 hours	3 hours	9 cups/4 pounds (2.25 lt/1.8 kg)
10 pounds (4.5 kg)	6½–7 hours	5–5½ hours	17 cups/7¾ pounds (4.25 lt/3.5 kg)
11–20 pounds (5–9 kg)	8–10 hours	6–7½ hours	32 cups/15 pounds (8 lt/7 kg)

Stove-Top *Ghee*
SADA GHEE

Because the procedure is the same for making 1 pound (455 g) or 10 pounds (4.5 kg) of *ghee*, the equipment will be the same. Only pan size, heat regulation and storing containers vary. For safety, allow at least 3 inches (7.5 cm) of empty pan above the surface of the melted butter, no matter how much you make at one time.

For example, to turn 5 pounds (2 kg) of butter into *ghee*, you will need a 5-quart/liter heavy casserole, pressure cooker or stockpot; a fine-mesh wire skimmer or large metal spoon; a small jar; a ladle; a large sieve, lined with a linen towel or four layers of cheesecloth, resting over another pan; and a clean jar, canister or earthenware crock with a tight-fitting lid.

1–5 pounds (½–2 kg) unsalted butter, preferably homemade (page 298)

1. Put the butter, in ¼-pound (115 g) pieces, in the casserole. Melt it over moderate heat, turning it about to ensure that it melts slowly and does not sizzle or brown at any time. When the butter has melted, increase the heat and bring it to a boil. When the surface is covered with a frothy foam, stir gently and reduce the heat to very low. Simmer, uncovered and undisturbed, until the gelatinous protein solids have settled on the bottom of the pan and turned from white to golden brown, and the thin crust on the surface of the near-motionless butterfat is transparent.

2. With the skimmer, remove the thin dry crust resting on the *ghee* and set it aside in the small jar. At this point, note the color and fragrance of the clear *ghee*. If the solids on the bottom of the pan are darker than golden brown, if the fragrance is intense, or if the color is dark—like toasted sesame oil—the butter has cooked too long or over too high a heat. If this is the case, I would suggest discarding the solids. The *ghee* is still usable, but next time adjust the heat or the cooking time.

3. Remove the pan from the heat and, without disturbing the solids on the bottom, ladle off the *ghee* and pour it through a the towel-lined sieve. When you have removed almost all of the *ghee*, ladle off as much as you can of the last 1 inch (2.5 cm) of *ghee*. Stop before you disturb the solids on the bottom. When the *ghee* has cooled somewhat, pour it into the storing container, label and, when at room temperature, cover with a tight-fitting lid.

4. Add the remaining small amount of *ghee* and golden solids to the thin crust you skimmed off. Some people love this mixed into sandwich spreads, moist vegetable dishes, stuffings, *uppma* and blended soups. Keep these solids covered and refrigerated, and use them within 3–4 days.

Oven-Method *Ghee*
CHOOLA GHEE

This is the best method for making a stockpile of *ghee*. Because the heat surrounds the *ghee*, rather than contacting only the bottom of the pan, the cooking is slower but almost effortless. More of a crust will harden on the surface, and the solids at the bottom of the pan will remain soft and somewhat gelatinous. Adjust the pan size to the quantity of butter you are turning into *ghee*. Always allow 3 inches (7.5 cm) of pan above the surface of the melted butter.

1. Preheat the oven to 300°F (150°C). Place the desired quantity of unsalted butter, in ¼-pound (115 g) portions, in a heavy-bottomed, thick-walled pan. Allow the butter to melt and slowly clarify, uncovered and undisturbed, until there is a layer of solid foam on the surface, clean amber-gold *ghee* in the middle and lumps of pale gold solids on the bottom. Remove the pan from the oven. Depending on quantity, 1 pound (455 g) could take as little as 1 hour; 30 pounds (15 kg) could take 12 hours or more.

2. Skim off the crusty foam on the surface with a fine-mesh wire skimmer or a large metal spoon. Place the foam in a small container.

3. Ladle the clear *ghee* into a strainer lined with a linen towel or four layers of cheesecloth. When you have removed as much as you can without disturbing the solids, skim off the last 1 inch (2.5 cm) with a large spoon. When the *ghee* has cooled somewhat, pour it into storage containers, label and, when at room temperature, cover with a tight-fitting lid.

4. Add the remaining *ghee* and lumps of golden solids to the reserved foam, and use it for anything from creamed soups to sandwich spreads. Keep covered and refrigerated for up to 3–4 days.

For information about unfamiliar ingredients or techniques, see A-to-Z

Cumin-Flavored *Ghee*
JEERA GHEE

The use of seasoned *ghee* is perhaps the subtlest way to introduce flavor to simple steamed, baked or raw foods. If you have ever tasted the brownish sesame oil used in Oriental cooking, you can get an idea of how even a few teaspoons of cumin *ghee* can lend flavor and aroma to unseasoned dishes. Because this *ghee* is not as strong as the thick sesame oil, you can use it both as a cooking oil and for subtle flavoring.

Prepare this *ghee* just as you would in the stove-top or oven method *ghee* in the previous two recipes, with the following additions for every 3 pounds (1.5 kg) of butter:

3 tablespoons (45 ml) cumin seeds
6–8 fresh or dried curry leaves

Wrap the seasonings in a small piece of cheesecloth to make a bouquet garni. When the butter has melted, add the bouquet garni, and then cook, strain and label as in the previous recipes.

Black Pepper *Ghee*
KALA MIRCH GHEE

Black and white pepper both come from the same plant. In large cities, one might purchase unripened dark green berries, which, as they dry, darken into black pepper. No matter what form you use, the volatile oil will lend a touch of pungency without heat.

Prepare *ghee* by either the stove-top or oven method, with the following addition for every 3 pounds (1.5 kg) of butter:

2 tablespoons (30 ml) black , white or dark green peppercorns

Wrap the pepper in a small piece of cheesecloth and add it to the melted butter. Cook, strain and label as directed on page 303.

Clove-Sesame *Ghee*
LAUNG GHEE

This is a delicately flavored *ghee* that I have found excellent for sautéed green vegetable dishes—broccoli, asparagus, green beans and spinach.

Prepare the *ghee* by either the stove-top or oven method, with the following additions for every 3 pounds (1.5 kg) of butter:

25 whole cloves
2 tablespoons (30 ml) whole sesame seeds
¼ whole nutmeg

Wrap the seasonings in a small piece of cheesecloth and add to the melted butter. Cook, strain and label as directed on page 303.

Ginger *Ghee*
ADRAK GHEE

My friend Saragini Devi, whose cooking has always fascinated me, includes ginger in many of her dishes. The first time she deep-fried pastries in ginger *ghee*, I became aware of the nuances possible with this wonderful oil. It is, hands down, my favorite of all seasoned *ghees*.

Prepare *ghee* by either the stove-top or oven method, with the following addition for every 3 pounds (1.5 kg) of butter:

2-inch (5 cm) piece of ginger root, peeled and sliced into 4 pieces

Add the ginger when the butter has melted, then cook, strain and label as directed on page 303.

For information about unfamiliar ingredients or techniques, see A-to-Z

HOMEMADE YOGURT, CHEESE AND OTHER MILK PRODUCTS

The following milk products are indispensable in Vedic cooking, for India utilizes homemade yogurt and cheese just as often as vegetables, grains and legumes. When it comes to milk products, one cannot overstate the merits of freshness: once made, they lose flavor and nutrients as rapidly as uprooted plants. The closer you are, therefore, to using fresh, homemade yogurt and cheese, the more vibrant and exciting your cooking will be. Though all of the following staples are made from milk, there is a wide diversity in flavors and textures, and it would take several cookbooks to cover the multitude of ingenious ways that milk products are used in the Vedic kitchen.

Homemade Yogurt

DAHI

When I refer to "plain yogurt" as an ingredient, I mean the kind that has been made for thousands of years in Vedic kitchens using whole milk, sometimes even thin cream or top milk, and a starter—nothing else. Most supermarket yogurt is made from low-fat milk, skimmed milk and even reconstituted powdered milk, and does not even resemble the custard-like smooth yogurt found in India, Greece and the Middle East. Yogurt is easy to make, it is economical, and it lends real character to a multitude of Vedic dishes. If you are pressed for time and prefer to use commercial yogurt, many health food stores and delicatessens carry whole milk yogurt, and some, like Brown Cow and Columbo, are very good. They also make the best starters.

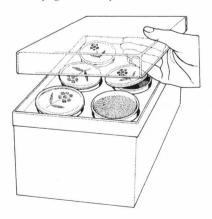

Because yogurt is no more than a transformation of milk, it possesses the same food value. Although the importance of fresh milk cannot be emphasized enough, it is the butterfat content that makes for the appreciable differences in body and texture. Whole cow's milk averages 3.25–3.8 percent butterfat, Guernsey and Jersey milk tops 4.2 percent, while half-and-half runs about 12 percent. In India today, buffalo milk, with about 8.2 percent butterfat, is widely used for commercial yogurt. Because I was never fond of its cloying strong taste, I preferred to make my own by boiling cow's milk to reduce it to three-quarters its original volume, ending up with a consistency similar to thick buffalo yogurt. Any yogurt made from unpasteurized milk has a creamy top layer of *malai*—a crust that solidifies on the surface of the milk—which is delicious and can be used a number of ways. When I want to make a firm-bodied yogurt, without the extra calories of whole milk, I add non-fat, non-instant powdered milk to 2 percent milk; the milk powder lends a touch of both sweetness and body. Homemade yogurt is not sweetened, but is both so mild and mellow that many refer to it as tasting sweet. It is a far cry from the often tangy, watery, tart commercial yogurt loaded with unnecessary stabilizers and fillers such as gelatin, locust bean gum, cellulose and carrageenan.

Yogurt has always been a guardian of good health. It is a source of calcium, protein, fat, carbohydrates, phosphorus, vitamin A, the B complex vitamins and vitamin D. It encourages the growth of benign intestinal bacteria that aid digestion and help to destroy the harmful bacteria that are alleged to spawn a variety of illnesses. The lactic acid content helps to digest and assimilate calcium and phosphorus, and yogurt is certainly easier to digest than milk. In one hour, 32 percent of milk can be digested, compared to 91 percent of yogurt. As a rule, yogurt beverages and salads are taken during the hot summer months, and when the fire of digestion increases in the winter, the frequency of milk dishes is increased in the diet.

The starter is nothing more than a little homemade or commercial plain yogurt. It is live bacteria, and must be fresh and sweet; tart and sour starters will yield tart and yogurt. Most starters combine *Lactobacillus bulgaricus* and *Streptococcus thermophilus*, but I prefer a culture including *L. acidolophilous*, which yields a mild yogurt known to be beneficial.

Yogurt not only flavors, it thickens, enriches and tenderizes. It is the basis of a multitude of Vedic dishes, from creamy chilled *lassi* beverages to nutritious yogurt salads called *raitas*. Drained of its whey, it turns into a low calorie cream cheese called *dehin*, which, sweetened, becomes an elegant Maharashtran dessert known as *shrikhand*.

Preparation time (after assembling ingredients): 20 minutes
Setting time: 4–10 hours
Makes: 1 quart/liter

½ cup (65 g) non-instant, non-fat dry milk powder (optional)
⅓ cup (80 ml) milk, at room temperature (optional)
1 quart/liter milk
3 tablespoons (45 ml) plain yogurt

1. If you want a spoonable firm yogurt, combine the milk powder with the room-temperature milk in a blender and process until lump-free and frothy. Set aside.

2. Bring the milk to a boil quickly in a heavy 3 quart/liter pan, stirring constantly to prevent it from sticking to the pan. Set aside to cool to about 118°F (48°C) or quick-cool by half-submerging the pan in a sink partially filled with cold tap water. While the milk is cooling, rinse a 1½–2-quart/liter container with boiling water, then dry. When the milk has cooled to about 115°F (46°C), pour ½ cup (120 ml) into the sterilized container, add the yogurt starter and whisk until smooth. Pour in the remaining milk and the powdered milk mixture, if you are using it, and blend well. The milk temperature should now be near 112°F (44°C), the ideal temperature for starting plain yogurt. Cover with a clean towel or lid and quickly put the container in a warm place, 85°–110°F (29°–43°C). If the environment is too warm, the yogurt will sour before it sets; if it is not warm enough, the yogurt will not set at all. I use an oven with a gas pilot light, or an electric oven preheated at 200°F (95°C) for 1½ minutes, then turned off. You could also use a large styrofoam picnic cooler, warmed with an open jar of hot water, then tightly covered. Another possibility is a heavy terry towel, blanket or foam rubber pouch resting near a central heater, boiler or heating duct. Any warm nook will do.

3. Check after 5–6 hours. It should be just thick and firm, for as it cools it will further set up considerably. The longer you allow the yogurt to set once it is firm, the stronger and more tart it will be. If it is not set, check every hour for up to 12 hours. If the yogurt has not set by then, there are several possible causes: stale or insufficiently sterilized milk, inadequate blending of starter in the milk, inadequate insulation during setting, or worn-out starter.

4. Refrigerate, covered, once it is set. It is best used within 3 days, though it will last for 4–5. After that, it is considered "old" yogurt and can be used in special recipes.

Sweetened Condensed Yogurt
KHASA MISTHI DAHI

The first time I had this exquisite, rich condensed milk yogurt, the temperature was near 120°F (50°C). In the depths of Calcutta's Chinatown, the temperature seemed over 130°F (55°C). My guide and shopping friend steered us mercifully toward a roadside café to rest weary feet and cool off. She ordered me this yogurt and icy sandalwood sherbet. The clay bowl was beaded from refrigeration, and with my first spoon I was addicted. Outside of Bengal, this dish never seemed to reach the same excellence, most likely because of the sweetener. It is made with freshly boiled-down date palm sugar or *jaggery*, almost like solid Vermont maple candy in texture, but with more of a molasses flavor—and most of the best *jaggery* never leaves Bengal. You can buy *jaggery* or *gur* at Indian grocery stores, and although it may look unappetizing, it is delicious. As an alternative, use grated maple candy or granules.

Due to the high sugar content in the yogurt, setting conditions and temperatures must be carefully regulated. I have found only two types of equipment that yield foolproof results in our test kitchens: the electric yogurt maker and the non-electric Devabridge or Solait type of yogurt maker. These last two are non-electric, wide-mouth thermos-like containers that have good insulation for maintaining steady setting temperatures.

The yogurt is classically served in individual throwaway or glazed clay cups as the finale to a luncheon or evening meal, as part of a special breakfast or as a light refreshment. You may want to reduce the sweetener to ½ cup (80 g), but by no more than that. This yogurt is meant to be sweet.

Preparation time (after assembling ingredients): 20 minutes
Setting time: 10–15 hours in a thermos or 4–7 hours in an electric yogurt maker
Makes: about 4 cups (1 liter)

8 cups (2 liters) whole milk, or
    4 cups (1 liter) evaporated milk
2-inch (5 cm) piece of vanilla bean, split down the center
¾ cup (115 g) lightly packed shredded or crumbled *jaggery* or maple sugar granules
3 tablespoons (45 ml) plain yogurt, at room temperature
¼ cup (35 g) non-instant, non-fat dry milk powder

1. If you use whole milk, pour it into a heavy 4-quart/liter pan over high heat. Stirring constantly with a wide wooden spoon, bring to a frothing boil. Reduce the heat slightly and boil with 1–2 inches (2.5–5 cm) of froth on the surface, stirring constantly until the volume is reduced by half, to 4 cups (1 liter).

2. Place the reduced milk or evaporated milk, vanilla bean and sweetener in a small saucepan and, stirring constantly, bring to just before the boiling point (do not boil, as many unrefined sweeteners tend to curdle milk). Remove the pan and begin cooling it in a sink partially full of icy cold tap water.

3. Meanwhile, combine the yogurt culture and milk powder in a small bowl and whisk with a fork until smooth. When the milk has cooled to 115°F (46°C), pour it through a fine-mesh strainer into a sterilized bowl, add the culture, and briefly beat with a wire whisk until thoroughly mixed.

4. Immediately pour into the 6 individual cups of an electric yogurt maker or the container insert for a non-electric yogurt maker and cover according to the manufacturer's directions. Incubate, undisturbed, for 4–6 hours in the yogurt maker or 10–12 hours in the thermos, then check to see if the yogurt has set. If it has not, check every hour until set. Refrigerate immediately, and serve in small dessert cups. Best used within 2–3 days.

Fresh Date Yogurt
KHAJAR DAHI

The potent ingredient in this rich yogurt is fresh dates. Just as smelling the perfume of ripe papaya or pineapple can be intoxicating, so can tasting the sweetness of plump fresh dates. Dates are always sweet; fresh, they contain more than 50 percent sugar and 7 percent protein, and drying increases the concentration. They are a high-energy food, rich in iron, that blends with any cultured milk product. In India, this yogurt is not made in throwaway cups or quart/liter jugs, but in shallow, paella-shaped unglazed clay dishes. The purpose is twofold: there is more surface room for rich *malai* to rise and firm up on the top of the yogurt, and any excess watery whey is absorbed into the porous clay, encouraging a firm-bodied yogurt. It is hard to find unglazed dishes like this, but you do occasionally come across them, sometimes sent in from Spain or Portugal. Any 1-quart/liter shallow, flat, ceramic quiche or lasagna dish will do.

Insulation is important for setting any yogurt with a sugar content, for it is more temperamental than plain cultured milk products. It also takes longer to set. You will also find it more difficult to set it in the winter, unless you have a spot that maintains an even temperature of between 90–100°F (32–38°F). Under or over that, the yogurt will either not set or sour before it firms up.

For information about unfamiliar ingredients or techniques, see A-to-Z

Preparation time (after assembling ingredients): about 30 minutes
Setting time: 8–15 hours
Makes: about 1 quart/liter

30 fresh ripe dates (about ½ pound/230 g)
    or soft pitted dates
5 cups (1.25 liters) whole milk, or 2½ cups
    (600 ml) each milk and half-and-half
2 whole green cardamom pods (optional)
3 tablespoons (45 ml) stirred plain yogurt,
    at room temperature
3 tablespoons (45 ml) blanched raw pistachio nuts,
    sliced or minced (optional)

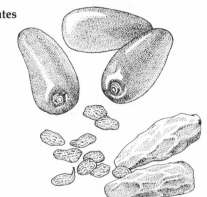

1. Wash, dry and pit the dates. Coarsely chop all but 2 dates, then mash them to a pulp, either in a food processor or with a mortar and pestle. Cut the remaining dates lengthwise into thin strips and set aside, covered, for a garnish.

2. Bring the milk and cardamom pods, if desired, to a boil in a heavy-bottomed 3-quart/liter pan, stirring constantly. Reduce the heat slightly and boil, stirring often, for 5 minutes. Add the date pulp, stir well, and turn off the heat. After 10 minutes, remove the cardamom pods and pour the milk through a fine-mesh sieve, pressing the dates to extract all of the juice. Discard the pulp. Using a thermometer, begin to cool the milk. Meanwhile, sterilize your 1-quart/liter "setting" container—ceramic, preferably unglazed clay—with a rinse of boiling water, then pour it out and dry well. While the container is warm but not too hot, smear 1 tablespoon (15 ml) of plain yogurt starter on the inner walls and bottom of the container.

3. When the milk has cooled to 115°F (46°C), whisk in the remaining 2 tablespoons (30 ml) yogurt until blended. Pour into the setting container, cover with a lid, and quickly insulate the container by wrapping it in a large heavy terry towel. Place in a warm location with a constant temperature of between 90°–100°F (32°–37°C). Check the yogurt after 8 hours, then every 1½ hours up to 14 hours. If it has not begun to firm up, place a covered baking dish filled with 2 inches (5 cm) of boiling water over the towel-wrapped yogurt container and carefully slip another one underneath. This will encourage setting within the next few hours.

The yogurt is best used within 3 days. Serve chilled in stemmed glass or fruit cups by cutting off spoonfuls of the firm yogurt and sprinkling them with pistachio nuts, if desired, and a few of the date strips.

Yogurt Cheese
DEHIN

Unlike some cultured milk products in this chapter, yogurt cheese is not yet sold commercially in America. I think it could become as popular as neufchatel or cream cheese. It is a revelation in light cheese, with an intriguing flavor. If you like yogurt, you will love *dehin*. It is nothing more than whole milk yogurt, or even low-fat yogurt, drained of whey and thickened until solid. It requires little more than a colander in the way of equipment, and requires only intermittent attention. Homemade, smooth whole milk yogurt makes the best cheese. If you prefer to use commercial yogurt, make sure it is sweet, and use well before the expiration date on the carton. Tart yogurt is often old, and as the yogurt flavor concentrates as it thickens, the cheese will become sharp and sourish as well. If you are using the cheese for a sweet dish, leave it plain; for eating or cooking, add up to ½ teaspoon (2 ml) of seasoned or herb salt.

Dehin is the basis of the elegant Maharastran dessert called *shrikhand* as well as *Yogurt Cheese Patties with Spicy Green Peas*. It is much less caloric than cream cheese, and offset with cracked black pepper, parsley, herb salt or fresh minced herbs, it is a delicious spread, dip and all-purpose accompaniment to crackers, fruit or flatbreads.

Preparation time (after assembling ingredients): a few minutes
Draining time: 12–18 hours for soft cheese or 24–36 hours for firm cheese
Makes: 2 cups (480 ml) soft cheese or 1½ cups (360 ml) firm cheese

6 cups (1.5 liters) plain whole milk yogurt
up to ½ teaspoon (2 ml) herb or sea salt (optional)

1. Line a colander with clean muslin or several thicknesses of cheesecloth and set it in a sink. If desired, stir the salt into the yogurt, then place it in the colander and spread it up the sides of the cloth to hasten the absorption of whey. Fold the ends of the cloth over the yogurt.

2. Set the colander on a rack in a dish at least 2 inches (5 cm) deep. (Leave at least 1 inch/2.5 cm between the rack and the bottom of the dish, for the drained-off whey.) Cover the whole unit with clear plastic wrap, sealing it to make it air tight.

3. Refrigerate to drain for 12–18 hours for a soft cheese or 24–36 hours for a firm cheese. Unwrap and store, sealed, for up to 3 days.

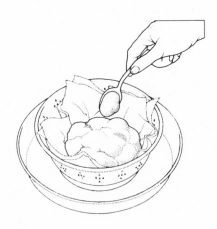

For information about unfamiliar ingredients or techniques, see A-to-Z

Panir Cheese
PANIR

Panir is to India's millions of vegetarians what tofu bean curd is to a similar number of Orientals. It is a versatile protein from a country that explores milk products perhaps more than any other. *Panir* is the simplest kind of unripened cheese. Whole milk is heated, an acid reagent is introduced, and milk protein coagulates to form a soft curd of casein. When drained of whey and compacted, it has a texture vaguely resembling tofu but with a delicious creamy taste, similar to pot cheese or farmers cheese. There are hundreds of ways to use *panir* in main-dish vegetables, breads, salads, dips and soups. The recipes in this book are only a sampling of the most popular regional dishes in India today, but the range is unlimited—enough to warrant a book of its own.

Panir, sold throughout India in bazaar cheese shops and grocery stores, is not available commercially in the West. Fortunately, it is quick and easy to make at home. I have lived and worked all around the world in the last 18 years, making *panir* in diverse kitchens, using available equipment, heat sources and acid reagents, and no two batches are ever exactly alike. Farm-fresh whole milk, especially rich Guernsey, Jersey or buffalo milk, and supermarket homogenized milk are handled differently and produce varying yields. There is a choice of acid reagents: strained fresh lemon or lime juice, a citric acid solution, or naturally soured *panir* whey from a previous batch. Each gives different body, texture and subtle flavor to the fresh curd. The more you practice making cheese, the more you will learn to control these variables to suit your preference. Experience is the best teacher, but the following tips will alert you to some of the subtleties in making both *panir* and *chenna* (a slightly moister version of the same fresh cheese) and help you achieve success, batch after batch.

Making each batch of cheese is different. You may find that your cheese forms before all of the curdling agent is added. If this happens, do not add the remaining curdling agent, because it would harden and toughen the delicate cheese curds. You may sometimes find that once the entire amount of curdling agent is added, the cheese curds will still not have sufficiently formed and whey will still be "milky." To finish the job, simply add a little more of the curdling agent until solid lumps of cheese separate from the whey.

A sour, acidic or lemony flavor in your cheese means that too much curdling agent was added or that the cheese was not sufficiently washed before draining and compressing.

Yeasty or "unclean" flavor in your cheese indicates that bacteria were introduced into the milk by using dirty utensils, or that the milk was soured or stale before being turned into cheese. Be impeccably clean! I keep a separate Silverstone 6-quart/liter pan reserved just for cheese making, and use stainless steel storage containers.

Tough or crumbly-textured cheese frequently results from using milk with a low fat content, or from allowing the cheese to remain too long over the heat once it has formed and separated from the whey, or from allowing the cheese to soak in the whey too long before washing.

Subtle differences in the texture of the soft cheese curds depend on the heat of the milk when the curdling agent is added, the type of heat used (electric, gas, coal and so on), the volume of milk in the pot and the thickness of the pot's walls. The fresh cheese curds should be soft and moist, not soggy and wet. The longer the cheese remains over heat, the firmer the texture becomes.

You do not need much by way of equipment: a 2–6 quart/liter pan (depending on the quantity of milk), a stirring spatula, a slotted metal spoon, a colander and some cheesecloth or a new handkerchief. You can use *panir* in many recipes, from *Royal Rice* and *Curried Red Kidney Beans with Panir Cheese* to *Stuffed Eggplant Supreme with Panir Cheese and Chickpeas* and *Vermicelli and Vegetable Uppma with Panir Cheese.*

Preparation and cooking time: 20–60 minutes, depending on quantity
Draining or compressing time: ¾–1¼ hours weighted or 2½–3½ hours hanging

1. Pour the milk into a heavy-bottomed pan that allows plenty of room for boiling. Set it over high heat and bring the milk to a full, foaming boil, stirring often to prevent scorching and sticking. Reduce the heat to low and, before the foam subsides, drizzle in the lemon juice or citric acid solution. Very gently and slowly move the spoon through the milk in one direction. After 10–15 seconds, remove the pan from the heat and continue to gently agitate the milk until large lumps of soft curd form. If the cheese has not formed after 1 minute, place the pan over the heat momentarily until the casein coagulates from pale yellow whey; if necessary, add a little more acid agent.

2. As soon as the cheese has formed, remove the pan from the heat, cover, and set aside for 10 minutes. If you want a very soft cheese, gently pour in 1–2 cups (240–480 ml) of hot water. When the cheese has settled under the surface of the whey, it is ready to drain.

3. Line a colander with 3 thicknesses of cheesecloth or a large white handkerchief that has been dipped in water and wrung dry. Drape the corners and edges of the cloth to hang over the sides of the colander. If you want to collect the whey for cooking or for making your next batch of cheese, set the colander over another pan; otherwise, place it in a sink. (Many sweetmakers in Bengal use this whey to make their daily cheese.) Curd made with whey is very soft, but you must use more whey than lemon juice. Use one part whey to four parts milk; for example, 1 cup (240 ml) whey for 4 cups (1 liter) milk. Remove the large lumps of cheese with a slotted spoon and place them in the colander. Gently pour the smaller pieces and remaining whey into the colander.

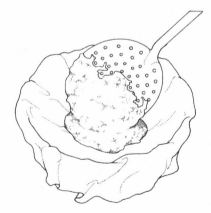

4. Gather up the corners of the cloth and twist 1–2 times around. Hold the cheese under a gentle stream of lukewarm tap water for 5–10 seconds to rinse off the cutting agent. Gently twist the cloth to squeeze out the excess whey.

5. You can slowly drain the whey, allowing the curd to compact under its own weight, or speed up the process by pressing the whey out with a weight. To drain the curd in the cloth, bind it with enough twine to hang it from a faucet over an empty sink or from a door handle on a kitchen cabinet. For small quantities, drain this way for 2½–3½ hours; for larger quantities, increase draining time. To drain under weight, bind the cloth around the curds, place in a colander, and rest a bowl of water, plastic-

For information about unfamiliar ingredients or techniques, see A-to-Z

wrapped brick or kitchen-scale weight on top of the cheese. Press for ¾–1½ hours, depending on the quantity of cheese.

6. Unwrap the cheese and use as directed in a recipe or wrap in paper-towel-lined plastic wrap, zip-lock bags or plastic containers for up to 4 days.

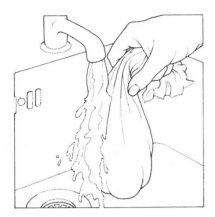

WHOLE MILK	STRAINED FRESH LEMON JUICE	APP. YIELD OF *PANIR*	CITRIC ACID SOLUTION IN HOT WATER
4 cups (1 lt.)	1½ Tbs. (22 ml)	4 oz. (115 g)	½ tsp. (2 ml) in ¼ cup (60 ml)
6 cups (1.5 lt.)	3 Tbs. (45 ml)	6 oz. (170 g)	¾ tsp. (3.5 ml) in ⅓ cup (80 ml)
8 cups (2 lt.)	4 Tbs. (60 ml)	10 oz. (285 g)	1 tsp. (5 ml) in ⅓ cup (80 ml)
10 cups (2.5 lt.)	5½ Tbs. (82 ml)	11–12 oz. (310–340 g)	1¼ tsp. (6 ml) in ½ cup (120 ml)
4 quarts (4 lt.)	8 Tbs. (120 ml)	18–20 oz. (510–570 g)	2 tsp. (10 ml) in ¾ cup (180 ml)

Chenna Cheese
CHENNA

All Indian cheeses are unripened—simply fresh casein curds or yogurt drained and compressed to extract whey. Cheese ripened with bacteria or mold has never been popular in India, perhaps because of the stress on absolutely fresh milk products or the intense heat. The two most popular cheeses are *chenna* and *panir*, both made the same way, just drained and compressed for different lengths of time. *Chenna* is freshly formed casein, very briefly drained, and often kneaded while still warm into a light, velvety smooth whipped cream cheese consistency. It is an essential ingredient for numerous Bengali sweets, such as *Sandesh Cheese Fudge* and juicy *rasgoola* sweets. Sometimes both the hot whey and cheese are used, as in *Griddle-Baked Chenna Whole Wheat Bread*.

Panir is the same cheese, compressed and drained until firm, with a texture something like Oriental tofu bean curd. It can be diced or cubed and sautéed before it is added to salads, vegetables, *dal* and grain dishes.

You will need very little by way of equipment: a 2–6-quart/liter pan (depending on the quantity of milk), a stirring spatula, slotted metal spoon, a colander and some cheesecloth or a new handkerchief. Use any quantity of milk, as you need the cheese; simply vary pan size and draining and pressing time accordingly.

Preparation and cooking time (after assembling ingredients): 20–60 minutes, depending on quantity of milk
Draining and compressing time: under 30 minutes

1. Pour the milk into a heavy-bottomed pan that allows room for boiling. Set it over high heat and bring the milk to a full, foaming boil, stirring often to prevent scorching and sticking. Reduce the heat to low, and before the foam subsides drizzle the lemon juice or citric acid solution over the milk. Very gently and slowly move the spoon through the milk, in one direction. After 10 seconds, remove the pan from the heat and continue to gently agitate the milk until large lumps of soft curd form. If the cheese has not formed after 1 minute, place the pan over the heat momentarily until the casein coagulates from pale yellow whey; if necessary, add a little more acid agent.

2. As soon as the cheese has formed, remove the pan from the heat and set aside, covered, for 10 minutes. If you want a very soft cheese, gently pour in 1–2 cups (240–480 ml) of hot water. When the cheese has settled unter the surface of the whey, it is ready to drain.

3. Line a colander with three thicknesses of cheesecloth or handkerchief that has been dipped in water and wrung dry; allow the corners and edges of the cloth to hang over the sides of the colander. If you want to collect the whey for cooking and making your next batch of cheese, set the colander over another pan; otherwise, place it in a sink. Remove the large lumps of cheese with a slotted spoon and place them in the colander. Gently pour the smaller pieces and remaining whey through the colander.

4. Gather up the four corners of the cloth and twist closed once or twice. Hold the cheese under a gentle stream of lukewarm water for 5–10 seconds to rinse off the cutting agent. Gently twist to squeeze out the excess water.

5. Place the wrapped cheese in a colander and rest a plastic-wrapped brick, pan of water, or stack of kitchen scale weights on top to exert weight on the cheese. Press and drain for 20–45 minutes (depending on the quantity of milk used). Unwrap the warm cheese, place it on a smooth, clean work surface, break it apart, and press with a clean cloth to extract any excess whey.

6. Knead the cheese by pressing and spreading it out, a small bit at a time, using the heel of your palm and the flat part of your hand. Gather up all of the cheese with a spatula and repeat the process again and again for up to 10 minutes or until the cheese is light and velvety smooth, losing any of its grainy texture. Use as directed in the recipe or in any number of dishes.

Note: You can add salt, pepper, minced green chilies, herbs and asafetida into the cheese, knead well and shape into 3-inch (7.5 cm) flat patties. Shallow-fried, they are the basis of a wonderful sandwich. Rolled into ½-inch (1.5 cm) balls and fried until golden, they make nutritious croutons for soup or salad. You can also roll the cheese into logs 4 inches (10 cm) long and 1½ inches (4 cm) in diameter and roll in minced fresh tarragon, parsley, basil, paprika or cracked black pepper for a cheese and cracker table. The cheese may be wrapped and refrigerated for 2–3 days.

For information about unfamiliar ingredients or techniques, see A-to-Z

WHOLE MILK	STRAINED FRESH LEMON JUICE	CITRIC ACID SOLUTION IN HOT WATER	APP. YIELD OF *CHENNA* (pressed less than 45 min.)
4 cups (1 liter)	1½ Tbs. (22 ml)	½ tsp. (2 ml) in ¼ cup (60 ml)	5 oz. (140 g)
6 cups (1.5 liters)	3 Tbs. (45 ml)	¾ tsp. (3.5 ml) in ⅓ cup (80 ml)	7½ oz. (215 g)
8 cups (2 liters)	4 Tbs. (60 ml)	1 tsp. (5 ml) in ⅓ cup (80 ml)	11 oz. (310 g)
10 cups (2.5 liters)	5½ Tbs. (82 ml)	1¼ tsps. (6 ml) in ½ cup (120 ml)	14 oz. (400 g)
4 quarts (4 liters)	8 Tbs. (120 ml)	2 tsps. (10 ml) in ¾ cup (180 ml)	21 oz. (600 g)

Fresh Curd Cheese
KHATTE PANIR

Commercial cottage cheese and ricotta often have such a small percentage of animal rennet or enzyme that manufacturers are not legally obliged to list it on the packages, though it is objectionable to vegetarians. Since both of these cheeses are nutritious and delicious and have numerous uses, you really should try making them with this simple recipe. When I cook at home, I make cheese about twice a week, along with yogurt and *panir*. The time spent is minimal and well worth the effort.

Use *khatte panir* in any recipe that calls for ricotta or cottage cheese. It is wonderful for a winter breakfast, sprinkled with chopped herbs, seasoned salt and freshly ground pepper. Well chilled, it is delicious sprinkled with sugar and accompanied by *Gingered Kiwi-Orange Medley* or any fresh fruit. It is also excellent in casseroles, stuffings and salads—from *Tomatoes Stuffed with Savory Green Pea Pilaf* and *Stuffed Eggplant Supreme with Panir Cheese and Chickpeas* to *Creamy Scrambled Chenna Cheese with Tomatoes and Snow Peas* and *Mixed Vegetable Salad*.

Preparation and cooking time (after assembling ingredients): 1–1¼ hours
Draining time: ½ hour–1½ hours
Makes: 1 quart/liter (2 pounds/1 kg) fresh curd cheese

4 quarts/liters whole milk
1 cup (240 ml) cream
1 quart/liter cultured buttermilk

1. Combine the milk, cream and buttermilk in a 6–8-quart/liter stockpot or kettle and stir until well blended. Set the pan over moderate heat and fix a candy thermometer on the side of the pan so that it is 1 inch (2.5 cm) into the milk. Warm the mixture, without stirring, until the temperature reaches 180°F (80°C). It will take about 40 minutes if the milk was cold.

2. Reduce the heat to low and gently cook, without stirring, for 25–30 minutes, carefully regulating the temperature of the milk at between 185°–200°F (85–95°C). (Remove the pan from the heat if the temperature goes above 200°F/95°C.) After 20 minutes of cooking, the curds will be soft. About 35 minutes more will yield firmer curd cheese. Though the bottom of the pan will probably show a small scorched area, stirring the mixture would break the curds and produce a smaller yield. If the heat remains moderate and low, the milk will never have a scorched flavor. To test the curd formation, gently press the top of the clot that forms—it should be like a firm baked custard, with the milky whey around it.

Place a colander in a clean sink and line it with four thicknesses of 16-inch (35 cm) square cheesecloth that has been dipped in water and squeezed dry. Very slowly pour the cheese and whey into the colander, without scraping the pan. Let the cheese curd drain for ½–1½ hours, or as desired. You can use it as is or add ¼ cup (60 ml) heavy cream, sour cream or yogurt for a creamier consistency. Store, covered and refrigerated, for 6–7 days.

Cultured Buttermilk
KHASA CHAACH

True buttermilk, known as *chaach*, is the cloudy, butter-flecked liquid remaining in the butter churn once the cream has solidified into butter. Cultured buttermilk is prepared like yogurt, by inoculating milk with a lactic acid culture and encouraging it to grow and transform the milk into buttermilk. The main difference is butterfat content: skimmed or 2-percent milk rather than whole milk is used to make buttermilk. I use it when I am calorie counting, and in many dishes it is excellent. I find an electric yogurt maker helpful in maintaining an even setting environment. The closer you can keep the setting temperature to between 70°–80°F (21°–26°C), the faster the buttermilk will set and the firmer it will be.

Buttermilk is the main ingredient in such diverse recipes as *Deep-Fried Buttermilk Whole Wheat Bread, Tender Chickpeas in Golden Karhi Sauce, Sweet Potatoes in Smooth Yogurt, Buttermilk Mung Dal Pancakes with Fennel Seeds*.

Preparation time (after assembling ingredients): 25 minutes
Setting time: 8–15 hours
Makes: 1 quart/liter

4 cups (1 liter) fresh skim or low-fat milk
⅔ cup (160 ml) commercial cultured buttermilk, at room temperature
½ cup (65 g) non-instant, non-fat dry milk powder

1. Pour the milk into a heavy-bottomed 2-quart/liter pan and place the pan over moderate heat. Stirring constantly, warm the milk until it reaches 108°F (42°C) on a thermometer. Remove the pan from the heat.

2. Place the buttermilk and milk powder in a food processor or blender, cover and process for about 15 seconds. While the machine is running, pour in the warm milk and process for another 15 seconds.

3. Immediately pour the mixture into a clean 1½-quart/liter jar, electric yogurt machine or insulated Solait crème fraîche container, and loosely cover. Wrap the container in a heavy terry towel or insulated wrapper and set aside at a temperature of 70°–80°F (21°–26°C) for 8–15 hours or until it reaches the firm consistency of whipped cream. Tightly cover the container and refrigerate for up to 1 week.

For information about unfamiliar ingredients or techniques, see A-to-Z

Homemade Sour Cream
KHASA MALAI

This cultured milk product can be made at home for a fraction of the cost of commercial sour cream, and the taste is ambrosial. Repeated success depends on the freshness of your culture and a well-controlled incubation and setting temperature. Nearly fool-proof are a wide-mouth thermos or an electric yogurt maker. The thermos will make 2 cups (480 ml), and the yogurt maker will make 1 quart/liter in neat ⅔-cup (160 ml) portions.

Use homemade sour cream in any recipe calling for sour cream. *Sour Cream Parsley Sauce* and *Cauliflower and Farina Uppma with Fenugreek Seeds* are outstanding with this ingredient.

Preparation time (after assembling ingredients): 15 minutes
Setting time: 12–15 hours in a thermos or 6–8 hours in an electric yogurt maker

Thermos Method:

1¾ cups (420 ml) light cream (18–30 percent butterfat)

Electric Yogurt Maker Method:

4 cups (1 liter) light cream (18–30 percent butterfat)
⅔ cup (160 ml) cultured buttermilk or sour cream, at room temperature, stirred until smooth

1. Slowly heat the cream in a small saucepan until it reaches 180°F (82°C) on a thermometer. Remove the pan from the heat and let cool to 100°F (37°C), stirring frequently. Add the buttermilk and whisk until blended.

2. Depending on the quantity, pour the mixture into a warmed wide-mouth thermos, then cover loosely with plastic wrap or a loose lid, or pour it into the plastic containers of the electric yogurt maker, loosely cover with the plastic lids, and place the cover on the unit. Incubate, undisturbed, for about 10 hours in the thermos or 6 hours in the electric yogurt maker, then check every hour or so until the sour cream is firm. Refrigerate immediately and, if possible, chill for a few hours before using.

Tart Cream
KHATTE MALAI

Mexico, England and America—several countries have their local variations on this recipe. Perhaps the most famous counterpart is French crème fraîche: a naturally mature, sour-flavored heavy cream. It is similar to sour cream but is made with heavy cream (about 40 percent butterfat).

I have only seen this type of soured cream in North India. I was taught to make it using buffalo milk, on the occasion of my first attempt at milking a buffalo. It is rarely if ever found in the marketplace. Use it as you would commercial crème fraîche or sour cream. Try it in such dishes as *Steamed Split Pea Dumplings in Milk Karhi Sauce, Sliced Bananas in Smooth Tart Cream* and *Lemon Stuffed with Almond-Chickpea Pâté.*

Preparation time (after assembling ingredients): about 15 minutes
Setting time: 8–24 hours
Makes: about 2 cups (480 ml)

2 cups (480 ml) heavy cream (36–40 percent butterfat)
1 tablespoon (15 ml) cultured buttermilk

1. Combine the cream and buttermilk in a heavy-bottomed 1-quart/liter pan and stir until thoroughly blended. Place the pan over low heat and, stirring gently but constantly, heat to 85°F (29°C).

2. Remove the pan from the heat and pour the cream into a sterilized 1-quart/liter jar. Loosely cover the jar and set aside at a room temperature of 60°–85°F (15°–29°C) until it has thickened to a consistency of lightly beaten cream—anywhere from 8 to 24 hours. Refrigerate, tightly covered, until you are ready to use it or up to 7 days.

Fresh Milk Fudge

KHOA

Just as in any French village the local bakers' loaves fill the cobblestone streets with hot wheat aromas, so in Indian villages the morning air is filled with the smell of sweetmakers' wood fires and condensing milk. The village *halwais* (sweet makers) are bent over giant, bowl-shaped iron pans, sometimes 3 feet (1 meter) wide, stirring rythmically and boiling their milk into fresh milk fudge. *Khoa* is simply whole milk that has been cooked down and condensed until nearly all of the water (37 percent by weight) has been driven off and an oyster-white unsweetened paste remains. As it cools it firms up into a thick, creamy milk fudge.

I strongly recommend that you take advantage of nonstick cookware while making *khoa*. I reserve two 5–6-quart/liter nonstick Silverstone pans exclusively for making milk sweets. These pans dramatically reduce the chances of scorching, burning and sticking. Especially during the last stages of reducing milk, heat distribution is crucial. Thin-walled pans are useless. Aside from the pot, a wide wooden spatula is also essential. When making small quantities, the task is neither time-consuming nor difficult, but it does require patient, rythmic stirring. When making *khoa* in quantity, pull up a stool and make yourself comfortable with your favorite tape.

Preparation and cooking time (after assembling ingredients): up to 1 hour
Makes: about 6 ounces (170 g) from 4 cups (1 liter) milk, about 12 ounces (340 g) from
**   8 cups (2 liters) milk**

1. Pour half of the milk into a heavy 4–6-quart/liter saucepan. Stirring constantly, bring to a full foaming boil over high heat. Continue to stir constantly with a wide wooden spatula to prevent it from sticking to the bottom of the pan and from forming a skin on the surface. If necessary, reduce the heat slightly to prevent the milk from spilling, and continue to boil the milk vigorously for 12–15 minutes.

For information about unfamiliar ingredients or techniques, see A-to-Z

2. Add the remaining half of the milk (2–4 cups/480–950 ml) and continue stirring to bring the milk to a full boil once again. Continue to stir and maintain at a full boil for 10–12 minutes.

3. Reduce the heat slightly, to moderate, and boil the milk until it thickens to the consistency of heavy cream.

4. Still stirring vigorously, lower the heat again and cook the milk until it is reduced to a slightly sticky, thick, pasty mass that draws away from the sides of the pan.

5. Remove the pan from the heat and use the *khoa* hot, as required, in a sweet recipe, or transfer to a platter. As it cools to room temperature, the paste firms up to a thick, fudge-like consistency.

Danedhar
DANEDHAR

Danedhar is the next stage of *khoa*. When a flat cake of the milk fudge is slowly baked until it dries and hardens, it can then be shredded or grated and sprinkled on anything, from sour dishes to sweets. I use it as I would ground almonds—to put a crust on fried cubed potatoes or a special rice pilaf. Grated, it is part of a powdered coating on elegant *Khoa- Flavored Cheese Balls Rolled in Coconut.*

Preparation time (after assembling ingredients): 30 minutes
Cooking time: 4–5 hours
Makes: 6 ounces (170 g) *khoa* yields about 4 ounces (115 g) *danedhar*; 12 ounces (340 g) *khoa*
   yields about 10 ounces (285 g) *danedhar*

1. Shape the milk fudge into a flat cake about 6 inches (15 cm) long and ½ inch (1.5 cm) thick. Bake slowly on a cake rack in a preheated 275°F (135°C) oven for 4–5 hours or until dry and hard. Let cool to room temperature on the rack.

2. Grate or shred as required for each recipe. May be refrigerated in an airtight container for up to 7 days.

Creamy Yogurt *Karhi*

Karhis are smooth yogurt-based dishes served with rice. Either yogurt or buttermilk is whisked with chickpea flour and then simmered into a creamy soup, sauce or custard-like gravy. The tartness of the yogurt greatly affects the flavor: fresh sweet yogurt yields a mellow flavor, and slightly soured yogurt lends a tangy flavor. If the yogurt is too sharp, the *karhi* will be excessively tart. The texture of *karhi* usually reveals its origin: in the western regions it is often souplike, with a hint of sweetness, and in the north it is thick sauce or gravy. Further, *karhis* are made plain, with vegetables, with steamed or fried dumplings and with cooked or sprouted whole beans.

Sautéed Bell Peppers in *Karhi* Sauce
SIMLA MIRCH KARHI

This recipe was an inspiration from the kitchen of the Panilal Pithi family of Hyderabad. During visits to Hyderabad, Srila Prabhupada was often a guest of Mr. Pithi, and during my first stay at his home I learned this South Indian variation. The household cooks explained that they preferred slightly sour yogurt, though I prefer to use it sweet and fresh. I also like the flavor of yellow and red bell peppers instead of green. Use whatever you have on hand or whatever is easily available. In South India, *karhi* is always served with rice. It is equally delicious with any whole grain pilaf: cracked wheat, millet, brown rice or buckwheat. Add a salad, and you have the basis of a nutritious quick meal.

Dal soaking time: 2 hours
Preparation time (after assembling ingredients): 15 minutes
Cooking time: 35–40 minutes
Serves: 4 to 6

Karhi Sauce:

3 tablespoons (45 ml) split *urad* or *moong dal,*
   without skins, soaked in water for 2 hours
¼ cup (25 g) sifted chickpea flour
   (sifted before measuring)
½ teaspoon (2 ml) turmeric
1 teaspoon (5 ml) salt
3¾ cups (890 ml) water or *panir* whey
1¼ cups (300 ml) plain yogurt
1 tablespoon (15 ml) *ghee* or unsalted butter
6–8 fresh or dried curry leaves

For information about unfamiliar ingredients or techniques, see A-to-Z

Vegetables:

2 tablespoons (30 ml) *ghee* or sunflower oil
1 teaspoon (5 ml) black mustard seeds
1 teaspoon (5 ml) cumin seeds
2 medium-sized green, red or yellow bell peppers
    (about 12 ounces/340 g), stemmed, seeded
    and cut lengthwise into thin strips
1 tablespoon (15 ml) ground coriander
¼ cup (25 g) shredded fresh or dried coconut
⅛ teaspoon (0.5 ml) freshly ground pepper
2 tablespoons (30 ml) chopped fresh coriander or basil
bell pepper chains for garnishing
1–2 tablespoons (15–30 ml) *Basil-Nutmeg Butter* (page 300) (optional)

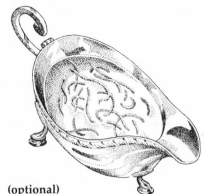

1. Drain the *dal* and pat dry with paper towels.
2. Combine the chickpea flour, turmeric and salt in a 1-quart/liter bowl. Add ½ cup (120 ml) of the water or *panir* whey, a little at a time, and whisk until smooth. Add the yogurt and whisk again until smooth and creamy. Finally, add the remaining 3¼ cups (770 ml) of water or whey and whisk until thoroughly blended. You could also blend the ingredients in a food processor or blender.
3. Heat the 1 tablespoon (15 ml) *ghee* or butter in a heavy 3-quart/liter saucepan over moderate heat. When it is hot but not smoking, add the *dal* and fry, stirring, until it turns reddish-brown. Pour in the yogurt mixture, and bring to a simmer, stirring often. Add the curry leaves, reduce the heat to low, cover and gently simmer for about ½ hour, stirring every 5 minutes or so.
4. Meanwhile, heat the 2 tablespoons (30 ml) *ghee* or oil over moderate heat in a large, preferably nonstick frying pan. When it is hot but not smoking, add the mustard seeds and cumin seeds, and fry until the mustard seeds turn gray, sputter and pop. Add the bell peppers and sauté, tossing occasionally, until almost tender, about 8 minutes. Sprinkle in the ground coriander, coconut and black pepper, toss, and set aside.
5. About 5 minutes before serving, add the peppers and coriander or basil to the *karhi* sauce and gently simmer. You may swirl in butter; I love to add a little *Basil and Nutmeg Butter*. Serve over rice, garnished with pepper chains, or in individual soup bowls.

Place a colander in a clean sink and line it with four thicknesses of 16-inch (40 cm) square cheesecloth that has been dipped in water and squeezed dry. Very slowly pour the cheese and whey into the colander, without scraping the pan. Let the cheese curd drain for ½–1½ hours, or as desired. You can use it as is or add ¼ cup (60 ml) heavy cream, sour cream or yogurt for a creamier consistency. Store, covered and refrigerated, for 6–7 days.

Creamy *Karhi* Sauce with Chickpea Flour Dumplings
PAKORA KARHI

I first learned a simple variation of this North Indian *karhi* while attending Srila Prabhupada's 1967 San Francisco cooking classes. It was such an ideal dish for quantity cooking that it quickly became a popular selection for holiday and Sunday feast menus. Recently, my younger sister Janaki surprised me by sending me the long-forgotten, hand-calligraphed original manuscript of my first cookbook attempt, and the 1967 recipe for this *karhi* was the same as here; it called for the sauce made with yogurt, water, turmeric, salt and chickpea flour. The dumplings are made only with chickpea flour, cayenne pepper, salt and turmeric. A fried seasoning, *chaunk*, is made with *ghee*, cumin seeds and dried red chili pods. Those were the ingredients as noted on February 20, 1967, in Srila Prabhupada's class.

On the whole, North Indian *karhis* are frequently thicker than their Gujarati or Marawadi counterparts. The *karhi* is simmered until rather thick and velvety and then, more often than not, flavored with aromatic fresh curry leaves. The chickpea flour dumplings vary from one kitchen to another. Some are fried, soaked in water, pressed dry and added as light and spongy dumplings, while others are crisp and crunchy and added just before serving to accentuate the contrast of crisp and velvety. In the Punjab, dried pomegranate seeds are a popular dumpling seasoning, and in Uttar Pradesh cumin and crushed red chilies are often favored. The variations are extensive.

Serve with rice and a vegetable salad for a nutritious everyday lunch or as part of a festive Sunday menu. A favorite menu in 1967 was rice, *Cauliflower and Potato Surprise*, *Gingered Chickpeas with Eggplant*, *Spinach and Tomato*, *Mixed Fruit Chutney*, *Zucchini Pakora with Crushed Peanuts* and *Nutty Farina Halva with Sliced Carrots*.

Preparation and batter resting time (after assembling ingredients): ½ hour–1 hour
Cooking time: 30–40 minutes
Serves: 4 to 6

Dumplings:

⅔ cups (60 g) sifted chickpea flour (sifted before measuring)
¼ teaspoon (1 ml) salt
⅛ teaspoon (0.5 ml) cayenne pepper or paprika
⅛ teaspoon (0.5 ml) yellow asafetida powder (*hing*)*
½ teaspoon (2 ml) dried pomegranate seeds (*anardana*) (optional)
about ⅓ cup (80 ml) warm water
ghee **or vegetable oil for frying**
¼ teaspoon (1 ml) baking powder

*This amount applies only to yellow Cobra brand. Reduce any other asafetida by three-fourths.

Karhi:

5 tablespoons (30 g) sifted chickpea flour (sifted before measuring)
3 cups (710 ml) water or whey
2 cups (480 ml) plain yogurt or cultured buttermilk, stirred until smooth
1 inch (2.5 cm) piece of cinnamon stick
6 peppercorns
4 whole cloves
6–8 curry leaves, preferably fresh
½ teaspoon (2 ml) turmeric
2–3 tablespoons (30–45 ml) chopped fresh coriander
3 tablespoons (45 ml) *ghee*, or 1 tablespoon (15 ml)
    peanut oil and 2 tablespoons (30 ml) unsalted butter
½ tablespoon (7 ml) cumin seeds
1–2 dried whole red chilies (or as desired)

1. Combine the chickpea flour, salt, cayenne or paprika, asafetida and pomegranate seeds (if desired). Gradually add enough water to make a smooth paste, whisking until smooth and light. Continue to add water to make a cake-like batter the consistency of heavy cream. Set aside to rest for ½ hour. If the batter sits for over 1 hour, it will thicken considerably and need more water. If you make the batter in a food processor, add the pomegranate seeds at the end, and rest the batter for only 5–10 minutes.

2. Pour enough *ghee* or oil into a 7–8-inch (17.5–20 cm) frying pan to fill to a depth of ¾ inch (2 cm). Place the pan over moderate heat and, while the oil is heating, stir the baking powder into the batter. When the oil is hot but not smoking, scoop up a scant teaspoonful (5 ml) of batter with a measuring spoon and carefully drop it into the oil. Fry about 12 at a time, never crowding the pan. If the heat is right, when the batter hits the oil it will immediately begin to swell and puff into a near balloon. Fry, stirring often, until all sides of the puffs are crisp and golden, then transfer to paper towels to drain. Repeat until all of the dumplings are fried. You can drop the fried dumplings in a bowl of warm water to soften for 10–15 minutes. Remove them with a slotted spoon and place in a strainer to drain. Alternately, you can leave the dumplings crisp and add them to the *karhi* at the last minute.

3. To make the *karhi*, place the chickpea flour in a 2-quart/liter bowl and add ½ cup (120 ml) of the water or whey, whisking to a smooth batter. Gradually whisk in the remaining liquid and the yogurt or buttermilk until smooth and creamy. Pour into a 3-quart/liter saucepan, add the cinnamon, peppercorns, cloves, curry leaves, turmeric and half of the chopped coriander and set over moderate heat. Bring to a gentle boil, stirring constantly. Reduce the heat to low and simmer for 20–25 minutes, stirring frequently as it thickens, and cook until it is reduced to a light, custard like consistency. (If desired, remove the whole spices.) Add the soaked or crispy dumplings, stir, cover, and remove from the heat.

4. Heat the *ghee* or oil in a small saucepan over moderate heat. When it is hot but not smoking, add the cumin seeds and red chilies and fry until the cumin darkens a few shades. Pour into the *karhi* and cover immediately. After 2–3 minutes, remaining coriander and butter if you used oil, and stir only to swirl it in. Serve piping hot.

Tender Chickpeas in Golden *Karhi* Sauce
KABLI CHANA KARHI

Srila Prabhupada was a self-taught cook: he said he learned cooking in early life by observing his mother, maternal aunt and street vendors. When I met him, he was seventy-one years old, and when he taught us the art of Lord Krishna's cuisine, it surpassed all the training I had ever received in cooking schools. As he taught it, cooking was an adventure, an art requiring few tools and usually little more than staple ingredients. This *karhi*, learned in 1966, is an example of basic ingredients transformed into home-style North Indian cooking at its best.

The dish includes two forms of *chana dal*: whole chickpeas (*kabli chana*) and chickpea flour made from *kala chana*. Both are very nutritious, and when combined with buttermilk provide a good portion of usable protein. I like to serve it with *Piquant Lemon Rice* or a celery and cracked wheat pilaf. This is a good dish to cook in quantity, one that I have often seen at Indian weddings. Try it with *White Radish and Chopped Radish Greens*, *Potato Pakora with Dried Pomegranate Seeds*, *Sweet Tomato Chutney with Fennel* and *Semolina Halva with Golden Raisins*.

Preparation time (after assembling ingredients and cooking the chickpeas): 10 minutes
***Dal* soaking time: 8 hours or overnight**
Serves: 6

Chickpeas:

1 cup (190 g) whole chickpeas, sorted
1 teaspoon (5 ml) salt
½ cassia or bay leaf
1½-inch (4 cm) piece of cinnamon stick
4 whole green cardamom pods

Karhi Sauce:

¼ cup (25 g) sifted chickpea flour (sifted before measuring)
2½ cups (600 ml) water or whey
2 cups (480 ml) buttermilk
1 teaspoon (5 ml) turmeric
½ tablespoon (7 ml) ground coriander
1 teaspoon (5 ml) salt
6–8 curry leaves, preferably fresh
2 tablespoons (30 ml) finely chopped fresh coriander

Seasoning:

1 dried red chili (or as desired)
½ tablespoon (7 ml) cumin seeds
3 tablespoons (45 ml) *ghee* or unsalted butter

1. Soak the chickpeas in 4 cups (1 liter) of water and the salt for 8 hours or overnight. (The salt helps the chickpeas absorb water evenly.) Drain and rinse. Place the soaked chickpeas and 3–3½ cups (710–830 ml) of water in a heavy 3-quart/liter saucepan. Bring to a boil over high heat, then add the cassia or bay leaf, cinnamon and cardamom. Reduce the heat and gently boil, partially covered, for 2–2½ hours or until tender. Check

For information about unfamiliar ingredients or techniques, see A-to-Z

occasionally to see if the water is evaporating too fast; if need be, add more. The beans should be soft but not broken down. Alternately, cook the chickpeas in a pressure cooker (at 15 pounds/8 kg pressure) for 20–25 minutes or until tender.

2. Drain the chickpeas through a strainer, reserving ½ cup (120 ml) of the cooking liquid. Remove the cardamom pods, bay or cassia leaf and cinnamon stick, and set aside.

3. Place the flour in a 1½-quart/liter bowl. Add enough water or whey to whisk into a smooth heavy batter. Slowly whisk in the remaining water or whey and the buttermilk, turmeric, ground coriander, salt, curry leaves, 1 tablespoon (15 ml) of the fresh coriander and the reserved cooking liquid until the mixture is smooth and blended.

4. Pour the *karhi* into a heavy 3-quart/liter saucepan and place over moderate heat. Stir constantly until the mixture comes to a boil. Reduce the heat slightly and simmer for 20–25 minutes, stirring every few minutes. When it has thickened to the consistency of a medium white sauce, add the cooked chickpeas and simmer for another 2–3 minutes. Cover, remove from the heat and set aside.

5. Finish the dish with a fried seasoning. Combine the red chili pod and cumin seeds in a small frying pan over moderate heat. Dry-roast, shaking the pan to brown evenly, until the seeds darken a shade or two. Add the *ghee* or butter, and when the seeds are richly browned or the butter froths, pour the seasonings into the *karhi*. Serve piping hot with the remaining 1 tablespoon (15 ml) coriander.

Thin *Karhi* Sauce with Sprouted Mung Beans
SABAT MOONG KARHI

This soup-like Gujarati *karhi* is usually served in small bowls on its own, rather than as a sauce over rice or vegetables. You can use any type of sprouted bean—mung, *urad*, muth or aduki—but only those barely sprouted, with ¼–½-inch (6 mm –1.5 cm) tails. They are easy to sprout at home, though I have seen them in some supermarkets. Avoid the giant, water logged mung sprouts sometimes used in Oriental cooking. To get the full protein value of this dish, accompany it with rice or a grain pilaf and steamed green vegetables with *Mint-Lime Butter*.

Preparation time (after assembling ingredients): 5 minutes
Cooking time: 20 minutes
Serves: 5 or 6

3 tablespoons (45 ml) chickpea flour (sifted before measuring)
1½ cups (360 ml) water or *panir* whey
2 cups (480 ml) plain yogurt, whisked until smooth
1 teaspoon (5 ml) salt
1 teaspoon (5 ml) sugar
½ teaspoon (2 ml) turmeric
1 teaspoon (5 ml) ground coriander
¼ teaspoon (1 ml) fenugreek seeds
1 cup (240 ml) sprouted mung beans (prepared from
    ½ cup/110 g whole mung beans, as directed on page 44)
1½ tablespoons (22 ml) *ghee* or vegetable oil
1 teaspoon (5 ml) cumin seeds
1–2 hot green chilies, seeded and minced
¼ teaspoon (1 ml) yellow asafetida powder (*hing*)*
1-inch (2.5 cm) piece of cinnamon stick
8–10 curry leaves, preferably fresh
2 tablespoons (30 ml) chopped fresh coriander or minced parsley

This amount applies only to yellow Cobra brand. Reduce any other asafetida by three-fourths.

   1. Place the chickpea flour in a 1-quart/liter bowl. Slowly add 3 tablespoons (45 ml) of the water or whey and whisk into a smooth paste. Stir in the remaining water and whisked yogurt until blended. Sprinkle in the salt, sugar, turmeric, ground coriander and fenugreek seeds, and whisk once again.
   2. Pour the mixture into a heavy-bottomed 2-quart/liter saucepan. Place over moderate heat and, stirring constantly, bring to a boil. Add the sprouted beans, reduce the heat to low, and simmer for 10 minutes, stirring every few minutes.
   3. Heat the *ghee* or oil in a small frying pan over moderate heat. When it is hot but not smoking, add all of the seasonings at once—cumin, green chilies, asafetida, cinnamon and curry leaves—and fry until the cumin seeds darken a few shades. Pour the fried seasonings into the *karhi* and immediately cover with a lid. Allow the *karhi* to sit for a few minutes before adding the fresh herbs, and then serve.

Mellow *Karhi* with Spicy *Paparh* Noodles
PAPARH KARHI

   These noodles are made from dried *dal* wafers and can be cut to any shape, from 1-inch (2.5 cm) squares to ½-inch (1.5 cm) wide ribbons. In North India the wafers are known as *paparh* and in the South as *pappadam*. Indian and Middle Eastern grocery stores and gourmet stores usually carry a few varieties. I suggest plain South Indian *pappadams* or black pepper or cumin-

For information about unfamiliar ingredients or techniques, see A-to-Z

flavored North Indian *paparhs*. Watch out for spiced *paparhs*: they are usually loaded with chilies and garlic. Keep in mind that the type of *paparh* you select will affect the finished flavor in the *karhi* sauce, and try a few varieties to see what best suits the occasion.

This is a simple and quick *karhi* and is always popular with dinner guests. You can serve it with practically anything except dishes containing yogurt. For a simple meal, serve with rice, *Sweet 'n' Sour Eggplant* and a green salad.

Preparation time (after assembling ingredients): 5 minutes
Cooking time: 15 minutes
Serves: 4 to 6

4 tablespoons (25 g) sifted chickpea flour
    (sifted before measuring)
1½ cups (360 ml) water or whey
2½ cups (600 ml) plain yogurt,
    whisked until smooth
½ teaspoon (2 ml) turmeric
2 teaspoons (10 ml) ground coriander
¼ teaspoon (1 ml) paprika
½ teaspoon (2 ml) *garam masala*
1 teaspoon (5 ml) salt
1 teaspoon (5 ml) honey (optional)
three 7-inch (17.5 cm) black pepper or cumin
    paparhs or four 5-inch (12.5 cm) plain
    ***pappadams*, cut into ½-inch (1.5 cm)**
    ribbons or 1-inch (2.5 cm) squares
½–1 whole dried red chili
4 whole cloves
1-inch (2.5 cm) piece of cinnamon stick
½ teaspoon (2 ml) black mustard seeds
2 tablespoons (30 ml) *ghee* or unsalted butter
2 tablespoons (30 ml) chopped fresh coriander or minced parsley

1. Place the chickpea flour in a 1-quart/liter bowl. Slowly add 4 tablespooons (60 ml) of the water or whey and whisk into a smooth paste. Add the remaining liquid and the whisked yogurt, stirring as you go, to thoroughly blend. Stir in the turmeric, ground coriander, paprika, *garam masala*, salt and honey, if desired.

2. Pour the mixture into a heavy-bottomed 2-quart/liter saucepan. Place over moderate heat and, stirring constantly, bring to a boil. Reduce the heat to low and simmer for 12 minutes, stirring every few minutes. Remove the pan from the heat and scatter half of the cut *paparh* into the *karhi* and stir until softened. Add the remaining *paparh* and stir again. Cover the pan.

3. Heat a small frying pan over moderate heat for 1 minute. Add the red chili, cloves, cinnamon and black mustard seeds and dry roast the spices, shaking the pan, for about ½ minute. Add the *ghee* or butter and roast the seasoning until the butter froths or the mustard seeds crackle and pop. Pour the seasoning into the *karhi* and immediately cover the pan. After 2–3 minutes, stir in the fresh herbs and serve.

Smooth *Karhi* Sauce with Homemade Chickpea Noodles
BESAN SEV KARHI

Though it does take time to shape these noodles by hand, it is worth the effort. You require such a small amount that a food processor or pasta machine would not be practical. Hands remain the most efficient tool in the kitchen.

It is difficult to give an exact flour-water measurement in such small quantities, so add sprinkles of liquid toward the end of making the dough. The dough must be firm but soft enough so that it does not crack when you roll it into thin ropes or noodles. The thinner your noodles, the better. If you have trouble rolling them out to an even thickness, handle a smaller portion at a time and cut into shorter lengths: instead of ½ inch (1.5 cm) long, cut them ⅓ inch (1 cm) long. The fresh noodles are cooked briefly in boiling water, then simmered slowly in the *karhi*.

This *karhi* is most frequently served as a gravy over *Sautéed Plain Rice*, but I have also thinned it down with additional water and served it as soup in small bowls.

Preparation time (after assembling ingredients): 30 minutes
Cooking time: 20 minutes
Serves: 6

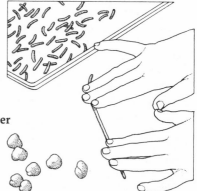

Noodles:

½ cup (50 g) sifted chickpea flour (sifted before measuring)
¼ teaspoon (1 ml) salt
½ teaspoon (2 ml) *ajwain* seeds
¼ teaspoon (1 ml) paprika or ⅛ teaspoon (0.5 ml) cayenne pepper
½ teaspoon (2 ml) melted unsalted butter
1 tablespoon (15 ml) plus ½–1½ teaspoons (2–7 ml) water

Karhi:

4 tablespoons (25 g) sifted chickpea flour (sifted before measuring)
½ teaspoon (2 ml) ground cumin
1 teaspoon (5 ml) ground coriander
1 teaspoon (5 ml) turmeric
¼ teaspoon (1 ml) cayenne pepper or paprika
1 teaspoon (5 ml) salt
2 cups (480 ml) water
2 cups (480 ml) plain yogurt, stirred until smooth
2 tablespoons (30 ml) *ghee* or coconut oil
1 teaspoon (5 ml) black mustard seeds
3 tablespoons (45 ml) chopped fresh coriander or minced parsley

1. Place the chickpea flour in a small mixing bowl. Add the salt, spices, melted butter and 1 tablespoon (15 ml) plus ½ teaspoon (2 ml) of water. Quickly gather the mixture into a stiff dough, adding additional sprinkles of water as necessary to make a workable noodle dough. Knead the dough until it is smooth, then divide into 10 balls.

2. Place a ball on a clean, smooth work surface. Using your palms or fingers, evenly roll the dough into a thin, long rope ¼–½-inch (6 mm–1.5 cm) thick. Cut with a sharp knife into ½-inch (1.5 cm) lengths. Repeat with the rest of the balls in the same way. Keep the noodles covered in a small dish.

For information about unfamiliar ingredients or techniques, see A-to-Z

3. Bring 2½–3 quarts/liters of lightly salted water to a rolling boil over high heat in a large saucepan. Strew in the noodles, taking care that they do not stick together. Reduce the heat to moderate and gently boil for 8–10 minutes. Remove the pan from the heat and drain the noodles through a fine-meshed sieve. Set them aside.

4. For the *karhi*, combine the chickpea flour, cumin, ground coriander, turmeric, cayenne or paprika and salt in a 4-cup (1 liter) bowl. Slowly add 4 tablespoons (60 ml) of the water and whisk into a smooth batter, then gradually add the remaining water and the yogurt and whisk to a smooth consistency.

5. Pour the *karhi* into a 2–3-quart/liter saucepan and place it over moderate heat. Stirring constantly, bring to a full boil. Reduce the heat to low and simmer for 10–12 minutes. Drop in the noodles and gently simmer for 3–4 minutes.

6. Heat the *ghee* or oil in a small saucepan over moderate heat. When it is hot but not smoking, toss in the mustard seeds and fry until they turn gray and pop. Immediately pour them into the *karhi*. Remove from the heat, gently stir, cover with a tight-fitting lid for 3–4 minutes, and serve, garnished with the fresh herbs.

Deep-Fried Mung *Dal* Dumplings in Creamy *Karhi*
MANGORHI KARHI

During my residence in Vrindavan, India, from 1972 through 1974, I was Srila Prabhupada's personal cook. On more than one occasion, however, I was needed elsewhere in the recently built temple community, and then other disciples would take my place. The following recipe comes from one of these, a Bengali Vaishnava named Vanamalini Devi. Srila Prabhupada commented favorably on the dish and asked me to note down the recipe—which I now pass on to you. This *karhi* sauce is thickened with wet-ground mung *dal* dumplings that are deep-fried and then simmered in the *karhi*. It is an outstanding Gujarati *karhi*, with a hint of sweetness and a velvety texture.

Dal **soaking time: 4 hours to overnight**
Preparation time (after assembling ingredients): 10 minutes
Cooking time: 30–40 minutes
Serves: 4 to 6

Dumplings:

½ cup (110 g) split *moong dal*, without skins, soaked
    in 2 cups (480 ml) water for at least 4 hours
2 tablespoons plus 1 teaspoon (35 ml) water
½ teaspoon (2 ml) salt
½ teaspoon (2 ml) turmeric
1 teaspoon (5 ml) cumin seeds
¼ teaspoon (1 ml) dried pomegranate seeds (*anardhana*), if available
⅛ teaspoon (0.5 ml) baking powder
ghee or vegetable oil for deep-frying
1 quart/liter warm water mixed with ½ tablespoon (7 ml) salt

Karhi:

1¾ cups (420 ml) plain yogurt or buttermilk
2¾ cups (650 ml) water or whey
1 tablespoon (15 ml) unbleached white flour or chickpea flour
½ tablespoon (7 ml) turmeric
⅛ teaspoon (0.5 ml) paprika or cayenne pepper
10 curry leaves, preferably fresh
½–1 teaspoon (2–5 ml) salt
1–2 fresh green jalepeño chilies
1–2 teaspoons (5-10 ml) scraped, minced fresh ginger root
1 teaspoon (5 ml) cumin seeds
½ teaspoon (2 ml) black mustard seeds
½ tablespoon (7 ml) raw sugar or maple sugar
2 tablespoons (30 ml) minced fresh coriander or parsley
1 teaspoon (5 ml) lemon juice

1. Blender method: Pour the soaked *moong dal* into a wire strainer, rinse and drain well. Place the *dal* in the blender, add the water, cover, and blend for a few seconds. Remove the feeder cap on the lid and scrape down the sides of the jar with a rubber spatula to place the beans near the blades. Cover and blend again, repeating this process for up to 5 minutes or until the beans are reduced to a fine, light, airy paste-batter.

Food processor method: Pour the soaked *moong dal* into a wire strainer, rinse and drain well. Attach the metal blade to the processor, add the *dal* and the water and process for 30 seconds. Scrape down the sides of the bowl and process again until the beans are reduced to a fine, airy batter, about 4 minutes.

2. Scrape the batter into a 4-cup (1 liter) bowl, then transfer ⅓ cup (80 ml) into a 2-quart/liter saucepan, cover, and set aside. Whisk the batter in the bowl to make it still lighter. Add the salt, turmeric, cumin seeds, pomegranate seeds and baking powder and gently mix. Place at least 1½ inches (4 cm) of *ghee* or oil in an electric frying pan or a 10–12-inch (25–30 cm) sauté pan and heat to 340°F (170°C). Using either your fingertips or a ½-teaspoon (2 ml) measuring spoon, drop small dollops of the batter into the hot oil. They will sink to the bottom of the pan and soon after bob to the surface, where they will swell into nice round balls. The batter should make 18–20 small dumplings. Deep-fry, stirring constantly with a slotted spoon, until the balls are golden brown and crispy. Lift them out of the *ghee* with the slotted spoon and place in the warm salted water. Soak the balls for 10–15 minutes or until spongy-soft. Gently press a few balls at a time between your palms and swish out the water; set aside on a plate.

3. Combine the yogurt, water or whey, flour, turmeric and paprika or cayenne in a bowl and beat until smooth. Pour this mixture into the reserved batter and thoroughly mix. Place the pan over moderate heat and, stirring constantly, bring the mixture to a gentle boil. Reduce the heat to low, drop in the curry leaves and salt, and gently simmer for 12–15 minutes. Add the fried soaked dumplings and simmer for 2–3 minutes; remove the pan from the heat and cover.

For information about unfamiliar ingredients or techniques, see A-to-Z

4. Heat 2 tablespoons (30 ml) of the frying *ghee* or oil in a small saucepan over moderate heat until hot but not smoking. Add the chilies, ginger, cumin seeds, mustard seeds and sweetener, and stir-fry until the sweetener turns reddish and the seasonings brown. Pour the fried seasonings into the *karhi*, cover immediately, and allow the flavor to penetrate into the gravy. Before serving, fold in the fresh herbs and lemon juice. Serve in small individual bowls.

Creamy *Karhi* with White Radishes
MOOLI KARHI

This Gujarati *karhi* can be made with any available radish—daikon, icicle or even red salad varieties. Serve with rice and salad for a simple meal.

Preparation time (after assembling ingredients): 5 minutes
Cooking time: 20 minutes
Serves: 4

4 tablespoons (25 g) sifted chickpea flour (sifted before measuring)
2 cups (480 ml) water
2 cups (480 ml) plain yogurt, stirred until smooth
¼ teaspoon (1 ml) fenugreek seeds
½ teaspoon (2 ml) cumin seeds
½-inch (1.5 cm) piece of cinnamon stick
1 cup (240 ml) shredded radishes, pressed dry
½ tablespoon (7 ml) sugar
1 teaspoon (5 ml) salt
6–8 curry leaves, if available
1 teaspoon (5 ml) black mustard seeds
2 tablespoons (30 ml) *ghee* or butter
1 dried red chili
½ tablespoon (7 ml) scraped, minced fresh ginger root
3 tablespoons (45 ml) chopped fresh coriander or minced parsley

1. Place the chickpea flour in a 1-quart/liter bowl. Add ¼ cup (60 ml) of the water slowly, whisking with a fork to a smooth paste. Add the remaining water and the yogurt, and whisk until thoroughly blended.

2. Pour the yogurt mixture into a heavy 2-quart/liter saucepan. Add the fenugreek seeds, cumin seeds, cinnamon stick, radishes, sugar, salt and curry leaves, and place over high heat. Stir constantly until the mixture comes to a boil. Reduce the heat to low and simmer, stirring every few minutes, for 12–15 minutes. Remove from the heat and cover.

3. Place the black mustard seeds in a small pan over moderate heat for ½ minute. Add the *ghee* or butter, chili pod and ginger root, and fry until the butter froths or the mustard seeds turn gray, crackle and pop. Pour the seasonings into the *karhi* and cover again immediately. Allow the seasonings to permeate the dish for 3–4 minutes before adding the fresh herbs and serving.

Steamed Split Pea Dumplings in Mild *Karhi* Sauce
TOOVAR KOFTA KARHI

Although this *karhi* appears time-consuming from start to finish, the time is mostly in soaking and preparation. I first had the dish made with *toovar dal*, but find it is equally delicious made with yellow split peas. The *dal* can be soaked, ground and steamed into dumplings ahead of time and assembled when required. Though not traditional, homemade crème fraîche is a pleasant alternative to plain yogurt.

This special-occasion *karhi* should be accompanied by some kind of rice—*Buttered Steamed Rice, Sautéed Plain Rice* or *Toasted Coconut Rice*. For vegetables, include a variety of colors and textures, such as *Buttery Spinach, Pineapple and Green Peas in Almond Broth* and *Bitter Melon Chips with Coconut*.

Dal soaking time: 4–6 hours
Dumpling steaming time: 10–15 minutes
Cooking time: 20 minutes
Serves: 6

Dumplings:

⅓ cup (70 g) *toovar dal* or yellow
    split peas, soaked in water for 4–6
    hours, then drained in a strainer
1-inch (2.5 cm) piece of scraped
    fresh ginger root, sliced
1 hot green chili, broken into bits
1½–2½ tablespoons (22–37 ml) water
1–2 tablespoons (15–30 ml) whole wheat flour
¼ teaspoon (1 ml) salt
¼ teaspoon (1 ml) baking powder
¼ teaspoon (1 ml) yellow asafetida powder (*hing*)*
½ tablespoon (7 ml) melted butter

*This amount applies only to yellow Cobra brand. Reduce any other asafetida by three-fourths.

Karhi:

2 tablespoons (30 ml) sifted chickpea flour
    (sifted before measuring)
1 cup (240 ml) water
2 cups (480 ml) plain yogurt or crème
    fraîche, whisked until smooth
½ teaspoon (2 ml) turmeric
¼ teaspoon (1 ml) paprika or
    ⅛ teaspoon (0.5 ml) cayenne pepper
1 teaspoon (5 ml) sugar
l teaspoon (5 ml) salt
3 tablespoons (45 ml) *ghee* or unsalted butter
1 teaspoon (5 ml) dry-roasted cumin seeds
2 tablespoons (30 ml) chopped fresh coriander or minced parsley

---

For information about unfamiliar ingredients or techniques, see A-to-Z

1. To make the dumplings in a food processor, first attach the metal blade. Put the drained *dal* or split peas, ginger and chili in the work bowl, along with 1½ tablespoons (22 ml) of water. Cover and process for 4–5 minutes (adding up to 1 tablespoon/15 ml more water if necessary to yield a light, fluffy paste). Take out ½ teaspoon (2 ml) and scoop it off with your fingertip onto the work surface. If it holds its shape, add only a touch of flour; if it spreads, add up to 2 tablespoons (30 ml). Add the flour, salt, baking powder, asafetida and melted butter, and pulse 3 or 4 times or until blended.

To make the dumplings in a blender, place the drained *dal* or split peas, ginger and chili in the blender jar. Cover and pulse several times. Add 1½ tablespoons (22 ml) of water and process for 1 minute. Uncover and scrape the mixture toward the blades with a thin rubber spatula. Cover and blend, adding only sprinkles of water to facilitate grinding into a thick paste, for about 5 minutes. Test the paste consistency as described above. Add the flour, salt, baking powder, asafetida and melted butter, cover, and pulse only until blended.

2. Set up steaming equipment, preferably with tiers to save time. You can use a 2-tiered bamboo steamer resting in a wok, a tiered stainless steel unit or even a canning rack or trivet in a large stockpot. Add at least 1 inch (2.5 cm) of water to the pan; the boiling-water level must be at least 1 inch (2.5 cm) below the bottom of the steamer. Butter two 8-inch (20 cm) cake tins. Using a ½-teaspoon (2 ml) measuring spoon or your fingertips, scoop off small dollops of dumplings and arrange them without touching in the buttered tins. Set in the steaming unit, cover, and steam over high heat for 8–10 minutes. Remove the pan from the heat and leave undisturbed for at least 5 minutes to firm up and cool.

3. To make the *karhi*, place the chickpea flour in a 1-quart/liter bowl. Slowly add 2 tablespoons (30 ml) of the water, whisking, and then add the yogurt or crème fraîche, turmeric, paprika or cayenne, sugar and the remaining salt. Pour into a heavy 2-quart/liter saucepan and place over moderately high heat. Stirring constantly, bring the mixture to a boil. Reduce the heat to low and simmer for 10–12 minutes. Cover, remove from the heat and set aside.

4. To finish the *karhi*, heat the *ghee* or butter in a heavy frying pan over moderate heat. Slip in the steamed dumplings and fry, gently shaking the pan or tossing with a wooden spatula, until they are golden brown. Pour into the *karhi*, stir, and sprinkle with the dry roasted cumin and fresh herbs.

YOGURT SALADS

All vegetarians know that a balanced, varied diet of grains (breads, cereals, rice), legumes (*dals*, dried beans and peas), dairy products (yogurt, buttermilk, cheese and tart cream) and fruits and vegetables is the necessary key to good health. *Raitas* are an excellent way to introduce cultured milk products into your meals. They are meant to be cool and refreshing on the palate alongside spicier, hot dishes. By yogurt I do not mean skimmed milk yogurt, which is too watery and thin to be authentic in these salads. Rather, if at all possible, make your own (it almost makes itself). Homemade yogurt is marvelously velvety, thick and delicate—a far cry from anything in a carton, which is often tangy and watery. You can appreciate it as a nutrition dynamo: ½ cup (120 ml) of whole milk yogurt has about 7 grams of protein, 10 grams of carbohydrates, 8 milligrams of cholesterol and only 83 calories. Some health food stores carry outstanding whole milk yogurts; just be sure to purchase them well ahead of the expiration date. If you want to add extra body, combine soured or tart cream (similar to crème fraîche) with the yogurt. If you must minimize calories, substitute a creamy cultured buttermilk, usually only 1 percent butterfat.

Rai means black mustard seeds, and for Gujaratis *raita* must contain them. In North India, *raita* usually has dry-roasted coarsely crushed cumin seeds. Fresh herbs are always a part of this dish; although fresh coriander is the most common, you can use those that best complement the menu.

Chopped Spinach in Smooth Yogurt
PALAK RAITA

This richly marbled yogurt salad is nutritious and very delicious. Blanched chopped spinach is combined with minced fresh herbs, fresh lemon juice, lemon zest and white pepper. You could use a mixture of greens instead of spinach—mustard greens, chard, watercress, kale or collards— each combination varying the taste. For a special light lunch or brunch, accompany it with *Griddle-Fried Radish-Stuffed Whole Wheat Bread* or *Griddle-Fried Potato-Stuffed Whole Wheat Bread* and soup.

Preparation time (after assembling ingredients): 15 minutes
Serves: 4 to 6

½ pound (230 g) fresh spinach, washed, patted dry, trimmed and coarsely chopped,
    or ½ package of frozen chopped spinach, defrosted and pressed dry (140 g)
1 tablespoon (15 ml) unsalted butter
2 cups (480 ml) plain yogurt, or 1½ cups (360 ml)
    yogurt and ½ cup (120 ml) tart cream (page 319)
3 tablespoons (45 ml) minced fresh herbs (coriander,
    dill, tarragon, chervil, parsley)
½ teaspoon (2 ml) grated lemon zest
2 teaspoons (10 ml) lemon juice
½ teaspoon (2 ml) salt
¼ teaspoon (1 ml) white pepper

1. Place the spinach, with any water clinging to the leaves or a sprinkle of water, in a large nonstick pot, add the butter, cover, and cook over moderate to moderately high heat for 5 minutes or until a sizzling sound comes from the pot. Turn the leaves over so the uncooked ones on top change places with the soft cooked ones on the bottom. Cover and cook for another 4–5 minutes. Take off the lid and cook off any excess water. Remove the spinach from the pan and let cool to room temperature. Alternately, cook the defrosted spinach in a dab of butter for a few minutes.

2. Meanwhile, combine the yogurt or yogurt–cream mixture, herbs, lemon zest, lemon juice, salt and pepper in a 1-quart/liter bowl and whisk with a fork until creamy. If you are ready to serve the salad, add the spinach and blend well. Otherwise, chill the yogurt mixture and spinach separately.

3. Just before serving, combine the yogurt mixture and spinach and stir to blend. Serve in small custard-cup-sized bowls or metal *katoris*.

Seasoned Potatoes in Smooth Yogurt
ALOO RAITA

This creamy potato salad is from the Maharashtra–Gujarat area in Southwest India. The yogurt should be very fresh and thick, never runny or tart. Rather than adding the calories of cream or sour cream to enrich the texture and flavor, you need only take the time to hang the yogurt for 2–3 hours in a cloth to drain off whey and condense the yogurt. You can bake, boil or steam potatoes. I like to cut them and bake them in a tin-foil packet with a few sprigs of fresh mint and a pat of butter. This dish is good any time of the year on almost any menu, Vedic or Western. Make sure that potatoes and yogurt are not ingredients in your other dishes. I like to serve this *raita* with *Flaky Biscuits with Black Pepper*, a flatbread selection and *Bottle Gourd and Green Peas in Tomato Broth* for a light lunch or dinner.

Preparation and draining time (after assembling ingredients): 2–3 hours
Serves: 4 to 6

2 cups (480 ml) plain yogurt
2 medium-sized all-purpose potatoes (about 10
    ounces/285 g), steamed, boiled or jacket-baked,
    peeled and cut into ¾-inch (2 cm) cubes
1 tablespoon (15 ml) *ghee* or vegetable oil
1 teaspoon (10 ml) black mustard seeds
1–2 hot green chilies, seeded and slivered
¾–1 teaspoon (3.5–5 ml) salt
2 tablespoons (30 ml) chopped fresh coriander or parsley
⅛ teaspoon (0.5 ml) paprika or *garam masala* for garnishing

1. Line a colander with three thicknesses of cheesecloth (about 16 inches/40 cm square) or a white handkerchief. Place the yogurt in the cloth, gather up the four corners, and tie closed with a piece of kitchen twine. Hang the yogurt where it can drip—from a knob on a kitchen cabinet or a sink faucet, for instance—and let it drain into a bowl or sink for 2–3 hours.

2. Place the yogurt in a 1-quart/liter bowl and stir with a fork until smooth and creamy. Gently stir in the cubed potatoes.

3. Heat the *ghee* or oil in a small pan over moderately high heat. When it is hot but not smoking, add the mustard seeds and green chilies and fry until the mustard seeds pop and turn gray. Immediately pour the fried seasonings into the yogurt-potato mixture and add the salt and most of the fresh herbs. Gently mix until blended.

4. Serve at room temperature or refrigerate, covered, for several hours. Transfer to metal *katoris* and garnish with paprika or *garam masala* and a touch of the remaining herbs.

Sliced Bananas in Smooth Tart Cream
KELA RAITA

Bananas are native to India and are one of the most popular commercial fruits of the nation. There are said to be a staggering 400 varieties, though they are divided into only two types: eating and cooking bananas. In India, my favorite selection for this dish is a yellow-skinned, finger-length banana, called, appropriately, a finger banana. If you live in tropical south Florida or Southern California, you can most likely find them at larger co-ops, fruit stores and Mexican or Indian grocery stores. Of course, you can use any firm ripe banana. Laced with fresh mint and fried seasonings, this *raita* is best served chilled. It can also be served as a fruit dessert. I enjoy it for a special summer brunch or lunch with fresh fruit juice and *Shallow-Fried Flaky Parathas* or *Savory Pounded Rice Uppma with Fried Nuts and Coconut*.

Preparation and cooking time (after assembling ingredients): a few minutes
Chilling time: 2–3 hours
Serves: 4 to 6

1¼ cups (300 ml) tart cream (page 319) or
   crème fraîche and ¾ cup (180 ml) plain
   yogurt, or 2 cups (480 ml) plain yogurt
½ teaspoon (2 ml) salt
2 tablespoons (30 ml) finely chopped fresh
   mint or ½ teaspoon (2 ml) dried mint
2 tablespoons (30 ml) shredded coconut
2 medium-sized firm ripe bananas,
   peeled and thinly sliced
1 tablespoon (15 ml) coconut or avocado oil
1 teaspoon (5 ml) black mustard seeds
1–2 hot green chilies, seeded and slivered
½ teaspoon (2 ml) *garam masala*

1. Put the tart cream-yogurt mixture or plain yogurt in a 1-quart/liter bowl; add the salt, mint and coconut, and whisk with a fork until creamy and smooth. Stir in the bananas, cover, and refrigerate for at least 2–3 hours.

2. Heat the oil in a small pan over moderate heat. When it is hot but not smoking, add the mustard seeds and green chilies and fry until the seeds turn gray, sputter and

---

For information about unfamiliar ingredients or techniques, see A-to-Z

pop. Pour the seasoning into the yogurt mixture and stir to mix.

3. Place the *raita* in a serving dish or individual custard-cup-sized bowls or metal *katoris* and garnish with *garam masala*.

Tomatoes in Smooth Yogurt
TAMATAR RAITA

Tomato is probably the most popular *raita* selection in India, vying for first position with cucumber. It is simple, unadorned refreshment, with each region having its own slight nuance in seasoning. The contrast between the brilliant red tomatoes and the snowy yogurt is vivid and appealing. To take advantage of the colors, use firm-fleshed or seeded tomatoes. I like to use marble-sized cherry or sugar-lump tomatoes, cut into quarters. You can use either fresh coriander, basil or dill for a garnish—a single leaf or feathery ½-inch (1.5 cm) pieces of dill. Try one of the most popular and loved lunches for Vedic vegetarians: a *raita*, *khichari*, *bhaji* menu. Accompany *tamatar raita* with *Easy Rice and Split Pea Khichari with Fried Cashews* and *Deep-Fried Shredded Plantain Clusters* and a hot flatbread selection.

Preparation and cooking time (after assembling ingredients): 10 minutes
Serves: 4 to 6

2 cups (480 ml) plain yogurt, or 1⅔ cups (400 ml)
    yogurt and ⅓ cup (80 ml) sour cream
¾ teaspoon (3.5 ml) salt
⅛ teaspoon (0.5 ml) white pepper
3–4 medium-sized firm ripe tomatoes or cherry
    tomatoes (about 1 pound/455 g), stems removed
1 tablespoon (15 ml) vegetable or peanut oil
1 teaspoon (5 ml) black mustard seeds
1 hot green chili, seeded and finely minced (or as desired)
1–2 sprigs fresh coriander, basil or dill for garnishing

1. Combine the yogurt or yogurt and sour cream, salt and pepper in a 1-quart/liter bowl. Whisk with a fork until smooth and creamy. Wash and dry the tomatoes and cut into ½-inch (1.5 cm) cubes, or quarter the cherry tomatoes; drop into the yogurt mixture, without stirring. The mixture can be covered and refrigerated for several hours or assembled at room temperature.

2. Heat the oil in a small pan over moderate heat. When it is hot but not smoking, add the mustard seeds and green chili and fry until the seeds crackle and turn gray. Pour into the salad and gently blend. Serve immediately, garnishing with fresh herb sprigs.

Fried Okra in Smooth Yogurt

BHINDI RAITA

Chilled yogurt salads are popular throughout India, and in Gujarati homes they are served with almost every summer lunch. This became one of my favorite dishes from the first time I tasted its delightful combination of textures and flavors. Though the ingredients can be prepared ahead of time, the salad is assembled just before serving. Crunchy fried okra is added to a toasted chickpea flour and yogurt sauce. The creamy sauce is seasoned with roasted cumin seeds and fresh coriander or parsley, and finally garnished with a dash of paprika. Since the okra softens as it sits in the sauce, and the chickpea flour both thickens and darkens the color, it can also double as a creamy room-temperature vegetable dish.

Though it does take a bit more time to clean, dry and fry okra than cut tomatoes, try this *raita* for a really special lunch or dinner. For light fare, try it with *Spiced Potato and Green Pea Samosa* and a dipping bowl of *Sweet 'n' Sour Tamarind Sauce* and the delicious main dish stew *Rice and Toasted Toovar Dal Khichari with Mixed Vegetables.* For a delicate sweet, add *Cheese Balls Stuffed with Nut Milk Fudge.*

Preparation and cooking time (after assembling ingredients): about 30 minutes
Serves: 4 to 6

ghee or vegetable oil for shallow-frying
1 pound (455 g) okra, washed, thoroughly dried, trimmed and cut
    into ¼-inch (6 mm) slices (about 1¼ cups/300 ml)
1 teaspoon (5 ml) *garam masala*
¼ teaspoon (1 ml) paprika or cayenne pepper
½ tablespoon (2 ml) ground coriander
1 teaspoon (5 ml) salt
2 cups (480 ml) plain yogurt, or 1¾ cups (420 ml)
    plain yogurt and ¼ cup (60 ml) sour cream
½ tablespoon (7 ml) dry-roasted coarsely crushed cumin seeds
1 teaspoon (5 ml) chopped fresh coriander or parsley
3 tablespoons (45 ml) sifted chickpea flour (sifted before measuring)

1. Pour the *ghee* or oil to a depth of 1 inch (2.5 cm) in an 8-inch (20 cm) frying pan. Set over moderate heat, and when it is hot but not smoking, add the sliced okra. Fry for 15–20 minutes or until crisp and browned. Remove with a slotted spoon and drain on paper towels. While the okra is hot, sprinkle it with *garam masala*, paprika or cayenne, ground coriander and ½ teaspoon (2 ml) of the salt. Toss to mix.

2. Place the yogurt or yogurt and sour cream in a 1-quart/liter bowl and add the remaining ½ teaspoon (2 ml) salt and all but ½ teaspoon (2 ml) each of the cumin seeds and fresh herbs. Whisk with a fork until smooth and creamy.

3. Dry-roast the chickpea flour in a small heavy pan over moderate heat, stirring constantly to prevent scorching. When it darkens a few shades and smells nutty, transfer to a bowl to cool.

4. If you do these steps 1–2 hours ahead of assembling the salad, refrigerate the yogurt and leave the okra uncovered in a 200°F (95°C) oven. Before serving, add the okra to the yogurt, sprinkle with the chickpea flour, and gently stir. Transfer to a serving dish or individual bowls, garnish with the remaining cumin seeds and fresh herbs and a dash of paprika, and serve immediately.

For information about unfamiliar ingredients or techniques, see A-to-Z

Deep-Fried Chickpea Flour Pearls in Creamy Yogurt
BOONDI RAITA

Most North Indian households keep a jar of fried *boondi* on hand to use in salads, snacks, sweets and soups, or as garnishes in a number of dishes. They are crispy fried drops of chickpea flour batter, no bigger than pearls. In this popular Punjabi selection, fried *boondi* are softened in water and then squeezed dry. These juicy little balls are delicious floating in a pistachio-coriander yogurt sauce. This *raita* makes a wonderful accompaniment to *Sautéed Cauliflower and Green Peas* or *Bitter Melon Vegetable Soup with Dal Badi* with rice or flatbreads for a typical Punjabi meal. You could serve it with stuffed *parathas* and a vegetable dish for an evening fireside dinner.

Preparation time (after assembling ingredients): 10–15 minutes
Cooking time: about 20 minutes
Serves: 4 to 6

½ cup (50 g) chickpea flour
    (sifted before measuring)
¾ teaspoon (3.5 ml) salt
⅛ teaspoon (0.5 ml) baking powder
4–5 tablespoons (60–75 ml) water
ghee or nut oil for shallow-frying
2 cups (480 ml) plain yogurt, or
    1 cup (240 ml) each buttermilk
    and tart cream (page 319)
½ tablespoon (7 ml) dry-roasted
    coarsely crushed cumin seeds
2 tablespoons (30 ml) raw pistachio nuts,
    blanched and chopped
2 tablespoons (30 ml) chopped fresh coriander,
    dill or minced parsley
paprika or cayenne pepper for garnishing

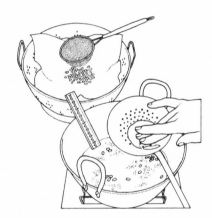

1. Combine the chickpea flour, ¼ teaspoon (1 ml) of the salt and the baking powder in a small bowl. Gradually whisk in enough water to make a smooth cake-like batter the consistency of heavy cream. Heat 1½ inches (4 cm) of *ghee* or oil in a deep-frying pan. Place the pan over moderate heat, and when it is hot (350°F/180°C) pour about 2 tablespoons (30 ml) of batter into a ladle or frying spoon with several ⅛-inch (3 mm) holes, hold the spoon just above the pan and press the batter through the holes with your finger or quickly tap the spoon with your hand so small drops of batter fall into the oil. (If the batter is too thin, they will fall as squiggles or globs; if it is too thick, they will not fall at all.) They will froth in the hot oil, then rise to the surface. Fry until crisp and golden yellow, 2–3 minutes; do not allow them to brown. Remove with a fine-meshed frying spoon and spread out on absorbent paper towels to drain. Repeat the process with all of the batter.

2. Place all but 2–3 tablespoons (30–45 ml) of *boondi* in a bowl of warm water. Leave them for a few minutes to soften, then gently squeeze between your palms to remove the water. Set aside in a dish.

3. Place the yogurt or buttermilk-cream mixture, the remaining ½ teaspoon (2 ml) salt, and the cumin seeds, nuts and fresh herbs in a 1-quart/liter bowl. Whisk with a fork until smooth and creamy. Stir in the soaked *boondi* and serve at room temperature, or chill for several hours. Garnish with the reserved crispy *boondi* and a sprinkle of paprika or cayenne.

Carrots, Cashews and Dates in Smooth Yogurt
GAJAR KAJU RAITA

This colorful *raita* comes from my good friend Mandakini Devi, an accomplished cook. The cashew and date combination can be replaced by almonds and golden raisins or pecans and currants. The yogurt is drained for 2–3 hours before being mixed into the salad to make a thick, rich sauce without the extra calories of added cream.

Preparation and draining time (after assembling ingredients): 2–3 hours
Serves: 4 to 6

2 cups (480 ml) plain yogurt, preferably homemade (page 307)
3 medium-sized carrots (about ½ pound/230 g), peeled and shredded
6 pitted dates, sliced into thin rounds, or 2 tablespoons (30 ml) raisins
    or currants soaked in hot water for 10 minutes, then drained
3 tablespoons (45 ml) dry roasted chopped cashews, almonds or pecans
1 teaspoon (5 ml) grated orange or lime zest
2 tablespoons (30 ml) fresh orange juice, strained
2 tablespoons (30 ml) granulated maple or date sugar
¼ teaspoon (1 ml) cardamom seeds, coarsely crushed

1. Line a colander with three thicknesses of cheesecloth (about 16 inches/40 cm square) or a white handkerchief. Place the yogurt in the cloth, gather up the four corners, and tie closed with a piece of kitchen twine. Hang the yogurt from a knob on a kitchen cabinet or a sink faucet where it can drip and drain into a bowl or sink. Let it drain undisturbed for 2–3 hours.
2. Press the carrots between your palms to extract excess juice. Place the drained yogurt in a 1-quart/liter bowl and whisk with a fork until smooth and creamy. Add the remaining ingredients, and stir until blended. Serve at room temperature or chill for 1–2 hours.

For information about unfamiliar ingredients or techniques, see A-to-Z

Sweet Potato Yogurt Salad with Dates and Almonds
SHAKARKAND RAITA

Orange zest, orange juice, dates and toasted almonds are added to a light blend of buttermilk and compressed yogurt in this outstanding *raita*. You can drain and compress the yogurt up to two days before assembling the *raita*. Sweet potatoes or yams can be used interchangeably, baked in their jackets until tender. You could even substitute baked butternut or acorn squash with equally pleasant results. For lunch or dinner, you might accompany this *raita* with plain rice, *Sautéed Brussels Sprouts with Coconut* and *Soft 'n' Savory Chickpea Kofta*.

Preparation and draining time (after assembling ingredients): 2–3 hours
Chilling time: at least 1 hour
Serves: 6

1 cup (240 ml) plain yogurt, drained for
    2–3 hours, and 1 cup (240 ml) cultured
    buttermilk; or a mixture of half plain
    yogurt and half sour cream
½ teaspoon (2 ml) grated orange zest
2 tablespoons (30 ml) fresh orange juice
2 tablespoons (30 ml) finely chopped dates
1–2 hot green chilies, seeded and minced
2 teaspoons (10 ml) dry-roasted
    coarsely crushed cumin seeds
¾ teaspoon (3.5 ml) salt
2 medium-sized sweet potatoes or yams
    (about ¾ pound/340 g), baked in
    their jackets just until fork-tender
2 tablespoons (30 ml) toasted sliced almonds for garnishing

1. Line a colander with three thicknesses of cheesecloth (about 16 inches/40 cm square) or a handkerchief. Place the yogurt in the cloth, gather the four corners, and tie closed with a piece of kitchen twine. Hang the yogurt from a knob on a kitchen cabinet or sink faucet where it can drain into a bowl or sink. Let it drain undisturbed for 2–3 hours.

2. Unwrap the thickened yogurt and place it in a 1-quart/liter bowl with the buttermilk. (Alternately use the yogurt–sour cream mixture). Add the orange zest, orange juice, dates, green chilies, cumin seeds and salt, and whisk with a fork until smooth and creamy. Refrigerate, covered, for at least 1 hour.

3. Peel the sweet potatoes or yams and cut into ½-inch (1.5 ml) dice. When you are ready to serve the dish, gently stir in the sweet potatoes. Garnish with toasted almonds.

Spiced Eggplant in Smooth Yogurt
BAIGAN RAITA

There are a number of ways to approach cooking eggplant for this *raita*, each method lending a different flavor and texture to the dish. Deep-frying is nice and festive; oven broiling lends a smoky, very delicious flavor; and steaming is simple and low in calories. No matter what your choice, three flavoring agents lend character and appeal to the eggplant: mustard seeds, turmeric and asafetida. If you want extra nutrition and texture, feel free to add toasted chopped peanuts, cashews, pecans or almonds. If you are deep-frying, reserve a few fried eggplant slices for garnishing, otherwise, use a few whole herb leaves.

Preparation and cooking time (after assembling ingredients): 1 hour
Serves: 5 or 6

1 medium-sized eggplant (about 1 pound/455 g), with stem intact
2½ tablespoons (37 ml) *ghee* or vegetable oil
½ teaspoon (2 ml) black mustard seeds
½ teaspoon (2 ml) cumin seeds
¼ teaspoon (1 ml) yellow asafetida powder (*hing*)*
1 teaspoon (5 ml) salt
⅛ teaspoon (0.5 ml) paprika or cayenne pepper
½ teaspoon (2 ml) *garam masala*
½ teaspoon (2 ml) turmeric
1¾ cups (420 ml) plain yogurt, or 1½ cups (360 ml) plain
    yogurt and ¼ cup (60 ml) tart cream (page 319), chilled
2 tablespoons (30 ml) chopped fresh coriander or sweet
    basil, plus a few whole leaves for garnishing

*This amount applies only to yellow Cobra brand. Reduce any other asafetida by three-fourths.

1. Cook the eggplant in any of these ways:
Cut into ¾-inch (2 cm) cubes and steam until butter-soft. Let cool.
Cut in half lengthwise, then quarter and slice crosswise into ¼-inch (6 mm) slices. Deep-fry at 365°F (185°C) until richly browned and tender. Remove with a slotted spoon and drain on paper towels. Let cool.
In six places pierce holes ½ inch (1.5 cm) deep and lay on a foil-lined baking tray. Place 5 inches (12.5 cm) away from a preheated gas or electric broiler and broil, slowly turning with tongs until all sides are shriveled and blackened and the pulp is fork-tender. Let cool slightly, then rinse under running water. Pat dry with paper towels, then coarsely chop.
2. Heat the *ghee* or oil in an 8-inch (20 cm) nonstick frying pan over moderate heat. When it is hot but not smoking, add the black mustard seeds and cumin seeds. Fry until the mustard seeds turn gray and pop, sprinkle in the asafetida, and in seconds add the eggplant. Sauté steamed or baked eggplant until browned, fried eggplant for only 1 minute. Sprinkle with ½ teaspoon (2 ml) of the salt and the paprika or cayenne, *garam masala* and turmeric, and toss. Let cool to room temperature.
3. Place the yogurt or yogurt–tart cream mixture into a 1-quart/liter bowl and stir until smooth. Stir in the seasoned eggplant, fresh herbs and remaining ½ teaspoon (2 ml) salt. Just before serving, garnish with fried eggplant slices or whole herb leaves.

For information about unfamiliar ingredients or techniques, see A-to-Z

Shredded Cucumbers in Smooth Mint-Flavored Yogurt
KHEERA RAITA

There are so many ways to make this, India's most popular *raita*, that I am presenting two of my favorite recipe variations. In this one, we discover how mint and cucumbers were made for each other. With a touch of lemon or lime zest, you have one of the most refreshing salads possible. Though avocado oil is not available in India, I find it perfect for delicate salads and *raitas*. You must use crisp, seedless young cucumbers. If all you can find are overgrown, out-of-season giants, seed them before shredding. This makes a terrific cold rice salad: simply fold it into room-temperature or chilled cooked rice and garnish with *Tomato Flowers* and a black mustard seed *chaunk*. For a workday lunch box, accompany with *Griddle-Fried Pea-Stuffed Whole Wheat Bread* and a thermos of *Quick Cream of Split Pea Soup with Sliced Carrots*.

Preparation time (after assembling ingredients): about 30 minutes
Chilling time: 1–2 hours
Serves: 5 or 6

2 medium-sized cucumbers (about 1 pound/455 g)
½ tablespoon (7 ml) salt
1½ cups (360 ml) plain yogurt, or 1¼ cups (300 ml)
**   plain yogurt and ¼ cup (60 ml) sour cream**
¼ teaspoon (1 ml) cayenne pepper or paprika
2 tablespoons (30 ml) finely chopped fresh mint
1 teaspoon (5 ml) grated lemon or lime zest
2 tablespoons (30 ml) avocado or sesame oil
1 teaspoon (5 ml) black mustard seeds
cucumber flowers and paprika for garnishing

1. Peel and coarsely shred the cucumbers, then place them in a bowl. Sprinkle with salt and toss. Let the cucumbers sit at room temperature for 20–30 minutes. Pour them into a strainer, press out the liquid, then pat them dry with paper towels.

2. Place the yogurt or yogurt–sour cream mixture, cayenne or paprika and mint in a 1-quart/liter bowl and whisk with a fork until smooth and creamy. Stir in the cucumbers. Heat the oil over moderate heat in a small pan. When it is hot but not smoking, add the mustard seeds. Fry until the seeds sputter and turn gray (if the oil is very hot, you may need to use a spatter screen to keep the seeds from jumping out of the small pan). Pour the fried seeds and oil into the cucumber–yogurt mixture, and stir to blend.

3. Refrigerate for 1–2 hours to allow the mint and seasoning to release their flavors. Serve with a garnish of twisted cucumber flowers and a sprinkle of paprika.

Cucumber and Coconut in Dill Yogurt-Cream
KHEERA NARIYAL RAITA

When cucumbers are blanched they become wonderfully crunchy and crisp, and they stay that way for hours. No matter what type of cucumber you use (I prefer the long European variety), they must be young and seedless or you must seed them. The crunchy cucumbers are folded into a thick dill yogurt-cream, then livened with a mustard seed *chaunk* and shredded hot chilies. Red chilies or capsicums lend color and flavor variation. For appetizers, I like to serve the *raita* in hollowed-out 1½ inch (4 cm) cucumber cups. *Raita* and hot *paratha* make a much loved spring or fall light lunch combination. If you want to expand, add a soup or *dal*. You could try hot *Sweet 'n' Sour Dal Soup with Fresh Vegetables* and room temperature *Lemon Stuffed with Almond-Chickpea Pâté*.

Preparation and cooking time (after assembling ingredients): 15 minutes
Chilling time: 1–2 hours
Serves: 5 or 6

2 medium-sized cucumbers (about 1 pound/455 g)
    or one 12–14 inch (30–35 cm) European cucumber
1 cup (240 ml) each plain yogurt and sour
    cream or tart cream (page 319)
½–1 teaspoon (2–5 ml) salt
1 tablespoon (15 ml) finely chopped parsley
2 tablespoons (30 ml) finely chopped fresh dill
    or 1½ teaspoons (7 ml) dried dill weed
2 tablespoons (30 ml) toasted chopped walnuts
⅓ cup (35 g) shredded fresh coconut
1 hot green or red chili, seeded and slivered,
    or 1 strip of red capsicum (½ x 3 inches/1.5 x 7.5 cm),
    slivered crosswise
2 tablespoons (30 ml) nut or coconut oil
1 teaspoon (5 ml) black mustard seeds
watercress for garnishing

1. Peel the cucumber and halve lengthwise. Scoop out the seeds with a melon baller. Slice crosswise ⅛ inch (3 mm) thick. Bring a 2-quart/liter pan of water to a boil, add the cucumbers, and blanch for 2 minutes. Pour through a strainer, shake off the water, then plunge them into a bowl of cold water. Strain again and pat dry with paper towels.

2. Combine the yogurt and sour or tart cream, salt, parsley, dill, walnuts, coconut and chili or capsicum in a 1-quart/liter bowl. Whisk with a fork until smooth and creamy, then stir in the cucumbers.

3. Heat the oil over moderate heat in a small pan. When it is hot but not smoking, add the mustard seeds. Fry until the seeds sputter and turn gray (if the oil is very hot, you may need to use a spatter screen to keep the seeds from jumping out of the small pan). Pour the fried seeds and oil into the salad and stir to blend.

4. Refrigerate for 1–2 hours to chill and allow the seasonings to release their flavors. Transfer to a flat serving dish and surround with watercress sprigs, or place in individual serving dishes and garnish each with 2–3 watercress leaves.

For information about unfamiliar ingredients or techniques, see A-to-Z

Raw Mixed Vegetables in Smooth Yogurt
SABJI RAITA

Here is a *raita* that could not be more colorful, nutritious or refreshing. It should be made from seasonal fresh vegetables—use whatever you wish, but include at least five or six kinds. The *raita* can be kept refrigerated for several hours prior to serving. Serve it with dishes that do not contain much of the vegetables you selected, or much yogurt. Other than that, anything from *uppma* to *dosa* to *paratha* is wonderful.

Preparation time (after assembling ingredients): about 10 minutes
Serves: 5 or 6

2 cups (480 ml) plain yogurt
1⅔–2 cups (400–480 ml) mixed vegetables: red, yellow or green bell peppers,
    diced cucumbers, celery, radishes or jicama, cut into ¼-inch (6 mm) dice;
    firm ripe tomatoes, fennel root, shelled fresh peas or frozen peas, defrosted,
    cut into ⅓-inch (1 cm) dice
1 tablespoon (15 ml) coriander seeds
1 tablespoon (15 ml) cumin seeds
½ teaspoon (2 ml) fennel seeds
1 teaspoon (5 ml) salt
¼ teaspoon (1 ml) cracked black pepper

    1. Place the yogurt in a 1-quart/liter bowl and whisk with a fork until smooth. Add the mixed vegetables and stir to blend.
    2. Combine the coriander seeds, cumin seeds and fennel seeds in a small frying pan and dry-roast over low heat until they darken a few shades. Coarsely crush in a coffee mill or with a mortar and pestle. When cool, add to the yogurt along with the salt and pepper. Serve at room temperature or chilled.

Buckwheat Flour Fritters in Lemon-Pepper Yogurt
EKADASEE KOTU PAKORA RAITA

Buckwheat is not a cereal grain. Rather, it is a seed that belongs to the same family as rhubarb and dock (*Polygonaceae*). Though the husked whole grains are available in many supermarkets, the flour is most often found in health food stores. If the grains have been roasted before milling, the flour is gray-brown; unroasted grains produce a grayish-tan flour. This is the most popular flour on *Ekadasee* days, used along with other non-cereal flours such as potato, water chestnut, cassava and tapioca.

Preparation and batter resting time (after assembling ingredients): about 30 minutes
Cooking time: about 15 minutes
Serves: 6

⅓ cup (50 g) buckwheat flour
    (sifted before measuring)
¼ teaspoon (1 ml) salt
¼ teaspoon (1 ml) sugar
about ⅓ cup (80 ml) water
¼ teaspoon (1 ml) baking powder
ghee or vegetable oil for frying
1¾ cups (420 ml) plain yogurt, chilled
¼–½ teaspoon (1–2 ml) salt
¼ teaspoon (1 ml) freshly cracked pepper
¼ teaspoon (1 ml) grated lime zest
½ teaspoon (2 ml) lime juice
a few whole coriander leaves for garnishing

1. Combine the buckwheat flour, salt and sugar in a small mixing bowl. Add the water and beat into a smooth, pouring-consistency batter. Cover the bowl with plastic wrap and set aside for ½ hour. Stir the batter, add the baking powder and check the consistency. It will have thickened slightly; you may have to add more water or flour to end up with a thin, cake like batter.

2. Pour *ghee* or vegetable oil into an 8-inch (20 cm) frying pan to a depth of ½ inch (1.5 cm). Place the pan over moderate heat, and when it is hot but not smoking, scoop up 1 teaspoon (5 ml) of batter and carefully drop it into the pan; shape as many as will fit easily without crowding. As they puff and turn reddish-brown, turn them over with a fork and brown on the other side. Remove with a slotted spoon and transfer to paper towels to drain. Shape and fry all of the batter. The puffs can be fried up to 3 hours before serving.

3. When you are ready to serve the *raita*, whisk together the yogurt, salt, pepper, lime zest and lime juice in a bowl. Add the puffs and gently mix. Pour into a serving bowl or individual custard-cup-sized bowls or *katoris*, and garnish with whole coriander leaves, laid flat on top of the dish.

PANIR AND *CHENNA* DISHES

I am hopeful that *panir* and *chenna* will become as popular as yogurt and crème fraîche in America. Unfortunately, there are no substitutes, and until they are available commercially, they have to be made at home. Fortunately, they are both quick and easy to make. *Panir* is widely used in North Indian cooking, while *chenna* is more popular in the eastern parts of the country. The following recipes include side- and main-dish vegetables and savory side dishes. The unripened cheese is very mild and invariably fried before it is served in a savory vegetable dish. For sautéed or pan-fried recipes, I strongly suggest using heavy nonstick cookware.

For information about unfamiliar ingredients or techniques, see A-to-Z

Chopped Spinach with *Panir* Cheese
PALAK PANIR SAK

One of the most popular vegetable dishes in North India is *palak panir sak*. Every temple and household has its own variation. Sometimes it is made exclusively with spinach, and at others with mixed greens—spinach and mustard, collard, fenugreek or beet greens. Some variations attain notoriety by puréeing cooked spinach and simmering it with cream and fried *panir* cubes. Other renditions remain textured, matching equal amounts of fried cheese with buttery, wilted chopped spinach. It is a moist, succulent dish that is delicious with hot flatbreads. Bite-sized pieces of flat bread are used to scoop up bits of cheese and spinach. Try *palak panir sak* with *Griddle-Baked Village-Style Corn Bread, Mixed Bean Salad with Fennel* or chopped tomatoes with herbs and oil and *Golden Pumpkin Toovar Dal Soup* for a delicious, nutritious meal.

Preparation time (after assembling ingredients): 5 minutes
Cooking time: about 30 minutes
Serves: 5 or 6

1–2 hot green chilies, cut into pieces
½-inch (1.5 cm) piece of fresh
    ginger root, sliced
4 tablespoons (60 ml) *panir* whey or water
½ tablespoon (7 ml) ground coriander
½ teaspoon (2 ml) turmeric
½ teaspoon (2 ml) ground cumin
¼ teaspoon (1 ml) paprika
6 tablespoons (90 ml) *ghee* or nut oil
fresh *panir* cheese (page 313) made from 6 cups
    (1.5 liters) milk, cut into ½-inch (1.5 cm) cubes
    (about 6 ounces/170 g)
2 pounds (1 kg) fresh spinach, washed, trimmed
    and finely chopped, or two 10-ounce (570 g)
    packages of frozen chopped spinach, defrosted
½ teaspoon (2 ml) *garam masala*
1 teaspoon (5 ml) salt
3 tablespoons (45 ml) cream or cream cheese,
    cut into small pieces

   1. Place the chilies, ginger and whey or water in a blender or food processor bowl fitted with the metal blade. Process to a smooth purée. Add the coriander, turmeric, cumin and paprika and pulse to blend well. Set aside.
   2. Heat the *ghee* or oil in a nonstick wok or 5-quart/liter saucepan over moderate heat until it is hot but not smoking. Gently add the *panir* cheese and fry for about 5 minutes, constantly turning the cubes with a gentle hand, to evenly brown them on all sides. (If you use a stainless steel pan, the cubes invariably stick to the pan and tend to spread apart.) When the cubes are golden brown, remove with a slotted spoon and set aside.
   3. Carefully add the wet spice *masala* to the hot oil and then pack in the fresh spinach leaves. Reduce the heat slightly, cover, and cook for 8 minutes. Using two forks, turn the spinach over so that the cooked leaves on the bottom change places with the leaves on top. Cover and cook for another 8 minutes. (If you are using frozen, defrosted spinach, cook it for only a total of 8 minutes.)

4. Add the *garam masala*, salt, fried *panir* and cream or cream cheese. Cover and continue to cook for about 5 minutes. Stir well before serving.

Panir Cheese and Green Peas in Mint Tomato Sauce
MATAR PANIR

Every Punjabi housewife has her version of this dish—and variations on her own version as well. Indeed, this dish is famed throughout India and has become popular around the world, largely from restaurant menus and cookbooks. The main ingredients—tomatoes, peas, *panir* cheese and whey—are supported by aromatics: cumin seeds, fennel seeds, coriander and mint. Unlike most vegetable dishes, it holds well and even improves in 1–2 hours after cooking. The fried *panir* cheese absorbs the sauce flavor as it sits.

The dish fits any type of menu, simple or elaborate. For a full Vedic dinner, you might try *Herbed Rice with Julienne Potatoes* or *Cracked Black Pepper Rice*. Add a *dal* such as *Double Dal Soup* or *Three-Dal Delight*. Side-dish vegetables should present varied colors and textures: perhaps *Green Beans in Spicy Tomato Glaze*, *Deep-Fried Shredded Plantain Clusters* and *Spiced Creamed Spinach*. Any griddle-baked or deep-fried bread goes wonderfully, but *pooris* and *matar panir* are a natural. Condiments could include a lemon wedge and a dab of fresh *Date and Raisin Chutney* or cooked *Simple Tomato Chutney*. The sweets could include *Creamy Saffron Yogurt Cheese* or *Maple Cream Simply Wonderfuls*.

Preparation time (after assembling ingredients): 5 minutes
Cooking time: about 40 minutes
Serves: 6 to 8

1–2 hot green chilies, broken in bits
1-inch (2.5 cm) piece of peeled fresh ginger root, sliced
4 tablespoons (60 ml) water
1 tablespoon (15 ml) ground coriander
1 teaspoon (5 ml) turmeric
½ teaspoon (2 ml) paprika
½ cup (120 ml) *ghee*, or 4 tablespoons (60 ml)
    vegetable oil and 4 tablespoons (60 ml) butter
fresh *panir* cheese (page 313) made from 8 cups
    (2 liters) milk, cut into ½ inch (1.5 cm) cubes (about 11½ ounces/325 g)
1¼ teaspoons (6 ml) cumin seeds
½ teaspoon (2 ml) black mustard seeds
¼ teaspoon (1 ml) fennel seeds
2 cups (480 ml) peeled and diced tomatoes (about 1½ pounds/685 g)
2½ cups (600 ml) whey
1½ cups (360 ml) fresh peas (about 1½ pounds/685 g in shell) or
    one 10-ounce (285 g) package of frozen baby peas, defrosted
1 teaspoon (5 ml) salt
½ tablespoon (7 ml) *garam masala*
2 tablespoons (30 ml) each chopped fresh coriander and mint
    or 1 tablespoon (15 ml) each dried coriander and mint

For information about unfamiliar ingredients or techniques, see A-to-Z

1. Fit a food processor with the metal blade or use a blender. Cover and turn on the machine, drop the green chilies and ginger through the feed cap and mince. Add the water, ground coriander, turmeric and paprika and process until smooth. Transfer to a cup.

2. Heat 4 tablespoons (60 ml) of *ghee* or oil in a 5-quart/liter nonstick saucepan over moderate heat. Carefully add the cheese cubes and fry, constantly turning the pieces until they are evenly browned on all sides. Remove them with a slotted spoon and set aside.

3. Add the cumin seeds, black mustard seeds and fennel seeds and fry until the black mustard seeds pop and turn gray. Add the remaining 4 tablespoons (60 ml) of *ghee* or the butter and the wet spice *masala*. Fry, stirring often, until most of the water evaporates. Add the tomatoes and continue to cook, stirring, until the mixture is dry and the oil separates from the tomato sauce (about 10 minutes).

4. Pour in the whey, add the fresh peas and bring to a boil. Reduce the heat to moderately low, cover and cook for about 15 minutes or until the peas are nearly tender. Add the fried *panir* cubes and defrosted frozen peas (if you are using them) and simmer on low heat for 5 minutes.

5. Add the salt, *garam masala* and fresh herbs when you are ready to serve.

Eggplant and Bell Pepper Stew with Fried *Panir* Cheese
BAIGAN PANIR TARKARI

This dish is a mélange of different cooking techniques: stir-frying, braising and stewing. Eggplant, bell peppers and tomatoes go well together and are outstanding when combined with fried *panir* cheese. I prefer using yellow bell peppers for visual impact, but red or green will do equally well, or a combination of all three. Serve as a main-vegetable dish on almost any menu, including rice or bread, *dal* and a salad for a well balanced Vedic lunch.

Preparation time (after assembling ingredients): 5 minutes
Cooking time: 20–25 minutes
Serves: 4 to 6

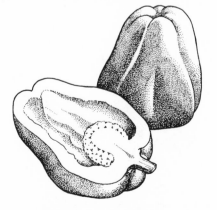

6 tablespoons (90 ml) *ghee*, or 4 tablespoons (60 ml)
  vegetable oil and 2 tablespoons (30 ml) butter
fresh *panir* cheese (page 313) made from 6 cups
  (1.5 liters) milk, cut into ½ inch (1.5 cm) cubes (about 6 ounces/170 g)
1 tablespoon (15 ml) scraped, minced fresh ginger root
1 hot green chili (or as desired)
1¼ teaspoons (6 ml) cumin seeds
½ teaspoon (2 ml) black mustard seeds
¼ teaspoon (1 ml) yellow asafetida powder (*hing*)*
10 curry leaves, preferably fresh, or ½ bay leaf
2 medium-sized bell peppers (about 12 ounces/340 g),
  stemmed, seeded and cut lengthwise into strips
3 medium-sized firm tomatoes (about 12 ounces/340 g), peeled and chopped
1 tablespoon (15 ml) ground coriander
4 tablespoons (60 ml) coarsely chopped fresh coriander or basil
1 teaspoon (5 ml) turmeric
1 teaspoon (5 ml) *garam masala*
1 medium-sized eggplant (about 1 pound/455 g), cut into
  1-inch (2.5 cm) cubes and steamed until tender
1 teaspoon (5 ml) salt
a few sprigs coriander or basil for garnishing (optional)

*This amount applies only to yellow Cobra brand. Reduce any other asafetida by three-fourths.

1. Heat 4 tablespoons (60 ml) of *ghee* or the oil in a nonstick 5-quart/liter saucepan or wok over moderate heat. When it is hot but not smoking, carefully add the cheese pieces and fry, constantly turning them until they are evenly browned on all sides. Remove them with a slotted spoon and set aside.

2. Add the remaining 2 tablespoons (30 ml) of *ghee* or the butter and immediately follow with the ginger, green chili, cumin seeds and black mustard seeds. Fry until the mustard seeds pop and turn gray. Drop in the asafetida and curry leaves or bay leaf, and in seconds add the bell peppers. Sauté for 3–4 minutes.

3. Stir in the tomatoes, ground coriander and turmeric and 2 tablespoons (30 ml) of the fresh herbs. Cook for about 10 minutes, stirring now and then, until the peppers are tender-crisp.

4. Add the *garam masala*, fried *panir* cheese, eggplant and salt, and gently mix. Reduce the heat to low, cover, and cook for 5–10 minutes, stirring now and then. Before serving, fold in the remaining chopped herb, and garnish with sprigs of coriander or basil, if desired.

Deep-Fried *Chenna* Cheese Balls in Fragrant Tomato Gravy
CHENNA RASEDAR

In 1972, I was cooking for Srila Prabhupada in Calcutta at the Shree Radha Govinda Temple. One day I served him a batter-coated stuffed baby tomato fritter, which inspired him to describe the ingredients and procedures for a dish he laughingly called *"chenna* chops." I followed his instructions but served the balls with a fragrant gravy. The anticipation of pleasing Srila Prabhupada through cooking was an experience I am inadequate to describe. Much to my delight, he approved with our signal indicating "first class": a wave of his palm over the top of his head!

This is a masterpiece for entertaining. It holds well in a bain-marie or warming tray and is visually dynamic. Turmeric-flavored mashed potatoes and mashed green peas are stuffed into kneaded, creamy white *chenna* cheese. The large globes are quickly deep-fried to put a crisp crust on the outside. They are then cut in half to reveal the green, gold and white bull's-eye within, and placed, cut side up, in a fresh tomato gravy. The success of the dish rests on the texture of the cheese. Once the curd forms, it is pressed for about 30 minutes or until it weighs 20 ounces (570 g). The warm cheese will feel firm and compact but still remain moist. If it is too soft or wet, the balls will disintegrate and fall apart during the deep-frying.

Preparation time (after assembling ingredients): 45 minutes
Cooking time: 45–60 minutes
Makes: 12 balls

Chenna Balls:

4 quarts/liters whole milk
about ½ cup (120 ml) lemon juice
1½ tablespoons (22 ml) unbleached flour
6 tablespoons (90 ml) *ghee* or unsalted butter
7 medium-sized potatoes (about 2 pounds/1 kg),
    cooked, peeled and mashed
1 teaspoon (5 ml) salt
¼ teaspoon (1 ml) turmeric
1½ cups (360 ml) fresh peas (1½ pounds/685 g
    in pods), cooked and mashed, or one 10-ounce (285 g)
    package of frozen baby peas, defrosted and mashed
¼ teaspoon (1 ml) *garam masala*
¼ teaspoon (1 ml) paprika or cayenne pepper
½ teaspoon (2 ml) each sugar and salt
2 tablespoons (30 ml) fresh coriander or parsley
about ¼ cup (25 g) sifted chickpea
    flour or whole wheat flour
ghee or vegetable oil for deep-frying

Gravy:

¼ cup (40 g) finely chopped almonds or cashews
1-inch (2.5 cm) piece of peeled fresh ginger root
1–2 hot green chilies
½ cup (120 ml) water
½ tablespoon (7 ml) ground coriander
1 teaspoon (5 ml) ground cumin
½ teaspoon (2 ml) turmeric
5 tablespoons (75 ml) *ghee,* or 2 tablespoons (30 ml)
    vegetable oil and 3 tablespoons (45 ml) butter
1 teaspoon (5 ml) cumin seeds
1-inch (2.5 cm) piece of cinnamon stick
4 whole cloves
3 cups (710 ml) peeled, seeded and finely chopped
    tomatoes (about 2¼ pounds/1 kg)
¾ cup (180 ml) *chenna* whey or water
1 teaspoon (5 ml) salt
2 tablespoons (30 ml) chopped fresh coriander or parsley

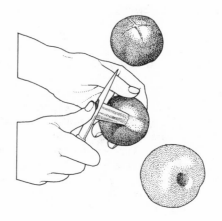

1. Bring the milk to a boil in a heavy-bottomed 5–6-quart/liter pan, stirring constantly over high heat. When the foam begins to rise, reduce the heat to moderately low and immediately add the lemon juice. Stir very slowly in one direction until large lumps of cheese form and separate from the yellowish whey. (If the cheese has not formed within 1 minute, add 1 tablespoon/15 ml more lemon juice.) Remove the pan from the heat. Moisten a triple-thick 15-inch (38 cm) square of cheesecloth and line a colander with it, then place the colander in the sink. Lift off the large pieces of cheese curd and transfer to the colander. When most of the cheese is transferred, pour the remaining whey and cheese through a strainer, collecting ¾ cup (180 ml) of whey for the sauce. Add the strainer contents to the colander. Gather the four corners and gently twist until tight, extracting some of the whey. Place the wrapped cheese back in the colander and set a weight directly on the cheese (such as a 2-quart/liter bowl or clean pan of water). Allow the weight to press the cheese for 20–30 minutes, then unwrap the cheese, check its weight, and if it is ready place it on a clean work surface. Break the cheese into large chunks and press with paper towels to extract any excess moisture.

2. While the cheese is warm, sprinkle in the flour and press across the work surface, using the heel of your palm, bit by bit until the cheese is smooth and fluffy, a grain-free cheese dough. Scrape the cheese into a mass with a spatula, cleaning all the bits off your hands, then wash and dry your hands. Roll the dough into a rope, then divide it into 12 portions. Roll each portion into a smooth ball and set aside on a plate.

3. Heat 3 tablespoons (45 ml) of the *ghee* or butter in a heavy nonstick frying pan over moderate heat. Add the mashed potatoes, salt and turmeric, and stir-fry for 3–4 minutes. Transfer to a plate. Heat the remaining 3 tablespoons (45 ml) of *ghee* or butter in the same pan. Add the mashed peas, *garam masala,* paprika or cayenne, sugar, salt and fresh herbs. Stir-fry for 2–3 minutes; transfer to another plate.

For information about unfamiliar ingredients or techniques, see A-to-Z

4. When the potatoes and peas are cooled, divide each into 12 portions. Flatten a portion of potatoes in the palm of your hand until it is about 3½ inches (9 cm) in diameter. Place a portion of peas in the center and bring up the sides to enclose the peas completely. Mold and press with your fingers to make a neat, smooth ball. Repeat with the remaining potatoes and peas.

5. Rub a film of oil over a clean work surface and your hands. Roll a ball of cheese into a round about 4½ inches (11.5 cm) in diameter. Place a potato ball in the center, then bring up the sides to enclose the potatoes completely. Mold and press with your fingers to make a smooth ball. Repeat with the remaining portions, then roll each ball in chickpea flour or whole wheat flour; shake off excess.

6. Pour enough *ghee* or vegetable oil to half fill a deep-frying vessel. Place over moderately high heat, and when the temperature reaches 350°F (180°C) on a thermometer, add one or two balls and fry until golden brown, turning as necessary (3–4 minutes). Drain on paper towels and fry the remaining balls.

7. To make the gravy, combine the nuts, ginger and chilies in a blender or food processor fitted with the metal blade. Process until the nuts are powdered, then add the water and process to a smooth purée. Add the ground coriander, cumin and turmeric and process until blended. Transfer the wet *masala* to a cup.

8. Heat the *ghee* or oil-butter mixture in a large heavy-bottomed pan over moderate heat. When it is hot but not smoking, add the cumin seeds and cloves and fry for 10–15 seconds. Add ½ cup (120 ml) of the tomatoes and the wet *masala*, and stir-fry until the liquid from the tomatoes is driven off and the oil separates from the tomato paste. Add the remaining tomatoes, the whey or water and the salt. Reduce the heat to low and simmer, covered, for 20–25 minutes until thickened slightly.

9. To serve, pour the sauce into a serving dish. Cut the balls in half and arrange cut side up in the sauce. Garnish with the fresh herbs.

Creamy Scrambled *Chenna* Cheese with Tomatoes and Snow Peas
CHENNA MALAI DALNA

I first had this dish at a Sunday brunch in New Delhi. It was a family recipe that the guests raved over, asking for more again and again, with fruits, hot *pooris* and homemade jam. Much to the host's amazement, the seemingly endless supply of cheese was finally depleted. In a spirit of fun, the guests demanded more of this scrumptious dish. So, en masse, the kitchen staff and guests traversed out to the family *gaushalla* (dairy) for an unscheduled milking, and after an hour the feast continued.

With the right equipment, this dish can be made from start to finish in under an hour. It is not practical for quantity cooking, but excellent for a small relaxed breakfast or brunch. The original Delhi recipe included only softened tomato bits, but I find tender-crisp snow peas and/or zucchini a nice addition. You can use one of several creamy milk products to finish it off: cream, cottage cheese, crème fraîche, cream cheese, *Yogurt Cheese* or *Fresh Curd Cheese*. Try it for a special occasion with *Deep-Fried Sesame Whole Wheat Bread*, your favorite jams or jellies and seasonal fresh fruits, or juice.

Preparation and cooking time (after assembling ingredients): about 1 hour
Serves: 4 to 6

4 quarts/liters whole milk
½ cup (120 ml) lemon juice
½ tablespoon (7 ml) cumin seeds
½ teaspoon (2 ml) black mustard seeds
4 tablespoons (60 ml) *ghee* or unsalted butter
6–8 curry leaves, preferably fresh
6 ounces (170 g) snow peas, tails and strings removed, each cut diagonally into
    3 pieces (about 1¾ cups/420 ml) and blanched, or 2 smallish zucchini,
    cut into ⅓ x 2-inch (1 x 5 cm) julienne, blanched
2 small firm ripe tomatoes, each cut into 8 pieces
¼ teaspoon (1 ml) turmeric
1 teaspoon (5 ml) salt
⅛ teaspoon (0.5 ml) each freshly ground pepper and cayenne pepper or paprika
½ cup (120 ml) cream (or above suggestions)
2 tablespoons (30 ml) coarsely chopped fresh coriander or minced fresh parsley

1. Prepare the cheese as directed in the previous recipe, but reduce the pressing time to 15 minutes. Unwrap the warm cheese and break it into 1–1¼-inch (2.5–3.5 cm) pieces.

2. Place a large heavy-bottomed nonstick frying pan over moderate heat for 30 seconds. Add the cumin and black mustard seeds, and shake the pan as they brown. After about 30 seconds, add the *ghee* or butter, and fry until the butter froths or the mustard seeds sputter and crackle.

3. Stir in the snow peas or zucchini and tomatoes and sauté, gently stirring, until the tomato skins soften and glisten yet the tomatoes still retain their shape. Add the *chenna* pieces, turmeric, salt, black pepper and cayenne or paprika, and gently stir. Add the cream and stir until warmed, but do not bring to a boil. Remove from the heat and stir in the fresh herbs. Serve on warmed plates.

Panir Cheese, Summer Squash and Red Bell Peppers
PANIR LOUKI TARKARI

Use whatever summer squash is available: yellow or green zucchini, yellow crookneck, patty-pan or immature Indian bottle gourd. This year I have grown a new squash from Park Seeds called *kuta*, and it is excellent in the dish. If possible, buy squash when it is young, with smooth glossy skin that needs no peeling and tight, seedless flesh. Contrast colors for visual impact: yellow zucchini and red bell peppers, or green squash and yellow bell peppers. For a midsummer lunch, try this main-dish vegetable with *Griddle-Baked Yogurt Whole Wheat Bread, Jicama Salad with Snow Peas, Avocado and Watercress* and *Sautéed Sprouted Mung Beans with Julienne Ginger Root.*

For information about unfamiliar ingredients or techniques, see A-to-Z

Preparation time (after assembling ingredients): 5 minutes
Cooking time: 25 minutes
Serves: 6

½ tablespoon (7 ml) ground coriander
½ teaspoon (2 ml) ground cumin
¼ teaspoon (1 ml) ground fennel
¼ teaspoon (1 ml) turmeric
¾ teaspoon (3.5 ml) *garam masala* or
    ¼ teaspoon (1 ml) each ground
    cloves, cardamon and cinnamon
¼ cup (25 g) unsweetened fresh or dried coconut
½ cup (120 ml) water
4 tablespoons (60 ml) *ghee* or a mixture
    of vegetable oil and butter
fresh *panir* cheese (page 313) made
    from 6 cups milk (1.5 liters), cut
    into ½-inch (1.5 cm) cubes (about 6 ounces/170 g)
1 whole dried red chili (or as desired)
½-inch (1.5 cm) piece of peeled ginger
    root, sliced into paper-thin rounds
7–8 small (5-inch/12.5 cm) zucchini or
    pattypan squash (about 1¼ pounds/570 g),
    or one 10-inch (25 cm) bottle gourd (*louki*)
2 small red, yellow or green bell peppers
    (about 8 ounces/230 g), stemmed, seeded
    and cut lengthwise into thin strips
1¼ teaspoons (6 ml) salt
1 medium-sized tomato, diced
3 tablespoons (45 ml) chopped fresh coriander or minced parsley

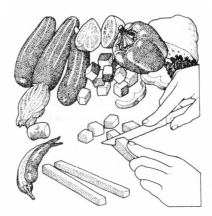

1. Combine the ground coriander, cumin, fennel, turmeric, *garam masala* or sweet spices, coconut and water in a small bowl and set aside.

2. Heat the *ghee* or oil-butter mixture in a heavy-bottomed 5-quart/liter nonstick pan or wok over moderate heat. When it is hot but not smoking, gently add the *panir* cheese cubes and fry for about 5 minutes, constantly turning the cubes to evenly brown them on all sides. (In anything but a nonstick surface, the cubes will tend to stick and break apart.)

3. Raise the heat a little, add the red chili and ginger, and fry until they darken a few shades. Stir in the squash and bell peppers and sauté for about 10 minutes or until the squash is tender crisp and the peppers are limp. Add the salt, spice paste *masala*, tomato and fried *panir* cubes, reduce the heat to low, and stir-fry until the tomatoes are soft and the dish is dry. Add the fresh herbs, stir and serve in a warmed dish.

Shallow-Fried Batter-Coated *Chenna* Cheese Patties
CHENNA TIKKA

I learned this dish from Srila Prabhupada's sister Pishima. She prepared it as a savory item on a full Bengali lunch *thali*. I have since made it on numerous occasions, and it seems to adapt itself to almost any type of menu. One variation I find pleasant is to knead fresh herbs into the *chenna* cheese: ¼ cup (60 ml) of either minced basil, summer savory, chervil, tarragon, coriander or parsley. The patties are delicious with a twist of lemon, but many people love them with a dipping sauce such as *Sour Cream Parsley Sauce, Fresh Tomato Sauce* or *Velvet Tomato Catsup*.

Preparation time (after assembling ingredients): 20 minutes
Cooking time: 20–25 minutes
Serves: 6 as a side-dish or 4 as a main-dish

fresh *chenna* cheese (page 315) made from
    10 cups (2.5 liters) milk, pressed under
    a weight for 20–25 minutes (about 14 ounces/400 g)
⅛ teaspoon (0.5 ml) freshly ground pepper
1 teaspoon (5 ml) salt
¼ cup (60 ml) fresh minced herbs (optional)
1½ tablespoons (22 ml) *ghee* or sunflower oil
1 tablespoon (15 ml) scraped, finely
    shredded or minced fresh ginger root
2 teaspoons (10 ml) cumin seeds
¼ teaspoon (1 ml) yellow asafetida powder (*hing*)*
½–⅔ cup (120-160 ml) water
1 cup (100 g) chickpea flour (sifted before measuring),
    spooned into a cup and leveled with a spatula
½ teaspoon (2 ml) salt
⅓ teaspoon (1.5 ml) turmeric
¼ teaspoon (1 ml) cayenne pepper or paprika
¼ teaspoon (1 ml) baking powder
ghee or vegetable oil for frying

*This amount applies only to yellow Cobra brand. Reduce any other asafetida by three-fourths.

    1. Unwrap the warm cheese and press it between several thicknesses of paper towels to extract excess moisture. Bray and knead the cheese on a clean work surface by spreading it out with the heel of your hand, a small bit at a time, until the texture is creamy smooth. Knead in the pepper, salt and optional herbs. (The kneading process takes 2½–5 minutes, depending on the texture of the fresh cheese.) Gather the cheese into a mass with a spatula, scraping up the odd bits on the work surface and your fingers. Wash and dry your hands and rub them with a film of oil. Divide the cheese into 12 portions and then roll into smooth round balls. Flatten them into patties about 2½ inches (6.5 cm) in diameter.

For information about unfamiliar ingredients or techniques, see A-to-Z

2. To make the batter, heat the 1½ tablespoons (22 ml) of *ghee* or oil in a small saucepan over moderate heat. Add the ginger and cumin seeds and fry until the seasonings brown. Remove the pan from the heat and add the asafetida powder. Carefully add ½ cup (120 ml) of the cold water to the hot seasonings.

3. Combine the chickpea flour, salt, turmeric, cayenne or paprika and baking powder in a 1-quart/liter mixing bowl. When the water has cooled to room temperature, pour them into the flour and whisk or beat, using a whisk or hand beater, into a light batter with a consistency similar to heavy cream. (You may need the full ⅔ cup/160 ml of water or even more to make the batter; add 1 tablespoon/15 ml at a time until it thins to the desired consistency.)

4. Pour *ghee* or oil into a large frying pan to a depth of ½ inch (1.5 cm). Heat over moderate to moderately high heat until it is hot but not smoking (345°–355°F/173°– 180°C). Hold each patty with your fingertips and dip into the batter. Hold it briefly above the bowl to let the excess drip off, and gently slip it into the hot oil. Fry only 4 or 5 patties at a time, so there is ample room for them to cook without touching. Fry for 4–5 minutes per side or until the batter is crisp and golden brown. Remove the patties with a slotted spoon and drain on paper towels. Continue with the remaining patties in the same way. Serve as soon as possible, or keep warm, uncovered, in a preheated 250°F (120°C) oven on paper towels for up to ½ hour. To serve as finger foods, serve on a tray with a dipping sauce. As a side dish allow 2 per person: as a main dish allow 3.

Pan-Fried *Chenna* Cheese Patties with Poppy Seeds
CHENNA KHAS-KHAS TIKKA

Like the previous recipe, I learned this dish from Pishima. She made it on an *Ekadasee* day, as a side-dish savory on a full Bengali *thali*. On *Ekadasee*, Vaishnavas abstain from all beans and grains. Vegetables, fruits, nuts, seeds and milk products, however, can be turned into hundreds of diverse dishes.

Poppy seeds vary considerably from the large blue-gray types used in poppy seed cakes and on Jewish breads to the much smaller pale cream seeds used in this dish. Purchased as white poppy seeds in Indian and Middle Eastern grocery stores, they are usually toasted when left whole. They have a pleasant nutty taste, similar to sesame seeds, that improves with toasting. Minced fresh ginger, chilies and toasted poppy seeds are kneaded into *chenna* cheese and pan-fried into delicate cutlets. I strongly suggest using a nonstick frying pan or griddle to brown the patties; they never stick, and the patties' crust is thin and feather-crisp. As an alternative, use a cast-iron skillet, but you will need a bit more *ghee* or oil for frying.

For an *Ekadasee* menu, accompany with *Sweet Potato Salad in Maple-Lemon Vinaigrette*, *Glazed Carrots*, *Spicy Okra with Coconut* and *Nut and Raisin Nibbler*. For a non-*Ekadasee* meal, add a *dal* dish and rice or bread.

Preparation time and soaking time (after assembling ingredients): 2 hours
Cooking time: 20–25 minutes
Serves 4 to 6

3 tablespoons (45 ml) white poppy seeds
fresh *chenna* cheese (page 315) made from 10 cups (2.5 liters)
   of milk, pressed under a weight for 20–25 minutes (about 14 ounces/170 g)
1 teaspoon (5 ml) seeded minced jalepeño chilies (or as desired)
1 teaspoon (5 ml) scraped, finely shredded or minced fresh ginger root
¼ teaspoon (1 ml) salt
up to ¼ cup (60 ml) *ghee*, or a mixture of vegetable oil and butter

1. Place the poppy seeds in a small frying pan over moderate heat. Toast, stirring frequently until they darken one or two shades. Some of them will pop if the heat is too high. Soak the toasted seeds in water for 1½–2 hours, then drain in a strainer.

2. Unwrap the warm cheese and press it between several thicknesses of paper towels to extract excess moisture. Bray and knead the cheese on a clean work surface by spreading it out with the heel of your hand, a small bit at a time, until the texture is creamy smooth. Knead in the poppy seeds, chili, ginger and salt. (The kneading takes 2½–5 minutes, depending on the texture of the fresh cheese.) Gather the cheese into a mass with a spatula, scraping up the odd bits from the work surface and your fingers. Wash and dry your hands and rub them with a film of oil. Divide the cheese into 12 portions and roll them into smooth, round balls. Flatten them into patties about 2½ inches (6.5 cm) in diameter.

3. Add 2 tablespoons (30 ml) of *ghee* or oil to a 12-inch (30 cm) nonstick griddle or frying pan or a cast-iron skillet. Place over moderate heat, and when the pan is warm, add the patties, reduce the heat to moderately low, and slowly brown until the crust is golden and crispy (about 8 minutes). Handle gently. Turn over and brown the other side. Fry in batches, adding more *ghee* or oil as necessary. Serve hot with a wedge of lemon, or try the variation below.

Pishima's Variation:

1. In step 3, add 1–2 additional tablespoons (15–30 ml) of *ghee* or butter to the pan, ⅔ cup (160 ml) water or *chenna* whey, 1 teaspoon (5 ml) raw sugar, ⅛ teaspoon (0.5 ml) each turmeric and yellow asafetida powder, ¼ teaspoon (1 ml) freshly ground black pepper and 2 tablespoons (30 ml) chopped fresh coriander or parsley.

2. Bring to a boil over moderate heat and reduce to ⅓ cup (80 ml). Add the patties, reduce the heat to low, and simmer for 2–3 minutes or until the liquid is reduced to a trace of glaze.

For information about unfamiliar ingredients or techniques, see A-to-Z

Salads

L ittle salads, loosely called *kachambers*, are light servings of freshness. Unlike Western main-dish or mixed-green salads, which are usually a rich composite of colors, tastes and textures, these are little more than one, two or three ingredients in a light coating of oil, lime or lemon juice and seasoning. They may be as simple as sun-ripe tomato wedges or cucumber spears sprinkled with salt and dry-roasted crushed cumin. In some regions, shredded white radish or red-orange carrots are favorites, bound only with a mustard-scented fried seasoning and traces of fresh herbs. Whether the vegetables and fruits are raw or blanched, diced, sliced or shredded, they are meant to be refreshing contrasts to the other dishes in the meal. Making successful *kachambers* depends more on obtaining really fresh, seasonal produce than on anything else. After glancing at the recipes, take advantage of the season's bounty and improvise. Keep it simple, and assemble it just before serving. *Kachambers* are not separate-course dishes: they go on the dinner plate in small 2–4-tablespoon (30–60 ml) amounts.

Chickpea and Ginger Root Salad
KABLI CHANA ADRAK KACHAMBER

Whole chickpeas are soaked overnight, sometimes even slightly sprouted, before being used in this salad. Two types of rhizomes are suitable here: young camphor ginger or ginger-like mango ginger (a member of the turmeric family). Their flesh should be virtually fiber-free, with a thin skin. Because they are only found sporadically, look for young or "green" fresh ginger at the corner produce store or supermarket.

This salad was a constant on my breakfast menus for Srila Prabhupada. He taught it to me in 1967 and commented that ginger root for breakfast aided his digestion all day. Eight years later, when I forgot to soak the chickpeas one day and had to omit the dish, he again reminded me how important this "digestive" breakfast salad was for his health. Later, another of his cooks, Palika Dasi, related that he also favored another variation using soaked mung *dal* instead of chickpeas—a variation he simply called chutney.

Try this dish with seasonal fresh fruits for a light breakfast, or include it as a "salad-chutney" with lunch or dinner.

Dal **soaking time: 8 hours or overnight**
Preparation time (after assembling ingredients): 10 minutes
Serves: 4 to 6

⅓ cup (50 g) whole chickpeas, sorted and soaked
    in 1½ cups (360 ml) water overnight
1½-inch (4 cm) piece of fresh ginger root
1½ tablespoons (22 ml) fresh lime or lemon juice
½ teaspoon (2 ml) *chat masala* (optional)
¼ teaspoon (1 ml) freshly ground black pepper

Drain the chickpeas. Peel the ginger and slice into paper-thin rounds, then paper-thin julienne. Combine all of the ingredients in a small bowl and toss well. Serve directly on the dinner plates in small mounds.

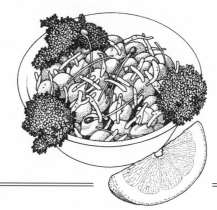

Banana and Pomegranate Salad
KELA ANAR KACHAMBER

This is an appropriate year-round *kachamber* to serve on a buffet or salad table. I first saw it at a North Indian wedding, among numerous small salads. The smooth and sweet golden banana slices make a vivid contrast with the sharp and sweet red pomegranate seeds.

Preparation time (after assembling ingredients): 15 minutes
Serves: 4

1 medium-sized pomegranate
2 medium-sized firm ripe bananas
2 tablespoons (30 ml) fresh lime juice
1 tablespoon (15 ml) maple or date sugar
¼ teaspoon (1 ml) salt (optional)

1. Cut the pomegranate into quarters and twist each wedge to loosen the cells. Gently shake, tap, scoop and coax the cells onto a serving plate and arrange them in a neat mound in the center.
2. Peel the bananas and slice them on the diagonal into ¼-inch (6 mm) rounds. Arrange them in a circle around the pomegranate cells. Sprinkle with the lime or lemon juice, sweetener and salt, if desired, and serve immediately.

For information about unfamiliar ingredients or techniques, see A-to-Z

Shredded Radish, Coconut and Carrot Salad
MOOLI NARIYAL KACHAMBER

Try this dish when you have leftover fresh coconut on hand, or if you have frozen shredded coconut. In large cities, frozen shredded coconut is sold in 1-pound (455 g) bags at many Cuban and Spanish grocery stores, and for occasional use it is a convenient alternative. Use any fresh radish—little round pinks as a vivid color contrast to the carrots, for example.

Preparation time (after assembling ingredients): 10 minutes
Serves: 6

½ cup (120 ml) shredded radishes
⅓ cup (35 g) shredded fresh coconut
⅓ cup (80 ml) shredded scraped carrots
¼ teaspoon (1 ml) salt
¼ teaspoon (1 ml) paprika or cayenne pepper
2 tablespoons (30 ml) chopped fresh coriander or parsley
1½ tablespoons (22 ml) *ghee* or avocado oil
¼ teaspoon (1 ml) *ajwain* seeds or celery seeds
¼ teaspoon (1 ml) fennel seeds
¼ teaspoon (1 ml) cumin seeds

1. Combine the radishes, coconut and carrots in a strainer and press out the excess liquid. Place them in a bowl and add the salt, paprika or cayenne and fresh herbs.

2. Heat the *ghee* or oil in a saucepan over moderate heat. When it is hot but not smoking, add the *ajwain*, fennel and cumin seeds and fry until they darken a few shades. Pour the seasoning into the salad and toss well.

Shredded Carrot and Cashew Nut Salad
GAJAR KAJU KACHAMBER

You can use almonds, hazelnuts or pistachios instead of cashews for this dish, and yellow bell peppers in place of red.

Preparation time (after assembling ingredients): 5 minutes
Serves: 6

1 cup (240 ml) scraped finely shredded carrots, pressed dry
⅓ cup (80 ml) finely chopped red bell peppers, stemmed and seeded
⅓ cup (50 g) chopped cashew nuts, toasted
½ teaspoon (2 ml) salt
2 tablespoons (30 ml) yogurt or crème fraîche (optional)
1½ tablespoons (22 ml) *ghee* or vegetable oil
1 teaspoon (5 ml) black mustard seeds
1 tablespoon (15 ml) coarsely chopped fresh coriander or minced parsley

1. Combine the carrots, bell peppers, nuts, salt, and yogurt or crème fraîche (if desired) in a mixing bowl.

2. Heat the *ghee* or oil in a small saucepan over moderate heat until it is hot but not smoking. Add the mustard seeds and fry until they sputter, pop and turn gray. Pour the seasoning into the salad, add the fresh herbs and toss to mix.

Apple Salad
SEB KACHAMBER

Outside of Kashmir, where most of India's apples are grown, the texture tends to be mealy—a sure sign of overripening due to long storage at warm temperatures. On the whole, I do not find them as good as most American varieties. Use any crisp salad or all-purpose apple: for example, Newton, Pippin or McIntosh, which are crisp, sweet and juicy, with a tangy overtone; anything from sweet Red or Golden Delicious to tart Granny Smith will do as well. With the grapes and mint-almond dressing, this is an elegant mid-winter fruit *kachamber*.

Preparation and chilling time (after assembling ingredients): 30 minutes Serves: 6

¼ cup (60 ml) plain yogurt or sour cream
2 tablespoons (30 ml) chopped fresh mint
3 tablespoons (45 ml) ground blanched almonds
¼ teaspoon (1 ml) cardamom seeds, crushed
2 tablespoons (30 ml) orange or lemon juice
3 medium-sized apples, cored and diced
½ cup (120 ml) seedless grapes, halved

Blend the yogurt or sour cream, mint, almonds, cardamom seeds and orange or lemon juice in a mixing bowl. Fold in the apples and grapes, cover, and chill for at least ½ hour before serving.

For information about unfamiliar ingredients or techniques, see A-to-Z

Cucumber and White Radish Salad
KHEERA MOOLI KACHAMBER

This simple salad contrasts crisp raw vegetables with a creamy pine nut dressing. Spooned into a shallow dish and garnished with a decorative pattern of paprika, minced parsley and roasted cumin and sesame seeds, this is an eye-catcher for a buffet.

Preparation and draining time (after assembling ingredients): 30 minutes
Serves: 6

2 small cucumbers (about 12 ounces/340 g), peeled, halved, seeded and coarsely shredded
salt
2 white icicle salad radishes (about 6 ounces/170 g), scraped and coarsely shredded
¼ cup (60 ml) sour cream or yogurt
2 tablespoons (30 ml) powdered pine nuts or almonds
1 tablespoon (15 ml) olive or sesame oil
¼ teaspoon (1 ml) paprika or cayenne pepper
2 tablespoons (30 ml) minced parsley
½ tablespoon (7 ml) dry-roasted coarsely crushed cumin seeds
2 tablespoons (30 ml) dry-roasted white sesame seeds

Place the cucumbers in a strainer resting over a bowl and sprinkle with salt. Drain for at least ½ hour and then press between your palms to extract excess liquid. Combine the cucumbers, radishes, sour cream or yogurt, nuts and oil in a mixing bowl and blend well. Transfer to a shallow serving dish and sprinkle decoratively with paprika or cayenne, parsley and cumin and sesame seeds. Serve at room temperature or chilled.

Simple Cucumber and Ginger Root Salad
ADRAK KHEERA KACHAMBER

This palate cleanser is appropriate any time of day, from breakfast through dinner. According to Palika Dasi, who used to cook for Srila Prabhupada, he loosely coined it as "mung chutney" and specified that it include "soaked mung *dal*, cucumbers and ginger root"—no quantities specified.

Dal **soaking time: at least 4 hours to overnight**
Preparation time (after assembling ingredients): 5–10 minutes
Serves: 6

¼ cup (55 g) split *moong dal*, without skins
1 cup (240 ml) water
1–1½-inch (2.5–4 cm) piece of peeled fresh ginger root, cut into fine julienne
salt
1 small cucumber (about 6 ounces/170 g)
6 lemon or lime slices

1. Sort through the *dal* and remove any foreign matter. Soak in the water for at least 4 hours or overnight. Rinse and drain, then combine with the ginger and a sprinkle of salt in a small dish and mix well.

2. Peel the cucumber, cut it into quarters lengthwise, and scoop out the seeds if they are developed. Cut crosswise into thirds to get 12 wedges. Arrange them artistically on a serving dish or directly on dinner plates, allowing 3 wedges, a citrus slice and a heaping spoonful of gingered *dal* per serving.

Mung *Dal*, Coconut and Cucumber Salad
MOONG NARIYAL KACHAMBER

In South India, this dish is relished with the onset of mango season; when made with sliced green mango instead of cucumber, it is called *vada pappu*. If you are fortunate enough to have mango trees in your yard, as I do when residing in Florida, by all means hand pick the fruit and give this variation a try. Another equally delicious alternative calls for firm, just ripe mango, available at supermarkets and greengrocers much of the year.

Dal **soaking time: 4 hours or overnight**
Preparation time (after assembling ingredients): 5–10 minutes
Serves: 6

½ cup (110 g) split *moong dal*, without skins
1½ cups (360 ml) water
½ cup (45 g) grated or finely shredded fresh coconut or
    ½ cup (75 g) grated frozen coconut, defrosted
¼ cup (60 ml) thinly sliced seeded cucumber or diced mango
1–2 hot green chilies, sliced crosswise into thin rounds
1 tablespoon (15 ml) fresh lime juice
½–1 teaspoon (2–5 ml) herb or sea salt
2 tablespoons (30 ml) *ghee* or coconut oil
1 teaspoon (5 ml) black mustard seeds
¼ teaspoon (1 ml) yellow asafetida powder (*hing*)*

*This amount applies only to yellow Cobra brand. Reduce any other asafetida by three-fourths.

1. Sort, wash and soak the *dal* in the water for 4 hours or overnight. Wash and drain in a strainer. Combine the *dal*, coconut, cucumber or mango, chilies, lime juice and salt in a bowl, and toss to mix.

2. Heat the *ghee* or coconut oil in a small pan over moderate heat. Add the black mustard seeds and fry until they sputter and turn gray. Remove the pan from the heat, sprinkle in the asafetida, and in seconds pour the seasoning into the salad. Toss and serve at room temperature, or chill slightly.

For information about unfamiliar ingredients or techniques, see A-to-Z

Minted Cucumbers and Strawberries
KHEERA KACHAMBER

Though mint and cucumber are a year-round favorite salad combination in India, strawberries are a rare treat. The first time I savored them, they were hand-delivered—carefully wrapped in a *khus* leaf parcel—and perhaps the importance of the occasion made them the sweetest I had ever eaten. Because they are such a rarity in India, they are almost always relished on their own or in this type of simple salad. In England I take advantage of red or black currants, and in America I might use golden raspberries, loganberries, lingonberries or blueberries. Though not available in India, hazelnut oil is perfect for a delicate fruit salad, but you could use almond or walnut oil, or leave out the oil entirely.

Preparation time (after assembling ingredients): 15–20 minutes
Serves: 6

2 long European-type cucumbers (about ½ pound/230 g each)
2 pints (480 ml) strawberries, rinsed and drained
2 tablespoons (30 ml) lemon juice
3 tablespoons (45 ml) orange juice
¼ cup (60 ml) finely chopped fresh mint
⅛ teaspoon (0.5 ml) cayenne pepper or paprika
2 tablespoons (30 ml) hazelnut or alternative oil

1. Peel the cucumbers and cut them crosswise into two or three pieces. Cut each piece lengthwise into four sections. Arrange the wedges in a pattern on a large salad plate. Remove the leaves and core from the strawberries by gathering up the leaves and stem cap and pulling away with a twist. Slice each one in half from cap to tip. Arrange in a decorative pattern between the cucumber wedges.

2. Whisk together the lemon juice, orange juice, mint, cayenne or paprika and oil until emulsified. Pour over the salad just before serving.

Crisp Lotus Root Salad
EKADASEE BHEN KACHAMBER

Popularly known as water lilies, lotus root grows in scores of species from Europe east through all of Asia. In India, they are loved for the majestic white, pink and bluish blossoms which grace the ponds of hundreds of temple and palace gardens. Not only are the plants cultivated for their beautiful flowers, but the seeds are popped like popcorn, the leaves are used as wrappers, and the rhizomes and flowers are cooked or used raw in salads.

Underneath the water, the lotus root looks like a series of finger-long sugar cane stalks connected on a string. After peeling, young roots are shredded or sliced and used in salads, while thick mature roots are boiled or stewed, sometimes mashed and deep-fried. Fresh lotus root is available at Chinese, Japanese and Indian grocery stores in large cities. Give a few stores a call to check on delivery dates; many will order a box if you need them for quantity cooking.

I like to arrange the lacy slices on a salad plate, along with other sliced fruits such as oranges, apples, banana, avocado or mango. For brilliant color contrast, nothing beats the addition of finely shredded beets. Sprinkle with toasted chopped nuts, currants and the orange-nut oil vinaigrette just before serving. This is a good selection for a salad buffet.

Preparation time (after assembling ingredients): 25 minutes
Cooking time: 1½ hours if steamed, 20 minutes if pressure-cooked
Serves: 6 to 8

6–8 links of tender lotus root (about 8 ounces/230 g)
2 smallish beets
2 tablespoons (30 ml) lemon juice
1 orange
1 red-skinned eating apple
2 firm ripe bananas
1 medium-sized avocado
3 tablespoons (45 ml) lime juice
6 large romaine lettuce leaves, trimmed and thinly sliced
3 tablespoons (45 ml) currants, soaked in hot water for 20 minutes and drained
3 tablespoons (45 ml) toasted chopped nuts
2 tablespoons (30 ml) sugar
2 tablespoons (30 ml) orange juice
2 tablespoons (30 ml) hazelnut, nut or vegetable oil

1. Separate the lotus links and cut off the beet tops, then scrub the root vegetables with a potato brush. If they are young and tender, it is best to leave them raw. If tough and mature, place them in a steaming basket over boiling acidulated water and steam just until tender-crisp, ¾–1½ hours. Alternately, cook under pressure at 15 pounds (7 kg) for about 15 minutes (according to the manufacturer's directions), depending on size. Let the vegetables cool, then peel the lotus root with a sharp knife and slice crosswise on the diagonal into ⅛-inch (3 mm) rounds; place in a bowl and toss with lemon juice. Rub the beet skins off under running water, dry the beets, and finely shred them with a rotary shredder; cover and set aside. If you prepare these ingredients ahead of time, refrigerate seperately, covered, until serving time.

2. When you are ready to assemble the salad, bring the lotus root and beets to room temperature. Using a serrated knife, peel and halve the orange, then cut into slices. Halve and core the apple, cut into thin slices, and dip each slice in the lime juice to prevent discoloration. Peel the bananas and slice them on the diagonal, dipping each piece in lime juice. Peel and pit the avocado and slice it into spears, then dip each piece in lime juice.

3. Lay the romaine lettuce on a large oval or round platter and arrange the lotus root slices, orange, apple, banana, avocado and beets in circles or another pattern on the lettuce. Sprinkle with currants and nuts. Whisk the sugar, orange juice and oil in a bowl until emulsified, then pour the dressing on the salad and serve.

For information about unfamiliar ingredients or techniques, see A-to-Z

Carrot and Water Chestnut Salad
GAJAR AUR SINGHARA KACHAMBER

Chinese and Indian water chestnuts are similar, floating water plants that grow in lakes and ponds. Indian chestnuts, called *singhara*, are not available in America, but the close relative, Chinese chestnuts, actually tubers, are frequently available at Japanese, Chinese and Asian greengrocers. Call ahead to check on availability.

The chestnut-colored flesh is sweet, vaguely resembling crisp bamboo shoots or South American jicama, a respectable substitute. Young chestnuts are often eaten raw, while older ones will improve with 10 minutes of simmering. The thick, horny green or brownish skins must be pulled off with your thumbs and a sharp paring knife. Like most *kachambers*, it is served in 3–4-table-spoon (45–60 ml) servings, more as a relish than as a salad. Water chestnuts are popular on *Ekadasee* menus.

Preparation time (after assembling ingredients): 15 minutes
Cooking time: 10 minutes (optional)
Serves: 6 to 8

12–14 fresh water chestnuts (about 6 ounces/170 g),
    scrubbed with a potato brush or peeled with a knife
2 medium-sized waxy boiling potatoes (about
    ½ pound/230 g), boiled until fork-tender
3 young carrots (about ½ pound/230 g),
    peeled and shredded
2 tablespoons (30 ml) sesame or peanut oil
1 tablespoon (15 ml) lemon juice
2 tablespoons (30 ml) chopped fresh coriander
¼ teaspoon (1 ml) cayenne pepper or paprika
¼ teaspoon (1 ml) *chat masala*, black salt
    or herb salt (optional)

1. Wash the water chestnuts, cut them into ⅛-inch (3 mm) slices and serve raw. Alternately, drop whole water chestnuts into boiling water, simmer for 10 minutes, then slice. Either raw or blanched, they should have a crisp, apple like texture. Place them in a mixing bowl.

2. Peel the potatoes and cut them into ½-inch (1.5 cm) cubes. Combine them with the water chestnuts and the remaining ingredients, and serve at room temperature or chilled.

SIDE-DISH SALADS

Whole Cauliflower Crowned with Creamy Avocado
GOBHI SALAAD

India's intense heat prevents the widespread use of salad greens—both for home gardeners and on a commercial scale. During northern winters, some green thumbs are successful with a few hardy types. In my search for salads with staying power, using available ingredients, I happened on this variation. It is eye-catching on a salad buffet, and often the first to disappear. For a backyard patio summer lunch, try it with *Flaky Biscuits with Black Pepper* or *Delicious Panir Cheese Pakora, Cold Minty Yogurt Soup* or *Cold Broth with Julienne Cucumbers* and iced glasses of *Fresh Orange Squash with Ginger*.

Preparation time (after assembling ingredients): 10 minutes
Cooking time: 25 minutes
Chilling time: 3 hours
Serves: 4 to 6

1 large cauliflower (2½ pounds/1.25 kg), trimmed
1 large tomato, peeled, seeded and finely chopped
2 teaspoons (30 ml) olive oil
1 tablespoon (15 ml) lemon or lime juice
½ teaspoon (2 ml) cayenne pepper or paprika
1 teaspoon (5 ml) ground coriander
¼ teaspoon (1 ml) salt
⅛ teaspoon (0.5 ml) freshly ground pepper
2 medium-sized avocados, peeled, pitted and mashed
3 tablespoons (45 ml) sour cream

1. Slice the base off the stem end of the cauliflower so it can sit on a flat surface. Fill a large pan with water to a depth of at least 1 inch (2.5 cm) and place a steaming rack or trivet inside. Bring the water to a boil and place the cauliflower in the steamer. Cover, reduce the heat slightly, and steam until the cauliflower is barely tender, ½ hour or more; avoid overcooking. Let cool, cover, and chill for 3 hours or more.

2. Combine the remaining ingredients in a bowl and mix well. Spread the mixture over the chilled cauliflower, and serve on a bed of cabbage or outer cauliflower leaves on a serving dish. Cut into wedges and serve.

Sprouted Mung Bean Salad with Water Chestnuts and Toasted Almonds
SABAT MOONG SALAAD

You can use any sprouted bean mixture for this salad, but avoid the supermarket, water-logged giant sprouts intended for oriental, stir-fry dishes. These beans should be barely sprouted (¼–½ inch/6 mm-1.5 cm) at most. Assemble this salad just before serving, as the sprouts soften and become watery once exposed to heat or combined with other ingredients.

Preparation time (after assembling ingredients): 10 minutes
Serves: 6

2 cups (80 ml) sprouted mung or aduki beans
    (made from 1 cup/195 g whole beans) (page 44)
¾ cup (180 ml) sliced water chestnuts
1 small yellow or red bell pepper (about
    4 ounces/115 g), stemmed, seeded and diced
½ cup (120 ml) chopped celery
2 tablespoons (30 ml) olive or avocado oil
1 tablespoon (15 ml) lemon juice
⅓ cup (80 ml) plain yogurt or a
    mixture of yogurt and sour cream
½ teaspoon (2 ml) herb or celery salt
1 teaspoon (5 ml) dry-roasted crushed cumin seeds
¼ teaspoon (1 ml) cayenne pepper or paprika
¼ cup (30 g) toasted sliced almonds
6 small tomatoes, cut into flower garnishes

Combine the sprouts, water chestnuts, bell pepper and celery in a salad bowl. (If you want to remove the raw taste from the sprouts, steam them for 5–7 minutes first.) Combine the remaining ingredients (except the almonds and tomatoes) in a screw-top jar, cover and shake until creamy. Just before serving, pour the dressing over the salad and gently toss. Sprinkle with toasted almonds and garnish with tomato flowers.

Mixed Bean Salad with Fennel
RAJMA KABLI CHANA SALAAD

This is an Indian west coast version of American three-bean salad. The cooking time for dried legumes varies from 1–3 hours, depending on their age, cooking water, dryness, and even the locality where they were grown. Check them frequently during the last ½ hour of simmering, and cook just to tenderness. Alternately, during the summer many greengrocers offer freshly hulled peas and beans: black-eyed peas, green peas, limas, fordhooks and more; pick any combination that suits the menu. This salad is a good make-ahead dish, as it keeps well under rerigeration for several hours.

Soaking time: 8 hours or overnight
Cooking time: up to 3 hours
Resting or chilling time: 2 hours
Serves: 4 to 6

½ cup (100 g) each dried chickpeas, black-eyed peas and
    kidney beans, soaked in water overnight, then drained
1-inch (2.5 cm) piece of peeled fresh ginger root, minced
1–2 minced hot green chilies
3 tablespoons (45 ml) each chopped fresh coriander and parsley
¼ cup (60 ml) olive oil
1 tablespoon (15 ml) fresh lemon juice
½ teaspoon (2 ml) herb or sea salt
¼ teaspoon (1 ml) freshly ground pepper
1½ tablespoons (22 ml) *ghee* or sunflower oil
1 teaspoon (5 ml) black mustard seeds
¼ teaspoon (1 ml) each *ajwain* and caraway seeds
1 fennel bulb, trimmed, cored and thinly sliced

    1. Place the drained legumes in a large heavy pan, add enough water to cover by 2 inches (5 cm), bring to a boil, and simmer for 1½–2 hours or until the beans are just tender; avoid overcooking. Drain and let cool.

    2. Combine the ginger, green chilies, herbs, olive oil, lemon juice, salt and pepper in a salad bowl. Heat the *ghee* or oil in a small pan over moderate heat. When it is hot but not smoking, add the mustard seeds, *ajwain* and caraway seeds and fry until the mustard seeds sputter and turn gray. Immediately pour the seasonings into the bowl, and whisk the dressing until emulsified. Gently stir in the cooked beans and fennel. Cover and refrigerate for at least 2 hours.

Lemon Stuffed with Almond-Chickpea Pâté
KABLI CHANA BADAAM SALAAD

    Inspired by a dish served at Robert Carrier's Hintelsham Hall in England, these appetizer salads are perfect for small parties, brunches or late-night dinners: hollowed-out lemons filled with hummous-like chickpea pâté, served with decorative vegetable crudités and/or crackers. You might try *Triangle Crisps* or *Flaky Biscuits with Black Pepper*, both of which can easily be made well ahead of time.

Preparation time (after assembling ingredients): 15 minutes
Chilling time: at least 1 hour
Serves: 4

4 large lemons
¾-inch (2 cm) piece of scraped fresh ginger root, sliced
1–2 seeded jalepeño chilies
3 ounces (85 g) cream cheese or fresh
    panir cheese, cut into small pieces
2 cups (480 ml) drained cooked chickpeas
    (1 cup/100 g when dried)
3 tablespoons (45 ml) toasted sesame seeds
6 tablespoons (90 ml) sour cream or crème fraîche
½ teaspoon (2 ml) salt
3 tablespoons (45 ml) olive oil or melted *ghee*
½ teaspoon (2 ml) yellow asafetida powder (*hing*)*
¼ teaspoon (1 ml) freshly ground pepper
1 teaspoon (5 ml) coarsely crushed dry-roasted cumin seeds
1 tablespoon (15 ml) minced fresh parsley or chervil
4 watercress sprigs
bibb lettuce leaves
crudités such as radish flowers , cucumber twists, or tomato flowers (optional)

*This amount applies only to yellow Cobra brand. Reduce any other asafetida by three-fourths.

    1. Cut off the tops of the lemons and reserve. Scoop out the pulp with a grapefruit spoon or knife until the shells are empty. Squeeze the pulp through a strainer and save the juice; discard the membranes and seeds. Trim a thin slice off the bottom of the lemons so they stand upright. Cover and chill until needed.

    2. Fit a food processor with the metal blade. Turn on the motor, drop the ginger and chilies through the feed tube and mince. Add the cheese and process until smooth. Drop in the chickpeas, sesame seeds, sour cream or crème fraîche, salt, oil or *ghee*, asafetida and pepper. Process until smooth, adding up to 2 tablespoons (30 ml) of the reserved lemon juice for flavor and to obtain a uniform, spoonable consistency. Add the cumin seeds and pulse 2 or 3 times to crush them.

    3. Fill the lemon cups, using a pastry bag fitted with a large star nozzle, or simply spoon in the pâté, slightly piling it up over the edge of the cup. Sprinkle with the fresh herbs and top with the reserved caps. Place some bibb lettuce on each plate and add the vegetable garnishes. Chill until you are ready to serve.

Spiced Chickpea Salad with Spinach
KABLI CHANA PALAK SALAAD

    As an alternative to spinach, try red or green Swiss chard leaves—they are delicious. Because chard is not as tender as spinach, blanch or steam it for a minute or two before assembling the salad.

Soaking time: 8 hours or overnight
Cooking time (after assembling ingredients): about 2 hours
Chilling time: at least 2 hours
Serves: 6

1½ cups (290 g) chickpeas, soaked in water
    8 hours or overnight, then drained
1 teaspoon (5 ml) black mustard seeds
½ teaspoon (2 ml) celery seeds
4 tablespoons (60 ml) lemon juice
6 tablespoons (90 ml) olive or nut oil
scant ½ teaspoon (2 ml) cayenne pepper or paprika
¼ teaspoon (1 ml) yellow asafetida powder (*hing*)*
2 tablespoons (30 ml) tomato paste
2 tablespoons (30 ml) maple syrup or honey
½ teaspoon (2 ml) salt
¼ teaspoon (1 ml) freshly ground pepper
1 large ripe tomato, diced
1 small cucumber, peeled, halved, seeded and diced
½ of a yellow bell pepper, seeded and diced
½ pound (230 g) fresh spinach, washed,
    trimmed, coarsely chopped and patted dry

This amount applies only to yellow Cobra brand. Reduce any other asafetida by three-fourths.

1. Place the chickpeas in a heavy saucepan with 4 cups (1 liter) of water and simmer over low heat for 1½–2 hours or just until tender. Keep an eye on the chickpeas during the last ½ hour to prevent them from overcooking. Drain and let cool.

2. Crush the mustard seeds and celery seeds with a mortar and pestle. Place them in a salad bowl with the lemon juice, oil, cayenne or paprika, asafetida, tomato paste, sweetener, salt and pepper, and beat with a fork or wire whisk until emulsified. Add the chickpeas, tomato, cucumber and bell pepper. Gently toss, cover and chill for 2–4 hours. Thirty minutes before serving, remove the salad from the refrigerator. Add the spinach, toss, and bring back to room temperature.

Jicama Salad with Snow Peas, Avocado and Watercress
KHASA SALAAD

You won't find this salad on a menu in Calcutta, Bombay or Delhi. It is a dish that fell into the salad bowl while I was working in Southern California. The greengrocers there seem to offer a limitless variety of salad fare, and a long hot spell spurred on this crisp vegetable salad. It is the basis of a delicious light lunch, accompanied by *Griddle-Baked Paper-Thin Whole Wheat Bread* and *Bubbly Lime Cooler Sweetened with Gur.*

For information about unfamiliar ingredients or techniques, see A-to-Z

Preparation time (after assembling ingredients): 15 minutes
Serves: 5 or 6

Dressing:

¼ cup (60 ml) chopped fresh parsley or coriander
2 tablespoons (30 ml) chopped watercress
2 tablespoons (30 ml) chopped walnuts
3 tablespoons (45 ml) lime juice
¼ avocado, peeled and chopped
½ teaspoon (2 ml) salt
1 tablespoon (15 ml) honey or maple syrup
scant ½ teaspoon (2 ml) dry mustard
¼ teaspoon (1 ml) paprika
⅓ cup (80 ml) fruity olive or avocado oil, or
     a mixture of 2 tablespoons (30 ml) walnut oil
     and 3 tablespoons (45 ml) safflower oil

Salad:

1 medium-sized jicama (about 14 ounces/400 g),
     peeled and cut into fine julienne
24 medium-sized snow peas (about 5 ounces/140 g),
     trimmed and cut on the diagonal into thin slices
1 small yellow or red bell pepper (about 4 ounces/115 g),
     cored, seeded and diced
2 bunches fresh watercress (about 6 ounces/170 g),
     rinsed, dried and stemmed
¾ avocado, peeled, seeded, diced and sprinkled with lemon juice
Boston or bibb lettuce leaves
6 sprigs fresh coriander
freshly ground pepper
salt

    1. Combine the parsley or coriander, watercress, walnuts, lime or lemon juice, avocado, salt, sweetener, mustard and paprika in a blender or a food processor fitted with the metal blade. Process until smooth. With the machine running, gradually add the oil in a slow stream until the dressing is thick and creamy. Transfer to a bowl and refrigerate, covered, until serving time.

    2. Combine the jicama, snow peas and bell pepper in a bowl and toss until blended. Reserve a few watercress leaves, and tear the rest into small pieces. Add them and the avocado to the bowl and gently toss.

    3. Arrange the lettuce leaves on a salad platter or on 6 individual plates and mound with the salad. Top with the reserved watercress leaves and the coriander and pour on the dressing. Serve with freshly ground black pepper and salt.

Cracked Wheat Salad

DALIA SALAAD

The South Indians' enthusiasm for rice dishes is equaled only by that of the North Indians for wheat. Wheat is eaten in some form every day in the North. During the India-Pakistan skirmish in 1971, I was residing in Vrindavan, tending a friend with a fever. Her resident homeopathic physician insisted that she recuperate on this salad. He knew nothing of Lebanese tabbouleh salad, yet this variation resembles it remarkably. It is full of flavor and nutrition (parsley is loaded with vitamin C). Cracked wheat and bulgur are processed differently but can be used interchangeably. They are available at gourmet, health food and Indian grocery stores. This room temperature salad is good in any season.

Preparation and cooking time (after assembling ingredients): 40 minutes
Serves: 4 to 6

1½ cups (360 ml) water
1 cup (240 ml) cracked wheat or bulgur
½ cup (120 ml) fresh peas or sliced snow peas
½ teaspoon (2 ml) salt
½ teaspoon (2 ml) freshly ground pepper
1 cup (240 ml) minced fresh parsley
¼ cup (60 ml) finely chopped fresh mint or
    1 tablespoon (15 ml) dried mint
2 medium-sized tomatoes, each cut into eighths
    or 8 tomatillos, husked and quartered
¼ cup (60 ml) olive or sesame oil
1–2 seeded and minced hot chilies,
    preferably yellow or red

Bring the water to a boil in a 2-quart/liter saucepan. Add the cracked wheat or bulgur, peas or snow peas, salt and pepper. Remove the pan from the heat and set aside for ½ hour. Most of the water will be absorbed into the grains. If there is any excess, drain it off or place the pan over low heat and cook until it is absorbed. When thoroughly cool, transfer to a serving bowl and gently toss with the remaining ingredients. Serve at room temperature or chill. If you want a showy presentation for a salad buffet, line the serving container with cabbage leaves, spoon in the salad and garnish with yellow bell pepper rings.

Papaya, Avocado and Jerusalem Artichoke Salad

PAPITA SALAAD

The creaminess of papaya and avocado and crispness of Jerusalem artichokes are pleasantly set off by the sweetish coriander-lime vinaigrette. You may prefer mango instead of papaya, or celeriac instead of Jerusalem artichokes. Also called sunchokes, the peeled Jerusalem artichokes

For information about unfamiliar ingredients or techniques, see A-to-Z

may be blanched before use or left raw, depending on your preference. This light salad goes well on any menu from lunch to late supper.

Preparation time (after assembling ingredients): 15 minutes
Serves: 4

3 tablespoons (45 ml) maple syrup or honey
¼ cup (60 ml) lime juice
⅓ cup (80 ml) olive oil, or a mixture of two
    parts almond oil to three parts sunflower oil
½ teaspoon (2 ml) salt
¼ teaspoon (1 ml) yellow mustard powder
¼ teaspoon (1 ml) freshly ground pepper
3 tablespoons (45 ml) chopped fresh coriander
1 medium-sized papaya (about 2½ pounds/1.5 kg),
    peeled, halved lengthwise, seeded, sliced
    crosswise into ⅓-inch (1 cm) slices and sprinkled with lemon juice
2 medium-sized ripe avocados, peeled, seeded, cut into
    ½-inch (1.5 cm) cubes and sprinkled with lemon juice
4 Jerusalem artichokes, peeled, cut lengthwise into
    julienne and sprinkled with lemon juice

1. Combine the sweetener, lime juice, oil, salt, mustard, pepper and coriander in a bowl and whisk until creamy.

2. Arrange the salad decoratively on a platter or individual plates; for example, overlap papaya slices around the edges, mound the avocado in the center and sprinkle the julienne artichokes between the two. Pour on the salad dressing and serve at once.

Mixed Vegetable Salad
SABJI SALAAD

Most Americans and Europeans exploring India without a package tour or four- star accommodations are overwhelmed by heat, dust, and the language barrier and long for familiar meals reminiscent of home. During my residence there, I tended many a weary traveler in search of stomach calming fare with recognizable ingredients. This satisfying dish seemed to bring around even a failing appetite and certainly fit the bill for any time of day. According to time and place, there are endless variations for this salad. It combines good nutrition with good taste: fresh and cooked vegetables with fried *panir* cheese and a creamy cashew nut dressing. Though fried *panir* cubes really do make the dish, for convenience or a change of pace, you might replace it with herbed tofu, farmer's cheese, pot cheese or *Fresh Curd Cheese*. The vegetable selections—inspired by available seasonal produce—should contrast colors, tastes and textures. Served with almost any flatbread selection and perhaps a frozen dessert, there is little that could be more satisfying after a challenging day on the go.

Preparation and cooking time (after assembling ingredients): 25 minutes
Serves: 6

Dressing:

1–2 hot green jalepeño chilies
½-inch (1.5 cm) piece of peeled fresh ginger root
½ cup (75 g) dry-roasted unsalted cashews
1 tablespoon (15 ml) raw sugar
⅓ cup (80 ml) yogurt or buttermilk
¼ cup (60 ml) light olive or sesame oil
1 cup (240 ml) water
1 teaspoon (5 ml) salt
⅛ teaspoon (0.5 ml) each paprika and black pepper
¼ cup (60 ml) chopped fresh coriander or parsley

Salad:

fresh *panir* cheese (page   313) made from 8 cups
　　　(2 liters) milk, cut into ½-inch (1.5 cm) cubes or
　　　10 ounces(285 gr) of the suggested alternatives on previous page
flour or cornstarch for dusting
ghee or vegetable oil for deep-frying
3 medium-sized boiling-type potatoes, boiled, peeled and sliced
½ pound (230 g) young green beans, cut into 1-inch (2.5 cm) lengths and parboiled for 7 minutes
3 medium-sized tomatoes, cut into wedges
2 celery stalks, sliced on the diagonal
3 medium-sized carrots, scraped and finely shredded
2 medium-sized avocados, peeled, seeded, diced and sprinkled with lemon juice
3 medium-sized beets, peeled and finely shredded
1 large green, yellow or red bell pepper, seeded and diced
2 medium-sized cucumbers, peeled, halved, seeded and sliced
2 tablespoons (30 ml) lime juice

1. Fit the food processor with the metal blade, or use a blender. Turn the machine on, drop in the chilies and ginger and mince. Add the cashews and grind. Add the remaining dressing ingredients and process until smooth and creamy. Set aside.

2. If the *panir* cheese or tofu is moist or crumbly, it will tend to spatter and stick together when fried. To counter this, place it on waxed paper and dust lightly with flour or cornstarch. Lift the corners of the paper and gently shake to coat evenly. Pour *ghee* or oil into a deep-frying pan to a depth of 2 inches (5 cm). Place over moderate heat and when the temperature reaches 350°F (180°C) on a thermometer, carefully add the *panir*. Do not stir the cheese immediately. After 1 minute, stir gently with a chopstick to keep the cubes from sticking together. Fry until the cheese is golden brown, then remove with a slotted spoon and set aside on paper towels. (If you use farmer's, pot or *Fresh Curd Cheese*, simply break or cut it into roughly small cubes and gently coat it with half of the dressing.)

3. To serve the salad, arrange the potatoes, green beans, tomatoes, celery, carrots, avocados, beets, bell pepper and fried *panir* cheese decoratively on a large serving plate. Line the edges of the plate with overlapping slices of cucumber. Sprinkle everything with lime juice. Serve with individual cruets or demi-bowls of dressing.

For information about unfamiliar ingredients or techniques, see A-to-Z

Whole Cabbage Stuffed with Carrot Coleslaw
BANDHGOBHI SALAAD

A large, crinkly-leafed Savoy cabbage makes an ideal cabbage bowl, though red or green cabbage can be used as well. In this variation, the cut-away inner portion is trimmed, shredded and jazzed up with herbs, spices, carrots and a creamy dressing. The outer shell serves as a salad bowl. For a summer backyard salad banquet, select several types of cabbage, vary the fillings and use small cabbages for dressings—they are sure crowd pleasers.

Preparation time (after assembling ingredients): 30 minutes
Serves: 6 to 8

1 oversized Savoy or stuffing-type cabbage
4 medium-sized carrots, scraped and shredded
1–2 hot green chilies, seeded and minced
½ tablespoon (7 ml) scraped fresh ginger root, minced
2 tablespoons (30 ml) chopped fresh coriander or dill
salt and freshly ground pepper
½ cup (120 ml) buttermilk or yogurt
½ cup (120 ml) heavy cream
3 tablespoons (45 ml) fresh lime juice
2 tablespoons (30 ml) *ghee* or vegetable oil
1 teaspoon (5 ml) black mustard seeds

1. Trim off all large bruised cabbage leaves and take a slice off the base so the cabbage stands flat on its own. Slice off the top third of the cabbage and cut around the edge, leaving a 1-inch (2.5 cm) border. Hollow out the center, and shred enough of it to equal the amount of carrots.

2. Combine the carrots, cabbage, chilies, ginger, fresh herbs, salt and pepper in a large bowl and toss to mix. In another bowl, combine the buttermilk or yogurt and the cream. Stirring constantly, slowly pour in the lime juice. Whisk until creamy, then pour over the carrot slaw.

3. Place the *ghee* or oil in a small pan over moderate heat. When it is hot but not smoking, add the black mustard seeds and fry until they sputter and turn gray. Pour the seasoning into the salad and toss well. Spoon the salad into the cabbage shell and serve at room temperature or chill.

Creamy Potato Salad Surprise
ALOO SALAAD

Global potato salad variations take many directions: warm and chilled, sweet 'n' sour, mustardy, rich and unadorned. The surprise in this "American-in-Delhi" salad is the addition of

crunchy bits of fried *moong dal badi*, sold at most Indian grocery stores or easily made at home·
This potato salad with a Punjabi twist is worth taking on any outing.

Preparation and cooking time (after assembling ingredients): about 45 minutes
Serves: 6

7–8 medium-sized red-skinned boiling potatoes (about 2 pounds/1 kg)
4 tablespoons (60 ml) *ghee* or peanut oil
⅓ cup (30 g) *moong dal badis* (cracked with a kitchen
    mallet into pea-sized bits) or cashew pieces
3 tablespoons (45 ml) each chopped fresh coriander and parsley
¼ teaspoon (1 ml) freshly ground pepper
1¼ teaspoons (6 ml) salt
2 tablespoons (30 ml) lime juice
½ tablespoon (7 ml) coarsely crushed dry-roasted cumin seeds
1 cup (240 ml) sour cream or rich yogurt
about ⅓ cup (80 ml) buttermilk
a sprinkle of cayenne pepper or paprika

1. Boil the potatoes in their skins until they are just fork-tender; take care not to overcook them. Cool slightly, peel and cut into ½-inch (1.5 cm) dice. Place in a salad bowl.

2. Heat the *ghee* or oil in a frying pan over moderate heat. Add the *badi* pieces or cashews and, stirring constantly, fry until golden brown. Pour them and the cooking oil over the potatoes. Add the remaining ingredients and gently mix, using your hands or a wooden spoon, until the salad is coated with dressing. Serve at room temperature or slightly chilled, sprinkled with cayenne or paprika.

Sweet Potato Salad in Maple-Lemon Vinaigrette
SHAKARKAND SALAAD

You can prepare this salad up to 8 hours before serving. Though it is light and healthy, it is also substantial and filling, perfect as a fall or winter salad. The maple-lemon dressing is barely sweet, pleasantly warmed by candied ginger.

For information about unfamiliar ingredients or techniques, see A-to-Z

Cooking time: about 45 minutes
Preparation and marinating time (after assembling ingredients): about 1 hour
Serves: 6

6 medium-sized sweet potatoes (about 2 pounds/1 kg), washed but not peeled
4 tablespoons (60 ml) maple syrup or honey
3 tablespoons (45 ml) orange or tangerine juice
3 tablespoons (45 ml) lemon or lime juice
¾ teaspoon (3.5 ml) salt
¼ teaspoon (1 ml) freshly ground black pepper or
    ⅛ teaspoon (0.5 ml) cayenne pepper
½ cup (120 ml) olive oil, or 2 tablespoons (30 ml)
    almond oil and 6 tablespoons (90 ml) sunflower oil
⅓ cup (80 ml) finely chopped fresh coriander or parsley
2 tablespoons (30 ml) chopped candied or stem ginger
3 medium-sized tomatoes, peeled, seeded and cut into ½-inch (1.5 cm) cubes

1. Prick the potatoes with a fork in 2 or 3 places, then wrap in aluminum foil. Bake in a preheated 400°F (205°C) oven for about 45 minutes or just until crushably soft. Cool, peel, cut into ½-inch (1.5 cm) cubes and place them in a large salad bowl. Alternatively, peel the potatoes, steam them, let them cool, and cube them.

2. Combine the sweetener, juices, salt, cayenne or black pepper, oil, fresh herbs and ginger in a jar, cover and shake until emulsified. Pour the dressing over the potatoes, toss gently, cover and set aside, refrigerated, for 1–8 hours.

3. Before serving, add the tomatoes, gently toss and serve on a bed of mixed greens.

Panir and Spinach Salad with Walnut-Coriander Dressing
PANIR PALAK SALAAD

In India, tossed green salads are rarely served—not because greens are unpopular, but because of the ever-present heat. Temperatures well over 100°F (38°C) prevent the growth of most greens; those that do make it suffer great losses without refrigeration. In India, consequently, an occasional family garden plot devoted to salad greens is a treasure. By far, spinach is the most widely used leafy green. Like Greek and Italian wilted salads with creamy mozzarella cheese, this variation on a theme became a favorite with many of my guests. If you want to cut calories, then, instead of frying the *panir*, toss it in 2–3 tablespoons (30–45 ml) of the dressing and marinate for at least 15 minutes.

Preparation and cooking time (after assembling ingredients): about 30 minutes
Serves: 6

Dressing:

¼ cup (60 ml) olive oil
2 tablespoons (30 ml) walnut or almond oil
2 tablespoons (30 ml) finely chopped walnuts or pine nuts
2 tablespoons (30 ml) each lime and orange juice
2 tablespoons (30 ml) minced fresh coriander or sweet basil
2 teaspoons (10 ml) sugar
½ teaspoon (2 ml) salt
¼ teaspoon (1 ml) each paprika and yellow mustard
⅛ teaspoon (0.5 ml) freshly ground pepper

Salad:

fresh *panir* cheese (page 313), made from 6 cups
        (1.5 liters) milk, (about 6 ounces/170 g) cut into pieces 1 inch
        (2.5 cm) long and ½ inch (1.5 cm) square
¾ cup (180 ml) *ghee* or vegetable oil for frying
3 cups (710 ml) hot water
8 cups (2 liters) fresh spinach (10–12 ounces/285–340 g),
        washed, trimmed, patted dry and torn into bite-sized pieces
1 medium-sized firm ripe avocado
1 teaspoon (5 ml) lemon juice
1 small red or yellow bell pepper, roasted and peeled
        or 2 whole pimentos, washed and patted dry
⅓ cup (50 g) coarsely chopped toasted walnuts or pine nuts

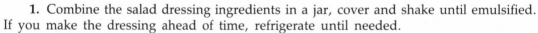

1. Combine the salad dressing ingredients in a jar, cover and shake until emulsified. If you make the dressing ahead of time, refrigerate until needed.

2. Spread the cut cheese on paper towels and let it dry out for 15 minutes. Heat the *ghee* or oil in a nonstick 10-inch (20 cm) frying pan over moderate heat. When it is hot, carefully add the cheese pieces and fry them for about 5 minutes, turning and tossing gently with a wooden spoon until they are golden brown on all sides. As they brown, transfer them to the bowl of hot water. Soak the cheese for 15–20 minutes, then drain well.

3. When you are ready to serve the salad, place the spinach in a large mixing bowl and add the fried or marinated *panir* cheese. Peel and seed the avocado and cut it into bite-sized pieces. Sprinkle them with lemon juice and add to the salad bowl. Slice the bell pepper or pimento into thin strips and add them.

4. Warm the salad dressing in a small pan, whisk with a fork, and pour it into the salad. Gently toss, either in the kitchen or at the table, and serve at once, garnished with chopped nuts.

For information about unfamiliar ingredients or techniques, see A-to-Z

Baked Buckwheat with Almonds
EKADASEE KOTU BADAAM SALAAD

Buckwheat is the seed of a starch plant that belongs to the same family as rhubarb, sorrel and dock (*Polygonaceae*). I researched this ingredient extensively to confirm its botanical identity, for unfortunately there is conflicting information in print. My first substantial information that it is a seed—not a cereal or grain—came from a beautifully illustrated eighteenth-century book in the Botanical Department of the British Museum Library in London. It not only described buckwheat in detail and gave its many species, but included its name in several languages, among them Hindi, Urdu and Sanskrit. To my relief, *phaphra*, *kotu* and *kutu* appeared in print next to the illustration—names of a triangular seed commonly used on *Ekadasee* fast days in place of wheat and other cereal grains (Vaishnavas strictly abstain from eating grains on *Ekadasee* days). Ground into a gritty flour, it is used for flat breads or fritter batters, and in cracked form, cooked as a grain pilaf.

From a health standpoint, buckwheat is the best source of available protein of all the grain-type foods. It is said to possess over 90 percent of the protein value of milk solids and is a rich source of iron, potassium, B vitamins and rutin. Unroasted, the shelled seed is called a groat, and roasted, it is known as *kasha*. If your local supermarket doesn't stock it, most health food stores do, in both roasted or unroasted groats and flour form. To toast the groats, dry-roast them in an ungreased pan over low heat until they pop and lighten in color.

Buckwheat has a subtle nutty flavor, and I find it lovely with herbs and olive oil as a room-temperature salad. You could also serve it hot, like a rice pilaf, with a simple or elaborate dinner.

Preparation (after assembling ingredients): 15 minutes
Cooking time: 45 minutes
Serves: 6

1 cup (240 ml) toasted buckwheat kernels (kasha)
2¼ cups (530 ml) boiling vegetable stock or water
⅓ cup (50 g) toasted almonds
2 tablespoons (30 ml) currants
2 tablespoons (30 ml) each chopped fresh coriander, parsley
    and sweet basil, or ½ teaspoon (2 ml) each dried herb
½ teaspoon (2 ml) salt
2 tablespoons (30 ml) butter or olive oil
6 large firm ripe tomatoes
bed of salad greens
1 medium-size firm ripe avocado
1 tablespoon (15 ml) lemon juice

1. Preheat the oven to 350°F (180°C). Place the buckwheat in a buttered baking dish, add the stock or water, almonds, currants, herbs, salt and butter or oil, and bake for about 45 minutes or until the kernels are soft. Fluff with a fork, adding an additional pat of butter or drizzle of oil if the pilaf is dry. Serve hot or let cool to room temperature.

2. Cut each tomato into eighths, leaving ½ inch (1.5 cm) at the base uncut. Place on a bed of salad greens. Peel and pit the avocado, dice it and sprinkle it with lemon juice. Add to the buckwheat pilaf. Spoon the salad into the tomato flowers and drizzle with your favorite dressing.

Chutneys

Chutneys, both fresh and cooked, are piquant, palate-teasing relishes that serve as accents to other dishes. From the simplest lunch of rice, vegetables and yogurt to a lavish spread of 108 preparations, a meal is often considered incomplete without a dab of chutney or pickle to liven it up. In some cases, chutneys play more than a supporting role, for they can be essential to the character of a dish. For example, South Indian *dosas* and *iddlis* are practically never served without some type of fresh coconut chutney, and North Indian *dahi baras* are inevitably served with a spoonful of sweet and sour tamarind chutney. Heat intensity ranges from fiery to pleasantly nippy; texture varies from thinnish sauces to jam like conserves; and taste spans spicy to mild.

In most Indian households, fresh chutneys are ground daily on large stone mortars. With a consistency similar to that of Genoese pestos, they are often little more than pounded fresh herb pastes or purées. Because fresh chutneys thicken and darken during storage, they are usually made within hours of use, even though they remain delicious for several days, and with the help of a food processor or blender one can make fresh chutneys effortlessly in minutes.

Supporting ingredients not only add flavor but also act as stimulating digestives. They include fresh ginger, hot green chilies, lemon juice, coconut, nuts, sour fruits and spice seeds. Glancing through the recipes, you will quickly note the absence of vinegar, curry powder, garlic or onions, ingredients often used in commercial Indian condiments but considered tamasic and therefore unacceptable to Vedic cooks.

Like fresh chutneys, cooked chutneys are invariably hot and spicy. Some, such as green tomato chutney, are unsweetened, while pineapple-raisin chutney is almost a hot, spicy conserve. Cooked chutneys keep well; covered and refrigerated, they can be used for a week or so. While fresh chutneys are everyday condiments, cooked chutneys are invariably served on holiday, festival, wedding and banquet menus. Jam-like cooked fruit chutneys are loved picnic and traveling companions, served with breads, pastries or crackers. Serving sizes for both are small and, depending on the selection, vary from 1–4 rounded spoonfuls. For example, a 2 teaspoon (10 ml) serving of nose-tingling hot coriander chutney will do for starters, while you could begin with ¼ cup (60 ml) of creamy cashew chutney.

Both types of chutney call for some type of hot chilies. How much and what kind you use are entirely matters of personal preference, though I would suggest that you allow enough for the heat to be recognizable. Indians like their chutneys hot, and I have seen many a cook drop two handfuls of fresh chilies and two spoons of cayenne into chutney meant to serve four! The recipes here have been tested with jalepeño chilies, unless stated otherwise. They are moderately hot and easy to seed. If your skin is sensitive, use rubber gloves when handling fresh chilies; normal skin will need little more than a film of oil for protection. Other chilies worth trying include tabasco, banana, cherry, poblano, serrano and Hungarian yellow, to name a few. The smallest varieties are usually the hottest.

Fresh Coconut and Mint Chutney
NARIYAL PODINA CHATNI

Most people become addicts with their first taste of coconut chutney, and several South Indian dishes are never served without it. In this variation, fresh mint lends both flavor and a soft green hue to the creamy consistency. This everyday chutney from Kerala is perfect with *Savory Urad Dal Doughnuts* or *Iddli with Cumin Seeds and Black Pepper*. Thinned with a little yogurt or milk, it serves as a delicious dipping sauce with North Indian *Bell Pepper Pakora with Nigella Seeds* or *Green Tomato Pakora with Cornmeal*. Frozen grated coconut is convenient and quite acceptable, and the only alternative to fresh. It is available at some supermarkets and many Hispanic grocery stores.

Preparation time (after assembling ingredients): 15 minutes
Makes: about 1¼ cups (300 ml)

1–2 hot jalepeño chilies, seeded and chopped
½-inch (1.5 cm) scraped fresh ginger root, sliced
10 whole almonds or cashews, blanched
⅓ cup (80 ml) water
2 tablespoons (30 ml) lemon or lime juice
1 tablespoon (15 ml) raw sugar or maple syrup
1 teaspoon (5 ml) salt
⅓ cup (80 ml) trimmed fresh mint, lightly packed
1 cup (85 g) grated fresh or defrosted (140 g)
     frozen coconut, lightly packed

Fit a food processor with the metal blade, or use a blender. With the machine running, drop in the chilies and ginger and process until minced. Add the nuts, pulse four or five times, then process until ground. Add the water, juice, sweetener, salt and mint, and process until smooth. Stop the machine, add the coconut, and continue to process until the chutney is creamy and smooth. (For a thinner consistency, add plain yogurt or milk as desired.) To accompany South Indian dishes, the consistency should be fairly thick; as a dipping sauce, it can be thinner. Serve at room temperature or chilled. Well covered and refrigerated, the chutney can be kept for 1–2 days.

For information about unfamiliar ingredients or techniques, see A-to-Z

Dry Coconut Chutney
KHOPRA CHATNI

In South Indian villages, whole coconuts are sun-dried by direct exposure to the intensely hot summer sun. The leathery smooth coconuts are sold by weight, both whole and in pieces, at outdoor bazaars. The oily dried coconut is then hand-grated on foot-operated iron *chekku* or *turapni*. In the West, commercial products are made by shredding coconut and drying it in a vacuum at 158°F (70°C) for an hour. Though desiccated coconut lacks the subtle flavor of fresh, it is convenient. Various types of unsweetened dried coconut—ribbon, flake, shredded and grated—are available at health food stores and gourmet shops. It is easy to powder in a coffee mill or food processor, so almost any type can be used in this recipe. Try this chutney with *Rice Flour Dosa with Cashews and Mustard Seeds* or *Chickpea Flour Pancakes with Mixed Vegetables*.

Preparation time (after assembling ingredients): 10 minutes
Makes: about 1½ cups (360 ml)

1 cup (85 g) unsweetened desiccated coconut, lightly packed
2–3 whole dried red chilies, broken into pieces and seeded
3 tablespoons (45 ml) dry-roasted chopped peanuts
½–1 teaspoon (2–5 ml) salt
about ⅓ cup (80 ml) plain yogurt
3 tablespoons (45 ml) chopped fresh coriander or minced parsley

Fit a food processor with a metal blade, or use a blender. Combine ½ cup (45 g) of the coconut, the red chilies and the peanuts, and process until powdered. Add the remaining coconut and the salt, and process until uniformly powdered. With the machine running, add the yogurt and pulse until light and fluffy. (To make a smooth purée, you can add more yogurt.) Add the fresh herbs and pulse four or five times, just to mix. Serve at room temperature or chilled. Well covered and refrigerated, the chutney can be kept for 1–2 days.

Toasted Fresh Coconut and Tomato Chutney
NARIYAL DAHI CHATNI

This toasted coconut chutney is more than a condiment for South Indian dishes: it is a flavor garnish that brings life to almost any fare. Coconut and *chana dal* or cashews are toasted before they are powdered along with herbs and seasonings. The finished consistency is slightly moist, from both the tomato and the yogurt. For a light repast, try this famous Bangalore coconut-tomato chutney with *Sweet 'n' Sour Dal Soup with Fresh Vegetables* and *Iddli with Cumin Seeds and Black Pepper*.

Preparation time (after assembling ingredients) and cooking time: 20 minutes
Makes: about 1¼ cups (300 ml)

3 tablespoons (45 ml) split *chana dal* or raw cashews
1 cup (85 g) grated fresh coconut, lightly packed
1 teaspoon (5 ml) cumin seeds
2–3 hot green chilies, cut into bits
3 tablespoons (45 ml) maple syrup
1–1¼ teaspoons (5–6 ml) salt
1 small tomato, blanched, peeled, seeded and cut into eighths
¼ cup (60 ml) plain yogurt
2 tablespoons (30 ml) each chopped fresh coriander and mint
3 tablespoons (45 ml) *ghee* or sesame oil
1 teaspoon (5 ml) black mustard seeds

1. Place the *dal* or cashews in a large heavy-bottomed frying pan over moderately low heat and slowly dry-roast until golden brown, then remove and set aside. Add the coconut, cumin seeds and chilies to the pan, and dry-roast, stirring frequently, until the coconut darkens a shade or two. Cool to room temperature.

2. Fit a food processor with the metal blade or use a blender. Add the *dal* or cashews and pulse to coarsely chop, then grind to a powder. Add half of the coconut and continue to process until the coconut is reduced to a powder. With the machine running, drop the remaining coconut through the feeder cap and continue to process until powdered. Add the maple syrup, salt, tomato, yogurt and herbs in the work bowl and pulse several times, then process continuously, stopping at intervals to scrape down the sides of the bowl with a rubber spatula, until the chutney is finely ground. Transfer to a bowl.

3. Heat the *ghee* or oil in a small saucepan over moderate heat. When it is hot but not smoking, add the black mustard seeds and fry until the *dal* turns brown and the black mustard seeds pop and turn gray. Pour the seasoning into the chutney and stir to mix. Serve at room temperature. Well covered and refrigerated, the chutney can be kept for 1–2 days.

Fresh Coconut and Tamarind Chutney with Fresh Coriander
NARIYAL IMLI CHATNI

Tamarind pulp has a fruity, sour taste and is frequently used in South Indian cooking. In this recipe, a touch of raw sugar is added to bring out a sweet and sour contrast of flavors. This chutney selection from Hyderabad goes well with virtually any savory, but is classic with *Delicate Rice and Urad Dal Dosa Pancakes* or *Paper-Thin Dosa Stuffed with Herbed Potatoes*.

Preparation time (after assembling ingredients) and cooking time: about 30 minutes
Makes: 1½ cups (360 ml)

For information about unfamiliar ingredients or techniques, see A-to-Z

1½-inch (37 g) ball of seeded dried tamarind pulp
½ cup (120 ml) hot tap water
2 tablespoons (30 ml) each chopped fresh mint and coriander
3 tablespoons (45 ml) crumbled *jaggery* or date sugar
2–3 hot green chilies, seeded and chopped
½ teaspoon (2 ml) salt
1¼ cups (105 g) grated fresh coconut, lightly packed
3 tablespoons (45 ml) *ghee* or sesame oil
1 teaspoon (5 ml) black mustard seeds
¼ teaspoon (1 ml) yellow asafetida powder (*hing*)*
10 curry leaves, preferably fresh

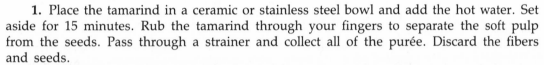

*This amount applies only to yellow Cobra brand. Reduce any other asafetida by three-fourths.

1. Place the tamarind in a ceramic or stainless steel bowl and add the hot water. Set aside for 15 minutes. Rub the tamarind through your fingers to separate the soft pulp from the seeds. Pass through a strainer and collect all of the purée. Discard the fibers and seeds.

2. Combine the tamarind purée, herbs, sweetener, chilies and salt in a food processor fitted with the metal blade, or a blender. Cover and process to a smooth purée. Add the coconut and process until well mixed. Transfer to a non-metallic bowl or ceramic dish.

3. Heat the *ghee* or oil in a saucepan over moderate heat. When it is hot but not smoking, add the black mustard seeds and fry until they begin to sputter and turn gray. Remove the pan from the heat, add the asafetida and curry leaves, and after several seconds pour the seasonings into the chutney. Stir well. Serve at room temperature or chilled. Tightly covered and refrigerated, the chutney can be kept for 1–2 days.

Date and Raisin Chutney
KHAJUR KISHMISH CHATNI

Dates are the candy-like fruits of date palm trees, and raisins are sun-dried grapes. Both are intensely sweet and, combined, have considerable nutritive value, especially in concentrated iron. Dates are sold in several states, from very soft and fresh to hard and dry. If possible, use soft organic dates in this recipe. Try a dab of this sweet and hot chutney with *Griddle-Fried Whole Wheat Bread* or *Pastry Puffs Stuffed with Spicy Urad Dal*.

Preparation time (after assembling ingredients): 2½ hours
Makes: about 1½ cups (360 ml)

½ teaspoon (2 ml) fennel seeds
1 teaspoon (5 ml) cumin seeds
½ tablespoon (7 ml) coriander seeds
1 cup chopped pitted dates (about 4 ounces/115 g)
⅓ cup (50 g) raisins, preferably muscat
¼ cup (60 ml) fresh lime juice
2 tablespoons (30 ml) fresh orange juice
½-inch (1.5 cm) piece of peeled fresh ginger root, sliced
2–3 hot green jalepeño chilies, seeded and chopped
¼ teaspoon (1 ml) salt
⅛ teaspoon (0.5 ml) freshly ground nutmeg
2 tablespoons (30 ml) chopped fresh coriander

1. Slowly dry-roast the spice seeds in a heavy pan over low heat. When they darken a few shades, remove from the heat and cool. Combine the dates, raisins and citrus juice in a small bowl and set aside for 2 hours.

2. Fit a food processor with the metal blade, or use a blender. With the machine running, drop the ginger and chilies through the feed cap and process until minced. Add the soaked fruits and juices and the spice seeds, and pulse several times until coarsely ground. Transfer to a bowl. Stir in the salt, nutmeg and fresh coriander. Covered tightly and refrigerated, the chutney can be kept for 5–6 days.

Fresh Tomato Chutney
TAZA TAMATAR CHATNI

This is a moderately hot chutney with a texture similar to that of Mexican salsa. Try it with almost any fried savory.

Makes: 1½ cups (360 ml)

4 small red or green tomatoes, peeled and diced
1-inch (2.5 cm) piece of peeled fresh ginger root, cut into fine julienne
2–3 fresh hot jalepeño chilies, halved lengthwise, seeded and slivered
1 teaspoon (5 ml) lime juice
1 tablespoon (15 ml) olive or sesame oil
¼ teaspoon (1 ml) salt
1 tablespoon (15 ml) currants
1 teaspoon (5 ml) each coarsely crushed dry-roasted cumin and coriander seeds
2 tablespoons (30 ml) chopped fresh coriander

Combine all of the ingredients in a bowl and gently mix. Let the chutney stand for at least 1–2 hours to merge the flavors, then serve at room temperature.

For information about unfamiliar ingredients or techniques, see A-to-Z

Fresh Ginger Root Chutney
ADRAK CHATNI

This fresh chutney is one of India's most loved digestives, for it fires up a failing appetite quite like nothing else. But for the newcomer, ginger as a main ingredient is biting and hot, and must be tempered by bland or sweet ingredients. A gamut of flavor directions can be explored, and in this variation I have chosen the tropical sweetness of dried papaya and coconut. You could also try any number of combinations using other dried fruits: currants, raisins, dates, figs, mangoes or apricots. Adjust the quantity of lime and orange juice accordingly, using only enough to reduce the chutney to a smooth purée. To cut down on food processor cleanup time when grinding dried fruits, rub a film of oil on the metal blade and the work bowl.

Preparation time (after assembling ingredients): 10 minutes
Makes: about 1½ cups (360 ml)

3 tablespoons (45 ml) fresh lime juice
⅓ cup (80 ml) fresh orange or tangerine juice
¾ cup (180 ml) peeled fresh ginger root,
    coarsely chopped
½ cup (120 ml) diced dried papaya or
    other above suggested dried fruit
½ cup (45 g) fresh or dried grated coconut
1½ teaspoons (7 ml) salt

Place 3 tablespoons (45 ml) of each fresh juice in a food processor fitted with the metal blade, or a blender. Add the remaining ingredients and process for about 1 minute. Uncover and scrape down the sides of the container with a rubber spatula, then blend again, using the remaining juice, or more if needed, until the ingredients are reduced to a smooth purée. Transfer to a ceramic or stainless steel bowl, and cover the chutney until you are ready to serve it. It can be kept refrigerated for a day or so.

Delicious Chickpea Chutney
KABLI CHANA CHATNI

Most people are unable to detect the main ingredient in this chutney (they invariably say it is some type of nut). In fact, it is a legume: toasted chickpeas, which have a remarkably nutty flavor. Bengalis prefer using *chana dal* over chickpeas, though to most the flavor distinction will not be discernible. A spoonable purée is standard chutney consistency; thinned down, it makes a good salad dressing.

Preparation time (after assembling ingredients): 10 minutes
***Dal* soaking time: 8 hours or overnight**
Makes: about 1½ cups (360 ml)

½ cup (100 g) dried chickpeas
2 cups (480 ml) water
2–3 dried red chilies, broken into pieces and seeded
1 cup (240 ml) plain yogurt or buttermilk
2 tablespoons (30 ml) sesame butter or almond butter
1 teaspoon (5 ml) salt
2 tablespoons (30 ml) *ghee* or sesame oil
1 teaspoon (5 ml) black mustard seeds
6–8 curry leaves, preferably fresh

1. Place the chickpeas in a heavy frying pan and dry-roast over moderately low heat until they darken one or two shades. Cover with the water and set aside for 8 hours or overnight. Drain.

2. Combine the chickpeas and chilies in a food processor fitted with the metal blade, or a blender. Pulse on and off several times to chop the chickpeas, then add the yogurt or buttermilk, tahini and salt, and process to a purée. Transfer to a bowl.

3. Heat the *ghee* or oil in a small pan over moderate heat. When it is hot but not smoking, add the black mustard seeds and fry until they turn gray and pop. Remove the pan from the heat, add the curry leaves, and in a few seconds pour the seasonings into the chutney. Stir well and cover until you are ready to serve. It can be kept in the refrigerator for 1–2 days; let it return to room temperature before serving.

Roasted Yellow Split Pea and Coconut Chutney
TOOVAR NARIYAL CHATNI

Dal chutneys, eaten over much of the South in numerous variations, are often made with *toovar dal*. Like coconut chutneys, they partner most rice dishes—from plain rice to *dosa* pancakes. I have come up with a variation using supermarket yellow split peas. You can vary the texture and serve it as a dipping sauce with *Chopped Spinach and Tomato Pakora*.

Preparation time (after assembling ingredients): 20 minutes
Resting time: at least 2 hours
Makes: about 1½ cups (360 ml)

2 tablespoons (30 ml) *ghee*, nut or vegetable oil
½ teaspoon (2 ml) black mustard seeds
¼ cup (50 g) yellow split peas or *toovar dal*
½ cup (45 g) unsweetened shredded dried coconut
⅔ cup (160 ml) warm water
2–3 hot green jalepeño chilies, chopped
⅓ cup (80 ml) yogurt
1 teaspoon (5 ml) salt
¼ teaspoon (1 ml) yellow asafetida powder (*hing*)*

*This amount applies only to yellow Cobra brand. Reduce any other amount by three-fourths.

For information about unfamiliar ingredients or techniques, see A-to-Z

1. Heat the *ghee* or oil in a large frying pan over moderate heat. Drop in the black mustard seeds and fry until they begin to jump in the pan. Add the split peas or *dal* and dry-roast, stirring often, until the color darkens one or two shades. Place the coconut in the pan and continue to stir-fry for 2–3 minutes.

2. Place the mixture in a food processor fitted with the metal blade, or a blender. Pulse on and off several times to chop the dried peas, then process to a powder. Add the remaining ingredients and process until smooth and creamy. Transfer to a bowl, cover, and set aside to thicken for at least 2 hours. Serve at room temperature. It can be kept in the refrigerator for 1–2 days.

Rich Tamarind Chutney
MEETHA IMLI CHATNI

In India, many parts of the tamarind tree are put to use. Fresh leaves are used as herbs, shiny polished fresh pods are cooked whole, and dried pods are ground into a meal called carob. If you can imagine it, the flavor of tamarind might resemble sour figs—sweet, sour and tangy. Small amounts of pulp accent many dishes, but tamarind chutney remains the most popular form. This variation is moderately accented with heat, spices and sweetness and textured with bits of dates, coconut and peanuts—the dates acting as both a natural sweetener and a flavor. Serve it with almost any dish you want to perk up, from rice and breads to sandwich spreads.

Preparation time (after assembling ingredients): about 40 minutes
Makes: 1¼ cups (300 ml)

¼ cup (60 ml) seeded dried tamarind, packed
1¼ cups (300 ml) boiling water
½ teaspoon (2 ml) *ajwain* seeds or 1 teaspoon (5 ml)
    cumin seeds
½ tablespoon (7 ml) scraped, minced fresh ginger root
¼–½ teaspoon (1–2 ml) cayenne pepper
¼ cup (35 g) finely chopped fresh dates
3 tablespoons (45 ml) chopped dry-roasted peanuts
3 tablespoons (45 ml) fresh or dried grated coconut
1 teaspoon (5 ml) salt
2 tablespoons (30 ml) finely chopped fresh coriander

1. Place the tamarind in a non-metallic bowl, add the boiling water, and set aside for at least ½ hour. Using your fingers or the back of a wooden spoon, mash and squeeze the tamarind until it separates from the fibers and turns into a pulpy sauce. Pour it into a sieve resting over a bowl, and press hard to force the purée through the sieve. Scrape the bottom of the sieve to collect as much as possible. Discard the roughage.

2. Add the remaining ingredients, cover, and set aside for at least 2–3 hours to let the flavors mingle. Covered and refrigerated, the chutney can be used for 3–4 days. Frozen, it keeps for several months.

Quick Tamarind–Raisin Chutney
IMLI KISMISH CHATNI

Along with compressed cakes of dried tamarind pods, most Indian grocery stores sell jars of thick, gelled tamarind purée concentrate. Shopkeepers often call it "instant tamarind." This fruit-sweetened chutney is delicious with *Spiced Potato and Green Pea Samosa* or *Flaky Mung Dal Kachori*.

Preparation time (after assembling ingredients): 15 minutes
Makes: about 1⅓ cups (320 ml)

⅔ cup (95 g) raisins
¾ cups (180 ml) water
1–2 hot green chilies
2 tablespoons (30 ml) chopped fresh coriander
1 tablespoon (15 ml) chopped fresh mint
⅓ cup (80 ml) tamarind, concentrated
¼ teaspoon (1 ml) cayenne pepper
½ teaspoon (2 ml) *garam masala*
¼ teaspoon (1 ml) *chat masala* or black salt
½ teaspoon (2 ml) salt

1. Combine the raisins and water in a small pan and quickly bring to a boil. Remove the pan from the heat and set aside to cool for 5 minutes.
2. Combine all of the ingredients in a food processor fitted with the metal blade, or a blender, and process to a smooth purée. Transfer to a non-metallic storage container, cover, and keep refrigerated for up to 3 days, or frozen for several months.

Fresh Coriander Chutney
DHANIYA CHATNI

Fresh herb chutney is as popular in the Punjab as pesto is in Genoa. In one of its simplest forms, fresh herb chutney might be a handful of trimmed leaves, several green chilies, salt, lemon juice and water, stone-ground to a wet pulp. This type of chutney is sharp, hot and nose-tingling. Chutney aficionados highly prize a subtle play of supporting flavors, balancing astringent, acid and sweet overtones. They might add unripened gooseberries or mango for a sharp contrast. Most newcomers prefer a tempered version, much like pine nut pesto, cut with coconut, nuts or sour cream to subdue the bite. Serve it as a dipping sauce for a fried savory such as *Cauliflower and Green Pea Samosa* or *Seasoned Potato Kachori*.

Preparation time (after assembling ingredients): 10 minutes
Makes: about 1 cup (240 ml)

1 teaspoon (5 ml) cumin seeds
3 tablespoons (45 ml) sesame seeds
¼ cup (25 g) freshly grated coconut or ¼ cup (40 g) chopped almonds
1 cup (240 ml) trimmed fresh coriander, slightly packed
1–2 hot green chilies, seeded
½-inch (1.5 cm) piece of peeled fresh ginger root, chopped
2 tablespoons (30 ml) water
¼ cup (60 ml) sour cream or yogurt (optional)
1 tablespoon (15 ml) raw sugar or *jaggery*
1 teaspoon (5 ml) salt

1. Combine the cumin seeds, sesame seeds and coconut or nuts in a heavy frying pan and place over low heat. Dry-roast, stirring frequently, until the coconut or nuts darken a few shades.

2. Combine the coconut mixture and the remaining ingredients in a food processor fitted with the metal blade, or a blender, and process until smooth. (The texture should resemble runny applesauce; you may need more water to reach this consistency.) Transfer to a bowl and serve, or cover well and keep refrigerated for up to 2 days.

Fresh Mint Chutney
PODINA CHATNI

Fresh mint chutney, like coriander chutney, is refreshingly sharp and bracing. Long recognized for its digestive properties, it is a very popular accompaniment to fried savories and highly spiced dishes. The overall character of the chutney depends on the type of mint you use, be it from the supermarket or freshly harvested from your herb garden. I have tested the recipe with numerous species and come up with different results. For example, the dappled cream and pale green leaves of pineapple mint (*Mentha suaveolens variegata*) has a fruity flavor, while the rounded downy leaves of Egyptian mint (*M. suaveolens*) has fresh apple overtones. For best all-around use, I prefer Bowles mint (*M. x villosa*), with its fresh scent and mild flavor. No matter what your source, if the mint is pungent, with a coarse flavor, temper it with coconut, nuts or dried fruits. Try the loved North Indian combination of *Cauliflower and Potato Samosa* or *Tangy Potato and Coconut Samosa Logs*.

Preparation time (after assembling ingredients): 10 minutes
Makes: about 1 cup (240 ml)

2 tablespoons (30 ml) each fresh lime juice and orange juice
2 tablespoons (30 ml) finely chopped dried papaya or honey
3 tablespoons (45 ml) water
1¾ cups (420 ml) trimmed fresh mint, packed
1–2 hot green chilies, seeded and chopped
¼ cup (25 g) fresh or dried coconut, lightly packed
1 teaspoon (5 ml) salt

Combine all of the ingredients in a food processor fitted with the metal blade, or a blender, and process until smooth. (The texture should resemble runny applesauce; you may need more water to reach this consistency.) Transfer to a bowl and serve or cover well and keep refrigerated for up to 2 days.

Creamy Cashew Chutney
KAJU CHATNI

This creamy chutney from Kerala, made from raw cashews, is versatile, wholesome and irresistible. It not only serves as a perfect accompaniment to traditional South Indian savories, but extends itself to accommodate a bowl of crunchy vegetable crudités or, thinned down, becomes an elegant salad dressing. Fresh cashews make the dish outstanding, for they are plump, white and sweet (stale nuts are gray and shriveled). Cashews are softer than most nuts, composed of about 47 percent oil, 22 percent carbohydrates and 21 percent protein, and provide excellent food value. This chutney is quickly assembled, keeps well and is easy to use. I have folded the last two tablespoons into a pan of stir-fried green beans, with smashing results.

Preparation time (after assembling ingredients): 10 minutes
Makes: about 1¼ cups (300 ml)

1 cup (140 g) raw cashews, bits or halves
¼ teaspoon (1 ml) lemon juice
1 teaspoon (5 ml) salt
½-inch (1.5 ml) piece of peeled fresh ginger root, sliced
1–2 hot green chilies, seeded and chopped
up to ⅓ cup (80 ml) water
2 tablespoons (30 ml) chopped fresh coriander

Combine the cashews, lemon juice, salt, ginger and chilies with ¼ cup (60 ml) of the water in a food processor fitted with the metal blade, or a blender, and process until smooth, adding more water as necessary to produce a loose purée. Transfer to a bowl, add the fresh coriander, and serve, or cover well and keep refrigerated for up to 3 days.
Note: This chutney thickens as it sits. Thin it with water to the desired consistency.

For information about unfamiliar ingredients or techniques, see A-to-Z

Roasted Peanut Chutney
MOONGFALLI CHATNI

Memories of my first arrival in Indore are hazy, but recollections of the B. Sharma estate, the friendly residents and elegant ambiance, are crystal clear. As the sun dipped into an endless expanse of peanut fields, our weary traveling *sankirtan* party reached its destination—a stately residence on one of the largest farms in Madya Pradesh. Our hosts showered us with Vaishnava hospitality. They whisked us to comfortable rooms, presented us with new clothes and, after we had bathed, ushered us to sprawling verandas, replete with wall-to-wall porch swings. Within minutes, twenty or so family members appeared, and in the twilight, animated exchanges ensued between new friends. Before long, an enthusiastic hand-clapping *kirtan* (chanting of spiritual songs) spontaneously began, followed by *pravachan* (discussion of scripture), and delicious *prasadam*. Our hosts served outstanding *prasadam* refreshment consisting of gingered fresh sugar cane juice, savory fried biscuits and crackers, finger bananas and peanut chutney. The fresh peanut chutney was so outstanding that Srila Prabhupada called me over and encouraged me to take advantage of the cooks' expertise. This recipe was one of the first I noted down.

Preparation and soaking time (after assembling ingredients): 45 minutes
Makes: 1½ cups (360 ml)

a walnut-sized ball of seeded dried tamarind pulp
⅔ cup (160 ml) boiling water
1 tablespoon (15 ml) *ghee* or peanut oil
1 cup (145 g) coarsely chopped raw peanuts,
     without skins
2 teaspoons (10 ml) coriander seeds
⅓ cup (35 g) fresh or dried shredded coconut
1 teaspoon (5 ml) salt
1–2 hot green chilies, seeded and chopped
1 tablespoon (15 ml) maple sugar or *jaggery*
¼ cup (60 ml) water

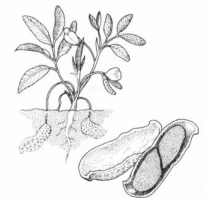

1. Soak the tamarind in the boiling water for ½ hour. Press the tamarind and rub it between your fingers to separate the pulp from the fibers. Pour it through a strainer and press, using the back of a wooden spoon or your fingers, to separate all of the purée from the fibers. Discard the fibers.

2. Heat the *ghee* or oil in a heavy frying pan over low heat. Drop in the nuts and coriander seeds and dry-roast, stirring now and then, for 3–4 minutes. Add the coconut and, still stirring, cook until the mixture begins to change color.

3. Combine the nut-coconut mixture, tamarind purée, salt, chilies, sweetener and water in a food processor fitted with the metal blade, or a blender. Process (adding more water if necessary to facilitate grinding) until creamy and smooth. Transfer to a bowl and serve at room temperature, or cover and refrigerate for 2–3 days.

Shredded Mango and Coconut Chutney

AAM NARIYAL CHATNI

Green mango makes delicious raw or cooked chutney. In this much loved South Indian variation, the rock-hard type is preferred. On the other hand, in the North fruit just short of ripe is favored. Use whatever is to your liking and convenient. The peppery orange–lime dressing beautifully sets off the near tart mango and sweet coconut–dried fruit mixture. This textured, nearly raw chutney has a character similar to *kachamber* and makes a pleasant contrast for soups, *dals* or stews. It is best assembled at least ½ hour before serving.

Preparation and marinating time (after assembling ingredients): 1–3 hours
Makes: 1½ cups (360 ml)

2 medium-sized firm unripe mangoes (about 2 pounds/1 kg)
¼ cup (25 g) dried or fresh coconut ribbons
1 tablespoon (15 ml) diced dried fruit, such as papaya or apricot
1 tablespoon (15 ml) each orange and lime juice
½ teaspoon (2 ml) salt
⅛ teaspoon (0.5 ml) cayenne pepper or paprika
1–2 hot green chilies, halved, seeded and slivered
2 tablespoons (30 ml) sesame or coconut oil
1 teaspoon (5 ml) black mustard seeds
2 tablespoons (30 ml) finely chopped fresh coriander

1. Peel the mangoes with a vegetable peeler or paring knife. Coarsely shred the fruit and discard the seed. Combine the mangoes with the coconut, dried fruit, juices, salt, cayenne or paprika and green chilies in a serving bowl, gently toss, cover, and marinate for ½ hour. It can be refrigerated for up to 6 hours before serving.

2. Heat the oil in a small pan over moderate heat until hot but not smoking. Drop in the black mustard seeds and fry until they turn gray and sputter (keep a lid handy to catch flying seeds). Pour the *chaunk* into the salad, add the fresh coriander, toss to mix, and serve.

COOKED CHUTNEYS

Simple Tomato Chutney

TAMATAR CHATNI

I was first introduced to one of Srila Prabhupada's famous tomato chutneys in 1966, and it still remains one of my favorites today. In my early days as his cook, I recall few feasts, banquets or journeys that did not include some variation or another. I have taken the liberty of approximating measurements, as Srila Prabhupada cooked without measuring tools. Try this chutney with any rice or dal, or vegetables that are compatible with tomatoes.

For information about unfamiliar ingredients or techniques, see A-to-Z

Preparation and cooking time (after assembling ingredients): about 25 minutes
Makes: about 1 cup (240 ml)

2 tablespoons (30 ml) *ghee*
1–2 whole dried red chilies
1 teaspoon (5 ml) cumin seeds
1-inch (2.5 cm) piece of cinnamon stick
1⅔ cups (about 1¼ pounds/570 g) coarsely chopped ripe tomatoes
3 tablespoons (45 ml) maple sugar, date sugar or *jaggery*
½ teaspoon (2 ml) salt

Heat the *ghee* in a large frying pan over moderate heat. When it is hot but not smoking, add the chilies, cumin seeds and cinnamon stick, and fry until the cumin seeds turn brown. Carefully add the tomatoes, sweetener and salt, and stir the sizzling ingredients for 10–15 minutes until the chutney is fairly dry. Serve warm, at room temperature or chilled. It can be kept, tightly covered and refrigerated, for 2–3 days.

Note: If you make this dish in quantity, cook it over moderately low heat, not moderate. The cooking time increases considerably because of the increased juice in the larger quantity of tomatoes.

Sweet Tomato Chutney with Fennel
MEETHA TAMATAR CHATNI

This dish, from a banquet at Calcutta's famous Radha Govinda Temple on Mahatma Gandhi Road, was served near the end of the meal. Depending on the number of courses, every regional cuisine has an order of serving, and sweet chutneys—often served with plain rice or toasted *pappadum*—are considered palate cleansers after other spicy dishes. This is a versatile chutney that complements many types of cuisine.

Preparation and cooking time (after assembling ingredients): about 30 minutes
Makes: about 1 cup (240 ml)

3 tablespoons (45 ml) *ghee* or mustard oil
½ teaspoon (2 ml) fennel seeds
¼ teaspoon (1 ml) nigella *kalonji*
¼ teaspoon (1 ml) cumin seeds
¼ teaspoon (1 ml) black mustard seeds
½ cassia or bay leaf
1–2 whole dried red chilies
1⅔ cups (570 g) firm ripe tomatoes,
    peeled and coarsely chopped
⅓ cup (50 g) maple sugar or *jaggery*
⅓ cup (50 g) golden raisins
¼ teaspoon (1 ml) turmeric
½ teaspoon (2 ml) salt

1. Heat the *ghee* or oil in a large heavy frying pan over moderate heat. (If you use mustard oil, bring it to the smoking point for about 5 seconds to make the pungent oil docile.) When it is hot but not smoking, add the fennel seeds, nigella, cumin seeds and black mustard seeds. When the fennel seeds darken one or two shades or the mustard seeds begin to pop, drop in the cassia or bay leaf and red chilies. Within 5 seconds, carefully add the chopped tomatoes and their liquid. Stir to mix, and cook over moderately low heat for 10 minutes.

2. Add the remaining ingredients and continue to cook for about 20 minutes or until the chutney is glazed and fairly thick. You should have about 1 cup (240 ml). Serve at room temperature, or cover and refrigerate for up to 4 days.

Zesty Green Tomato Chutney
KACHA TAMATAR CHATNI

Bengalis love green tomato chutney—either sweet or sweet 'n' sour—for although it is made from a plebeian ingredient, it has a wonderfully delicate flavor. In this century-old recipe from Bir Nagar, saffron and lime juice beautifully set off a green tomato–papaya combination. Bengalis are fond of both unripened mango and papaya, and many cooks might toss in a handful of diced fruit about halfway through the cooking. A relative newcomer to greengrocers' shelves and roadside stalls, yellow tomatoes make a fine golden variation in summer. For a small informal meal, serve a dish of *basmati* rice, green tomato chutney and fried *bhaji*.

Preparation time (after assembling ingredients): about 30 minutes
Makes: about 1 cup (240 ml)

4 medium-sized green or yellow tomatoes (about 1¼ pounds/570g)
3 tablespoons (45 ml) *ghee*, or corn or mustard oil
1 tablespoon (15 ml) minced yellow banana chilies,
    or 1–2 seeded and minced hot serrano chilies
½ teaspoon (2 ml) black mustard seeds
8–10 curry leaves, preferably fresh
⅛ teaspoon (0.5 ml) saffron threads
2 tablespoons (30 ml) each finely chopped candied ginger and papaya
½ cup (120 ml) peeled and diced green papaya or mango or other slightly underripe fruit
½ teaspoon (2 ml) salt
2 tablespoons (30 ml) coarsely chopped fresh coriander

1. Plunge the tomatoes into a pan of boiling water for 30 seconds. Drain immediately and peel the tomatoes. Cut each in half crosswise and squeeze out most of the seeds. Dice the tomatoes.

2. Heat the *ghee* or oil in a heavy frying pan over moderate heat until it is hot but not smoking. (If you use mustard oil, bring it to the smoking point for about 5 seconds

to make the pungent oil docile.) Drop in the black mustard seeds and fry until they turn gray and sputter. Add the curry leaves, and in seconds carefully add the tomatoes and saffron. Stir and cook for about 15 minutes over moderately low heat.

3. Add the candied fruit, diced green fruit and salt. Stirring often toward the end, cook for about 15 minutes or until fairly thick. Remove the pan from the heat, stir in the fresh coriander, and let cool. Serve at room temperature, or cover and refrigerate for up to 2 days.

Fresh Pineapple and Raisin Chutney
ANANAS KISMISH CHATNI

Within India's districts, even towns and villages have their own distinct cuisines. Mayapur, in West Bengal, is associated with foods loved by Shree Chaitanya Mahaprabhu, the founder of Gaudiya Vaishnavism, and on his birthday, called *Gour Purnima*, thousands of dishes are made in his honor. On Srila Prabhupada's first *Gour Purnima* in America, he taught his students to make a handful of dishes loved by Lord Chaitanya, including *laphra*, *charchari*, *payasa*, *bhaji* and this chutney. Its character is outstanding, and although over the years many imitations have come to my attention, none match the original. It makes even a humble meal an event.

Preparation and cooking time: about 1 hour
Makes: about 2 cups (480 ml)

3 tablespoons (45 ml) *ghee*
1–2 whole dried red chilies
½ tablespoon (7 ml) cumin seeds
½ tablespoon (7 ml) coriander seeds
1 large ripe pineapple (about 2½ pounds/1.5 kg)
    peeled, quartered, cored, and cut into pieces
    ¾ x ¼ x ¼ inch (2 cm x 6 mm x 6 mm);
    reserve the juice
½ teaspoon (2 ml) cardamom seeds, slightly crushed
½ teaspoon (2 ml) *garam masala* or ¼ teaspoon (1 ml)
    each ground cloves and cinnamon
⅔ cup (100 g) maple sugar, brown sugar or *jaggery*
⅓ cup (50 g) raisins or currants

1. Heat the *ghee* in a 2-quart/liter heavy-bottomed pan (preferably nonstick) over moderate heat until it is hot but not smoking. Add the red chilies, cumin seeds and coriander seeds and fry until they darken a few shades. Carefully add the pineapple and its juice (they tend to splatter), cardamom seeds and *garam masala*. Stirring now and then, gently boil over moderate to moderately low heat until the fruit is tender and the juice has cooked off. Toward the end, stir constantly to keep the fruit from scorching in the nearly dry pan.

2. Add the sweetener and raisins or currants, reduce the heat slightly and cook, stirring frequently, until the chutney is glazed and thick. Serve at room temperature, or cover and refrigerate for 3–4 days. Bring to room temperature before serving.

Cranberry Chutney
TOPOKUL CHATNI

Topokul is not a cranberry but a sour berry that makes a chutney similar to whole-berry American cranberry sauce. There are two main types of cranberries: small wild European berries and the larger red cultivated American berries. Indian *topokul* is like a cross between the two. Because fresh berries freeze well, this selection can be made on short notice, especially in the fall.

Preparation and cooking time (after assembling ingredients): about 45 minutes
Makes: about 3 cups (710 ml)

3-inch (7.5 cm) piece of cinnamon stick
3–4 whole green cardamom pods, crushed open
1 teaspoon (5 ml) whole cloves
1–2 hot green chilies, seeded
3-inch (7.5 cm) piece of orange zest
1½ cups (360 ml) white grape juice or water
¾ cup (120 g) raw sugar or maple syrup (180 ml)
½ cup (80 g) pitted dates, sliced
1 pound (455 g) cranberries

1. Tie the cinnamon, cardamom pods, cloves, green chilies and orange zest in a small piece of cheesecloth. Combine the juice or water, sweetener, dates and spice bag in a heavy-bottomed, 2-quart/liter saucepan over moderate heat, and cook, stirring, until the sugar dissolves. Reduce the heat to low and simmer for ½ hour.

2. Remove the spice bag, pressing it to extract the flavor. Stir in the cranberries and cook for 7–10 minutes or until the mixture thickens and the berries pop. Serve at room temperature, or cover and refrigerate for up to a week.

Crab Apple or Green Apple Chutney
SEB CHATNI

In India, I have only seen this chutney made in Kashmir, where small tart apples and quinces are used interchangeably. In many locations worldwide, Granny Smiths are a third option that yields excellent results. For those fortunate enough to have access to English Cox's Pippins, the chutney enters celestial realms.

Preparation and cooking time (after assembling ingredients): about 40 minutes
Makes: about 1½ cups (360 ml)

For information about unfamiliar ingredients or techniques, see A-to-Z

2 tablespoons (30 ml) *ghee* or unsalted butter
½ teaspoon (2 ml) cumin seeds
½ teaspoon (2 ml) coriander seeds
½ teaspoon (2 ml) fennel seeds
6 medium-sized tart apples, peeled,
    cored and thinly sliced
¾ cup (110 g) date sugar or maple sugar
⅛ teaspoon (0.5 ml) each ground mace,
    nutmeg, cinnamon and cardamom
¼ teaspoon (1 ml) cayenne pepper
⅓ cup (80 ml) orange juice
¼ cup (25 g) fresh or dried ribbon coconut
¼ cup (40 g) coarsely chopped toasted walnuts

1. Heat the *ghee* or butter in a large nonstick frying pan over moderate heat. Add the cumin, coriander and fennel seeds, and fry until the butter froths or the seeds darken a few shades. Add the apples, sugar, ground spices, cayenne and juice. Stir until the sugar dissolves, and bring to a boil.

2. Reduce the heat to moderately low and, stirring frequently during the last 10 minutes, cook for about ½ hour, or until the chutney is thick and glazed. Remove the pan from the heat and stir in the coconut and nuts. Serve warm or at room temperature, or cover and refrigerate for up to a week.

Pear Chutney with Dates and Pecans
NASHPATI CHATNI

While residing in the vale of Evesham, I had the opportunity to sample some of England's best produce. Every day for weeks on end I took on the challenge of coming up with a different cooked chutney, and in due course this recipe emerged from the test kitchen as everyone's favorite.

Preparation and cooking time (after assembling ingredients):   about 1 hour
Makes: about 1½ cups (360 ml)

¼–½ teaspoon (1–2 ml) crushed dried red chilies
1 tablespoon (15 ml) scraped, finely shredded or minced fresh ginger root
½ tablespoon (7 ml) grated orange zest
¼ teaspoon (1 ml) crushed cardamom seeds
2-inch (5 cm) piece of cinnamon stick
2 tablespoons (30 ml) *ghee* or unsalted butter
½ cup (120 ml) fresh orange juice
¼ cup (40 g) maple sugar or brown sugar, packed
6–7 medium-sized Bosc pears (about 2½ pounds/1.5 kg), peeled, quartered,
    cored and cut crosswise into ⅓-inch (1 cm) slices
½ cup (95 g) pitted soft dates, snipped into ⅓-inch (1 cm) pieces
⅓ cup (40 g) chopped toasted pecans

1. Combine the red chilies, ginger, orange zest, cardamom seeds and cinnamon on a saucer. Place the *ghee* or butter in a 3-quart/liter saucepan over low heat. Before the *ghee* is hot or the butter froths, add the combined spices. Fry for 1–2 minutes to release flavors. Add the orange juice and sugar, and stir until the sugar dissolves. Stir in the pears, bring to a gentle boil, and cook until syrupy and thick, about 30 minutes. Stir often during the last 5 minutes to prevent scorching.

2. Remove the pan from the heat, stir in the dates and pecans, and cool to room temperature. Serve, or cover and refrigerate for 3–4 days.

Golden Papaya Chip Chutney
KACHA PAPITA CHATNI

I was introduced to this dish at a lavish Bengali feast in the suburban Calcutta estate of Mr. Tarun Kunti Ghosh, the publisher of *Amrita Patrika Bazaar*, Calcutta's largest newspaper. The memorable *prasadam* repast contained some of the finest Bengali cuisine I have ever tasted, made with great care in a newly constructed kitchen equipped with freshly made clay stoves, by a fleet of Brahman cooks decked out in new clothes, and using mountains of fresh produce, grains and milk products. The end result of this kitchen army included 108 exquisite preparations served to the 100-plus guests dining village style: seated on an open veranda behind newly picked throw-away banana leaf plates and clay cups. Before I stopped counting, more than forty servers had brought in relay after relay of indescribably delicious *prasadam*—and this chutney, made from unripened papaya, caught my attention at the first bite. Inquiring after the recipe in the kitchen, I was laughingly told in halting pidgin English that I was eating Tarun Baba's famous "plastic chutney": when shavings of green fruit are simmered in an acidulated syrup, they become transparent, and to the Bengali cooks, resembled chips of plastic.

Unripened, green papaya has very hard, white flesh and is frequently used in Bengali and Oriyan chutneys, *dals* and vegetables. It is available at Indian, Chinese and Latin greengrocers. Because most supermarket papaya is picked quite green, to ripen in transit and in the stores, half-ripe fruit is more than acceptable. The thin papaya slices rest in a glistening golden sauce. Try it as a relish with a formal full-course meal or as a jam with hot *Griddle-Fried Whole Wheat Bread*.

Preparation time (after assembling ingredients): 15 minutes
Cooking time: 30 minutes
Makes: 1½ cups (360 ml)

2 pounds (1 kg) unripe green papaya (about
    2½ cups/600 ml of thinly sliced fruit)
1¼ cups (265 g) sugar
⅓ cup (80 ml) water
¼ cup (60 ml) strained lime juice
¼ teaspoon (1 ml) salt
1 hot green or dried red chili (or as desired)

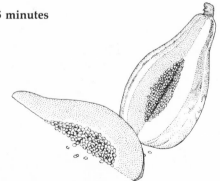

1. Quarter the papaya lengthwise, peel with a paring knife, and scoop out the center seeds and fibers. Cut each quarter in half lengthwise, then slice the papaya wedges crosswise into thin wafers.

2. Combine the sugar and water in a 2-quart/liter saucepan. Place over moderately low heat and stir until the sugar is dissolved; then add the papaya, raise the heat slightly, and gently boil until the fruit is soft.

3. Remove the papaya slices with a slotted spoon and set aside. Continue to boil the sugar–water mixture for about 20 minutes or until it is reduced to a one-thread consistency. When it is thick, add the papaya, lemon juice, salt and whole chili. Cook until the papaya is translucent and the texture jam-like.

Mixed Fruit Chutney
PHAL CHATNI

When summer fruits are abundant, this is a perfect chutney to make in quantity.

Preparation and cooking time (after assembling ingredients): about 1 hour
Makes: about 1⅔ cups (400 ml)

3 tablespoons (45 ml) *ghee* or unsalted butter
1 tablespoon (15 ml) scraped, finely shredded or minced fresh ginger root
1–2 hot green or dried red chilies, broken into small bits
½ tablespoon (7 ml) cumin seeds
1 large cooking apple, peeled, cored, quartered and thinly sliced
1 large firm ripe pear, peeled, cored, quartered and thinly sliced
2 large firm ripe peaches, peeled, seeded and diced
4 firm ripe apricots, peeled, seeded and diced
2 tablespoons (30 ml) raisins or currants
1¼ cups (180 g) brown, date or maple sugar
⅓ cup (80 ml) fresh orange juice or water
¼ cup (25 g) unsweetened shredded dried coconut
1 teaspoon (5 ml) *garam masala*
½ teaspoon (2 ml) salt

1. If you are using *ghee*, heat it in a 2-quart/liter saucepan over moderate heat until it is hot but not smoking. Drop in the ginger, chilies and cumin seeds, and fry until the cumin seeds darken a shade or two. If you are using butter, drop the cumin seeds into a dry pan and toast over moderately low heat until they begin to change color. Add the butter and ginger, and stir until the butter froths.

2. Add the remaining ingredients, reduce the heat to moderately low, and simmer, stirring occasionally, for 40–60 minutes or until the chutney is thick and glazed. Serve at room temperature, or refrigerate, covered, for 3–4 days.

Gooseberry Chutney
AMLA CHATNI

I have been told that gooseberries are not popular in America because they are not a good commercial crop. Evidently, they are susceptible to pests and nasty American gooseberry mildew. They are, nonetheless, available in the wilds—in damp woods, valleys and mountain regions from Maine to Oregon, as well as at roadside stalls and co-ops in season. In India they are widely used, both ripe and unripe, in jams, chutneys and sweet syrups. This chutney resembles a preserve in texture but is characteristically Bengali in seasoning.

Preparation and cooking time: 10 minutes
Makes: about 2½ cups (600 ml)

4 cups (1 liter) gooseberries, stemmed and washed
½ cup (120 ml) water
2–3 cups (425–635 g) sugar
¼ teaspoon (1 ml) cayenne pepper
½ cassia or bay leaf
½-inch (1.5 cm) piece of peeled fresh ginger root
¼ teaspoon (1 ml) *panch puran* (optional)
¼ teaspoon (1 ml) salt

1. Place the gooseberries in a 3-quart/liter heavy saucepan, add the water and bring to a boil over high heat. Add the remaining ingredients, reduce the heat, and simmer until the berries are clear and the juice is thick, about 15–20 minutes.

2. Remove the pan from the heat and lift out the cassia or bay leaf and ginger with fork tongs. Cool to room temperature and serve as a sweet chutney, even as a jam, or cover well and refrigerate for 2–3 days.

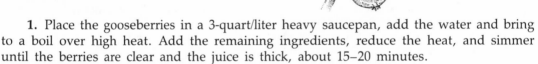

Mild Plum Chutney
SADA ALOO BOOKHARA CHATNI

Most California residents take full advantage of local produce, and when plums are at their peak—vibrant yellow, purple and red fruit with equally vivid flavors—they are irresistible, for both eating and cooking. One hot August, way back in 1967, I came up with this chutney for a celebration in honor of Srimati Radharani, Lord Krishna's eternal consort. Immediately coined "Radha Red," because of its ruby color, it has remained a favorite among devotees for over two decades.

Though hard-fleshed Damsons are generally preferred for cooking, almost any smooth-textured eating plum works well in this chutney. For color continuity, couple red grape juice with red- or purple-fleshed fruit, and white grape juice with yellow fruit. Sweet chutneys traditionally accompany griddle- or deep-fried breads or crackers for small meals, though they can also be a part of any full meal.

For information about unfamiliar ingredients or techniques, see A-to-Z

Preparation and cooking time: about 50 minutes
Makes: about 1½ cups (360 ml)

3 tablespoons (45 ml) *ghee* or unsalted butter
½ tablespoon (7 ml) peeled fresh ginger root, minced
1–2 hot green or yellow chilies, seeded and slivered
3-inch (7.5 cm) strip of orange zest, slivered
1½ pounds (685 g) firm ripe plums, halved,
    pitted and quartered
¼ teaspoon (1 ml) each ground mace, cloves,
    cinnamon, coriander and turmeric
½ cup (120 ml) grape juice
1½ cups (315 g) sugar or equivalent sweetener
pinch of salt

1. Heat the *ghee* or butter in a heavy 3-quart/liter saucepan over low heat. When the *ghee* is hot, or the butter froths, stir in the ginger, chilies and orange zest, and cook for a minute or so. Add the remaining ingredients, raise the heat slightly, and, stirring constantly, bring to a boil.

2. Reduce the heat to moderately low and cook until the chutney is fairly thick and glazed, about ½ hour. Serve at room temperature, or refrigerate, covered, for up to 4 days.

Spicy Plum Chutney
ALOO BOOKHARA CHATNI

This sweet plum chutney, laced with crystallized ginger and fennel seeds, is nose-tinglingly hot and spicy.

Preparation and cooking time (after assembling ingredients): about 45 minutes
Makes: about 1⅔ cups (400 ml)

3 tablespoons (45 ml) *ghee* or a mixture of butter and corn oil
½ teaspoon (2 ml) fennel seeds
¼ teaspoon (1 ml) *kalonji*
½ teaspoon (2 ml) black mustard seeds
2 hot green chilies, sliced very thin (or as desired)
1½ pounds (685 g) Italian plums, pitted and quartered
½ cup (70 g) raisins, preferably muscat
1½ cups (315 g) sugar or equivalent sweetener
¼ teaspoon (1 ml) salt
¼ cup (40 g) coarsely chopped toasted walnuts
¼ cup (25 g) fresh or dried ribbon coconut
2 tablespoons (30 ml) minced crystallized or stem ginger

1. Place the *ghee* or butter-oil mixture in a 3-quart/liter saucepan over moderately low heat. When it is hot but not smoking, add the fennel seeds, *kalonji*, black mustard seeds and chilies, and fry until the mustard seeds pop and turn gray or the butter froths. Stir in the plums, raisins, sugar and salt and simmer until thick, about 30–40 minutes.

2. Remove the pan from the heat and stir in the remaining ingredients. Serve at room temperature or refrigerate, well covered, for 2–3 days.

Currant and Date Chutney
KISHMISH KHAJUR CHATNI

Like gooseberries and cranberries, fresh currants are highly acidic, and therefore quite tart and sour. Though they can be eaten raw, most people prefer them transformed into sugar-sweetened cooked jams, chutneys, fruit syrups or desserts. Red and white currants are less well known than black—famous in England as a vitamin C–rich, delicious beverage called Ribena. I prefer red currants for this chutney.

Preparation and cooking time: about 30 minutes
Makes: about 2¼ cups (530 ml)

2 cups (245 g) fresh red currants,
   washed and stemmed
½ cup (120 g) *jaggery* or maple sugar
¾ cup (120 g) chopped soft dates
¼ cup (40 g) monukka or muscat raisins
¼ cup (60 ml) white grape juice
¼ teaspoon (1 ml) cayenne pepper
¼ teaspoon (1 ml) each ginger,
   nutmeg, cloves and cinnamon
½ teaspoon (2 ml) salt

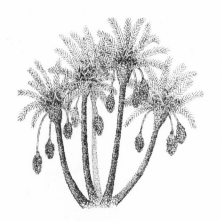

Combine all of the ingredients in a 3-quart/liter heavy stainless steel or enamel saucepan, place over moderate heat, and, stirring occasionally, bring to a gentle boil. Reduce the heat to moderately low and cook for about 20 minutes or until the liquid is thick. (It should reach 215°F/101°C on a thermometer.) Serve at room temperature, or refrigerate, covered, for 3–4 days.

For information about unfamiliar ingredients or techniques, see A-to-Z

Apricot Chutney with Currants
KHUMANI CHATNI

This is an outstanding chutney, especially when the apricots are tree-ripened, sweet and fragrant. For those of us resorting to fruits sold at supermarkets or corner grocers, look for barely ripened fruit with a fragrant smell. If they are absolutely without smell, use dried apricots which require an overnight soaking in lime juice and water and a slight increase in cooking time. American dried apricots little resemble their shriveled Indian counterpart, *aloo bookhara*, but they are almost as tasty as the fresh fruit.

Preparation and cooking time for fresh apricots: 30 minutes
Preparation, soaking and cooking time for dried apricots: overnight
Makes: 1½ cups (360 ml)

½ pound (230 g) dried apricot halves,
    quartered and soaked overnight in 3
    tablespoons (45 ml) lime juice and
    2 cups (480 ml) hot water; or
2 pounds (1 kg) fresh apricots, seeded
    and sliced, plus 3 tablespoons (45 ml)
    lime juice and ½ cup (120 ml) water
2 tablespoons (30 ml) *ghee* or butter
3-inch (7.5 cm) piece of cinnamon stick
½ teaspoon (1 ml) *kalonji* or black sesame seeds
½ tablespoon (7 ml) scraped fresh ginger root, minced
⅔ cup (85 g) dark raisins or currants
½ cup (75 g) maple sugar or brown sugar, packed
¼ teaspoon (1 ml) salt
⅛–¼ teaspoon (0.5–1 ml) cayenne pepper

    1. If you are using dried apricots, drain the soaked fruit in a strainer and collect the liquid.
    2. Heat the *ghee* or butter over moderate heat in a 3-quart/liter stainless steel or enamel saucepan. When it melts, add the cinnamon, *kalonji* or black sesame seeds and ginger, and fry for about ½ minute. Stir in the remaining ingredients, raise the heat slightly, and bring to a boil. Reduce the heat to moderately low and simmer, stirring now and then, especially in the last 10 minutes, until the chutney is thick and glazed, about 30 minutes for fresh apricots and 45 minutes for dried. Serve at room temperature, or refrigerate, covered, for 2–3 days.

Sauces
and
Relishes

Until recently, many Americans regarded "curry sauce" as little more than a béchamel, velouté or Mornay sauce flavored and hued with curry powder. Going for a menu with international flair, my mother might have served this over converted white rice with *sambal* toppings of raisin, peanut, and shredded coconut. Still others equated "curry" with Indian restaurant fare: assertive, almost undecipherable brown sauces coating yesterday's vegetables. The explanation for this dates back to the colonial period, when servant-cooks of expatriate merchants would try to recreate some of the flavors and colors of India's cuisines back in their English kitchens, but without a sound knowledge of seasoning techniques. Often they resorted to a sprinkle of the turmeric-colored powder, used occasionally in South India, called *kari podi*—now Anglicized to "curry powder." Similarily, *karhi*—a light, delicate yogurt sauce barely thickened with chickpea flour—became a medium white sauce with curry powder.

The Vedic approach to saucery is quite a different matter, however, similar to the Asian and lighter variations of classic sauces popular today, low-calorie and given body through reduction instead of thickeners. More often than not, the Vedic approach produces sauces that are flavor-enriched and thickened as they cook into a dish, becoming inseparable from it. Sauce-like accompaniments generally fall into the catagory of chutneys, and are meant to be served with or on other dishes. There are always exceptions to the rule, dishes that can be served on their own or coupled with sauce-like *kofta* with *sas* or *karhi* sauce with vegetables.

The recipes that follow are designed to show some of the variety in flavors, colors and textures possible in sauces. They can be used in a number of ways to turn the ordinary into the extraordinary.

Sour Cream Parsley Sauce
KHATTE MALAI SAS

While most Indians prefer deep-fried pastries served with zesty chutneys or dipping sauces, Americans have a penchant for creamy, blander sauces. While this sauce is not traditional fare in a Calcutta or Bombay residence, I have known many expatriates who love it. More of a dip than sauce, it goes well with numerous dishes, from *pakoras* and *dal badas* to fresh vegetable crudités. With a tartar sauce consistency, it can be made from any number of low-fat milk products with equally delicious results: plain kefir or yogurt, or cottage cheese or *panir* cheese processed with enough buttermilk to reach a sour cream consistency.

The character of the sauce-dip depends largely on asafetida, and to obtain the best results, use only powdered yellow asafetida. Virtually all Indian grocery stores sell Cobra brand or a reasonable facimile. Other forms of strong-smelling asafetida means overpowering flavor, so take note.

Preparation time (after assembling ingredients): 5 minutes
Resting time: at least 10 minutes
Makes: 1 cup (240 ml)

¼ cup (60 ml) minced fresh parsley, coriander, dill or chervil
1 cup (240 ml) sour cream or as above
1 tablespoon (15 ml) sesame, almond or cashew butter
¼ teaspoon (1 ml) salt
¼ teaspoon (1 ml) coarsely ground pepper
⅓ teaspoon (1.5 ml) yellow asafetida powder (*hing*)*

*This amount applies only to yellow Cobra brand. Reduce any other asafetida by three-fourths.

Combine all of the ingredients in a bowl, stir well, and set aside for at least 10 minutes (or up to several hours) to allow the flavors to mingle. To make a salad dressing, add up to one-third of the total volume of peeled and seeded cucumbers, finely shredded and pressed dry, to the food processor and thin further to the desired consistency. Either dip or dressing can be made up to 8 hours before use; keep it refrigerated and well sealed.

Fresh Tomato Sauce
TAZA TAMATAR SAS

Spectacular fresh tomato sauce depends on the quality and type of tomatoes used, and many feel nothing equals locally grown, garden-ripened plum tomatoes. These pear-shaped fruits should still be firm to the touch, with an intense red color. The pulpy plum tomatoes are less watery than salad varieties and are ideal for sauces. When you need a terrific sauce in the dead of winter, and your freezer's summer bounty is depleted, try a newly arrived alternative—strained plum tomato pulp. Available in supermarkets, under brand names like Bertolli and Hunt's, it is packaged in fruit-juice-sized cartons. The pulp is velvety smooth and delicate, and in most cases preferable to freshly made pulp from supermarket salad tomatoes. This all-purpose light sauce goes well with almost any type of cuisine and is especially delicious with fried savories.

For information about unfamiliar ingredients or techniques, see A-to-Z

Preparation time (after assembling ingredients): 15 minutes
Cooking time: 15 minutes
Makes: about 2 cups (480 ml)

8–10 medium-sized plum tomatoes (about 2 pounds/1 kg)
3 tablespoons (45 ml) *ghee* or a mixture
    of olive oil and unsalted butter
1-inch (2.5 cm) piece of peeled fresh
    ginger root, cut into 4 slices
½ teaspoon (2 ml) yellow asafetida powder (*hing*)*
8–10 curry leaves, preferably fresh
1 teaspoon (5 ml) salt
½ teaspoon (2 ml) brown sugar or *jaggery*
½ teaspoon (2 ml) paprika or ¼
    teaspoon (1 ml) cayenne pepper

*This amount applies only to yellow Cobra Brand. Reduce any other asafetida by three-fourths.

1. To peel the tomatoes, dip them in boiling water for 10–30 seconds, then plunge into cold water. Ease off the skins. Halve the tomatoes and, using a small paring knife, core them and gently squeeze out the seeds. Cut the tomatoes into chunks, place them in a blender or a food processor fitted with the metal blade, cover, and process until smooth.

2. Place the *ghee* or oil-butter mixture in a heavy saucepan over moderate heat. When it is hot but not smoking, add the ginger and let it sizzle for about 30 seconds. Drop in the asafetida and curry leaves, and in seconds, carefully stir in the tomato pulp (keep a lid nearby to minimize spattering). Add the remaining ingredients and bring to a gentle boil. Reduce the heat slightly, then simmer for 5–10 minutes or until the sauce has thickened slightly. Remove the ginger slices before serving.

Velvet Tomato Catsup

MEETHA TAMATAR SAS

India's equivalent to tomato catsup would be a tie between zesty tamarind chutney and fresh coriander chutney—both condiments traditionally served with fried pastries, fritters and cutlets. A notable exception worth including here is this catsup-like relish made by the chefs in Jaipur's famous Radha Govinda Temple. Serve it as you might any tomato catsup; it is especially delicious with fried *dal badas* and stuffed pastries.

Preparation and cooking time: 25 minutes
Makes: about 1⅔ cups (400 ml)

1 teaspoon (5 ml) ground cumin
½ tablespoon (7 ml) ground coriander
1 teaspoon (5 ml) *garam masala*
⅛ teaspoon (0.5 ml) each ground nutmeg, ginger and cloves
¼ teaspoon (1 ml) cayenne pepper or paprika
½ teaspoon (2 ml) yellow asafetida powder (*hing*)*
2 tablespoons (30 ml) brown sugar or *jaggery*
3 tablespoons (45 ml) water
1½ tablespoons (22 ml) *ghee* or vegetable oil
½ cassia or bay leaf
¾ cup (180 ml) tomato paste and 1 cup (240 ml) water, or
    1¾ cups (420 ml) seeded tomato pulp or purée, or
    2⅔ cups (630 ml) peeled, seeded, diced tomatoes
½ teaspoon (2 ml) salt

*This amount applies only to yellow Cobra brand. Reduce any other asafetida by three-fourths.

Combine the ground spices, sweetener and water in a bowl and whisk well. Heat the *ghee* or oil in a 2-quart/liter saucepan over moderate heat. Before it is hot, add the cassia or bay leaf and wet spice mixture, and, stirring constantly, fry for about 1 minute. Carefully add the selected tomato product and salt. Bring the sauce to a boil, reduce the heat to low and simmer for about 20 minutes or until thickened to a catsup consistency. Serve at room temperature, or bottle, cover, and refrigerate for up to 2 days.

Hot Green Chili Sauce
HARI MIRCH SAS

In rural West Bengal, chili sauce is often a fiery combination of green tomatoes, hot chilies and fresh coriander. The distinctive acid flavor in green tomatoes is further heightened by splashes of lime juice—a delightful flavor contrast to roasted chilies. Despite the obvious heat in fresh chilies, aficionados relish subtle flavor variations as well. For newcomers, I suggest starting out with easy-to-handle, medium-hot poblano chilies, available at supermarkets. As an alternative to green tomatoes, you can use lime-sized tomatillos, available at Cuban and Mexican greengrocers. This low-calorie sauce goes well with almost any savory, from chips to stuffed pastries. It is traditionally married with *Shredded Radish and Mung Dal Patties*, a combination I first tasted in West Bengal's idyllic village of Bir Nagar.

Preparation and cooking time: about 30 miinutes
Makes: about 2 cups (480 ml)

For information about unfamiliar ingredients or techniques, see A-to-Z

4 poblano chilies, (5–7 inches/12–17 cm long) or
    3–5 hot green serrano or jalapeño chilies or
    one 4-ounce (115 g) can of green chili peppers
3 medium-sized green tomatoes or 6–8 tomatillos, husked
½ tablespoon (7 ml) scraped fresh ginger root, chopped
¼ cup (60 ml) trimmed fresh coriander, lightly packed
½–1 teaspoon (2–5 ml) salt
1 tablespoon (15 ml) *ghee* or vegetable oil
½ teaspoon (2 ml) cumin seeds
¼ teaspoon (1 ml) yellow asafetida powder (*hing*)*
¼ teaspoon (1 ml) freshly ground black pepper
1 teaspoon (5 ml) fresh lime juice

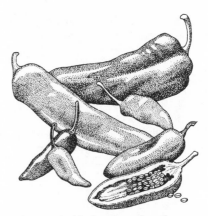

*This amount applies only to yellow Cobra brand. Reduce any other asafetida by three-fourths.

    1. To prepare poblano chilies, place them on a baking sheet 3–4 inches (7.5–10 cm) from a broiler. Turn them occasionally with a pair of tongs and broil until they are blistered on all sides. Transfer to a paper bag, close it up, and let them steam for 10 minutes. Peel off the loosened skin with your fingers or a small knife. Scoop out the seeds and coarsely chop the chilies. If you are using serrano or jalapeño chilies, coarsely chop them. If you are using canned chilies, wash them, seed, and then, coarsely chop.

    2. Put the tomatoes or tomatillos in a heavy saucepan and cover with cold water. Place the pan over moderately high heat and bring the water to a boil. Remove the pan from the heat and set aside for 2 minutes. Drain and cool them, then cut them into chunks.

    3. Combine the chilies, tomatoes or tomatillos, ginger, coriander and salt in a blender or a food processor fitted with the metal blade. Pulse the machine on and off until the ingredients are finely chopped.

    4. Heat the *ghee* or oil in a saucepan over moderately low heat. When it is hot but not smoking, add the cumin seeds and fry until they darken a few shades. Sprinkle in the asafetida and within a few seconds, carefully stir in the tomato-chili mixture. Cook until pulpy, about 10 minutes. Transfer to a serving container and sprinkle with pepper and lime juice. Serve at room temperature, or refrigerate, well covered, for up to 2 days.

Chickpea, Almond, Sesame Sauce
KABLI CHANA TIL SAS

    Recipe testers coined this dish "The Endless Miracle" because, simply by varying the consistency, your use of it is limited only by your creativity. As is, it serves as an all-temperature sauce. I have also used it as a flavor coating for steamed vegetables, a flatbread or sandwich spread, a party dip and a salad dressing. Strongly influenced by Middle Eastern hummous, the sauce is healthful and a source of complete protein when served with another grain like rice or a bread. It is equally delicious made with cashews.

Preparation time (after assembling ingredients): 10 minutes
Makes: about 2 cups (480 ml)

¼ cup (40 g) sesame seeds
1 teaspoon (5 ml) cumin seeds
½ teaspoon (2 ml) black mustard seeds
¼ cup (40 g) chopped almonds
2 cups (480 ml) cooked chickpeas, drained
3 tablespoons (45 ml) fresh lemon or lime juice
¼ teaspoon (1 ml) cayenne pepper or paprika
½ teaspoon (2 ml) yellow asafetida powder (*hing*)*
1 teaspoon (5 ml) salt
about ¼ cup (60 ml) water or stock
3 tablespoons (45 ml) olive or sesame oil

*This amount applies only to yellow Cobra brand. Reduce any other asafetida by three-fourths.

1. Combine the sesame seeds, cumin seeds, black mustard seeds and almonds in a large heavy frying pan and place over moderately low heat. Slowly dry-roast until the sesame seeds darken one or two shades.
2. Fit a food processor with the metal blade. Add the toasted seeds, cover, and pulse on and off for about ½ minute or until coarsely powdered. Add the remaining ingredients and process until creamy smooth, pausing now and then to scrape the ingredients toward the blades with a spatula. (You can vary the texture and flavor by adding more or less liquid; also, try using buttermilk, yogurt or sour cream, either warmed or at room temperature.) If you want a sandwich spread, leave the consistency spreadable; for a salad dressing, thin it down. Serve warm or at room temperature. It can be kept for up to 2 days, covered and refrigerated.

Creamy Almond Sauce with Horseradish
BADAAM MALAI SAS

The horseradish tree, *Moringa oleifera*, which grows wild in the forests of the Himalayan foot-hills, is also cultivated in India for its edible pods, leaves and roots. The long pods are called drumsticks, and though it is mostly ribs and skin, the cooked pulp is every bit as delicious as artichoke bottoms. The small, pungent leaves and gnarled roots are used primarily in eastern regional cuisines, though I have seen them used ocasionally in Kashmiri and Assamese dishes. With a pungency similar to that of the root of another hardy plant called horseradish (*Armoracia rusticana*, the nose-tingling root used in European condiments for centuries), grated fresh horserad-ish adds life to dips and sauces. In the last few years, more and more greengrocers are stocking fresh roots. If you cannot find them, use ground dried horseradish sold near the spice shelves at many supermarkets. Avoid prepared bottled sauces made with vinegar. This sauce goes well with *Crunchy Chana Dal Patties with Coconut and Sesame Seeds* or *Crunchy Urad Dal Patties with Black Pepper*.

For information about unfamiliar ingredients or techniques, see A-to-Z

Preparation and cooking time (after assembling ingredients): 20 minutes
Makes: about 2¼ cups (530 ml)

1 tablespoon (15 ml) chickpea flour or
    unbleached white flour
¼ teaspoon (1 ml) each ground cardamom,
    nutmeg and white pepper
½ teaspoon (2 ml) ground coriander
a pinch of both cayenne pepper and turmeric
2 tablespoons (30 ml) finely chopped fresh coriander
2 tablespoons (30 ml) *ghee* or unsalted butter
⅔ cup (60 g) ground almonds
2 cups (480 ml) half-and-half
½ teaspoon (2 ml) lemon juice
½ teaspoon (2 ml) salt
2 tablespoons (30 ml) grated peeled fresh horseradish
    or ½ tablespoon (7 ml) ground dried horseradish
½ teaspoon (2 ml) dry-roasted coarsely
    crushed cumin seeds for garnishing

1. Combine the flour, ground spices and fresh coriander in a dish. Melt the *ghee* or butter in a heavy-bottomed 3-quart/liter saucepan over moderately low heat. Add the flour mixture and cook, stirring, for 2–3 minutes.

2. Stir in the nuts and half-and-half and slowly bring to a boil, stirring constantly. Reduce the heat slightly and simmer, stirring frequently, until the sauce has thickened enough to coat a spoon, about 12–15 minutes.

3. Remove the pan from the heat and stir in the lemon juice, salt and horseradish. Transfer to a serving dish, or spoon it over another dish—such as *dal* patties—and garnish with the crushed cumin seeds.

Fragrant Tomato and Yogurt Gravy
TAMATAR DAHI SAS

I first had this sauce at the Delhi residence of Kenneth Keating, America's ambassador to India in the early 1970s. It was served at dinner with *Cauliflower Koftas*, though it goes equally well with *Radish Kofta Patties*. This versatile sauce can be served with a number of dishes, from grilled eggplant to steamed rice.

Preparation and cooking time (after assembling ingredients): about 45 minutes
Makes: 2½–3 cups (600–710 ml)

2 tablespoons (30 ml) sesame or sunflower seeds
¼ cup (40 g) chopped blanched almonds
2 tablespoons (30 ml) fresh or dried grated coconut
1–2 hot jalapeño chilies, seeded and chopped
½-inch (1.5 cm) piece of peeled fresh ginger root, chopped
⅔ cup (160 ml) water
1½ tablespoons (22 ml) ground coriander
½ tablespoon (7 ml) ground cumin
1 teaspoon (5 ml) turmeric
1 tablespoon (15 ml) *jaggery* or brown sugar
4 tablespoons (60 ml) *ghee* or 2 tablespoons (30 ml)
   each sunflower oil and unsalted butter
1 teaspoon (5 ml) black mustard seeds
6 curry leaves, preferably fresh
10 medium-sized plum tomatoes (about 1½ pounds/685 g),
   peeled, seeded and quartered
⅔ cup (160 ml) plain yogurt or crème fraîche
½ tablespoon (7 ml) salt
¼ cup (60 ml) chopped fresh coriander
about 1¼ cups (300 ml) water

1. Combine the sesame or sunflower seeds, almonds and coconut in a blender or a food processor fitted with the metal blade. Cover and pulse the machine on and off until the ingredients are coarsely powdered. Add the chilies, ginger, water, ground coriander, cumin, turmeric and sweetener. Cover and process until smooth and thoroughly blended.

2. Heat the *ghee* or 2 tablespoons (30 ml) oil in a heavy-bottomed, large sauté pan over moderate heat. When it is hot but not smoking, add the black mustard seeds and fry until they begin to sputter, pop and turn gray. Toss in the curry leaves, and in a few seconds carefully add the spice *masala* and the butter, if you are using it. (The *masala* tends to spatter and bubble when the oil is hot; keep a spatter screen handy.) Fry the *masala* until it separates from the oil, 2–3 minutes. Stir in the tomatoes, yogurt or crème fraîche, salt and half of the fresh coriander. Reduce the heat to moderately low and simmer for 12–15 minutes or until the sauce has slightly thickened.

3. Pour in the water and remaining coriander and continue to simmer for 10 minutes. If you serve this sauce with *koftas*, allow them to simmer in the sauce for a few minutes before serving, or keep them warm in the sauce in a gratin-type serving dish in a preheated 250°F (120°C) oven for up to 20 minutes.

For information about unfamiliar ingredients or techniques, see A-to-Z

Seasoned Tomato Gravy

MASALA TAMATAR SAS

The quality of this dish comes from the sweetness, freshness and texture of red tomatoes. Many tomatoes cultivated for commercial purposes are machine-picked, still green, and ripened (or at least made to turn red in ethylene chambers) before thousands of miles of transportation. Finally, wrapped in plastic, they sit on shelves awaiting purchase. It is worthwhile searching out local vine-ripened tomatoes. If you can get plum, pear or Italian tomatoes, so much the better. These are almost seedless and excellent for cooking. This recipe was inspired from the Bengali kitchens of Mr. Tarun Kunti Ghosh. The gravy was served with *Cabbage Kofta*, though it is also irresistible with *Zucchini Kofta*.

Preparation and cooking time (after assembling ingredients): about 1 hour
Makes: 2½ cups (600 ml)

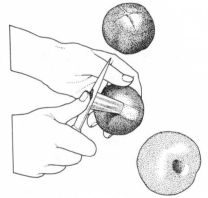

4 or 5 large red tomatoes or 16 Italian plum tomatoes
    or 20 tomatillos (about 2 pounds/1 kg)
3 tablespoons (45 ml) chopped blanched almonds or cashews
¼ teaspoon (1 ml) fennel seeds
1 teaspoon (5 ml) cumin seeds
1–2 hot green chilies, seeded and broken into bits
½-inch (1.5 cm) piece of peeled fresh ginger root, sliced
½ tablespoon (7 ml) *jaggery* or brown sugar
½ teaspoon (2 ml) turmeric
1 tablespoon (15 ml) tomato paste
4 tablespoons (60 ml) *ghee* or olive oil
3 tablespoons (45 ml) chopped fresh coriander or parsley
½ cup (120 ml) vegetable stock or water
1 teaspoon (5 ml) salt

1. Cut a shallow cross in each tomato, then plunge them into boiling water for several seconds. Slip off the skins. Cut each tomato in half and squeeze the seeds and juice into a strainer, pressing out all of the liquid into a bowl. Dice the tomatoes and reserve the tomato juice.

2. Place the nuts, fennel seeds and cumin seeds in a blender or a food processor fitted with the metal blade. Pulse on and off until coarsely powdered. Add the reserved tomato juice, green chilies, ginger, sweetener, turmeric, tomato paste and enough water to yield ⅔ cup (160 ml) of seasoned tomato liquid. Process until smooth.

3. Heat the *ghee* or oil over moderate heat in a heavy, 3-quart/liter saucepan. When it is warm, carefully add the tomato liquid. Partially cover and cook until a seasoned tomato purée separates from the oil. Stir in the diced tomatoes, half of the fresh herbs and the stock. Reduce the heat to low and simmer, partially covered, for about 30 minutes or until gravy like. Add the salt and remaining fresh herbs. This gravy can be kept, covered and refrigerated, for 2–3 days.

Pistachio Cream Sauce with Sesame Seeds
PISTA MALAI SAS

This elegant sauce is given *du corps* or body through reduction—the slow evaporation of seasoned cream. Though pistachios or almonds are traditional, walnuts or pecans may better complement the flavors in accompanying dishes. The desired texture is attained by the length of cooking, and, unlike sauces thickened with a roux, the flavors are clear and delicate. This sauce is wonderful with any type of *kofta* or steamed green vegetable. Try it with *Cabbage Kofta* or *Soft 'n' Savory Chickpea Kofta*.

Preparation and cooking time (after assembling ingredients): about 20 minutes
Makes: 2½ cups (600 ml)

⅓ cup (80 ml) *ghee* or unsalted butter
1 teaspoon (5 ml) black mustard seeds
½ tablespoon (7 ml) sesame seeds
1 teaspoon (5 ml) hot green chilies, seeded and minced
1 cup (125 g) blanched raw pistachios, toasted and
    powdered in a coffee mill or food processor
2 cups (480 ml) heavy cream
¼ teaspoon (1 ml) turmeric
1 teaspoon (5 ml) ground coriander
½–1 teaspoon (2–5 ml) salt
¼ teaspoon (1 ml) ground white pepper
2 tablespoons (15 ml) minced fresh coriander or basil
paprika

1 Melt the *ghee* or butter in a heavy 3-quart/liter saucepan over moderately low heat. When it is hot, drop in the black mustard seeds and fry until they begin to pop. Add the sesame seeds and green chilies, and, stirring often, cook until the sesame seeds darken a few shades.

2. Add the nuts, cream, turmeric and ground coriander. Raise the heat and, stirring constantly, bring to a boil. Reduce the heat to low and simmer, stirring frequently, until the sauce is thick enough to coat a spoon, about 15 minutes. (Do not try to rush the reduction which causes the milk sugar to sweeten the sauce.) Stir in the salt, pepper and fresh herbs. Serve with or over *kofta*, garnished with a sprinkle of paprika.

Sweet 'n' Sour Tamarind Sauce
MEETHA KHATTE IMLI SAS

Every North Indian has several favorite variations of tamarind sauce. This one is a very popular accompaniment for fried savories, often served with North Indian *Seasoned Potato Samosa* or *Feather-Soft Urad Dal Doughnuts with Seasoned Yogurt*.

For information about unfamiliar ingredients or techniques, see A-to-Z

Preparation and resting time (after assembling ingredients): at least 6 hours
Makes: about 1½ cups (360 ml)

walnut-sized (50 g) ball of seeded tamarind pulp
1–2 hot ancho chilies, seeded and broken into bits
1¼ cups (300 ml) boiling water
1 tablespoon (15 ml) butter or almond oil
½ cup (75 g) monukka raisins or currants
¼ cup (35 g) chopped pitted dates
½-inch (1.5 cm) piece of peeled fresh ginger root, sliced
1 teaspoon (5 ml) *garam masala*
½ teaspoon (2 ml) *chat masala*, if available
2 teaspoons (10 ml) salt

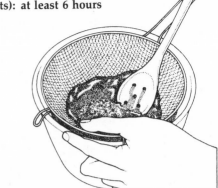

1. Place the tamarind pulp and hot chilies in a bowl and add the boiling water. Set aside for ½ hour. Meanwhile, place a small pan over moderate heat and warm the butter or oil. Add the raisins or currants and fry until they are roasted, turning a few shades lighter and puffing. Remove the pan from the heat and add the remaining ingredients. Mash the softened tamarind with the back of a spoon or with your fingers to release a pulpy sauce. Pour it through a sieve resting over a bowl. Press out as much sauce as you can and discard the fibers and chili bits.

2. Combine the tamarind sauce and the fried raisin mixture in a blender or a food processor fitted with the metal blade. Process until smooth. Transfer to a bowl and set aside to let the flavors mingle for 5–6 hours. This sauce keeps well, sealed and refrigerated, for 4–5 days.

PICKLES

The village of Vrindavan, about 90 km from Delhi, is the birthplace of Lord Krishna and a pilgrimage site of great spiritual significance for Vaishnavas. Srila Prabhupada lived there as a resident of the Radha-Damodar Temple for several years in the 1960s, and I accompanied him back there in 1971. One morning, while I was building coal fires for the noonday cooking, he called from his veranda and pointed out the activities of a group of Rajasthani pilgrims. Four women had set up a makeshift kitchen in an open field nearby and were busily engaged in rolling bread balls. Their children sat perched above them in a *neem* tree, quietly watching the goings on, contentedly sucking on little pieces of pickle. Observing them, Srila Prabhupada asked, "Do you know what *aam achar* is? It is mango pickle. When one is traveling, he can always take some *pooris* and *achar*."

"Formerly," he continued, "when people used to travel by bullock cart, they would stop in a shady place, collect some wood and *gobar* (dried cow patties), make a small fire and cook simple *dal* soup. While the *dal* was cooking, they would mix some flour, *ghee* and water into a soft dough, roll it into balls and place them on dying embers to cook. Next, they would flavor the *dal* with spices fried in *ghee*. Finally, they would remove the cooked bread balls, called *baati*, from the embers, dip them in warmed *ghee* and toss them into the *dal*. This was their simple noon meal: *pooris* and *achar*, which they brought from home, and hot *dal baati*. Rich or poor was no consideration in the life of the village.''

Prabhupada then inquired if I could prepare a meal as the village women did, starting from scratch in an open field. He said that an expert cook was one who could cook well under any circumstances, be it in a field or a marble kitchen. This experience inspired me to delve into outdoor cooking—starting from scratch in an open field.

Many serious cooks will agree that certain dishes prepared on electric or gas stoves cannot compare with the same dishes prepared in clay pots over open heat. Village equipment may be unsophisticated, but village cooks are masters of their craft, and I am acquainted with several Bombay residents who make yearly sojourns to their village birthplace in Rajasthan just to feast on homemade pickles and outdoor-cooked *dal batti*.

In some regions, a new bride is requested to show her cooking skills to her in-laws by presenting them with pickles. She might serve four kinds with her best flatbreads: salty, fiery hot, sour and hot, and sweet and hot. Taking advantage of India's intense heat, cooks leave pickles in the summer sun to mature. Sunlight is not only antiseptic and helps to speed up the pickling reaction, it also helps to keep fermentation in check. During the first three or four weeks, the jars are brought in every night and set out the next morning. Many pickles are ready to serve two or three weeks after they are made; some take six months to mature but keep well for several years. I have tasted lemon pickle purported to be eleven years old!

The two most popular kinds of pickles are lemon and green mango. Also well liked are such varieties as carrot, gooseberry, hot chili, fresh ginger root, white radish and turnip—virtually any fruit or vegetable that is without a mushy texture. Whatever you prefer, obtain garden-fresh, high-quality produce, a shade underripe and free from blemishes and soft or decayed spots. The lemons or limes should be smallish in size, with smooth, thin skins and plenty of juice. Since the type of sour, small green mango required for mango pickle is available only in tropical Florida, I have concentrated on pickles made easily from local produce.

Pickles are preserved in sufficient oil, salt or lemon juice to ensure that they keep well. Mustard oil is the first choice, not only for flavor, but because pickles made with it seem to keep miraculously. As a second choice, I suggest peanut or sesame oil.

The recipes that follow have been put together with the Western palate in mind. Consequently, while sharp and exhilarating, even the chili pickle is mild by some standards. The ingredients fill a pint (500 ml) jar to the lid, yet when mature the yield will be considerably less: 1–1½ cups (240–360 ml) on the average. This should enable you to sample the different types and find your personal favorites.

For information about unfamiliar ingredients or techniques, see A-to-Z

Sour Lemon or Lime Pickle
NIMBU ACHAR

In India, limes are small (no more than 1½ inches/4 cm in diameter) and very sour. This is an example of lemon pickle at its simplest. Use Key limes if they are available, or small lemons or limes. The citrus must be washed and thoroughly dried, in the sun if possible. Any moisture will cause the pickle to spoil. You may serve it after a month, although it is better after three months, and better still after six.

Makes: enough to fill a pint (500 ml) jar

4 or 5 small smooth skinned lemons or limes (about 12 ounces/340 g)
3 tablespoons (45 ml) sea salt
½ cup (120 ml) sesame or peanut oil

1. Wash and thoroughly dry the lemons or limes. Set them in the sun or air-dry in a warm oven for 5 minutes. Slice each one lengthwise into 8 wedges and save any juice. Squeeze 2 wedges of citrus slightly and mix with the salt and reserved juice.
2. Heat the oil over low heat in a large non-metallic pan. Carefully add the citrus and stir for about 1 minute. Remove the pan from the heat and stir in the salt–lemon juice mixture. Transfer to a sterilized pint (500 ml) jar and cool to room temperature. Cover with a non-metallic lid.
3. Set in the sun every day for 3 weeks, bringing the jar inside every night. Give the jar a shake 2 or 3 times a day. After the third week, you do not have to set the pickle in the sun, but continue to shake the jar daily for another week before use.

Sweet Lemon or Lime Pickle
MEETHA NIMBU ACHAR

Nearly every family in India has its own recipe for this syrupy, thick pickle. If you can find it, *jaggery* or *gur* lends an authentic flavor to the dish, but I find maple sugar equally delicious. Though maple sugar is expensive, you need to make pickles only once or twice a year. This selection needs to mature a good two months before use but is still delicious two years later.

Makes: enough to fill a pint (500 ml) jar

4 or 5 small smooth-skinned lemons or limes (about 12 ounces/340 g)
2 tablespoons (30 ml) sea salt
½ tablespoon (7 ml) crushed fennel seeds
½ tablespoon (7 ml) crushed cumin seeds
½ teaspoon (2 ml) cracked black pepper
1 cup (155 g) shredded *jaggery* or (145 g) maple sugar
⅓ cup (80 ml) fresh lemon or lime juice

1. Wash and thoroughly dry the lemons or limes. Set them in the sun or air-dry in a warm oven for 5 minutes. Slice each one lengthwise into 8 pieces, reserving any juice. Combine the salt, fennel seeds, cumin seeds and black pepper in a small bowl and mix well.

2. Arrange a layer of citrus, cut side up, in a pint (500 ml) jar or crock. Sprinkle with the salt-spice mixture. Alternate the two ingredients until the jar is full.

3. Combine the sweetener with the citrus juice in a small saucepan. Bring to a boil over high heat, stirring constantly, then reduce the heat to low and simmer for 2–3 minutes. Cool to lukewarm then pour over the citrus in the jar. Cool to room temperature and cover with a non-metallic lid.

4. Set in the sun every day for 5 weeks; bring the jar inside every night. Give the jar a shake two or three times a day. After this time, you do not need to set the pickle in the sun, but continue to shake the jar for another 1–2 weeks before use (it is worth the wait).

Whole Lemon or Lime Pickle
MASALA BHARA NIMBU ACHAR

This is a pungent, hot pickle. I had this variation in Madras, though it could easily have been Mayapur or Surat, as it is popular throughout all the regions of India. You can use the pickle after 5 weeks, but it is better after 10 weeks.

Makes: enough to fill a pint (500 ml) jar

4 or 5 small Key limes or lemons
    (about 12 ounces/340 g)
½ teaspoon (2 ml) fenugreek seeds
1 teaspoon (5 ml) black mustard seeds
scant ½ teaspoon (2 ml) cayenne pepper
¼ teaspoon (1 ml) yellow asafetida powder (*hing*)*
1½ tablespoons (22 ml) sea salt
4 tablespoons (60 ml) lemon or lime juice
⅓ cup (80 ml) mustard or sesame oil

*This amount applies only to Cobra brand. Reduce any other asafetida by three-fourths.

1. Wash and thoroughly dry the limes or lemons. Set them in the sun or air-dry in a warm oven for 5 minutes. Meanwhile, dry-roast the fenugreek seeds and black mustard seeds in a heavy pan over low heat. When the fenugreek seeds turn reddish-brown, remove the seeds and coarsely powder with a mortar and pestle or in a coffee mill. Combine them with the cayenne, asafetida and salt in a small bowl and mix well.

2. Quarter the citrus from the top to within ¼ inch (6 mm) of the bottom. The sections should remain attached to the bottom. Using a small knife, spread a little of the spice mixture on the surface of each cut. Squeeze the citrus closed and place them, cut side up, in a sterilized jar or crock. Pour the lemon or lime juice over the stuffed citrus. Drape a piece of cheesecloth over the top and secure it with a rubber band. Set the jar in sunshine for four days, bringing it in every night.

3. On the fifth day, place the oil in a small pan over moderate heat; bring the mustard oil to the smoking point for 5 seconds (the sesame oil only requires to be heated). Cool slightly, then pour the oil over the lemons. When the oil has cooled to room temperature, cap the jar with a non-metallic lid, shake the jar, then set it in the sun daily for 4 weeks, bringing it in every night. Give the jar a shake two or three times daily. The pickle may be used after 5 weeks, though it is better after 10 weeks.

Pickled Green Chilies
SADA HAR MIRCH ACHAR

Srila Prabhupada was fond of these pickles and once asked me if I knew how to make them. At the time I had never even ventured to taste a chili pickle, let alone make one, so he directed me to a shop in old Delhi to purchase them. I made several inquiries from the proprietor, and though he was initially hesitant, he reluctantly offered the following recipe—purported to be a secret family recipe passed on for generations. These pickles are meant to be fiery hot, a challenge that the Cajun aficionados should welcome. I have made them with easy-to-handle jalapeño chilies; if you use serrano chilies, they will be hotter.

Makes: enough to fill a pint (500 ml) jar

1¾ cups hot green jalapeño chilies,
    packed (about 7 ounces/200 g)*
1 tablespoon (15 ml) salt
¼ cup (60 ml) mustard or sesame oil
1-inch (2.5 cm) scraped fresh ginger root, minced
2 tablespoons (30 ml) fresh lemon juice

If you have sensitive skin or are not used to handling green chilies, take the precaution of wearing thin rubber gloves. The volatile oils in chilies will definitely burn your face and eyes if you inadvertantly touch them. Alternately, rub a film of oil on your hands before handling the chilies and be sure to wash your hands with soap and water when you are finished.

1. Wash the chilies and spread them out on a tray lined with paper towels. Dry in the sun or air-dry in a warm oven for 15 minutes. Stem the chilies, slice them ¼ inch (6 mm) thick, and place in a bowl. Sprinkle with salt and toss well.

2. Heat the mustard oil in a small saucepan over moderate heat until it reaches the smoking point. (The sesame oil need only be heated.) Remove the pan from the heat and toss in the ginger. Let it sizzle and then cool for 1–2 minutes. Stir in the chilies and lemon juice and mix well. When they have cooled to room temperature, transfer the chilies to a sterilized pint (500 ml) glass jar or crock and seal with a non-metallic lid.

3. Set the jar in the sun every day for a week; bring it back inside every night. Give the jar a shake two or three times a day. This pickle is ready for use after a week, but its heat-giving quality will continue to intensify as the weeks pass.

Spicy Green Chili
HAR MIRCH ACHAR

This second green chili pickle variation is spicy and fiery hot.

Makes: enough to fill a pint (500 ml) jar

1¾ cups (420 ml) hot green jalapeño chilies,
    packed (about 7 ounces)*
1 tablespoon (15 ml) black mustard seeds
1 teaspoon (5 ml) cumin seeds
½ teaspoon (2 ml) fenugreek seeds
⅓ teaspoon (1.5 ml) yellow asafetida powder (*hing*)
1 teaspopon (5 ml) *garam masala*
½ teaspoon (2 ml) tumeric
1 ½ tablespoons (22 ml) sea salt
½ cup (120 ml) mustard oil or sesame oil
2 tablespoons (30 ml) lemon juice

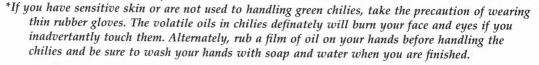

*If you have sensitive skin or are not used to handling green chilies, take the precaution of wearing thin rubber gloves. The volatile oils in chilies definately will burn your face and eyes if you inadvertantly touch them. Alternately, rub a film of oil on your hands before handling the chilies and be sure to wash your hands with soap and water when you are finished.

*This amount applies only to yellow Cobra brand. Reduce any other asafetida by three-fourths.

1. Wash the green chilies and trim off all but ¼ inch (6 mm) of the stems. Spread them out on a tray lined with paper towels and dry in the sun or air-dry in a warm oven for 15 minutes.

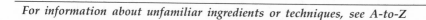

For information about unfamiliar ingredients or techniques, see A-to-Z

2. Meanwhile, combine the black mustard seeds, cumin seeds and fenugreek seeds in a small pan and place over moderately low heat. Dry-roast, stirring often, until the fenugreek seeds turn golden brown. Transfer to a mortar or a coffee mill and powder. Combine the roasted powder with the asafetida, *garam masala*, turmeric and salt, and mix well.

3. With a sharp paring knife, cut a slit lengthwise in each chili from cap to point and spread some of the spice mixture in it. Pack the chilies into a sterilized pint (500 ml) jar.

4. Heat the mustard oil to the smoking point, the sesame oil only until it is hot. Cool for 3–4 minutes, then add the lemon juice and whisk with a fork. Pour this mixture over the chilies and cover tightly with a non-metallic lid.

5. Set in the sun every day for 5 days; bring the jar inside every night. Give the jar a shake two or three times daily. The pickle is ready for use at this time, but its heat-giving quality will continue to intensify as the weeks pass.

Cauliflower Pickle
GOBHI ACHAR

The cauliflower flowerets must be blanched and then dried out before use. This pickle matures quickly (within two weeks) and is pleasantly sour.

Makes: enough to fill a pint (500 ml) jar

3 cups (710 ml) water
8 ounces (230 g) trimmed cauliflower flowerets (½ of a small head), cut
    into pieces 1½ inches (4 cm) long and no more than ½ inch (1.5 cm) thick
1½-inch (4 cm) piece of peeled fresh ginger root, thinly sliced
½ teaspoon (2 ml) cayenne pepper (or as desired)
½ teaspoon (2 ml) turmeric
1 tablespoon (15 ml) dry-roasted cumin seeds
1 teaspoon (5 ml) sea salt
½ cup (120 ml) mustard or sesame oil

1. Boil the water in a 2-quart/liter saucepan. Add the cauliflower and ginger and blanch for 1 minute. Drain, then spread them out on a towel-lined cookie tray and sun-dry or air-dry in a warm oven (about 200°F/95°C) for 1 hour.

2. Mix the cayenne, turmeric, cumin seeds and salt in a mixing bowl. Add the cauliflower and ginger and toss to mix. Transfer to a sterilized pint (500 ml) glass jar or crock.

3. Place the mustard oil in a small saucepan over moderate heat. Just before it reaches the smoking point, remove the pan from the heat. (The sesame oil need only be heated.) Cool the oil for 4 minutes, then pour it over the cauliflower and cover with a non-metallic lid.

4. Set the jar in sunlight for 12–14 days, bringing it indoors every night. Give the jar a shake two or three times daily. Refrigerate after opening.

White Radish Pickle
MOOLI ACHAR

Any type of white radish will make a crunchy pickle, but the snappy flavor of Indian white cooking radish (*mooli*) makes a noticeable difference in the overall character of this pickle. Japanese daikon radish is my second choice.

Makes: enough to fill a pint (500 ml) jar

3 cups (710 ml) water
2 cups (480 ml) white radishes (about 8 ounces/230 g), peeled and diced
1½ tablespoons (22 ml) black mustard seeds, coarsely crushed
½ teaspoon (2 ml) cayenne pepper
2 teaspoons (10 ml) salt
½ cup (120 ml) mustard or sesame oil

1. Boil the water in a 2-quart/liter saucepan. Add the white radishes and blanch for 1 minute. Drain, then spread them out on a towel-lined cookie tray and sun-dry or air-dry in a warm oven (about 200°F/95°C) for 1 hour.

2. Mix the black mustard seeds, cayenne and salt in a mixing bowl. Add the radishes and toss to mix. Transfer to a sterilized pint (500 ml) glass jar or crock.

3. Place the mustard oil in a small saucepan over moderate heat. Just before it reaches its smoking point, remove the pan from the heat. (The sesame oil need only be heated.) Cool the oil for 4 minutes, then pour it into the jar and cover with a non-metallic lid.

4. Set the jar in sunlight for 12–14 days, bringing it indoors every night. Give the jar a shake two or three times daily. Refrigerate after opening.

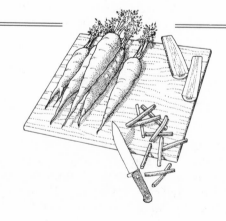

Carrot Pickle
GAJAR ACHAR

You can substitute almost any crunchy vegetable—parsnips, turnips, turnips, kohlrabi or jicama—for the carrots.

Makes: enough to fill a pint (500 ml) jar

For information about unfamiliar ingredients or techniques, see A-to-Z

3 cups (710 ml) water
½ pound (230 g) carrots, scraped
   and cut into sticks 2 inches (5 cm)
   long and ½ inch (1.5 cm) thick
1½ tablespoons (22 ml) black mustard seeds
½ teaspoon (2 ml) cayenne pepper (or as desired)
⅛ teaspoon (0.5 ml) each ground mace,
   cloves and cardamom
2 teaspoons (10 ml) sea salt
¼ cup (40 g) shredded *jaggery*, maple
   or brown sugar
⅓ cup (80 ml) mustard oil or sesame oil

1. Boil the water in a 2-quart/liter saucepan. Add the carrots and blanch for 1 minute. Drain, then spread them out on a towel-lined cookie tray and sun-dry or air-dry in a warm oven (about 200°F/95°C) for 1 hour.

2. Mix the black mustard seeds, cayenne, mace, cloves, cardamom, salt and sweetener in a mixing bowl. Add the carrots and toss to mix. Transfer to a sterilized pint (500 ml) glass jar or crock.

3. Pour the mustard oil into a small saucepan and place it over moderate heat. Just before the oil begins to smoke, remove the pan from the heat. (The sesame oil need only be heated.) Cool the oil for 4 minutes, then pour it into the jar and cover with a non-metallic lid.

4. Set the jar in sunlight for 12–14 days, bringing it indoors every night. Give the jar a shake two or three times daily. Refrigerate after opening.

JAMS AND PRESERVES

Like all Vedic condiments, jams, preserves and butters are spicy and, more often than not, hot. They are made in small quantities, as cooked chutneys are, and are not kept for more than a week or two. If you are in the habit of preserving and canning, and you have an abundance of fruits, by all means process them for long-term storage. Seal them with rubber-edged sealing lids in sterilized wide mouthed canning jars, and complete with a water bath. This allows a taste of September in January.

Select perfect, slightly underripe fruits for maximum flavor and to ensure a good gel. Heavyweight stainless steel or enameled saucepans help to prevent discoloration, scorching and loss of flavor. Follow cooking times carefully; in some cases, the liquid may appear thin in the pan but will thicken as it cools. Making double batches completely changes the balance of natural pectins with sugar and acid, and therefore cooking times cannot just be doubled proportionately.

Spicy Guava Jam
MASALA AMROOD MURABBA

In November 1973, Srila Prabhupada came to Vrindavan for a short stay. The morning before his departure, he requested me to purchase ripe guavas for jam. That afternoon, he came into the kitchen and set up his brass steaming unit. As he began cutting the fruit, he related how this jam was a childhood favorite of his and how his mother frequently brought it along on family outings. Although I noted down the ingredients and procedures, there were no exact measurements, as he used no measuring tools. The end product is a cross between a spicy fruit butter and a jam—thick, hot and sweet.

Preparation and cooking time: 1¼–1½ hours
Makes: about 2 cups (480 ml)

1¼ pounds (570 g) just-ripe guavas
2–3 whole dried red chilies
6–8 whole cloves
1 teaspoon (5 ml) coriander seeds
½ teaspoon (2 ml) cumin seeds
3-inch (7.5 cm) piece of cinnamon stick
½ teaspoon (2 ml) cardamom seeds
¼ teaspoon (1 ml) *kalonji*
2 cups (425 g) sugar
½ tablespoon (7 ml) lime juice

1. Cut the guavas into eighths and place them in a steamer basket over boiling water. Steam for about 45 minutes.

2. Meanwhile, combine the red chilies, cloves, coriander seeds, cumin seeds, cinnamon stick, cardamom seeds and *kalonji* in a heavy skillet and dry-roast over low heat until the cumin seeds darken a few shades. Crush the cinnamon stick with a kitchen mallet, then coarsely grind, along with the roasted spices, with a mortar and pestle or in a spice mill.

3. Transfer the guavas to a heavy 3-quart/liter saucepan and mash to a smooth purée (you can pass it through a food mill instead). Place over low heat, add the sugar, and stir until it is dissolved. Increase the heat, add the lime juice, and, stirring often, cook until thick or until it reaches 218°–221°F (103°–105°C) on a candy thermometer.

4. Remove the pan from the heat, stir in the powdered spices, and cool to room temperature. Transfer to glass jars or crocks and seal well. Store, refrigerated, for up to 2 weeks.

For information about unfamiliar ingredients or techniques, see A-to-Z

Rich Guava Jam

AMROOD MURABBA

Srila Prabhupada taught this second guava jam recipe to Palika Devi in 1977, stressing the importance of adding enough chili powder to produce noticeable heat. It is not too sweet and has distinctive flavor overtones of fennel seeds and ginger.

Preparation and cooking time: 1¼–1½ hours
Makes: about 2 cups (480 ml)

1¼ pounds (570 g) just-ripe guavas
1 cup (210 g) sugar
3 tablespoons (45 ml) *ghee*
1½ tablespoons (22 ml) peeled fresh ginger root, minced
½ tablespoon (7 ml) cumin seeds
½ teaspoon (2 ml) fennel seeds
½–1 teaspoon (2–5 ml) cayenne pepper or chili powder
¼ teaspoon (1 ml) salt (optional)

1. Cut the guavas into eighths and place them in a steamer basket over boiling water. Steam for about 45 minutes.

2. Combine the guavas and sugar in a heavy 3-quart/liter saucepan and mash the fruit to a coarse pulp. Place the pan over low heat and stir until the sugar is dissolved. Remove from the heat.

3. Heat the *ghee* in a small frying pan over moderate heat. When it is hot but not smoking, add the ginger, cumin seeds and fennel seeds, and fry until nicely browned. Pour this seasoning into the guavas, along with the cayenne or chili powder and salt, if desired, and stir well.

4. Cool to room temperature, transfer to glass jars or crocks and seal well. Store, refrigerated, for up to 2 weeks.

Mango Jam

AAM MURABBA

Mangoes have been cultivated in India for over fifty centuries, and there are countless ways to appreciate them. Many varieties flourish there, but experts agree that the Alphonsos are one of the finest. In America, Hayden mangoes are among the best, but they never seem to match the perfumed acid-sweet balance of the smooth Alphonsos. This recipe is from the kitchen of B. Jariwala in Gujarat.

Preparation and cooking time: about 40 minutes
Makes: about 1⅔ cups (400 ml)

½ teaspoon (2 ml) each whole cloves, cumin seeds,
    black peppercorns and cardamom seeds
2-inch (5 cm) piece of cinnamon stick
½-inch (1.5 cm) piece of peeled fresh ginger root, sliced
2 medium-sized firm ripe mangoes (about 1 pound/455 g each)
2 cups (425 g) sugar
¼ cup (60 ml) water or fresh orange juice
3 tablespoons (45 ml) fresh lime juice

1. Tie the whole spices, cinnamon stick and sliced ginger in a small piece of cheese-cloth. Wash, peel and dice the mangoes, scraping as much pulp and juice as possible off the seed. Combine the fruit, sugar and water or orange juice in a heavy 3-quart/liter saucepan and place over low heat. Stir until the sugar dissolves, raise the heat to moderate, and bring to a boil. Gently boil until the mango is just tender.

2. Add the spice bag and lime juice and cook until thick or until the temperature reaches 218°–220°F (103°–105°C) on a candy thermometer. Cook, bottle, seal, and store, refrigerated, for up to 2 weeks.

Gooseberry Jam
AMLA MURABBA

Gooseberries grow wild everywhere in the British countryside, and during my residence there I made them a number of ways—fools, jellies, sweet dried pastes and jams. They are not quite the same varieties as found in America or India, but whether they are green, white or rosy red, if they are ripe, they make good jam.

Preparation and cooking time: 25 minutes
Makes: about 2 cups (480 ml)

1 pound (455 g) gooseberries
¼ cup (60 ml) water
2 cups (425 g) sugar
1 teaspoon (5 ml) coarsely crushed cardamom seeds
¼ teaspoon (2 ml) turmeric
½ cassia or bay leaf
2-inch (5 cm) piece of cinnamon stick

1. Wash and stem the berries. Combine with the water in a heavy saucepan and place over high heat. When the water boils, add the sugar and stir constantly until the sugar dissolves.

2. Reduce the heat to low, add the remaining ingredients, and simmer until the berries are clear and the juice is thick, about 15 minutes. Remove the whole spices. Cool, bottle, seal, and store, refrigerated, for up to 2 weeks.

For information about unfamiliar ingredients or techniques, see A-to-Z

Rose Petal and Fruit Jam
GULAB MURABBA

In Bengal, rose water and rose essence play important roles in flavoring beverages and sweets. In this dish, fresh flowers take center stage. You will need pesticide-free flowers. When you are gathering roses to make this colorful and unusual jam, cut them when the dew has dried but before the day becomes hot. Clip off the upper, colored portion of the petals, discarding the white base which tends to be bitter-tasting. Rinse the petals in a colander and pat dry with paper towels. Generally, dark red roses have a strong taste, while the light pink varieties are delicately flavored. Whichever you choose, use them as soon as they have been picked and cleaned, to preserve their flavor. For a special treat, try a spoonful of this jam over ice cream, or as often served in Bengal, with hot flatbreads.

Preparation time (after assembling ingredients): 20 minutes
Soaking time: 8 hours or overnight
Cooking time: about 30 minutes
Makes: 2 cups (480 ml)

1 cup rose petals, tightly packed
    (about 3½ ounces/100 g)
1½ cups (360 ml) thinly sliced trimmed
    rhubarb (about 7 ounces/200 g)
1½ cups (360 ml) sliced strawberries
    (about 8 ounces/230 g)
2 cups (480 ml) water
1½ tablespoons (22 ml) lemon juice

1. Prepare the rose petals as described above. Combine all of the ingredients in a glass, enamel, stainless steel or nonstick pan, cover, and let stand at room temperature for 8 hours or overnight.
2. Place the pan over moderately high heat and, stirring constantly, bring to a boil. Reduce the heat to moderately low and gently boil, stirring constantly, for 25–30 minutes or until the jam is thick. Cool, bottle and seal, and keep refrigerated for up to 7 days.

Fig and Cranberry Conserve
ANGEER MURABBA

Cranberries are available year-round in America, and this is a pleasant alternative to berry jams or conserves.

Preparation and cooking time: about 1 hour
Makes: about 2 cups (480 ml)

2-inch (5 cm) piece of cinnamon stick
6 whole cloves
½ teaspoon (2 ml) cardamom seeds
1 hot jalapeño chili, seeded (optional)
¾ cup (180 ml) white grape juice
¾ cup (160 g) sugar
½ cup (95 g) sliced figs, fresh or dried
1½ cups (360 ml) cranberries
¼ cup (40 g) coarsely chopped toasted almonds or pecans

1. Tie the cinnamon stick, cloves, cardamom seeds and green chili, if desired, in a piece of cheesecloth. Combine the grape juice and sugar in a 3-quart/liter heavy saucepan and place over low heat. Stir until the sugar dissolves, then add the spice bag and figs. Increase the heat to moderate and simmer for 20 minutes. Cover, remove from the heat, and set aside for 20 minutes. Remove the spice bag.

2. Bring the liquid to a boil over moderate heat. Add the cranberries and cook until they pop and the mixture thickens, about 8 minutes. Stir in the almonds or pecans and remove the pan from the heat. Cool slightly and transfer into a jar or crock. Seal well and keep refrigerated for up to a week.

Apricot Jam

KHUMANI MURABBA

Fresh peaches and apricots are not everyday fruits for most Indians; if used at all, they are in the dried form. I came up with with this spicy jam when a friend brought me a large basket of freshly dried Kashmiri fruits. Dried peaches can be substituted for the apricots.

Soaking time: overnight
Cooking time: about 45 minutes
Makes: about 3 cups (710 ml)

½ cup (100 g) dried apricots
1 cup (240 ml) water
¼ cup (60 ml) fresh orange juice
¼ cup (60 ml) fresh lemon juice
1½ cups (315 g) *jaggery* or sugar
1 bay leaf
⅓ cup (50 g) toasted chopped walnuts or almonds

1. Wash and dry the apricots, then cut each piece in half, discarding the seed. Place them in a heavy medium-sized saucepan and cover with the water, orange juice and lemon juice. Soak for 8 hours or overnight.

2. Place the pan over high heat and bring the liquid to a boil. Reduce the heat to low and simmer for 30 minutes or until the fruit is soft.

3. Add the sugar, bay leaf and nuts, and stir until the sugar has dissolved. Bring to a boil over moderate heat, stirring frequently to prevent sticking. Boil until the jam reaches 221°F (105°C) on a candy thermometer. Cool to room temperature, cover, and store, refrigerated, for up to a week.

Light Meals
and
Savories

Early one afternoon on an autumn day in 1970, my spiritual master, Srila Prabhupada, was the honored guest of a well-to-do Indian family in Bombay. He sat with fifteen of his disciples in an elegant white marble dining room, eating his lunch. Toward the end of the meal he called me over.

"Can you make them just like this?" he said, pointing to a dish of deep-fried stuffed juicy *dal* cakes nestled in creamy yogurt.

"No, not this version," I admitted.

"Go into the kitchen and find out how," he replied.

I walked into the kitchen and, with the chef's permission, began filling my notebook with drawings, ingredients, procedures and variations of *Marawadi Dahi Bada*, a dish that I found out was as old as the Vedic literature, written many centuries ago.

Dahi badas are only one of a wide array of classic light-meal dishes that are divided into seven general categories. There are deep-fried fritters called *pakoras*; deep-fried stuffed pastries such as *samosas*, *singharas* and *kachoris*; thin pancakes known as *dosas*; cake-like dumplings called *iddlis*; deep-fried ground *dal* patties and puffs called *badas*; fried vegetable patties known as *tikkis*; and assorted other fried grain and vegetable combinations like *uppma*, *chidwas* and *churas*. What all these dishes have in common is that they can be served at any time of the day or night. With assorted fresh fruits, they are a breakfast dish. Just as easily, they can be a side dish at a holiday feast or special luncheon. At five o'clock they are a snack with juice and chutney, and with a fresh flatbread they are a light meal before bed.

PAKORAS: VEGETABLE FRITTERS

In India, *pakoras* are almost a national passion. Anywhere people congregate—from bustling city street corners to remote village railway stations—it is a common sight to see a small crowd encircling a hand-pushed *pakora* cart. In snack houses, they are favorites with little more than soup or a beverage. And in the home, from late breakfast to late supper, they are simple, inexpensive, easy-to-make finger foods for drop-in company or a relaxing family break.

Whether you make the fried fritters with vegetables, *panir* cheese or even fruits, there are two methods to choose from: batter-dipped or spoon-fried. The vegetables or other ingredients can simply be cut into rounds, sticks, fan shapes or slices, dipped in seasoned chickpea flour batter and deep-fried, or they can be coarsely chopped or shredded, mixed into a thick batter and spooned into hot oil. Either way, *pakoras* are served piping hot.

There is a choice of batter consistency as well, though the basic principle is to make a texture thick enough to envelop the foods in a thorough coating. A thin batter is used to put a crisp, delicate coating on irregularly-shaped items such as spinach leaves, watercress or Swiss chard leaves. A thick batter is recommended for coating moist foods such as tomatoes or *panir* cheese. A medium-consistency batter will do for such items as eggplant, bell peppers, zucchini, potatoes, blanched cauliflower flowerets and countless more. If you prefer a noticeably crisp outside crust, a little *ghee* or oil is added to the batter and the *pakoras* are fried at a temperature slightly lower than usual, sometimes even double-fried.

To make *pakoras* that are soft and cake-like on the outside, a little baking powder in the batter will suffice. Like Japanese tempura, one batter will do for almost any vegetable, but to show a sample of regional variations, I have suggested eight different seasoned batters. Whether you mix your batter in a food processor or blender or by hand, do not add all of the liquid to the flour at once. Add only two-thirds to three-quarters of the liquid and blend until smooth, then slowly add the remaining liquid until the batter is thinned to the desired consistency.

Unlike crumb-coated ice cream, cheese or butter or delicate phyllo pastry—which is deep-fried at high temperatures and only long enough to toast the coating—*pakoras* are fried at lower temperatures to both cook the vegetables and brown the batter. Healthy deep-frying depends on the quantity of oil in relation to frying items and temperature control. Foods that are correctly fried are neither greasy nor soggy, but crispy outside and sufficiently cooked on the inside. *Ghee* begins to smoke at a relatively low temperature—365°–370°F (185°–187°C), while light vegetable oils begin much higher—440°F (226°C) for peanut oil and 465°F (240°C) for soybean oil. Since most *pakoras* are fried at 345°–355°F (173–180°C), most nut and vegetable oils can be used without the risk of smoking. Recently a new light olive oil has reached the market which can be used for deep frying. Darker, fruity virgin oils smoke at low temperatures and are best reserved for salads.

Avoid crowding the frying pan with too many *pakoras*: the temperature will drop, foods may stick together, and, most of all, they will absorb unwanted excess oil. Many temple kitchens, even white tablecloth restaurants, will not use a frying oil a second time, encouraging chefs to fry carefully with attention to the quantity of oil in relation to frying demands. If you choose to deep-fry in *ghee*, cost efficiency and waste should be a natural concern. Frugal homecooks will likely re-use oil a second, even third time. No matter what your choice, it is best to strain still warm *ghee* or oil through a fine sieve before storage, and refrigerate when cool. With the exception of mustard oil, if the oil has been allowed to reach its smoking point, it begins to chemically decompose and darken and must soon be discarded.

A Batter for All *Pakoras*

Mixed vegetable *pakoras* are one of the most popular of all finger-food snacks. At home, they are not only a late-afternoon favorite at tiffin time, but are also frequently served on entertainment menus, from holidays to wedding buffets. If you are frying several types of vegetables with one batter, here is a good choice. Made with chickpea flour, ground spices and ice water, the batter puts a crisp crust on fried foods. If you prefer a cake-like, light crust, add baking powder. You need a medium consistency batter that will thoroughly coat moist foods like *panir* cheese or tomatoes, but will not be too thick for delicate foods such as spinach or Swiss chard.

One flour absorbs water differently than another, and one cook's measurement of flour varies from another's. For 1⅓ cups (135 g) of sifted chickpea flour (3½ ounces/135 g), 8 tablespoons (120 ml) of ice water yields a thickish batter; 10 tablespoons (150 ml) a thinnish one. Add water in small amounts toward the end of mixing to achieve the desired results.

Try any of the following *pakora* suggestions, allowing 25–35 cut pieces for this amount of batter. Depending on the accompanying dishes, allow 4–5 *pakoras* per person.

For information about unfamiliar ingredients or techniques, see A-to-Z

Preparation time (after assembling ingredients): 10 minutes
Resting time: 10–15 minutes
Cooking time: about 30 minutes
Serves: 6

1⅓ cups (135 g) sifted chickpea flour (sifted before measuring)
2 teaspoons (10 ml) melted *ghee* or vegetable oil
1 tablespoon (15 ml) lemon juice
¼ teaspoon (1 ml) cayenne pepper
½ teaspoon (2 ml) turmeric
1 teaspoon (5 ml) *garam masala* or ¼ teaspoon (1 ml)
    each ground cardamom, cumin, cinnamon and cloves
2 teaspoons (10 ml) ground coriander
1–1½ teaspoons (5–7 ml) salt
9 tablespoons (135 ml) cold water, or as needed
⅓ teaspoon (1.5 ml) baking powder (optional)

Pakora Suggestions:

underripe banana, cut into rounds ⅓ inch (1 cm) thick
cauliflower flowerets, 1½ inches (4 cm) long
    and ½ inch (1.5 cm) square, half-cooked
panir cheese, 1-inch (2.5 cm) cubes sprinkled
    with paprika, *chat masala* and ground pepper
eggplant, cut into rounds ¼ inch (6 mm) thick
potato or yam, peeled and cut into rounds ⅛ inch (3 mm) thick
lotus root, washed, peeled, steamed for ½ hour, cut
    on the diagonal ¼ inch (6 mm) thick, and patted dry
pumpkin, cut into 2-inch (5 cm) squares ¼ inch (6 mm) thick
Swiss chard, small leaves, stemmed, washed and dried
spinach, medium-sized leaves, stemmed, washed and dried
bell peppers (red, yellow or green), sliced crosswise
    ¼ inch (6 mm) thick, seeded and ribbed
green tomatoes, cut into rounds ⅓ inch
    (1 cm) thick and thoroughly patted dry
zucchini, cut on the diagonal ¼ inch (6 mm) thick
bitter melon, cut into rounds ¼ inch (6 mm) thick,
    salted for ½ hour, rinsed and thoroughly patted dry
asparagus tips, blanched and dried
ghee or vegetable oil for deep-frying

1. Combine the flour, melted *ghee* or oil, lemon juice, spices and salt in a bowl and mix well. Add 5 tablespoons (75 ml) of water slowly, beating with an electric beater or wire whisk until the batter is smooth and free of lumps. Slowly add 3 tablespoons (45 ml) more water, continuing to beat until well mixed. Check the consistency, and if necessary, slowly add the remaining water until the batter resembles the consistency of heavy cream and easily coats a wooden spoon.

Alternately, place the batter ingredients in a food processor fitted with the metal blade, or a blender, process until smooth, then transfer to a bowl. Cover the batter and set aside for 10–15 minutes.

2. Again beat with an electric beater, wire whisk or your hand for 2–3 minutes to further lighten the batter. (Check the batter consistency: if it is too thin, moist foods will

spatter as they fry; if it is too thick, they will not cook properly. Add flour or water as necessary.) Stir in the baking powder at this time if you prefer a cake-like crust. Set all of the items to be fried next to the stove. They should be patted dry and at room temperature.

3. Heat 2½–3 inches (6.5–7.5 cm) of fresh *ghee* or vegetable oil in a *karai*, wok or deep-frying pan until the temperature reaches 355°F (180°C). Dip 5 or 6 of your selected ingredients in the batter and, one at a time, carefully slip them into the hot oil. The temperature will fall but should then be maintained at between 345°–355°F (173°–180°C) throughout the frying. Fry until the *pakoras* are golden brown, turning to brown evenly. Leafy greens may take as little as 1 or 2 minutes per side, while potatoes may take up to 5 minutes per side. Remove with a slotted spoon and drain on paper towels. Serve immediately, or keep warm, uncovered, in a preheated 250°F (120°C) oven until all the *pakoras* are fried, for up to ½ hour.

Note: It is convenient to keep a bowl of water and a tea towel near the frying area. After batter-dipping the items to be fried, rinse and dry your hands before continuing your frying.

Zucchini *Pakora* with Crushed Peanuts
LOUKI PAKORA

Any type of summer squash can be substituted for green zucchini: yellow crookneck, patty-pan, yellow zucchini or Indian bottle gourd (*louki*). Cut them into rounds ¼ inch (6 mm) thick straight across or on the diagonal. The batter should be thick enough to completely coat the slices and keep the peanut bits from sliding off. Stir the batter before dipping each batch of zucchini.

Preparation time (after assembling ingredients): 10 minutes
Resting time: 10–15 minutes
Cooking time: about 30 minutes
Serves: 6 as a snack or 8 at a meal

1⅓ cups (135 g) sifted chickpea flour (sifted before measuring)
1½ teaspoons (7 ml) melted *ghee* or vegetable oil
1 tablespoon (15 ml) lemon juice
1 teaspoon (5 ml) crushed cumin seeds
1–2 hot green chilies, seeded and minced
1 teaspoon (5 ml) salt
up to 9 tablespoons (135 ml) cold water or enough
    to make a medium-consistency batter
¼ teaspoon (1 ml) baking powder
3 tablespoons (45 ml) finely chopped peanuts
2 medium-sized zucchini (about ½ pound/230 g),
    cut into 30–35 slices ¼ inch (6 mm) thick
ghee or vegetable oil for deep frying

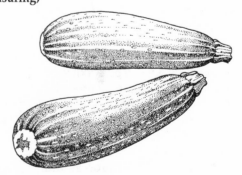

For information about unfamiliar ingredients or techniques, see A-to-Z

1. Combine the flour, melted *ghee* or oil, lemon juice, cumin seeds, chilies and salt in a bowl and mix well. Add 8 tablespoons (120 ml) of water slowly, beating with an electric beater or wire whisk until the batter is smooth and free of lumps. Slowly add the remaining water until the batter consistency is similar to cream and easily coats a wooden spoon. Alternately, place the batter ingredients in a food processor fitted with the metal blade, or a blender, process until smooth, then transfer to a bowl. Cover the batter and set aside for 10–15 minutes.

2. Again beat with an electric beater, wire whisk or your hand for 2–3 minutes to further lighten the batter. (Check the batter consistency: if it is too thin, moist foods will spatter as they fry; if it is too thick, they will not cook properly. Add flour or water as necessary.) Stir in the baking powder and peanuts. Set the zucchini, a bowl of water, tea towels and paper towels for draining near the stove.

3. Heat 2½–3 inches (6.5–7.5 cm) of fresh *ghee* or vegetable oil in a *karai*, wok or deep-frying pan until the temperature reaches 355°F (180°C). Dip 6–8 pieces of zucchini in the batter and carefully slip them into the hot oil. Avoid crowding the pan, which would make the temperature of the oil drop. Fry the zucchini *pakoras* 3–4 minutes per side or until golden brown. Remove with a slotted spoon and drain on paper towels. Serve immediately, or keep warm, uncovered, in a preheated 250°F (120°C) oven until all of the *pakoras* are fried, up to ½ hour.

Note: After batter-dipping each batch of squash rounds, rinse your hands and dry them on a tea towel before you continue frying.

Potato *Pakora* with Dried Pomegranate Seeds
ALOO PAKORA

Pomegranate seeds, used predominantly in North Indian cooking, are dried from wild pomegranate or *daru* that grow in the Himalayan foothills. The pleasantly sour flavor of the seeds are best for complementing potatoes and other starchy vegetables. Potato slices are handsomely jacketed in a medium-consistency batter that puts a crunchy crust on the soft potatoes. The food processor crushes the seeds while whisking the batter until it is light and airy. This is one *pakora* that lends itself to double-frying: the first frying may be done several hours before serving time, the second one warms the thin fritters and gives them their final crunch.

Preparation time (after assembling ingredients): 10 minutes
Resting time: 10–15 minutes
Cooking time: 30 minutes
Serves: 6 as a snack or 8 at a meal

1⅓ cups (135 g) sifted chickpea flour (sifted before measuring)
2 teaspoons (10 ml) melted *ghee* or vegetable oil
½ tablespoon (7 ml) dried pomegranate seeds
¼ teaspoon (1 ml) cayenne pepper or paprika
¼ teaspoon (1 ml) turmeric
1½ teaspoons (7 ml) salt
up to 9 tablespoons (135 ml) cold water, or enough
    to make a medium-consistency batter
1 large baking potato (about ½ pound/230 g), peeled, cut into a rectangle
    and sliced ⅛ inch (3 mm) thick (cut just before frying)
ghee or vegetable oil for deep-frying

1. Place the flour, melted *ghee* or oil, pomegranate seeds, cayenne or paprika, turmeric and salt in a blender or a food processor fitted with the metal blade. Pulse on and off 3 or 4 times. With the machine running, slowly pour in ½ cup (120 ml) of water and process for 2–3 minutes until smooth and airy. In 1 teaspoon (5 ml) amounts, add water until the batter consistency is similar to heavy cream. Transfer to a bowl, cover and set for 10–15 minutes. (Check the batter consistency: if it is too thin, moist foods will spatter as they fry; if it is too thick, they will not cook properly. Add flour or water as necessary.)

2. Place the sliced potatoes (about 30–35 pieces), a bowl of water, tea towels and paper towels for draining near the stove. Heat the *ghee* or vegetable oil in a *karai*, wok or deep-frying pan until the temperature reaches 355°F (180°C). Fry 6–7 potato *pakoras* at a time, maintaining the temperature at 345°–355°F (173°–180°C), for about 2 minutes per side if you will be serving them later, or 4–5 minutes per side until golden brown if you are frying them for serving now. Remove with a slotted spoon and drain on paper towels. If not serving immediately, fry a second time for about 2 minutes or until hot, crispy and golden brown. Serve hot.

Note: After batter-dipping each batch of the potato rounds, rinse your hands and dry with a tea towel before you continue frying.

Bell Pepper *Pakora* with Nigella Seeds
SIMLA MIRCH PAKORA

Nigella seeds, or *kalonji*, have a peppery, lemon flavor and are widely used in Bengali cooking, on their own or as part of the five-seed spice blend known as *panch puran*. Unfortunately, they are sometimes called "onion seeds" in Indian grocery stores, even though they have nothing to do with onions. The nigella seeds should be left whole, so if you make the batter in a blender or food processor, stir them in after you transfer the batter to a bowl. Yellow, red or green bell peppers can be used with this *pakora* batter.

For information about unfamiliar ingredients or techniques, see A-to-Z

Preparation time (after assembling ingredients): 10 minutes
Resting time: 10–15 minutes
Cooking time: about 30 minutes
Serves: 6 as a snack or 8 at a meal

1⅓ cups (135 g) sifted chickpea flour
    (sifted before measuring)
½ tablespoon (7 ml) salt
2 teaspoons (10 ml) melted *ghee* or vegetable oil
1–2 hot green chilies, seeded and minced
½ tablespoon (7 ml) nigella seeds (*kalonji*)
½ teaspoon (2 ml) turmeric
9 tablespoons (135 ml) cold water, or enough
    to make a medium-consistency batter
⅛ teaspoon (0.5 ml) baking powder (optional)
25–35 long strips or rounds of seeded
    bell pepper (3 medium-sized peppers)
ghee or vegetable oil for deep-frying

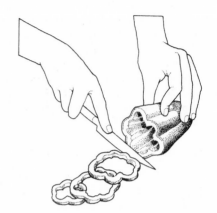

1. Combine the flour, salt, melted *ghee* or vegetable oil, green chilies, nigella seeds and turmeric in a bowl and mix well. Add ½ cup (120 ml) of water slowly, beating with an electric beater or wire whisk until the batter is smooth and free of lumps. Slowly add the remaining water until the batter consistency is similar to cream and easily coats a wooden spoon. Alternately, place the above ingredients in a food processor fitted with the metal blade, or a blender, adding the nigella seeds after the mixture is transferred to a bowl. Cover the batter and set aside for 10–15 minutes.

2. Again beat with an electric beater, wire whisk or your hand for 2–3 minutes to further lighten the batter. (Check the batter consistency: if it is too thin, moist foods will spatter as they fry; if it is too thick, they will not cook properly. Add more flour or water as necessary.) Stir in the baking powder at this time if you prefer a cake like crust. Set the bell peppers to be fried next to the stove. They should be patted dry and at room temperature.

3. Heat 2½–3 inches (6.5–7.5 cm) of fresh *ghee* or vegetable oil in a *karai*, wok or deep-frying pan until the temperature reaches 355°F (180°C). Dip 5 or 6 bell pepper rings in the batter and, one at a time, carefully slip them into the hot oil. The temperature will fall but should be maintained at 345°–355°F (173°–180°C) throughout the frying. Fry for 3–4 minutes on each side until the *pakoras* are golden brown. Remove with a slotted spoon and drain on paper towels. Serve immediately, or keep warm, uncovered, in a preheated 250°F (120°C) oven until all the *pakoras* are fried, for up to ½ hour.

Note: It is convenient to keep a bowl of water and a tea towel near the frying area. After batter-dipping the items to be fried, rinse and dry your hands before continuing your frying.

Pumpkin *Pakora* with Crushed Coriander Seeds
KADDU PAKORA

Any type of winter squash—butternut, acorn, turban or Indian wax gourd (*petha*)—as well as yams or sweet potatoes may be substituted for pumpkin. This is a good batter to make in a food processor, for along with crushing whole coriander seeds, the processor makes the batter light and smooth. If you make the batter by hand, add freshly crushed coriander seeds.

Preparation time (after assembling ingredients): 10 minutes
Resting time: 10–15 minutes
Cooking time: about 30 minutes
Serves: 6 as a snack or 8 at a meal

1⅓ cups (135 g) sifted chickpea flour (sifted before measuring)
1½–2 teaspoons (7–10 ml) salt
2 teaspoons (10 ml) melted *ghee* or vegetable oil
½ teaspoon (2 ml) turmeric
¼ teaspoon (1 ml) yellow asafetida powder (*hing*)*
1 tablespoon (15 ml) crushed coriander seeds
2 tablespoons (30 ml) yogurt
½ cup (120 ml) cold water, or enough to make a batter of medium consistency
¼ teaspoon (1 ml) baking powder (optional)
25–35 pieces of trimmed, peeled ripe pumpkin, cut into
    2-inch (5 cm) squares ¼ inch (6 mm) thick
ghee or vegetable oil for deep-frying

*This amount applies only to yellow Cobra brand. Reduce any other asafetida by three-fourths.

1. Place the flour, salt, melted *ghee* or vegetable oil, turmeric, asafetida, crushed coriander seeds and yogurt in a bowl and mix well. Add ½ cup (120 ml) of water slowly, beating with an electric beater or wire whisk until the batter is smooth and easily coats a wooden spoon. Alternately, place the batter ingredients in a food processor fitted with the metal blade, or a blender, and process until the coriander seeds are crushed and the texture is smooth, then transfer to a bowl. Cover the batter and set aside for 10–15 minutes.

2. Again beat with an electric beater, wire whisk or your hand for 2–3 minutes to further lighten the batter. (Check the batter consistency: if it is too thin, moist foods will spatter as they fry; if it is too thick, they will not cook properly. Add water or flour as necessary.) Stir in the baking powder at this time if you prefer a cake-like crust. Set the pumpkin pieces to be fried next to the stove. They should be patted dry and at room temperature.

3. Heat 2½–3 inches (6.5–7.5 cm) of fresh *ghee* or vegetable oil in a *karai*, wok or deep-frying vessel until the temperature reaches 355°F (180°C). Dip 5–6 pieces of pumpkin in the batter and, one at a time, carefully slip them into the hot oil. The temperature will fall but should then be maintained at between 345°–355°F (173°–180°C) throughout the frying. Fry until the *pakoras* are golden brown, turning to brown evenly, 3–4 minutes per side. Remove with a slotted spoon and drain on paper towels. Serve immediately, or keep warm, uncovered, in a preheated 250°F (120°C) oven, until all of the *pakoras* are fried, for up to ½ hour.

For information about unfamiliar ingredients or techniques, see A-to-Z

Note: It is convenient to keep a bowl of water and a tea towel near the frying area. After batter-dipping the items to be fried, rinse and dry your hands before continuing your frying.

Eggplant *Pakora* with Poppy Seeds
BAIGAN PAKORA

Whole white poppy seeds or *khas-khas* are quite different from the blue-black seeds used in the West. Raw, the flavor is a cross between pine nuts and sesame seeds. Subjected to dry-roasting, nutty flavor overtones prevail. Raw and roasted seeds are popular in Bengali cooking for thickening gravies or adding a crust on steamed and fried vegetables. They are wonderful in *pakora* batter, though they need to be soaked for several hours before use; otherwise, they tend to sink to the bottom of the thin batter and often remain rock hard.

In Bengal, eggplant is generally cut into thin rounds or wedges for *pakoras*. Inspired by a recipe for eggplant *tempura* by Jacques Pépin, I have also cut thin Japanese eggplants into fans and shallow-fried them, a visually attractive presentation for entertaining family or company dinners. Select very slender eggplants, about 1½ inches (4 cm) in diameter and no more than 4–5 inches (10–12.5 cm) long. Trim off the cap and slice lengthwise 7 or 8 times, leaving the slices attached at the stem end. Press down on the eggplants to fan out the slices.

Soaking time: 4 hours or overnight
Preparation time (after assembling ingredients): 10 minutes
Cooking time: 20 minutes
Makes: 30–40 rounds or wedges, or 6–8 eggplant fans

3 tablespoons (45 ml) white poppy seeds (*khas-khas*), soaked
in warm water for 4 hours or overnight, then drained
1⅓ cups (135 g) sifted chickpea flour (sifted before measuring)
2 teaspoons (10 ml) melted *ghee* or vegetable oil
½ teaspoon (2 ml) each cayenne pepper, turmeric and salt
¼ teaspoon (1 ml) sugar
up to 10 tablespoons (150 ml) ice cold water, or enough to make a thin batter
***ghee* or vegetable oil for frying**
1 medium-sized eggplant (about 1½ pounds/685 g), cut in half
lengthwise and sliced ¼ inch (6 mm) thick, or 6–8 very thin
Japanese eggplants, about 1½ inches (4 cm) in diameter

1. Combine the poppy seeds, flour, *ghee* or vegetable oil, cayenne, turmeric, salt, sugar and 8 tablespoons (120 ml) of water in a bowl and whisk until smooth. Add enough of the remaining water to make a thinnish batter and whisk for 15 seconds.

2. If you are deep-frying eggplant slices, heat 2½–3 inches (6.5–7.5 cm) of fresh *ghee* or vegetable oil in a *karai*, wok or deep-frying pan until the temperature reaches 365°F (185°C). Dip 5 or 6 eggplant slices in the batter and, one at a time, lift each piece, allow the excess to drain off momentarily, and, in a fluid motion, carefully slip it into the hot oil. The temperature will fall but should then be maintained at between 345°–355°F (173°–180°C) throughout the frying. Fry for about 3–4 minutes per side until golden brown. Remove with a slotted spoon and drain on paper towels.

To fry eggplant fans, heat ½ inch (1.5 cm) of fresh *ghee* or vegetable oil in a large cast-iron skillet or frying pan until it is hot but not smoking. Working one at a time, pick up an eggplant fan by the base and dip it in the batter, lift it up momentarily to let the thinnish batter drain off, and carefully place it flat in the hot oil. Fry 2 or 3 at a time, without crowding the pan, for 4–5 minutes on each side or until golden brown and cooked throughout. Remove with a slotted spatula and drain on paper towels. Serve with lemon or lime wedges.

Spinach *Pakora* with *Ajwain* Seeds
PALAK PAKORA

This is a wafer-thin, crunchy *pakora*. Because the batter is assembled just before frying, with ground rice and ice water, the *pakoras* turn out crispy and delicate. The batter should be thin enough to allow the irregularly shaped leaves to get a good coating of flavor. The predominant seasoning is *ajwain* seeds. The seeds and flour are available at Indian grocery stores, and they lend a spicy, lemony twist to the otherwise plain batter. Try to use spinach leaves of similar size, and trim off all but 1 inch (2.5 cm) of the stem.

Preparation time (after assembling ingredients): 10 minutes
Resting time: 10–15 minutes
Cooking time: about 20 minutes
Serves: 6 as a snack or 8 at a meal

1 cup (100 g) sifted chickpea flour (sifted before measuring)
¼ cup (40 g) rice flour
1½ teaspoons (7 ml) *ajwain* seeds
scant ½ teaspoon (2 ml) cayenne pepper or paprika
1 teaspoon (5 ml) salt
¼ teaspoon (1 ml) baking powder
9–10 tablespoons (135–150 ml) ice cold water, or enough to
    make a thin batter similar in consistency to light cream
25–30 medium-sized fresh spinach leaves, trimmed,
    washed and patted dry (about ½ pound/230 g)
ghee or vegetable oil for deep-frying

1. Combine the flours, *ajwain* seeds, cayenne pepper or paprika, salt, baking powder and ½ cup (120 ml) of ice water in a bowl and work with a whisk until smooth. Slowly whisk in the remaining water or enough to make a crèpe-like batter, similar to cream.

2. Next to the stove, set out the spinach leaves, a bowl of hand rinsing water and drying towel, and paper towels for draining the finished fritters. Heat the *ghee* or vegetable oil in a *karai*, wok or deep-frying pan until the temperature reaches 350°F (175°C). Dip a spinach leaf in the batter so it is lightly coated, lift it and drain off the excess momentarily, then carefully slip it into the oil. Batter-coat only 4 or 5 leaves per batch, maintaining the oil at 350°F (175°C). Quickly rinse and dry your hands, then fry the leaves on both sides for 1–2 minutes or until crisp and pale gold. Remove with a slotted spoon and drain on paper towels. Serve immediately or keep warm, uncovered, in a preheated 200°F (120°C) oven until all the *pakoras* are fried, for up to 30 minutes.

For information about unfamiliar ingredients or techniques, see A-to-Z

Panir Cheese *Pakora*
PANIR PAKORA

Of all North Indian *pakoras*, these stand out as utterly irresistible. For those times when you are planning a special-occasion menu and you want to serve an easy-to-make deep-fried savory, try this variation. Like all *pakoras*, they are best served immediately after frying—plain, sprinkled with lime juice or accompanied by a fresh dipping chutney.

Though the cheese is usually cut into ¾-inch (2 cm) cubes, you can also make other shapes— sticks, slices, smooth kneaded balls, or even julienne pieces of cheese mixed into the batter and fried like potato pancakes. The chickpea batter should be fairly thick, one that will thoroughly envelop the moist cheese and prevent it from sputtering during frying. The fritters will be pleasantly crisp on the outside and soft and light on the inside.

Panir cheese is not yet available commercially in America but is easy to make at home. You can make herb cheese by adding one of the following fresh herbs into 8 cups (2 liters) of milk: 2 tablespoons (30 ml) minced summer savory, basil, marjoram, parsley, coriander, chervil, dill or mustard cress. Make the cheese as directed, and the herb variations will lend yet another dimension of elegance to the *pakora*.

Preparation and resting time (after assembling ingredients): 45 minutes
Cooking time: about 25 minutes
Serves: 6 as a snack or 8 at a meal

1⅓ cups (135 g) sifted chickpea flour (sifted before measuring)
1½ teaspoons (7 ml) salt
½ tablespoon (7 ml) coriander seeds
1 teaspoon (5 ml) cumin seeds
1–2 hot green chilies, seeded and minced
⅓ teaspoon (1.5 ml) yellow asafetida powder (*hing*)*
2 teaspoons (10 ml) melted *ghee* or vegetable oil
8 tablespoons (120 ml) cold water, or enough to make a thickish batter
1 tablespoon (15 ml) chickpea flour or all-purpose flour mixed with
    ½ teaspoon (2 ml) *chat masala, amchoor* powder or paprika
fresh *panir* cheese (page 313) made from 8 cups (2 liters) milk,(about 10 ounces/285 g),
    cut into ¾ inch (2 cm) cubes, or sticks 2 inches (4 cm) long
    and ½ inch (1.5 cm) square, or kneaded and rolled into smooth
    cumquat-sized balls, or cut into julienne for pancake fritters
½ teaspoon (2 ml) baking powder
ghee or vegetable oil for frying

**This amount applies only to yellow Cobra brand. Reduce any other asafetida by three-fourths.*

1. Combine the 1⅓ cups (135 g) flour, salt, coriander seeds, cumin seeds, green chilies, asafetida, melted *ghee* or oil and 6 tablespoons (90 ml) of water in a food processor fitted with the metal blade. Process for about 1 minute, stopping to scrape down the sides of the work bowl once or twice. Add the remaining 2 tablespoons (30 ml) cold water, or enough to make a thickish batter. Cover and set aside for 10–15 minutes.

2. Meanwhile, mix the 1 tablespoon (15 ml) flour with the ground spice. Arrange the cheese on a large plate, sprinkle with the seasoned flour and gently coat the cheese. Let the cheese air-dry while the batter rests. After ½ hour, mix the baking powder into the batter. (Check the batter consistency: if it is too thin, moist foods will spatter as they fry; if it is too thick, they will not cook properly. Add flour or water as necessary.) Stir in the baking powder.

3. If you are frying cubes, sticks or balls, pour 2½–3 inches (6.5–7.5 cm) of *ghee* or vegetable oil into a *karai*, wok or deep-frying pan and heat to 345°–355°F (173°–180°C). Dip 6 or 7 *panir* pieces in the batter and, one at a time, carefully slip them into the hot oil. The temperature will fall but should then be maintained at between 345°–355°F (173°–180°C). Fry until the *pakoras* are golden brown on all sides, up to 5–6 minutes. If you are frying pancakes, pour ¼–½ inch (6 mm–1.5 cm) of *ghee* or oil into a heavy frying pan and heat to 350°F (175°C). Combine the batter and julienne *panir* cheese. Gently add the cheese-batter mixture in 3-tablespoon (45 ml) amounts, making 5 or 6 pancakes at a time. Fry on both sides until golden brown, then remove with a slotted spoon and drain on paper towels.

Cauliflower *Pakora*
GOBHI PAKORA

North Indians frequently serve this luscious *pakora* selection at wedding feasts. It adds a festive touch to almost any occasion, from brunch to late-night supper. Unless the cauliflower flowerets are cut very small, parboil or half-steam them before deep-frying. Make certain that the pieces are thoroughly patted dry and at room temperature before batter-dipping. If you are making the batter by hand, rather than in a food processor or blender, use ground coriander or fenugreek instead of the whole seeds.

Preparation and resting time (after assembling ingredients): 40 minutes
Cooking time: about 30 minutes
Makes: 25–35 pieces

1⅓ cups (135 g) sifted chickpea flour (sifted before measuring)
1½ teaspoons (7 ml) salt
2 teaspoons (10 ml) melted *ghee* or vegetable oil
2–4 hot green chilies, seeded and minced
1 inch (2.5 cm) piece of scraped, finely shredded or minced fresh ginger root
1 teaspoon (5 ml) dry-roasted fenugreek seeds or 1 tablespoon (15 ml) coriander seeds
2 tablespoons (30 ml) coarsely chopped fresh fenugreek or coriander
about 9 tablespoons (135 ml) cold water, or enough to make a
    medium-consistency batter
¼–½ teaspoon (1–2 ml) baking powder
ghee or vegetable oil for deep-frying
25–35 cauliflower flowerets, 1½ inches (4 cm) long and
    ½ inch (1.5 cm) thick, parboiled or half-steamed

1. Combine the flour, salt, 2 teaspoons (10 ml) *ghee* or vegetable oil, chilies, ginger, fenugreek or coriander seeds, fresh herbs and 7 tablespoons (105 ml) of cold water in a blender or a food processor fitted with the metal blade. Cover and process until smooth. (If you mix the batter by hand, substitute ground spices for the seeds and work with a balloon whisk until smooth.) Gradually add the remaining water, or enough to make a batter the consistency of heavy cream. Cover and set aside for 10–15 minutes.

2. Again beat with an electric beater, wire whisk or your hand for 2–3 minutes to further lighten the batter. (Check the batter consistency: if it is too thin, moist foods will spatter as they fry; if it is too thick, they will not cook properly. Add flour or water as necessary.) Stir in the baking powder.

3. Heat 2½–3 inches (6.5–7.5 cm) of fresh *ghee* or vegetable oil in a *karai*, wok or deep-frying vessel until the temperature reaches 355°F (180°C). Dip 5 or 6 flowerets in the batter and, one at a time, carefully slip them into the hot oil. The temperature will fall but should then be maintained at between 345°–355°F (173°–180°C) throughout the frying. Fry until the *pakoras* are golden brown, turning to brown evenly. Remove with a slotted spoon and drain on paper towels. Serve immediately, or keep warm, uncovered, in a preheated 250°F (120°C) oven until all of the *pakoras* are fried, for up to ½ hour.

Note: It is convenient to keep a bowl of water and tea towels near the frying area. After batter-dipping the items to be fried, rinse and dry your hands before continuing your frying.

Buckwheat Flour–Potato Fritters
EKADASEE KOTU ALOO PAKORA

Buckwheat is the fruit of a plant related to rhubarb and sorrel. Though it is not a cereal grain, it is cooked like one and milled into a grainy, low-gluten flour. The flour, known as *kotu* or *phaphra atta*, is used on the *Ekadasee* day, when all cereals and grains are avoided by Vaishnavas. These chocolate-brown potato fritters are one of the most popular *Ekadasee* dishes in North India, where little street stalls sell them piping-hot and crunchy in leaf cups to passers-by.

Preparation time and batter resting time (after assembling ingredients): 30 minutes
Frying time: 15 minutes
Serves: 6

1 cup (140 g) buckwheat flour
½ tablespoon (7 ml) cracked black pepper or seasoned pepper
½ teaspoon (2 ml) salt
¼ cup (60 ml) finely chopped fresh coriander or minced parsley
about 1¼ cups (300 ml) cold water
3 medium-sized baking potatoes (about 1¼ pounds/570 g),
    boiled whole for 10 minutes or until half-cooked
¾ teaspoon (3.5 ml) baking powder
ghee or vegetable oil for deep frying

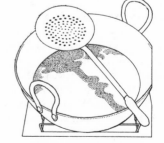

1. Combine the flour, pepper, salt and fresh herbs in a mixing bowl and mix well. Add 1 cup (240 ml) of water and, working with a whisk, beat into a smooth batter. Add the remaining water (you may need more or less than the stated amount) and continue whisking until the batter is the consistency of cream. Cover and set aside for at least 20 minutes.

2. When the potatoes are cool enough to handle, peel and slice each one on the diagonal into 8 slices. You should have about 24 slices. Stir the batter, add the baking powder, and stir again.

3. Pour *ghee* or vegetable oil to a depth of 2 inches (5 cm) in a deep-frying pan over moderate heat until it reaches 355°F (180°C) on a thermometer. Put a few slices of potato in the batter and cover them completely. One at a time, lower each slice of batter-coated potato into the hot oil. Fry as many slices as will float on the surface of the oil without touching. Maintaining the oil at between 345°–355°F (173°–180°C), fry on both sides, using a fork to turn the fritters, until reddish-gray and crisp. As the fritters color, remove with a slotted spoon and drain on paper towels. Continue to dip and fry until all of the potatoes and batter have been used. Keep an eye on the consistency of the batter; it quickly thickens near heat. You may have to add water from time to time so you do not run short. Serve hot—the fritters soften as they cool.

Green Tomato *Pakora* with Cornmeal
TAMATAR PAKORA

If you have a tomato patch or even one plant on the patio, harvest 3 or 4 tomatoes when they are green and try this delicious dish. Alternately, you can purchase green or firm red tomatoes, but if they are soft and ripe, they will exude too much moisture when heated. Though cornmeal makes the most flavorful coating, a mixture of half semolina and half chickpea flour is also pleasant. Semolina flour is sold at Indian grocery stores, large health food stores and in supermarket gourmet aisles. If you wish, season the coating with 1 teaspoon (5 ml) of any dried herb, such as crushed summer savory, marjoram, oregano, chervil or basil.

Preparation and drying time: 15 minutes
Cooking time: 15 minutes
Serves: 4 to 6

4 medium-sized green tomatoes
⅔ cup (95 g) yellow or white cornmeal, preferably stone-ground,
    or ⅓ cup each semolina (70 g) and chickpea flour (30 g)
1½ teaspoons (7 ml) salt
½ teaspoon (2 ml) cracked black pepper
⅛ teaspoon (0.5 ml) cayenne pepper or paprika
2 teaspoons (10 ml) coarsely crushed cumin seeds
4 tablespoons (60 ml) *ghee* or a mixture of vegetable oil and unsalted butter

1. Slice the tomatoes, unpeeled, about ½ inch (1.5 cm) thick and save the ends for another use. Pat the slices dry with paper towels. Combine the cornmeal or semolina–chickpea flour mixture, salt, pepper, cayenne or paprika and crushed cumin seeds in a pie dish, and mix well. Press both sides of each tomato slice in the coating and set on a cake rack to air-dry for 5–10 minutes.

For information about unfamiliar ingredients or techniques, see A-to-Z

2. Place 2 tablespoons (30 ml) of the *ghee* or oil–butter mixture in a large heavy nonstick or cast-iron skillet over moderately high heat. When it is hot but not smoking, place in the pan as many coated slices as will easily fit. Fry until the bottoms are lightly browned, about 1½ minutes, then turn with tongs or a spatula and brown the second side. Remove and fry the remaining coated slices, adding *ghee* or the oil–butter mixture as necessary. Serve hot.

Crispy-Fried Eggplant Slices
BAIGAN BHAJI

In Bengal, *bhaji* is almost any fried flour-dredged vegetable. Srila Prabhupada once commented that his aunt used to make delicious savories with little more than flour and mustard oil, and this was one such dish. Mustard oil has a pungent flavor until it is tamed. Unlike other oils, you must bring it to its smoking point for a few seconds. This renders the oil docile and very pleasant. You can cut the eggplants into rounds, sticks or almost any shape you desire.

Preparation and drying time: 45 minutes
Frying time: about 20 minutes
Serves: 4 to 6

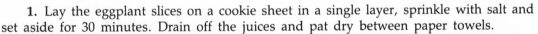

1 medium-sized eggplant (about 1½ pounds/685 g), peeled
   and sliced into rounds ⅓ inch (1 cm) thick
1 teaspoon (5 ml) salt
½–⅔ cup (50–60 g) chickpea flour or whole wheat flour (65–85 g)
¼–½ teaspoon (1–2 ml) cayenne pepper
¼ teaspoon (1 ml) turmeric
ghee **or mustard oil for deep-frying**

1. Lay the eggplant slices on a cookie sheet in a single layer, sprinkle with salt and set aside for 30 minutes. Drain off the juices and pat dry between paper towels.
2. Place the flour, cayenne and turmeric in a paper bag, add the cut eggplant, close the bag and shake. Heat enough *ghee* or oil to half-fill a *karai*, wok or deep-frying pan over moderately high heat until it reaches 360°F (182°C). (If you are using mustard oil, bring it to the smoking point for a few seconds.)
3. Remove several eggplant pieces from the bag and one by one slap them on the outside of the bag to shake off excess flour. Fry without crowding the pan (crowding makes the temperature drop) until they are reddish-brown on all sides and crispy. Remove with a slotted spoon and drain on paper towels. Serve immediately or keep warm in a 250°F (120°C) oven until the remaining eggplant is fried.

Herbed Cornmeal *Pakora*
MAKKAI PAKORA

With a texture similar to hush puppy or cornmeal muffin batter, these shallow-fried *pakoras* are made from stone-ground corn, either white or yellow.

Preparation time (after assembling ingredients): 5 minutes
Cooking time: 10 minutes
Serves: 4

½ cup (75 g) stone-ground cornmeal
½ cup (65 g) unbleached white flour,
    chapati, or whole wheat pastry flour
1¼ teaspoons (6 ml) baking powder
½ teaspoon (2 ml) salt
½ teaspoon (2 ml) sugar
a generous ¼ teaspoon (1 ml) of crushed red chilies
2 teaspoons (10 ml) chopped fresh dill or
    1½ teaspoons (7 ml) dried dill
½ cup (120 ml) milk
2 tablespoons (30 ml) melted *ghee* or vegetable oil
ghee or vegetable oil for shallow-frying

1. Blend the cornmeal, flour, baking powder, salt, sugar, crushed red chilies and dill in a mixing bowl. Whisk together the milk and *ghee* or oil in a small bowl, then pour into the cornmeal mixture and stir just until blended.

2. Heat ½ inch (1.5 cm) of *ghee* or oil in a large frying pan until it is hot but not smoking. Scoop up roughly 1 tablespoon (15 ml) amounts of the batter and carefully lower into the hot oil. Fry until golden brown on both sides (3–4 minutes per side), and serve immediately.

Batter-Coated Mashed Potato Balls
ALOO BONDA

This finger food is popular as the focal point of a late afternoon tiffin or as the savory part of a late night supper. The ginger-flavored mashed potatoes are dipped in an herbed chickpea flour batter and deep-fried into golden globes. One note of caution: be sure to thoroughly coat the balls with batter; exposed areas of mashed potatoes tend to splatter and disintegrate in the hot oil.

Preparation and frying time (after assembling ingredients): about ½ hour
Serves: 6

For information about unfamiliar ingredients or techniques, see A-to-Z

Potato Balls:

2 cups (480 ml) warm mashed potatoes
2 tablespoons (30 ml) finely chopped toasted almonds, peanuts or cashews
½ teaspoon (2 ml) *amchoor* or ½ tablespoon (7 ml) lemon juice
¼ teaspoon (1 ml) cayenne pepper or paprika
2 tablespoons (30 ml) scraped, finely shredded or minced fresh ginger root
½ teaspoon (2 ml) salt
2 tablespoons (30 ml) whole wheat flour

Batter:

1¼ cups (125 g) sifted chickpea flour (sifted before measuring)
1 tablespoon (15 ml) arrowroot
½ teaspoon (2 ml) each baking powder, salt, turmeric,
    garam masala and ground coriander
3 tablespoons (45 ml) finely chopped fresh coriander
9 tablespoons (135 ml) cold water or enough
    to make a medium-consistency batter
ghee or vegetable oil for deep-frying

1. Mix the mashed potatoes with the remaining potato-ball ingredients and roll into 16 balls.

2. Place the flour, arrowroot, baking powder, salt, turmeric, *garam masala*, ground coriander and fresh coriander in a mixing bowl. Working with a wire whisk, make a smooth batter, adding 7 tablespoons (105 ml) of water initially and then 2 more tablespoons (30 ml) or enough to make a smooth, slightly thick, crêpe-like batter.

3. Heat 2½–3 inches (6.5–7.5 cm) of *ghee* or vegetable oil in a *karai*, wok or deep-frying pan over moderately high heat until it reaches 350°F (180°C). Dip 5 or 6 balls in the batter and, one at a time, lift out with two fingers. Let the excess batter drip back into the bowl and, with a twist of the wrist, carefully slip the ball into the hot oil. Fry without crowding the balls (crowding makes them stick together and makes the oil temperature drop). Cook, turning gently after they float to the surface, until golden brown or for about 4–5 minutes. Remove and drain on paper towels. Keep warm in a 250°F (120°C) oven until all the *bondas* are fried, or serve immediately.

Chopped Spinach and Tomato *Pakora*
PALAK TAMATAR PAKORA

I made this *pakora* at Srila Prabhupada's request on several occasions, always making subtle changes in a basic recipe for variety. The substitution of freshly ground *moong dal* or *chana dal* for the chickpea flour is a popular variation. If green tomatoes can be found, they add a wonderful taste dimension. Whichever way you choose to make these *pakoras*, serve them immediately after frying.

Though some variations of this dish may be deep-fried, this one is shallow-fried. This is an example of a spoon-fried *pakora* made by folding vegetables into a thick paste-like batter and scooping the mixture into shallow *ghee* or oil. Regulate the heat during frying so that the insides cook in the same time it takes to put a crackling-crisp crust on the outside. When the *pakoras* are put in the oil, the temperature will drop but should again gradually be raised back to 350°F (180°C) by the end of frying. They are cooked to a reddish, golden-brown color.

Preparation and cooking time (after assembling ingredients): 40 minutes
Serves: 4 to 6

1¼ cups (125 g) sifted chickpea flour
    (sifted before measuring)
½ teaspoon (2 ml) turmeric
¼-½ teaspoon (1-2 ml) cayenne pepper
    or crushed dried red chilies
½ tablespoon (7 ml) ground coriander
½ tablespoon (7 ml) dry-roasted crushed cumin seeds
scant 1 teaspoon (5 ml) salt
¾ teaspoon (3.5 ml) baking powder
2 tablespoons (30 ml) melted *ghee* or unsalted butter
1 cup (240 ml) firmly packed fresh spinach (about 8 ounces
    /230 g), washed, stemmed, patted dry and shredded
1 large firm red or green tomato (about ½ pound/230 g), diced
ghee or vegetable oil for shallow-frying

    1. Blend the chickpea flour, turmeric, cayenne or crushed chili, ground coriander, cumin seeds, salt and baking powder in a mixing bowl. Add the melted *ghee* or butter, spinach and tomato, and gently mix. The juice from the tomato should bind the ingredients together, but you may need an additional sprinkle of water. You should have a muffin-like batter, neither too moist nor too dry.

    2. Heat 2 tablespoons (30 ml) of *ghee* or vegetable oil in a large heavy frying pan over moderately high heat until it is hot but not smoking. Half-fill a ¼-cup (60 ml) measuring cup with batter and carefully add to the hot oil. Depending on pan size, fry 5 or 6 *pakoras* at a time for about 4 minutes per side until both sides are crisp and reddish-brown. Remove with a slotted spoon and drain on paper towels. Shape and fry the remaining *pakoras* in the same way. Serve piping hot with a lemon wedge or fresh chutney.

    Note: Once the batter is assembled, it should be used immediately. As the mixture sits, it tends to become sticky and wet, and will require additional flour to thicken.

For information about unfamiliar ingredients or techniques, see A-to-Z

The Great Shallow-Fried Vine Leaf Rissole
ANGOOR PATTA PAKORA

Fresh vine leaves are a rarity, unless you have an arbor in your yard. Most likely you will purchase them preserved in water, salt and citric acid, in 6–8-ounce (170–230 g) jars or plastic pouches. They are available at most gourmet stores or Greek groceries. The leaves are blanched, drained, finely shredded and folded into a seasoned, herbed batter. The mixture is then poured into an 8 or 9-inch (20–22.5 cm) sauté pan and shallow-fried into a large round rissole that is golden brown and crunchy on the outside and soft on the inside. Cut the rissole into pie-shaped wedges for serving and accompany with a wedge of lemon or a seasoned sauce.

Preparation time (after assembling ingredients): 30 minutes
Cooking time: 10–15 minutes
Makes: 6 or 8 wedges

2 cups (205 g) sifted chickpea flour
    (sifted before measuring)
1½ teaspoons (7 ml) salt
1 cup (85 g) shredded fresh or dry
    unsweetened coconut, lightly packed
1 teaspoon (5 ml) paprika or a scant
    ½ teaspoon (2 ml) cayenne pepper
1 tablespoon (15 ml) cumin seeds
½ teaspoon (2 ml) yellow asafetida powder (*hing*)*
1 cup (240 ml) cold water
1 teaspoon (5 ml) baking powder
1 6–8-ounce (170–230 g) package of grapevine
    leaves, blanched for 5 minutes, rinsed,
    drained thoroughly and finely shredded
1 cup (240 ml) *ghee* or light vegetable oil
a few sprigs of fresh parsley for garnishing

*This amount applies only to yellow Cobra brand. Reduce any other asafetida by three-fourths.

1. Blend the flour, salt, coconut, paprika or cayenne, cumin seeds and asafetida in a large bowl. Add the water and, working with a wire whisk, blend into a smooth, light batter. Add the baking powder and vine leaves, and stir with a few swift strokes, until mixed.
2. Heat the *ghee* or vegetable oil in an 8–9-inch (20–22 cm) sauté pan over moderately low heat until it is hot but not smoking. Gently transfer the mixture into the hot oil, quickly spreading it evenly to the edges of the pan, into a flat cake. After 4–5 minutes, when one side is golden brown, lift the rissole with a wide spatula or two small spatulas and flip it over to brown the other side. When golden brown, transfer to paper towels to drain momentarily, then to a serving tray. Garnish with minced parsley and serve hot, cut into wedges. (Cut with a sharp serrated knife. If the vine leaves are not sufficiently blanched, they tend to tear when cut.)

Batter-Coated Stuffed Baby Tomatoes
TAMATAR BONDA

For entertaining, it is hard to top this hot-off-the-flame *pakora*—cherry tomato cups stuffed with herbed *chenna* cheese. They can be stuffed well ahead of serving time and fried just before they are required. It is important to fully cover the tomato with batter, especially the stuffing, as it sputters and tends to fall apart in the frying oil. They must be served piping-hot and crisp, for as they cool they soften from the moisture in the stuffing. If you make the dish in quantity, organize carefully and collect a few helping hands.

Hollowed-out tomato cups are ideal containers for a number of stuffings, and you may want to include low calorie variations along with the fried *pakora*. Try stuffing small tomato cups, 1½–2 inches (4–5 cm) in diameter, with yogurt, puréed vegetables, cracked wheat or rice salad. Pasta salad also makes a good stuffing, dressed with pesto: use very fine fedelini (vermicelli), soup stars or any small pasta shape you might use in a broth.

Preparation and cooking time (after assembling ingredients): 30–40 minutes
Serves: 6 as hors d'oeuvres or 8 as a side dish

24–28 cherry tomatoes (about ¾–1 pound/340–455 g)
freshly made *chenna* cheese (page 315) made from
    4 cups/1 liter milk (about 5 ounces/140 g)
¼ teaspoon (1 ml) each freshly ground black pepper,
    yellow asafetida powder (*hing*)* and turmeric
2 tablespoons (30 ml) finely chopped fresh herbs, such as dill
    coriander, parsley, summer savory, basil or chervil
⅔ cup (60 g) sifted chickpea flour (sifted before measuring)
¼ teaspoon (1 ml) each cayenne pepper, salt and baking powder
about ¼ cup (60 ml) cold water
ghee or vegetable oil for deep-frying

*This amount applies only to yellow Cobra brand. Reduce any other asafetida by three-fourths.

1. Slice the stem off each cherry tomato and carefully hollow out with a small melon baller. Drain upside down on paper towels or a rack.

2. Bray and knead the *chenna* cheese, spices and herbs until fairly smooth. Divide into 24–28 portions and stuff into the tomato cups.

3. Combine the flour, cayenne, salt and baking powder in a bowl and mix well. Add 3 tablespoons (45 ml) of water slowly, beating with a wire whisk until the batter is smooth and free of lumps. If necessary, slowly add the remaining water until the consistency is similar to that of cream. It must be thick enough to seal in the cheese filling and thoroughly coat the tomatoes.

4. Heat 2½–3 inches (6.5–7.5 cm) of *ghee* or oil in a *karai*, wok or sauté pan to 350°F (180°C). Place 4 or 5 tomatoes in the batter, lift them up one by one with a chocolate dipping fork, drain off excess batter momentarily, then slip into the hot oil. Fry until golden brown on all sides, turning gently once they rise to the surface, or for about 3 minutes. Remove with a slotted spoon and drain on paper towels. Serve immediately, or keep warm in a 250°F (120°C) oven until the remaining tomatoes are fried. Allow 4 each for hors d'oeuvres or 3 as a side-dish savory.

For information about unfamiliar ingredients or techniques, see A-to-Z

KOFTA: FRIED VEGETABLE BALLS

Though *koftas* are almost always served in small bowls with a succulent sauce as part of a banquet or formal Vedic meal, they can also be served in large portions and make an ideal main-dish entrée for a three-course meal. There are innumerable varieties of *koftas* popular in regional cuisines. They are made from raw or cooked vegetables, sometimes fresh cabbage or cooked *dals*, combined with herbs and spices and usually bound together with chickpea flour. Shapes vary from balls to patties or logs, and cooking techniques include deep- and shallow-frying as well as baking. Seven varieties are considered classics: potato, cauliflower, cabbage, radish, lotus root, spinach and *panir* cheese. While most *koftas* are served with a gravy or sauce, some are simmered slowly to absorb the sauce fragrance and soften. Others are only drizzled with sauce for hinted flavors. Each sauce that I have suggested complements the seasonings in its specific *kofta* recipe. Still, feel free to select another sauce if you find it better complements accompanying dishes.

Cauliflower *Kofta*
GOBHI KOFTA

In North India, both cauliflower and lotus root *koftas* are favorites. They are not everyday foods, but it would not be surprising to find shredded cauliflower *koftas* on a Punjabi wedding menu, or lotus root *koftas* in a Kashmiri Sunday dinner. Since cauliflower is widely available much of the year, this is a perfect dish for entertaining: not only is it easy to make, but it holds up especially well in a bain-marie for up to an hour after frying. Cauliflower *koftas* are most frequently served with a spicy tomato sauce, but I find this pumpkin seed–cream sauce a pleasant alternative.

Four or five balls can be placed on hot rice, pasta or *paparh* noodles and served with a chunky vegetable sauce. Little more than soup or salad is needed to complete a full meal.

Preparation and cooking time (after assembling ingredients): about 45 minutes
Serves: 4 to 6

Sauce:

¾ cup (180 ml) toasted shelled pumpkin seeds
⅔ cup (160 ml) water or vegetable stock
1–2 green jalepeño chilies
½ teaspoon (2 ml) *garam masala*
½ teaspoon (2 ml) ground coriander
¼ teaspoon (1 ml) raw sugar
¼ teaspoon (1 ml) turmeric
1 tablespoon (15 ml) chickpea flour
1 teaspoon (5 ml) salt
1 cup (240 ml) cream or half-and-half

Kofta:

3½ cups (830 ml) finely shredded cauliflower
    flowerets (about 1 pound/455 g)*
1 tablespoon (15 ml) scraped, minced fresh ginger root
1 teaspoon (5 ml) turmeric
1 tablespoon (15 ml) dry-roasted crushed cumin seeds
1 teaspoon (5 ml) *garam masala*
3 tablespoons (45 ml) minced fresh coriander or parsley
about 1 cup (100 g) sifted chickpea flour
    (sifted before measuring)
1 teaspoon (5 ml) baking powder
¾ teaspoon (3.5 ml) salt
ghee or vegetable oil for deep-frying
chopped toasted pumpkin seeds or minced herbs for garnishing

*To shred the cauliflower in a blender, half-fill the container with water. Add 1 cup (240 ml) of chopped cauliflower, cover, and pulse 5 or 6 times until finely shredded. Pour into a strainer and drain, then press out all the excess water. Repeat until all the cauliflower is shredded. Alternately, shred in a food processor or Mouli machine with a fine shredding disc.

    1. To make the sauce, combine the pumpkin seeds, water or stock and chilies in a food processor fitted with the metal blade, or a blender. Cover and process until smooth. Add the remaining ingredients and process once again briefly to mix. Transfer to a heavy saucepan and place over moderate heat. Stirring constantly, bring to a boil. Reduce the heat and simmer for 6–8 minutes or until slightly reduced and thickened to the consistency of a thin cream sauce.

    2. Combine the cauliflower, ginger, turmeric, cumin seeds, *garam masala* and fresh coriander or parsley in a mixing bowl and toss to mix. In a smaller bowl, blend the chickpea flour with the baking powder and salt.

    3. When you are ready to fry the *koftas*, begin warming 2½–3 inches (6.5–7.5 cm) of *ghee* or vegetable oil in a *karai*, wok or deep-frying pan over moderate heat. While the oil is heating, add the flour mixture into the cauliflower and knead by hand until the ingredients are bound together. (The cauliflower should have enough moisture to hold the ingredients together. You may need to add sprinkles of water or chickpea flour to achieve this texture. As it sits, the mixture will become looser. For this reason, the flour is added just before shaping and frying.) Shape into 20 balls or logs.

For information about unfamiliar ingredients or techniques, see A-to-Z

4. Raise the heat to moderately high, and when the frying oil reaches 355°F (180°C), slip in 6–8 balls at a time, depending on pan size, maintaining the temperature at between 335°–340°F (168°–171°C). After the *koftas* bob to the surface, turn them frequently and fry for 8–10 minutes or until evenly browned to a reddish-gold color and crispy texture. Remove with a slotted spoon and drain on paper towels. Keep warm in a 250°F (120°C) oven while frying the remaining *koftas*. Allow the temperature to reach 355°F (180°C) before frying the second batch. Before serving, place the balls in a heated shallow serving dish and cover with hot sauce. Garnish with chopped toasted pumpkin seeds or minced herbs.

Zucchini *Kofta*
LOUKI KOFTA

Louki and *tinda*, fine-grained summer-type squash, are popular in *koftas*. *Louki*, also known as bottle gourd, is available in larger cities at Indian or Chinese grocery stores. *Tinda*, actually a melon but known as round gourd, is more difficult to locate and is often tough-skinned and over mature. The recipe has also been tested using three types of seedless American squash—young zucchini, pattypan and cocozelle—all yielding excellent results. These are moist *koftas*, slightly heavier than the previous cauliflower variation, and should be heated in sauce, over the lowest possible heat, for 4 or 5 minutes to soften them and absorb supporting flavors. Try them with *Fragrant Tomato and Yogurt Gravy*.

Preparation and cooking time (after assembling ingredients): about 30 minutes
Serves: 4 to 6

3 cups (710 ml) coarsely shredded seedless summer squash (about 1 pound/455 g)
1–2 hot green chilies, seeded and minced
½-inch (1.5 cm) piece of scraped, minced fresh ginger root
3 tablespoons (45 ml) finely chopped fresh coriander or minced parsley
1 teaspoon (5 ml) salt
½ teaspoon (2 ml) baking powder
ghee or vegetable oil for deep-frying
about 1 cup (100 g) sifted chickpea flour (sifted before measuring)
a few sprigs of coarsely chopped fresh coriander or minced parsley for garnishing

1. Squeeze the shredded squash between your palms to extract excess moisture, then blend with the green chilies, ginger, fresh herbs, salt and baking powder in a mixing bowl.
2. When you are ready to fry the *koftas*, begin warming 2½–3 inches (6–7.5 cm) of *ghee* or vegetable oil in a *karai*, wok or deep-frying pan over moderate heat. While the oil is heating, add the flour into the zucchini mixture and knead by hand until the ingredients are bound together. (The zucchini should have enough moisture to hold the ingredients together. As it sits, the mixture will become looser. For this reason, the flour is added just before shaping and frying.) Divide into 20 portions and press them into round balls.

3. Raise the heat to moderately high, and when the oil reaches 355°F (180°C), slip in 6–8 balls at a time, depending on pan size, maintaining the temperature at between 335°–340°F (168°–171°C). After the *koftas* bob to the surface, turn them frequently and fry for 8–10 minutes or until evenly browned to a reddish-gold color and crispy texture. Remove with a slotted spoon and drain on paper towels. Keep warm in a 250°F (120°C) oven while frying the remaining *koftas*. Allow the temperature to reach 355°F (180°C) before frying the second batch.

4. Before serving, place the balls in a heated shallow serving dish and serve in *Fragrant Tomato and Yogurt Gravy*. Garnish with the minced fresh herbs.

Cabbage *Kofta*
BANDHGOBHI KOFTA

The Bengali chefs in the home of Tarun Kunti Ghosh, a sprawling country residence just outside Calcutta, are some of the finest in the area. Though many of them have never left Bengal, they are artists in regional Bengali Vaishnava cooking. The first time I sampled their artistry, nearly 80 guests had assembled for a 108 course feast—an intoxicating experience that lasted several hours. Their cabbage *koftas* were served with a room-temperature tamarind dipping sauce, rather than with a hot gravy. Try with either *Sweet 'n' Sour Tamarind Sauce* or *Seasoned Tomato Gravy*.

Preparation and cooking time (after assembling ingredients): about 30 minutes
Serves: 4 to 6

3½ cups (830 ml) finely shredded trimmed cabbage (about 1 pound/455 g)
1–2 hot green chilies, seeded and minced
½-inch (1.5 cm) piece of peeled fresh ginger root
¼ cup (25 g) grated fresh or dried coconut
1 teaspoon (5 ml) each turmeric and *garam masala*
3 tablespoons (45 ml) finely chopped fresh coriander,
    parsley or mixed herbs
1 teaspoon (5 ml) salt
1 teaspoon (5 ml) baking powder
ghee or vegetable oil for deep-frying
about 1 cup (100 g) sifted chickpea flour (sifted before measuring)
a few sprigs of coarsely chopped fresh coriander or minced
    parsley for garnishing
1 tablespoon (15 ml) toasted choppped pumpkin seeds for garnishing

1. Squeeze the shredded cabbage between your palms to extract excess moisture, then blend with the green chilies, ginger, coconut, turmeric, *garam masala*, herbs, salt and baking powder in a mixing bowl.

2. When you are ready to fry the *koftas*, begin warming 2½–3 inches (6.5–7.5 cm) of *ghee* or vegetable oil in a *karai*, wok or deep-frying pan over moderate heat. While the oil is heating, add the flour into the cabbage mixture and knead by hand until the ingredients are bound together. (The cabbage should have enough moisture to hold the ingredients together. As it sits, the mixture will become looser. For this reason, it is important to add the flour just before shaping and frying. You may need to add sprinkles of water or more chickpea flour to ensure a mixture that can be pressed into logs. If you make this recipe in quantity, mix the ingredients in batches.) Divide into 8 portions and press into logs about 1½ inches (4 cm) long.

3. Raise the heat to moderately high, and when the oil reaches 355°F (180°C), slip in 6–8 logs at a time, depending on pan size, maintaining the temperature at between 335°–340°F (168°–171°C). After the *koftas* bob to the surface, turn them frequently and fry for 8–10 minutes or until evenly browned to a reddish-gold color and crispy texture. Remove with a slotted spoon and drain on paper towels. Keep warm in a 250°F (120°C) oven while frying the remaining *koftas*. Allow the temperature to reach 355°F (180°C) before frying the second batch. Before serving, place the logs in a heated shallow serving dish and cover with one of the above suggested sauces. Garnish with the fresh minced herbs and chopped toasted pumpkin seeds.

Radish *Kofta* Patties
MOOLI KOFTA

I have made this *kofta* often over the last fifteen years, and each time four out of every five people who tried it were unable to guess that radish was the main ingredient. The more pungent the radish, the more authentic the taste. In India, a white cooking radish called *mooli* is used, and you will likely be able to find them in large cities at Indian or Chinese grocery stores. At supermarkets and greengrocers, Japanese *daikon* radishes are becoming popular. Failing that, use icicle or even rosy-red salad radishes. This *kofta* is delicious with *Pistachio Cream Sauce with Sesame Seeds*.

Preparation and cooking time (after assembling ingredients): about 30 minutes
Serves: 6

2 tablespoons (30 ml) coriander seeds
1 tablespoon (15 ml) cumin seeds
½ teaspoon (2 ml) fennel seeds
3½ cups (830 ml) finely shredded radishes
½ teaspoon (2 ml) crushed dried red chilies
1 tablespoon (15 ml) scraped, finely shredded or minced fresh ginger root
1 teaspoon (5 ml) salt
2 tablespoons (30 ml) finely chopped fresh coriander or parsley
ghee **or vegetable oil for shallow-frying**
about 1 cup (100 g) sifted chickpea flour (sifted before measuring)
¾ teaspoon (3.5 ml) baking powder

1. Combine the coriander seeds, cumin seeds and fennel seeds in a small heavy pan and place it over moderately low heat. Dry-roast the spice seeds, tossing often, until they darken a few shades, or for about 5 minutes. Remove and coarsely crush in a spice mill or a mortar and pestle.

2. Squeeze the shredded radishes between your palms to extract excess moisture, then combine with the crushed spice seeds, red chilies, ginger, salt and fresh herbs in a mixing bowl.

3. When you are ready to fry the *koftas*, begin warming ½ inch (1.5 cm) of *ghee* or vegetable oil in a heavy large frying pan over low heat. While the oil is heating, add the flour and baking powder to the radish mixture and knead with your fingers until the mixture holds together. (The radish should have enough moisture to hold the ingredients together. As it sits, the mixture will become looser. For this reason, the flour is added just before shaping and frying.) Divide into 12 portions and flatten into smooth patties ½-inch (1.5 cm) thick.

4. Raise the heat to moderately high and, when the oil reaches 355°F (180°C), slip in 6 patties at a time, without crowding the pan, maintaining the temperature at between 335°–340°F (168°–171°C). Fry until evenly browned on both sides to a reddish-gold color and a crispy texture. Remove with a slotted spoon and drain on paper towels. Keep warm in a 250°F (120°C) oven while frying the remaining *koftas*. Allow the temperature to reach 355°F (180°C) before frying the second batch.

Chenna Cheese *Kofta* with Shredded Spinach
CHENNA PALAK KOFTA

When fried at just the right temperature, the outside crust on this marbled *kofta* is crisp and thin, and the spinach-cheese filling is succulent and moist. The light balls are delicious with little more than a sprinkle of lime juice, but they also go well with *Creamy Almond Sauce with Horseradish*.

Preparation and cooking time (after assembling ingredients): about 25 minutes
Serves: 4 to 6

1 pound (455 g) fresh spinach, washed, trimmed,
    finely chopped and steamed for 5 minutes
freshly made *chenna* cheese (page 315)
    made from 6 cups (1.5 liters) milk (about 7½ ounces/215 g)
1 tablespoon (15 ml) scraped, finely
    shredded or minced fresh ginger root
1–2 hot green chilies, seeded and minced
¼ teaspoon (1 ml) turmeric
¼ teaspoon (1 ml) yellow asafetida powder (*hing*)*
⅛ teaspoon (0.5 ml) freshly ground nutmeg
½ teaspoon (2 ml) *garam masala*
1 teaspoon (5 ml) salt
¾ cup (75 g) sifted chickpea flour (sifted before measuring)
ghee or vegetable oil for deep-frying

This amount applies only to yellow Cobra brand. Reduce any other asafetida by three-fourths.

For information about unfamiliar ingredients or techniques, see A-to-Z

1. When the spinach is cool enough to handle, press handfuls between your palms to remove as much liquid as possible.

2. Unwrap the warm *chenna* cheese, break it apart, and press with a clean tea towel to extract excess moisture. Knead on a marble slab or clean countertop by pushing small amounts across the work surface with the heel of your palm, spreading the cheese into a thin film. Knead and bray the cheese for a few minutes until it is creamy and smooth. Add the ginger, chilies, turmeric, asafetida, nutmeg, *garam masala*, salt and ⅔ cup (60 g) of chickpea flour, and knead until well blended. Scrape off as much as you can from your hands, then wash your hands and dry them.

3. Using a spatula, gather the cheese into a neat mound on the work surface. Rub your hands with a film of oil, then divide the cheese into 16–18 even portions and roll into smooth balls. Dust the balls with the remaining chickpea flour and again roll out the balls between your palms. (The balls can be made up to this point and set aside, covered, for several hours in the refrigerator. Bring to room temperature before frying.)

4. Heat 2½–3 inches (6.5–7.5 cm) of *ghee* or oil to 345°F (173°C) on a thermometer. One by one, slip 5 or 6 balls into the oil. Once they bob to the surface, turn gently and constantly until they are crisp and evenly browned, anywhere from 6 to 8 minutes per batch. Remove with a slotted spoon and drain on paper towels. Fry the remaining balls and serve piping hot, or keep warm in a 250°F (120°C) oven for up to ½ hour.

Potato and *Panir* Cheese *Kofta*
ALOO PANIR KOFTA

There are numerous variations of this *kofta*. One popular North Indian recipe combines crumbled herb *panir* cheese with par-boiled shredded potatoes. Another, a Gujarati favorite, combines firm, shredded *panir* with coarsely mashed potatoes. This *kofta* is traditionally batter-coated and deep-fried. As a low-calorie alternative, skip the batter and bake them. For a brunch buffet, try it both ways, and accompany with creamy, stirred yogurt, a touch of *Hot Green Chili Sauce* and *Seasoned Tomato Gravy*.

Preparation time (after assembling ingredients): about 15 minutes
Baking time: 25–30 minutes (15–20 minutes if frying)
Serves: 6

Koftas:

fresh *panir* cheese (page 313) made from 6 cups (about 6 ounces/170 g)
3 large baking potatoes (about 1½ pounds/685 g), peeled, steamed and mashed
3 tablespoons (45 ml) coarsely chopped fresh coriander or minced parsley
3 tablespoons (45 ml) finely chopped mixed nuts
½ teaspoon (2 ml) turmeric
¼ teaspoon (1 ml) yellow asafetida powder (*hing*)*
1 tablespoon (15 ml) scraped, finely shredded or minced fresh ginger root
1–2 hot green chilies, seeded and minced
½ teaspoon (2 ml) *amchoor* powder or 1 teaspoon (5 ml) lemon juice
1½ teaspoons (7 ml) salt

Optional Batter:

1⅓ cups (135 g) chickpea flour (sifted before measuring)
¼ teaspoon (1 ml) salt
½ tablespoon (7 ml) ground coriander
1 teaspoon (5 ml) melted *ghee* or vegetable oil
1 cup (240 ml) cold water
ghee or vegetable oil for shallow-frying

*This amount applies only to yellow Cobra brand. Reduce any other asafetida by three-fourths.

1. Place the fresh firm *panir* cheese on a large countertop or marble slab and knead it by pushing small bits across the surface with the heel of your hand until the texture is smooth and creamy, anywhere from 3 to 5 minutes. Add all of the remaining *kofta* ingredients and repeat the kneading until they are thoroughly mixed in. Wash and dry your hands. Rub your palms with a film of oil and divide into 12 pieces. Roll the mixture into balls then flatten slightly into patties ½-inch (1.5 cm) thick. Set all of the pieces on a plate lined with plastic wrap.

2. If you are baking the *koftas*, heat the oven to 350°F (180°C). Arrange on a buttered baking sheet and bake for 12–15 minutes. Turn the patties over and bake for another 12–15 minutes. Serve hot or at room temperature.

3. If you are deep-frying the *koftas*, combine the chickpea flour, salt, ground coriander and melted *ghee* or vegetable oil in a mixing bowl. Pour in ½ cup (120 ml) of water and whisk until smooth, then slowly add enough water to make a thick crêpe-like batter.

4. Heat about 1 inch (2.5 cm) of *ghee* or oil in a large sauté pan or skillet until the temperature reaches 345°F (173°C). One by one, slip 4 or 5 of the *koftas* into the batter and carefully lower into the hot oil. Do not overcrowd the pan or the temperature will drop. Cook on both sides until golden brown. Remove and drain on paper towels. Keep warm in a 250°F (120°C) oven until all of the *koftas* are fried. Serve hot or at room temperature.

Soft 'n' Savory Chickpea *Kofta*
KABLI CHANA KOFTA

This *kofta* resembles a Middle Eastern snack food called falafel. Though it is more often a part of a Vedic meal than a light snack, try it with a drizzle of *Creamy Almond Sauce with Horseradish* as part of a dinner or at lunch as a sandwich filling for *chapatis*, with a shredded salad, cheese and *Simple Tomato Chutney.*

Preparation time (after assembling ingredients): 15 minutes
Cooking time: about 20 minutes for baking, 15 minutes for frying
Serves: 6

For information about unfamiliar ingredients or techniques, see A-to-Z

2 cups (480 ml) cooked chickpeas, well drained
1 medium-sized baking potato (about 8 ounces/230 g), cooked, peeled and mashed
½–1 tablespoon (7–15 ml) ground coriander
½ teaspoon (2 ml) yellow asafetida powder (*hing*)*
1 teaspoon (5 ml) each paprika and ground cumin
⅛ teaspoon (0.5 ml) cayenne pepper
½ tablespoon (7 ml) salt
3 tablespoons (45 ml) olive or sesame oil
½ teaspoon (2 ml) baking powder
¼ cup (25 g) ground sesame seeds, pumpkin seeds or almonds
2 tablespoons (30 ml) yogurt
¼ cup (60 ml) coarsely chopped fresh coriander or minced fresh parsley, slightly packed
ghee or vegetable oil for frying (optional)

This amount applies only to yellow Cobra brand. Reduce any other asafetida by three-fourths.

1. Attach the metal cutting blade to a food processor. Add the chickpeas and process, stopping to scrape down the sides of the work bowl with a spatula, until the texture resembles coarse bread crumbs. Transfer two-thirds of the ground chickpeas to a mixing bowl, along with the mashed potato.

2. Add the remaining ingredients, except the *ghee* or oil, to the ground chickpeas in the food processor and blend until smooth. Add this paste to the mixing bowl and mix well. Wash and dry your hands, then rub them with a film of oil. Shape the mixture into about 20 balls, patties or logs. (If the mixture is too loose, add breadcrumbs, wheat or chickpea flour to facilitate easy shaping.)

3. The *koftas* can be baked or fried. To bake, place on a well-greased baking sheet and bake in a preheated 350°F (178°C) oven for about 20 minutes, turning once for even browning. To fry, heat about 2 inches (5 cm) of *ghee* or vegetable oil in a sauté pan or *karai*, and when the temperature reaches 355°F (180°C), add 6 or 7 *koftas*. Do not crowd the pan or the temperature will drop too suddenly. Fry until golden reddish-brown on all sides, or for 4–5 minutes. Transfer with a slotted spoon and drain on paper towels. Keep warm in a 250°F (120°C) oven until all the *koftas* are cooked.

DEEP-FRIED SAVORY STUFFED PASTRIES

Pastries the world over are made from three basic materials: flour, butter and liquid. An elaborate array of textures results from combining different techniques and heat sources with varying proportions of these ingredients. The hallmark doughs in Western cooking—shortcrust, puff pastry and pâte brisée—are assembled with two rules of thumb: use cold ingredients, work surfaces and tools; and handle the dough as little and as rapidly as possible. These rules are topsy-turvy in the case of strudel dough, which is made with melted butter and vigorously kneaded before being stretched into gossamer-thin sheets.

Like strudel dough, Vedic pastry doughs must be strong and elastic, so that they can be rolled thin. These characteristics are acquired from the preparation technique known as *moyan dena*, ''rubbing into.'' Melted butter and flour are rubbed between fingers and warm palms to evenly incorporate the ingredients. The doughs are then kneaded to activate the gluten network and, after resting, easily respond to shaping. Properly fried, the pastries are slightly more flaky than crisp.

For the recipes in this pastry section, please note that for accurate flour measurements you should spoon the flour into a measuring cup and level off with a spatula. Though quicker, the "dip-and-sweep" method and the practice of shaking a cup to level it will not give accurate results. For further suggestions on measuring flour, check *A–Z General Information*.

Samosas

These triangular pastries are a national passion, and all over India one can buy them in snack houses and from hand-pushed carts and roadside stalls even in remote villages. *Samosa* dough has a high proportion of flour to butter and is firm, slightly resembling Italian cannoli dough.

Samosas are usually fried just before serving as a snack or meal savory. They are also delicious at room temperature in a lunch box or on a picnic. To reheat *samosas*, place them on a baking tray in a 350°F (176°C) oven for 10 minutes. *Samosas* can also be partially fried (about two-thirds cooked), cooled and kept frozen in a single layer in flat plastic containers for up to 2 weeks. Defrost and air-dry, then fry again at 350°F (176°C) until golden brown, warmed and crisp.

Kachoris

The first time I assisted Srila Prabhupada in the kitchen, he sat in front of me with flour, unsalted butter and a pitcher of water and deftly made *kachori* dough. For five hours he engaged me in shaping more than 100 potato *kachoris*, while he personally fried them in his kitchen. He informed me every time one burst from improper sealing or a thin spot formed on the crust. That was my introduction to one of the most elegant of Vedic pastries. The occasion was my younger sister's wedding, and of all the dishes prepared by Srila Prabhupada for this fifteen-course feast, *kachoris* were one of the most popular. It was only later that I learned the art of frying *kachoris*.

Kachoris come in two types: flat patties about 1½ inches (4 cm) in diameter and ¼ inch (6 mm) thick, popular as tiffin snacks (a custom similar to British high tea), traveling and lunch box companions and feast foods; and thin *kachoris*, also called *dal poori*, which are winter favorites for brunch or late supper.

Here, even more than with other fried pastries, care must be paid to temperature, for *kachoris* are fried at very low temperatures. Initially, they are placed in *ghee* heated to at least 300°F (150°C). (At this temperature the gluten proteins in the flour begin to coagulate, along with the starches and sugars, to form a coating that protects the inside of the food from absorbing excess oil.) The temperature will immediately drop to near 225°F (107°C), and should be slowly brought back up to near 300°F (150°C), which means that each batch will take about 25 minutes to fry. For this reason, very large *karais* (bowl-shaped frying pans) are used for quantity cooking. I have attended wedding feasts where three-foot (one meter) wide *karais* were busy from dawn to dusk for three days turning out thousands of *kachoris*!

For those new to *kachori* frying, the following temperatures and corresponding times may be helpful.

Low to moderately low heat After 1 minute: 220°–225°F (104°–107°C) Faint bubbles rising.	Low to moderately low heat After 7 minutes: 235°–245°F (113°–118°C) Almost all have risen to the surface.
Moderate range heat After 14 minutes: 255°–265°F (124°–129°C) All have swelled. Turn over at this time.	Moderate range heat After 21 minutes: 270°–275°F (132°–135°C) Surface becomes hard; faint gold color.

Moderately high heat After 27 minutes: 290°–295°F (143°–146°C) Pale, buff-gold color on both sides; crisp crust.

Note: Let the *ghee* cool to 300°F (150°C) before frying the second batch. Strain the *ghee* after frying, cool, and refrigerate it until needed for further deep-frying.

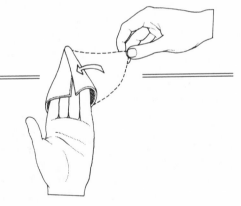

Seasoned Potato *Samosa*
ALOO SINGHARA

In Bengal, *samosa* and *singhara* are synonymous—an outstanding pastry. One temple chef in Vishakapatnam informed me there are "as many variations for potato *samosa* as there are stars in the sky!" Suffice it to say that there is ample room for improvisation. This one is part traditional, part inspirational: potatoes are the predominant flavor, supported by green chilies, black mustard seeds, raw sugar, powdered spices and *Mint–Lime Butter*. The crust is thin, light and fried until flaky. Try these *samosas* with a dab of *Fresh Mint Chutney*.

Preparation time (after assembling ingredients): about 1 hour
Frying time: about 20 minutes
Makes: 28 *samosas*

1½ cups (175 g) unbleached white flour
¼ cup (45 g) fine semolina or regular (non-instant) farina (35 g)
½ teaspoon (2 ml) salt
4 tablespoons (60 ml) *Mint–Lime Butter* (page 300)
   or unsalted butter, softened
6–7 tablespoons (90–105 ml) ice water
1½ teaspoons (7 ml) black mustard seeds
2 tablespoons (30 ml) *Mint–Lime Butter, ghee* or unsalted butter
2–3 hot green chilies, seeded and minced
½-inch (2 cm) piece of scraped, finely shredded or minced fresh ginger root
¼ teaspoon (1 ml) yellow asafetida powder (*hing*)*
6 medium-sized potatoes (1½ pounds/675 g), boiled,
   peeled and cut into ¼-inch (6 mm) dice
1¼ teaspoons (6 ml) *garam masala* or *chat masala*
2 teaspoons (10 ml) salt
1 teaspoon (5 ml) raw sugar
2 tablespoons (30 ml) chopped fresh coriander or lemon basil
flour for dusting
ghee or vegetable oil for deep-frying

*This amount applies only to yellow Cobra brand. Reduce any other asafetida by three-fourths.

   1. Blend the flour, semolina or farina, and salt in a mixing bowl. Add the softened butter and rub it in with your fingertips until it is fully incorporated and the mixture resembles fresh bread crumbs. Add 6 tablespoons (90 ml) of ice water and work until the ingredients can be gathered into a ball. (Add the remaining water in dribbles as necessary to form a non-sticky, kneadable firm dough.) Knead on a clean surface for about 8 minutes or until the dough is smooth and pliable. Shape it into a ball, rub it with oil, cover with plastic, and set aside to rest for ½–1 hour while making the filling. (The dough can be made up to 2 days in advance, well sealed, and refrigerated. Bring it to room temperature before rolling out and shaping the *samosas*.)
   Alternately, fit a food processor with the metal blade, combine the flour, semolina or farina and salt, and pulse twice. Add the softened butter and 6 tablespoons (90 ml) of ice water and pulse about 10 times. Add the remaining water slowly, with the machine running, just until the dough forms into a mass. Do not allow the dough to form into a ball; avoid overprocessing. Remove and shape into a ball of dough, place it in a plastic bag and refrigerate while making the filling.
   2. Place the black mustard seeds in a large frying pan over moderate heat. When they begin to jump around in the pan, add the seasoned butter, *ghee* or unsalted butter, green chilies, ginger and asafetida. Fry until the mustard seeds turn gray and pop. Immediately add the potatoes, *garam masala* or *chat masala*, salt and sugar, and stir-fry for 2–3 minutes. Remove the pan from the heat, stir in the fresh herbs and let the mixture cool to room temperature. Divide it into 28 portions.
   3. Knead the dough briefly, roll it into a rope about 14 inches (35 cm) long, and cut it into 14 equal pieces. Shape them into smooth balls and set aside on a plate, without touching, then cover with a damp kitchen towel or plastic wrap. Collect the equipment you need for shaping: a bowl of water, sharp paring knife, dusting flour and a rolling pin. Divide the dough into 28 equal portions. Working on one piece of dough at a time, flatten the ball into a patty, then roll it out on a lightly floured work surface into a thin, 6-inch (15 cm) round.

For information about unfamiliar ingredients or techniques, see A-to-Z

Cut the round in half to make two semicircles. Dip a fingertip in water and moisten half of the straight edge of one semicircle; then pick it up and bring the other half over it to form a cone, making a ¼-inch (6 mm) seam of a dry edge over a moistened edge. Press securely to seal the seam well. Fill the cone ⅔–¾ full with filling, moisten the inside of the opening, then pinch the top closed, allowing a good ¼-inch (6 mm) seam. (All seams must be well sealed. If they are weak, filling will fall out during frying and, worse, hot oil will seep into the pastry and the *samosa* will become heavy and greasy.)

The top edge can be left plain, crimped with a fork or plaited with your fingers. Set the *samosa*, seam side down, on a baking tray in a cool place. Make all 28 *samosas* in the same way. (The *samosas* may be kept on trays in a cool nook, loosely covered, for 3–4 hours, or refrigerated for up to 8 hours and removed 30 minutes before frying.)

5. Heat 2½–3 inches (6.5–7.5 cm) of *ghee* or oil to 365°F (185°C) in a *karai* or deep sauté pan over moderate heat. Slip 3 or 4 *samosas* into the oil and fry for 4–5 minutes or until golden brown. Drain on paper towels and serve hot.

Cauliflower and Green Pea *Samosa*
GOBHI HARI MATAR SAMOSA

Srila Prabhupada's 1967 cooking classes in San Francisco were the most exciting I have ever known in any cooking school: the who, what, when, where, why and how of Vedic cooking. When he gave us this recipe, he suggested only the techniques required and main ingredients. Spices were measured in the palm of the hand, and the quality of flour was determined by feel. Each student came out of the class with his or her version of a good cauliflower *samosa*. This is mine. Try it with *Quick Tamarind–Raisin Chutney*.

Preparation time (after assembling ingredients): about 1 hour
Frying time: 30–40 minutes
Makes: 24 *samosas*

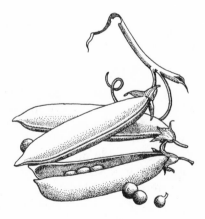

2 cups (235 g) unbleached white flour
¾ teaspoon (3.5 ml) salt
4 tablespoons (60 ml) melted *ghee* or unsalted butter
⅓ cup (80 ml) plain yogurt
2 tablespoons (30 ml) cold water, or as needed
½ tablespoon (7 ml) cumin seeds
1 tablespoon (15 ml) coriander seeds
½ teaspoon (2 ml) fennel seeds
4 whole cloves
1-inch (2.5 cm) piece of cinnamon stick,
    crushed into small pieces
2 tablespoons (30 ml) *ghee* or vegetable oil
½ teaspoon (2 ml) yellow asafetida powder (*hing*)*
1 small cauliflower (1 pound/455 g), cored, trimmed,
    coarsely diced and steamed until tender
1¼ cups (300 ml) new peas or frozen baby peas, steamed
½ teaspoon (2 ml) turmeric
1 teaspoon (5 ml) salt
ghee or vegetable oil for deep-frying

This amount applies only to yellow Cobra brand. Reduce any other asafetida by three-fourths.

1. Blend the flour and salt in a mixing bowl. Add the softened butter and rub it in with your fingertips until it is fully incorporated and the mixture resembles fresh bread crumbs. Add the yogurt and 1 tablespoon (15 ml) of cold water and work until the ingredients can be gathered into a ball. Add the remaining tablespoon (15 ml) of water in dribbles, or as necessary, to form a nonstick, kneadable firm dough. Knead on a clean surface for about 8 minutes or until the dough is smooth and pliable. Shape it into a ball, rub it with oil, cover with plastic, and set aside to rest for ½–1 hour while making the filling. (The dough can be made up to 2 days in advance, well sealed, and refrigerated. Bring it to room temperature before rolling out and shaping the *samosas*.)

Alternately, fit a food processor with the metal blade, combine the flour and salt, and pulse twice. Add the butter, yogurt and 2 tablespoons (30 ml) of water and pulse about 10 times, adding additional water if necessary. The mixture should not form a ball, but should resemble coarsely chopped soft cheese. It can be easily gathered into a ball and briefly kneaded until smooth and round. Gather into a smooth ball, place in a plastic bag, and refrigerate while making the filling.

2. Place the cumin seeds, coriander seeds, fennel seeds, cloves and cinnamon in a heavy frying pan over moderately low heat. Dry-roast until the seeds darken a few shades, then remove and coarsely grind in a spice mill or stone mortar. Heat the *ghee* or oil in the frying pan over moderate heat until it is hot but not smoking. Drop in the asafetida, and a few seconds later add the steamed cauliflower, peas, turmeric and salt. Stir-fry for 2–3 minutes, then remove from the heat and cool to room temperature. Divide into 24 portions.

3. Knead the dough briefly, roll it into a rope about 12 inches (30 cm) long, and cut it into 12 equal pieces. Shape them into smooth balls and set aside on a plate, without touching, then cover with a damp kitchen towel or plastic wrap. Collect the equipment you need for shaping: a bowl of water, sharp paring knife, dusting flour and a rolling pin. Working on one piece of dough at a time, flatten it into a patty, then roll out on a lightly floured work surface into a thin, 6-inch (15 cm) round. Cut the round in half to make two semicircles. Dip a fingertip in water and moisten half of the straight edge of one semicircle; then pick it up and bring the other half over it to form a cone, making a ¼-inch (6 mm) seam of a dry edge over a moistened edge. Press securely to seal the seam well.

4. Fill the cone ⅔–¾ full with stuffing, moisten the inside of the opening, pinch the top closed, allowing a good ¼-inch (6 mm) seam. (All seams must be well sealed. If they are weak, stuffing will fall out during frying and, worse, hot oil will seep into the pastry and the *samosa* will become heavy and greasy.)

The top edge can be left plain, crimped with a fork or plaited with your fingers. Set the *samosa*, seam side down, on a baking tray in a cool place. Make all 24 *samosas* in the same way. (The *samosas* may be kept on trays in a cool nook, loosely covered, for 3–4 hours, or refrigerated for up to 8 hours. Remove 30 minutes before frying.)

5. Heat 2½–3 inches (6.5–7.5 cm) of *ghee* or oil to 365°F (185°C) in a *karai* or deep sauté pan over moderate heat. Fry 3 or 4 *samosas* at a time for 4–5 minutes or until they are crisp and golden brown. Remove with a slotted spoon and drain on paper towels. Keep warm in a 250°F (120°C) oven while frying the remaining *samosas*.

Note: *Samosas* are usually fried just before serving as a snack or meal savory. They are also delicious at room temperature in a lunch box or on a picnic. To reheat *samosas*,

---

For information about unfamiliar ingredients or techniques, see A-to-Z

place them on a baking tray in a 350°F (176°C) oven for 10 minutes. *Samosas* can also be partially fried (about two-thirds cooked), cooled and kept frozen in a single layer in flat plastic containers for up to 2 weeks. Defrost and air-dry, then fry again at 350°F (180°C) until golden brown, warmed and crisp.

Cauliflower and Potato *Samosa*
GOBHI ALOO SAMOSA

Though *samosas* are usually made with unbleached flour and deep-fried, I created this baked, whole wheat *samosa* when I was catering for a vegetarian health club. The pastries resemble miniature Cornish pasties more than traditional *samosas*. Like pasties, it goes very well with *Velvet Tomato Catsup.*

Preparation, cooling and rolling out time (after assembling ingredients): about 1 hour
Cooking time: 20 minutes for frying, 20–25 minutes for baking
Makes: 26 *samosas*

2 cups (210 g) well-sieved whole wheat pastry flour or *chapati* flour
⅛ teaspoon (0.5 ml) baking powder
2 tablespoons (30 ml) powdered sunflower seeds
2 tablespoons (30 ml) minced fresh herbs, such as coriander, parsley or basil
3 tablespoons (45 ml) cream cheese, well chilled
3–4 tablespoons (45–60 ml) unsalted butter or *ghee*, well chilled and cut into small pieces
½ cup (120 ml) yogurt or buttermilk
water as needed
2 tablespoons (30 ml) *ghee* or vegetable oil
1 tablespoon (15 ml) scraped, minced fresh ginger root
2–3 hot green chilies, seeded and minced
1 teaspoon (5 ml) black mustard seeds
2 medium-sized tomatoes, peeled, seeded and chopped
½ tablespoon (7 ml) ground coriander
½ teaspoon (2 ml) turmeric
1 teaspoon (5 ml) *garam masala*
3½ cups (830 ml) diced cauliflower, steamed until tender
2¼ cups (530 ml) diced potatoes, steamed until tender
¼ cup (60 ml) minced fresh herbs such as coriander, parsley or basil
1 tablespoon (15 ml) lemon juice
ghee or oil for deep-frying (optional)

1. Place the flour, baking powder, sunflower meal and fresh herbs in a bowl and blend well. Add the chilled cream cheese and butter and rub them in with your fingertips until they are fully incorporated and the mixture resembles fresh bread crumbs. Pour in the yogurt or buttermilk and sprinkles of water until the ingredients can be gathered into a non-sticky, kneadable firm dough. Knead on a clean surface for about 8 minutes or until the dough is smooth and pliable. Shape it into a ball, rub it with oil, cover with plastic, and set aside to rest for 1 hour while making the filling. (The dough can be made up to 2 days in advance, well sealed, and refrigerated. Bring it to room temperature before rolling out and shaping.)

Alternately, fit a food processor with the metal blade, combine the flour, baking powder, sunflower meal and fresh herbs, and pulse twice. Add the cream cheese and butter and process until the texture resembles the size of small peas. With the motor running, add the yogurt or buttermilk and cold water in dribbles until the mixture holds together when pressed into a ball. Shape it into a ball, cover with plastic, and set aside while making the stuffing.

2. Heat the *ghee* or vegetable oil in a large frying pan over moderate heat until it is hot but not smoking. Add the ginger, green chilies and black mustard seeds, and fry until the seeds pop and turn gray. Stir in the tomato, ground coriander, turmeric and *garam masala*, and fry until the mixture is thick and pulpy. Add the cauliflower and potatoes, mashing lightly, and fry for 3–4 minutes. Remove the pan from the heat, stir in the ¼ cup (60 ml) fresh herbs and the lemon juice, and cool to room temperature. Divide the filling into 26 portions.

3. Knead the dough briefly, roll it into a rope 13 inches (17.5 cm) long and cut it into 13 equal pieces. Shape them into smooth balls and set aside on a plate without touching, then cover with a damp kitchen towel or plastic wrap. Collect the equipment you need for shaping: a bowl of water, sharp paring knife, dusting flour and a rolling pin. Working on one piece at a time, flatten the ball into a 5½ inch (14 cm) circle. Cut the round in half to make two semicircles. Place a portion of stuffing (about 1½ table-spoons/22 ml) on half of a semicircle. Moisten the edges of the pastry with water and fold the unfilled side over the filling. Press the edges together, then pick up the *samosa* and pinch the straight and rounded edge firmly closed. Trim off the excess and crimp the edges with a fork. Repeat the process with the remaining *samosas*. All seams must be well sealed.

5. Bake on a cookie sheet in a preheated 350°F (176°C) oven for 20–25 minutes, or deep-fry as directed in the previous recipe. Serve hot.

Tangy Potato and Coconut *Singhara* Logs
ALOO NARIYAL SINGHARA

In 1976, I had the opportunity to observe the mastery of the resident chef of the C.L. Bajoria household, Mr. S.B. Sharma. Daily I stood, notebook in hand, studying and questioning the Marawadi master chef as he turned out elaborate menus from breakfast to late dinner. One day he supervised the making of 250 of these *singharas*, carefully arranging the pastries in leaf-lined shallow baskets, each basket covered with a monogrammed, new linen napkin. In an elaborate procession of 20 bearers, each balancing three baskets, a lavish array of fried nibblers, pastries, sweets and fruits was presented before the family Deity of Lord Krishna and then relished at a late-afternoon garden party.

This *singhara* has a thin, crisp crust and a moist, buttery potato filling. It is excellent with *Rich Tamarind Chutney* or *Fresh Coriander and Gooseberry Chutney*.

For information about unfamiliar ingredients or techniques, see A-to-Z

Preparation, cooking and shaping time (after assembling ingredients): about 1 hour
Frying time: about 30 minutes
Makes: 16 *singhara* logs

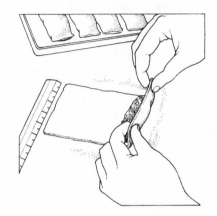

1½ cups (175 g) unbleached white flour
½ teaspoon (2 ml) salt
⅛ teaspoon (0.5 ml) baking powder
3 tablespoons (45 ml) melted *ghee* or butter
5–6 tablespoons (75–90 ml) ice water, or as needed
ghee or vegetable oil for deep-frying
2½ cups (600 ml) peeled potatoes, cut
    into ¼-inch (6 mm) dice
2 tablespoons (30 ml) *ghee* or vegetable oil
1¼ teaspoons (6 ml) cumin seeds
⅓ teaspoon (1.5 ml) yellow asafetida powder (*hing*)*
½ cup (120 ml) new peas or frozen baby peas, steamed
⅔ cup (160 ml) shredded fresh or defrosted
    frozen shredded coconut
2–3 hot green chilies, seeded and minced
½-inch (1.5 cm) piece scraped minced fresh ginger root
1 teaspoon (5 ml) turmeric
¼ teaspoon (1 ml) paprika or cayenne pepper
1½ teaspoons (7 ml) salt
1¼ teaspoons (6 ml) *garam masala*
1 tablespoon (15 ml) lemon juice
1 teaspoon (5 ml) sugar
2 tablespoons (30 ml) chopped fresh coriander

This amount applies only to yellow Cobra brand. Reduce any other asafetida by three-fourths.

    1. Blend the flour, salt and baking powder in a large mixing bowl. Drizzle in the melted *ghee* or butter and rub it in with your fingertips until it is fully incorporated and the mixture resembles fresh bread crumbs. Add 5 tablespoons (75 ml) of ice water and work until the ingredients can be gathered into a ball. Add the remaining tablespoon (15 ml) of water in dribbles, or as necessary, to form a non-sticky, kneadable firm dough. Knead on a clean surface for about 8 minutes or until the dough is smooth and pliable. Shape it into a ball, rub it with oil, cover with plastic and set aside to rest for ½ hour–1 hour while making the stuffing. (The dough can be made up to 2 days in advance, well sealed, and refrigerated. Bring it to room temperature before rolling and shaping the *singharas*.)
    Alternately, fit a food processor with the metal blade, combine the flour, salt and baking powder, and pulse twice. Add the butter and 5 tablespoons (75 ml) of water and pulse about 10 times. Add the remaining water slowly, with the machine running, just until the dough forms into a mass. Avoid overprocessing. Do not allow the dough to form into a ball. Remove the dough and shape into a ball. Place it in a plastic bag and refrigerate briefly while making the stuffing.
    2. Heat 2½–3 inches (6.5–7.5 cm) of *ghee* or vegetable oil in a *karai* or sauté pan until the temperature reaches 365°F (185°C) on a thermometer. Carefully add half of the diced potatoes and fry for about 5 minutes or until they are three-quarters cooked but not crispy or brown. They will be a few shades darker than crisp white, a buff-tan color.

Remove with a large slotted spoon and drain in a sieve resting over another pan. Fry the remaining potatoes in the same way, then remove the pan from the heat and set aside to cool.

3. Place 2 tablespoons (60 ml) *ghee* or vegetable oil in a large nonstick frying pan over moderate heat. When it is hot but not smoking, add the cumin seeds and asafetida, and fry until the spice seeds darken a few shades. Stir in the potatoes, steamed peas, coconut, chilies, ginger, turmeric, paprika or cayenne, salt, and *garam masala*, and mix well. Reduce the heat to moderately low, partially cover, and cook for 8–10 minutes or until the potatoes are soft and the stuffing is dry. Lightly mash some of the potatoes, then add the lemon juice, sugar and fresh herbs, remove the pan from the heat, and let the mixture cool to room temperature. When it is easy to handle, divide into 16 portions and compress them into logs about 2½ inches (6.5 cm) long.

4. Briefly knead the dough and divide into 2 pieces. Roll each into a rope 8 inches (20 cm) long and cut each into 8 equal pieces. Shape into smooth balls and set aside on a plate, without touching, then cover with a damp kitchen towel or plastic wrap. Collect the equipment you need for shaping: a bowl of water, sharp paring knife, dusting flour and a rolling pin. Working with one piece at a time, flatten a ball into a patty and roll it out on a lightly floured work surface into a thin rectangle or oblong shape about 6½ inches (16.5 cm) long and 4½ inches (11.5 cm) wide. Trim the edges with a knife to make a 6 x 4-inch (15 x 10 cm) pastry. Dip your fingers in water and moisten all the edges. Place a portion of the filling about 1¼ inches (3.5 cm) from one end. Roll the log up to the other end, pressing to firmly close the seams. Lay each log on a cookie sheet, seam side down, and crimp the edges with the tines of a fork. Roll, fill and close the remaining pieces.

7. Heat the *ghee* or oil in the frying vessel over moderate heat until it reaches 355°F (179°C). Fry 5 or 6 pieces at a time at about 340°F (171°C) until they turn a pale golden brown color and are nicely crisped. Remove and drain on paper towels. Serve immediately, or keep warm on a paper-towel-lined baking dish in a pre-heated 250°F (120°C) oven.

Spicy Green Pea *Kachori*
MATAR KACHORI

Kachoris are served on special occasions such as weddings, birthdays and holidays. Try pea *kachoris* with *Fresh Mint Chutney*, sliced mango or papaya with fresh lime and *Dainty Chenna Cheesecakes with Almond Frosting* for a late morning brunch or late afternoon tiffin.

Preparation and shaping time (after assembling ingredients): 1¼ hours
Frying time: about 1 hour
Makes: 18 *kachoris*

For information about unfamiliar ingredients or techniques, see A-to-Z

2 cups (235 g) unbleached white flour
1 teaspoon (5 ml) salt
⅛ teaspoon (0.5) sugar
4 tablespoons (60 ml) *ghee* or unsalted butter, softened
7–9 tablespoons (105–135 ml) ice water
1⅔ cups (400 ml) new peas or frozen baby peas, steamed
1 tablespoon (15 ml) *ghee* or unsalted butter
2–3 hot green chilies, seeded and minced
1-inch (2.5 cm) piece of scraped, minced fresh ginger root
¼ teaspoon (1 ml) yellow asafetida powder (*hing*)*
1 teaspoon (5 ml) *garam masala*
½ tablespoon (2 ml) lemon juice
⅛ teaspoon (0.5 ml) baking soda
1 teaspoon (5 ml) sugar
ghee for deep-frying

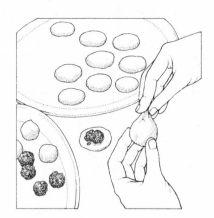

This amount applies only to yellow Cobra brand. Reduce any other asafetida by three-fourths.

   1. Blend the flour, salt and sugar in a mixing bowl. Add the softened *ghee* or butter and rub it in with your fingertips until it is fully incorporated and the mixture resembles coarse bread crumbs. Add a scant ½ cup (120 ml) of ice water and quickly work the ingredients to moisten the flour evenly until it can be gathered into a rough dough. If necessary, add the remaining water or as needed to make a non-sticky, kneadable soft dough. Knead on a clean surface for about 8 minutes or until the dough is smooth and pliable. Shape it into a ball, wrap with plastic and set aside in a cool nook to rest for ½ hour–1 hour while making the stuffing. (The dough can be made up to 2 days in advance, well sealed, and refrigerated. Bring it to room temperature before shaping and stuffing the *kachoris*.)

   Alternately, fit a food processor with the metal blade, combine the flour, salt and sugar, and process until mixed. Add the softened *ghee* or butter and pulse about 10 times or until fully incorporated. With the motor running, slowly pour in a scant ½ cup (120 ml) of ice water and process until the dough forms a ball. Remove it, shape it into a ball, wrap in plastic, and set aside in a cool place while making the stuffing.

   2. Place the peas in a bowl and mash with a fork until pulpy. Heat the 1 tablespoon (15 ml) *ghee* or butter in a heavy nonstick frying pan over moderate heat. Add the green chilies and ginger and fry for about ½ minute, then follow with the asafetida. After frying for 5 seconds, add the peas, *garam masala*, lemon juice, baking soda and sugar, and stir-fry for about a minute. Remove the pan from the heat and cool to room temperature. Divide the stuffing into 18 portions.

   3. Divide the dough in half and roll each piece into a log about 9 inches (22.5 cm) long. Cut both to yield 18 pieces. Shape each piece into a smooth patty and set them aside on a plate, without touching. Cover with a damp towel or plastic wrap. Working with one piece of dough at a time, flatten it into a 2½-inch (6.5 cm) patty. Gently press around the edges with your thumb and forefinger to thin slightly. Place a portion of stuffing in the center of the dough, then bring the sides of the dough over the filling to enclose it completely. Pinch the seams together until thoroughly sealed and smooth. With the pastry resting in the right palm, seam side up, press it with the heel of your left hand and flatten into a 2¼-inch (6 cm) patty, about ½ inch (1.5 cm) thick. (Try to avoid thin spots in the pastry casing, for they easily burst during frying. This allows oil to enter the *kachori*, which makes it heavy and greasy.) Place the pastry, seam side down, on a baking tray and cover with plastic wrap or a moist towel. Shape and stuff the remaining pieces.

4. Slowly heat 2½ inches (6.5 cm) of *ghee* to 300°F (150°C) in a 10–12-inch (25–30 cm) *karai* or sauté pan over moderately low heat. Slip in 9 pastries, seam side down. The *ghee* will automatically fall to about 225°F (107°C). Slowly fry the pastries for 24–27 minutes or until they sound hollow when tapped and turn a pale gold color. The crust should be delicately blistered and crisp. Use a wooden spoon for turning the delicate pastries (even chopsticks, if you are adept at using them). Remove them with a slotted spoon and drain on paper towels. Keep warm in a 250°F (120°C) oven while frying the remaining pastries. *Kachoris* may be made several hours ahead and reheated, uncovered, in a 350°F (180°C) oven for 10 minutes.

Seasoned Potato *Kachori*
ALOO KACHORI

Aside from festival, holiday and wedding menus, *kachoris* are good traveling or picnic companions. Try this variation with a dipping chutney such as *Fresh Coriander Chutney*, *Rich Tamarind Chutney* or *Velvet Tomato Catsup*.

Preparation and shaping time (after assembling ingredients): about 1¼ hours
Frying time: about 1 hour
Makes: 18 *kachoris*

2 cups (235 g) unbleached white flour (measured by spooning
    into a cup and leveling off with a spatula)
1 teaspoon (5 ml) salt
4 tablespoons (60 ml) *ghee* or butter, softened
2 tablespoons (30 ml) plain yogurt
7 tablespoons (105 ml) ice water, or as needed
2 tablespoons (30 ml) *ghee* or unsalted butter
2-3 hot green chilies, seeded and minced
½ tablespoon (7 ml) scraped, minced fresh ginger root
1¼ cups (300 ml) coarsely mashed potatoes
½ tablespoon (7 ml) ground coriander
1 teaspoon (5 ml) ground cumin
½ teaspoon (2 ml) ground fennel
1 teaspoon (5 ml) *garam masala*
¼ teaspoon (1 ml) turmeric
1 tablespoon (15 ml) lemon juice
1 teaspoon (5 ml) salt
2 tablespoons (30 ml) minced fresh coriander or parsley
ghee for deep-frying

1. Blend the flour and salt in a mixing bowl. Add the softened *ghee* or butter and rub it in with your fingertips until it is fully incorporated and the mixture resembles coarse bread crumbs. Add the yogurt and 6 tablespoons (90 ml) ice water, and quickly work the ingredients to moisten the flour evenly until it can be gathered into a rough dough. If necessary, add the remaining water or as much as needed to make a non-sticky, kneadable soft dough. Knead on a clean surface for about 8 minutes or until the dough is smooth and pliable. Shape it into a ball, wrap with plastic and set aside in a cool nook to rest for ½ hour–1 hour while making the stuffing. (The dough can be made up to 2 days in advance, well sealed, and refrigerated. Bring it to room temperature before shaping and stuffing the *kachoris*.)

Alternately, fit a food processor with the metal blade, combine the flour and salt, and process until mixed. Add the softened *ghee* or butter and pulse about 10 times or until fully incorporated. With the motor running, slowly pour in the yogurt and ice water and process until the dough forms a ball. Remove it, shape it into a smooth ball, wrap in plastic, and set aside in a cool place while making the stuffing.

2. Combine the remaining ingredients, except the *ghee* for deep-frying, in a mixing bowl and knead with your hands until well blended. Divide into 18 portions and set aside on a covered plate.

3. Divide the dough in half. Roll each half into a log about 9 inches (22.5 cm) long and cut them into 18 even pieces. Shape each piece into a smooth patty and set them on a plate, without touching. Cover well with a damp towel or plastic wrap. Working with one patty at a time, flatten it into a 2½-inch (6.5 cm) circle. Gently press around the edges with your thumb and forefinger to thin slightly. Place a portion of stuffing in the center of the dough, then bring the sides of the dough over the filling to enclose it completely. Pinch the seams together until thoroughly sealed and smooth. With the pastry resting in your right palm, seam side up, press with the heal of your left palm and flatten into a 2¼-inch (6 cm) patty, about ½ inch (1.5 cm) thick. (Try to avoid thin spots in the pastry casing, for they easily burst during frying. This allows oil to enter the *kachori*, which makes it heavy and, worse, greasy.) Place the pastry, seam side down, on a baking tray and cover with plastic wrap or a moist towel. Shape and stuff the remaining pieces.

4. Slowly heat 2½ inches (6.5 cm) of *ghee* to 300°F (150°C) in a 10-12-inch (25-30 cm) *karai* or sauté pan over moderately low heat. Slip in 9 pastries, seam side down. The *ghee* will automatically fall to about 225°F (107°C). Slowly fry the pastries for 24-27 minutes or until they sound hollow when tapped and turn a pale gold color. The crust should be delicately blistered and crisp.

Note: For those new to *kachori* frying, refer to cooking time chart on page 477.

Pastry Puffs Stuffed with Spicy *Urad Dal*
RADHABALLABHI KACHORI

In North India, winter mornings often reach freezing temperatures. As the sun begins to bring its warmth, many people gather around outdoor snack houses watching batches of these *kachoris* frying. They are served piping-hot along with filled leaf cups containing a steaming-hot potato stew called *aloo dum*. This is also a popular mid-morning brunch throughout the Punjab and Uttar Pradesh.

The dough is frequently made with a mixture of *chapati* and unbleached flour, although you could also use all *chapati* flour or a mixture of whole wheat pastry flour and unbleached flour. Also called *dal poori*, the *toovar dal* stuffing is delicious. These *kachoris* are rolled into flat rounds that look like small, thick *pooris*. They balloon during quick frying, but soon deflate and become soft.

Dal soaking time: 3-5 hours
Preparation and shaping time (after assembling ingredients): about 1 hour
Frying time: 20 minutes
Makes: 18 *kachoris*

2 cups (260 g) well-sieved *chapati* flour, or 1 cup (120 g) unbleached
    white flour and 1 cup (105 g) whole wheat pastry flour
1 teaspoon (5 ml) salt
5 tablespoons (75 ml) melted *ghee* or vegetable oil
7-10 tablespoons (105-150 ml) warm water, or as needed
½ cup (105 g) split *urad dal*, without skins,
    or *toovar dal*, soaked for 3-5 hours
1½ teaspoons (7 ml) cumin seeds
1½ tablespoons (22 ml) coarsely crushed coriander seeds
1 teaspoon (5 ml) fennel seeds
½ teaspoon (2 ml) crushed red chilies
½ teaspoon (2 ml) yellow asafetida powder (*hing*)*
½ teaspoon (2 ml) coarsely ground black pepper
⅔ cup (160 ml) water or vegetable stock
¾ teaspoon (3.5 ml) salt
ghee or vegetable oil for deep-frying

*This amount applies only to yellow Cobra brand. Reduce any other asafetida by three-fourths.

1. Blend the flour and salt in a large mixing bowl. Add 3 tablespoons (45 ml) of the *ghee* or oil and rub it in with your fingertips until it is fully incorporated and the mixture resembles coarse bread crumbs. Add 7-8 tablespoons (105-120 ml) of water and quickly work the ingredients to moisten the flour evenly until it can be gathered into a rough dough. If necessary, add the remaining water, or as needed, to make a non-sticky, kneadable soft dough. Knead on a clean surface for about 8 minutes or until the dough is smooth and pliable. Shape it into a ball, wrap with plastic, and set aside in a cool nook to rest for ½ hour–1 hour while making the stuffing. (The dough can be made up to 2 days in advance, well sealed, and refrigerated. Bring it to room temperature before shaping and stuffing the *kachoris*.)

Alternately, fit a food processor with the metal blade, combine the flour and salt, and process until mixed. Add the *ghee* or oil and pulse about 10 times or until fully incorporated. With the motor running, slowly pour in the water and process until the dough forms a ball. Remove it, shape it into a smooth ball, wrap in plastic, and set aside in a cool place while making the stuffing.

2. While the dough is resting, drain the *dal* and coarsely grind in a blender or a food processor fitted with the metal blade, pulsing the machine 5 or 6 times. Heat the remaining 2 tablespoons (30 ml) *ghee* or oil in a medium-sized saucepan over moderate

For information about unfamiliar ingredients or techniques, see A-to-Z

heat. When it is hot but not smoking, add the cumin seeds, crushed coriander seeds and fennel seeds and fry until the cumin seeds begin to brown. Drop in the crushed red chilies and asafetida, and after 5 seconds add the black pepper, water or stock and *dal*. When the liquid comes to a boil, reduce the heat to low and simmer, partially covered, until it is absorbed and the *dal* has softened but is still slightly firm. The texture should be moist enough to form into soft balls; if it is too dry or hard, add additional liquid and simmer for a few more minutes. Cool to room temperature, add the salt, and divide into 18 portions.

3. Divide the dough in half and roll each piece into a log about 9 inches (22.5 cm) long. Cut them into 18 pieces. Shape each piece into a smooth patty and set aside on a plate, without touching. Cover well with a damp towel or plastic wrap. Working with one piece of dough at a time, shape it into a patty about 2½ inches (6.5 cm) in diameter. Gently press around the edges with your thumb and forefinger to slightly thin it. Place a portion of stuffing in the center and bring the edges of the dough up over the filling to enclose it completely. Pinch the excess dough together, then press it back into the center of the patty. Flatten slightly, then dip in flour on both sides and roll out, seam side down, into a 3½-inch (9 cm) round. (Use even pressure and only enough flour to facilitate shaping. Excess flour will fall into the *ghee* and burn during frying.) Fill and roll out the remaining pieces, laying them in a single layer, without touching, on baking trays. Keep covered with plastic wrap.

4. When you are ready to fry the *kachoris*, heat 2½ inches (6.5 cm) of *ghee* or vegetable oil to 350°–355°F (175°–180°C) in a *karai* or sauté pan. Carefully slip 2 *kachoris* into the hot oil. First they will sink to the bottom of the pan, then bob to the surface. Press the surface of the *kachoris* with a slotted spoon to keep them below the surface of the hot oil. They will swell and fill with hot air within 30 seconds. Fry until lightly browned on one side, about 2 minutes, then turn over and fry on the second side for another 1-2 minutes. Remove with a slotted spoon and drain on a triple thickness of paper towels. Serve hot, or keep warm in a 250°F (120°C) oven while frying the remaining *kachoris*.

Note: For those new to *kachori* frying, refer to cooking time chart on page 477.

Flaky Mung *Dal Kachori*
KHASTA KACHORI

In popularity, *kachoris* are the Indian equivalent of Italian calzone—for children of all ages. As a child, Srila Prabhupada liked to watch the street vendors cooking on the busy roadside and accepted *kachoris* from them until all the inside and outside pockets of his vest were filled. That pastime won him the name "Kachori-mukhi" or "Kachori-mouth" from his grandmother. He predicted that *kachoris* would become almost as popular in America as they were in India, and I have noted that no matter how many I make, there are never leftovers.

The stuffing for this *kachori* is peppery and spicy, accentuated noticeably with flavor from fennel seeds and fresh coriander. It is very pleasant offset with *Pear Chutney with Dates and Pecans* or *Roasted Peanut Chutney*.

Dal soaking time: 3-5 hours
Preparation and shaping time (after assembling ingredients): about 1¼ hours
Frying time: about 1 hour
Makes: 18 *kachoris*

1½ cups (175 g) unbleached white flour, measured by
    spooning into cup and leveling off with a spatula
½ cup (70 g) *chapati* flour or whole wheat pastry flour
½ teaspoon (2 ml) salt
6 tablespoons (90 ml) *ghee*, softened
7-9 tablespoons (105-135 ml) ice water
½ cup (110 g) split *moong dal*, without skins, soaked for 3-5 hours
1 teaspoon (5 ml) cumin seeds
¾ teaspoon (3.5 ml) caraway seeds
1½ teaspoons (7 ml) fennel seeds
1½ tablespoons (22 ml) coriander seeds
¾ teaspoon (3.5 ml) coarsely ground black pepper
⅔ cup (160 ml) water or vegetable stock
¾ teaspoon (3.5 ml) salt or ½ teaspoon (2 ml) black salt
ghee or vegetable oil for deep-frying

1. Blend the flours and salt in a mixing bowl. Add 4 tablespoons (60 ml) of the softened *ghee* and rub it in with your fingertips until it is fully incorporated and the mixture resembles coarse bread crumbs. Add a scant ½ cup (120 ml) ice water and quickly work the ingredients to moisten the flour evenly until it can be gathered into a rough dough. If necessary, add the remaining water, or as needed, to make a non-sticky, kneadable soft dough. Knead on a clean surface for about 8 minutes or until the dough is smooth and pliable. Shape it into a ball, wrap with plastic, and set aside in a cool nook to rest for ½ hour–1 hour while making the stuffing. (The dough can be made up to 2 days in advance, well sealed, and refrigerated. Bring it to room temperature before shaping and stuffing the *kachoris*.)

Alternately, fit a food processor with the metal blade, combine the flours and salt, and process until mixed. Add the softened *ghee* and pulse about 10 times until fully incorporated. With the motor running, slowly pour in the scant ½ cup (120 ml) cold water and process until the dough forms a ball. Remove it, shape it into a smooth ball, wrap in plastic, and set aside in a cool place while making the stuffing.

2. While the dough is resting, drain the soaked *dal* and coarsely grind in a blender or food processor fitted with the metal blade by pulsing the machine 5 or 6 times. Heat the remaining 2 tablespoons (30 ml) of softened *ghee* in a medium-sized saucepan over moderate heat. When it is hot but not smoking, add the cumin seeds, caraway seeds, fennel seeds and coriander seeds, and fry until they darken a few shades. Add the black pepper, water or stock and coarsely ground *dal*, and bring the water to a boil. Reduce the heat to low and simmer, partially covered, until the water is absorbed and the *dal* has softened but is still slightly firm. The texture should be moist enough to form into soft balls; if it is too dry or hard, add additional water and simmer for a few more minutes. Cool to room temperature, add the salt and divide into 18 equal portions.

3. Divide the dough in half and roll each piece into a log about 9 inches (22.5 cm) long. Cut them into 18 pieces. Shape each piece into a smooth patty and set them aside on a plate, without touching. Cover well with a damp towel or plastic wrap. Working

For information about unfamiliar ingredients or techniques, see A-to-Z

with one piece of dough at a time, flatten into a 2½-inch (6.5 cm) patty. Gently press around the edges with your thumb and forefinger to thin slightly. Place a portion of stuffing in the center of the dough, then bring the sides of the dough over the filling to enclose it completely. Pinch the seams together until thoroughly sealed and smooth. With the pastry resting in your right palm, seam side up, press with the heel of your left hand and flatten into a 2½-inch (6.5 cm) patty, about ½ inch (1.5 cm) thick. (Try to avoid thin spots in the pastry casing, for they easily burst during frying. This allows oil to enter the *kachori*, which makes it heavy and, worse, greasy.) Place the pastry, seam side down, on a baking tray and cover with plastic wrap or a moist towel. Shape and stuff the remaining pieces.

4. Slowly heat 2½ inches (6.5 cm) of *ghee* to 300°F (150°C) in a 10-12-inch (25-30 cm) *karai* or sauté pan over moderately low heat. Slip in 9 pastries, seam side down. The *ghee* will automatically fall to about 225°F (107°C). Slowly fry the pastries for 24-27 minutes or until they sound hollow when tapped and turn a pale gold color. The crust should be delicately blistered and crisp.

Note: For those new to *kachori* frying, see the chart on page 477.

Corn *Kachori*
MAKKAI KACHORI

Kachori dough will never be as flaky as a pâte brisée, but will rather be a buttery, moist, layered crust with a crisp outside surface. In this dish, a small amount of fine cornmeal is added to both white and wheat flour to complement the fresh corn stuffing nestled inside. Try this *kachori* with *Fresh Coriander and Gooseberry Chutney*.

Preparation and shaping time: 1¼ hours
Frying time: 1 hour
Makes: 18 *kachoris*

1½ cups (175 g) unbleached white flour, measured by
    spooning into a cup and leveling off with a spatula
¼ cup (35 g) *chapati* flour or whole wheat pastry flour
¼ cup (35 g) fine cornmeal
1 teaspoon (5 ml) salt
¼ teaspoon (1 ml) sugar
4 tablespoons (60 ml) unsalted butter or *ghee*, softened
7-9 tablespoons (105-135 ml) ice water
1¼ cups (300 ml) fresh corn kernels (about
    3 small ears), cooked until tender
½ teaspoon (2 ml) *garam masala*
1 teaspoon (5 ml) ground coriander
¼ teaspoon (1 ml) cayenne pepper
½ teaspoon (2 ml) salt
2 tablespoons (30 ml) grated fresh or dried coconut
½ tablespoon (7 ml) wheat flour
ghee for deep-frying

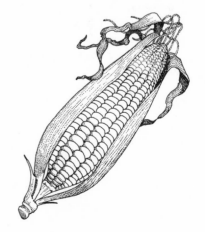

1. Combine the flours, cornmeal, salt and sugar in a large bowl. Add the softened *ghee* or butter and rub it in with your fingertips until it is fully incorporated and the mixture resembles coarse bread crumbs. Add a scant ½ cup (120 ml) of cold water and quickly work the ingredients to moisten the flour evenly until it can be gathered into a rough dough. If necessary, add the remaining water, or as needed, to make a non-sticky, kneadable soft dough. Knead on a clean surface for about 8 minutes or until the dough is smooth and pliable. Shape it into a ball, wrap with plastic, and set aside in a cool nook to rest for ½ hour–1 hour while making the stuffing. (The dough can be made up to 2 days in advance, well sealed, and refrigerated. Bring it to room temperature before shaping and stuffing the *kachoris*.)

Alternately, fit a food processor with the metal blade, combine the flours, cornmeal, salt and sugar, and process until mixed. Add the softened *ghee* or butter and pulse about 10 times or until fully incorporated. With the motor running, slowly pour the scant ½ cup (120 ml) of cold water and process until the dough forms a ball. Remove it, shape it into a ball, wrap in plastic, and set aside in a cool place while making the stuffing.

2. Mash the corn kernels in a small bowl or pulse 10 times in a food processor fitted with the metal blade. Add the remaining ingredients, except the *ghee*, and divide into 18 portions.

3. Divide the dough in half and roll each piece into a log about 9 inches (22.5 cm) long. Cut them into 18 pieces. Shape each piece into a smooth patty and set them aside on a plate, without touching. Cover well with a damp towel or plastic wrap. Working with one piece of dough at a time, flatten it into a 2½-inch (6.5 cm) patty. Gently press around the edges with your thumb and forefinger to thin slightly. Place a portion of stuffing in the center of the dough, then bring the sides of the dough over the filling to enclose it completely. Pinch the seams together until thoroughly sealed and smooth. With the pastry resting in your right palm, seam side up, press with the heel of your left hand and flatten into a 2¼-inch (6 cm) patty, about ½ inch (1.5 cm) thick. (Try to avoid thin spots in the pastry casing, for they burst easily during frying. This allows oil to enter the *kachori*, which makes it heavy and, worse, greasy.) Place the pastry, seam side down, on a baking tray and cover with plastic wrap or a moist towel. Stuff and shape the remaining pieces.

4. Slowly heat 2½ inches (6.5 cm) of *ghee* to 300°F (150°C) in a 10-12-inch (25-30 cm) *karai* or sauté pan over moderately low heat. Slip in 9 pastries, seam side down. The *ghee* will automatically fall to about 225°F (107°C). Slowly fry the pastries for 24-27 minutes or until they sound hollow when tapped and turn a pale gold color. The crust should be delicately blistered and crisp.

Note: For those new to *kachori* frying, please refer to the cooking time chart on page page 477

For information about unfamiliar ingredients or techniques, see A-to-Z

Dried Fruit *Kachori*

BESAN KACHORI

This sweet *kachori* stuffing can be made with many different fruits: apricots, dates, figs, prunes, apples, pears or raisins. Because the dried fruits and nuts rest in a chickpea flour fudge that is firm at room temperature, this *kachori* is particularly pleasant for outings and traveling. There is a distinctive contrast between the flaky crust and crumbly sweet filling.

Preparation and shaping time (after assembling ingredients): 1¼ hours
Frying time: 1 hour
Makes: 18 *kachoris*

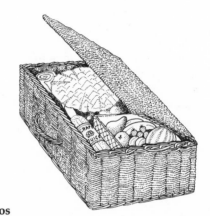

1 cup (120 g) unbleached white flour, measured by
    spooning into a cup and leveling off with a spatula
1 cup (105 g) whole wheat pastry flour, measured by
    spooning into a cup and leveling off with a spatula
½ teaspoon (2 ml) salt
½ tablespoon (7 ml) sugar
4 tablespoons (60 ml) *ghee*, softened
7–9 tablespoons (105–135 ml) ice water
3 tablespoons (45 ml) *ghee*
½ cup (50 g) sifted chickpea flour
    (sifted before measuring)
2 tablespoons (30 ml) finely chopped walnuts or cashews
2 tablespoons (30 ml) finely chopped almonds or pistachios
¼ cup (35 g) finely chopped dried fruit
⅓ cup (30 g) sifted maple sugar or powdered sugar
2 tablespoons (30 ml) honey or maple syrup
ghee for deep-frying

1. Combine the flours, salt and sugar in a large bowl. Add the softened *ghee* and rub it in with your fingertips until it is fully incorporated and the mixture resembles coarse bread crumbs. Add a scant ½ cup (120 ml) cold water and quickly work the ingredients to moisten the flour evenly until it can be gathered into a rough dough. If necessary, add the remaining water, or as needed, to make a non-sticky, kneadable soft dough. Knead on a clean surface for about 8 minutes or until the dough is smooth and pliable. Shape it into a ball, wrap with plastic, and set aside in a cool place to rest for ½ hour–1 hour while making the stuffing. (The dough can be made up to 2 days in advance, well sealed, and refrigerated. Bring it to room temperature before shaping and stuffing.)

Alternately, fit a food processor with the metal blade, combine the flours, salt and sugar, process until mixed, then add the softened *ghee* and pulse about 10 times or until fully incorporated. With the motor running, slowly pour in a scant ½ cup (120 ml) cold water and process until the dough forms a ball. Remove, shape it into a smooth ball, wrap in plastic, and set aside in a cool place while making the stuffing.

2. Melt the *ghee* in a heavy frying pan over moderate heat. When it is hot but not smoking, add the chickpea flour and cook, stirring constantly, for about 8 minutes or until the flour darkens a few shades. Add the remaining ingredients, except the *ghee*, and fry for 1–2 more minutes. Remove the pan from the heat, cool to room temperature, and divide into 18 portions.

3. Divide the dough in half and roll each piece into a log about 9 inches (22.5 cm) long. Cut them into 18 even-sized pieces. Shape each piece into a smooth patty and set them aside on a plate, without touching. Cover well with a damp towel or plastic wrap. Working with one piece of dough at a time, flatten it into a 2½-inch (6.5 cm) patty. Gently press around the edges with your thumb and forefinger to flatten slightly. Place a portion of stuffing in the center of the dough, then bring the sides of the dough over the filling to enclose it completely. Pinch the seams together until thoroughly sealed and smooth. With the pastry resting in your right palm, seam side up, press with the heal of your left hand and flatten into a 2½-inch (6.5 cm) patty, about ½ inch (1.5 cm) thick. (Try to avoid thin spots in the pastry casing, for they burst easily during frying. This allows oil to enter the *kachori*, which makes it heavy and, worse, greasy.) Place the pastry, seam side down, on a baking tray and cover with plastic wrap or a moist towel. Finish shaping and stuffing the remaining pieces.

4. Slowly heat 2½ inches (6.5 cm) of *ghee* to 300°F (150°C) in a 10–12-inch (25–30 cm) *karai* or sauté pan over moderately low heat. Slip in 9 pastries, seam side down. The *ghee* will automatically fall to about 225°F (107°C). Slowly fry the pastries for 24–27 minutes or until they sound hollow when tapped and turn a pale gold color. The crust should be delicately blistered and crisp. Use a wooden spoon or chopstick to turn the delicate pastries. Remove with a slotted spoon and drain on paper towels. Keep warm in a 250°F (120°C) oven while frying the remaining pastries. *Kachoris* can be made several hours ahead and reheated, uncovered, in a 350°F (180°C) oven for 10 minutes.

Note: For those new to *kachori* frying, please refer to the chart on page 477.

THIN *DOSA* PANCAKES

Some type of unleavened, thin pancake is made in most cuisines the world over— French crêpes, Dutch pannekoeken, Chinese mandarin pancakes, Russian blinchki and Italian socca. India is no exception, though to call them pancakes is somewhat of a misconception. Each region in India has its favorite versions and they are noticeably different: paper-thin crisp *dosa* from Tamil Nadu and Karnataka, vegetable laden *poora* from Maharastra and Gujarat and velvety smooth *cheela* from Uttar Pradesh and Madhya Pradesh. These versatile dishes are eaten from breakfast to late dinner.

In South India, where rice and *dal* play a predominant role in the diet, *dosas* are eaten as much as pasta is in Italy. They are made from pastes of wet-ground *urad dal* and rice, fermented slightly for flavor, and spread on hot iron griddles into parchment-thin rounds, sometimes 20 inches (50 cm) in diameter. The cooked side is smooth and golden-red while the top side is off-white with darker concentric circles from spreading the batter. Nourishing and easily digested, *dosas* are low calorie and quite addictive. Served with one of a myriad of fresh coconut chutneys and a cup of vegetable *dal* soup, they provide a gourmet meal for the most discerning palate.

For information about unfamiliar ingredients or techniques, see A-to-Z

Other *dosas* are made with batter. *Moong dal* or black-eyed pea *poora* batters are laced with spices and herbs—often with shredded vegetables—and spread a little thicker than *dosas*. Further, they are smaller and with a softer, finished crust. *Pooras* are made with a silky batter of chickpea flour and wheat or other *dal* flour. The finished pancake is soft and smooth, and, in the case of sweet Bengali *pullis*, crisp and waferlike. Gujarati *pudlas* most resemble Italian socca. While some batters require resting and fermenting, others can be whipped up on the spot. With few exceptions, most batters can be successfully refrigerated for several days, so they can be cooked just before serving. Like crêpes, some *dosas* freeze well for future use.

There are many opinions as to the perfect pans for cooking these delicacies. Indian cooks have long relied on well-seasoned iron griddles. However, even in rural areas, other pans are finding their way into the kitchens. Nature's contribution to nonstick surfaces is organic soapstone. Though they generally are small, expensive, and take considerable time to heat, they are excellent for some *dosas*. Upkeep is minimal—an occasional scouring with salt will suffice. Highly seasoned and well-used iron griddles and skillets are lifelong friends. Heavy-bottomed skillets offer good heat distribution and are inexpensive. Iron griddles are my personal favorites for yielding a crisp crust on the *dosas*. Soapstone, by contrast, yields a smoother, slightly softer, crust. Unlike crêpes and pancakes, which are under 8 inches, even household *dosas* are large: standard size is 18 inches (45 cm) long and 10 inches (25 cm) wide. For showy restaurant presentation, they may reach 24 inches (60 cm) in diameter. To duplicate these giants you will need either a double-burner iron griddle or restaurant griddle. The iron griddles reserved for *dosas* in South Indian restaurant kitchens are virtually nonstick because they are in constant use. You may not find this the case if your iron griddles or skillets are used infrequently. I find that greasing the heated pan before and after each use, along with adding a film of vegetable spray before shaping each *dosa*, usually does the trick.

For most other *dosas*, *cheelas* and *pooras*, nonstick griddles or omelette pans work well. Our testing kitchens rated Silverstone on heavy aluminum their unanimous first choice, with T-Fall last because its surface was too slippery. Recently Super Silverstone has reached the market with the promise of extended life expectancy and more durability. Like the original Silverstone surface, our test kitchens preferred its "grabbing" quality over other nonstick cookware. Because the pan's surface is more porous than cast iron, *dosas* cooked on it are softer and will usually brown more quickly.

The following selections are smaller than traditional *dosas*, anywhere from 6–10 inches (15–25 cm) in diameter, so you can use standard cookware and fit three or four pans easily on a household stove top, cutting cooking time to a minimum. Where preferred pans are suggested, they will be mentioned in the forewords to the recipes.

Delicate Rice and *Urad Dal Dosa*
SADA DOSA

These classic *dosas* are to South Indians what crêpes are to the French. But unlike crêpes, which are made from an egg, flour and milk batter, *dosas* are made from an airy purée of ground rice and *urad dal*. More like a spoonable cake batter than pourable crêpe batter, this mixture is spread out on the griddle with the back of a ladle instead of turning the pan with a flick of the wrist.

The Tamil word *pattu* (silky) best describes the texture of the batter and bottom crust. The hallmark of this *dosa* is its paper thin crust: silky smooth and crisp on the bottom with faint concentric ridges on its ivory-colored top.

Our test kitchens favored well-used iron pans over all others, not for ease during cooking, but because of even browning and a crisp and smooth underside. If you have a restaurant griddle or use two or three cooking pans, *dosas* take very little time to make; each one cooks in a few minutes. Preparing the batter is effortless in a food processor, but you will have to allow 24–36 hours resting time to achieve a sourdough flavor.

Dosas are served on large metal *thalis* (stainless steel trays) or are folded and placed on regular dinner plates with the crisp ends extending out over the edge of the plate.

Plain *dosas* are best hot off the griddle. For a light meal, try them with a cup of *Sweet 'n' Sour Dal Soup with Mixed Vegetables* and *Fresh Coconut and Mint Chutney*.

Soaking time: 4–6 hours
Preparation time: 15 minutes
Batter resting time: 24–30 hours
Cooking time: 30 minutes
Serves: 6 to 8

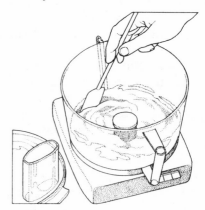

⅔ cup (145 g) split *urad dal*, without skins
1½ cups (130 g) *basmati* or other long grain white rice
scant ½ tablespoon (7 ml) salt
about ¾ cup (180 ml) *ghee* or vegetable oil

1. Sort through the *dal* and remove any foreign matter, then wash in several changes of water, drain, and place in a bowl. Add 3 cups (710 ml) of cold water to the *dal* and loosely cover. In a separate bowl, wash the rice in several changes of water, drain, and cover with 3 cups (710 ml) of cold water. Loosely cover the rice, and allow both to soak for 4–6 hours.

2. Drain the *dal* and place it in a food processor fitted with the metal blade, or a blender. Process for about 1½ minutes, adding ½ cup (120 ml) warm water in tablespoon (15 ml) amounts. Stop now and then to push the *dal* down toward the blades to facilitate even grinding. Slowly feed in another ¼ cup (60 ml) warm water and continue to process for 1–2 minutes until the batter is light and frothy. Using a rubber spatula, transfer all of the *dal* batter into a large ceramic or glass bowl. Drain the rice and add it to the food processor or blender. Cover and process for 1½ minutes, stopping now and then to push the rice down toward the blades, until it is ground into a meal similar to Cream of Wheat cereal.

For information about unfamiliar ingredients or techniques, see A-to-Z

Add ½ cup (120 ml) of water and process for 1 minute, then add another ¼ cup (60 ml) of water and process for another 3–4 minutes into a fine paste-like batter with only a trace of texture. Scrape the rice batter into the bowl with the *dal* batter and gently stir to mix. Drape a cloth napkin over the bowl and loosely cover with a plate. Set aside in a warm place (85–90°F/29–32°C is ideal) for 22–24 hours or until the batter has slightly expanded in volume, pleasantly fermented, and the surface is a mass of tiny bubbles. (Batter resting time will vary according to temperature and humidity and may take up to 30 hours.) Once the batter has fermented, add the salt and thin with warm water until the consistency is similar to a light cake batter, anywhere from ¾–1 cup (180–240 ml). The batter can also be kept for 2 or 3 days, well covered and refrigerated. Bring it to room temperature before use.

3. Collect the paraphernalia you will need for cooking the *dosas*: at least one (two or three to save time) iron griddle or skillet, 10 inches (25 cm) or more in diameter; a ⅓-cup (80 ml) measuring scoop or ladle; a large round-bottomed spoon; a wide spatula; a bowl of melted *ghee* or oil and a teaspoon; and a covered platter large enough for the cooked *dosas*. Pre-heat the griddle or skillet over moderate heat until it is hot. Brush the hot surface with *ghee* or oil and wipe off the excess. (To test griddle temperature, sprinkle a few drops of water on the surface. If it is too hot, the water will vanish immediately; if it is not hot enough, the water will sit on the surface and boil off. When the griddle is the right temperature, the drops of water will dance and sputter, then vanish.)

4. With the measuring cup or ladle, place ⅓ cup (80 ml) of batter in the center of the pan. Immediately place the bottom of a ladle or large soupspoon in the center of the batter and, pressing lightly, spread it outward in a continuous spiral motion. Make the *dosa* as thin as possible, in either a round or oval, until it is roughly 8 inches (20 cm) in diameter. Drizzle 1-2 teaspoons (5–10 ml) of *ghee* or oil over the surface and around the edges of the *dosa*, then cover the pan. Cook for 2–2½ minutes on the first side or until the bottom is golden-red and small holes appear on the top. Ease a flexible metal spatula around the edge to loosen the *dosa*, then flip it over. Cook, uncovered, for another minute or so on the second side, then flip it over again. Fold it in half and serve immediately or slip it onto a warm platter, the brown side on top. Place the platter in a warm oven (250°F/120°C) or place it on a food warmer, loosely covered, while making the remaining *dosas*.

Paper-Thin *Dosa* Stuffed with Herbed Potatoes
MASALA DOSA

A good paper *dosa* is so thin and crisp that it crumbles when broken and literally melts in your mouth. It is made from a plain *dosa* batter, but once shaped, the top surface is scraped away with a spatula, leaving only a paper-thin layer of batter on the griddle. Immediately after the cooked sheaf is loosened from the griddle, it is eased into a hollow log shape and the center garnished with a generous spoon of herbed potatoes and a dollop of soft herb butter. Stuffed *dosas* are always accompanied by a moist coconut chutney. *Creamy Fresh Coconut Chutney* is a good choice, or you can thin down any other selection with water or buttermilk.

It is impractical to use anything but your hands when eating this dish. If you are new to this practice, custom dictates that you use the right hand, breaking off bite-sized pieces of crisp *dosa*, scooping up a bite of potatoes and dipping both in the chutney.

Soaking time: 4–6 hours
Batter preparation time: 15 minutes , Batter resting time: 22–24 hours
Prepartion time for stuffing and cooking *dosas*: 30 minutes
Serves: 6 as a main dish or 8 as a side dish

Dosas:

⅔ **cup (145 g) split *urad dal*, without skins**
1½ **cups (130 g) *basmati* or other long grain white rice**
warm water as needed
1 **teaspoon (5 ml) salt**
1 **teaspoon (5 ml) ground cumin**
¼ **teaspoon (1 ml) yellow asafetida powder (*hing*)***

Stuffing and Cooking:

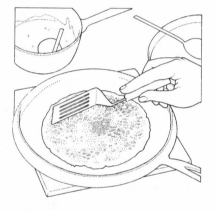

2 **tablespoons (30 ml) *ghee* or vegetable oil**
1 **teaspoon (5 ml) black mustard seeds**
½ **tablespoon (7 ml) seeded and minced hot green chilies**
2 **medium-sized boiling potatoes (about 12 ounces/340 g),**
    boiled, peeled and coarsely chopped
¼ **teaspoon (1 ml) turmeric**
½ **teaspoon (2 ml) *garam masala***
½ **teaspoon (2 ml) *chat masala* or black salt**
¼ **teaspoon (1 ml) ground coriander**
2 **tablespoons (30 ml) water**
1 **tablespoon (15 ml) lemon juice**
3 **tablespoons (45 ml) coarsely chopped fresh coriander or herbs**
up to ¾ cup (180 ml) *ghee* or vegetable oil

*This amount applies only to yellow Cobra brand. Reduce any other asafetida by three-fourths.

1. Sort through the *dal* and remove any foreign matter, then wash in several changes of water, drain, and place in a bowl. Add 3 cups (710 ml) of cold water and loosely cover. In a separate bowl, wash the rice in several changes of water, drain it, and cover with 3 cups (710 ml) of cold water. Loosely cover the rice, and allow both to soak for 4–6 hours.

2. Drain the *dal* and place it in a food processor fitted with the metal blade, or a blender. Process for about 1½ minutes, adding ½ cup (120 ml) warm water in tablespoon (15 ml) amounts. Stop now and then to push the *dal* down toward the blades and facilitate even grinding. Slowly feed in another ¼ cup (60 ml) warm water and continue to process for 1–2 minutes until the batter is light and frothy. Using a rubber spatula, transfer all of the *dal* batter into a large ceramic or glass bowl. Drain the rice and add it to the food processor or blender. Cover and process for 1½ minutes, stopping now and then to push the rice down toward the blades, until it is ground into a meal similar to Cream of Wheat cereal.

For information about unfamiliar ingredients or techniques, see A-to-Z

Add ½ cup (120 ml) of water and process for 1 minute, then add another ¼ cup (60 ml) of water and process for another 3–4 minutes into a fine paste-like batter with only a trace of texture. Scrape the rice batter into the bowl with the *dal* batter and gently stir to mix. Drape a cloth napkin over the bowl and loosely cover with a plate. Set aside in a warm place (85–90°F/29–32°C is ideal) for 22–24 hours or until the batter has slightly expanded in volume, pleasantly fermented, and the surface is a mass of tiny bubbles. (Batter resting time will vary according to temperature and particularily with humidity. It may take up to 30 hours.) Once the batter has fermented, add the salt and thin with warm water until the consistency is similar to a light cake batter, anywhere from ¾–1 cup (180–240 ml). The batter can also be kept for 2 or 3 days, well covered and refrigerated. Bring it to room temperature before use.

3. To make the potato stuffing, heat the 2 tablespoons (30 ml) *ghee* or oil in a large frying pan over moderate heat. When it is hot but not smoking, add the black mustard seeds and partially cover. When the seeds sputter, pop and turn gray, stir in the chilies and potatoes. Add the turmeric, *garam masala*, *chat masala*, ground coriander and 2 tablespoons (30 ml) water. Stir-fry for 2–3 minutes, then reduce the heat to very low and stir in the lemon juice and fresh herbs.

4. Collect the paraphernalia you will need for cooking the *dosas*: at least one (two or three to save time) iron griddle or skillet, 10 inches (25 cm) or more in diameter; a ⅓-cup (80 ml) measuring scoop or ladle; a large round-bottomed spoon; a wide spatula; a bowl of melted *ghee* or oil and a teaspoon; and a covered platter large enough for the cooked *dosas*. Pre-heat the griddle or skillet over moderate heat until it is hot. Brush the hot surface with *ghee* or oil and wipe off the excess. (To test griddle temperature, sprinkle a few drops on the surface. If it is too hot, the water will vanish immediately; if it is not hot enough, the water will sit on the surface and boil off. When the griddle is the right temperature, the drops of water will dance and sputter, then vanish.)

4. With the measuring cup or ladle, place ⅓ cup (80 ml) of batter in the center of the pan. Immediately place the bottom of a ladle or large soupspoon in the center of the batter and, pressing lightly, spread it outward in a continuous spiral motion. Make the *dosa* as thin as possible, in either a round or oval, until it is roughly 8 inches (20 cm) in diameter. When the bottom of the *dosa* has set but the top surface is still moist, gently pull a wide spatula across the surface and scrape off all but a paper thin layer of batter. This scraped-off portion of the batter is discarded. When the *dosa* has cooked for about 1 minute, drizzle 1–2 teaspoons (5–10 ml) of *ghee* or oil over the surface and around the edges, then cover the pan. Cook for about 2 minutes on the first side or until the bottom is golden-red. Ease a flexible metal spatula around the edge to loosen the *dosa*, and when it is free, carefully ease it into a hollow jellyroll. Because this *dosa* is exceptionally thin and crisp, it will crack if handled with anything but a light touch. Carefully transfer to a warm plate or platter.

5. To serve, place about 2 tablespoons (30 ml) of herbed potatoes into the hollow center of the *dosa* and add a dab of soft herb butter on top. Serve piping hot with room temperature chutney or keep warm, uncovered, in a 250°F (120°C) oven while shaping the remaining *dosas*.

Coconut *Dosa*

NARIYAL DOSA

In Kerala and Tamil Nadu, coconut seems to find its way into hundreds of dishes, sometimes prominently and at other times almost undetected. In these households, several coconuts are shredded daily and the preparation of coconut milk, even coconut oil, is a daily standard. This dish is a happy medium: a featured ingredient, but in small quantity. For most busy Western cooks, even shredding an occasional coconut is bothersome and far too time consuming. Fortunately, supermarkets now carry shredded or grated frozen coconut so the process is eliminated altogether. Try this *dosa* with *Simple Fresh Coconut Chutney*.

Dal soaking time: 4–6 hours
Preparation and batter resting time: 8–12 hours
Cooking time: 30 minutes
Serves: 6 to 8

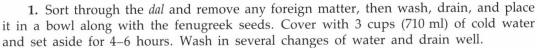

1 cup (210 g) split *urad dal*, without skins
¼ teaspoon (1 ml) fenugreek seeds
2 cups (300 g) ground rice or Cream of Rice cereal
warm water as needed
½ tablespoon (7 ml) salt
1 small hot red, yellow and green chili, halved, seeded
    and minced, or 2 dried red chili pods, halved, seeded
    and finely chopped
¾ cup (65 g) fresh or frozen grated coconut, defrosted (115 g)
about ½ cup (120 ml) melted *ghee* or coconut oil

1. Sort through the *dal* and remove any foreign matter, then wash, drain, and place it in a bowl along with the fenugreek seeds. Cover with 3 cups (710 ml) of cold water and set aside for 4–6 hours. Wash in several changes of water and drain well.

2. Place the drained *dal* and fenugreek seeds in a food processor fitted with the metal blade, or a blender. Process for about 1½ minutes, adding 1 cup (240 ml) warm water in ¼ cup (60 ml) amounts. Stop now and then to push the *dal* down toward the blades to facilitate even grinding, for 2–3 minutes. Slowly feed in another ¼ cup (60 ml) warm water and continue to process for an additional 2 minutes until the batter is light and frothy. Using a rubber spatula, transfer all of the *dal* batter into a large ceramic or glass bowl. Place the ground rice or Cream of Rice and 2 cups (480 ml) warm water in the container and process for about 2 minutes, stopping once or twice if necessary, to incorporate the dry ingredient with the water. When the mixture is smooth and light, add it to the *dal* batter and stir to mix. Drape a cloth napkin over the bowl, loosely cover with a plate, and set aside in a warm place (85–90°F/29–32°C is ideal) for 8–12 hours. (Batter resting time varies with temperature and humidity. When it is ready, it will have expanded in volume and will appear light and frothy with a pleasant sour smell.) When the batter has sufficiently fermented, stir in the salt, chilies, and coconut.

3. Collect the paraphernalia you will need for cooking the *dosas*: at least one (two or three to save time) iron or nonstick griddle, 10 inches (25 cm) or more in diameter; a ⅓-cup (80 ml) measuring scoop or ladle; a large round-bottomed spoon; a wide spatula; a

---

For information about unfamiliar ingredients or techniques, see A-to-Z

bowl of melted *ghee* or oil and a teaspoon; and a covered platter large enough for the cooked *dosas*. Pre-heat the griddle or skillet over moderate heat. Brush the hot surface with *ghee* or oil and wipe off the excess. (To test griddle temperature, sprinkle a few drops of water on the surface. If it is too hot, the water will vanish immediately; if it is not hot enough, the water will sit on the surface and boil off. When the griddle is the right temperature, the drops of water will dance and sputter, then vanish.)

4. With the measuring cup or ladle, place ⅓ cup (80 ml) of batter in the center of the pan. If you use an iron griddle, immediately place the bottom of a ladle or large soup spoon in the center of the batter and, pressing lightly, spread it outward in a continuous spiral motion. (If you use a nonstick pan, allow the batter to sit in the pan for a few seconds before attempting to shape it). Make the *dosa* as thin as possible, in either a round or oval, until it is roughly 8 inches (20 cm) in diameter. Drizzle 1-2 teaspoons (5–10 ml) of *ghee* or oil over the surface and around the edges of the *dosa*, then cover the pan. Cook for 2–2½ minutes on the first side or until the bottom is golden-red and small holes appear on the top. Ease a flexible metal spatula around the edge to loosen the *dosa*, then flip it over. Cook, uncovered, for another minute or so on the second side, then flip it over again. Fold in half or quarters, or serve without folding. Slip onto a warm platter, the brown side on top. Place the platter in a warm oven (250°F/120°C) or on a food warmer, loosely covered, while making the remaining *dosas*.

Urad and Rice Flour *Dosa* with Cracked Black Pepper
KHARA DOSA

Commercial rice flours vary in granularity, because any kind of rice can be ground into flour, and in many cases, the type is not specified. The rice flour used in oriental cooking is usually ground from short-grain starchy polished rice, and though it is excellent for baking biscuits and scones, it is not well suited for *dosas*. You need a coarse rice flour, made from long-grain rice. In England, this product is called ground rice and is available in most supermarkets. Both coarse rice flour and *urad dal* flour are available at Indian grocery stores in America.

Though the batter is quickly assembled with *dal* and rice flour, it is fermented slowly in the same way as classic batters. Because these flours absorb water in different proportions, recipe liquid suggestions are more guidelines than fixed recommendations. You will have to fine-tune amounts as you go. This *dosa* is traditionally laced with cumin seeds and black Malabar pepper, cultivated on the Malabar coast since Vedic times. A pleasant alternative is a currently popular mix of black, white, green and pink peppercorns. No matter what your choice, avoid pre-ground pepper. Try cooking this *dosa* in coconut oil, offset with pleasantly nippy *Fresh Coconut and Tamarind Chutney with Fresh Coriander* and stir-fried seasonal vegetables.

Preparation time (after assembling ingredients): a few minutes
Batter resting time: 20–24 hours
Cooking time: 30–40 minutes
Serves: 6 to 8

1½ cups (225 g) coarse rice flour (ground rice)
⅔ cup (85 g) *urad dal* flour
2⅓ cups (550 ml) warm water (l00°F/38°C) or as needed
2 tablespoons (30 ml) self-rising flour
½ tablespoon (7 ml) salt
¼ teaspoon (1 ml) yellow asafetida powder (*hing*)*
½ tablespoon (7 ml) medium-ground cracked pepper
½ tablespoon (7 ml) dry-roasted coarsely crushed cumin seeds
about ½ cup (120 ml) melted *ghee*, coconut or vegetable oil

*This amount applies only to yellow Cobra brand. Reduce any other asafetida by three-fourths.

1. Combine the rice flour and *ural dal* flour with 2 cups (480 ml) of warm water in a ceramic bowl or other non-metallic container and whisk until lump-free and smooth. Cover and set aside in a warm place (85–90°F/29–32°C is ideal) for 20–24 hours. (Batter resting time varies with temperature and humidity. When it is ready, it will have expanded in volume and will appear light and frothy with a pleasant sour smell.) When the batter has sufficiently fermented, stir in the self-rising flour, salt, asafetida, cracked pepper, and cumin seeds. Check batter consistency: it should resemble a pourable cake batter; add water as necessary to achieve the desired consistency.

2. Collect the paraphernalia you will need for cooking the *dosas*: at least one (two or three to save time) nonstick griddle or omelette pan, 10 inches (25 cm) or more in diameter; a ½ cup (120 ml) measuring scoop or ladle; a large round-bottomed spoon; a wide spatula; a bowl of melted *ghee* or oil and a teaspoon; and a covered platter large enough for the cooked *dosas*. Pre-heat the griddle or skillet over moderate heat for 2–3 minutes. Brush the hot surface with *ghee* or oil, avoiding excess. (To test griddle temperature, sprinkle a few drops on the surface. If it is too hot, the water will vanish immediately; if it is not hot enough, the water will sit on the surface and boil off. When the griddle is the right temperature, the drops of water will dance and sputter, then vanish.)

3. With the measuring cup or ladle, place a scant ½ cup (120 ml) of batter in the center of the pan. Allow the batter to sit in the pan for a few seconds before attempting to shape it. Place the back of the ladle or a round-bottomed spoon in the batter, and using gentle pressure, spread the batter outward in a continuous spiral motion until it is 6–7 inches (15–17.5 cm) in diameter. Drizzle 2 teaspoons (10 ml) of *ghee* or oil over the surface and around the edges of the *dosa*, then cover the pan. Cook for 2–3 minutes on the first side or until the bottom is reddish-brown and small holes appear topside. Ease a spatula around the edge to loosen the *dosa*, then flip it over. Cook, uncovered, for 1–2 minutes on the second side, then flip it over again. Slip the *dosa* onto a warm platter and place it in a warm oven (250°F/120°C) or on a food warmer, loosely covered, while making the remaining *dosas*.

For information about unfamiliar ingredients or techniques, see A-to-Z

Rice Flour *Dosa* with Cashews and Mustard Seeds
MAIDA DOSA

This *dosa* batter is effortless to assemble, and it is rested no longer then crêpe batter. Because it is made with a high proportion of rice flour and bound with yogurt as well as water, the finished crust is soft instead of crisp. Nonstick cookware makes shaping a breeze. All in all, this is a quick and easy selection when you are short of kitchen time. These *dosas* are perfect for any light meal, from breakfast to late dinner. Try them with an avocado and orange salad tossed with endive, *Savory Chickpeas in Tangy Tomato Glaze* and a frosty glass of *Rhubarb and Pomegranate Refresher*.

Preparation time (after assembling ingredients): a few minutes
Batter resting time: 15–20 minutes
Cooking time: 20 minutes (using 2 griddles)
Makes: 12 *dosas*

⅓ cup (50 g) chopped raw cashews or almonds
½ cup (65 g) unbleached white flour
¼ cup (35 g) cornstarch
¾ cup (115 g) coarse rice flour (ground rice)
⅔ cup (160 ml) plain yogurt
⅔ cup (160 ml) water, or as needed
1¼ teaspoons (6 ml) salt
¼ teaspoon (1 ml) cayenne pepper or paprika
½ teaspoon (2 ml) freshly ground black pepper
1 teaspoon (5 ml) poppy seeds or black mustard seeds
½ cup (120 ml) melted *ghee* or vegetable oil

1. Place the cashews or almonds in a food processor fitted with the metal blade, or a blender and process until they are finely minced. Add the flour, cornstarch and rice flour and process for 1 minute. Add the yogurt, ½ cup (120 ml) of the water, and the salt, cayenne or paprika and black pepper, cover, and process for 10 seconds more. Uncover and scrape down the sides of the work bowl with a rubber spatula, then cover and process until smooth. Check the batter consistency. It should resemble barely whipped cream. Add water or additional flour as necessary. Scrape the batter into a mixing bowl, loosely cover, and set aside for 15–20 minutes.

2. If you are using poppy seeds, add them to the batter. If you are using black mustard seeds, heat 1 tablespoon (15 ml) of *ghee* or oil in a small pan over moderate heat. When it is hot but not smoking, drop in the seeds. Cover partially and fry until the seeds crackle, sputter and turn gray. Remove the pan from the heat, and in a few seconds, pour the seeds into the batter. Stir to mix.

2. Collect the paraphernalia you will need for cooking the *dosas*: at least one (two or three to save time) nonstick griddle or omelette pan, 10 inches (25 cm) or more in diameter; a ½ cup (120 ml) measuring scoop or ladle; a large round-bottomed spoon; a wide spatula; a bowl of melted *ghee* or oil and a teaspoon; and a covered platter large enough for the cooked *dosas*. Pre-heat the griddle or skillet over moderate heat for 2–3 minutes. Brush the hot surface with *ghee* or oil, avoiding excess. (To test griddle temperature, sprinkle a few drops on the surface. If it is too hot, the water will vanish immediately; if it is not hot enough, the water will sit on the surface and boil off. When the griddle is the right temperature, the drops of water will dance and sputter, then vanish.)

3. With the measuring cup or ladle, place ⅓ cup (80 ml) of batter in the center of the pan. Allow the batter to sit in the pan for a few seconds before attempting to shape it. Place the back of the ladle or a round-bottomed spoon in the batter, and using gentle pressure, spread the batter outward in a continuous spiral motion until it is roughly 8 inches (20 cm) in diameter. Drizzle 1–2 teaspoons (5–10 ml) of *ghee* or oil over the surface and around the edges of the *dosa*, then cover the pan. Cook for 2–3 minutes on the first side or until the bottom is reddish-brown and small holes appear on the top. Ease a spatula around the edge to loosen the *dosa*, then flip it over. Cook, uncovered, for a minute or so on the second side, then flip it over again. Slip the *dosa* onto a warm platter, and place it in a warm oven (250°F/120°C) or on a food warmer, loosely covered, while making the remaining *dosas*.

Lacy Semolina *Dosa* with Cumin Seeds and Bell Pepper
SOOJI DOSA

Fine-grain semolina or semolina flour is not yet available at Western supermarkets, but largely due to the recent fascination with homemade pasta, it is now easy to find in health food stores, specialty gourmet stores, and Indian or Middle Eastern grocery stores. Plain semolina—a cream-colored, finely milled durum wheat product—gives excellent body to *dosa* batter. Carrot, tomato and spinach semolina pasta flour is also available. The alternative choice is farina, a slightly more granular processed product available at supermarkets.

Both are protein-rich meals, made from hard wheat, but because they are processed in different ways, they absorb water differently. You need a batter consistency similar to that of heavy cream, one that, when poured from about 8 inches (20 cm) above the pan, will splatter into lacy patterns. A batter that is too thick will yield a tough, chewy *dosa*; one that is too thin will not hold its shape at all or will yield a flimsy, easily torn *dosa*. Because the batter is poured from above the pan to create a lacy effect, you will need to use a pan with walls—either a well-used cast-iron or nonstick skillet or sauté pan.

Laced with fresh mint, lime juice, and cumin seeds, this *dosa* is delicious topped with a dab of *Mint-Lime Butter*. For a light breakfast or brunch, serve with seasonal fruits and herb tisaine.

Preparation time (after assembling ingredients): 5 minutes
Batter resting time: 20–30 minutes
Cooking time (using 2 skillets): 30 minutes
Makes: 10–12 *dosas*

For information about unfamiliar ingredients or techniques, see A-to-Z

¾ inch (2 cm) piece of peeled fresh ginger root, sliced
2–3 seeded hot chilies (preferably yellow banana)
½ of a medium-sized yellow bell pepper, seeded,
    cored and cut into ½-inch (1.5 cm) pieces
2 tablespoons (30 ml) minced fresh mint
⅔ cup (160 ml) plain yogurt
2 tablespoons (30 ml) fresh lime juice
¾ cup (180 ml) water, or as needed
1 cup (170 g) fine-grain semolina (semolina flour)
    or quick-cooking farina
½ cup (80 g) coarse rice flour
    or Cream of Rice cereal
3 tablespoons (45 ml) unbleached white flour or *chapati* flour
½ tablespoon (7 ml) salt
½ teaspoon (2 ml) dry-roasted, coarsely crushed cumin seeds
about ½ cup (120 ml) melted *ghee* or vegetable oil

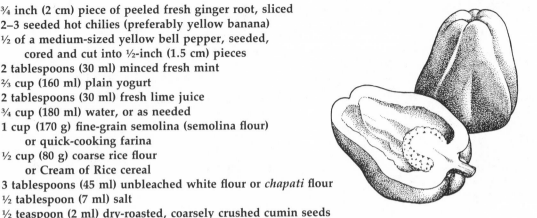

1. Fit a food processor with the metal blade, or use a blender. With the motor running, drop in the ginger and chilies and, when they are minced, add the bell peppers. Add the mint, yogurt, lime juice and water, and blend until smooth. Add the semolina or farina, rice flour or rice cereal, and the flour, and pulse 5 or 6 times. Scrape the batter toward the blades with a rubber spatula, cover again, and process until smooth. Using a rubber spatula, scrape the batter into a bowl, loosely cover with a cloth napkin, and set aside for 20–30 minutes.

2. Stir in the salt and cumin seeds. Check the batter consistency. Add additional flour or water as needed to make a texture similar to that of heavy cream. Collect the paraphernalia you will need for cooking the *dosas*: at least one (two or three to save time) nonstick skillet or sauté pan, 10 inches (25 cm) or more in diameter; a ⅓ cup (80 ml) measuring scoop or ladle; a large round-bottomed spoon; a wide spatula; a bowl of melted *ghee* or oil and a teaspoon; and a covered platter large enough for the cooked *dosas*. Pre-heat the pan(s) over moderate heat for 2–3 minutes. Brush the hot surface with *ghee* or oil, avoiding excess. (To test griddle temperature, sprinkle a few drops on the surface. If it is too hot, the water will vanish immediately; if it is not hot enough, the water will sit on the surface and boil off. When the griddle is the right temperature, the drops of water will dance and sputter, then vanish.)

3. With the measuring cup or ladle, place ⅓ cup (80 ml) of batter in the center of the pan. Allow the batter to sit in the pan for a few seconds before attempting to shape it. Place the back of the ladle or a round-bottomed spoon in the batter, and using gentle pressure, spread the batter outward in a continuous spiral motion until it is roughly 8 inches (20 cm) in diameter. Drizzle 1–2 teaspoons (5–10 ml) of *ghee* or oil over the surface and around the edges of the *dosa*, then cover the pan. Cook for 2–3 minutes on the first side or until the bottom is reddish-brown and small holes appear on the top. Ease a spatula around the edge to loosen the *dosa*, then flip it over. Cook, uncovered, for a minute or so on the second side, then flip it over again. Slip the *dosa* onto a warm platter, and place it in a warm (250°F/120°C) oven or on a food warmer, loosely covered, while making the remaining *dosas*.

Quick 'n' Easy Sweet *Dosa* with Mango Butter
MEETHA DOSA

Because these sweet *dosas* are made from a thin milk batter, they are shaped like a crêpe. Once removed from the pan, they quickly cool and become brittle and crisp—almost like dessert tuiles. While still warm, they can be rolled around wooden spoon handles, folded in quarters, or draped over custard cups. Served with mango butter, they are left flat, sandwiched between mango slices and sprinkled with slivered pistachio nuts. In fluted cup shapes, they are delicious filled with a scoop of ice cream.   In summer, serve with tropical fresh fruits.

Preparation time (after assembling ingredients): 25 minutes
Cooking time: about 25 minutes (using 2 pans)
Makes: 14 *dosas*

Mango Butter:

¼ **cup (55 g) sugar**
4 strips of lime zest, each ½ x 3 inches (1.5 x 7.5 cm)
½ **cup (120 ml) unsalted butter, at room temperature, cut into 6 pieces**
one 3½ ounce (95 g) package of cream cheese, at room temperature, cut into 6 pieces
1 large mango, peeled, seeded and cut into 1-inch (2.5 cm) cubes
¼ **teaspoon (1 ml) freshly ground nutmeg**

Dosas:

1½ **cups (360 ml) milk**
½ **cup (80 g) lightly packed shredded *jaggery*, *gur* or equivalent sweetener**
1 tablespoon (15 ml) fennel seeds
1 cup (135 g) *chapati* flour or a mixture of cake flour and whole wheat flour
2 tablespoons (30 ml) cornstarch
2 tablespoons (30 ml) farina or semolina
⅓ **cup (80 ml) melted butter or vegetable oil**
¼ **teaspoon (1 ml) salt**
¼ **cup (60 ml) maple syrup or golden syrup, warmed (optional)**

1. To make the mango butter, fit a food processor with the metal blade. Add the sugar, cover, and with the machine running, drop in the citrus zest and process until finely minced. Add the butter pieces and process until smooth and creamy. Add the cream cheese and process in the same manner. Finally, add the mango and nutmeg and pulse repeatedly until finely chopped. Refrigerate, well sealed.

2. Combine the milk, sweetener and fennel seeds in the food processor or blender, and process until the seeds are ground. Feed in the flour, cornstarch, farina or semolina, melted butter or oil and salt, and process into a smooth pouring-consistency batter. (You may need to add additional flour or milk to achieve the right consistency.) Transfer to a pouring jug or large measuring cup with a spout and set aside for 15 minutes before cooking.

3. Use two 8-inch (20 cm) nonstick omelette pans to save time. Brush the pans with a film of melted *ghee* or oil and warm over moderate heat. When hot, pour in about ¼ cup (60 ml) of the batter, or enough to cover the base of the pan, and immediately tilt it around to spread the batter into a thin 6-inch (15 cm) *dosa*. Cook until the edges brown

---

For information about unfamiliar ingredients or techniques, see A-to-Z

and the bottom turns golden-brown in patches, about 3 minutes. Flip over and cook for another 1½–2 minutes. Flip the cooked *dosa* onto a clean plate and either serve it flat or, if you want to shape it, fold it into quarters, roll it around a rolling pin or wooden spoon handle, or lay it over an upside-down custard cup and press down the sides to make a basket. Make all of the *dosas* in the same way, stirring the batter occasionally. These dessert *dosas* are served at room temperature, with a spoonful of mango butter or sliced fresh fruits, either plain or drizzled with warmed maple syrup or golden syrup.

Herbed Mung *Dal Cheela*
CHEELA

When we visited Surat in 1970, Mr. Bhagubhai Jariwala hosted Srila Prabhupada and 25 guests. Day after day the giant kitchen hummed with continuous cooking, and each meal was a culinary treat. The guests sat on fluffy cushions on the spotless marble floor. As each person sat down, a small individual ornamented table, called a *chaunki*, was placed before him or her and then the meal was served with pomp and ceremony. These *cheelas* were featured at one evening meal and were so much appreciated by Prabhupada and the guests that I learned the recipe and here share it with you. I also pass on the entire menu for that meal so that you can sample fine Gujarati cuisine. The hot *cheelas* were served with *Roasted Peanut Chutney* and a spoonful of *Shredded Radish, Coconut and Carrot Salad*. The main dish was *Light 'n' Easy Pounded Rice Uppma with Potatoes and Green Peas*. The sweets included and seasonal fresh fruits.

There is bound to be more than one opinion on what is the perfect pan for *cheelas*. A cast-iron griddle is excellent for distributing even heat—the *cheelas* always seem thinner and crispier. I find Silvertone the nonstick choice—it seems to have a better grabbing surface than T–fal. You can make the batter at your convenience and refrigerate it; just bring it to room temperature before cooking. Stir the batter before shaping each pancake.

Dal soaking time: 4 hours
Preparation time (after assembling ingredients): 5 minutes
Cooking time: about 30 minutes (using 2 griddles)
Makes: 10 *cheelas*

1 cup (215 g) split *moong dal*, without skins
1-inch (2.5 cm) piece of peeled fresh ginger root, cut into 4 pieces
1–2 hot green chilies, seeded
1 cup (240 ml) water, or as needed
⅓ cup (45 g) whole wheat flour
1 teaspoon (5 ml) salt
¼ teaspoon (1 ml) yellow asafetida powder (*hing*)*
¼ teaspoon (1 ml) turmeric
¼ teaspoon (1 ml) baking powder
1 tablespoon (15 ml) each minced fresh chervil, tarragon and coriander or parsley,
    or 3 tablespoons (45 ml) minced fresh coriander
about ¼ cup (120 ml) melted *ghee* or vegetable oil

This amount applies only to yellow Cobra brand. Reduce any other asafetida by three-fourths.

1. Sort through the *dal* and remove any foreign matter. Wash in several changes of water, then drain. Place the drained *dal* in a bowl and cover with 3 cups (710 ml) of hot tap water. Soak for at least 4 hours, then drain well.

2. Fit a food processor with the metal blade, or use a blender. With the machine running, drop in the ginger and chilies, and when they are minced, stop the machine and add the *dal* and ½ cup (120 ml) water. Cover and process until the *dal* is pulverized into a thick paste. Stop the machine and add the remaining ½ cup (120 ml) water and the flour, salt, asafetida, turmeric, baking powder and fresh herbs. Cover and again process for 1–2 minutes or until smooth. Stop the machine, scrape down the sides of the work bowl with a rubber spatula and check the batter consistency. You want a thickish batter, something like lightly whipped cream. If necessary, add up to ⅓ cup (80 ml) more water or additional flour to reach this consistency.

3. Collect the paraphernalia you will need for cooking the *cheelas*: at least one (two or three to save time) nonstick skillet or sauté pan, 10 inches (25 cm) or more in diameter; a ¼ cup (60 ml) measuring scoop or ladle; a large round-bottomed spoon; a wide spatula; a bowl of melted *ghee* or oil and a teaspoon; and a covered platter large enough for the cooked *cheelas*. Pre-heat the pan(s) over moderate heat for 2–3 minutes. Brush the hot surface with *ghee* or oil, avoiding excess. (To test griddle temperature, sprinkle a few drops on the surface. If it is too hot, the water will vanish immediately; if it is not hot enough, the water will sit on the surface and boil off. When the griddle is the right temperature, the drops of water will dance and sputter, then vanish.)

4. Remove ¼ cup (60 ml) of the batter and place it in the middle of the pan. Let the batter sit for 3–4 seconds, then place the bottom of a ladle or large soupspoon in the center of the batter and, pressing lightly, spread outward in a continuous spiral motion. You should be able to make a thin, uniformly round or oval pancake roughly 8 inches (20 cm) in diameter. After about a minute, drizzle 1 teaspoon (5 ml) of *ghee* or oil over the surface and around the edges of the *cheela*, then cover the pan. Cook for 3–4 minutes on the first side. When small holes appear on top of the *cheela* and the bottom is golden to reddish-brown, loosen the edges with a wide spatula and turn the *cheela* over. Fry, uncovered, for another minute or so on the second side, then flip it over again, fold it in half, slip it onto a serving plate and serve hot; or keep the *cheelas* warm, covered, until the remaining *cheelas* are cooked. Cook the remaining batter in the same way, rubbing a film of *ghee* or oil on the surface and sprinkling it with water before shaping each *cheela*. These *cheelas* can be wrapped in aluminum foil and reheated in a preheated 350°F (180°C) oven for 15 minutes.

Buttermilk Mung *Dal Cheela* with Fennel Seeds
MASALA CHEELA

This Gujarati *cheela* recipe features coriander, fennel and asafetida and goes well with *Shredded Mango and Coconut Chutney* or *Creamy Cashew Chutney*. If you serve *cheelas* for a luncheon or dinner, add *Golden Pumpkin Toovar Dal Soup* and *Baby Potatoes with Seasoned Tomato Sauce* or any seasoned steamed vegetable with *Cumin-Flavored Ghee*. For a sweet, add *Shredded Carrot Milk Pudding*.

For information about unfamiliar ingredients or techniques, see A-to-Z

Dal soaking time: 3–4 hours
Preparation time (after assembling ingredients): 5 minutes
Cooking time: about 30 minutes (using 2 griddles)
Makes: 10 *cheelas*

1 cup (215 g) split *moong dal*, without skins
2 tablespoons (30 ml) coriander seeds
1 tablespoon (15 ml) fennel seeds
½ cup (120 ml) cultured buttermilk or plain yogurt
1 teaspoon (5 ml) salt
¼ teaspoon (1 ml) turmeric
½ teaspoon (2 ml) yellow asafetida powder (*hing*)*
⅓ cup (80 ml) water, or as needed
½ teaspoon (2 ml) crushed dried red chilies (or as desired)
½ cup (120 ml) melted *ghee* or vegetable oil

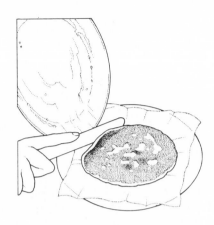

*This amount applies only to yellow Cobra brand. Reduce any other asafetida by three-fourths.

1. Sort through the *dal* and remove any foreign matter. Wash in several changes of water, then drain. Place the drained *dal* in a bowl and cover with 3 cups (710 ml) of cold water. Soak for 3–4 hours, then drain in a strainer.

2. Fit a food processor with the metal blade, or use a blender. Add the *dal* and process for 1½ minutes, stopping the machine now and then to push the *dal* down toward the blades with a rubber spatula. Add the coriander seeds, fennel seeds, buttermilk or yogurt, salt, turmeric and asafetida and process for another minute. You want a thickish batter, something like lightly whipped cream. If necessary, add up to ⅓ cup (80 ml) water or additional flour to reach this consistency. Scrape into a bowl and add the crushed chilies.

3. Collect the paraphernalia you will need for cooking the *cheelas*: at least one (two or three to save time) nonstick skillet or sauté pan, 10 inches (25 cm) or more in diameter; a ¼ cup (60 ml) measuring scoop or ladle; a large round-bottomed spoon; a wide spatula; a bowl of melted *ghee* or oil and a teaspoon; and a covered platter large enough for the cooked *cheelas*. Pre-heat the pan(s) over moderate heat for 2–3 minutes. Brush the hot surface with *ghee* or oil, avoiding excess. (To test griddle temperature, sprinkle a few drops on the surface. If it is too hot, the water will vanish immediately; if it is not hot enough, the water will sit on the surface and boil off. When the griddle is the right temperature, the drops of water will dance and sputter, then vanish.)

4. Remove ¼ cup (60 ml) of the batter and place it in the middle of the pan. Let the batter sit for 3–4 seconds, then place the bottom of a ladle or large soupspoon in the center of the batter and, pressing lightly, spread it outwards in a continuous spiral motion. You should be able to make a thin, uniformly round or oval pancake roughly 8 inches (20 cm) in diameter. After about 1 minute, drizzle 1 teaspoon (5 ml) of *ghee* or oil over the surface and around the edges of the *cheela*, then cover the pan.

Cook for 3–4 minutes on the first side. When small holes appear on top and the bottom is golden to reddish-brown, loosen the edges with a wide spatula and turn the *cheela* over. Fry, uncovered, for another minute or so on the second side, then flip it over again, fold it in half, and slip it onto a serving plate. Serve hot or keep the *cheelas* warm, covered, until the remaining *cheelas* are cooked. Cook the remaining batter in the same way, rubbing a film of *ghee* or oil on the surface and sprinkling it with water before shaping each *cheela*. These *cheelas* can be wrapped in aluminum foil and reheated in a preheated 350°F (180°C) oven for 15 minutes.

Chickpea Flour *Poora* with Mixed Vegetables
BESAN POORA

This dish resembles a quiche in as much as it sets like a custard and is cut into pie-shaped servings. But there the similarities end. Rather than being baked, the herbed chickpea flour–vegetable batter is fried in a skillet over low heat until the bottom becomes crisp and the center is smooth and firm. For added flavor and texture, the large pancake is then flipped over to crisp the other side. There are numerous regional variations of these thickish pancakes, and all are usually accompanied by a fresh chutney. Try it with either zesty *Quick Tamarind–Raisin Chutney*, *Fresh Coriander Chutney* or *Sour Cream Parsley Sauce*, and serve from breakfast through late dinner.

Preparation time (after assembling ingredients): 30 minutes
Cooking time: 25 minutes (using 3 nonstick pans)
Serves: 6 to 8

2 cups (205 g) sifted chickpea flour (sifted before measuring)
½ cup (120 ml) fresh corn kernels
½ cup (120 ml) bell peppers, seeded and diced
½ cup (120 ml) fresh snow peas, trimmed and thinly sliced
½ cup (120 ml) fresh peas or frozen baby peas, defrosted
¼ cup (60 ml) coarsely chopped fresh coriander or a mixture of minced parsley, chervil and basil
½ teaspoon (2 ml) turmeric
¼ teaspoon (1 ml) cayenne pepper
1 teaspoon (5 ml) salt
1 teaspoon (5 ml) baking powder
¼ teaspoon (1 ml) baking soda
½ teaspoon (2 ml) freshly ground black pepper
½ teaspoon (2 ml) *ajwain* seeds (optional)
1⅓ cups (320 ml) peeled and seeded tomatoes, diced
¼ cup (60 ml) plain yogurt
¼ cup (60 ml) water
½ cup (120 ml) melted *ghee* or unsalted butter

1. Place the chickpea flour in a heavy frying pan and dry-roast over low heat, stirring frequently. When it has darkened a few shades and loses its raw smell (10–15 minutes), set aside to cool.

2. Bring 4 cups (1 liter) of water to a boil in a saucepan. Add the corn, bell peppers, snow peas and fresh peas, if you are using them, and boil for 3 minutes. Drain.

3. Combine the chickpea flour, vegetables (add the defrosted peas here if using them), fresh herbs, turmeric, cayenne, salt, baking powder, baking soda, black pepper, optional *ajwain* seeds and diced tomatoes in a mixing bowl and toss with a fork to blend. Whisk the yogurt and water together in another bowl and then stir into these ingredients.

4. Place at least one, but preferably two or three, 8-inch (20 cm) omelette pans or skillets over low heat and add 2 tablespoons (30 ml) of *ghee* or butter to each. Divide the batter into three portions. If using three pans, pour each portion in and spread evenly over the bottom of the pan. If using one pan, remove ⅓ of the batter, keeping the rest covered in the mixing bowl. Cover with a lid and let the pancake cook for about 10 minutes or until it is firm and the bottom crust is golden-brown. To turn the *poora*, invert it onto the flat side of the lid and then back into the pan. Cook, covered, for

For information about unfamiliar ingredients or techniques, see A-to-Z

another 10 minutes on the second side or until golden-brown. Transfer the pancake to a cutting board and let cool for 5 minutes before cutting into wedges. Serve piping hot, warm, or at room temperature. If you want to reheat the *pooras*, wrap them in paper-towel-lined aluminum foil and heat for 10–15 minutes in a preheated 350°F (180°C) oven.

Savory Black-Eyed Pea *Poora*
CHOWLA POORA

Sometimes called *cheela*, at other times *pulli* and *poora*, this substantial, nourishing pancake can be served flat, or can be stuffed and rolled up jellyroll fashion. These Gujarati delicacies are good any time of the day from breakfast to late supper, or can be made small, as finger-food appetizers. To save time, use two or even three pans at once. Try *pooras* with *Creamy Cashew Chutney*, *Sautéed Eggplant and Bell Peppers* and a green salad for lunch or dinner. If you want to stuff the *pooras*, try *Okra Supreme*, *Green Beans with Coconut* or *Cubed Potatoes with Fresh Fenugreek*. For a sweet, add *Date Rice Pudding*.

Dal soaking time: 14 hours for whole black-eyed peas, 8 hours for split *chowla dal*
Preparation time (after assembling ingredients): 15 minutes
Batter resting time: 30 minutes
Cooking time: about 30 minutes (using 2 pans)
Makes: 12 *pooras*

1¼ cups (265 g) whole dried black-eyed peas or split *chowla dal*, without skins, cleaned, washed and drained
2 pieces of lime zest, 2 x ½ inch (5 x 1.5 cm)
½-inch (1.5 cm) piece of peeled fresh ginger root, sliced
1–2 hot green chilies, seeded and quartered
3 tablespoons (45 ml) chopped fresh mint or coriander
1¼ cups (300 ml) water, or as needed
¼ cup (35 g) *chapati* flour or unbleached white flour
¼ teaspoon (1 ml) freshly grated nutmeg
¼ teaspoon (1 ml) turmeric
¼ teaspoon (1 ml) yellow asafetida powder (*hing*)*
1 teaspoon (5 ml) salt
⅔ cup (160 ml) *ghee* or vegetable oil

This amount applies only to yellow Cobra brand. Reduce any other asafetida by three-fourths.

1. Soak the black-eyed peas or *dal* in 3 cups (710 ml) water for at least 14 hours for the black-eyed peas or 8 hours for the *dal*. If you are using whole black-eyed peas, drain and place them in a bowl of fresh water. Rub them between your palms to loosen the skins and pour out the skins with the water. Add more fresh water and repeat the process until most of the skins are removed. Drain. If you are using *chowla dal*, simply rinse and drain.
2. Fit a food processor with the metal blade, or use a blender. With the motor running, drop in the lime zest, ginger, chilies and fresh herbs. When they are minced,

stop the machine and add the drained black-eyed peas or *dal*. Cover and process until the texture is paste-like. Add 1 cup (240 ml) of water slowly through the feed tube, then follow with the flour, nutmeg, turmeric, asafetida and salt. Process for another 2–3 minutes or until the batter is smooth and fluffy with a consistency similar to lightly whipped cream. (Add more water as necessary to reach this consistency.) Scrape the batter into a bowl.

3. Collect what you will need for cooking the *pooras*: two or three 8-inch (20 cm) nonstick griddles; a wide rubber spatula, a ⅓-cup (80 ml) measuring scoop, a large round-bottomed spoon, a bowl of melted *ghee* or oil and a teaspoon, two large platters, one inverted over the other for keeping the *pooras* warm, and a clean kitchen towel to line the platter. Heat the griddle over moderately low heat. Brush the surface with a film of *ghee* or oil, then test the temperature. If it is too hot, water sprinkled on the surface will vanish immediately; if it is not hot enough, the water will sit on the surface and boil. When the griddle is the right temperature, the drops will dance and sputter, then vanish.

4. Remove ⅓ cup (80 ml) of the batter and place it in the middle of the pan. Immediately place the round-bottomed spoon in the center of the batter and, pressing lightly, spread it outward in a continuous spiral motion. You should be able to make a thin, uniformly round or oval pancake roughly 7½ inches (17.5 cm) in diameter. After about a minute, drizzle 1 teaspoon (15 ml) of melted *ghee* or oil over the surface and around the edges, then cover the pan. Cook for 3–4 minutes on the first side. When small holes appear on top of the *poora* and the bottom is golden to reddish-brown, loosen the edges with a wide spatula and turn the *poora* over. Fry, uncovered, for another minute or so on the second side, then flip it over again, fold it in half, slip it onto a serving plate and serve hot; or keep the *pooras* warm, covered by the inverted plate, until the remaining *pooras* are cooked. Cook the remaining batter in the same way, rubbing a film of *ghee* or oil on the surface and sprinkling it with water before shaping each *poora*. These *pooras* can be wrapped in aluminum foil and reheated in a preheated 350°F (180°C) oven for 15 minutes.

CAKE-LIKE *IDDLI* DUMPLINGS

Iddlis, made from almost the same batter as *dosas*, are unequivocally South India's most popular breakfast and tiffin treat and, because they have no similar counterpart in the West, they are difficult to define. To call an *iddli* a dumpling is as inadequate as calling a *dosa* a pancake—for this spongy steamed rice and *dal* delight, moist like a dumpling and light like a muffin, is in fact, quite unlike either.

For information about unfamiliar ingredients or techniques, see A-to-Z

Many things contribute to the uniqueness of the *iddli*. Its flavor and aroma—redolent of sourdough—is its most beautiful quality. Classic *iddlis* are made from a batter of two parts parboiled rice and one part *urad dal*. The batter is left to ferment until it expands and is covered with tiny bubbles. This fermentation is not only for enhanced flavor but also increases nutritive value and encourages easy digestion.

Because *iddlis* are made in individual molds that are deep in the center and tapered at the edges (something like smooth Madeleine molds), they will be smooth and glossy on one side and slightly textured on the other. Each steamed *iddli* is about 1 inch (2.5 cm) thick in the middle and 3 inches (7.5 cm) in diameter. Several *iddlis* can be steamed at once in a South Indian tiered *iddli* tree. This utensil consists of 3–5 disks, each holding 4 molds spaced 1½ inches (4 cm) apart on a central trunk. Traditionally the molds are lined with damp cotton; alternatively, you can use parchment cup papers. The entire *iddli* tree—housing 12, 16 or 20 molds—is placed in a large pan filled with 1 inch (2.5 cm) of water, covered, and then steamed. *Iddli* trees are available at most Indian grocery stores in both aluminum and stainless steel.

Though not as popular as the individual molds, *iddlis* are also steamed in other sizes and shapes. The famous Vaishnava temple of Sri Simhachalam in Orissa, for example, prepares a special type of spiced *iddli*. Each piece weighs 1 pound (455 g) and is almost 10 inches (25 cm) in diameter. It is cut into slices or squares and is offered to guests as *prasadam*.

If you do not have a tiered *iddli* tree, improvise with available kitchen equipment. Small *iddlis* can be steamed using individual stainless steel *katoris* set in a 6-cup (1.5 liter) muffin tray, or in triple-thick parchment cupcake cups, each brushed with a film of *ghee* or a coat of vegetable spray. To make one large *iddli*, use a Cuisinart vegetable steaming basket with a triple-thick square of moist cheesecloth. Spoon in the batter to a depth of ½ inch (1.5 cm), cover with a tight-fitting lid, and pull the excess cheesecloth over the top of the lid. Some Americanized South Indian cooks will use a covered 6-quart/liter pressure cooker without the rocker weight on the lid, letting a thin stream of steam escape through the vent. No matter what your choice, the bottom of your steaming equipment must rest at least 1 inch (2.5 cm) above the surface of the boiling water.

How long *iddlis* should be steamed depends on two things: the size of the *iddli* molds and the batter consistency. In principle, if the batter is too thin, the *iddlis* will be sticky; if it is too thick, they will be hard and tough. The batter should be light and airy and slightly fermented, with a texture similar to that of half-whipped cream. A tiered *iddli* tree has small holes in each mold which lets in steam to further lighten the batter and allow it to breath. When placed in the mold, a spoonful of batter should be stiff enough to hold its own without dripping through the perforations. Small *iddlis* should be steamed for 12–15 minutes; a 10-inch (25 cm) *iddli* may take as long as 25 minutes.

Rice and *Urad Dal Iddli*

SADA IDDLI

Wet-grinding *urad dal* and rice prior to the advent of food processors was a labor of love carried out on stone mortars—laboriously time-consuming and tricky to execute. Since technology has rendered wet-grinding an effortless task, it is now easy to achieve the first requirement for ideal *iddli* cooking: a finely-ground batter. The second requirement is a properly fermented batter. Depending on temperature and even relative humidity, batters will take different times to ferment. During the summer in a Key West or Bombay kitchen, 12 hours is sufficient, while in Oregon's Rogue Valley or England's Cornwall, up to 36 hours can be required. The batter must expand in volume and be light and airy, with hairline cracks and tiny bubbles on the surface. The smell should be pleasantly sour, not pungent.

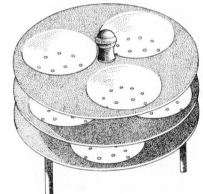

Soaking time: 6–8 hours or overnight
Preparation and resting time: 12–36 hours
Steaming time: up to ½ hour (depending on equipment)
Serves: 8 to 10

1 cup (95 g) *basmati* or other long-grain white rice
½ cup (110 g) *urad dal*, without skins
1 cup (240 ml) warm water, or as needed
1 teaspoon (5 ml) salt
scant ¼ teaspoon (1 ml) baking soda
melted *ghee*, light vegetable oil or
    vegetable spray for brushing the molds
¼ cup (60 ml) seasoned *ghee* or butter (optional)

1. If you are using *basmati* rice, sort out any foreign matter. Place the rice in a bowl, cover it with water, and rub the grains between your palms. When the water is cloudy, drain it and cover the grains again with water. Repeat the washing and draining process until the water is almost clear, then drain and set aside in a bowl. Sort, wash, and drain the *dal* in the same way. Place the rice and *dal* in separate bowls, add 3 cups (710 ml) of water to each, then soak them for 6–8 hours, or overnight.

2. Drain the rice then place it in a food processor fitted with the metal blade and process until it resembles coarse cornmeal. Add a scant ½ cup (120 ml) of warm water and continue to process for 1 minute. Scrape down the sides of the work bowl with a rubber spatula and continue to process for 3–4 minutes or until the purée is smooth. Scrape the rice purée into a 2-quart/liter glass or ceramic bowl. Place the drained *dal* into the food processor, add a scant ½ cup (120 ml) of warm water, and process in the same way as the rice, for 3–4 minutes or until the purée is light and airy. Combine the *dal* with the rice, add the salt, and mix well. Cover with plastic wrap and set aside in a warm place (90–95°F/32–35°C is ideal) for 12–14 hours. If your room is cold or the humidity high, it may have to rest for up to 36 hours. When the batter has expanded in volume and is covered with bubbles, it is ready.

3. Gently stir the batter to remix and then test batter consistency. Place 1½ tablespoons (22 ml) of batter in a buttered *iddli* mold. It should spread out slowly and be thick enough not to fall through the perforations. If the batter is too thin, the steamed *iddli* will be sticky; if it is too thick, it will be hard and tough. If necessary, add 1–2

For information about unfamiliar ingredients or techniques, see A-to-Z

tablespoons (15–30 ml) of water or additional self-rising flour to reach the desired consistency. Just before steaming, gently fold the baking soda into the batter. Rough handling will disturb the light foamy batter and prevent the *iddli* from rising properly.

4. To prepare the *iddli* molds, cut new voile handkerchiefs slightly larger than the *iddli* tiers with a small hole in the center for the support pole. Moisten the handkerchiefs and lay them on the tiers. Liberally brush the handkerchiefs with melted *ghee* or oil or a film of vegetable spray. Heat water to a depth of 1 inch (2.5 cm) in an *iddl* steamer, a 6-quart/liter pressure cooker or a stockpot over high heat. Place 2–3 tablespoons (30–45 ml) of batter in each small *iddli* mold, or spread batter to a depth of ½ inch (1.5 cm) in a larger container.

Assemble the tiered rack and place it in the steaming pot. Cover securely and steam small molds for 12–15 minutes or larger molds (10 inches/25 cm) for 22–25 minutes, or until a toothpick inserted into an *iddli* comes out clean. Properly made *iddlis* will have a soft well-rounded surface. Remove the steaming pot from the heat, lift out the tiered rack, and disassemble. Ease out the *iddlis* with a rubber spatula and transfer to a napkin-lined second steamer while you make the remaining *iddlis*.

5. Check the water level in the cooking pot and add water, as necessary, to a depth of 1 inch (2.5 cm). Lay the clean side of the handkerchiefs up, brush them again with *ghee* or oil, and repeat the steaming procedure using the remaining batter. Serve the *iddlis* piping hot with the smooth side up and a dab of seasoned *ghee* or butter on top. Cut large *iddlis* into slices, squares or diamonds. *Iddlis* keep well for one or two days refrigerated, or up to a month frozen. To reheat, line a steaming basket with a napkin and steam, covered, for about 10 minutes.

Iddli with Cumin Seeds and Black Pepper
MASALA IDDLI

This recipe was inspired by spiced *iddlis* made in two famous Vaishnava temples: Jagannath Mandir in Puri and Sri Simhachalam near Vishakhapatnam, both in Orissa. If you prefer less spice, eliminate all but the cumin seeds and black pepper. Grind the rice and *dal* in as little water as possible, adding yogurt to make the batter consistency similar to that of half-whipped cream. Serve with *Fresh Coconut and Mint Chutney*.

Soaking time: 6–8 hours or overnight
Preparation and resting time: 12–36 hours
Steaming time: up to ½ hour
Serves: 8 to 10

1⅓ cups (115 g) *basmati* or other long-grain white rice
1 teaspoon (5 ml) fenugreek seeds
⅔ cup (145 g) split *urad dal*, without skins
1-inch (2.5 cm) piece of scraped fresh ginger root, sliced
warm water, as needed
1½ tablespoons (22 ml) dry-roasted coarsely crushed cumin seeds
1½ teaspoons (7 ml) coarsely ground black pepper
½ teaspoon (2 ml) yellow asafetida powder (*hing*)*
2 teaspoons (10 ml) salt
3 tablespoons (45 ml) melted *ghee* or butter
about 3 tablespoons (45 ml) plain yogurt, at room temperature
¼ teaspoon (1 ml) baking soda
melted *ghee*, light vegetable oil or vegetable spray for brushing the molds
¼ cup (60 ml) seasoned *ghee* or butter

This amount applies only to yellow Cobra brand. Reduce any other asafetida by three-fourths.

1. If you are using *basmati* rice, sort out any foreign matter. Place the rice in a bowl, cover it with water, and rub the grains between your palms. When the water is cloudy, drain and cover with water again. Repeat the washing process until the water is almost clear, then drain. Add the fenugreek seeds to the rice and soak in 3 cups (710 ml) water for 6–8 hours. Sort, wash and drain the *dal* in the same way. Place the *dal* in a separate bowl, add 3 cups (710 ml) of water, and soak for 6–8 hours. Drain separately.

2. Fit a food processor with the metal blade. With the motor running, drop the fresh ginger through the feed tube and process until minced. Add the rice and process until the consistency resembles coarse cornmeal. Add ⅓ cup (80 ml) warm water and process for 1 minute. Scrape down the sides of the work bowl with a rubber spatula, then continue to process for 3–4 minutes, adding dribbles of additional water, as necessary, to make a smooth thick purée. Scrape the purée into a 2-quart/liter glass or ceramic bowl. Place the drained *dal* into the food processor, add 7 tablespoons (105 ml) of water, and process in the same way as the rice, or until the purée is light and airy.

Add the cumin seeds, black pepper, asafetida and salt, and continue to process for about 20 seconds or until the cumin seeds and black pepper are coarsely ground. Combine with the rice and mix well. Cover with plastic wrap and set aside in a warm place (90–95°F/32–35°C) for 12–24 hours. If your room is cold or the humidity high, it may have to rest for up to 36 hours. The batter is ready when it has increased in volume, is covered with tiny bubbles and hairline cracks and has pleasantly fermented.

3. Gently stir in the melted *ghee* or butter and enough yogurt (you may need less than 3 tablespoons/45 ml) to make a batter similar in consistency to that of half-whipped cream. To check batter consistency, place 1½ tablespoons (22 ml) of batter in a buttered *iddli* mold. It should spread out slowly and be thick enough not to fall through the perforations. (If the batter is too thin, the steamed *iddli* will be sticky; if it is too thick, it will be hard and tough. If necessary, add 1–2 tablespoons/15–30 ml water or self-rising flour to achieve the desired consistency.) Just before steaming, gently fold the baking soda into the batter. Rough handling will disturb the light foamy batter and prevent the *iddlis* from rising properly.

4. To prepare the *iddli* molds, cut new voile handkerchiefs slightly larger than the tiers with a small hole in the center for the support pole. Moisten the handkerchiefs and lay them on the tiers. Liberally brush the handkerchiefs with melted *ghee*, oil or vegeta-

---

For information about unfamiliar ingredients or techniques, see A-to-Z

ble spray. Heat water to a depth of 1 inch (2.5 cm) in an *iddli* steamer, a 6-quart/liter pressure cooker or a stockpot over high heat. Place 2–3 tablespoons (30–45 ml) of batter in each small *iddli* mold, or spread batter to a depth of ½ inch (1.5 cm) in a larger container. Assemble the tiered rack and place it in the steaming pot. Cover securely and steam small molds for 12–15 minutes, larger molds (10 inches/25 cm) for 22–25 minutes, or until a toothpick inserted into an *iddli* comes out clean. Properly made *iddlis* will have a soft well-rounded surface. Remove the steaming pot from the heat, lift out the rack and disassemble. Using a rubber spatula, ease out the *iddlis* and transfer them to a napkin-lined steaming unit to keep them warm while you make the remaining *iddlis*.

5. Check the water level in the steaming pot and add water, as necessary, to a depth of 1 inch (2.5 cm). Lay the clean side of the handkerchiefs up, brush them with melted *ghee* or oil, and repeat the steaming procedure using the remaining batter. Serve the *iddlis* piping hot with the bottom side up and a dab of seasoned *ghee* or butter on top. Cut large *iddlis* into slices, squares or diamonds. *Iddlis* keep well for 1–2 days refrigerated, or up to a month frozen. To reheat, line a steaming basket with a napkin and steam, covered, for about 10 minutes.

Semolina *Iddli* with Cashews and Coconut
SOOJI KAJU IDDLI

For this famous Kanchipuram *iddli*, semolina is substituted for the rice and the *dal* is dry-roasted and coarsely ground instead of puréed. If the menu needs a boost of color, use spinach semolina flour, which lends a very slight spinach flavor and a lovely hue of green. Another alternative is to use regular or quick Cream of Wheat or farina, though our testers preferred the fine texture of semolina *iddlis*. I have also used almonds, hazelnuts, and pecans, instead of the cashews. For breakfast or tiffin, this dish is invariably accompanied with coconut chutney. For lunch or dinner, a spicy vegetable soup or broth is added.

Dal soaking time: 6–8 hours or overnight
Preparation and resting time: 1 hour ,Steaming time: up to ½ hour
Serves: 8 to 10

½ cup (100 g) split *chana dal*
water as suggested
2 hot green chilies, seeded and broken into bits, or
        a scant ½ teaspoon (2 ml) cayenne pepper
½ inch (1.5 cm) piece of peeled fresh ginger root, sliced
1⅓ cups (320 ml) plain yogurt
½ tablespoon (7 ml) salt
½ cup (120 ml) warm water
3 tablespoons (45 ml) coconut oil, light sesame oil or nut oil
1 teaspoon (5 ml) black mustard seeds
⅓ cup (50 g) chopped raw cashew nuts
¼ cup (25 g) shredded fresh or dried coconut
1⅓ cups (250 g) semolina
¼ cup (60 ml) chopped fresh coriander
¼ teaspoon (1 ml) baking soda

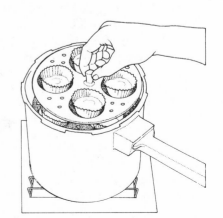

1. Sort out any foreign matter in the *dal*. Place the *dal* in a heavy-bottomed skillet and dry-roast over low heat, stirring to brown evenly, until the color darkens a few shades, about 5 minutes. Transfer to a bowl, cover with water, and rub the grains between your palms. When the water is cloudy, drain and cover with water again. Repeat the washing process until the water is almost clear, then drain. Add 3 cups (710 ml) of water and soak for 6–8 hours or overnight. Drain well.

2. Fit a food processor with the metal blade. With the machine running, feed in the green chilies (if you are using them) and ginger, and process until minced. Add the yogurt, cayenne (if you are using it), salt, *dal* and the warm water, and process until the *dal* is coarsely chopped. Transfer the mixture to a mixing bowl.

3. Heat the oil in a heavy saucepan over moderate heat. When it is hot but not smoking, drop in the black mustard seeds and fry until they sputter and pop. Remove the pan from the heat and stir in the nuts. In a minute, again place the pan over the heat and fry the nuts until golden. Add the coconut and semolina and, stirring frequently, fry for about 5 minutes. Remove the pan from the heat and cool, stirring once or twice as it sits.

4. Stir the fried semolina into the yogurt mixture, cover, and set aside for ½–1 hour. Check batter consistency. It should resemble a light cake batter. Place 1½ tablespoons (22 ml) of batter into a buttered *iddli* mold. It should spread out slowly and be thick enough not to fall through the perforations. (Add self-rising flour or water, as necessary, to achieve the desired consistency.) Fold in the fresh coriander and baking soda and set aside while preparing the steaming apparatus.

5. To prepare the *iddli* molds, cut new voile handkerchiefs slightly larger than the tiers with a small hole in the center for the support pole. Moisten the handkerchiefs and lay them on the tiers. Liberally brush the handkerchiefs with melted *ghee*, oil or vegetable spray. Heat water to a depth of 1 inch (2.5 cm) in an *iddli* steamer, a 6-quart/liter pressure cooker or a stockpot over high heat. Place 2–3 tablespoons (30–45 ml) of batter in each small *iddli* mold, or spread batter to a depth of ½ inch (1.5 cm) in a larger container. Assemble the tiered rack and place it in the steaming pot. Cover securely and steam small molds for 12–15 minutes, larger molds (10 inches/25 cm) for 22–25 minutes, or until a toothpick inserted into an *iddli* comes out clean. Properly made *iddlis* will have a soft well-rounded surface. Remove the steaming pot from the heat, lift out the rack and disassemble. Using a rubber spatula, ease out the *iddlis* and transfer them to a napkin-lined steaming unit to keep them warm while you make the remaining *iddlis*.

6. Check the water level in the steaming pot and add water, as necessary, to a depth of 1 inch (2.5 cm). Lay the clean side of the handkerchiefs up, brush them with melted *ghee* or oil, and repeat the steaming procedure using the remaining batter. Serve the *iddlis* piping hot with the bottom side up and a dab of seasoned *ghee* or butter on top. Cut large *iddlis* into slices, squares or diamonds. *Iddlis* keep well for 1–2 days refrigerated, or up to a month frozen. To reheat, line a steaming basket with a napkin and steam, covered, for about 10 minutes.

For information about unfamiliar ingredients or techniques, see A-to-Z

Urad Flour and Ground Rice *Iddli*
KHATTE IDDLI

This batter, made entirely from flour and cereal, is very quick to assemble. Because ground rice is only available in America at Indian grocery stores or through some mail order sources, we have substituted Cream of Rice cereal with delightful results. If you do have an Indian grocery nearby, make sure you specify ground rice or coarse rice flour. The silky-smooth fine rice flour used in Oriental cooking will not produce good results in this *iddli* .

Batter resting time: 20–22 hours
Steaming time: up to ½ hour
Serves: 8 to 10

2 hot green chilies, seeded and quartered
½-inch (1.5 cm) piece of scraped fresh ginger root, sliced
1½ cups (225 g) ground rice or Cream of Rice cereal
water as needed
¾ cup (100 g) *urad* flour
2 teaspoons (10 ml) salt
2 tablespoons (30 ml) melted butter or *ghee*
¼ teaspoon (1 ml) baking soda

1. Fit a food processor with the metal blade. With the machine running, add the green chilies and ginger and process until minced. Remove the lid, add the ground rice or cereal, the *urad* flour and salt, then pulse 3 or 4 times. Pour in 1⅓ cups (320 ml) water and process for 3–4 minutes. You should have a thick muffin-consistency batter. If necessary, add additional water or rice cereal to achieve the desired consistency. Scrape the batter into a ceramic bowl, cover with plastic wrap, and set aside in a warm place (90–95°F/32–35°C) for 20–22 hours. (Depending on humidity, it may have to rest for up to 36 hours.) The batter is ready when it has increased in volume, has tiny bubbles on the surface, and has pleasantly fermented.

2. Gently stir and then test batter consistency. It should be light and frothy, like a cake batter. Place 1½ tablespoons (22 ml) of batter in a buttered *iddli* mold. It should spread out slowly and be thick enough not to fall through the perforations. If necessary, add water or self-rising flour to achieve the desired consistency. Fold in the melted butter or *ghee* and the baking soda.

3. To prepare the *iddli* molds, cut new voile handkerchiefs slightly larger than the tiers with a small hole in the center for the support pole. Moisten the handkerchiefs and lay them on the tiers. Liberally brush the handkerchiefs with melted *ghee*, oil or vegetable spray. Heat water to a depth of 1 inch (2.5 cm) in an *iddli* steamer, a 6-quart/liter pressure cooker or a stockpot over high heat. Place 2–3 tablespoons (30–45 ml) of batter in each small *iddli* mold, or spread batter to a depth of ½ inch (1.5 cm) in a larger container. Assemble the tiered rack and place it in the steaming pot. Cover securely and steam small molds for 12–15 minutes, larger molds (10 inches/25 cm) for 22–25 minutes, or until a toothpick inserted into an *iddli* comes out clean. Properly made *iddlis* will have a soft well-rounded surface. Remove the steaming pot from the heat, lift out the rack and disassemble. Using a rubber spatula, ease out the *iddlis* and transfer them to a napkin-lined steaming unit to keep them warm while you make the remaining *iddlis*.

4. Check the water level in the steaming pot and add water, as necessary, to a depth of 1 inch (2.5 cm). Lay the clean side of the handkerchiefs up, brush them with

melted *ghee* or oil, and repeat the steaming procedure using the remaining batter. Serve the *iddlis* piping hot with the bottom side up and a dab of seasoned *ghee* or butter on top. Cut large *iddlis* into slices, squares or diamonds. *Iddlis* keep well for 1–2 days refrigerated, or up to a month frozen. To reheat, line a steaming basket with a napkin and steam, covered, for about 10 minutes.

Cornmeal *Iddli* with Sesame Seeds
MAKKAI IDDLI

I first had this dish in Hyderabad at a lavish feast at the Radha Govinda Mandir. The cooks in this temple were expert in all types of South Indian cuisine, but this vegetable *iddli*, laced with sesame seeds, was outstanding. It was served with moist *Roasted Yellow Split Pea and Coconut Chutney*.

Preparation and resting time: 12 hours
Steaming time: up to ½ hour
Serves: 6 to 8

¼ cup (50 g) semolina
¼ cup (40 g) Cream of Rice cereal
⅓ cup (50 g) fine cornmeal
⅔ cup (85 g) *urad* flour
1 cup (240 ml) plain yogurt or buttermilk
½ tablespoon (7 ml) salt
2 tablespoons (30 ml) light sesame or nut oil
1 teaspoon (5 ml) black mustard seeds
3 tablespoons (45 ml) sesame seeds
1–3 hot yellow banana chilies or jalapeño
    chilies, seeded and minced
a few fresh curry leaves
⅓ cup (80 ml) finely chopped yellow or
    green bell peppers, or cooked green peas
1½ tablespoons (22 ml) brown sugar or *jaggery*
2 tablespoons (30 ml) chopped fresh coriander
½ teaspoon (2 ml) baking soda

1. Place the semolina in a heavy pan over moderate heat. Dry-roast, stirring frequently, until golden brown. Transfer to a ceramic mixing bowl and cool slightly. Add the rice cereal, cornmeal and *urad* flour, and mix well. Stir in the yogurt and salt, and blend well. Cover with plastic wrap and set aside in a warm place (90–95°F/32–35°C) for 12 hours.

2. Heat the oil in a saucepan over moderate heat. When it is hot but not smoking, add the black mustard seeds and fry until they turn gray and sputter. Remove the pan from the heat and add the sesame seeds. Within a minute, return the pan to the heat and fry until the seeds turn golden brown. Stir in the hot chilies and curry leaves and, a

For information about unfamiliar ingredients or techniques, see A-to-Z

few seconds later, stir in the bell peppers or peas and the brown sugar or *jaggery*. Fry for about 4 minutes or until the peppers are limp. Cool to room temperature, then gently mix into the *iddli* batter. Check the batter consistency. It should resemble half-whipped cream. If necessary, add a little warm water or self-rising flour to achieve the desired consistency. Just before steaming, gently stir in the herbs and baking soda.

3. To prepare the *iddli* molds, cut new voile handkerchiefs slightly larger than the tiers with a small hole in the center for the support pole. Moisten the handkerchiefs and lay them on the tiers. Liberally brush the handkerchiefs with melted *ghee*, oil or vegetable spray. Heat water to a depth of 1 inch (2.5 cm) in an *iddli* steamer, a 6-quart/liter pressure cooker or a stockpot over high heat. Place 2–3 tablespoons (30–45 ml) of batter in each small *iddli* mold, or spread batter to a depth of ½ inch (1.5 cm) in a larger container. Assemble the tiered rack and place it in the steaming pot. Cover securely and steam small molds for 12–15 minutes, larger molds (10 inches/25 cm) for 22–25 minutes, or until a toothpick inserted into an *iddli* comes out clean. Properly made *iddlis* will have a soft well-rounded surface. Remove the steaming pot from the heat, lift out the rack and disassemble. Using a rubber spatula, ease out the *iddlis* and transfer them to a napkin-lined steaming unit to keep them warm while you make the remaining *iddlis*.

4. Check the water level in the steaming pot and add water, as necessary, to a depth of 1 inch (2.5 cm). Lay the clean side of the handkerchiefs up, brush them with melted *ghee* or oil, and repeat the steaming procedure using the remaining batter. Serve the *iddlis* piping hot with the bottom side up and a dab of seasoned *ghee* or butter on top. Cut large *iddlis* into slices, squares or diamonds. *Iddlis* keep well for 1–2 days refrigerated, or up to a month frozen. To reheat, line a steaming basket with a napkin and steam, covered, for about 10 minutes.

═══ FRIED *DAL* PATTIES, PUFFS AND BALLS ═══

The word *bada* does not translate well. Phrases such as "*dal* cakes," "*dal* balls" and "*dal* puffs" do not begin to capture the qualities of the dish. Even in India, they are known by a confusing number of names, such as *wada*, *boorah* and *ballah*. Notwithstanding, this family of savories includes some of the Vedic cuisine's best light-meal entrées. *Badas* are served throughout the day: for breakfast, lunch, again for late-afternoon tiffin, and on through to a light supper. As with other fried savories, *badas* are served with some kind of fresh chutney—coconut in the South, and mint, coriander or tamarind in the North.

A cook studying regional cuisines in India learns old methods and techniques passed down through generations. To make *badas*, you acquire the skill to wet-grind *dals* on a heavy stone mortar and pestle, called a *sil-batta*. Wet-grinding is good exercise and yields excellent results but is quite time-consuming and involves considerable clean up. Fortunately, the Western cook can perform the job equally well with a food processor, which performs a number of tasks quickly and efficiently—including wet-grinding *dals*. The metal cutting blade not only reduces soaked *dal* to a smooth, fine texture but also beats necessary air into the mixture at the same time. This encourages the *badas* to expand as they fry, rendering them light and airy. If you grind *dal* in a blender, the mixture must be further wire-whisked or hand-beaten to incorporate air into the dense batter.

   Dal pastes and batters are formed into a wide range of shapes and sizes. The simplest are balls, best made by slipping a portion of seasoned *dal* batter from your fingertips into hot *ghee*. Among the most challenging are thin mung *bada* and doughnut-shaped *urad bada*, both requiring considerable skill in transfering the shaped pieces from your fingers into the frying oil. When any type of fried *bada* is combined with creamy yogurt, the result is called *dahi bada*. Some *badas* are added to yogurt while they are still crisp and warm; others are soaked in water until spongy-soft, then squeezed dry and folded into chilled yogurt. Marawadi *badas* are stuffed with chopped pistachios and raisins. Whatever their degree of complexity, *badas* require attention to basics such as adjusting *dal* consistency and controlling frying temperature.

Crunchy *Urad Dal* Patties with Black Pepper
URAD DAL BADA

   Lord Krishna's birthday, called *Janmastami* or *Sri Krishna Jayanti*, is the single most important Vaishnava holiday. It is an occasion honored with elaborate religious ceremonies and grand festivities. Devotees of Lord Krishna decorate their homes, temples and villages with lamps and flowers, and there is much exchanging of gifts of *prasadam*. Preparations begin many days in advance with the greatest of care and attention to detail.

   My second *Janmastami* with Srila Prabhupada was in Montreal, Canada, in 1969. He supervised every aspect of preparation for this great event and on the day of the celebration cooked this dish for 150 people. Though Srila Prabhupada did not use measuring tools for his ingredients, he did state that "only three seasonings are required for this *urad bada*: black pepper, asafetida and cayenne." The *badas* were shallow-fried until reddish-brown and crisp and then folded into room-temperature sour cream.

For information about unfamiliar ingredients or techniques, see A-to-Z

Dal soaking time: 4–6 hours
Preparation time (after assembling ingredients): 30 minutes
Cooking time: about 20 minutes
Serves: 4 to 6

¾ cup (160 g) split *urad dal*, without skins
water, as needed
1 teaspoon (5 ml) coarsely ground black pepper
½ teaspoon (2 ml) yellow asafetida powder (*hing*)*
½ teaspoon (2 ml) cayenne pepper or paprika
½ tablespoon (7 ml) salt
ghee or vegetable oil for frying

This amount applies only to yellow Cobra brand. Reduce any other asafetida by three-fourths.

1. Place the *dal* on a plate and sort out any foreign matter. Transfer the *dal* to a bowl, cover with water, and rub the legumes between your palms. When the water is cloudy, drain and rinse again. Repeat the washing process until the water is almost clear, then drain and set aside in a bowl. Add 3 cups (710 ml) of water and soak for 4–6 hours. Drain well.

2. To grind the *dal* in a food processor, fit the work bowl with the metal blade. Add half of the drained *dal* and 6 tablespoons (90 ml) of water, then process for 2–3 minutes, turning the machine off every minute or so to scrape down the sides of the work bowl with a rubber spatula. When the paste is smooth and fluffy, transfer it to a mixing bowl. Add the remaining *dal* and 5 tablespoons (75 ml) of water and process until the mixture is reduced to a coarse paste. There should be some texture left in the *dal*. Add to the bowl. Stir in the black pepper, asafetida, cayenne or paprika and salt, and mix well.

To grind the *dal* in a blender, first combine half of the drained *dal* and 1½ tablespoons (22 ml) of water in the blender jar, cover, and blend on high for 30 seconds. Process for 3–4 minutes, turning the machine off every 15–20 seconds, adding 4½ tablespoons of water (67 ml) and scraping down the container jar to push the ingredients toward the blades. When the *dal* paste is smooth, transfer it to a mixing bowl. Add the remaining *dal* and about 5 tablespoons (75 ml) of water and blend on high speed until the mixture is reduced to a coarse paste. Transfer it to the bowl and add the black pepper, asafetida, cayenne or paprika and salt, and blend until mixed in.

3. Rub the inside of a ¼-cup (60 ml) measuring cup with melted *ghee* or oil. Heat about ¾ inch (2 cm) of *ghee* or oil in a large frying pan or sauté pan over moderate heat. When it is hot (340°F/170°C), scoop up a scant portion with the measuring cup and carefully pour it into the hot oil, flattening the surface to make a patty about ½ inch (1.5 cm) thick. Shape about 6 patties per batch, without crowding the pan, and fry until the bottom is reddish-brown and crisp, or 4–5 minutes. Turn over and fry on the second side until evenly browned. Remove with a slotted spoon and drain on paper towels. Keep warm in a 250°F (120°C) oven while frying the remaining pieces. Allow 2–3 per person, depending on accompanying dishes. Fold into whisked sour cream, crème fraîche or thick yogurt, or place on a platter and drizzle with the cultured milk product.

Urad Dal Balls with Bitter *Neem* Leaves
URAD NEEM BADA

Bitterness is not a quality that can be smelled; it is known only by the palate and in India is achieved with any of a number of leaves, vegetables or seeds used to flavor bitter dishes. The most easily obtained and popular in India is *neem* leaves. A few cooks may have friends or relatives in India who do them the favor of drying a branch of *neem* leaves and sending them off. If you are not one of these, the alternative is to use bitter-tasting fenugreek seeds.

Dal soaking time: 4–6 hours
Preparation and cooking time: 45 minutes
Serves: 8 to 10

½ cup (105 g) split *urad dal*, without skins
½-inch (1.5 cm) piece of peeled fresh ginger root, sliced
2 hot green chilies, seeded and quartered
water, as needed
1–2 teaspoons (5–10 ml) powdered bitter *neem* leaves
    or 1 teaspoon (5 ml) fenugreek seeds
1½ tablespoons (22 ml) *ghee* or vegetable oil
2 tablespoons (30 ml) fresh or dried shredded coconut
1¼ teaspoons (6 ml) salt
ghee or vegetable oil for deep-frying

1. Place the *dal* on a plate and sort out any foreign matter. Transfer the *dal* to a bowl, cover with water, and rub the legumes between your palms. When the water is cloudy, drain and rinse again. Repeat the process until the water is almost clear, then drain and set aside in a bowl. Add 3 cups (710 ml) of water and soak for 4–6 hours. Drain well.

2. To grind the *dal* in a food processor, fit the work bowl with the metal blade. With the machine running, feed the ginger and green chilies through the feed tube and process until minced. Remove the lid, add the drained *dal* and ½ cup (120 ml) water, then process for 3–4 minutes or until the thick batter is light and airy, turning the machine off every minute or so to scrape down the sides of the work bowl with a rubber spatula. If you are using powdered *neem*, add it now, along with the *ghee* or vegetable oil, shredded coconut and salt. Pulse to mix. If you are using fenugreek seeds instead, heat the *ghee* or oil in a small saucepan over moderate heat. When it is hot but not smoking, add the seeds and fry until reddish-brown. Pour the seeds, along with the shredded coconut and salt, into the work bowl. Process for about 20 seconds to mix well and coarsely grind the seeds. Using a spatula, scrape the batter into a mixing bowl.

To grind the *dal* in a blender, with the machine on high, feed the ginger and chilies through the cap and blend until minced. Add the drained *dal* and ½ cup (120 ml) water. Blend on high for about 30 seconds. Turn the machine off and scrape down the sides of the container jar to push the ingredients toward the blades. Blend for 3–4 minutes, stopping every 15–20 seconds, until the ingredients are reduced to a smooth batter. If you are using powdered *neem*, add it now, along with the *ghee* or oil, coconut and salt. (If you are using fenugreek seeds instead, proceed as above.) Transfer to a mixing bowl, then whisk by hand or electrically for 1–2 minutes to put air in the batter.

For information about unfamiliar ingredients or techniques, see A-to-Z

To test the batter consistency, drop ½ teaspoon (2 ml) into a cup of lukewarm water. If it floats to the surface, it is ready to use. If it remains on the bottom of the cup, it requires additional beating. You may need to add additional water or a touch of self-rising flour to make a batter consistency similar to that of half-whipped cream.

3. Heat 2½–3 inches (6.5–7.5 cm) of *ghee* or vegetable oil in a *karai* or other deep-frying pan until the temperature reaches 355°F (180°C). To make each *bada*, gently lower about 1 tablespoon (15 ml) of the batter into the hot *ghee* or oil, shaping 6 or 7 at a time (or as many as will fit in the pan without crowding). Once the *badas* float to the surface, they will begin to expand and you can gently move them about to ensure even browning. Fry for 3–4 minutes or until puffed up, crisp and golden brown on all sides. Remove with a slotted spoon and drain on paper towels. Keep warm in a 250°F (120°C) oven while frying the remaining *badas*. Toss them in a bowl of whisked yogurt, crème fraîche or a sauce, or serve with chutney.

Urad Dal Balls with Coriander Leaves
URAD DHANIYA BADA

This variation of *urad bada* differs from the previous recipe in texture, flavor and shape. The *dal* is ground to a thinner consistency, more a thick batter than a paste, and is laced with fresh coriander and roasted cumin seeds. It is deep-fried into small puffs, with a soft spongy center and thin golden crust. These *badas* are always served with a moist dipping sauce or chutney. The simplest accompaniment would be plain whisked yogurt or crème fraîche. For a more tingly contrast, try *Fresh Coconut and Mint Chutney* or *Fresh Coriander Chutney*. For a more subdued sauce, try simple *Fresh Tomato Sauce*.

Dal soaking time: 4–6 hours
Preparation and frying time: 40 minutes
Serves: 4 to 6

½ cup (105 g) split *urad dal*, without skins
½-inch (1.5 cm) piece of peeled fresh ginger root, sliced
2–3 hot green chilies, seeded and quartered
water, as needed
¼ cup (60 ml) chopped fresh coriander
1½ tablespoons (22 ml) dry-roasted cumin seeds
1¼ teaspoons (6 ml) salt
¼ teaspoon (1 ml) yellow asafetida powder (*hing*)*
ghee or vegetable oil for deep-frying
2 cups (480 ml) yogurt or crème fraîche, whisked (optional),
    or a chutney or sauce

This amount applies only to yellow Cobra brand. Reduce any other asafetida by three-fourths.

1. Place the *dal* on a plate and sort out any foreign matter. Transfer the *dal* to a bowl, cover with water, and rub the legumes between your palms. When the water is cloudy, drain and rinse again. Repeat the washing process until the water is almost clear, then drain and set aside in a bowl. Add 3 cups (710 ml) of water and let soak for 4–6 hours. Drain well.

2. To grind the *dal* in a food processor, fit the work bowl with the metal cutting blade. With the machine running, feed the ginger root and green chilies through the feed tube and process until minced. Remove the lid, add the drained *dal*, ½ cup (120 ml) of water and the fresh coriander, then process for 3–4 minutes, turning the machine off every minute or so to scrape down the sides of the work bowl with a rubber spatula. (You may need to add up to 1 tablespoon/15 ml more water to make a medium-consistency batter.) When the batter is smooth and airy, add the cumin seeds, salt and asafetida and process for about 20 seconds or until the cumin seeds are coarsely ground. Using a spatula, scrape the batter into a mixing bowl.

To grind the *dal* in a blender, with the machine on high, feed the ginger and green chilies through the cap and blend until minced. Add the drained *dal*, ½ cup (120 ml) of water and the fresh coriander, and blend on high for about 30 seconds. Turn the machine off and scrape down the sides of the container jar to push the ingredients toward the blades. Blend for 3–4 minutes, stopping every 15–20 seconds, until the ingredients are reduced to a smooth batter. (You may need to add up to 1 tablespoon/15 ml more water to make a medium consistency batter.) Add the cumin seeds, salt and asafetida and blend until the seeds are coarsely ground. Transfer to a mixing bowl, then whisk by hand or electrically for 1–2 minutes to put air in the batter and make it light and airy.

To test the batter consistency, drop ½ teaspoonful (2 ml) into a cup of lukewarm water. If it floats to the surface, it is ready to use. If it remains on the bottom of the cup, it requires additional beating. You may need to add additional water or a touch of self-rising flour to make a batter consistency similar to that of half-whipped cream.

3. Heat 2½–3 inches (6.5–7.5 cm) of *ghee* or vegetable oil in a *karai* or other deep-frying pan until the temperature reaches 355°F (180°C). To make each *bada*, gently lower about 1 tablespoonful (15 ml) of the batter into the hot or oil, shaping 6 or 7 at a time (or as many as will fit in the pan without crowding). Once the *badas* float to the surface, they will begin to expand and you can gently move them about to ensure even browning. Fry for 3–4 minutes or until puffed up, crisp and golden brown on all sides. Remove with a slotted spoon and drain on paper towels. Keep warm in a 250°F (120°C) oven while frying the remaining *badas*. Toss in a bowl of whisked yogurt, crème fraîche or a sauce, or serve with a chutney.

Crunchy *Chana Dal* Patties with Coconut and Sesame Seeds
MASALA CHANA BADA

Serve these *badas* with *Zesty Mint and Green Mango Chutney* or *Fresh Tomato Chutney*.

Dal **soaking time: 5–6 hours**
Preparation time (after assembling ingredients): 15 minutes
Frying time: 25 minutes
Serves: 4 to 6

For information about unfamiliar ingredients or techniques, see A-to-Z

⅔ cup (130 g) split *chana dal*
water, as needed
2 hot green chilies, seeded and minced
¾-inch (2 cm) piece of peeled fresh ginger root, minced
½ teaspoon (2 ml) coarsely crushed fennel seeds
1 teaspoon (5 ml) salt
½ cup (45 g) fresh or dried shredded coconut, lightly packed
3 tablespoons (45 ml) sesame seeds
3 tablespoons (45 ml) finely chopped fresh coriander
3 tablespoons (45 ml) *urad* flour or arrowroot
½ teaspoon (2 ml) baking powder
ghee or vegetable oil for frying

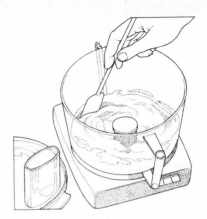

1. Place the *chana dal* on a plate and sort out any foreign matter. Place the *dal* in a bowl, cover with water and rub the legumes between your palms. When the water is cloudy, drain and rinse again. Repeat the washing process until the water is almost clear, then drain. Add 3 cups (710 ml) of water and soak for 4–6 hours. Drain well.

2. To grind the dal in a food processor, fit the work bowl with the metal blade. Add half of the drained *dal* and 2½ tablespoons (37 ml) of water. Then process for 2–3 minutes, turning the machine off every minute or so to scrape down the sides of the work bowl with a rubber spatula. When the paste is smooth and fluffy, transfer it to a mixing bowl. Process the remaining *dal* with 2½ tablespoons (37 ml) of water until the mixture is reduced to a coarse paste. There should be some texture left in the *dal*. Add it to the mixing bowl.

To grind the *dal* in a blender, first combine half of the *dal* and 2½ tablespoons (37 ml) of water in the blender, cover, and blend on high for 30 seconds. Process for 3–4 minutes, turning the machine off every 15–20 seconds to scrape down the container jar and push the ingredients toward the blades. When the *dal* paste is smooth, transfer it to a mixing bowl. Blend the remaining *dal* and about 2½ tablespoons (37 ml) of water on high speed until the mixture is reduced to a coarse paste. Add it to the mixing bowl.

3. Combine the minced chilies, ginger, fennel seeds, salt, coconut, sesame seeds and fresh coriander in a bowl. Combine the flour and baking powder in a small cup. Sprinkle the flour mixture into the *dal* paste, then add the seasonings and gently stir to blend (do not handle the mixture roughly). The mixture must be thick enough to hold its shape when pressed between your palms. If necessary, add additional water, flour, or arrowroot.

4. Heat about ¾ inch (2 cm) of *ghee* or vegetable oil to 345°F (173°C) in a large frying pan or sauté pan over moderate heat. Moisten your fingers or a metal spatula with a film of oil and scoop up about 1½ tablespoons (22 ml) of the mixture. Flatten it into a patty ½ inch (1.5 cm) thick and carefully slip it into the hot oil. You can fry 5 or 6 at a time (depending on the size of your pan), but avoid overcrowding. Fry for about 5 minutes per side or until crisp and reddish-brown. The temperature will fall to near 300°F (150°C) when the patties are added but should slowly rise back up to 345°F (173°C). Remove with a slotted spoon and drain on paper towels. Keep warm in a 240°F (115°C) oven while frying the remaining *badas*.

Seasoned *Chana Dal* Patties with Tomatoes
CHANA TAMATAR BADA

Bhavatarini Devi, Srila Prabhupada's sister, was born in Calcutta in 1898, and when I met her she was in her seventies. Respectfully known as "Pishima" (Aunt), she was a great Vaishnavi and an inspiration in many ways. When she cooked, she sat immobile in the center of the kitchen floor and placed her work around her in every direction, pivoting here and there to execute a task. For me, she was a primary influence—the Julia Child of Bengali vegetarian cooking—and I cannot recall a dish she made that I did not like. She thoroughly delighted in making, teaching and serving this dish and it offers us a fine example of Bengali *bada*. Accompany with a moist, zesty chutney such as mint or coriander.

Dal soaking time: 5–6 hours
Preparation and frying time (after assembling ingredients): about 45 minutes
Serves: 4

½ cup (100 g) split *chana dal*
1½ tablespoons (22 ml) *ghee* or vegetable oil
1–2 hot green chilies, seeded and minced
½ tablespoon (7 ml) minced fresh ginger root
½ tablespoon (7 ml) coriander seeds
1 teaspoon (5 ml) cumin seeds
½ teaspoon (2 ml) fennel seeds
2 medium-sized tomatoes, peeled, seeded and diced,
    or 2½ tablespoons (37 ml) tomato paste
¼ teaspoon (1 ml) turmeric
water, as needed
2 tablespoons (30 ml) arrowroot
1¼ teaspoons (6 ml) salt
ghee or vegetable oil for frying

1. Place the *chana dal* on a plate and sort out any foreign matter. Transfer the *dal* to a bowl, cover with water, and rub the legumes between your palms. When the water is cloudy, drain and rinse again. Repeat the washing process until the water is almost clear, then drain. Add 3 cups (710 ml) of water and soak for 5–6 hours. Drain well.

2. Heat the *ghee* or oil in a heavy nonstick saucepan over moderate heat. When it is hot but not smoking, add the chilies, ginger, coriander seeds, cumin seeds and fennel seeds, and fry until the seeds darken a few shades. Add the diced tomatoes and turmeric and cook, stirring frequently, until the tomatoes are reduced to a paste. (If you are using tomato paste, fry the spice seeds and then stir in the tomato paste.) Remove the pan from the heat and cool to room temperature.

3. To grind the *dal* in a food processor, first fit the work bowl with the metal blade. With the machine running, feed the ginger and chilies through the feed tube and process until minced. Remove the lid, add the *dal* and 3½ tablespoons (52 ml) of water, and process for 3–4 minutes, turning the machine off every minute or so to scrape down the sides of the work bowl with a rubber spatula. When the batter is smooth and airy, add the seasoned tomato paste, arrowroot and salt, and process for about 20 seconds or until the spice seeds are coarsely ground. Using a spatula, scrape the batter into a mixing bowl.

For information about unfamiliar ingredients or techniques, see A-to-Z

To grind the *dal* in a blender, with the machine on high, feed the ginger and green chilies through the cap and blend until minced. Add the *dal* and 3½ tablespoons (52 ml) of water and blend on high for about 30 seconds. Turn the machine off and scrape down the sides of the container jar to push the ingredients toward the blades. Blend for 3–4 minutes, stopping every 15–20 seconds, until the ingredients are reduced to a smooth batter. Add the seasoned tomato paste, arrowroot, salt and spice seeds, and blend until the seeds are coarsely ground. Transfer to a mixing bowl, then whisk by hand or electrically for 1–2 minutes to put air in the batter.

4. Heat 2½–3 inches (6.5–7.5 cm) of *ghee* or vegetable oil to 355°F (180°C) in a *karai* or other deep-frying pan. To make each *bada*, gently lower about 1 tablespoonful (15 ml) of the batter into the hot oil, shaping 6 or 7 at a time (or as many as will fit in the pan without crowding). Once the *badas* float to the surface, they will begin to expand and you can gently move them about to ensure even browning. Fry for 3–4 minutes or until puffed up, crisp and golden brown on all sides. Remove with a slotted spoon and drain on paper towels. Keep warm in a 250°F (120°C) oven while frying the remaining *badas*. Toss in a bowl of whisked yogurt, crème fraîche or sauce, or serve with a chutney.

Shallow-Fried Cabbage and Mung *Dal* Patties
BANDHGOBHI MOONG BADA

Cabbage *badas* are very pleasant for a special winter breakfast or brunch. I have tried this variation with finely shredded carrots or Brussels sprouts with equally good results. No matter what your choice of shredded vegetable, press it between your palms to extract excess moisture. If you like to serve *badas* with a contrasting sauce, try *Creamy Almond Sauce with Horseradish.*

Dal soaking time: 5–6 hours
Preparation and frying time: about 40 minutes
Serves: 4 to 6

½ cup (110 g) split *moong dal*, without skins
2 tablespoons (30 ml) water
2 cups (480 ml) coarsely shredded cabbage
3 tablespoons (45 ml) chopped fresh coriander
1 tablespoon (15 ml) ground coriander
1 teaspoon (5 ml) *garam masala*
scant ½ teaspoon (2 ml) turmeric
½ teaspoon (2 ml) medium grind pepper
¼–½ teaspoon (1–2 ml) crushed dried red chilies
1¼ teaspoons (6 ml) salt
¼ teaspoon (1 ml) baking powder
ghee or vegetable oil for shallow-frying

1. Place the *dal* on a plate and sort out any foreign matter. Transfer the *dal* to a bowl, cover with water and rub the legumes between your palms. When the water is cloudy, drain and rinse again. Repeat the process until the water is almost clear, then drain and set aside in a bowl. Add 3 cups (710 ml) of water and soak for 4–6 hours. Drain well.

2. Place the *dal* in a food processor fitted with the metal blade, or a blender, add the water, and grind for 5 minutes or until the purée is light and airy. Scrape the purée into a 2-quart/liter glass or ceramic bowl.

3. Press a handful of shredded cabbage between your palms and extract as much liquid as possible. When the cabbage is dry, add it along with all of the remaining ingredients, except the *ghee* or oil, to the *dal* purée.

4. Rub the inside of a ¼-cup (60 ml) measuring cup with melted *ghee* or vegetable oil. Heat about ¾ inch (2 cm) of *ghee* or oil in a large frying pan or sauté pan over moderate heat. When it is hot, about 340°F (170°C), scoop up a scant portion with the measuring cup and carefully pour it into the hot oil, flattening the surface to make a patty about ½ inch (1.5 cm) thick. Fry about 6 patties per batch, without crowding the pan, until the bottom is reddish-brown and crisp (4–5 minutes). Remove with a slotted spoon and drain on paper towels. Keep warm in a 250°F (120°C) oven while frying the remaining pieces. Allow 2–3 per person, depending on accompanying dishes. Delicious with whisked sour cream, crème fraîche or thick yogurt.

Mung *Dal* Patties with Chopped Spinach
MOONG PALAK BADA

This *bada* can be made with any leafy green vegetable. I find that both red and green Swiss chard yield excellent results, as does spinach with a handful of fresh fenugreek greens. Add a bowl of yogurt and you have a nutrition extravaganza.

Dal soaking time: 5–6 hours
Preparation and frying time: about 40 minutes
Serves: 4 or 5

½ cup (110 g) split *moong dal*, without skins
¾-inch (2 cm) piece of peeled fresh ginger root, sliced
2–3 hot green chilies, seeded and quartered
2 tablespoons (30 ml) water
½ pound (230 g) fresh spinach, washed and trimmed
¼ teaspoon (1 ml) freshly ground nutmeg
1 teaspoon (5 ml) ground coriander
½ teaspoon (2 ml) turmeric
¼ cup (25 g) sifted chickpea flour (sifted before measuring)
1 teaspoon (5 ml) salt
½ teaspoon (2 ml) baking powder
ghee or vegetable oil for frying

1. Place the *moong dal* on a plate and sort out any foreign matter. Put the *dal* in a bowl, cover with water, and rub the legumes between your palms. When the water is cloudy, drain and rinse again. Repeat the washing process until the water is almost clear, then drain. Add 3 cups (710 ml) of water and soak for 5–6 hours. Drain.

2. To grind the *dal* in a food processor, fit the work bowl with the metal blade. With the machine running, feed the ginger and chilies through the feed tube and process until minced. Remove the lid, add the *dal* and the water, then process for 3–4 minutes, turning the machine off every minute or so to scrape down the sides of the work bowl with a rubber spatula. Process until light and airy. Using a spatula, scrape the batter into a mixing bowl.

To grind the *dal* in a blender, with the machine on high, feed the ginger and green chilies through the cap and blend until minced. Add the *dal* and the water and blend on high for about 30 seconds. Turn the machine off and scrape down the sides of the jar to push the ingredients toward the blades. Blend for 3–4 minutes, stopping every 15–20 seconds, until the ingredients are reduced to a smooth batter. Transfer to a mixing bowl, then whisk by hand or electrically for 1–2 minutes to put air in the batter.

3. Half fill a 5-quart/liter saucepan with water. Bring it to a boil over high heat. Add the spinach and wilt for about 3 minutes. Pour into a strainer and drain. When the spinach is cool enough to handle, squeeze it between your palms to remove as much water as possible, then finely chop.

4. Add the spinach and the remaining ingredients, except the *ghee* or oil, to the batter, and mix well. (You may need to add a sprinkle of water or a little more chickpea flour to make the mixture a soft dropping consistency.)

5. Rub the inside of a ¼ cup (60 ml) measuring cup with melted *ghee* or vegetable oil. Heat about ¾ inch (2 cm) of *ghee* or oil in a large frying pan or sauté pan over moderate heat. When it is hot, about 340°F (170°C), scoop up a scant portion with the measuring cup and carefully pour it into the hot oil, flattening the surface to make a patty about ½ inch (1.5 cm) thick. Shape about 6 patties per batch, without crowding the pan, and fry until the bottom is reddish-brown and crisp (4–5 minutes). Remove with a slotted spoon and drain on paper towels. Keep warm in a 250°F (120°C) oven while frying the remaining pieces. Allow 2–3 per person, depending on accompanying dishes. Delicious with whisked sour cream, crème fraîche or thick yogurt.

Shredded Radish and Mung *Dal* Patties
MOOLI MOONG BADA

This exceedingly delicious *bada*, popular from Uttar Pradesh to Bengal, was one of Srila Prabhupada's favorite late evening or breakfast meals—and with good reason, for it is nutritious and warming. Radishes vary in pungency from mild to hot, and the type most often used in cooking is a white radish called *mooli*. (Because the flavor and heat of the *bada* changes with your radish selection, regulate chilies accordingly.) Any type of radish can be used, from moderately warm Japanese daikon to mild rosy-red salad variety.

Dal soaking time: 5–6 hours
Preparation and frying time: about 40 minutes
Serves: 4 to 6

½ cup (110 g) split *moong dal*, without skins
2 tablespoons (30 ml) water
1½ cups (360 ml) shredded radishes
1½ tablespoons (22 ml) coriander seeds
½ teaspoon (2 ml) fennel seeds
½–1 teaspoon (2–5 ml) crushed red chilies
½ teaspoon (2 ml) yellow asafetida powder (*hing*)*
¼ cup (25 g) sifted chickpea flour (sifted before measuring)
1¼ teaspoons (6 ml) salt
½ teaspoon (2 ml) baking powder
2 tablespoons (30 ml) finely chopped fresh coriander
ghee or vegetable oil for shallow-frying

*This amount applies only to yellow Cobra brand. Reduce any other asafetida by three-fourths.

1. Place the *dal* on a plate and sort out any foreign matter. Transfer the *dal* to a bowl, cover with water, and rub the legumes between your palms. When the water is cloudy, drain and rinse again. Repeat the process until the water is almost clear, then drain and set aside in a bowl. Add 3 cups (710 ml) of water and soak for 4–6 hours. Drain well.

2. To grind the *dal* in a food processor, fit the work bowl with the metal blade. Add the mung *dal* and the water, then process for 3–4 minutes, turning the machine off every minute or so to scrape down the sides of the work bowl with a rubber spatula. When the thick batter is light and airy, scrape it into a mixing bowl.

To grind the *dal* in a blender, add it and the water to the blender jar and blend on high for about 30 seconds. Turn the machine off and scrape down the sides of the jar to push the ingredients toward the blades. Blend for 3–4 minutes, stopping every 15–20 seconds, until the ingredients are reduced to a smooth batter. Transfer to a mixing bowl, then whisk by hand or electrically for 1–2 minutes to put air in the batter.

3. Squeeze the radishes between your palms to remove as much liquid as possible, then add them to the batter.

4. Place a small pan over moderate heat and drop in the coriander seeds and fennel seeds. Dry-roast until they darken a few shades, then coarsely crush. Add them and the remaining ingredients, except the *ghee* or oil, to the batter and gently stir to mix.

5. Rub the inside of a ¼ cup (60 ml) measuring cup with melted *ghee* or vegetable oil. Heat about ¾ inch (2 cm) of *ghee* or oil in a large frying pan or sauté pan over moderate heat. When it is hot, about 340°F (170°C), scoop up a scant portion with the measuring cup and carefully place it in the hot oil, flattening the surface to make a patty about ½ inch (1.5 cm) thick. Shape about 6 patties per batch, without crowding the pan, and fry until the bottom is reddish-brown and crisp, or 4–5 minutes. Remove with a slotted spoon and drain on paper towels. Keep warm in a 250°F (120°C) oven while frying the remaining pieces. Delicious with whisked sour cream, crème fraîche or thick yogurt.

For information about unfamiliar ingredients or techniques, see A-to-Z

Spicy Mixed *Dal* Patties

MASALA BADA

The texture of wet-ground *dals* varies considerably: a spoonful of *urad dal* paste dropped into a cup of water floats, while white *chana dal* paste tends to disintegrate. Ground *urad* is glutinous and has a velvety texture, while *chana* remains moist and loose. *Urad* should be the constant *dal* ingredient in this recipe, but feel free to use any other *dals* you wish—*chana, toovar, moong* or even supermarket split peas—and if the mixture is loose, bind it with arrowroot.

Dal **soaking time: 6 hours or overnight**
Preparation and frying time (after assembling ingredients): about 40 minutes
Serves: 6 to 8

½ **cup (105 g) split** *urad dal*, **without skins**
¼ **cup (50 g)** *moong dal* or *toovar dal*
¼ **cup (50 g)** *chana dal* or **split peas**
¾-**inch (2 cm) piece of peeled fresh ginger root, sliced**
2 **hot green chilies, seeded and quartered**
water, as needed
3 **tablespoons (45 ml) fresh or dried shredded coconut**
1¼ **teaspoons (6 ml)** *garam masala*
¼ **teaspoon (1 ml) each turmeric and yellow asafetida powder (***hing***)***
1 **teaspoon (5 ml) ground coriander**
1¼ **teaspoons (6 ml) salt**
½ **teaspoon (2 ml) baking powder**
ghee **or vegetable oil for frying**

**This amount applies only to yellow Cobra brand. Reduce any other asafetida by three-fourths.*

1. Sort through the *dals* and remove any foreign matter. Place them in a bowl of water and rub the legumes between your palms. When the water is cloudy, drain and rinse again. Repeat the washing process until the water is almost clear, then drain. Cover with 4 cups (1 liter) of cold water and soak for 6 hours or overnight. Drain well.

2. To grind the *dal* in a food processor, fit the work bowl with the metal blade. With the machine running, feed the ginger and green chilies through the feed tube and process until minced. Remove the lid, add the *dal* and ¾ cup (180 ml) of water, then process for 3–4 minutes, turning the machine off every minute or so to scrape down the sides of the work bowl with a rubber spatula. When the batter is light and airy, scrape it into a mixing bowl.

To grind the *dal* in a blender, with the machine on high, feed the ginger and green chilies through the cap and blend until minced. Add the *dal* and ¾ cup (180 ml) of water and blend on high for about 30 seconds. Turn the machine off and scrape down the sides of the jar to push the ingredients toward the blades. Blend for 3–4 minutes, stopping every 15–20 seconds, until the ingredients are reduced to a smooth batter. Transfer to a mixing bowl, then whisk by hand or electrically for 1–2 minutes to put air in the batter.

3. Add the remaining ingredients, except the *ghee* or oil, and gently mix. Heat 2½–3 inches (6.5–7.5 cm) of *ghee* or vegetable oil to 245°F (120°C) in a *karai* or other deep-frying pan. To make each *bada*, gently lower about 1 tablespoonful (15 ml) of the batter into the hot oil, shaping 6 or 7 at a time (or as many as will fit in the pan without crowding). Once the *badas* float to the surface, they will begin to expand and you can gently move them about to ensure even browning. Fry for 3–4 minutes or until puffed up, crisp and golden brown on all sides. Remove with a slotted spoon and drain on paper towels. Keep warm in a 250°F (120°C) oven while frying the remaining *badas*.

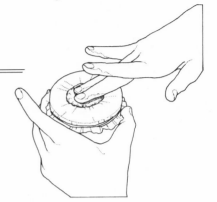

Golden Mung *Dal* Puffs
MOONG BADA

These are not easy *badas* to shape or deep-fry. They require a confident, experienced hand and a good sense of timing. If you have had experience in deep-frying, this recipe is a challenge well worth the effort. The first four pieces will likely be mediocre, the fifth will be an improvement, and the tenth a total success. The first step is to carefully read the instructions, decide on the shaping method, and collect the necessary equipment.

Success, however, will depend on three things: the consistency of the *dal* mixture, the shaping technique, and maintaining an even frying temperature. Add enough flour to the ground mung *dal* to make a thick paste if you are an experienced fry cook, or enough to make a dough if you are a novice. If the mixture is not stiff enough to hold its shape, the flat *badas* will fall apart before hitting the frying oil. Since your fingertips must come to within ¼ inch (6 mm) of the hot frying oil, do not try to attempt the first shaping technique without frying experience. An electric frying pan will be helpful in maintaining an even oil temperature. Because it takes time to shape each piece, the *ghee* tends to overheat; your heat source will thus need frequent adjustment.

This is a classic savory for a special late-afternoon tiffin. Accompany it with *Fresh Mint Chutney*, *Heart-Shaped Cheesecakes with Saffron Frosting* and seasonal fresh fruits.

Dal soaking time: 4-6 hours
Preparation and frying time: about 45 minutes
Serves: 6 to 8

¼ cup (55 g) split *urad dal*, **without skins**
¾ cup (75 g) split *moong dal*, **without skins**
¾-inch (2 cm) piece peeled fresh ginger root, sliced
2 fresh green chilies, seeded and quartered
 water, as needed
1¼ teaspoons (6 ml) salt
½ teaspoon (2 ml) yellow asafetida powder (*hing*)*
¼ teaspoon (1 ml) each ground coriander,
     cumin, fennel and turmeric
⅓-½ cup (45-70 g) well-sieved *chapati* or wheat pastry flour
ghee or vegetable oil for deep-frying

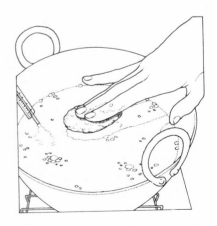

*This amount applies only to yellow Cobra brand. Reduce any other asafetida by three-fourths.

1. Combine the *dals* on a plate and sort out any foreign matter. Transfer the *dals* to a bowl, cover with water, and rub the legumes between your palms. When the water is cloudy, drain and rinse again. Repeat the washing process until the water is almost clear, then drain. Add 3 cups (710 ml) of water and soak for 4–6 hours. Drain well.

2. To grind the *dal* in a food processor, fit the work bowl with the metal blade. With the machine running, feed the ginger and green chilies through the feed tube and process until minced. Remove the lid, add the drained *dal* and 4 tablespoons (60 ml) of water, and process for 3–4 minutes, turning the machine off every minute or so to scrape down the sides of the bowl with a rubber spatula. Transfer to a bowl and mix in the remaining ingredients, except the *ghee* or oil. (The *dal* mixture should be quite stiff and easily hold its shape. If necessary, add more flour or water.)

To grind the *dal* in a blender, with the machine on high, feed the ginger and green chilies through the feed cap and blend until minced. Add the drained *dal* and 4 tablespoons (60 ml) water and blend on high for 30 seconds. Turn the machine off and scrape down the sides of the container jar every 15–20 seconds, until the ingredients are reduced to a thick batter. Transfer to a mixing bowl and add the remaining ingredients, except the *ghee* or oil. (The *dal* mixture should be quite stiff and easily hold its shape. If necessary, add more flour or water.)

3. When you are ready to fry the *badas*, prepare a simple apparatus for shaping. First, drape a piece of damp cotton cloth (handkerchief voile will do fine) over the top of a cup, and cover that with a double thickness of plastic wrap. Secure with a wide rubber band, then pull the surface taut. Brush the wrap with a film of *ghee* or coat with vegetable spray. Heat 2½–3 inches (6.5–7.5 cm) of *ghee* or vegetable oil in a *karai* or deep-frying pan over moderate heat until the temperature reaches 340–345°F (170–175°C).

4. Rub your hands with a film of oil. To shape each *bada*, place about ½ tablespoon (7 ml) of the *dal* mixture on the plastic wrap and flatten into a disk about ⅛ inch (3 mm) thick and 1½ inches (4 cm) in diameter. Pick up the cup with your left hand, tilt it onto its side, and slip the disk onto the fingertips of your right hand. In a rhythmic motion, turn your hand over and lower it to within ¼ inch (6 mm) of the hot oil. Slip the *bada* into the oil. (If your fingers are held too far from the oil, the disk tends to wrinkle or tear before reaching the oil, and the oil will splash. Heed the warning!)

An alternative shaping method would be to cut a stack of silicone-coated parchment paper 3 inches (7.5 cm) square. Coat one side of the paper with vegetable spray and after shaping a *bada* on the cup, transfer it to a paper square. Shape all of the *badas* and lay them out, without stacking, on baking trays. To fry each piece, invert and lower the paper momentarily in the frying oil, dislodge the *bada* and discard the paper. It will sink to the bottom of the pan, then rise to the surface and, if all goes well, puff into a balloon. Try to shape and fry 5 or 6 pieces at a time, maintaining the frying oil at 340–345°F (170–175°C). Fry on both sides until golden brown, then remove with a slotted spoon and drain on paper towels. Keep warm in a preheated 250°F (120°C) oven while shaping and frying the remaining pieces, then serve hot.

Note: The first time you make these *badas*, it is a good idea to have two cooks on the project: one to shape, the other to fry. In time, you will pick up the rhythm of shaping and frying.

Spongy *Dal Bada* with Creamy Yogurt and Tamarind Chutney
MARAWADI DAHI BADA

Known as *dahi boorah* in the North, *dahi vadai* in the South, and *dahi bada* in the East or West, this is one of the most loved tiffin dishes in India. It is served in homes, snack houses and street stalls, with scores of regional variations. This outstanding version, from the Bombay home of Mr. Kailash Seksaria, is a fine example of the Marawadi cuisine of Maharashtra. Marawadis, originally from Rajasthan but now settled in India's largest areas of commerce, are from the *bania* or business community. Their cuisine exhibits simplicity and purity, with refined taste—in this case exploring sweet, salty, sour and hot dimensions.

In India, this dish is served on a 4-inch (10 cm) stainless steel dish called a *dahi bada* plate. A creamy white yogurt sauce lines the bottom of the plate and two or three soft *badas* are placed in the center. Sweet 'n' sour tamarind chutney is drizzled or spooned over the *badas* and they are finally garnished with a sprinkle of dry-roasted cumin seeds, cayenne pepper and chopped fresh coriander. You can easily serve the dish in a shallow fruit dish or even a bread plate. For late afternoon tiffin or morning brunch, accompany with flaky *Savory Butter Crackers with Lemon*, munchy *Nut Medley* and assorted sparkling mineral waters—lemon, lime, grape or apple. It can also be served as a side-dish savory on a full course meal.

Dal **soaking time: 5–6 hours**
Preparation and frying time (after assembling ingredients): 1½ hours
Chilling time: at least 3 hours
Serves: 8 to 12

Bada:

⅔ **cup (145 g) split** *urad dal*, **without skins**
⅔ **cup (145 g) split** *moong dal*, **without skins**
½-**inch (1.5 cm) piece of peeled fresh ginger root, sliced**
2 hot green chilies, seeded and quartered
1 teaspoon (5 ml) caraway seeds
up to ⅔ cup (160 ml) water, as needed
1¼ teaspoons (6 ml) salt
3 tablespoons (45 ml) finely chopped raisins
2 tablespoons (30 ml) finely chopped raw pistachios
2 tablespoons (30 ml) finely chopped blanched almonds
scant ¼ teaspoon (1 ml) baking soda
ghee **or vegetable oil for frying**

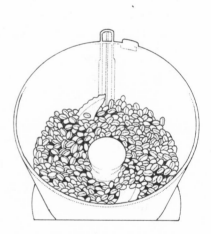

Yogurt Sauce:

2 cups (480 ml) plain yogurt, chilled
¼ **cup (60 ml) sour cream or crème fraîche**
2 tablespoons (30 ml) unsweetened grated fresh or dry coconut
¼ **teaspoon (1 ml) salt**

For information about unfamiliar ingredients or techniques, see A-to-Z

Tamarind Chutney:

4 tablespoons (60 ml) thick tamarind purée or
    2½ tablespons (37 ml) tamarind concentrate
    mixed with 1½ tablespoons (22 ml) boiling water
⅓ cup (50 g) chopped seeded dates
2 tablespoons (30 ml) date or maple sugar
½ teaspoon (2 ml) *garam masala*
¼ teaspoon (1 ml) salt
¼ teaspoon (1 ml) each cayenne pepper
    or paprika and dry ginger powder
4 tablespoons (60 ml) boiling water

Garnish:

1 tablespoon (15 ml) dry-roasted coarsely crushed cumin seeds
1 tablespoon (15 ml) homemade *garam masala* or
    dry-roasted coarsely crushed coriander seeds
¼ teaspoon (1 ml) each cayenne pepper and paprika, mixed well
several fresh coriander leaves for garnishing

To Make the Badas:

1. Place the *dals* on separate plates and sort out any foreign matter. Transfer both to a bowl, cover with water, and rub the legumes between your palms. When the water is cloudy, drain and rinse again. Repeat the washing process until the water is almost clear, then drain. Cover with 4 cups (1 liter) of cold water and soak for 5–6 hours. Rinse and drain well.

2. To grind the *dal* in a food processor, fit the work bowl with the metal blade. With the machine running, feed the ginger and green chilies through the feed tube and process until minced. Remove the lid, add the drained *dal* and process for 1 minute. Add ½ cup (120 ml) water, caraway seeds and salt, then process for 3–4 minutes, turning the machine off every minute or so to scrape down the sides of the work bowl with a rubber spatula. The batter should be light and fluffy; if necessary add the remaining water. Using a spatula, scrape the batter into a mixing bowl and cover with plastic wrap. (If time permits, set the batter aside in a warm nook for 5–6 hours to further lighten the consistency.)

To grind the *dal* in a blender, with the machine on high, feed the ginger and green chilies through the feed cap and blend until minced. Add the drained *dal*, a scant ⅔ cup (160 ml) water, and the caraway seeds and salt, and blend on high for about 30 seconds. Turn the machine off and scrape down the sides of the jar to push the ingredients toward the blades. Blend for 3–4 minutes, stopping every 15–20 seconds, until the ingredients are reduced to a smooth, light batter. Transfer to a mixing bowl, then whisk by hand, with a balloon whisk or electrically for 1–2 minutes to put air in the mixture. (If time permits, set the batter aside in a warm nook for 5–6 hours to further lighten the consistency.)

3. When you are ready to fry the *badas*, fold in the raisins, pistachios, almonds and baking soda. (Use a gentle hand to keep air in the batter; rough handling will make the *badas* heavy and dense.) Collect the equipment you will need for shaping and frying and place it near the stove: a cookie sheet lined with waxed paper, a small cup of vegetable

oil and a pastry brush, a bowl of cold water for rinsing your hands and a hand drying towel, a nonstick cooking spatula, a slotted frying spoon and a 2-quart/liter bowl of lightly salted warm soaking water.

4. This recipe makes about 24 *badas*, 4 frying batches with 6 pieces in each. If you are experienced, shape the *badas* as you fry them. For newcomers, shape 6 pieces beforehand. Brush the waxed paper with a film of oil. Dip you hand in water, scoop up a scant 3 tablespoons (45 ml) of batter and place it on waxed paper. Flatten slightly into a patty, then shape 5 more pieces.

5. Heat *ghee* or oil to a depth of 2½–3 inches (6.5–7.5 cm) to 340–345°F (170–175°C) in a *karai* or other deep-frying pan. To fry each piece, dip the cooking spatula in oil, carefully lift up a *bada* and ease it into the hot oil. (If you shape the *badas* as you fry, moisten your hands with water, scoop up the batter, roll it around your palm and slip it into the hot oil.) Fry one side for about 3 minutes or until puffed and golden, then turn over with a slotted spoon and fry for another 3 minutes on the other side. Remove the *badas* with a slotted spoon and carefully drop them into the warm soaking water. Repeat the procedure for the remaining batches. (When not in use, be sure to remove the pan from the heat to avoid overheating the oil.) Soak each batch of fried *badas* for 15–20 minutes or until they lighten in color and become spongy-soft.

6. Taking care not to break them, gently press each *bada* between your palms to swoosh out the soaking water. Place them on a plate, cover with plastic wrap, and refrigerate for at least 3 hours. (The *badas* can be made up to this stage 12 hours in advance.)

To Assemble the Badas:

7. Combine the yogurt, sour cream or crème fraîche, coconut and salt in a mixing bowl and whisk until smooth. Combine the tamarind chutney ingredients in a blender and blend on high until smooth. Scrape the chutney into another small bowl. Place the garnishes in little mounds on a plate.

8. To serve, ladle 3–4 tablespoons (45–60 ml) of yogurt sauce into a saucer or shallow fruit bowl, place 2 or 3 *badas* in the center, and drizzle with a generous spoon of chutney. Sprinkle with crushed cumin, coriander or *garam masala* and the cayenne–paprika mixture. Crown with 1 or 2 whole coriander leaves.

Savory *Urad Dal* Doughnuts
MEDU URAD BADA

Throughout Karnataka and Tamil Nadu, this dish is likely to be served any time of day. Made entirely from an *urad dal* batter, seasoned with cumin seeds, Malabar black pepper, asafetida and curry leaves, these *badas* are roughly the size of cake doughnuts, but the resemblance ends there.

For information about unfamiliar ingredients or techniques, see A-to-Z

Also called *medu vadai*, which indicates a silky-light texture, they possess a cloud-like interior with a crisp, thin crust. To serve as a snack or appetizer, accompany with *Fresh Coconut and Mint Chutney*. To serve as *rasawade*, soak briefly in piping-hot, spicy *rasam* broth.

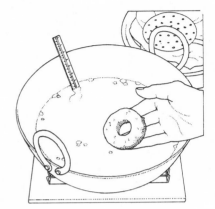

Dal soaking time: 5–6 hours
Preparation time: about 10 minutes
Batter resting time: 6 hours or overnight
Serves: 8

¾ cup (160 g) split *urad dal*, without skins
1-inch (2.5 cm) piece of peeled fresh ginger root, sliced
2 jalapeño chilies, seeded and quartered
9 tablespoons (135 ml) water, or as needed
½ tablespoon (7 ml) dry-roasted cumin seeds
1 teaspoon (5 ml) Malabar black peppercorns or
    green peppercorns
scant ½ teaspoon (2 ml) yellow asafetida powder (*hing*)*
1¼ teaspoons (6 ml) salt
10–12 fresh or dried curry leaves, coarsely chopped or crushed
⅛ teaspoon (0.5 ml) baking soda
ghee or vegetable oil for deep-frying

This amount applies only to yellow Cobra brand. Reduce any other asafetida by three-fourths.

   1. Place the *urad dal* on a plate and sort out any foreign matter. Transfer the *dal* to a bowl, cover with water, and rub the legumes between your palms. When the water is cloudy, drain and rinse again. Repeat the washing process until the water is almost clear, then drain. Add 3 cups (710 ml) of water and soak for 5–6 hours. Rinse and drain well.
   2. To grind the *dal* in a food processor, fit the work bowl with the metal blade. With the machine running, feed the ginger and chilies through the feed tube and process until minced. Remove the lid, add the drained *dal* and process for 1 minute. Add 9 table-spoons (135 ml) of water, then process for 3–4 minutes, turning the machine off every minute or so to scrape down the sides of the work bowl with a rubber spatula. When the batter is light and airy, add the cumin seeds, peppercorns, asafetida and salt and process until the peppercorns are coarsely ground. Using a spatula, scrape the mixture into a mixing bowl.
   To grind the *dal* in a blender, with the machine on high, feed the ginger and green chilies through the feed cap and blend until minced. Add the drained mung *dal* and 9 tablespoons (135 ml) of water and blend on high for about 30 seconds. Turn the machine off and scrape down the sides of the jar to push the ingredients toward the blades. Blend for 3–4 minutes, stopping every 15–20 seconds, until the ingredients are reduced to a smooth batter. Add the cumin seeds, peppercorns, asafetida, and salt and blend until the peppercorns are coarsely ground. Transfer to a mixing bowl, then whisk by hand or electrically for 1–2 minutes to put air in the batter.
   To test batter consistency, drop ½ teaspoonful (2 ml) into a cup of cold water. If it floats to the surface, it is ready to use. If it remains on the bottom of the cup, it requires additional beating. You may need to add more water or self-rising flour to make a dropping consistency paste-batter. Cover with plastic film and set aside in a warm nook for 6 hours or overnight or until the batter has expanded in volume slightly.

3. When you are ready to fry the *badas*, gently stir in the baking soda and curry leaves. Collect the equipment you will need for shaping and frying and place it near the stove. If you are an experienced fry-cook, you will only need a bowl of water for rinsing your hands and a hand drying towel, a slotted frying spoon, and paper towels for draining the *badas*. If you are a newcomer to making *badas*, add a small cup of oil and a pastry brush, sixteen 3 x 3-inch (7.5 x 7.5 cm) squares of waxed paper, a cookie sheet and a cooking spatula. To shape all of the pieces before cooking, brush each piece of paper with oil. Dip your hand in water and scoop up a walnut-sized portion of paste-batter. Roll it around your palm, then place it on a piece of waxed paper. Poke a hole in the center with your thumb. Shape 15 more pieces.

4. Heat 2½–3 inches (6.5–7.5 cm) of *ghee* or oil to 345°F (175°C) in a *karai* or deep-frying pan over moderate heat. If your *badas* are already shaped, lift up a piece of waxed paper and place it just over the pan. With the help of a spatula, ease it into the hot oil. Fry 5 or 6 in a batch.

To shape and fry the *badas* simultaneously, moisten your hands with a film of oil, scoop up a walnut-sized ball of *dal* paste, and place it in your left palm. Open your palm and flatten the ball into a 2¼-inch (6 cm) patty. With the thumb of your right hand, press a hole in the center of the patty to form a doughnut. Gently transfer the doughnut to the fingertips of your right hand and bring your hand to within 1 inch (2.5 cm) of the surface of the frying oil, turn it over, and carefully slip the doughnut into the pan. (Please take care: if you release the *bada* from more than ½ inch/1.5 cm above the surface of the oil, it will splash unnecessarily and burn.) Shape and fry 5 or 6 pieces at a time, without crowding the pan.

Once the *badas* float to the surface, they will begin to swell and expand. Fry for 3–4 minutes on each side or until the crust is crisp and reddish-brown. Remove with a slotted spoon and drain on paper towels. Keep warm in a 250°F (120°C) oven while frying the remaining pieces. Serve piping hot, warm or at room temperature.

Feather-Soft *Urad Dal* Doughnuts with Seasoned Yogurt
URAD DAHI BADA

This type of *dahi bada* might be served anywhere in Bengal or Bihar. Fenugreek seeds give the *bada* a particularily spongy texture, while the mustard seeds and ginger lend warmth to the cashew yogurt. You could make a South Indian version, called *dahi vadai*, by soaking a batch of *badas* from the previous recipe in yogurt laced with coconut, cayenne and chopped fresh coriander. Because the *badas* are added to the yogurt while they are still warm, they soak up sauce flavors as they soften.

Dal soaking time: 5–6 hours
Shaping and frying time: about 40 minutes
Chilling time: at least 1 hour
Serves: 5 or 6

For information about unfamiliar ingredients or techniques, see A-to-Z

⅔ cup (145 g) split *urad dal*, without skins
generous ¼ teaspoon (1 ml) fenugreek seeds
2 jalepeño chilies, seeded and quartered
1 teaspoon (5 ml) green or white peppercorns
⅓ cup (80 ml) water, or as needed
1¼ teaspoons (6 ml) salt
⅛ teaspoon (0.5 ml) baking soda
ghee or vegetable oil for deep-frying
1 teaspoon (5 ml) black mustard seeds
¼ cup (35 g) raw cashew bits
2½ cups (600 ml) plain yogurt and ½ cup (120 ml) water or
   3 cups (710 ml) buttermilk
1½ tablespoons (22 ml) *ghee* or sesame oil
2 tablespoons (30 ml) chopped fresh coriander
½ teaspoon (2 ml) scraped and grated fresh ginger root
a sprinkle of cayenne pepper or paprika

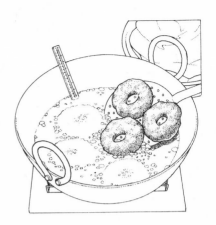

1. Place the *urad dal* on a plate and sort out any foreign matter. Transfer the *dal* to a bowl, cover with water, and rub the legumes between your palms. When the water is cloudy, drain and rinse again. Repeat the process until the water is almost clear, then drain and set aside in a bowl. Add the fenugreek seeds and 3 cups (710 ml) of water and soak for 5–6 hours. Rinse and drain well.

2. To grind the *dal* in a food processor, fit the work bowl with the metal blade. With the machine running, feed the chilies through the feed tube and process until minced. Remove the lid, add the drained *dal* and process for 1 minute. Add 5 tablespoons (75 ml) of water, then process for 3–4 minutes, turning the machine off every minute or so to scrape down the sides of the work bowl with a rubber spatula. When the batter is light and airy, add the peppercorns and salt and process until the peppercorns are coarsely ground. Using a spatula, scrape the mixture into a mixing bowl.

To grind the *dal* in a blender, with the machine on high, feed the chilies through the feed cap and blend until minced. Add the drained mung *dal* and 5 tablespoons (75 ml) of water and blend on high for about 30 seconds. Turn the machine off and scrape down the sides of the jar to push the ingredients toward the blades. Blend for 3–4 minutes, stopping every 15–20 seconds, until the ingredients are reduced to a smooth batter. Add the peppercorns and salt and blend until the peppercorns are coarsely ground. Transfer to a mixing bowl, then whisk by hand or electrically for 1–2 minutes to put air in the batter.

To test batter consistency, drop ½ teaspoonful (2 ml) into a cup of cold water. If it floats to the surface, it is ready to use. If it remains on the bottom of the cup, it requires additional beating. You may need to add more water or self-rising flour to make a dropping consistency paste-batter.

3. When you are ready to fry the *badas*, gently stir in the baking soda. Collect the equipment you will need for shaping and frying and place it near the stove. If you are an experienced fry-cook, you will only need a bowl of water for rinsing your hands and a hand drying towel, a slotted frying spoon, and paper towels for draining the *badas*. If you are a newcomer to making *badas*, add a small cup of oil and a pastry brush, fifteen 3 x 3-inch (7.5 x 7.5 cm) squares of waxed paper, a cookie sheet and a cooking spatula. To shape all of the pieces before cooking, brush each piece of paper with oil. Dip your hand in water and scoop up a generous tablespoon (15 ml) of paste-batter. Roll it around your palm then place it on a piece of waxed paper. Poke a hole in the center with your thumb. Shape 14 more pieces.

4. Heat 2½–3 inches (6.5–7.5 cm) of *ghee* or oil to 345°F (175°C) in a *karai* or deep-frying pan over moderate heat. If your *badas* are already shaped, lift up a piece of waxed paper and place it just over the pan. With the help of a spatula, ease it into the hot oil. Fry 5 in a batch.

To shape and fry the *badas* simultaneously, moisten your hands with a film of oil, scoop up a generous tablespoon (15 ml) of *dal* paste, and place it in your left palm. Open your palm and flatten the ball slightly. With the thumb of your right hand, press a hole in the center of the patty to form a doughnut. Gently transfer the doughnut to the fingertips of your right hand and bring your hand to within 1 inch (2.5 cm) of the surface of the frying oil, turn it over, and carefully slip the doughnut into the pan. (Please take care: if you release the *badas* from more than ½ inch/1.5 cm above the surface of the oil, they may splash and burn.) Shape and fry 5 pieces at a time, without crowding the pan.

Once the *badas* float to the surface, they will begin to swell and expand. Fry for about 3 minutes on each side or until the crust is crisp and golden-red. Remove with a slotted spoon and drain on paper towels while frying the remaining pieces.

5. Combine ½ teaspoon (2 ml) of the mustard seeds and cashew nuts in a blender or food processor and pulse until powdered. Add half of the yogurt and water or buttermilk and process until smooth. Add the remaining yogurt or buttermilk and process briefly. Pour the yogurt sauce into a shallow serving dish, add the warm *badas*, and gently stir. Cover and refrigerate until chilled, from 1–6 hours.

6. Heat the *ghee* or oil in a small pan over moderate heat. When it is hot, drop in the remaining mustard seeds and fry until they sputter and pop. Pour the seasoning on the chilled *bada* and garnish with fresh coriander, cayenne or paprika.

Mung *Dal* Balls in Herbed Yogurt
MOONG DAHI BADA

North Indian *chat* or snack houses—half sidewalk café, half open restaurant—specialize in both North and South Indian light meals. Near one entrance, a 20-foot (7 meter) long refrigerated case brims with all sorts of colorful, decorated sweet confections. Near another door, a man sits cross-legged, surrounded by a never-ending pyramid of golden fried *mung badas*, chilled yogurt and various garnishes. An innocent passer-by is lured inside just by glancing at the sweet case or watching the *dahi bada* man assemble plate after plate of this dish. This is one of North India's most refreshing summer pick-me-ups, nutritious and cooling. Every Indian temple, home and restaurant has several variations.

Dal **soaking time: 5–6 hours**
Preparation and frying time (after assembling ingredients): about 40 minutes
Chilling time: at least 1 hour
Serves: 6 to 8

For information about unfamiliar ingredients or techniques, see A-to-Z

⅔ cup (145 g) split *moong dal*, without skins
2 tablespoons (30 ml) split *urad dal*, without skins
4–5 tablespoons (60–75 ml) water, or as needed
½ tablespoon (7 ml) cumin seeds
½ teaspoon (2 ml) caraway seeds
¼ teaspoon (1 ml) *ajwain* seeds
¼ teaspoon (1 ml) yellow asafetida powder (*hing*)*
⅓ teaspoon (1.5 ml) cayenne pepper
1½ teaspoons (7 ml) salt
⅛ teaspoon (0.5 ml) baking soda
ghee or vegetable oil for deep-frying
2 cups (480 ml) plain yogurt
2 tablespoons (30 ml) finely chopped fresh coriander
    or 1 tablespoon (15 ml) minced fresh dill
paprika or freshly ground pepper

*This amount applies only to yellow Cobra brand. Reduce any other asafetida by three-fourths.

   1. Combine the *dals* on a plate and sort out any foreign matter. Place the *dals* in a bowl, cover with water, and rub the legumes between your palms. When the water is cloudy, drain and rinse again. Repeat the washing process until the water is almost clear, then drain. Add 3 cups (710 ml) of water and soak for 5–6 hours. Drain well.
   2. To grind the *dal* in a food processor, fit the work bowl with the metal blade. Add the drained *dal* and 3–4 tablespoons (45–60 ml) water, then process for 3–4 minutes, turning the machine off every minute or so to scrape down the sides of the work bowl with a rubber spatula. When the batter is smooth and airy, transfer it into a mixing bowl.
   To grind the *dal* in a blender, add the drained *dal* and 3–4 tablespoons (45–60 ml) water and blend on high for about 30 seconds. Turn the machine off and scrape down the sides of the container jar to push the ingredients toward the blades. Blend for 3–4 minutes, stopping every 15–20 seconds, until the ingredients are reduced to a smooth batter. Transfer to a mixing bowl, then whisk by hand or electrically for 1–2 minutes to put air in the batter.
   3. Just before frying, stir in the cumin seeds, caraway seeds, *ajwain* seeds, asafetida, cayenne, 1¼ teaspoons (6 ml) of the salt and the baking soda. (The consistency should resemble that of half-whipped cream; if necessary, add additional water or whole wheat flour.) Heat 2½–3 inches (6.5–7.5 cm) of *ghee* or oil to 345°F (175°C) in a *karai* or other deep-frying pan over moderate heat. Using your fingertips or a spoon, scoop up cherry-sized portions of the *dal* mixture and slip them into the hot oil. Shape up to 10 *badas* per batch (depending on the size of your pan), but do not overcrowd.
   As the *badas* float to the surface of the oil, they will begin to swell. Turn the balls constantly with a slotted spoon to ensure even browning. Fry for 3–4 minutes or until they are golden brown and crisp, then remove with a slotted spoon and drop into a bowl of slightly salted lukewarm water. Continue to shape and fry all the remaining pieces, then soak for ½ hour.
   4. Gently press each *bada* between your palms to swoosh out the soaking water. Whisk the yogurt, fresh herbs and remaining ¼ teaspoon (1 ml) of salt in a shallow serving bowl, and fold in the drained *badas*. Cover and chill for at least an hour and serve with a sprinkle of paprika or freshly ground pepper.

PAN-FRIED VEGETABLE PATTIES

Just as people enjoy watching pizzas being made with dexterity right before their eyes in a typical Western pizza parlor, so in many quaint Indian restaurants you can watch the experts making *tikkis*. These delightful fried vegetable patties are cooked with practiced skill, exactly as they have been made for centuries. The patties lie, cooking ever-so-slowly, in the center of a large, flat, heavy iron griddle. As a paper-thin brown crust forms on the *tikki*, testifying that they are done, the cook adroitly scoots them to the sides of the griddle. There they remain, thoroughly soft and warm, ready for takers.

These tantalizing patties are not difficult to make at home. The formula consists of maximizing the cooking time and minimizing the cooking medium, which is *ghee* or vegetable oil. Using a cast-iron frying pan will put a wafer-thin crust on *tikki*, but non-stick Silverstone is less bothersome. Brush the pan with just enough *ghee* or vegetable oil to prevent the patties from sticking, use the lowest possible heat, and simply let the *tikkis* cook for about 15 minutes on each side. Too much *ghee* or oil, or hasty cooking, will cause the delicate patties to break apart. One of the best things about *tikkis* is that they cook effortlessly, except for a brief turn over, and thus make for an ideal breakfast or brunch. The last two *tikki* recipes given here differ from the others in that the *tikkis* are shallow-fried over moderately high heat. These, of course, require full attention while cooking.

Tikkis are classically served with a dab of seasoned yogurt, fresh chutney or sauce just before serving.

Herbed Potato Patties
ALOO TIKKI

Tikkis can be compared in popularity to American hash-browns. Though they are most popular at breakfast, they are also eaten at almost any time of the day as a light meal. Serve with a spoonful of yogurt and *Quick Tamarind–Raisin Chutney* or *Velvet Tomato Chutney*.

Preparation and cooking time (after assembling ingredients): about 1 hour
Serves: 4

For information about unfamiliar ingredients or techniques, see A-to-Z

3 large boiling potatoes (1¼ pound/570 g)
1 tablespoon (15 ml) *ghee* or unsalted butter
1¼ teaspoons (6 ml) salt
¼ teaspoon (1 ml) freshly ground pepper
⅛ teaspoon (0.5 ml) freshly ground nutmeg
¼ teaspoon (1 ml) turmeric
1 tablespoon (15 ml) lemon juice
½ tablespoon (7 ml) minced or puréed hot chilies, or ¼ teaspoon (1 ml) cayenne pepper
2 tablespoons (30 ml) finely chopped fresh coriander or minced parsley
3–4 tablespoons (45–60 ml) dry-roasted chickpea flour or whole wheat pastry flour
ghee or vegetable oil for pan-frying

1. Boil the potatoes in their skins just until fork-tender. When they are cool enough to handle (between hot and warm), peel them and force them through a potato ricer or coarse sieve to produce smooth mashed potatoes.

2. Add the remaining ingredients, except the *ghee* or oil. Knead until blended, then divide into 8 portions. Wash and dry your hands and rub them with a film of oil. Roll each portion between your palms to make a ball, then flatten into a smooth round patty about ½ inch (1.5 cm) thick.

3. Brush a well-seasoned 12-inch (30 cm) cast-iron griddle or nonstick pan with a film of *ghee* or oil. Place over the lowest possible heat, and when the pan is hot, add the patties in a single layer. Pan-fry for 15–20 minutes per side or until a crisp reddish brown crust forms. Serve hot.

Potato Patties with Crunchy Bitter Melon Chips
ALOO KARELA TIKKI

Bitter melons, also called bitter gourds, are found at Oriental and Italian grocery stores. If they are not available, use chopped pecans. This *tikki* is excellent with a light soup and salad for lunch.

Preparation and cooking time (after assembling ingredients): about 1 hour
Serves: 4

3 large boiling potatoes (1¼ pounds/570 g)
3 tablespoons (45 ml) *ghee*, or 1 tablespoon (15 ml) sunflower
    oil and 2 tablespoons (30 ml) unsalted butter
2 small bitter melons (4 ounces/115 g), trimmed and coarsely chopped
    or ¼ cup (35 g) toasted pecan pieces
1¼ teaspoons (6 ml) salt
⅓ teaspoon (1.5 ml) cayenne pepper
1 teaspoon (5 ml) freshly grated horseradish or
    ½ teaspoon (2 ml) powdered horseradish
2 tablespoons (30 ml) fresh or dried grated coconut
½ tablespoon (7 ml) lime juice
2–3 tablespoons (30–45 ml) whole wheat pastry flour
ghee or vegetable oil for pan-frying

1. Cover the potatoes with cold water in a saucepan and bring to a boil. While they are gently boiling, heat the *ghee* or oil–butter mixture in a frying pan over moderately high heat. When it is hot but not smoking, add the bitter melon and stir-fry until brown and crispy. Set aside.

2. When the potatoes are fork tender, drain and cool slightly. Peel while quite warm, and coarsely mash in a bowl. Add the fried bitter melon or pecans and the remaining ingredients, except the *ghee* or oil, and mash only until blended. Divide into 10 portions. Wash and dry your hands, roll the portions into balls, and flatten them into smooth 2½-inch (6.5 cm) patties.

3. Brush a well-seasoned 12-inch (30 cm) cast-iron griddle or nonstick pan with a film of *ghee* or oil. Place over the lowest possible heat, and when the pan is hot, add the patties in a single layer. Pan-fry for 15–20 minutes per side or until a crisp reddish-brown crust forms. Serve hot.

Potato Patties Stuffed with Green Peas
ALOO HARI MATAR TIKKI

Pea-stuffed *tikkis* are as well loved in North India as *iddlis* and *dosas* are in the South. *Tikkis* are usually pan-fried, but once—out of necessity and a lack of equipment—I was obliged to bake *tikkis* for 150 people. The crust was not as delicate as when pan-fried, but baking is a time saving alternative that yields pleasing results.

Preparation and cooking time (after assembling ingredients): about 1 hour
Serves: 4 or 5

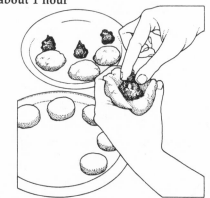

3 large boiling potatoes (1¼ pounds/570 g)
1 teaspoon (5 ml) salt
¼ teaspoon (1 ml) freshly ground black pepper
⅔ cup (160 ml) cooked peas or frozen baby peas, defrosted
½ tablespoon (7 ml) scraped and minced fresh ginger root
¼ teaspoon (1 ml) yellow asafetida powder (*hing*)*
¼ teaspoon (1 ml) *garam masala*
¼ teaspoon (1 ml) salt
1 teaspoon (5 ml) dry-roasted coarsely crushed cumin seeds
ghee or vegetable oil for pan-frying

*This amount applies only to yellow Cobra brand. Reduce any other asafetida by three-fourths.

1. Boil the potatoes in their skins just until fork-tender. When they are cool enough to handle (between hot and warm), peel them and force them through a potato ricer or coarse sieve to produce smooth mashed potatoes. Add salt and pepper, knead until blended, then divide into 10 portions. Wash and dry your hands and rub them with a

---

For information about unfamiliar ingredients or techniques, see A-to-Z

film of oil. Roll each portion between your palms to make a ball, then flatten into a smooth round patty about ½ inch (1.5 cm) thick.

2. Using a fork, coarsely mash the peas. Add the remaining ingredients, except the *ghee* or oil, mash briefly, then divide into 10 portions.

3. Shaping one at a time, place a portion of peas in the center of a potato patty and fold the edges together so the peas are nestled inside. Gently flatten into a 2½-inch (6.5 cm) patty. Shape all the pieces in this way.

3. Place 1 teaspoon (5 ml) of *ghee* or oil in a 12-inch (30 cm) nonstick pan and preheat slowly over low heat for 2 minutes. Slip in the patties, without crowding, and reduce the heat to the lowest possible setting. Pan-fry for 15–20 minutes per side, adding *ghee* or oil if necessary, or until a crisp reddish-brown crust forms. Serve hot.

Note: If you are baking the *tikkis*, place them on a well-buttered baking tray without crowding. Place in a 350°F (180°C) oven for 15 minutes, brush with melted *ghee* two or three times during browning, turn over, and brown for another 15 minutes.

Savory Mashed Yam Patties
SURAN TIKKI

You can also use sweet potatoes. Ground nuts and seeds, also called nut and seed meals, are available at health food stores.

Preparation and cooking time (after assembling ingredients): about 1 hour
Serves: 4

3 medium-sized yams (1 pound/455 g)
3 tablespoons (45 ml) ground almonds or cashews
3 tablespoons (45 ml) ground sunflower seeds
3 tablespoons (45 m) fresh or dried grated coconut
¼–½ teaspoon (1–2 ml) cayenne pepper
½ teaspoon (2 ml) ground cumin
1 teaspoon (5 ml) ground coriander
1 tablespoon (15 ml) maple sugar or granulated *jaggery*
1 teaspoon (5 ml) salt
3 tablespoons (45 ml) dry-roasted chickpea flour or
    1 tablespoon (15 ml) arrowroot
ghee or sunflower oil for pan-frying

1. Place the yams in boiling water, cover and gently boil for 20–30 minutes or until tender when pierced with a fork. Drain, peel while still warm, and mash.

2. Mix in the remaining ingredients, except the *ghee* or oil, and knead until thoroughly blended. Divide into 8 portions. Wash and dry your hands and rub them with a film of oil. Roll each portion between your palms to make a ball, then flatten into a smooth round patty about ½ inch (1.5 cm) thick.

3. Brush a well-seasoned 12-inch (30 cm) cast-iron griddle or nonstick pan with a film of *ghee* or oil. Place over the lowest possible heat, and when the pan is hot, add the patties in a single layer. Pan-fry for 15–20 minutes per side or until a crisp reddish-brown crust forms. Serve hot.

Yogurt Cheese Patties with Spicy Green Peas
DEHIN HARI MATAR TIKKI

Yogurt cheese is every bit as delicious as cream cheese, but much lower in calories. Though it is not yet available commercially, it is very easy to make, as it is simply whole yogurt drained of whey and compacted. You need a dry yogurt cheese for this dish, so allow extra time to drain off the whey if necessary. You cannot press water from yogurt; it must slowly drip off. The combination of yogurt cheese and roasted chickpea flour is very delicious and, combined with peas, a powerhouse of nutrition.

Preparation and cooking time (after assembling ingredients): about 45 minutes
Serves: 4

½ cup (50 g) sifted chickpea flour (sifted before measuring)
2 tablespoons (30 ml) whole wheat pastry flour
1 teaspoon (5 ml) salt
¼ teaspoon (1 ml) *garam masala*
2 tablespoons (30 ml) finely chopped fresh coriander
2 tablespoons (30 ml) finely chopped toasted pecans
⅓ cup (80 ml) cooked fresh or frozen baby peas, mashed
⅛ teaspoon (0.5 ml) freshly ground pepper
1 teaspoon (5 ml) finely minced or puréed green chilies
1 teaspoon (5 ml) peeled, minced or puréed fresh ginger root
¾ cup (180 ml) dry yogurt cheese (page 311), unsalted,
    made from 3½ cups (830 ml) whole milk yogurt
    (about 4½ ounces/130 g)
⅔ cup (60 g) fresh or dried grated coconut
2 tablespoons (30 ml) *ghee* or sunflower oil for pan-frying

1. Place the chickpea flour in a heavy frying pan over moderately low heat and dry-roast, stirring constantly, until it darkens a few shades and becomes aromatic. Transfer to a mixing bowl, add the wheat flour, salt, *garam masala*, fresh coriander and chopped pecans, and mix well.

2. Mix the peas, black pepper, green chilies, ginger and yogurt cheese in a separate bowl, then add to the flour mixture and knead with your hands to mix well. (You may have to add additional flour or a sprinkle of water, depending on the moisture content of the yogurt cheese.) The mixture should be stiff and dough-like. Divide it into 8 portions. Wash and dry your hands then rub them with a film of oil. Shape each portion into a ball, then flatten into a 2¼-inch (6 cm) patty. Dip each patty in coconut on both sides.

3. Heat 1 tablespoon (15 ml) of *ghee* or oil in a 12-inch (30 cm) nonstick frying pan over low heat. Adding 1 tablespoon (15 ml) additional *ghee* when you turn them over, slowly fry the patties for 12–15 minutes per side, or until golden brown.

Note: Should the cheese mixture be too moist or the heat too high, the patties tend to disintegrate during pan-frying.

For information about unfamiliar ingredients or techniques, see A-to-Z

Mixed Vegetable Cutlets

SABJI TIKKI

Snack house and railway restaurant vegetable cutlets, bound together with milk-soaked bread, are popular throughout India. Prior to the British presence in India, white yeast bread was almost nonexistent. Though Western bakeries are constantly popping up in large cities, most bread is better suited for crumbs, stuffing or cutlets than for sandwiches or toast.

This Bengali version, made without bread, is the type eaten in Vaishnava homes. The potatoes and garbanzo beans bind the cutlets together, *chenna* cheese, nuts and seeds offer easily substantial protein, and fresh vegetables and herbs fill in with necessary vitamins and minerals. White poppy seeds adds a thin, crunchy crust on the cutlets; for a meeting of both traditions, use breadcrumbs. Serve with a lemon wedge, fresh chutney, or sauce.

Preparation and cooking time (after assembling ingredients): about 1¼ hours
Makes: 12 cutlets

1 cup (240 ml) coarsely chopped cauliflower flowerets
1 cup (240 ml) peeled and diced boiling potatoes
1 cup (240 ml) fresh or frozen peas, defrosted
1 cup (240 ml) green beans cut into ¼-inch (6 mm) pieces
1 cup (240 ml) finely shredded carrots
½ cup (120 ml) finely shredded beets
¼ cup (60 ml) finely chopped celery and tops
2 hot green chilies, seeded and quartered
⅔ cup (160 ml) cooked garbanzo beans (wash and drain canned beans)
freshly made *chenna* cheese (page 315) made from 4 cups
       (1 liter) milk (about 5 ounces/140 g)
3 tablespoons (45 ml) each chopped walnuts and almonds
3 tablespoons (45 ml) sunflower or pumpkin seeds
1½–2 teaspoons (7–10 ml) salt
⅛ teaspoon (0.5 ml) freshly ground pepper
¼ teaspoon (1 ml) turmeric
1 teaspoon (5 ml) *garam masala*
3 tablespoons (45 ml) each chopped fresh coriander and parsley
¾ cup (180 ml) buttermilk
2 tablespoons (30 ml) each cornstarch and whole wheat flour
⅔ cup (90 g) white poppy seeds or 1 cup (110 g) toasted
       bread crumbs
ghee or vegetable oil for shallow-frying

1. Place the cauliflower, potatoes, fresh peas and green beans in the bottom of a steaming unit and cover them with water. Put the carrots, beets and celery in the steaming basket, cover and cook until the vegetables are tender-crisp; do not overcook. Drain the lower vegetables through a strainer, collecting the water. Add the defrosted peas to the top steamed vegetables.

2. Fit a food processor container with the metal blade, and with the machine running, drop in the chilies and mince. Add the garbanzo beans, *chenna cheese*, nuts and seeds and process until the beans and cheese are mashed. (If necessary, add sprinkles of vegetable cooking water to facilitate grinding.) Add the cauliflower, potatoes, fresh peas and green beans and pulse on and off until the vegetables are coarsely mashed. Transfer the mixture to a mixing bowl, add the steamed vegetables, salt, pepper, turmeric and *garam masala*, and mix well. Divide into portions.

3. Line a baking sheet with waxed paper. Rub your hands with a film of oil and flatten a portion into an almond-shaped cutlet about ¾ inch (2 cm) thick. Shape the remaining pieces, setting them on the waxed paper, cover, and refrigerate for at least 30 minutes. (These can be made to this point several hours in advance.)

4. Whisk the buttermilk, cornstarch and flour in a flat bowl until a smooth batter forms. Dip each cutlet in the batter, allowing the excess to drip back into the bowl, then roll in white poppy seeds or bread crumbs, coating completely. Set aside on waxed paper to air-dry.

5. Heat *ghee* or oil to a depth of ¾ inch (2 cm) in a large frying pan or sauté pan over moderate heat until the temperature reaches 350°F (180°C). Fry 4–6 cutlets per batch, without crowding the pan, for 1½–2 minutes per side. The poppy seeds should not turn brown, but the bread crumbs should turn golden brown. Drain on paper towels. Fry the remaining cutlets and serve hot.

Tapioca and Potato Patties with Roasted Peanuts
EKADASEE SABU ALOO TIKKI

Although once a regional specialty of Maharashtra, today this dish is served in households around the country, especially on *Ekadasee* fast days. This variation is from a farmhouse kitchen in Indore. Made with little more than tapioca, potatoes and peanuts, the recipe ingredients hide the really delicious results. Pearl tapioca, available on the deli-gourmet shelves of most supermarkets, is sold in three sizes: small, medium and large pearls. Use small or medium, but avoid the quick-cooking variety, which is used for instant creamy puddings. With a hint of sugar and lime juice, this *tikki* is meant to be hot—with flavor from both fresh chilies and cayenne. Serve this dish as a savory on a full meal or as finger foods for holiday parties.

Soaking time: 30 minutes
Preparation time: 15 minutes
Cooking time: about 15 minutes
Serves: 6 to 8

⅔ **cup (95 g) raw peanuts with skins or**
   dry-roasted peanuts, without skins
½ **cup (65 g) pearl tapioca**
4–5 **medium-sized potatoes (about 1½ pounds/685 g),**
   boiled, peeled and coarsely mashed
⅓ **cup (80 ml) chopped fresh coriander**
3–4 **hot green chilies, seeded and minced**
scant 1 tablespoon (15 ml) fresh lime or lemon juice
2 **teaspoons (10 ml) sugar**
1½ **teaspoons (7 ml) salt**
⅛ **teaspoon (0.5 ml) each black pepper and cayenne pepper**
peanut or vegetable oil for frying

For information about unfamiliar ingredients or techniques, see A-to-Z

1. If you are using raw nuts, spread them on a baking sheet and roast in a low oven (250°F/120°C) until the reddish skins are brittle and easily flake off and the nuts turn a pale brown color. Remove and cool them, then rub between your fingers to remove the skins. (In India, a small woven hand fan is used to blow away the skins.) Chop the nuts and place them in a mixing bowl.

2. Place the tapioca in a strainer and rinse it under a stream of tap water, swishing the grains with your hand, for about 1 minute or until the starchy water runs clear. Submerge the strainer in a bowl of water so that the tapioca is covered and let it soak for 30 minutes. Again rinse under tap water and drain well.

3. Add the tapioca and remaining ingredients to the nuts and, using your hands, knead the mixture until well mixed. Wash and dry your hands and rub them with oil. Divide the mixture into 24 portions, then flatten them into smooth patties about 2 inches (5 cm) in diameter. Set aside on waxed paper.

4. Pour oil to a depth of 2 inches (5 cm) in a *karai* or deep fryer. Place over moderately high heat, and when the oil reaches 370°F (190°C), slip in 6 patties or as many as will fit the pan without crowding. Fry for about 3 minutes on each side, turning with a slotted spoon, until they turn reddish-brown. Drain on paper towels and fry the remaining pieces. It is best served piping hot. To reheat, place in in a moderately hot oven for 10 minutes.

LIGHT-MEAL FAVORITES

Semolina *Uppma* with Bell Peppers and Cabbage
SOOJI UPPMA

Uppma is regarded with great affection in India. In its simplest form—semolina, cashews, fried spices and water—it resembles a fluffy version of Italian *polenta*. In its more elaborate forms, it takes on some of the elements of North African couscous. Until the 1980s, semolina was not easy to find, but with the popularity of pasta in America, it is now sold at a number of places: Italian, Indian and Middle Eastern grocery stores, health food stores, mail order gourmet shops and even large supermarkets. If you have a choice between coarse- and fine-grained, choose the latter, which makes a lighter, fluffy-textured *uppma*. Coarse semolina is better for a moist, pudding like *uppma*—often set in ramekin-sized cups. Though not as authentic, you can substitute quick Cream of Wheat or farina cereal.

Preparation and cooking time (after assembling ingredients): ½ hour
Serves: 4 to 6

1 cup (170 g) fine-grained semolina
¼ cup (60 ml) *ghee* or a mixture of peanut oil and unsalted butter
2 hot green chilies, seeded and minced
1 teaspoon (5 ml) cumin seeds
1 teaspoon (5 ml) black mustard seeds
2 teaspoons (10 ml) split *urad dal*, if available
1 red or green bell pepper (about 6 ounces/170 g),
      stemmed, seeded and cut lengthwise into thin strips
2 cups (480 ml) finely shredded cabbage (about 6 ounces/170 g)
½ cup (120 ml) fresh peas or frozen baby peas, defrosted
½ teaspoon (2 ml) turmeric
1 teaspoon (5 ml) salt
2 cups (480 ml) water
2 tablespoons (30 ml) chopped fresh coriander
1 tablespoon (15 ml) lemon juice

1. Place the semolina in a large heavy frying pan over moderate heat. Stir-fry for 6–8 minutes or until the grains darken a few shades. Transfer to a Pyrex measuring cup and set aside.

2. Heat the *ghee* or oil–butter mixture in a heavy 4 or 5-quart/liter casserole over moderately high heat. When it is hot, add the green chilies, cumin seeds, black mustard seeds and *urad dal*, and fry, partially covering the pan with a lid or spatter screen, until the mustard seeds pop and the *urad dal* turns reddish-brown. Stir in the bell pepper, cabbage, fresh peas, and turmeric, and sauté for 2–3 minutes. Reduce the heat to moderate and continue to cook for 4–5 minutes or until the vegetables are limp, but still tender-crisp.

3. Carefully pour in the water and bring to a boil. While stirring, slowly sprinkle in the semolina. Add the salt, stir, and reduce the heat to moderately low and cook, stirring occasionally, until all the liquid is absorbed and the *uppma* is light and fluffy—about 10–12 minutes for semolina and 6–8 minutes for Cream of Wheat. If you are using defrosted peas, fold them in now, along with the fresh coriander. Sprinkle with lemon juice before serving.

Cauliflower and Farina *Uppma* with Fenugreek Seeds
GOBHI SOOJI UPPMA

Farina is a granular meal made from hard, but not durum, wheat. Cream of Wheat brand sells three types: Instant, Quick-Cooking and Regular, while Malt-O-Meal and Farina brands are only sold in the Quick-Cooking form. Malt-O-Meal is a pre-roasted grain, so it saves you the roasting time necessary to bring out a nutty flavor in the grain and helps make the finished dish light and fluffy.

For information about unfamiliar ingredients or techniques, see A-to-Z

Preparation and cooking time (after assembling ingredients): ½ hour
Serves: 6

5 tablespoons (75 ml) *ghee* or a mixture of
    light sesame oil and unsalted butter
2 whole dried red chilies, halved and seeded
½ tablespoon (7 ml) minced fresh ginger root
½ tablespoon (7 ml) cumin seeds
½ teaspoon (2 ml) fenugreek seeds
2 tablespoons (30 ml) sesame seeds
10–12 curry leaves, preferably fresh
1 small cauliflower (¾–1 pound/340–455 g),
    trimmed, cored and cut into pieces roughly
    1 x ½ x ½ inch (2.5 x 1.5 x 1.5 cm)
scant ½ teaspoon (2 ml) turmeric
1 teaspoon (5 ml) ground coriander
1 cup (180 g) Malt-O-Meal brand farina
⅔ cup (160 ml) buttermilk mixed with
    1½ cups (360 ml) hot water
1¼ teaspoons (6 ml) salt
2 tablespoons (30 ml) finely chopped fresh fenugreek or coriander

    1. Heat the *ghee* or oil-butter mixture in a 4–5-quart/liter casserole over moderately high heat. When it is hot but not smoking, add the chilies, ginger, cumin seeds and fenugreek seeds, and fry until the fenugreek seeds darken slightly. Add the sesame seeds and fry until the fenugreek turns reddish-brown. Drop in the curry leaves, and a few seconds later add the cauliflower. Stir-fry for 2–3 minutes, then reduce the heat to moderate, add the turmeric and ground coriander, and cook, stirring frequently, until the cauliflower is almost fork-tender.

    2. Add the pre-roasted farina and gently stir to coat the vegetable. Pour in the buttermilk–water mixture and salt and, stirring, bring to a boil over high heat, then cook for 1 minute. Cover, remove the pan from the heat, and set aside for 4 minutes so the grains can expand and absorb the liquid. Fluff with a spoon and sprinkle with the fresh herbs before serving.

Farina *Uppma* with Cashews and Coconut
SOOJI KAJU UPPMA

    Use any of the following brand names of quick-cooking farina: Cream of Wheat, Farina or Malt-O-Meal. The first two require toasting before use; Malt-O-Meal is a pre-roasted cereal. This dish is very quick to assemble, but to soften the split *dals* for the seasoning, soak them 1 hour ahead of time.

Dal soaking time: 1 hour
Preparation and cooking time (after assembling ingredients): ½ hour
Serves: 4 to 6

2 cups (480 ml) water
2 tablespoons (30 ml) split *chana dal*
½ tablespoon (7 ml) split *urad dal*
4 tablespoons (60 ml) *ghee* or a mixture
      of peanut oil and unsalted butter
½ cup (75 g) cashew pieces
⅓ cup (35 g) ribbon coconut
1 teaspoon (5 ml) black mustard seeds
10–12 curry leaves, preferably fresh
generous ¼ teaspoon (1 ml) yellow asafetida powder (*hing*)*
¾ cup (135 g) quick-cooking Cream of Wheat,
      Farina or pre-roasted Malt-O-Meal
1¼ teaspoons (6 ml) salt
½ tablespoon (7 ml) lemon juice

*This amount applies only to yellow Cobra brand. Reduce any other asafetida by three-fourths.

1. Bring the water to a boil in a small saucepan and add the *dals*. Boil for 1 minute, remove the pan from the heat and set aside for 1 hour. Remove the *dals* with a slotted spoon and pat dry on paper towels.

2. Heat the *ghee* or oil-butter mixture in a heavy 4–5-quart/liter casserole over moderate heat. Add the cashews and fry until golden. Remove with a slotted spoon and set aside. Fry the coconut until golden, remove, and set aside.

3. Add the black mustard seeds and drained *dals* to the casserole and fry until the *urad dal* turns reddish-brown and the mustard seeds pop and turn gray. Toss in the curry leaves and asafetida, and in a few seconds follow with the Cream of Wheat or farina. Stir-fry for 6–8 minutes or until the grains darken slightly and turn a pale gold color. (If you use Malt-O-Meal, fry it for 1 minute.)

4. Slowly add the hot water, ¼ cup (60 ml) at a time, stirring until all the water is absorbed. The texture should be light and fluffy. Sprinkle in the fried nuts, coconut and salt and gently stir to mix. Sprinkle with lemon juice. Cover and set aside for 4–5 minutes before serving.

Vermicelli and Vegetable *Uppma* with *Panir* Cheese
SEVIYA PANIR UPPMA

The Punjab, in northwestern India, is famous for its creamy toasted vermicelli milk pudding. The whole wheat vermicelli is as fine as angel hair and pre-roasted until golden brown. On occasion, this vermicelli is combined with seasonal vegetables into a pasta-based *uppma*. You will find the noodles at Indian grocery stores in 8-ounce (230 g) boxes, usually called *seviya*, sometimes *sev*. If you want to make a copy of the dish with Italian pasta, be sure it is the finest vermicelli or thin spaghettini. To save time on vegetable cutting, I prepare the vegetables in a food processor. This dish sticks in stainless steel or enamel pans with thin walls; for worry-free, excellent results, use a heavy-bottomed nonstick saucepan.

Preparation time (after assembling ingredients): 15 minutes
Cooking time: ½ hour
Serves: 4 to 6

½ yellow, green or red bell pepper,
    seeded and cut into 6 pieces
2 celery stalks, fibers removed and
    cut into 1-inch (2.5 cm) pieces
2 medium-sized carrots, peeled and cut to fit the
    feed tube horizontally (about 8 ounces/230 g)
2 small zucchinis, ends trimmed, and cut
    to fit the feed tube horizontally
1 small tomato, diced
¼ cup (60 ml) *ghee* or sunflower oil
5 ounces (140 g) fresh *panir* cheese (page 313)
    made from 6 cups (1.5 liters) milk
    cut into ⅓-inch (1 cm) dice
1 teaspoon (5 ml) cumin seeds
1 teaspoon (5 ml) black mustard seeds
¼ teaspoon (1 ml) *ajwain* seeds
2 hot green chilies, seeded and finely sliced
¼ teaspoon (1 ml) yellow asafetida powder (*hing*)*
10–12 small *neem* leaves, preferably fresh
½ cup (120 ml) diced eggplant
1½ cups (285 g) very thin Italian vermicelli
    noodles broken into 1-inch (2.5 cm) pieces,
    or 1½ cups (85 g) Indian pre-roasted noodles
1⅔ cups (400 ml) water or unsalted vegetable stock
1¼ teaspoons (6 ml) salt
3 tablespoons (45 ml) minced mixed fresh herbs (parsley,
    coriander, basil) or 1 tablespoon (15 ml) dried herbs
¼ teaspoon (1 ml) freshly ground black pepper

This amount applies only to yellow Cobra brand. Reduce any other asafetida by three-fourths.

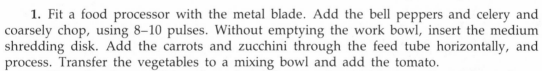

1. Fit a food processor with the metal blade. Add the bell peppers and celery and coarsely chop, using 8–10 pulses. Without emptying the work bowl, insert the medium shredding disk. Add the carrots and zucchini through the feed tube horizontally, and process. Transfer the vegetables to a mixing bowl and add the tomato.

2. Heat the *ghee* or oil in a large heavy-bottomed nonstick pan over moderate heat. When it is hot, add the cheese pieces and fry, stirring frequently with a wooden spatula, until they are an even golden-brown color and crisp. Transfer the cheese to a plate with a slotted spoon.

3. Raise the heat to moderately high. Drop in the cumin seeds, black mustard seeds, *ajwain* seeds and green chilies, and fry until the cumin seeds brown and the mustard seeds pop. Add the asafetida and *neem* leaves, and in a few seconds stir in the eggplant. Stir-fry for 2 minutes, then add the vegetables and continue to cook for 5 minutes, stirring frequently to ensure even browning, until the vegetables soften and partially cook.

4. Add the noodles, *panir* cheese, water or vegetable stock, salt and half of the fresh herbs. (If you use dried herbs, add them all now.) When the water comes to a boil, cover, reduce the heat to low, and simmer for 12–15 minutes.

5. Remove the lid, raise the heat and cook until all the water has evaporated and the noodles are soft and the vegetables tender. Sprinkle the dish with the remaining fresh herbs and black pepper.

Note: If you make this dish in quantity, boil the vermicelli in salted water separately, then add it to fully cooked vegetables, fried cheese and herbs; omit the 1⅔ cups (400 ml) water or vegetable stock.

Herbed Cracked Wheat *Uppma* with Fried Vegetables
DALIA UPPMA

If you have the luxury of a kitchen herb garden, feel free to add your favorites. I enjoy summer savory, coriander, parsley, mint and marjoram. If you must resort to dried herbs, at least feature fresh parsley, a year-round staple even in supermarkets. Cracked wheat and bulgur can be used interchangeably and are available at supermarkets, specialty stores and many co-ops. Bulgur is a wheat that has been boiled, dried and cracked, with outstanding whole grain food value and a delicious, nutty taste. With a tossed green salad and a light soup, you have a complete lunch. If you want to elaborate on a menu for company or family, add *Rice Flour Dosa with Cashews and Mustard Seeds, Creamy Fresh Coconut Chutney* and a seasonal salad.

Preparation time and cooking time (after assembling ingredients): about ½ hour
Serves: 4 to 6

3 tablespoons (45 ml) *ghee* or vegetable oil
1 teaspoon (5 ml) split *urad dal*, if available
1½ teaspoons (7 ml) cumin seeds
½ teaspoon (2 ml) black mustard seeds
1–3 fresh green chilies, finely sliced
½ cup (120 ml) finely chopped cored and seeded red bell peppers
½ cup (120 ml) finely chopped celery stalks with tops
⅔ cup (160 ml) zucchini, cut into ¼-inch (6 mm) dice
1 cup (155 g) cracked wheat or bulgur
2 cups (480 ml) water
1 cup (240 ml) packed chopped spinach
½ cup (120 ml) chopped fresh herbs (coriander, parsley, basil, summer savory, mint, marjoram, as
    desired) or ⅓ cup (80 ml) chopped fresh parsley and ½ tablespoon (7 ml) mixed dried herbs
1½ teaspoons (7 ml) salt
tomato flower garnish (optional)

1. Heat the *ghee* or oil over moderate heat in a heavy nonstick saucepan. When it is hot, add the *urad dal*, and in a few seconds follow with the cumin seeds, black mustard seeds and green chilies. Fry until the *dal* turns reddish-brown and the mustard seeds pop.

For information about unfamiliar ingredients or techniques, see A-to-Z

2. Stir in the bell peppers, celery and zucchini and fry for 2–3 minutes. Pour in the cracked wheat or bulgur and stir-fry to toast it for another 2–3 minutes.

3. Add the water, spinach, half of the fresh mixed herbs or parsley and all of the dried herbs, and the salt, cover, and reduce the heat to low. Simmer for about 15 minutes or until the liquid is absorbed into the grains and the dish is light and fluffy.

4. Fold in the remaining herbs and serve garnished with optional tomato flowers.

Light 'n' Easy Pounded Rice *Uppma* with Potatoes and Green Peas
GUJARATI CHURA UPPMA

This dish is in Gujarat what *usal* is in Maharastra: an exceedingly popular breakfast and light meal dish. It is made with pounded (flat) or beaten rice, available at Indian grocery stores, usually under the name *poha*. Of the two types sold—thick and thin—thick is the preferred selection as it holds its shape during washing. Fragile, thin *poha* is used in deep-fried munchie mixtures. The opaque flat rice sold in Britain for pudding cannot be substituted for thick *poha*. For a warm weather breakfast or brunch, try this flat rice pilaf with seasonal cut fruits and *Minty Yogurt Shake*.

Preparation and cooking time (after assembling ingredients): 40 minutes
Serves: 6

2½ cups (155 g) thick-type pounded rice (*poha*)
⅓ teaspoon (1.5 ml) turmeric
½ tablespoon (7 ml) dry-roasted coarsely crushed cumin seeds
1 teaspoon (5 ml) salt
½ tablespoon (7 ml) lemon or lime juice
¼ cup (60 ml) *ghee* or a mixture
    of sunflower oil and unsalted butter
2 hot green chilies, seeded and minced
½ tablespoon (7 ml) peeled fresh ginger root, minced
1¼ teaspoons (6 ml) black mustard seeds
½ teaspoon (2 ml) fennel seeds
generous ¼ teaspoon (1 ml) yellow asafetida powder (*hing*)*
10–12 curry leaves, preferably fresh
1 baking potato, peeled and cut into ⅓-inch (1 cm) dice
½ cup (120 ml) fresh peas or frozen baby peas, cooked
¼ cup (40 g) raisins, soaked in hot water for 10 minutes, then drained
1 teaspoon (5 ml) sugar
2 tablespoons (30 ml) chopped fresh coriander or parsley
lemon or lime wedges

*This amount applies only to yellow Cobra brand. Reduce any other asafetida by three-fourths.

1. Sort through the flat rice and remove any foreign matter. Place it in a large strainer under running water for 10–15 seconds. Lower the strainer into a pan of water and swish the grains with your fingers, then rinse again. Drain in the strainer for a few minutes. (Thin flat rice is delicate, and the grains easily break; clean with a gentle touch, briefly, for no more than 15–20 seconds. If left too long in water, the rice will literally disintegrate.) Spread the drained rice on a plate to air-dry, and sprinkle with turmeric, cumin seeds, salt and citrus juice.

2. Heat the *ghee* or oil–butter mixture in a 4-quart/liter pan over moderately high heat. When it is hot but not smoking, add the green chilies, ginger, black mustard seeds and fennel seeds in quick succession. Partially cover and fry until the mustard seeds crackle and pop. Uncover. Drop in the asafetida and curry leaves, and in a few seconds add the potatoes. Cook the potatoes, stirring now and then, until they are golden brown and tender.

3. Reduce the heat to low, add the peas, raisins, sugar, fresh herbs and flat rice, stir gently, partially cover and cook for 10–12 minutes. Serve with lemon or lime wedges.

Savory Pounded Rice *Uppma* with Fried Nuts and Coconut
KHASA CHURA UPPMA

Ahmedabad, the capital of Gujarat, is famed for exquisite vegetarian cuisine and qualified chefs. Very slightly sweet and sour, this simple dish is a favorite in almost every household and family restaurant in the city. Since fresh coconut is important for flavor and few Western cooks keep it on hand, grated frozen coconut is a convenient substitute. It is sold at Cuban or Latin American grocery stores and in large cities is even found in supermarkets. If you open a fresh coconut, grate and freeze what remains for further use. It keeps well for 3–4 months in a freezer and is a time saver for coconut chutneys. For a special brunch or late breakfast, accompany the *uppma* with *Sliced Oranges with Maple Cream* and iced herb tea.

Preparation and cooking time (after assembling ingredients): 40 minutes
Serves: 4 to 6

2 cups (120 g) thick pounded rice (*poha*)
½ teaspoon (2 ml) turmeric
generous ¼ teaspoon (1 ml) coarsely cracked pepper
2 teaspoons (10 ml) fresh Key lime or lemon juice
1¼ teaspoons (6 ml) salt
1 tablespoon (15 ml) date sugar
3 tablespoons (45 ml) *ghee* or light sesame oil
½ tablespoon (7 ml) black mustard seeds
2 fresh green chilies, seeded and minced
⅓ cup (45 g) cashew pieces
⅓ cup (50 g) split raw peanuts
3 x 3-inch (7.5 x 7.5 cm) piece of peeled fresh coconut, cut into
    thin slices, or ½ cup (75 g) grated frozen coconut, defrosted
2 tablespoons (30 ml) chopped fresh coriander

For information about unfamiliar ingredients or techniques, see A-to-Z

1. Sort through the flat rice and remove any foreign matter. Place it in a large strainer under running water for 10–15 seconds. Lower the strainer into a pan of water and swish the grains with your fingers, then rinse again. Drain in the strainer for a few minutes. (Thin flat rice is delicate, and the grains easily break; clean with a gentle touch, briefly, for no more than 15–20 seconds. If left too long in water, the rice will literally disintegrate.) Spread the drained rice on a plate to air-dry and sprinkle with turmeric, pepper, salt, lemon or lime juice and sugar.

2. Heat the *ghee* or vegetable oil in a heavy 4-quart/liter casserole over moderate heat. When it is hot but not smoking, add the mustard seeds and chilies, and fry until the seeds crackle and pop. Stir in the cashews and peanuts and fry, stirring constantly until the nuts are golden brown. Stir in the coconut and flat rice, gently toss, then partially cover and cook over low heat for 10–12 minutes, stirring occasionally. Garnish with fresh coriander.

Crispy Puffed Rice Snack with Fried Cashews and Green Peas
KAJU MOORI CHIDWA

In Indian bazaars, it is a familiar sight to see men puffing rice. A sand-filled *karai* is placed over glowing coals, and when the coarse sand is hot, rice is added. Using a long paddle, the sand is patiently stirred, until one by one, the rice grains pop into long pointed puffs. With nothing more than straining it through a fine sieve, hot puffed rice, called *moori*, is ready to be sold in recycled newspaper bags. Like everything in India, you have to search for quality and then haggle for it—and even if you pay dearly, much of the puffed rice tastes a little dusty. Homemade puffed rice is always more delectable. Par-boiled rice is stir-fried in a dry pan until very hot, and immediately dropped into hot oil where it expands into puffs. This is the basis of numerous munchy snacks, much like this one.

This dish can be made with any puffed grain—from *moori* sold at Indian grocery stores, to supermarket Quaker puffed rice or a health food store puffed brown rice. Serve for breakfast or a light snack.

Preparation and cooking time (after assembling ingredients): 30 minutes
Serves: 4 to 6

¼ cup (60 ml) *ghee* or a mixture of
    sunflower oil and unsalted butter
⅓ cup (50 g) split raw peanuts
⅓ cup (45 g) cashew pieces
½ tablespoon (7 ml) minced fresh ginger root
1–2 fresh green chilies, seeded and minced
½ teaspoon (2 ml) turmeric
1 teaspoon (5 ml) ground coriander
1 teaspoon (5 ml) ground cumin
¼ teaspoon (1 ml) yellow asafetida powder (*hing*)*
¾ cup (180 ml) steamed fresh peas or
    frozen baby peas, defrosted
2½ cups (45 g) puffed rice
½ teaspoon (2 ml) fine popcorn salt
1 teaspoon (5 ml) date or maple sugar (optional)

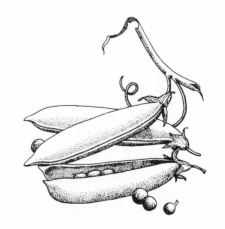

*This amount applies only to yellow Cobra brand. Reduce any other asafetida by three-fourths.

1. Heat the *ghee* or oil-butter mixture in a heavy 5-quart/liter pan over moderate heat for about 1 minute. Add the peanuts and fry until they turn golden brown. Remove with a slotted spoon and drain on paper towels. Fry the cashew nuts until golden brown, then remove and set aside with the peanuts.

2. Drop in the minced ginger, chilies, turmeric, coriander, cumin and asafetida, one after another in quick succession, and fry for no more than 3–4 seconds. Immediately add the peas, raise the heat to moderately high, and cook for 2 minutes.

3. Add the puffed rice and, stirring constantly, cook until it is slightly crisp and well coated with powdered spices. Add the nuts, salt and sugar. Mix well. Serve hot and crisp.

Spicy Puffed Rice Snack with Crispy Fried Noodles and Almonds
MOORI SEV CHIDWA

The first time you make this dish, it will take longer than the second, and so on. The only time-consuming job is making the *sev* noodles, but once you have the hang of using the machine, it takes little time. Looking much like fried Chinese noodles, they are shaped with a brass utensil called a *seviya* machine. This inexpensive utensil will last a lifetime and is available at Indian grocery stores. The noodles will keep for up to a week. Assemble the snack just before serving.

Preparation and cooking time (after assembling ingredients): 45 minutes
Serves: 6 to 8

Noodles:

½ cup (50 g) unsifted chickpea flour
¼ teaspoon (1 ml) salt
⅛ teaspoon (0.5 ml) cayenne pepper
½ teaspoon (2 ml) vegetable oil
water, as needed
ghee or vegetable oil for deep-frying
4 tablespoons (60 ml) *ghee* or unsalted butter
½ tablespoon (7 ml) cumin seeds, crushed
½ tablespoon (7 ml) fennel seeds, crushed
½ cup (55 g) sliced almonds
⅓ cup (35 g) shredded coconut
3 tablespoons (45 ml) currants
2½ cups (45 g) puffed rice
¼ teaspoon (1 ml) cayenne pepper
1½ teaspoons (7 ml) *chat masala*
2 teaspoons (10 ml) *garam masala*
1½ teaspoons (7 ml) salt

For information about unfamiliar ingredients or techniques, see A-to-Z

1. Combine the flour, salt, cayenne, and oil in a small bowl and add 4 tablespoons (60 ml) of water, or enough to mix into a medium-stiff paste. Knead well. Scrape into a *seviya* utensil fitted with the finest noodle disk. Screw on a lid and set aside.

2. Heat 2–3 inches (5–7.5 cm) of *ghee* or vegetable oil in a *karai* or deep-frying utensil over moderate heat until the temperature reaches 355°F (180°C). Force the noodle paste through the holes, rotating the machine in a complete circle over the pan. As the noodles fall into the hot oil, they will first sink and then rise and float. Stir gently with a knife blade to keep the noodles from sticking together. Fry for about 1–1½ minutes on each side or until golden brown and crisp. Remove with a slotted spatula and drain on paper towels. Fry the remaining batter in batches. When the noodles are cool and crisp, break them into small pieces about 1½-inches (4 cm) long.

3. Heat the *ghee* or butter in a 4-quart/liter pan over moderate heat. Add the cumin seeds, fennel seeds and almonds, and slowly fry for 5–6 minutes or until the nuts turn golden brown.

4. Add the coconut, currants, puffed rice, cayenne, *chat masala*, *garam masala* and salt. Stir-fry for 4–5 minutes or until the puffed rice is slightly crisp. Just before serving, mix in the noodles. Serve hot.

Puffed Rice and Nut Snack with Raisins
MOORI KISHMISH CHIDWA

Though not widely available in India, sunflower and pumpkin seeds help to make this a nutritious snack. Recently, seven-grain puffed cereal packaged as Kashi has reached health food stores shelves. It is wonderfully crunchy and flavorful, a wonderful alternative to puffed rice—and to popcorn.

Preparation and cooking time (after assembling ingredients): 20 minutes
Serves: 6

¼ teaspoon (1 ml) cayenne pepper
¼ teaspoon (1 ml) turmeric
¼ teaspoon (1 ml) freshly ground nutmeg
¼ teaspoon (1 ml) freshly ground black pepper
⅛ teaspoon (0.5 ml) each ground cloves and cinnamon
1¼ teaspoons (6 ml) salt or herb salt
2 tablespoons (30 ml) confectioner's sugar
¼ cup (60 ml) *ghee* or a mixture of vegetable oil and unsalted butter
⅓ cup (45 g) sunflower seeds
⅓ cup (45 g) pumpkin seeds
⅓ cup (50 g) raisins
2 tablespoons (30 ml) chopped fresh coriander or parsley
2½ cups (45 g) puffed rice or Kashi

1. Combine the ground spices, salt and sugar in a small bowl. Heat the *ghee* or oil–butter mixture in a heavy 4-quart/liter pan over moderate heat. Fry the sunflower seeds until they pop and brown. Remove with a slotted spoon and drain on paper towels. Fry the pumpkin seeds in a similar way and add to the sunflower seeds. Add the raisins and fry until they plump and begin to brown. Remove and drain. Finally, add the fresh herbs and fry until crisp. Sprinkle half of the seasoning mixture on the fried items and toss to mix.

2. Add the remaining seasoning and puffed rice to the remaining oil and stir-fry until warm and a little crispy. Add the remaining seasonings and fried things and toss to mix. Serve hot.

Snacks
and
Nibblers

The Vedic culture places great importance on hospitality. Anyone, whether a casual visitor or an old friend, is immediately offered refreshment on entering even the most humble home. No gathering, whether of friends, acquaintances or business associates, is complete without offering and receiving food. It is socially imperative.

If you know beforehand that someone is coming over, you will usually have time to make one of the savory snacks described in the previous chapter that can be assembled just before serving and then served piping hot. The "nibbling" varieties in this chapter are the kind you might want to keep on hand for the unexpected guest. These between-meal foods, generally deep-fried and salty, have a diverse range of exquisite textures and flavors. They are either ready to eat at room temperature or easily warmed. Either way, they go well with a cool drink, fresh cut fruits or a sweet. They also make excellent traveling companions.

Triangle Crisps
SAKARPARA

"With only flour, water and a little mustard oil", Srila Prabhupada used to say, "my maternal aunt made wonderful dishes." It wasn't until I tasted this fried pastry in Bir Nagar, Bengal, that I fully appreciated this achievement. The finest mustard oil was used, almost the color of almond oil, and the pastry was coated with a thin sugar glaze. This variation, fried in *ghee* and left unglazed, is classically flavored with *kalonji*, a black spice seed with a lemon pepper flavor. The crisps will keep well for up to four weeks.

Preparation and resting time: 40 minutes
Frying time: 35–45 minutes
Makes: 16 *sakarparas*

1½ **cups (175 g) unbleached white flour**
¾ **teaspoon (3.5 ml) salt**
1¼ **teaspoons (6 ml) *kalonji* or lemon pepper**
3 **tablespoons (45 ml) melted *ghee* or unsalted butter**
4½–5½ **tablespoons (67–82 ml) lukewarm water**
ghee **or vegetable oil for deep-frying**

1. Combine the flour, salt and *kalonji* or lemon pepper in a large bowl and mix well. Add the melted *ghee* or butter and rub it in with your fingertips to evenly distribute. Pour 4½ tablespoons (67 ml) of water over the flour and quickly mix into a rough, shaggy dough. If necessary, add the remaining tablespoon (15 ml) of water, a few drops at a time, until the mass can be kneaded into a stiff dough. Knead on a clean work surface for about 8 minutes or until the dough is firm but pliable. Cover with a damp towel or plastic wrap and allow it to rest for ½ hour.

Alternately, fit a food processor with the metal blade and pulse the flour and salt twice. Add the melted *ghee* or unsalted butter and pulse 8–10 times to mix. With the motor running, pour 4½ tablespoons (67 ml) of water through the feed tube and process until pea-sized bits form in the mixture. Add the *kalonji* or lemon pepper and pulse twice. You may need to add up to 1 tablespoon (15 ml) more water to make a stiff dough. (The mixture should not form a ball in the bowl, but should easily form into a ball with your hands.) Gather the dough into a ball, cover it with a damp towel or plastic wrap, and set aside for at least ½ hour.

2. Divide the dough in half and roll each piece into a log 8 inches (20 cm) long. Cut each log into 8 portions and flatten each portion into a smooth patty. Drape the dough with a damp towel as you work. Roll out each patty on a lightly oiled countertop into a thin, 5-inch (12.5 cm) circle. Using a pastry brush or your fingers, brush the surface with a film of melted *ghee* or oil and fold in half. Brush the semicircle with *ghee* or oil and fold into a triangle. Press lightly with your fingers, then roll out again into a thin 5-inch (12.5 cm) triangle. Place the pastries on a plastic-wrap-lined baking tray, without touching as you roll and shape them.

3. Heat *ghee* or oil to a depth of 2½–3-inches (6.5–7.5 cm) in a *karai* or deep-frying pan over moderate heat until the temperature reaches 335–340°F (168–171°C) on a deep-frying thermometer. Slip one pastry into the hot oil. First it will sink, then bob toward the surface. Immediately hold the back of a slotted spoon over the pastry to keep it submerged in the oil. It will blister and puff in places. Fry for 1½–2 minutes on each side or until crisp and pale gold. Remove with a slotted spoon and drain on paper towels. Fry the remaining pieces. Cool to room temperature. They can be kept for up to 4 weeks in a tightly sealed container.

For information about unfamiliar ingredients or techniques, see A-to-Z

Thin 'n' Crisp Chickpea Flour Noodles
MASALA SEV

Sev rivals peanuts as India's most popular munching snack. Anywhere people gather, a *sev* vendor is sure to appear with an assortment of freshly made fried noodles. Some noodles are spicy and spaghetti-thick, while others are very fine and unseasoned.

Sev noodles are shaped with a *seviya* machine, a unique brass utensil equipped with an assortment of interchangeable disks. A fine-holed disk is attached to the container and filled with dough, which is then pressed into hot oil where it fries into crisp crunchy noodles. This utensil has two *sev* disks—thick and thin—with additional disks for several other fried snacks. It is available at most Indian grocery stores. You can use a potato ricer as a substitute.

Preparation and frying time: 25 minutes
Serves: 10–12

2¼ cups (230 g) sifted chickpea flour
    (sifted before measuring)
½ tablespoon (7 ml) salt
½ teaspoon (2 ml) cayenne pepper
½ teaspoon (2 ml) turmeric
1 tablespoon (15 ml) vegetable oil
½ tablespoon (7 ml) lemon juice
¾ cup (180 ml) water
ghee or vegetable oil for deep-frying

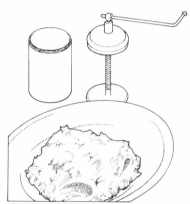

    1. Blend the chickpea flour, salt, cayenne and turmeric in a mixing bowl. Add the oil and lemon juice to the water and pour into the flour. Mix into a thick paste, adding additional flour as necessary so that the mixture is not sticky. It should resemble the texture of mashed potatoes. Divide into three portions, then fill the *seviya* machine with one portion, or place that amount in a potato ricer.

    2. Heat *ghee* or oil to a depth of 2½ inches (6.5 cm) in a *karai* or deep-frying pan over moderate heat until it reaches 345°F (175°C). Holding the utensil over the hot oil, force the mixture through the holes by turning the handle. As the noodles fall, slowly move the machine around in a circular motion so that they do not clump together. Fry for 1½ minutes per side or until crisp and lightly browned. Remove with a slotted spoon and drain on paper towels. Fry the remaining paste in the same way. Cool to room temperature, then break into uniform pieces. They can be kept in airtight containers for 2 weeks. To reheat, place in a 250°F (120°C) oven for 8 minutes.

Golden Pastry Chips
NIMKIN

In Bengal, this snack is sold everywhere, from shops and roadside hand-pushed carts to vendors carrying baskets on their heads and wandering from place to place. They are seasoned with one of three spice seeds: caraway, fennel or *kalonji*. For a typical late afternoon Bengali tiffin, serve *nimkin* with *Cheese Balls Stuffed with Nut Milk Fudge* and *Minty Lemon–Lime Refresher*.

Preparation and cooking time (after assembling ingredients): 30 minutes
Serves: 8 to 10

1½ cups (175 g) unbleached white flour
½ teaspoon (2 ml) salt
⅛ teaspoon (0.5 ml) baking soda
1 teaspoon (5 ml) either caraway seeds, fennel seeds or *kalonji*
2½ tablespoons (37 ml) melted unsalted butter or *ghee*
4½–5½ tablespoons (67–82 ml) water
ghee or vegetable oil for deep-frying

1. Combine the flour, salt, baking soda and caraway seeds in a large bowl and mix well. Add the melted butter or *ghee* and rub between your palms to evenly distribute. Pour 4½ tablespoons (67 ml) of water over the flour and quickly mix into a rough, shaggy dough. If necessary, add the remaining water, a few drops at a time, until the mass can be kneaded into a stiff dough. Knead on a clean work surface for about 8 minutes or until the dough is firm but pliable. Cover with a damp towel or plastic wrap and allow it to rest for at least ½ hour.

Alternately, fit a food processor with the metal blade, add the flour, salt, baking soda and caraway seeds and pulse twice. Add the melted butter and pulse 8–10 times to mix. With the motor running, pour 4½ tablespoons (67 ml) of water through the feed tube and process until the mixture masses together. You may need to add up to 1 tablespoon (15 ml) more water to make a stiff dough. (The mixture should not form a ball in the bowl, but should easily form into a ball with your hands.) Gather the ingredients into a ball, cover with a damp towel or plastic wrap, and set aside for at least ½ hour.

2. Roll the dough into a log 14 inches (35 cm) long, cut into 12 pieces, and flatten each piece into a patty. Drape a damp towel over the patties.

3. Pour *ghee* or oil into a *karai* or deep-frying pan to a depth of 2½ (6.5 cm) inches and place over moderate heat. Roll a patty into a 5½-inch (14 cm) round on a lightly floured board. Cut with a sharp knife into strips ½ inch (1.5 cm) wide and again cut across into ½ inch (1.5 cm) strips, to yield squares. Brush off the excess flour with a pastry brush. When the temperature of the *ghee* or oil reaches 335°F (170°C), fry the squares, stirring constantly, until they turn almond brown and are crisp on all sides. Remove with a slotted spoon and drain on paper towels. Shape and fry the remaining patties in this way.

3. Cool to room temperature, then store in a container with a tight-fitting lid for up to 2 weeks.

Flaky Biscuits with Black Pepper
MATHRI

This savory fried munchy—a cross between salty shortbread and a pastry—is popular in Uttar Pradesh and the Punjab. It is made with a combination of semolina and unbleached white flour

For information about unfamiliar ingredients or techniques, see A-to-Z

and flavored with either crushed black pepper or *ajwain* seeds. If you can't find semolina flour, use 2¼ cups (265 g) unbleached flour. The biscuits are fried over moderately low heat until pale gold, tender and flaky.

Preparation and resting time: 45 minutes
Cooking time: ½ hour
Makes: 36 *mathris*

2 cups (235 g) unbleached white flour
¼ cup (45 g) fine semolina flour
2 teaspoons (10 ml) salt
½ tablespoon (7 ml) whole black or
**   green peppercorns, coarsely cracked**
⅛ teaspoon (0.5 ml) baking soda
4 tablespoons (60 ml) melted *ghee* or oil
2 tablespoons (30 ml) plain yogurt
6–7 tablespoons (90–105 ml) warm water
***ghee* or vegetable oil for frying**

1. Place the flours, salt, cracked pepper and baking soda in a large bowl and mix well. Add the *ghee* or oil and rub between your palms until the texture resembles coarse bread crumbs. Combine the yogurt with the water and pour slowly into the flour until the ingredients can be gathered into a shaggy mass. Knead on a clean work surface into a pliable but firm dough, about 8 minutes. Cover with a damp cloth or plastic wrap and set aside for ½ hour.

Alternately, place the flours, salt and baking soda in a food processor fitted with the metal blade. Pulse 6 times. Add the *ghee* or oil and process for 30 seconds. Combine the yogurt, crushed pepper and water, and, with the machine running, slowly pour the liquid through the feed tube. It will not form into a ball, but can be gathered into a ball on the countertop. Shape into a ball, drape with a damp towel or plastic wrap, and set aside for ½ hour.

2. Divide the dough into three portions, cover two of them, and roll out the remaining one into a circle or rectangle ⅛ inch (3 mm) thick. Cut into 2-inch (5 cm) rounds with a cookie cutter or into any other desired shape. Roll out all of the dough, including the scraps, until it is used up. Place the rounds on a large tray and prick each one in three or four places with a fork or knife.

3. Pour *ghee* or oil to a depth of 1 inch (2.5 cm) in a large frying pan and heat over moderate heat until the temperature reaches 310–320°F (154–160°C) on a deep-frying thermometer. Add about 12 rounds to the pan and fry slowly for about 4 minutes per side, maintaining an even 300–310°F (150–155°C) temperature. Do not allow the rounds to become brown; they should remain pale gold in color. Remove with a slotted spoon and drain on paper towels. Repeat the process for frying all of the biscuits. Well sealed, they will keep for 2–3 weeks.

Note: After frying is completed, allow the oil to cool for 15 minutes and, while still warm, strain through a fine sieve to remove any bits of flour or seasonings.

Savory Butter Crackers with Lemon

NUN GAJA

In Bengal, there are two types of *gaja*: salty and sweet. Within these two types, several shapes and flavors are possible: poppy seed cubes, sesame seed oblongs, *kalonji* curls and this variation: lemon zest diamonds. These crackers are somewhat crumbly, with a faintly sour taste. They are a much-loved delicacy throughout Orissa and Bengal, popular at late afternoon tiffin with contrasting sweet *gaja* and tropical fresh fruits.

Preparation and resting time (after assembling ingredients): 45 minutes
Cooking time: 50 minutes
Makes: about 60 *gajas*

2 cups (235 g) unbleached white flour
1¼ teaspoons (6 ml) salt
⅛ teaspoon (0.5 ml) baking soda
½ teaspoon (2 ml) finely grated lemon zest
4½ tablespoons (67 ml) unsalted butter, chilled and cut into small pieces
2 tablespoons (30 ml) cold yogurt, stirred until smooth
1 tablespoon (15 ml) ice water
¼ cup (60 ml) strained fresh lemon juice
ghee or vegetable oil for deep-frying

1. Place the flour, salt, baking soda and lemon zest in a large bowl and mix well. Add the butter and rub between your palms until the texture resembles coarse bread crumbs. Blend the yogurt, ice water and lemon juice and pour slowly into the flour until the dough can be gathered into a shaggy mass. Knead for only 2–3 minutes.

Alternately, fit a food processor with the metal blade. Place the flour, salt, and baking soda in the processor bowl and pulse 6 times. Add the lemon zest and butter and process for one minute or until the mixture resembles fine breadcrumbs. Blend the yogurt with the water, and while the machine is running, slowly pour in the liquid and process until the consistency is the size of peas. Do not allow a ball of dough to form. Gather the dough into a ball by hand and cover it with a damp towel or plastic wrap. Set aside for at least ½ hour.

2. Divide the dough into 5 balls. Cover 4 balls with a damp towel and roll the remaining one out on a lightly floured work surface into a 7-inch (17.5 cm) round. With a sharp knife, cut into diamond shapes—cutting across from east to west into 1-inch (2.5 cm) strips, then on the diagonal, from northeast to southwest, in 2-inch (5 cm) strips. This will form diamonds about 1 inch (2.5 cm) wide and 2 inches (5 cm) long. Prick the diamonds with a fork at 1-inch (2.5 cm) intervals and remove any small scraps of dough. Roll the scraps into a final ball of dough.

3. Pour *ghee* or oil to a depth of 2 inches (5 cm) into a *karai* or deep-frying pan and place it over moderate heat. When the temperature reaches 320°F (160°C), slip in all of the crackers. Fry, maintaining the heat at between 310–320°F (155–160°C), for about 5 minutes on each side or until they are pale gold (not brown) and crispy. Remove with a slotted spoon and drain on paper towels. Roll out, cut and fry the remaining dough in the same way. Can be kept, well sealed, for 2–3 weeks.

For information about unfamiliar ingredients or techniques, see A-to-Z

Munchy Chickpea Flour Spirals with Sesame Seeds
CHAKLI

This snack could easily become as popular as pretzels. It is a crunchy spiral, made from roasted chickpea flour and rice flour, shaped by forcing soft dough through a star-shaped nozzle or disk. A *seviya* machine is used to shape this and several other fried snacks in this chapter. It is available at Indian grocery stores. Because any star shape will do, you can also use a pastry bag fitted with a 5-star nozzle or a continuous-flow cookie gun, like the *sawa*, available through the William Sonoma mail order catalogue.

This savory, with a beverage, is good for drop-in company or for a Gujarati-style late afternoon refreshment. Try it with *Creamy Almond Pudding*, cut papaya with lime wedges and *Barley Tonic*.

Preparation time (after assembling ingredients): 20 minutes
Frying time: 15 minutes
Makes: about 24 *chaklis*

1½ cups (145 g) sifted chickpea flour
    (sifted before measuring)
½ cup (80 g) coarse rice flour or ground rice
1¼ teaspoons (6 ml) salt
1¼ teaspoons (6 ml) cayenne pepper
¼ teaspoon (1 ml) yellow asafetida powder (*hing*)*
⅛ teaspoon (0.5 ml) baking soda
¼ cup (40 g) sesame seeds
3 tablespoons (45 ml) grated fresh coconut
    or dry coconut, unsweetened
1 tablespoon (15 ml) vegetable oil
¾ cup (180 ml) water
ghee or vegetable oil for deep-frying

*This amount applies only to yellow Cobra brand. Reduce any other asafetida by three-fourths.

1. Place the chickpea flour in a heavy pan over moderate heat and dry-roast, stirring constantly, for 3–4 minutes or until the color darkens one or two shades.

2. Transfer to a large bowl, add the rice flour, salt, cayenne, asafetida, baking soda, sesame seeds and coconut, and stir to mix. Pour in the oil and then rub between your palms until the mixture resembles coarse bread crumbs. Add the water and work into a soft dough (similar in texture to cold mashed potatoes) that can easily be forced through a star nozzle. If necessary, add sprinkles of flour or water. Divide the dough into 2 or 3 portions.

3. Brush oil on the inside of one of the suggested utensils and add a portion of dough. Line a baking tray with aluminum foil and brush the foil with vegetable oil. Force the dough out of the utensil. Starting at the center and using steady pressure, force the dough out of the utensil in a continuous outward spiral until the diameter is 2 inches (5 cm). Shape all of the *chaklis* in this way.

4. Heat 2½ inches (6.5 cm) of *ghee* or oil in a *karai* or deep-frying pan over moderate heat until the temperature reaches 335°F (170°C). Using a spatula, transfer 8–10 *chakli* spirals to the hot oil, or as many as will float on the surface without crowding. Fry for 3–4 minutes on each side or until crispy and golden brown. Remove with a slotted spatula and drain on paper towels. Fry the remaining pieces in this way. Serve at room temperature. Can be stored in an air-tight container for 2–3 weeks.

Munchable Chickpea Flour Ribbons with *Ajwain* Seeds
GIANTHA

Just as the West has shops that sell only candy or ice cream, India has shops devoted to the fried snacks in this chapter. The array of delectable snacks, displayed in glass cases, lures the casual passerby in for a purchase. Some shops are so famous, people wait in line for up to an hour to be served. This savory, also called *papadi gianthiya*, is as popular as potato chips are here, with as many flavor variations. Like the previous snack, it is shaped by forcing soft dough through a star-shaped disk, but instead of being crunchy, the texture is light and crisp.

Preparation and resting time: 45 minutes
Frying time: 20 minutes
Serves: 8

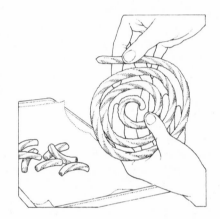

2⅓ cups (235 g) sifted chickpea flour
   (sifted before measuring)
1¼ teaspoons (6 ml) salt
½ tablespoon (7 ml) *ajwain* seeds,
   coarsely crushed
¾ teaspoon (3.5 ml) baking soda
¼ teaspoon (1 ml) freshly ground black pepper
3 tablespoons (45 ml) melted *ghee* or vegetable oil
½ cup (120 ml) plain yogurt and up to
   ½ cup water (120 ml), or as needed
ghee or vegetable oil for deep-frying

1. Combine the flour, salt, *ajwain* seeds, baking soda and black pepper in a large bowl. Add the *ghee* or oil and rub between your palms until the consistency resembles coarse bread crumbs. Whisk the yogurt with three-fourths of the water until smooth, then add to the dry mixture and work into a soft but not sticky dough, similar in texture to mashed potatoes. (If necessary, add more flour or water.) Divide into 2 or 3 portions, cover, and set aside for ½ hour.

2. Brush a film of oil on the inside of a *seviya* machine or a continuous-flow cookie press like the *sawa*. Attach the star-shaped nozzle, add a portion of dough to the container, and cover. Heat *ghee* or oil to a depth of 2½ inches (6.5 cm) in a *karai* or deep-frying pan over moderate heat until the temperature reaches 350°F (180°C). Hold the machine 2–3 inches (5–7.5 cm) above the surface of the oil and force out the dough. Simultaneously, move your hand in a circle as large as the outside of the pan and spiral inwards until you reach the center. Fry the large spiral for about 2 minutes on each side or until it is golden brown. Remove it with a slotted spoon and drain on paper towels. Fry all of the dough in this way.

3. When the spirals are cool, break into 3-inch (7.5 cm) pieces. Serve at room temperature. Can be kept in well-sealed containers for 2–3 weeks.

For information about unfamiliar ingredients or techniques, see A-to-Z

Dal Munchies
MOONG DALMOT

Just as fried peanuts, cashews and almonds are Westerners' favorite choices, Indians love fried mung *dal*, *chana dal* and chickpeas, and, as with nuts, these are eaten anytime and anywhere. If one has an edge over the others in popularity, it is probably mung *dal*. Though it needs nothing more than a sprinkle of plain salt, it is also pleasant with seasoned, smoked or herb salt. If you do not eat salt, try it with a sprinkle of a salt-free herb blend and lemon juice.

Preparation and soaking time: 8 hours or overnight
Frying time: 20 minutes
Makes: 1⅔ cups (400 ml)

1 cup (215 g) split *moong dal*, without skins
1 teaspoon (5 ml) baking soda
½ teaspoon (2 ml) salt
vegetable oil for deep-frying

1. Sort through the *dal* and remove any foreign matter. Wash in several changes of water until it is clear. Drain, then soak in 4 cups (1 liter) of water and the baking soda for 8 hours or overnight. Rinse well, drain in a strainer for several minutes, then pat completely dry with paper towels. Air-dry for 15–30 minutes.
2. Heat oil to a depth of 2½ inches (6.5 cm) in a *karai* or deep-frying pan over moderate heat. Line a baking tray with several thicknesses of paper towels. When the temperature reaches 365°F (185°C), place ½ cup (110 g) of *dal* in a wire mesh strainer and lower it into the pan. The oil will immediately froth and bubble; as it subsides, the *dal* will float to the surface. Fry for about 2 minutes or until the *dal* is crispy and pale gold. Do not allow it to brown. Remove the strainer and pour the *dal* onto the paper towels. Fry the remaining batches. Blot with clean paper towels to remove excess oil on the fried *dal*. While still hot, toss in the salt. Cool to room temperature. Can be kept in a well sealed container for up to 4 weeks.

Chickpea Chips
KABLI CHANA DALMOT

In this fried *dal* selection, chickpeas are half-cooked and flattened before they are deep-fried into crispy chips.

***Dal* soaking time: 10 hours or overnight**
Preparation and cooking time: 2 hours
Makes: about 2 cups (480 ml)

1¼ cups (235 g) whole chickpeas
4 cups (1 liter) water
1 teaspoon (5 ml) baking soda
vegetable oil for deep-frying
½ teaspoon (2 ml) fine salt
¼ teaspoon (1 ml) cayenne pepper
½ teaspoon (2 ml) *chat masala* or *amchoor* powder

1. Wash the chickpeas in running water, drain, then soak in 4 cups (l liter) of water with the baking soda for 10 hours or overnight.

2. Wash and drain the chickpeas. Gently boil them in 4 cups (1 liter) of fresh water for 1¼ hours. Drain well in a strainer, then spread out on a oiled aluminum-foil-covered baking tray. Using the bottom of a smooth bowl or custard cup, half-smash and flatten the chickpeas. Allow them to air-dry for at least ½ hour.

3. Heat 2½ inches (6.5 cm) of oil in a *karai* or deep-frying pan over moderate heat. Line a baking tray with several thicknesses of paper towels. When the temperature reaches 365°F (185°C), place ½ cup (100 g) of the chickpeas in a wire mesh strainer and lower it into the pan. The oil will immediately froth and bubble, but as it subsides the chickpeas will float to the surface. Fry for about 2 minutes or until crispy and pale gold. Do not allow it to brown. Remove the strainer and pour the fried chickpeas onto the paper towels. Blot with clean paper towels to remove the excess oil. Fry the remaining batches in the same way. While still hot, sprinkle with salt, cayenne and *chat masala* or *amchoor*, and gently toss. Cool to room temperature. Can be kept in a well-sealed container for 2–3 weeks.

Nut Medley

BHONA BADAAM KAJU

Hot peanuts, cashews, pistachios, Brazil nuts, almonds and hazelnuts are mouth watering when properly fried. They require a controlled heat source and must be well drained before salting. If you are going to serve an assortment of fried nuts, contrast sizes and colors.

Preparation and cooking time: 25 minutes
Makes: 2 cups (480 ml)

sunflower or vegetable oil for frying
2 cups (275 g) of 3 or 4 of the following:
    whole peanuts, with skins;
    half peanuts, without skins;
    whole cashews;
    cashew halves;
    whole almonds, with skins;
    whole almonds, blanched;
    whole pistachios, with skins;
    whole Brazil nuts, with skins;
    whole hazelnuts, without skins
¼–½ teaspoon (1–2 ml) salt

Heat the oil to a depth of 1 inch (2.5 cm) in a heavy large frying pan or sauté pan over moderately low heat. When the temperature reaches 310°F (155°C), add the nuts. Fry at 300–310°F (150–155°F), stirring often, for 10–12 minutes or until golden brown. Remove with a slotted spoon and drain in a strainer resting over a cake pan, then transfer to several thicknesses of paper towels. Blot off the excess oil with more paper towels. While still warm, toss in the salt and mix.

Spicy Nuts
MASALA BADAAM KAJU

These are best served warm and are a popular snack with drop-in guests. Serve with hot or cold beverages.

Preparation time (after assembling ingredients): a few minutes
Makes: 2 cups (480 ml)

2 cups (275 g) freshly fried *Nut Medley* (page 574)
½ teaspoon (2 ml) salt
1 teaspoon (5 ml) *garam masala*
¼ teaspoon (1 ml) cayenne pepper
½ teaspoon (2 ml) *amchoor* powder
1 tablespoon (15 ml) confectioners' sugar (optional)

Toss the nuts with the salt, spices and sugar, if desired. Keep warm in a 200°F (95°C) oven until serving. Can be kept for 2–3 weeks. To rewarm, place in a 250°F (120°C) oven for 7–8 minutes.

Nut and Raisin Nibbler
KAJU KISHMISH CHIDWA

You can vary the formula—cashews and currants, peanuts and golden raisins, almonds and raisins—in this nutritious snack. Srila Prabhupada recommended this combination on *Ekadasee* fasting days.

Preparation time (after assembling ingredients): a few minutes
Serves: 10

1 teaspoon (5 ml) fine salt
½ tablespoon (7 ml) ground coriander
2 teaspoons (10 ml) ground cumin
¼ teaspoon (1 ml) each freshly ground pepper or grated
    nutmeg, ground cardamom, ground cinnamon and cayenne pepper
⅛ teaspoon (0.5 ml) ground cloves
2 tablespoons (30 ml) finely crushed rock candy or date sugar
2 cups (275 g) freshly fried *Nut Medley* (page 574)
½ cup (65 g) currants or raisins

Combine the salt, spices and sweetener in a small dish and blend well. Sprinkle half of the seasoning on the hot nuts and half on the currants or raisins and toss separately. Mix together before serving.

Deep-Fried Batter-Coated Mixed Nuts
BHONA BADAAM

Use large plump nuts—cashews, almonds and Brazils—for ease in handling. The chickpea flour–rice flour batter puts a crisp crust on the nuts.

Preparation and cooking time: about 40 minutes
Makes: 1½ cups (360 ml)

3 tablespoons (45 ml) sifted chickpea flour
    (sifted before measuring)
1 tablespoon (15 ml) rice flour
¼ teaspoon (1 ml) turmeric
½ teaspoon (2 ml) ground cumin
¼ teaspoon (1 ml) cayenne pepper
⅛ teaspoon (0.5 ml) yellow asafetida powder (*hing*)*
⅛ teaspoon (0.5 ml) baking powder
¾ teaspoon (3.5 ml) salt
3 tablespoons (45 ml) water
1½ cups (210 g) mixed raw cashews, almonds and Brazil nuts
vegetable oil for deep-frying

*This amount applies only to yellow Cobra brand. Reduce any other asafetida by three-fourths.

1. Combine the flours, spices, baking powder and salt in a bowl and blend well. Add the water and whisk with a fork until smooth. Stir in the nuts.
2. Heat 2½ inches (6.5 cm) of oil in a *karai* or deep-frying pan over moderate heat. When the temperature reaches 340°F (170°C), one by one slip about 15 of the batter-coated nuts into the oil. Fry, stirring gently once the batter firms up, until they are crisp and golden brown. Remove and drain on paper towels. Fry the remaining nuts in the same way. Serve warm.

For information about unfamiliar ingredients or techniques, see A-to-Z

Spicy Matchstick Potatoes
MASALA ALOO LATCHE

Potatoes are a good vegetable for deep-frying and can be cut a number of ways for dramatic effects: shavings, spirals, waffles, chips and fine sticks. For this recipe you need a fine matchstick cut, with a maximum width of ⅛ inch (3 mm). You can produce fine strips by hand cutting them into slices ⅛ inch (3 mm) thick and then cutting them again lengthwise into strips about ⅛ inch (3 mm) wide. Save considerable time by using the fine julienne slicing blade of a mandoline or food processor. My late friend and mentor Pishima, a great Bengali Vaishnava cook, often combined carrots and potatoes in this spicy nibbler.

Preparation and soaking time (after assembling ingredients): up to 1½ hours
Frying time: 10–15 minutes
Serves: 6

2 large baking potatoes (about 1 pound/455 g)
ghee or nut or vegetable oil for deep-frying
½–1 teaspoon (2–5 ml) fine salt
¼ teaspoon (1 ml) cayenne pepper
1 teaspoon (5 ml) ground coriander
½ teaspoon (2 ml) ground cumin
½ teaspoon (2 ml) *amchoor* powder or *chat masala*

1. Peel the potatoes and cut into fine matchsticks. Soak in cold water for at least 1 hour, changing the water twice. Drain and pat dry with paper towels.
2. Pour *ghee* or oil to a depth of 2½–3 inches (6.5–7.5 cm) into a *karai* or deep-frying pan and place over moderate heat. (Do not fill the pan more than half-full.) When the temperature reaches 375°F (190°C), add a handful of potatoes and stir to prevent them from sticking together. Fry until golden brown, then remove with a slotted spoon and drain on paper towels. Fry the remaining batches in the same way. Place the salt and spices in a bowl, mix together, and sprinkle on the hot potatoes. These nibblers can be kept in airtight containers for up to a week.

Yam *Chidwa*
SHAKARKAND LATCHE

Naturally sweet yams or sweet potatoes are brought to life in this recipe with freshly ground sweet spices, seeds and dried fruits.

Preparation and soaking time (after assembling ingredients): 1½ hours
Cooking time: 40 minutes
Serves: 10 to 12

2 medium-sized yams or sweet potatoes (12 ounces/340 g), peeled
ghee or nut oil for deep-frying
⅓ cup (45 g) cashew halves
⅓ cup (50 g) pine nuts
¼ cup (45 g) sunflower seeds
2–3 hot green chilies, seeded and cut lengthwise into thin strips
¼ cup (35 g) chopped dates
¼ cup (40 g) golden raisins
½ tablespoons (7 ml) *amchoor* powder
½ tablespoons (7 ml) *garam masala*
1 tablespoon (15 ml) date sugar or maple sugar
1¼ teaspoons (6 ml) salt

1. Shred the yams or sweet potatoes through the large holes of a four-sided hand grater, holding them at a 45° angle to shape long, thin straws. Rinse, and soak in cold water for 45 minutes, changing the water twice. Drain well, then pat thoroughly dry with paper towels.

2. Heat *ghee* or oil to a depth of 2½ inches (6.5 cm) in a *karai* or deep-frying pan over moderate heat until the temperature reaches 375°F (190°C). (Do not fill the pan over half-full.) Drop a handful of potato straws into the oil and fry for about 1½ minutes or until they are golden brown and crispy. Remove with a slotted spoon and drain on paper towels. Fry the remaining potatoes in the same way.

3. Reduce the heat slightly and allow the temperature to fall to 330°F (165°C). Place the cashews in a wire strainer, lower it into the oil, and fry until they are golden brown. Remove and transfer the nuts onto paper towels to drain. In separate batches, fry the pine nuts, sunflower seeds and chilies, and drain.

4. Combine the potatoes, nuts, seeds, chilies, dates and raisins in a mixing bowl. Sprinkle with the spices, date or maple sugar and salt, and gently toss. Cool to room temperature before storing in airtight containers. Keeps well for up to 2 weeks.

Potato Straw, Cashew, Raisin and Coconut Snack
GUJARATI ALOO CHIDWA

The following *chidwa* (pronounced *chur-ah*) recipes hail from Gujarat. Potatoes, nuts and dried fruits are the foundations for a multitude of versatile snacks. Few cuisines have explored the possibilities of these ingredients more than those of central and western India. Although diverse in texture and flavor, *chidwa* always has a balance of contrasts. This is an *Ekadasee* or grainless snack, typical of those served throughout Gujarat.

Preparation and soaking time (after assembling ingredients): at least 1½ hours
Cooking time: about ½ hour
Serves: 10

For information about unfamiliar ingredients or techniques, see A-to-Z

2 large baking potatoes (about 1 pound/455 g)
ghee or nut or vegetable oil for deep-frying
2–3 hot green chilies, sliced crosswise into thin rounds
½ cup (75 g) cashew pieces or halves
½ cup (45 g) dried ribbon coconut
10–15 curry leaves, preferably fresh
1 tablespoon (15 ml) fennel seeds
½ cup (70 g) raisins
1 teaspoon (5 ml) ground cumin
1 teaspoon (5 ml) *garam masala*
½ teaspoon (2 ml) turmeric
¼ teaspoon (1 ml) cayenne pepper
1¼ teaspoons (6 ml) salt
1½ tablespoons (22 ml) crushed rock
    candy (*misri*) or date sugar

1. Peel the potatoes and then shred them using one of the methods described on page 578. Soak them in cold water for at least an hour, changing the water twice. Drain and pat dry with paper towels.

2. Pour *ghee* or oil to a depth of 2½–3 inches (6.5–7.5 cm) into a *karai* or deep-frying pan and place over moderate heat. (Do not fill the pan more than half-full.) When the temperature reaches 375°F (190°C), add a handful of the shoestring potatoes and stir to prevent them from sticking together. Fry until golden brown, then remove with a slotted spoon and drain on paper towels.

3. Reduce the temperature of the frying oil to 345–350°F (173–180°C). Place the sliced chilies in a wire mesh strainer and lower it into the pan. Fry until the chilies become crispy and golden brown. Remove the strainer, shake off the excess oil, and drain on paper towels. In separate batches, fry the nuts, coconut, curry leaves and fennel seeds. When each is crisp and golden brown, transfer to paper towels to drain.

4. Soak the raisins in hot water for 5 minutes, then drain and pat dry with paper towels. Combine the spices, salt and rock candy or date sugar in a small dish. Sprinkle 1 teaspoon (5 ml) of this mixture on the raisins and toss to coat. While still warm, combine the ingredients in a large bowl, sprinkle with the remaining spice mixture, and toss to mix.

Crisp Pounded Rice with Potato Straws, Peanuts and Raisins
GUJARATI ALOO POHA CHIDWA

This *chidwa* variation includes pounded, or flat, rice, called *poha*, in India. There are two types of *poha* available at Indian grocery stores: thick *poha* and thin *poha*. The thick is preferable for deep-frying as it holds up well without crumbling and tends to puff. If you want to try this recipe and do not have flat rice, Rice Crispies cereal may be substituted. To save time during preparation, collect all of the ingredients and equipment you will need before frying. Serve anytime, anywhere. This *chidwa* can be kept, well sealed, for up to two months.

Preparation and soaking time: 1¼ hours
Frying time: 30 minutes
Serves: 10

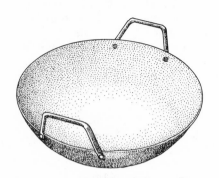

½ teaspoon (2 ml) turmeric
⅓ teaspoon (1.5 ml) cayenne pepper
1¼ teaspoons (6 ml) salt
1 tablespoon (15 ml) powdered rock candy or maple sugar
⅔ cup (95 g) peanuts
½ cup (70 g) raisins or sultanas
1¼ cups (75 g) thick flat rice (*poha*)
1 tablespoon (15 ml) fennel seeds
½ tablespoon (7 ml) cumin seeds
1 large baking potato (8 ounces/230 g), peeled, coarsely
    shredded, soaked 1 hour in ice water, drained and patted dry
2 hot green chilies, halved, seeded and cut into long thin strips
nut or vegetable oil for deep-frying

1. Combine the turmeric, cayenne, salt and sweetener in a bowl and mix. Arrange mounds of peanuts, raisins or sultanas, flat rice, fennel seeds, cumin seeds, shredded potatoes and chilies near the frying area. Line two large baking trays with several thicknesses of paper towels and keep nearby.

2. Heat oil to a depth of 2½ inches (6.5 cm) in a *karai*, wok or deep-frying pan over moderately high heat until the temperature reaches 375°F (190°C). (Do not fill the pan over half-full.) Drop in a handful of shredded potatoes, stir with a knife, and fry until crisp and golden brown. Remove with a slotted spoon and drain on paper towels. Fry the remaining potatoes in the same way.

3. Reduce the heat slightly and allow the temperature to drop to 360°F (180°C). Place a handful of flat rice in a wire-mesh strainer and lower it into the hot oil. The oil will immediately froth and then, within a minute, settle; the flat rice is finished when crisp but not brown. Remove the strainer, shake off the excess oil and place on paper towels to drain. Fry the remaining flat rice in this way.

4. One after another, fry each of the ingredients in batches, placing them in the strainer, then in the oil, and frying until crisp and golden brown. (The raisins should be fried only until they plump.) Drain on paper towels. Combine all of the ingredients in a large bowl. While warm, sprinkle with the seasoning mixture. Cool to room temperature before storing in airtight containers.

Chickpea Flour Pearls with Nuts and Currants
BOONDI CHIDWA

Crisp, golden yellow chickpea flour pearls contrast with soft black currants in this *chidwa* from Maharastra. Though almonds and cashews are traditional nut selections, I have substituted split macadamia nuts and pistachios with excellent results.

For information about unfamiliar ingredients or techniques, see A-to-Z

Preparation and cooking time: 45 minutes
Makes: about 3 cups (710 ml)

1 cup (100 g) sifted chickpea flour
    (sifted before measuring)
¼ teaspoon (1 ml) turmeric
½ teaspoon (2 ml) salt
⅛ teaspoon (0.5 ml) baking soda
cold water, as needed
ghee or vegetable oil for deep-frying
½ cup (75 g) cashew pieces or raw pistachios
⅓ cup (40 g) sliced almonds or macadamia halves
½ cup (65 g) currants
½ tablespoon (7 ml) *amchoor* powder
½ tablespoon (7 ml) *garam masala*
½ teaspoon (2 ml) cayenne pepper
½ teaspoon (2 ml) salt

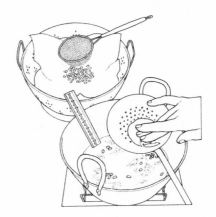

1. Combine the chickpea flour, turmeric, salt and baking soda in a bowl and blend well. Slowly pour in ½ cup (120 ml) cold water, beating with a whisk until the batter is smooth. (The batter should be slightly thick and cake like; add more water or flour as necessary.) Line a large baking tray with several thicknesses of paper towels and place it near the frying area.

2. Heat *ghee* or oil to a depth of 2½ inches (6.5 cm) in a *karai* or deep-frying pan over moderate heat until the temperature reaches 345°F (175°C). Hold a frying spatula with ⅛-inch (3 mm) holes over the pan, place 2 or 3 tablespoons (30–45 ml) of batter on it, and rub it through the holes with the help of a rubber spatula. Cover the surface of the frothing *ghee* with chickpea flour pearls. (If the batter is too thin, it will fall through the holes into irregular-shaped globs or squiggles; add additional flour as necessary. If it is too thick, add water.) The *ghee* will subside within a minute. Fry for an additional minute or until the pearls are crisp and golden-yellow in color. Remove with a wire strainer and drain on paper towels. Fry the *boondi* in this way until the batter is finished.

3. Reduce the heat slightly and allow the frying temperature to fall to 330°F (165°C). Fry the nuts until they are golden brown. Remove with a slotted spoon and drain on paper towels.

4. Combine the warm *boondi*, nuts and currants in a bowl. Sprinkle in the spices and salt, and toss to mix. Cool before storing in airtight containers. Will keep for up to a month.

Special Blend Nibbler
BOMBAY CHIDWA

The diversity of *chidwa* seems boundless; one shop in Bombay's Crawford Market boasts of over 100 varieties. A cook need never make two batches exactly the same. Each one should be assembled in a play of contrasts: colors, textures and flavors. This recipe, one of Srila Prabhupada's favorites, is based on nuts and dried fruits, and extended with fried seeds, noodles, *dals* and herbs. Though this elaborate mixture is time-consuming, it is not difficult to make. It is a very light and satisfying fried snack, just the thing for special times, friends or places. Feel free to substitute other nuts or seeds for those suggested, but keep in mind that they are best halved and must, of course, be raw.

Preparation and cooking time: about 1 hour
Makes: about 2 quarts/liters

vegetable oil for deep-frying
⅓ cup (50 g) peanut halves
⅓ cup (45 g) cashew halves
¼ cup (30 g) whole almonds
¼ cup (35 g) blanched pistachios
¼ cup (45 g) pumpkin seeds
¼ cup (35 g) pine nuts
2–3 hot green chilies, sliced crosswise into thin rounds
1 tablespoon (15 ml) fennel seeds
15 curry leaves, preferably fresh
3 tablespoons (45 ml) fresh coriander leaves
⅔ cup (45 g) thick pounded flat rice (*poha*)
¼ cup (40 g) golden raisins
¼ cup (35 g) currants
¼ cup (35 g) chopped dates
scant ½ teaspoon (2 ml) salt
2 tablespoons (30 ml) maple or date sugar
⅓ cup (65 g) deep-fried *moong dal*
1 cup (190 g) deep-fried *sev* noodles

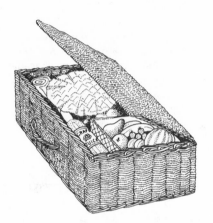

1. Line a few large baking trays with several thicknesses of paper towels. Pour *ghee* or oil to a depth of 2½ inches (6.5 cm) into a *karai* or deep-frying pan and place over moderate heat until the temperature reaches 330°F (165°C). (Do not fill over half-full.) Place the peanuts in a wire-mesh sieve and lower it into the oil. Fry until the peanuts are golden brown, lift out the sieve, and transfer the nuts to paper towels to drain. In separate batches, fry the cashews, almonds, pistachios, pumpkin seeds and pine nuts until golden brown, and drain on paper towels. Pat the nuts dry with more paper towels to blot off any excess oil. Transfer all of the nuts to a bowl. Reline the baking trays with fresh paper towels.

2. Raise the temperature of the oil to 350°F (180°C). Place the green chilies in the sieve, lower it into the oil, and fry until blistered and crispy. Lift out the sieve and transfer the chilies to paper towels to drain. Add the fennel seeds, curry leaves and fresh coriander to the sieve and fry in the same way until the leaves are dark green and crisp and the seeds darken a few shades. Drain on paper towels. Add half of the flat rice to the sieve, lower it into the oil, and fry for 1–1½ minutes or until the frothing oil subsides and the *poha* floats. It should not brown, only turn golden yellow. Remove and drain on paper towels. Fry the remaining flat rice. Pat the flat rice dry with fresh paper towels to blot up any excess oil. Add all of the fried flat rice to the nuts and toss to mix.

3. Combine the raisins, currants and dates in one small bowl and the sweetener, salt and spices in another bowl. Sprinkle ½ of the spice mixture into the dried fruit and

the remaining spices into the nuts; toss well. Finally, combine all the ingredients and toss to mix. Cool to room temperature before storing in airtight containers. Keeps well for up to 2 months.

Thin Chickpea Flour Noodles with *Muth Dal*
MUTH DAL CHIDWA

Whole *muth dal*, available at Indian grocery stores, must be soaked before it can be fried. The noodles, called *sev*, are very thin, like fedelini, a fine form of Italian vermicelli. They are shaped in a brass *seviya* machine. An *ajwain*-flavored dough is forced through pin-like holes into hot *ghee*. Once fried, the crispy noodles are broken into 1-inch (2.5 cm) lengths and mixed with fried *dal*.

Preparation and *dal* soaking time (after assembling ingredients): 8 hours or overnight
Cooking time: about 30 minutes
Makes: 1 quart/liter

1 cup (210 g) whole *muth dal*
½ tablespoon (7 ml) baking soda
water, as needed
½ cup (50 g) sifted chickpea flour (sifted before measuring)
½ teaspoon (2 ml) *ajwain* seeds, crushed
⅛ teaspoon (0.5 ml) salt
pinch of baking soda
5 tablespoons (75 ml) cold water
½ teaspoon (2 ml) cayenne pepper
1¼ teaspoons (6 ml) fine salt
½ tablespoon (7 ml) *garam masala*
1 teaspoon (5 ml) sugar
vegetable or nut oil for deep-frying

1. Sort through the *dal* and remove any foreign matter. Wash in several changes of water until it is clear. Drain, then soak in 4 cups (1 liter) of water and the baking soda for 8 hours or overnight. Rinse well, drain in a strainer for several minutes, then pat completely dry with paper towels. Air-dry for 60 minutes.

2. Meanwhile, blend together all of the remaining ingredients, except the frying oil, and mix into a thick paste, adding additional flour, if necessary, so the mixture is not sticky. It should resemble mashed potatoes in texture. Fill the *seviya* machine with a portion of the paste.

3. Heat oil to a depth of 2½ inches (6.5 cm) in a *karai* or deep-frying pan over moderate heat until it reaches 345°F (175°C). Holding the utensil over the hot oil, force the paste through the holes by turning the handle, so the noodles drop into the oil. As they fall, slowly move the machine around in a circular motion so the noodles do not clump together and cover the surface. Fry for about 1½ minutes per side or until crisp and lightly browned. Remove with a slotted spoon and drain on paper towels. Fry the remaining paste in the same way.

4. Raise the temperature of the oil to 365°F (185°C), then place ½ cup (100 g) of the *dal* in a wire mesh strainer and lower it into the pan. The oil will immediately froth and bubble, but as it subsides, the *dal* will float to the surface. Fry for about 2 minutes or until the *dal* is crispy and pale gold. Remove the *dal* with a strainer and pour onto paper towels to drain.

5. Break the noodles into 1-inch (2.5 cm) lengths. Combine the fried noodles and *dal* in a bowl and toss to mix. Cool to room temperature before storing in airtight containers. May be kept for up to 2 months.

Sweets

India is a nation with a penchant for sweets. This is not a new phenomenon but one which dates back to Vedic times. The living art of preparing sumptuous sweets, puddings and desserts has been preserved largely by successive generations of temple cooks and professional sweetmakers, known as *halwais*. Today, as in centuries past, presenting sweets conveys gratitude, affection, respect, joy or reward. Even an unexpected visitor is welcomed with a sweet beverage, fruit or confection.

While this chapter is not exhaustive, it does include more than 60 recipes—traditional specialties and personal favorites—that illustrate the diversity of regional cooking styles. To simplify matters, the chapter is divided into several sections. The first covers easy-to-make confections, candies and *halvas*. The second and third parts focus on Bengali confections and desserts made from fresh *chenna* cheese. Nutritious, low-calorie and uncomplicated to make, these sweets are considered by many to be the finest India has to offer. The fourth section deals with North Indian milk fudges, including ancient dishes rarely made outside of Vaishnava temple or home kitchens. In the fifth section you will learn how to make an elegant range of fried pastries with, or soaked in, flavored syrups. They include national favorites sold in sweet shops throughout India. The chilled milk puddings in the sixth section are light and delicate, often served with a meal to contrast with other dishes that are hot and spicy. The last section is devoted to delectable fruit desserts, from exotic combination fruit platters to fruit dishes that are baked, poached or broiled.

Unearthing the treasures of milk in this chapter will likely be a new or only vaguely familiar experience for many. Milk is a versatile liquid food and the basis for a number of exquisite homemade products such as plain and sweetened yogurt, condensed milk fudge (*khoa*), fresh *chenna* and *panir* cheeses, *ghee* and clotted creams. If you have access to pasteurize fresh milk from a nearby farm or dairy, you are among a fortunate few. Because milk, in the form of *khoa* or *chenna* cheese, is the primary ingredient in confections and fudges, its flavor, butterfat content, processing and handling are of primary importance in these dishes. Most of us will use store-bought homogenized milk; and, while the recipes here have been tested with both raw and homogenized milk, yields are based on store-bought homogenized milk and cream.

The type of sweetener used in a recipe will greatly affect its finished taste and appearance. The word sugar is derived from the Sanskrit word *sarkar*. Since Vedic times, sugar cane has been cultivated in India's western regions, and various date palm trees have flourished along the eastern coast. Both sugar cane and date palm trees were treasured for their sweet sap which was cooked down and concentrated to make fudge-like brown sugars known as *jaggery* and *gur*. India's epic tale *Mahabharata* describes that these solid sweeteners were used in sophisticated and artful toffees, fudges, confections and boiled-sugar candies at the time of Lord Krishna's appearance 5,000 years ago.

For information about unfamiliar ingredients or techniques, see A-to-Z

Of less importance were liquid sweeteners made from grains. In the arid farming regions of Central and Northwest India where sorghum (a tall grass of the millet family), corn and barley have been cultivated since Vedic times, sweet syrups were made to provide an alternative to solid sugars. Today these sweeteners, along with *jaggery* syrup, are not available commercially in India and often never leave the areas where they are produced. However, several grades of maple syrup, barley, wheat, corn, sorghum and rice syrup are sold in most Western health food stores. Sweetening power, flavor and consistency vary in these liquid sugars: dark, strong-flavored syrups can be used with grains; light, mild-flavored ones should be used in milk-based sweets.

Though much of the ancient world is supposed to have used honey as a sweetener, India tapped other sources for cooking. *Ayur Veda*, the science of herbal medicine, warns against letting honey boil, as it purportedly affects the flavor and develops toxicity. Therefore, honey is rarely if ever used in sweetmaking. Exceptions are using it as a binder in uncooked confections or in instances where temperatures are kept below the boiling point.

Many recipes specify a particular unrefined sugar—most often *jaggery* or *gur*—not only because they have origins dating back centuries and are traditional, but because they work well and taste better than the alternatives. Unfortunately, todays *gur* production is limited, making it rare outside of Bengal and Orissa. Though labeled *gur* or *goodh* at Indian grocery stores, the aromatic sweetener you purchase is most likely *jaggery*. If purchased in lump form, coarsely grate or sliver it to facilitate accurate measuring and dissolving. Two equally delicious sugars to use in sweetmaking are maple sugar and date sugar, both sold at health food and specialty stores. Relative newcomers on the market, both of these sugars are expensive but contain a flavor worth showcasing. If circumstance dictates a substitution for these solid sugars, use light brown sugar.

Before the turn of the century, refined sugars were all but nonexistant in kitchens the world over; however, like elsewhere, they have become a part of contemporary Vedic cooking. Granulated white sugar, superfine sugar, large preserving sugar crystals, powdered or confectioners' sugar and rock candy sugar—made from either sugar cane or sugar beets—lend no flavor to a dish, only pure sweetness. White sugar is especially suited to some types of *rasgoolas* and *burfis* where flavorings are subtle and a milk-white color is important. Surprisingly, the vitamin, mineral and iron content of refined and unrefined sugars are similar, though the sweetening power, consistency and flavor vary.

In comparison with the same dish made in India, the quantity of sugar in these recipes is greatly reduced. Indian sweet shops often use inordinate amounts of sugar because it costs a fraction of the cost of other raw ingredients such as nuts, seeds, *chenna* cheese or *khoa*. For example, a Delhi cook might add ¾–1 cup (160–210 g) of sugar to 8 cups (2 liters) of milk for a rice pudding called *chaval kheer*; a similar recipe in this book calls for ⅓ cup (70 g) sugar and is pleasantly sweet. While the ratio of sugar to *khoa* for a milk fudge *burfi* might be 1 to 4 in Bombay, this book suggests a 1 to 5 or 6 ratio. Through a personal quest to create healthful variations of classic dishes, I have sweetened some confections entirely with dried fruit purées, fruit concentrates or date sugar.

A well-stocked sweetmaking kitchen should contain a supply of flavoring agents such as green cardamom pods, whole nutmegs, cloves, good quality saffron, black peppercorns and pure camphor. Liquid essences such as rose, *khus*, *kewra* and sandalwood, though not essential, bring Bengali syrup sweets and confections to life. Fresh coconut, nuts, seeds and dried fruits are important for flavor, nutrition and texture. Most sweets are garnished in some way: either with a dusting of powdered nuts or sugar or royally topped with a small piece of paper-thin gold or silver foil, called *varak*. All of these ingredients are available at Indian grocery stores.

QUICK AND EASY SWEETS

Simply Wonderfuls
KHARA PERA

My spiritual master, Srila Prabhupada, called this mock milk fudge a "simply wonderful sweet." Some varieties include a dash of essence such as vanilla, almond, lemon or lime. This version resembles firm, uncooked fondant in texture and is so easy to assemble that kindergarten children can turn out a successful batch for grown-up treats.

I have made this sweet around the world, using different processed ingredients. Health-food-store non-instant skim milk powder yields the creamiest consistency; whole milk powder has a firm fudge-like consistency; and Milkman brand instant non-fat milk powder is somewhere in-between and slightly granular. If you use a granulated sugar—raw or white—process it in a blender until superfine. Because these ingredients are processed and stored under varied conditions, you may need to use more or less milk powder to achieve the desired texture.

Preparation time (after assembling ingredients): 10 minutes
Makes: 24 *Simply Wonderfuls*

½ cup (120 ml) unsalted butter, at room temperature
⅔ cup (60 g) confectioners' sugar
1¾ cups (220 g) dry milk powder, or as needed
1 teaspoon (5 ml) milk or cream, or as necessary
a few drops of flavoring essence (as suggested above), or
    2 tablespoons (30 ml) grated nuts or dried fruit purée

1. Cream the butter and sugar in a mixing bowl until light and fluffy. Using your hands, work in the milk powder and milk or cream, (adjusting proportions as necessary) to make a medium-soft fondant. Flavor with essence, nuts or fruit purée and continue to work until well blended.

2. Wash and dry your hands, then roll the fondant into smooth balls. (You can also roll the fondant around whole nuts or sandwich a pellet between nut halves.) Place the confections in paper candy cases and keep refrigerated in a well sealed container for up to 4 days. Serve chilled or at room temperature.

For information about unfamiliar ingredients or techniques, see A-to-Z

Coconut and Cream Cheese Simply Wonderfuls
KHARA NARIYAL PERA

This mock milk fudge takes only minutes to assemble. I find homemade yogurt cheese a pleasant alternative to cream cheese because it has fewer calories and adds its own distinctive flavor.

Preparation time (after assembling ingredients): 10 minutes
Makes: 24 *peras*

¼ cup (60 ml) unsalted butter, at room temperature
¼ cup (60 ml) neuchatel or cream cheese at room temperature,
    or fresh yogurt cheese (page 311)
¼ cup (60 ml) frozen apple concentrate, thawed
½ cup (45 g) toasted grated coconut
1⅓ cups (165 g) dry milk powder, or as needed
generous ¼ teaspoon (1 ml) freshly ground nutmeg

Cream the butter, cheese and apple concentrate in a mixing bowl until light and fluffy. Add the coconut and blend well. With your hands, work in powdered milk until it forms a medium-stiff dough. Wash and dry your hands, then roll the fondant into smooth balls and place them in paper candy cases. Sprinkle with ground nutmeg. Keep refrigerated, in a well sealed container, for up to 4 days.

Maple Cream Simply Wonderfuls
KHARA JAGGERY PERA

A friend introduced me to the wonder of maple sugar as a sweetener, and we never tire of exchanging new ways to showcase its delicate flavor. It is the closest counterpart to Bengal's exquisite *nalin gur*, an ingredient rarely found outside of West Bengal. The confection is equally delicious sweetened with date sugar or date purée, all of them available at health food stores or mail order suppliers.

Preparation time (after assembling ingredients): 10 minutes
Makes: 24 *peras*

½ cup (120 ml) unsalted butter, at room temperature
½ cup (75 g) sieved and lightly packed maple or date sugar,
    or ⅓ cup (80 g) seeded and puréed soft dates, or
    ½ cup (85 g) light brown sugar with 4 drops of maple extract
½ teaspoon (2 ml) coarsely crushed cardamom seeds
a pinch of freshly ground white pepper
1⅔ cups (205 g) non-fat skim milk powder, or as needed

Cream the butter and sweetener in a mixing bowl until light and fluffy. Add the cardamom seeds, pepper and milk powder and work into a medium-soft dough. Wash and dry your hands and roll the fondant into 24 round balls. Place the balls in paper candy cases and refrigerate, well sealed. They will keep for up to 4 days.

Quick and Easy Milk Fudge
KHARA BURFI

For centuries, Vedic cooks have been making milk fudge *burfi* from the same ingredients: milk reduced to a pasty-dough, and unrefined sugars—either cane *jaggery* or palm *gur*. *Burfi* has changed very little since its beginnings, but with the twentieth century came powdered milk and shortcut procedures. Rather than boiling milk to reduce it to a paste, modern cooks can stir powdered milk into a flavored syrup and cook it very briefly until thick. The hot mixture is spread out, garnished, and when it sets, cut into decorative shapes. Plain milk fudge is receptive to additions; for this recipe, try adding ⅓ cup (50 g) of chopped toasted hazelnuts, pecans, walnuts, almonds, dried figs, dried apricots or dried mangoes.

This quick milk fudge can be made with several sweeteners, but each will yield a different result. Granulated white sugar allows the flavor from supporting ingredients to shine through and lends no color or flavor of its own. Liquid sweeteners such as rice, barley, malt and maple syrup vary in sweetening power and color, making the finished texture chewy instead of creamy.

Preparation time (after assembling ingredients): 30 minutes
Makes: 24 pieces

½ cup (110 g) white or brown sugar
  plus 1 cup (240 ml) water, or
  ¾ cup (180 ml) liquid sweetener
3 tablespoons (45 ml) *ghee* or unsalted butter
1⅓ cups (165 g) low-fat milk powder,
  or as necessary
⅓ cup (50 g) chopped nuts or dried fruits
dried fruit pieces for garnishing

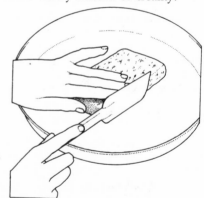

1. Combine the sugar and water, or liquid sweetener, in a heavy-bottomed 3-quart/liter nonstick saucepan and place over moderately low heat. Stir until the sugar dissolves, then raise the heat slightly and gently boil for 8 minutes. Remove the pan from the heat and let the syrup cool for 10 minutes or until the temperature reaches 110°F (45°C).

2. Add 1 tablespoon (15 ml) of *ghee* or butter and, stirring constantly, pour in the milk powder. When the mixture is smooth, place the pan over moderate heat and cook, constantly stirring and scraping the sides and bottom of the pan with a wooden spatula, for up to 4 minutes. When the mixture is reduced to a thick paste that draws away from the sides of the pan, remove the pan from the heat and stir in the remaining 2 tablespoons (30 ml) *ghee* or butter and the ⅓ cup (50 g) chopped nuts or dried fruit.

For information about unfamiliar ingredients or techniques, see A-to-Z

3. Using a rubber spatula, scrape the sticky paste onto a buttered cookie sheet. Spread out, pat and mold the hot mixture into a smooth square cake about ¾ inch (2 cm) thick. Depending on the finished shape of the fudge pieces, press nut halves or dried fruit pieces into the surface at regular intervals. When the fudge is thoroughly cool, cut it into 24 pieces with a knife dipped into hot water and dried before each cut. This fudge is best used within 4 days. Keep refrigerated in an airtight container and bring to room temperature before serving.

Pistachio Milk Fudge
KHARA PISTA BURFI

Plain milk fudge marries well with chopped pistachios and rose water. The mixture can be left just marbled with nuts or tinted a pistachio green color. For a classic look, garnish with a piece of edible silver foil (*varak*) and slivered pistachios.

Preparation time (after assembling ingredients): 30 minutes
Makes: 24 pieces

½ cup (110 g) sugar
1 cup (240 ml) water
3 tablespoons (45 ml) *ghee* or unsalted butter
¼ teaspoon (1 ml) powdered cardamom seeds
½ cup (75 g) raw pistachio nuts,
    blanched and finely chopped
1⅔ cups (165 g) low-fat or whole milk powder
1 teaspoon (5 ml) rose water or a few drops rose essence
2 drops green plus 1 drop yellow food coloring (optional)
one 4-inch (10 cm) piece of edible silver foil (*varak*) for garnishing, if available
3 tablespoons (45 ml) blanched pistachios, slivered

1. Combine the sugar and water in a heavy-bottomed 3-quart/liter nonstick saucepan and place over moderately low heat. Stir until the sugar dissolves, then raise the heat and gently boil for 8 minutes. Remove the pan from the heat and allow the syrup to cool for 10 minutes or until it reaches 110°F (45°C).

2. Add 1 tablespoon (15 ml) *ghee* or butter and the cardamom seeds and pistachio nuts, and, stirring constantly, mix in the milk powder. When the mixture is smooth, place the pan over moderate heat and cook, stirring constantly and scraping the sides and bottom of the pan with a wooden spatula, for up to 4 minutes. When the mixture is reduced to a thick paste that draws away from the sides of the pan, remove the pan from the heat, add the remaining 2 tablespoons (30 ml) *ghee* or butter and the rose water or essence and optional food coloring and stir until thoroughly incorporated.

3. Using a rubber spatula, scrape the sticky paste onto a buttered cookie sheet. Spread out and pat the hot mixture into a smooth-surfaced square cake about ¾ inch (2 cm) thick. When thoroughly cool, press the silver foil on the surface, cover with waxed paper and gently secure with a rolling pin. Cut with a hot knife into 24 squares and press slivered pistachios into each square. This quick fudge is best used within 4 days. Refrigerate in an airtight container. Bring to room temperature before serving.

Coconut Milk Fudge Log
KHARA NARIYAL BURFI

This uncooked confection is quick to assemble and power-packed with nutrition.

Preparation time (after assembling ingredients): 15 minutes
Makes: 24 pieces

½ cup (120 g) honey, rice or maple syrup
½ cup (120 g) almond, cashew or peanut butter
½ cup (80 g) finely chopped dates
⅔ cup (85 g) low-fat or whole milk powder
1½ cups (130 g) grated fresh coconut, lightly packed
    or 1½ cup (215 g) frozen coconut, defrosted
½ tablespoon (7 ml) rose water or *kewra* water

1. Combine the sweetener, nut butter, dates and milk powder in a bowl, and, using your hands, work into a soft, non-sticky dough. (You may have to add additional milk powder or a sprinkle of water.) Wash and dry your hands and roll the dough into a log about 20 inches (50 cm) long.

2. Place the coconut on a large square of waxed paper, sprinkle with the rose or *kewra* water and toss to mix. Cut the log in half and roll each half in the coconut to cover well. Slice each log into 10 pieces and place them in candy cases, if desired. This confection keeps well for up to 7 days. Keep refrigerated, well covered in an airtight container. Bring to room temperature before serving.

Carrot Milk Fudge
KHARA GAJAR BURFI

This yellow-orange marbled fudge is beautiful as well as delicious. You can substitute pecans for the walnuts, if desired.

Preparation time (after assembling ingredients): 30 minutes
Makes: 24 pieces

3 tablespoons (45 ml) unsalted butter or *ghee*
2 medium-sized carrots, shredded and pressed dry (about 1¼ cups/300 ml)
¼ teaspoon (1 ml) freshly grated nutmeg
¼ teaspoon (1 ml) cardamom seeds, coarsely powdered
1 cup (240 ml) hot water
½ cup (110 g) sugar
1⅔ cups (165 g) low-fat or whole milk powder
2 tablespoons (30 ml) chopped toasted walnuts

For information about unfamiliar ingredients or techniques, see A-to-Z

1. Heat 2 tablespoons (30 ml) of butter or *ghee* in a heavy-bottomed 3-quart/liter nonstick saucepan over moderate heat. When it is hot, add the carrots, nutmeg and cardamom seeds and sauté for 2–3 minutes. Add the water and sugar and stir constantly until the sugar is dissolved. Raise the heat to moderately high and boil for 8 minutes. Remove the pan from the heat and let the syrup cool for 10 minutes or until the temperature falls to 110°F (45°C).

2. Add ½ tablespoon (7 ml) butter or *ghee* and, stirring constantly, pour in the milk powder. When the mixture is smooth, place the pan over moderate heat and cook, stirring constantly and scraping the sides and bottom of the pan with a wooden spatula, for up to 4 minutes. When the mixture is reduced to a thick paste that draws away from the sides of the pan, remove the pan from the heat and stir in the remaining ½ tablespoon (7 ml) butter or *ghee*.

3. Scrape the sticky paste onto a buttered cookie sheet, using a rubber spatula to scrape it out. Spread out, pat and mold the hot mixture into a smooth-surfaced square cake about ¾ inch (2 cm) thick. When thoroughly cool, cut with a hot knife into 24 squares. Press chopped walnuts into each square. This quick fudge is best used within 4 days. Keep it refrigerated in an airtight container and bring to room temperature before serving.

The Grand Caramel Milk Fudge Cake
KHARA KALAKAND

This dish is a specialty of the Vrindavan–Mathura area of Uttar Pradesh. The local *halwais* (sweetmakers) proudly display this oversized "cake" on pedestals. The cakes are often as large as 16 inches (40 cm) in diameter and 10 inches (25 cm) in height, purchased by weight and sliced into wedges that reveal their glistening moist interior. The outside of the cake is a golden honeycomb color, and the inside is richly browned from caramelized sugar. This quick version is a uniform peanut butter color, but the texture is very similar to that of the classic version. You will need a small amount of citric acid crystals, available at most pharmacies. The hot fudge is poured into a decorative copper mold to set; any 3½ cup (830 ml) turret, rosette mold or smooth bowl can be used.

Preparation time (after assembling ingredients): 40 minutes
Setting time: at least 4 hours
Makes: 14 wedges

4 cups (1 liter) milk
¹⁄₁₆ teaspoon (0.25 ml) citric acid crystals
1¼ cups (180 g) light brown sugar or maple sugar granules
2 tablespoons (30 ml) maple syrup
3 tablespoons (45 ml) unsalted butter or *ghee*
3½ cups (345 g) instant dry milk powder
1 teaspoon (5 ml) ground cardamom seeds
one 4-inch (10 cm) piece of edible silver foil for garnishing (optional)

1. Pour the milk into a heavy-bottomed 5-quart/liter nonstick pan and, stirring constantly, bring to a frothing boil over high heat. Boil for 3 minutes, then add the citric acid. Stirring constantly with a wooden spatula, boil until the milk is reduced to 2 cups (480 ml). (Small flecks of clotted milk will appear from the addition of the citric acid.) Remove the pan from the heat and cool for 12 minutes.

2. Add the sugar, maple syrup, 1 tablespoon (15 ml) of the butter or *ghee* and the powdered milk, and blend until the mixture is smooth. Place the pan over moderate heat and cook, constantly stirring and scraping the sides and bottom of the pan with a wooden spatula until the mixture becomes thick and sticky, about 5–8 minutes. When the mass draws away from the sides of the pan, remove it from the heat and stir in the remaining 2 tablespoons (30 ml) butter or *ghee* and the cardamom.

3. Pour the mixture into a buttered 3½-cup (830 ml) mold and smooth the surface with a rubber spatula. Drape a clean tea towel over the mold and cover with a plate. Allow the cake to set for at least 4 hours or until firm. To unmold, dip into a pan of boiling water for 45 seconds to loosen the cake. Invert the mold and ease the cake onto a serving tray. If desired, press silver foil over the fudge. Cut into wedges with a sharp knife that has been dipped in hot water and dried before each cut.

Creamy Saffron Yogurt Cheese
SHRIKHAND

Dehin, a yogurt cheese with a consistency vaguely resembling whipped cream cheese, is the basis of this Gujarati dish. Sweetened and flavored with aromatic saffron and cardamom, the cheese is beaten until silken and light. Served in small cups with a simple garnish of pistachio slivers or delicate charoli seeds, it is much-loved when accompanied with fragrant fresh mango slices and deep-fried puffed *Luchi*.

Preparation time (after assembling ingredients): 15 minutes
Yogurt draining time: 12–16 hours
Serves: 6

a pinch of high-quality saffron threads
½ tablespoon (7 ml) scalding hot milk
½ teaspoon (2 ml) ground cardamom seeds
4 cups (1 liter) whole milk yogurt
½ cup (50 g) confectioners' sugar
2 tablespoons (30 ml) blanched raw pistachios, slivered,
    or charoli seeds, toasted

1. Line a colander with a triple thickness of cheesecloth. In a heavy pan, dry-roast the saffron threads over low heat until they are brittle. Powder them in a small porcelain or marble mortar and pestle, add the hot milk, and stir. Add the cardamom and saffron milk to the yogurt, and blend well.

2. Spoon the yogurt into the cheesecloth-lined colander, gather the four corners and

---

For information about unfamiliar ingredients or techniques, see A-to-Z

tie the yogurt into a bundle with a piece of kitchen twine. Hang the bundle somewhere in the refrigerator or in a cool cupboard where it can drain undisturbed for at least 12 hours. (Be sure to place a dish beneath the yogurt to catch the whey.) When the cheese is reduced to about 2 cups (480 ml), it should have a consistency like firm (rather than thick) sour cream. Transfer to a bowl, add the sugar and beat until light and fluffy. Serve chilled or at room temperature, garnished with pistachios or charoli seeds.

Sweet Yogurt Ambrosia
AMRITA MADHURA

Vedic cooking is kept alive, in part, by temple chefs. Each temple has a few dishes—often sweets—that have been traditional for centuries. This hallmark dish is from the kitchens of a temple called Sri Radha Banabihari Mandir. Taken from the ancient text *Chaitanya Charitamrta*, it is a cousin dish to *shrikhand*, but with more flavor and a different texture. Surrounded by seasonal fruits, this is a light dish that fits well into several types of menus.

This recipe calls for pure raw camphor crystals, an infrequently used, intense flavoring agent. Used since Vedic times, it is obtained by a steam distillation process from the bark of an evergreen tree native to the Himalayas. Called *karpoor*, this salt-like substance is used in minute quantities (a pinhead amount will flavor this entire dish). Unfortunately, raw camphor is difficult to find today. Once commonly sold in pharmacies and botanical stores, it has been all but phased out and replaced with a synthetic form impossible to use in cooking. Raw camphor is sometimes still to be found in Chinese and Indian grocery stores.

Draining time: 18–24 hours
Preparation and setting time (after assembling ingredients): 12–24 hours
Serves: 8

2 quarts/liters whole milk yogurt
4 each white and black peppercorns
¼ teaspoon (1 ml) cardamom seeds
5 whole cloves
¼ teaspoon (1 ml) fennel seeds
1 teaspoon (5 ml) rose water or orange flower water
4 tablespoons (60 ml) unsalted butter, at room temperature
enough raw camphor crystals to cover the head of a pin
¼ cup (55 g) rock sugar candy, powdered in a coffee mill
fresh seasonal berries or cut fruits (optional)

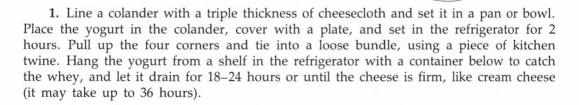

1. Line a colander with a triple thickness of cheesecloth and set it in a pan or bowl. Place the yogurt in the colander, cover with a plate, and set in the refrigerator for 2 hours. Pull up the four corners and tie into a loose bundle, using a piece of kitchen twine. Hang the yogurt from a shelf in the refrigerator with a container below to catch the whey, and let it drain for 18–24 hours or until the cheese is firm, like cream cheese (it may take up to 36 hours).

2. Combine the peppercorns, cardamom seeds, cloves and fennel seeds, and with a mortar and pestle or spice mill, reduce them to a powder. Place the spices, rose water or orange flower water, butter and camphor in a mixing bowl and beat until light and fluffy. Add the yogurt cheese and sweetener and beat with a wooden spoon until thoroughly blended and smooth.

3. Transfer the mixture to any double-cheesecloth-lined 1-quart/liter mold (such as a clay flowerpot or heart-shaped *paskha* mold) or into individual molds. Fold the ends of the cheesecloth over the cheese, cover with a flat plate, and weigh the plate down with anything weighing 2 pounds (1 kilo). Stand the mold in a bowl or pan and refrigerate for 12–24 hours.

4. Unfold the cheesecloth, place a serving dish on the top of the mold, and turn it over. Carefully remove the mold and cheesecloth. If desired, serve with fresh fruit— blueberries, sliced strawberries, mangoes—or a sprinkle of slivered nuts.

Sesame–Nut Nibbler
GAJJAK

I learned how to make several kinds of boiled-sugar candies from a sweetmaker in Vrindavan, India. Every afternoon for a fortnight, I sat, notebook and thermometer in hand, and scribbled down the B.K. Sharma family secrets. His leather-like hands seemed heat-resistant as he toasted sesame seeds or patted out soft-crack syrups without tools. Though he used peanuts in this sweet, I retested the recipe using hazelnuts, pecans and walnuts with equal success.

Preparation and cooking time (after assembling ingredients): ½ hour
Makes: about 1¼ pounds (570 g)

1 cup (160 g) sesame seeds
1 cup (about 4 ounces/115 g) coarsely chopped peanuts or
    mixed nuts
1½ cups (360 ml) maple syrup
1 tablespoon (15 ml) strained fresh lemon juice

1. Place the sesame seeds and nuts in a heavy frying pan over moderate heat and, stirring constantly, cook for about 10 minutes or until toasted.

2. Lightly oil the inside of a heavy-bottomed 3-quart/liter saucepan. Combine the sesame–nut mixture, maple syrup and lemon juice in the pan, place over moderate heat and bring to a boil. Stirring constantly with a wooden spoon, boil until the temperature reaches 280°F (140°C).

3. Immediately pour the mixture onto an oiled marble slab or into a jelly roll pan. Place a piece of buttered parchment or waxed paper over the candy and, using a rolling pin, roll the mixture into a layer about ¼ inch (6 mm) thick. While the candy is still warm, remove the paper and, using a sharp knife, cut into 2 x 4-inch (5 x 10 cm) bars. When cool, separate the pieces, wrap individually, and store in airtight containers.

For information about unfamiliar ingredients or techniques, see A-to-Z

Melt-in-Your-Mouth Chickpea Flour Confection
BESAN LADOO

This is the most popular flour-based confection in North India, where several versions are sold in sweet shops. You could use any type of solid or liquid sweetener, bearing in mind that each varies in sweetening power and that adjustments in cooking time will be necessary. This version, served at the home of the late Prime Minister of India, Indira Gandhi, is one of my favorites.

Cooking and preparation time (after assembling ingredients): about 20 minutes
Makes: 2 dozen balls

¾ cup (180 ml) *ghee* or unsalted butter
2 cups (205 g) sifted chickpea flour
    (sifted before measuring)
2 tablespoons (30 ml) grated dried coconut
2 tablespoons (30 ml) chopped pecans or walnuts
¼ teaspoon (1 ml) freshly ground nutmeg
¾ cup (110 g) brown sugar or maple sugar, packed

1. Melt the *ghee* or butter in a heavy-bottomed frying pan over moderately low heat. Add the chickpea flour, coconut, nuts and nutmeg and cook, stirring constantly with a wooden spoon, for about 5 minutes. Add the sweetener and continue to cook for 10–15 minutes or until the mixture is thick and deep golden brown.

2. Scrape it onto a marble surface or countertop, and, while hot, spread it into an even slab with a buttered spatula. When cool enough to handle, roll into 24 balls, or cool until set and cut into squares.

Coconut Candy
RASKARA

In Bengal, this sweet is barely flavored with black pepper and raw camphor, while in Uttar Pradesh it is perfumed with rose essence and cardamom. As a substitute for white sugar, I suggest trying unrefined *jaggery*.

Preparation and cooking time (after assembling ingredients): 45 minutes
Makes: about 10 ounces (285 g)

1 tablespoon (15 ml) unsalted butter or *ghee*
¾–1 cup (160–210 g) sugar
2½–3 cups (215–255 g) grated fresh coconut
a pinch of freshly ground black pepper with
    a pinhead amount of raw camphor, or
    ¼ teaspoon (1 ml) freshly ground cardamom seeds with
    a few drops of rose essence, or
    1 teaspoon (5 ml) rose water

1. Heat the butter or *ghee* in a heavy-bottomed frying pan over low heat. Mix the sugar with the coconut and add it to the pan. Cook slowly, stirring frequently at first and constantly toward the end, for about 30 minutes or until the mixture forms a soft, sticky paste.

2. Remove the pan from the heat, add one of the suggested flavorings, and mix well. Pour the mass onto a buttered marble slab or into a flat dish. When it is cool enough to handle, oil your hands and roll the mixture into walnut-sized balls. When completely cool, store in a well-sealed container, for up to 3 weeks refrigerated, or 2 weeks at room temperature.

Cardamom Shortbread Cookies
ELAICHE GAJA

This buttery cookie bears some resemblance to Scottish shortbread. To the basic recipe, try one of the following additions: ¼ cup (25 g) ground pecans, cashews, almonds, pistachios or walnuts; or 3 tablespoons (45 ml) purée of dried mango, apples, cherries or papaya.

Preparation time (after assembling ingredients): 15 minutes
Baking time: 1 hour
Makes: 2 dozen small bars

1 cup (240 ml) unsalted butter, at room temperature
1 teaspoon (5 ml) crushed cardamom seeds or
   2 teaspoons (10 ml) fresh ginger paste
½ cup (110 g) superfine sugar or *jaggery*
2½ cups (300 g) unbleached white flour
½ cup (85 g) fine semolina (pasta flour)
¼ teaspoon (1 ml) salt
¼ teaspoon (1 ml) baking powder

1. Preheat the oven to 250°F (120°C). Cream the butter and cardamom or ginger in a mixing bowl, then gradually add the sugar and beat until light and fluffy. (If you are using a dried fruit purée, work it into the sugar–butter mixture.) Combine the flour, semolina, salt and baking powder on a sheet of waxed paper and mix well. (If you are using nuts, add them to the dry ingredients.) Add the dry mixture to the butter and work with your hands until thoroughly blended into a dough. Alternatively, place all of the ingredients in an electric mixer, and with a dough hook, mix on low speed until thoroughly blended.

2. Press into an 8 x 10-inch (20–25 cm) rectangle on an ungreased baking tray. Score the surface to make 24 cookies, and prick the surface with fork tines at 1-inch (2.5 cm) intervals. Bake for about 1 hour or until pale gold but not brown. Cool for 10 minutes in the pan. Carefully cut again over the scored markings. (If you want to sprinkle the surface with sugar, do it as soon as it comes out of the oven.)

For information about unfamiliar ingredients or techniques, see A-to-Z

HALVA PUDDINGS

To many Westerners, *halva* means a chewy Middle Eastern candy made with crushed sesame seeds bound with honey. Though these recipes bear the same name, they differ considerably. More like fluffy puddings, these *halvas* are made with grains, vegetables, fruits, seeds or legumes. The most popular *halva* is little more than a fusion of toasted semolina and flavored sugar syrup with nuts and dried fruits added for texture.

In the most enduring vegetable *halvas*—carrot, winter melon, yam or *louki* summer squash—shredded vegetables are cooked in cream and reduced to a paste-like fudge. In North India, these dense *halvas* are served as desserts, snacks and even late morning brunches. Fruit *halvas*—more cooked fruit purées than puddings—are the sweetest of all, served in small quantity with fried biscuits or breads.

Srila Praphupada's maxim, "Good *halva* means good *ghee*," underscores the importance of the one ingredient used in all types of *halva*. Connoisseurs insist on it, perhaps adding a flavor dimension with clove- or ginger-flavored *ghee*. However, I feel that the recipes work best using unsalted butter. For many, it will be much more convenient. By varying sweeteners, the flavor cornucopia increases.

Semolina *Halva* with Golden Raisins
SOOJI HALVA

A popular item on a wedding or banquet menu, I have seen this *halva* made in enormous bowl-shaped iron pans with two or three pairs of hands steadily stirring the semolina while it plumps to tenderness. With stoves and pans large enough for the job, this dessert can be made from start to finish in one hour—for 300 people. It is best served hot, or at least warm; as the butter cools to room temperature, the consistency firms up and loses its fluffy texture. Served as a dessert, it can be dressed up with a dollop of whipped cream or even a spoonful of custard.

For a festive holiday or wedding menu, accompany it with *Jicama Salad with Snow Peas, Avocado and Watercress, Butter Soft Zucchini and Tomatoes, Fried Okra in Smooth Yogurt, Deep-Fried Buttermilk Whole Wheat Bread, Panir Cheese Pakora* and *Cake-Like Fried Milk Balls in Scented Syrup.*

Preparation and cooking time (after assembling ingredients): about 25 minutes
Serves: 6 to 8

2 cups (480 ml) water
¾ cup (160 g) sugar
¼ teaspoon (1 ml) each ground
    cloves, nutmeg and cinnamon
1 teaspoon (5 ml) crushed cardamom seeds
¼ teaspoon (1 ml) saffron threads
3 x ½-inch (7.5 x 1.5 cm) strip of orange zest
⅓ cup (50 g) golden raisins
½ cup (120 ml) *ghee* or unsalted butter
1 cup (185 g) fine-grained semolina (pasta flour)
¼ cup (40 g) sliced almonds or chopped Brazil nuts
1 cup (240 ml) whipped cream (optional)

1. Combine the water, sugar, ground spices, cardamom seeds, saffron and orange zest in a heavy 2-quart/liter saucepan over low heat and, while stirring, dissolve the sugar. Raise the heat and bring the mixture to a boil. Gently boil for a few minutes, then add the raisins. Strain through a sieve and set aside, covered.

2. Heat the *ghee* or butter in a large nonstick saucepan over moderately low heat. When it is hot, add the semolina and rhythmically stir-fry until the grains swell and darken to a warm golden color, about 10 minutes. (To make white *halva*, reduce the heat to a very low setting and cook for about ½ hour, stirring now and then until the grains expand, invisibly toast, and slightly color.) Remove the pan from the heat.

3. Stirring steadily, gradually pour syrup into the semolina. At first the grains may sputter, but will quickly cease as the liguid is absorbed. Place the pan over very low heat and, stirring steadily, cook uncovered until the the grains absorb the liquid and the texture is fluffy, up to 10 minutes. Serve in dessert cups or stemmed glasses, garnished if desired. If necessary, reheat slowly in a double boiler, mashing and stirring to lighten the texture.

Nutty Farina *Halva* with Sliced Carrots
SOOJI GAJAR HALVA

Supermarket farina replaces semolina in this *halva*. This enriched wheat cereal is available in most supermarkets in three types: instant, quick-cooking, and regular. For convenience, you can use one of two types: pre-toasted Malt-O-Meal farina or Cream-of-Wheat brand quick-cooking farina. For additional fiber, nutrition, texture and flavor, a mélange of nuts, seeds, dried fruits, bran and wheat germ can be added. If you do not have all these items, replace the missing ones with substitutes. For example, you could use granola instead of bran or wheat germ. This dish is a power-packed way to warm up an icy winter morning, or celebrate a fire-side evening.

Preparation and cooking time (after assembling ingredients): 15–20 minutes
Serves: 8

For information about unfamiliar ingredients or techniques, see A-to-Z

1 cup (240 ml) maple, barley or rice syrup
1½ cups (360 ml) water
2-inch (5 cm) piece of cinnamon stick
4–5 cloves
2 medium-sized carrots, scraped and thinly sliced
½ cup (120 ml) unsalted butter or *ghee*
1 cup (185 g) Malt-O-Meal brand pre-toasted farina or
    quick-cooking farina, dry-roasted over low heat for 10 minutes
2 tablespoons (30 ml) each chopped walnuts, cashews and almonds
2 tablespoons (30 ml) each sesame seeds and sunflower seeds
3 tablespoons (45 ml) each bran flakes and wheat germ
2 tablespoons (30 ml) each currants, golden raisins and grated coconut

1. Place the sweetener, water, cinnamon, cloves and carrots in a heavy saucepan over moderate heat. Stirring occasionally, bring to a boil. Gently boil for about 5 minutes, or until the carrots are just tender. Remove from the heat and set aside, covered.

2. Place the butter or *ghee* in a large saucepan over moderate heat. When it is hot but not smoking, stir in farina, nuts, seeds, bran and wheat germ. Stir-fry for a few minutes, then remove the pan from the heat. Stirring constantly, pour the carrots and syrup into the hot grains. At first the grains may sputter but will quickly cease as the liquid is absorbed. Place the pan over low heat and simmer, stirring often, for about 2 minutes. Stir in the dried fruits and coconut. Turn off the heat, cover and let the pan rest undisturbed for 2–3 minutes. Uncover and fluff with a spoon. (If the *halva* is dry, add water. If it is still liquid, place over heat and cook until thickened.) Serve hot.

Semolina and Chickpea Flour *Halva* with Almonds and Saffron
SOOJI BESAN HALVA

In Bengal this *halva* is called *mohan bhog*, "captivating dish," and is a personal favorite. Flavored with warm aromatics—saffron, black pepper, fennel seeds and cassia leaves—it is rib-sticking fare for a cold winter day.

Preparation and cooking time (after assembling ingredients): about 30 minutes
Serves: 6 to 8

2¼ cups (540 ml) milk or a mixture of 1 cup
    (240 ml) milk and 1¼ cups (300 ml) water
1 cup (210 g) sugar
¼ teaspoon (1 ml) good-quality saffron threads
¼ cup (35 g) currants
½ cup (120 ml) *ghee* or unsalted butter
1 cassia or allspice leaf, or ½ bay leaf
½ teaspoon (2 ml) fennel seeds
½ cup (50 g) sifted chickpea flour
    (sifted before measuring)
¾ cup (125 g) fine-grained semolina (pasta flour)
½ cup (55 g) sliced or slivered almonds
⅛ teaspoon (0.5 ml) freshly ground black pepper
¼ teaspoon (1 ml) freshly ground nutmeg

1. Combine the milk or milk–water mixture and sugar in a heavy saucepan and, stirring constantly, bring to a boil over moderately high heat. Reduce the heat to the lowest setting, add the saffron and currants, and cover.

2. Place the *ghee* or butter in a heavy pan over moderate heat. When it is hot, add the cassia, allspice or bay leaf and fennel seeds, and fry for several seconds. Stir in the chickpea flour, semolina or farina and almonds. Reduce the heat to moderately low and, stirring constantly, toast the ingredients for 10–12 minutes. It is ready when the chickpea flour and semolina darken a few shades to a warm golden color; they should not be allowed to brown.

3. Remove the pan from the heat. Stirring constantly, slowly pour in the sweet liquid into the grains. At first the grains may sputter but will quickly cease as the liguid is absorbed. Place the pan over low heat and, while stirring, simmer until all of the liquid is absorbed and the grains are swollen, from 5–8 minutes. Garnish each serving with a sprinkle of black pepper and nutmeg.

Shredded Carrot *Halva* with Pistachios
GAJAR HALVA

In some Western cities, to coax customers into their shops, bakers vent aromas from the ovens out onto the sidewalk. With a slightly different twist, the same holds true for sweetmakers in Old Delhi's Chandi Chowk market. *Halwais* bring pans and paraphernalia outside the sweet stall, and, before the eyes of passersby, prepare carrot *halva* on the spot. Further, a well garnished pan of hot *halva* sits nearby, beckoning foot traffic to stop and enjoy one of the area's favorite sweets.

Large, brilliant orange-red carrots are used in this *halva*, making the finished dish a vibrant color. It makes little difference what type you use as long as they are sweet and fresh. For best results, hold the carrots at a 45-degree angle to the shredding surface of a box shredder; you want long shreds, neither too thin nor too thick.

Not an everyday dessert, this North Indian dish is served hot or warm, with or without cream, and is regally garnished with silver or gold foil, fried almonds, cashews and puffed lotus pods. Use whatever suits the occasion.

Preparation and cooking time (after assembling ingredients): 1 hour
Serves: 10 to 12

For information about unfamiliar ingredients or techniques, see A-to-Z

9 medium-sized carrots (1½ pounds/685 g),
    washed, peeled, shredded and pressed dry
1½ cups (360 ml) half-and-half
2½ cups (600 ml) whole milk
8 whole black peppercorns
½ cup (110 g) sugar
½ cup (85 g) light brown sugar, lightly packed
1 teaspoon (5 ml) cardamom seeds, coarsely powdered
⅓ cup (80 ml) *ghee* or unsalted butter
¼ cup (30 g) sliced or slivered raw almonds
¼ cup (40 g) raisins or currants
½ cup (40 g) chopped walnuts
¼ teaspoon (1 ml) ground cloves
¼ teaspoon (1 ml) freshly ground nutmeg
¼ teaspoon (1 ml) ground cinnamon
2 tablespoons (30 ml) golden syrup or light honey
two 4-inch (10 cm) squares of edible silver or
    gold foil (*varak*) for garnishing (optional)

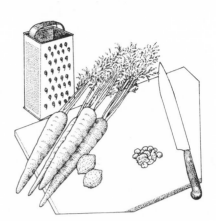

1. Combine the carrots, half-and-half, milk and peppercorns in a heavy 5–6 quart/liter nonstick saucepan and, stirring constantly, bring to a full boil over high heat. Reduce the heat to moderately high and, stirring frequently, cook for about 25–35 minutes, reducing the heat to moderately low toward the end of cooking, until the milk is reduced to a pasty fudge and the mixture is nearly dry.

2. Add the sugars and half of the cardamom and, stirring steadily to prevent scorching, cook for about 10–12 minutes or until the mixture is again nearly dry. Remove the pan from the heat and set aside.

3. Heat the *ghee* or butter in a small pan over moderately low heat, add the almonds and fry until golden. Remove with a slotted spoon and set aside. Add the hot butter to the carrot mixture along with the raisins or currants, walnuts, and ground spices, and again place the pan over moderately low heat. Cook until the mixture begins to pull away from the sides of the pan. Remove the pan from the heat, extract the peppercorns, if desired, and stir in the golden syrup or honey. Transfer the *halva* to a decorative serving bowl or tray and garnish with the optional silver or gold foil, remaining cardamom and any of the above suggested garnishes.

CHENNA CHEESE CONFECTIONS

In India, mango is considered the king of tropical fruits. And *sandesh* is regarded as the king of Bengali sweets. In its simplest form, this remarkable fudge is little more than fresh *chenna* cheese and a sweetener. Yet the resulting flavor and texture of this aristocratic confection are superbly elegant. Fortunately, *sandesh* is relatively quick to make and, once you have learned the technique, easy as well.

Repeated success in making *sandesh* comes from producing a fresh cheese that is neither too wet nor too dry, kneading it until silky-smooth, and maintaining a very low temperature during cooking. *Sandesh* must be cooked over very low heat. If your heat source cannot be set at low temperatures, use a heat diffuser or cook it in a double boiler. If your heat is too high, silky-smooth cheese will again become granular.

Today, nearly all of the *sandesh* sold in sweet houses is made with white sugar. The pure sweetness of sucrose does not affect the color or interfere with the subtle flavoring. Though only moderately sweet compared to other types of milk-based confections and fudges, *sandesh* as prepared according to traditional cookbooks and professional *halwais* requires a ratio of 1 part sugar to 3 parts *chenna*. I find a 1 to 4 or 5 ratio sufficient even for a sweet tooth, though you may find a happy medium somewhere in-between. Seasonal specialties are made with unrefined *gur* that rival the delicate flavor of the finest maple candy.

Though not traditional, the sugar-free *sandesh* variations I have come up with are sweetened and flavored with dried fruit pastes. Candied ginger, dried papaya, dates, pineapple, mangoes and apricots are all low in moisture, firm in texture and make excellent sweeteners. These natural sweeteners also lend subtle color and character to the confection. For quantity cooking, prepare fruit pastes in a food grinder fitted with a fine disk; for smaller amounts, reduce it to a paste in a food processor. You can then add the cheese and bray it together with the fruit paste.

Sandesh can be quite artistic. It can be shaped into a cake and cut into diamonds, squares or rectangles, or colored and layered in rainbow contrasts. It is pliable enough to be pressed into decorative molds. Classic carved wooden and clay molds are not easy to find in America, but candy molds—roses, wreaths, pineapples—are acceptable substitutes.

For information about unfamiliar ingredients or techniques, see A-to-Z

Creamy Cheese Fudge
SANDESH

You can use powdered vanilla sugar, maple sugar or even date sugar as a substitute for cane sugar in this *sandesh*. If you want to use the fruit pastes, substitute 4 tablespoons (60 ml) of dried papaya, mango, pineapple, apricot, dates or figs for every 10 to 11 ounces (285–310 g) of cheese. Plain *sandesh* is often pressed into decorative confection molds.

**Preparation and cooking time (after the *chenna* is made,
    drained and pressed for 15 minutes): 30 minutes**
Makes: ¾ pound (340 g)

**freshly made *chenna* cheese (page 315)
    made from 2 quarts/liters whole milk
    (about 12 ounces/340 g)**
**⅓–½ cup (70–110 g) superfine sugar,
    or above-suggested sweeteners**

1. Unwrap the pressed cheese and transfer to a clean countertop, thoroughly blend in the sweetener, and bray the cheese until it is without a touch of graininess.

2. Place a heavy-bottomed pan over the lowest possible heat, add the cheese, and, stirring constantly with a wooden spoon, cook for 10–15 minutes or until the surface becomes slightly glossy and the texture is slightly thickened. (The cheese will continue to firm up as it cools.)

3. Scrape it onto a buttered tray and press into a flat ¾-inch (2 cm) thick cake, or set it aside on a plate to cool. When it is cool enough to handle, roll the *sandesh* into balls, logs or egg shapes. Alternately, press into decorative confection molds, carefully unmold, and set aside on a plate. When completely cool, store in single layers, separated with parchment or waxed paper in an airtight storage container. Refrigerated, they may be kept for up to 4 days.

Lemon–Lime Cheese Fudge
NIMBU SANDESH

Citrus zest is an excellent flavoring for *sandesh*. Use zest in long strips so that it can be easily removed after cooking. When exposed to heat, the volatile citrus oils burst to life, leaving subtle flavor without even a trace of texture. This dish is a beautiful sweetmeat: once the fudge has cooled, it is divided into two portions and tinted yellow and green. They are sandwiched and rolled into a log of concentric circles, then sliced into rounds, revealing the contrasting colors.

**Preparation and cooking time (after the *chenna* is made,
    drained and pressed for 15 minutes): 40 minutes**
Makes: about ¾ pound (340 g)

freshly made *chenna* cheese (page 315) made from
  2 quarts/liters whole milk (about 12 ounces/340 g)
⅓ cup (70 g) superfine sugar
one 3-inch (7.5 cm) strip each lemon and lime zest
natural green and yellow food coloring*

*A pinch of powdered saffron threads dissolved in a teaspoon (5 ml) of boiling water makes a
  yellow food coloring. The juice from puréed fresh spinach that has been cooked and drained of
  excess liquid makes a green food coloring.*

  1. Unwrap the warm *chenna* cheese and transfer it to a clean countertop, thoroughly blend in the sugar and citrus zest, and bray the cheese until it is without a touch of graininess.
  2. Place a heavy-bottomed pan over the lowest possible heat, add the cheese, and, stirring constantly with a wooden spoon, cook for 10–15 minutes or until the surface becomes slightly glossy and the texture is slightly thickened. (The cheese will continue to firm up as it cools.)
  3. Scrape the fudge onto a plate and cool to room temperature. Remove the zest and divide the cheese into two portions, one twice the size of the other. Thoroughly knead 4 drops of green food coloring and 2 drops of yellow food coloring into the larger portion and divide it in half. Knead 3 drops of yellow food coloring into the remaining smaller portion.
  4. With your palms, roll out the green portion into a log 9 inches (22.5 cm) long. Roll and pat out the other two portions into narrow rectangles 9 inches (22.5 cm) long, with the green sheet slightly thinner and wider than the yellow sheet. Place the green log on one long edge of the yellow rectangle and roll it up until the log is just covered; trim off any overlap. Pinch the seam closed and trim off the ends. Slice across the log at ½-inch (1.5 cm) intervals and place each slice in a single layer on waxed paper. When completely cool, store in single layers, separated with parchment or waxed paper, in an airtight storage container. Refrigerated, they may be kept for up to 4 days.

Almond Cheese Fudge Delights

BADAAM SANDESH

  Blanched ground almonds (called almond meal at health food stores) are a supermarket staple in Europe. To grind the nuts in a rotary grater, attach the finest grating cylinder, fill the chopper with blanched almonds, and rotate the handle. A mini-food processor also does the trick. Place dry blanched nuts in the work bowl and fit it with the metal blade. Pulse the machine in short bursts to powder the nuts (continuous processing makes the nuts excessively oily). Scrape down the sides of the bowl frequently to ensure an evenly ground consistency. These sweets are elegant garnished with whole almonds covered with edible silver foil, available at Indian grocery stores.

Preparation and cooking time (after the *chenna* is made,
  drained and pressed for 15 minutes): 40 minutes
Makes: about ¾ pound (340 g)

For information about unfamiliar ingredients or techniques, see A-to-Z

freshly made *chenna* cheese (page 315)
    made with 2 quarts/liters whole milk
    (about 12 ounces/340 g)
⅓–½ cup (70–110 g) superfine sugar
⅔ cup (100 g) blanched whole almonds,
    powdered or finely ground
20 blanched almond halves
three 3-inch (7.5 cm) squares of edible
    silver foil (*varak*) (optional)
a large spoon of warmed honey or golden syrup

1. Unwrap the pressed *chenna* cheese and transfer it to a clean countertop, thoroughly blend in the sugar, and bray the cheese until it is without a touch of graininess. Add the ground almonds and mix in thoroughly.

2. Place a heavy-bottomed pan over the lowest possible heat, add the cheese, and, stirring constantly with a wooden spoon, cook for 10–15 minutes or until the surface becomes slightly glossy and the texture is slightly thickened. (The cheese will continue to firm up as it cools.)

3. Scrape the *sandesh* onto a buttered tray and press it out into a 3 x 5-inch (7.5 x 10 cm) smooth rectangle. When thoroughly cool, chill for ½ hour. With a sharp knife, cut it into 3 strips, 5 inches (12.5 cm) long and 1¼ inches (3.5 cm) wide. Then cut diagonally across the strips in alternate directions to make 6 small triangles per strip. Mold the trimmings by hand into triangles.

4. One by one, spear an almond half with a straight pin and paint it with a thin layer of warm honey or golden syrup. Set aside on waxed paper. In a windless spot, cut the silver foils into 20 squares. Cover each almond half with foil and then press it into a *sandesh* triangle. When completely cool, store in single layers, separated with parchment or waxed paper, in an airtight storage container. Refrigerated, they may be kept for up to 4 days.

Creamy Saffron Cheese Fudge
KESAR SANDESH

High-quality saffron is available at specialty food shops, gourmet food departments and good mail-order food suppliers, but it is expensive. If you come across a bargain, be wary as it may not be saffron but the stigma of a similar flower. Powdered saffron may be adulterated, lending only color, but none of the distinct aroma of this unparalleled ancient spice. You will need only a healthy pinch, about ¼ teaspoon (1 ml), to flavor this entire dish. A smooth cake of the *sandesh* is painted with saffron milk and then cut into 1-inch (2.5 cm) squares.

Preparation and cooking time: (after the *chenna* is made,
    drained and pressed for 15 minutes): 30 minutes
Makes: about 1 pound (455 g)

¼ teaspoon (1 ml) good-quality saffron threads
½ tablespoon (7 ml) scalding hot milk
freshly made *chenna* cheese (page 315) made from
    10 cups (2.5 liters) whole milk (about 1 pound/455g)
½ cup (110 g) superfine sugar

1. Toast the saffron threads in a dry pan over low heat until they are brittle. Powder them in a small porcelain mortar and pestle, then add the hot milk and set aside.

2. Unwrap the pressed *chenna* cheese and transfer it to a clean countertop, thoroughly blend in the sugar, and bray the cheese until it is without a touch of graininess.

3. Place a heavy-bottomed pan over the lowest possible heat, add the cheese, and, stirring constantly with a wooden spoon, cook for 10–15 minutes or until the surface becomes slightly glossy and the texture is slightly thickened. (The cheese will continue to firm up as it cools.)

4. Scrape the *sandesh* onto a buttered tray, press it into a flat 1-inch (2.5 cm) thick cake and cool to room temperature. Using a delicate brush or the flat of your palm, paint the top of the cake with a film of the orange–saffron milk. Cut the cake into 1-inch (2.5 cm) squares. When completely cool, store in single layers, separated with parchment or waxed paper, in an airtight container. Refrigerated, they may be kept for up to 4 days.

Pistachio Cheese Fudge with Rose Water
KASTURI SANDESH

Known as "Royal *Sandesh*," this sweetmeat is popular throughout Bengal, flavored and colored with four distinctive ingredients: crushed cardamom seeds, saffron threads, minced pistachios and rose water. The cardamom and saffron are kneaded into the cheese along with the sugar, and after sitting for 24 hours, the flavors intensify. The pistachios provide a pale green blanket of color. Before serving, the cake is sprinkled with rose water, then cut into squares. Each square is garnished with a small piece of a brilliant pink or red rose petal.

Preparation and cooking time (after the *chenna* is made,
    drained and pressed for 15 minutes): 45 minutes
Makes: about 1 pound (455 g)

freshly made *chenna* cheese (page 315)
    made from 10 cups (2.5 liters) whole
    milk (about 1 pound/455 g)
½ cup (110 g) superfine sugar
½ tablespoon (7 ml) cardamom seeds,
    coarsely crushed
a pinch of good-quality saffron threads
¼ cup (35 g) blanched raw pistachios, minced
½ tablespoon (7 ml) rose water
a few insecticide-free garden pink
    or red rose petals (optional)

For information about unfamiliar ingredients or techniques, see A-to-Z

1. Unwrap the warm pressed *chenna* cheese and transfer to a clean countertop, thoroughly blend in the sugar, cardamom seeds and saffron, and bray the cheese until it is without a touch of graininess.

2. Place a heavy-bottomed pan over the lowest possible heat, add the cheese, and, stirring constantly with a wooden spoon, cook for 10–15 minutes or until the surface becomes slightly glossy and the texture is slightly thickened. (The cheese will continue to firm up as it cools.)

3. Scrape the *sandesh* onto a buttered tray and press it into a flat 1-inch (2.5 cm) thick cake. Set it aside to cool. While still warm, sprinkle with nuts and secure them in place by gently rolling the top with a rolling pin. When cool, cut the cake into 1-inch (2.5 cm) squares. When completely cool, store in single layers, separated with parchment or waxed paper, in an airtight container. Refrigerated, they may be kept for up to 4 days.

Cheese Balls Stuffed with Nut Milk Fudge
MANOHARA LADOO

In Bengal this confection is called *Ganga-Yamuna Ladoo*. *Ganga* represents the cheese fudges famous in Bengal, and *Yamuna* represents the milk fudge loved in North India. Despite their contrasting qualities, these two regional sweets combine successfully. Though they are beautiful when plain, you can further embellish these fudge balls with a coating of powdered nuts.

Preparation and cooking time (after the *chenna* is made,
    drained and pressed for 15 minutes): 1 hour
Makes: about 1 pound (455 g)

2⅓ cups (550 ml) half-and-half
¼ cup (55 g) sugar
½ teaspoon (2 ml) ground cardamom
freshly made *chenna* cheese (page 315)
    made from 10 cups (2.5 liters) whole
    milk (about 1 pound/455 g)
½ cup (110 g) superfine sugar
2 tablespoons (30 ml) minced walnuts, pecans,
    hazelnuts, almonds or pistachios

1. Combine the half-and-half, sugar and cardamom in a heavy-bottomed, nonstick saucepan over high heat and, stirring constantly, bring to a full boil. Cook, stirring frequently, until the milk has been reduced by half. Lower the heat to moderate and, stirring constantly, reduce the milk to a semi-solid fudge that pulls away from the sides of the pan. Set aside and cool to room temperature.

2. Unwrap the pressed *chenna* cheese and transfer it to a clean countertop, thoroughly blend in the superfine sugar and bray the cheese until it is without a touch of graininess.

3. Place a heavy-bottomed pan over the lowest possible heat, add the cheese, and, stirring constantly with a wooden spoon, cook for 10–15 minutes or until the surface becomes slightly glossy and the texture is slightly thickened. The cheese will continue to firm up as it cools.

4. Knead the nuts into the cooled milk fudge. Divide it into 16 portions and roll each into a smooth ball. Divide the cheese into 16 portions and pat each into a smooth 2-inch (5 cm) patty. Place a ball of the nut fudge in the center of a cheese patty and bring up the edges to enclose the stuffing. Pinch and press the seams together, rolling the ball between your palms and exerting slight pressure. When the ball is free of all seams, exert more pressure on one end of the ball and mold it into an egg shape. If desired, dip one end (or the whole sweet) in additional powdered or ground nuts. When completely cool, store in single layers, separated with parchment or waxed paper, in an airtight container. Refrigerated, they may be kept for up to 4 days. Serve in candy papers.

Rainbow-Layered Cheese Fudge Bar
GOURAHARI SANDESH

This colorful confection combines differently flavored and colored layers of *sandesh* into an artful and delicious sweet.

Preparation and cooking time (after the *chenna* is made,
    drained and pressed for 15 minutes): 1 hour
Makes: about 1 pound (455 g)

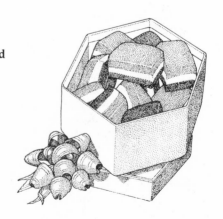

¼ teaspoon (1 ml) good-quality saffron threads
½ tablespoon (7 ml) scalding hot milk
2 handfuls of fresh spinach leaves, washed and trimmed
freshly made *chenna* cheese (page 315)
    made from 10 cups (2.5 liters) whole
    milk (about 1 pound/455 g)
⅔ cup (140 g) superfine sugar
¼ cup (35 g) blanched raw pistachios,
    powdered or finely grated
¼ cup (25 g) blanched almonds or cashews,
    powdered or finely grated
two 3-inch (7.5 cm) sheets of edible silver
    foil (*varak*) (optional)

1. Toast the saffron in a pan over low heat until it is brittle. Grind it to a powder with a small porcelain mortar and pestle or the back of a spoon. Add the hot milk, stir and set aside.

2. Process the spinach in a mini-food processor fitted with the metal blade, or pound with a large mortar and pestle, until reduced to a paste. Transfer all of the spinach paste to the center of a clean muslin square, gather the ends, and wring out all of the juice into a small saucepan. Cook the juice over low heat until it separates into solid pulp and liquid. Strain it through a fine sieve and discard the liquid. Pat the pulp dry with paper towels. Set aside.

3 . Unwrap the pressed warm *chenna* cheese and transfer it to a clean countertop, add the sugar, knead the cheese briefly, and divide it into three portions. Knead a generous teaspoon (5 ml) of spinach solids and the ground pistachios into one portion. (If necessary, add additional solids to make the cheese a pistachio-green color.) Knead the saffron milk into another portion, and knead the powdered or ground almonds or cashews into the last portion.

4. Using your palms, roll out each portion into a 14-inch (35 cm) long cylinder. Place each cylinder on a piece of waxed paper and, using your fingers, press and mold it into a narrow rectangle 1 inch (2.5 cm) wide and 14 inches (35 cm) long. Lay the yellow rectangle over the green rectangle, and the almond or cashew rectangle over the yellow rectangle. Gently firm the top and sides with a long spatula to even up the edges. With a long sharp knife, trim the shavings off the uneven edges. Pat the decorative foil on the top of each strip. Cut into pieces at ½-inch (1.5 cm) intervals. When completely cool, store in single layers, separated with parchment or waxed paper, in an airtight container. Refrigerated, they may be kept for up to 4 days. Serve in candy cases.

Coconut Cheese Fudge
KANCHAGOLLA

I first made this dish in the San Francisco kitchen of Asha Dhar, an inspired cook. Typical of many recipes from expatriate Indians, hers was a modified version of a classic Bengali sweet. Presented here, it is made with ricotta cheese, though you could also use farmer cheese or home-made *chenna*. Baked instead of cooked on the stove, it is quick and easy.

Unlike most *sandesh*, this one is meant to be grainy and textured even further with shredded coconut. In this variation, coconut is added to the cheese mixture before it is baked and, for contrast, the cake is turned onto a bed of toasted coconut.

Preparation and cooking time (after assembling ingredients): about 1¼ hours
 Resting time: 8 hours or overnight
Serves: 10 to 12

2 pounds (910 g) whole milk ricotta cheese, or freshly
    made *chenna* cheese (page 315) made from 10 cups
    (2.5 liters) whole milk (about 1 pound/455 g)
    pressed briefly and mixed with 1 cup (240 ml) sour cream
¾ cup (165 g) superfine sugar
2 tablespoons (30 ml) arrowroot
1 teaspoon (5 ml) crushed cardamom seeds
1 cup (85 g) fresh coconut, or 1 cup
    (140 g) frozen grated coconut, defrosted
⅓ cup (35 g) toasted, grated dried coconut
one 3-inch (7.5 cm) piece of edible silver or gold foil (*varak*) (optional)

1. Preheat the oven to 325°F (165°C). Combine the ricotta or *chenna* or sour cream, sugar, arrowroot, cardamom and coconut in a bowl and blend well. Transfer the mixture to a buttered 8-inch (20 cm) square or round springform pan. Pack and smooth the surface with a spatula. Cut a round of parchment for the surface, gently pat into place and bake for about 1 hour. Cool in the pan, then cover well with plastic film and refrigerate overnight.

2. Dry-roast the coconut in a heavy-pan over moderately low heat until golden brown. Loosen the *sandesh* using a spatula, and turn onto a serving tray. Sprinkle the toasted coconut around the edges. To serve, cut in wedges or squares.

JUICY *CHENNA* CHEESE SWEETS

Juicy *chenna* cheese sweets, called *rasgoola*, are made with two basic ingredients: milk and sugar. Subtle variations in treatment determine the character of each variety. It matters little what catalyst you use to prepare the cheese: a citric acid solution, lemon juice or soured whey. Once made, the solid curds are immediately pressed to compact them, and then kneaded while still warm. Professional Bengali *halwais* turn out immense quantities daily. Consequently, the cheese is kneaded with traces of fine semolina, flour or arrowroot which act as binders—a precautionary measure that helps keep the sweets in perfect shape while they are cooking. If the moisture content of untreated *chenna* is not within a suitable range, the *rasgoolas* often crack, deflate or even crumble while they vigorously boil in syrup. Because I am attempting to present the finest standard of Bengali sweetmaking, none of the following *rasgoola* recipes call for binders. They rely instead on precise weight information and clear instructions.

For assured success in these recipes, you will need an accurate scale to weigh the warm *chenna*, but little else in the way of ingredients or equipment. Several small-sized, high accuracy scales with ¼ or ½-ounce (7–15 g) gradations, such as Terraillon, Cuisin-art, or Soehnle, are available at better cookware stores or through mail order outlets. Unless otherwise specified, *chenna* made from 8 cups (2 liters) of whole milk should be pressed until it weighs 9½–10 ounces (270–285 g). Alternatively, follow the instructions carefully, and to be on the safe side, bray the cheese along with ½ tablespoon (7 ml) arrowroot or white flour to minimize excess moisture content.

In Calcutta's Dalhousi Square, the firm of K.C. Das specializes in *rasgoolas*, *sandesh*, and other Bengali delicacies. Shipping the sweets around the nation and selling thousands at the shop on a busy day, their production operation is impressive. During the night, huge quantities of milk are turned into cheese, and scores of cooks—comfortably squatting on low floor seats—hand-roll smooth, white cheese balls and slip them into caldrons of heaving sugar syrup. After each batch, the syrup is replenished with more, keeping an even flow of activity batch after batch and never wasting a drop. (If you make *rasgoolas* in quantity, you need a strong heat source, large stoves and giant pans; but the procedures remain similar to those mentioned in this chapter.)

For information about unfamiliar ingredients or techniques, see A-to-Z

There are many different textures of *rasgoolas*. For example, one texture is achieved by momentarily pressing cheese made from raw milk and cut with a sour whey agent under a weight, then braying the cheese until smooth while still hot to the touch, and vigorously boiling it in a thin syrup. Once cooked, it might then be soaked in a per-fumed medium-heavy syrup—one part sugar to one part water—to intensify the flavor. Another texture is achieved by hanging cheese made with store bought milk and cut with a citric acid solution in cheesecloth and slowly draining it of whey for one or two hours. A third texture is achieved by slowly boiling the cheese in a heavy syrup—say two parts sugar to one part water—and then soaking it in the same syrup. Further, sweets are sometimes cooked in two, three, even four successive syrups of different consistencies before soaking. Whatever your preference for syrup consistency, it must be maintained consistently throughout the entire cooking period.

In an attempt to present the most respected versions of *rasgoola*, I offer the following guidlines:

1. Add strained lemon juice only until solid cheese curds form; you may need more or less than the amount suggested.

2. Use an accurate scale to weigh the cheese; it should weigh 9½–10 ounces (270 –285 g).

3. Use the recommended pan size to take full advantage of the quantity of sugar syrup and select a burner with the strongest heat.

4. Keep a clock nearby and use it when adding thinning water to the syrup to maintain a uniform consistency throughout the cooking.

Rasgoolas are served in Bengal for any festive occasion.

Classic Juicy *Chenna* Balls
RASGOOLA

Every Bengali *halwai* and household has at least one or two favorite recipes for plain *rasgoolas*. Over the years, I have made hundreds of batches, trying scores of recipes from around the world. Most recipes follow a similar procedure, but subtle variations are endless. Though experts agree that raw milk yields the best *rasgoola*, it is not available to most cooks. This recipe is especially composed for store-bought whole milk.

Preparation and cooking time (after assembling ingredients): 1¼ hours
Soaking time: at least 4 hours
Serves: 8

8 cups (2 liters) whole milk
4 tablespoons (60 ml) strained lemon juice
8 cups (2 liters) water
7 cups (1.5 kg) sugar
1 tablespoon (15 ml) cornstarch dissolved
    in 2 tablespoons (30 ml) water
½ teaspoon (2 ml) *khus* or *kewra* essence or
    1 tablespoon (15 ml) *khus* or *kewra* water

1. Place the milk in a heavy 5-quart/liter pan over high heat and, stirring constantly, bring to a frothing boil. Reduce the heat to moderate, pour in the lemon juice, and ever-so-gently stir. Within 1 minute, soft white cheese curds should separate from the yellowish whey. If the cheese has not formed by then, add up to a tablespoon (15 ml) more lemon juice. Remove the pan from the heat and set aside for 10 minutes.

2. Line a colander with three thicknesses of moist cheesecloth and place it in the sink. With a slotted spoon, transfer the large pieces of cheese into the colander. Pour the whey and small pieces of cheese through a strainer and add the cheese to the colander. Gather the four corners of the cheesecloth and rinse the bundle of cheese under a stream of lukewarm tap water for 10 seconds. Gently twist the cloth to extract excess moisture, then place the cheese in a colander resting in a 2-quart/liter bowl. Flatten the top, rest a salad plate on the cheese, and then balance a large bowl or pan filled with water on the plate. You may also use any other method that will exert weight on the cheese and allow it to drain. Press the cheese for 20–45 minutes. or until it weighs 9½–10 ounces (270–285 g).

3. While the cheese is draining, combine the water and sugar in a heavy 5-quart/liter pan and bring it to a boil over moderate heat, stirring until the sugar dissolves. Increase the heat to high and cook, uncovered, for about 5 minutes or until the temperature reaches 220°F (105°C). Reduce the heat to the lowest possible setting.

4. Unwrap the cheese and place it on a clean work surface. Roughly break it apart and press with white paper towels to extract excess moisture. Using the heel of your hand, spread a small amount at a time across the work surface. Gather the cheese into a mass with a wide spatula and repeat the process again and again for up to 5 minutes or until the cheese is smooth and fluffy and without a trace of graininess. Gather the cheese into a mass. Wash and dry your hands, then rub them with a film of oil. Divide the cheese into 16 portions and roll each into a uniformly round ball.

5. Bring the syrup to a boil over moderate heat. Add the balls, one by one, and gently cook for 1 minute. Raise the heat to high and boil vigorously, covered, for 20 minutes. To keep the syrup at the same consistency throughout the boiling, pour ¼ cup (60 ml) of hot water down the sides of the pan (not on the balls) at 4 minute intervals. After the first 4 minutes, add the cornstarch–water mixture along with the ¼ cup (60 ml) of plain water. The syrup should be a mass of frothing bubbles, the *rasgoolas* only visible when water is added to the syrup. The balls will swell and double, triple, sometimes quadruple in size. During the last 3 minutes, sprinkle the surface of the syrup with water every minute. Turn off the heat.

6. Cool for 10 minutes, then sprinkle with the *khus* or *kewra* flavoring. Gently shake the pan to cover the balls with syrup. Soak *rasgoolas* at room temperature for at least 4 hours. The longer they sit, the more they take on a new dimension, firming up and intensifying in flavor. They may be stored, refrigerated and well covered, for up to 36 hours, though they are served at room temperature. Serve 2 *rasgoolas* per person in a small bowl with a few tablespoons (45 ml) of syrup.

For information about unfamiliar ingredients or techniques, see A-to-Z

Orange Zest *Chenna* Balls in Orange Flower Syrup
KAMALA RASGOOLA

The center of these *rasgoolas* is stuffed with a small bead of homemade, candied orange zest. Across Europe, you can purchase wonderful orange sugar candies made by Troubat. As the balls cook, the sugar inside melts and turns to a syrup. You can make this variation equally well with lemon or lime zest or anise seeds.

Preparation and cooking time: 1¼ hours
Serves: 8

For the Stuffing:

3 tablespoons (45 ml) sugar
1 tablespoon (15 ml) grated orange, lemon or lime zest
3 drops melted butter
1 tablespoon (15 ml) water
3 drops edible citrus oil or essence

For the Chenna Balls:

8 cups (2 liters) whole milk
4 tablespoons (60 ml) strained lemon juice
8 cups (2 liters) water
7 cups (1.5 kg) sugar
1 tablespoon (15 ml) cornstarch dissolved
    in 2 tablespoons (30 ml) water
1 tablespoon (15 ml) orange flower water

1. Mix the sugar, citrus zest, butter and water in a small heavy saucepan over moderate heat and, stirring constantly, cook until the sugar melts and the syrup begins to thicken. Boil for 3–4 minutes until quite thick. Remove the pan from the heat, add the oil or essence and cool slightly. When you can handle the syrup, form into 16 small balls.

2. Place the milk in a heavy 5-quart/liter pan over high heat and, stirring constantly, bring to a frothing boil. Reduce the heat to moderate, pour in the lemon juice, and every-so-gently stir. Within 1 minute, soft white cheese curds should separate from the yellowish whey. If the cheese has not formed by then, add up to 1 tablespoon (15 ml) more lemon juice. Remove the pan from the heat and set aside for 10 minutes.

3. Line a colander with three thicknesses of cheesecloth and place it in the sink. With a slotted spoon, transfer the large pieces of cheese into the colander. Pour the whey and small pieces of cheese through a strainer and add the cheese to the colander. Gather the four corners of the cheesecloth and rinse the bundle of cheese under a stream of lukewarm tap water for 10 seconds. Twist the cloth to extract excess moisture, then place the cheese in a colander resting in a 2-quart/liter bowl. Flatten the top, rest a salad plate on the cheese, and balance a large bowl or pan filled with water on the plate. (You can also use any other method that will exert weight on the cheese and allow it to drain.) Press the cheese for 20–40 minutes. The cheese is ready when it weighs 10 ounces (285 g).

4. While the cheese is draining, combine the water and sugar in a heavy, 5-quart/liter pan and bring it to a boil over moderate heat, stirring until the sugar dissolves. Increase the heat to high and cook, uncovered, for about 5 minutes or until the temperature reaches 220°F (105°C). Reduce the heat to the lowest possible setting.

5. Unwrap the cheese and place it on a clean work surface. Roughly break it apart and press with white paper towels to extract excess moisture. Using the heel and palm of your hand, spread a small bit at a time across the work surface. Gather the cheese into a mass with a wide spatula and repeat the process again and again for up to 5 minutes until fluffy and without a trace of graininess. Gather the cheese into a mass. Wash and dry your hands, then rub them with a film of oil. Divide the cheese into 16 portions, roll them into balls, and flatten them into patties 1¼ inches (3.5 cm) in diameter. Place a citrus candy in the center of each patty and pull the edges closed. Smooth into seamless balls.

6. Bring the syrup to a gentle boil over moderate heat. Add the balls, one by one, and cook slowly for 1 minute. Raise the heat to high and boil vigorously, covered, for 20 minutes. To keep the syrup at the same consistency throughout the boiling, pour ¼ cup (60 ml) of water down the sides of the pan (not on the balls) at 4-minute intervals. After the first 4 minutes, add the cornstarch paste along with the first ¼ cup (60 ml) of hot water. The syrup should be a mass of frothing bubbles, the *rasgoolas* visible only when water is added. The balls will swell and nearly double in size. During the last 3 minutes, sprinkle the surface of the syrup with water every minute. Turn off the heat.

7. Cool for 10 minutes, then sprinkle with orange flower water. Shake the pan to cover the balls with syrup. Soak the *rasgoolas* at room temperature for at least 4 hours. The longer they sit, the more they take on a new dimension, firming up and intensifying in flavor. They may be stored, well covered and refrigerated, for up to 36 hours. Serve 2 *rasgoolas* per person in a small bowl with a few tablespoons (45 ml) of syrup. (The soaking syrup can be saved and used in *Semolina Halva with Golden Raisins*.)

Nut-Stuffed *Chenna* Balls in Rose Syrup
RAJBHOG

These white globes are about the size of jam-filled fried doughnuts: that is, two or three times the size of *rasgoolas*. *Rajbhog* literally means "a sweet fit for a king," and this elegant variation lives up to its name, for nestled inside each ball is cardamom–pistachio fudge.

Preparation and cooking time (after assembling ingredients): 1¼ hours
Serves: 8

For the Stuffing:

1⅓ cups (320 ml) whole milk
2 tablespoons (30 ml) sugar
3 tablespoons (45 ml) raw pistachio nuts,
    powdered or grated
½ teaspoon (2 ml) cardamom seeds, crushed

For information about unfamiliar ingredients or techniques, see A-to-Z

For the Chenna Balls:

8 cups (2 liters) whole milk
4 tablespoons (60 ml) strained lemon juice
8 cups (2 liters) water
7 cups (1.5 kg) sugar
1 tablespoon (15 ml) cornstarch dissolved
    in 2 tablespoons (30 ml) water
1 tablespoon (15 ml) rose water or
    ½ teaspoon (7 ml) rose essence
1 tablespoon (15 ml) minced pistachios for garnishing
one 3-inch (7.5 cm) sheet of edible silver
    or gold foil (*varak*) (optional)

1. To prepare the stuffing, place the milk and sugar in a large heavy-bottomed nonstick pan over high heat and, stirring constantly, bring to a boil. Reduce the quantity of milk to ½ cup (120 ml), then add the nuts and cardamom seeds, lower the heat to moderate, and cook until the mixture pulls away from the sides of the pan and forms a ball. Scrape the paste onto a plate and set aside to cool.

2. Place the milk for the *chenna* balls in a heavy 5-quart/liter pan over high heat and, stirring constantly, bring to a frothing boil. Reduce the heat to moderate, pour in the lemon juice, and ever-so-gently stir. Within 1 minute, soft white cheese curds should separate from the yellowish whey. If the cheese has not yet formed by then, add up to 1 tablespoon (15 ml) more lemon juice. Remove the pan from the heat and set aside for 10 minutes.

3. Line a colander with three thicknesses of cheesecloth and place it in the sink. With a slotted spoon, transfer the large pieces of cheese into the colander. Pour the whey and small pieces of cheese through a strainer and add the cheese to the colander. Gather the four corners of the cheesecloth and rinse the bundle under a stream of lukewarm tap water for 10 seconds. Gently twist the cloth to extract excess moisture, then place the cheese in a colander resting in a 2-quart/liter bowl. Flatten the top, rest a salad plate on the cheese, and balance a large bowl or pan filled with water on the plate. (You can also use any other method that will exert weight on the cheese and allow it to drain.) Press the cheese for 20–40 minutes. The cheese is ready when it weighs 10 ounces (285 g).

4. While the cheese is draining, combine the water and sugar in a heavy 5-quart/liter pan and bring it to a boil over moderate heat, stirring until the sugar dissolves. Increase the heat to high and cook, uncovered, for about 5 minutes or until the temperature reaches 220°F (105°C). Reduce the heat to the lowest setting possible.

5. Unwrap the cheese and place it on a clean work surface. Roughly break it apart and press with white paper towels to extract excess moisture. Using the heel and palm of your hand, spread a small bit at a time across the work surface. Gather the cheese into a mass with a wide spatula and repeat the process again and again for up to 5 minutes until fluffy and without a trace of graininess. Gather the cheese into a mass. Wash and dry your hands, then rub them with a film of oil. Divide the cheese into 8 large balls and flatten them into patties 1¼ inches (3.5 cm) in diameter. Divide the nut fudge into 8 balls, place one in the center of each patty, and pull the edges closed. Smooth into seamless balls.

6. Bring the syrup to a gentle boil over moderate heat. One by one, add the balls and cook for 1 minute. Cover the pan, raise the heat to high, and boil vigorously for 20 minutes. To keep the syrup at the same consistency throughout the boiling, pour ¼ cup (60 ml) of hot water down the sides of the pan (not on the balls) at 4-minute intervals. After the first 4 minutes, add the cornstarch paste along with the first ¼ cup (60 ml) of hot water. The syrup should be a mass of frothing bubbles, the *rasgoolas* visible only when water is added. The balls will swell and nearly double in size. During the last 3 minutes, sprinkle the syrup with water every minute. Turn off the heat.

7. Cool for 10 minutes. Add the rose water or essence and shake the pan to cover the balls with syrup. Soak the *rasgoolas* at room temperature for at least 6 hours, then drain on a screen for 1 hour. Place them in pastry cups, sprinkle with minced nuts, and garnish each ball with a piece of silver or gold foil.

Dainty *Chenna* Cheesecakes with Almond Frosting
MALAI CHUM CHUM

Chum chums are made in various shapes: logs, boats and diamonds. Some are halved horizontally, the bottom piece frosted and the top piece gently placed over the filling. In this recipe, I have chosen to leave them whole and pipe a milk fudge frosting on top using a shell nozzle. You can also frost the cakes with a spatula, smoothing the sides to slightly crest the frosting down the center.

Preparation and cooking time (after assembling ingredients): 1½ hours
Serves: 8

For the Frosting:

4 cups (1 liter) half-and-half
⅓ cup (70 g) sugar
⅓ cup (35 g) ground almonds, blanched
3 drops almond oil or essence
sprinkles of milk, as necessary
3 drops natural red food coloring (optional)

For the Chum Chums:

8 cups (2 liters) whole milk
4 tablespoons (60 ml) strained lemon juice
7 cups (1.75 liters) water
5 cups (1 kg) sugar
2 teaspoons (10 ml) cornstarch dissolved
    in 2 tablespoons (30 ml) water
4 tablespoons (60 ml) blanched raw pistachios, minced

1. Place the half-and-half in a large heavy-bottomed nonstick pan over high heat and, stirring constantly, bring to a boil. Cook, stirring often, until it is reduced to ¾ cup (180 ml), then lower the heat to moderate. Add the sugar and, stirring constantly, cook until the mixture forms a ball that pulls away from the sides of the pan. Scrape the milk paste into a bowl and set aside to cool.

2. To make the *chum chums*, place the milk in a heavy 5-quart/liter pan over high heat and, stirring constantly, bring to a frothing boil. Reduce the heat to moderate, pour in the lemon juice, and every-so-gently stir. Within 1 minute, soft cheese curds should separate from the yellowish whey. If the cheese has not formed by then, add up to 1 tablespoon (15 ml) more lemon juice. Remove the pan from the heat and set aside for 10 minutes.

3. Line a colander with three thicknesses of cheesecloth and place it in the sink. With a slotted spoon, transfer the large pieces of cheese into the colander. Pour the whey and small pieces of cheese through a strainer and add the cheese to the colander. Gather the four corners of the cheesecloth and rinse the bundle under a stream of lukewarm tap water for 10 seconds. Gently twist the cloth to extract the excess moisture, then place the cheese in a colander resting in a 2-quart/liter bowl. Flatten the top, rest a salad plate on the cheese, and balance a large bowl or pan filled with water on the plate. (You can also use any other method that will exert weight on the cheese and allow it to drain.) Press the cheese for 20–40 minutes. The cheese is ready when it weighs 10 ounces (285 g).

4. While the cheese is draining, combine the water and sugar in a heavy 5-quart/liter pan and bring to a boil over moderate heat, stirring until the sugar dissolves. Increase the heat to high and cook, uncovered, for about 5 minutes or until the temperature reaches 220°F (105°C). Reduce the heat to the lowest setting possible.

5. Unwrap the cheese and place it on a clean work surface. Roughly break it apart and press with white paper towels to extract excess moisture. Using the heel and palm of your hand, spread a small bit at a time across the work surface. Gather the cheese into a mass with a wide spatula and repeat the process again and again for up to 5 minutes until fluffy and without a trace of graininess. Gather the cheese into a mass. Wash and dry your hands, then rub them with a film of oil. Divide the cheese into 8 portions, roll them into balls, and then flatten and mold each piece into a boat-shaped sweet—roughly 3 inches (7.5 cm) long, 2 inches (5 cm) wide and ½ inch (1.5 cm) thick. Round off the pointed ends and continue to pinch and mold until the sweets are smooth and seamless. Set aside on a plate and loosely drape with plastic wrap.

6. Rub a film of oil on a work surface and on your hands. Add the optional food coloring to the milk fudge and then combine the milk fudge with the ground almonds and almond essence or oil. On a clean work surface, bray a small bit at a time with the heel of your hand until it is smooth and creamy. Transfer the mixture to a bowl and add enough milk to whisk into a consistency similar to that of confectioners' cake frosting. Using a rubber spatula, transfer to a pastry bag fitted with a shell or star nozzle. Keep refrigerated until ready to use.

7. Bring the syrup to a gentle boil over moderate heat. Add the cheese boats, one by one, and cook for 1 minute. Raise the heat to high and boil vigorously, covered, for 20 minutes. To keep the syrup at the same consistency throughout the boiling, pour ¼ cup (60 ml) of hot water down the sides of the pan, not on the *chum chums*, at 4-minute intervals. After the first 4 minutes, add the cornstarch paste along with the first ¼ cup (60 ml) of hot water. The syrup should be a mass of frothing bubbles, the *chum chums* only visible when water is added to the syrup. The sweets will considerably swell in size. During the last 3 minutes, sprinkle the syrup with water every minute. Remove from the heat.

8. Soak the *chenna* boats in the syrup for 6 hours or up to 24 hours. Carefully remove each piece and drain on a cake rack. When you are ready to decorate them, remove the frosting from the refrigerator and bring it to room temperature. Hold the pastry bag at a 45-degree angle, ¼ inch (6 mm) from the pointed end. Pipe a short line toward yourself, then move the bag a little to your left; reverse the direction and pipe a second short line to the right, close to the first. Keep piping from left to right to form a thick zig-zag of icing, widest at the center and narrowing to a point at the other end. Leave a ¼-inch (6 mm) border around the edges. This will produce a tightly woven cable over the top of the *chum chum*. To finish garnishing, sprinkle a ¼-inch (6 mm) border of minced pistachios around the boat shape, bordering the frosting and meeting the edge of the cake. Once assembled, these sweets can be stored in a single layer in airtight containers, refrigerated, for up to 2 days.

Pistachio-Stuffed *Chenna* Patties in Cardamom Cream Sauce
RAS MALAI

In *Ras Malai*, simple milk and sugar are transformed into something celebratory. This dish is actually little more than flattened sponge *rasgoolas* and a sauce of milk boiled down to one-fourth its original volume (called *malai kheer*). The dish is then infused with aromatics like cardamom, saffron, rose and *kewra* flavoring, and elegantly garnished with pistachios, almonds and gossamer-thin edible foil.

This recipe is from the head chef at the Royal Palace of Bharatpur, in Uttar Pradesh. I observed him at a festival during which he oversaw an entire crew of cooks. They worked nonstop for two days, filling hundreds of red clay dishes with beautiful individual portions. This dish may be served any time of the day, from brunch to late-night supper.

Preparation and cooking time (after assembling ingredients): 1½ hours
Serves: 8

For the Sauce:

4 cups (1 liter) whole milk
1 cup (240 ml) heavy whipping cream
¼ cup (55 g) sugar
1 teaspoon (5 ml) crushed cardamom seeds

For the Stuffing:

a pinch of high-quality saffron threads
1½ tablespoons (22 ml) cream, or as necessary
1 tablespoon (15 ml) blanched raw pistachios, minced
1 tablespoon (15 ml) blanched almonds, minced
1 tablespoon (15 ml) golden raisins, minced
½ tablespoon (7 ml) honey or golden syrup

For information about unfamiliar ingredients or techniques, see A-to-Z

For the Rasgoolas:

8 cups (2 liters) whole milk
4 tablespoons (60 ml) strained lemon juice
6 cups (1.5 liters) water
5 cups (1 kg) sugar
2 teaspoons (10 ml) cornstarch mixed with 2 tablespoons water

For the Garnishes:

1½ tablespoons (22 ml) slivered raw pistachio nuts
1½ tablespoons (22 ml) slivered blanched almonds
1 tablespoon (15 ml) rose water or
  ½ teaspoon (2 ml) rose essence
1 tablespoon (15 ml) *kewra* water or
  ½ teaspoon (2 ml) *kewra* essence
two 3-inch (7.5 cm) sheets of edible silver
  or gold foil (*varak*) (optional)

1. To make the sauce, place the milk in a 5-quart/liter heavy-bottomed, nonstick pan over high heat and, stirring constantly, bring to a full boil. Continue to boil the milk vigorously, stirring occasionally, until it has been reduced to 1 cup (240 ml). Add the cream, sugar and cardamom seeds and, stirring constantly, boil for 4 minutes. Pour the sauce into a shallow serving dish at least 8 inches (20 cm) square and 1½ inches (4 cm) deep.

2. Dry-roast the saffron threads in a heavy pan over low heat until they are brittle. Powder with the back of a spoon. To make the filling, combine up to 1½ tablespoons (22 ml) cream (as necessary), nuts, raisins and sweetener in a small bowl and mash with your fingers or a fork. Wash and dry your hands, rub them with a film of oil, and divide the stuffing into 16 portions. Set aside.

3. Place the milk for the *rasgoolas* in a heavy 5-quart/liter nonstick pan over high heat and, stirring constantly, bring to a frothing boil. Reduce the heat to moderate, pour in the lemon juice, and ever-so-gently stir. Within 1 minute, soft cheese curds should separate from the yellowish whey. If the cheese has not formed by then, add up to 1 tablespoon (15 ml) more lemon juice. Remove the pan from the heat and set aside for 10 minutes.

4. Line a colander with three thicknesses of moist cheesecloth and place it in the sink. With a slotted spoon, transfer the large pieces of cheese into the colander. Pour the whey and small pieces of cheese through the strainer and add the cheese to the colander. Gather the four corners of the cheesecloth and rinse the bundle under a stream of lukewarm tap water for 10 seconds. Gently twist the cloth to extract excess moisture, then place the cheese in a colander resting in a 2-quart/liter bowl. Flatten the top, rest a salad plate on the cheese, and balance a large bowl or pan filled with water on the plate. (You can also use any other method that will exert weight on the cheese and allow it to drain.) Press the cheese anywhere from 20–45 minutes. The cheese is ready when it weighs 9½–10 ounces (270–285 g).

5. While the cheese is draining, combine the water and sugar in a heavy 5-quart/liter pan and bring to a boil over moderate heat, stirring until the sugar dissolves. Increase the heat to high and cook, uncovered, for about 5 minutes or until the temperature reaches 220°F (105°C). Reduce the heat to the lowest setting possible.

6. Unwrap the cheese and place it on a clean work surface. Roughly break it apart and press with white paper towels to extract excess moisture. Using the heel and palm of your hand, spread a small bit at a time across the work surface. Gather the cheese into a mass with a wide spatula and repeat the process again and again for up to 5 minutes or until fluffy and without a trace of graininess. Gather the cheese into a mass. Wash and dry your hands, then rub them with a film of oil. Divide the cheese into 16 portions, roll them into balls, and flatten into patties 1¼ inches (3.5 cm) in diameter. Place a portion of the pistachio stuffing in the center of each patty and pull the edges closed. Shape into seamless balls by rolling between your palms, assisting the process by pinching any seams closed, then flatten slightly into patties.

7. Bring the syrup to a boil over moderate heat. Add the patties, one by one, and gently cook for 1 minute. Raise the heat to high and then boil vigorously, covered, for 20 minutes. To keep the syrup at the same consistency throughout the boiling, pour ¼ cup (60 ml) of hot water down the sides of the pan (not on the patties) at 4-minute intervals. After the first 4 minutes, add the cornstarch paste along with the first ¼ cup (60 ml) of hot water. The syrup should be a mass of frothing bubbles, the *rasgoolas* only visible when water is added to the syrup. The balls will swell and double, triple or even quadruple in size. During the last 3 minutes, sprinkle the syrup with water every minute. Turn off the heat.

8. Very gently lift out the hot *rasgoolas* with a slotted spoon, drain momentarily, and slip them into the cardamom–cream sauce. When the balls have cooled to room temperature, cover and refrigerate for at least 6 hours or up to 3 days. Just before serving, turn the balls over, sprinkle them with nuts, rose and *kewra* flavoring, and press silver or gold foil in a few places on top. Serve in small flat dishes with the cream sauce.

Heart-Shaped Cheesecakes with Saffron Frosting
DILBHAR

Dilbhars are heart-shaped *rasgoolas*, either white or tinted yellow. They vary in size. If you prefer smaller pieces, like the size of candy, divide the cheese into 16 parts; for larger sweets, served like *patisseries*, divide the cheese into 8 portions. The cheese fudge frosting may be decoratively piped on with a pastry bag or smoothed over the top with a palate knife. This is an example of the best in Bengali sweetmaking.

Preparation and cooking time (after assembling ingredients): 1½ hours
Serves: 8

For the Frosting:

4 cups (1 liter) half-and-half
¼ cup (55 g) sugar
¼ teaspoon (1 ml) saffron threads
¼ teaspoon (1 ml) ground cardamom

For the Dilbhars:

8 cups (2 liters) whole milk
¼ cup (60 ml) strained lemon juice
a few drops natural yellow food
    coloring (optional)
7 cups (1.75 liters) water
6 cups (1.25 kg) sugar
1 tablespoon (15 ml) cornstarch, dissolved
    in 2 teaspoons (10 ml) water
raw pistachio halves for garnishing, blanched

1. Place the half-and-half and sugar in a heavy-bottomed large pan over high heat and, stirring constantly, bring to a boil. Continue to vigorously boil, stirring often, until it is reduced to 1 cup (240 ml). Powder the saffron threads and add, along with the cardamom, to the pan. Reduce the heat to moderate and, stirring constantly, cook until a thick paste forms in the middle of the pan. Transfer the saffron frosting to a plate to cool, then refrigerate, covered.

2. Place the milk in a heavy 5-quart/liter pan over high heat and, stirring constantly, bring to a frothing boil. Reduce the heat to moderate, pour in the lemon juice, and every-so-gently stir. Within a minute, soft cheese curds should separate from the yellowish whey. If the cheese has not formed by then, add up to 1 tablespoon (15 ml) more lemon juice. Remove the pan from the heat and set aside for 10 minutes.

3. Line a colander with three thicknesses of cheesecloth and place it in the sink. With a slotted spoon, transfer the large pieces of cheese into the colander. Pour the whey and small pieces of cheese through a strainer and add the cheese to the colander. Gather the four corners of the cheesecloth and rinse the bundle under a stream of lukewarm tap water for 10 seconds. Gently twist the cloth to extract excess moisture, then place the cheese in a colander resting in a 2-quart/liter bowl. Flatten the top, rest a salad plate on the cheese, and balance a large bowl or pan filled with water on the plate. (You can also use any other method that will exert weight on the cheese and allow it to drain.) Press the cheese for 20–45 minutes. The cheese is ready when it weighs 9½–10 ounces (270–285 g).

4. While the cheese is draining, combine the water and sugar in a heavy 5-quart/liter pan and bring to a boil over moderate heat, stirring until the sugar dissolves. Increase the heat to high and cook, uncovered, for about 5 minutes or until the temperature reaches 220°F (105°C). Reduce the heat to the lowest setting possible.

5. Unwrap the cheese and place it on a clean work surface. Roughly break it apart and press it with white paper towels to extract excess moisture. Using the heel and palm of your hand, spread a small bit at a time across the work surface. Gather it into a mass with a rubber spatula and continue to spread and bray again and again for about 5 minutes or until it is fluffy and silky smooth and without a trace of graininess. Add the yellow coloring, if desired, near the end. Gather the cheese into a mass. Wash and dry your hands, then rub them with a film of oil. Divide the cheese into 8 or 16 portions, as desired, and roll them into balls. Keeping your hands clean and moistened with oil, press a ball in your palm and mold it into a seamless heart shape. Round off the pointed tip slightly. Finish all the pieces in the same way.

6. Bring the syrup to a gentle boil over moderate heat. Add the patties, one by one, and cook slowly for 1 minute. Raise the heat to high and boil vigorously, covered, for 20 minutes. To keep the syrup at the same consistency throughout the boiling, pour ¼ cup

(60 ml) of water down the sides of the pan (not on the patties) at 4-minute intervals. After the first 4 minutes, add the cornstarch paste along with the first ¼ cup (60 ml) of hot water. The syrup should be a mass of frothing bubbles, the patties only visible when water is added to the syrup. The hearts will swell in size. During the last 3 minutes, sprinkle the syrup with water every minute. Remove from the heat.

7. Soak the *chenna* hearts in the syrup for at least 6 hours or up to 24 hours. Carefully remove each piece with a slotted spoon and drain on a cake rack for ½ hour. When you are ready to frost the sweets, bring the frosting to room temperature. If necessary, add enough milk to thin the mixture to a spreadable consistency. Whisk vigorously with a fork to mix well. If you use a pastry bag, fit it with a medium-sized plain nozzle. Hold the bag perpendicular to the cakes and pipe dots or flourishes according to your preference. Alternately, spread the frosting with a cold palate knife. Garnish each piece with half a pistachio nut. Serve at room temperature or chilled.

Khoa-Covered Cheese Balls Rolled in Coconut
RASKADAMBA

Raskadambas are *khoa*-frosted *rasgoolas* that have been flavored and colored with saffron and then rolled in grated coconut, *danedhar* or almonds. They are one of the most loved sweets of Bengal.

Preparation and cooking time (after assembling ingredients): 1½ hours
Serves: 8

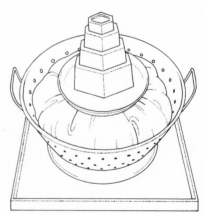

4½ cups (1 liter) half-and-half
5 tablespoons (60 g) sugar
3 drops of natural yellow food coloring (optional)
8 cups (2 liters) whole milk
¼ cup (60 ml) strained lemon juice
6 cups (1.5 liters) water
5 cups (1 kg) sugar
⅛ teaspoon (0.5 ml) powdered saffron
1 tablespoon (15 ml) cornstarch mixed
    with 2 teaspoons (10 ml) water
½ cup (45 g) grated fresh coconut, or
    ½ cup (75 g) frozen coconut,
    grated *danedhar* or almonds

1. Place the half-and-half in a large heavy-bottomed nonstick pan over high heat and, stirring constantly, bring to a boil. Cook, stirring often, until it is reduced to ¾ cup (180 ml), then lower the heat to moderate. Add the 5 tablespoons (60 g) of sugar and, stirring constantly, cook until the mixture forms a sticky mass that pulls away from the sides of the pan. Scrape all of the frosting into a bowl and, if desired, work in the food coloring with a fork until the color is uniform. Set aside to cool, then refrigerate, covered. Before using it, bring it to room temperature.

For information about unfamiliar ingredients or techniques, see A-to-Z

2. Place the milk in a heavy 5-quart/liter pan over high heat and, stirring constantly, bring to a frothing boil. Reduce the heat to moderate, pour in the lemon juice, and ever-so-gently stir. Within a minute, soft cheese curds should separate from the yellowish whey. If the cheese has not formed by then, add up to 1 tablespoon (15 ml) more lemon juice. Remove the pan from the heat and set aside for 10 minutes.

3. Line a colander with three thicknesses of moist cheesecloth and place it in the sink. With a slotted spoon, transfer the large pieces of cheese into the colander. Pour the whey and small pieces of cheese through a strainer and add them to the colander. Gather the four corners of the cheesecloth and rinse the bundle under a stream of lukewarm tap water for 10 seconds. Gently twist the cloth to extract excess moisture, then place the cheese in a colander resting in a 2-quart/liter bowl. Flatten the top, rest a salad plate on the cheese, and balance a large bowl or pan filled with water on the plate. (You can also use any other method that will exert weight on the cheese and allow it to drain.) Press the cheese for 20–45 minutes. The cheese is ready when it weighs 9½–10 ounces (270–285 g).

4. While the cheese is draining, combine the water and sugar in a heavy 5-quart/liter pan and bring to a boil over moderate heat, stirring until the sugar dissolves. Increase the heat to high and cook, uncovered, for about 5 minutes or until the temperature reaches 220°F (105°C). Reduce the heat to the lowest setting possible.

5. Unwrap the cheese and place it on a clean work surface. Roughly break it apart and press it with white paper towels to extract excess moisture. Using the heel and palm of your hand, spread a small bit at a time across the work surface. Gather the cheese into a mass with a wide spatula and repeat the process again and again for up to 5 minutes or until fluffy and without a trace of graininess. Knead in the saffron. Gather the cheese into a mass. Wash and dry your hands, then rub them with a film of oil. Divide the cheese into 8 portions and roll each one into a seamless ball.

6. Bring the syrup to a boil over moderate heat. Add the balls, one by one, and gently cook for 1 minute. Raise the heat to high and then boil vigorously, covered, for 20 minutes. To keep the syrup at the same consistency throughout the boiling, pour ¼ cup (60 ml) of hot water down the sides of the pan (not on the balls) at 4-minute intervals. After the first 4 minutes, add the cornstarch paste along with the first ¼ cup (60 ml) of hot water. The syrup should be a mass of frothing bubbles, the balls only visible when water is added. The balls will substantially swell in size. During the last 3 minutes, sprinkle the syrup with water every minute. Remove from the heat.

7. Soak the balls in syrup for at least 6 hours or up to 24 hours. Drain the balls in a colander for ½ hour. Check the consistency of the frosting; it should resemble a butter frosting. If necessary, add milk to thin it. Place the grated coconut, *danedhar* or ground almonds on a sheet of waxed paper. Spear a ball with the tip of a fork. Using a spatula, spread the frosting over the surface. When it is coated, hold it over the coconut, *danedhar* or ground almonds and sprinkle the coating over the surface. It will adhere to the frosting. Place the ball in a paper case for serving. Cover the remaining balls with frosting and coating. Refrigerate in a single layer in airtight containers for up to 2 days.

MILK FUDGES

Milk that has been cooked down until all of the water has evaporated, leaving a creamy white fudge, is called *khoa* and is the basis of the distinctive milk confections included here. Though *khoa* is somewhat time-consuming to prepare, those who take the time will find the culinary techniques fascinating and the exquisite finished dishes ample reward for their endeavors. The recipe and complete instructions for preparing *khoa* are on page 320.

Dainty Milk Fudge Confection
PERA

When milk is cooked down quickly, the *khoa* remains white; when milk is cooked down slowly, the lactic sugar caramelizes and the fudge darkens several shades. Because *pera* is nothing but *khoa* and sugar, its flavor depends on the special handling of these ingredients. *Pera* balls are often rolled in sugar while warm.

Preparation and cooking time (after assembling ingredients): 20 minutes
Makes: 24 *peras*

12 ounces (340 g) *khoa* (page 320)
      made from 8 cups (2 liters) milk
½ cup (110 g) sugar
½ teaspoon (2 ml) ground cardamom seeds
1 teaspoon (5 ml) unsalted butter or *ghee*
sugar for garnishing (optional)

1. If the *khoa* has been refrigerated, bring it to room temperature. Combine all of the ingredients, except the optional sugar for garnishing, on a marble slab or countertop and knead until thoroughly mixed and sticky. Gather up the mixture with a spatula and place it in a large heavy-bottomed nonstick frying pan over moderate heat. Stirring constantly, cook until the fudge pulls away from the sides of the pan into a soft ball.

2. Scrape the *pera* mixture onto a plate and cool until it is easy to handle. Wash and dry your hands and rub them with a film of oil. Divide the fudge into 24 portions and roll each into a smooth ball. Roll each ball in sugar, if desired, and place it in a candy case. Store in airtight containers, refrigerated, for up to 4 days.

For information about unfamiliar ingredients or techniques, see A-to-Z

Cardamom-Flavored Caramel Milk Fudge
VRINDAVAN PERA

This *pera* possesses the flavor of caramel toffee and the texture of grainy fudge. It is a specialty of Vrindavan, India, the birthsite of Lord Krishna and a Vaishnava township that boasts more than 5,000 temples. Traditionally, this variation is made with raw sugar and pressed into a 1½ inch (4 cm) diameter mold with a scrolled edge, but any candy mold of a similar size will do. It is important to shape the fudge while it is warm and pliable, because as it cools it becomes difficult to handle.

Preparation and cooking time (after assembling ingredients): 20 minutes
Makes: 24 *peras*

⅔ cup (100 g) maple or brown sugar
12 ounces (340 g) *khoa* (page 320)
    made from 8 cups (2 liters) milk
1 tablespoon (15 ml) honey or golden syrup
½ teaspoon (2 ml) ground cardamom
⅛ teaspoon (0.5 ml) freshly ground nutmeg
1 teaspoon (5 ml) unsalted butter or *ghee*

1. Place the sugar in a coffee mill or blender and grind to a powder. Combine all of the ingredients on a marble slab or countertop and knead until smooth and sticky. Gather the mass together with a spatula and transfer to a large heavy-bottomed nonstick frying pan. Place over moderate heat and cook, stirring constantly, until the mixture thickens into a soft ball that pulls away from the sides of the pan.

2. Scrape the *pera* mixture onto a plate and cool until it is easy to handle. Wash and dry your hands and rub them with a film of oil. Divide the fudge into 24 portions and roll each into a smooth ball. While still warm, press into decorative molds and set on waxed paper. When cool, store in airtight containers, refrigerated, for up to 4 days.

Pistachio Nut Milk Fudge
PISTA BURFI

Equal amounts of nuts and milk combine in this easy-to-make fudge. It is beautifully garnished with gossamer-thin sheets of edible silver foil.

Preparation and cooking time (after assembling ingredients): 30 minutes
Makes: about 1 pound (455 g)

2 cups (250 g) unsalted raw pistachios, blanched
2 cups (480 ml) milk
¾ cup (160 g) superfine sugar
1 tablespoon (15 ml) unsalted butter or *ghee*
3 drops *kewra* essence or almond oil
natural green food coloring (optional)
two 3-inch (7.5 cm) sheets of edible silver foil (*varak*) (optional)

1. Place the pistachios in a food processor fitted with the metal blade. Pulse on and off until they are powdered. (Constant processing will make the pistachios oily.) Alternately, powder the pistachios in a rotary nut grinder.

2. Combine the milk and sugar in a 5-quart/liter heavy-bottomed nonstick pan over high heat. Stirring constantly, bring to a boil and cook vigorously until it is reduced to ½ cup (120 ml). Lower the heat to moderate, add the nuts and the butter or *ghee*, and cook, stirring rhythmically and steadily, until the mixture forms a soft ball that pulls away from the sides of the pan. Remove the pan from the heat and mix in the *kewra* essence or almond oil and green food coloring, if desired.

3. Scrape the fudge onto a buttered tray and, working quickly with a buttered spatula, press and pat the mixture into a 7 x 7-inch (17.5 x 17.5 cm) square. Press the silver foils over the fudge. When it is cool, cut it into 1¼-inch (3.5 cm) squares with a sharp cold knife, wiping the knife clean after each cut. Store in airtight containers, refrigerated, for up to 2 weeks.

Coconut Toffee Balls with Nutmeg
NARIYAL DHOOD LADOO

Though Bengalis grind coconut on foot-held iron scrapers and Western cooks use electric blenders or food processors, the cooking procedure is the same and the results are equally satisfying. This recipe, from Calcutta's Sri Radha Govinda Mandir, is not actually a toffee but toffee-flavored from the sweetener (unrefined *gur*). If unavailable, substitute equal amounts of molasses and raw brown sugar.

Preparation and cooking time (after assembling ingredients): 30 minutes
Makes: about 1¼ pounds (570 g)

1½ cups (315 g) sugar
½ cup (120 ml) corn syrup
½ cup (120 ml) half-and-half
¼ cup (40 g) shredded *jaggery* or *gur*, or
    half molasses and half light brown sugar
1¼ cups (105 g) grated fresh coconut
2 tablespoons (30 ml) unsalted raw pistachios, minced
2 tablespoons (30 ml) blanched raw almonds, minced
⅓ teaspoon (1.5 ml) freshly ground nutmeg
3 tablespoons (45 ml) *ghee* or unsalted butter

1. Combine the sugar, corn syrup, half-and-half and *gur* or molasses–brown sugar mixture in a heavy medium-sized pan and place over moderate heat. Stir until the sugars dissolve, then bring to a boil, cover, and cook for 3 minutes. Reduce the heat, uncover and cook, without stirring, until the temperature reaches 238°F (114°C).

2. Remove the pan from the heat and stir in the remaining ingredients. Pour the toffee onto a buttered marble slab or platter. When it is cool enough to handle, roll into small balls.

For information about unfamiliar ingredients or techniques, see A-to-Z

Sesame Seed Toffee Balls
TILKUTA

These sesame–coconut-studded balls are specialties of the Vrindavan–Mathura district in North India, and are much sought after by pilgrims visiting the area. Further, they are seasonal—appearing on menus and in sweet shops only from November through January. It is considered a warming, nutritious dish for colder months.

Preparation and cooking time (after assembling ingredients): 30 minutes
Makes: about 1¼ pounds (570 g)

½ cup (80 g) white sesame seeds
½ cup (45 g) fresh coconut or
    ½ cup (75 g) dried grated coconut
12 ounces (340 g) *khoa* (page 320)
    made from 8 cups (2 liters) milk
1 cup (210 g) sugar
1 teaspoon (5 ml) coarsely crushed cardamom seeds
½ tablespoon (7 ml) *ghee* or butter

1. Place the sesame seeds and coconut in a heavy frying pan and fry over moderate heat, stirring constantly, until the seeds turn pale gold. Transfer to a food processor fitted with the metal blade, or a blender (divide into two batches if you use a blender), and pulse on and off until the seeds are coarsely crushed. Do not reduce to a powder.

2. Combine the *khoa*, sugar, cardamom seeds and ⅔ cup (90 g) of the sesame–coconut mixture on a marble slab or countertop and knead until thoroughly blended. (You may need to add up to 2 tablespoons/30 ml of milk to the *khoa* if it is too stiff or thick to knead into a paste.) Scrape up the sticky mass with a dough scraper or spatula and place it in a large heavy-bottomed nonstick frying pan. Add the *ghee* or butter and cook over moderate heat, stirring constantly and vigorously, until the mixture pulls away from the sides of the pan and forms a soft ball.

3. Pour the mixture onto a buttered tray. When it is cool enough to handle, roll into about 20 balls. Place them on waxed paper and sprinkle with the remaining ⅓ cup (35 g) of the sesame–coconut mixture. Place in candy papers. Store in airtight containers, refrigerated, for up to 2 weeks.

Gingered Milk Fudge Confections
ADRAK DHOOD LADOO

Here is a ginger aficionado's dream confection. You can make it creamy-smooth by using fresh ginger juice or create a textured consistency by using stem or candied ginger. The best tool for extracting ginger juice is a Japanese ginger grater, sold in either glazed stoneware or stainless steel in Japanese and better cookware stores. If you use stem ginger, flavor and sweeten the *ladoo* with a small amount of thick ginger syrup.

Preparation and cooking time (after assembling ingredients): 50 minutes
Makes: about ¾ pound (340 g)

1-inch (2.5 cm) piece scraped fresh ginger root
    (about 2 ounces/60 g), or 2 tablespoons
    (30 ml) minced, stem or candied ginger
½ teaspoon (2 ml) water
3 cups (710 ml) heavy cream
3 cups (710 ml) whole milk
⅔ cup (140 g) superfine sugar, or
    ¼ cup (60 ml) stem ginger syrup
    and ½ cup (110 g) sugar

    1. Grate the fresh ginger, catching all of the juice and pulp in a dish. Remove the pulp clinging on the grater with fork tines. Add the water and filter through a piece of muslin, squeezing out all of the juice; discard the pulp.

    2. Pour the cream and milk into a 5–6 quart/liter nonstick pan and place over high heat. Stirring rhythmically and constantly, bring the milk to a full boil. After boiling for 20 minutes, add the sweetener, reduce the heat slightly, and cook for about 15 minutes or until reduced to a thick cream sauce.

    3. Reduce the heat to moderate and, stirring vigorously and constantly, cook until the mass pulls away from the sides of the pan and is sticky. To test consistency, remove about ¼ teaspoon (1 ml) of the mixture and place it in a shallow saucer of cool water. If it holds its shape, it requires no additional cooking; if it still disintegrates, cook for a few minutes more.

    4. Remove the pan from the heat, stir in the fresh ginger juice and stem or candied ginger, if using it, and beat the thickened mass until it is velvety smooth and light-textured. Cool the mass until it is firm enough to mold. Divide into about 18 pieces, roll them into smooth balls, logs or patties, or press into decorative molds. Store in an airtight containers for up to 4 days.

Milk Fudge Cake Supreme
KULIYA

    This is not a sweet for fans of the *I Hate to Cook Book*. It is rather for those cooks who enjoy culinary challenges, who can unwind by stirring a pot of milk and listening to a favorite record. In Indian sweetshops, you pay dearly for *kuliya*; not because the ingredients are costly—mostly just milk and sugar—but because it takes time and attention to prepare. Twice a week, Vrindavan *halwais* position themselves at the front of their shops and begin the day's work of condensing huge quantities of milk. When I resided there, I would take my place among the throngs of early-evening shoppers waiting to buy the prized sweet.

    Proper equipment will keep cooking time to a minimum. For this quantity, a heavy 8-quart/liter nonstick pan is best; otherwise, the milk fudge can be condensed using two 5-quart/liter pans. You will need a pinch of citric acid crystals, available at most pharmacies. The finished result is a stately, rich milk cake with a divine flavor and texture you have likely never sampled.

For information about unfamiliar ingredients or techniques, see A-to-Z

Preparation and cooking time (after assembling ingredients): 1½–2 hours
Resting time: 8–12 hours
Makes: about 1½ pounds (685 g) or 8–12 servings

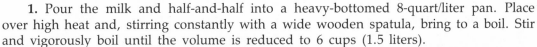

2 quarts/liters whole milk
1 quart/liter half-and-half
⅛–¼ teaspoon (0.5–1 ml) citric acid crystals, powdered
    with a small mortar and pestle or the back of a spoon
1⅓ cups (285 g) superfine sugar
1 teaspoon (5 ml) coarsely crushed cardamom seeds
one 3-inch (7.5 cm) sheet of edible gold or silver foil (*varak*) (optional)
1 tablespoon (15 ml) blanched, raw, unsalted pistachios, slivered

1. Pour the milk and half-and-half into a heavy-bottomed 8-quart/liter pan. Place over high heat and, stirring constantly with a wide wooden spatula, bring to a boil. Stir and vigorously boil until the volume is reduced to 6 cups (1.5 liters).

Alternately, pour 4 cups (1 liter) milk and 2 cups (480 ml) half-and-half into a heavy 5–6 quart/liter nonstick pan, place over high heat, and, stirring constantly with a wide wooden spatula, bring to a boil. Stir and vigorously boil the milk until it is reduced to 3 cups (710 ml); transfer to another container. Repeat with the remaining 4 cups (1 liter) milk and 2 cups (480 ml) half-and-half, reducing it to 3 cups (710 ml).

2. Transfer the condensed milk to a heavy 5-quart/liter nonstick pan over moderately high heat and, stirring constantly, sprinkle in ⅟₁₆ teaspoon (0.25 ml) of the citric acid. After 3 minutes, add another ⅟₁₆ teaspoon (0.25 ml), and continue to add in ⅟₁₆-teaspoon (0.25 ml) amounts at 3-minute intervals until very small granules of clotted cheese fleck the milk (no more than ¼ teaspoon/1 ml of citric acid in all). If the citric acid powder becomes wet, it may become ineffective, forming small pieces of cheese rather than cheese flecks. If so, remove the pan from the heat and beat with a wire whisk to break up the cheese.

3. Add the sugar and cardamom and continue to condense the milk over moderate heat, stirring rhythmically and steadily, until it is reduced to a very thick, sticky paste that begins to pull away from the sides of the pan. (The heat should be regulated to reduce the milk as rapidly as possible without scorching.) Pour into a buttered 3½-cup (830 ml) rosette mold or 1-quart/liter stainless steel bowl. Wrap the container in a heavy tea towel and set aside in a cool place for 8–12 hours.

4. To unmold the *kuliya*, loosen by partially submerging the mold in a pan of boiling water for 10–15 seconds. Gently slip a spatula or palate knife down the walls of the mold and invert onto a small serving tray or cake stand.

5. Garnish the top of the cake with edible gold or silver foil, pressing them until the surface is smooth. Sprinkle with slivered pistachios and pat gently to secure them over the foil. Cut into small wedges and serve chilled or at room temperature. Store, refrigerated, in an airtight container for up to 2 weeks.

Crème de la Crème
RABRI

Literally "cream of the cream", this is one of India's most versatile sweets. Whether eaten chilled or mixed with diced tropical fruits such as mangoes, bananas, sapodillas or custard apples, it is unforgettably delicious.

Many classic Indian recipes are based on weight or volume relationships. For example, a classic ratio for *Rabri* is 1 part sugar to 8 parts milk. No matter what the quantity, the ratio remains the same. *Rabri* is best made in a bowl-shaped pan—a wok or *karai*—preferably with a nonstick surface. The pan's broad surface area helps in rapid evaporation. Serve in small shallow bowls and sip, or eat with dessert spoons.

Preparation and cooking time (after assembling ingredients): about 30 minutes
Chilling time: at least 2 hours
Serves: 4

4 cups (1 liter) whole milk
4 tablespoons (55 g) sugar
½ teaspoon (2 ml) crushed cardamom seeds
3 tablespoons (45 ml) *kewra* essence
    or 1 tablespoon (15 ml) rose water
2 tablespoons (30 ml) blanched, raw,
    unsalted pistachios, finely chopped

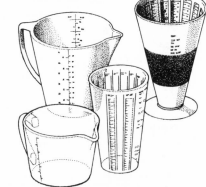

   1. Pour the milk into a bowl-shaped pan and place it over high heat. Stirring constantly, bring to a full boil. Boil briskly for about 5 minutes.

   2. Reduce the heat to moderate and, without stirring, allow the milk to boil gently. While fanning the surface of the milk with the left hand, pull a wooden spoon across the surface to collect the thin skins of cream that form from time to time. Pull them up the side of the pan above the surface of the milk and collect them all around the top sloping edges of the pan. Stir the bottom of the pan occasionally to keep the milk from sticking. As the milk condenses, stir more frequently. Continue fanning and collecting the skins of cream until the volume is only one-quarter of the original. Add the sweetener and cardamom seeds and let the milk simmer for about 3 minutes more.

   3. Remove the pan from the heat, cool, and scrape all the layers of cream from the sides of the pan into the sweetened condensed milk. Mix well. Cool the mixture to room temperature, stir in the *kewra* or rose water, and refrigerate until cold. Garnish the servings with a sprinkle of pistachios.

SYRUP SWEETS

Jalebis are just one of many amazing syrup sweets descending from the ancient Vedic cuisine. These sweets vary widely in texture, taste and appearance. Some, such as *jalebis*, are saffron-colored, light, juicy and slightly crunchy. Others are golden brown and so soft that they literally melt in your mouth. Still others have pale golden crusts and are stuffed with nuts and dried fruit and then drizzled with a trace of scented syrup.

What these uncommon sweets have in common is, first, sugar syrup. Unlike more dense candy syrups with a standard ratio of 8 parts sugar to 1 part water, they are fairly low in sugar content. There are four standard syrups: light syrup (1 part sugar to 2 parts water); medium syrup (1 part sugar to 1½ parts water); medium-heavy syrup (1 part sugar to 1 part water); and heavy syrup (2 parts sugar to 1 part water). These are often called stock syrups, or *sops*. More often than not, they are infused with aromatic scents such as cardamom, rose, saffron, *kewra*, *khus*, or sandalwood. Secondly, the sweets are almost always cooked in *ghee*. Many purists will not even consider making these dishes in anything but *ghee*—no more than a French baker would ever layer croissants with vegetable shortening. If you do wish to delve into the use of an alternative light vegetable or nut oil, it must be fresh and not previously used.

Sweet Rose-Flavored Crêpes with Fennel Seeds
MALPOORA

Classic North Indian *malpooras* bear a faint resemblance to French crêpes, though they are shallow-fried, slightly smaller and thicker, and made from an egg-free batter. Once cooked, they are handled something like *crêpes suzettes* in that they are briefly heated in a sweet sauce, suffusing them with delicate aromatic flavors. In the winter, this dish is made in front of sweet shops, beckoning passersby with its buttery sweet aromas.

A lighter, more contemporary version—made with less butter and sugar—is becoming increasingly popular. This lighter batter combines *chapati* or whole wheat pastry flour, unbleached white flour, cornstarch and semolina for flavor and ease in handling, yet still incorporates the traditional flavors of fennel and cardamon for authenticity. *Malpooras* are cooked like crêpes, in a barely-buttered omelet or crêpe pan over high heat. Instead of soaking the *malpooras* in syrup, a spoonful of sliced fruit is placed just off the center, and then they are then folded in half or rolled up, placed in a gratin dish, drizzled with rose-flavored syrup, and briefly warmed before serving.

Preparation time (after assembling ingredients): 5 minutes
Batter resting time: 1 hour
Cooking time: 20–30 minutes
Makes: 12 *malpooras*

⅔ cup (95 g) sieved *chapati* flour
    or ⅔ cup (75 g) whole wheat pastry flour
⅓ cup (60 g) fine semolina
4 tablespoons (30 g) cornstarch
4 tablespoons (30 g) unbleached flour
2 tablespoons (30 ml) dried milk powder
½ tablespoon (7 ml) fennel seeds
¼ teaspoon (1 ml) cardamom seeds
⅛ teaspoon (0.5 ml) salt
2 tablespoons (30 ml) melted *ghee* or butter
1¼ cups (300 ml) water, or as needed
about 1½ cups (360 ml) coarsely mashed
    mangoes, papayas or nectarines, or
    thinly sliced apples sautéed until soft
1 tablespoon (15 ml) rose water
½ cup (120 ml) warm maple syrup,
    golden syrup or light honey

1. Combine the *chapati* or wheat flour, semolina, cornstarch, unbleached flour, milk powder, fennel seeds, cardamom seeds and salt in a food processor fitted with the metal blade, or a blender. Cover and process until the spice seeds are coarsely crushed. Add 1 tablespoon (15 ml) *ghee* or butter and, with the motor running, slowly pour in the water (you may need to use more or less) and process to a smooth batter with a cream-like consistency. Transfer to a large glass measuring cup, cover with plastic wrap, and set aside for at least 1 hour. It may be refrigerated for up to 8 hours and returned to room temperature before use.

2. Check the batter consistency; it should put a thin coating on a spoon. Place a 7-inch (18 cm) nonstick omelet pan over moderate heat. Working with two pans at a time will speed up the process. Using a folded paper towel or a pastry brush, spread a film of *ghee* or butter in the pan. When it is hot, pour a scant ¼ cup (60 ml) of batter into the pan. Immediately tilt and roll the pan back and forth until the base is covered with a thin 6-inch (15 cm) film of batter; pour the excess back into the bowl. Replace the pan over the heat and cook until the upper surface looks dry and the edges begin to curl (30–40 seconds).

Using your fingers or a spatula, flip it over and cook until brown flecks mark the surface. While still in the pan, place 1½ tablespoons (22 ml) of fruit just off of the center of the *malpoora*, fold it over to make a half circle, and slip it directly onto a buttered gratin or shallow serving platter. Finish cooking the remaining *malpooras* in the same way. They can be made up to this point several hours before serving. Cover and refrigerate, then bring to room temperature before warming.

3. Add the rose water to the warmed syrup or honey and spoon it over the *malpooras*. Bake in a 350°F (180°C) oven for about 10 minutes to warm. Serve immediately.

For information about unfamiliar ingredients or techniques, see A-to-Z

Cake-Like Fried Milk Balls in Scented Syrup
GULAB JAMUN

The dough for this dish takes only minutes to assemble, but the balls must be fried very slowly under carefully controlled temperatures. Some recipes increase the flour content in order to minimize the importance of the heat regulation; but the less flour there is in the dough, the better the quality of the *gulab jamun*. If the balls are browned too quickly or not fried long enough, they tend to collapse in the sugar syrup. Because the balls must be constantly agitated while they fry, unplug the phone, pull up a stool, and put on your favorite record.

Gulab jamuns are good sweets for festive moments, such as holidays and entertaining. They may be served warm or at room temperature.

Preparation and cooking time (after assembling ingredients): about 45 minutes
Makes: 24 *gulab jamuns*

2½ cups (600 ml) water
2¼ cups (480 g) sugar
1 tablespoon (15 ml) rose water or
    ½ teaspoon (2 ml) rose essence
ghee for deep-frying
2 cups (195 g) instant nonfat dried milk powder
1½ tablespoons (22 ml) self-rising flour
½ cup (120 ml) warm milk, or as needed
1 teaspoon (5 ml) *ghee* or unsalted butter

1. Combine the water and sugar in a 3-quart/liter pan over moderate heat and stir constantly until the sugar is dissolved. Raise the heat to high and boil for 5 minutes. Remove the pan from the heat, stir in the rose water or essence, and set aside.

2. Pour *ghee* to a depth of 2½–3 inches (6.7–7.5 cm) in any deep-frying vessel at least 10 inches (25 cm) in diameter. (A bowl-shaped *karai* or wok makes the best use of the frying medium.) Place over very low heat while making your dough.

3. Brush a plate with a film of oil. Place the milk powder and flour on a sheet of waxed paper or in a small bowl and mix thoroughly. Combine the warm milk and 1 teaspoon (5 ml) *ghee* or butter in a large mixing bowl. While sprinkling in the dry mixture with one hand, stir with your other hand to quickly mix into a pliable dough. Working quickly, wash and dry your hands and rub them with a film of oil. Divide the dough into 24 portions and, exerting gentle pressure, roll each portion between your palms into a smooth ball. Place the balls on a plate.

4. Raise the heat to moderately low and when the *ghee* reaches 215°F (102°C), slip in the balls, one by one. They will sink to the bottom of the pan, but do not try to move them. Instead, gently shake the pan to keep the balls from browning on just one side. After about 5 minutes, the balls will rise to the surface. Now they must be gently and constantly agitated with a wooden spoon to ensure even browning. After 5 minutes, the temperature should increase to 220°F (104°C); after 10 minutes, to 225°F (107°C); after 15 minutes, to 230°F (110°C). After 25 minutes, the balls should be golden brown and the temperature between 245°–250°F (118°–121°C).

Remove one ball and slip it into the syrup. If it does not collapse within 3 minutes, add the remaining balls. Otherwise, fry the balls for about 5 minutes more. The balls should soak in the syrup for at least 2 hours before serving and may be stored, well sealed and refrigerated, for up to 4 days. Return to room temperature or warm before serving.

Chenna and Powdered Milk Pastries in Cardamom Syrup
PANTOAH

The success of this dish lies in the moisture content and weight of the fresh *chenna*. Six cups (1.5 liters) of milk should yield 6½ ounces (185 g) of *chenna* cheese.

Preparation and cooking time (after assembling ingredients): 1½ hours
Makes: 18 logs

6 cups (1.5 liters) whole milk
3 tablespoons (45 ml) strained lemon juice
2 cups (480 ml) water
2 cups (425 g) sugar
1 teaspoon (5 ml) crushed cardamom seeds
1 cup (100 g) instant nonfat dried milk powder
1½ tablespoons (22 ml) self-rising flour
ghee for deep-frying

1. Place the milk in a heavy 5-quart/liter pan over high heat and, stirring constantly, bring to a frothing boil. Reduce the heat to moderate, pour in the lemon juice, and ever-so-gently stir. Within a minute, soft white cheese curds should separate from the yellowish whey. If the cheese has not formed by then, add up to 1 tablespoon (15 ml) more lemon juice. Remove the pan from the heat and set aside for 10 minutes.

2. Line a colander with three thicknesses of cheesecloth and place it in the sink. With a slotted spoon, transfer the large pieces of cheese into the colander. Pour the whey and small pieces of cheese through a strainer and add the cheese to the colander. Gather the four corners of the cheesecloth and rinse the bundle under a stream of lukewarm tap water for 10 seconds. Twist the cloth to extract excess moisture, then place the cheese in a colander resting in a 2-quart/liter bowl. Flatten the top, rest a salad plate on the cheese, and balance a large bowl or pan filled with water on the plate. (You can also use any other method that will exert weight on the cheese and allow it to drain.) Press the cheese for 20–30 minutes or until it weighs 6½ ounces (185 g).

3. While the cheese is draining, combine the water, sugar, and cardamom seeds in a heavy 5 quart/liter pan and bring to a boil over moderate heat, stirring until the sugar dissolves. Increase the heat to high and cook, uncovered, for about 5 minutes or until the temperature reaches 220°F (105°C). Remove the pan from the heat.

4. Combine the milk powder and flour and mix well. Unwrap the cheese and place it on a clean work surface. Roughly break it apart and press it with white paper towels to extract excess moisture. Using the heel and palm of your hand, spread it out across the work surface, a small bit at a time. Gather the cheese into a mass with a wide spatula and repeat the process again and again for about 5 minutes. Gather all of the cheese into a mass. Knead in the dry ingredients. Wash and dry your hands and rub them with a film of oil. Divide the cheese into 18 portions and roll each into a seamless log 2 inches (5 cm) long.

5. Pour *ghee* to a depth of 3 inches (7.5 cm) in a deep-frying pan at least 10 inches (25 cm) in diameter. Place over very low heat, and when the temperature reaches 230°F (110°C), slip in the logs, one by one. They will sink to the bottom of the pan. Do not try to move the logs. Instead, gently shake the pan to keep them from browning on just one

---

For information about unfamiliar ingredients or techniques, see A-to-Z

side. After about 5 minutes, the logs will rise to the surface. Now they must be gently and constantly agitated with a wooden spoon to ensure even browning. Every 5 minutes, the temperature should increase: after 10 minutes, to 235°F (113°C); after 15 minutes, to 240°F (116°C). After 20–25 minutes, the logs should be golden brown and the temperature between 250°–255°F (121°–124°C).

Remove one log and slip it into the syrup. If it does not collapse within 3 minutes, add the remaining logs. Otherwise, fry the logs for about 5 minutes more. The logs should soak in the syrup for at least 2 hours before serving and may be stored, well sealed and refrigerated, for up to 4 days. Return to room temperature or warm before serving.

Deep-Fried Pretzel-Shaped Loops in Saffron Syrup
JALEBI

Jalebis are a striking dessert with their impressive shape, brilliant color and intriguing texture. Though the fried loops do not take long to cook, the batter must be started at least 18 hours before it is required. A simple flour–water mixture is allowed to ferment slightly and become what the French call *en ruban*—when the batter falls from a spoon, it flows in a broad solid band, without breaking. The consistency appears gooey and somewhat gelatinous when whisked.

The batter is forced through a plain nozzle of a pastry bag, the arm and hand rhythmically moving over the surface of the hot *ghee*, forming interlocking three-ring spirals or double figure-eights, either individually or in a chain. After they are fried on both sides until golden and crisp, the *jalebis* are submerged for several seconds in a hot saffron-scented syrup, which saturates their hollow insides.

Although skill is required to master the uniform shapes of *jalebis*, novice squiggles will taste just as good. If you are new to making *jalebis*, call in a helper to soak the sweets while you shape them and keep the heat regulated. This is a wonderful dessert for buffet entertaining. With only two burners and two people, batch after batch can be turned out in no time.

Preparation time (after assembling ingredients): 15 minutes
Batter resting time: 18–24 hours
Cooking time: 25–30 minutes
Serves: 6 to 8

2 cups (235 g) unbleached white flour
1½ tablespoons (22 ml) fine-grained
    semolina or rice flour
¼ teaspoon (1 ml) baking powder
2 tablespoons (30 ml) plain yogurt
1¼ cups (300 ml) warm water (100°F/38°C)
½ teaspoon (2 ml) saffron threads,
    slowly dry-roasted and powdered
3 cups (635 g) sugar
2⅔ cups (630 ml) water
1½ tablespoons (22 ml) *kewra* water,
    rose water or orange flower water
ghee or vegetable oil for deep-frying

1. Combine the white flour, semolina or rice flour, baking powder, yogurt and ¾ cup (180 ml) of the warm water in a ceramic bowl. Mix well with a whisk, then add the remaining water and ⅛ teaspoon (0.5 ml) of the powdered saffron, and whisk until smooth. Cover with a clean tea towel and set aside in a warm nook (80°-85°F/26°-32°C) for 18–24 hours. The batter should ferment slightly and appear *en ruban*, as described above.

2. Combine the sugar, remaining saffron powder and water in a 3-quart/liter sauté pan and place over moderate heat. Stir until the sugar dissolves, then raise the heat to high and boil for 8 minutes. Remove the pan from the heat and stir in the scented water.

3. Arrange a cake rack resting on a baking tray near the frying area. Heat *ghee* or oil to a depth of 1½ inches (4 cm) in a large electric frying pan, *paella* pan or skillet until it reaches 355°F (180°C). While it is heating, pour 1–1½ cups (240–360 ml) of batter into a pastry bag or squeeze bottle. To shape the *jalebis*, hold the pastry bag in one hand and direct it with the other. Squeezing the batter into the hot oil, shape three-ring connecting spirals or loose double figure-eights, each piece about 2 x 3-inches (5 x 7.5 cm) wide. Fry for about 30 seconds on the first side and 20–30 seconds on the second side or until they turn crisp and just begin to brown. (You will have to turn them the moment you finish shaping them. Do not allow the loops to brown.)

Using a slotted spoon, lift the fried *jalebis* out of the oil and drop them into the hot syrup. With another slotted spoon, submerge them for 15–20 seconds in the syrup to allow the hollow centers to fill with syrup while the outsides remain crisp. (If they soak too long, they will become limp.) Transfer with a slotted spoon to a cake rack to drain. Shape, fry, soak and drain the remaining *jalebis*. Serve immediately.

Super-Flaky Pastry Swirls with Cardamom Glaze
BALUSHAI

Unlike their western counterparts, Vedic pastries are fried, not baked, and the proportions of their butter–flour content determine how the pastries should be cooked. For example, kneaded doughs with a low butter content should be rolled thin and fried quickly. Richer pastry doughs with a higher butter content can be rolled thicker and fried more slowly.

This North Indian pastry is very flaky. It is given a boost of lightness by the combination of yogurt (an acid) and soda (a leavening agent). When these two ingredients combine, they form one of the lightest of pastry crumbs. Though *balushais* are often coated with a thick sugar syrup, I have suggested a light milk glaze instead, more like the type that coats glazed doughnuts.

Preparation time (after assembling ingredients): 20 minutes
Dough resting time: 30 minutes
Frying time: 20–25 minutes
Makes: 12 *balushais*

For information about unfamiliar ingredients or techniques, see A-to-Z

2 cups (235 g) unbleached white flour
½ teaspoon (2 ml) salt
½ tablespoon (7 ml) sugar
½ teaspoon (2 ml) baking powder
1 teaspoon (5 ml) baking soda
⅛ teaspoon (0.5 ml) each freshly ground
    pepper and nutmeg
4 tablespoons (60 ml) melted *ghee*
    or unsalted butter
⅓ cup (80 ml) plain yogurt or thick
    buttermilk, at room temperature
water, as needed
ghee or vegetable oil for deep-frying
⅔ cup (60 g) confectioners' sugar
1 tablespoon (15 ml) hot milk
1 teaspoon (5 ml) rose or *kewra* water
two 3-inch (7.5 cm) sheets of edible silver
    foil (*varak*) for garnishing (optional)
2 tablespoons (30 ml) blanched, unsalted
    pistachios, slivered

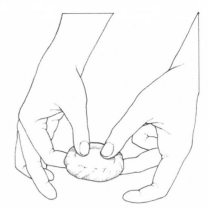

1. Mix the flour, salt, sugar, baking powder, baking soda, black pepper and nutmeg in a mixing bowl. Sprinkle in the melted *ghee* or butter and rub the mixture between your fingers until it resembles the consistency of dry oatmeal. Blend the yogurt and ¼ cup (60 ml) of water in a small cup and pour it into the dry ingredients with one hand, mixing it in with the other. Gather the ingredients into a ball, adding sprinkles of warm water, if necessary, until the dough adheres into a rough mass. Knead it until you have a smooth medium-soft dough. Divide the dough into 12 pieces. Drape the pieces with a damp cloth during shaping to prevent them from drying out.

2. To shape the pastries, roll each piece of dough between your palms into a ball. Continue rolling, exerting firm pressure so that the outside edges begin to slightly crease into tiny ridges, from the center of the ball. Using your thumb and forefinger, slightly flatten the center of each patty so it is thinner than at the edges.

3. Heat *ghee* or oil to a depth of 3 inches (7.5 cm) in a *karai*, wok or deep-frying pan over moderate heat until the temperature reaches 375°F (190°C). Remove the pan from the heat and immediately slip in 6 pastries or as many as will fit in the pan in a single layer without crowding. Allow the pastries to fry heat until the temperature drops to 320°F (160°C) and the oil stops boiling. Place the pan over moderately low heat and fry slowly, maintaining the temperature at 320°C (160°C), for 10–12 minutes. As the *balushais* turn golden brown, turn them over. Remove with a slotted spoon and drain on a cake rack resting over a baking tray. Fry the remaining pieces in the same way.

4. To make a glaze, mix the sugar, milk and rose or *kewra* water in a small dish until smooth. Spoon it over the pastries while still warm. Press a small piece of edible silver foil in the center and sprinkle with pistachio slivers. Air-dry until the glaze sets and is no longer tacky. Store between layers of waxed paper or parchment in a well sealed container for up to 1 week.

Glazed Flower Blossom Pastries
KHAJA

This classic Bengali pastry is made with a thin, strudel-type dough. Rather than encasing a filling, the sheet of dough is brushed with a cardamom and rose-flavored butter and rolled up into a tight, multi-layered scroll. Small pieces are cut off and flattened into patties. As they shallow-fry, the layers open up and blossom. When they are brown and crispy, they are hand-dipped in thick *kewra* syrup and garnished with minced pistachios.

The dough is best made with bread flour milled from hard wheat, or unbleached white flour. The *khajas* must be fried in *ghee*; a pound (455 g) is needed for this recipe. Finally, the flavoring agents—cardamom, rose essence (*ruh gulab*) and *kewra* essence (*ruh kewra*)—are available at Indian and Middle Eastern grocery stores. In a pinch, you could substitute a cardamom and orange flower water mixture.

No guest is allowed to leave a Vaishnava home without relishing a taste of this loved treat. It is a tradition I thoroughly recommend introducing into the Western world.

Preparation time: 1½ hours
Dough resting time: 2 hours
Cooking time: 40 minutes
Makes: 36 pieces

3 cups (355 g) bread flour or
    unbleached white flour
½ teaspoon (2 ml) each sugar and salt
1 tablespoon (15 ml) warm *ghee*
¾ cup (180 ml) lukewarm water
6 tablespoons (90 ml) unsalted butter,
    at room temperature
5 tablespoons (40 g) cornstarch,
    plus additional for dusting
¼ teaspoon (1 ml) baking soda
1 teaspoon (5 ml) ground cardamom
½ teaspoon (2 ml) rose essence or
    1½ teaspoons (7 ml) rose water
1¼ cups (300 ml) rose water or water
1½ cups (315 g) sugar
3 tablespoons (45 ml) honey or golden syrup
¼ teaspoon (1 ml) *kewra* essence or
    ½ teaspoon (2 ml) *kewra* water
2 cups (480 ml) *ghee* for deep-frying
4 tablespoons (35 g) blanched raw pistachios, minced
two 3-inch (7.5 cm) pieces of edible silver
    or gold foil (*varak*) (optional)

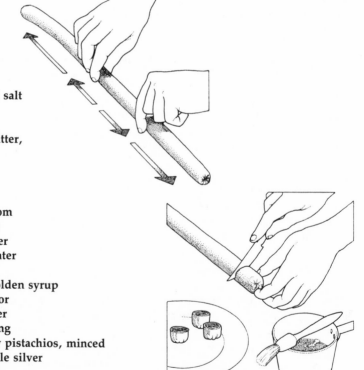

1. Blend the flour, sugar and salt in a bowl. Mix 1 tablespoon (15 ml) *ghee* with the water, pour it into the dry ingredients, and quickly stir to gather it into a ball. (If necessary, sprinkle in up to 2 additional tablespoons/30 ml of water to make a medium-stiff dough.) Knead the dough for about 15 minutes until silky smooth.

Alternately, fit a food processor with the metal blade, add the flour, sugar, salt and *ghee*, and pulse several times until blended. With the machine running, slowly pour in

For information about unfamiliar ingredients or techniques, see A-to-Z

the water (you may need approximately ¾ cup/180 ml more to make a medium-stiff dough) until the dough partially forms a ball with pea-sized globules around the edges. Redistribute the dough and process two or three more times, until it is satiny.

2. Cream the butter, cornstarch, baking soda, cardamom and rose essence well.

3. Divide the dough into three equal portions and roll each into a smooth ball. Cover two portions. Working on a cool countertop or marble slab, roll out a portion into an evenly thin sheet about 10 x 16 inches (25 x 40 cm), using an occasional dusting of flour, as necessary, to facilitate the rolling. Dust both sides with a thin layer of corn-starch and continue to ease the dough into a 12½ x 18½-inch (31.5 x 46.5 cm) thin rectangle. (Roll the dough from the center outward in all directions.) Trim the edges with a sharp knife to make a 12 x 18-inch (30–45 cm) rectangle. Using a pastry brush, carefully spread one-third of the flavored butter mixture to within ½ inch (1.5 cm) of the edges. Roll the dough into a tight scroll 12 inches (30 cm) wide. Gently squeeze the cylinder from the center toward the ends, stretching and compacting it into a rope 18 inches (45 cm) long. (Work slowly to avoid tearing the thin dough.) Slightly moisten your fingertips with water and pinch both ends closed. Cover the rope with a damp towel and shape the remaining two portions of dough.

4. Score a pastry log into 12 portions, each about 1½ inches (4 cm) long. Using a sharp knife, cut off a piece and set it, pinched side down, on a plate. To make the second piece, pinch the left end (the edge just cut) closed and cut on the second score mark. Set it on the plate, pinched side down. Continue to pinch and cut each piece, shaping 36 pieces from the three ropes. Press each piece between your thumbs and forefingers to ease the pastry into a patty 2 inches (5 cm) in diameter. Cover with plastic

5. To make the syrup, combine the rose water or water and sugar in a heavy-bottomed pan and place over moderate heat. Stir until the sugar dissolves. With a pastry brush dipped in hot water, brush the sides of the pan to dissolve any sugar crystals. Raise the heat slightly and bring the syrup to a boil. Cook for 12–15 minutes or until the temperature reaches 244°C (117°C). Remove the pan from the heat and add the honey or golden syrup and the *kewra* essence or water. Keep warm over the lowest possible heat.

6. Set two cake racks over two plates. Heat the *ghee* in a frying pan over moderate heat. When it reaches 240°F (115°C), slip in 6 of the pastries, seam side down. Fry for 3–4 minutes on each side or until crisp and golden brown. Drain on a cake rack. While the next 6 pastries are frying, dip each piece in the syrup and soak for 1 minute, then lift it out and drain it on the second cake rack. While the syrup is sticky, dip the pastries in the minced nuts and garnish the top with a tiny piece of silver foil. Fry, soak, and garnish the remaining pastries. Store in pastry cases in airtight containers, at room temperature, for up to 2 weeks.

Stuffed Pastries with Lemon Milk Glaze
KANTI

In Bengal, there are many ways to make *kanti*. Shapes vary from half-moons or triangles to full pleated circles. They can be filled with cooked fresh fruits, honeyed dry fruit and nut mixtures, or fluffy semolina-based *halvas*. This classic variation from the town of Navadwipa features flaked fresh coconut and crumbled *khoa*. After frying, the top is drizzled with a sweet lemon zest–milk glaze.

Preparation and frying time (after assembling ingredients): 1 hour
Makes: 14 pieces

1¼ cups (150 g) unbleached white flour
¼ teaspoon (1 ml) salt
¼ teaspoon (1 ml) sugar
⅛ teaspoon (0.5 ml) baking soda
3 tablespoons (45 ml) melted *ghee*
    or unsalted butter
about ⅓ cup (80 ml) water
1½ cups (130 g) grated fresh coconut or
    frozen coconut (215 g), defrosted, lightly packed
½ cup (110 g) sugar
2 tablespoons (30 ml) finely chopped almonds
2 tablespoons (30 ml) chopped raisins
1 teaspoon (5 ml) lemon zest
½ teaspoon (2 ml) crushed cardamom seeds
3 ounces (85 g) fresh *khoa* (page 320)
    made from 2 cups (480 ml) milk
⅓ cup (30 g) confectioners' sugar
½ tablespoon (7 ml) strained lemon juice
½ teaspoon (2 ml) grated lemon zest
½ tablespoon (7 ml) milk
ghee or vegetable oil for deep-frying

1. Place the flour, salt, ¼ teaspoon (1 ml) sugar and baking soda in a food processor fitted with the metal blade. Pulse three times. Add the *ghee* or butter and process for 8–10 seconds or until the mixture resembles coarse crumbs. (To mix by hand, combine the dry ingredients in a large mixing bowl. Using your fingers, cut in the *ghee* or butter until the mixture resembles coarse crumbs.) With the processor running, add the water in a slow stream just until the dough holds together; do not process for more than 40 seconds. You want a firm dough, not one that is soft or wet. Transfer the dough to a piece of plastic wrap and form into a smooth ball. Wrap tightly and set aside while making the stuffing and glaze.

2. Combine the coconut, sugar, almonds, raisins, 1 teaspoon (5 ml) lemon zest and cardamom seeds in a nonstick frying pan and cook until the mixture is dry and sticky. Remove the pan from the heat and cool to room temperature. If the *khoa* is firm, shred it through the large holes of a hand grater; if it is soft, crumble it into small bits. Add it to the coconut mixture and blend well. Divide into 14 portions and mold them into patties. Set aside, covered with plastic wrap.

For information about unfamiliar ingredients or techniques, see A-to-Z

3. Combine the confectioners' sugar, lemon juice, ½ teaspoon (2 ml) lemon zest and milk in a small bowl and mix until smooth.

4. To make the stuffed pastries, divide the dough into 28 pieces. Roll them into smooth balls and cover with a damp towel. One by one, pat each ball into a patty, dip it in flour on both sides, and roll it into an evenly thick round about 3½ inches (9 cm) in diameter. Place a portion of stuffing in the center, easing it to within ½ inch (1.5 cm) of the edges. Dip your finger in water and moisten the ½-inch (1.5 cm) border. Place another pastry round over the flling and press well to seal the edges. Pleat by hand or press the edges with fork tongs. (If the edges are not well sealed, the stuffing will ooze out during the frying.) Set aside on a wax paper-lined cookie sheet and roll, stuff and seal the remaining pieces.

6. Pour *ghee* or vegetable oil to a depth of 2 inches (5 cm) in a deep-frying vessel. Place over moderate heat until the temperature reaches about 360°F (180°C). Carefully slip in 4 pastries or as many as will float on the surface without crowding. The temperature will fall to about 330°F (165°C). Slowly raise the temperature again to 360°F (180°C) and fry until the pastries are golden brown on both sides.

7. Transfer the pastries to paper towels to drain. Fry the remaining pieces, and, while still warm, brush or spoon the tops with the glaze.

Melt-in-Your-Mouth Chickpea Flour Fudge
MYSORE PAK

This elegant, rich fudge is one of South India's most famous sweets. Its distinction is its crumbly texture, achieved by slowly adding toasted chickpea flour into a buttery sugar syrup and rhythmically stirring to the point of frothing.

Preparation and cooking time (after assembling ingredients): about 40 minutes
Makes: about 1¼ pounds (570 g)

⅔ cup (60 g) chickpea flour (sifted before measuring)
2 cups (425 g) sugar
1 cup (240 ml) cold water
1 cup (240 ml) *ghee* or unsalted butter
1 teaspoon (5 ml) cardamom seeds, coarsely crushed
2 tablespoons (30 ml) toasted sliced almonds
2 tablespoons (30 ml) sliced raw pistachios

1. Butter a 9-inch (22.5 cm) square or 6 x 12-inch (15 x 30 cm) baking pan. Place the chickpea flour in a heavy-bottomed nonstick frying pan over moderate heat. Toast, stirring constantly, until the flour darkens one or two shades and gives off a nutty smell, about 5–6 minutes. Sift again, then transfer to a pyrex glass measuring cup.

2. Combine the sugar, water and *ghee* or butter in a heavy-bottomed 3-quart/liter pan and place over moderate heat. Stir constantly until the sugar dissolves, then raise the heat and bring to a boil. Cook until the syrup reaches 240°F (115°C).

3. Reduce the heat to moderately low, and, stirring constantly and rythmically, sprinkle in the chickpea flour, a small amount at a time, over a period of 5 minutes. Add the crushed cardamom. From this point on, the mixture continues to thicken and begins to froth in places, taking on a lighter color. Continue to cook, stirring constantly, for another 5–8 minutes until the mixture foams and appears thick and silky smooth.

4. Immediately pour the mixture into the buttered pan, smooth the surface with a spatula, and sprinkle with almonds and pistachios. Cool for about 4 minutes, then cut it into 1¼-inch (3.5 cm) squares before it hardens. Store at room temperature in an airtight container for up to a month.

Flaky Pastry Diamonds with Fennel Milk Glaze
GAJA

Bengali *gajas*, both salty and sweet, are diamond-shaped deep-fried pastries. The two most popular flavorings are *kalonji* and fennel seeds, though sesame seeds, caraway seeds and black pepper are also used. In Vrindavan, during the *Kartikka* season (October-November), this is a traditional sweet to offer guests, and when Srila Prabhupada spent *Kartikka* there, I always arranged for them to be on hand for him to distribute.

Resting time: ½ hour
Preparation and cooking time (after assembling ingredients): 45 minutes
 Makes: 2 dozen

1⅔ cups (200 g) unbleached white flour,
   or 1 cup (120 g) white flour and ⅔ cup
   (75 g) whole wheat pastry flour
1¼ teaspoons (6 ml) baking powder
3 tablespoons (45 ml) sugar
¼ teaspoon (1 ml) salt
½ tablespoon (7 ml) coarsely cracked pepper
1 tablespoon (15 ml) crushed fennel seeds
3 tablespoons (45 ml) *ghee* or unsalted butter
½ cup (120 ml) milk, or as needed
¾ cup (70 g) confectioner's sugar
½ teaspoon (2 ml) each ground
   cardamom seeds and fennel seeds
2 tablespoons (30 ml) milk
ghee or vegetable oil for frying

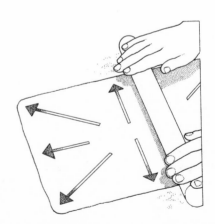

1. Combine the flour(s), baking powder, sugar, salt, crushed pepper and fennel seeds in a large bowl. Add the *ghee* or butter and rub the mixture between your palms until the texture resembles coarse bread crumbs. Add the milk, stirring briskly, and gather the mixture into a rough dough. Knead the dough, adding additional sprinkles of milk or flour, as necessary, until you have a medium-consistency, smooth dough. Gather the dough into a round ball, cover, and set aside to rest for ½ hour.

For information about unfamiliar ingredients or techniques, see A-to-Z

2. Place the sugar, ground cardamom, ground fennel and milk in a bowl and mix until smooth. Roll the dough on a lightly floured work surface until it is about ¼ inch (6 mm) thick. Cut it into 1 x 2-inch (2.5 x 5 cm) long diamonds. Heat *ghee* or oil to a depth of 2 inches (5 cm) over moderate heat in a large sauté pan until the temperature reaches 360°F (180°C). Remove the pan from the heat, add the diamonds (as many as will fit in a single layer) and, when the temperature reaches 310°F (155°C), place it back over the heat. Maintaining the temperature at about 320°F (160°C), fry until golden brown on both sides, 5–6 minutes in all. Transfer to a cake rack resting on a plate. Using a fork, place the diamonds in a single layer. While they are warm, spoon the frosting over them and then cool to room temperature. Store in an airtight container for up to 2 weeks.

CLASSIC MILK PUDDINGS

The most popular name for India's condensed milk puddings is *kheer*, though regional variations are also known as *payasa, basundi, kushmanda, payesh* and *phirni*, to name a few. The ancient Sanskrit scriptures relate that some of these classic dishes were offered to Lord Krishna thousands of years ago. Today, temples across the subcontinent prepare these same recipes, passed from generation to generation for centuries.

The Sanskrit word for *kheer* is *ksira*. (There is a Deity of Lord Krishna in Remuna known as *"Ksira-cora Gopinath,"* or *"Krishna, the Sweet Rice Thief,"* because He once "stole" a pot of *ksira* as a gift for his devotee Madhavendra Puri.) The simplest form of *kheer* is nothing more than milk that has been sweetened and reduced by boiling to one-half or one-third its original volume. When further cooked down to one-fourth its original volume, it is known as *rabri*. Sometimes plain *kheer* or *rabri* is the basis for nut or fruit puddings, while at other times grains, legumes or vegetables are added to the milk as it is condensed.

The most sought-after type of *kheer* is made with rice—as both a flavoring agent and thickener—but it is quite unlike the often starchy, oversweet rice puddings in the West. A medium-consistency rice, *kheer* is made with a ratio of 1 part rice to 3 or 4 parts milk; baked rice *kheer* is made with 1 part rice to 12 parts milk. More often than not, *kheer* is thickened by reduction rather than by the starch in supporting ingredients. Flavoring agents such as cardamom, saffron, rose essence, *kewra* essence, almonds and pistachios preserve the classic flavors.

Because the milk is reduced quickly at first, you will need a pan that can handle two- or even three-times the volume of milk called for in the recipe. For example, if a recipe calls for 8 cups (2 liters) of milk, use a 5- or 6-quart/liter pan. This allows you to initially reduce the milk at a full frothing boil which ensures a light color for the finished *kheer*. If it is reduced slowly, the color will be deeper. I highly recommend heavy-walled nonstick pans to minimize sticking and scorching, particularly during the final stages of cooking. No matter what type of pan you use, it must be heavy; thin pans are useless for *kheer*. Aside from a wide round-cornered spatula, you will need no additional equipment. The only technique required is rhythmic, thorough stirring, being particularly attentive to avoid scorching in the final stages of cooking.

In most of the recipes, I have omitted a specific cooking time, choosing instead to suggest observable checkpoints such as "when it thickens enough to coat a spoon" or "when it is reduced to one-half or one-third of its original volume." Specified cooking times vary according to the type and size of your heat source, and no two burners burn exactly the same. In the case of *kheer*, the finished consistency just off the heat should be only slightly thickened, because it will further thicken as it cools to room temperature, and more so if it is chilled. This is especially true when grains or starchy items are added.

There is a *kheer* selection suited to every occasion and season. Well-chilled fruit or nut puddings are refreshing in the hot summer months, while wholesome grain, legume or vermicelli puddings, frequently served warm, are welcome during cold winter months. To keep the color of the *kheer* light, use raw turbinado sugar or granulated sugar. Darker raw sugars—*gur*, *jaggery*, maple sugar and date sugar—will not only affect the finished color and taste, but will frequently cause *kheer* to curdle. Add these sweeteners after the pudding is removed from the heat. They will dissolve before the *kheer* has cooled. The same is true for maple syrup or honey.

Often, the first portion of *kheer* is garnished before serving. On special occasions, small sheets of gossamer-thin silver foil, called *varak*, are placed on top of the puddings. This edible foil is made from pure silver, which is hammered so thin between pieces of paper that the slightest hint of a breeze will tear it to shreds. While this garnish is regal and showy, it is also tasteless and odorless. *Varak* is available at Indian grocery stores and is reasonably priced. To apply *varak*, remove the top piece of protective paper. Lift up the bottom sheet of paper with the *varak* on it and, in a windless place, invert it onto the surface of the *kheer*. The foil will immediately stick to the pudding and the paper can be peeled off. Store *varak* in airtight containers to prevent tarnishing. Other popular garnishes include slivered pistachios or almonds or a few pieces of scattered fresh fruits.

Rich Rice Pudding
BENGALI BHAT PAYASA

Rich rice puddings are served throughout East India from Bangladesh to Orissa. This variation is a specialty at the famous Jagannath Temple in Jagannath Puri, about 80 miles south of Calcutta. The form of Krishna in this temple is called Jagannath, and the practice here is to offer the Jagannath Deity opulent meals fifty-four times a day. The remnants of these elaborate ceremonies are distributed to the thousands of visitors who travel there daily. This dish is wonderful topped with a spoonful of puréed sweetened raspberries, strawberries or red currants.

Preparation and cooking time (after assembling ingredients): about 1 hour
Serves: 4 to 6

2 tablespoons (30 ml) *ghee* or unsalted butter
¼ cup (25 g) *basmati* or other long-grain
    white rice, washed, drained and air-dried
½ of a cassia or bay leaf (optional)
8 cups (2 liters) whole milk, or a mixture of 6 cups
    (1.5 liters) milk and 2 cups (480 ml) half-and-half
½ cup (110 g) sugar or rock candy, pulverized
¼ cup (35 g) currants
½ teaspoon (2 ml) ground cardamom
enough pure camphor powder to cover the
    head of a straight pin (optional)
1 tablespoon (15 ml) toasted *charoli* or
    pine nuts for garnishing

1. Heat the *ghee* or butter in a heavy-bottomed nonstick 5-quart/liter pan over moderate heat. Add the rice and stir-fry until it darkens one or two shades, then add the cassia or bay leaf and milk or milk–half-and-half mixture. Raise the heat to high and, stirring constantly, bring it to a frothing boil. (This will take about 15 minutes.) Reduce the heat slightly and let the milk boil, stirring slightly, until it is reduced to about half of its original volume.

2. Add the sweetener, currants and cardamom, and reduce the heat to moderately low. Simmer, stirring attentively to avoid scorching, until the liquid is reduced to a fourth of its original volume. It will become thick and creamy. Stir in the optional camphor and cool to room temperature. The pudding will continue to thicken as it cools. If you prefer it chilled, refrigerate for at least 3 hours. Serve garnished with toasted *charoli* or pine nuts.

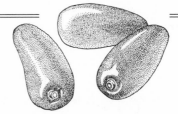

Date Rice Pudding
KHAJUR PAYASA

The date palm tree is recognized as being one of the oldest cultivated fruit trees; there are scriptural references to it that date back more than 7,000 years. It is also famous for its exceptional longevity; certain trees are purported to have been producing fruits for the past 2,000 years. Both the sap and fruit—exquisitely sweet and nutritious—can be used in this type of *payasa*, if you have access to them. Alternately, you can use date sugar as a sweetener.

Preparation and cooking time (after assembling ingredients): about 1 hour
Serves: 6

1 cup (95 g) *basmati* or other long-grain white rice
2 cups (480 ml) date palm sap, or 1¾ cups (420 ml)
    water mixed with ⅔ cups (100 g) date sugar
6 cups (1.5 liters) milk
1 cup (155 g) pitted fresh or soft dates, chopped
¼ teaspoon (1 ml) ground cinnamon

1. If you are using *basmati* rice, clean, wash and drain well (see page 6). If you are using date palm sap, bring it to a boil in a heavy pan and skim the impurities off the surface. If you are using water and date sugar, bring it to a boil. Add the rice, reduce the heat to low, cover, and gently simmer for 2 minutes. Remove the pan from the heat and set aside.

2. Pour the milk into a heavy-bottomed nonstick 5-quart/liter pan. Place it over high heat and, stirring constantly, bring to a frothing boil. (This will take about 10 minutes.) Reduce the heat slightly and allow the milk to boil, stirring occasionally, until it is reduced to about one-third of its original volume, about 2½ cups (600 ml).

3. Stir in the dates, cinnamon and cooked rice, reduce the heat to low, and simmer, stirring often, for about 15 minutes. Cool to room temperature, then chill well before serving.

Toasted Vermicelli Milk Pudding
SEVIYA KHEER

This quick-cooking pudding, also called *kheer korma*, is very popular throughout North India, especially in Pakistan and the Punjab. It is made with very fine vermicelli noodles, sold as both *sev* and *seviya* at Indian grocery stores. Two types are available: pre-toasted and plain. For this dish, purchase plain *seviya*. Elephant brand is a good choice, if available, as it is very fine and made with wheat flour. In a pinch, you can use extra fine Italian vermicelli, broken into 1½-inch (4 cm) lengths.

Preparation and cooking time (after assembling ingredients): ½ hour
Chilling time: a few hours
Serves: 6 to 8

3 tablespoons (45 ml) *ghee* or unsalted butter
1 cup (190 g) *seviya* (vermicelli),
    broken into 1½-inch (4 cm) bits
5 cups (1.25 liters) milk
½ cup (110 g) sugar
⅓ cup (40 g) sliced almonds
¼ cup (35 g) unsalted blanched pistachios, slivered
½ tablespoon (7 ml) rose water
two 3-inch (7.5 cm) sheets of edible silver or gold foil
    (*varak*) or a few garden rose petals

1. Melt the *ghee* or butter in a heavy-bottomed, 5-quart/liter nonstick pan over moderate heat. When it is hot, add the *seviya* noodles and fry, stirring to ensure even browning, until they turn a golden brown.

2. Pour in the milk, sugar, almonds and pistachios and, stirring constantly, bring to a boil. Cook for about 20 minutes or until the pudding is slightly thickened and creamy. Cool to room temperature, add the rose water and chill thoroughly. Stir well, then serve in individual bowls or goblets topped with a piece of edible silver or gold foil or a rose petal.

For information about unfamiliar ingredients or techniques, see A-to-Z

Creamy Milk Pudding with Juicy Tangerine Segments
BENGALI KAMALA PAYASA

In Bengal, *kamalas* or temple oranges, are something between tangerines and sweet oranges. In the West, they are most often called tangors or clementines. Regardless of what citrus you select—loose-skinned mandarines, satsumas or tight-skinned dessert oranges—they are peeled and segmented in a similar way. Only the juicy cells are used; save the juice and zest for other purposes. This is a visually dynamic *kheer*, served in stemmed goblets and garnished with raspberries.

Preparation and cooking time: about 1 hour
Chilling time: at least 3 hours
Serves: 6 to 8

2 tablespoons (30 ml) *basmati* or other long-grain
**   white rice, washed and soaked in water for 4 hours**
8 cups (2 liters) milk
⅓ cup (70 g) sugar
5 loose-skinned tangerines or 3 seedless dessert oranges
¼ teaspoon (1 ml) orange flower water
a few fresh raspberries for garnishing

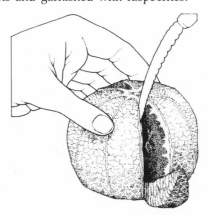

1. Drain the rice, then combine it with 1 cup (240 ml) of milk in a blender. Cover and blend until smooth, about 4 minutes. Pour the remaining milk into a heavy-bottomed 5-quart/liter nonstick pan and bring to a boil over high heat. (This will take about 15 minutes.) Add the rice–milk mixture and again bring to a boil. Reduce the heat slightly and gently boil, stirring occasionally, until the mixture is reduced to half its original volume.

2. Add the sugar and cook, stirring frequently, for another 5 minutes. Remove the pan from the heat and cool to room temperature. Stir in the orange flower water, transfer to a bowl, and chill for at least 3 hours.

3. To segment the citrus, remove the peel and white pith with a sharp serrated knife (rotate the fruit and cut the skin away in a long spiral strip). Hold the citrus over a plate, slice down to the core on either side of a segment and let the juice fall into the bowl. Place the segments on a plate. Drain off excess juices. Before serving, fold the segments into the chilled pudding. Serve in goblets with a few raspberries for a fresh fruit garnish.

Creamy Almond Pudding
BADAAM KHEER

This *kheer* is popular throughout South India, and there are numerous variations that are excellent. This particular version is based on a recipe from the Sri Sita–Rama Temple in Udupi on southwest India's Malabar coast (according to the Sanskrit text *Adhyatma Ramayana*, the Deities of Rama and Sita have been worshipped in this temple from the time of King Iksvaku, dating back before recorded history).

Traditionally, the temple cooks cool the pudding in clay jugs resting in cool water. I find it best well-chilled, though it is also very pleasant at just above room temperature. Raw turbinado sugar, now sold at many health food and grocery stores, is the best unrefined sweetener for this dish. Many of the other solid, unrefined sugars tend to make the *kheer* curdle during cooking.

Soaking and preparation time (after assembling ingredients): 3 hours
Chilling time: a few hours
Serves: 6

⅔ cup (100 g) blanched almonds
1 cup (240 ml) boiling water
5 cups (1.25 liters) milk
1 cup (240 ml) light cream or half-and-half
2 tablespoons (30 ml) semolina flour
¼ teaspoon (1 ml) good-quality saffron threads, crushed
½ teaspoon (2 ml) cardamom seeds, crushed
½ cup (100 g) turbinado sugar or granulated sugar
2 tablespoons (30 ml) toasted almond slivers for garnishing

1. Place the almonds in a bowl, add the boiling water and soak for 2 hours. Pour the nuts and soaking water into a blender or food processor fitted with the metal blade, cover, and process until smooth. Slowly pour in 1 cup (240 ml) of milk and process into a smooth almond milk.

2. Combine the remaining milk and light cream or half-and-half in a heavy-bottomed 5-quart/liter nonstick pan and bring to a boil over high heat. (This will take about 10 minutes.) While stirring constantly, sprinkle in the semolina, then pour in the almond milk. Reduce the heat to moderately low, add the saffron, cardamom and sugar, and simmer, stirring attentively, until the pudding is reduced to one-third of its original volume. Remove the pan from the heat and beat with a wire whisk to smooth out the somewhat clotted texture. Cool to room temperature, stir with a whisk again, then chill, covered, for a few hours. Serve in individual *katoris* or goblets, garnished with toasted almonds.

Royal Milk Pudding with *Chenna* Cheese
BENGALI CHENNA PAYASA

The high standard of sweets and desserts in West Bengal is recognized throughout India. While some of these sweet recipes are difficult to master, others are elegant yet simple to make. In this pudding, soft, fresh *chenna* cheese is stirred into creamy pistachio *kheer* and served ice cold, sipped rather than eaten with a spoon.

Preparation and cooking time (after assembling ingredients): 1½ hours
Chilling time: at least 4 hours
Serves: 6 to 8

For information about unfamiliar ingredients or techniques, see A-to-Z

For the Chenna Cheese:

3 cups (710 ml) milk
2 tablespoons (30 ml) strained lemon or lime juice

For the Kheer:

8 cups (2 liters) milk, or 6 cups (1.5 liters)
      milk and 2 cups (480 ml) half-and-half
⅓ cup (70 g) sugar
⅓ cup (80 ml) water
4 tablespoons (35 g) unsalted blanched
      pistachios, slivered
¼ teaspoon (1 ml) rose essence or
      1 tablespoon (15 ml) rose water
a few garden rose petals for garnishing (optional)

1. Pour the 3 cups (710 ml) of milk for the *chenna* cheese into a heavy-bottomed nonstick saucepan over high heat and, stirring constantly, bring to a boil. Reduce the heat to low and pour in the lemon or lime juice. Stir very gently in one direction until lumps of cheese form and separate from the yellowish whey. Remove the pan from the heat and set aside. Place a colander over a bowl or in the sink and line with two or three thicknesses of damp cheesecloth. Pour the cheese and whey through the colander, gather up the four corners of the cheesecloth and tie into a loose bundle. Rinse the cheese under a stream of lukewarm tap water for about 10 seconds. Hang the bundle of cheese over the sink or a bowl and drain while making the *kheer*.

2. Pour the milk for the *kheer* into a heavy-bottomed 5-quart/liter nonstick pan. Place over high heat and, stirring constantly, bring to a frothing boil. (This will take about 15 minutes.) Reduce the heat slightly and allow the milk to boil, stirring occasionally, until it is reduced to one-third of its original volume. Let cool.

3. Combine the sugar and water in a small saucepan and place over moderate heat. Stirring constantly, bring to a boil, then cook for 5 minutes. Remove the pan from the heat. Unwrap the *chenna* cheese and break it into roughly ½-inch (1.5 cm) pieces. Pat them dry on paper towels. Add to the sugar syrup and gently boil for 2 minutes. Pour the syrup and cheese into the cooled *kheer*, add the nuts and rose essence or rose water, and transfer to a bowl. Cover and chill thoroughly. Serve in individual shallow bowls or *katoris*, or in a large dish resting on cracked ice. Garnish with rose petals, if desired.

Creamy Almond and Rice Dessert
BADAAM PHIRNI

In this irresistible pudding, the almonds are soaked along with the rice and then both are ground into a purée. Once filtered, this mixture is used as both a flavoring agent and a thickener, making a texture similar to the consistency of blancmange or British custard. It is beautiful garnished with a sprinkle of toasted almonds and richly hued blueberries, loganberries or currants.

Preparation and cooking time (including soaking time): 1½ hours
Chilling time: a few hours
Serves: 8

½ cup (75 g) blanched almonds
⅓ cup (30 g) *basmati* or other long-grain white rice
1 cup (240 ml) boiling water
4 cups (1 liter) half-and-half
⅔ cup (140 g) sugar
¼ teaspoon (1 ml) rose essence or *khus* essence
¼ cup (30 g) slivered almonds, toasted
½ cup (120 ml) blueberries, loganberries or currants

1. Combine the almonds, rice and boiling water in a bowl and soak for ½–1 hour. Pour the almonds, rice and soaking water into a blender and process until smooth. Strain through a double layer of cheesecloth into a pouring cup, squeezing out all of the liquid possible.

2. Combine the half-and-half and sugar in a nonstick saucepan. Place over moderately high heat and, stirring constantly, bring to a full boil. Reduce the heat to moderately low and, stirring constantly, slowly pour in the almond milk. (The stirring must be constant to prevent lumping.) Cook, still stirring, for 10–12 minutes or until thick enough to fall *"en ruban"* from a spoon. Remove the pan from the heat and cool to room temperature. Pour into the dessert dishes—*katoris* or goblets—cover, and chill thoroughly. Garnish each serving with toasted almonds and berries.

FRESH FRUIT DESSERTS

A simple dessert in England might be fruit and cream. In France, it might be fruit and cheese. In India, it would be several types of fruits cut in their prime of ripeness, served plain or with a sprinkle lime juice, salt, pepper, or a spice blend called *chat masala*. This would not be the finale to the menu, however, for in India all desserts, sweets and fruits are served along with the entire meal—acting as "palate cleansers" or cool contrasts to hot foods.

From the cook's point of view, nothing could be easier to serve than fruits. I remember one sunny day when Srila Prabhupada was cooking lunch in his kitchen. My sister came in with an unexpected gift: a large bowl of fresh whipped cream. Srila Prabhupada graciously accepted the offering, and into the cream he adroitly folded some powdered spices, sweetener, raisins, buttered rice and lots of fresh pineapple. This ambrosial dessert won instant praise,and we began making it and serving it regularly during the open-house feasts we held each Sunday.

For information about unfamiliar ingredients or techniques, see A-to-Z

With the revived popularity of fresh fruits and vegetables, the opportunity to serve special produce is becoming a reality even in large cities. There are, for example, exotic imported fruits available from gourmet green grocers. I have found Indian alphonso mangoes—hand-picked just before they are ripe and carefully packed in straw—air-shipped to England with exquisite taste intact.

Fresh Fruit Plate
PHAL CHAT

There are no separate courses in a Vedic meal, though for a full-scale feast menu—more than 30 dishes—there is an order of serving. Fruits may be served at any time in the meal, from beginning to sweet conclusion. For breakfast, cut fruits often make up the entire meal. As a snack, a combination of three or four fruits is infinitely satisfying. Fruit combinations are endless, limited only by availability and imagination. Try specialty fruits such as cherimoyas, guavas, kiwis, carambolas, persimmons and fresh figs.

Chat plates require no preparation except the peeling and cutting of the fruits. Fruits are served in large pieces with a lime wedge and an optional sprinkle of either *chat masala* or black salt. To enhance the flavor of the fruits, I have suggested two fruit dressings: *Crème Fraîche–Cardamom* and *Fruit Juice*. The following recipes make about 1 cup (240 ml) of dressing. Simple combine all of the ingredients in a bowl and whisk until blended.

Fruit Combinations:

tangerines, blueberries and cherimoyas
orange and papaya slices with pineapple cubes
avocado slices,* grapefruit segments and stuffed fresh dates
sweet cherries, bananas* and yellow peaches*
sliced pears*, seedless green grapes and prickly pears
guava cubes, kiwi slices and persimmons
apple slices,* raspberries and fresh figs
cucumber slices, strawberries and blue plum slices
passion fruit, lychees and cape gooseberries
carambolas, tangelos and pomegranates
casaba melon, cantaloupe and crenshaw melon

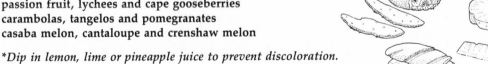

*Dip in lemon, lime or pineapple juice to prevent discoloration.

For the Crème Fraîche–Cardamom Dressing:

1 cup (240 ml) *crème fraîche*, yogurt or sour cream
2 tablespoons (30 ml) honey
2 tablespoons (30 ml) strained fresh orange juice
1 teaspoon (5 ml) ground cardamom

For the Fruit Juice Dressing:

⅓ cup (80 ml) strained fresh lime juice
⅓ cup (80 ml) strained fresh orange juice
3 tablespoons (45 ml) honey
2 tablespoons (30 ml) olive oil
2 tablespoons (30 ml) finely chopped fresh mint

Sliced Oranges with Maple Cream
SANTARA MITHAI

If you can find candy-like lumps of *gur* in Indian grocery stores, buy it, for it is hard to come by. It is made in a similar fashion to maple candy—syrups are boiled down until a solid cake remains. Grated, shredded or powdered, their flavor is similar and elegant. Though expensive, equally delicious alternatives are maple sugar granules or date sugar, both available at health food stores and specialty shops.

Preparation time (after assembling ingredients): 15 minutes
Chilling time: 1 hour
Serves: 5 or 6

4 large navel or blood oranges
1 tablespoon (15 ml) rose or *kewra* water
2 tablespoons (30 ml) honey
¼ cup (60 ml) lime juice
1 cup (240 ml) whipping cream, chilled
¼ cup (40 g) of one of the above suggested sweeteners
8 orange segments for garnishing

1. With a sharp serrated knife, peel the oranges and cut them into ¼-inch (6 mm) slices. Remove any seeds with the tip of a knife. Reserve the juice in a small bowl.

2. Add the rose water or *kewra* water, honey and lime juice to the reserved orange juice. Decoratively arrange the orange slices in overlapping rows in a shallow round or rectangular serving dish, then sprinkle with the juice mixture. Chill for at least 1 hour.

3. Whip the cream and spread it over the surface of the oranges with an icing spatula. Just prior to serving, sprinkle the cream with maple sugar or *gur*. If desired, make a starburst of peeled orange segments in the center as a garnish.

Broiled Bananas with Toasted Almonds
KELA MITHAI

You can try this dish with a date sugar–citrus juice topping or with an apple juice–apricot purée. Both are excellent contrasts to the banana halves. This quick, natural dessert should be assembled just before serving, for it takes only a few minutes to prepare. To make the apricot purée, place 8 peeled apricot halves and 2 tablespoons (30 ml) apple juice in a blender and reduce to a purée.

Preparation and cooking time (after assembling ingredients): 15 minutes

Serves: 4

1 tablespoon (15 ml) fresh lime juice
¼ cup (60 ml) strained fresh orange juice
¼ teaspoon (1 ml) freshly ground nutmeg
¼ teaspoon (1 ml) ground cardamom
2 tablespoons (30 ml) melted *ghee* or butter
4 firm bananas
¼ cup (40 g) date sugar or maple sugar granules
2 tablespoons (30 ml) blanched sliced almonds

1. Combine the lime juice, orange juice, nutmeg and cardamom in a small dish. Preheat the grill. Brush a film of *ghee* or butter on a small cookie sheet. Peel the bananas, split them lengthwise in half, and lay them, cut side up, on the cookie sheet.
2. Spoon the juice over the banana halves, drizzle with the remaining *ghee* or butter, then evenly sprinkle with the sugar. Grill the bananas for 3–4 minutes or until the surface is bubbly and lightly browned. Remove from the grill, sprinkle the almonds evenly over the banana halves, and grill again until the almonds are toasted and golden brown. Serve piping hot.

Stuffed Dessert Grapes
BHARA ANGOOR MITHAI

Large black grapes and cheese are made for each other, both for taste and appearance. In this version, pepper and saffron bring warmth to the cheese. While living in South Cornwall with acres of garden and orchard at my disposal, I sweetened the cheese with fresh mashed figs, crushed and drained raspberries and wild dewberries. In New York, I love to use strawberry farmers cheese from Ben's Cheese Shop. As finger foods for entertaining, these stuffed grapes look wonderful set out on a bed of geranium leaves. On a dinner menu, arrange 2 or 3 grapes in a cluster and set them on a fresh vine leaf.

Preparation time (after assembling ingredients): 25 minutes
Chilling time: 3–4 hours
Serves: 3 or 4

freshly made *chenna* or *panir* cheese (pages 313–315)
    made from 3 cups (710 ml) milk (about 3 ounces/85 g)
2 tablespoons (30 ml) superfine sugar or
    sugar-free apple butter
⅛ teaspoon (0.5 ml) freshly ground pepper
¼ teaspoon (1 ml) good quality saffron threads
4 ounces (115 g) large firm dessert grapes

1. Place the cheese on a smooth countertop or marble slab and, working with the heel of your hand, knead and bray the cheese until it is creamy smooth without a trace of graininess. Sprinkle in the sugar, black pepper and saffron, and knead until the ingredients are blended. Place in a bowl and chill until firm.

Alternately, fit a food processor with the metal cutting blade. Break the cheese into 1-inch (2.5 cm) pieces. Combine the cheese, sugar, pepper and saffron in the work bowl and process until light and creamy smooth. Scrape the mixture into a bowl and chill until firm.

2. Slice the grapes lengthwise about three-quarters through and remove the seeds with the tip of a knife. Stuff each grape with the cheese filling; smooth the edges and wipe the grapes clean. Chill before serving.

Creamy Pineapple and Rice Jubilee
ANANAS CHAVAL MITHAI

This dish goes well on a festive holiday menu but does not keep well. It should be made within a few hours of serving.

Preparation time (after assembling ingredients): 10 minutes
Chilling time: at least ½ hour
Serves: 6 to 8

2 cups (260 g) freshly cooked *basmati* or other long-grain white rice
1 tablespoon (15 ml) unsalted butter or *ghee*
¼ teaspoon (1 ml) ground cinnamon
½ teaspoon (2 ml) freshly ground nutmeg
½ teaspoon (2 ml) freshly ground cardamom seeds
⅛ teaspoon (0.5 ml) ground cloves
½ cup (65 g) currants
¼ cup (30 g) toasted sliced almonds
2 cups (480 ml) whipping cream, chilled
3 cups (710 ml) fresh pineapple, well drained and cut
    into 1 x ½ x ¼-inch (2.5 x 1.5 x 6 mm) pieces
⅓ cup (70 g) sugar
pineapple rings for garnishing (optional)

For information about unfamiliar ingredients or techniques, see A-to-Z

1. Spread the hot rice onto a baking tray, dot with butter or *ghee*, and add the spices, currants and 3 tablespoons (45 ml) of almonds. Cool to room temperature and transfer to a bowl.

2. Chill a mixing bowl and a whisk or beater in the freezer for 10 minutes. Whip the cream into soft peaks, add it to the rice along with the pineapple and sugar, and gently fold to mix. Chill for ½ hour. Mound on a flat serving dish, sprinkle with the remaining almonds, and, if desired, garnish with pineapple rings.

Melon Bowl Supreme with Honey–Lime Dressing
CARBOOJ MITHAI

This is a good dish for summer entertaining—a buffet showstopper, an appetizer at a party, or a fruit dessert for a garden party. Watermelons are best at the height of the summer season. Vine-ripened sweet melons have a glossy thick skin with juicy scarlet or yellow flesh. Honeydew, casaba, Ogden, *charentais* and cantaloupe are excellent choices. The fruit is served in a melon bowl—a hollowed-out watermelon with a zig zag or ruffed cut edge. A 3–4-pound (1.5–2 kg) round melon will form the basis of a serving bowl; a 10-pound (5 kg) oblong melon can hold up to 20 servings.

Preparation time (after assembling ingredients): 40 minutes
Chilling time: at least 1 hour
Serves: 4 to 6

one 3–4-pound (1.5–2 kg) round watermelon
1 small cantaloupe or Ogden melon
1 small honeydew or *charentais* melon
⅓ cup (80 ml) honey
¼ cup (60 ml) lime juice
2 tablespoons (30 ml) orange juice
2 tablespoons (30 ml) lemon juice
¼ teaspoon (1 ml) ground ginger or ½ tablespoon (7 ml)
**   scraped, finely chopped fresh ginger root**
½ teaspoon (2 ml) cardamom seeds
2 tablespoons (30 ml) olive oil or almond oil
2 cups (480 ml) blueberries
a few sprigs of mint for garnishing

1. Using a large sharp knife, cut off the top third of the watermelon. Using a melon baller or a large spoon, scoop balls from the large section of the melon. Remove the seeds and refrigerate the balls. Spoon out the remaining melon flesh, leaving a melon shell. With a small sharp knife, cut a saw-toothed or scallop design around the top edge of the melon shell. Cut a thin slice of rind from the base of the shell so it will stand without tipping. Cover with plastic wrap and refrigerate until required.

2. Halve the other melons and scoop out the flesh with a melon baller. Combine these balls in a bowl, mix, cover and refrigerate.

3. Combine the honey, lime juice, orange juice, lemon juice, ginger, cardamom seeds and oil in a blender and process into a smooth sauce. Just before serving, drain the melon balls, mix well with the blueberries, and spoon into the watermelon bowl. Pour the honey sauce over the top and garnish with fresh mint.

Pineapple Tower Surprise
ANANAS MITHAI

Here is an ideal summer fruit dessert for entertaining. It is important that, aside from being sweet and juicy, the pineapple you select should be unbruised, unblemished and uniformly shaped. The spiny leaves atop the crown should flower out symmetrically. To prepare this dish, the fruit from the pineapple is removed from the shell and cubed, marinated in lime juice, folded in whipped cream, and again spooned into the pineapple shell. Topped with the pineapple crown and garnished, this showy after-dinner treat always elicits praise.

Preparation time (after assembling ingredients): 30 minutes
Chilling time: at least 1–2 hours
Serves: 5 or 6

1 medium-sized ripe pineapple
grated zest of 1 lime
⅓ cup (80 ml) strained lime juice
⅓ cup (35 g) shredded coconut, lightly packed
¼ cup (25 g) confectioner's sugar
1 cup (240 ml) whipping cream, chilled
2 tablespoons (30 ml) slivered almonds or pistachios
6 orange twists and 6 whole grapes for garnishing

1. To make the pineapple shell, cut off the top about 1 inch (2.5 cm) from the leaves and reserve. Using a sharp knife, cut down the insides of the shell, leaving sturdy walls about ½ inch (1.5 cm) thick.

2. To remove the fruit, make three slits 1 inch (2.5 cm) from the bottom of the pineapple. In each slit, work the knife from left to right, taking care not to enlarge the slit, so the fruit is loosened from the base and side of the shell. Carefully try to remove the fruit in one piece.

3. Cut the pineapple into 10 slices, core each slice, and cut them into even-sized ¾-inch (2 cm) segments. Combine the lime zest, lime juice, coconut and sugar in a bowl and chill, along with the shell, for at least 1–2 hours or up to 6 hours.

4. Just before serving, whip the cream and fold it into the fruit. Spoon the mixture into the chilled pineapple shell. Sprinkle the slivered nuts over the fruit and replace the pineapple top. Place the pineapple on a serving platter and garnish at the base with orange twists and whole grapes.

Beverages

As elsewhere in the world, hospitality in India is expressed by offering a beverage to guests. This custom is mandatory etiquette in all Indian homes, and the beverage can be as simple as cool, clear water. In fact, from the Southern tropics to the Himalayan foothills, India is a nation of water connoisseurs. Ideally, drinking water is fetched twice daily and stored in unglazed earthenware jugs. These vessels cool water by evaporation, keeping the temperature at 48°–54°F (9°–12°C), ideal for Indian tastes. Some temples store water in silver or copper jugs, used traditionally in temple worship and known to destroy some forms of bacteria.

In India, surface water (run-off from melting glaciers, snow or rain) is used primarily for washing and cleaning. Spring and well water, saved for drinking and cooking, is graded by its mineral and salt content—"sweet water" is almost tasteless, while "salty water" has enough salt to be easily detected. Sweet water wells are a prized and cherished commodity. Pilgrims will travel thousands of miles to temples famous for their sweet clear water, bringing bottles home for special occasions. For example, the seventeenth-century well at the foot of Vrindavan's Madanmohan Temple is a mecca for thousands of pilgrims yearly. Other temple wells are famed for medicinal or healing properties, much in the same way as Lourdes in France.

Going beyond the humble offering of water, there is a wonderful variety of non-alcoholic beverages to be had in India. Vaishnavas, devout worshippers of Lord Krishna, avoid caffeine, alcohol and other intoxicants completely. Historically, coffee was introduced by the Moguls and tea crops (as recently as the nineteenth century) by the British. To this day, followers of Vedic tradition abstain from these drinks, preferring a host of alternative liquid refreshments.

Fresh juices and flavored liquids can be extracted from raw ingredients in a number of ways—by squeezing, crushing, cooking, infusing and the use of centrifugal force. Before my first trip to India in 1970, I would never have considered hand-crushing fruits to extract juice, but in 115°F (45°C) temperatures, with no electricity, you become resourceful. Besides, it proved to be a more than adequate method for extracting the juice from soft fruits—all types of berries, grapes, currants or melons. These juices can be slowly strained through a jelly bag to obtain a clear juice or effectively squeezed through cheesecloth for fruit nectar. Undeniably, the quickest and easiest method for juicing hard vegetables and fruits like celery, carrots, beets and apples is a centrifugal juicer or a food processor with a juice attachment. In the absence of abundant fruit and fresh homemade juice, take advantage of the many organic unsweetened juices available at health food stores. Knudsen, Westbrae, Lakewood and Wagner's are just a few high-quality products.

For information about unfamiliar ingredients or techniques, see A-to-Z

Still another means for extraction of a host of other dry ingredients is infusion. Coconut, nuts, grains, seeds, citrus zest, even sandalwood chips and flowers, can be infused in boiling water, sweetened, and strained to yield delicately flavored liquids. Citrus need only be squeezed against a reamer to release abundant juice. Some fibrous or firm-fleshed fruits require heat to release moisture and break down tissue. Rhubarb, cranberries and quinces need to be simmered before filtering for a clear juice. Finally, fruits with a low liquid content—bananas, guavas, papayas and mangoes—are best puréed in a food processor or blender before being strained for juice.

Chilled beverages frequently include milk products and some form of ice. They are blender or food processor drinks, puréed and aerated until frothy. Serve immediately in iced glasses or chilled fruit cups. A few garnishes lend visual appeal to cold drinks—citrus twists, mint sprigs, whole or cubed fruits on skewers or even sprinkles of freshly ground cardamom, coriander or nutmeg. The most popular chilled dairy drink in India is *lassi*. It is the equivalent of a smoothie and provides a low-calorie alternative to frothy milk shakes. *Lassis* can be as simple as sugar, yogurt and crushed ice; or fruit-sweetened using, for example, bananas instead of sugar.

The forefunner of punch is called *panchamrita*. While these are not exclusively dairy beverages, they generally contain the five ingredients milk, yogurt, honey, sugar and *ghee*. (The Sanskrit word *panch* means "five", and *amrita* means "nectar." More recently, "punch" has come to mean more or less any sweetened juice, served hot or cold.) There can be many variations on this theme, such as *thandai*—a luxurious amalgamation of nuts, raisins and fennel-flavored milk—which lends nutrition and imposing flavor to any light meal.

To make a delightful Vedic chilled punch, try any of the following combinations:

Punch Combinations:

Papaya nectar, pineapple juice, orange juice, guava nectar,
    yogurt, lime juice and crushed ice
Pineapple juice, coconut milk, apple juice, orange juice,
    ground cardamom and crushed ice
Passion fruit nectar, pineapple juice, orange juice,
    lemon and lime juice and crushed ice
Orange juice, apricot juice, powdered milk, crushed ice,
    a few drops of vanilla extract
Pineapple juice, pear nectar, coconut milk, orange juice,
    crushed ice and nutmeg
Buttermilk, banana, papaya concentrate
    and crushed ice
Apple juice with a little fresh ginger purée,
    fresh mint leaves and crushed ice
Banana, yogurt, minced dates, orange juice
    and lime juice
White grape juice, diced papaya, coconut milk,
    tangelo juice and crushed ice

Combine all of the ingredients in a blender or food processor and process until smooth and airy. Raisins or dried fruits need plumping and softening in hot water before use. Whole fruits should be chopped. Bananas and apples need a sprinkle of lemon juice to prevent discoloration. Proportions of the ingredients will determine the punch's flavor.

Warm drinks need little more than fresh or dried fruits, nuts, herbs and spices. The warming drinks in this chapter are variations on hot milk. In addition to these, try the following fruit juice and dried fruit combinations for wonderful warm punch pick-me-ups:

White grape juice offset with whole allspice,
    white peppercorns and Key lime zest
White grape juice offset with chopped dates,
    cardamom seeds and lemon zest
Red grape juice offset with chopped figs, cinnamon stick,
    apple slices and orange zest
White grape juice and water with fresh ginger root,
    cinnamon stick, honey and a pinch of cayenne
Apple juice offset with cloves, orange slices,
    fresh ginger root and cardamom pods
Red currant juice with raisins, cloves
    and orange zest
White grape juice with fennel seeds,
    cinnamon stick and lemon juice
Blackberry juice, grape juice and apple juice with
    allspice, lemon zest and cinnamon stick

When juices are simmered, their flavors intensify. If you prefer a more delicate beverage, heat the liquid to simmering and keep it there—a process generally called mulling. As a rule of thumb, allow the beverage 10–25 minutes over heat, then 5 minutes, covered, off the heat. Unprocessed juices should not come in contact with copper, iron or almunum utensils because they cause discoloration and impair flavor.

FRUIT JUICES AND SYRUPS

Maple Syrup and Lime Crush
EKADASEE KARA NIMBU PANI

The Vaishnava calendar notes scores of holidays on which some type of fasting preceeds feasting. Many are half-day fasts, some last until dusk or moonrise, and on a few *Ekadasees* a full-day fast is recommended. On the holy day of *Gour Purnima* in 1967, Srila Prabhupada introduced a variation of this beverage, which he simply called a "break-fast drink." It was made with both lemon and lime juice, black pepper, sugar, water and a pinch of salt. Over the years I have enjoyed numerous break-fast drinks, and this is one of the nicest. Aside from being delicious, it is healthful—fresh lime juice, maple syrup and a little cayenne to help dissolve and eliminate toxins in the digestive system.

Preparation time (after assembling ingredients): a few minutes
Makes: about 2 quarts/liters

For information about unfamiliar ingredients or techniques, see A-to-Z

¾ cup (180 ml) maple syrup, slightly warmed
¾ cup (180 ml) strained fresh lime juice
⅛–¼ teaspoon (0.5–1 ml) cayenne pepper
6 cups (1.5 liters) water

Whisk the maple syrup with the lime juice in a jug. Add the cayenne and water and stir well. Serve at room temperature or chilled over ice.

Lime or Lemon Syrup
NIMBU CHAUSNI

Nimbu Pani, India's most popular cold drink (see next recipe), can be made with lime syrup or fresh juice. Most street vendors make the drink from syrups, and though the ingredients are common knowledge, the recipes remain guarded secrets. Though it is most often made with water, club soda or carbonated mineral water is also refreshing.

Preparation time: 40 minutes
Makes: about 6 pints (3 liters)

8–9 large juicy lemons
9 cups (2 generous liters) water
7 cups (1.5 kg) sugar

1. Juice the lemons, strain the juice, and peel away the zest in long strips. Bring the lemon zest and water to a boil in a large pan and cook for 20 minutes, then strain it into another pan.
2. Add the sugar and, stirring constantly, dissolve over low heat. Raise the heat to high and boil for 10 minutes.
3. Remove from the heat and stir in the fresh lemon juice. Cool to room temperature, then bottle, or refrigerate for up to a month.

Lemon Drink
NIMBU PANI

I was introduced to this traditional recipe in the home of Mrs. Sumati Morarji, director of Bombay's Scindia Steamship Lines. It was Mrs. Morarji who provided Srila Prabhupada with his passage to America in 1965. I first met this refined and religious woman in 1970 at Scindia House, near Juhu Beach, where she had arranged a program of lecture and *kirtan* for Srila Prabhupada. She served this beverage before the full *prasadam* feast, and it has since remained a favorite recipe of mine.

Preparation time: 15 minutes
Infusion and chilling time: 8–12 hours or overnight
Makes: 2 quarts/liters

4 juicy lemons or large limes
8 cups (2 liters) water
10 dates, (55 g) pitted and halves
⅔ cup (160 ml) honey

1. Cut the citrus in half crosswise, remove the zest from 6 of the halves and squeeze out the juice. Slice the remaining half into thin rounds.

2. Place the water and dates in a saucepan and gently boil for 10 minutes. Add the zest and boil for another 2–3 minutes. Remove the pan from the heat, stir in the honey, citrus juice and citrus slices, and set aside, loosely covered, for 8–12 hours.

3. Strain through a muslin-lined sieve. Serve chilled.

Minty Lemon–Lime Refresher
PODINA NIMBU PANI

A perfect choice for entertaining—before, during or even after a special meal. If you like, freeze it to a slush in an ice-cream machine and serve in iced stemmed goblets at a meal presented in courses—say, between soup and the main course.

Preparation time (after assembling ingredients): 15 minutes
Serves: 6

25 fresh mint leaves, trimmed
¼ teaspoon (1 ml) cardamom seeds
¼ cup (55 g) sugar
½ cup (120 ml) boiling water
2 cups (480 ml) white grape juice, chilled
2 cups (480 ml) sparkling water, chilled
¼ cup (60 ml) strained lemon juice
¼ cup (60 ml) strained lime juice
24 seedless green grapes
6 mint sprigs for garnishing

1. Bruise the mint leaves, cardamom and sugar with a mortar and pestle. Transfer to a small saucepan, add the boiling water and, stirring constantly, dissolve the sugar over low heat. Simmer for about 5 minutes, then strain through a muslin-lined strainer. Cool to room temperature and chill well.

2. Combine the mint syrup, grape juice, sparkling water, lemon juice and lime juice in a pitcher. Serve in goblets, each garnished with 4 green grapes and a sprig of mint.

For information about unfamiliar ingredients or techniques, see A-to-Z

Dainty Rose Water Drink

RUH GULAB SHARBAT

Homemade rose syrup, lemon or lime juice and fresh pomegranate juice make this pale pink beverage elegant and exotic. In India, a container made from freshly tinned metal is recommended for soaking the petals because the metal preserves their color. Be sure your garden roses are free of insecticides.

Infusion and chilling time: 8 hours or overnight
Makes: about 3 pints (1.5 liters)

1½ cups (360 ml) freshly picked rose petals, lightly packed
¾ cup (180 ml) boiling water
¼ teaspoon (1 ml) cardamom seeds
¾ cup (160 g) sugar or ¾ cup (180 ml) honey
¼ cup (60 ml) strained fresh lemon or lime juice
⅔ cup (160 ml) pomegranate juice
5 cups (1.25 liters) cold water

1. Crush the rose petals with a mortar and pestle and place them in a large bowl. Add the boiling water, then pour the mixture into a metal container and add the cardamom seeds. Set aside 8 hours or overnight to infuse.

2. Pour the rose–cardamom water through a muslin-lined strainer set over a bowl. Add the sweetener, and float the bowl in a hot-water-filled sink until the sugar dissolves. Remove from the hot water and filter once again. Cool to room temperature.

3. Combine all of the ingredients in a pitcher and stir well. Serve in goblets half-filled with crushed ice.

Fresh Orange Squash with Ginger

ADRAK SANTARA SHARBAT

This tropical refresher vies with freshly squeezed sugar cane juice as a tried and true thirst quencher.

Preparation and cooling time: 1 hour   Makes: about 2 quarts/liters

12 oranges
2 limes
1 cup (210 g) sugar or 1 cup (240 ml) liquid sweetener
2 quarter-sized slices of fresh ginger root
6 cups (1.5 liters) water

1. Wash the oranges and limes and, using a small paring knife, remove the zest from the fruit. Combine the zest, sugar, ginger and water in a pan and place over low heat. Stir constantly until the sugar has dissolved. Press on the zest to release the oil into the syrup. Remove from the heat and set aside to cool.

2. Cut the oranges and limes in half, remove the juice, and then strain the juice into a large bowl. When the infusion of citrus zest has cooled to room temperature, strain it through a sieve into the bowl of citrus juice. Mix well. Chill thoroughly in a pitcher and serve in tall glasses half-filled with ice cubes.

Bubbly Lime Cooler Sweetened with *Gur*
KHAJUR GUR NIMBU JAL

In Bengal this beverage is made with still water, though I prefer the the added zest of a carbonated water. Perrier or San Pellegrino are excellent for this drink. *Gur* and *jaggery* are available at Indian grocery stores.

Preparation time: 30 minutes
Infusion time: 8 hours or overnight
Makes: about 5 pints (2.5 liters)

8 limes
1 cup (155 g) *gur* or *jaggery* plus 2 cups (480 ml) water, or
    1 cup (240 ml) maple syrup plus ½ cup (120 ml) water
8 cups (2 liters) still water or
    a mixture of still and carbonated water
¼ teaspoon (1 ml) salt

1. Juice the limes, strain the juice, and remove the zest. Place the *gur* or *jaggery* and 2 cups (480 ml) water in a saucepan and cook, stirring constantly, over moderately low heat until the sugar dissolves. Raise the heat to high and boil for 2 minutes, without stirring. Remove the pan from the heat and pour through a fine strainer. Alternately, warm the maple syrup and ½ cup (120 ml) water in a small saucepan.

2. Combine the sweet syrup, lime juice, lime zest, 4 cups (1 liter) of the still water and salt, stir, and set aside for 8 hours or overnight to infuse. Strain through a muslin-lined sieve and chill well. Mix with the remaining water and serve over ice.

Gingered Watermelon Cooler
TARBOOJ SHARBAT

In Vrindavan, watermelon season—April and May—provides a much-welcomed relief from the scorching heat of India's summer. The melons grow on the sandy banks of the Yamuna river, and I remember watching the *sadhus* swim out to retrieve melons that were floating down the sacred waters. This thirst quencher is also delicious using gold watermelons.

For information about unfamiliar ingredients or techniques, see A-to-Z

Preparation time: 15 minutes
Chilling time: a few hours
Makes: about 1 quart/liter

1 pint (0.5 liters) strawberries
3 cups (710 ml) fresh watermelon juice
½ teaspoon (2 ml) puréed fresh ginger root
3 tablespoons (45 ml) superfine sugar

1. Wash and stem the berries in cold water. Force through a food mill to separate the purée from the seeds. Alternately, place a nylon sieve over a bowl and, using a pestle or outstretched fingers, push to extract the fruit purée; discard the seeds.

2. Combine all of the ingredients in a jug, stir well, and refrigerate for a few hours. Stir and serve in chilled glasses with crushed ice.

Honeydew Drink Flavored with *Khus*
CARBOOJ SHARBAT

This drink is popular throughout Bengal and Orissa, and there are as many variations as there are types of melon. The melon shells provide a beautiful receptacle to drink the juice from.

Preparation time: 15 minutes
Chilling time: a few hours
Serves: 4

4 small or 2 large honeydew melons
½ cup (120 ml) strained fresh orange juice
¼ cup (60 ml) strained fresh lime juice
4 drops *khus* essence

1. If you are using small melons, slice off the top of each as a lid; if you are using large ones, cut them in half. Cut the edges in a zig-zag pattern. Cut a thin slice off the bottom so that the melon stands firmly upright without tipping. (Take care not to cut through the shell.) Scoop out the seeds and discard. Scoop out the flesh and process in a blender or food processor, along with the remaining ingredients, until smooth.

2. Chill well and serve in the shells, if desired, with the reserved lids and straws.

Perfumed Sandalwood Crush
VRINDAVAN GOSWAMI SHARBAT

Before Srila Prabhupada left India for America in 1965, he lived in Vrindavan, Lord Krishna's birthplace. When he visited the S. K. Joshi family in their Vrindavan home, Mrs. Joshi frequently served him this beverage in the late afternoon. She explained that this recipe originated from the famous Radha Ramana Temple of Gopal Bhatta Goswami in Vrindavan and was centuries old. This exotic beverage, known for its cooling effect on a scorching afternoon, can be served on its own or with cut seasonal fruits.

Pure sandalwood is sold in small bars—about 1½ inches (4 cm) diameter and 3–4 inches (7.5–10 cm) long. You will have to saw or chip off slices to make an infusion. Alternately, use sweetened sandalwood syrup, but eliminate the sweetener entirely or reduce it as desired. Both sandalwood and its syrup are available at Indian grocery stores. Camomile is a pleasant alternative.

Preparation time (after assembling ingredients): about 30 minutes
Infusion time: 6–8 hours or overnight
Chilling time: several hours
Makes: about 2½ pints (1.5 liters)

12 green cardamom pods
3 quarter-sized slices of pure sandalwood or
    ½ cup (120 ml) sandalwood syrup
6 cups (1.5 liters) spring or well water
2½ x 1-inch (6.5 x 2.5 cm) strip of orange zest
1½ x 1-inch (4 x 2.5 cm) strip of lime zest
⅔–¾ cup (140–165 g) sugar candy, crushed,
    or *gur* (100–115 g)
3 tablespoons (45 ml) dried *malati* or camomile flowers

1. Combine the cardamom pods, sandalwood slices, if using them, and water in a saucepan and bring to a boil. Reduce the heat to the lowest possible setting, cover, and let it steep, without simmering, for 25 minutes. Remove the pan from the heat, cover with a tea towel, and set aside in a cool place to infuse flavors for 6–8 hours or overnight.

2. Strain into a clean pan. Bring to a near boil, turn off the heat and add the remaining ingredients. Cover and steep for 5 minutes. Strain and cool to room temperature. If you are using sandalwood syrup, stir it in. Chill well. Serve in goblets over crushed ice.

For information about unfamiliar ingredients or techniques, see A-to-Z

Zesty Grape Juice Cooler

ANGOOR SHARBAT

Homemade juices are more pure and fresh in flavor than their store-bought counterparts. Concord, Emperor and Cardinal red-purple grapes yield outstanding juice. Even if you do not have a juicer, it is relatively easy to pass the fruit through the fine disk of a food mill or simply purée it and press it through a fine sieve. Both methods produce a juice purée that takes well to the addition of sparkling water.

Preparation time (after assembling ingredients): 20 minutes
Makes: 2 quarts/liters

½ x 3-inch (1.5 x 7.5 cm) piece of orange zest
¼ teaspoon (1 ml) cardamom seeds
4 whole cloves
6 cups (1.5 liters) grape juice
¼ cup (60 ml) honey or maple syrup (optional)
3-inch (7.5 cm) piece of cinnamon stick
2 cups (480 ml) sparkling water

1. Tie the zest, cardamom seeds and cloves in a small piece of cheesecloth. Place the juice and optional honey or maple syrup in a large enamel or stainless steel pan and bring to near the boiling point over moderate heat.

2. Remove the pan from the heat, add the spice bag and cinnamon stick, cover, and set aside until the juice has cooled to tepid. Remove the spice bag and cinnamon stick and chill. Add the sparkling water before serving.

Green Mango Drink
GUDUMBA

Unlike the intensely sweet ripe mango, green mangoes are firm and tart. They are usually used for pickles or fresh chutneys for the pleasant astringent edge they contribute to a dish. Because this Gujarati beverage is sweetened, you can use either green or just-ripening mangoes. Traditionally, the mangoes are roasted on the dying embers of an open heat before being puréed, which gives them an especially enjoyable flavor, though they may also be either baked or boiled with excellent results. Not only is this drink a great thirst quencher, it is also respected as a curative for the heat boils that seem to afflict residents in the tropics.

Preparation time (after assembling ingredients): about 45 minutes
Makes: about 1 quart/liter

1 large or 2 medium-sized green mangoes
¼ cup (55 g) sugar or (60 ml) liquid sweetener
⅛ teaspoon (0.5 ml) good-quality saffron threads,
    toasted and powdered
¼ teaspoon (1 ml) ground cardamom
3 cups (710 ml) water
1 teaspoon (5 ml) dry-roasted crushed fennel seeds

1. Bake the fruit in a 300°F (150°C) oven, boil it in water, or slowly roast it over dying embers until soft, 30–40 minutes. Cool to room temperature, then peel, seed, and place the fruit in a blender or food processor fitted with the metal blade. Purée until smooth.

2. Add the sugar, saffron, cardamom and water, and pulse until mixed. Strain the mixture through a gauze-lined sieve. Chill well and serve in glasses, garnished with a pinch of crushed fennel seeds.

Rhubarb and Pomegranate Refresher
CHINARCHA SHARBAT

While rhubarb squash is relatively unknown in India, fresh pomegranate juice is a popular repast. This pleasant combination of freshly squeezed juices is brilliant in color. As both juices are fairly acidic, avoid utensils made from iron, copper or aluminum, which tend to cause discoloration and impair flavor.

Much depends on your choice of sweetener—superfine sugar lends little more than sweetness to the drink. Different honeys produce varied flavors, and maple syrup gives a woodsy, sweet taste as well as deepened color. If you have it on hand, rose syrup is a pleasant addition.

Preparation time (after assembling ingredients): 30 minutes
Makes about: 1½ quarts (1.5 liters)

1 pound (455 g) rhubarb, washed, trimmed and
    cut into 1-inch (2.5 cm) lengths
2 cups (480 ml) water
¾–1½ cups (160–315 g) sugar or equivalent sweetener
2 cups (480 ml) fresh pomegranate juice
¼ cup (60 ml) strained orange juice or rose syrup

1. Place the rhubarb, water and sugar in a saucepan and bring to a boil over moderate heat. Cover, reduce the heat to low, and simmer for 15 minutes. Strain the juice through a fine nylon sieve resting over a bowl. Discard the pulp.

2. Add the remaining ingredients and cool to room temperature. Chill well and serve over crushed ice or in chilled glasses.

For information about unfamiliar ingredients or techniques, see A-to-Z

Lime Ginger Ale
ADRAK SHARBAT

I first served this beverage to Srila Prabhupada in Vrindavan, India, where the well water is distinguished by a slightly salty taste. He commented that his mother had made this summer thirst quencher with effervescent quinine water. It is pleasant with most carbonated mineral waters—from the gentle fizz of San Pellegrino to the brisk fizz of Perrier.

Double-boiling the ginger stretches the flavor of fresh ginger root. India's *nimbu* is a cross between Key limes and lemons, though any type of lime will do. You may or may not want to use peppercorns. I find that a blend of allspice and white, green and Malabar peppercorns lends pleasant spunk to the beverage.

Preparation time (after assembling ingredients): 15–20 minutes
Makes: 2 quarts/liters

1 x 2-inch (2.5 x 5 cm) piece of peeled fresh
    ginger root (about 1 ounce/30 g)
8 cups (2 liters) still water, or 4 cups (1 liter)
    still water and 4 cups (1 liter) carbonated water
1 teaspoon (5 ml) whole peppercorns (optional)
2⅓ cups (495 g) sugar or equivalent sweetener
12 limes, juiced and strained

1. Grind the ginger to a paste in a food processor or with an Oriental ginger grater or mortar and pestle. Mix with 2 cups (480 ml) of still water and the optional peppercorns. Bring the water to a boil over moderately high heat, then reduce the heat and simmer for 4–5 minutes. Strain the mixture through muslin and again place it in the saucepan. Add 2 more cups (480 ml) of water and repeat the process. After straining the liquid again, add the sweetener and stir until dissolved. Finally, mix in the lime juice. Chill well.

2. Before serving, top off with the remaining 4 cups (1 liter) still water or the 4 cups (1 liter) carbonated water. Serve over ice cubes.

Barley Tonic
JAWAR SHARBAT

Barley water is famed as a thirst quencher—a real hot-weather beverage. This Gujarati version is served much like lime tonic: over ice and frequently. The rather bland flavor of simmered barley and water is heightened by infusing lemon zest into the hot liquid. Just before serving, the beverage is topped off with fresh lemon juice and orange juice. Further, you can macerate fruits such as cherries, grapes or red currants in sugar and lime juice and add them to the punch bowl or cups for added color.

Preparation and cooking time (after assembling ingredients): 15 minutes
Makes: about 1 quart/liter

¼ cup (55 g) pearl barley
3 cups (710 ml) cold water
10 black or green peppercorns
three 3-inch (7.5 cm) pieces of lemon or lime zest
½–⅔ cup (110–140 g) sugar or equivalent sweetener
2 tablespoons (30 ml) fresh lemon or lime juice
1 cup (240 ml) fresh orange juice

1. Wash the barley in several changes of water. Drain, and place it in a saucepan with the cold water. Bring to a boil over moderate heat, reduce the temperature, and simmer for 10 minutes. Remove the pan from the heat and add the peppercorns, lemon zest and sweetener. Stir, cover, and cool to room temperature.

2. Strain the juice and then chill well. Before serving, blend in the lemon or lime and orange juices. Pour over ice and garnish with a citrus twist.

═══════CHILLED DAIRY DRINKS═══════

Sweet Yogurt Shake
MEETHA LASSI

India's yogurt-based shakes or smoothies are both nutritious and thirst-quenching. Of the three most popular flavors—sweet, salty-mint and fruit-flavored—the first is by far the most popular. In milk and cheese shops, yogurt is made at least three times daily: early morning, mid-day and late afternoon. During the summer months, a *lassi* maker positions himself at the shop entrance and whips off cup after clay cup of this frosty sweet treat.

As a rule of thumb, plain sweet *lassi* is made with a 4 to 1 yogurt-water ratio while salty or fruit-based *lassi* is thinner—a 3 or even 2 to 1 ratio. Also, the yogurt is traditionally made from extra-rich buffalo or cow's milk, the thick layer of "yogurt cream" that forms on its surface used as a finishing garnish. Commercial Brown Cow yogurt—made from pasturized, but not homogenized, whole milk—is perfect for sweet *lassi*. Its flavor is mild and the "yogurt cream" thick and rich. For this *lassi*, homemade yogurt should be made with 3 parts milk to 1 part light cream or from rich whole milk, preferably from Jersey or Guernsey cows.

Preparation time: 10 minutes
Makes: 1 quart/liter

3 cups (710 ml) Brown Cow plain or vanilla yogurt, with
    "yogurt cream" from the top reserved as a garnish, or 2½ cups
    (600 ml) plain yogurt plus ½ cup (120 ml) sour cream
⅔ cup (140 g) sugar or equivalent sweetener
½ cup (120 ml) ice water
8–10 ice cubes, crushed or partially cracked

For information about unfamiliar ingredients or techniques, see A-to-Z

1. If you have access to it, spoon off 4 pieces of firm "yogurt cream" from the top of yogurt made with non-homogenized milk, and set aside on waxed paper for a garnish.

2. Place the yogurt (and sour cream, if you are using it) and the sweetener in a 2-quart/liter mixing bowl and whisk with a balloon whip until frothy. Add the ice water and again whisk briefly. Stir in the crushed ice.

Alternately, fit a food processor with the metal blade or use a blender. Divide the yogurt–sweetener mixture into two batches. Place one batch, ¼ cup (60 ml) water and half of the cracked ice in the processor or blender, cover, and process for 1–2 minutes. Transfer and repeat for the second batch.

3. Pour the beverage into 4 chilled glasses. Carefully place a piece of "yogurt cream", if desired, on each drink and garnish with a sprinkle of sweetener. Serve immediately.

Cumin-Flavored Yogurt Shake
KARA JEERA LASSI

This is my variation on a much-loved Rajasthani beverage popular from the Bikaner desert to the mountains of Udaipur. It is subtly flavored with dry-roasted cumin seeds and limes or lemons. The zest is added to milk before it is heated for homemade yogurt; as the milk warms, the citrus oils infuse it with a delicate bouquet. Strain the milk and proceed as you would for plain yogurt. As an alternative, Brown Cow Farm or Colombo lemon yogurt will produce good results.

This beverage is sometimes made with slightly tangy yogurt, but I prefer it fresh and mild—a clear foundation allows the citrus flavor to dominate, whether you use a light touch of herb salt or none at all. The dry-roasted cumin should be coarsely powdered—if only crushed, it will sink to the bottom of the glasses; if finely powdered, you lose pleasant bursts of flavor.

Preparation time (after assembling ingredients): 10 minutes
Makes: 1 quart/liter

3 cups (710 ml) lemon-flavored whole or low-fat yogurt
2 tablespoons (30 ml) cream (optional)
2 tablespoons (30 ml) lime or lemon juice
⅓ cup (80 ml) ice water
½ teaspoon (2 ml) herb salt or sea salt, or as desired
6 ice cubes
½ tablespoon (7 ml) dry-roasted cumin seeds, coarsely powdered

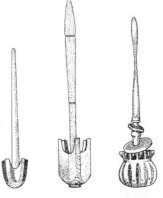

Place the yogurt, cream, citrus juice, ice water and salt in a blender or food processor fitted with the metal blade. Process for 2 minutes. Add the ice cubes and process for another minute. Add all but a few pinches of cumin and process for 5 seconds. Pour into chilled glasses, sprinkle with the remaining cumin, and serve immediately.

Minty Yogurt Shake
KARA PODINA LASSI

In India, mint follows coriander and *neem* leaves as the most widely used herb. It is an important flavoring in soups, savories, vegetables, rice, *dals* and beverages. American seedsmen offer herb gardeners a good selection of scented hybrids, from apple mint to cinnamon mint, each type with a different flavor. My favorite mint *lassi* combines homemade vanilla yogurt with licorice mint and coarsely powdered fennel seeds. These hinted sweet ingredients are offset with a splash of rose water for a very refreshing summer thirst quencher.

For a special Maharastran breakfast, try this drink with two or three varieties of seasonal fresh fruits and *Bombay Chidwa*.

Preparation time (after assembling ingredients): 10 minutes
Serves: 4

2 cups (480 ml) homemade or Brown Cow vanilla yogurt or
    Dannon low-fat vanilla yogurt
3 tablespoons (45 ml) sour cream, cream, or half-and-half
¼ cup (60 ml) trimmed fresh mint, loosely packed
1 teaspoon (5 ml) dry-roasted fennel seeds, coarsely powdered
½ cup (110 g) superfine sugar or equivalent sweetener
½ tablespoon (7 ml) rose water
¼ cup (60 ml) ice water
8–10 ice cubes, cracked
4 sprigs fresh mint or rose petals for garnishing

Combine all of the ingredients, except the ice cubes and garnish, in a blender or food processor fitted with the metal blade, cover, and process for 2 minutes. Add the ice and process for another minute. Pour into frosted glasses and garnish with fresh mint or rose petals.

Papaya Yogurt Shake
PAPITA LASSI

This is a quick and healthy meal-in-a-glass for those occasions when you are too rushed to prepare a meal or just want a fast pick-me-up. Though fresh papayas are preferred for this *lassi*, you can also use sugar-free Wagner's creamed papaya concentrate, available at health food stores.

Preparation time: 10 minutes
Serves: 4

For information about unfamiliar ingredients or techniques, see A-to-Z

1 tablespoon (15 ml) fresh ginger root purée or pulp
1 cup (240 ml) finely chopped fresh papaya or
    ¾ cup (180 ml) papaya concentrate
8 ice cubes, cracked
2 cups (480 ml) fresh or unfiltered apple juice
⅔–1 cup (160–240 ml) plain or maple-flavored yogurt

Place the ginger, papaya and ice cubes in a blender or food processor fitted with the metal blade and process for 2–3 minutes. Add the remaining ingredients and process for about 1 minute or until the *lassi* is light and frothy. Serve in iced glasses. For a colorful garnish, place papaya cubes and mint sprigs on long skewers and drop it into the glasses.

Banana Yogurt Shake
KELA LASSI

This is a perfect low-calorie alternative to rich banana milk shakes made with heavy cream. Bananas lend both body and natural fructose sweetener to yogurt drinks and complement almost any other fruit. In India, banana *lassi* is little more than banana, lime juice, yogurt and ice, but in the West I have made scores of exciting variations. For natural sweeteners, try blending in a few soaked raisins, currants, dates or figs. The beverage can also be made with apple, pineapple, coconut or peach juice. Since bananas are available year-round, this is a good all-season *lassi*. You might try it for a special breakfast or brunch, accompanied by *Crispy Puffed Wheat with Seasoned Vegetables* or *Spicy Puffed Rice Snack with Fried Noodles and Almonds*.

Preparation time (after assembling ingredients): 10 minutes
Serves: 4

2 ripe bananas, peeled and sliced
2 tablespoons (30 ml) fresh lime or lemon juice
½ cup (120 ml) ice-cold white grape juice or water
3 tablespoons (45 ml) clear honey or maple syrup, optional
1 cup (240 ml) plain yogurt or buttermilk
6–8 ice cubes, cracked
¼ teaspoon (1 ml) ground cardamom
½ tablespoons (7 ml) *kewra* water or a few drops of *kewra* essence
⅛ teaspoon (0.5 ml) freshly ground nutmeg
grated lime zest for garnishing

Place the bananas, lime or lemon juice, grape juice or water, optional sweetener and yogurt or buttermilk in a blender or food processor fitted with the metal blade. Process for about 2 minutes, then add the ice, cardamom and *kewra* and process for another minute. (The ice does not need to be fully crushed.) Pour into glasses, sprinkle with nutmeg and lime zest, and serve.

Lemon-Flavored Yogurt Shake
NIMBU LASSI

In India, this beverage is popularly made with four ingredients: sugar cane juice, lime juice, fresh ginger pulp and yogurt. The flat sweetness of fresh cane juice pleasantly complements the acidity in the citrus juice. Indian limes, called *nimbu*, are something between lemons and limes, quite like Key limes from South Florida. You can use lemon and lime juice instead of *nimbu* and white grape juice instead of sugar cane juice. If you have access to green coconut, it is also delicious, although it needs additional sweetener.

Preparation time (after assembling ingredients): a few minutes
Serves: 4

2 cups (480 ml) sugar cane juice or white grape juice
1 cup (240 ml) plain yogurt
½ teaspoon (2 ml) grated lemon zest
¼ cup (60 ml) Key lime juice or 2 tablespoons
    (30 ml) each lemon and lime juice
8 ice cubes, cracked
½ tablespoons (7 ml) ground raw pistachio nuts

Combine the sugar cane or grape juice, yogurt, lemon zest and citrus juice in a blender and process for 1 minute. Pour over cracked ice in chilled glasses and sprinkle with ground pistachios. Serve immediately.

Frosty Mango Milk Shake
AAM LASSI

India is a paradise for mango lovers. During the growing season, dozens of varieties reach the marketplace—some fruits as large as footballs. One of the most loved and outstanding varieties, Alphonso, is nearly fiber-free, rose-pineapple-perfumed and a brilliant orange-red in color. It is an excellent choice for any fruit dessert or beverage that stands on its own. Though this shake is traditionally made with rich milk, it is equally delicious with yogurt or buttermilk. If fresh mangoes are not available or are of poor quality, you can purchase good Alphonso mango pulp at Indian groceries. Because it is usually sweetened, omit or cut down on the sweetener. Serve this elegant treat at a special gathering of friends or family, with *Potato Straw, Cashew, Raisin and Coconut Snack*.

Preparation and chilling time: 30 minutes
Serves: 4

1 cup (240 ml) diced fresh mango (about 1 pound/455 g)
    or ¾ cup (180 ml) mango pulp
½ cup (120 ml) chilled orange juice
3–4 tablespoons (45–60 ml) clear honey or vanilla sugar
2 cups (480 ml) rich milk, chilled in the freezer for 15 minutes
a few garden rose petals for garnishing (optional)

For information about unfamiliar ingredients or techniques, see A-to-Z

1. Combine the mango, orange juice and sweetener in a food processor fitted with the metal blade and process for 1½ minutes. Pour it into a bowl and set in the freezer for 15 minutes.

2. Pour the milk into the food processor and process until it has expanded in volume and become frothy. Add the mango purée and process for about a minute, then pour into chilled glasses. Garnish with rose petals, if desired, and serve immediately. (Made with milk, this drink is light and airy, but it will thin down within a few minutes. Assemble just before serving.)

Honeyed Peach Shake
AROO LASSI

Peach trees dot the slopes of the Himalayan foothills and specialties made from peaches almost invariably come from the North because few of the prized fruits ever reach South India. The unripened fruits are sometimes cooked with whole *dals* into hot tart gravy dishes, while ripe fruits are usually savored plain or in chutneys and beverages. American nectarines are equally delicious in this smooth delight, as are apricots and papayas.

Preparation time (after assembling ingredients): 10 minutes
Serves: 4

2 ripe peaches or nectarines, peeled, pitted and chopped
1 pear, peeled, cored and chopped
1 tablespoon (15 ml) lime juice
4 tablespoons (60 ml) clear honey or sugar
6–8 ice cubes, cracked
1 cup (240 ml) coconut milk or apple juice
1 cup (240 ml) yogurt or buttermilk
a few pomegranate cells for garnishing

Combine the peaches or nectarines, pear, lime juice and sweetener in a blender or food processor fitted with the metal blade and purée until smooth. Add the cracked ice and pulse several times. Finally, add the coconut milk or apple juice and yogurt or buttermilk. Process for 1½ minutes or until frothy and light. (The ice need not be crushed.) Pour into glasses and garnish with a few pomegranate cells.

Zesty Buttermilk Cooler
CHAACH PIYUSH

American buttermilk is a cultured product, like yogurt and sour cream, and, though made from low-fat milk, it has a creamy consistency. Its Indian counterpart, called *chaach*, is quite different. It is the liquid that separates from butter as it is churned. In America, butter is usually made from sweet fresh cream, and the *chaach* is therefore mild and sweetish. Indian butter is generally made from slightly soured clotted cream or yogurt, and its *chaach* possesses tart overtones. *Piyush* or *meetha* is the chilled beverage made with *chaach*, and, whether sweetened or salty, it is served ice cold.

A good alternative for homemade *chaach* is thinned-down commercial buttermilk with butter flakes. It makes a delicious low-calorie refresher for summer breakfast or brunch.

Preparation time (after assembling ingredients): a few minutes
Serves: 4

2 cups (480 ml) buttermilk
½ cup (120 ml) yogurt
½ teaspoon (2 ml) salt
1 teaspoon (5 ml) dry-roasted cumin seeds, powdered
1 tablespoon (15 ml) lemon or lime juice
2 tablespoons (30 ml) sugar or equivalent sweetener
6–8 ice cubes, slightly crushed

Place all of the ingredients in a blender or food processor fitted with the metal blade and process until frothy, about 2 minutes. (The ice need not break down completely.) Pour into chilled glasses and serve immediately.

Five-Nectar Milk Bowl
PANCH AMRITA

Jaipur, the famed Pink City in Rajasthan, houses several remarkable palaces. One of the largest, City Palace—literally a small city within a city—is the present home of the Maharani of Jaipur. In the center of the compound, surrounded by gardens, sits the spectacular Sri Radha Govinda Temple, the citadel residence of the original Deities of the sixteenth-century Vaishnava saint Srila Rupa Goswami.

In 1971 the Maharani, Gayatri Devi, hosted Srila Prabhupada's *sankirtan* party for a fortnight of lectures and *kirtan* programs, and the stay was memorable. Daily our party feasted on *prasadam* from Radha Govinda's expert temple cooks. This is one of the beverages served to the Deities in the late afternoon. In Sanskrit, *panch* means five and *amrita* means nectar. This version features five ingredients that make it nectarean: milk, yogurt, coconut milk, honey and mango purée. Served in deep silver or glass punch bowls garnished with rose petals, exotic fried lotus pods and coconut, it makes a wonderful banquet beverage. To keep the beverage well chilled, fresh pieces of fruit and sweetened milk can be combined in a *savarin*-type tube tin and frozen until solid. Once in the punch bowl, the melting frozen milk will not dilute the beverage.

For information about unfamiliar ingredients or techniques, see A-to-Z

Preparation time (after assembling ingredients): about 30 minutes
Infusion time: 1 hour
Chilling time: several hours
Serves: 15

¾ cup (180 ml) milk
¾ cup (180 ml) water
¼ cup (60 ml) warmed honey
1½ cups (360 ml) mixed fruits, such as grapes,
        strawberries, raspberries and cubed mangoes
1 coconut, husked, peeled and coarsely shredded
3 cups (710 ml) boiling water
1 quart/liter milk
two 3-inch (7.5 cm) strips of orange zest
1-inch (2.5 cm) piece of vanilla bean
½ teaspoon (2 ml) cardamom seeds, crushed
4 cups (1 liter) plain or vanilla yogurt
1 cup (240 ml) chopped mango
up to ¾ cup (180 ml) honey or liquid sweetener
¼ cup (60 ml) rose water
ghee for shallow-frying
12 puffed lotus pods, halved
¼ cup (25 g) dried ribbon coconut
a few garden rose petals for garnishing

1. Combine ¾ cup (180 ml) milk, ¾ cup (180 ml) water, and ¼ cup (60 ml) honey in a small pan and warm until the honey is dissoved. Pour into a tube tin and add the fruits. Freeze until solid.

2. Place the coconut in a bowl and cover with the boiling water. Set the infusion aside for at least 1 hour.

3. Pour 3 cups (710 ml) milk into a pan and add the orange zest, vanilla bean and cardamom seeds. Place over moderate heat and, stirring frequently, bring to a boil. Remove the pan from the heat, cover, and set the infusion aside for about 45 minutes.

4. Combine 2 cups (480 ml) of yogurt, the chopped mango, and sweetener in a blender, cover, and process until smooth. Place the remaining yogurt in a large bowl and whisk until smooth. Pour in the mango yogurt and stir well.

5. Place a sieve lined with a dampened cloth over a bowl and pour the shredded coconut and soaking water into the sieve. When the liquid has drained through the sieve, gather the corners of the cloth and squeeze it tightly to extract as much liquid as possible. Add the liquid to the yogurt mixture.

6. When the flavored milk has set for at least ½ hour, pour it through a sieve. Add it with the remaining 1 cup (240 ml) milk and the rose water to the yogurt mixture and whisk well. Cover and refrigerate thoroughly.

7. Just before serving, heat ½ inch (1.5 cm) of *ghee* in a small frying pan over moderate heat. Fry the lotus pods until golden brown, remove with a slotted spoon, and set aside on paper towels. Add the coconut and, tossing to ensure even browning, fry until golden. Remove with a slotted spoon and drain.

8. Pour the chilled beverage into a punch bowl. Remove the frozen fruit milk ring from the tube mold and float it, fruit side up. Place the lotus puffs and coconut in the center and the rose petals on the outside of the ice.

Scented Almond Milk Cooler
BADAAM DHOOD

Phool Bhag, the palace compound of Pratapkumar, Crown Prince of Alwar, is an example of spiritual management and nature's perfect arrangements. Situated in Rajasthan's northeastern arid desert, the complex encompasses acres of flower-spangled gardens and lakes and offers sanctuary to numerous bird and animal species—elephants, camels, cows, buffaloes, deer, horses, peacocks, sheep, rabbits, goats, lions and tigers. Pratapkumar attributes his wealth and success in life to his dedicated daily worship in the Sri Janaki-Vallabha Temple. This statement reflects his personal lifestyle and philosophy: "In India, the temple is the center of activity in the royal palace. Worship of the Lord must personally be performed by the king before he can accept worship in the palace." The Janaki-Vallabha Temple kitchens engage nearly 20 expert cooks in the service of the Deities. Though they excel in local Rajasthani cuisine, they are proficient in numerous others. This is one of the cooling beverages served during the hot summer months.

Preparation and nut soaking time : about 1 hour
Serves: 4

⅔ cup (100 g) blanched almonds
½ teaspoon (2 ml) cardamom seeds
4 whole peppercorns
2 cups (480 ml) boiling water
¼ cup (60 ml) honey
2 cups (480 ml) white grape juice
½ tablespoon (7 ml) rose water
2 cups (480 ml) still water or sparkling water

1. Place the almonds, cardamom seeds and peppercorns in a bowl and add 1¼ cups (300 ml) boiling water. Set aside for 1 hour. Pour into a blender, cover, and reduce the nuts to a fine paste. Add the remaining ¾ cup (180 ml) boiling water and the honey and blend for ½ minute.

2. Line a sieve with three thicknesses of cheesecloth. Pour the nut milk through the sieve, then extract as much liquid as possible. (The nut pulp can be saved for cutlets or salad dressing.) Add a little grape juice to the blender and process briefly to release any almonds sticking to the sides of the jar. Add to the sieved nut milk.

3. Pour the remaining grape juice, rose water and water into the nut milk and blend well. Chill before serving.

Raisin and Nut Milk Laced with Fennel
THANDAI

This summer punch is made from sugar-free nut milk. Raisins, almonds, pistachios and melon seeds are steeped in a fennel seed tea until their oils and flavors have been released. This infusion is then blended and strained—a once time-consuming task made easy with a blender. Finally, the nut milk is enriched with low-fat saffron-flavored milk, resulting in a healthful and refreshing beverage. *Thandai* is served ice cold—an ideal Vedic drink for holidays and celebrations, whether for 8 or 80.

Preparation and soaking time (after assembling ingredients): 1½–3 hours
Serves: 8

2½ cups (600 ml) water
2 tablespoons (30 ml) fennel seeds
½ teaspoon (2 ml) cardamom seeds
4 whole cloves
⅔ cup (95 g) raisins
½ cup (50 g) almonds, blanched and chopped
¼ cup (35 g) blanched pistachios, chopped
¼ cup (35 g) melon seeds, sunflower seeds or pine nuts
1 quart/liter low-fat or whole milk
¼ teaspoon (1 ml) good-quality saffron threads, dry-roasted and powdered

1. Bring the water to a boil in a small saucepan. Add the fennel seeds, cardamom and cloves, cover, and remove from the heat. Set aside for 10 minutes.

2. Place the raisins, almonds, pistachios and melon seeds, sunflower seeds or pine nuts in a bowl and add the fennel tea. Cover and set aside for at least 1 hour.

3. Transfer the infusion to a blender, cover, and blend until the nuts and spices are reduced to a smooth texture. Pour into a strainer lined with a dampened cloth and set over a clean bowl. When some of the liquid has drained through the sieve, gather the corners and squeeze tightly to extract the maximum amount of liquid. (The pulp may be saved for nut cutlets, sauces or fudges.)

4. Heat 2 tablespoons (30 ml) of milk and add the saffron. Combine the nut milk, saffron milk and remaining low-fat milk in a large jug or pitcher and chill well. Serve over cracked ice.

WARMING DRINKS

Pistachio Milk
PISTA DHOOD

In India, hot milk beverages are served like Italian *cappuccino*—covered with a creamy frothy topping. For the Italian beverage, milk is frothed by steam in a costly espresso machine. Indians simply pour the milk from one pot to another; an expert spans 2–3 feet (60–75 cm) without spilling a drop! Americans can take advantage of a food processor or blender. They do the job wonderfully. Pistachio milk is served in the morning or late evening, as a toddy during the winter months.

Preparation time: 15 minutes
Serves: 4

3 tablespoons (45 ml) unsalted raw pistachios, blanched
3½ cups (830 ml) milk
6–8 good-quality saffron threads
2 tablespoons (30 ml) sugar or honey, or as desired

1. Cut 4 pistachios into slivers and set aside. Place the remaining nuts in a blender, cover, and pulse several times to coarsely grind. Add ½ cup (120 ml) of milk and blend until smooth, stopping the machine now and then to scrape down the sides of the jar with a spatula to free the nuts. Slowly add another 1 cup (240 ml) milk and blend for ½ minute.

2. Place the nut milk, remaining milk and saffron in a heavy-bottomed pan over high heat. Stirring constantly, bring to a full boil. Froth the milk two more times, then remove it from the flame and stir in the sweetener until dissolved.

3. Place a strainer over the blender and pour in the milk. Partially cover and blend, starting at a low speed and increasing to high, until the milk is frothing. Pour into cups, sprinkle with the pistachio slivers, and serve at once.

Spiced Coconut Milk Tonic

NARIYAL DHOOD

This restorative is smooth and satisfying, but milk-free. It is a good beverage to toast a wintry evening or cheer a recovering patient.

Preparation and cooking time (after assembling ingredients): 15
      minutes
Serves: 6 to 8

2 cups (170 g) shredded fresh coconut
6 whole peppercorns
8 whole cloves
3 cups (710 ml) boiling water
2 cups (480 ml) white grape juice
1 cup (240 ml) pear juice or nectar
1 tablespoon (15 ml) lime juice
grated nutmeg for garnishing

1. Place the coconut, peppercorns and cloves in a bowl and cover with the boiling water. Set aside for 1 hour, or overnight for stronger flavor.

2. Set a sieve lined with a dampened cloth over a clean bowl. Slowly pour the coconut and liquid into the sieve. When all of the liquid has drained off, gather the edges of the cloth and sqeeze tightly to extract as much liquid as possible. (The coconut can be ground for chutneys or savories.)

3. Place the coconut milk and the remaining ingredients, except the nutmeg, in a large pan over moderate heat and bring to the boiling point. Pour into cups or mugs and sprinkle with nutmeg.

For information about unfamiliar ingredients or techniques, see A-to-Z

Sweet Milk
MEETHA DHOOD

In India, a cup of unadorned hot milk receives some of the care afforded to brewing *tisanes* in the West. The pan must be scrupulously clean, the milk absolutely fresh, and careful attention paid to heating and aerating. Srila Prabhupada could tell if milk had been carelessly allowed to boil for even a few minutes or if it was one or two days old. He preferred a little rock candy as a sweetener, but more often than not, took it plain. Whether you like tupelo honey, molasses or sugar, hot milk is a pleasant tonic or relaxer for a sleepless winter night.

Preparation and cooking time: under 10 minutes
Serves: 2

2 cups (480 ml) fresh milk
2 teaspoons (10 ml) crushed rock candy or other sweetener

1. Heat the milk in a heavy-bottomed pan over high heat. Stirring constantly, bring it to a fierce frothing boil. Remove the pan from the heat and allow the foam to subside. Repeat the procedure a second time. Add the sweetener, bring the milk to a full boil a third time, and remove from the heat.
2. To aerate the milk, pour it back and forth from one pan to another until it is frothy. Immediately pour the milk into warmed mugs or cups and serve.

Cardamom Milk
ELAICHI DHOOD

Milk, nature's nearly perfect food, receives a protein boost from the added nuts and poppy seeds in this variation. This beverage, popular in Bengal, is delicious both hot and chilled. (Simply process ice-cold milk in a food processor until it has nearly doubled in volume.)

Preparation and cooking time (after assembling ingredients): 15 minutes
Serves: 4

3 tablespoons (45 ml) white poppy seeds
2 tablespoons (30 ml) minced raw cashews or almonds
3 tablespoons (45 ml) fresh or dried shredded coconut
1 cup (240 ml) water
3 cups (710 ml) whole or low-fat milk
⅓ cup (70 g) sugar or equivalent sweetener, or as desired
½ teaspoon (2 ml) freshly ground cardamom seeds

1. Place the poppy seeds in a heavy frying pan over moderately low heat and dry-roast, turning often, for about 5 minutes. Combine the poppy seeds, cashews or almonds, coconut and water in a blender or food processor fitted with the metal blade and process for 2–3 minutes or until the nuts are reduced to a fine purée. Add 2 cups (480 ml) of milk and process on low speed for 15 seconds.

2. Pour the mixture through a strainer over a pan. Press out as much liquid as possible, then add the remaining milk and the cardamom seeds. Stirring constantly, bring to a boil over moderately high heat. Reduce the heat to low and simmer for 2 minutes. Add the sweetener.

3. Pour the milk back and forth from one pan to another until it is frothy. Serve immediately in warmed cups or mugs.

Banana Nutmeg Milk
KELA DHOOD

Bananas tend to toughen when they are simmered in milk. In this version, rather than being placed over heat, they are puréed with scalded milk just before serving.

Preparation time: 10 minutes
Serves: 2

2 cups (480 ml) milk
1 firm ripe banana
2 tablespoons (30 ml) sugar or
    equivalent sweetener (optional)
1 teaspoon (5 ml) softened unsalted butter
¼ teaspoon (1 ml) freshly ground nutmeg

1. Place the milk in a heavy-bottomed pan over high heat. Bring it to a full boil, stirring constantly, then reduce the heat and simmer for 2 minutes.

2. While the milk is simmering, place the banana, sweetener, if desired, softened butter and nutmeg in a blender or food processor fitted with the metal blade and process until puréed. Pour 1 cup (240 ml) of milk into the blender or processor and process for another minute. Add the remaining milk and process for ½ minute or until the milk is foamy.

3. Pour the milk into warmed mugs or cups and serve immediately.

Almond Honey Milk
BADAAM MADHUR DHOOD

This drink is as much a morning ritual in North India as *cafe au lait* is in Normandy. Protein-rich almonds lend both nutrition and a boost of flavor to this much-loved beverage. Select a clear mild honey to avoid overpowering both the color and the delicate milk taste.

For information about unfamiliar ingredients or techniques, see A-to-Z

Preparation and cooking time: 15 minutes
Serves: 2

¼ cup (30 g) blanched almonds
2 cups (480 ml) milk
¼ teaspoon (1 ml) cardamom seeds or a 1-inch (2.5 cm)
    piece of vanilla pod, slit to expose the seeds
3 tablespoons (45 ml) mild honey

1. Place the nuts in a blender or food processor fitted with the metal blade and pulse until finely chopped. Add ⅔ cup (160 ml) of milk and process until smooth. Pour the milk into a heavy-bottomed pan and whisk in the remaining milk.

2. Place the milk over moderately high heat and, stirring contantly, bring it to a full frothing boil. Remove the pan from the heat, allow the foam to subside, and add the cardamom seeds or vanilla pod. Place the pan over moderately high heat and again bring to a boil. Remove the pan from the heat and add the honey.

3. Again place the pan over the heat, bring the milk to just the boiling point, and pour it through a strainer resting over a clean pan. Pour the milk back and forth from one pan to another for at least a minute or until frothy. Pour it into warm mugs and serve immediately.

Spiced Apple Cider Cup
SEB RAS

Fruit juice vendors in India sell freshly pressed juice by the glass or liter. Since the quality of Indian apples in general is poor, I sometimes made a clear pale apple juice from an infusion and, more often than not, served it hot and spiced. Whether you use freshly pressed juice or a supermarket special, this is a wonderful beverage for a wintry setting.

Preparation time (after assembling ingredients): 20–25 minutes
Serves: 8

2 quarts/liters apple juice or apple cider
two 3-inch (7.5 cm) pieces of cinnamon stick
½ tablespoon (7 ml) whole cloves
½ teaspoon (2 ml) freshly grated nutmeg
½ teaspoon (2 ml) whole cardamom seeds
½ teaspoon (2 ml) whole coriander seeds
2 tablespoons (30 ml) honey (optional)
8 lemon slices

Pour the juice into a heavy-bottomed large pan, add the cinnamon stick, cloves, nutmeg, cardamom seeds and coriander seeds and bring to a gentle boil over high heat. Cover, reduce the heat to low, and simmer for 20–25 minutes. Strain out the whole spices and stir in the optional honey. Serve in mugs with a slice of lemon.

A–Z GENERAL INFORMATION

Most cooks are eager to expand their knowledge through personal experience, observation and books and to share their knowledge with others. Before you resolve to explore a new cuisine, you must be inspired by at least a few of the following elements: a sense of adventure, history, health, pleasure or convenience. The following information addresses these topics as well as basic questions asked by cooks since time immemorial: what, when, where, why and how.

The following alphabetical entries cover such diverse topics as cooking fundamentals, specific regional cuisines, menu planning, recipe conversion, entertaining and serving. Special attention is given to unfamiliar ingredients, equipment, procedures and techniques. Each entry includes practical information about appearance, availability, preparation, nutrition, storage and sources. Because an ingredient is often known by several names in Indian grocery stores, scientific terms have been included to eliminate any confusion. Moreover, much can be lost in translation: a black cumin seed is often mistaken for a black onion seed, or an anise seed for a fennel seed. The Hindi references will help you in purchasing the item at an Indian or Middle Eastern grocery store.

Fruits and vegetables are a vital means of expression in any cuisine, but in a vegetarian diet they are an essential nutrition—four or more vegetable servings and two or more fruit servings are daily adult requirements. Clearly, the closer they are to the garden, the more vibrant their flavor and nutritive value.

Several reference libraries and books were consulted to assure the accuracy of the information that follows. Of valued assistance were the Botanical Reference section of the British Museum Library in London; the New York Public Library, Reference Service; the University of Pennsylvania Reference Library; and the Philadelphia Horticultural Society. At deskside was George Usher's *Dictionary of Plants Used By Man*; Sterdivant's *Edible Plants of the World*; Tom Stobart's *The Cook's Encyclopedia*, and Asa Gray's *Manual of Botany*. (Special thanks to Dr. Ludo Rochner and Mrs. Rama Karamcheti for their time and research.)

ADUKI BEAN: Also called *adzuki* and *feijao*. Small, oblong, reddish-brown beans (*Phaseolis angu-laris*) native to Japan and China. The sweet beans are pleasant when sprouted and can be used in place of whole *urad* or mung beans in virtually any recipe. Available from some health food stores and all Oriental grocers.

AJWAIN SEED: Also known as *ajowan* or bishop's weed. A celery-sized spice seed (*Carum ajowan*) closely related to caraway and cumin. The assertive flavor resembles thyme, with pepper and oregano overtones. Popular in North Indian vegetable cooking, especially with root vegetables such as potatoes, parsnips and radishes. Also used in fried snacks and nibblers. Available at Middle Eastern and Indian grocery stores.

ALL-PURPOSE FLOUR, Bleached or Unbleached: A blend of both hard and soft wheat flour. Milled from the central portion of the wheat grain, called the endosperm. During milling, both the bran and germ are removed. Most white flour is bleached to increase its whiteness and enriched to replace a few of the nutrients removed during the milling process. I prefer unbleached flour which closely resembles India's *maida* (wheat flour) though you can use bleached or un-bleached all-purpose flour interchangeably.

ALMOND OIL: The pressed oil from the nuts of almond trees (*Prunus amygdalus*). As with most nut oils—cashew, walnut or hazelnut—almond oil must be kept in a cool, dark place to keep it from going rancid. In India, the sweet oil is only available custom-pressed from an old-fashioned oil press and is quite expensive. It is used sparingly for brushing *sandesh* molds in sweetmaking or is sometimes added to *ghee* and brushed on hot flat breads. Available in health food and gourmet specialty stores.

AMCHOOR: A tan-colored powder made from sun-dried, tart, unripe mango slices. Seen in several regional cuisines, primarily in the North, *amchoor* is used, like pomegranate seeds, tama-rind or lemon juice, to bring pungency to a dish. Available at Indian grocery stores.

ANARDANA: The sun-dried kernals of wild pomegranate fruit, called *daru*. The trees flourish in the Himalayan foothills and, though the fruits are not edible, the dried seeds are an important souring agent in Vedic cooking. Used either whole or ground, *daru* lends piquancy to vegetables, *karhis* and *dals* and is especially popular in Northwestern cuisines. Available at Indian grocery stores.

ANCHO CHILI: The sun-dried pod of ripe poblano chili. With relatively mild heat and a rich flavor, it is a good selection for *chaunks* (fried spice seasonings). The dried pods—3–5 inches (7–12 cm) long—are chocolate-brown colored, but, once soaked in water, they turn brick-red. This soaking procedure tempers the heat somewhat and is a common practice in Rajasthani regional cuisine. Available at supermarkets and specialty stores.

ARHAR DAL: See *TOOVAR DAL*

ARROWROOT: A fine powdery-white starch obtained from the rhizomes of the tropical plant *Maranta arundinacea*, native to Central and South America. The original plant is named *aru* root of the Aruac Indians, but several other sources of the starch are also called arrowroot. Arrowroot can be used much like cornstarch in sauces and glazes, but, unlike cornstarch, it thickens at a lower temperature and does not have to be cooked to remove its "raw taste." It is not used in Vedic sauces, but may be used as a binding agent in *Ekadasee* dishes; for example, to bind seasoned mashed potatoes into cakes for pan- or shallow-frying.

ASAFETIDA: Known as *hing*. Obtained from several species of *Ferula* (fennel-related plants), asafetida is a dried gum resin, virtually odorless in its solid form. When the stems of the giant perennials are cut, a milk-like sap flows out which is sun-dried into a solid mass. The intensity of flavor and color varies considerably from its source, but generally the fresh resins are pearly-tan-colored and, with age, darken to a chocolate-black.

When bulk quantities of solid resins are ground, they release a strong to overpowering smell. In Delhi's Red Fort area, famous for its concentration of spice milling shops, a cloud of the heady asafetida smell pervades the area for blocks. Indeed, I have purchased costly and pure asafetida in crushed crystal form which must be double-jar-stored in the kitchen to encase the odor emanating from its sulphur compounds. Indian commercially ground asafetida varies considerably in texture, color and purity. For the most part, only two types are available in the West: a finely-ground mustard-yellow powder; and a coarser, sandy-brown grind. Both types are combined with small quantities of rice, wheat or barley flour as well as gum arabic to prevent lumping and to cut the strong flavor.

I have tested all of the recipes in this book with mild, yellow-colored Cobra Brand asafetida compound, and I strongly recommend it. If you use any other form, reduce the quantities substantially, to one-half or three-quarters of the suggested amount. Often said to resemble the flavor of shallot or garlic, asafetida is almost unknown to American and European cooks, though it was popular in Roman times and is used extensively in all of the regional cuisines of India. Available at Indian and Middle Eastern grocery stores.

AVOCADO OIL: Extracted from avocados, sometimes called Alligator pears, this oil has a nutty full-bodied flavor. Like other vegetable oils, it is unsaturated and therefore does not adversely affect blood cholesterol levels. Its high smoking point makes it excellent for sautéing, though I find it most enjoyable in salad dressings. Because it is expensive, reserve it for dishes that let the flavor shine through. Once opened, the bottle should be kept in a cool, dark place to lengthen shelf life. Available at health food and gourmet stores.

BAKING: In Vedic cooking, baking has been given a limited role, most likely because Indian kitchens are primitive by Western standards. Even today, most cooking is carried out on portable, bucket-sized, one-burner stoves, or slightly larger two-burner stoves—both called *choolas*. The portable model is little more than a galvanized five gallon bucket with a palm-sized vent hole cut near the base and an iron grate near the middle; the tiny chamber beneath the grate serves as the oven. An installed stove—with either one or two burners—is constructed of bricks with vents on the hearth and iron grates to support the solid fuel. The smoke from wood and coal stoves fills village and city streets round the clock. Only recently in India have propane and electric stoves or ovens become viable cooking alternatives.

The partially closed chambers of clay stoves have limited baking capabilities. Whole ash-baked potatoes, eggplants and squash develop wonderful smoky flavors and are traditionally used in vegetable purées called *bhartas*. Flat bread *chapatis* are placed on dying coal embers in the oven chambers to balloon and give them a charcoal flavor. In some regions, foods are wrapped in pliable fresh banana leaves and baked in the oven chamber.

BANANA FLOUR: Ground from varieties of dried cooking bananas or plantains (*M. paradisiaca*). It is a very digestible flour primarily used on *Ekadasee* fasting days when Vaishnavas refrain from eating beans, legumes and grains. As a non-cereal flour, it is low-gluten and, hence, difficult to handle when making flat breads. Popular in an *Ekadasee halva* mixed with *ghee* and in sugar syrups offset with spices and dried fruits. Available at some health food stores and Latin American grocers.

BARLEY and BARLEY FLOUR: One of the world's first domesticated cereal grasses, it has been cultivated in India since Vedic times. Husk-covered barley grains are obtained from the barley · grass (*Hordeum vulgare*), called *jawar* in India. Once the husk is removed, the whole grain is called hulled barley and is brownish in color from a thin germ and protein layer called aleurone. When stripped of the brown layer, it is ivory colored and is called pearled barley, the type most commonly sold in the West today. When toasted and cracked, they are called barley grits and are cooked much like bulgur. In India, the barley flour which is perhaps the most popular is milled from whole hulled grains. In America, the flour is most commonly milled from pearled barley. The low-gluten flour is routinely mixed with *chapati* (wheat) flour and used in both griddle-baked and shallow-fried flat breads. Call Indian and health food stores for availability before shopping.

BASIL: An herb appreciated worldwide by cooks, basil (*Ocimum basilicum*) has tender green leaves and delicate flowers. Cultivated in warm climates such as the Mediterranean, it has long been the basis of delicate favorites such as French *pistou* and Italian *pesto*. In America, seed catalogs offer home growers uniquely scented varieties rarely sold commercially. Park's Seeds, for example, offers Italian basil (*Ocimum basillicum neapolitaneum*), lemon basil (*Ocimum basilicum citriodorum*), licorice basil and cinnamon basil.

Holy basil (*Ocimum sanctum* and *Ocimum album*), called Krishna and Rama *tulasi*, is grown extensively in India but never used in cooking or dried for tisanes. Krishna *tulasi* has purple-tinged green leaves and flowers while Rama *tulasi* has green leaves and white flowers. These plants are worshipped in virtually every Krishna, Vishnu and Rama temple in India, as well as in the homes of all Vaishnavas. The flowers and leaves are offered daily in the worship of the Deities. The only basil used in Vedic cooking is camphor basil (*Ocimum kilimandscharicum*), known as *karpoor* basil. It is used in the regional cuisines of Bihar and West Bengal as an accent to rice, *dals* and vegetables. Fresh basil can be used in any tomato-based dish and is wonderful as a flavor accent on numerous salads. Available at some supermarkets (perhaps by special request) and at any good greengrocer.

BASMATI RICE: A long-grain scented rice that has been cultivated in the Himalayan foothills for thousands of years. The rice grains (*sali*) are milk-white, pointed at the ends, and four or five times as long as they are wide. Literally translated as the "queen of fragrance", well-aged *basmati* rice is considered by many cooks as the world's finest. Even when served unadorned or with only a drizzle of *ghee*, it exudes a perfumed, nutty aroma. Though *basmati* rice was traditionally a favorite in North Indian regional cuisines, today it is used extensively, not only throughout India, but all over the world—anywhere memorable rice dishes are made. Available in the United States in three varieties: Dehradhun and Patna *basmati* from North India, and Pakistani *basmati* from Pakistan. Unless otherwise specified, all recipes in the book are made with *basmati* rice. Available at Indian and specialty grocers.

TO BASTE: To moisten food with *ghee*, nut or vegetable oil (usually when cooking over dry heat) to prevent it from drying out and also to enhance the flavor. Foods cooked by moist heat are basted with cooking juices or sauces to prevent scorching and burning. Deep-fried breads are basted on the surface to encourage them to balloon during frying.

BATTER: An uncooked mixture of grain or *dal* flour, liquid and seasonings, beaten until it is of smooth dropping or pouring consistency. When batter is used as a coating over foods, the consistency should be thick enough to adhere to the surface that it will coat. Batters are also made by soaking *dals* in water, then draining and wet-grinding them into a smooth paste as a coating for sweets or savories.

BAY LEAVES, also called SWEET BAY and SWEET LAUREL: The leaves of an aromatic tree or bush (*Laurus nobilis*). The fresh or dried leaves are powerful and are used sparingly in vegetarian cooking. Some cookbooks recommend them as substitutes for cassia leaves, which are used extensively in Bengali and Eastern regional cuisines, but they bear little or no resemblance in flavor.

BEANS, Dried: Known as *dal*, dried legumes are classified into three groups: beans, peas and lentils. They are eaten either whole and unhulled (with the skin still intact) or split in half (both hulled and unhulled). Unlike the long-cooking selections popular in America, India's two favorites—mung (*moong dal*) and black gram (*urad dal*)—cook quickly and are easy to digest because they are low in the complex sugars that are not easily broken down by digestive enzymes. For more information on *dals*, see individual entries.

BITTER MELON: Also known as *karela* and bitter gourd, it is harvested while young from a climbing annual (*Momordica charantia*) noted for its beautiful foliage and yellow flowers. Like its close relative, Balsam apple (*Memordica muricata*), bitter melon has been cultivated in India for millenia. Four to eight inches (10–20 cm) long, thick in the middle (tapering to pointed ends), with a distinctive wrinkled green skin, bitter melon easily stands out in a vegetable market. Best harvested when slightly immature, it should be firm to the touch with white seeds. Avoid overripe bitter melon that is soft to the touch with a yellowish skin; it is not fit for cooking.

From the Punjab east to Orissa, bitter melon dishes are considered a delicacy. Known to be an antidiabetic and a stimulant to even the most listless appetite, bitter melon dishes are commonly served to elderly or sickly persons. Bengalis relish a bitter melon vegetable stew while Punjabis love them whole: nut-stuffed and pan-fried. Though bitter melon is an acquired taste, it is one worth exploring. Even in India, some cooks routinely salt or blanch the bitter melons to remove some of the bitterness before cooking. Sliced and dehydrated into thin brittle chips, bitter melon can be kept on hand for a moment's notice. Dehydrated fried bitter melon chips are very mild and every bit as tasty as potato chips. Available at Oriental and Indian grocery stores.

BITTER MELON

BLACK CUMIN SEED or ROYAL CUMIN: Known as *shahi* or *siyah jeera*, it is the spice seed of a wild annual plant (*Cuminum nigrum*) which grows profusely in North India's mountainous regions. The seed is blackish in color and slightly thinner than its close relative, cumin seed (*Cuminum cyminum*), known as *safed jeera* or *jeera*. While cumin seed is extensively used in all regional cuisines, black or royal cumin remains almost unknown outside of Kashmir, Punjab and Uttar Pradesh. In many Indian cookbooks, the seeds are mistakenly called *kala jeera* (literally black cumin or *kalonji*), being confused with the black variety of true cumin seed mentioned above. Further, *kalonji* is sold in many Indian groceries as black onion seeds, though it has no connection with the onion plant. Black or royal cumin is available at Indian and Middle Eastern grocery stores.

BLACK-EYED PEAS: Also called cowpeas in the United States, it is the kidney-shaped grayish seed from the pod of the plant *Vigna unguiculata*. Cultivated in India for thousands of years, it is popular both whole, known as *lobiya*, or split and husked, as *chowla dal*, and used extensively in Southwestern regional cuisines. The whole beans soften quickly and cook in about the same time it takes to cook yellow split peas. The whole beans are especially popular in a chili-like dish served, appropriately, with rice. Split *chowla dal* is delicious simmered in a tomato-flavored *chaunk* or loaded with vegetables and herbs. *Chowla dal* is also ground, milled into flour or soaked and wet-ground into batters for *dosas* and *badas*. Available whole at supermarkets and split at Indian groceries.

BLACK SALT or *KALA NAMAK:* It is not actually black but reddish-gray, due to the presence of small quantities of trace minerals and iron. Like pure sodium chloride, black salt is available either in lump form or ground, and is best stored, well sealed, in a cool dry place. It is not used interchangeably with sea salt or table salt because it has a distinct flavor—some say like hard-boiled egg yolks. It is a major ingredient in the spice blend called *chat masala*, a popular blend usually sprinkled on snack foods, from cut fruits to fried nuts.

TO BLANCH: To loosen the outer coverings of foods such as tomatoes, peaches, almonds or pistachios by scalding them briefly in boiling water. They may be cooled in cold water before draining and removing the skins.

   To blanch almonds and pistachios, pour boiling water over the shelled nuts and let them sit for up to 1 minute. Drain them, cool them slightly, and slip off the skins individually. Alternately, place the blanched nuts on one end of a tea towel. Fold the towel over the nuts and rub your hands lightly back and forth over the towel so that the nuts roll inside it. (Most of the skins will loosen within a minute or two). Place the skinned nuts on a cookie sheet and dry them out in a 250°F (120°C) oven for 20 minutes.

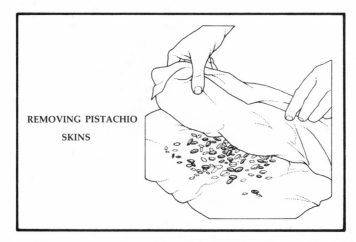

REMOVING PISTACHIO
SKINS

TO BLEND: To mix or stir two or more ingredients into a homogenous mixture.

TO BOIL: Known as *obalna*, boiling may be roughly divided into two catagories: full and gentle boiling. A full boil occurs when a liquid reaches 212°F (100°C) at sea level and the surface bursts into bubbled activity, releasing steam vapors above the pan. Foods are plunged into rapidly boiling water to parboil—set colors, or to blanch—and loosen skins. With limited usage, a full boil evaporates liquids quickly, concentrates flavors or reduces volume. In the early stages of preparing milk fudge *khoa*, milk is rapidly boiled to quickly reduce the volume and ensure a white color.

When the liquid is heated until slowly rising bubbles gently burst onto the surface, it is called a gentle boil. The pace is not as fast and furious as a full boil—an effective measure for cooking soft root vegetables with minimal bruising or disintegration. Split *dals* are gently boiled until they break down and are reduced to smooth soups or thin purées.

BOTTLE GOURD: Called *louki*, *ghiya* and *dhoodhi*, it is an outstanding vegetable from the quick-growing annual plant *Lagenaria siceraria* , also appreciated for its large yellow ornamental flowers. A much-loved vegetable, bottle gourd has been cultivated in India for millenia and references to its cooking are found in ancient Vedic texts.

Bottle gourd is best used when immature—as are zuchinni and other summer squash—while the skin is still paper-thin and the seeds undeveloped. In this state, they are 8–12 inches (20–30 cm) in length, heavy for their size and pale green in color. *Louki* flesh is outstanding—a cross between baby zuchinni and chayote—with a texture that holds its shape during cooking. If you must purchase older vegetables, they must be peeled and seeded before use and will never have the sweetness of the young crop.

Renowned for its versatility, *louki* is delicious in a light tomato broth for relief from indigestion. Check availability at good Indian groceries, and at Oriental groceries under the name *hula*.

BOTTLE GOURD

BRAISING: Known as *korma*, this moist cooking method is a combination of two procedures: browning, and then steaming or stewing. This method of cooking brings out rich, intense flavors in both vegetables and sauces. The food is first browned in seasoned *ghee* or oil over moderately high heat, then small quantities of a liquid, such as cream, tomato sauce, *dal*, yogurt–nut purées or water are added and slowly cooked over very low heat. The cooking may be done on the top of the stove or in an oven at between 300°–350°F (150°–175°C).

TO BRAY: To repeatedly spread an ingredient into a thin layer and again gather it into a mass using the heel and palm of your hand until the consistency is light and creamy-smooth. For example, to bray *chenna* cheese for Bengali confections, fresh cheese is spread out, bit by bit, in long strokes across a marble slab. Repeating this movement will break down even the most granular cheese. In large quantities, it is preferable to use a food processor to break down a coarse or granular *chenna* cheese, both for convenience and speed.

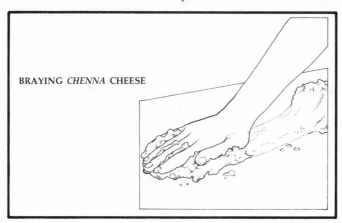

BRAYING *CHENNA* CHEESE

BROWN *BASMATI* or CALMATI RICE: Both are newcomers to American shoppers and should prove very popular. They are hybrids, made by crossing long-grain *basmati* rice from India with short-grain brown rice from America. The result is a nutritious and delicious, essentially brown rice with a moderately long grain. Calmati rice is grown in the earthy red soil of Northern California in a climate similar to the Punjab region of India. Brown *basmati* rice is offered by Arrowhead Mills and is sold in health food stores. Calmati is available at good gourmet shops. Dean and DeLuca in New York sell it by mail order.

BROWN RICE: Like white rice, brown rice is obtained from a cereal grass (*Oryza sativa*) but is unpolished, each grain retaining its valuable germ and yellow-brown outer layer containing the bran. Like polished rice, brown rice is available in short, medium and long-grain, but compared with the flavor of most white rice, it is nutty, chewy and sweet. Nutritionally, it has a balanced ratio of sodium and potassium. There is also a balance of minerals to protein and protein to carbohydrates that releases energy slowly and smoothly. Compared to other whole grains, it is high in much-needed B-complex vitamins—a positive plus for vegetarians. When cooked or served with *dal*, the nutrition is further boosted, providing nearly all of the essential amino acids. Many whole food enthusiasts consider brown rice a nearly perfect grain and, therefore, a superior food.

Health food stores and grain co-ops offer quality organic and non-organic brown rice. Lundberg Farms from California sells a wonderfully smoky-tasting short-grain brown rice. Lone Pine Farm from Louisiana offers superior medium- and long-grain rice. Eden products have long been considered a marvelous source of nutritional goodness. For further information about the processing of rice and comparisons between brown and white rice, see RICE.

BROWN SUGAR: Today, supermarket brown sugars—light and dark—are little more than white sugar with molasses added for flavor. True brown sugars are by-products from the process of refining white sugar from sugar cane or sugar beet and are not sold by American refineries. Though difficult to find in many locations, two types of relatively unrefined brown sugars are available: honey-brown turbinado sugar and date-brown muscavado sugar. Of the two, muscavado is the darkest with nearly all of the molasses still intact. The product called "Sugar in the Raw," sold in many supermarkets, resembles turbinado; but it is entirely unclear from the package how it is made. Two brown-colored sweeteners that are natural and unrefined are powdered date sugar and maple sugar granules and may be used in place of raw or brown sugar whenever suggested. It is important to note that date sugar is not really a sugar, but a pulverized dried fruit, often the only sugar allowed for diabetics. It burns at a much lower temperature than supermarket brown sugar—don't try to caramelize it when making a *chaunk*.

BUCKWHEAT and BUCKWHEAT FLOUR: Known as *kutu* or *phaphra*, it is the triangular-shaped seed from any plant of *Genus fagopyrum*. Native to Siberia, China and Nepal, there are two prominant species: *esculentum* (*faafar*) and *tataricum* (*kutu*). As a member of the *polyganaceae* family—like rhubarb, sorrel and dock—buckwheat has nothing to do with wheat and is not a true grain, though it is treated as such. As defined in George Usher's *Dictionary of Plants Used by Man*, it is botanically a "whole hulled fruit" but practically a "notched-seed." Sterdivant's, *Edible Plants of the World* states that in summer, wild *tataricum* has been spotted in rocky crevices as high as 11,000 feet in the Himalayas. The cold-climate plant, with branching heart-shaped leaves and fragrant white or pink flowers, little resembles the reedy grasses that produce most grains.

Of grain-type foods, the nutrient value of buckwheat is only surpassed by a similar seed called *quinoa*. Its 11.7 percent protein content is considered outstanding, posessing a good balance of the amino acids often lacking in the plant kingdom. Low in calories and purported to have over 90 percent of the value of milk solids, buckwheat is a rich source of fiber, iron, phosphorus and potassium.

With the hard outer shell removed, the triangular seed is called a groat. When roasted to bring out nutty flavor, it is known as *kasha*—either left whole or cracked into two sizes: coarse and medium. Buckwheat grits are finely cracked unroasted groats. The gritty flour, called *kutu atta* in India, is made from unroasted groats with gray flecks of the hull showing up in the sand-colored flour. In fact, the color of buckwheat flour varies from tan to gray-brown according to its percentage of roasted or unroasted hull.

In Russian and Jewish cooking, coarse and medium *kasha* is used for pilaf-type dishes like *kasha varnishkas* (a combination of *kasha* and noodles). Because of its popularity with these ethnic communities, *kasha* is sold in the gourmet food section of many supermarkets. Buckwheat groats, grits and flour are sold at health food stores and Indian grocery stores. In India, the low gluten flour is used primarily on *Ekadasee* days for *pakora* batter, *poori* dough and even sweet *halva*.

Even many Vedic cooks I questioned about buckwheat sustained the notion that it was a grain. Unfortunately, even good publications mistakenly call it a grain or cereal. To dispell this misnomer, I launched into extensive research. For those readers interested in my information sources, I am listing them, and encourage you to contact them if you are still in question: The National Buckwheat Institute in New York; the British Museum Reference Library, Botanical Section; the Horticultural Society of Philadelphia; and the Academy of Natural Sciences in Philadelphia.

BULGUR: This wheat product is to Middle Eastern cooking what cracked wheat is to Indian cooking. It is steamed and dried wheat that has been cracked or crushed into three grades: fine, medium and coarse. Because it is parboiled, it cooks quickly. In fact, in some Middle Eastern dishes, it is added to boiling water and softens off the heat in about an hour. Available at health food stores, Indian and Middle Eastern groceries, gourmet stores or grain co-ops.

BUTTERMILK: Known as *chaach*, real buttermilk is the liquid left in the churn when cream or yogurt is turned into butter. It has a flavor reminiscent of its source; when made from ripened cream, it is mildly tart; when made from yogurt, it is distinctly pungent. American cultured buttermilk is made from low-fat milk that has been innoculated with a starter, much like yogurt, and is mild and creamy. It can be used in chilled beverages, chilled soups, bread doughs and vegetables.

CAMPHOR: Pure edible camphor, called *kacha karpoor*, is a crystalline compound that looks like coarse salt. It is obtained by steam distillation of the aromatic leaves and wood of the evergreen tree *Cinnamomum camphora* that grows in India and China. Unlike inedible synthetic camphor, which is used in everything from insect repellents to explosives, raw camphor is used in minute quantity as a flavoring agent in milk puddings and confections, especially in Bengal and Orissa. Like bitter *neem* leaves, it is almost impossible to ferret out in America and is best forwarded by friends in India.

CARAMBOLA (STARFRUIT): Known as *kamrakh*, carambola is the star-shaped fruit of a tropical evergreen tree (*Averrhoa carambola*) native to India, China and Indonesia. The ovoid fruits are a translucent greenish-yellow color, 3–5 inches (8–12 cm) long, with five clearly defined ridges running down its sides lengthwise. Cut crosswise, the star-like slices add dramatic appeal to any fruit presentation. When ripe, they are juicy and almost sweet; when unripe and firm, they are used in cooking as a souring agent, much like tamarind. Carambola have appeared in supermarkets and greengrocers only recently and, like kiwi, are sure to catch on.

TO CARAMELIZE: To heat sugar until it melts and turns a reddish-brown color (about the shade of grade A maple syrup). To make a caramelized *chaunk*, heat 2–3 tablespoons (30–45 ml) of *ghee* in a heavy saucepan over moderate heat. When it is hot, add 1 tablespoon (15 ml) sugar, 1 teaspoon (5 ml) cumin seeds and one or two dried red chilies. Cook until the sugar caramelizes and the cumin seeds darken. The caramelized *chaunk* can be used to coat steamed vegetables or spice *dals*, stews or soups.

CARAWAY: The aromatic spice seed of the plant *Carumcarvi* which grows wild in the Himalayan foothills. Though popular in Europe, in India it is rarely used outside of Kashmir. Many Indian cookbooks mistakenly call them cumin seeds, though they bear little resemblance and cannot be used interchangeably.

CARDAMOM, Green Pods: The spice seed harvested from the tropical plant *Elettaria cardamomum*, native to South India. The small brownish-black seeds are encased in oval pods which turn a sandy to creamy-white color when sun-dried and a soft-green when air-dried. Green pods are much preferred to bleached white ones because the volatile oils in the seeds have more potency. The flavor of cardamom may be likened to a cross between lemon zest and eucalyptus. It is a very important ingredient in Vedic sweets.

For subtle flavor, whole pods can be added to syrups, puddings and rice pilafs. More often than not, however, the seeds are removed from the pods, coarsely crushed or powdered, and used in virtually any sweet—from cheese fudge to *halva*. If the seeds are fresh, they will be plump and a uniform dark color; if stale, they will appear shriveled and brownish-gray. Generally, four green pods yield about ¼ teaspoon (1 ml) cardamom. Green cardamom pods, cardamom seeds and ground cardamom are available at Indian and Middle Eastern grocery stores, gourmet and specialty food stores, and ground cardamom at most supermarkets.

CARDAMOM, Large Black Pods: Large oval-shaped black pods about 1 inch (2.5 cm) long, from a plant in the ginger family. The pods are rarely, if ever, used in sweets. The whole pods are slightly crushed and added to rice pilafs to release a warm, aromatic flavor with eucalyptus overtones. Available at Indian grocery stores.

CAROLINA RICE: Almost all American rice is called Carolina rice, though it is grown in Texas, Louisiana, Arkansas, and even California. Rice was first cultivated in the United States in 1695, near Charleston, South Carolina, and the name has stuck for centuries. It is a nondescript, moderately long-grain medium-thick rice widely available at supermarkets. Follow the cooking instructions on the package for best results.

CARROT FLOWER GARNISH: An eye-catching garnish that can be made with either a sharp paring knife or a canelle knife. (The cutting edge on this tool is a V- or U-shaped tooth that lies on a horizontal slot near the tip of the blade.) Cut V-shapes from one end of the carrot to the other in long strips about ¼ inch (6 mm) apart, then slice crosswise, into flowers. The attractive slices are fine for crudités or as garnishes on salad trays. They are also beautiful as a glazed carrot vegetable.

CASEABEL CHILI: A round, brownish-red colored dried chili with a nutty flavor when toasted. Regarded as medium-hot, it is suitable for sauces, *dals* or vegetables. Available at Latin and Mexican grocery stores.

CASSIA LEAVES: Known as *tejpatta*, the leaves of the tree *Cinnamomum cassia*, native to South India and Sri Lanka. Dried, the leaves are tan with an olive green tinge and are 7–8 inches (17–20 cm) long. In most cases, the leaves are fried briefly before cooking, releasing a strong, woodsy flavor. They are used extensively in Eastern regional cuisines, particularly in Bengal and Orissa, in dishes such as *shukta*, *charchari*, or even sweet *payasa*. Available at Indian and Middle Eastern grocery stores.

FRESH CASSIA LEAVES

CAYENNE PEPPER: Known as *puissi lal mirch*, this red powder is made from sun-dried red chili peppers (*Capicum annuum L.* or *Capsicum frutescens*). The chilies are very hot, with few seeds and thin skins, and are often roasted lightly before being ground into a powder. Several types of chilies are used, making some powders brick-red and others reddish-yellow, but all of them are very hot by Western standards. India is a large supplier of cayenne. In Rajasthan alone, tons of red chilies are dried yearly for export, and it is not uncommon to see acre upon acre of chilies drying in the scorching heat.

The Ayurvedic system of medicine maintains that red chilies help to reduce the presence of *kapha* (mucus) in the system. A disturbance of *kapha* accounts for disorders such as sinus problems, bronchitis and colds. The *Ayur Veda* recommends that these conditions be treated with *pitta* (forces of heat). In India today, a host of cayenne and herb mixtures are still used quite effectively to treat these disorders. Cayenne is respected as an aid in reducing inflammation, relieving lung congestion and increasing muscular strength. Widely available at supermarkets and almost anywhere quality ingredients are sold.

CELERY CURL GARNISH: A garnish that pleases the eye on any entertainment menu. You might see it at a luxury hotel banquet in Bombay or Delhi, but you will rarely see it elsewhere in India. Cut trimmed celery stalks into 2 or 3-inch (5–8 cm) pieces. Using a small garnishing knife, make cuts (1/16-inch apart) along the grain from the end of the piece to about one-third of the way toward the middle. Repeat the process at the other end, leaving one-third of the piece uncut in the middle. With care, cut through the center of the tiny cuts so that you have a double fringe effect at both ends of the celery piece. Soak the celery pieces in cold water with several ice cubes until the cut ends twirl and fan out. Drain, place them on trays, cover with plastic wrap, and refrigerate until needed. Before serving, bring to room temperature to regain flavors.

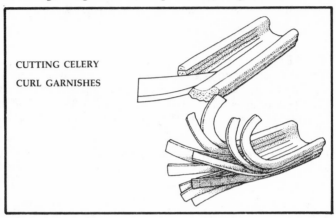

CUTTING CELERY
CURL GARNISHES

CENTRAL CUISINES: The cooks in India's Central Provinces, including Madhya Pradesh and Bihar, have made the most of whatever the land produced, most notably grains and *dals*. Spanning a distance of nearly 900 miles (500 kilometers), the region presents an eclectic diversity in everything from its topography, culture, dress and dialects to its variegated cuisines. Bhopal, the capital of Madhya Pradesh, exemplifies culinary diversity through its acceptance of dishes from bordering states into its own cuisine—Gujarati chutneys and Rajasthani *dals* are popular examples.

CHANA DAL: A split and husked relative of chickpeas (*Cicer grietinum*), perhaps the most popular legume in India. Nearly round, they are just over ¼ inch (6 mm) in diameter and pale gold in color. *Chana dal* is said to make up over one-half of India's pulse production. The reason for its popularity lies in the fact that not only is *chana dal* exceptionally delicious, nutritious and easily digested, but, aside from its usage both in *dal* dishes and savories, the legumes are also roasted and milled into chickpea flour (*besan*), another widely used ingredient in nearly every regional cuisine. (Calcutta's ricshaw-*walas* practically exist on a paste of chickpea flour mixed with water, hot green chilies, fresh ginger and salt, with an occasional raw vegetable, usually onion.) In South India, it is often dry-roasted and used in spice blends or chutneys as a nutty-flavored seasoning like *urad dal* or fenugreek seed. Available at Indian and Middle Eastern grocery stores.

CHAPATI **FLOUR:** Known as *atta*, this type of wheat flour has been used in India for over 5,000 years. By far, most of the wheat grown in India today is this low-gluten, soft-textured wheat (*Triticum gestivum*), golden buff-white in color. *Atta* is particularly suited to flat breads because the doughs made with this flour offer little resistance during kneading and rolling.

Atta is the entire kernal of wheat—endosperm, bran and germ—milled to a very fine powder. One of the finest wheat strains, known as *pisi lahore*, yields exquisite, buff-gold flour which makes silky smooth doughs. Even though the bran and germ are powdered, *atta* is routinely passed through a very fine sieve, called a *chalni* , to remove traces of roughage. *Chapati* flour is available at Indian and Middle Eastern grocery stores.

CHAPATI **ROLLING PIN:** Though any well-sanded hardwood rolling pin can be used for shaping flat breads, a tapered pin is especially suited for rolling out thin, perfectly round breads. The pins are slightly flared in the center, tapering out to the ends. By rolling a patty of dough in a back and forth motion and adding a subtle, side to side rocking motion, the dough actually rotates clockwise as it is thinned out and the patty is eased into an evenly thick disk. This procedure is difficult to do without a tapered rolling pin. Tapered pins from Europe are too long for ordinary flat breads: they average 21 inches (52 cm), while the type sold at Indian grocery stores is about 14 inches (35 cm) long. Not all Indian rolling pins are perfectly smooth. Request a perfect one with a gentle swell in the center.

INDIAN ROLLING

PIN AND BOARD

CHAROLI SEED: Known as *chironji*, these nut-like seeds are harvested from a tree (*Buchanania lazan*). The flavor so much resembles almonds that they are often regarded as an almond substitute. Charoli is a lens-shaped, brown seed about ¼ inch (6 mm) wide. They are frequently toasted before use and are a classic garnish for Gujarati *shrikhand*—a creamy yogurt cheese dessert. Like other nuts and seeds with a high oil content, they are best refrigerated in a warm climate. Available at Indian or Middle Eastern grocery stores.

CHAT MASALA: A sand-colored powdered spice blend containing several ingredients, but predominantly flavored with mango powder, black salt and asafetida. It is a traditional companion to a light fresh fruit snack called *phal-ki-chat*—four or five fresh fruit selections sprinkled with lime juice and *chat masala*. Two ready-made *chat masalas* available in America are quite good: Bedekar's and M.D.H., both available at Indian grocery stores.

The following recipe for homemade *chat masala* is uncomplicated, made from only a few ingredients, but with a characteristic sour twist that complements the flavor of fruits.

2 tablespoons (30 ml) cumin seeds
½ tablespoon (7 ml) fennel seeds
1 tablespoon (15 ml) *garam masala*
1 tablespoon (15 ml) mango powder (*amchoor*)
1 tablespoon (15 ml) black salt (*kala namak*)
1 teaspoon (5 ml) cayenne pepper
½ teaspoon (2 ml) yellow asafetida powder (*hing*)*
¼ teaspoon (1 ml) ground ginger

*This amount applies only to yellow Cobra brand. Reduce any other asafetida by three-fourths.

Combine the cumin seeds and fennel seeds in a heavy frying pan and dry-roast over low heat for about 5 minutes or until the cumin seeds darken a few shades. Grind in a coffee mill until powdered. Add the remaining ingredients and pulse to mix. Store in a tighly covered jar.

CHAUNK: Also known as *baghar* and *tadka*, a key seasoning technique used throughout India whereby selected seasonings are fried in *ghee* or oil and added to a dish to lend a distinctive flavoring. Typical seasonings include whole spice seeds, fresh ginger root, fresh green chilies or dried red chilies, *chana dal* or *urad dal*, cassia leaves, cinnamon or cloves. The *chaunk* may be made at the beginning or end of a dish, and, along with the endless possible combinations of ingredients, the cooking oils you choose also play a prominent role.

Different types of pans and heat sources affect the sequence of activity in a *chaunk*. The size of the pan in relation to burner size, as well as the shape and thickness of the pan, affect timing. In principle, the seasoning is made by heating *ghee* or oil until it is hot but not smoking. Depending on the heat intensity and the choice of seasonings, they may be added to the pan all at once or consecutively. Keep in mind that it is far easier to control the dimensions of flavor over moderate, rather than high, heat.

How long the seasoning is fried depends on the ingredients and desired flavor intensity. More specifically, black mustard seeds should pop and turn gray, cumin seeds should turn from tweedy-green to brown or reddish-brown and whole red or green chilies should blister. Spice seeds release dormant oils over heat, bringing flavors to life. A spatter screen is handy for preventing spice seeds from jumping out of small pans. Mustard seeds are the worst culprits; when they turn gray and pop, they also tend to leap from the pan. Moist paste *masalas* cause various degrees of spattering. You can also use a pot lid, set slightly ajar, to do the trick.

CHENNA CHEESE: An unripened fresh cheese used extensively in Bengali sweets such as *ras-goola*, *sandesh* and *pantoah*. Unfortunately, there is no commercial equivalent, except to say that, like uncured cheeses such as farmer's cheese, pot cheese, ricotta and mascarpone, it is simple to make. When whole cow's milk is treated with acid culture—lemon juice, yogurt or soured whey—the protein in the milk coagulates to form a curd of casein—hence the cheese is sometimes referred to as "curd" or "casein". Once made, *chenna* is immediately ready for use, though for some recipes it is compressed for up to an hour to release whey.

CHICKPEA FLOUR: Known as *besan* or gram flour and often sold under these names in Indian grocery stores. It is a finely milled, almost pale yellow flour made from roasted *chana dal* (*Cicer arietinum*) and is used extensively in batters for vegetable fritters (*pakoras*) and savories. Often, the chickpea flour sold in health food stores has not been roasted prior to milling and, therefore, has a raw taste. A light pan roasting will improve its flavor.

CHICKPEAS: Cultivated since Vedic times, they remain one of the most popular legumes in India today. Immature green peas removed from the plant *Cicer arietinum* are known as *har chana*, while peas allowed to mature on the plant are known as *kabli* or *safed chana dal*. Crisp and crunchy like water chestnuts, green chickpeas are exceedingly delicious in salads or stir-fried vegetables. Indian village children munch on them as a healthful snack. Unfortunately, both fresh and dried green chickpeas are not yet available in America. Mature dried chickpeas are about ⅓ inch (1 cm) in diameter and biscuit to light-brown colored, with a wrinkled surface. Also called garbanzo beans and ceci beans, they are available at supermarkets. Before use, they must be soaked at least 8 hours or "quick soaked" by placing 2 cups (380 g) of chickpeas in a pan with 6 cups (1.5 liters) of water, bringing it to a boil for 2 minutes, removing the pan from the heat, and letting it stand, covered, for 1 hour before use. They take 2½–3 hours to cook in a saucepan; pressure-cooked, they take only about ½ hour.

CHILIES, Dried Red: Sun-dried pods of various capsicum plants, they vary from red to black-ish-brown in color and are 1–3 inches (2–8 cm) long. Numerous varieties are available, ranging from hot to volcanic. Much of the intense heat is concentrated in the seeds, and, once removed, the chilies are slightly tamed. Whole dried chilies are sometimes soaked before being used in a recipe. For example, soaking and quick-blanching caseabel and ancho chilies softens the skins and disarms the pungency. As a rule, crushed chilies are very hot because the dried seeds are mixed in equal proportions with the dried skins. Both whole and crushed chilies are often fried in *ghee* or oil with other spices and added to cooked dishes as a distinctive *chaunk* seasoning. Dried whole and crushed chilies are found in most supermarkets, both in bottles and cellophane packages. There are many names for the same chilies and labels are often confusing and misleading. For use in small quantity, almost any type of chili will do.

CHILIES, Hot Green: The immature green pods of various peppers, including *Capsicum annum* and *Capsicum frutescens*. They range in heat-giving quality from mild to devilishly hot. Though most start green and turn red when ripe, some are yellow or brown in color. As a rule, small chilies with pointed tips and narrow shoulders are the most pungent. Chilies with a rounded base and broad shoulders indicates moderate heat with sweet overtones.

Chilies are a mainstay ingredient in a Vedic kitchen, valued for their color, flavor and heat. They are rich in vitamins A and C, renowned for stimulating the digestive process and in helping to relieve heat fatigue in hot climates by inducing perspiration. Many inhabitants in the tropics seem to be able to tolerate an inordinate amount of chilies. It is not unusual to see a dish for four persons prepared something like this: a handful of soaked and drained whole dried chilies, two spoonfuls of cayenne pepper, two spoonfuls of chopped fresh chilies and a bowl of whole green chilies on the table for munching. With that in mind, it is interesting to note that the trend in many Indian kitchens today is towards moderation—neither spices nor chilies are excessive. When handled like this, chilies enliven the flavor of a dish, much like salt or lemon juice.

Unless otherwise specified, all of the recipes in this book have been tested with moderately hot jalapeño chilies. According to the Waverly Root system, chilies are graded on a hotness scale from 1 to 120, with jalapeño registering at a mere 15.

While the flavor in the chili lies in the flesh and skins, much of the heat potency rests in the seeds and veins and can easily be removed. One note of caution: if you are handling a quantity of chilies or have sensitive skin, wear disposable, surgical-type rubber gloves. Avoid touching your face when working with chilies; the volatile oils can cause serious irritation. To seed the chilies, slice them in half lengthwise with a small sharp knife and rinse them under running water to remove the loose seeds. To remove veins, scrape away the light-colored veins with the sharp side of the small knife. To remove the seeds and veins from whole chilies, cut through the top of the chili around the stem, and, with a twisting motion, grasp the stem and pull out the seed core. Wash your hands after handling chilies. Hot chilies are available in most supermarkets and green-grocers.

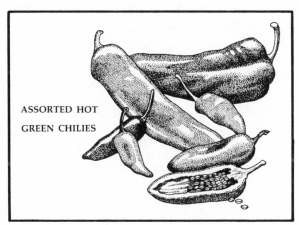

ASSORTED HOT GREEN CHILIES

CHINESE PARSLEY: see **CORIANDER LEAVES (CILENTRO)**

TO CHOP: To cut foods into irregular, ⅛–¼-inch (3–6 mm) pieces with a chef's knife or chopper. Foods are chopped when uniform shapes are not important. Finely chopped foods, cut into slightly smaller pieces, are also called minced or *émincé*.

CINNAMON: Known as *dalchini*, the dried bark of the tree *Cinnamomum cassia*. Cultivated in South India, both the bark, as cinnamon, and the leaves, as *cassia*, are used extensively in Eastern and Southern regional cooking. In most cases, the type of cinnamon used in India is sold interchangeably with true cinnamon, obtained from the bark of the tree *Cinnamomum zeylanicum*. Though *cassia* cinnamon quills are thicker and more pungent than *zeylanicum* quills, either type can be used.

Cinnamon quills are made from stripped-off bark which is flattened and planed away, then dried. Cassia quills do not splinter as easily as true quills and are, therefore, easier to use whole, without breaking. Quills or sticks, as they are referred to, are tossed into pilafs, *dals* or vegetables for sweet aromatic flavor. Freshly ground, cinnamon is an important part of *garam masala*, a North Indian spice blend. Available at supermarkets and at Indian and Middle Eastern groceries.

CITRIC ACID: Known as *nimbu-ka-sat*, these salt-like white crystals contain a concentration of the acid present in citrus fruits, predominantly from lemon juice. In a solution with water, it is an effective and convenient starter in making homemade *panir* or *chenna* cheese. A citric acid solution can also be brushed onto the surface of cut fruits, such as bananas and pears, to prevent them from darkening. In its crystal form, it is often powdered, along with white sugar, salt, even mango powder, then sprinkled on fried Gujarati *chidwa* snacks or nibblers. Like green mango powder, powdered citric acid crystals can be used as a souring agent when moisture must be avoided. Available at pharmacies and Indian grocery stores.

CITRUS GARNISHES: Citrus, sliced virtually any way, can add visual embellishment to drinks, salads, rice, vegetables and entrées. They are also indispensible flavor garnishes that can be used a number of ways. To make lemon or lime roses, using a sharp paring knife, cut a piece off to make a flat surface at the base and then continue to peel off a long, very thin 3-inch (7.5 cm) long strip of skin. Take off a second strip about 4 inches (10 cm) long in the same way. To make the rose, coil the first strip loosely around the flat base; coil the second strip more tightly and place it in the center. Using a toothpick, adjust the skin to resemble a rose in bloom. To make decorative shapes, using a paring knife, slice oranges crosswise ¼ inch (6 mm) thick. To decorate each round, cut through the white skin and rind removing small wedges, triangles and other decorative shapes and float them in a citrus punch.

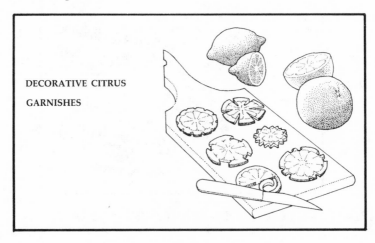

DECORATIVE CITRUS
GARNISHES

TO CLARIFY: To separate and remove impurities from liquids, thus making a clear product. *Ghee* is made by slowly heating unsalted butter to separate the water and solids from the clear butterfat. The clear butter is further filtered through cheesecloth to remove any traces of impurities. Nothing compares with the flavor of slowly cooked *ghee*, and, unlike butter, which burns at about 250°F (120°C), it may be heated as high as 360°–365°F (180°–185°C) before reaching its smoking point.

CLOVES: Known as *laung*, cloves are the nail-shaped dried buds from a sea-loving evergreen tree (*Eugenia aromatica*). Freshly dried cloves are quite oily, brownish-red in color, with a pungent sweet taste. If they are shriveled, black in color and limp, this indicates an outdated spice. Because it is a powerful spice, it is better to understate, using only a pinched-off head for subtle flavor. A popular ingredient in some North Indian *garam masalas*, cloves are sometimes offered as a chewable refreshment after meals—definitely a cultivated taste. Available at supermarkets and Indian grocery stores.

COCONUT: Swaying palm trees (*Cocos nucifera*) are a source of many products used in India, especially in the regions bordering the Bay of Bengal and Indian Ocean, where the trees grow on virtually all of the beaches. The unripened green nuts, called *dobs*, are large (sometimes 18 inches/ 45 cm long), and when the top is hacked off with a machete, a sweet juice is straw-sipped for pure refreshment. The insides house a gelatinous pulp which is used in savories and steamed cakes.

The date palm tree is tapped much like a sugar maple tree, but the coconut palm must be climbed to reach the tip of the shoot that bears flowers, and a cut is then made. An earthen pot is placed underneath the cut to catch steady drips. Because this liquid ferments quickly, the pots are changed at least twice a day and its contents bottled immediately. As one of the nation's favorite beverages, date palm sap is routinely dispatched by the government to State Emporiums throughout the country, where it is sold ice cold. When the sap is boiled and reduced to a solid form, it is relished as a candy-like, unrefined sweetener, similar to date palm *gur*.

While nuts are the dried fruits of trees, coconut is botanically a drupe—a fruit with a hard kernal—like the cherry or peach. Once the fibrous husk is removed, what remains is a hard brown shell encasing moist white meat and a sweet milky liquid called coconut water. A fresh coconut should feel heavy for its size with a generous quantity of coconut water inside. Do not purchase one with a cracked shell or any sign of greenish-gray mold around the three holes (called "eyes"). Coconuts are available year round and will keep for a few months.

To open a fresh coconut, pierce the two softest "eyes" and shake the water into a cup. Place the coconut in a preheated 400°F (205°C) oven for about 15 minutes, or until the shell cracks. Remove with oven mits and set aside on a cutting board. Tap the coconut sharply to crack it into two pieces. Using a small knife, pry out large pieces of flesh, then peel the brown skin off with a vegetable peeler. Once peeled, it can be sliced, grated, shredded, used to prepare coconut milk, or stored in the refrigerator for several days. Fresh coconut also freezes well with minimal loss of texture.

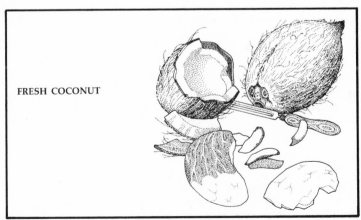

FRESH COCONUT

COCONUT OIL: Extracted from coconut meat and known as *nariyal ka tel*, this is a creamy-white fat which is hard at room temperature but clear when heated. It is used extensively in South India and is made in many households by soaking freshly grated coconut in water and then boiling it until the oil rises to the surface. Skimmed off and strained, the oil resembles a commercial product. Coconut oil is high in saturated fat, nearly 95 percent by most accounts. I have used it sparingly in this book, only in small quantity to lend regional authenticity to a dish. Available at Indian and Middle Eastern grocery stores.

CORIANDER LEAVES, Fresh: Known as *har dhania*, this is a zesty herb from the annual plant *Coriandrum sativam*, grown and used extensively in warm climates worldwide. It is purported to be the world's most used herb. Certainly, it is at least to Indian cuisines what basil is to Italian. The fan-shaped leaves are delicate, looking something like flat leaf Italian parsley but bearing no resemblance in flavor. The unique warm-bodied taste of fresh coriander lends itself well to the highly seasoned regional cuisines of Maharastra, Rajasthan, Gujarat and the Punjab, and to be authentic, it should not be overlooked either as a flavoring or as a colorful garnish.

Until recently, when California's chefs began using fresh coriander in restaurants, it was only available for the shopper as *cilentro* in Mexican or Latin grocery stores and as Chinese parsley in Oriental grocery stores. Today, it is found in ethnic and greengrocer stores nationwide, and even in some supermarkets. Coriander stores well for up to two weeks with the root ends in a glass of water and the leaves covered with a plastic bag. Use only the leaves from the coriander, never the stems.

CORIANDER SEED: Known as *dhania*, the spherical dried spice seed of the plant *Coriandrum sativum*. Used extensively in one of three ways (whole, ground or coarsely crushed), the flavor complements many foods and never masks the presence of other ingredients. Left whole, the ridged, off-white seeds are fried in *ghee* or oil to release volatile oils and darken a few shades before use. Before grinding or crushing, they must be slowly dry-roasted until brittle, otherwise, after grinding, you get more roughage than powder. Commercially ground coriander should have a pleasant sweet smell; if it is musty and nondescript, it is stale. Both ground and whole seeds are sold in plastic bags at Indian and Middle Eastern grocery stores; ground is also sold at supermarkets.

CORN FLOUR: Known as *makkai atta*, certain types of corn are milled into a granular, cream-colored flour, similar in texture to semolina. It is used primarily in North India, along with other flours and creamed fresh corn, in village-style flat breads. Corn flour has no gluten so it should not replace more than 40 percent of the *chapati* flour in flat bread doughs. It should not to be confused with cornstarch, a pure starch extracted from corn, similar in consistency to arrowroot.

In America, both corn flour and corn meal are generally ground from a type of corn called *dent* corn. The stalks are allowed to fully mature on the plant and are then dried before grinding. Because the germ in corn is rich in oils and spoils under certain conditions, it is often removed before milling. This type of corn product, called degermed or degerminated, is enriched to again reach its full nutritive value. It is best to seek out stone ground corn products—both flour and meal—and keep them refrigerated in a warm climate for extended shelf life. Available at Indian and gourmet grocery stores.

CORN OIL: An oil pressed from the germ of *maize* (corn). It is very pleasant for stir-fried vegetables and can be used in any type of cooking. Heated with minced fresh herbs, then mixed with lemon juice, olive oil, salt, pepper and *garam masala*, it is a pleasant vinaigrette for salads. From the cook's point of view, this is also a good frying oil because of its high smoking point, between 470°–485°F (245°–250°C). Cold-pressed corn oil is amber colored, with a toasted corn flavor, but many refined supermarket brands have been stripped of both color and flavor.

CRACKED WHEAT: Known as *dalia*, made by crushing or cracking raw whole wheat kernals (*Triticale aestivum*). Indian *dalia* needs to cook nearly three times as long as bulgur (which is already parboiled, steamed and dried), though, with time and adjustments, they can be used interchangeably. Usually available in three grinds: fine, for *tabbouli*-like salads; medium, for creamy milk puddings; and coarse, for rice-like pilafs. Sold in 8- and 16-ounce (230 and 455 g) packages at Indian and Middle Eastern grocery stores and, in bulk, at health food stores.

TO CRIMP: 1) To pinch very firm pastry dough between your fingertips at regular intervals to produce artistic patterns, or to pleat and twist two edges of dough together as done in some *samosa* recipes. When the pastries are fried, the crimping remains decoratively intact.

2) To score—for instance, the outside of a peeled or unpeeled cucumber—by pulling fork tongs from one end to the other, incising the surface with evenly spaced marks. When sliced crosswise, the pieces will have a frilled edge.

TO CUBE: In this book, to cut foods into uniform squares ½–1 inch (1.5–2.5 cm) on each side.

CUCUMBER FLOWER TWIST: Pull a canelle knife from one end to the other of a long, peeled or unpeeled, seedless European cucumber at ½-inch (1.5 cm) intervals. Cut halfway through the length, then slice crosswise into thin rounds. Twist and set upright as garnishes.

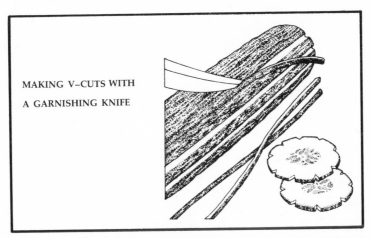

MAKING V–CUTS WITH
A GARNISHING KNIFE

CUMIN SEED: Known as *jeera* and sometimes as *safed jeera*, this relative of caraway is from the annual plant *Cuminum cyminum*. The seeds are yellow-brown in color and slightly ridged and curved, like caraway. It has been an important element in Vedic cooking for millenia and remains so today, used widely in North, East, West and Central cuisines. The seed—either whole, coarsely crushed or ground—is almost always exposed to heat before use to bring out its rich, exceedingly agreeable flavor. Dry-roasted until they darken a few shades and coarsely crushed, cumin seeds are used as a flavor garnish on steamed vegetables, *raitas*, *kachambers*, *dals* and rice. Once cumin is ground, it has a relatively short shelf life, so purchase a good brand and a small quantity. Available whole and ground at supermarkets and Mexican and Indian grocery stores.

CURRY LEAF: Known as *meetha neem* or *kadhi patta*, the powerfully fragrant small leaf of the plant *Murraya koenigii*. These look like miniature lemon leaves. In fact, Florida's Dade County Fruit and Spice Park has experimented with grafting it onto other citrus trees. In India, the plants have grown wild since Vedic times in almost all forest regions, from the Himalayas to Kanniya Kumari.

South of Hyderabad, it would be rare to find a kitchen that does not use *meetha neem* daily. A typically South Indian *chaunk* includes tossing a sprinkle of mustard seeds, 6–8 curry leaves and a pinch of asafetida into hot *ghee* and frying until the mustard seeds pop and turn gray. This could flavor anything from a dish of yogurt to a pot of *dal* soup. Freshly dried leaves lend characteristic flavor to the Tamil Nadu spice blend called curry powder.

Fresh curry leaves are sold at most Indian grocery stores. They keep well in an airtight container, refrigerated, for up to 2 weeks. If you cannot use all that you purchased, air-dry them on a towel until shriveled and brittle. Storebought dry leaves lack flavor, much like dried parsley does, and moreover, because they are delicate and rarely packaged in jars, they are usually crushed and past their prime. If the bulk of the leaves are not whole, with a noticeably olive-green tint, avoid them; they will lend little more than bulk to a homemade curry powder.

CURRY POWDER: Generally referred to as *masalas*, regional spice blends are composed of ingredients grown locally. Resourceful cooks combine spice seeds, herbs, twigs, leaves and weeds in endless combinations, though some loosely defined formulas become legends. The most popular spice blend to leave South India is undoubtedly curry powder; but what is obtainable in our supermarkets little resembles the blend that is stone ground daily in nearly every South Indian household.

In Tamil Nadu, the word *kari* means sauce, and in the last 200 years—most likely because these dishes were seasoned with curry leaves—curry has become a catch-all term for almost any gravy-like dish originating from India. Restaurant menus and cookbooks abound with curries—any number of hot spicy dishes. Unfortunately, many of the commercial curry powders sold today are stamped with the flavor of raw turmeric and spice seeds. The following recipe is flavored predominantly with curry leaves, coriander and cumin, with warm heat from both red chilies and black pepper.

Tamil Nadu Curry Powder:

2 tablespoons (30 ml) cumin seeds
2 tablespoons (30 ml) black mustard seeds
½ tablespoon (7 ml) fenugreek seeds
½ tablespoon (7 ml) split *urad dal* or yellow split peas
6–8 whole dry chili pods
25–30 curry leaves, preferably fresh
1 teaspoon (5 ml) black peppercorns, preferably Malabar
⅓ cup (30 g) ground coriander
2 tablespoons (30 ml) ground turmeric

   1. Combine the cumin seeds, black mustard seeds, fenugreek seeds, split *dal* and fresh curry leaves in a heavy frying pan. Dry-roast over low heat, stirring frequently, for about 10 minutes or until the seeds and *dal* darkens a few shades. (If you use dried curry leaves, heat for only one or two minutes.) Remove the pan from the heat and add the peppercorns.
   2. In small batches, grind the roasted spices in a coffee mill or spice grinder until it is reduced to a fine powder. Add the coriander and turmeric, and mix well. Store in an airtight container for up to 4 months.

CUSTARD APPLE or CHERIMOYA: Known by several names including *sitaphal*, *ramphal* and *sharifa*, India's custard apple comes from two trees related to papaya: *Annona reticulata* and *Annona squamosa*. There are several fruits in the family *anonaceae* which resemble the types that grow in India. Flavors range from intensely sweet to quite sour. Indian custard apple is roughly heart-shaped, with green to olive-black skin. The scaly skin houses a creamy-white flesh that is slightly granular and divided into segments, each one enveloping a large black seed. Properly ripened, the skin should yield slightly to pressure; overripened, the flesh yellows and becomes mushy. These delicious fruits are very sweet and taste something like a cross between banana, papaya and pineapple. Serve them plain, cut in quarters, or pass the flesh through a sieve and blend with yogurt, cracked ice and sugar for a delicious beverage. Available sporadically at Latin grocery stores.

DAL: In India, any type of dried bean, pea or lentil is called *dal*. Like rice, it is sold according to color, uniformity, flavor and processing. A high percentage of the *dal* eaten in India is split and husked—*urad, moong, chana* or *toovar*—because it is quick to cook, easy to digest and provides a valuable source of protein in the diet. *Dal* is split in one of two ways: dry, without soaking; and wet-split. In the Southwest and North, it is split, without soaking. Though it is more costly to the consumer because of waste in processing, this method yields the best flavor. It is easy to recognize this *dal* in the market, for both the flat inside and rounded outer curve are smooth. In the South, Central and East, where high yields and economy in processing are priorities, the *dal* is soaked, husked, sun-dried and then split. Wet-split *dal* generally has a depression on the flat side due to shrinkage. Much, if not all, of the mung *dal* that reaches American and European consumers is not from India but from Southeast Asia, specifically Indonesia, and is wet-split.

Good *dal*, whether split or whole, husked or unhusked, should have a uniform color, with a minimal amount of shriveled grains and foreign matter. For more information, see individual *dal* entries.

DANEDHAR: Made from homemade *khoa* which is slowly baked for several hours (8 ounces/230 g of *khoa* should bake for 4–5 hours) until it is firm and dried-out. When cool, it is easy to grate or finely shred and is used in sweets, frozen desserts, elegant rice dishes and even vegetable dishes.

DATE SUGAR: This natural sweetener is not really a sugar but rather coarse brown crystals obtained from dehydrated dates. Pitted and sliced dates are dried until rock hard and ground into a "sugar" that looks and tastes much like raw brown sugar. It is delicious sprinkled on desserts, yogurt or bland fruits, but is not ideal for creamy consistency foods or when cooking temperatures are high. This is because it does not dissolve easily and burns quickly. Look for date sugar in health food stores or order by mail. Store, well sealed, on a cool dry shelf, or refrigerate.

DATE PALM TREE

DEEP-FRYING: Known as *talna*, this is the most important dry-heat cooking method in India. Moreover, it is one of the culinary techniques that captures the attention of serious cooks the world over. The temperature range for deep-frying in Vedic cooking is broad—as low as 240°F (115°C) for slow-frying pastries, or as high as 385°F (195°C) for browning previously cooked foods. Properly cooked fried foods are often less caloric than improperly cooked pan-fried foods. The most important factor in deep-frying is to maintain the right temperature for the job. Using an accurate thermometer will prove invaluable.

Foods can be fried in any type of deep-walled container, from a thermostat-controlled deep-fryer to a casserole. Traditionally, in India, a bowl-shaped iron pan called a *karai* is used for deep-frying. Quantity cooking *karais* can reach 5 feet (1.5 meters) in diameter, requiring specially constructed outdoor stoves to support them. Home-size pans are usually 10–12 inches (25–30 cm) wide at the top and about 4 inches (10 cm) deep in the center. Much like a wok, this pan makes the best use of oil—you may have to use twice the amount of oil to fill a flat-bottomed pan to the same depth. If you use an electric stove, use a wok ring or collar to support the pan and prevent it from tipping.

TO DICE: To cut foods into uniform small cubes; in this book, under ½ inch (1.5 cm) but no smaller than ⅛ inch (3 mm) on each side. To obtain uniform pieces, cut the food into strips of the desired thickness, then bundle them together and cut crosswise into even pieces. Diced foods, of course, cook more quickly than cubed foods.

DOUGH: A pliable mixture of flours, combined with water, milk or yogurt, that is kneaded until the consistency is smooth and silky. Hard or stiff doughs require very little liquid and a long, determined kneading period to produce the desired finished texture. A soft or medium-consistency dough is sticky in the early mixing stages; when it has been kneaded until smooth and pliable, it will easily show the imprint from your fingertip.

TO DREDGE: To coat foods lightly with flour, or to garnish foods with a light dusting of confectioner's sugar or seasonings.

TO DRIZZLE: To pour sauce, sweetener or melted butter over the surface of foods in a very fine stream.

DROPPING CONSISTENCY: A term used to describe the desired texture of ground *dal* purées or the thickish flour batters used in deep-frying. To test dropping consistency, fill a spoon with the batter, turn it on its side above the bowl, and, in one or two seconds, the mixture should drop from the spoon.

TO DRY, also TO DEHYDRATE: To evaporate all of the water from certain foods by setting them on trays or wire screens under the hot sun. This is the most ancient method of preserving vegetables and fruits. Special dishes are made from *dal* flour doughs or wet-ground *dal* pastes, such as sun-dried thin wafers, called *paparhs* or *pappadams* and the dried *dal* cakes, called *badis*. In India's northern region of Kashmir, summer and autumn vegetables—turnips, pumpkin, radish, greens, tomatoes, chilies and lotus root—are routinely dried on every available rooftop and courtyard for use during the long cold winters.

TO DRY-ROAST: Known as *bhona* or *bhun-ana*, this technique refers to the process of slowly browning whole spice seeds, split *dals*, nuts, and some types of flour. It is best done on a heavy *tava* or cast-iron griddle that has been pre-warmed over low heat. The ingredients are stir-fried without the addition of any *ghee*, oil or liquid, until lightly browned, releasing flavorful volatile oils and aromatic fragrances. Most spice seeds benefit from dry-roasting before grinding; in fact, in North Indian *garam masala*, it is essential for authenticity. Kashmiri's prepare a very hot spice blend called *ver* by first dry-roasting the spices, grinding them, and adding enough mustard oil to shape the mixture into patties. *Ver* is air-dried until brittle and dry, then small bits are broken off and used as needed.

EASTERN CUISINES: In the East, Bengali and Orissan cuisines are characterized by vivid lively seasonings, a few special ingredients, and outstanding sweet delicacies. From Calcutta to Gopalpur-on-Sea, coconut palms overhang the Bay of Bengal's sandy beaches, while inland there seems to be an endless expanse of green or yellow fields from rice or yellow mustard plants. As a rule, Eastern cuisines are hot and spicy, typically seasoned with freshly ground wet spice *masalas* containing ginger root, hot red chilies, fresh coconut, and perhaps, white poppy seeds—a "digestive" balance of ingredients long considered helpful in combatting the effects of the intense tropical heat. Cassia leaves and asafetida, along with *panch puran*—a five spice blend of whole fennel seeds, cumin, nigella, fenugreek and black mustard seeds—are routinely fried in *ghee* or mustard oil to season with pizzazz.

Though local produce does play an important role in vegetable cookery, authentic regional flavors can be obtained with substitute produce outside of India. Indian grocery stores and health food stores in large cities carry such staples as cold pressed mustard oil, coconut cream and oil, *jaggery* and spices. Eastern produce can also be found in Chinese and gourmet greengrocers: plantains, unripened papayas and mangoes, *portals*, drumsticks, sponge gourds, and bitter melons.

EKADASEE: The twice-monthly fast day observed by Vaishnavas. Literally, the eleventh day of the waning and waxing moon, *Ekadasee* is honored by minimizing physical activity and increasing devotional activity. The fast requires that no grains or beans be eaten.

EQUIPMENT: see KITCHEN EQUIPMENT

ESSENCES: Known as *ruh*, these concentrated flavorings can be extracted from herbs and spices, fruits and flowers, even the roots, leaves or wood of trees. A few essences have been used in India since Vedic times, and they are made today much as they have been for centuries. Unlike Western extracts, usually extracted by a steam distillation process and bottled in an ethyl alcohol solution, these essences are usually made by a water distillation process and are devoid of alcohol. Out of the hundreds of available natural flavors, and many more artificial selections, only four essences are used extensively in regional cuisines: rose (*ruh gulab*), from scented rose petals ; vetiver (*ruh khus*), from the plant's roots; screw pine (*ruh kewra*), from flowers; and sandalwood (*ruh chandan*), from sandalwood chips. These essences are also diluted and sold as rose water or *kewra* water and can be used interchangeably, simply by increasing the quantity four times. Anyone delving into Vedic cooking should have these essences on the kitchen shelf; they are essential to making authentic sherbets and sweet dishes. Indian essences are sold in small bottles at Indian and Middle Eastern grocery stores.

Essences are added either toward the end of cooking or after the cooking is completed, once it has been removed from the heat. In some cases, one or two minutes of delicate simmering will help to release the full-bodied flavor of the esssence; high heat inevitably evaporates its flavoring potency. See individual entries for further information.

FARINA: Though the term can mean almost any type of flour or fine meal, in America it is most often refers to a creamy-colored granular product made from hard wheat. The berries are hulled and contain the germ, but no bran. It is a passable alternative ingredient for semolina, called *sooji* in India, though it is processed and enriched in a different way. Farina is available at supermarkets as both Farina and Cream of Wheat, including Regular, Quick-Cooking and Instant varieties.

FENNEL SEED: Known as *saunf*, this is the spice seed from the perennial plant *Foeniculum vulgare*. The plants are large, something like dill, and are cultivated mainly for their seeds. Less frequently, they are cultivated as an herb and for their thick, bulbous leaf stalks used much like celery stalks. Fennel seeds are greenish-yellow, resembling a large curled cumin seed in shape. The seed, herb and bulb possess an agreeable licorice flavor, slightly less sweet than anise. Whole seeds play subordinate roles in seasoning Kashmiri and Punjabi dishes and are one of the five spices used in Bengali *panch puran*.

Fennel seeds are used to flavor numerous vegetables, *dals*, syrup pastries and beverages. Perhaps its greatest use is as an after dinner digestive, offered much as we do thin dinner mints. Dry-roasted and served in one teaspoon (5 ml) amounts, candy-coated or combined with shredded coconut, toasted melon seeds and sugar candy, fennel seeds have long been respected as a natural breath freshener.

Anise seeds and star anise are not good substitutes for fennel; they are much more pungent and licorice-like. Fennel seeds are available in small jars in many supermarkets, or in bulk at Indian grocery stores. The best quality is called *lakhnavi saunf*, cultivated in Lucknow, India.

FENUGREEK LEAF: Known as *methi sak*, these are the edible green leaves from the leguminous spice seed *Trigonella foenumgracum*. Native to India since Vedic times, the greens possess a marked bitter taste but are much loved when combined with potatoes or spinach and used in wheat-based flat breads, both minced and mixed into the dough or as an herbed stuffing. Unfortunately, much of the fresh fenugreek sold during the summer at Indian grocery stores is not at its best but is overgrown and pungent. It is, however, very easy to sow seeds in kitchen window boxes and grow them to a height of 3–4 inches (7–10 cm). The flavor of the greens is pleasantly bitter at this stage and add distinction to a green salad bowl.

Sun-dried fenugreek leaves, called *kasoori methi* are sold at Indian grocery stores and can be used, in a pinch, for flavoring cooked dishes. It is necessary, however, to carefully separate the dried leaves from the thick brittle stems, soak them in water for about 30 minutes, and reduce the quantity called for by one-fourth.

FRESH FENUGREEK LEAVES

FENUGREEK SEED: Known as *methi*, this is actually a small legume (*Trigonella foenumgracum*) widely used as a spice seed. Brownish-yellow and rectangular, the seed is used both whole and ground. To develop its best flavor, it must be dry-roasted or fried, but only until lightly roasted. It should not be allowed to turn to reddish-brown shades because, at this point, the taste becomes intensely bitter. In some regions cooks allow the seeds to turn nearly black, as blackened seeds turn docile, with almost no pungency, and give off a pleasant charred flavor. Whole, the seeds are used in *dals* and pickles and play an important part in the Bengali five spice mixture called *panch puran*. Both whole and ground fenugreek are available in Indian and Middle Eastern grocery stores.

TO FILTER: To strain any liquid through fine-meshed paper filters, layers of finely woven cotton cloth or cheesecloth in order to remove impurities or other unwanted residue.

TO FOLD: To delicately mingle light and airy ingredients with heavier ingredients. Using a flat, shallow spoon, the ingredients are blended using an "over and over" circular motion so that the air in the light ingredient is not released by the mixing. For example, freshly whipped cream is folded into a mango purée by very gently mixing the two items to preserve the light, airy volume of the whipped cream.

FROTHING MILK: 1) To rapidly bring milk to a full boil and allow a 1–2 inch (2–5 cm) lacy foam to rest on the heaving surface. For example, to keep milk a white color when preparing the fresh milk fudge called *khoa*, it is allowed to froth in the early stages of reduction.

2) To froth or aerate hot milk for drinking by pouring it back and forth, from the pan to another vessel, for about 1 minute, until it is frothy. In India, experts pour the milk a distance of 2–3 feet (30–60 cm), managing never to spill a drop. Milk is always served hot in India because it is considered a liquid food, to be sipped rather than drunk and served very hot to minimize the gulping tendency and allow slow digestion.

GARAM MASALA: An aromatic blend of several dry-roasted and ground "warm" spices. The ancient Sanskrit medical work *Ayur Veda* suggests that "warm" spices generate internal body heat, whereas "cool" spices help remove internal heat. Originating in the colder climates of North India, *garam masala* routinely combines such "warm" spices as cinnamon, cloves, coriander, cumin, black pepper, dried chilies, cardamom or mace. Most households have a few favorite recipes, some only using three ingredients, others using twelve or more. Unless otherwise specified, *garam masala* is added toward the end of cooking, a concluding garnish of flavor like paprika or seasoned pepper. If you buy it ready-made in an Indian grocery store, purchase the type sold in vacuum-packed tins and, once opened, use for no more than 4–5 months; when stale, it loses its impact.

Homemade *garam masala* is easy to make and—in conjunction with other spices, herbs and seasonings—imparts exhuberant flavor to a host of dishes. Even if you are only dabbling in Vedic cookery, it is well worth it to try out one or two recipes. Every region has a few classic combinations. All of the ingredients mentioned below, and where to find them, are dealt with in this reference section. The procedure is the same in each recipe. Before they are ground to a powder, whole spice seeds and *dals* are toasted to release flavor and lengthen shelf life. All you need is a large, heavy-bottomed frying pan or cookie sheet, an electric coffee mill or spice grinder, and a fine-meshed sieve.

To pan-toast the spices on the stove, keep the heat low and stir every 5 minutes or so, for about 15 minutes. Alternately, oven-toast the ingredients in a preheated 200°F (95°C) oven for about 30 minutes. (Using a kitchen mallet or rolling pin, crush the toasted whole cinnamon sticks, cassia or bay leaves or blades of mace into small bits before grinding them with the remaining ingredients. Also, tap the whole cardamom pods to release the black seeds inside, and discard the pods.) Grind small amounts of the toasted spices until they are reduced to a powder. Pass them through a fine sieve and mix well with the already powdered ingredients. Cool thoroughly, label and date the containers, then store, well sealed, away from heat and light.

Rajasthani-Style:

3 dried whole chili pods
4 black cardamom pods
1⅓ cups (160 g) cumin seeds
½ cup (40 g) coriander seeds
1 teaspoon (5 ml) *ajwain* seeds

Delhi-Style:

⅓ cup (35 g) whole cloves
five 3-inch (7.5 cm) cinnamon sticks
½ cup (50 g) green cardamom pods
1 cup (120 g) cumin seeds
¾ cup (55 g) coriander seeds

My Version:

1 dried whole chili pod
½ teaspoon (2 ml) saffron threads
5 cloves of mace
¼ cup (30 g) whole cloves
three 3-inch (7.5 cm) cinnamon sticks
15 black cardamom pods
⅓ cup (30 g) cardamom pods
½ cup (65 g) cumin seeds
⅔ cup (50 g) coriander seeds
¼ cup (25 g) fennel seeds
1½ tablespoons (22 ml) ground nutmeg

Maharastra-Style:

4 dried whole chili pods
2 tablespoons (30 ml) sesame seeds
1½ tablespoons (22 ml) green peppercorns
1½ tablespoons (22 ml) white peppercorns
¼ cup (30 g) whole cloves
four 3-inch (7.5 cm) cinnamon sticks
22 black cardamom pods
⅔ cup (80 g) cumin seeds
¼ cup (20 g) coriander seeds
2 cassia or bay leaves
1 teaspoon (5 ml) ground ginger
2 tablespoons (30 ml) ground nutmeg

Uttar Pradesh Style:

3 dried whole chili pods
2 tablespoons (30 ml) pomegranate seeds
⅛ teaspoon (0.5 ml) saffron threads
5 cloves of mace
2 tablespoons (30 ml) green peppercorns
2 tablespoons (30 ml) black peppercorns
2 tablespoons (30 ml) whole cloves
⅓ cup (40 g) cumin seeds
⅔ cup (50 g) coriander seeds
1 tablespoon (15 ml) fennel seeds
2 cassia or bay leaves
1 tablespoon (15 ml) ground nutmeg
2 tablespoons (30 ml) white peppercorns

Punjabi-Style:

6 cloves of mace
¼ cup (35 g) black peppercorns
3 tablespoons (45 ml) whole cloves
four 3-inch (7.5 cm) cinnamon sticks
⅓ cup (30 g) green cardamom pods
½ cup (65 g) cumin seeds
⅔ cup (50 g) coriander seeds
½ teaspoon (2 ml) *ajwain* seeds
½ teaspoon (2 ml) ground ginger
2 tablespoons (30 ml) ground nutmeg
2 cassia or bay leaves

Bengali-Style:

3–4 dried whole chili pods
3 tablespoons (45 ml) sesame seeds
2 tablespoons (30 ml) green peppercorns
2 tablespoons (30 ml) black peppercorns
2 tablespoons (30 ml) white peppercorns
1 tablespoon (15 ml) whole cloves
three 3-inch (7.5 cm) cinnamon sticks
20 green cardamom pods
¼ cup (35 g) cumin seeds
¾ cup (55 g) coriander seeds
3 cassia or bay leaves
1 teaspoon (5 ml) ground ginger

Gujarati-Style:

3 tablespoons (45 ml) grated coconut
1 tablespoon (15 ml) sesame seeds
2 tablespoons (30 ml) black mustard seeds
¼ teaspoon (1 ml) saffron threads
¼ cup (15 g) green peppercorns
¼ cup (15 g) white peppercorns
⅔ cup (60 g) green cardamom pods
¾ cup (95 g) cumin seeds
¼ cup (25   g) ground nutmeg

GARNISHES: The way a formal Vedic meal is served precludes the need for garnishes on individual portions of a dish. This is because, unlike a Western meal where the dishes are served in courses and arranged on different plates in the kitchen, a Vedic meal is served to the guest on a large tray called a *thali*. Depending on the menu, each diner sits down in front of the carefully arranged empty *thali* (14–18 inches/35–45 cm in diameter) with various size metal bowls (*katoris*) strategically placed around the edges of the plate. One after another, portions are placed into the bowls or on the plate and the meal begins.

To bring visual excitement to a meal, the dishes can be decorated with items as simple as a few feathery coriander leaves, a sprinkle of roasted crushed spices, pistachio slivers or *charoli* nuts. Sweets and elegant rice pilafs are often garnished with paper-thin sheets of edible silver foil, called *varak*. For summer meals, when you have access to the bounty of garden produce, take the time to be creative and set aside a few minutes to make radish flowers, celery curls or carrot flowers.

GHEE **and SEASONED** *GHEE: Ghee* in the North is known as *usli ghee*. Though oils are playing an increasingly large part in today's regional cuisines—sesame, peanut, mustard and coconut oil are standard favorites—*ghee* is undeniably the preferred cooking medium for many dishes. It begins like French clarified butter but is cooked until fully clarified, driving off all moisture and separating all of the milk solids from the clear butterfat. Unlike butter, *ghee* is excellent for sautéing and frying, as it can be brought to 170°F (75°C) without reaching its smoke point. In previous ages, cooks thought nothing of using a pot of fresh *ghee* each time they deep-fried whole wheat flat breads or pastries—a practice currently limited to temple kitchens, fine restaurants and affluent homes.

Today, *ghee* is costly in India, the majority of the rural population preferring to use their hard earned *paisas* (pennies) for nutrition in the form of milk, vegetables or fruit. The best commerical *ghee* is from Holland, though Scandanavia and Australia also offer very good *ghee*. Sold at most Indian and Middle Eastern grocery stores, store-bought *ghee* is convenient but expensive. Flavored *ghee* is not yet sold commercially, though it is effortless to make at home. It simply includes the addition of flavor enhancing spices during the clarifying process and can do wonders for any number of dishes. Any type of *ghee* can be frozen and stored for up to a year, or, well-sealed in the refrigerator, for up to 6 months. Even left at room temperature, *ghee* has the marked advantage of a shelf life of several weeks. For detailed information on making plain or seasoned *ghee*, see pages 302–306.

GINGER ROOT, Fresh: The underground creeping rhizome of the tropical plant *Zingiber officinale* is native to most of Asia. Relished for its invigorating sharp taste, digestive properties and cleansing effect on the body, it is used extensively in every region, not only as a flavoring but as a food, much as shallots are used in the West. Shoppers in India can be choosy on their ginger selections, ferreting out different varieties with camphor or mango overtones and always purchasing tender, young "green" ginger. This type of fiberless ginger has a paper-thin pinkish skin and greenish-ivory flesh. It is sporadically available in the spring and summer at specialty greengrocers, Indian groceries and Oriental markets. The flavor is milder than mature ginger root and is excellent in a fresh ginger chutney or as a relish, cut into paper-thin julienne strips and sprinkled with herb salt and lime juice, or used in cooking. Mature ginger root, available in nearly all supermarkets, should be purchased firm to the touch, with a smooth, unwrinkled skin. Its skin must be peeled off before use, then it is either minced, julienned, sliced, shredded or puréed, as required.

Many recipes in the book call for puréed, finely shredded or minced fresh ginger root. Once prepared for cooking, it can be kept refrigerated for several days use: mix up to 1 cup (240 ml) of puréed ginger with a small spoon of oil, store it in a tightly sealed container, and refrigerate.

GRAPE LEAVES: Also known as vine leaves, they are the ragged edged leaves of grape vines used as wrappers for stuffings. Though grape vines are not cultivated in India, I have used the leaves in place of one of India's most popular wrappers, called *arbi patta*—leaves from the colocasia plant, also known as "elephant ears." If you have a backyard grape vine, select the third or fourth leaf from the top; larger ones have tough stalks and veins on the back of the leaf and are not suitable for stuffing. Before use, blanch fresh leaves in boiling water, without overcrowding, until soft and pliable. Bottled or plastic-wrapped leaves must be rinsed in warm water before use to remove the brine solution. They are available in supermarket deli aisles and at Middle Eastern grocery stores.

FRESH VINE LEAVES

TO GRATE: Hand-turned rotary graters such as the Mouli, or food processors, are effective for grating in any quantity. In the case of grating oily nuts, the hand-held machine is superior to a food processor as it produces a fluffy powder without clogging from the released nut oil. Non-greasy grated fresh coconut is best made in a hand-operated Indian implement called a *turapni* or *nariyal kas*, available at Indian grocery stores.

GREEN MANGO: Known as *kacha aam*, this is the unripened fruit of any type of mango tree (*Mangifera indicia*). Native to India, there are several varieties, some especially grown for eating ripe, others cultivated for using raw. While ripe mango is recognized by many to be the world's finest fruit, Indians hold the green unripened fruit in the highest esteem. Green mango is picked long before ripening, while it is still very hard. The firm green skin is cut off, revealing a fine-grained, ivory flesh. The fruit is grated and added to *dals* or vegetables for a pleasant, tart flavor. Green mango is available sporadically at Indian or Latin greengrocers, usually in the spring when they are harvested and shipped out of Florida, the Bahamas or Mexico.

TO GRIND: Known as *peesna*, this technique usually refers to dry-grinding spices or flavorings, but it can also include wet-grinding such items as *dal*, herbs, nuts, fresh ginger, chilies or coconut. Whether the ingredients are reduced to powders or pastes, a number of utensils can be used. In India, hand-held mortar and pestles are used daily for grinding. Depending on the region, shapes differ. In the North, it is a flat slab with a smaller, round stone, called a *sil batta*. In the South, the *himan dasta* is more popular: a thick, bowl-shaped base made either of stone or metal, accompanied by a heavy, oblong pestle. When grinding small quantities, these tools are hard to beat—fast and efficient. Children are taught at an early age how to use each tool, effortlessly using the right pressure and motion for each ingredient. Most of us will use electric tools such as coffee grinders for powdering roasted spices, little Seb or Moulinex electric mincers or a mini food processor for small batches of herb paste *masalas*, and a full-sized food processor or blender for grinding *dals*.

GROUND RICE: Also called rice flour and rice powder. Its texture depends on the degree of fineness of the rice and its origin. Oriental markets sell two types of rice flour: sweet and waxy, both milled from short grain rice and both unsuitable for Vedic dishes. England's supermarket ground rice is the best commercial product available for home use. It is made from long grain rice and is slightly granular. Americans can use almost any rice flour or ground rice sold at Indian grocery stores in the few recipes calling for this ingredient. White rice flour is richer in starch than wheat flour and, during mixing, requires more time to absorb liquid. Brown rice flour, sold in health food stores, can be used for the nutrition-minded, but it will yield a darker, heavier *dosa* or *iddli*. The oil in rice bran tends to turn rancid quickly, so brown rice flour should be purchased in small quantities and used rapidly, or refrigerated during storage.

GUAVA: Known as *amrood*, the tropical fruit of the small tree or shrub *Psidium guajava*. The acid-sweet fruit is quite popular throughout India. During the season, street vendors stand near perfectly arranged mounds of freshly-picked guavas and entice passersby with a small plate of cut fruit sprinkled with lime juice. It is unlikely that you have ever had a good guava unless you live where they grow, for they are best eaten within 24 hours of picking. If you live near a Latin, West Indian or Indian greengrocer who flies in fresh produce, look for fruits that are scented. If the fruit is overripe, the skin is usually greenish-yellow and noticeably soft and smooth. Though the flesh ranges in color from creamy to pinkish-red, most fruits contain tiny edible seeds in the center. If you are making a purée for jellies or beverages, strain out the seeds. Guavas are an excellent source of vitamin C, containing ten times the amount found in oranges.

GUR: see *JAGGERY*

HONEY: Known as *madhur* or nectar. According to the *Ayur Veda*, honey should not be exposed to high temperatures or the boiling point because, aside from losing essential flavor, it becomes slightly toxic. Consequently, while honey is taken as a medicinal cleanser or as a sweetener, it is not used to cook. If, for example, you use honey to sweeten tisaines or custards, simply add it immediately after the herbal infusion or the completion of the cooking, then stir until dissolved. There are scores of choices for honey, ranging from runny, clear and golden, to thick and nearly black.

HORSERADISH ROOT: Cultivated primarily in Bengal and Orissa, horseradish roots and leaves, from the plant *Armoracia rusticana*, are most popular combined with root vegetables such as potatoes or yams. While only young leaves are desirable as greens, larger roots are preferable for grating or shredding. The gnarled roots must be scrubbed and the skin peeled off before use. Large roots have a woody inner core which is not used at all; only the outer portion contains the volatile oils which give horseradish its pungency. Further, the desired pungency in fresh horseradish fades within a few hours of grating or when exposed to heat for any length of time. Fresh roots are finding their way on to more and more supermarket produce shelves and, once purchased, can be kept for at least two or three weeks.

JAGGERY **and** *GUR:* In India's villages, these unrefined sugars are made today much as they have been for thousands of years. *Jaggery*, made from the juice crushed out of sugar cane stalks (*Saccharum officinarum*), accounts for over 50 percent of the sugar currently eaten in India. *Gur*—made from the sap drained from various palm trees, such as date, coconut or palmyra—is used primarily in the cuisines of the East and South, usually in the areas of its origin. West Bengal's *tal gur*, from *tal* palms, rivals the best grade A maple candy as a delicacy. Much of the high quality *gur* made in India never reaches distant market places; it remains in the villages where it is made. Affluent families work around a fluctuating market by outright purchasing the tapping rights to a variety of palms, thus assured of a shipment of the first *gur* of the season. It is not uncommon for a family Deity to be offered six or eight types of *gur*, much as one might offer a fruit, nut or confection tray.

The reduction process resembles the "sugaring off" of maple sap. It is boiled down to about one-fourth of its original volume into a thick, dark brown syrup. As the syrup thickens further, and more liquid evaporates off, it is scooped out and placed on palm leaves. Some of the molasses drains off in the cooling process, leaving varying textures from that of raw peanut butter to firm lumps.

Moist, slightly syrupy *gur* is used like jam—spread on *parathas*, *chapatis*, confections and cereals. Firm, candy-like *gur* is, in fact, regarded as a confection—often poured into decorative molds and served like American maple candy. Bengalis and Gujaratis make some of the world's most delectable boiled-sugar candies with *gur*: almond brittle, butterscotch, sesame toffee and ginger caramels.

With today's trends toward natural unrefined ingredients, both sweeteners are meritorious. Alternate liquid sweeteners are made from grains, such as barley, rice, wheat and corn—available at health food stores but expensive. Other relatively unrefined concentrated sweeteners include honey and maple syrup. Like all unrefined sugars, *gur* and *jaggery* tend to curdle milk. If you use them, add them towards the end of cooking or, in the case of hot milk, just after frothing. These sweeteners are available in Indian and Middle Eastern grocery stores.

JALAPEÑO CHILI: The medium-hot fresh green chili named after the capitol of Veracruz in Mexico, Jalapa. They average about 2 inches (5 cm) in length and are about 1 inch (2.5 cm) in diameter at the base. Good chilies are firm, with a waxy dark green skin and a blunt tip. Jalapeño chilies were used for all of the recipe testing in this book, not only because they are medium-hot, but because they are easily seeded. They are widely available at supermarkets and greengrocers.

TO JULIENNE: To cut firm ingredients—vegetables, fruits, citrus zest, chilies or ginger root to name a few—into long thin strips. A professional stainless steel mandoline has a blade that cuts 29 julienne strips at a time, while a food processor julienne disc produces as many as 18 strips each time the disc revolves. Julienne strips range from 1–3 inches (2.5–7.5 cm) long and can also be cut by hand. Using a chefs knife, cut any round ingredient in half to create a flat surface. Core, peel or trim, as necessary, then, placing each piece cut side down, slice the food lengthwise into ¼-inch (1 cm) strips. Stack two or three slices on their side and cut in the same size strips lengthwise. Trim the ends to make them the desired length. In this book, there are two further subdivisions: "matchsticks" are 1/16 inch (1.5 mm) on a side and "shoestrings" are ¼ inch (6 mm).

KALA CHANA DAL: Known in English as Bengal gram, this is a small variety of chickpea from the plant *Cicer arietinum*. Though similar in color to supermarket yellow split peas, the flavor is quite different. Whole *kala chana*, with a brown skin, is popular in North Indian dishes, but split and husked, the *dal* is eaten throughout India, particularly in the East. The flour, milled from hulled and roasted *kala chana* and called variously chickpea flour, gram flour or *besan*, is second only to wheat flour in popularity. It is not only protein-rich, but flavorsome, adding distinctive character to *pakora* batter, vegetable *koftas* and yogurt *karhi* sauce. Whole and split *kala chana dal* is available at Indian and Middle Eastern grocery stores.

KALONJI: Known as *nigella* or black onion seed, this small, jet-black spice seed from the plant *Nigella sativa* has enough names in print to confuse even the most committed reader. While Middle Eastern grocery stores often sell the seeds under the label "black seeds" or "*siyah daneh*," many Indian grocers incorrectly sell the spice as black onion seed. *Kalonji* has no connection to the onion plant, but because the seeds resemble onion seeds, the name has found its way onto packages. Vedic vegetarians, who do not eat onions, need not be misled by the labeling.

The tear-drop seed has a peppery taste and, when heated, an aroma reminiscent of oregano. It is used sporadically in *dals*, vegetables and pickles, sprinkled on *naan* in North India, and, in the East, is an important ingredient in the whole five spice blend known as *panch puran*.

KARAI: A bowl-shaped pan similar to the Chinese wok, with high sloping walls and a rounded bottom. It is usually made of iron and varies in size from 12–14 inches (30–35 cm) for home use, or 3–4 feet (1 meter) for restaurant use. Indian *karais* should be seasoned and handled much as one would a cast-iron pan. Available at Indian and Middle Eastern grocery stores. Better cookware stores sell Silverstone-coated woks and Chinese woks, both suitable replacements for the *karai*.

KATORI: A small metal bowl 1½–3 inches (4–7.5) in diameter served on *thalis*. A typical dinner *thali* may require three or four *katoris* for liquid *dals*, vegetables, *raitas*, salads or sweets. An entertainment menu *thali* may require eight or ten *katoris*. Today, they are most often made from stainless steel.

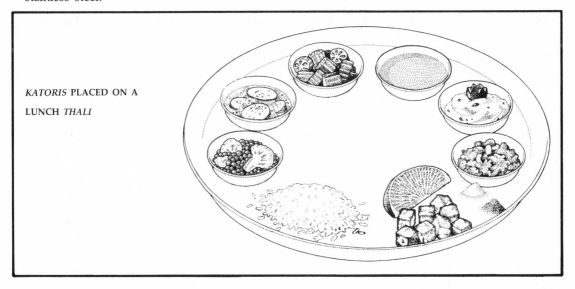

KATORIS PLACED ON A
LUNCH *THALI*

KEWRA ESSENCE: Known as *ruh kewra* or *kevda*, this essential flavoring is obtained from screw pine shrubs and trees of the genus *Pandanu tectorius* and is one of the four most important flavorings in sweets and beverages. The tree grows in much of South India's tropical areas and sometimes also in the North. It is loved for its highly perfumed flowers, called *tayai*, and its sweet fruits. Both *kewra* essence and *kewra* water are used to flavor Bengali sweets such as *pantoah* and *rasgoola* and are even sprinkled over festive rice pilafs. Available at Indian and Middle Eastern grocers.

KHOA: When milk is boiled down until much of the water (87 percent by weight) has evaporated, the solid, dough-like mass (about one-sixth of the total volume) that remains is *khoa*. It is the basis of many North Indian milk fudges such as *pera*, *burfi* and *mewa ladoo*—much loved in nearly all of India. If milk is reduced quickly and stirred constantly, the color remains nearly white; if it is reduced slowly, the lactose sugar caramelizes and the color darkens to golden. *Khoa* is not available commercially in America, but made in household quantities, and, with the right equipment, is a simple task.

KHUS ESSENCE: Also known as *khas* and *khas khas*, obtained from the roots of vetiver, an aromatic grass (*Vetiveria zizanioides*) grown in India, South America, Java and other tropical climates. The web-like roots of the grass are dried and bound into screens for windows or hand-held fans. When moistened, the roots give off a cooling, deliciously fragrant smell. Both *khus* essence and *khus* water are used to flavor syrup sweets and beverages, especially in Bengal. Pure *khus* oil has a heavy, woodsy scent and is used in such well known perfumes as Missoni and Jean Patou 1000. *Khus* essence is available at Indian grocery stores.

KIDNEY BEAN: Known as *rajma dal*, this kidney-shaped, red-skinned bean is a seed from the plant *Phaseolus vulgaris*. Kidney beans are almost unknown in India outside of the Punjab, where they are popular in a spicy gravy—a type of Punjabi chili—often laced with cubes of succulent *panir* cheese. Because the *dal* is recognized as an inducer of flatulence, it is assisted by adding liberal splashes of fresh ginger root, a digestive seasoning. Northerners, who work long days in a cold climate, appreciate the nutritionally sustaining combination of *rajma*, rice, yogurt and vegetable—a power-packed menu, by any standard. Kidney beans are sold at almost all supermarkets.

KITCHEN EQUIPMENT: If you cook, you most likely have enough equipment to carry you through the bulk of recipes in this book. If you don't already have a wok and a heavy-bottomed griddle, or, if you intend to take up Vedic cooking on a daily basis, you might want to purchase a *karai* (a bowl-shaped iron pan) and a *tava* (a concave iron griddle) for convenience at an Indian grocery store. Of course, any wide, heavy deep-frying casserole, with walls 3–4 inches (7.5–10 cm) high can be used instead of a *karai*, and a griddle or frying pan can take the place of a *tava*.

TO KNEAD: Any type of Vedic bread dough can be made by hand or, more conveniently, in a food processor. Kneading by hand involves rubbing flour moistened with liquid ingredients into smooth, satiny doughs. You can use almost any procedure of applying pressure with the palms, knuckles and fingers in a rhythmic pressing, folding and turning motion. All wheat-based bread doughs require a good kneading to make the final product light, smooth and easily digestible.

KOSHER SALT: A coarse-grained sea salt possessing natural iodine and trace minerals that is very pleasant used in cooking. Choosing this coarser-textured salt is a matter of personal preference. Available at health food stores.

KRISHNA: The name for God given in the Sanskrit Vedic texts of India. Historically, Krishna appeared in the village of Vrindavan 5,000 years ago. Revered in the *Vedas* as the original form of the Godhead, Krishna is the speaker of India's paramount spiritual text *Bhagavad Gita*.

LEMONS and LIMES: Both lemons (*Citrus limon*) and limes (*Citrus aurantifolia*) are versatile and valuable ingredients. They impart tart flavors, act as preservatives, bring life to even salt-free foods, make wonderful garnishes and are thirst quenchers. There are numerous varieties of both citruses, with varying degrees of sourness and oil in the zest.

India's most popular citrus is called *kagzee nimbu*. It is less acid then Persian or Key limes, but with a very sour juice. Rather small—only 1½–2 inches (4–5 cm) in diameter—the yellow-green skin is very thin, but both skin and flesh are powerfully sour. Most Indian *nimbu* that reach the market are tree-ripened, with an oily skin and rich flavor. Even the simplest lunch—one or two dishes—is incomplete without a juicy wedge of *nimbu* to perk up flavors.

Unfortunately, most commercial citrus in the West is picked green and likely dyed and treated with preservatives to store well. Skin color often masks content. Pick fruits heavy for their size with a firm skin and free of bruises. They are best stored, uncovered, in a cool nook, or refrigerated.

LENTIL BEANS: As one of three types of legumes called *dal* in India, lentils, along with beans and peas, are used extensively. Americans and Europeans are most familiar with an unhulled lens-shaped brown variety from the plant *Lens culinaris*. In India, only two types are eaten: yellow lentils, known as *toovar dal* or *arhar dal*, from the plant *Cajanus cajan*; and tiny pink lentils, called *masoor dal*, hulled seeds also hulled from the *Lens culinaris*. While hulled yellow *toovar dal* is widely used, pink lentils are eaten in the North and are a staple in Muslim kitchens. For further information on *toovar dal*, see individual entries.

LYCHEE: Also called litchi, the succulent fruit of the small tree *Litchi chinensis*, native to Southern China, but more recently introduced into subtropical areas of India and Southeast Asia. The fruit is picked in clusters and, when ripe, the red skin is brittle and leathery. More often than not, litchi is relished on its own—raw, unadorned and deliciously sweet.

The peeled fruit resembles a giant, creamy-white peeled grape, housing a single large black seed in the center. The fruits store well for up to two weeks, refrigerated. Available fresh, in mid summer, at specialty greengrocers and Chinese grocery stores.

LOTUS SEED, Puffed: Known as *makhana*, this creamy-white puff with a brown-speckled surface is an exotic ingredient used primarily in the North. Several varieties of lotus, water lilies and aquatic plants florish in the lakes of Kashmir, and, in July and August, boat farmers harvest various edibles—lotus stems, pods and leaves (just after the flowers wither), tender white fruits from the water bamboo, and water chestnuts floating just beneath the lake's surface.

Removed from the pods, peeled lotus seeds are off-white and crispy with a delicate flavor. Once dried, the hazelnut-sized seeds are dropped into a giant *karai* filled with hot sand. In time, they swell and burst into 1-inch (2.5 cm) oval puffs with a texture like hull-less popcorn.

On *Janmastami*, Lord Krishna's birthday, Vrindavan residents make a delicious candy from powdered butter-toasted *makhana*, sugar, ground coriander and water. It is also popular in *kheer*—boiled down in milk—where it disintegrates but lends an herby flavor to the dish. As a garnish, crisp butter-fried *makhana* and rose petals look smashing floating in a punch bowl of *panchamrita* or sprinkled on a mound of succulent carrot *halva*. Available at Indian grocery stores. Store in airtight containers.

PUFFED LOTUS SEEDS

LOTUS ROOT: Known by various names—*kamal*, *bhain* and *bhen* in Gujarat—the underground rhizome of the lotus plant *Nelumbium nuciferium*, native to the ponds and lakes of Kashmir, China and Japan. Though it is cultivated as a vegetable in much of India, it is also grown for its magnificent lotus flowers (*kamala*)—blue or pink petals reaching skyward in many temple compounds and formal gardens and considered by many to be the most beautiful flower on earth. In Rishikesh, I was served a marvelous tea from the stamens of the flowers. The seeds are sometimes sliced and served with fruit, dried and ground into flour, or parched and puffed up, like popcorn.

The gray-brown skinned rhizome grows in links and can reach a length of 3 feet (1 meter). Inside, the creamy-white flesh is crisp and has several large and small perforations running lengthwise. Cut crosswise, the holes create a lacy pattern. Young roots can be eaten raw, peeled, sliced and soaked in acidulated water to prevent discoloration, and then tossed into a fried seasoning. Mature roots are cooked, though they never become soft, just tender-crisp. These are used in stir-fried dishes, soups, or, more popularly, mashed and combined with chickpea flour to become a delicious fried *kofta*. Lotus root has an elusive flavor, with hints of asparagus, artichoke and cucumber. The fresh root is available from late summer through the fall at Chinese greengrocers.

MACE: A special bonus from the nutmeg tree (*Myristica fragrans*), known as *javitri*. It is the aril or fibrous membrane that covers the nut of the nutmeg fruit, tangerine-red colored when fresh, but sandy-brown when dried. In its dried form, it is sold as blades of mace and used, for example, to infuse a spicy sauce. The blades are removed before serving. As mace is difficult to grind because it is oily, it is slowly roasted to become brittle and crisp and then ground with other spices, usually for the spice blend known as *garam masala*. The flavor is similar to, but more delicate than, nutmeg. In a pinch, you can use nutmeg, but, in simple milk fudges, the subtlety of mace shows its colors. Mace blades and ground mace are available at specialty food shops and at Indian and Middle Eastern grocery stores and supermarkets.

MANGO: The mango has held a special place in India for millenia. Known as *aam*, it is often called the "king of fruits." Its succulent, distinctively sweet-and-acid flesh is second to none. There are several hundred species cultivated in India, and their flavors, colors and sizes vary enormously. In my mind, two Indian species rate as superior: the Alphonso or *apus* mango, from the Konkan coast region; and the *dassheri* mango, from the Lucknow area. Many aficionados feel that the Hayden mango is one of America's best, while Mexico's apple-mango has the distinction of both apple and peach flavor overtones. Most supermarket mangoes are picked while still firm and pale green, but as they soften they develop orange-red, pink and yellow tones. The best eating mango is fiber-free, but even a stringy mango can be sweet and juicy.

South Florida supplies America with its best mangoes; the soil and climate are ideal. If you want a good quality mango at a remarkably low price, write to Ira Ebersole Farms. A lifetime vegetarian dedicated to organic farming, Ira has farmed his land for many years. He will hand-care for your order and ship anywhere in the U.S. and Canada. His mangoes are available from June 15 through September 15. For further information write to: Ira Ebersole and Earl Ebersole Farms, 25295 S. W. 194 Ave., Homestead, Florida 33031.

MANGO POWDER: See *AMCHOOR*

MAPLE SYRUP and MAPLE SUGAR: "Sugar bushes" or the maple groves of rock and sugar maple (*Acer saccharum*) and black maple (*Acer nigrum*) have long been a source of sweeteners for North America. Maple sap is watery and tasteless, but when it is boiled down to about one-ninth of its original volume, its sweet and woodsy flavor becomes manifest. Today, the syrup is graded according to area. Light amber "first run" syrup (the first sap of the season) has the most delicate flavor and is called Grade AA. Most residents of Vermont and New Hampshire consider this syrup the highest quality. However, many people prefer the slightly less expensive medium amber or dark amber pure syrup (Grade A and B) from later runs; it contains more nutrients and has a more robust flavor. Old-fashioned maple sugar candy is made by simply boiling down the syrup until all of the water has evaporated.

Free-flowing granules or maple sugar grains can be substituted, measure for measure, for white sugar. It is, however, the most expensive sweetener I have found yet; small fourteen ounce (400 g) bags can cost as much as one hundred dollars.

Maple sugar and syrup are wonderful sweeteners for fruits, flat bread doughs, vegetables, *dals*, chutneys and beverages. Maple sugar has as much calcium as milk and only one-tenth of the sodium of honey. It is also richer in minerals, potassium, magnesium, phosphorous and manganese than honey.

Containers of maple syrup are sold at supermarkets and health food stores. If you purchase it in quantity, you will get better prices ordering directly from the source. Write to any of the following mail order sources for current price lists: Green Mountain Endeavors, P.O. Box 53, Jericho Center, Vermont 05465; Dan Johnson, Route 1 Box 265, Jeffrey, New Hampshire 03452; American Spoon Foods, Inc., 411 East Lake Street, Petrosky, Michigan 49770.

TO MARINATE: A procedure during which foods are soaked in a liquid mixture (marinade) to either preserve the foods, infuse them with flavor, or tenderize them. Practically speaking, the only marinade used by Vedic vegetarians consists of salt and lemon juice or sour fruit juice. For example, julienned fresh ginger root is marinated in seasoned lemon juice, turning the flesh pink, infusing it with flavor, and softening the tough fiber.

MASA: Also called tortilla flour and masa harina, it is made from parched corn that is simmered in a lime solution until the skins are loosened. The skins are rubbed off and the treated corn is called nixtamal. Masa is the finely ground corn flour from nixtamal. It is used as the basis for Mexican tortillas, and, in Vedic cooking, it is a pleasant flour to mix with *atta* or sifted whole wheat flour, yielding very soft, flexible flat breads. Because corn does not contain any protein capable of producing gluten, a straight masa dough is tricky to handle: flat breads break apart, crumble and crack in the hands of a novice. However, when it is combined with wheat, the rolling-out becomes easy. Make the dough slightly firmer than for an all-wheat dough; it softens considerably upon resting. Instant masa is available in Latin, Spanish and Mexican grocery stores and even at some supermarkets. It is an acceptable alternative to North Indian corn flour.

MASALA: This term refers to any number of spice, herb and seasoning combinations, each containing from two to twenty or more ingredients. A *masala* is the key that unlocks individuality and expression in your kitchen, and its contents, proportions and applications are limitless. *Masala* refers to powders, whole spice blends, dry-roasted and crushed seeds, herbs, and wet-ground seasonings including spices and herbs, as well as yogurt, tomatoes, tamarind pulp and lemon or lime juice. Not only ginger root and hot chilies, but coconut, seeds, nuts and dried fruits can be added to wet-ground *masalas*.

There are numerous commercial brands of powdered *masala* blends available at Indian grocery stores: Punjabi *garam masala*, Maharastran *dhana jeera*, Delhi's *chat masala*, Kerala's *dal masala*, Mysore's *sambar masala*, and many more. While bulk blends are the cheapest, brand names, like Bedekers and MDH, with visible expiration dates, are of better quality. My personal preference in ready-made *masalas* and ground spices is Rajah brand, sold in vacuum-packed resealable tins. The quality and flavor is superior to *masalas* sold in bulk or in cellophane-wrapped boxes. For further information on *masalas* and *masala* recipes, see individual entries.

MENU PLANNING: To most people, India'a religions, habits and customs appear highly complex. The history of India's ancient Vedic culture dates back thousands of years to a time when India was ruled by honorable and chivalrous kings and was culturally and spiritually unified. Unfortunately, little is left of this once flourishing Vedic culture. Through centuries of conquering foreign armies and internecine conflicts, modern India is today divided into seventeen states, each with an indigenous "culture," and houses fifteen major languages and more than 1,000 local dialects. Spiritually, India is home to practitioners of four major religions, with a seemingly limitless amount of disparate sects and offshoots. The fact that India has traditionally been, and still remains today, a predominantly vegetarian country, has ensured that at least the country's culinary history is still very much present.

Although it is important to understand the rich heritage from which this cuisine has evolved, it is more important to understand how to use the recipes practically—as a framework for exploring the world's oldest high fiber, high carbohydrate vegetarian diet. With a little foresight, these dishes can easily be worked into a well-balanced eating plan. No matter what your situation or location, you can create convenient menus from this book that are nutritious and delicious.

In addition to the suggestions below, there are also menu suggestions accompanying many of the rice, *dal* and vegetable recipes in the first three chapters. The suggestions I have made are either classic combinations from city, state or regional cuisines or personal favorites, inspired by classical principles and then experimenting and embellishing to achieve the desired result. The suggestions cover numerous occasions such as a family dinner, light lunch, company breakfast, backyard outing, buffet, or late night supper. Many are seasonal menus, centered around available fresh produce. They will provide the groundwork and then inspire you to experiment on your own.

The following menu suggestions meet the requirements of an adult lacto-vegetarian diet and are based on dishes included in this book. Julie Sahni's *Classic Indian Vegetarian and Grain Cooking* could be of assistance for additional dishes in menu planning, though Vaishnava vegetarians will want to drop the onions and garlic from the recipes. Though the menus will not fit the needs of a macrobiotic or vegan vegetarian who does not eat milk products, they can still be inspirational.

BREAKFAST/BRUNCH:

No matter what your activities or sleeping schedule, keep in mind that within three to five hours after rising, your body needs nutrition. Ideally, breakfast should contain protein from milk or its products, legumes, nuts or seeds. Vitamins are contained in fresh fruits, while necessary carbohydrates are obtained from whole grains and cereal dishes. In the summer, you might be able to enjoy four or five types of fresh fruit, while in the winter, it might be apple sauce and orange juice. If you serve your meal on a *thali*, place the cut fruits either in small *katoris* or directly on the plate. One popular means of adding *dal* protein to the meal is in the form of a ginger-laced salad. Try to build on breakfast ideas from the following suggestions:

Fall Breakfast/Brunch:

Chickpea and Ginger Root Salad with a wedge of lime
Light 'n' Easy Pounded Rice Uppma with Potatoes and Green Peas
Herbed *panir* cheese cubes marinated in herbed olive oil
Assorted seasonal fruits
Hot beverage

Winter Breakfast:

Urad and Rice Flour Dosa with Cracked Black Pepper
Roasted Yellow Split Pea and Coconut Chutney
Seasonal fresh fruit
Cardamom Milk **or other hot beverage**

Spring Breakfast:

Sautéed Sprouted Mung Beans with Julienne Ginger Root
Minted Cucumbers with Strawberries
Griddle-Fried Whole Wheat and Corn Bread
Rhubarb and Pomegranate Refresher

Summer Breakfast:

Puffed Rice and Nut Snack with Raisins
Seasonal fresh fruit
Griddle-Baked Whole Wheat Bread with Cashew Butter
Minty Yogurt Shake

LUNCH or MAIN MEAL

As with breakfast, the main meal should contain substantial protein, vitamins and complex carbohydrates. When whole grains and legumes are combined together, their food value increases, receiving even a further boost with the addition of a milk product. Lunch also includes two, three or four seasonal vegetables, served either separately or combined. Finally, a full meal is served with relishes or chutneys to stimulate digestion and round out flavors.

One serving: rice or whole grain and/or bread
One serving: *dal* **soup purée, stew or dry-textured dish**
Two to five vegetable servings. You might steam them individually
    or make dishes with contrasting textures: a vegetable in
    broth, a dry-textured vegetable, a moist and succulent
    vegetable, a stir-fried vegetable, a blanched vegetable or
    shredded raw vegetable.
One serving: yogurt, yogurt salad or cheese equivalent Small touch of cooked or raw chutney,
    pickle or relish
Lemon or lime wedge

The above meal might seem a far cry from a brown-bag sandwich or deli-salad, but, with a little planning and the right equipment, a full meal like this can be cooked within an hour using a tiered steamer. Quick-cooking *dal* is gently boiled in the bottom unit, with vegetables in the center unit and a rice or grain selection slowly steaming in the top chamber. If whole wheat, triticale, buckwheat, barley or rye is soaked overnight, it can be slowly steamed along with, or instead of, rice in the top chamber. Moving clockwise from the one o'clock position, a full-scale lunch might resemble this:

Vishakha's Cream of Vegetable Dal Soup
Plain yogurt or any yogurt salad
Any type of cooked or raw chutney, relish or pickle
Small mound of salt and pepper with a lemon wedge
Cucumber cubes sprinkled with dry-roasted crushed cumin seeds
    and cracked pepper or cayenne pepper
Piquant Lemon Rice
Sautéed Cauliflower with Green Peas
Buttersoft Zuchinni and Tomatoes
Okra Supreme

A streamlined nutritious lunch can also be concentrated into a one dish meal, *khichari*, served with yogurt and a relish. *Khichari* combines the needed serving of rice, *dal* and vegetables in one pot, and its variations are endless. The yogurt can be served plain; or it can be used in a raw vegetable salad, condensed into cheese, sweetened with fruit purée and whipped into an airy fool, or frozen into a not-too-sweet dessert. Any number of ready-made relishes, chutneys or pickles completes the meal.

METRIC MEASUREMENTS: Cooks on several continents use the metric system for weights and measurements. Many American manufacturers of measuring cups and scales are already including dual measurement markings, and most packages are sold with dual weights. By comparison to the metric system, American measuring is inaccurate and can often be confusing. For example, cookbooks differ considerably in their approach to measuring flour. To prevent a major disappointment, a cook should ferret out the type of system used in each book. In the last decade, the dip and sweep method—dipping a measuring cup into flour and leveling it off with a knife—has often been replaced by spooning the flour into the measuring cup and leveling it off. If the flour is sifted before being measured, the measurement can be off by as much as 2–3 tablespoons (30–45 ml), even for only one cup of flour.

In the kitchen, metric measurements relate to each other in units of ten. Grams, liters and meters are preceeded with prefixes that expand the system to accomodate large and tiny amounts: milli/1000 (one thousandth), deka x 10 (10 times); centi/100 (one hundredth), hecto x 100; deci/10 (one tenth), kilo x 1000. Each unit is multiplied or divided by ten to the next larger or smaller unit.

Centimeters are the unit used to measure anything from pans to pastries, while Celsius replaces Fahrenheit to measure baking temperatures. Liquid measurements are most commonly defined in terms of liters, though liquids can also be weighed on a scale as well. In this book, whether solid or liquid, all measurements under ¼ cup are in teaspoons and tablespoons (ml for metric users) and should suffice in any kitchen, from Canada to New Zealand.

After listing the American measurement in a recipe, we have decided to add metric measurements in parentheses. While many cookbooks with dual measurements round off the second type of measurement—sometimes to the nearest increment increase or decrease of twenty-five—we have chosen not to do so, preferring instead to give you the most precise information possible. In principle, measuring by weight is more accurate than measuring by volume, but everything rests on the quality of your scale. Of the two types of scales available, balance and spring balance, balance is the most efficient and exacting (an ingredient is placed on a platform at one end, and weights are placed on the other). In England, two sets of weights are used, iron metric weights and brass imperial weights. Every dry ingredient used in this book has been weighed on a balance scale with five gram increments and then double-checked by a second person using a good spring balance scale with ten gram increments.

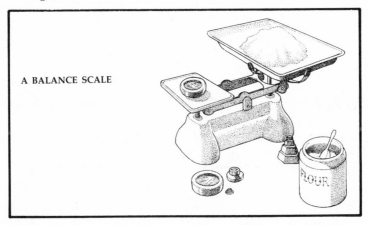

A BALANCE SCALE

Liquids are measured in various types of beakers and jugs. They, too, are available with varying degrees of accuracy. The best liquid measuring utensil I have found in America is made by Wecolite Co., Inc. and is called "The Metric Wonder Cup." It offers the user 10 ml increments from 10 to 500 (roughly one-half liter).

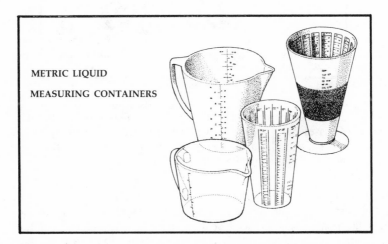

METRIC LIQUID

MEASURING CONTAINERS

MILLET: Known as *bajra* in North India and *ragi* in South India, millet is a widely cultivated grain harvested from several grasses. Two species are important: widely used pearl millet (*Pennisetum typhoideum*) and finger millet (*Eleusine coracana*). After rice and wheat, millet follows as the third most used grain in India, growing well in Rajasthan's sandy soil, hot climate and limited rainfall. In Northern India and Gujarat, the flour is routinely mixed with *atta* and turned into vegetable and chili-laced flat breads. It is also made into a pilaf, with a texture similar to fine bulgar.

Nutritionally, millet is a good source of B vitamins, phosphorus, iron and lecithin. It is also known to possess more protein than rice, corn or oats. Hulled millet groats—tiny buff-colored kernals the size of large mustard seeds—are perfect for pilafs. To cook, fry whole millet in a little *ghee* or oil until golden, add water at the ratio of 2 to 1, and simmer in a covered saucepan for 25–30 minutes or until light and fluffy. Millet groats, flour and puffed millet are sold at health food stores.

MINCING: To cut foods into very fine irregular-shaped pieces from one-sixteenth to one-thirty second inch.

MINT LEAF: Known as *podina*, mint, along with curry leaves and fresh coriander, is widely used throughout India. Available nearly year round, it is part of a *sabji wala's* (greengrocer's) standard stock. There are many species of mint (*meetha*) that grow in warm climates. While American nurseries offer many varied flavors and colors in mints—including peppermint, stone mint, water-mint and spearmint—many of us are quite happy with any crisp bunch sold at supermarkets. Mint has an affinity for vegetables, *dals*, pilafs, beverages and is prominantly used in fresh chutneys. Dried mint, like parsley, is lacking in flavor, as the flavor in mint depends on the vibrant volatile oils in the leaves. Many supermarkets are stocking fresh mint now; if yours does not, request it. Most are anxious to oblige.

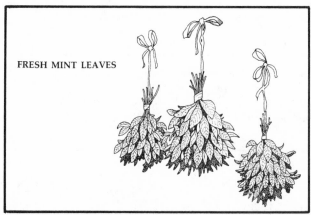

FRESH MINT LEAVES

MOLASSES: The thick brown syrup produced in refining sugar cane. It comes in three grades: light, dark and blackstrap molasses, respectively from the first, second and third extractions in reducing cane juice. Molasses has a strong flavor and may overpower many dishes, but it is quite tasty in whole bean dishes and in the occasional bread dough. It is an excellent source of digestible iron for vegetarians and is widely available at supermarkets.

MOONG DAL: Known as green gram, the split bean of the plant *Vigna aureus* or *Phaseolus aureus*, widely used in two forms: split and husked (*moong dal*) and split with skins (*chilke moong dal*). Like *urad* and *arhar*, split *moong* does not need soaking prior to cooking and, of the three, it is the easiest to digest. Further, the flavor is delicate, lending itself to virtually any supporting seasonings or ingredients.

When you are shopping, look for uniform, pale gold *dal* with minimal foreign matter. Since India does not export *moong dal*, some of the *dal* that reaches the U.S. is of inferior quality and the package usually states "product of several countries." Depending on its origins, the flavor and freshness will vary.

Made into a soup or broth, *moong dal* is considered a perfect light food for those suffering from colds or flu, or for babies or the elderly. Wet-ground *moong dal* can be used in a number of ways, including *badas*, *pakora* or *dhokra* batter, as a stuffing for *pooris* and as the basis of *halva*. Available at Indian and Middle Eastern grocery stores.

MORTAR and PESTLE: This equipment is a bonus for the serious cook, for it performs basic kitchen functions like grinding (*peesana*), crushing (*musulana*) and mashing or wet-grinding, quite like nothing else. Shapes and materials vary worldwide with many ancient versions still in use today, each design evolving from the particular needs of a regional cuisine. For example, traditional equipment is likely made from blackish earthenware in Thailand; marble in Italy; the *surikogi* and *suribachi*—a wooden pestle and unglazed pottery bowl—in Japan; or the porcelain apothecary-style English mortar and pestle remommended by Mrs. Beeton and used in much of Europe.

No Indian kitchen is complete without at least one mortar and pestle. The most popular type is called a *sil batta*. The flat stone bed (*sil*), from 12–18 inches (30–60 cm) long and 1½–2 inches (4–5 cm) thick rests on the work surface. The *batta* is a hand-held stone roller which is worked back and forth across the base. Usually made of sandstone or granite, the surface of the *sil* is cut with a pattern of shallow ridges or a design to create friction for the *batta*. The friction efficiently coaxes maximum flavor from the essential oils locked in dry-roasted *dals* or hard spices such as peppercorns, cloves, cinnamon sticks, mace blades, cumin seeds, cardamom seeds or ridged coriander seeds. The speed of the rotating metal cutting blades of an electric spice grinder, blender or food processor cannot match the control of hand-pulverizing. They are marvelous for whipping-up green chili and ginger pastes or any pounded wet-spice *masala*.

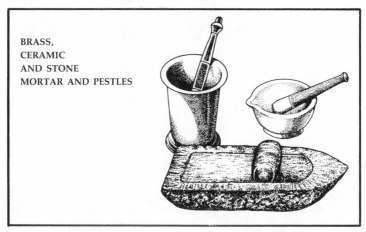

BRASS,
CERAMIC
AND STONE
MORTAR AND PESTLES

Though any mortar and pestle will do, a few Indian grocery stores do sell special models: the *sil batta*, described above, or a brass cup-shaped mortar with a bat-shaped pestle; and the *himan dasta*, a large bowl-shaped stone mortar and pestle. On the whole, most wood equipment is too absorbent for use with many seasonings and the surface too smooth to create good friction. Heavy equipment is the most efficient. Available sporadically at Indian, Oriental and Middle Eastern grocery stores and better houseware stores.

MULATO CHILI: Considered a Mexican chili but readily available at Latin and Mexican markets, it is a deep brownish-black color, sometimes heart-shaped. The tough skin softens and turns red after soaking. The flavor is mild, a bit sweeter than ancho chilies and, some say, chocolate-flavored.

MUNG BEAN and MUNG SPROUTS: BB-sized beans known as *sabat moong* from the plant *Vigna aureus* or *Phaseolus aureus*. Very popular in North India, they are prepared in a number of ways: simmered to tenderness without soaking, or soaked, husked and wet-ground into smooth batters or pastes. When soaked and sprouted with about ¼-inch (6 mm) tails, they are called *ugadela kathar*. Stir-fried mung sprouts laced with julienne ginger root and slivered hot chilies are very nutritious and popular in Gujarat and Maharastra as a breakfast. The whole beans are available at health food stores, specialty stores and Indian grocery stores.

MUSTARD OIL: Known as *sarson ka tel*, this amber-colored oil is pressed from the seed of Indian mustard plants (*Brassica juncea*). It is widely used in cooking in many regional cuisines of Eastern and Northern India, particularly in Bengal and the Punjab. In its raw state, the oil has a pungent mustard scent and is used externally. For example, a mustard oil massage and morning sun promotes warmth and relief from minor arthritis, or mustard oil rubbed between the palms and massaged into the scalp encourages a healthy glow and good hair roots.

As a cooking medium, mustard oil is handled quite unlike other oils; it is always brought to its smoking point momentarily before use. This brief exposure to the high temperature softens the harsh mustard flavor, making it pleasantly docile and easy to digest. Mustard oil stores well, unlike many unrefined oils, and is therefore preferred for pickles. It is delicious in stir-fried dishes—spinach, bitter melon, squash or yams—and is often used for deep-frying Bengali crackers and wafers. Available at Indian and Middle Eastern grocery stores.

MUSTARD SEED, Black: Known as *rai*, the tiny round brownish-black or purplish-brown seed obtained from the annual Indian mustard plant *Brassica juncea*. Slightly smaller than true black mustard (*Brassica nigra*), *rai* is less pungent and hot. It is widely used in Eastern and Southern cuisines and its popularity has spread into numerous other regions, especially Gujarat and Maharastra. Only in Bengal are the seeds used raw, ground with water, ginger and chilies and used to flavor nose-tingling dishes such as *laphra* and *shukta*. In the South, mustard is the most frequently used spice seed, and in the East, it is an important part of the five spice blend called *panch puran*. When mustard seeds are added to hot *ghee* or oil, they pop, sputter and turn gray, developing a nutty taste in the process. For a weak digestive system, too much mustard causes flatulence. Available at Indian or Middle Eastern grocery stores.

MUTH DAL: Known as dew bean or tepary, the cylindrical bean of the vine *Vigna acontifolius* in India and *Phaseolus acutifolius* in Mexico. The flavor is similar to mung beans, though they are smaller and olive-brown. In North India, the unhulled whole beans are simmered with seasonal vegetables, tomatoes, ginger and chilies into a thick purée and seasoned with a zesty *chaunk*. Soaked and drained, they are also deep-fried until crispy and eaten as a snack. *Muth* is sold in Indian and Middle Eastern grocery stores.

NEEM: Known also as *vapu*, the margosa (*Azadirachta indica*) is one of India's most loved trees. It is to the arid wilds of Punjab and Rajasthan what coconut palm is to Bengal and Orissa: a source of solace and sustenance. The entire tree is used, the bulk of the wood for fuel, the finger-thick branches for disposable toothbrushes (the ends are crushed to release antiseptic juices which act as gum stimulators), and the leaves and flowers in cooking as bitter seasonings. Bitter-flavored vegetables—including those made with *neem*, *karela* or *methi*—are not only popular main dishes but are also served as antipastos at the beginning of a meal to sharpen the palate or stimulate a failing appetite.

Dried *neem* leaves are rarely, if ever, available at Indian grocery stores, though *neem* flowers are occasionally seen. If you have friends in India, have them dry and powder a branch of leaves and send a care package. Though they pale in comparison to the fresh leaves, dry *neem* leaves are a convenient and effective seasoning.

NORTHERN CUISINES: The varied cuisines of the North are full-bodied and nourishing, noticeably influenced by climate, land cultivation and cow protection. The temperature extremes—from the subfreezing winters of the Himalayan foothills to the furnace-like heat of the Rajasthani deserts—have greatly influenced crop selections. Since ancient times, farmers have been cultivating wheat, barley, mung and *urad dals* in the fertile plains along the Ganges and Yamuna Rivers, while millet is the primary crop in the arid Rajasthani desert. In the colder but still temperate area of the Northeast Indus Valley, corn, oats, rye, *basmati* and similar rice crops, chickpeas and buckwheat flourish. North India is undoubtably the country's granary.

To help stave off the effects of cold temperatures, Northerners often incorporate "warm" seasonings into their cooking: saffron, cloves, cassia leaf, black cardamom, mace, dried red peppers and vine peppercorns. *Garam masala*, literally a blend of powdered "warm" spices, is widely used in North India, and has become popular in other major cuisines. Exotic flavor accents from rose and *khus* essences garnish many sweet dishes.

Respect for tradition in Vaishnava temple kitchens has contributed greatly to preserving ancient Northern cuisines, especially in Vrindavan temples such as Shree Radha Raman, Shree Radha Govinda, Shree Radha Damodar, Shree Radha Shyamasundar and the newly established Shree Krishna Balaram Temple. Recipes from these temples, as well as from the varied kitchens of other Northerners (from government officials and diplomats to the royalty of Alwar and Jaipur) are included in this book.

NUT CURL GARNISH: Soak whole blanched nuts in boiling water for 3–4 minutes, drain, and pat them dry. Remove curled shavings with a vegetable peeler. Fresh large nuts, such as brazil nuts and almonds, are the easiest to work with, though you can also use pistachios and cashews. Handle them carefully and, if you are storing them, thoroughly dry them before sealing in airtight containers.

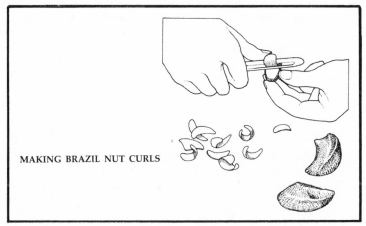

MAKING BRAZIL NUT CURLS

NUTMEG: Known as *jaiphal*, the fragrant nut found in the center of the fruit of the evergreen tree *Myristica fragrans*. The hard nut is brown, slightly cylindrical in shape, and about 1 inch (2.5 cm) in diameter. Nutmeg is used occasionally in milk-based sweets in Bengal and Gujarat and is often part of the North Indian spice blend known as *garam masala*. Since nutmeg loses its vitality soon after grinding, its best to use a nutmeg grinder (sold at better cookware stores) and grind just what you need directly into your dish. Nutmeg has an affinity for spinach and, as it has sweet-fruity overtones, is wonderful with winter squash, yams or sweet potatoes. Whole nutmeg is available at some supermarkets, better health food stores and most mail order spice firms.

OILS: From Vedic literature, we know that *ghee* was the primary cooking medium in ancient India, and, for many uses, it still remains so today. Whether homemade or purchased, *ghee* is easily detected in cooking, and for those who wish to delve into a taste tradition, it is essential. That is not to say that *ghee* is used exclusively, or that it is well suited for all culinary applications. Four vegetable oils—sesame, peanut, mustard and coconut—have been used in India for millenia. Recently, sunflower oil, safflower oil and even soy oil have become popular. Shops specializing in oil pressing offer selections so fresh that they are still warm, with a head on top. You bring in jugs, have them weighed when empty and then when full, and pay for the difference.

A cook must be aware of the temperature at which a particular oil begins to smoke. Generally, unrefined oils have a much lower smoking point than refined oils and, in some cases, this may prevent you from using it for deep-frying. Further, an oil's smoking point varies from brand to brand. Oil is best heated slowly and, should you near its smoking point, add more oil to lower the temperature. Many cooks will not re-use oil or *ghee*, but if you do, be sure to strain it through a fine meshed sieve or cheesecloth to remove stray food particles. Remember that after holding an oil at its smoking point, it begins to decompose. This chemical breakdown is permanant and researchers suggest the loss is in more than just flavor: decomposed oil is difficult to digest, it may cause diarrhea and is devastating on a weak liver. Overused oil shows noticeable signs of wear: it begins to smoke at lower and lower temperatures and gives off a strong odor, even when cold. Discarding this type of oil is never a loss.

From a health standpoint, fats and oils are either saturated or unsaturated. Saturated oils, such as *ghee*, butter, coconut, and palm oil, are known to increase the amount of cholesterol carried in the blood. Unsaturated oils, such as sunflower, safflower, cottonseed, and corn oils, include monounsaturates and polyunsaturates and are reported to actually lower the cholesterol level in the blood. Those with heart disease or health concerns should limit fat consumption in general and try to eat only unsaturated vegetable oils.

Regional cuisines are characterized by the types of oil used. Sesame oil is used in Western cuisines, peanut oil in Northern and Central cuisines, mustard oil in Eastern cuisines and coconut oil in much of the South. Olive oil, clearly the world's favorite salad oil, has a strong flavor even without being heated and adds its very distinct flavor to uncooked dishes. Experiment with the wide range of oils available today; it will enliven and expand your culinary expression. For further information, see individual entries.

OLIVE OIL: Pressed from the ripe olives of a semi-tropical evergreen tree *(Olea europaea)*, the flavor nuances in olive oil are as broad as the spectrum of their gold-to-olive hues. Once only available to cooks in the Mediterranean, it is now used the world over.

The choice of olive oil depends on its prospective usage: as an unheated oil for salad dressings, fresh chutneys or poured on grain pilafs, or as a heated oil for use as a cooking medium. Further, colors vary from blond to jade-green and flavors from mild to fruity. Labels are often confusing because French, Italian and Spanish producers have different standards for explaining grades. Generally speaking, the first cold-pressing of the olives yields a full-bodied, greenish oil and is labeled extra virgin or virgin oil. It is graded according to its acidity (perceived as the quality of sharpness on the back of the tongue). Cold pressed oil is, more often than not, used unheated because its smoking point is low—often under 300°F (150°C). For cooking, you will need the grade labeled pure oil. It has been chemically refined from the skins, pits and pulp of the first pressing, yielding a mild blond oil with a smoking point of over 380°F (195°C)—well within the range needed for making a *chaunk* or for stir-frying vegetables.

Selection is a matter of personal preference, but for use in Vedic dishes that are not cooked, I would suggest sticking to mild extra virgin French oils: James Plagniol, Louis de Regis, J.B. and A. Artaud Frères and Crabtree and Evelyn are a few excellent selections found in specialty shops or by mail order. For cooking, pure grade Italian Bertolli, Berio or Progresso are all excellent and available at most supermarkets.

ORANGE FLOWER WATER: Though not used in India, orange flower water is a wondeful flavoring agent. Most of it is imported from France and can be found at specialty stores and from mail order sources. It is pleasant added to *rasgoola* syrup or sprinkled on shredded carrot rice pilaf.

PAN-FRYING: Though this term can technically refer to frying any ingredient in a small amount of oil, in this book it generally refers to very slowly frying *tikkis* on a heavy griddle that has been coated with a film of oil. Well-seasoned cast-iron *tavas* are used in India, but I find nonstick frying pans trouble-free and an excellent replacement.

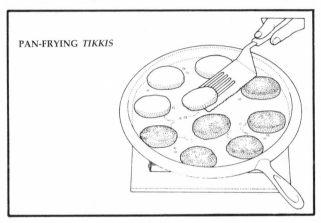

PAN-FRYING *TIKKIS*

PANCH PURAN: A blend of five whole spices most often associated with Bengali cuisine but also popular in neighboring Orissa and Bangaladesh. Most Bengalis combine the whole seeds—cumin seeds, black mustard seeds, fennel seeds, nigella (*kalonji*) and fenugreek seeds—in equal amounts. For newcomers, cut down on the fenugreek a bit; it lends a distinct bitter flavor to everything except root vegetables, which seem to tame its bite. *Panch puran* is always fried in *ghee* or oil before use to release the dormant flavor in the seeds.

Though Bengalis balance the five spices in every conceivable proportion, if you buy it ready-made at an Indian grocery store, there is no telling what the balance will be. As it is easy to put together, newcomers are advised to try the following recipe with just a hint of bitter overtones: three parts each cumin seed, black mustard seeds and fennel seeds, two parts nigella and one part fenugreek seeds. Store in an airtight container for up to 8 months.

PANIR **CHEESE:** In much of India, *panir* is the only word for cheese. It is the simplest type of unripened fresh cheese, and, though not available commercially in America, is easy to make at home. Much like the consistency of soft Japanese *tofu* bean curd, with a flavor like farmers cheese, *panir* is alabaster-white and sweet-smelling. While firm *tofu* is somewhat custard-like, *panir* is creamier and less rubbery. It provides a valuable source of protein for Indian vegetarians, supplying 18–20 grams of protein per 100 grams of cheese. More often than not, *panir* is cubed, fried until brown and then added to other dishes such as vegetables, stews, soups, rice or salads. For *pakoras*, it is left raw and can be sprinkled with powdered spices before being batter-coated and fried.

Over the years, I have experimented with *panir* in dishes from other world cuisines such as Mexican, Italian, Greek and Chinese. It can be introduced into soups, salads, main or side dishes, breads and desserts, instead of other unripened cheeses such as *requeson*, mozzarella or *feta*. No matter what the menu, it is terrific sliced, marinated in herbed oil or a tahini-based marinade, and baked until slightly crisp in a nonstick pan. It might be kneaded with minced herbs, vegetables or both, rolled into balls, rested in a lemon–oil marinade and served from breakfast to dinner. Combined with flour, spices and milk, it serves as a batter for anything from vegetables to bread for french toast.

***PAPARH* and *PAPPADAM*:** Also known as *papad* in the North and *puppadum* in the South, sun-dried parchment-thin brittle disks, usually made from a wet-ground *moong* or *urad dal* paste. In North India, they are anywhere from 6–10 inches (15–25 cm) in diameter and are laced with salt, soda and one or several crushed spices. The South Indian version is much smaller, 3–5 inches (7.5–12.5 cm) in diameter and is usually unspiced. More often than not, the disks are deep-fried or open-flame toasted until they swell into delicate wafers. No matter what the region, they are a popular accompaniment to a full meal, as in-between-meal snacks, and even fingerfood for enter-taining. Though unconventional, they can also double as a protein-rich pasta. Cut into ribbons or other shapes and dropped into a seasoned broth or moist vegetable, they soften in seconds and can replace any number of delicate pastas. Blanched cut *paparhs* or *pappadams* are delicious added to stir-fried greens or vegetables for a low-calorie warm salad or side dish.

Paparhs are also made from soaked tapioca or mashed potatoes, especially popular on grain-free *Ekadasee* menus. Several types are available at Indian grocery stores.

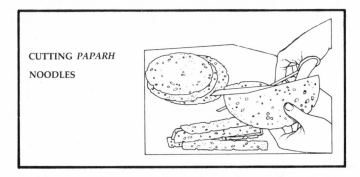

CUTTING *PAPARH* NOODLES

PAPRIKA: Known as *deghi mirch*, this red-orange to brilliant red powder is made by drying and grinding ripe sweet chili peppers. Grown mostly in Kashmir, these chilies, like those used in Hungarian paprika, lend virtually no heat to a dish but only a bright red color. It is used in *dals* and sauces throughout the North. Available at Indian grocery stores.

PAR-BOILING: While blanching briefly exposes an ingredient to boiling water, usually to loosen skins, par-boiling involves partially or even half-cooking an ingredient. Par-boiled foods are usually finished off by frying or baking: for example, green peppers or bitter melons are routinely par-boiled, drained, cooled and stuffed before being pan-fried until brown.

PARSLEY LEAF, Fresh: Parsley is to America and much of Europe what coriander is to India and much of the world: its most commonly used herb. The two most prominent varieties of the plant (*Petroselinum crispum*) are Italian flat-leafed and ornamental curly-leafed. Widely available most of the year at supermarkets, parsley not only perks up the appearance of almost any dish that is not sweet but is also rich in vitamin C, A and calcium. Parsley has a strong flavor of its own, and when minced it fits into a dish like salt or pepper. You can add half of it during cooking and half just before serving. It is colorful, delicious and a pleasant addition to many dishes.

PASILLA CHILI: A Mexican dried chili, about 6 inches (15 cm) long, with a brownish-black color and wrinkled skin. Quite hot and piquant (slightly hotter than the famous ancho chili), it is a flavorful chili to toast and grind for table use and is especially pleasant in tomato-based sauces. If you want to soften the chilies for use in a *chaunk* at the end of a dish, soak them in water or milk for 15 minutes, drain, and then use as needed. Available at corner grocery stores or supermarkets with Latin or Mexican produce.

PASTE *MASALA:* A mixture of seasonings in paste form, made by pounding or wet-grinding spice seeds, ground spices, fresh ginger, hot chilies and herbs, until the consistency is smooth and creamy. For more information on spice blends, see *MASALA*.

PATNA **RICE:** There are at least two types of rice available with *patna* in its name: long-grain *patna* rice and *patna basmati* rice (*basmati* rice from the Patna area of India). Both are sold at Indian grocery stores and though they are quite different, they can be used interchangeably in the recipes.

PEANUT OIL: Known as *moongfalli ka tel* and in Europe as ground nut oil, this is the most widely used oil in many of the Central and Northern cuisines of India, particularly in western Madhya Pradesh where peanuts are a major crop. The first time I saw peanut oil freshly-pressed from nuts, it was almost murky, containing bits of peanut sediment. Yet, compared to anything I had previously tasted, the flavor was intense and alive. The peanut oil labeled "cold pressed" and sold at health food stores most resembles the type sold in India but is more refined and can be heated to higher temperatures (up to 385°F/200°C). The peanut oil sold at supermarkets is the best choice for deep-frying because it has a smoking point of 425°–450°F (220°–230°C) and a bland flavor.

PECAN RICE: A partially hulled, long-grain rice with a smooth grain and a pale gold color. Grown near groves of wild pecan trees (*Carya illinoensis*) in Louisiana, it has a nutty flavor that is subtley reminiscent of walnuts or pecans. It is best shown off alone, perhaps sprinkled with toasted chopped pecans and orange flower water and orange twist garnishes for a special occasion. A newcomer, now available at both supermarkets and specialty mail-order firms like Dean and Deluca.

PEPPER CHAIN GARNISH: Slice off the top and bottom of a bell pepper. Using a sharp paring knife, remove the seeds and core, then make one cut through the flesh lengthwise. Cut crosswise into thin rounds, then interlink and use as a garnish.

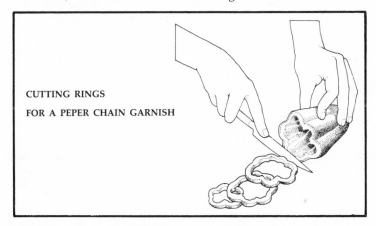

CUTTING RINGS
FOR A PEPER CHAIN GARNISH

PEPPERS, Fresh Green: see **CHILIES**

PEPPERS (VINE), Black, White and Green: These three forms of peppercorns are obtained from the same source, a tropical vine native to India (*Piper nigrum*), which grows plentifully along the coast region of Southwest India. As the world's most used spice, peppercorns are available in several qualities, varying in size, aroma, pungency and color. Today, home cooks desirous of quality and flavor can easily ferret out peppercorns by their place of origin (for example, Malabar or Tellicherry peppercorns, both from the Malabar coast in South India).

Black peppercorn, known as *kali mirch*, is the dried fruit or berry of the vine, harvested unripe and usually sun-dried until the skin becomes wrinkled and black. White peppercorn, known as *safed mirch*, is obtained by allowing the berries to nearly ripen on the vine. After harvesting, the outer skin is removed and then dried. Green peppercorn is simply a soft immature berry, traditionally either preserved in brine or, more recently, freeze-dried. Clusters of green peppercorns are sometimes available at gourmet greengrocers and, in England, in supermarkets like Waitrose or Sainsburys.

Though it is pre-ground and convenient to use, cracked pepper does not compare with the flavor and aroma of freshly-ground pepper. Pepper's highly volatile oils and components begin to pale the moment they are broken; so a good peppermill is essential in a discriminating kitchen. Black pepper, like other warm spices—coriander, cloves, cinnamon, or cumin—has long been regarded as stimulating for the digestion.

PLANTAIN: Known as *kacha kela*, a cooking banana (*Musa paradisiaca*) used frequently in Eastern and Southern cuisines. Compared to supermarket eating bananas, plantains are larger, 9–12 inches (22–30 cm) long, with a thick green skin. Plantains are treated more like vegetables than fruits and contain more starch than sugar and never sweeten, even when fully ripe. They are cooked in several ways, most popularly peeled, shredded or sliced, and then fried until crispy. Bengalis love them simmered in *shukta*, while South Indians love them baked with coconut. Plantains are available year round at Latin American grocery stores and some Indian and Oriental greengrocers.

POBLANO CHILI: This fresh chili, usually greenish-black, is large, about 5 inches (12.5 cm) long. It is roughly triangular, broad at the base, with a pointed tip, but color, shape and size vary according to where it is grown. Compared to jalepeño (the hot chili used in all recipe testing), poblano is more often available at supermarkets as it is used in making chili *rellenos*, a popular cheese-stuffed Mexican dish.

POMEGRANATE SEED, Dried: Known as *anardhana*, the dried seed of a variety of wild pomegranate (*Punica granatum*). Native to the Himalayan foothills of Kashmir and Jammu, *daru* or wild pomegranate, has a distinct sour, rather than sweet taste. When fresh, the sun-dried seeds are somewhat sticky to the touch, with a blackish-wine color; when old or stale, the seeds are dry and shriveled. Pomegranate seeds are popular in some Northern dishes: *karhis*, *pakoras* and stuffings for *parathas* or *kachoris*. Available at Indian grocery stores.

POPPY SEED, White: Known as *khas khas* and *posta* in Bengal, the ripe seeds of the poppy plant (*Papaver somniferum*). The creamy-white seeds used in India are much smaller than the blue-gray seeds sprinkled on cakes and breads in Europe and America, though the flavor is similar. Like sesame seeds, white poppy seeds are oily and protein-rich and are used in several regional cuisines, especially in Gujarat. Wet-ground poppy seeds are indispensible in some types of Bengali *shukta* and *laphra*. Powdered, wet-ground or whole, the seeds are routinely baked, dry-roasted or fried to bring out a dormant nutty flavor. Perhaps its most outstanding use is as a thickener for sauces and gravies. Powdered poppy seeds combined with crushed spices add a wonderful flavor-crust to pan-fried steamed potatoes, green beans or bell peppers. Like other nuts and seeds with a high oil content, they are best stored in a cool nook. Available at Indian and Middle Eastern grocery stores.

POTATO FLOUR: A nutritious flour made by either grinding steamed, dried baking-type potatoes like Idaho or Burbank, or by extracting the starch by pulverizing and repeated washings. The starch found in potatoes is similar to that found in grains; therefore, it is a good thickener for people on gluten-free diets. Potato flour is nutritious—rich in vitamin C, iron and potassium—and slightly sweeter than white flour. It is particularly delicious in flat breads, yielding a crisp crumb and moist inside. To prevent lumping as a thickener, it is best to use potato starch; cream it into soft butter and make a mock *beurre manie*: a mixture of 1½ tablespoons (22 ml) unsalted butter and 1½ tablespoons (22 ml) potato starch will moderately thicken a cream soup. Potato flour is available at health food, gourmet and specialty stores.

POUNDED RICE: Known as *poha*, flat or flaked rice, this ingredient is only available at Indian grocery stores and is sold in two varieties: thick *poha* and thin *poha*. While thick *poha* is most often used in a light meal dish called *chura*, thin *poha* is almost always reserved for deep-frying in a nibbler called *chidwa*; they are not used interchangeably. Thick *poha* grains are about the size of a sunflower seed, with a creamy-gray color. They must be washed and softened before use, then gently pressed dry. Depending on the quality, flat rice requires different handling. If the grains are very firm and thick in the middle, they will take several quick rinsings in water and then a brief soaking. If they are thinner, the grains will swell during the rinsings and further soaking will cause them to disintegrate. The best policy is to work quickly: place the grains in a sieve and dip them in clear water only long enough to swish them around a few seconds. Drain and change the water several times, repeating the rinsing, then test by pressing a grain between your thumb and forefinger. It should be *al dente*, like pasta. The thick, softened *poha* is now ready to use in any *chura* recipe.

In England, supermarkets sell a type of pounded rice made from a starchy, medium-grain rice. While it is not suitable for deep-fried savories, it is excellent for baked *kheer*. Follow the package directions for baked pudding with the following adjustments: start by reducing the quantity of flat rice suggested by one-fourth. Add a pinch of crushed cardamom during the baking and sprinkle with rose water just before serving.

PRABHUPADA, SRILA: See *Appendix* on His Divine Grace A.C. Bhaktivedanta Swami.

PRASADAM: A newcomer in India will likely hear three words used in relation to food: *prasadam*, *bhoga* and *bhojana*. For the most part, food which has been offered to God before being eaten is called *prasadam* or "God's mercy," whether in an established temple with formal worship or at home with a simple prayer. Depending on the name of the Deity it is being offered to, *prasadam* is prefixed by names such as *Govinda*, *Damodar*, *Banabehari* or any one of thousands of other names. Temples become well known for their special *prasadams*. For example, Vrindavan's temple of Radha Ramana is famous for a sweet called *kuliya*. *Bhoga* is a collective term meaning almost any food ingredient that is to be used for offering to God. *Bhojana* simply means either cooked or uncooked food.

PRESSURE COOKING: The process can cut cooking time by up to seventy percent and it can be used for foods that are steamed, stewed, boiled or cooked by the *dum* process. Pressure cookers are particularly well suited for cooking dried beans and peas, soups, beets, and hearty vegetables which normally take a seemingly interminable time to cook. Follow the manufacturer's instructions for care, usage and cooking timetables.

TO PURÉE: To reduce foods to a smooth consistency using a food mill, masher, ricer or a food processor or blender. A food mill is particularly effective for removing fiber, seeds and skins from fruits or tomatoes. A ricer is effective when you want a dryish smooth pulp, perhaps for yams or potatoes.

QUINOA: *Quinoa* (pronounced keen-wa) has been cultivated in the South American Andes for 5,000 years. Given the name "the mother grain" by ancient farmers, it was revered as sacred due to its hardiness, nutritional value and versatility. Like buckwheat, it is called a grain, but it is technically the fruit of a plant in the *Chenopodium* family. The annual plant is 3–6 feet (1–2 meters) high with large seed clusters at the end of the stalk, similar to millet. The strain most popular in America today is the pale yellow, a cross between the size of millet and yellow mustard seeds; other species vary from oyster to pink, orange, red and purple.

So far as its food value is concerned, one researcher has said that "while no single food can supply all of the essential life-sustaining nutrients, it (*quinoa*) comes as close as any other in the vegetable or animal kingdoms." It contains more protein than any other grain: an average of 16.2 percent, compared with 7.5 percent for rice, 9.9 percent for millet, 8.2 percent for barley and 14 percent for wheat. It has a good balance of the amino acids that make up the protein and is high in lysine, an amino acid not overly abundant in the vegetarian diet. It is cooked like rice and blends well with other grains or whole grain pilafs. The cooked consistency is light and the flavor described as nutty. It makes a good stuffing for cabbage or grape leaves, can be used instead of bulgar for *tabooli*-type salads and mixed with buckwheat for wonderful croquettes. For Vedic vegetarians, *quinoa* is a welcome food for *Ekadasee* menus. It is available at health food and grain stores.

RADISH ROSE GARNISH: To shape each flower, cut a thin slice off the base. Using a small sharp knife, make vertical paper-thin cuts through to the base. Make the vertical slices both lengthwise and crosswise. Chill in ice water for several hours until the blossoms open up.

RAW SUGAR and NATURAL SWEETENERS: In many regions in India, the unrefined sweeteners used millenia ago are still in use today. Two of these sweeteners, *gur*, from palm trees and *jaggery*, from sugar cane, account for most of the sugars used.

Several relatively unrefined sweeteners are available at health food stores. Sugar maple trees in Canada and Northeast America are the source of both maple syrup and maple sugar granules. During March, usually with snow still on the ground, sap in the trees begins to flow and is collected in buckets. The sap is boiled down until it is reduced to a sweet syrup.

Sorghum molasses or syrup is obtained from sorghum, a tall grass in the millet family. The sweet juice is extracted from stalks, much like sugar cane, and boiled down into a dark syrup. Other liquid sweeteners include those made from barley, corn, wheat and rice. The grains are sprouted, sometimes malted, and allowed to ferment to convert starches into natural liquid sweeteners. Rice syrup, perhaps the most expensive, is the lightest in color and flavor, while barley malt is dark brown and relatively inexpensive.

Mexican *panocha* or *piloncillo*, molded into the form of bottle corks, is an unrefined brown sugar available at many Cuban, Latin and Mexican grocery stores. Some health food stores and supermarkets sell a product called "Sugar in the Raw"—though it is never entirely clear how unrefined it is because legally "raw sugar" cannot be manufactured in America. Dean and Deluca, Zabar's and other good mail order sources offer unrefined sugars such as Muscovado sugar from Malawi, Africa (heralded as "a raw cane sugar containing all of its molasses"). Less powerful, and only partially cleansed of impurities, is honey-blond turbinado sugar, containing only fifteen percent molasses. Though pleasant for the table and for baking, the granules are large and do not dissolve if creamed with butter for cakes or pastries. It is best to powder turbinado in a coffee mill before most use.

Before I met Jeanne Jones, nutritionist and author of several books for special diets and diabetics, I was not aware of the benefits of date sugar. It is a granular sweetener made by pulverizing rock-hard dried dates—actually a fruit rather than a sugar. A highly concentrated sweet, it is an unrefined carbohydrate, the most "natural" of all sugars—rich in fiber, calcium, iron, vitamin A, and some trace minerals. Since it burns at low temperatures, it is not well-suited for baking or cooking; better to sprinkle it on foods where it can be seen as well as appreciated for its delicious taste. Date sugar is one sweetener allowed in limited quantity on sugar-restricted and diabetic diets.

Perhaps the most obvious and overlooked natural sweetener is fruit: fresh purées, frozen and bottled concentrates, fresh juices, and dried fruit pastes. Granted, it cannot be used for everything, but it can easily be worked into healthful baked goods, beverages and frozen desserts. Sugar-free frozen fruit juice concentrates such as orange, pineapple, apple, white and red grape, as well as numerous blends, offer a tremendous sweet flavor dimension to many dishes. Health food stores sell bottled concentrates of pear, peach, apple, cranberry, black cherry and on. Any type of dried fruits, alone or in tandem, can be used as sweeteners. Puréed bananas are wonderful in frozen fruit desserts and cold milk- or yogurt-based shakes.

Once, when I was requested to come up with a sugar-free Bengali *sandesh* for a catered function, I made several *nouvelle* variations sweetened with dried mango and papaya pastes. With today's increased nutritional awareness, exploring natural sweeteners is not only easy but guaranteed to enrich your cooking expression as well. A partial or full switch from refined to alternative sweeteners is painless, and depending on taste preference, dietary needs, cost and usage, there are many choices. The following chart is meant to guide you in determining how much of a particular sweetener is equivalent to white sugar, and whether a liquid proportion of ingredients should be modified, especially in Western baking.

ASSORTED SWEETENERS

ALTERNATIVE SWEETENER	SUBSTITUTE THIS AMOUNT FOR EACH CUP OF SUGAR	REDUCE TOTAL LIQUID BY THIS AMOUNT PER CUP
maple syrup	¾ cup (180 ml)	2 tablespoons
maple sugar granules	1 cup (145 g)	
date sugar	1 cup (150 g)	
honey	¾ cup (180 ml)	2 tablespoons
barley malt	1¼ cups (300 ml)	6 tablespoons
rice syrup	1¼ cups (300 ml)	6 tablespoons
fruit juice concentrate	1½ cups (360 ml)	½ cup (360 ml)
molasses	½ cup (120 ml)	

RECIPE CONVERTER: When you increase recipes for quantity cooking, adjust pan size, regulate heat source, and keep in mind that spices will need to be adjusted accordingly.

TO MULTIPLY A RECIPE			
Amount	**x 2**	**x 3**	**x 4**
¼ t	½ t	¾ t	1 t
½ t	1 t	1½ t	2 t
¾ t	1½ t	2¼ t	1 T
1 t	2 t	1 T	4 t
1¼ t	2½ t	3¾ t	1⅔ T
1½ t	1 T	1½ T	2 T
1¾ t	3½ t	5¼ t	2⅓ T
2 t	4 t	2 T	2⅔ T
½ T	1 T	1½ T	2 T
1 T	2 T	3 T	¼ c
1½ T	3 T	¼ c − ½ T	⅜ c
2 T	¼ c	⅜ c	½ c
2½ T	¼ c + 1 T	½ c − ½ T	⅝ c
¼ c	½ c	¾ c	1 c
⅓ c	⅔ c	1 c	1⅓ c
½ c	1 c	1½ c	2 c
⅔ c	1⅓ c	2 c	2⅔ c
¾ c	1½ c	2¼ c	3 c
1 c	2 c	3 c	4 c
1¼ c	2½ c	3¾ c	5 c
1⅓ c	2⅔ c	4 c	5⅓ c
1½ c	3 c	4½ c	6 c
1⅔ c	3⅓ c	5 c	6⅔ c
1¾ c	3½ c	5¼ c	7 c
2 c	4 c	6 c	8 c

TO DIVIDE A RECIPE				
Amount	**÷ ¼**	**÷ ⅓**	**÷ ½**	**÷ ⅔**
¼ t	4 d	5 d	⅛ t	10 d
½ t	⅛ t	10 d	¼ t	⅓ t
¾ t	12 d	¼ t	⅓ t	½ t
1 t	¼ t	⅓ t	½ t	⅔ t
1¼ t	¼ t + 3d	⅓ t + 5 d	½ t + 5 d	¾ t + 5 d
1½ t	⅓ t	½ t	¾ t	1 t
1¾ t	½ t	⅜ t	⅞ t	1⅛ t
2 t	½ t	⅔ t	1 t	1⅓ t
½ T	⅓ t	½ t	¾ t	1 t
1 T	¼ T	1 t	½ T	2 t
1½ T	⅜ T	½ T	¾ T	1 T
2 T	½ T	2 t	1 T	4 t
2½ T	2 t	2½ t	3¾ t	1⅔ T
¼ c	1 T	4 t	2 T	2⅔ T
⅓ c	4 t	5⅓ t	2⅔ T	3½ T
½ c	2 T	2⅔ T	¼ c	⅓ c
⅔ c	2⅔ T	3⅔ T	⅓ c	½ c − 2 t
¾ c	3 T	¼ c	⅜ c	½ c
1 c	¼ c	⅓ c	½ c	⅔ c
1¼ c	¼ c + 1 T	⅜ c + 2 t	⅝ c	⅞ c − 2 t
1⅓ c	⅓ c	½ c − 1 T	9 c	1c − 2 t
1½ c	⅜ c	½ c	¾ c	1 c
1⅔ c	⅜ c + 2 t	½ c + 1 T	¾ c + 4 t	1 c + 2 T
1¾ c	⅜ c + 1 T	½ c + 4 t	⅞ c	1⅛ c + 2 t
2 c	½ c	⅔ c	1 c	1⅓ c

ABBREVIATIONS

t = teaspoon　　　T = tablespoon　　　c = cup　　　d = drop

TO REDUCE: To boil down liquids, evaporating some of the water content, to concentrate volume, flavor and consistency. Most Vedic sauces and gravies are thickened by reduction rather than by the addition of starches.

RICE: Known as *chaval*, rice (*Oryza sativa*) is India's most important food grain, and, along with wheat, barley and millet, it has been cultivated since Vedic times. Paddy rice, grown in water, is planted in most of the fertile plains of tropical South India, while hill rice, grown on dry land, is grown in the temperate northern regions of Pakistan and Uttar Pradesh. The yearly rice crop is fed today as it has been for millenia, by the downpour of the monsoon rainy season (*varsa*). From July through September, the parched land is refreshed, and, aided by the scorching heat of the season, crops flourish. By fall (*sarad*), the rains stop and the land begins to dry out for harvest.

Since most cooks in India know what they want in a rice and how to select it, finding it is the greatest task. Out of the thousands of varieties grown in India alone, there are relatively few sources with over thirty qualities available for sale. Still, by Western standards, that amount is almost unheard of. I was quite awed at my first visit to one of Bombay's finest purveyors of grains in bustling Bhuleshwar marketplace. Walking between rows of neatly bagged cereals, I counted no less than sixty-seven qualities and strains of rice—my guide feeling and smelling the grains and heralding one type over another with flair.

Rice is selected considering such factors as the length and breadth of the grains, whether it is raw or par-boiled, unpolished or polished, and, of course, by its color, smell, translucency, uniformity and age. All rice is classified into length—long, medium or short-grain—and by breadth—extra-fine, fine or coarse.

Like other grains, rice is composed of a starchy endosperm and germ embryo, covered by a bran layer and finally encased in a husk. In its natural state, with the inedible husk removed, a rice kernal, covered with its yellow-brown bran covering, is called *ukad*—unpolished or brown rice. While brown rice is coveted in the West for its obvious nutritional edge over *arwa chaval*—polished or white rice—in India, *ukad* is considered coarse and inferior. Well over ninety percent of the rice eaten in India is white, preferred for its appealing looks, significantly longer storage life and its ability to exibit its inherent subtle nutty or sweet flavor. Raw white rice, husked and polished, is called *kacha*, *atapa* or *sukla chaval*. It is the most expensive rice in India and accounts for over one-third of India's production.

Par-boiled white rice, known as *pakkha*, *siddha* or *sela chaval*, accounts for over one-half of India's rice. In America, par-boiled or converted rice is a nutritional consideration; the process of steaming or boiling the grains before milling forces some of the vitamins and minerals towards the center of the endosperm, locking in food value which would otherwise be removed with the bran. In India, par-boiling is more of a practical consideration: the process firms up soft new rice grains encouraging a high yield during milling and therefore minimal costs. There is a third type of rice called doubly-boiled rice generally shunned by rice connoisseurs.

For the Vaishnava temple chef, the selection of rice is clear: *sali anna*—extra-fine, fragrant, raw white rice, with long, pointed, unbroken grains. This type of rice is offered to temple Deities daily, steamed and accompanied with *ghee*, much as it has been for over fifty centuries. My personal favorite, which was also the favorite of my spiritual preceptor, Srila Prabhupada, is Dehradun *basmati* rice, aged one or two years, though this quality rice is even difficult to find in many areas of India. Any fragrant *basmati* rice sold at Indian grocery stores is preferred over other long-grain rice.

There is no harm adding variety to rice offerings in the temple, provided the traditional selection of *sali anna* is always present. Experiment with organic whole seeds and grains—barley, millet, wheat, corn, rye, buckwheat, and *quinoa*. Along with wild rice and the currently popular cross-strains of Indian *basmati* and American long-grain brown rice or Carolina rice, called Texmati and Calmati, an innovative Vedic cook can come up with elegant and nutritious fare. For further information on specific ingredients or strains, see individual entries.

RICE FLOUR: See **GROUND RICE**

RICING: To press or force food through the perforations of a ricer or strainer.

RIDGED GOURD: Also known as club gourd, sponge gourd and silk squash, and as *toray*, *jhingha* and *tori* in India, this popular vegetable belongs to a plant in the cucumber family (*Luffa acutangula*). Harvested when anywhere from 8–12 inches (20–30 cm) long, the green-skinned gourd has long ridges running along its entire length. It is best served when still immature and, even then, the ridges are spiny and must be removed. Mature vegetables develop a fiberous core and lose succulence. The buttery flesh is off-white and has a flavor somewhere between zucchini and cucumber. It is loved in Bengali dishes and has an affinity for peas, tomatoes and peppers. Available at Indian and Oriental grocery stores; I have even seen it occasionally at good supermarkets.

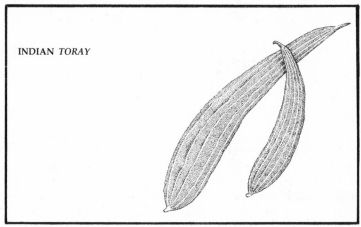

INDIAN *TORAY*

RISSOLE: A British version of Bengali vegetable or nut cutlets. They are usually round and about half as thick as they are in diameter. Pan- or shallow-fried, they are well-browned and served warm.

ROLLING OUT: Though you can use any one of several makeshift implements—a 1-inch (2.5 cm) dowel, a segment of broom handle or certain flat-surfaced bottles—good pins are not expensive. Though there are several special pins available, two will cover most needs: a 20-inch (50 cm) straight beechwood pin and a 15-inch (37.5 cm) tapered Indian *chapati* pin. A possible source of difficulty in a tapered pin is the angle of the center swell; avoid a tapered pin with a pointed center.

ROSE ESSENCE or ROSE WATER: Known as *ruh gulab* and *gulab jal*, these flavorings are particularly important to the cuisines of Bengal, Uttar Pradesh and Punjab. Both are diluted forms of pure rose oil, made from any highly scented rose petals, but most often from the intensely perfumed damask rose (*Rosa damascena*).

For centuries, rose oil has been made by a simple steam distillation of fresh rose petals and water. Diluted rose water is often sprinkled about the home or temple room as a refresher, especially in the summer. Rose essence or water is used in milk-based dishes and beverages such as sweet *lassi*, *gulab jamun*, *rasgoola* and rice *kheer*. In some temples, the drinking water offered to the Deity is rose-flavored: fresh petals are added to well water, left to sit for twenty-four hours and then strained off. This water is also delicious in lemonade or herb teas. Both *ruh gulab* and *gulab jal* are available at Indian grocery stores.

RUBBING IN: The process of incorporating butter, *ghee* or oil into flour when preparing short-ened pastry dough. The butter and flour can be rubbed between the thumbs and fingers or between open palms until the butter is evenly distributed and the texture resembles oatmeal.

SAFFLOWER OIL: Pressed from the seed of the flowering saffron thistle or safflower plant (*Carthamus tinctorius*), this oil was only occasionally used in India before the early 1970s. When it appeared in the bazaar—attractively tinned and widely available—it met with instant approval. Numerous city vegetarians in India enjoy a versatile oil like safflower because, compared to the widely used mustard, coconut, peanut and sesame oils, it is very low in saturated fatty acids (only ten percent) and therefore welcome to those concerned about cholesterol. The mild oil has a very high smoking point (from 450°–510°F/232°–265°C depending on processing) and can be used equally well in salads or in cooking. It blends well with *ghee*, making it a pleasant and economical alternative to deep-frying in pure *ghee*. Available at supermarkets and health food stores.

SAFFRON: Known as *kesar*, the hand-picked stigmas, called threads, collected from the flowers of the saffron crocus (*Crocus sativas*), cultivated in the Mediterranean, Asia Minor, India and China. Today, most cooks agree that the best saffron is from Spain or Kashmir—deep red-brown threads, best under a year old and still soft to the touch. Saffron is expensive no matter where you buy it, because good quality saffron, properly sealed, dated and labeled to prevent adulteration, is pack-aged in small amounts—usually two grams or less. To collect only one pound (455 g) of saffron, up to 250,000 flowers must be harvested of stigmas the moment the blossoms open up.

As powdered saffron is easily adulterated, most cooks prefer the threads. They are customarily soaked in a small amount of hot milk before wet-grinding or slightly dry-roasted over very low heat to become brittle before powdering. Saffron's flavor is difficult to describe: sharp yet slightly sweet, with a strong perfume, and, when used discreetly, it lends a wonderful color and flavor to a dish. Only ¼ teaspoon (1 ml) is needed for a dish serving 4 to 6 persons. *Kesar sandesh* is one of the most outstanding sweets of Bengal and saffron rice pilafs are made for special occasions. Inquire for quality saffron at Indian and Middle Eastern grocers, gourmet stores and good mail order firms.

SALT and SEASONED SALTS: Common table salt (*Sambar namak*), sodium chloride, is the most important of many salts in sea water, though several other mineral combinations do exist. Today, it is obtained in three principal ways: through vacuum pan production, rock salt mining, and solar evaporation.

Rock salt or halite is known as *sendha namak* and is most often mined in its crystalline state, much like coal is, from underground dry sea beds. Indian black salt or *kala namak* is actually reddish-gray when it is mined but turns gray-brown when ground. Because of the various miner-als present in the salt, with noticeable calcium chloride, it has a flavor faintly resembling hard boiled eggs.

Our daily biological need for salt is minute: about ¹⁄₁₆th teaspoon (0.25 ml). While fresh peas or carrots may require little or no salt to be appreciated, other foods, such as grains and *dals*, are brought to life with salt. Most of us feel that salt sharpens our awareness of fine food. Unless you have high blood pressure or a doctor's order to avoid it entirely, a safe daily intake falls within the range of ½–1½ teaspoons (1,100 to 3,300 milligrams). Today's average American is said to consume considerably more than this—2–4 teaspoons (10–20 ml) daily—and if you eat a large amount of commercially prepared foods, the quantity is likely to increase.

Ultimately, how much salt you use is a personal matter. Our recipe testers rated the salt content in the recipes as moderately-low, and, more often than not, a recipe instructs you to add salt toward the completion of cooking, making full use of its vitality. If you are on a salt-free regimen or are cooking for others who are, stimulate foods by adding fresh herbs or different types of peppers. Lemon juice brings out the best in just about everything.

SANDALWOOD, in its Various Forms: The wood, known as *chandan*; the oil, known as *chandan tel*; and the essence, as *ruh chandan*—all are obtained from the yellowish-brown sandalwood tree (*Genus santalum*; in India, *S. album*). Native to the southern districts of Mysore and Tamil Nadu, sandalwood also grows in the Malaya Hills and Nilagiri Hills in the Western Ghat.

Sandalwood, India's most prized wood, is not only used in temple carvings and paraphernalia but is also the source of one of the world's most expensive fragrant oils. Some of the finest French perfumers turn to India for sandalwood oil, and, like gold, the market prices fluctuate according to demand, flow and yields. Further, oils extracted from different parts of the tree have different values—the core of the tree yields the most concentrated powerful fragrance and is therefore the most expensive.

Sandalwood is also used in cooking and, in addition to its delicate fragrance, is also considered "cooling" and hence used widely in the summer season. Sandal *sharbat*—made from a sandalwood essence and sugar syrup—is the basis of wonderful iced drinks or frappées. In Vrindavan's medieval temple of Shree Radha Madhan Mohan, I met a temple chef who kindly supplied me with an ancient recipe for sandalwood *burfi*. A walnut-sized chunk of sandalwood is sliced, combined with a few crushed green cardamom pods on a small muslin square, and a parcel made with a secure knot. The flavor parcel is added to 8 cups (2 liters) of milk and then boiled down into *rabri*. About ½ cup (110 g) of sugar is then added and the milk continued to be reduced into a thick paste. The paste is then cooled, kneaded on a marble slab and shaped into bite-sized confections. The result is a *burfi* infused with exquisite flavor.

Fresh ground sandalwood pulp has long been used externally to counteract the ill effects of intense tropical heat. Sandalwood is sold in Indian *bazaars* and Indian grocery stores in easy to handle pieces. Also available are flat round slabs of coarse sandstone for grinding. Any one of several varieties of perfumed water—rose, *khus*, *kewra* or even orange flower water—can be used as a lubricant. Pour a few drops onto the sandstone. Clench a piece of the sandalwood firmly in your hand and, pressing it against the grinding stone, work it around in a continuous circular motion to produce a fine wet paste.

For millenia, this type of fragrant sandalwood paste has been used in Deity worship. Depending on the circumstance, a touch of ground camphor or saffron can be added while grinding the paste. A temple *pujari* or priest might dip a *tulasi* flower or leaf in the sandal paste, offer it to the Deity and then distribute it as *prasadam*. Small sandalwood logs, chips, pure powder, oil, essence and syrups are sometimes available at Indian grocery stores.

SAPODILLA (SAPOTA): Known as *chickoo*, the honey-brown-skinned fruit of the tree *achras sapota*. It looks like a large kiwi fruit on the outside with a slightly smoother skin, while the fruit is yellow-brown. It is very sweet, slightly grainy in texture and honey-maple flavored. In India, *chickoo* is eaten as it is, as a finale to a meal or with other fruits of contrasting colors, textures and flavors. In Gujarat, it is often sliced into *rabri* or plain *kheer*, perhaps with diced mango and banana, for a richer sweet.

One giant sapodilla tree growing in my neighbor's Key West garden supplied fruits for ten families. Further, the fruits can be picked unripe 4–6 weeks before ripening with little, if any, effect on the quality. They should feel like a ripe kiwi before use, firm yet soft to the touch. *Chickoo* is famed in India as one of Lord Krishna's favorite fruits. Available at Latin American grocery stores throughout most of the late summer.

SCALD: In this book, to scald refers either to the heating of milk or cream to just before the boiling point, or the plunging of vegetables or fruits into boiling water momentarily to facilitate removal of skins.

SCORE: To scrape or make shallow incisions—often in a cross-hatched pattern—on the top of a pastry or sweetmeat, either to roughen or decorate the surface. For example, the surface of a flat slab of milk fudge (*burfi*) is scored with a fork before adding a garnish of minced nuts or silver foil (*varak*).

To score well-defined marks on the side of a cucumber, carrot or citrus, pull a canelle knife along the sides from top to bottom to remove a groove from the skin. Leave about ¼ inch (6 mm) between the cuts, then slice into rounds crosswise. This creates a shaped or ridged pattern when cut, adding a touch of artistry to the dish.

SCREW PINE ESSENCE: Known by various names—*ruh kewra*, *ruh kevda* and *ruh keora*—this essential flavoring is obtained from the exquisitely perfumed flowers and petal-like leaves of the tropical screw pine (*Pandanus tectorius* or *P. odoratissimus*). Native to the humid, swampy canal regions of South India and Asia, the beauty of the blossoms is legendary and its fragrance rivals jasmine, gardenia or tube roses. The flower petals themselves, known as *tayai* in Kerala, might be floated in a silver dish for a formal table setting. On special Vaishnava holidays, a giant latticework trellis might be covered with an elaborate screw pine flower decoration and placed around an altar for the pleasure of the temple Deity and visitors. A similarly decorated walk-in trellis might serve as a "flower bungalow" for an affluent wedding ceremony.

Both *kewra* water and *kewra* essence are used extensively throughout India—primarily in sweet dishes—but they might also act as flavor garnishes in elaborate rice *briyanis* or pilafs. Almost any sweet syrup dish could be accented by *kewra*—from Bengali *pantoah* to North Indian *balushai*. If you are interested in exploring the exotic flavorings used in India's regional cuisines, keep a supply of *kewra*, rose, vetiver and sandalwood essences on hand. Available at Indian and Middle Eastern grocery stores.

SEMOLINA: Known as *sooji*, this wheat product, very popular in India and parts of Europe (particularly Italy), consists of the creamy-colored granules of hard endosperm sifted out of durum wheat (*Triticum durum*) during the milling process. In India, *sooji* is available in three grinds: fine, medium and coarse. The texture of fine Indian *sooji* is very similar to the widely available product sold at health food stores as semolina flour. Equally suitable is one of the plain or flavored Italian semolina pasta flours sold at specialty food stores.

Sooji is used in unusual ways. It can be simmered until fluffy for savory vegetable *uppmas* or sweet *halvas*, or used in bread and pastry doughs. Italian semolina and Indian *sooji* can be used interchangeably in any grind, though I prefer the fine grind over the others. Semolina is available as *sooji* at Indian grocery stores and as semolina flour at health food and gourmet grocery stores.

Farina, also sold as instant, quick-cooking or regular "Cream of Wheat" and "Malt O' Meal", is a similar wheat products, but made from hard, not necessarily durum, wheat. They are all processed in different ways, absorbing liquids in varying amounts and therefore, affecting cooking times. Farina products are generally coarse and do not "fluff" quite as much as semolina, though they are acceptable substitutes in a pinch. Unless you use the exact farina product mentioned in a recipe, follow the manufacturer's instructions for adjusting the liquid content and alter cooking times accordingly.

SERRANO CHILI: About 1½ inches (4 cm) long—at first bright green but ripening to bright red—they are thin and narrow, even at the base. Though available at many supermarkets, they are smaller and hotter than jalepeño chilies, and more time consuming to seed. If you use them unseeded, cut down on the quantity considerably. If you use the smaller Indian serrano-type chilies, reduce the quantity even more.

SERVING and ENTERTAINING: No matter what the occasion, entertaining requires fore-thought and planning, and when it is effective, everyone—hosts, helpers and guests—enjoy themselves. Once a guest enters your home, resolve to create a smooth continuity in your serving and entertaining. For an authentic Indian atmosphere, nothing sets the scene like traditional stain-less steel dinnerware, available at better Indian grocery stores.

Dinnerware:

In terms of traditional place settings, formal and informal meals are uncomplicated and re-markably similar, no matter what the occasion. Instead of separate courses, the entire meal is served at once, including the dessert. Traditional plates are called *thalis*—anywhere from 8–20 inches (20–50 cm) in diameter—and the individual bowls are called *katoris*—from 1½–3½ inches (4–9 cm) in diameter. The number of bowls and their placement on the plate depends upon the menu and time of day. Western cutlery and silverware—with the exception of a spoon or two placed to the right of the plate—is rejected in favor of using the fingertips of the right hand with finesse. While this may seem unusual at first, it is a pleasing experience once you are used to it. A water glass is placed just above the spoons, slightly to the right of the plate. Though a stainless steel alloy containing an 18 percent chrome to 8 percent nickel ratio is the most popular metal for dinnerware and serving utensils, villagers still prefer a tin and copper alloy called bell metal, while royal and wealthy households use full settings of either silver or gold.

Another type of *thali*, made only in stainless steel, is indented with as many as fourteen hollows—in an array of sizes—that conveniently serve as small bowls. This type is practical for both family dinners and any type of entertaining, saving in both set-up and clean-up time. The advantage of this plate on a standup buffet spread is obvious: it precludes the need for oversized wobbly bowls and cuts down on balancing-act disasters.

Dining Room and Place Settings:

Compared to a Western dining room, the ambiance of its Indian counterpart is understated and serene in its simplicity. If the setting is traditional, as in a Japanese home, shoes are not worn and diners sit on low stools called *patlas* or cushions on floors made of polished marble or, in villages, satin-smooth concrete slabs or sandstone. *Thalis* might be placed directly on the immaculately clean floors or on individual *chonkis* (dining tables) set before each diner. If there are an equal number of men and women guests, they would be seated in rows facing each other, with room in the center for servers. If there is a guest of honor, he or she would sit at one end. The guest of honor, elder, host or hostess is served first.

Worn like a fine ornament, a Vedic host or hostess proudly displays entertaining etiquette. While Western protocol extends itself to heads of state and officials, the warmth of Vaishnava hospitality crosses all boundaries to welcome any guest who enters the home—be they guests of recognition or total strangers. The first royal dinner I attended at the palace of the late Rajah Pratap Kumar of Alwar was, to my embarrassment, personally served to me by the Maharaja himself, though scores of servants stood in waiting. After several such occasions, I came to under-stand that respect and honor are expressed through either serving or receiving *prasadam*, no matter what one's social position.

Special Occasions and Order of Serving:

Most Vedic festivities—religious or social—are held at mid-day, between noon and 2 p.m. A formal dinner or evening supper is held between 7 and 9:30 p.m. The presentation, menu and order of service vary from one region to another. Three menus and their order of serving are illustrated on the following pages.

Of the Western vegetarian regional cuisines, the Marawadi community in Maharashtra is regarded as the finest, and their presentation, the most refined. While the following meals from the East and South are served on an empty plate, one dish after another, the Marawadi *thali* is presented to the diner with several dishes already on the plate. The *thali* is further divided into an imaginary right and left side and each item on the menu is placed in a designated area. With the *thali* representing an imaginary timepiece, one o'clock to six o'clock is the right side, and seven o'clock to twelve o'clock the left side. The rice, drizzled with *ghee* or seasoned fresh butter, is placed just below center. Within this traditional framework, cooks have worked their magic in limitless ways.

Moving clockwise down the right side of the *thali* from one o'clock to six o'clock are the main- and side-dish vegetables, *dal* and sweet: *Cauliflower Kofta, Green Beans with Water Chestnuts, Steamed Split Pea Dumplings in Mild Karhi Sauce* or *Sautéed Bell Peppers in Karhi* Sauce, *Toovar Dal with Chopped Spinach* or *Rice and Toasted Toovar Dal Khichari with Mixed Vegetables, Tender-Crisp Sprouted Urad Beans in Sesame–Yogurt Sauce, Super-Flaky Pastry Swirls with Cardamom Glaze* or *Deep-Fried Pretzel-Shaped Loops in Saffron Syrup.*

At the eleven-thirty to twelve o'clock position on the *thali* are a lime wedge and a tiny mound of both salt and pepper. Moving counter-clockwise down the left side of the *thali* are the chutneys, relishes, pickles and savories, in this case: *Apricot Chutney with Currants, Shredded Mango and Coconut Chutney, Fried Bitter Melon with Ground Almonds* or *Deep-Fried Shredded Plantain Clusters, Dessert Grapes Stufed with Herbed Soft Cheese, Savory Butter Crackers with Lemon, Tapioca and Potato Patties with Roasted Peanuts.*

Eastern Cuisine Wedding Feast:

The menu items are presented in the order they should be served. Design your *thali* or plate(s) ahead of time for the most colorful and practical positioning of the foods.

Royal Milk Pudding with Chenna Cheese, lemon or lime wedge and a small spoon of salt, *White Radish Pickle* or *Sweet Lemon or Lime Pickle, Sautéed Rice, Greens and Plantain with Toasted Almonds, Bitter Melon Chips with Coconut, Bitter Melon Vegetable Stew in Poppy Seed Gravy, Mung Dal Purée with Sliced White Radishes, Pumpkin Wafers, Rice and Cauliflower Pilaf, Crispy Diced Eggplant with Bitter Neem Leaves,* Stir-fried or steamed seasonal vegetable with *Ginger Ghee, Deep-Fried Golden Puffs, Sweetened Condensed Yogurt, Cake-Like Fried Milk Balls in Scented Syrup,* seasonal fruits (cut mangoes, papayas, finger bananas).

Southern Cuisine Banquet:

Again, the items are listed in the order of serving. Plan ahead to insure the best use of space on your *thalis* or plates, and make them aesthetically pleasing with clever color contrasts.

Fresh Coconut Pudding, lemon or lime wedge, *Carrot Pickle*, *Crispy Plantain Wafers*, *Savory Urad Dal Doughnuts*, *Fresh Coconut and Mint Chutney*, *Seasonal Stir-Fried Vegetables* with *Clove–Sesame Ghee*, *Buttered Steamed Rice*, *Sweet 'n' Sour Dal Soup with Mixed Vegetables*, *Sweet Potato Yogurt Salad with Dates and Almonds*, *Green Beans with Crunchy Fried Mung Badis*, *Crackling-Crispy Dal Wafers*, seasonal cut fruits, *Semolina Halva with Golden Raisins*.

The End of The Meal:

Regardless of whether the occasion is formal or informal, diners rinse their hands and finish the meal with a selection of spice seed mixtures as mouth refreshers or digestives—equivalent to offering chocolate mints in the West. For formal entertaining, three servers in quick succession pass each guest: one with a pitcher of scented warm water and a receiving bowl, a second with drying napkins and a third with the refreshers. The diner holds his or her hand over the bowl and water is poured over it. The server moves along while the second server offers a drying towel. The third offers the guest a selection of digestive mixtures, spooning a little into the palm of the right hand. For less formal occasions, hands are washed away from the table and refreshers as simple as toasted fennel seeds can be offered.

The following spice refreshers—one sweet and one salty—are classics, and hopefully they will inspire you to create your own blends. The ingredients are available at Indian grocery stores. Several other mixtures are available ready-made.

Sweet After-Dinner Refresher:

Makes: About 2½ cups

½ tablespoon (7 ml) each beet juice and water
   or 5–6 drops red food coloring mixed with ½ tablespoon (7 ml) water
1½ cups (130 g) unsweetened or sweetened shredded coconut, lightly packed
2 tablespoons (30 ml) silver-covered cardamom seeds
   or silver dragées (silver-covered sugar balls)
¼ cup (35 g) dry-roasted fennel seeds, preferably *Lucknavi*
½ cup (75 g) cantaloupe seeds, honeydew seeds (magaz),
   sunflower seeds or pumpkin seeds, toasted
½ cup (115 g) rock candy, crushed to a coarse powder

Place the selected red food coloring in a plastic bag and add the coconut. Close and shake well until the liquid is absorbed, then rub the mixture between your palms until the coconut turns pale pink. Combine with the remaining ingredients and mix well. Store in a well-sealed container for up to 6 months.

Sweet and Salty Fennel Seed Refresher:

Makes: about 1½ cups

¾ cup (95 g) dry-roasted fennel seeds
¼ cup (35 g) dry-roasted cumin seeds
3 tablespoons (45 ml) silver-coated candy balls (dragées)
¼ cup (35 g) cantaloupe seeds, honeydew seeds (magaz)
    or pine nuts, toasted and chopped
¼ teaspoon (1 ml) fine salt
2 tablespoons (30 ml) date or maple sugar

Combine the ingredients and toss to mix. Store in a well sealed container for up to 6 months.

SESAME OIL: Known as *til-ka-tel*, this golden oil is pressed from the oil-rich seeds of the sesame plant (*Sesamum indicum*), used in India for thousands of years. The depth of color and flavor in the oil depends on the color of the seeds—from off-white to gray-black. A good-quality oil should smell slightly sweet with a clear taste. Also known as gingelly oil, it is widely used in regional dishes from Tamil Nadu and is a preferred oil in many kitchens throughout the South and Southwest. The smoking point averages 420°F (215°C) but may be higher or lower depending upon the brand.

SESAME SEED: Known as *til*, this is the flat, pear-shaped seed of the sesame plant (*Sesamum indicum*) which has been a staple crop in India since Vedic times. The seeds range in color from off-white to grayish-black, and, amazingly enough, light-colored seeds contain over fifty percent oil. They are also a good source of incomplete proteins, and when combined with rice, milk or *dal*, the protein volume is strengthened—one reason the seeds are popular in so many regional cuisines. Gentle roasting brings out a nutty flavor in the almost tasteless seeds—a good idea before most usage. Though black sesame seeds are used in Oriental dishes, most Vedic cooks prefer them white. They are an important ingredient in Deity worship in the temples and in Ayurvedic medicine. *Tahini*, a semi-liquid sesame butter used in Middle Eastern cooking, is a wonderful staple in the kitchen. You might want to make up a batch of not-too-salty *Cumin–Sesame Salt*—five parts crushed toasted sesame seeds, two parts dry-roasted crushed cumin seeds and one part sea salt.

SEVIYA NOODLES: Also known as *sevian*, a form of very fine, thread-like vermicelli made from durum wheat. It is used primarily in a creamy, raisin-nut-studded milk pudding called *seviya kheer*, popular in the Punjab, from Delhi to Amritzar. Available at Indian grocery stores, the best commercial brand is "Elephant" in cellophane-wrapped one pound (455 g) boxes.

SEVIYA or MOROKOO PRESS: A brass, stainless steel or wood noodle press sold with an assortment of decoratively patterned metal discs. It is most often used to make *sev*—spicy chickpea noodles something like fried chinese noodles. The dough is placed in the main chamber and forced out by turning a mechanism at the top. To make thin *sev* noodles, the press is rotated slowly over a pan of hot oil. To make *giantha*, the press is fitted with a star-shaped disc, and the implement is rotated to make individual spirals 2 inches (5 cm) in diameter. Each piece is carefully slipped into hot oil to keep its shape in tact. In a pinch, you might use a *churro* press, pastry bag or continuous-flowing cookie press. The *seviya* implement is available at Indian grocery stores.

SHALLOW-FRYING: To cook and brown foods that are one-quarter to one-half covered in hot *ghee* or oil. Shallow-fried flat breads, such as *parathas*, are efficiently cooked in a specially designed concave griddle called a *tava*; available at Indian grocery stores. Though any griddle can be used, the slight curve of the *tava* griddle allows the oil to remain under the bread, where it is needed.

TO SIEVE: See *TAMIS and CHALNI.*

TO SIMMER: To cook foods in a liquid at below the boiling point. At sea level, a high simmer is 210°F (98°C), a medium simmer is 195°F (90°C), and a low simmer is 180°F (82°C).

SNOWPEA: Also called *mangetout* and sugar pea, a special type of pea (*Pisum saccaratum*), eaten while young and sweet, still encased in its tender pod. The pods are harvested before they develop any fiber, while the row of peas protrudes only slightly. The flavor is delicate, akin to perhaps new asparagus tips. The pods must be topped and tailed, with the strings pulled away from the edge if necessary. Once only available at Chinese grocery stores where they were known as Chinese peas, snowpeas are now available at many supermarkets.

SOUR CREAM: Known in India as *khatte malai*, made by culturing fresh cream with a butterfat content of at least eighteen percent. Once sterilized or pasteurized, the cream is cooled to about 80°F (25°C) before adding either a *Lactobacillus acidophilus* or *L. bulgarious* culture. Within 12–15 hours, keeping the cream near 85°F (29°C), it will thicken and develop a pleasant tart taste.

SOUR SALT: See **CITRIC ACID**

SOUTHERN CUISINES: Many outstanding regional cuisines make up the larger tapestry of the South. If there is one similarity between all of the regional cuisines, it is in their prodigious use of rice and *dal*—making it the best high-fiber, high-carbohydrate diet in the nation. One ingredient usually plays counterpoint to the other: bland against spicy, sour against sweet, etc. When rice and *dals* are combined together, amazing things happen. They are simmered, wet-ground, steamed, fried, fermented, and more. Further, "dry" dishes, such as *iddlis*, *dosas* and *badas*, are invariably offset with moist or liquid ones, like coconut chutneys, consommés and vegetable soups.

A South Indian *chaunk* might be made in a number of oils such as sesame, coconut, *mowra* butter, or *ghee*. It more than likely would include black mustard seeds, split *urad dal*, red chilies and fresh curry leaves. Yogurt, fresh grated coconut, tamarind purée and lime juice are frequently-used ingredients, both as foods and condiments.

The *brahmanas*, or priests who oversee the Deity worship in ancient South Indian temples, are called *pancha-daksinatya-brahmanas* and come from the old areas known as Andhra, Karnata, Gujara, Dravida and Maharastra. The temples are famous for their chefs and massive *prasadam* distributions. Yearly, hundreds of thousands of pilgrims battle the elements for just one taste of these special sanctified foods. Many South Indian Temples kindly revealed their recipes for this book, while others served as inspirations. Special thanks to: Sree Krishna Matha in Udupi; Sree Balaji Mandir in Tirupati; B.V. Puri Maharaj's Ashram Temple in Visakhapatnam, and Sree Simhachalam Temple.

SPROUTED BEANS: Known as *ugadela kathar*, sprouting increases the nutrient content in foods. The most popular sprout today in India, as in much of the world, is the mung bean sprout. Its mild, slightly sweet flavor is compatible with many ingredients. In India, however, the tails barely appear—only about ¼-inch (6 mm) long—yielding a crispier texture and more compact appearance.

Mung sprouts are most popular in a ginger-laced dish called *usal*, but could, of course, be added to *kachambers*, *raitas*, even *karhis*. The water-logged mung sprouts sold in supermarkets have little in common with those made at home. Sprouting procedures are described on page 44.

STAPLES: The dry goods in this entry can be worked into any number of recipes in this book. To substantiate nutrition in a high-fiber, high-carbohydrate diet, add plenty of seasonal fresh fruits and vegetables. Milk and yogurt will do on the dairy front, though other excellent products are available.

Grains and Cereals:

basmati rice
Patna long-grain rice
brown rice: long and short grain; Calmati; Texmati
pounded or flaked rice; cream of rice; puffed rice; rice flour
oat groats; oat flakes; oat flour
whole barley; pressed barley; barley grits
whole rye groats; rye grits; rye flakes; light and dark flour
whole winter wheat; whole spring wheat
cracked wheat or *bulgar*; semolina; farina; couscous; bran
    flakes; wheat germ; puffed wheat
chapati flour or *atta*; wheat pastry flour; hard wheat bread
    flour; graham flour; gluten flour;
all-purpose flour; unbleached flour; cake flour; unbleached
    bread flour; self-raising flour
popcorn, corn flour; yellow corn meal; blue corn meal; coarse
    grain, high lysine corn meal; *masa harina*; yellow and white
    corn grits; hominy grits; puffed corn
whole hulled millet groats; puffed millet; millet flour
whole triticale berries; triticale flakes; triticale flour
wild rice

Pseudo-Cereals or Flours for Ekadasee:

Kutu: buckwheat groats or whole seeds, roasted or unroasted;
    buckwheat grits; light and dark buckwheat flour
Rajgira: whole amaranth seeds, flour and puffs
Quinoa (pronounced keenwa): whole seeds and flour
potato flour; banana flour; tapioca granules and flour;
    arrowroot starch

Nuts and Seeds:

whole almonds; blanched almonds; sliced and slivered almonds;
    almond meal; chopped almonds
whole cashews; cashew halves; cashew bits or pieces; chopped cashews; cashew meal
raw pistachios; macadamia nuts; walnut halves, pieces and
    chopped; pecan halves, pieces and chopped; Brazil nuts;
    filberts; pignoli (pine nuts); peanuts
nut and seed butters: peanut; almond; cashew; sesame; sunflower
charoli seeds *chironji*; melon seeds *magaz*; pumpkin seeds;
    sunflower seeds; sesame seeds; white poppy seeds

Oils, Butter and Ghee:

corn; sunflower; safflower; sesame and toasted sesame; peanut;
    coconut; mustard; palm; rape seed; poppy seed; cotton seed
Italian, French and California olive oils
avocado; almond; hazelnut; walnut; grape seed
vegetable oil cooking spray
sweet and unsalted fresh butter; *ghee*; homemade
    flavored *ghee*

Dried Fruits:

apples; light raisins or sultanas; dark raisins; pears; peaches;
    currants; mango; papaya; banana chips; pineapple rings
coconut ribbons, thin and thick shredded coconut; creamed
    coconut
blond dates; brunette dates; deglet dates; medjool dates;
    date sugar
Calmyrna figs; Black Mission figs
Sunray prunes; Moyers prunes
Turkish apricots; semi-moist apricots

Sugars and Sweeteners:

jaggery or *gur*; turbinado sugar; muscovado sugar; light and
    dark brown sugar
maple sugar or granules; maple syrup; maple cream; maple candy
light rice syrup; *amasake* (sweet brown rice syrup); sorghum syrup;
    barley malt syrup; molasses; corn syrup; golden syrup; honey
white granulated; superfine; powdered or confectioner's sugar;
    barley sugar; rock candy *misri*

Legumes:

lentils: *toovar* or *arhar dal*; brown lentils
beans: mung beans—whole, split with skins, split and husked;
    urad beans—whole, split with skins, split and husked;
    whole *muth* beans; whole butter beans; kidney beans;
    adzuki beans; navy beans; lima beans; pinto beans; black beans
peas: whole chickpeas; black-eyed peas; soybeans; yellow and
    green split peas

STEAMING: Known as *bhap dayana*. Any pot with a tight-fitting lid becomes a suitable steaming vessel when a steaming rack is placed inside. A Chinese bamboo-lidded steamer (three tiered) is efficient in that it can be set over boiling water in any shape of pan and accomodates a quantity of food. Stainless steel steamers are a good investment .

    Indian steamers are not available in America; for the most part they are tinned brass and, if used frequently, need re-tinning. More and more mail order firms offer good-quality two-, three- and four-tiered European stainless steel steaming units. These space and energy savers are practical for anyone on a schedule, and can cook a rice, *dal* and two vegetable lunch in under an hour.

STEWING: The closest equivalent to the slow cooking method known as *dum dayna* in India. Often using earthenware, the lid is sealed into place with a thin rope of *chapati* dough, locking flavors inside. The rice, *dal* or vegetable dish is very gently boiled or simmered, preserving the shape and texture of the ingredients. A classic example of this type of stewing is a famous North Indian dish called *aloo dum*. Baby potatoes are fried or steamed until about three-quarters cooked, then stewed in a flavorful broth until just tender.

STOCK: The liquid strained from a mixture of vegetables, spices, and herbs that have simmered for a long time in water. Used as a base for soups and sauces.

TO STUD: To insert whole blanched nuts or whole spices into the surface of a foodstuff.

SUGAR, CANE and BEET: Sugar obtained from sugar cane grass (*Saccharum officinarum*) and sugar beet (*Beta vulgaris*) accounts for most of the sugar consumed worldwide. Though the word sugar may refer to any of several water-soluble crystalline carbohydrates—glucose, fructose, maltose or lactose—it most frequently refers to sucrose: what we know as table sugar. Sugar cane and sugar beet provide us with nearly pure sucrose. Honey and grapes supply us with the sugar called glucose. Lactose is the sugar contained in milk, while fructose is present in many ripe fruits. Almost all refined sugar products used in India are obtained from native sugar cane; some is from the recently introduced sugar beet in North India.

Unrefined cane and date sugar—*jaggery* and *gur*—have been used in India since Vedic times. Along with American maple sugar granules and Columbian *panella*, they are good choices when a recipe calls for "raw" or unrefined sugar. Refined sugars became popular the moment refineries were established in the eighteenth century, and today Americans are reported to consume nearly 100 pounds (50 kg) a year per person—too much by most acounts. No matter what your choice of sweeteners, bear in mind the characteristics and attributes of each, and keep in mind that solid and liquid sweetener cannot be used interchangeably without adjusting the liquid content.

White granulated sugar, known as *chini*, has no "flavor," but an intense sweet taste. The only recipes in this book that require it are delicate milk fudges, *chenna* cheese confections and some syrup sweets. As an alternative to the bleached white sugar sold in supermarkets, health food stores sell "sugar in the raw" or turbinado sugar which is refined, but not pure white—more a buff or tan color. It must be ground in a coffee mill before some usage, especially when superfine sugar is called for.

Superfine sugar, called castor sugar in England, is quick-dissolving and an all-around good choice for refined sugar. When sugar is further pulverized and mixed with up to three percent cornstarch, it is known as powdered sugar, confectioner's sugar or 10X in America, and icing sugar in England. Though it tends to lump in the box, once passed through a sieve, it is good for dusting on confections or uncooked candies, such as *Simply Wonderfuls*.

Brown sugar, known in India as *shakkar*, most resembles the type of brown or dark sugars available in America in the early half of the century. Often named after its place of production, like Demerara, from a district in Guyana, or Barbados, from an island in the West Indies, they were only partially refined, granulated but still moist, with a dark color and rich flavor. Today's brown sugar, whether light or dark, is almost always white sugar with molasses added for flavor. Most Americans have never had real brown sugar, though in England Tate and Lyle offers a modern version of the originals.

Sugar candy or rock candy, known as *misri*, is quite popular in India, for unlike granulated sugar which can easily be adulterated, it is in crystal form and therefore more pure. It is purchased on a string and sold by weight. Rock candy is made by growing strands of crystals on a string or wooden stick in a super-saturated sugar syrup. It takes about a week for the crystals to form. They are then rinsed and air-dryed until free of moisture and will store indefinitely.

SUNFLOWER OIL: The golden oil pressed from the seeds of the sunflower plant (*Helianthus annuus*) is not only light and delicate, but an excellent choice for the health conscious, for it contains one of the lowest percentages of saturated fatty-acids (about five percent) of any oil. It is a versatile oil, excellent for both cooking and salads. Only recently available in India, it met with instant popularity. Readily available at supermarkets and health food stores.

TAMARIND: Known as *imli*, the pulp obtained from the hanging pods of the tamarind tree (*Tamarindus indica*), native to India. The magnificent tamarind tree often rises dramatically from soil seemingly incapable of growth, offering shelter and fruit. One of the most famous trees in India is an ancient tamarind tree in Vrindavan, situated on the banks of the Yamuna river. Known simply as *Imli Tala* (the tamarind tree), it is revered as the spot where Shri Chaitanya sat in meditation for days, finally revealing many lost locations of Lord Krishna's pastimes. Thereafter, tree became a kind of mecca for Vaishnava pilgrims.

Fresh tamarind pods—anywhere from 4–6 inches (10–15 cm) long—are cinnamon-brown colored and fuzzy. The fresh pulp is piquant with a sour, date-apricot flavor, and the entire pod can be split and dropped into a rice *pilau* or vegetable to impart a suggested, rather than aggressive, sour flavor. Dried tamarind is sold commercially in two forms: pressed l-pound (455 g) bricks of pulp (peeled and pitted or unpitted) called tamarind pulp, and jelly-like tamarind concentrate, sold in l-pound (455 g) jars under the label Tamcon. Tamarind purée, made from dried pulp or concentrate, has a distinct, fruity sweet-and-sour flavor and is widely used in all regional cuisines. Tamarind dipping sauce or chutney is used for drizzling over savories and pastries.

To make tamarind purée, break up one half-pound (230 g) of dried, seeded tamarind pulp and place it in a ceramic or stainless steel bowl. Cover it with 2 cups (480 ml) of boiling water and set aside for at least 4 hours or overnight, partially covered. Squash the softened pulp through your fingers to release as much pulp as possible from the fibers. Pour into a sieve resting over a second bowl and, using the back of a spoon, mash as much purée from the fiber as possible. Scrape the pulp from the underside of the strainer; discard the fiber. You should have about 1¼ cups (300 ml). Store, well covered, in a crock for up to ten days or freeze in an ice cube tray, unmold, and store in freezer bags for up to 2 months.

TAMIS **and** *CHALNI:* The French *tamis* and Indian *chalni* are both drum-shaped sieves, excellent for a number of sieving and straining tasks. The wooden-rimmed *tamis* range from 6–16 inches (15–45 cm) in diameter, fixed with either nylon or wire mesh in varying gauges. The mesh is stretched over the inner wooden hoop and held in place by the outer hoop. A flat-surfaced wooden *champignon* masher or plastic dough scraper is effective for forcing purées through the mesh.

The Indian *chalni* is similarly drum-shaped, but instead of a wooden rim, it is either stainless steel or tinned steel. It is sold with five interchangeable mesh sieves of varying gauges—from very fine to very coarse. Averaging 8–10 inches (20–25 cm) in diameter, this implement was designed to efficiently remove the fine particles of bran from finely-milled *chapati* flour as well as any number of other straining jobs.

DRUM-SHAPED
INDIAN *CHALNI* SIEVES

TAPIOCA and SAGO: Known as *sabu* or *sabudana*, both ingredients are used similarly in Vedic cooking. Tapioca is a starchy bead processed from tubers of the cassava plant (*Manihot utilissima*), while sago is obtained from the sago palm (*Metroxylon sagu*). Unless tapioca is precooked and called instant, it is usually called pearl tapioca—small, medium or large size—and like sago, it is routinely softened before use: ½ cup (65 g) medium pearl tapioca soaked in 1 cup (240 ml) of water will soften in about 20 minutes; large pearls will take 45 minutes. *Sabu* is made into sun-dried wafers, *pakoras* and *badas* in Southern and Southwestern cuisines and is a popular binding agent, thickener or flour used on *Ekadasee* grain fasting days. Available at supermarkets and Indian grocery stores.

TAVA: A slightly concave iron griddle, 9–12 inches (23–30 cm) in diameter, used for cooking flat breads. A good-quality *tava* should be at least ¼-inch (6 mm) thick with a glassy-smooth surface. Like all iron cookware, it must be seasoned and cannot be put away wet. A *tava* is especially well-suited for cooking griddle-fried *parathas* because they are cooked in a small amount of *ghee* or oil. The concave shape keeps the oil at the bottom of the pan where it is needed. *Tavas* are sold at Indian grocery stores.

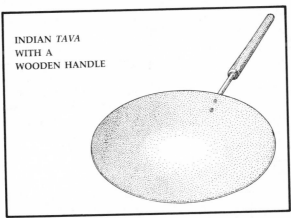

INDIAN *TAVA*
WITH A
WOODEN HANDLE

THALI: A rimmed, circular tray—anywhere from 12–18 inches (30–45 cm) in diameter—used as a dinner plate. *Thalis* are available in a number of metals, most commonly stainless steel. Gold or silver might be used at a well-appointed formal dinner table; bell-metal (an alloy of tin and copper) is favored at village dinner tables. A table setting is completed with small bowls called *katoris*, varying in size from 1½–3 inches (4–7.5 cm) in diameter. The *katoris* are placed around the edge of the plate with as many used as neccessary (8 to 10 is common). One or two beverage containers complete the service.

TOMATO FLOWERS: Choose small to medium tomatoes. Use a small sharp knife or a V-shaped garnishing knife and make a series of V-cuts around the equator of the tomato so that you have a continuous saw-toothed line all around. Carefully pull the two halves apart and use as is or squeeze out the seeds and fill with a salad. Oranges, limes, lemons, grapefruits and melons may also be separated in this way.

TOMATO ROSE GARNISH: Use a small sharp knife. Cut a flat surface at the blossom end and continue to peel off a thin strip of skin about 4 inches (10 cm) long. Cut a second strip about 3 inches (7.5 cm) long. To make a rose, coil the first strip loosely around the flat base. Coil the second strip tightly and place it in the center of the outside coiled strip. Using a toothpick, adjust the peels to resemble a rose in bloom.

TOOVAR DAL: Also called *arhar dal* and *tur dal*, a split lentil from the plant *Cajunus cajan*. Known in English as pigeon pea, it looks something like a slightly flat split pea, but with a creamy-gold color. *Toovar dal* has a slightly sweet flavor and is delicious simmered into a purée, seasoned with ginger, hot chilies, a little turmeric, lime juice and salt. It is widely used in Western and Southwestern cuisines and is easily detected in two loved South Indian dishes: *sambar* and *rasam*.

Toovar dal is available in two types: plain and oil-coated. Castor oil is routinely used to coat grains or *dals* in the villages as it acts as a bug repellent. One of several oils are used for *dal* sold commercially. Before use, the oil is removed by rinsing it in several changes of hot water. Both types of *toovar dal* are available at Indian and Middle Eastern grocery stores.

TRITICALE: Deriving its name from scientific terms, this relatively new grain is a hybrid cross between wheat (*triticum*) and rye (*secale*). With a taste similar to rye, with sweet wheat overtones, it is also described as nutty. Its protein content averages 11.5 percent but its biological value is considered higher than soybeans or wheat because it contains the valuable amino acid lysine. Use it in tandem with *chapati* flour for delicious flat breads. Whole berries need to be soaked overnight before use and then cooked for about 40 minutes, like brown rice. Cracked like bulgar, it is best fried and then cooked for 25–35 minutes. The flakes make a delicious hot breakfast cereal. Distributed through Arrowhead Mills at health food stores.

TURMERIC: Known as *haldi*, an underground rhizome from the perennial plant *Curuma longa*, native to humid areas of South India and Southeast Asia. Like ginger root, it is dug up and can be used either fresh or dried. Unfortunately, fresh turmeric root is rarely, if ever, available outside of Indian grocery stores. It is at its prime when young and immature, with thin skin, tender offshoots and firm yellow flesh. If you find it, by all means buy a supply. It is moderately easy to reduce it into a smooth purée on a Japanese ginger grater and it freezes well.

To produce ground turmeric, the cleaned rhizomes are boiled and sun-dried until thoroughly dehydrated, sometimes taking two to three weeks. The outer skin is scraped off before the rhizomes are powdered. The one and only time I was forced to hand-grind dried rhizomes was exhausting and difficult. Unless absolutely necessary, don't bother. Fortunately, good-quality ground turmeric is inexpensive, and, if kept well-stored, has a long shelf life.

Turmeric is an essential ingredient in almost all regional cuisines. It is used extensively in vegetables, legumes, beans and *dal* dishes. The powder ranges from a brilliant yellow to reddish-yellow color but, properly used, adds little more than warm flavor and a delicate yellow-orange hue to a dish. Like asafetida, too much turmeric devastates a dish; the color will be excessive and the flavor slightly bitter. Use it sparingly until you are aware of its potency.

The *Ayur Veda* recognizes turmeric for its health-giving properties, internally as a blood purifier and externally for use in ointments or poultices.

Ground turmeric is available at supermarkets bottled in small jars or tins. It is also available at specialty stores and Indian or Middle Eastern grocery stores.

***URAD DAL*, *URAD* FLOUR and *URAD* BEANS:** Known as black gram in English, the dried bean from the plant *Phaseolus mungo*, a close relative of the mung bean. Whole *urad* beans, called *sabat urad*, are BB-sized cylinders with a grayish-black skin and creamy-white interior. Dry split *urad* beans, with the skins still intact, are called *chilke urad*, while the split and husked beans are simply called *urad dal*. Each type is used extensively in North India, while in the South, whole *urad* bean dishes are less popular. Southerners use split *urad dal* in endless ways, even as a seasoning in a fried *chaunk*. Like fenugreek seeds, it takes on a nutty flavor when it is fried.

Urad dal is substantially protein-rich: ⅔ cup (145 g) of cooked beans yields about twenty percent of a woman's daily requirement, more, when it is combined with whole grains and milk products. *Urad* purée or soup is complemented by certain seasonings: ginger root, black pepper, asafetida, red chilies and turmeric, along with fresh coriander, curry leaves or fresh mint. It also has an affinity for leafy greens, tomatoes, radishes, eggplant and yogurt. Rice and *urad*-based batter—made from *urad* flour or wet-ground *urad dal*—is particularly delicate and airy and is the basis of feather-light steamed dumplings (*iddlis*), silky *dosa* pancakes or pillow-soft fried *bada* savories. The whole beans, split *dals* and flour are available at Indian and Middle Eastern grocery stores.

VANILLA: The flavoring agent obtained from the seed pod of a flowering orchid plant (*Vanilla planifolia*) native to the Americas. The pod is harvested in its immature state while still yellow—the color of the orchid. It is tightly packed into boxes and allowed to dry out and develop its vanilla flavor and color. Good vanilla is deceptive: long, narrow, shriveled blackish pods speckled with a powdery-white coating. The pods contain thousands of minute seeds—the source of the vanilla flavor. Because plant cultivation cannot satisfy more than ten percent of the demand, most commercial products contain synthetic vanillin. Though whole pods are expensive, they can be used several times; after each use, such as steeping in milk, wash the pod well and dry before storage.

VARAK: Also called *vark*, this is no doubt the most opulent garnish used in the world: exceptionally thin sheets of edible pure silver or gold. Since ancient times, Ayurvedic physicians have used powdered precious metals, jewels, even conch shells, in herbal medicines. The miracle drug known as *Hiranya-garbha*, used in the treatment of chronic illness, was made with pure gold and pearls. *Varak* is tasteless and odorless, and visibly stunning as a garnish.

Each *varak* sheet is made by placing a small portion of moistened precious metal dust between two sheets of parchment. The papers are encased in a protective pouch which is hand-hammered until the dust is compressed into a piece of gossamer-thin foil. The *varak* foils are sold by the dozen at Indian grocery stores and are relatively inexpensive. Usually saved for special religious or social holidays, they add elegance to sweets, confections and elaborate rice dishes.

Apply *varak* in a windless place, as a breeze can cause the delicate foils to be swept away. Remove the top sheep of paper, holding the foil on the bottom sheet in an open palm. Invert your hand and gently press the foil onto the food.

WALNUT OIL: This expensive but exquisite oil seems to be tailor-made for outstanding salad dressings. Pressed from oil-rich walnuts, the flavor and color of the oil varies from one place to another. French oils seem more aromatic and vibrant than the ones I have sampled from America. The strongest are from the Dordogne region; the mildest, from the Loire region. Even though I have seen it recommended straight, I find it better to mix half walnut oil with half olive oil or bland vegetable oil. Unfortunately, this oil has a short life once opened. As with all oil, keep it in a dark bottle or can, well sealed, in a cool, dry cupboard. Available at gourmet and health food stores and mail order firms.

WATER CHESTNUT and WATER CHESTNUT FLOUR: Known as *singhara* or *paniphal* and the flour as *singhar atta*. Both are from the fruit of the underwater plant *Trapan bispinosa*, native to Kashmir and much of the Orient. The horned, blackish case covers a fruit that is much loved, both raw or briefly cooked, throughout the North. Sun-dried water chesnuts are ground into a flour used not only in batters and flat bread doughs, but also in sweet puddings. Both water chestnuts and water chestnut flour are widely used on *Ekadasee* fast days. They are often easier to obtain at Oriental grocery stores than at Indian grocery stores.

WESTERN CUISINES: In the Western provinces of India, contemporary Marawadi and Maharastran cuisines are regarded as superior, largely due to their creative artistry. Almost everywhere in India, formal dinners are served on *thalis*, but here particular attention is paid to the placement and order of the dishes. The meal must be pleasing to the eye first, then the nose, and finally the palate. Temperature, taste, texture and appearance are meant to counterpoint: hot dishes are taken after chilled, spicy offsets mild, crunchy contrasts creamy, and sour enhances sweet.

Vegetable cooking in Western cuisines is particularily healthy and fits into today's trend towards light menus. Single vegetables are often cooked in their own juices in a little seasoned *ghee* while vegetable combinations in sauces are enriched by reduction rather than flour sauces. Nutrition-rich cashews, almonds, sesame seeds and white poppy seeds are frequent supporting ingredients.

The present State of Gujarat houses the largest concentration of vegetarians in India. Ahmedabad, Surat and Dwaraka are all cities respected for vegetarian specialties, dishes once hidden in private homes are now eaten around the world. Many light meal dishes are characterized by the addition of the seasoning combination of curry leaves, green chilies, lime juice and and a little sugar. A typical fried *chaunk* would likely be made in *ghee* and contain black mustard seeds, cumin seeds, asafetida, and coriander leaves.

WHEY: The watery liquid that is a by-product of the *panir* cheese-making process or that separates from yogurt during storage. It may be used in making bread doughs, yogurt-based beverages or *karhi* sauces. Families in India with an excess of whey routinely feed it to small animals to stimulate their growth.

TO WHISK: To vigorously move a whisk with a quick sweeping motion to obliterate lumps in a mixture, to blend ingredients, or to add a final gloss to a sauce. A sauce whisk is rigid and elongated rather than springy and bulbous. A batter whisk is nothing more than a slightly flattened balloon whisk—an excellent design for beating fairly-liquid batters until smooth and well-blended. To whisk light mixtures, hold the wire handle as you would a pencil, with the rounded balloon end pointing away from you. To whisk a stiff mixture, grasp your palm around the wire handle and point the rounded balloon end towards you; this is less tiring, especially in quantity.

WHOLE WHEAT FLOUR: One hundred percent whole wheat flour contains all of the wheat grain, including its nutritious bran and germ. The relatively coarse texture of the bran and its high oil content makes a heavier dough than that of *atta* or *chapati* flour. The crumb of a flat bread made with whole wheat flour, even mixed with unbleached white flour, is coarser than that made with *chapati* flour. Graham flour, like whole wheat flour, is made only from wheat kernals but is more finely powdered, so the bran is less discernable. Still, the texture of the wheat flour depends upon two factors: the milling process and the variety of wheat used. Keep in mind that non-yeast bread doughs and pastries are best made with soft red or gold wheat because it has more starch than hard wheat. Whole wheat flour should be stored in a cool place, or, in hot humid climates, refrigerated.

WILD RICE: The seed of an aquatic grass (*Zizania aquatica*) that grows in shallow muddy ponds, lakes, even sluggish waterways, in Eastern and Central North America, Ontario and Canada. Not actually a grain, but treated as such, this is a year-round crop, long a staple in the diets of native American Sioux, Chippewa and Fox Indians. Only recently has wild rice received interest from other sources. Up until the 1970s, almost all of the grains were obtained by ancient, hand-harvesting Indian methods, both tedious and time-consuming. Commercial farming methods have raised the yield from about 300 pounds (150 kg) per acre to nearly 800 pounds (400 kg). Still, the precarious onslaughts of nature—bad weather, disease, birds and other insects—have kept wild rice expensive; at this writing it is upwards of fifteen dollars per pound.

The long, thin grains, ash-brown to blackish in color, cook into a chewy, slightly smoky delight, prized not only for its distinctive taste, but also for its nutritional assets. Wild rice is high in protein, low in calories, and respectable in potassium, phosphorous and B vitamin content. Further, one pound goes a long way—25 to 30 servings—with each plain portion averaging a comfortable seventy calories. Wild rice keeps almost indefinitely, well-covered and kept in a cool, dry nook.

Plain, buttered *basmati* rice and wild rice pilaf—with an optional touch of currants, fried pine nuts or slivered, toasted pecans and minced parsley and basil—is elegant on any Vedic menu. Experiment with up to one-fourth wild rice in many whole grain pilafs. A versatile and epicurian treat, available in better grocery stores nationwide.

WOK: A gently sloping, bowl-shaped metal pan from China now used world-wide for stir-frying, deep-frying and steaming. Designed for use over a live or gas flame, the base of the pan is supported on a metal ring set over the heat. The sloping walls allow you to quickly cook ingredients in the bottom of the pan and move them up the sides when cooked, leaving the bottom free for new ingredients. For deep-frying, a semi-circular rack rests around the rim. Fried foods are not only drained there, but kept warm while others cook in the frying oil. The wok is an ideal pan for supporting a Chinese bamboo-lidded steamer. Purchase a size that corresponds with the wok. The base should rest well above the boiling water. Like all steel and iron pans, the wok must be seasoned and re-seasoned, as necessary. Widely available at better cookware stores and department stores.

YOGURT: Known as *dahi*, Indian yogurt is thick and creamy, not from thickening agents, but because it contains a substantial butterfat content (ten percent and upwards). Like sour cream (with an eighteen percent butterfat content), *dahi* is firm—the consistency of well-set custard. Commerical yogurt used as a starter should not contain preservatives; this tends to kill the yogurt culture and lessen nutritional benefits. In America, Brown Cow Farm produces an outstanding line of yogurts containing three living cultures: *Lactobacillus acidophilus*, *L. bulgaricus* and *S. thermophilus*. When living bacteria enter the intestines, they create an acid environment that helps in the manufacturing of B and K vitamins and, more importantly, assist the body in assimilating nutrients, especially phosphorus and needed calcium. Although yogurt has the same food value as milk, it is more easily digested, and is therefore a natural choice for those with digestive problems. My personal preferences in commercial American yogurts are Brown Cow, Nancy's (available only on the west coast) and Columbo. All three brands are available at health food stores. These products not only serve as starter cultures for most of my homemade yogurt, but they were occasionally used in recipe testing as well.

Indian milk is pasteurized but not homogenized. This allows the cream to rise during setting and form a rich, solid "yogurt layer" on the surface. If you live in a state that sells pasteurized raw milk, by all means use it for your homemade yogurt. To imitate the consistency of Indian *dahi*, either boil down whole milk to three-fourths or two-thirds its original volume, or use three parts whole milk to one part cream before adding the culture. This thick yogurt will lend body and character to your dishes.

YOGURT CHEESE: Known as *dehin*, plain yogurt, drained of its whey and compacted until the flavor is slightly sharp and the texture resembles cream cheese. I have made this cheese around the world, using many types of milk and yogurt, and no two batches are ever the same; I have noted that low-fat yogurt cheese usually has a more pronounced sour flavor than cheese made from rich yogurt. The most important thing to keep in mind is that, as the cheese compacts, its flavors intensify. Over the years, I have experimented with a few variations on yogurt cheese spreads. While they are not traditional fare in India, they go very well with flat breads, raw vegetable crudités and savory biscuits or crackers. Though the spreads can be served at room temperature in a bowl, they are festive when chilled and molded into shapes—square cakes, round cakes, logs or balls.

Yogurt Cheese Recipes:

The following ingredient combinations should be added to 1 cup (240 ml) of firm yogurt cheese. Simply cream all of the ingredients well and refrigerate, covered, for at least 3 hours.

¼ cup (60 ml) softened butter
¼ cup (60 ml) minced dried mango, papaya or apricots
¼ teaspoon (1 ml) powdered orange zest

1 tablespoon (15 ml) minced and seeded hot green chilies
½ tablespoon (7 ml) each ground horseradish and cracked pepper
salt as desired

Special Shapes for Yogurt Cheese:

To make a log, spoon the mixture into the center of a sheet of waxed paper. Fold the near end of the paper over the cheese, and, with the assistance of a spatula or scraper, tuck it toward the cheese and then press the tool against the cheese to compress it into a uniform log. Roll it up, tuck in the ends, and chill until firm.
To make a ball, line a 1–1½ cup (240–360 ml) round-bottomed bowl with buttered wax paper, spoon in the mixture, and pack, lining the top with additional waxed paper. Refrigerate until firm. Repeat the same procedure for a round cake, substituting a buttered 1 cup ramekin for the bowl.
To make a flat cake, place the cheese on a square of buttered wax paper and cover with a second piece. Using your hands or a pastry scraper, pat and mold into a smooth block as thick as you wish. Tuck in the edges and chill until firm.
Any of these shapes can be garnished with flavor coverings that contrast textures but marry flavors. Try one of these: minced raw pistachios or minced toasted almonds; a coat of paprika (brushing off the excess with a pastry brush); cracked black pepper; minced parsley or summer savory; a toasted sesame and cumin seed mixture; pecan halves

ZEST: 1) The oily outer portion of citrus peel. 2) To cut off citrus strips or shavings or grate citrus zest with a knife or zester tool. 3) To infuse a preparation such as *sandesh* with citrus strips to release their essential oil, and then remove them.

ABOUT HIS DIVINE GRACE
A.C. BHAKTIVEDANTA SWAMI PRABHUPADA

His Divine Grace A.C.Bhaktivedanta Swami (1896–1977), known to his disciples as Srila Prabhupada, arrived in America in 1965 at the age of seventy. The following year, he founded the International Society for Krishna Consciousness and subsequently established more than 100 temples for the study of Vaishnava spirituality and culture. In his lifetime, he traveled the globe fourteen times, wrote more than sixty books and initiated some 8,000 disciples, introducing them to India's meditational practice known as *Bhakti-yoga* ("union with God through devotion").

Prabhupada was born Abhay Charan De on September 1, 1896, in Calcutta, India. His father, Gour Mohan De, was a well-respected Vaishnava who infused the devotional worship of Lord Krishna into the lives of his family. By the time he was six years old, Abhay had his own Deity of Lord Krishna and performed worship—chanting, playing instruments and observing Vaishnava festivals—that he would carry on throughout his life.

In 1922, in his fourth year at Scottish Churches' College, he met his spiritual master, Srila Bhaktisiddhanta Saraswati Goswami. A prominent religious scholar in Calcutta, Srila Bhaktisiddhanta was the founder of the Gaudiya Matha, a *Bhakti-yoga* society with sixty-four teaching institutes around India. At their first meeting, Bhaktisiddhanta liked the educated young man and convinced him of the importance of spreading the philosophy of *Bhakti-yoga* throughout the world and, more specifically, through the use of the English language.

In the years that followed, Srila Prabhupada wrote a commentary on the *Bhagavad Gita*, assisted the Gaudiya Matha in its work, and, in 1944, started *Back to Godhead*, an English fortnightly magazine, distributed by his disciples to this day in more than thirty languages.

Recognizing Abhay's learning and devotion, the Gaudiya Vaishnava Society honored him in 1947 with the title "Bhaktivedanta," meaning "one who has realized the import of the *Vedas* through devotion to God." In 1950, at the age of fifty-four, he retired from business and family life in order to devote his full time to studies and writing. Traveling to the holy city of Vrindavan, he resided in humble circumstances in the medieval temple of Radha Damodar. There he engaged in deep study for several years, single handedly writing, publishing and distributing his *Back to Godhead* magazines. He became known as Bhaktivedanta Swami when he accepted the renounced order of life (*sannyasa*) in 1959.

At Radha Damodar temple, he also began work on his life's masterpiece: a multi-volume translation of and commentary on the eighteen-thousand-verse *Srimad Bhagavatam*, India's epic historical narrative. After publishing three volumes of the *Srimad Bhagavatam* in India, he traveled to America in 1965 to fulfill the request of his spiritual master. Arriving in New York City practically penniless, after almost a year of great difficulty he established his Society in July, 1966.

By his demise in November, 1977, A.C. Bhaktivedanta Swami Prabhupada had accomplished the mission given him half a century before by his spiritual master. He had brought the message of *Bhagavad Gita* to Western shores and impressed upon the hearts of many the spirit of its teachings: that life's glory lies in our ability to rise above the ignorance of matter through a life of devotion to God.

GLOSSARY OF HINDI TERMS
AND PRONUNCIATION GUIDE

Aam	AHM	ripe mango
Aam Paparh	AHM PAH-paar	dried sheets of mango pulp
Achar	ah-CHARR	pickle
Adrak	AH-druk	ginger root
Ajwain	aj-WINE	ajowan or carom seeds
Aknor Jhol	ak-NEER JOAL	a Bengali seasoned broth
Akhroot	ak-ROHT	walnut
Aloo	AH-loo	potato
Aloo Bokhara	AH-loo bok-AH-rah	dried plum
Aloo Chidwa	AH-loo CHID-vah	deep-fried savory snack
Aloo Tikki	AH-loo TEE-kee	potato patty
Amchoor	AHM-CHOOR	mango powder
Amla	AHM-la	green gooseberries
Amrood	AHM-rood	guava
Ananas	ah-NAH-nus	fresh pineapple
Anar	ah-NAHR	fresh pomegranate
Anardana	ah-NAHR-dah-nah	dried pomegranate seeds
Angoor	AHN-goor	fresh grapes
Angeer	ahn-JEER	figs
Arbi	AHR-bee	starchy root vegetable
Arbi ki Patta	AHR-bee kee PAHT-tah	leaves of the *arbi* plant
Arhar Dal	AHR-HAHR DAHL	pigeon peas
Aroo	AHR-roo	fresh peaches
Arwa Chaval	AHR-wah CHA-vul	long-grain rice
Atta	AH-tah	finely powdered wholewheat flour
Avatara	AH-vah-TAHR	an incarnation of the Lord
Ayur Veda	AH-yoor VAY-dah	a system of medicine based on the *Vedas*

Baasi	BAH-see	stale
Bada	BAH-duh	deep-fried *dal* dumplings
Badaam	bah-DAHM	almond
Badi	BAH-dee	dried *dal* cakes
Baigan	BAY-gun	eggplant
Bajri	BAHJ-ree	millet
Balushai	BAH-loo-SHY	deep-fried pastry swirls
Bandhgobhi	BANDH-go-bee	cabbage
Barbatti	BAHR-bah-tee	snap or green beans
Bari Hari Mirch	BAH-ree HAH-ree MEERCH	mild paprika
Basmati	bas-MAH-tee	superior long-grain rice
Belna	BELL-nah	tapered rolling pin
Besan	BAY-sahn	chickpea
Bhagavad Gita	BAH-guh-VAHD GEETA	the paramount scripture of the Vedic tradition
Bhaktiyoga	BAHK-tee-yoh-gah	the science of devotion to God
Bhap Dayna	BAHP DAY-nah	steaming
Bharta	BHAR-tah	oven-baked vegetables that are mashed or puréed
Bhatura	bah-TOO-rah	a deep-fried flat bread
Bhelpoori	BELL-POOR-ee	deep-fried pastry wafers
Bhen	BEN	lotus root
Bhindi	BIN-dee	okra
Bhona	BOO-nah	fried
Bhopla	BHOP-lah	ash pumpkin
Bhujia	BOO-jee-ah	stir-fried vegetables
Boondi	BHUN-je	deep-fried chickpea flour balls
Brahmana	BRAH-mun-ah	a person qualified to instruct others on spiritual life
Burfi	BUR-fee	a milk fudge confection
Chaach	CHAACH	natural buttermilk
Chaitanya Charitamrita	chay-TAAN-yah char-ee-TAAM-ree-tah	the biography of Shri Chaitanya Mahaprabhu
Chaitanya Mahaprabhu	chay-TAAN-yah ma-HA-prah-BOO	the avatara of Lord Krishna for the present age
Chakki	CHAH-kee	a large stone grain mill
Chakli	CHAH-klee	deep-fried chickpea spirals
Chalni	CHAL-nee	sieves in varying meshes
Chana dal	CHAH-na DAHL	a variety of split chickpea
Chandan	CHAN-dun	sandalwood
Chapati	chah-PAH-tee	griddle-baked flat bread
Charchari	CHAR-char-ee	smoky-flavored vegetable
Chat	CHAAT	a fruit or vegetable snack
Chaunk	CHAUNK	spice blend fried in *ghee*
Chaunk gobhi	CHAUNK GO-bee	Brussels sprouts
Chaval	CHAH-vul	rice
Cheekoo	CHEE-koo	sapodilla or sapota fruit
Chenna	CHEN-nah	a soft-textured fresh cheese
Chidwa	CHID-vah	a spiced snack
Chini	CHEE-nee	granulated sugar
Chironji	cheer-OHN-jee	charoli seeds

Chole	CHOAL-ee	savory chickpea/vegetable dish
Chowla dal	CHOW-lah DAHL	black-eyed peas
Chukandar	choo-KAHN-dahr	beet root
Chum chum	CHUM CHUM	a delicate fresh cheese sweet
Dahi	duh-HEE	plain yogurt
Dahi bara	dah-HEE BAR-ah	*dal* dumplings with yogurt sauce
Dal	DAHL	dried legumes, peas and beans
Dalchini	dahl-CHEE-nee	cinnamon
Dalia	DUL-ee-ah	cracked wheat
Dhania	DUN-ee-ah	coriander seeds
Dhokla	DHOK-lah	savory steamed cake
Dilbhar	DILL-bhar	cake-like cheese confection
Dhoodh	DHOODT	milk
Dosa	DOH-sha	crisp paper-thin pancake
Ekadasee	ee-KAH-duh-see	a fasting day for Vaishnavas
Elaichi	ee-LIE-chee	cardamom
Firni	FEER-nee	rice flour and almond pudding
Foogath	FOO-gath	mixed vegetable dish
Gaja	GAH-jah	flaky fried savory nibbler
Gajar	GAH-jar	carrot
Garam masala	ga-RAHM ma-SAH-lah	blend of powdered spices
Gehun	GAY-hun	wheat berries
Ghee	GHEE	clarified unsalted butter
Ghiya	GHEE-yah	bottlegourd; also *Louki*
Gobhi	GO-bee	cauliflower
Goswami	GO-SWAH-mee	one who controls his senses
Gulab jal	goo-LAHB JAHL	rose water
Gulab jamun	goo-LAHB JA-mun	milk fudge balls in scented syrup
Gur	GOOR	raw date palm sugar
Guru	GUH-RUH	a spiritual master
Haldi	HAUL-dee	turmeric
Halva	HAUL-vah	dessert made with cereals, vegetables or fruits
Halwai	HAUL-why	professional sweetmaker
Har dhania	HAR DUN-ee-yah	fresh coriander (cilentro)
Hari gobhi	HAH-ree GO-bee	broccoli
Hari mirch	HAH-ree MEERCH	green bell pepper
Hari matar	HAH-ree mah-tar	green peas
Hing	HEENG	asafetida
Iddli	ID-lee	steamed bread made of rice and *dal*
Imli	IM-lee	tamarind
Jaggery	JUG-er-ee	raw cane sugar
Jaiphal	JIE-fall	nutmeg
Jaitun ka tel	JIE-tun kah tell	olive oil
Jalebi	jul-AY-bee	deep-fried syrup sweet

Jamikand	JUM-ee-khand	yam
Javitri	jah-VIH-tree	mace
Jawar	JAH-wahr	barley
Jeera	JEE-rah	cumin seeds
Kabli chana	KAH-blee CHAH-nah	dried chickpeas
Kacha	KAH-CHA	raw
Kacha aam	KAH-CHA AAM	green mango
Kacha kela	KAH-CHA KAY-lah	plantain
Kachamber	kah-CHUM-bur	small salad
Kachori	kah-CHOOR-ee	deep-fried stuffed savory pastries
Kaddu	kah-DOOH	pumpkin
Kaju	KAH-joo	cashew nut
Kala chana	KAH-lah CHA-nah	black or brown dried chickpeas
Kala elaichi	KAH-lah ee-LIE-chee	large black cardamom pods
Kala mirch	KAH-lah MEERCH	black pepper
Kala namak	KAH-lah NEH-mek	black salt
Kalonji	kah-LONE-jee	nigella seeds
Kamarakh	kah-MAHR-ak	starfruit; carambola
Karai	kah-RIE	deep-frying vessel
Karela	kah-RELL-ah	bitter melon or bitter gourd
Karhi	kah-REE	yogurt/chickpea flour gravy or soup
Karhi patta	kah-REE pah-tah	curry leaves; also sweet *neem*
Karpoor	KAHR-poor	edible camphor
Katori	kah-TOOR-ee	small metal bowl
Kela	KAY-lah	banana
Kesar	KAY-sar	saffron
Kewra ruh	KAY-rah ROOH	screw pine essence
Khara	KAHR-ah	made with little seasoning
Khas-khas	KUS KUS	white poppy seeds
Khatte	KAH-teh	sour
Kheer	KEER	condensed milk dessert
Kheera	KEER-ah	cucumber
Khichari	KITCH-er-ee	wholesome stew made with *dal*
Khoa	KOH-ah	milk cooked down until fudge-like
Khopra	KOH-prah	dried coconut
Khumani	koo-MAH-nee	apricot
Khus ruh	KUSS ROOH	essence used in sweets
Kirtan	KEER-tahn	singing in praise of God
Kishmish	KISH-mish	raisin
Kofta	KOFF-tah	deep-fried vegetable balls
Krishna	KRISH-nah	Supreme Personality of Godhead
Kulfi	KULL-fee	Indian ice cream
Ladoo	LAH-doo	round sweetmeat
Lal mirch	LAL MEERCH	cayenne or red pepper
Lanka	LAN-kah	dried whole red chilies
Laphra	LAAF-rah	Bengali vegetable soup
Lassi	LAH-see	chilled yogurt drink

Latche	LAHT-chee	deep-fried potato sticks
Laung	LONG	cloves
Louki	LOH-kee	bottlegourd
Luchi	LOO-chee	deep-fried white flour flatbread
Madhur	MAHD-hur	honey
Maida	MIE-dah	unbleached white flour
Makhan	MAH-kahn	butter
Makkai	MAH-KIE-ee	corn
Malai	mah-LIE	cream
Malpoora	mal-POOH-rah	crêpes served with syrup
Marawadi	mar-WAH-dee	a Southwestern Indian cuisine
Masala	mah-SAHL-ah	spice and spice blends
Matar dal	MAH-tur DAHL	dried split green peas
Mathri	MAH-tree	deep-fried salty biscuits
Meetha	MEE-tah	sweet
Methi	MAY-tee	fenugreek seeds
Misri	MEE-shree	old-fashioned sugar candy
Mithai	MIT-hie	sweets
Mooli	MOO-lee	white radish
Moong badi	MOONG BAH-dee	dried mung *dal* dollaps
Moong dal	MOONG DAHL	dried split mung beans
Moongfalli	MOONG-fahl-ee	peanuts
Moori	MOO-ree	puffed rice
Mosambi	mo-SAHM-bee	orange
Murabba	MUR-ah-bah	preserves
Muth dal	MUTH DAHL	dried dew beans; tepary beans
Mysore pak	MIE-sore PAHK	chickpea flour fudge
Namak	NAH-muk	table salt
Nariyal	NAH-RIE-yel	coconut
Nariyal kash	NAH-RIE-yel KAASH	coconut grater
Nariyal tel	NAH-RIE-yel tayl	coconut oil
Naspati	NASH-pah-tee	pear
Neem	NEEM	margosa tree
Nimbu	NEEM-boo	cross between lemon and lime
Nimbu ka sat	NEEM-boo	citric acid crystals
Obla	OH-blah	boiled
Pakora	pah-KOOR-ah	batter-coated deep-fried vegetables
Palak	PAH-lek	spinach
Panch puran	punch POOR-ahn	Bengali spice blend
Pani	PAH-nee	water
Panir	pah-NEER	pressed fresh *chenna* cheese
Paparh	PAH-par	*dal* wafer
Papita	pah-PEE-tah	papaya
Pappadam	PAH-pah-dum	*dal* wafers from South India
Paratha	pah-RAH-tah	griddle-fried whole wheat bread

Payasa	PIE-ah-sah	rice pudding
Pera	PEH-rah	milk fudge
Phal	PHAAL	fruits
Phulka	PUHL-kah	griddle-baked flat bread
Pista	PEE-stah	pistachio
Podina	poh-DEE-nah	mint
Poha	POH-ha	flat or pounded rice
Poori	POOR-ee	deep-fried bread
Prabhupada	PRAH-boo-pod-ah	honorific title of A.C. Bhaktivedanta Swami
Prasadam	prah-SHAH-dum	foods offered to God before eating
Pulau	POO-la-oh	rice pilaf
Pushpanna	push-PAH-nah	rich rice pilaf
Rabri	RAH-bree	cooked clotted cream
Rai	RIE	black mustard seeds
Raita	RIE-tah	seasoned yogurt salad
Rajma	RAAJ-mah	red kidney beans
Ras	RAHS	vegetable stock or broth
Rasedar	rah-seh-DAAR	vegetable dish in thin gravy
Rasgoola	raas-GOO-lah	*chenna* cheese balls in syrup
Roti	ROH-tee	griddle-baked flat breads
Ruh	ROO	essence
Sabat moong	SAH-baat MOONG	whole mung beans or mung dishes
Sabat urad	SAH-baat OOH-rud	whole *urad* beans or dishes
Sabji	SAAB-zee	vegetables
Sabu or *Sabudana*	SAH-boo/SAH-boo-duh-nah	tapioca
Sahijan	SAH-hee-jun	horseradish root
Sag or *Sak*	SAAG/SAAK	spinach
Salat	SAH-laat	salad
Sambar	SAAM-bahr	spicy vegetable and *dal* stew
Sambar masala	SAAM-bahr ma-SAH-la	spice blend for *sambar*
Samosa	sah-MOE-sah	vegetable-filled pastries
Sandesh	SAAN-desh	fresh cheese fudge
Sankirtan	saan-KEER-taan	congregational chanting of the Lord's names
Santara	SAAN-tah-rah	orange
Sarson	saar-SOHN	mustard greens
Sarson tel	saar-SOHN TELL	mustard oil
Saunf	SONF	fennel seeds
Seb	SEB	apple
Sem	SAYM	thin green beans
Sev	SAYV	chickpea noodle snack
Seviya	SAY-vee-yah	fine vermicelli noodles
Shakarkand	shah-KAAR-kaand	sweet potato
Shakkar	SHAH-kaar	brown sugar
Shalgam	SHAL-gam	turnip
Sharbat	SHER-beht	fruit juice punch
Shorba	SHOOR-bah	soup
Shrikhand	shree-KAAND	sweetened yogurt cheese

Shukta	SHOOK-tah	Bengali bitter-flavored stew
Sil batta	SIL BAH-tah	grinding stone with pestle
Simla mirch	SIM-lah MEERCH	green bell pepper
Sitaphool	see-TAH-PHOOL	custard apple
Sonth	SAWNT	dry ginger powder
Sooji	SOO-jee	semolina or farina
Srimad	SREE-mahd	18,000 verse history of
Bhagavatam	BAH-ga-vah-TAHM	Lord Krishna and incarnations
Suran	SOOR-ahn	yam
Tal Gur	TAHL GOOR	raw sugar from the *tal* palm
Talna	TELL-nah	deep-frying
Tamatar	tah-MAH-tahr	tomato
Tarbooj	TAAR-booj	watermelon
Tari	TEH-ree	gravy
Tava	TAH-vah	curved cast iron griddle
Tej patta	TAYJ PAH-tah	cassia leaf
Tel	TAYL	oil
Thali	TAH-lee	metal dinner plate
Thandai	tahn-DIE-ee	cold milk punch
Tikki	TEE-kee	pan-fried vegetable patties
Til	TIHL	sesame seeds
Toovar dal	TOOR DAHL	dried pigeon peas
Topokul	TOP-oh-kuhl	fruit similar to cranberry
Ubalna	ooh-BAHL-nah	boiling
Urad dal	OOH-rahd DAHL	split *urad* beans
Uppma	OOP-mah	savory semolina dish
Vaishnava	VIESH-NAH-vah	devotee of Lord Vishnu/Krishna
Varak	VAH-ruk	edible silver or gold foils
Vedas	VAY-dahs	four ancient revealed scriptures
Vedic	VAY-dik	based on the *Vedas*
Vrindavan	vrin-DAH-vahn	village where Lord Krishna appeared
Wada	WAH-dah	deep-fried *dal* paste savory

GENERAL INDEX